OXFORD DICTIONARY OF CURRENT IDIOMATIC ENGLISH

Volume 1:

Verbs with Prepositions & Particles

OXFORD DICTIONARY OF CURRENT IDIOMATIC ENGLISH

Volume 1: Verbs with Prepositions & Particles

A P COWIE & R MACKIN

London Oxford University Press 1975

Oxford University Press, Ely House, London W.1.
GLASGOW NEW YORK TORONTO MELBOURNE WELLINGTON CAPE TOWN IBADAN
NAIROBI DAR ES SALAAM LUSAKA ADDIS ABABA DELHI BOMBAY CALCUTTA MADRAS
KARACHI LAHORE DACCA KUALA LUMPUR SINGAPORE HONG KONG TOKYO

First published 1975

Computer typeset in Times and Univers by
George Overs Ltd, Oxford University Press,
Unwin Brothers Ltd and Tradespools Ltd.
Printed in Great Britain at the University Press, Oxford
by Vivian Ridler, Printer to the University.

Contents

Acknowledgments

We are grateful to all those who have supported our work on this dictionary with their encouragement, specialist advice and practical help. Particular thanks are due to Dr Frans Liefrink, formerly on the staff of the School of English, University of Leeds, whose own research interests in grammar were an invaluable stimulus to our thinking when the framework of reference for the dictionary was first being developed. We should also like to express our indebtedness to Miss Loreto Todd, of the School of English, who undertook the exacting task of checking the entire cross-reference system for the dictionary, and to Mrs Hilary Gilfoy, a former postgraduate student at Leeds, who made the detailed analysis of that system on which our treatment in the Introduction is based.

The task of typing over 7,000 entry slips in their original and revised forms was shared by Mrs Ethel Bacon, Mrs Moira Halloways and Mrs Florence Herstell. Mrs Nicky Cabuzet and Mrs Halcyon McLaren typed the final draft of the Introduction and explanatory tables. We are indebted to them all for their patient and meticulous work, much of it undertaken at short notice and under great pressure.

Finally we express our appreciation to the editorial staff of the Oxford University Press for the expert attention they have given to the technical complexities of computer setting and to matters of typography and design.

A P Cowie and R Mackin

General Introduction

Familiarity with a wide range of idiomatic expressions, and the ability to use them appropriately in context, are among the distinguishing marks of a native-like command of English. Expressions such as **step up** (supplies), **lay on** (transport) and **take up** (the story) are part of the common coin of everyday colloquial exchange, and the tendency, especially in casual or informal contexts, to prefer the Anglo-Saxon combination to its single Romance equivalent – **increase**, **provide**, **continue** – helps to explain the widely-held view that idioms such as these are among the most characteristically 'English' elements in the general vocabulary.

To say that such expressions are in common use is not however to say that their meanings are always self-evident: a French speaker would surely understand **continue** more readily than **take up**, while a native speaker might have difficulty in explaining the sense of the combination in terms of its constituent parts. In fact, a close study of various kinds of idiomatic items brings to light many curious anomalies of form and meaning. While we can equally well talk of **angling for** or **fishing for** compliments, where the verbs are as freely interchangeable as when they are used in a literal sense, we should not say of a friend that he had difficulty in **making up his thoughts** (as distinct from **his mind**). And while we might want to say of him that he found it hard to **hit the nail on the head**, we should not substitute **strike** for **hit** unless we were thinking literally of his skill with the hammer rather than figuratively of his inability to say precisely what he meant. Among collocational pitfalls of this kind the mature speaker of the language picks his way with unconscious ease. The foreign student, however, or the native speaker of English whose control of idiom is not yet sure, looks for explicit guidance on a wide variety of expressions in current use, and often to a considerable depth of detail. As far as we are aware, no specialized dictionary of idiomatic usage at present exists which is sufficiently broad in scope to answer the various practical requirements of the learner, and it is chiefly with a view to meeting this need that the *Oxford Dictionary of Current Idiomatic English* has been designed and is being compiled.

When complete, the Dictionary will consist of two volumes. The present volume deals with only part of the total range of idiomatic expressions in English; other types of idiom will be treated in a second volume, which is in preparation. An important feature of the whole Dictionary is that the grammatical and semantic treatment of headphrases is supported by citations from a variety of contemporary sources, both written and spoken. Most of the quotations are drawn from an analysis of works of fiction, biography, history etc which was specially undertaken to provide illustrative material for the Dictionary. As the drafting of entries proceeded this archive of upwards of 30,000 recorded excerpts was added to from time to time, especially from such sources as the daily and weekly press and radio and television broadcasts.

The scope of the present volume is explained in some detail below (0.1). We set out the main idiom patterns represented here, discuss the problem of idiomaticity as it affects the question of what to include and what to exclude, and outline our reasons for adopting the particular grammatical framework used in the entries. The second part of the Introduction (0.2) touches upon some features of the entries which are specifically designed to encourage the use of the dictionary as a learning and teaching aid.

The scope of the dictionary

0.1 One feature of idiomatic usage in English which complicates the task both of the lexicographer and of the student is that idioms correspond to a wide range of grammatical types, or patterns. Idioms are found for example in the phrase patterns 'article + adj + noun' – *the last straw, a live wire, a lame duck*; 'article + present participle + noun' – *a parting shot, a sitting duck*; and 'article + past participle + noun' – *a foregone conclusion, a close-run thing*. Idiomatic expressions also span sentences of various structural types, as in *break the bank, fill the bill, make sb's day, jump the gun*; *give him an inch and he'll take a mile, spare the rod and spoil the child*. This is but a small sample of the great diversity of grammatical patterns in which idiomatic expressions may occur. The spread is enormous but there is one outstandingly large category that does permit coverage in depth and uniformity of treatment within a single volume, and that is the subject of this part of the dictionary.

The basic requirement that expressions have to meet for inclusion in the present volume is a simple one: all consist of, or include, a verb and a particle or preposition (i e one of the words **down**, **for**, **in**, **off**, **on**, **up**, **with** etc). This restriction explains the 'verbs with prepositions and particles' of the subtitle. The simple combinations of verb + particle (or verb + preposition) – **back away**, **fall through**, **size up**; **abide by**, **run into**, **take to** – account for the bulk of the entries, but there is an important sub-type containing both a particle and a preposition – **put up with**, **set up as**, **take out on**. A considerable number of entries, too, are devoted to more complex types, many having nouns (and sometimes also adjectives) as fixed elements in addition to the verb and preposition or particle: **lose track of**, **make a mental note of**, **put one's best foot forward**, **take to one's heels**.

In this brief survey of the grammatical types represented in the dictionary the question of idiomaticity has not been directly raised. Though various expressions have been cited as examples of each type, we have yet to say what it is that entitles us to refer to them as idioms. In turning now to consider this central question of idiomaticity it will be best to break down under separate heads the rather complex issues that are raised.

1 How in practice do we determine whether a given expression is idiomatic or not? We may sense for example that **put up** as used in the sentence

They're having a memorial ***put up*** *to him by public subscription.*

is not idiomatic, whereas **put up** in

A well-wisher had ***put up*** *the money (for the scheme).*

is idiomatic. What kinds of criteria can we call upon in support of our intuitions?

2 Is the distinction between non-idioms and idioms clear-cut, or does the one type shade off gradually into the other?

3 What criteria in particular determine the inclusion of some items in the dictionary and the exclusion of others?

4 Finally, what is the bearing of the conclusions we reach upon the grammatical labels we attach to idioms? If an expression such as put up (in the second example) is shown to be a unit of *meaning*, should we not describe it as a grammatical unit also, and generally abandon the 'verb + particle' labelling in idiomatic cases?

In considering these questions, unnecessary complications will be avoided if the complex items (e g **turn one's back on**) are considered separately from the simple two-word combinations (e g **turn on**). The immediate discussion will centre particularly on combinations of transitive verb + particle; we shall return later to the more complex cases.

Discussions of idiomaticity are sometimes confused by introducing inappropriate grammatical criteria into an area where considerations of meaning carry particular weight. A question which is often raised in treatments of the verb + particle combination, but from the discussion of which the wrong conclusions are sometimes drawn, has to do with the different grammatical functions of **on** in such pairs of sentences as

The machine **turns** (= rotates) ***on*** *a central pivot.*
Pop music **turns on** (= stimulates, excites) *many young people.*

There is certainly a difference of function here: we cannot shift the final noun phrase to precede **on** in the first sentence, but we can in the second:

The machine* **turns *a central pivot* ***on***.
Pop music **turns** *many young people* ***on***.

Further evidence of the difference is the contrastive positioning of 'it' and 'them' (as replacements for the noun phrases) in the two sentences

The machine **turns on** *it.*
Pop music **turns** *them* ***on***.

It is on the basis of such criteria that **on** can be said to function as a *preposition* in the first example and as a *particle* (or adverbial particle) in the second. At the same time, we cannot use this grammatical evidence of contrastiveness in support of a claim that **turn on** (= 'excite') is a unit of meaning, and thus an idiom. If we did, we should have to explain why it is that **turn on** as used in the sentence

The caretaker **turns on** *the hall lights.*

appears, and can be shown to be, *less* idiomatic, while at the same time displaying the *same* characteristics with regard to the particle. Compare:

The caretaker **turns** *the hall lights* ***on***.
The caretaker **turns** *them* ***on***.

We should also have to account for the fact that, whereas **turn on** (verb + preposition) in

The machine **turns on** *a central pivot.*

is intuitively less idiomatic than its homonym in the following sentence, **on** is equally 'prepositional' in both cases:

Our conversation **turned on** (= had as its main topic) *what was to be done when the battle was over.*

The evidence of such examples points to the conclusion that whereas the particle/preposition contrast is a valid and important one, it has no bearing on whether expressions are idiomatic or not. The idiom/non-idiom contrast is different in kind and must be established by different means. Having said that, it is true that grammatical support of another type can sometimes be found for treating items such as **turn on** (in the sense of 'excite') as units of meaning. Whether we shall wish to argue from this that such expressions should be described as *grammatical* units (i e words) in the dictionary is a question we shall take up again when various (largely semantic) criteria of idiomaticity have been examined.

We can begin the discussion of idiomaticity with a simple and familiar assumption: an idiom is a combination of two or more words which function as a unit

* marks sentences that are considered unacceptable.

of meaning. This assumption can be tested: if a verb + particle expression (for instance) is a semantic unit we should be able to substitute for it a number of single words (in this case verbs) of equivalent meaning. By this criterion, **step up** as used in the sentence

His promotion has **stepped up** *their social status.*

is clearly idiomatic, since it is synonymous with 'improve', 'enhance'. By the same token, **take off** is an idiom in the sentence

Bill **took off** *Winston Churchill to perfection.*

since it is equivalent in meaning to 'mimic', 'imitate'.

We can test our intuitions about idiomaticity in another way. If **step up** and **take off** are units of meaning, it should not be possible to break that unity either by removing the particle component or by replacing the verb component with other verbs of like meaning. The 'particle deletion' test shows both expressions to be idiomatic: the effect of applying it is to make nonsense of the example sentences:

His promotion has* **stepped *their social status.*
Bill* **took *Winston Churchill to perfection.*

'Verb replacement' also applies negatively in both cases: there are no precise equivalents to **step** and **take** as they are used here:

His promotion has **stepped up** *their social status.*
? ***pushed***
? ***bumped***

Bill **took off** *Winston Churchill to perfection.*
* ***grabbed***
* ***snatched***

(? marks choices which are acceptable in the context but doubtful synonyms, and * marks choices that are totally unacceptable.)

The semantic unity which is characteristic of idioms tends to make them behave as single *grammatical* words also. This tendency is reflected for example in the fact that some verb + particle expressions which are idiomatic can be converted into *nouns*. So **to make up** (one's face) has a corresponding noun **make-up**, and **to break down** (the accounts, the figures) has the corresponding form **breakdown**. This characteristic suggests a further test – of 'noun formation' – which applies positively to both our examples. In parallel with the cases just cited, we find that **to step up** (someone's status) can be changed into **a step-up** (in someone's status) and **to take off** (Churchill) into **a take-off** (of Churchill).

Idiomatic expressions are units of meaning; non-idiomatic expressions, conversely, are made up of distinct meaningful parts. We should expect this assumption about non-idioms to be borne out when they are tested in the same ways as idioms. This time however the tests should apply in reverse. Consider the item **draw out**, as in the example

Robert **drew out** *twenty pounds from his savings account.*

We note first that there is no corresponding noun in this case: we shall not attest ***a draw-out** (of twenty pounds) to parallel **a step-up** (in status). We find too that we can equally well use **take** or **draw** in this context: the verbs are synonymous here. Again, the particle **out** can be deleted without affecting sense or acceptability:

Robert **drew** *twenty pounds from his savings account.*

The examples we have been looking at tend to suggest that there is a sharp contrast between idioms and non-idioms – that there are items like **take off** (a politician) to which all the tests apply, positively or negatively as appropriate, and other combinations like **draw out** (money) to which the same tests apply in reverse. In reality, the picture is not so clear-cut: even **draw out**, which on most counts seems unidiomatic enough, has a one-word equivalent in **withdraw** (suggesting semantic unity):

Robert ***withdrew*** *twenty pounds from his savings account.*

In fact, the more individual cases that we examine the more does it appear that the boundary between highly idiomatic items and the rest is not sharply drawn but hazy and imprecise. We shall do better to think in terms of a *scale* of idiomaticity, with the 'true' idioms (**step up**, **take off**) clearly established at the upper end and **draw out** appearing near the bottom, but with many items representing varying degrees of semantic and grammatical unity spaced out in between. Among the intermediate types, or 'semi-idioms', we find items like **put up**, as used in the sentence

Increased transport costs will ***put up*** *the prices.*

and **muck up**, as in the example

The weather really ***mucked up*** *our weekend.*

What gives such items their special status is that when the tests used to identify idioms (or non-idioms) are applied, the results are not conclusive either way. We find for example that whereas **put up** and **muck up** are unitary according to one criterion ('raise' or 'increase' can be substituted for the first expression and 'spoil' or 'ruin' for the second), they are separable according to another criterion (replacement of the verb component by a verb, or verbs, of equivalent meaning). Thus we can say

Increased transport costs will ***send up*** *the prices* (or: *cause the prices to* ***go up***).

where **send** and **go** replace **put** in the original sentence; and we can also say

The weather really ***messed up*** *our weekend.*

where the synonymous **mess** has replaced **muck**.

What has been said about the nature of the relationship between idioms and non-idioms applies also to more complex expressions – those containing a noun and an adjective, for example. Here too there is a gradual shading-off from absolutely fixed expressions, such as **make an honest woman of** or **make a clean breast of**, through those which allow the replacement of certain words by others of related meaning – **make effective/good use of, put a bold/brave/good face on it/things** – down to expressions of which an adjective (etc) is not an essential part – **keep a (careful, close, watchful etc) eye on, take (strong, instant, particular etc) exception to**. As these examples suggest, the distinctive character of each complex expression (as more or less idiomatic) is brought out by applying the same simple tests of replacement and deletion that were demonstrated earlier.

We have discussed at some length the nature of idiomaticity chiefly to throw light on the special problems raised when deciding what to include in a dictionary which has 'idiomatic' as part of its title. Clearly all those items which are demonstrably units of form and meaning must be recorded. Equally, there are expressions at the lower end of the scale for which an adequate case cannot be made. But as regards the central area – the semi-idioms – where is the line to be drawn? On the whole we have tended to be accommodating to marginal cases, drawing the line low rather than high. There are certain criteria, too, to which we have given special weight. These we explain below with reference to a number of recurrent types of semi-idiom.

1 We have tended on the whole to include any expression, simple or complex, from which the preposition(s) or particle(s) cannot be deleted (i e without making nonsense of, or changing the sense of, the wider context in which the expression is used). This tendency explains the inclusion of pairs such as the following, which in terms of meaningful links between their verbs are less than idiomatic:

angle for	**fasten on/upon**	**jack in** (= abandon)
fish for	**seize on/upon**	**pack in**

2 The weighting given to this criterion also in part explains the inclusion of many semi-idiomatic expressions containing one of the major verbs **come**, **go**, **put**, **take** etc. Because of the relationship of 'intransitive' to 'transitive' which exists between **come down** (for example) in certain of its senses and **bring down**, these expressions are often not full idioms. The fixity of the particle ensures their inclusion. In many such cases, we have also been guided by the need to include items which, while not idioms themselves, may throw light on the meanings of items which are. So **put aside** (a book, one's knitting) is included because it is related in sense to **put aside** (money, cash) and **put aside** (a grievance, one's differences).

3 Even when an expression contains a preposition which can be removed without affecting the meaning of the sentence in which the whole item appears, it may none the less be recorded, provided that the preposition has a strong tendency to co-occur with the verb. Similarly, if a verb combines in a predictable way with two particles (or prepositions), such a combination is also included. The decision to deal with such expressions in the dictionary explains the presence of many verbs of Romance origin, whose meanings are often understood in isolation:

abstain (from)	**develop (from) (into)**
agitate (for)	**transfer (from) (to)**

4 Verbs of motion such as **march**, **run**, **walk** combine with a wide range of particles and prepositions of direction to form sets of expressions – **march through**, **march up**; **run across**, **run back**; **walk away**, **walk in**, **walk out** – whose meanings can be easily grasped. We have not attempted to account for these many possibilities in the dictionary. But when any such combination is used in a specialized way – as **march past** is when it means 'move ceremonially past sb' (i e on parade), or as **walk on** is when it means 'have a small part, appear briefly, in a play' – then that expression is recorded, even though the specialized meaning may sometimes be readily understood.

5 Verbs such as **puff**, **steam** and **zoom** also combine freely with particles and prepositions to give such expressions as **puff across**, **puff past**; **steam along**, **steam into**; **zoom down**, **zoom out** etc. Such combinations have a different status from those containing **walk**, **run** or **march**, however. Since **steam**, for example, in combination with a particle of direction is interpreted as a verb of motion (**steam across** = 'move across under steam power' etc) the particle cannot be removed without changing the sense of the verb. Compare:

The train ***steamed out*** *noisily.*
The train ***steamed*** *noisily.*

It is for this reason that we have indicated in the dictionary the possible combinations in which verbs such as **steam** can occur (though in a special kind of entry; ⇨ *The headphrase*, 1.5, for fuller details).

Finally, we can take up again the grammatical questions raised earlier. We have seen that items that are highly idiomatic tend to function in certain ways as grammatical units (i e as single words). Should this kind of unity be reflected in the way items are grammatically described in the dictionary?

One approach would be to say that it should, and to use the familiar term 'phrasal verb' (in itself indicative of unity) when referring to idiomatic expressions of the verb + particle type, and the rather less familiar 'prepositional verb' to designate idioms of the verb + preposition type. Dividing the 'phrasal' category to take account of the difference between transitive and intransitive would give the following general scheme:

phrasal verb (transitive)	*phrasal verb* (intransitive)
make up (one's face)	(of a witness) **come forward**
take off (a politician)	(of an actor) **walk on**

prepositional verb
run into (difficulties)

This scheme of three unitary 'verbs' will be familiar to many users of this dictionary; there are however serious criticisms to be made of it. We shall not go into the linguistic questions that are raised, but confine ourselves to practical arguments for not adopting it as a descriptive framework for the dictionary. As we have seen, there is no clear dividing line between idioms and non-idioms: they are the end points of a scale. This being so, the question is raised of how 'semi-idioms' are to be described in terms of the above scheme. To call such expressions 'phrasal verbs' or 'prepositional verbs' would imply that they are unities, which is inconsistent with the facts. A second practical objection is that the dictionary contains many complex items – **push the boat out** and **bring the house down** for example – which the scheme does not provide for. While both these expressions contain a verb and a particle it would not make sense to speak of them as 'phrasal verbs'. Finally, if we were to adapt and enlarge the scheme so that it took account both of the scale of idiomaticity *and* of the difference between simple and complex expressions we should end up with a system that was both cumbersome to operate and difficult to interpret. These considerations have led us to look elsewhere for a grammatical framework of reference for the dictionary.

Throughout the Introduction we have referred *separately* to the grammatical structure of expressions (i e in such terms as 'verb + particle', 'verb + preposition') and to their idiomatic status (as 'idioms', 'semi-idioms' etc). This separation is in line with our view that idiomaticity is largely, though not wholly, a question of meaning. This approach has the descriptive advantage of enabling us to speak of **make up** (one's face) etc as a unit of meaning while at the same time leaving us free to speak of the grammatical separability, or mobility, of its parts (as in **make up** one's face/**make** one's face **up**).

This general view governs the way expressions are described in the entries. Whether idioms or not, they are treated *grammatically* as combinations of verb + particle etc functioning in sentence patterns. The item **make up** (one's face) for instance is identified as 'verb + particle in a transitive sentence pattern'. In practice, the identification is by means of a simple code – here [B1i] – which refers the user to a full treatment of the pattern in tabular form (⇨ *Content and arrangement of the entries*, 3.4).

When in addition to being verb + particle etc an expression is *also* idiomatic, this information is conveyed separately. Idiomaticity may be reflected by the definition (⇨ 5.2), or shown by cross-referencing the expression to its synonyms

(⇨ 5.3), or indicated by specifying possible *changes* to the sentence pattern(s) in which the item is used (⇨ 3.2).

Just as the idiomaticity of an item does not affect its basic structural description, so no distinction is drawn between simple expressions (**make up**) and more complex ones (**make one's mind up**) *on grounds of complexity alone* when deciding what pattern to assign them to. Since these two items both contain a verb and a particle, and both are used transitively, they are described exactly alike in their respective entries. The analysis is reinforced in this case by the fact that the expressions have the same passive pattern:

Her face is ***made up.*** ***His mind*** *is* ***made up.***

As well as being in accord with the facts, this approach to the grammatical treatment of complex idioms has the great practical merit of keeping to the minimum the number of distinct structural types in the overall scheme for the dictionary. All the expressions recorded, whether idiom or non-idiom, simple or complex, are accounted for by a system of six basic patterns (⇨ 3.1).

The dictionary and the practical needs of the learner

0.2 Although the dictionary is not intended simply as a practical work of reference for the student of English, we have taken special account of his needs in deciding what information to include in the entries and how best to arrange it. In particular, we have incorporated certain special features which are designed to encourage the confident use of idiomatic expressions in grammatical patterns and lexical contexts beyond those which the student has already met. It is in this sense that the dictionary is designed as a practical learning and teaching aid.

Three related features are singled out for special mention here: the design of the *headphrases* (as embodying limited ranges of lexical choice); the inclusion in most entries of the habitual *collocations* in which headphrase items occur; and the extensive *cross-reference system* by means of which intransitive verbs (for example) are explicitly linked to their appropriate transitives.

A problem commonly facing the would-be user of an idiomatic item is that of deciding how fixed it is. Take, for example, the complex expression **buck one's ideas up**. How invariable is this? Can **up** be deleted? Is **thoughts**, say, freely substitutable for **ideas**? The student needs clear guidance on fine points of lexical detail such as those, as also on the question whether singular **idea** is as acceptable as plural **ideas**, since without it he may produce such variants as ***buck one's ideas** or ***buck one's notions up**. When the lexical shape of an expression is perfectly fixed, as it is here, the help can be given simply and straightforwardly through the headphrase itself (i e the form in which the expression is conventionally represented in **bold type** at the head of the entry). Examples of headphrases which represent *fixed* expressions are:

buck one's ideas up **take the gilt off the gingerbread**
let the side down

Sometimes a very limited range of options is available to the speaker: he can choose to say, for example, either **drag** (sb's name etc) **through the mire**, or **drag** (sb's name etc) **through the mud**, where **mire** and **mud** are permitted alternatives, but ***slime** is not. This restricted range of choice can again be conveyed through the headphrase, by the use of the oblique. The single oblique in the following headphrases shows that the choice of noun in each case is limited to two:

drag through the mire/mud **take sb's mind/thoughts off**
put the cat among the canaries/pigeons

As the examples show, there is often a clear relationship of meaning between the words marked off by the oblique in this kind of headphrase: **canaries** and **pigeons** are both kinds of birds. But this awareness does not help us to determine what the acceptable choices are in any particular case.

The problems which the learner faces in handling the meanings of such complex expressions (and those of the more numerous two-word combinations) are well known. He may have difficulties of understanding or interpretation (especially when the form of an expression is a poor guide to its meaning). He may have trouble in discriminating accurately between various meanings of the 'same' item – those of **put out**, for example, or **take in**. And again, he may need help in distinguishing between expressions which are related in form (cf **level off** and **level up**) though not necessarily in meaning. Among the features we have included in the dictionary to help the student deal with such problems is the regular listing in entries of 'collocating' words. We can consider briefly the special advantages of this guidance here.

The collocates of an expression are the particular words which are commonly combined with it to form sentences. Among the words which regularly appear (as subjects) in the same sentences as **bring to blows**, for example, are disagreement, difference and rivalry, and among those habitually associated (as direct objects) with **bring to attention** are troops, platoon, company. The learner normally becomes aware of these word associations, or collocations, one by one through meeting them in books or hearing them in conversation, and as one association builds upon another he gradually develops a firm understanding of the meanings of **bring to blows** and **bring to attention**. The advantage of bringing together a number of these associated words in one place – as in the entries shown just below – is that the student is made aware of several at the same time. As a result the learning process can be greatly speeded up.

bring to attention ... **S:** sergeant, officer. **O:** troops; platoon, company ...

bring to blows ... **S:** disagreement, difference (of opinion): rivalry, enmity. **O:** (two) sides, parties ...

Another advantage, of course, is that the student can make up sentences of his own on the basis of the collocates recorded in such entries, so strengthening still more his grasp on the meanings of the headphrases themselves.

Illustrative sentences in dictionary entries can serve much the same purpose as lists of collocates. If the illustrations are carefully chosen, they too will contain words that are characteristically and unambiguously associated with the headphrase, and which help to develop the learner's understanding of its meaning. But collocates and examples have different and complementary parts to play in the definition of meaning. In a list of collocates some of the more important clues to our understanding of an expression are abstracted from their real contexts and presented in a highly condensed form. In illustrations, various kinds of information – grammatical and stylistic as well as lexical – are combined in actual instances of language use, though the most important clues to meaning may be rather thinly spread.

A further advantage of indicating the collocates of headphrases, and it is related to the first, is that it enables the learner to distinguish, more precisely than he might otherwise be able to do, between items that are pronounced or spelt alike but which differ in meaning. Take for example the two items entered and defined in the dictionary as:

come down[1] [A1 emph] collapse, drop; fall.
come down[3] [A1 emph] fall, be reduced.

These items have the same grammatical patterns, and their definitions are related, but their *collocations* are quite unalike, and indicate clearly and economically the difference in sense between 1 and 3:

come down[1] ... **S:** ceiling, wall; curtain, picture; rain, sleet ...
come down[3] ... **S:** prices, costs, expenditure ...

(where **S** in each case indicates that the collocates function as subjects.)

Yet another practical application of collocate lists has to do not so much with the learning of new meanings as with indicating and suggesting to the student fresh contexts in which a partially known item can be acceptably used. Take for example the sets of words shown to function as Subjects (**S**), Direct Objects (**O**) and prepositional objects (**o**) in the following entry:

lend (to)[3] ... make (more) significant, believable etc. **S:** event, development. **O:** meaning, significance; credibility, genuineness. **o:** view, interpretation, analysis ...

The student may already 'know' this sense of **lend (to)**, in that he can confidently use the expression in some of the collocations indicated, e g

*(This) event ... **lend(s)** ... meaning ... **to** ... (his) view.*

The statement of other likely collocates in itself extends this capacity, so that for example he can now in addition construct the sentence:

*This development **lends** significance **to** the analysis (already made by economists).*

But as well as being directly available for use in this way, the collocates view, interpretation, analysis (for example) can also suggest – perhaps to the more advanced student – the area in which other suitable choices should be sought (study, account, statement, narrative).

Statements of likely or probable collocates are in an important way linked to the special cross-references which are given at the end of many entries, especially those where the verb in the headphrase is one of the 'heavy-duty' group **come**, **go**, **bring**, **take** etc. Consider the collocates and cross-references in:

bring to fruition ... cause sth to be fulfilled or realized. ... **O:** hope, dream, ambition; plan ... ⇨ come to fruition.

The cross-reference to **come to fruition** indicates that the latter is the 'intransitive' equivalent of the 'transitive' headphrase, a correspondence which is reflected in the tendency for the *same* words to collocate with both expressions. The matching collocates appear in the **come to fruition** entry, as follows:

come to fruition ... be realized, fulfilled. ... **S:** hope, dream, ambition; plan, scheme ... ⇨ bring to fruition.

How can the student make use of this information in a productive way? First of all, he can be confident that when a **bring** entry is cross-referenced to a **come** entry the two normally correspond as transitive to intransitive. He can check that there is a close correspondence in particular cases by comparing collocates and definitions. Having grasped the relationship between the expressions, he can practise it systematically, drawing on his awareness of the shared collocates:

*Their hopes were never **brought to fruition.***
*Their hopes never **came to fruition.***

Once again, the illustrative sentences in the entries are a further source of clarification and practice. Since the **bring/come** correspondence applies to many pairs of simple and complex expressions recorded in the dictionary (cf **bring to the ground/come to the ground**), the learner's exploitation of it in one case can be extended to the numerous parallel cases.

The content and arrangement of the entries

In the following set of entries, the user is referred from a number of features which are often found in the dictionary itself to the detailed explanations provided in sections 1–9 of *The content and arrangement of the entries*.

alternative preps in headphrase **1.1.2**	**centre on/round** [A2 emph rel B2 pass emph rel] have, fix, as its centre; (cause to) revolve about/around (q v). **S:** [A2] **O:** [B2] movement, activity; commerce, industry. **o:** (key) figure, personality; port, capital city □ *She became involved in the whirlpool of activity which* ***centred round*** *Joe.* AITC □ *To give access to markets, the new industries had been* ***centred on*** *a motorway junction.* □ some purists object to the use of round with the v centre.	basic patterns **3.1**; codes repeated before collocates **6.3.1**; usage note **8**
alternative nouns in headphrase **1.1.3**; cross-reference to synonym **5.3**	**dart a glance/look at** [B2 pass emph rel] look suddenly, sharply, at sb; shoot a glance (at) (q v). **adj:** furtive, anxious, hostile. **o:** stranger, visitor; watch, clock □ *She* ***darted an*** *interested* ***glance at*** *the handsome newcomer from under lowered eyelids.* □ *The villagers were guarded in their reception. So many suspicious* ***looks*** *were* ***darted at*** *him.*	transforms **3.2, 3.4**
'anomalous' transform **3.3, 3.4**; headphrase picked out in illustration **7.3**	**flashback** [nom (A1)] (cinema) a return during a film either to events that have already been shown, or to events that occurred before the main action of the film began □ *The main action of the film portrayed the hero's adult life; scenes from his boyhood were shown in* ***flashback***.	register marking **4.2**
optional prep in headphrase **1.2**; codes preceding each illustration **3.1.2**; cross-reference to other major verbs **9.1**	**go across (to)** [A1 A2 A3] pass from one side to the other (of); go over (to) (q v). **o:** (***across***) road, bridge; river; Channel; (***to***) shop; other bank; France □ [A2] *Planks were laid so that the villagers could* ***go across*** *the marshy area.* □ [A3] *'I'm just* ***going across to*** *the pub for half an hour.'* ⇨ **get across¹; send across (to), take across (to).**	definition **5**; preps repeated before collocates **6.2**
reference to set of adjs **1.4, 7.3.5**	**make a good etc job of** [B2 pass pass(o) rel] (informal) perform a task well, ill etc (esp make repairs or decorations to sth well, badly etc). **adj:** good, excellent, satisfactory; poor, dreadful. **o:** car, cooker; bathroom, kitchen □ *Many machines wash, rinse, spin-dry — but the new Acme Twin-Speed Combination* ***makes a better job of*** *all three.* (DM)	style marking **4.1**; grammatical functions of collocates **6.3**
source of quotation **7.2**		
	spray on/onto [B2 pass rel] send liquid in a stream of tiny drops (onto sth). **O:** paint, varnish; perfume; disinfectant, weed-killer. **o:** wall; skin; plant □ *The gardener* ***sprayed*** *insecticide* ***on*** *the rose-bushes* (or: ***sprayed*** *the rose-bushes* ***with*** *insecticide*). □ *Insect repellent should be* ***sprayed onto*** *the skin to discourage mosquitoes* (or: *The skin should be* ***sprayed with*** *insect repellent* etc).	internal arrangement of collocate lists **6.4**; transform shown in illustration **7.4**
'dummy' entry **9.3**	**spray with** [B2 pass rel] ⇨ previous entry.	
restricted set of collocates **6.5**	**turn in**① [A1 B1i pass adj] face or curve inwards (naturally); cause to face inwards. **S:** [A1] **O:** [B1] ⚠ one's toes, feet, knees □ *His big toe* ***turns in*** (i e towards the other toes on that foot). □ *His feet* ***turn in*** (i e towards each other).	numbered headphrase **1.6**

The headphrase

1 The headphrase of an entry (i e the expression which the entry defines and illustrates) is printed in **bold type** and set slightly to the left of the column of text. The form of the verb normally given in the headphrase is the 'base' form – the infinitive without *to*:

blow down **make eyes at** **take up the slack**

The use of the base form indicates that the verb has its full range of inflected forms, finite and non-finite. Expressions in which the verb is restricted to the *to*-infinitive, the present tense etc, appear in those forms in the headphrase:

to begin with[1] **pride goes before a fall**
to start with[1] **money doesn't grow on trees**

A few idiomatic expressions conform to subordinate clauses of time, condition etc. In their headphrases the verb is given in the present tense to indicate the possible use of this tense *and* the past simple:

when it comes down to **when one's ship comes in**

In those few cases recorded in which a verb + particle combination forms part of a longer expression containing another verb, the *first* verb is given in the base form:

(have) one's head screwed on
tell sb where he gets off/where to get off

When a noun, pronoun etc forms an integral part of an expression and functions as Subject, it is placed before the verb in the headphrase. If the verb in such expressions has the normal range of tense forms, it is entered in the base form:

one's blood be up **it fall on/upon sb to do sth**
the game be up

Expressions which are transformationally anomalous, in that they function in passive sentence patterns, or as 'nominalized' forms, but not in active sentence patterns, are given headphrases of an appropriate form (for a detailed treatment of 'transforms' ⇨ *Grammatical codes and tables*, 3.2, 3.4):

accustomed to **washed up** **hangover/hung over**
used to **burn-up** **runabout**

In many expressions of which a *noun* is an integral part, the noun may – whether the expression is in other respects fixed or not – be used in both the singular and plural forms. In others again, the form of the noun cannot be varied. The different possibilities are dealt with in the following ways:

(i) When the noun can only be singular, it appears in the appropriate form in the headphrase and illustration(s):

come into season ... *Tomatoes* ***come into season*** *much earlier in Italy than in Northern Europe.*

(ii) When the noun can only be used in the plural form, it appears in that form in the headphrase and illustration(s):

get to grips with ... *It's time you* ... ***got to grips with*** *the basic trouble* ...

(iii) When the noun can function in both the singular and plural forms, the singular form is given in the headphrase, and both forms are illustrated:

bring a charge (against) ... *you might feel justified in* ***bringing charges against*** *him.* □ *'Of course, you could* ***bring a charge*** *of dangerous driving* ***against*** *him ....'*

(iv) When the noun tends to occur more frequently in the plural form, but is sometimes met in the singular, the headphrase and example(s) show the noun in the plural, while a note at the end of the entry explains that the singular ma[y] also be used:

make allowances (for) ... *The jury were asked to* ***make*** *all* ***allowances fo[r]*** *the age of the accused.* ... □ allowances occasionally sing, as in: *When ever[y]* ***allowance*** *has been* ***made for*** *his inexperience* ...

(v) Where special circumstances require it, the headphrase may includ[e] singular *and* plural forms:

keep a tab/tabs/a tag on

(where **tab** can be either singular or plural, while **tag** must be singular).

The possessive adjectives **my**, **his**, **her**, **one's**, **its**, **our**, **your** and **their** ar[e] usually represented in headphrases by one of the forms **one's**, **his**, **sb'[s]** (⇨ *Illustrations* 7.3.1). These three headphrase forms are used to indicat[e] differences in the way the possessive in *examples* is related to other parts of th[e] sentence:

make one's way in the world ... *If he hasn't* ***made his way in the worl[d]*** *by now, he never will.* MM

Here **one's** is used in the headphrase because the possessive in the exampl[e] (**his**) refers to the same person as the Subject (**he**).

bring to his feet ... *A jolt nearly threw me from the bed, and a second jo[lt]* ***brought*** *me* ***to my feet.*** SD

Here **his** is used (rather than **one's** or **sb's**) because the possessive in th[e] illustration (**my**) refers to the same person as the Object (**me**).

take off sb's hands ... *I should be glad if a buyer* ***took*** *the entire block* (i[e] of flats) ***off our hands.***

In this headphrase, the form **sb's** is used because in the illustration the perso[n] referred to by the possessive (**our**) is different from either the Subject (a buye[r]) *or* the Object (the entire block).

1.1 An oblique / is used to separate parts of a headphrase which can be substitute[d] for each other. In many cases, though not in all, the use of the oblique als[o] indicates that the substitutable words etc have the same sense (i e are synonyms[)] so that they can be used in place of each other without affecting the meaning o[f] the headphrase as a whole:

come into sight/view

(where **come into sight** has the same meaning as **come into view**).

The use of the oblique always indicates a *limited* range of alternative words et[c] it usually occurs once, and seldom more than twice, at a given point in th[e] headphrase:

carry all/everything before one
fall on/upon evil days/hard times
scatter about/around/round

In the notes which follow, the kinds of alternatives most frequently recorde[d] in the headphrases are dealt with in turn.

1.1.1 The *particle* **in** and the *preposition* **into** (which are closely similar in for[m] and meaning) commonly alternate in expressions of which the other constitue[nt] is a verb. In the same way, **on** alternates with **onto** and **out** with **out of**. Th[us] we have **break in** (or: **into** a bank etc) and **opt out** (or: **out of** a scheme etc[)] In such cases, the particle and preposition are normally treated, together wit[h] the verb, in the same entry, with the oblique separating the variant forms in the headphrase.

break in/into **dab on/onto** **opt out/out of**

1.1.2 When two or more synonymous particles (e g **about**, **around**, **round**) or prepositions (e g **on**, **over**, **upon**) alternate in forming an expression with a particular verb, they are allocated with the verb to the same entry, and are separated from each other by the oblique in the headphrase:

look around/round **dote on/upon**
muck about/around **muse on/over/upon**

The same convention is used when particles (or prepositions) which are not generally equivalent in meaning are equivalent alternatives in a given expression:

brick in/up **centre in/on/upon**
fill in/out/up **hanker after/for**

1.1.3 In certain longer expressions one *noun* can be substituted for another without affecting the meaning of the whole. In such cases, the alternatives are marked off by the oblique in the headphrase:

come into being/existence **run to earth/ground**
make a hash/mess of

The same convention has been adopted for expressions containing alternative equivalent *articles*, *adjectives* or *adverbs*:

run an/one's eye over **never/not think of**
have a soft/weak spot for

Adjectives, adverbs etc which are alternatives but *opposite* in meaning are indicated in the same way:

get off on the right/wrong foot **do badly/well for**

It should be borne in mind, however, that when two *particles* (or *prepositions*) which are opposite in meaning can combine with a verb used in a particular sense, they are regarded as forming parts of different expressions and treated in separate entries:

leave down i e allow to remain in a lowered position
leave up i e allow to remain in a raised position
put back[2] i e move the hands of a clock back
put forward[3] i e move the hands of a clock forward

1.2 Parentheses **(in)** are used to enclose a part or parts of a headphrase which, though closely related to the whole, may under certain conditions be deleted. The classes of word, phrase etc most commonly marked as deletable (or 'optional') in the headphrases will be considered in turn.

1.2.1 *Prepositions* are frequently enclosed by parentheses:

cope (with) **miss out (on)** **take out (against)**

Each preposition here is closely tied to the verb (or verb + particle) in the sense that when **cope**, **miss out** or **take out** occurs at the end of a piece of text, one can confidently predict that, if a preposition is to follow, it will be **with**, **on** and **against** respectively, rather than any other:

Our collection of antiques reached such proportions that we were barely able to ***cope*** *...* ***with*** *it.*

If he finds that his paper (= newspaper) *has* ***missed out*** *...* ***on*** *some important fact, his day is soured to begin with.*

The police have decided to ***take out*** *a summons ...* ***against*** *the drivers of both cars involved in the accident.*

At the same time, it is possible to *omit* the prepositions (and their objects) altogether and still be left with intelligible sentences which are related in meaning to the fuller ones:

Our collection of antiques reached such proportions that we were barely able to ***cope****.*

If he finds that his paper has ***missed out****, his day is soured to begin with.*

The police have decided to ***take out*** *a summons.*

If is in these respects that the prepositions in the headphrases given here can be said to be 'optional'.

In headphrases such as

strike up (with)

the preposition **with** is optional under different conditions, however. From a sentence such as

I'd first ***struck up*** *an acquaintance* ***with*** *him while waiting for a train.*

the preposition + object (***with*** *him*) is not normally deleted. At the same time, the sentence can be paraphrased as:

We'd first ***struck up*** *an acquaintance while waiting for a train.*

To the extent that this sentence is close in meaning to the first, and **with** is now omitted, the preposition may be regarded as optional. The dictionary contains many headphrases with the same characteristics as **strike up (with)**:

agree (with) **fall in love (with)** **make it up (with)**

The paraphrase relationship referred to above is illustrated in many of the entries for such expressions (usually in parentheses after one or more of the example sentences).

1.2.2 From certain (usually complex) expressions a particle, adjective, adverbial phrase etc can be deleted under conditions similar to those described for the preposition in **cope (with)** etc (⇨ 1.2.1). The optional item is highly predictable in the context; it can be removed without making nonsense of the remainder; the meanings of the expression with and without the particle etc are closely allied. In these cases too, the optional part is placed within parentheses in the headphrases. Consider these headphrases and the examples given below them:

foist (off) on... *He* ***foisted off*** *a few cases of inferior scotch* ***on*** *a too eager customer.* □ *I'm sorry all this has been* ***foisted on*** *you.* EHOW

make up a four (at bridge) ... *Ask old Mr Smith if he'd mind* ***making up a four.***

and compare with those examples these possible variants:

He ***foisted*** *a few cases of inferior scotch* ***on*** *a too eager customer.*

I'm sorry all this has been ***foisted off on*** *you.*
Ask old Mr Smith if he'd mind ***making up a four at bridge.***

1.2.3 A reflexive pronoun or phrase is sometimes placed within parentheses in the headphrase:

adjust (oneself) to **work (one's way) through**

The reflexive item can be omitted from these expressions under the conditions outlined above (⇨ 1.2.1 and 1.2.2). Thus one meets:

I don't think I shall ever ***adjust to*** *this hot climate.*
He was ***working through*** *an enormous steak.*

as well as:

I don't think I shall ever ***adjust myself to*** *this hot climate.*
He was ***working his way through*** *an enormous steak.*

A different case is represented by the headphrases:

burn (oneself) out **content (oneself) with**

The reflexive pronoun may not be deleted from these expressions in *active* sentences. One may not say:

If you don't give up this evening work, you'll* ***burn out**.* (cf ... *you'll* ***burn yourself out****.*)

It is however deleted in *passive* sentences. One says (in the active):

We can't go abroad this year so we'll have to ***content ourselves with*** *a family holiday in London.*

but in the passive:

We can't go abroad this year so we'll have to be ***contented with*** etc.

Note that in the appropriate entries (as here) this active/passive relationship is often clarified by means of examples.

1.2.4 In the headphrase

change over (from) (to)

two prepositions are put in separate sets of parentheses. Each preposition is related to the verb + particle in much the same way as **on** is related to **miss out** in **miss out (on)** (⇨ 1.2.1). Given a context such as this, for example:

My wife doesn't like the cooking arrangements. She wants to ***change over*** ...

we can predict as possible continuations:

... ***from*** *gas.* or: ... ***to*** *electricity.*

We could, however, also continue by using *both* prepositions:

... ***from*** *gas* ***to*** *electricity.*

This is what is indicated by placing **from** and **to** in separate sets of parentheses. It will be clear that in the cases of:

She wants to ***change over*** .
She wants to ***change over from*** *gas.*
She wants to ***change over to*** *electricity.*
She wants to ***change over from*** *gas* ***to*** *electricity.*

the meaning of **change over** (verb + particle) is unaffected in the context of 'cooking arrangements'.

1.3 In some headphrases parentheses and the oblique are used together. In all such cases, the words etc marked as alternatives by the oblique are *enclosed* by the parentheses:

congratulate (on/upon)
make a song and dance (about/over)
tackle (about/on/over)

The use of *parentheses* here indicates that everything enclosed by them may be omitted and that, if this is done, the meaning of the rest of the expression is unaffected (⇨ 1.2). The oblique is used to mark off words – in these examples prepositions with the same meaning (⇨ 1.1.2) – from which a choice can be made.

In the case of **tackle (about/on/over)** for instance, the conventions can be taken to mean that the following variations on a single sentence are all acceptable, and all related in meaning:

'He's always playing his radio at full blast: it's time we ***tackled*** *him'*
... *we* ***tackled*** *him* ***about*** *it.'*
... *we* ***tackled*** *him* ***on*** *it.'*
... *we* ***tackled*** *him* ***over*** *it.'*

1.4 In certain complex expressions in which a noun is a fixed element, the noun *must* be modified by one from a small selection of adjectives. When the number of alternative adjectives is limited to two or three, they can be shown in the headphrase and marked off by the oblique (as explained above, 1.1.3):

have a soft/weak spot for **make effective/good use of**

Sometimes, however, the list of adjectives from which a choice must be made is more extensive:

make a good, an excellent, a satisfactory, a poor, a dreadful job of
take the easy, simplest, quickest, coward's way out/out of

To put so much information in the headphrases would invite confusion. In particular, the dictionary user might lose sight of the *fixed* elements in each expression – **make a** ... **job of** and **take the** ... **way out/out of** respectively. In such cases one commonly occurring adjective (+**etc**) is included in the headphrase:

make a good etc job of **take the easy etc way out/out of**

and this adjective is repeated, and other possible choices indicated, in the body of the entry:

adj: good, excellent, satisfactory, poor, dreadful.
adj: ⚠easy, simplest, quickest, coward's.

The use of the ⚠ in the second entry indicates that the number of options, while more than three, is still *limited* (though it may not be exhausted by the words listed). The absence of this sign from the entry **make a good etc job of** indicates a more open range of choice (⇨ also *Collocations*, 6.5). The same conventions are used when a *particle* must be modified by one of a small set of adverbs of degree:

be well etc off (for) .. **m:** ⚠ (very, fairly) well, comfortably, badly.

(where **m** = adverbial modifier. For a detailed treatment of words listed after **adj, m** etc in dictionary entries, ⇨ *Collocations*, 6.2.)

1.5 Such verbs as **puff**, **steam**, **stump** and **zoom** combine freely with a number of particles and prepositions of *direction* (e g **across**, **along**, **back**) to form such expressions as **puff across** (the bridge), **puff along** (the track), **steam into** (Newcastle), **steam through** (the tunnel) etc. Characteristically, these combinations are equivalent in meaning to a verb of *motion* + a particle of *direction* + an adverbial phrase of *manner*. Thus

puff across = move across sending out smoke etc and/or panting noisily.

These special features of combination and meaning are dealt with in the dictionary, though no attempt is made to list *in separate entries* all the possible combinations of particles with any *one* verb. This would entail wasteful duplication, since one headphrase for each verb can indicate an appropriate choice of particles, and one general definition can embrace the particular meanings:

stump across, along, away etc ... move across etc heavily (and often in anger or irritation).

zoom across, along, away etc ... move across etc swiftly, with engine(s) roaring.

In the form of headphrase used here, **across, along, away etc** refer to the following list of directional particles and prepositions which, because of their frequency, the user can with reasonable confidence combine with the verbs in question. The exclusion of one item from the list does not, of course, imply that it cannot combine with one or several of the verbs (for a full list, ⇨ *Alphabetical list of prepositions and particles*, p. lxxx):

across, along, away, back, behind, by, down, from, in, into, off, on, onto, out, out of, over, past, through, to, towards, under, up.

The user will note, finally, that when **zoom** etc is part of a verb + particle expression with a more specialized, and, in some cases technical sense, this expression is dealt with in an entry of its own:

zoom out ... (cinema, TV) by adjusting the 'zoom' lens on a camera, move gradually from a close-up to a longer shot.

1.6 Expressions which have the same form but quite different meanings are given separate, *numbered*, headphrases:

be over[1] ... be ended, be finished. ... *work* **was over** *for the weekend.*

be over[2] ... remain, be left. ... *A small piece of flannel* **was over** *when the tailor had finished cutting out my suit.*

deal in[1] ... include sb in a game by dealing him a hand of cards ... *Peter arrived late for our bridge party, but ... we* **dealt** *him* **in**.

deal in[2] ... handle, do business in. ... *Most foreign trading companies ...* **deal in** *rubber, cocoa and vegetable oils.*

Expressions with the same form whose meanings are related, the one being literal and the other figurative, are usually given separate numbered headphrases, and invariably so when their grammatical patterns, and/or transforms, are different:

see through[1] [A2 nom pass] (be able to) see from one side to the other of sth (because it is transparent). ...

see through[2] [A2] (informal) understand the true nature of sb beneath a pleasant, deceptive appearance. ...

Expressions with the same form and related meanings are usually assigned to different entries when they are used in different *styles* or *registers* of English:

burn out[1] [A1 B1i pass adj](technical) (cause to) damage and stop working (through electrical burning). ...
burn out[2] [A1](space technology) use up its fuel. ...
burn out[3] [B1i pass adj] gut, reduce to a shell by fire. ...

Where there is a lengthy series of numbered entries, the headphrases are, as far as possible, arranged in an order which reflects differences and similarities of meaning:

blow up[1] ... (informal) lose one's temper. ...
blow up[2] ... (informal) lose one's temper with, reprimand severely. ...
blow up[3] ... arise, work towards a crescendo or crisis. **S:** storm, gale; political storm, crisis. ...
blow up[4] ... (cause to) explode or smash to pieces. ...
blow up[5] ... inflate, pump air or gas into. ...
blow up[6] ... (photography) make bigger, enlarge. ...
blow up[7] ... (informal) inflate, exaggerate. ... **O:** reputation, achievements; story, affair. ...

Order of headphrases

2 The headphrases in this dictionary are *not* arranged in strict alphabetical sequence. Instead, principles of arrangement are followed which take account first of the *verb*, then of the *particle(s)* or *preposition(s)*, and only subsequently of *nouns, adjectives* etc. The most important reason for favouring this procedure is that it tends to draw together many headphrases which are related in grammatical structure and sense, without at the same time presenting too many problems for the user who wishes simply to look up individual entries. One instance of a series of headphrases which is ordered relative to other series by the verb and preposition, and afterwards ordered internally by particular nouns, is as follows:

take care (of)
take charge (of)
take control (of)
take heed (of)
take one's leave (of)

It happens that these headphrases are related in meaning, as all can be given the generalized definition 'change one's role or attitude towards sb or sth'. Moreover, the preposition **of** is optional in each case. This arrangement of the headphrases has the merit of leading the user quickly and easily from one entry that he may wish to consult at a particular time to a number of other related entries. It is also in keeping with a more general aim – that the design of the dictionary, as well as favouring ease of reference, should promote active language use. That aim would not be served if a series such as the one shown were interrupted by 'extraneous' items such as the following, as a strictly alphabetical approach would require:

take down[1,2,3]
take down a peg (or two)
take (for)

At the same time, the need to ensure quick access to individual entries has not been overlooked. Those headphrases which consist of the verb + particle (or verb + preposition) alone, and which make up the bulk of the total, pose few problems in this respect. As regards the more complex entries, the user will find that if he spends a little time in studying the following notes, he should have little difficulty in locating headphrases with an included noun, adjective or adverb. In addition, special help has been provided for users who wish to look up an expression containing a noun, adjective etc and who are uncertain about the verb (or preposition) which would enable them to locate the appropriate headphrase in the usual way. This help takes the form of an *Index of nouns etc used in headphrases and collocations* and is the first of two indexes at the end of the dictionary.

2.1 The alphabetical order of *verbs* takes precedence over that of all other classes of word in determining the sequence of headphrases:

carve up	**pick up with**	**rave-up**
cash in (on)	**picture to oneself**	**raze to the ground**
cast about for	**piece out**	**reach down**

This rule is followed even when a noun, adverb etc comes *before* the verb in a headphrase:

the sky cloud over
club together

2.2 The sequence of headphrases is *next* decided by the alphabetical order of the *particle* or *preposition*:

hand in	**talk at**	**work towards**
hand off	**talk back**	**work under**
hand on	**talk down**	**work up**

2.2.1 The location of headphrases consisting of a 'regular' past participle form of the verb (plus a particle or preposition) depends first on the alphabetical order of the verb:

enroll in	**indulge in**
ensconced in	**infatuated (with)**
enshrined in	**infect with**

and afterwards on that of the particle or preposition:

deceived in	**used to**
deceive into	**use up**

When the verbs and particles in two headphrases are the same, except that the verb form in one is the (regular) past participle, the headphrase with past participle is placed *second*:

button up	**tuck away**[2]	**wash up**[2]
buttoned up	**tucked away**	**washed up**

'Irregular' past participles are given a strict alphabetical location:

cater to	**fear for**
caught up in[1]	**fed up (with)**
caught up in[2]	**feed back (into/to)**[1]

For purposes of alphabetical arrangement, headphrases consisting of a 'nominalized' form, e g **come-hither**, **flashback**, **runabout**, are as a general rule treated as if they were 'normal' verb + particle combinations:

come from/of[2]	**flash at**	**rumour about/abroad**
come-hither	**flashback**	**runabout**
come home to	**flash into**	**run across**

Note, however, these sequences, where the 'nominalized' form *follows* an almost identical 'verbal' form:

burn up[3]	**drive in**	**push over**
burn-up	**drive-in**	**push-over**

2.2.2 When a headphrase contains a particle *and* a preposition, e g **live up to**, **move in (on)**, **buy oneself in/into** the *particle* determines its position before or after headphrases containing the same verb and a *single* particle (or preposition):

live it up	**move in**	**buy in**
live up to	**move in (on)**	**buy oneself in/into**
live with[1]	**move into**	**buy off**

Similarly, when a headphrase contains *two prepositions*, the alphabetical order of the *first* preposition decides whether the headphrase follows or precedes one containing the same verb and *one* preposition:

act for	**convert (from) (to)**	**work up (into)**
act on/upon[1]	**convert (into)**	**work up (into/to)**

When a number of headphrases contain a particle and a preposition, and the particle and the verb are the same in each case, sequencing is determined by the alphabetical order of the *prepositions*:

build up (from)	**line up (against)**	**let in for**
build (up) into	**line up alongside/with**	**let in/into**
build up to[1]	**line up behind**	**let in on**

As these examples show, the use of parentheses or the oblique in a headphrase does not affect the ordering of headphrases when they are *in any case* different by virtue of the particles etc which they contain. When two headphrases have the *same* form apart from parentheses, the headphrase with parentheses precedes:

agree (with)	**bring round (to)**[2]
agree with	**bring round to**

2.3 The alphabetical order of noun(s), adjective(s) etc is taken into account *after* the headphrases have been placed in sequence according to the verb and particle/preposition:

be out of[4]	**do with**	**keep in**[6]
be out of action	**do business with**	**keep in check**[1]

Several headphrases containing the *same* verb and particle/preposition but *different* nouns etc are placed in sequence according to the alphabetical order of the nouns:

bring into focus	**take care of**
bring into force	**take charge of**
bring into play	**take control of**

When establishing the order of headphrases according to their nouns, the indefinite and definite articles and the possessive adjectives (**one's**, **sb's**, **his**) are ignored:

bring into force	**get into the act**
bring into the open	**get into sb's black books**
bring into play	**get into deep water**

However, when the article or possessive helps to distinguish two headphrases which are otherwise the same, the article etc determines their order:

go out of one's mind	**make (a) peace (with)**
go out of sb's mind	**make one's peace with**

None of the parts of speech, noun, adjective, adverb etc is given priority over the others when establishing the order of entries. Alphabetical order *alone* governs the location of a headphrase containing (say) a noun before or after one containing an adverb. When a headphrase contains *two* nouns (or an adjective + noun etc) the *first* of these words decides the location of the headphrase:

	order determined by:
be at attention	**attention** (noun)
be at a dead end	**dead** (adjective)
be at an end	**end** (noun)
be at a halt/standstill	**halt** (noun)
be hard at it/work	**hard** (adverb)
be at it	**it** (pronoun)
be at pains to do sth	**pains** (noun)
what be at	**what** (interrog pronoun)

The relative positions in a headphrase of the noun etc and the preposition/particle do not affect the alphabetical placement of that headphrase. Neither does the use of parentheses (when the headphrases are in other respects different):

take at (his/its) face value
take a look (at)
take offence (at)
take umbrage (at)

2.3.1 Except for the articles and possessives, 'grammatical' words are given the same weight as 'lexical' words in determining the order of headphrases. The grammatical classes most frequently met with are *negative adverbs* and *indefinite adjectives*, especially **never**, **not**; **no** and *indefinite* and *personal pronouns*, especially **anything**, **nothing**, **something**; **it**, **me**, **us**, **you**. Note the order of headphrases in:

have a flair/gift for
have no fears/terrors for

(where **flair** and **no** decide the order)

lay one's hands on[3]
never/not lay a finger on

(where **hands** and **never** decide the order)

make a note (of)
make nothing of
make a nuisance of

(where **note**, **nothing** and **nuisance** decide the order).

2.3.2 Since particles or prepositions take precedence over nouns, pronouns etc in determining overall arrangements, such headphrases as

be in fashion/vogue
be in focus
be in force

form part of a series which is placed *above*

be in at the finish/kill

since **in** precedes **in at**. In the same way, the headphrases

be in charge (of)
be in control (of)

are placed earlier in the general arrangement than

be in accord/harmony/tune (with)
be in collision (with)
be in collusion (with)

because **in (of)** precedes **in (with)**.

Grammatical codes and tables

3 Verbs and particles/prepositions are elements in the structure of sentences. They are preceded, interrupted and followed by other elements – Subject, Direct Object, prepositional object, and so on – which may not themselves form part of the idiomatic expression. As we show with reference to the particle/preposition contrast itself (⇨ *General Introduction*, 0.1, and 3.1.1) important differences of *function* cannot be made clear except by placing an expression in the sentence pattern (or patterns) in which it regularly occurs. Again, we cannot indicate the 'transformational' possibilities of such items as **bring up** (children), **try out** (a machine), **fill in** (an application) etc except by reference to this wider context. It is for these reasons that each item recorded in the dictionary is described in terms of the sentence pattern (or patterns) in which it normally appears.

These patterns (and their transformations) are not specified in detail, or named in full, in the entries themselves. Instead, we make use of a small set of symbols and abbreviations which for each entry make up a *grammatical code*. The code refers the user to a full treatment in tabular form (to be found below, 3.4) of the appropriate pattern or patterns. The guidance provided by the codes is of two kinds. A letter/number code, which generally comes first, indicates the simple, active sentence pattern, or patterns, to which the headphrase conforms:

cave in[1] [A1 ...] **blow up**[6] [B1i ...]

One or more abbreviations, generally given after the letter/number code, indicate which of the structural transformations associated with the basic patterns can be applied to that particular headphrase:

cave in[1] [A1 nom] **blow up**[6] [B1i nom pass adj]

The basic patterns and their transformations are fully illustrated in the tabular treatment. The tables are largely self-explanatory and reference can quickly be made to them when the dictionary is being consulted, but the user may find these preliminary notes helpful, as they set out the general principles underlying the scheme.

Basic patterns

3.1 With very few exceptions, the items treated in the dictionary can be shown to function in one or more of six simple, active sentence patterns. These 'basic' patterns can be divided into two groups according to *transitivity* (i e according to whether or not they contain a Direct Object). Intransitive sentences are labelled [A] and transitive sentences [B]. Within each of [A] and [B] the sentence patterns are further subdivided into [1], [2] and [3] according to whether they contain a particle, a preposition, or a particle *and* a preposition. The whole system of basic patterns can be represented schematically, and illustrated, as follows:

	Intransitive	Transitive
Particle	[A1]	[B1]
Preposition	[A2]	[B2]
Particle + Preposition	[A3]	[B3]

[A1] *The electricity supply* ***went off***.
[A2] *We were* ***banking on*** *a change of heart.*
[A3] *The committee* ***fell back on*** *an earlier plan.*
[B1] *Fred* ***tipped*** *the police* ***off***.
[B2] *Peter* ***foists*** *all his problems* ***on*** *his unfortunate friends.*
[B3] *You can* ***put*** *the shortage* ***down to*** *bad planning.*
([B1] sentences can be further subclassified, as will be shown, but these finer distinctions do not affect the others made in the scheme.)

3.1.1 This simple scheme of sentence patterns embodies the contrast between 'particles' (sometimes called adverbial particles) and 'prepositions'. The terms particle and preposition are used throughout the dictionary to reflect the ways in which words such as **away**, **back**, **off**, **on**, **with** etc are used in sentences (i e their syntactic functions). In other words 'particle' and 'preposition' refer to use and not to form. We can see that in the sentences

[A1] *The electricity* ***went off***.
[B1] *Fred* ***tipped*** *the police* ***off***/*Fred* ***tipped*** *them* ***off***.

the word **off** does not introduce a noun phrase, noun or pronoun. To this extent it functions independently – as a *particle*. We can contrast

[A2] *John* ***went off*** *his food.*
[B2] *The instructor* ***put*** *me* ***off*** *driving.*

where **off** does introduce a noun phrase or noun – 'his food' and 'driving' respectively. In these sentences, **off** functions, and is described, as a *preposition* (the noun phrases themselves are used, and referred to, as prepositional *objects*). Or consider again the sentences

[A3] *The committee* ***fell back on*** *an earlier plan.*
[B3] *You can* ***put*** *the shortage* ***down to*** *bad planning.*

In the first of these, **back** has the function of a particle (no dependent noun phrase), while **on** has that of a preposition (it introduces the phrase 'an earlier plan'). In the same way, **down** is used as a particle in the second example, and **to** as a preposition.

This whole question is complicated for the student by the fact that certain words (**on**, **off**, **up**, for example) are at times used as particles and at others as prepositions. Other words function only as particles (**away**, **back** etc) while others again are used only as prepositions (**into**, **with** etc). The fact that some words may have a *double* function, however, does not affect the way they are described in the dictionary. The user may find it helpful to remember that the way a word such as **off** or **on** is labelled in a particular context depends entirely on its use *in that context*, and not on its potentiality of use.

3.1.2 When, as frequently happens, a headphrase functions in two or more basic patterns (e g in a transitive as well as an intransitive one) these differences of use are indicated in the grammatical code, and often illustrated as well:

turn against [A2 B2 pass] (cause to) oppose, be hostile to. ... *He had the distinct impression that everyone was* ***turning against*** *him.* □ *'What* ***turned*** *her* ***against*** *me, do you think? The child, I suppose, horrid little creature.'* DC

When a grammatical code refers to *four* basic patterns, it is often the case that the headphrase contains an optional preposition (⇨ *The headphrase*, 1.2), and that the headphrase form *without* the preposition functions in two of the patterns, while the form *with* the preposition functions in the other two. In such complex entries, each illustration is preceded by the appropriate code (or codes):

keep away (from) [A1 A3 B1ii ... B3 ...] ... not go near; prevent from going near, touching, using etc ... □ [B1 B3] *It's the job of the police to* ***keep*** *the spectators* ***away*** *(****from*** *the players).* □ [B3] *Children should be* ***kept away from*** *the river.* □ [A1 A3] *The spectators have to* ***keep away*** *(****from*** *the players).*

3.1.3 The headphrases of a few entries do not conform exactly to *any* of the basic patterns. Examples of such headphrases are:

bring to grips with **fall in love (with)**

If these headphrases did not contain the preposition **with** they would fit the [B2] and [A2] patterns respectively; as it is, they do not correspond directly with *any* of the six patterns. Nevertheless, the principle is followed of describing as [A2], [A3], [B2] or [B3] all headphrases which would exactly match those patterns if it were not for an additional preposition. To do otherwise would have meant greatly complicating the scheme of basic patterns. The codes allocated to the two example headphrases are therefore:

bring to grips with [B2 ...] **fall in love (with)** [A2 ...]

Transforms

3.2 A good deal of grammatical information about headphrases can be stated quite economically if some patterns are regarded as being 'transformationally' related to others. But what precisely is meant by grammatical transformation? In a sentence such as

The prices ***came down****.*

the order of words can be rearranged to give

Down came *the prices.*

This structural rearrangement is a 'transformation' of the original sentence (for convenience we can refer to the *result* of the rearrangement as a 'transform'). Transformations may involve not simply a change of word order but also the corresponding replacement of one word (or phrase) by another. Compare the last sentence with:

Down *they* ***came****.*

They may also include corresponding changes in the *form* of a word or phrase, as when an active sentence is transformed into a passive one. Compare:

The travel agent ***messed up*** *our bookings completely.*

Our bookings were ***messed up*** *completely (by the travel agent).*

(where **messed** → **were messed**). Transformation, then, is a matter of structural change, and the changes may be of various kinds.

Sentences which are transformationally related are often closely related in *meaning* also. As a general rule the transforms which are referred to and illustrated in the dictionary are close in meaning to the sentences from which they derive. Again, it is usual to regard some sentences as more 'basic' or fundamental than others for purposes of describing transformations. As has already been suggested when introducing the simple, active patterns referred to as [A1], [A2] etc, this is the procedure which we adopt here. It should perhaps be added that the decision to treat some kinds of sentence pattern as being derived from others has been made for reasons of descriptive convenience. It does not imply a commitment to the view that some patterns are more abstract, or 'deeper' than others, nor does it require a technical understanding of the rules of a transformational grammar.

3.2.1 Whether or not a particular transformation can be applied to the sentence pattern of any given headphrase is shown by including the appropriate abbreviation in the code for that entry. The code in the entry for

make room for [B2 pass ...]

shows, for example, that a *passive* sentence can be derived from an *active* sentence in which that headphrase appears. Compare:

We will have to ***make*** *more* ***room*** *on the programme* ***for*** *these performers.*
More ***room*** *will have to be* ***made*** *on the programme* ***for*** *these performers.*

Information about the transformational *restrictions* of certain 'idiomatic' expressions is of special importance to the foreign user of the dictionary, who might without such guidance modify the structure of sentences in ways regarded by the native speaker as abnormal or unacceptable. In any given entry, this guidance of course takes the form of omitting from the grammatical code any reference to a transformation which is *not* applied to that entry.

3.2.2 A particularly difficult transform to handle, and to explain by means of a table alone, is that referred to in the dictionary as the 'nominalized form' (abbreviated in the notes which accompany the tables to 'nom form'). Put in general terms, a nominalized form is a noun derived from a verb + particle combination – **break-in**, **flypast**, **upkeep**, **outpouring** – or from a combination of verb + preposition – **glance-through**, **skim-through**. As the examples show, however, nouns which originate as verb + particle expressions may have quite different internal patterns (cf **flypast**, **upkeep**, **outpouring**): there is a variety of nominalized *forms*, rather than a single *form*. Secondly, nouns which are composed of the same elements occurring in the same order may be hyphenated or not (cf **break-in**, **flypast**). Thirdly, two nouns which are formed on the same model (and are both hyphenated) may function in different sentence patterns. While a sentence such as

She gave the place a thorough ***clean-out****.*

is normal, the sentence

He gave the arrangements a thorough* ***mess-up**.*

is decidedly abnormal. We deal with these questions in turn below, beginning with a simple classification of nominalized forms on the basis of differences in their internal structure. At this stage we disregard differences of spelling and stress.

We start with the class represented by **break-in**, **flypast**, **holdup**, **mess-up** etc. This is the class most frequently recorded in the dictionary (as can quickly be seen by referring to the *Index of nominalized forms* at the end of the dictionary). Most members of the class are derived from verb + particle combinations functioning in the [A1] and [B1] patterns and have the structure 'base form (of verb) + particle'. It should be noted that most nouns derived from combinations of verb + preposition (i e as used in the [A2] basic pattern) have a similar structure, thus: **glance-through**, **look-over**, **look-through**, and are treated as falling within the same major class. Whatever their source (i e as verb + particle or verb + preposition) all nouns of this type are pluralized in the same way: (two) **break-ins**, (several) **mess-ups** (a couple of quick) **flick-throughs** etc. Only nouns of this commonly occurring and highly productive class are identified in the appropriate grammatical codes as[... nom], though other types are illustrated, and listed in the *Index*.

A second category includes such examples as **downpour**, **offprint**, **outbreak**, **upkeep**, derived in all cases from verb + particle combinations and having the structure 'particle + base form'. The plural is formed in the same way as for the major class: (two successive) **downpours**, (three) **offprints** etc. A small number of nouns formed on this pattern are paired with 'standard' forms originating in the same verb and particle (cf **print-off/offprint**; **turndown/downturn**).

A third type, of which the dictionary records very few examples, is represented by **outpouring** and **upbringing**. Both are derived from verb + particle combinations and have the pattern 'particle + *-ing* form'. Their plurals parallel those of the other classes: **outpourings**, **upbringings**.

It is possible to give firm guidance on how nouns in the two *minor* categories are regularly written or printed. British and American practice is to write them fully joined, as in **downturn**, **offprint**; **outpouring**, **upbringing**, and they appear in that form in the dictionary. As regards the major class, some uncertainty is inevitable in making recommendations to users. The difficulty arises from the fact that many of the nouns exist in two written forms (fully linked and hyphenated) in British English, and individual users and printing houses differ in the conventions that they favour. On the whole, we have tended to prefer the hyphenated forms in the illustrations we provide ourselves, though where citations are used we record the authors' own usage (and in some cases where this is at variance with our own, add an explanatory note: ⇨ **black out**[2,4]).

Nominalized forms of all three types carry principal stress on the *first* element. In the major class the placement of stress does not vary with the choice of the solid as distinct from the hyphenated form:

`downpour, `offprint, `upkeep
`outpouring, `upbringing
`break-in, `flypast, `glance-through

This general rule is departed from only in cases such as the following, where an *unlinked* form exists side by side with, and may sometimes be preferred to, a *hyphenated* one:

a quick **look `round** (cf a quick **`look-round**)
a quick **thumb `through** (cf a quick **`thumb-through**)

Such unlinked alternatives, in which principal stress falls on the final element (particle/preposition) are recorded in the *Index* and often illustrated in the entries themselves.

Finally, we can consider the various sentence (and other) patterns in which nouns derived from (finite) verb + particle etc are used. Many nominalized forms have a diversity of syntactic functions. The form **make-up** (in one of its senses) can be used attributively – as in **make-up** box, **make-up** girl – or as direct object – You're using too much **make-up** – or as Subject – Your **make-up**'s running. In certain cases, the noun may be associated with a particular sentence pattern which is a paraphrase of the 'basic' pattern in which the corresponding finite verb + particle operates. Compare, for example:

The pilot **took off** *smoothly / The pilot made a smooth* **take-off**.

Building workers **walked out** */ Building workers staged a* **walk-out**.

Each paraphrase of this kind may be regarded as a transform of the whole of the corresponding 'basic' sentence. Where a particular type of paraphrase occurs sufficiently often in relation to a basic pattern we explain and illustrate it in the form of a table (⇨ 3.4, [A1 nom], [B1i nom]).

It should be made clear however that the 'basic' sentences in which individual verb + particle combinations occur are not all paraphrased in the same way. We shall not find

* *Violence made/staged a sudden* **flare-up**.

to parallel the sentence

The pilot made a smooth **take-off**.

We have not attempted to deal with these complexities through the grammatical code (which indicates simply whether the noun itself – **take-off**, **flare-up** – occurs). As far as space allows, however, the characteristic syntactic uses of particular nouns are displayed in the illustrations.

3.2.3 In practice it is difficult to draw a sharp line between *passive* sentences and those in which a participial adjective follows a 'copula' or 'linking verb'. While a sentence such as:

John is **worn out** *by an over-demanding boss.*

clearly falls into the first category and:

John seems utterly **worn out**.

into the second, there are various intermediate possibilities. A sentence in which there is no explicit reference to a human agent such as:

John is being progressively **worn out**.

may none the less indicate a process, or activity, rather than a state, while a sentence which appears to indicate John's condition may contain a reference to its cause (or causer):

John seems thoroughly **worn out** *by all the demands being made of him.*

It is the difficulty of separating sentences which are partially passive from those which are fully so, and also the need to keep the grammatical indications in entries simple and manageable for the user, which have prompted us to use the *one* abbreviation [... pass] to refer to a range of different (though related) 'passive' constructions. This variety is reflected in the following examples from the dictionary. It will be noted that only the first contains an agentive phrase ('by Ernest Bevin') as well as indicating a process. The third is ambiguous. Is it an instruction to someone to ensure (i) that he seals the parcel up (action), or (ii) that it is already sealed up (state)?

[B2 pass] *This offer was* **seized** *by Ernest Bevin* **with both hands**.

[A2 pass] *His personal papers have all been* **searched through**.

[B1i pass] *Make sure the parcel of examination scripts is properly* **sealed up**.

3.3 Transformational anomalies

There are several nominalized forms, participial adjectives etc in everyday use which are 'anomalous' in the sense that there are no corresponding verb + particle expressions from which they can be derived in the usual way. While we can say, for example

John is suffering from a bad ***hangover*** *this morning*
(or: *John is badly* ***hung over*** *this morning*).

there is no corresponding active sentence

Drinking all those double whiskies* ***hung* *John* ***over*** *badly this morning.*

to which that nominalized form, and that passive construction, are transformationally related. In the same way, there is no acceptable sentence of the form

Mary has been* ***running* *John* ***around****.*

of which the commonly occurring pattern

Mary has been giving John the ***run-around*** (= making life difficult for him).

can be said to be a paraphrase.

A certain number of anomalous transforms arise indirectly as specialized extensions of the meaning of an existing (and 'regular') transform. The item **wash-out** ('failure', 'disappointment') is a case in point, as its meaning is recognizably related to that of a noun with the same spoken and written form (**wash-out**, in the sense 'an end to play, brought about by rain, etc'). The latter is however derived from a finite verb + particle, as is shown in this example:

Heavy rain completely ***washed out*** *the game* (or: *made the game a complete* ***wash-out***).

In all such cases the grammatical code for the 'anomalous' entry is made to reflect its own special character and the connection with the 'regular' entry:

wash out[2] [B1i nom ...] bring play to an end ...
wash-out [nom (B1)] ... failure; disappointment.

Anomalous transforms which are not closely related in meaning and form to other entries are given codes which (i) identify the transform itself (as 'nom', 'pass' etc) (ii) indicate the usual functions of its verb etc (as intransitive etc):

come-back[1] [nom (A1)]
hangover/hung over [nom pass (B1)]

3.4 Tables of patterns

The order in which the tables of basic patterns and transforms are set out below is as follows:

[A1] intransitive pattern with a particle; [A1 nom]; [A1 emph].

[A2] intransitive pattern with a preposition; [A2 nom] (*explanatory note only*); [A2 pass]; [A2 pass(o)] (*explanatory note only*); [A2 adj]; [A2 emph]; [A2 rel].

[A3] intransitive pattern with a particle and preposition; [A3 pass]; [A3 adj]; [A3 emph]; [A3 rel].

[B1i] transitive pattern with a particle (i) (*Tables A and B*); [B1i nom]; [B1i pass]; [B1i adj].

[B1ii] transitive pattern with a particle (ii); [B1ii nom] (*explanatory note only*); [B1ii pass].

[B1iii] transitive pattern with a particle (iii); [B1iii nom] (*explanatory note only*); [B1iii pass].

[B2] transitive pattern with a preposition; [B2 pass]:[B2 pass(o)];[B2 emph]; [B2 rel].

[B3] transitive pattern with a particle and preposition; [B3 pass]; [B3 emph]; [B3 rel].

The tables of basic patterns and transforms have been arranged in the same order as the symbols and abbreviations which refer to them in the grammatical codes. The arrangement indicated above can be compared with codes for the following entries:

compensate (for) [A2 pass emph rel B2 pass emph rel]
fade out [A1 nom B1i pass adj]
welcome in/into [B1i pass B2 pass]

When referring to the various tables set out below, the user will notice that the examples appear in the same typographical form as in the entries themselves, with the headphrase picked out in each example sentence in ***bold italic***. He should note especially that when an example illustrates a 'complex' headphrase such as **get off to a good start**, where the adjective and the noun are integral parts of an idiomatic whole, the full headphrase is printed in bold italic: *The match* ***got off to a good start***.

[A1] intransitive pattern with a particle

	subject		verb phrase	particle	(adv phrase etc)
			verb		
1	*A gang of thieves*		***broke***	***in***	*last night.*
2	*A squadron of jet fighters*		***flew***	***past.***	
3	*Laurence Olivier*		***makes***	***up***	*for the part of Othello.*
4	*Students*	*are*	***sitting***	***in***	*at the university.*
5	*The module*		***splashed***	***down***	*perfectly.*
6	*The pilot*		***took***	***off***	*smoothly.*
7	*Moore*		***throws***	***in***	*near the half-way line.*
8	*The runners*	*are*	***warming***	***up***	*quickly before the race.*
9	*Building workers*		***walked***	***out***	*during the morning.*
10	*The snow*		***came***	***down***	*thick and fast.*
11	*The electricity supply*		***went***	***off.***	
12	*The sun*		***went***	***in.***	
13	*The prices*		***came***	***down.***	
14	***The balloon***		***went***	***up***	*in 1944 with the invasion of Europe.*

Notes

(a) There is a general relationship of intransitive to transitive between this pattern and [B1]. This is borne out by the particular correspondences of many items, e g:

[A1] *Moore* ***throws in*** *near the half-way line.*
[B1ii] *Moore* ***throws the ball in*** *near the half-way line.*

(b) An adverb is not normally inserted between the verb and particle. But note:

11 *The electricity supply* ***went*** *straight* ***off*** *(when the cable was cut).*
13 *The prices* ***came*** *right* ***down*** *(when people started buying elsewhere).*

[A1 nom] nominalized form of verb + particle

	subject	do/make	object	(adv phrase etc)
1	*A gang of thieves*	*did*	***a break-in***	*last night.*
2	*A squadron of jet fighters*	*did/staged*	***a fly-past.***	
3	*Laurence Olivier*	*does*	***his make-up***	*for the part of Othello.*
4	*Students*	*are staging*	***a sit-in***	*at the university.*
5	*The module*	*made*	***a perfect splash-down.***	
6	*The pilot*	*made*	***a smooth take-off.***	
7	*Moore*	*takes*	***a throw-in***	*near the half-way line.*
8	*The runners*	*are having*	***a quick warm-up***	*before the game.*
9	*Building workers*	*staged*	***a walk-out***	*during the morning.*

Notes

(a) Various 'nominalized' forms are derived from verb + particle expressions as used in the [A1] basic pattern. The form referred to as [A1 nom] in the code consists of the base form of the verb plus the particle, which in writing may be hyphenated, thus: **break-in**, **make-up**, **sit-in**, **take-off**, or fully linked, thus: **flypast**, **splashdown**. The nouns are pronounced with principal stress on the verbal element:

`break-in, `make-up, `flypast, `splashdown

(b) Nominalized forms commonly function in sentence types which stand in a paraphrase relationship to the basic [A1] pattern. In one such sentence type, the nom form occurs as direct object, while the verb is one of a small set which includes, 'do', 'make' and 'take'.

(c) The nominalized form also functions as the complement of the verb 'to be' in a sentence introduced by 'there':

1 *There was a* ***break-in*** *last night.*
2 *There was a* ***flypast*** *(by jet fighters).*
4 *There is a* ***sit-in*** *(by students) at the university.*
7 *There is a* ***throw-in*** *near the half-way line.*
9 *There was a* ***walk-out*** *(by building workers) during the morning.*

[A1 emph] emphatic transform

	particle	verb phrase	subject	(adv phrase etc)
10	***Down***	**came**	*the snow*	*thick and fast.*
11	***Off***	**went**	*the electricity supply.*	
12	***In***	**went**	*the sun.*	
13	***Down***	**came**	*the prices.*	

Notes

(a) In this transform, the particle precedes the verb (or verb phrase) and the subject follows. Compare:

[A1] *The prices* ***came down.***
[A1 emph] ***Down came*** *the prices.*

(b) In some sentences in which the subject is a noun, or noun phrase, it may precede the verb:

10 ***Down*** *the snow* ***came.***
12 ***In*** *the sun* ***went.***

(c) When the subject of the 'emphatic' sentence is a *pronoun*, however, it *must* precede the verb:

***Down** they **came**.*

(d) The verbs and particles in sentences 1–9 of the [A1] table are not normally transposed:

?***Down splashed** the module perfectly.*
****Off took** the pilot smoothly.*

In fact, it is generally the case that when verb + particle expressions are idiomatic – as here – the emphatic transformation cannot be applied.

[A2] intransitive pattern with a preposition

	subject	verb phrase		prepositional phrase		(adv phrase etc)
			verb	prep	object	
1	*He*		***glanced***	***through***	*the article*	*quickly.*
2	*He*		***ran***	***through***	*the main points*	*briefly.*
3	*We*	*were*	***banking***	***on***	*a change of heart.*	
4	*You*	*can*	***cope***	***with***	*these few extra people*	*easily.*
5	*He*	*has*	***provided***	***for***	*his family*	*well.*
6	*We*	*'ve*	***talked***	***about***	*this topic*	*endlessly.*
7	*A gang of thieves*		***broke***	***into***	*Smith's warehouse*	*last night.*
8	*Olive*		***gets***	***at***	*her husband*	*frequently.*
9	*The Chancellor*	*would*	***go***	***into***	*these proposals*	*very carefully.*
10	*He*	*can*	***reckon***	***on***	*a safe political future*	*with some confidence.*
11	*I*		***got***	***through***	*the written papers*	*with special coaching.*
12	*The question of a reprieve*	*may*	***turn***	***on***	*the age of the accused.*	
13	*All our hopes*		***rested***	***upon***	*this venture.*	
14	*He*		***went***	***off***	*driving*	*altogether.*
15	*The company*	*has*	***fallen***	***into***	*disrepute*	*in recent years.*

Notes

(a) Some of the expressions appearing here have transitive equivalents (compare nos 11 and 14 in this table with nos 8 and 10, [B2] table).

(b) In many cases, an adverb or adverbial phrase can be inserted between the verb phrase and the prepositional phrase:

4 *You can **cope** easily **with** these few extra people.*
10 *He can **reckon** with some confidence **on** a safe political future.*

There may be restrictions when the expression is highly idiomatic, though not in every case. Compare:

8 **Olive **gets** frequently **at** her husband.*
9 *The Chancellor would **go** very carefully **into** these proposals.*

[A2 nom] nominalized form of verb + preposition

Notes

(a) Nouns referred to in grammatical codes as [A2 nom] have the internal pattern 'base form + preposition'. The dictionary does not record any case where they are written as fully joined. The hyphenated form corresponds to the stressing in speech of the verbal element:

`glance-through, `run-through

The user should note that hyphenated nouns derived from some verb + preposition items have a corresponding unlinked form, with principal stress falling on the final element. Compare:

a quick **`flick-through**/a quick **flick `through**
another **`skim-through**/another **skim `through**

(b) These 'nom' forms occur in a number of sentence patterns, some of which are paraphrases of the basic [A2] pattern:

1 *He gave the article a quick* ***glance-through****.*
2 *He did a brief* ***run-through*** *of the main points.*

[A2 pass] passive transform

	subject	verb phrase			(adv phrase etc)
			verb	prep	
1	*The article*	*was*	***glanced***	***through***	*quickly.*
2	*The main points*	*were*	***run***	***through***	*briefly.*
3	*A change of heart*	*was being*	***banked***	***on.***	
4	*These few extra people*	*can be*	***coped***	***with***	*easily.*
5	*His family*	*has been*	***provided***	***for***	*well.*
6	*This topic*	*has been*	***talked***	***about***	*endlessly.*
7	*Smith's warehouse*	*was*	***broken***	***into***	*last night.*
8	*Her husband*	*is*	***got***	***at***	*frequently.*
9	*These proposals*	*would be*	***gone***	***into***	*very carefully.*
10	*A safe political future*	*can be*	***reckoned***	***on***	*with some confidence.*

Notes

(a) The transform is derived from the active pattern by moving the prepositional object to initial position (with corresponding modification of the verb phrase). Compare:

[A2] *The Chancellor would* ***go into*** *these proposals very carefully.*
[A2 pass] *These proposals would be* ***gone into*** *very carefully.*

An 'agentive' prepositional phrase – 'by the Chancellor' – is an optional constituent:

[A2 pass] *These proposals would be* ***gone into*** *very carefully (by the Chancellor).*

(b) There is no simple one-to-one correspondence between idiomaticity and the application of this transform. Some sentences containing an idiom may be passivized:

8 *Olive* ***gets at*** *her husband frequently.*
Her husband is ***got at*** *frequently.*

but the same is true of many sentences containing less idiomatic items:

1 *He* ***glanced through*** *the article quickly.*
The article was ***glanced through*** *quickly.*

(c) Sentences in which the prepositional object is part of a complex idiom are generally not passivized:

15 ****Disrepute*** *has been* ***fallen into*** *in recent years.*

(d) Some expressions are recorded in the dictionary which function in *passive* sentences of the [A2] type though not in the corresponding *active* patterns. A curious and highly irregular group is made up of such items as **unaccounted for**, **uncalled for** and **unguessed at**. Certain of these combinations have a corresponding finite form without the negative prefix, thus **account for**, **call for**, **guess at**, and this can be used in both active and passive sentences. Compare:

These missiles are ***unaccounted for*** *by the authorities.*
These missiles are ***accounted for*** *by the authorities.*
The authorities have ***accounted for*** *these missiles.*

However, there is no such sentence as

The authorities have* ***unaccounted for* *these missiles.*

to correspond, as active, to the first of the set of three.

[A2 pass(o)] passive transform, with the object of a second preposition becoming the subject of the passive sentence

Notes

(a) A small number of idiomatic expressions, such as **get to the bottom of** or **get to grips with**, form their passives in a special way. It will be noted that the expressions contain a verb and *two* prepositions, and that the object of the first preposition is an integral part of the idiom.

(b) In this special passive transform, the object of the *second* preposition is transposed to front position in the sentence (where it functions as Subject of the passive construction):

[A2] *I'll* ***get to the bottom of*** *this whole business.*
[A2 pass(o)] *This whole business will be* ***got to the bottom of.***
[A2] *You* ***got to grips with*** *the basic trouble inside an hour.*
[A2 pass(o)] *The basic trouble was* ***got to grips with*** *inside an hour.*

[A2 adj] noun phrase with a participial adjective

	noun phrase			
	article	(adv)	participial adj	noun etc
1	*The*	*quickly*	***glanced-through***	*article ...*
3	*A*		***banked-on***	*change of heart ...*
4	*These*	*easily*	***coped-with***	*extra people ...*
5	*His*	*well*	***provided-for***	*family ...*
6	*This*	*endlessly*	***talked-about***	*topic ...*
7	*A (An)*	*(easily)*	***broken-into***	*warehouse ...*
9	*These*	*carefully*	***gone-into***	*proposals ...*

Notes

(a) Here, the noun phrase is drawn from the basic sentence as a whole and the participial adjective from the verb and preposition which function in that sentence. The grammatical link between the sentence and the phrase is most clearly shown by relating both to the passive:

[A2] *He* ***glanced through*** *the article quickly.*

[A2 pass] *The article was quickly* ***glanced through****.*

[A2 adj] *The quickly* ***glanced-through*** *article …*

(b) The connection of meaning between this transform and the passive is particularly close when the latter indicates a *state* (not a process). Compare:

His family seems well ***provided for****.*

His seems a well ***provided-for*** *family.*

[A2 emph] emphatic transform

	prepositional phrase		subject	verb phrase		(adv phrase etc)
	prep	object			verb	
4	***With***	*these few extra people*	*you*	*can*	***cope***	*easily.*
5	***For***	*his family*	*he*	*has*	***provided***	*well.*
10	***On***	*a safe political future*	*he*	*can*	***reckon***	*with some confidence.*
12	***On***	*the age of the accused*	*the question of a reprieve*	*may*	***turn.***	
13	***Upon***	*this venture*	*all our hopes*		***rested.***	

Notes

(a) This transform is the result of a simple change of order: the prepositional phrase of the basic pattern is transposed to initial position (cf [B2 emph]):

[A2] *He can* ***reckon on*** *a safe political future with some confidence.*

[A2 emph] ***On*** *a safe political future he can* ***reckon*** *with some confidence.*

(b) When the subject is a *pronoun* it must precede the verb phrase in this transform (cf [A1 emph]). The following sentence is unacceptable:

5 **For* *his family has* ***provided*** *he well.*

When the subject is a noun, or noun phrase, it will precede the verb phrase in some sentences (as could be the case in nos 4, 5 and 10 above) but may precede *or* follow in others (nos 12 and 13). Compare the following sentences with the corresponding ones in the table:

12 ***On*** *the age of the accused may* ***turn*** *the question of a reprieve.*

13 ***Upon*** *this venture* ***rested*** *all our hopes.*

The expressions in both these examples, it should be noted, represent formal usage.

(c) In some examples of this transform, a contrast is implied between the noun in the prepositional phrase and another unspecified noun. This noun may be made explicit, as follows:

5 ***For*** *his family he has* ***provided*** *well (but not* ***for*** *his employees).*

[A2 rel] relative transform

noun phrase		relative clause				
article	noun	prep	rel pron	subject	verb phrase	(ad phrase etc)
1 *The*	*article*	**through**	*which*	*he*	**glanced**	(*so*) *quickly…*
3 *A*	*change of heart*	**on**	*which*	*we*	*were* **banking . . .**	
4 *These*	*people*	**with**	*whom*	*you*	*can* **cope**	*easily …*
5 *The*	*family*	**for**	*which*	*he*	*has* **provided**	*well …*
6 *This*	*topic*	**about**	*which*	*we*	*'ve* **talked**	*endlessly …*
10 *A*	*safe political future*	**on**	*which*	*he*	*can* **reckon**	*with some confidence …*
12 *The*	*factor*	**on**	*which*	*the question of a reprieve*	**turns . . .**	
13 *This*	*venture*	**upon**	*which*	*all our hopes*	**rested . . .**	

Notes

(a) In this transform a noun (etc) originating in the *prepositional object* of the basic pattern is modified by a relative clause (part of which derives from the subject and verb phrase of the same basic pattern):

[A2] *We were* **banking on** *a change of heart.*
[A2 rel] *A change of heart* **on** *which we were* **banking***…*

(b) Sentences in which highly idiomatic expressions occur are not normally relativized as shown above. We shall not find:

8 **The husband* **at** *whom Olive* **gets** *regularly …*

(c) As the transform is associated with formal written usage, items which are normally in colloquial use tend not to occur in this transform:

7 ?*A warehouse* **into** *which a gang of thieves* **broke** *last night …*

A more common type of relative construction in everyday informal use is:

7 *A warehouse which a gang of thieves* **broke into** *…*

[A3] intransitive pattern with a particle and preposition

subject	verb phrase		particle	prepositional phrase		(adv phrase etc)
		verb		prep	object	
1 *The coaster*		**went**	**aground**	**on**	*a sandbank.*	
2 *He*		**scraped**	**along**	**on**	*a low salary.*	
3 *He*		**sent**	**away**	**for**	*a free fisherman's almanac.*	
4 *The office staff*	*are*	**looking**	**forward**	**to**	*his retirement*	*very much.*
5 *They*	*had*	**done**	**away**	**with**	*this piece of legislation*	*reluctantly.*
6 *She*	*is*	**facing**	**up**	**to**	*the responsibilities*	*badly.*
7 *We*		**put**	**up**	**with**	*these interruptions*	*cheerfully.*
8 *An outsider*	*had*	**come**	**in**	**on**	*our private arrangement.*	
9 *The family*		**came**	**up**	**against**	*fresh problems.*	
10 *The match*		**got**	**off**	**to**	*a good start.*	

Notes

(a) Here we must distinguish between the expressions **go aground (on)**, **scrape along (on)** and **send away (for)** (nos 1, 2, 3), from which the preposition (and its object) can be deleted, and the remaining expressions, where the preposition is a fixed element. Whether or not the preposition is removable tends to affect the transformational possibilities of the whole.

(b) This pattern is the intransitive equivalent of [B3], in terms of the correspondences of particular examples. Compare:

[A3] *The family* ***came up against*** *fresh problems.*
[B3] *The move* ***brought*** *the family* ***up against*** *fresh problems.*

(c) In some cases, an adverb or adverbial phrase may be inserted between the particle and the prepositional phrase. As the following examples show, it is possible to separate particle and preposition in this way even when the latter cannot be removed:

5 *They had* ***done away*** *reluctantly* ***with*** *this piece of legislation.*
7 *We* ***put up*** *cheerfully* ***with*** *these interruptions.*

(d) The verb may sometimes be divided from the particle, though generally only by the adverbs 'right' or 'straight':

5 *They had* ***done*** *right* ***away with*** *this piece of legislation.*
9 *The family* ***came*** *straight* ***up against*** *fresh problems.*

(Occasionally, we find such adverbs of degree as 'completely', 'totally', 'entirely' in the position of 'right' in no 5.)

[A3 pass] passive transform

subject	verb phrase		particle		(adv phrase etc)
		verb		prep	
3 *A free fisherman's almanac*	*was*	***sent***	***away***	***for.***	
4 *His retirement*	*is being*	***looked***	***forward***	***to***	*very much.*
5 *This piece of legislation*	*had been*	***done***	***away***	***with***	*reluctantly.*
6 *The responsibilities*	*are being*	***faced***	***up***	***to***	*badly.*
7 *These interruptions*	*were*	***put***	***up***	***with***	*cheerfully.*

Notes

(a) In this transform the object of the preposition is transposed forward (cf [A2 pass]), and the form of the verb phrase modified:

[A3] *We* ***put up with*** *these interruptions cheerfully.*
[A3 pass] *These interruptions were* ***put up with*** *cheerfully.*

(b) This transform tends to be restricted to cases where the preposition + object are *not* deletable (though see no 3, above).

(c) Sentences in which the prepositional object is part of a complex idiom are generally not passivized:

10 ?***A good start*** *was* ***got off to.***

(d) Note the placing of stress in this pattern:

*... **looked 'forward to***
*... **done 'away with***
*... **faced 'up to***

[A3 adj] noun phrase with a participial adjective

noun phrase			
article etc	adv	participial adj	noun
4 *His*	*very much*	***looked-forward-to***	*retirement …*
5 *This*	*reluctantly*	***done-away-with***	*piece of legislation …*
6 *The*	*badly*	***faced-up-to***	*responsibilities …*
7 *These*	*cheerfully*	***put-up-with***	*interruptions …*

Notes

(a) This noun-phrase transform derives from the basic [A3] pattern as a whole, and the adjective from the verb + particle + preposition which functions as part of that basic pattern. Note the connection provided by the passive between the basic pattern and this transform:

[A3] *She is **facing up to** the responsibilities badly.*

[A3 pass] *The responsibilities are being badly **faced up to**.*

[A3 adj] *The badly **faced-up-to** responsibilities …*

(b) This transform is generally restricted to verb + particle + preposition items from which the last element is not removable. The following is an unusual (though possible) phrase:

2 ?*His **scraped-along-on** salary …*

[A3 emph] emphatic transform

prepositional phrase		subject	verb phrase	particle	(adv phrase etc)
prep	object		verb		
1 ***On***	*a sandbank*	*the coaster*	***went***	***aground.***	
2 ***On***	*a low salary*	*he*	*just* ***scraped***	***along.***	

Notes

(a) In this transform, the prepositional phrase of the basic pattern has been moved to the front (cf [A2 emph]).

(b) Sentences from which the preposition + object are *not* removable are less likely to be transformed in this way than those (like 1 and 2 above) in which they are, though some speakers may find the following acceptable:

7 ?***With*** *these interruptions we* ***put up*** *cheerfully.*

8 ?***On*** *our private arrangement an outsider had* ***come in***.

[A3 rel] relative transform

noun phrase						
		relative clause				
article	noun	prep	rel pron	subject	verb phrase	particle
1 *A*	*sandbank*	***on***	*which*	*the coaster*	***went***	***aground . .***
2 *A*	*low salary*	***on***	*which*	*he*	***scraped***	***along . . .***
3 *A*	*free fisherman's almanac*	***for***	*which*	*he*	***sent***	***away . . .***

Notes

(a) Here, a noun (etc) derived from the *prepositional object* of the basic pattern is modified by a relative clause (part of which derives from the subject, verb phrase and particle of the same basic pattern (cf [A2 rel])):

[A3] *The coaster* **went aground on** *a sandbank.*

[A3 rel] *A sandbank* **on** *which the coaster* **went aground** ...

(b) Sentences from which preposition + object cannot be removed (i e without affecting the meaning of the whole) are less likely to be relativized, though we may hear, or read:

5 *This piece of legislation* **with** *which they had* **done away** ...

(c) Since this transform (like [A2 rel]) is generally associated with formal styles, expressions normally found in colloquial use – whether the preposition is fixed or not – will tend not to be relativized in this way. Instead, a relative pattern will be used in which the preposition is *final.*

2 *A low salary which he* **scraped along on** ...

5 *This piece of legislation which they had* **done away with** ...

[B1] transitive pattern with a particle

General note

Verb + particle expressions which are used in transitive sentences can be sub-classified according to whether (i) a noun or noun phrase Object can be placed on either side of the particle; (ii) such an Object must appear between the (main) verb and the particle; (iii) it must be placed after the particle. To account for these differences in Object placement, we recognize three types of [B1] transitive patterns, distinguished in the code as [B1i], [B1ii], [B1iii]. We deal with these types, and their transforms, in turn, beginning with two tables for [B1i].

[B1i] transitive pattern with a particle (i) *Table A*

	subject	verb phrase		object	particle	(adv phrase etc)
			verb	noun(pronoun)		
1	*The studio*	*will*	**blow**	*your photographs (them)*	**up**	*well.*
2	*The accountant*		**broke**	*expenditure (it)*	**down**	*as follows ...*
3	*The travel agent*		**messed**	*our bookings (them)*	**up**	*completely.*
4	*We*	*can*	**play**	*the recorded programmes (them)*	**back.**	
5	*Bill*		**took**	*the premier (him)*	**off**	*to perfection.*
6	*The daily help*		**cleaned**	*the whole place (it)*	**out.**	
7	*Fred*		**tipped**	*the police (them)*	**off.**	
8	*I*	*will*	**try**	*the machine (it)*	**out**	*thoroughly.*
9	*You*	*have*	**brought**	*your children (them)*	**up**	*well.*
10	*You*	*have*	**filled**	*the application (it)*	**in**	*incorrectly.*
11	*These entertainers*		**make**	*their stories (them)*	**up.**	
12	*You*		**thought**	*the scheme (it)*	**out**	*carefully.*
13	*The shops*		**put**	*the prices (them)*	**up.**	

[B1i] transitive pattern with a particle (i) *Table B*

	subject	verb phrase		particle	object	(adv phrase etc)
			verb		noun	
1	*The studio*	*will*	**blow**	**up**	*your photographs*	*well.*
2	*The accountant*		**broke**	**down**	*expenditure*	*as follows …*
3	*The travel agent*		**messed**	**up**	*our bookings*	*completely.*
4	*We*	*can*	**play**	**back**	*the recorded programmes.*	
5	*Bill*		**took**	**off**	*the premier*	*to perfection.*
6	*The daily help*		**cleaned**	**out**	*the whole place.*	
7	*Fred*		**tipped**	**off**	*the police.*	
8	*I*	*will*	**try**	**out**	*the machine*	*thoroughly.*
9	*You*	*have*	**brought**	**up**	*your children*	*well.*
10	*You*	*have*	**filled**	**in**	*the application*	*incorrectly.*
11	*These entertainers*		**make**	**up**	*their stories.*	
12	*You*		**thought**	**out**	*the scheme*	*carefully.*
13	*The shops*		**put**	**up**	*the prices.*	

Notes

(a) This sub-pattern accounts for the great majority of verb + particle expressions which function in transitive sentences. It is thus the standard or 'regular' sub-pattern.

(b) A combination of verb + particle is classified as [B1i] when a noun or short noun phrase functioning as Object can either precede the particle (as in Table A) or follow it (as in Table B). A personal pronoun substituted for such an Object will always *precede* the particle (note the pronouns in parentheses in Table A).

(c) If a short Object (as illustrated in Tables A and B) is *extended* there are two possibilities: either the *extension* of the Object follows the particle:

We can **play** *the programmes* **back** *that you recorded last week.*

or the *whole* of the extended Object follows:

We can **play back** *the programmes that you recorded last week.*

(d) A verb + particle combination whose Object is a *clause* is classified as [B1i] if it can *also* occur with noun or noun phrase Objects functioning as in Tables A and B. An expression of this kind is **work out** (meaning 'calculate'). Compare the examples:

We have computers to **work out** *what we earn, these days.*
We have computers to **work** *our salaries* **out**, *these days.*
We have computers to **work out** *our salaries, these days.*

(e) Expressions such as **sew on** or **saw off**, which can take an Indirect as well as a Direct Object, are assigned to this sub-pattern when a short Direct Object, as shown in the following examples, can be placed on either side of the particle:

'The zip has broken. Will you **sew** *me a new one* **on**?'
... **sew** *a new one* **on** *(for me)?'*
... **sew on** *a new one (for me)?'*

(here the Direct Object is 'a new one'.)

'Would you **saw** *me a piece* **off**?'
saw *a piece* **off** *(for me)?'*
saw off *a piece (for me)?'*

(here the Direct Object is 'a piece'.)

(f) Adverbs other than 'straight' or 'right' seldom appear between the verb phrase and the particle (cf [A1]). These sentences are therefore unacceptable:

The studio will* ***blow* *well* ***up*** *your photographs.*

The studio will* ***blow* *your photographs well* ***up****.*

'Straight' and 'right' are themselves not usually inserted when the verb + particle expression is idiomatic:

Bill* ***took* *the premier right* ***off****.*

This rule is relaxed when the item is not highly idiomatic:

The shops ***put*** *the prices straight* ***up****.*

The daily help ***cleaned*** *the place right* ***out****.*

But note that in these examples the order is (main) verb + object + adverb + particle; this order is invariable and the following is unacceptable:

The daily help* ***cleaned* *right* ***out*** *the place.*

[B1i nom] nominalized form of verb + particle

Notes

(a) Nouns referred to as [B1i nom] are formed on the 'base form + particle' model and may be written as fully joined or hyphenated (occasionally as two separate words). The verbal element carries principal stress:

`breakdown, `mess-up, `take-off

(b) These nominalized forms are often used in sentence patterns which are paraphrases of the basic [B1i] pattern. In one type of paraphrase, the 'nom' form functions as (part of) the Direct Object of the verb 'do' (or 'make'), as in this table:

	subject	do/make	object
1	*The studio*	*will do*	*a good* **blow-up** *of your photographs.*
2	*The accountant*	*did*	*a* **breakdown** *of expenditure as follows ...*
3	*The travel agent*	*made*	*a complete* **mess-up** *of our bookings.*
4	*We*	*can do*	*a* **play-back** *of the recorded programmes.*
5	*Bill*	*did*	*a perfect* **take-off** *of the premier.*

(c) In some cases, an Indirect Object pattern with 'give' is used, as in this table:

	subject	give	indirect object	direct object
6	*The daily help*	*gave*	*the whole place*	*a* **clean-out.**
7	*Fred*	*gave*	*the police*	*the* **tip-off.**
8	*I will*	*give*	*the machine*	*a thorough* **try-out.**

(d) This sentence type can in turn be related to one containing 'get':

6 *The whole place got a* ***clean-out****.*

7 *The police got the* ***tip-off*** *from Fred.*

8 *The machine will get a thorough* ***try-out****.*

[B1i pass] passive transform

	subject	verb phrase		particle	(adv phrase etc)
			verb		
1	*Your photographs*	*will be*	***blown***	***up***	*well.*
2	*Expenditure*	*was*	***broken***	***down***	*as follows …*
3	*Our bookings*	*were*	***messed***	***up***	*completely.*
4	*The recorded programmes*	*can be*	***played***	***back.***	
5	*The premier*	*was*	***taken***	***off***	*to perfection.*
6	*The whole place*	*was*	***cleaned***	***out.***	
7	*The police*	*were*	***tipped***	***off.***	
8	*The machine*	*will be*	***tried***	***out***	*thoroughly.*
9	*Your children*	*have been*	***brought***	***up***	*well.*
10	*The application*	*has been*	***filled***	***in***	*incorrectly.*
11	*Their stories*	*are*	***made***	***up.***	
12	*The scheme*	*was*	***thought***	***out***	*carefully.*
13	*The prices*	*were*	***put***	***up.***	

Notes

(a) The passive pattern is derived from the active by transposing the Direct Object to the front position and by changing the form of the verb phrase (*will* ***blow*** → *will be* ***blown***; *can* ***play*** → *can be* ***played***). The particle now immediately follows the (main) verb. Compare:

[B1i] *Fred* ***tipped off*** *the police.*

[B1i pass] *The police were* ***tipped off***.

A prepositional phrase, 'by Fred', originating as the subject of the active sentence, is optional in the passive:

[B1i pass] *The police were* ***tipped off*** *(by Fred).*

(b) When the Object of the active sentence is a *clause*, it remains in the final position in the transform and 'it' is introduced initially. Compare:

We ***worked out*** *that we should need £100.*

It was ***worked out*** *that we should need £100.*

(c) There may be two types of passive sentence when the active pattern contains an Indirect (as well as a Direct) Object. Compare these acceptable transforms:

I was ***sent down*** *a list of missing stock.*

A list of missing stock was ***sent down*** *to me.*

with the unacceptable

A list of missing stock was* ***sent down* *me.*

(d) There is a close similarity (in terms of word order) between this passive transform and that of the [A2] pattern. However, the transforms are in most cases differentiated by stress placement. Compare:

[A2 pass] *The doctor's been* ***ˋsent for***.

[B1i pass] *The student's been* ***sent ˋdown*** (i e from a university).

(e) Several expressions recorded in the dictionary (e g **fed up (with)**, **run down**) function in [B1] *passive* sentences but not in the *active* sentences from which such passives are regularly derived. While we find such examples as these:

I'm ***fed up with*** *being wholesome. I long to be seductive …*

He's thoroughly ***run down*** *(by all this extra work).*

they have no corresponding active in common use:

Being wholesome* **feeds *me* **up**. *I long to be seductive …*
All this extra work* **ran *him* **down** *thoroughly.*

(For a more detailed treatment of this topic, ⇨ 3.3.)

[B1i adj] noun phrase with a participial adjective

noun phrase				
	article	(adv)	participial adj	noun
1	*Your*	*well*	***blown-up***	*photographs …*
3	*Our*	*completely*	***messed-up***	*bookings …*
4	*The*		***played-back***	*programmes …*
8	*The*	*thoroughly*	***tried-out***	*machine …*
9	*Your*	*well*	***brought-up***	*children …*
10	*Your*	*incorrectly*	***filled-in***	*application …*
11	*Their*		***made-up***	*stories …*
12	*Your*	*carefully*	***thought-out***	*scheme …*

Notes

(a) The noun phrase of this transform is derived from the basic pattern as a whole, and the participial adjective from the verb + particle (e g **blow up**, **mess up**) which functions in it. Note the link between the basic pattern and this transform provided by the *passive*:

[B1i] *You* **thought** *the scheme* **out** *carefully.*
[B1i pass] *The scheme was carefully* **thought out**.
[B1i adj] *Your carefully* **thought-out** *scheme …*

(b) The pattern indicates 'completed action' and not 'action in progress':

Those **played-back** *programmes are not a success.*

(implying that they have already been **played back**).

A close connection of meaning between this transform and the passive can only be established when the latter expresses a state also. Compare:

Your children were well **brought up** *by their mother.*
Your children seem well **brought up**.
Yours seem well **brought-up** *children.*

(c) Idiomaticity appears to have no bearing on whether this transform is possible or not.

[B1ii] transitive pattern with a particle (ii)

	subject	verb phrase		object	particle	(adv phrase etc)
			verb	noun/pronoun		
1	*The comedian*	*doesn't*	**get**	*his jokes* (*them*)	**across.**	
2	*The police*		**moved**	*spectators* (*them*)	**along.**	
3	*The technician*	*will*	**run**	*that bit of tape* (*it*)	**through**	*again.*
4	*The government*	*will*	**see**	*the thing* (i e crisis) (*it*)	**through.**	
5	*I*	*'ll*	**knock**	***his block***	**off.**	
6	*Moore*		**throws**	***the ball*** (*it*)	**in**	*near the half-way line.*

Notes

(a) In this sub-pattern there is a restriction upon the placing of an Object consisting of a noun or short phrase. This must *precede* the particle, as is shown in the table. A personal pronoun substituted for such Objects also precedes, as is the general rule for the whole [B1] pattern.

(b) If a short object is lengthened (say, by the addition of a clause) the *extension* may follow the particle, or the *whole* Object may:

The comedian doesn't ***get*** *the jokes* ***across*** *that he prepares in advance.*
The comedian doesn't ***get across*** *the jokes that he prepares in advance.*

(though the second pattern is more unusual: see the next note).

(c) This sub-pattern is often preferred for such verbs as **move**, **run**, **get**, **see** and such particles as **across**, **over**, **through** because if a short Object were free to *follow* those particles, the particle might, in particular cases, be mistaken for a preposition, and the expression misinterpreted. Compare the examples:

[B1ii] *He* ***saw*** *the crisis* ***through*** (i e he survived it).
[A2] *He* ***saw through*** *the crisis* (i e he didn't really believe there was one).

(d) Items such as **work (oneself) out** (= 'reach the point where one is no longer creative, etc') belong to this sub-pattern because the only object possible is a *reflexive pronoun*, and such pronouns must precede the particle. The head-phrase and grammatical code for this item are therefore:

write (oneself) out [B1ii ...]

We can compare in this respect:

fix up (with) [B1i ... B3] ... arrange for sb to have ...

Here, **fix up** is described as [B1i] because, although the expression can be used reflexively, it can also be used with short Objects which both precede and follow the particle. Compare:

He's ***fixed*** *the whole family* ***up*** *(****with*** *good jobs).*
He's ***fixed up*** *the whole family (****with*** *good jobs).*
He's ***fixed*** *himself* ***up*** *(****with*** *a good job).*

[B1ii nom] nominalized form of verb + particle

Note

Though only one example has been given in the main [B1ii] table above of a verb + particle combination from which a noun can be derived (i e **throw in**, yielding **throw-in**), there is no general restriction on noun formation for expressions which occur in the sub-pattern [B1ii]. The following entry provides a further example:

send off [B1ii nom pass] bid sb farewell ... *He was given a good* ***send-off*** (or: *got a good* ***send-off***) *when he left for America.*

and several others are recorded. The code [B1ii nom] should be taken to mean – as here – that the noun is of the 'base-form + particle' type (for fuller details see the notes and tables at [B1i nom], above).

[B1ii pass] passive transform

	subject	verb phrase		particle	(adv phrase etc)
			verb		
1	*His jokes*	*aren't*	***got***	***across.***	
2	*The spectators*	*were*	***moved***	***along.***	
3	*That bit of tape*	*will be*	***run***	***through***	*again.*
6	***The ball***	*is*	***thrown***	***in***	*near the half-way line.*

Notes

(a) This passive transform and that of the 'major' [B1i] sub-pattern are in all essential respects – word-order, form of the verb phrase, treatment of clause objects, stress placement – exactly the same, and users seeking a fuller explanation of those features as they apply *here* are referred to the notes at [B1i pass].

(b) Since some of the words functioning as particles in the [B1ii] pattern (e g **across**, **over**, **through**) can also be used as prepositions, the passive treated here and the [A2] passive may resemble each other in individual cases to the point where misinterpretation is possible. In speech, however, the two types are often (though not always) differentiated by the placing of nuclear stress. Compare:

[B1ii pass] *The man's references have been carefully* ***looked `through*** (= inspected).

[A2 pass] *The morning papers were quickly* ***`looked through*** (= surveyed, scanned).

(c) When the direct object of this sub-pattern is a reflexive pronoun (and no other kind of direct object is possible), we shall not find:

He had been* ***written out* *by the age of thirty.*

as a passive of:

He had ***written himself out*** (= had nothing new to write) *by the age of thirty.*

though the following passive-like construction is acceptable:

He was/seemed ***written out*** *by the age of thirty.*

[B1iii] transitive pattern with a particle (iii)

	subject	verb phrase		particle	object
			verb		
1	*The cavalry*	*will*	***bring***	***up***	***the rear.***
2	*The search party*	*has*	***given***	***up***	***all hope*** *of finding the missing aircraft.*
3	*Jeremy*		***put***	***in***	*a brief* ***appearance.***
4	*The hedgerows*		***put***	***forth***	*new buds.*
5	*Many households*		***take***	***in***	*lodgers.*
6	*The authorities*		***trumped***	***up***	*a case against Smith.*

Notes

(a) In this sub-pattern an Object consisting of a noun, or short noun phrase, is placed *after* the particle.

(b) Following the general rule for the whole [B1] group, a substituted pronoun object, if there is one, *precedes* the particle. Compare:

Many households ***take in*** *lodgers.*
Many households ***take*** *them* ***in****.*

(c) Combinations of verb + particle whose Object is a *clause* but which cannot have a noun or noun phrase Object are classified as [B1iii] because the clause must, following the general rule, be placed *after* the particle. Consider:

find out[2] [... B1iii] discover a mistake, a loss, sb's dishonesty etc ... *One day someone will start asking questions and* ***find out*** *precisely why we've been losing so much money.*

If an expression can take a clause or a short noun phrase as Object, and the latter *must* follow the particle, the item will be described as [B1iii]:

find out[1] [... B1iii ...] learn by calculation, study or inquiry ... *Do you feel a need to* ***find out*** *what you have done with it?* (cf *Do you feel a need to* ***find out*** *its whereabouts?)*

[B1iii nom] nominalized form of verb + particle

Note

Though we provide no example in the table just above of a verb + particle expression from which a 'nom' form derives, there is no general restriction on the transform here, provided that the expression is not complex (as **bring up the rear** and **put in an appearance** are). When an entry has the code [B1iii nom], as in the following entry, this is to be taken to mean that the noun in question is of the 'base form + particle' type (for further details see the notes and tables at [B1i nom], above).

make up[5] [B1iii nom ...] form, compose, constitute ...*There are plans to change the* ***make-up*** (=composition) *of the Board.* □ *There is something in his* ***make-up*** (=nature, character) *that repels people.*

[B1iii pass] passive transform

subject	verb phrase		particle	(agentive prep phrase)
		verb		
1 ***The rear***	*will be*	***brought***	***up***	*(by the cavalry).*
2 ***All hope*** *of finding the missing aircraft*	*has been*	***given***	***up***	*(by the search party).*
3 ***A*** *brief* ***appearance***	*was*	***put***	***in***	*(by Jeremy).*
4 *New buds*	*are*	***put***	***forth***	*(by the hedgerows).*
5 *Lodgers*	*are*	***taken***	***in***	*(by many households).*
6 *A case against Smith*	*was*	***trumped***	***up***	*(by the authorities).*

Note
As regards word order, the form of the verb phrase, the treatment of clause objects and the placing of stress, the passives of the sub-patterns [B1i] and [B1iii] are alike. The user is referred to the notes at [B1i pass] for an explanation of these features.

[B2] transitive pattern with a preposition

	subject	verb phrase		object	prepositional phrase	
			verb		prep	object
1	*He*		**makes**	*rather too* **much**	**of**	*his aristocratic connections.*
2	*The governor*		**made**	**an example**	**of**	*these prisoners.*
3	*I*	*have*	**taken**	*careful* **note**	**of**	*your remarks.*
4	*We*		**take**	*strong* **exception**	**to**	*the attack on Mr Mackay.*
5	*Peter*		**foists**	*all his problems*	**on**	*his unfortunate friends.*
6	*Some*		**pinned**	**their faith**	**on**	*a religious revival.*
7	*Warning cries*		**cheated**	*the cat*	**of**	*its prey.*
8	*Special coaching*		**got**	*me*	**through**	*the written papers.*
9	*I*	*don't*	**hold**	*his past feelings*	**against**	*him.*
10	*The instructor*		**put**	*him*	**off**	*driving altogether.*

Notes
(a) Some of the expressions classified as [B2] – and illustrated here – are related to [A2] items in terms of the transitive/intransitive contrast. Compare:

[B2] *Special coaching* **got** *me* **through** *the written papers.*

[A2] *I* **got through** *the written papers with special coaching.*

[B2] *The instructor* **put** *him* **off** *driving altogether.*

[A2] *He* **went off** *driving altogether.*

(see examples 11 and 14 in the [A2] table.)

(b) In many cases, an adverb or adverbial phrase can be placed between the Direct Object and the prepositional phrase. This may be possible even when the item is idiomatic:

2 *The governor* **made an example**, *only last week*, **of** *these prisoners.*

5 *Peter* **foists** *all his problems, year in and year out,* **on** *his unfortunate friends.*

(c) When the Object is relatively long and the prepositional phrase relatively short, they are often transposable, as follows:

10 *The instructor* **put off** *driving every student who came his way.*

When the Object – or part of it – is an element in a complex expression, however, this kind of transposition is usually not possible:

4 ?*We* **take to** *this attack the strongest possible* **exception**.

though we do sometimes meet acceptable transpositions of this kind as in:

1 *He* **makes of** *these connections rather too* **much**, *I feel.*

(d) Sometimes a long Object can be *divided*, with part of it – usually a relative clause – following the prepositional phrase:

9 *I don't* **hold** *past failings* **against** *him for which he can't really be held responsible.*

[B2 pass]

	subject	verb phrase		prepositional phrase	
			verb	prep	object
1	*Rather too* ***much***	*is*	***made***	***of***	*his aristocratic connections.*
2	***An example***	*was*	***made***	***of***	*these prisoners.*
3	*Careful* ***note***	*has been*	***taken***	***of***	*your remarks.*
4	*Strong* ***exception***	*is*	***taken***	***to***	*the attack on Mr Mackay.*
5	*All his problems*	*are*	***foisted***	***on***	*his unfortunate friends.*
6	***Their faith***	*was*	***pinned***	***on***	*a religious revival.*
7	*The cat*	*was*	***cheated***	***of***	*its prey.*
8	*I*	*was*	***got***	***through***	*the written papers.*
9	*His past failings*	*are not*	***held***	***against***	*him.*
10	*He*	*was*	***put***	***off***	*driving altogether.*

Notes

(a) This passive pattern is derived from the active by transposing the Direct Object of the latter to front position and by changing the form of the verb phrase. The prepositional phrase remains in final position. Compare:

[B2] *Warning cries* ***cheated*** *the cat* ***of*** *its prey.*

[B2 pass] *The cat was* ***cheated of*** *its prey.*

A prepositional phrase, 'by warning cries', which originates from the subject of the active pattern, is optional:

[B2 pass] *The cat was* ***cheated of*** *its prey (by warning cries).*

(b) There is a general parallel between this passive and those of the [B1] sub-patterns. This is particularly evident when the *same* expression functions in the [B2] pattern and, say, the [B1ii] pattern. Compare

[B2] *I was* ***got through*** *the written papers (by special coaching).*

[B1ii] *I was* ***got through*** *(by special coaching).*

(c) A [B2] expression may take as Object a clause introduced by 'that', 'how' etc:

You should ***bear in mind*** *that he wasn't present*
(cf *You should* ***bear*** *that fact* ***in mind***).

The passive of a [B2] sentence with a clause as Object is:

It should be ***borne in mind*** *that he wasn't present.*

though the following alternative construction is found:

That he wasn't present (at the time) should be ***borne in mind.***

(d) A number of expressions recorded as main entries (e g **enshrined in**, **used to**) function only in *passive* sentences of the [B2] type. While we find sentences such as

The glorious history of the regiment is ***enshrined in*** *the official records.*

By now I'm ***used to*** *sudden changes of plan.*

there are no corresponding *active* sentences from which they can be said to derive. Such sentences as the following are unacceptable:

The archivist has* ***enshrined* *the glorious history of the regiment* ***in*** *the official records.*

Experience has* ***used* *me* ***to*** *sudden changes of plan by now.*

(For a fuller treatment of this topic, ⇨ 3.3.)

[B2 pass(o)] passive transform, with the prepositional object of the active pattern becoming the subject of the passive

	subject	verb phrase		object	
			verb		prep
1	*His aristocratic connections*	*are*	***made***	*rather too* ***much***	***of.***
2	*These prisoners*	*were*	***made***	***an example***	***of.***
3	*Your remarks*	*have been*	***taken***	*careful* ***note***	***of.***
4	*The attack on Mr Mackay*	*is*	***taken***	*strong* ***exception***	***to.***

Notes

(a) This transformation only applies when there is a close idiomatic link between parts of a complex expression functioning as (main) verb, Direct Object and preposition. It will be noted, for example, that nothing can be removed from **make an example of** or **take exception to** without making the remainder unacceptable. In the [pass(o)] transform these parts remain together and a subject is introduced originating in the *prepositional object* of the active pattern:

[B2] *The governor* ***made an example of*** *these prisoners.*

[B2 pass(o)] *These prisoners were* ***made an example of*** *(by the governor).*

(b) Note that in this transform it is the pronoun or noun forming (part of) the Direct Object which bears principal stress, and not the main verb:

His aristocratic connections are ***made*** *rather too* ***ˋmuch of.***
Your remarks have been ***taken*** *careful* ***ˋnote of.***

[B2 emph] emphatic transform

	prepositional phrase		subject	verb phrase		object
	prep	object			verb	
1	***Of***	*his aristocratic connections*	*he*		***makes***	*rather too* ***much.***
2	***Of***	*these prisoners*	*the governor*		***made***	***an example.***
3	***Of***	*your remarks*	*I*	*have*	***taken***	*careful* ***note.***
4	***To***	*the attack on Mr Mackay*	*we*		***take***	*strong* ***exception.***
5	***On***	*his unfortunate friends*	*Peter*		***foists***	*all his problems.*
6	***On***	*a religious revival*	*some*		***pinned***	***their faith.***

Notes

(a) This transform results from a simple change of order, with the prepositional phrase shifted to initial position (cf [A2 emph]):

[B2] *Peter* ***foists*** *all his problems* ***on*** *his unfortunate friends.*

[B2 emph] ***On*** *his unfortunate friends Peter* ***foists*** *all his problems.*

(b) In some of the examples, a contrast may be implied between a noun etc in the prepositional phrase and other unspecified words. These words may be made explicit. Consider:

4 ***To*** *the attack on Mr Mackay we* ***take*** *strong* ***exception*** *(though not* ***to*** *your other remarks).*

(c) In some cases adjustments in vocabulary and style will affect the extent to which the emphatic transform can be acceptably applied. Compare:

****Of*** *its prey warning cries* ***cheated*** *the cat.*
Of *all these benefits a sudden fall in share values* ***cheated*** *the hopeful investors.*

[B2 rel] relative transform

noun phrase					
	relative clause				
(article) + noun	prep	rel pron	subject	verb phrase	object
1 *Aristocratic connections*	**of**	*which*	*he*	**makes**	*rather too* **much**...
2 *These prisoners*	**of**	*whom*	*the governor*	**made**	**an example** ...
3 *Remarks*	**of**	*which*	*I*	*have* **taken**	*careful* **note** ...
4 *The attack*	**to**	*which*	*we*	**take**	*strong* **exception** ...
5 *The friends*	**on**	*whom*	*Peter*	**foists**	*all his problems* ...
6 *A religious revival*	**on**	*which*	*some*	**pinned**	**their faith** ...

Notes

(a) In this transform the article + noun (etc), which originates in the prepositional phrase of the basic pattern, is modified by a relative clause (which itself contains the subject, verb phrase and object of that same pattern):

[B2] *The governor* **made an example of** *these prisoners.*

[B2 rel] *These prisoners* **of** *whom the governor* **made an example** ...

(b) Sentences in which idiomatic items occur are not normally relativized as shown above. Consider:

9 **A man* **against** *whom I don't* **hold** *his past failings* ...

(c) Restrictions on relativization (i e of the above type) often have to do with the formality of the item. A colloquial expression (whether highly idiomatic or not) would not be relativized as in this example:

8 **The written papers* **through** *which special coaching* **got** *me* ...

though it might be used as follows:

The written papers which special coaching **got** *me* **through** ...

[B3] transitive pattern with a particle and preposition

subject	verb phrase		object	particle	prepositional phrase	
		verb			prep	object
1 *We*		**brought**	*them*	**around**	**to**	*a different way of thinking.*
2 *The women*	*had*	**decked**	*themselves*	**out**	**in**	*satin frocks.*
3 *They*		**filled**	*me*	**in**	**on**	*the latest developments.*
4 *Some trickster*	*had*	**fobbed**	*him*	**off**	**with**	*this story.*
5 *Someone*	*had*	**let**	*an outsider*	**in**	**on**	*our private arrangement.*
6 *The move*		**brought**	*the family*	**up**	**against**	*fresh problems.*
7 *The referee*		**got**	*the match*	**off**	**to**	**a good start.**
8 *You*	*can*	**put**	*the shortage*	**down**	**to**	*bad planning.*
9 *They*		**put**	*him*	**up**	**to**	*some mad escapade.*
10 *You*	*shouldn't*	**take**	*your resentment*	**out**	**on**	*me.*

Notes

(a) In each of nos 1–4 the preposition (and its object) can be removed withou changing the meaning of the remainder of the sentence. To some extent th affects possibilities of transformation.

(b) The pattern has an intransitive equivalent in [A3]. Compare nos 5, 6 and here with nos 8, 9, 10 in the [A3] table.

(c) In the table, the Direct Object is placed before the particle. In some case it can, when it is a noun or short noun phrase, follow the particle:

3 *They* ***filled in*** *their colleagues* ***on*** *the latest developments.*
10 *You shouldn't* ***take out*** *your resentment* ***on*** *me.*

(d) In most of the examples here, an adverb or adverbial phrase may be place between the particle and the prepositional phrase:

2 *The women had* ***decked*** *themselves* ***out*** *gaudily* ***in*** *satin frocks.*
7 *The referee* ***got*** *the match* ***off***, *despite the incident on the terraces,* ***to a goo start*** .

(The idiomaticity of items does not appear to affect adverb insertion in a genera way.)

[B3 pass] passive transform

	subject	verb phrase		particle	prepositional phrase	
			verb		prep	object
1	*They*	*were*	**brought**	**around**	**to**	*a different way of thinking*
2	*The women*	*were*	**decked**	**out**	**in**	*satin frocks.*
3	*I*	*was*	**filled**	**in**	**on**	*the latest developments.*
4	*He*	*had been*	**fobbed**	**off**	**with**	*this story.*
5	*An outsider*	*had been*	**let**	**in**	**on**	*our private arrangement.*
6	*The family*	*was*	**brought**	**up**	**against**	*fresh problems.*
7	*The match*	*was*	**got**	**off**	**to**	***a good start.***
8	*The shortage*	*can be*	**put**	**down**	**to**	*bad planning.*
9	*He*	*was*	**put**	**up**	**to**	*some mad escapade.*
10	*Your resentment*	*shouldn't be*	**taken**	**out**	**on**	**me**

Notes

(a) In transforming an active [B3] sentence into the passive, the same genera rule applies as to sentences in the [B1] and [B2] categories: the Direct Objec (noun, noun phrase or pronoun) of the basic pattern shifts to front position an becomes the subject of the passive construction:

[B3] *Someone had* ***let*** *an outsider* ***in on*** *our private arrangement.*
[B3 pass] *An outsider had been* ***let in on*** *our private arrangement.*

(b) A *clause* is occasionally found as Object of a [B3] sentence:

[B3] *We* ***put*** *it* ***up to*** *the committee* (i e proposed to them) *that Frank should b made secretary.*

This sentence is transformed as follows:

[B3 pass] *It was* ***put up to*** *the committee that Frank should be made secretary.*

(c) When an expression functioning in the [B3] pattern has a *deletable* preposition + object (e g **bring around (to), deck out (in)**), and those constituents are removed, the passive is of the [B1] type. Compare these passive sentences:

[B3 pass] *They were **brought around to** our way of thinking (eventually).*
[B1ii pass] *They were **brought around** (eventually).*

[B3 emph] emphatic transform

prepositional phrase		subject	verb phrase	object	particle
prep	object		verb		
4 **With**	*this story*	*some trickster*	*had **fobbed***	*him*	***off.***
5 **On**	*our private arrangement*	*someone*	*had **let***	*an outsider*	***in.***

Notes

(a) The transform results from a simple change of order, with the prepositional phrase being shifted to front position (cf [B2 emph]):

[B3] *Someone had **let** an outsider **in on** our private arrangement.*
[B3 emph] ***On** our private arrangement someone had **let** an outsider **in** .*

(b) In some cases, there may be an implied contrast between part of the prepositional phrase and other unspecified words. These words may on the other hand be specified in the context:

***With** that kind of excuse you could **fob** her **off** (but don't pretend that your mother was ill).*

[B3 rel] relative transform

noun phrase						
	relative clause					
article + noun	prep	rel pron	subject	verb phrase	object	particle
1 *A different way of thinking*	**to**	*which*	*we*	***brought***	*them*	***around*** …
4 *This story*	**with**	*which*	*some trickster*	*had **fobbed***	*him*	***off*** …
5 *The private arrangement*	**on**	*which*	*someone*	*had **let***	*an outsider*	***in*** …

Notes

(a) The 'article + noun' of this transform is derived from the prepositional phrase of the basic pattern. The relative clause itself contains the subject, verb phrase, object and particle of the original pattern (cf [B2 rel]):

[B3] *Some trickster had **fobbed** him **off with** this story …*
[B3 rel] *This story **with** which some trickster had **fobbed** him **off** …*

(b) This transform, in common with other relative transforms, is often associated with formal styles, and expressions commonly found in colloquial use will *tend* not to be relativized on this model. A common alternative in everyday informal use is as follows (note the preposition in *final* position):

4 *This story which some trickster had **fobbed** him **off with** …*

Style and Register

4 The expressions recorded in this dictionary represent the idiomatic usage[1] c educated British speakers in the latter part of the present century. This is nc to say that the dictionary confines itself to usages which are not found outsid Great Britain – to British English, that is, in the narrow sense. Very many c the expressions are also readily understood, and commonly used, in othe countries where English is spoken as a mother tongue or firmly established a a second language. Thus the dictionary describes idiomatic items which ar peculiarly British and those which, while also British, are widely diffuse throughout the English-speaking world.

While no attempt has been made to list and describe expressions which ar solely, or largely, American, the dictionary does include a few items – marke (US) or (esp US) – which have a marginal status in British English. These ar items which though not fully established among British speakers, and sti regarded as 'American' by some, are none the less used sufficiently often t merit inclusion in a dictionary of British usage. Examples are:

get to first base with ... (esp US informal) make significant progress to wards achieving an objective ...

run (for) ... (esp US) offer oneself as a candidate (for) ...

want out/out of ... (US informal) wish to be freed from sth unpleasant, nc wish to be involved any longer ...

Within the wide range of British idiomatic usage which the dictionary aims t cover, certain items can be singled out as being associated with particular *style* of use, or as belonging to the languages of professional groups or specialize fields of activity, i e to particular *registers*. The native speaker knows, fo instance, that items such as:

ascribe to **give credence to** **make application (to**

are more likely to be found in an official document or a set speech than to cro up during relaxed conversation among friends. In a similar way, the expression

find against (the prisoner) **set aside** (a decision, verdic
pass sentence (on the accused)

unmistakably suggest the specialized language, or register, of court proceedings

Since the foreign learner often finds it difficult to identify, or use in the righ contexts, items which are restricted in style or register, a scheme of marking has been devised to provide the necessary guidance. When an expression ca be clearly identified as having a restricted use, the appropriate marking i entered in parentheses after the grammatical code:

ascribe to [B2 ...] (formal) **find against** [A2] (lega

Styles of use: formal, informal, slang, taboo

4.1 For purposes of marking entries in the dictionary, the *style* of an idiomati expression is seen as the reflection of certain factors in the situations in whic that expression is habitually used. Among the most important of these factor are:

(i) the relationship between the speakers, or correspondents (remote and officia or intimate and relaxed)

[1] By usage we mean not only those expressions which an educated person may 'produce' in speec or writing, in a variety of styles, but those which he may readily understand when used by others though he himself might never use them. For example, the taboo expressions given in the Dictionar would never be used by many people who nevertheless must often hear or read them, with unde standing.

(ii) whether one is speaking or writing (compare a spoken commentary on a football match with a newspaper report of it).
(iii) the level of seriousness, detachment etc suggested or imposed by the occasion (compare a speech at an official banquet with one given at a farewell party for a personal friend).

Four categories are set up to indicate differences of style in the dictionary: *formal*, *informal*, *slang* and *taboo*. Each category places a different emphasis on aspects of the factors outlined just above.

4.1.1 *formal* – more likely to reflect a distant than a close relationship; more likely to be met in writing than in speech; often suggesting a serious or elevated tone:

call forth ... (formal) ... *The dark days of 1940* ***called forth*** *the best in the character of the British people.*

(the rhetorical tone of the example suggests a public speech, or perhaps a statesman's memoirs).

4.1.2 *informal* – intimate rather than distant; spoken rather than written; modest rather than grand or imposing:

cheer up... (informal) ... *'You must* ***cheer up****, Mrs Gaye. You'll soon be walking again.'* DC

(an example of speech in a modern novel)

4.1.3 *slang* – usually met in (and invariably derived from) the spoken language; suggesting an easy and intimate relationship between the speakers; serving to establish and reinforce the 'togetherness' of particular sub-groups in society, e g the police, criminals, schoolboys etc, and their distinctness from other groups; tending to date quickly, and therefore needing to be used with care by foreign speakers:

chat up ... (slang) ... *Mary was being* ***chatted up*** *by a bearded youth when I arrived on the scene.*

4.1.4 *taboo* – 'swear words'; highly informal; generally avoided by educated male speakers when in the company of women and children, though conventions vary greatly from speaker to speaker, as well as from one social group to another; often expressing tension, irritation, anger, etc; best avoided by foreign speakers:

cock up[2] ... (taboo) ... *Trust Smith to* ***cock*** *the whole thing* ***up***. □ *Don't let him organize your trip; he completely* ***cocked up*** *ours.*

The user should note that it is impossible to assign fixed stylistic values to most items which call for a marking of some kind. The boundary between 'formal' and 'informal' usage is constantly shifting, and the conventions observed by individual speakers and writers differ very considerably. We can only attempt to give general guidance here.

Registers of use

4.2 The occupational or professional fields with which certain expressions are particularly associated are much more numerous than the stylistic categories, and more clearly separated from each other. The following examples show a selection of the register markings used in the dictionary. As will be seen, the labels are largely self-explanatory:

blast off [A1 ... B1i ...] (space technology)
fold in/into [B1i ... B2 ...] (cooking)
cut back[1] [B1i ...] (horticulture)
walk out[2] [A1 ...] (industrial relations)
convict (of) [B2 ...] (legal)
come to attention [A2] (military)
cast off[1] [A1 ...] (nautical)

Definitions

5 In framing definitions, the aim has been to provide concise and readily intelligible statements of meaning which do not assume an understanding of (and therefore do not contain) expressions given elsewhere in the dictionary as headphrases. Where it is helpful to draw the user's attention to another headphrase which is a synonym of the one being defined, this cross-reference is not made part of the definition proper, but is placed after it (⇨ 5.3).

Position of the definition

5.1 The definition is placed after the grammatical code, or if there is an indication of style or register, after that indication:

come to rest [A2] stop, reach a final position ...
come to something [A2] (informal) be surprising, strange ...

Form of the definition

5.2 In some entries, the verb(s) etc constituting the definition can be substituted for the headphrase in the illustrations given, and in other possible sentences also.

set up[4] [B1iii pass] cause, produce. ... □ *Smoking* ***sets up*** *an irritation in the throat and bronchial passages.* □ *The doctor has no idea how the condition was first* ***set up***.

In other entires, the definition is expanded to include words which refer to the subject, object etc of the illustrations (and other possible sentences):

flock together [A1] (esp of people with common interests or loyalties) gather, come together, in a crowd. ... □ *Brighton was full of Conservative Party stalwarts,* ***flocking together*** *for their annual conference.*

tap off [B1i pass adj] draw liquid from a cask etc through a tap. ... □ *He keeps a barrel of the local red wine in his cellar and* ***taps off*** *a couple of bottles every day.*

In other entries again, the definition goes on to specify some of the wider connotations of the headphrase:

ham up [B1i pass adj] (informal) act on the stage in a crude or exaggerated way (either through inexperience or for deliberate effect). ...

school (in) [B2 pass emph rel] teach sb the elements or principles of sth (usu the teaching is informal and by example; its purpose may be sinister or antisocial). ...

5.2.1 If a particular headphrase has two clearly distinguishable senses, it is given two definitions, separated by a semi-colon:

cater for [A2 pass rel] serve the public, by providing refreshments; aim to satisfy (the needs of) particular groups. ...

look through[4] [A2] not see sb or sth that is clearly visible; deliberately ignore sb whom one can plainly see. ...

Some headphrases have two meanings which are related (and can be combined in a definition) in a special way. The headphrase **light up**[4], for instance, has the related meanings 'become bright or flushed with emotion' and 'make (sb) bright or flushed with emotion'. These meanings can be combined in *one* statement, as in the definition for the entry:

light up[4] [A1 B1i ...] become, make, bright or flushed with emotion. ...

There are many headphrases whose meanings are related in much the same way (i e as 'change, act' is related to '*cause to* change, act'), and the connection is conveyed in the definitions either by using 'become, make', as above, or by using '(cause to)' or '(make sb)', as in the following entries:

line up[1] [A1 B1i ...] (cause to) form into lines or ranks. ...
tank up [A1 B1i ...] (slang) (make sb) drink a great deal of alcohol. ...

5.3 Cross-references to other entries

An entry may contain a cross-reference to another headphrase which is a *synonym* of the headphrase being defined. This cross-reference is placed at the end of the definition proper, and usually separated from it by a semi-colon. Cross-references of this kind are always identified by the abbreviation '(q v)':

talk about[3] ... propose, consider, a possible course of action (though usu without acting in fact); talk of[2] (q v). ...

Idiomatic expressions are closely synonymous when they are interchangeable in many sentences without both the cognitive and emotive meanings of those sentences being thereby affected. When headphrases in the dictionary are synonyms in this *strict* sense, care has been taken to cross-refer them *to each other*, thus indicating their close equivalence. Compare the entry just given with:

talk of[2] ... consider, discuss, a possible plan of action (though usu without following it); talk about[3] (q v). ...

Note too, the following pair of entries, and how each of the headphrases can be used in the illustrations provided for the other:

adapt (oneself) to ... change one's outlook or behaviour to suit; adjust (oneself) to (q v). ... □ *I don't think I shall ever* **adapt myself to** *this hot climate.* □ *The new teacher was slow to* **adapt to** *the unusual rules of the school.*

adjust (oneself) to ... change one's outlook or behaviour to suit; adapt (oneself) to (q v). ... □ *I don't think I shall ever be able to* **adjust myself to** *life in this remote place.* □ *Jenkins was well* **adjusted to** *the society in which he lived.*

Such close equivalence is rare, however. More often, headphrases are found to be *cognitively* equivalent (i e they express 'the same ideas'), but not to share the same emotive or stylistic overtones.

For example, the expressions **balls up**, **cock up**, **mess up**, **muck up**, **screw up** can all be given the same generalized definition – 'mishandle, mismanage, spoil, ruin' etc – but they have different connotations, different *shades* of meaning. The procedure generally followed with such sets of expressions is to cross-refer those which have special associations (and possibly special stylistic markings) to the one which is the most neutral (in this case, **mess up**):

balls up ... (taboo) ruin, mishandle; mess up (q v). ...
cock up[2] ... (taboo) spoil, ruin; mess up (q v). ...
mess up ... (informal) mishandle, mismanage; confuse, disarrange. ...
muck up ... (informal) spoil, ruin; mess up (q v). ...
screw up[4] ... (slang) mishandle, mismanage; mess up (q v). ...

5.3.1 In some entries with *two* definitions, *one* of the definitions will have a cross-reference to another entry. The cross-reference is positioned accordingly:

deal with[1] ... trade with, do business (with) (q v); talk with in order to reach a settlement etc. ...

get into[1] ... get dressed in, put on[1] (q v); force sb or sth into. ...

In other entries again, a single definition may be followed by references to two (or more) other entries:

dally with[2] [A2] appear to show an interest in sb (without intending a serious relationship); play with[2] (q v), toy with[2] (q v). ...

5.3.2 Finally, it is important for the user to keep in mind the different purposes served by the kind of cross-referencing explained in this section, and those cross-references which often appear at the *end* of entries (⇨ 9: The cross-reference system). The former kind is intended to draw the user's attention to sameness (or close similarity) of meaning between headphrases. The latter system is largely confined to the major, or 'heavy duty' verbs such as **be**, **come**, **go** and **take** and points to important relationships of meaning between them, though not as a general rule to synonymy.

Collocations

6 As has already been explained in the General Introduction (⇨ 0.2), an important aim of the dictionary is to foster skill in producing new and acceptable sentences by indicating particular words which regularly *collocate* with the expressions entered as headphrases. Information about collocating words is set out in the entries in a way which is designed to make clear the relationship between collocations on the one hand and grammatical patterns (and their transforms) on the other.

Position of the collocates in entries

6.1 Words which collocate with the headphrase of an entry are arranged in sets preceded by a letter or other abbreviation in **bold type** and are placed immediately after the definition:

crop up[1] ... be mentioned. **S:** topic, subject, theme □ ...

fade up ... gradually make louder (esp in a radio or TV studio). **S:** technician, sound effects man. **O:** music, voice; announcer □ ...

The words given in such sets may be repeated lower down in the illustrations, but if the range of possible collocates is large, those used in one or more illustrations are often chosen to extend the list(s) already given:

add up to[2] ... mean; amount to[2] (q v). **S:** refusal, statement, attitude. **o:** what (in initial position); the fact that □ *What your statement **adds up to** is that you helped to kill the old woman.* □ *Your evidence, then, really **adds up to** this – that you were nowhere near the scene of the crime?*

Abbreviations used

6.2 The abbreviations which introduce sets of collocates are generally single letters representing the major constituents of the basic sentence patterns (as displayed in the tables in Section 3.4). The letters are printed in **bold type**:

S = Subject (all basic patterns)
O = (Direct) Object ([B1i] [B1ii] [B1iii] [B2] [B3])
o = object of a preposition ([A2] [A3] [B2] [B3])
A = Adverbial phrase or clause, adverb (all basic patterns)

When **S** introduces a set of collocating words in an entry, this indicates that any of the words can function as (part of) the Subject in a sentence formed on the pattern given in the grammatical code for that entry:

shrivel up [A1] dry and curl up through old age, heat, frost etc. **S:** leaf, shoot, blade (of grass); skin; face □ *In the long drought, the leaves* ***shrivelled up*** *and died.*

The same principle governs the use of the other letters introducing collocates:

act on/upon[2] [A2 emph rel] affect; have an effect on. ... **o:** organ; heart, liver, spleen, gland □ *These pills* ***act on*** *the liver.*

6.2.1 The following abbreviations refer to parts of sentences (or parts of phrases) which are not dealt with in the tables of basic patterns:

Inf = Infinitive (either standing alone or introducing a non-finite clause)

adj = adjective (usu modifying the noun in an expression of which the noun is a fixed part)

m = adverbial modifier of a particle

The usual grammatical functions of the collocates introduced by these abbreviations are shown in the illustrations in the following entries:

bring up[2] ... teach, persuade, sb in the course of his upbringing to do sth. ... **Inf**: to scorn convention, to respect his parents, to be courteous to strangers □ *He had been* ***brought up*** *to think that in business matters his likes and dislikes didn't count.*

make a mockery of ... bring to a low level, be a travesty of. ... **adj**: complete, total. ... □ *The conduct of the elections* ***made an*** *absolute* ***mockery of*** *democratic processes.*

be out[12] ... be inaccurate, be wrong. ... **m:** (some) way, not far, five minutes, well, miles. ... □ *His forecast of rapid growth in the public sector of industry* ***was*** *some way* ***out****.*

In a few entries (especially entries whose headphrases are 'nominalized forms') the unabbreviated word **Verb** introduces a set of collocating verbs:

come-back[1] [nom (A1)] a (successful) return (to a profession etc). ... **Verb:** make, stage; attempt, try □ *After many years of obscurity, the once-famous film-star made an unexpected* ***come-back****.*

This form of entry indicates that 'make' etc can function as main verb in a sentence of which **come-back** is Object – as in the illustration.

6.2.2 Some headphrases contain *two prepositions* and therefore do not strictly conform to any of the basic patterns, though in practice they are given the codes [A2] and/or [B2] (⇨ *Grammatical codes and tables*, 3.1.3):

develop (from) (into) [A2 ... B2 ...]
lodge (against) (with) [B2 ...]

To help the user to distinguish between the words collocating with *each* preposition in such entries, the procedure is followed of setting each preposition (in ***bold italic***) in front of its particular collocates:

develop (from) (into)... **o:** (***from***) principality, village; small-holding, family business; ordinary, simple beginnings; (***into***) major power, metropolis; estate, vast complex; the best, most advanced of its kind □ ...

Collocations and grammatical patterns

6.3 Collocating items always have grammatical functions (e g as Subject, Object etc, as indicated above), and those functions may well alter when the pattern of a sentence is changed (e g from 'active' to 'passive'). Consider the example:

write up[1] [B1i pass adj] rewrite sth in a fuller, better organized way; ... **O:** note, observation; experiment, project □ ...

Here, the words 'note, observation' etc can function in the *active* pattern [B1i] as *Objects*, as in the example:

'For homework you can ***write up*** *your rough notes.'*

When this sentence is transformed into the *passive*, however, 'notes' functions as (part of) the *Subject*:

'For homework, your rough notes can be ***written up****.'*

Awareness of such systematic changes of function adds to the resources of the dictionary user who wishes to construct sentences of his own. He can safely assume that when a grammatical code shows that a passive transform (for instance) is possible, he can use the *same* set of collocating words *twice* – as the Object (or prepositional object) in active sentences, and as the Subject in passive ones. (For a description of the transforms themselves, ⇨ the appropriate tables in 3: *Grammatical codes and tables*.)

6.3.1 In entries with two *basic* patterns, a single set of collocates may have different functions in the two patterns. The set of collocating words is introduced in a special way to show that this is the case:

move in [A1 B1i pass] (cause to) occupy, take possession of, a house etc. **S:** [A1] **O:** [B1] family, couple. **S:** [B1] council, church □ ...

Here two abbreviations, and two codes, are placed together before 'family, couple' to show that those words can function both as the Subject of the 'intransitive' pattern *and* as the Object of the 'transitive', thus:

[A1] *The family are* ***moving in*** *on the first of the month.*

[B1] *The Council are* ***moving*** *the family* ***in*** *on the first of the month.*

Conversely, 'council, church' can function only as the Subject of the transitive pattern. Hence, **S:** [B1]. It should be noted that the same kind of relationship between intransitive and transitive is represented by the following entry, even though there are *four* basic patterns:

build up (to)[2] [A1 ... A3 ... B1iii ... B3 ...] develop, increase, intensify. **S:** [A1 A3] **O:** [B1 B3] pressure, tension; opposition, resistance. **S:** [B1 B3] overwork, stress; decision, attitude □ ...

In other entries with two (or more) basic patterns, the Subject of an intransitive pattern [A1] may *also* be the Subject of a transitive one [B1]. Compare:

[A1] *If you don't* ***wind on*** *after taking a picture, your negative will be double-exposed.*

[B1] *If you don't* ***wind*** *the film* ***on*** *after taking a picture ....*

In such entries the Subject and Object collocates are kept separate, and there is no reference before those lists to sentence patterns. The user can assume that what are Subject collocates for the [A1] pattern are also Subject collocates for the [B1] pattern:

wind on [A1 B1i ...] move a film forward (so as to expose, or show, the next portion). **S:** photographer, cameraman. **O:** film, film-strip, tape □ ....

Internal arrangement of lists of collocates

6.4 Various principles govern the arrangement of collocates within the lists in which they appear:

(i) When collocates within a single list belong to different word classes (parts of speech) the classes are separated off by the semi-colon:

make up[7] ... **O:** himself; face, nose, eyes ....
take to heart ... **O:** disappointment, setback, loss; things; it, everything ....

(ii) Words, phrases and clauses are kept separate in the same way:

rope in/into ... **o:** group, organization; forming sth, being a member. ...
work out[2] ... **O:** pay, allowance, pension; cost; that it will cost £100, how much to pay him. ...

(iii) Different sub-classes of noun (e g common, abstract, proper) are separated:

engrave on ... **o:** presentation cup, plate; memory, mind. ...
work on ... **o:** book, play; Milton, Tolstoy; radio, rocket motor; improvement. ...

(iv) General, or inclusive, terms precede and are separated from particular, or included terms:

chug along ... **S:** (old) ship, boat; steamer, tug, tramp(-steamer). ...
act on/upon[2] ... **o:** organ; heart, liver, spleen, gland. ...

(v) Words which are closely related in sense are placed together and divided by a semi-colon from others which are more remote in meaning:

prepare (for) ... **O:** oneself; pupil, class; follower, subject; article, book; room. ...

saturate (with)... **O:** ground, soil; cloth, rag. ...

(vi) When one part of a set of words etc collocates closely with one part of another set, the semi-colon is used in each set to mark this part off. In certain entries, a set of words may be divided into several groups according to the relations which those groups contract with parts of other sets:

take over (from) ... **S:** (new, younger) man; pilot, skipper; specialist, expert; runner, car. **O:** management, direction; controls, helm; case, inquiry; lead, first place. **o:** (retiring) director; crew member; assistant; competitor. ...

The particular lay-out of this entry may be interpreted as meaning that (among other collocations) 'skipper' collocates with 'helm' and 'crew member', to give the sentence:

*The skipper **took over** the helm **from** a crew member.*

'Open' and 'restricted' sets of collocates

6.5 A distinction can be drawn between sets of collocates to which other words can be added at will, and sets which virtually exhaust all the possibilities of choice open to the speaker. The difference between the first, or *open* kind of set and the second, or *restricted*, kind is of course not clear-cut but a gradual progression. An example of the first kind is found in the entry:

come in[1] ... become fashionable. **S:** long hair, whiskers; short skirts, full sleeves. ...

Since a wide variety of styles of dress, ways of wearing one's hair, and so on, can become the fashion, the suggested collocates far from exhaust the range of suitable items, but simply indicate the general areas in which *many* appropriate choices can be made.

The kind of set which represents a severely *limited* range of choice is marked in a special way – with the sign ⚠:

keep an/one's eye on ... observe and if necessary take appropriate action; watch over (q v). **adj:** ⚠ (a) careful, professional, sharp, watchful, weather. ...

Here this sign warns the user that the set is highly restricted: other adjectives are unlikely to collocate with the headphrase. This set, like similarly marked sets in other entries, does not *exhaust* the speaker's options: he might, for special effect, choose 'vigilant' or 'amateurish'. But these are unusual choices, and the foreign learner would be wise to regard this sign as a warning to confine himself for some time to the choices indicated.

All such restricted sets of collocates marked with this sign are listed, together with collocates used in headphrases, in the *Index of nouns etc used in headphrases and collocations* at the end of the dictionary, and referred back to the entry or entries in which they occur.

Illustrations

Sources

7.1 The illustrative material in the dictionary is of two kinds: *citations* from written or spoken texts and *made-up examples.*

In 1959, work began on the collection of idiomatic expressions of all types as a prelude to the writing of this dictionary. A substantial collection of excerpts from texts of various kinds, chiefly written, was thus available from which suitable illustrations for the dictionary entries could be selected. As the writing-up and the editing of the dictionary proceeded, however, the material was supplemented by more recently observed occurrences from both spoken and written sources. All the original sources date from about the end of the Second World War to 1965; we can thus claim that the dictionary represents English usage of the latter part of the twentieth century. (⇨ *List of Sources* pp lxxv–lxxix.)

Examples *not* drawn from texts are made to reflect, as closely as possible, the natural and normal conditions of use of the headphrases which they illustrate. They also cover the full range of basic patterns and transforms which in our view particularly needed exemplification.

Position of illustrations in entries

7.2 Illustrations are placed after the collocations, or where there are no collocations, after the definition, and preceded by a box □, thus:

dive (one's hand) into ... **o:** pocket, purse, handbag □ *He* ***dived into*** *his jacket pocket to make sure his wallet was still there.*

Where two or more illustrations are given they are divided from each other by a smaller box □:

wait up (for) ... **S:** parent, wife □ *The old folks always go to bed about ten. They don't* ***wait up for*** *me.* TC □ *'I shan't get in till after midnight, so don't bother to* ***wait up****.'*

When an illustration is quoted from a text, the title of the book, newspaper etc is given in abbreviated form at the end of the illustration:

usher in ... □ *It is the happy custom for the Viennese to* ***usher in*** *the New Year with a concert of music by Strauss.* RT □ *It would be unwise to assume that the July elections will* ***usher in*** *a new millennium.* OBS

(where RT = *Radio Times* and OBS = *The Observer*; ⇨ *List of Sources*, pp lxxv–lxxix.)

In a few entries in the dictionary only one quotation is used from a text. In these cases the work is printed in full (author and title) at the end of the illustration quoted:

defect (from) (to) ... □ *'So you're the man who is going to make Semitsa* ***defect from*** *the Moscow Academy of Sciences and come to work in the West.'* L DEIGHTON: FUNERAL IN BERLIN

Illustrations and the headphrase

7.3 Illustrations are printed in *italic*. To help the user to pick out the headphrase in example sentences, it is printed there in ***bold italic***. In most entries, when allowance has been made for inflection of the verb, there is a close similarity between the headphrase as it appears at the top of the entry and the particular form it takes in the illustration(s).

start up ... □ (order to aircraft mechanic) *'All right, **start** her **up**!'* □ *He **started up** a successful car hire firm.* □ *There was no danger of **starting up** some stumbling conversation with them.* CON

In certain entries there are differences between the *forms* of adjectives, nouns etc given in the headphrase and those appearing lower down in the illustration(s). In some entries it is a matter of the choice of different words. The user should note in particular the following conventions.

7.3.1 Generally speaking, the use of **one's**, **sb's** or **his** in a headphrase represents the full set of possessive adjectives – **my**, **his**, **her**, **its**, **one's**, **our**, **your**, **their**. The appropriate choice from this set is given, according to context, in the illustrations, and printed there in bold italic (for the difference between **one's**, **sb's**, **his**, ⇨ 1, *The headphrase*):

come into one's own ... *The Lotus car **came into its own** when Jim Clark won the great American race at Indianapolis.*

get on sb's nerves ... *She **gets on my nerves** the way she never stops talking about her brilliant son.*

bring to his feet ... *A jolt nearly threw me from the bed, and a second jolt **brought** me **to my feet**.* SD

The use of **sb's** in a headphrase can also represent the possessive form of nouns and possessive phrases introduced by 'of'. In order to avoid typographical complexity the whole of the possessive noun is printed in bold italic, but only the 'of' introducing the possessive phrase is. Compare:

get into sb's black books ... *I **got into Lady Whatsit's black books** as soon as I mentioned that I was a Labour supporter.*

bring to sb's attention/notice ... *An inspector first **brought** these deficiencies **to the attention of** the management.*

7.3.2 In general, the use in headphrases of the reflexive forms, **himself** or **oneself** represents the following set of reflexive pronouns:

myself, **himself**, **herself**, **itself**, **oneself**, **ourselves**, **yourself**, **yourselves**, **themselves**.

Again, the appropriate choice from this list is made, according to context, in the illustrations:

bring to himself ... *This sound **brought** me **to myself** ...* UTN

draw oneself up ... *He **drew himself up** portentously, walked stiff-legged over to the table, and sat down.* DC

The form **itself** in a headphrase may stand for **itself** or **themselves** in the actual example sentences:

wreathe (itself) around/round ... *Creeping plants had **wreathed themselves around** the trellis ...*

7.3.3 A noun given in the singular form in the headphrase often means that both the singular *and* plural forms may be used. In such cases both forms are illustrated (⇨ 1, *The headphrase*).

7.3.4 Where one article or indefinite adjective (usu **a** or **no**) is given in the headphrase, and other similar adjectives are listed as collocates (after **adj**), then *whichever* indefinite adjective etc appears in the illustrations is treated as part of the headphrase, and printed in bold italic:

make a fuss of ... **adj:** much, a lot of; (not) any. □ ... *We were* ***made*** *so* ***much fuss of*** *by the welcoming committee.* □ *Too* ***much fuss*** *can be* ***made of*** *very young children.* □ *We* ***made*** *such* ***a fuss of*** *them. Gave them cigarettes and mugs of tea.* CSWB

7.3.5 When a selection of adjectives (or particles) is indicated by means of the following conventions in the headphrase, then whichever adjective(s) or particle(s) are chosen for purposes of illustration are treated as part of the headphrase, and printed in bold italic:

take a poor etc view of ... **adj**: poor, dim, sombre, pessimistic; optimistic, sanguine, bright ... □ *The federation* ***takes a gloomy view of*** *the prospects for the economy in the months to come.* T □ *Most other road-users* ***take a stern view of*** *the private motorist.* SC

file across, along, away etc ... □ *The men* ***filed across*** *a narrow footbridge.* □ *The staff* ***filed into*** *the canteen for their mid-morning break.*

Coverage of various patterns in the illustrations

7.4 When the grammatical code in an entry refers to two basic patterns, the entry will often illustrate them both:

draw in/into [A1 A2] ... □ *As I reached the ticket barrier the London train was just* ***drawing in.*** □ *The 'Cornish Riviera'* ***drew into*** *Plymouth a few minutes ahead of schedule.*

Sometimes, the connection between two grammatical patterns (or two alternative forms of the headphrase) is shown by means of additional illustrative material inserted within parentheses:

team up (together/with) [A1 A3]... □ *John then* ***teamed up with*** *a boat builder (*cf *They* ***teamed up (together)****) and began making cabin cruisers.*

When alternatives are given inside examples from recorded sources, the abbreviation indicating the source is placed last:

trust (for that)... □ *Alec got the house rebuilt when licences were almost unprocurable –* ***trust*** *him* ***for*** *that (*or: ***trust*** *him to do that)!* PW

In every entry with a complex grammatical code, the need to illustrate basic patterns has to be balanced against the desirability of providing examples of *transforms.* Very unusual transforms are always illustrated, and care has been taken to provide examples of 'nominalized' forms whenever they occur:

call up[2] ... *The* ***call-up*** *of the 40–42 age-group was announced on the radio last night.*

The grammatical and collocational patterns associated with these forms are often illustrated:

walk out[2] ... *Building workers* ***walked out*** *(*or: *staged a* ***walk-out****) during the morning in protest at the sacking of a bricklayer.*

7.4.1 A number of transformational relationships which are not accounted for in the grammatical code (or tables of patterns) are dealt with, as they arise, in the illustrations. Certain of these relationships recur quite often. The connection between:

*Don't **splash** any paint **on** your clothes.*
*Don't **splash** your clothes **with** paint.*
for example, also holds for
*The gardener **sprayed** insecticide **on** the rose-bushes.*
*The gardener **sprayed** the rose-bushes **with** insecticide.*
The fact that this relationship is found repeatedly makes a consistent treatment possible, as follows:

spread on ... □ *An embroidered blanket was **spread on** the sofa (*or: *The sofa was **spread with** an embroidered blanket).* □ ***Spread** the butter thickly **on** the rolls (*or: ***Spread** the rolls thickly **with** butter).*

– where the alternative **with** pattern is given in parentheses after the **on** pattern. In all such cases, the verb + **with** expression is itself listed as a headphrase and referred back to the main entry:

spread with ... ⇨ spread on.

Grammatical and other notes

8 When the user's attention needs to be drawn to special features of form, grammatical function or meaning which cannot conveniently be pointed out elsewhere in the entry, they are explained in a note placed after the illustrations (and separated from them by a box – □). The notes are printed in ordinary type, except for collocational material, or further illustrations, which are printed in *italic* and the headphrase (or any part(s) of it), which are printed in ***bold italic*** in the illustrative material:

accustom oneself to ... □ often preceded by *find it difficult/easy/hard to.*

make allowances (for)... □ allowances occasionally sing, as in: *When every **allowance** has been **made for** his inexperience.* ...

Among the various special features which the notes are used to point out and explain are the following:

(i) special restrictions of *tense* or *aspect* applying to an expression:

finish with[3] ... finish chastising or punishing ... □ with perfect tenses.

(ii) the extension of the basic pattern of an expression by relating it to a larger syntactic pattern of which it forms a part:

lean over backwards ... try one's hardest to help ... □ followed by *-ing* form or *to*-inf.

(iii) the tendency for one or more of the transforms of an expression to be used more frequently than the basic pattern(s):

let down[4] [B1i nom pass adj]... make sb's spirits sink, depress. ... □ usu passive and nom.

punch up[2] [A1 nom] ... have a (fist) fight, exchange punches ... □ usu nom.

(iv) any special, restricted, meaning or context of use of an expression:

account to ... give an explanation to; be responsible to ... □ usu with the implication that failure to do sth will be punished.

The cross-reference system

9 As is explained in 5, *Definitions*, a headphrase which has the *same* meaning as another is cross-referenced to it in a special way: the synonym referred to is placed near the *beginning* of the entry, and is marked (q v). In many entries, however, a different kind of cross-reference is found. This appears at the *end* of the entry, as follows:

turn back[2]... fold one (smaller) part of sth over another (larger) part. ... ⇨ turn down[1].

Very often – as in this case – there will be a reference back from the entry to which attention is directed:

turn down[1]... fold one part of sth over another (esp over sth which is lower down). ...: ⇨ turn back[2].

When one entry follows immediately on another, the form of cross-reference is as follows:

palm off (on) ... ⇨ next entry.
palm off (with) ... ⇨ previous entry.

An entry may contain a number of cross-referenced items. When these are of the same pattern (e g verb + particle) they are arranged alphabetically:

take before ... ⇨ be before[2], bring before, come before[2], go before[2], put before[2].

When reference is made to two (or more) headphrases which are alike except for their verbs (e g **be down (from), come down (from)** the headphrases are combined, as follows:

send down ... ⇨ be/come down (from); go down[8].

When numbered items (which are never themselves combined) are included in the same cross-referenced set as combined ones, the types are separated as in the entry just shown, and as follows:

be in fashion/vogue ... ⇨ bring/come into fashion/vogue; be in[1], come in[1].

The general purpose of these kinds of cross-reference is to indicate special grammatical connections between entries, or to point out important relationships of meaning (other, that is, than *sameness* of meaning). Headphrases which are explicitly linked in this way fall into two main groups: those containing 'major' verbs (**come**, **go**, **bring**, **send** etc) and those featuring other verbs. To simplify the presentation, these groups are dealt with in separate sub-sections (9.1 and 9.2), beginning with the major verbs. Sub-section 9.3 is concerned with 'dummy' entries – those whose purpose is simply to direct the user's attention to main entries.

Cross-references and the 'major' verbs

9.1 A 'major' verb is one which (like **come** or **go**) combines readily with a wide range of particles and prepositions and also enters freely into more complex expressions containing nouns (and possibly adjectives). Both the simple and the complex expressions are often highly idiomatic. The verb **put** is a highly productive example of the type. Not only do we find **put down**, **put in**, **put through**, **put up** etc, but we also meet **put at a premium**, **put in a nutshell** and **put one's thinking cap on**. Another characteristic of this aptly-named 'heavy-duty' class is that a particular combination of major verb and particle is likely to display (and continue to develop) a range of separate meanings. For **put up** alone, the dictionary records no less than ten distinct senses. A further significant feature of these verbs is that they are found, in their various combinations with prepositions, nouns etc, to correspond to each other. It is these correspondences which are reflected by the cross-references in entries for major verbs. Thus the cross-references in the entry **put into force**, for example, show a correspondence between **put**, **be**, **bring** and **come**:

put into force ... ⇨ be in/bring into/come into force.

while those in the entry **put up for auction/sale** indicate a connection between **put**, **be** and **come**:

put up for auction/sale ... ⇨ be/come up for auction/sale.

As these examples suggest, the relationship which is most frequently indicated by the cross-reference system for major-verb entries is the contrast between intransitive verbs (e g **come**) and transitive verbs (e g **bring**, **put**). Another connection which is commonly reflected by the system is that between either or both these types of verb and the 'copula' **be**. In the following entries these three classes of verb are again brought together:

be in play ... ⇨ bring/come into play.
be on to[1] ... ⇨ be talking to ... ⇨ get on to[1], put on to[1]

There is a strong tendency (as shown by certain of the examples already given) for **come**, **go**, **get** and **stay** (to name only the most common of the major intransitives) to be associated with some transitives rather than others. Those intransitives, and the verbs with which they tend to be linked, are considered in turn below. Comments on entries with more complex cross-references (i e those which show association between several verbs, intransitive and transitive) are reserved until the end.

9.1.1 In very many of the combinations (of verb + particle, verb + preposition etc) in which it occurs, **come**, as intransitive, is found to correspond with **bring**, as transitive:

come back[3]... return (to the memory). ... ⇨ bring back[2].
come in[5]... be received as income. ... ⇨ bring in[2].

There may be additional links between each of these verbs and the copula:

come into focus ... ⇨ be in/bring into focus.
come out[4] ... flower, blossom. ... ⇨ be out[4], bring out[4].

A common and important connection also exists between **come** and **take** (most especially in expressions where **take** can have the generalized meaning 'cause (sth) to move towards one'); once again there may be a further correspondence with **be**:

take off[1] ... remove, detach (esp sth fastened to a surface or edge). ... ⇨ be off[2], come off[2].
take off[8] ... reduce a price ... ⇨ come off[8].

Connections between **come** and other transitive verbs (e g **let**, **put**) are also found, but such cases are rare:

come out[2] ... leave, be released from, prison. ... ⇨ be out[2], let out/out of.
come up for ... be considered as an applicant ... ⇨ be up for, put up (for)[1].

9.1.2 For expressions with **go**, the most commonly recorded transitive equivalents contain **put** (with or without a further link to **be**):

go in[3] ... fit. ... ⇨ put in[4].
go out[2] ... become unconscious. ... ⇨ be out[9], put out[9].
go out of action ... ⇨ be/put out of action.
go up[4] ... be constructed. ... ⇨ put up[3].

Other links (less frequently recorded in the dictionary) are with **send** and **take** (especially in the generalized sense 'move (sb or sth) *away* from the speaker'):

go up[5] ... be destroyed ... ⇨ send up[2].

go up the wall ... go nearly mad. ... ⇨ send up the wall.

go around/round (with) ... keep company (with). ... ⇨ take around/round (with).

go through[5] ... review, rehearse ... ⇨ take through.

Apart from these usual, or 'regular' correspondences, there are equivalent transitive verbs of which only a few examples are found:

go aground (on) ... become stuck on mud ... ⇨ run aground (on).

Again, for many expressions containing **go** there is no matching transitive at all – and thus no cross-reference:

go round[4] ... be sufficient (for). ...

9.1.3 When **get** is used as a verb of motion (as distinct from a possessive verb) it may, in the various expressions where it occurs, have both an intransitive *and* a transitive function. These two functions are usually handled in the *same* entry, with no need for a cross-reference:

get off on the right/wrong foot [A3 B3 ...] (cause to) make a good/bad start ...

In a few expressions in which **get** is used intransitively, however, it corresponds to a distinct transitive verb, especially **put**. In these cases, the user is referred from the **get** entry to the **put** entry (and to the **be** entry, if there is one) in the usual way:

get on to[2] [A3] trace, find, detect ... ⇨ be on to[2], put on to[2].

When **get** is used as a possessive verb (i e in the senses 'receive', 'recover' etc) it may have links with **give** and **have**. Such connections are shown as follows:

get back[4] ... recover possession of ... ⇨ give back (to)[1], have back[1].

9.1.4 Several expressions containing the intransitive verb **stay** are matched by expressions containing transitive **keep** (= 'cause to stay'):

stay in[1] ... remain at school after others have left, as a punishment ... ⇨ keep in[3].

It should be noted that since **keep** can have an intransitive as well as a transitive function, there may sometimes be a reference from a **stay** entry to an intransitive use of **keep**:

stay ahead/ahead of ... not lose one's position in front ... ⇨ keep ahead/ahead of.

keep ahead/ahead of ... not lose one's position in front ... ⇨ stay ahead/ahead of.

An important transitive equivalent of **stay**, though less commonly found than **keep**, is **leave** (= 'allow to stay'):

stay down ... remain in a lowered position. ... ⇨ leave down.

9.1.5 Certain entries whose headphrases contain a major verb refer the user to *several* other headphrases, which may be related in grammar and meaning in quite complex ways. Some cross-references, for example, may direct the user to a number of intransitive and transitive verbs:

be back[1] ... return; have returned. ... ⇨ bring back[1], come back[1], get back[1], go back[1], take back[1]

Because of the special links that have been shown to exist between **come** and **bring** (⇨ 9.1.1, above), and **go** and **take** (when the verb has the generalized meaning 'move (sth) away from the speaker'; ⇨ 9.1.2), it seems reasonable to suppose that those connections are also strong here. We can assume, too, that in the following set of cross-references **come before** has as its particular transitive **bring before**, and that correspondingly **go before** is matched by **put before** and **take before**.

be before[2] ... appear, be presented for a decision, the judgment of a court, etc. ... ⇨ bring before, come before[2], go before[2], put before[2], take before.

Other cross-references

9.2 Cross-references between entries whose headphrases do *not* include a major verb serve a variety of purposes. The commonest of these are as follows.

9.2.1 Expressions which are close in meaning (and possibly also in form) but which need to be carefully distinguished are usually cross-referenced to each other, with additional explanatory notes where necessary:

sell (at) ... give in exchange at a particular price level. ... □ one sells at a point on a scale (e g of loss or gain); one sells for (q v) a particular amount or sum of money.

sell (for) ... give in exchange for a particular sum of money. ... ⇨ (footnote at) sell (at).

work at ... give thought, energy etc to getting rid of or solving sth. ... ⇨ work on.

work on ... give thought, effort etc to making or discovering sth. ... ⇨ work at.

9.2.2 When a complex headphrase (i e one containing a noun or nouns) is clearly related in meaning to a simpler headphrase, and it is helpful to point to this connection, the entry for the complex expression is cross-referenced to the entry for the simpler one, as follows:

see beyond ... (be able to) foresee and understand events etc which are at some distance in space or time; be farsighted. ...

see beyond the end of one's nose ... (be able to) understand more than is present and obvious ... ⇨ previous entry.

9.2.3 When two expressions are opposite in meaning, the entries for them may be cross-referenced to each other:

switch off[2] ... make sb dull, lifeless, unresponsive ... ⇨ switch on[2].

switch on[2] ... make sb lively, excited ... ⇨ switch off[2].

9.2.4 When two expressions are related in such a way that the Subject of one corresponds to the prepositional object of the other (and perhaps vice-versa), the entries for the expressions are cross-referenced to each other:

break out in[1] ... suddenly become covered in. **S**: patient; face, body. **o**: spots, pimples, sores; rash ... ⇨ break out on.

break out on ... appear suddenly upon. **S**: spots; rash. **o**: face, arm ... ⇨ break out in[1].

run out[1] ... be finished, exhausted. **S**: supply, stock (of wines, cigarettes etc); patience; time ... ⇨ run out/out of.

run out/out of ... finish, exhaust. **o**: supply, stock (of commodities); ideas; patience ... ⇨ run out[1] ...

9.2.5 If two expressions are related to each other in such a way that the Direct Object of one corresponds to the prepositional object of the other (and vice-versa) the connection is shown by means of a cross-reference in each entry:

weave (up) (from) ... make cloth from threads by weaving them together. **o**: length, piece; (cotton, woollen) cloth. **O**: yarn, thread ... ⇨ next entry.
weave (up) (into)... make threads into cloth by weaving them together. **o**: yarn, thread; cotton, wool. **o**: cloth; blanket, covering ... ⇨ previous entry.

9.2.6 Some expressions containing a transitive verb (such as **raise**) are closely matched by expressions containing the corresponding intransitive verb (thus, **rise**). The matching entries are cross-referenced, as follows:

raise from the dead ... ⇨ rise from the dead/grave.
rise from the dead/grave ... ⇨ raise from the dead.

(For transitive/intransitive correspondences between the heavy-duty verbs, ⇨ 9.1, above.)

Cross-references from 'dummy' entries

9.3 Entries such as

spatter with [B2 pass rel] ⇨ previous entry.

contain a minimum of information about the headphrase. They are empty or 'dummy' entries, designed simply to direct the user to a main entry – in this case the immediately preceding one – where fuller information is provided. Dummy entries perform two main functions in the dictionary. In the case of the entry just quoted and also of

splash with [B2 pass rel] ⇨ splash on/onto².
spread with [B2 pass rel] ⇨ spread on.

their purpose is to refer the user to main entries in which the verb + **with** pattern is illustrated side by side with the verb + **on** (or **onto**) pattern. (This relationship is dealt with in more detail in *Illustrations*, 7.4.1.)

Many headphrases in the dictionary contain two or more alternative prepositions or particles, divided by the oblique. Others contain two optional prepositions or particles, within separate sets of parentheses:

come along/on² ... make progress. ...
take around/round (with) ... take as a companion. ...
stand (as) (for) ... be a candidate ... (for sth). ...

Each of these headphrases introduces a main entry, with a definition and examples. However, a user meeting **come on**, **take round (with)** or **stand (for)** – in the senses indicated – for the first time in speech or writing, and is not aware that there are alternative prepositions, might without help have difficulty in locating the main entries he needs. To guide him, the following dummy entries are provided (at the appropriate alphabetical places):

come on² ... make progress. ⇨ come along/on².
take round (with) ... ⇨ take around/round (with).
stand (for) ... ⇨ stand (as) (for).

The user will notice that the numbered entry **come on²** (like the main entry **come along/on²**) contains the definition 'make progress'. The additional information is given so that this dummy entry can be distinguished from other members of a **come on** series (some of which are not dummy entries).

List of sources

This list records the original texts and subsequent additional texts used as a basis for some of the illustrative quotations (⇨ General Introduction, p vi and The content and arrangement of entries, 7, *Illustrations*).

It is arranged in alphabetical order according to the reference initials of the title (the first column on the left) that are used in the text of the dictionary to identify the source. The author, if known, and the full title of the work follow in the second and third columns. The last column gives the edition used with the date of the publication or impression and, in parentheses below it, the name of the original publisher and date of first publication in England if they differ from the edition used.

Reference initials	*Author*	*Title*	*Edition used (+ original publisher and date of first publication)*
AH	William Plomer	At Home	Penguin 1961 (Jonathan Cape 1958)
AITC	Monica Dickens	The Angel in the Corner	Penguin 1960 (Michael Joseph 1956)
ARG		Argosy (magazine)	September 1958
ART	N F Simpson	A Resounding Tinkle	Penguin 1960 in New English Dramatists 2
ASA	Angus Wilson	Anglo-Saxon Attitudes	Penguin 1958 (Secker & Warburg 1956)
B	Alan Clark	Barbarossa	Penguin 1967 (Hutchinson 1965)
BB	Gerald Durrell	The Bafut Beagles	Reprint Society 1956 (Rupert Hart-Davis 1954)
BBCR		BBC Radio	programmes 1973–1974
BBCTV		BBC Television	programmes 1967–1974
BFA	H E Bates	A Breath of French Air	Penguin 1962 (Michael Joseph 1959)
BM		Blackwood's Magazine	July 1960
BN	Alan Moorhead	The Blue Nile	Heron Books 1965 (Hamish Hamilton 1962)
CON	John Wain	The Contenders	Penguin 1962 (Macmillan 1958)
CSWB	Arnold Wesker	Chicken Soup with Barley	Penguin 1959

list of sources

CWR	Laurie Lee	Cider with Rosie	Penguin 1962 (Hogarth Press 1959)
DBM	H E Bates	The Darling Buds of May	Penguin 1961 (Michael Joseph 1958)
DC	Dorothy Eden	Darling Clementine	Penguin 1959 (MacDonald 1955)
DF	Gerald Durrell	The Drunken Forest	Penguin 1961 (Rupert Hart-Davis 1956)
DIL	Richard Gordon	Doctor in Love	Penguin 1961 (Michael Joseph 1957)
DM		Daily Mirror (newspaper)	21 June 1960
DOP	Aldous Huxley	The Doors of Perception	Penguin 1960 (Chatto & Windus 1954)
DPM	Bernard Kops	The Dream of Peter Mann	Penguin 1960
E	Samuel Beckett	Embers	Faber & Faber 1959
EGD	John Osborne & Anthony Creighton	Epitaph for George Dillon	Penguin 1960 (Faber & Faber 1958)
EHOW	Doris Lessing	Each His Own Wilderness	Penguin 1959
EM	Cyril Hare	An English Murder	Penguin 1960 (Faber & Faber 1951)
FFE	Peter Shaffer	Five Finger Exercise	Penguin 1962 (Hamish Hamilton 1958)
G		The Guardian (newspaper)	April–October 1967
H		Honey (magazine)	August 1960
HAA	Angus Wilson	Hemlock and After	Penguin 1957 (Secker & Warburg 1952)
HAH	Aldous Huxley	Heaven and Hell	Penguin 1960
HAHA	Jennifer Dawson	The Ha-Ha	Penguin 1962 (Blond 1961)
HD	John Wain	Hurry On Down	Penguin 1960 (Secker & Warburg 1953)
HOM	Graham Greene	The Heart of the Matter	Penguin 1962 (William Heinemann 1948)
HSG	Bernard Kops	The Hamlet of Stepney Green	Penguin 1959

ILIH	Kingsley Amis	I Like It Here	Four Square 1961 (Gollancz 1958)
ITAJ	Arnold Wesker	I'm Talking About Jerusalem	Penguin 1960
ITV		(various) Independent Television Companies	programmes 1967
JFTR	Stanley Price	Just for the Record	Penguin 1962 (Michael Joseph 1961)
L		The Listener (periodical)	14 February & 4 April 1963
LBA	John Osborne	Look Back in Anger	Faber & Faber 1960 (1957)
LF	William Golding	Lord of the Flies	Penguin 1960 (Faber & Faber 1954)
LLDR	Alan Sillitoe	The Loneliness of the Long-distance Runner	Pan 1962 (W H Allen 1959)
LWK	Laurens van der Post	The Lost World of the Kalahari	Penguin 1962 (Hogarth Press 1958)
MFF	Ian M L Hunter	Memory: Facts and Fancies	Pelican 1961 (1957)
MFM	Field-Marshal Montgomery	The Memoirs of Field-Marshal Montgomery	Fontana 1961 (Collins 1958)
MM	Muriel Spark	Memento Mori	Penguin 1961 (Macmillan 1959)
NDN	W R Geddes	Nine Dayak Nights	Oxford University Press 1957
NM	C P Snow	The New Men	Penguin 1961 (Macmillan 1954)
NS		The New Scientist (periodical)	17 September 1959, 10 March 1960
OBS		The Observer (newspaper)	1960–1974
OI	Marghanita Laski	The Offshore Island	May Fair Books 1961 (Cresset Press 1959)
OMIH	Graham Greene	Our Man in Havana	Penguin 1962 (William Heinemann 1958)
PE	Hugh Clevely	Public Enemy	Penguin 1961 (Cassell 1953)
PL	C Northcote Parkinson	Parkinson's Law,	John Murray 1961 (1958)
PM	William Golding	Pincher Martin	Faber & Faber 1960 (1956)
PP	Robert Harling	The Paper Palace	Reprint Society 1952 (Chatto & Windus 1951)

list of sources

PTLB	Andre Maurois	Prometheus: The Life of Balzac	Penguin 1971 (Bodley Head 1965)
PTTP	Martha Gellhorn	Pretty Tales for Tired People	Michael Joseph 1965
PW	L P Hartley	A Perfect Woman	Penguin 1959 (Hamish Hamilton 1955)
QA	Graham Greene	The Quiet American	Penguin 1962 (William Heinemann 1955)
R	Arnold Wesker	Roots	Penguin 1959
RATT	John Braine	Room at the Top	Penguin 1960 (Eyre & Spottis-woode 1957)
RFW	Nevil Shute	Requiem for a Wren	Reprint Society 1956 (William Heinemann 1955)
RM	Compton Mackenzie	The Rival Monster	Penguin 1959 (Chatto & Windus 1952)
RT		Radio Times (periodical)	Scottish edition, 29 December 1960
SC		The Scotsman (newspaper)	6–29 April 1960, 6 January 1972
SD	Sir Mortimer Wheeler	Still Digging	Pan Books 1958 (Michael Joseph 1955)
SKOG	Robin Jenkins	Some Kind of Grace	Corgi Books 1962 (MacDonald 1960)
SML	William Cooper	Scenes from Married Life	Macmillan 1961
SNP	H J Eysenck	Sense and Nonsense in Psychology	Pelican 1961 (1957)
SPL	William Cooper	Scenes from Provincial Life	Penguin 1961 (Jonathan Cape 1950)
ST		The Sunday Times (newspaper)	1967–1974
T		The Times (newspaper)	1960–1974
TBC	Fred Hoyle	The Black Cloud	Penguin 1960 (William Heinemann 1957)
TC	Harold Pinter	The Caretaker	Methuen 1960
TCB	Agatha Christie	They Came to Baghdad	Fontana 1960 (Collins 1951)
TCM		The Cornhill Magazine	Summer 1960
TES		The Times Educational Supplement (periodical)	15 February, 29 March, 9 August 1963

TGLY	Kingsley Amis	Take a Girl Like You	Penguin 1962 (Gollancz 1960)
THH	John Arden	The Happy Haven	Penguin 1962
TK	Arnold Wesker	The Kitchen	Penguin 1960
TLG	Raymond Chandler	The Long Good-bye	Penguin 1959 (Hamish Hamilton 1953)
TO		Today (magazine)	25 June 1960
TOH	Shelagh Delaney	A Taste of Honey	Methuen 1960
TST	John Wyndham	The Seeds of Time	Penguin 1960 (Michael Joseph 1956)
TT	G W Target	The Teachers	Penguin 1962 (Duckworth 1960)
UL	Richard Hoggart	The Uses of Literacy	Pelican 1959 (Chatto & Windus 1957)
US	Pamela Hansford Johnson	The Unspeakable Skipton	Penguin 1961 (Macmillan 1959)
UTN	Iris Murdoch	Under the Net	Penguin 1960 (Chatto & Windus 1954)
WDM	Angela Thirkell	What Did It Mean?	Hamish Hamilton 1954
WI		Woman's Illustrated (magazine)	16 July 1960
WTR	Bruce Michael Cooper	Writing Technical Reports	Penguin 1964
YAA	Michael Hastings	Yes, and After	Penguin 1962

Alphabetical list of particles and prepositions

The lists below gather together all those particles and propositions that are used to form part of the headphrases in the dictionary.

Particles

aback
aboard
about
above
abreast
abroad
across
adrift
after
aground
ahead
aloft
along
alongside
apart
around
aside
astray
away
back
backwards
before
behind
below
between
beyond
by
counter

down
downhill
downstairs
forth
forward(s)
home
in
indoors
in front
inside
near
off
on
on top
out
outside
over
overboard
past
round
through
to
together
under
underground
up
upstairs
without

Prepositions

aboard
about
above
across
after
against
ahead of
along
alongside
among
around
as
as far as
astride
at
before
behind
below
beneath
beside
between
beyond
by
down
for
from

in
in front of
inside
into
like
near
of
off
on
onto
on top of
out of
outside
over
past
round
through
to
toward(s)
under
underneath
up
upon
with
within
without

Note: **in front** (cf **before**; **behind**) and **on top** (cf **under**) are regarded as the equivalent of *particles* which are written as a single word; **ahead of**, **as far as** (cf **to**), **in front of**, **on top of** and **out of** (cf **from**; **into**) are regarded as the equivalent of *prepositions* which are written as a single word.

Abbreviations and symbols used in the dictionary

(For the initials used to identify the source of quotations ⇨ *List of sources*, pp lxxv–lxxix; for the coding system used in the grammatical patterns ⇨ *Grammatical codes and tables*, pp xxxiv–lvii.)

Abbreviations

A	Adjunct (adverbial phrase)	n	noun
adj	adjective, adjectival; participial adjective	neg	negative
		nom	nominalized (noun) form
adv	adverb (phrase, clause)	no, nos	number, numbers
alt	alternative (construction, form, spelling)	O	Direct Object
		o	object of a preposition
attrib	attributive(ly)	pass	passive (transform)
cf, cp	compare	pl	plural
e g	for example	pp	past participle
emph	emphatic (transform)	prep	preposition
esp	especially	q v	which may be referred to
etc	and the rest of these	reflex	reflexive
fig	figurative(ly)	rel	relative (transform)
GB	British (usage)	S	Subject
i e	that is	sb	somebody
imper	imperative	sing	singular
Inf, inf	infinitive	sth	something
-ing form	non-finite verb form in *-ing* (e g *eating*, *drinking*)	*to*-inf	infinitive preceded by *to* (e g *to eat*, *to drink*)
interr	interrogative	US	American (usage)
lit	literal(ly)	usu	usually
m	(adverbial) modifier of a particle	v	verb

Symbols

□	separates collocated words (or definitions) and grammatical information from illustrative quotations (⇨ 7, *Illustrations*)
□	separates individual illustrations from each other (⇨ 7, *Illustrations*)
⚠	marks words in the lists of collocations (after **S**, **O**, **o** etc) that are part of a 'restricted' set (⇨ 6.5, *Collocations*)
⇨	see (the entry for, etc)
=	is equivalent to, means the same thing as
*	marks an unacceptable phrase, sentence etc
?	marks an unlikely phrase, sentence etc

A

abide by [A2] accept; act in accordance with. **S:** contestants, parties, sides, members. **o:** rules, regulations; decision, verdict □ *The two men agreed to* ***abide by*** *the referee's decision.* □ *Unless they* ***abide by*** *the rules of the club, they will have to leave.*

abound in [A2 rel] be full of. **S:** place, institution, area of learning. **o:** opportunities; difficulties, snags; examples (of) □ *Modern industry* ***abounds in*** *opportunities for young men with imagination.* □ *This language* ***abounds in*** *difficulties for the foreign learner.* □ *The countryside* ***abounds in*** *wild life of every kind.* □ occasionally abound with.

abscond (from) [A2 emph rel] (formal) go away (from), leave (unlawfully). **S:** boy, prisoner. **o:** remand home, detention centre; custody □ *'You have twice* ***absconded from*** *an open prison, where you had every opportunity of living a reasonable, if restricted, life,' said the magistrate. 'I now have no alternative to sending you to a closed prison for the completion of your sentence.'*

abscond with [A2 rel] (formal) go away, disappear, taking property to which one has no right. **o:** family jewels, firm's secret plans □ *The accountant, after serving the company faithfully for twenty-odd years,* ***absconded with*** *at least ten thousand pounds, accompanied by the boss's attractive secretary!*

absent oneself (from) [B2 emph rel] (formal) not attend, not be present (at); stay away (from)[1] (q v) □ *The Chairman of the housing committee deliberately* ***absented himself from*** *the meeting, realizing that he could not face up to the criticisms of his opponents.*

absolve from [B2 pass emph rel] (legal, formal) declare free from, release (from) (q v). **S:** priest; court, investigating commission, judge. **O:** dying man, repentant woman; accused person, company, jury. **o:** sin, guilt; blame, responsibility, obligation □ *Having been* ***absolved*** *by the court* ***from*** *all responsibility in the death of the pedestrian, the man went to the nearest pub and got drunk by way of celebration.* □ *After a trial lasting for three weeks and ending in the conviction of all the accused, the jury were* ***absolved from*** *all further service for the rest of their lives.*

absorbed in [pass (B2)] have one's attention totally occupied by. **o:** book, story; what was going on outside □ *The children were so* ***absorbed in*** *their game that they did not notice the passage of time.* □ passive with *be, get, seem.*

abstain (from) [A2] not do something; refrain (from) (q v). **o:** alcohol, sex; criticism □ *Patrons are requested to* ***abstain from*** *smoking in the restaurant.* □ *Several MPs* ***abstained from*** *voting at the end of the debate.* □ often followed by an *-ing* form.

abut on [A2 rel] (formal) touch the boundary of, border on □ *The residence of the Archbishop* ***abuts on*** *the medieval walls of the city.*

accede to [A2 pass emph rel] (formal) grant, meet. **S:** company; manager, doctor, principal. **o:** request, demand, application □ *The Committee regrets that it cannot* ***accede to*** *your request for a month's unpaid leave.* □ *My application for a change of department was readily* ***acceded to.***

accord with [A2] (formal) match, be in agreement with; correspond (to/with) (q v). **S:** information, statement, claim, account. **o:** facts, data, our records □ *My information does not* ***accord with*** *what this report states.* □ *His behaviour does not* ***accord with*** *my idea of a gentleman.* □ usu neg or interr.

account for[1] [A2 pass] give a satisfactory record of. **S:** cashier, accountant. **o:** expenses, payments, outlay □ *He was unable to* ***account for*** *the deficit in the firm's bank balance.* □ *I'm afraid that you'll have to* ***account for*** *every penny of the money that was entrusted to you.*

account for[2] [A2 pass] explain. **S:** he etc; his state of mind; fact. **o:** presence, absence; attitude; surprise, shock; position □ *Peter must be ill; it's the only thing that will* ***account for*** *his strange behaviour.* □ *'The record-player's out of order.' 'Oh, that would* ***account for*** *the strange noise it's making.'*

account for[3] [A2 pass] be responsible for killing, destroying, knocking out etc. **S:** gunner; ack-ack fire, fighter aircraft; guard, policeman. **o:** raider, bomber, tank; intruder, bandit □ *The fighter screen* ***accounted for*** *three of the enemy aircraft.* □ *Two masked intruders were* ***accounted for*** *by security men.*

not account for preferences/tastes [A2] not be able to explain why sb prefers one thing to another □ *One simply can* ***not account for tastes*** (or: *There's simply* ***no accounting for tastes***).

account to [A2] give an explanation to; be responsible to; answer to (for) (q v). **o:** superior, manager; parent □ *You'll have to* ***account to*** *me if anything happens to this girl while she is in your care.* □ usu with the implication that failure to do sth will be punished.

accuse (of) [B2 pass rel] say that sb is guilty (of). **S:** police, prosecution; mother-in-law. **o:** stealing a car; theft, robbery; treason, perjury □ *Alfred's teacher* ***accused*** *him* ***of*** *cheating in the examination.* □ *I've been* ***accused of*** *many things in my life, but never of cowardice.* □ (ironic) *'You can never* ***accuse*** *Cyril* ***of*** *overwork.'* □ often followed by an *-ing* form.

accustom oneself to [B2 rel] learn to accept; get used to. **o:** (new) conditions, situation; one's changed position; retirement, different kind of life; doing sth. **A:** quickly, slowly, with difficulty, at last □ *The old man slowly* ***accustomed himself to*** *life without companionship.* □ *You'll just have to* ***accustom yourself to*** *the new conditions, and stop complaining.* □ *She thought she would never* ***accustom herself to*** *eating nothing but fruit and vegetables.* □ often preceded by *find it difficult/easy/hard to.* ⇨ next entry.

accustomed to [pass (B2)] have learned to expect or accept; (be) used to (q v). **o:** conditions, situation; food, weather, light □ *Conditions here are not what she's* ***accustomed to****.* □ *You'll soon get* ***accustomed to*** *the change of climate.* □ *He'd become* ***accustomed to*** *having his meals brought to him.* ⇨ previous entry.

acquaint with [B2 pass rel] (formal) (help to) learn, discover. **O:** oneself; pupil; colleague, wife. **o:** facts, details, circumstances □ *When I was a teacher I always made a point of* ***acquainting*** *myself* ***with*** *the home background of all my pupils.* □ *You should try to* ***acquaint*** *yourself* ***with*** *the facts, before you express an opinion.* □ *Are you* ***acquainted with*** *the works of Maria Edgeworth?*

acquiesce (in) [A2 pass emph rel] (formal) offer no opposition (to); agree (to) (q v). **o:** arrangement, action, change □ *He said he would never* ***acquiesce in*** *his lifelong enemy being made a director of the company.* □ *I was annoyed to find that their proposal to take control had been weakly* ***acquiesced in****.*

acquit (of) [B2 pass rel] (legal) find not guilty (of). **S:** magistrate, judge, jury, court. **O:** prisoner, accused. **o:** charge; aiding and abetting, causing grievous bodily harm, loitering with intent; murder, manslaughter □ *After a trial of several days the jury* ***acquitted*** *the man (****of*** *the charge of murder).* □ *The accused was* ***acquitted of*** *manslaughter but found guilty of dangerous driving.*

act for [A2 rel] represent; perform sb's duties etc on his behalf. **S:** solicitor; union, professional organization. **o:** private citizen, member □ *Since old Mr Smith fell ill, his son has been* ***acting for*** *him in all his affairs.* □ *During the sergeant-major's absence on a training course, the senior sergeant* ***acted for*** *him.*

act on/upon[1] [A2 pass emph rel] follow, take; take action (on) (q v). **o:** advice; (recent, the latest) information, news; one's own initiative; intuition □ ***Acting on*** *your recommendation, I have decided to emigrate to Australia.* □ *If my advice had been* ***acted upon****, the firm would not have gone bankrupt.*

act on/upon[2] [A2 emph rel] affect; have an effect on. **S:** medicines, pills, drugs. **o:** organ; heart, liver, spleen, gland □ *These pills* ***act on*** *the liver.* □ ***On*** *which part of the brain does this drug* ***act****?*

act out [B1i pass] act or play a part to a conclusion (usu in a real-life situation). **O:** part, role; drama, comedy; scene □ *She looked at the boy* ***acting out*** *his injured innocence and stared at him until he looked down.* TT □ *In the enclosed life of this small village, many passions are brought to the surface and* ***acted out****.*

act up[1] [A1] (informal) react, respond appropriately to sth □ *'The young lady's rather easily upset,' the landlord said. 'When the chaps tease her she doesn't quite know how to* ***act up****.'* PW

act up[2] [A1] (informal) behave in an annoying way □ *'You look a bit down in the mouth* (= depressed). *Boy friend* ***acting up****?' 'Oh yes, he* ***acts up****.'* TGLY □ *Don't take any notice of the baby. If you scold him, he'll only start* ***acting up****.*

adapt (for) [B2 pass rel] rewrite, rearrange, modify (for). **O:** novel, play, story; machine. **o:** stage, radio, TV; children; use in; a special purpose. **A:** specially; skilfully □ *The author is going to* ***adapt*** *his play* ***for*** *television.* □ *It's surprising that this novel hasn't yet been* ***adapted for*** *the cinema.* □ *These tractors have been* ***adapted for*** *use in very cold climates.* □ adapt (for) and adapt (from) (⇨ next entry) may be combined: *He appeared in a series* ***adapted for*** *radio* ***from*** *a French original.*

adapt (from) [B2 pass rel] translate, change, modify (from). **O:** novel, play, story. **o:** French, Spanish; the original □ *This play has been skilfully* ***adapted from*** *the original.* ⇨ previous entry.

adapt to [B2 pass rel] modify, rearrange, make fit, for. **O:** building; ship, bus, plane. **o:** new conditions; the special needs of; the use of □ *We'll have to* ***adapt*** *this building* ***to*** *the needs of the old people who are going to live in it.* □ *The ships were found to be unsuitable for the conditions* ***to*** *which they had supposedly been* ***adapted****.*

adapt (oneself) to [A2 pass rel B2 rel] change one's outlook or behaviour to suit; adjust (oneself) to (q v). **o:** (new) circumstances, situation, conditions; way of life; environment, climate □ *I don't think I shall ever* ***adapt myself to*** *this hot climate.* □ *The new teacher was very slow to* ***adapt to*** *the unusual rules of the school.*

add in [B1i pass] put or pour in; include. **O:** flour, butter, egg. **A:** while, before, after, mixing, heating, stirring etc □ *Should you* ***add in*** *the lemon juice before or after mixing the flour and sugar?* □ often used in recipes, in the imper form.

add on [B1i pass] include; attach □ *'Here's your bill, sir. I've* ***added on*** *the ten per cent service charge.'* □ *She wrote me rather a cold letter; even the inquiry about my health looked as if it had been* ***added on*** *as an afterthought.*

add to [A2 pass B2 pass rel] increase in extent or quantity; supplement. **S:** discovery, work, research. **O:** much, a good deal, something, nothing. **o:** (store of) knowledge, wealth, enjoyment, understanding, appreciation; difficulties, problems □ [A2] *The recent excavations have* ***added*** *greatly* ***to*** *our knowledge of life in Britain during the Stone Age.* □ [A2] *The palace had been* ***added to*** *from time to time, and as a result incorporated various styles of architecture.* □ [B2] *Nothing has been* ***added to*** *our understanding of this disease by all the cruel experiments on animals.* □ [B2] *Will you* ***add*** *your name* ***to*** *this petition against abortion?*

add up[1] [A1] (informal) make sense, present a reasonable picture; lead to an obvious conclusion. **S:** facts, evidence; their behaviour; it □ *Sometimes she would greet him happily; sometimes he found her in tears. It just didn't* ***add up****.* □ *The murder had obviously been committed in the house, yet the snow around the house was smooth and undisturbed: it didn't* ***add up****.*

add up[2] [A1 B1i pass] find the sum (of); combine, take together. **O:** figures, numbers, score; the effects (of sth) □ *Try* ***adding up*** *this time instead of subtracting.* □ *Every time I* ***add*** *these figures* ***up*** *I get a different answer.* □ *The practical connections of Britain with her fellow-members are numerous and important, and when* ***added up*** *comprise a good part of Britain's external relations.* SC

add up to[1] [A3] (informal) have a certain value, be equal to; amount to[1] (q v). **S:** information, news; contribution, discovery, acquisition. **o:** (not) much, (not) a lot; very little □ *Their knowledge of how other people live doesn't* **add up to** *much.* □ *Sir Percy said he was surprised that the annual leakage by theft, smuggling and illicit digging did not* **add up to** *more than the figures given to him.* DS □ *The entertainment is most notable for its male dancing, yet in total it* **adds up to** *little more than a fiesta of classical dancing.* T □ usu neg or interr.

add up to[2] [A3] (informal) mean; amount to[2] (q v). **S:** refusal, statement, attitude. **o:** what (in initial position); the fact that □ *'What your statement* **adds up to** *is that you helped to kill the old woman.'* □ *'Your evidence, then, really* **adds up to** *this — that you were nowhere near the scene of the crime?'*

addicted (to) [pass (B2)] have formed, (be) devoted to, as a strong, almost unbreakable habit. **o:** smoking, cigarettes; alcohol, drink; drugs, opium, LSD, heroin; women, sex; reading, television. **A:** hopelessly, strongly, desperately □ *He became* **addicted to** *drugs at quite an early age.* □ *The two things that Appleby is most* **addicted to** *are big cars and big cigars.* □ *He was* **addicted to** *Westerns through regular attendance at the Saturday-morning shows for children.*

address oneself to [B2 emph rel] (formal) tackle; give one's full attention to. **o:** (urgent) task, job, problem; matter, business in hand. **A:** with vigour, with (some) misgivings; energetically, single-mindedly □ *When his father died, Paul had to* **address himself to** *the business of earning his own living.* □ *There are two questions* **to** *which I will* **address myself** *in this lecture.*

adhere to[1] [A2 emph rel] (formal) remain attached to, stick to. **S:** material, preparation; paste, paint. **o:** surface, wall; wood, metal, glass, paper. **A:** firmly, securely □ *This paint will* **adhere to** *any surface, whether rough or smooth.*

adhere to[2] [A2 pass emph rel] (formal) maintain; not depart from. **o:** plan, original programme; (one's) principles, ideas; promise, offer; demand(s), proposal(s), suggestion(s). **A:** firmly, resolutely; through thick and thin; come what may □ *He resolutely* **adhered to** *what he had said at the meeting: he had not changed his mind in any way.* □ *We decided to* **adhere to** *our original plan, in spite of the appalling weather.*

adjourn to [A2 rel] interrupt proceedings in order to resume them at (another place) □ *'Well, gentlemen, if you've all finished, may we* **adjourn to** *the lounge for coffee?'* □ *The judge decided to* **adjourn to** *the scene of the crime so that the jury could see for themselves whether the arguments put forward by the defence were valid in terms of the actual lie of the land.*

adjust (oneself) to [A2 pass rel B2 pass rel] change one's outlook or behaviour to suit; adapt (oneself) to (q v). **o:** new circumstances, environment, situation, condition(s). **A:** quickly, slowly, (im)perfectly, (in)completely, gradually □ *I don't think I shall ever be able to* **adjust myself to** *life in this remote place.* □ *Jenkins was well* **adjusted to** *the society in which he lived.*

admit of [A2] (formal) allow; leave room for. **S:** word(s), statement; facts, evidence. **o:** (only one) meaning, interpretation; no contradiction □ *His problems did not really* **admit of** *any solution.* HD □ *His statement* **admits of** *one interpretation only: that he was fully aware of what he was doing.* □ *These facts* **admit of** *no contradiction.*

admit (to) [B2 pass rel] allow to enter, or join. **S:** ticket, letter. **O:** the bearer; one, two. **o:** (football) match; tournament; ground, arena; museum, zoo, palace; membership □ *This ticket* **will admit** *three* (**to** *the concert*). □ *He was* **admitted to** *the local branch of the Bird Watchers' Association.*

admit to [A2 pass rel] (formal) not deny; confess to (q v). **o:** weakness, taste, liking for; doing sth; everything, nothing. **A:** willingly, reluctantly, readily □ *Mr Pearson* **admitted** *readily* **to** *a great liking for horror films.* □ *'Do you* **admit to** *taking these goods without paying for them?'* □ *Mrs Cross* **admits to** *being easily annoyed.* □ *She* **admits to** *being forty, so she must be about forty-five.*

adorn (with) [B2 pass rel] (formal) make beautiful by decoration (with). **O:** oneself; maiden; (her) hair, body; building, temple, statue, boat. **o:** garlands, flowers; jewels, gold □ *The girl* **adorned** *herself* **with** *flowers and garlands before she entered the hall.* □ *The Goddess's head was* **adorned with** *a crown of many jewels.*

advance on/towards/upon [A2 rel] move in the direction of, e g in order to attack □ *We were ordered to* **advance on** *the enemy's position under cover of darkness.* □ *As I* **advanced towards** *the trapped animal, it snarled and struck at me with its free paw.* □ *The villages* **upon** *which they now* **advanced** *had been turned into veritable fortresses.*

advertise (for) [A2 pass rel] make known one's need (for), try to obtain, by means of notices in newspapers etc. **o:** house, bedsitter; daily help, gardener; second-hand bicycle, washing-machine □ *It's no use just* **advertising for** *a 'secretary' these days. You've got to* **advertise for** *a 'girl-Friday', or a 'personality-girl' and you may even have to hint at office-romance.* □ *'I suppose a suitable flat will turn up. It's been* **advertised for** *enough, hasn't it?'*

advise on [A2 B2 pass] give advice about □ *John makes a good living* **advising on** *interior decoration and lighting.* □ *'Have you ever been* **advised on** *the best way of exploiting your talents as a singer?'*

affiliate (to) [B2 pass rel] connect (with), perhaps as a branch □ *This college is* **affiliated to** *the University of London.* □ *The Committee regrets that it cannot at present* **affiliate** *your group* **to** *our Society.* □ usu passive.

affix (to) [B2 pass rel] add (to); attach (to) (q v). **O:** label, sticker, seal. **o:** letter, parcel □ *Please* **affix** *your signature* **to** *the enclosed form and return it to us at once.* □ *Unless stamps to the correct value are* **affixed** (**to** *your letter*), *it will be sent by surface mail.*

afflict with [B2 pass rel] cause to suffer or be preoccupied with; bother with. **O:** teacher, employer. **o:** (one's) troubles, worries, complaints □ *I wish you wouldn't* **afflict** *me* **with** *your constant complaints.* □ *The poor boy was* **afflicted with** *diabetes.* □ *It's awful to be* **afflicted with** *a sense of inferiority.*

agitate (for) [A2 pass emph rel] demand in an

organized, sometimes disruptive, manner. **S:** movement, party; women, students. **o:** reform, change (in the law etc); freedom, independence; higher wages, lower taxes, better pensions, improved conditions; shorter hours □ *Women had to* ***agitate for*** *the vote for many years before they finally got it.* □ *These were reforms* ***for*** *which they were prepared to* ***agitate****.*

agree (on/upon) [A2 pass emph rel] reach or make an agreement concerning; find (sth) which is mutually acceptable. **o:** price; date; position; cease-fire; terms □ *It seemed as though the two sides would never* ***agree*** *(****on*** *an end to hostilities).* □ *Once the price for the land has been* ***agreed upon****, we can go ahead and build the house.* □ ***On*** *this we can* ***agree****: no sale before January.*

agree (to) [A2 pass rel] accept; fall in with[2] (q v). **o:** terms, suggestions, proposals; plan, arrangement; conditions; what you say □ *I find it impossible to* ***agree to*** *your terms.* □ *After much argument, his proposal was finally* ***agreed to****.*

agree (with) [A2 emph rel B2 emph rel] have the same opinion as. **o:** you; what he says; John's father □ *I entirely* ***agree with*** *you: that road is very dangerous.* □ *I'm afraid I shall never* ***agree with*** *you* (or: *we shall never* ***agree****) about corporal punishment in schools.* □ *Do you* ***agree with*** *me that fox-hunting is a cruel sport?* □ followed by a *that*-clause in [B2] pattern.

agree with [A2] suit sb's digestion, health, temperament or character. **S:** food, fish, meat; climate; conditions, altitude □ *I don't feel well. That meat pie hasn't* ***agreed with*** *me.* □ *That hot, damp climate didn't* ***agree with*** *him — he always felt tired or unwell.* □ *'Does the sea-air* ***agree with*** *you?' 'Rather! I thrive on it.'* □ usu neg or interr.

aim at[1] [A2 B2 pass emph rel] try to hit, have as one's target. **O:** rifle, fire, stone, missile; remarks, criticism. **o:** target; man, animal, bird; young people, the privileged few □ *Mr Appleby* ***aimed at*** *a rabbit, but hit a bird.* □ *He* ***aimed*** *his gun* ***at*** *a policeman, and fired.* □ *I don't know* ***at*** *which union the Minister's remarks were* ***aimed****, but he ought not to say such things.*

aim at[2] [A2 rel] have as one's objective, whether stated or not. **o:** goal, objective, position, job □ *It isn't just a seat in the Cabinet* ***at*** *which he's* ***aiming****, but the Prime Ministership itself!* □ *I don't understand that girl's behaviour. What's she* ***aiming at****?*

alienate from [B2 pass rel] (formal) cause to be estranged from. **o:** society, former friends, workmates □ *The man's unsociable behaviour gradually* ***alienated*** *him* ***from*** *all his friends.* □ *The MP's views on Britain's joining the European Economic Community* ***alienated*** *him still further* ***from*** *some of his colleagues.*

alight (from) [A2 rel] get off, out or down (from). **o:** horse, train, bus, taxi □ *As the old lady was* ***alighting from*** *the car a child on roller-skates collided with her.* □ *The carriage* ***from*** *which the guests were now* ***alighting*** *had the royal coat-of-arms emblazoned on the doors.*

alight on[1] [A2 rel] descend from the air and come to rest on. **S:** bird, bee, spider □ *A long-tailed tit* ***alighted on*** *the window-ledge and began to peck at the nuts that had been placed there.* □ *Every evening the seagulls returned from their feeding-grounds,* ***alighted on*** *the rocks and settled down for the night.*

alight on[2] [A2] encounter, find by chance. **o:** solution, answer to the problem; truth □ *Sir Alexander Fleming* ***alighted on*** *the antibiotic properties of penicillin while he was engaged on research of a quite different nature.*

align (oneself) with [B2 pass rel] adopt a common position with, come or bring into agreement. **S:** (political) party; minority; country; (party) leader. **o:** the Opposition, the Government; the West, Russia □ *The Communist Party unexpectedly* ***aligned itself with*** *the Christian Socialists.* □ *This small country is now* ***aligned with*** *a major power.*

allied (to) [pass adj (B2)] (be) associated (with), (be) similar to; sharing certain characteristics (with). **S:** organism; disease; humour. **o:** creativity; aggression. **A:** closely, clearly, in no way □ *This disease is closely* ***allied to*** *malaria.* □ *Love is* ***allied to*** *hatred* (or: *Love and hatred are* ***allied****).*

allocate (to) [B2 pass emph rel] give (to), earmark (for), reserve (for). **S:** government, committee, council, company. **O:** funds, duties, shares. **o:** building, education □ *The Government has* ***allocated*** *ten million pounds* ***to*** *the stricken area.* □ *Half of the medical supplies have already been* ***allocated*** *(****to*** *the victims of the earthquake).*

allot (to) [B2 pass rel] decide who shall receive sth; make available (for). **S:** as for allocate (to). **O:** as for allocate (to); also: time; house, accommodation; work □ *Where is the family* ***to*** *which the big house was* ***allotted****?* □ *How much time has been* ***allotted to*** *this work?*

allow for [A2 pass emph rel] include in one's calculations etc; take into account/consideration (q v). **S:** he etc; measurement; instructions; estimate. **o:** expansion; (unexpected) difficulty; (any possible) delay, error, factor, miscalculation, eventuality; the fact that... □ *Don't forget to* ***allow for*** *a little shrinkage when you're making that material up.* □ *He missed the target because the wind hadn't been* ***allowed for****.*

allow of [A2] (formal) permit, leave room for. **S:** situation, position; attitude, behaviour, principles. **o:** no discussion, argument; (only one) interpretation; no relaxation (in, of); (no) deviation (from) □ *His responsible position* ***allowed of*** *no unseemly behaviour in public.* □ *Mr Pearson's income* ***allows of*** *no extravagance in his way of living.* □ *The cult of success by which he lived could* ***allow of*** *no tolerance of his parents.* HD □ usu neg.

allude to [A2 pass emph rel] (formal) mention, refer to[1] (q v) (indirectly or directly). **S:** book, article, letter, paper □ *In the course of his lecture Sir Basil* ***alluded*** *many times* ***to*** *the work of his predecessors.* □ *If the question of his bequest must be* ***alluded to****, you will be discreet, won't you?* □ *This is the building* ***to*** *which I have often* ***alluded*** *in my broadcasts.*

ally (oneself) with [B2 pass rel] have a close political or military link with; combine with. **S:** country, (political) party □ *Britain has been* ***allied with*** *Portugal for many centuries.* □ *At one time the Blue Party was on the point of* ***allying itself with*** *the Green Party.* □ *His accident,* ***allied with*** *the news of his bankruptcy, caused* *him to suffer a complete nervous breakdown.*

allied (to) [pass adj (B2)] ⇨ entry after align (oneself) with.

alternate (with) [A2 rel] happen, arrange, perform, by turns. **S:** (good) weather, fortune, times; success; tears. **o:** (bad) weather etc; failure; laughter. **A:** over a long period, throughout his career □ *While they were on holiday sunshine* ***alternated*** *regularly* ***with*** *wintry conditions* (or: *sunshine and wintry conditions* ***alternated***). □ *The cheerfulness* ***with*** *which his bad moods* ***alternated*** *brought welcome relief to his family.*

amalgamate (with) [A2 rel B2 pass rel] combine with, unite (with) (q v). **S:** [A2] **O:** [B2] group, company, organization, society. **S:** [B2] director, board. **o:** an American company, former rivals □ *If the ABC company* ***amalgamates with*** *XYZ, they will form the biggest shipbuilding organization in Britain.* □ *We've just been* ***amalgamated with*** *a Birmingham company.*

amount to[1] [A2] be equal to, reach, a total; add up to[1] (q v). **S:** bill(s), debt(s), liabilities, assets. **o:** sum, total; quantity; very little; (not) much; nothing □ *The British National Debt* ***amounts to*** *many thousands of millions of pounds.* □ *His total wordly possessions* ***amounted to*** *little more than the clothes he stood up in.* □ often neg.

amount to[2] [A2] mean; add up to[2] (q v). **S:** it; statement, suggestion, proposal, offer, idea(s). **o:** this; (not) much; very little □ *He always has a lot to say, but when you analyse it it never* ***amounts to*** *much.* □ *What it* ***amounts to*** *is simply that he is not willing to give us his support.* □ *Whether I pay or whether my wife pays* ***amounts to*** *the same thing, because we share all our money.*

amount to[3] [A2] become successful, make progress, in life. **o:** ⚠ (not) very much, (not) anything □ *Jimmy doesn't know where he is or where he's going. He'll never do anything, and he'll never* ***amount to*** *anything.* LBA □ usu neg.

angle for [A2 pass adj rel] (informal) try to obtain by means of hints; fish for (q v). **o:** compliment; promotion; useful information; invitation □ *I wish that woman wouldn't* ***angle for*** *compliments in such an obvious way.* □ *The promotion* ***for*** *which he had long been* ***angling*** *eventually came his way.* □ *On the very day of the ball the long* ***angled-for*** *invitation at last arrived.*

animadvert on/upon [A2 rel] (formal) express opinions on, often in a reflective or philosophical manner □ *Old Sergeant is the classic bore: there is hardly a subject that you can mention that will not make him* ***animadvert upon*** *some aspect of human nature, usually in a series of unbearable clichés.*

annex (to) [B2 pass] add to the territory of a country, estate etc □ *In the years immediately preceding the outbreak of war in 1939, Hitler succeeded in* ***annexing*** *various parts of Europe (****to*** *Germany) without firing a shot.*

answer back[1] [A1 B1ii pass] speak or interrupt in a rude manner when being scolded. **S:** child; servant; private. **O:** mother; employer; officer, NCO □ *When your mother scolds you, you shouldn't* ***answer*** *(her)* ***back.*** □ *'Don't* ***answer*** *(me)* ***back****, or I'll put you on a charge.'* □ *She longed to assert herself, and found herself being impertinent in small matters, almost* ***answering back.*** PW

answer back[2] [A1 B1ii pass] defend oneself; speak up for oneself (perhaps impudently) □ *Cressett complains of an injustice and John criticizes in public a man whose position forbids him to* ***answer back.*** ASA □ *It's unfair to attack a person in the newspaper when he can't* ***answer*** *(you)* ***back.***

answer for[1] [A2] be responsible for, be blamed for. **o:** actions, behaviour, madness, failure; the consequences □ *Don't forget that one day you'll have to* ***answer for*** *your foolish behaviour—perhaps to the police, even.* □ *If you insist on carrying out this mad experiment I won't* ***answer for*** *the consequences.* □ *That poor woman seems to be more neurotic every time I see her: her husband's got a lot to* ***answer for.***

answer for[2] [A2 rel] speak, or accept responsibility, on behalf of. **o:** others, anyone else; (my) brother; our allies □ *My opinion is that you are the best man for the job, but I can't* ***answer for*** *the other members of the committee, of course.* □ *They all agree with me except one person: Mr Johnson is the one* ***for*** *whom I can't* ***answer.***

answer (to) [A2] obey; be controlled by; respond (to) (q v). **S:** boat, car, aircraft. **o:** rudder, steering-wheel; movement, jerk, tug; wind, breeze □ *The horse* ***answers to*** *the slightest pull on the rein.* □ *The boat seemed very slow to* ***answer to*** *any movement of the helm.*

answer to (for) [A2] try to explain, and probably receive punishment (for); account to (q v) (for). **o:** (***to***) father, employer, police; (***for***) crime, misdeed, mistake □ *You'll have to* ***answer to*** *me if any harm comes to this child.* □ *One day you will have to* ***answer to*** *a higher authority* ***for*** *your sins of omission and commission.*

answer to the description (of) [A2] fit, match; correspond to. **S:** (stolen) car, handbag; (wanted) man □ *This car exactly* ***answers to the description of*** *the stolen vehicle.* □ *Pearson was arrested because he seemed to* ***answer to the description of*** *the escaped prisoner.*

answer to the name of [A2] (informal) be called, named □ *They had an old goat that* ***answered to the name of*** *Smelly.* □ *There's no one here* ***answering to that name.***

apologize (to) (for) [A2 pass rel] express regret (to sb) (for sth). **o:** being late, forgetting his name; offence, inconvenience, delay □ *She* ***apologized*** *profusely* ***for*** *treading on my toe.* □ *You'd better* ***apologize to*** *Mary* ***for*** *not writing to her earlier.* □ *He's not used to being* ***apologized to.*** □ *That's not something that has to be* ***apologized for.*** □ two passive forms: be apologized to/for.

appeal (to) (for) [A2 pass rel] earnestly request (sb) (to give or grant sth). **S:** prisoner; manager, steward; mountaineer. **o:** (***to***) court, tribunal, crowd; workers, employees; rescue team, Red Cross; (***for***) clemency; quiet; assistance □ *The condemned man* ***appealed to*** *the court* ***for*** *mercy.* □ *The police saw that the two sides might come to blows, and* ***appealed for*** *calm.* □ *The help* ***for*** *which the drifting ship had* ***appealed*** *seemed an age arriving.* □ two passive forms: be appealed to/for.

appear for [A2] (legal) represent in court, at an inquiry etc □ *Mr Peebles* **appeared for** *the defence in the case brought by the Crown against the alleged conspirators.* □ *The residents decided to invite a local solicitor to* **appear for** *them in the inquiry concerning the proposed establishment of a new airport near the village.*

append (to) [A2 pass emph rel] (formal) make a part of, affix (to) (q v). **O:** rider, codicil. **o:** document; lease, will □ **To** *the original agreement between the parties an important clause concerning the disposal of assets had been* **appended**.

appertain to [A2] (formal) properly concern; rightfully belong to. **S:** right to do sth; conditions. **o:** post; holder (of post) □ *The duties and privileges* **appertaining to** *the post of warden of the students' residence have never been officially stated.*

apply (for) [A2 pass emph rel] ⇨ apply (to) (for).

apply (to)[1] [A2 rel] concern; include. **S:** rules, restrictions, instructions; remarks, criticisms; what I say; taxes □ *'Do these regulations* **apply to** *me?' 'Yes, they* **apply to** *everyone, without exception.'* □ *The categories* **to** *whom the charges do not* **apply** *are: persons under the age of 21 and old age pensioners.*

apply (to)[2] [B2 pass rel] put on, spread on (q v). **O:** paint, emulsion; cream, ointment, lotion; plaster, poultice. **o:** surface; burns, sore, cut. **A:** evenly, generously; sparingly, promptly □ *Do not* **apply** *this ointment* **to** *the affected parts until all dirt has been removed.* □ *The lotion should be* **applied** *sparingly* **to** *the skin.* □ *The surface* **to** *which the paint was to be* **applied** *was full of cracks and dirt.* □ often imper.

apply oneself to [B2 emph rel] put all one's energy and time into. **o:** work, task, job, passing one's exams; business, matter in hand. **A:** with a will; enthusiastically, wholeheartedly; with zest □ *If you* **apply yourself to** *the job in hand, you'll soon finish it.* □ *Had he* **applied himself** *as enthusiastically* **to** *work as* **to** *pleasure he might have been very successful.*

apply (to) (for) [A2 pass emph rel] make a request (to sb), usu in writing (for sth). **o:** (*to*) manager, secretary; address; branch, head office; post office, police station; (*for*) position, vacancy, promotion, increase (in salary); visa, permit, permission □ *Miss O'Hara has just* **applied to** *the Coal Board* **for** *a job.* □ **For** *further information,* **apply to** *the Secretary of the Company.* □ *'***To** *whom should I* **apply for** *a licence?'* □ *Those over fifty need not* **apply**. □ often imper.

appoint (to) [B2 pass rel] select (as the person to occupy a post); choose (as). **S:** employer, selection board. **O:** applicant, candidate. **o:** post; vacancy □ *Mr Pearson was* **appointed to** *the Chairmanship of the Committee.*

apprise of [B2 pass emph rel] (formal) make aware of; inform of. **o:** (true, grave) situation, facts; (sb's) feelings, intentions; peril, danger □ *Nobody was willing to* **apprise** *the President* **of** *the great danger in which the country stood.* □ *It was only when he was twenty-one that he became* **apprised of** *his true origin.*

approach (about) [B2 pass rel] talk to sb (concerning sth); put a request to sb. **O:** director, headmaster; Information Department, Inquiries (office). **o:** grievance, complaint, loss. **A:** informally, privately, confidentially □ *Have you* **approached** *the manager* **about** *taking a day off next week?*

appropriate (for) [B2 pass rel] (formal) make available (for); take, earmark (for). **O:** money; the best bedroom; area of land. **o:** the repair of the defective houses; one's own use; artillery practice □ *The committee* **appropriated** *£5 000* **for** *the provision of better sporting facilities in the local schools.* □ *The army* **appropriated** *some of the best houses in the district* **for** *the use of the senior officers.*

appropriate to oneself/one's own use [B2 pass] (formal) take for one's own use, as one's own property □ *The relatives of the dead man were extremely angry when they discovered that his executor had* **appropriated** *the Rolls Royce* **to himself**.

approve of[1] [A2 pass rel] like, admire; consider to be acceptable. **o:** him etc; attitude, behaviour; manner, appearance □ *'His new mother-in-law doesn't exactly* **approve of** *him, does she?'*

approve of[2] [A2 pass rel] accept; support. **o:** proposal, plan, scheme, policy; new-fangled ideas, ways of doing sth □ *If my plan isn't* **approved of** *by the Committee, all my work will have been wasted.* □ *Don't expect him to* **approve of** *your design straight away.*

approximate to [A2 rel] (formal) come near to; be nearly. **S:** account, description (of the event, proposal); cost of the completed building. **o:** facts, truth; (original) version, intention; estimate. **A:** roughly, on the whole, closely □ *Your latest design* **approximates** *much more closely* **to** *what I understood the building to be like.* □ *His original conception,* **to** *which this sketch* **approximates** *roughly, was for a five-door saloon car.*

arbitrate (between) [A2 rel] (legal) seek an agreement which is acceptable (to two contending persons etc). **S:** judge, referee, umpire □ *An experienced lawyer has been asked to* **arbitrate between** *the contending parties.* □ *There is no statutory body whose duty it is to* **arbitrate between** *these workers and their employers.*

arch over [A2 pass rel] overhang; form a sort of cover over □ *At this part of the river, the trees on both banks* **arch over** *the water, affording an atmosphere of calm and seclusion which is a welcome relief from the bustle of the nearby city.* □ *The drive was* **arched over** *with thick foliage.*

argue about [A2 pass rel] discuss in a controversial way; express disagreement about. **o:** meaning, origin (of); the best way to do sth; who should do it; size, weight, colour (of) □ *'What are you two* **arguing about***?'* □ *While they were* **arguing about** *who should cook the dinner, the dog ran off with the meat.* □ *He's a crook; and that's not something that can be* **argued about**.

argue against[1] [A2 rel] advance arguments opposed to. **o:** (proposed) plan, action; appointment, nomination; award □ *Father* **argued** *fiercely* **against** *any increase in expenditure for the children's annual party.* □ *The scheme* **against** *which I had* **argued** *turned out to be a great success.*

argue against[2] [A2 rel] (formal) indicate, suggest, the opposite conclusion of. **S:** information, evidence, previous experience □ *All the evidence* ***argued against*** *the theory that the disease was transmitted by water.*

argue (with) [A2 pass rel] try to persuade sb to change his mind; protest to sb against instructions he has given □ *'Don't* ***argue*** *(****with*** *me)! Just do as I tell you.'* □ *Mrs Burns is a very stubborn woman: she isn't to be* ***argued with****.*

arise from [A2 rel] (formal) have its origin in; be due to, be caused by. **S:** problem, misunderstanding, difficulty; (his) poor condition, state of health. **o:** (poor) communications, distance; neglect, isolation, malnutrition □ *The company's losses this year* ***arise*** *almost entirely* ***from*** *the new taxes.* □ *His condition will not improve until the cause* ***from*** *which it* ***arises*** *is removed.*

arm (oneself) against [A2 B2 pass rel] (formal) prepare to resist and render ineffective. **o:** subversion, the undermining of the country's morale, the erosion of our rights □ *It is up to every citizen to understand the motives of the anarchists in our midst and* ***arm*** (himself) ***against*** *their insidious propaganda.*

arm (against) (with) [B2 pass rel] supply, or provide with, weapons etc, as a precaution or defence. **O:** oneself; friends, allies; the people. **o:** (***against***) invasion, threat; attack, subversion; (***with***) sword, gun; information, religious faith □ *I* ***armed*** *myself* ***with*** *a poker and hid behind the curtain.* □ *It is not enough to condemn aggression: we must take steps to* ***arm*** *ourselves* ***against*** *invasion* ***with*** *guns, ships and planes.* □ *The students' leaders arrived at the inquiry* ***armed with*** *an impressive collection of facts and figures to prove that their grants were quite inadequate.*

arouse (from) [B2 pass rel] (formal) make conscious; awaken (from) (q v). **o:** sleep, slumber; stupor, lethargy, apathy, indifference. **A:** gently, roughly, hurriedly □ *Mr Murray was* ***aroused from*** *his slumber by his wife whispering urgently in his ear, 'There's a burglar downstairs!'* □ *The spread of disease among the refugees at last* ***aroused*** *local people* ***from*** *their indifference towards these unhappy people.*

arrange (for)[1] [B2 pass rel] fix, set in order, on sb's behalf. **S:** secretary, receptionist; (travel) agency. **O:** appointment, meeting; trip, excursion, outing. **o:** employer, visitor, guest □ *Ring up, and try to* ***arrange*** *an appointment* ***for*** *me with the dentist.* □ *You'll find that everything will have been* ***arranged for*** *you when you arrive.*

arrange (for)[2] [B2 pass rel] make suitable for use (by). **O:** piece, composition. **o:** string quartet, chamber orchestra □ *The composer has* ***arranged*** *Chopin's nocturnes* ***for*** *the full orchestra.*

arrange for [A2] make plans for. **o:** sth to happen or be done; sb to do sth □ *I'll* ***arrange for*** *the parcel to be delivered first thing tomorrow.* □ *They have* ***arranged for*** *the old man to be buried alongside his wife.* □ *I've* ***arranged for*** *a car to pick them up at the station.*

arrive at [A2 pass rel] reach. **o:** hotel, town, village; coast, river; destination, goal; result, decision, conclusion □ *We* ***arrived at*** *the station just as the train was leaving.* □ *The two scientists* ***arrived at*** *the same conclusion quite independently.*

ascribe to [B2 pass emph rel] (formal) consider to be the result of sth or the work of sb; attribute to[1,2] (q v). **O:** failure, success, achievement; mistake; illness; death, recovery. **o:** (good, bad) luck; fortune; tenacity, determination; carelessness; malnutrition, war wounds; a healthy life, sensible living □ *His success as a novelist can be* ***ascribed to*** *the simple formula of sex, violence and suspense.* □ *For many years these poems were wrongly* ***ascribed to*** *Marlowe.*

ask after [A2 pass] seek news of (the health of); inquire after (q v) □ *Don't forget to* ***ask after*** *your uncle when you see Mary this afternoon.* □ *I met John yesterday: he was* ***asking after*** *you.* □ *They all seemed very concerned; and your health was* ***asked after****.*

ask (for) [A2 pass rel] request. **o:** food, drink, shelter; help, sympathy; sth to be done □ *If you get into difficulties, don't hesitate to* ***ask for*** *advice.* □ *I only wanted a little equipment for my research, but it was like* ***asking for*** *the moon.* □ *When he was found guilty, he* ***asked for*** *fifteen other offences to be taken into consideration.*

ask for it/trouble [A2] (informal) invite or provoke punishment, retaliation etc □ *You'd better not touch the apples in that orchard: if you do, you're just* ***asking for trouble****.* □ *'You* ***asked for it****', the mother said as she slapped the child, 'and now you've got it!'*

ask (of) [B2 pass rel] request sb to behave, hope he will behave, in a certain way; expect (of) (q v). **O:** a lot, a great deal, too much. **o:** anyone; such a (young) person □ *You can't expect the man to work seven days a week: that's too much to* ***ask*** *(****of*** *anyone).* □ *'Aren't you* ***asking*** *rather a lot* ***of*** *your son — expecting him to be top of his class in every subject?'* □ *'May I* ***ask*** *a favour* ***of*** *you? Would you lend me your lecture notes?'* □ the phrase does not necessarily imply a specific request.

ask out (to) [B1ii pass B3 pass rel] invite to go out (usu for a treat of some kind, whether stated or not). **O:** girl, neighbour. **o:** dinner, a dance, the theatre □ *I've been* ***asked out*** *for the evening by the boy next door.* □ *When Mrs Hughes discovered that her husband had* ***asked*** *his secretary* ***out to*** *dinner, she was furious.*

aspire to [A2 pass rel] (formal) desire, be ambitious, to obtain sth or become sth. **o:** fame, fortune; eminence, distinction □ *My father never* ***aspired to*** *the job of managing director, and was very surprised when it was offered to him.* □ *The fame* ***to*** *which Mr Hastings* ***aspired*** *was quite beyond his reach.*

assail with [B2 pass rel] (formal) trouble by asking, pester with □ *As soon as the young man returned home, his parents* ***assailed*** *him* ***with*** *questions about the interview.*

assent (to) [A2 pass rel] (formal) give one's approval (to), agree (to) (q v). **o:** suggestion, proposal, plan, scheme; (his) doing sth. **A:** willingly, readily, unhesitatingly □ *My father will never* ***assent to*** *my spending a holiday abroad before I'm 16.* □ *The marriage,* ***to*** *which their parents finally* ***assented****, turned out to be a complete failure.*

assess (at) [B2 pass rel] estimate to be. **S:** judge; Inspector of Taxes; valuer, surveyor. **O:** income, expenditure, value. **o:** sum, figure □ *The Inspector of Taxes has* ***assessed*** *your income for the year 1974–5* ***at £3 000****.* □ *The value of the* *property has been* ***assessed at*** *£20 000.*

assign to [B2 pass rel] (formal) reserve for the use of; give to. **O:** room, building; task, duty, work. **o:** staff, guest; office, department □ *The Director* ***assigned*** *a wing of the building* ***to*** *the important visitors.* □ *The defence of the oil installation had been* ***assigned to*** *my regiment* (or: *My regiment had been* ***assigned to*** *its defence*).

assimilate (into/with) [A2 B2 pass] (formal) (help to) become like, become indistinguishable from and a part of □ *The great obstacle that prevents European immigrants* ***assimilating*** *quickly* ***with*** *the rest of the Australian population is that of language.* □ *In less than a century the Huguenot refugees had become fully* ***assimilated into*** *the local community.*

associate with[1] [A2 rel] (formal) keep company with; spend a lot of time with. **o:** thieves, prostitutes, riff-raff; the rich, the successful □ *I wouldn't trust him any further than I could see him — he* ***associates with*** *all sorts of undesirable characters.* □ *The people* ***with*** *whom Mr Smart* ***associates*** *are all highly respectable.*

associate with[2] [B2 pass emph rel] (formal) connect with (often mentally). **O:** him etc; place, experience; sound, smell, feel (of sth). **o:** plan, proposal, activity; childhood, school; failure, success □ *I always* ***associate*** *the smell of jasmine* ***with*** *Uruguay.* □ *The doctor was always* ***associated*** *in the child's mind* ***with*** *injections and pain.* □ *'Do you wish your name to be* ***associated with*** *our fund-raising scheme?' 'No, it's something* ***with*** *which I'd rather not* ***associate*** *myself.'*

assure of [B2 pass rel] (formal) give certainty or confidence to sb; promise. **o:** (one's) willingness, readiness; (great, warm, enthusiastic) reception, welcome; (careful, sympathetic) consideration of sth □ *I can* ***assure*** *you* ***of*** *my full support for your plan.* □ *As soon as they adopted the new procedures, they were* ***assured of*** *success.* □ *Peter* ***assured*** *me* ***of*** *his continued interest in my work.*

atone for [A2 pass rel] (formal) make repayment for; make amends (to) (for) (q v). **o:** offence, injury; failure to do sth □ *Your son is doing his best to* ***atone for*** *his bad behaviour last night.* □ *I think you can now consider your unfortunate mistake to be fully* ***atoned for.***

attach (to) [B2 pass rel emph] fix (on or to). **O:** handle; buckle; codicil. **o:** door; belt; will □ *Is it possible to* ***attach*** *this bracket (****to*** *the wall)?* □ ***To*** *the bridegroom's car his friends had* ***attached*** *a lot of old boots and empty tin cans.*

attach to[1] [B2 pass emph rel] consider as having. **O:** (too much) importance, significance, meaning. **o:** news, report; what the papers say; announcement □ *Too much importance should not be* ***attached to*** *the reports of impending revolution in Ruritania.* □ *You* ***attach*** *altogether too much significance* ***to*** *the Prime Minister's words.*

attach to[2] [B2 pass emph rel] (formal) consider as being attributable or applicable to. **S:** court, crown. **O:** blame, suspicion; charge of neglect. **o:** accused, prisoner □ *The court said that it could* ***attach*** *no possible blame* ***to*** *the driver of the lorry.* □ *No suspicion can be* ***attached to*** *the accountant.*

attach to[3] [A2] (formal) be applicable or attributable to. **S:** (great, considerable) importance; credit for doing sth; (no) suspicion. **o:** decision, vote, outcome of the discussions; the Prime Minister, the Union leaders; accountant □ *Far-reaching implications* ***attach to*** *the railwaymen's decision to go on strike.* □ *The main credit for the party's electoral success* ***attaches to*** *the coolness and confidence of its leader.*

attach oneself to [B2 rel] join, sometimes in an unwelcome manner □ *A stray dog* ***attached itself to*** *me while I was out walking and would not leave me.* □ *By* ***attaching himself to*** *a secret society he satisfied the sensation-seeking side of his nature.*

attain to [A2 rel] (formal) reach, succeed in getting. **o:** (great) prominence, eminence, distinction; riches, wealth, prosperity; perfection; high office, power; stardom □ *Mr Singleton's aim in life is quite modest. He wants to be moderately successful, but does not expect to* ***attain to*** *very great heights.* □ *The perfection* ***to*** *which the pianist had* ***attained*** *was achieved only by years of hard work.*

attend (on/upon)[1] [A2 pass rel] (formal) tend; look after (q v). **S:** servant, doctor, physician, nurse. **o:** patient, sick man □ *Two nurses* ***attended*** *night and day* ***on*** *the dying statesman.* □ *He was called out to a patient* ***(on)*** *whom he had* ***attended*** *some years previously.*

attend (on/upon)[2] [A2 pass] (formal) accompany. **S:** dangers, consequences, hazards, difficulties. **o:** enterprise, adventure □ *Many difficulties and dangers* ***attended upon*** *Sir Francis Chichester's single-handed voyage round the world.* □ in the passive form on/upon are not required: *The mission was* ***attended (upon)*** *by many risks.*

attend (to) [A2 rel] listen carefully (to), pay attention (to) (q v). **o:** teacher, parent; advice, counsels; what people say □ *If she had* ***attended to*** *what her mother told her, she wouldn't be in trouble now.* □ *If you don't* ***attend*** *(****to*** *your teacher), you'll never learn anything.*

attend to [A2 pass rel] tend, manage; look after (q v), take care (of) (q v). **o:** invalid; client, customer; shop, office □ *If you go out, who will* ***attend to*** *the baby?* □ *He foolishly left an inexperienced young assistant to* ***attend to*** *some very important customers.* □ *'Don't worry, everything will be* ***attended to*** *in good time!'*

attire (oneself) (in) [B2 pass rel] (formal) dress in (usu for formal occasions). **S:** magistrate, judge, official; king, queen; the bride. **o:** formal dress, crimson, purple; robes of state, office; white. **A:** from head to foot, splendidly □ *The Lords were* ***attired in*** *their ceremonial robes for the opening of Parliament.* □ usu passive.

attract (to) [B2 pass emph rel] cause to move forwards; draw to. **S:** activity; noise; light, smell. **O:** crowd; onlooker(s), spectator(s), customer(s). **o:** market; fight, accident; stall, shop □ *The bright lights and the noisy music* ***attracted*** *the children* ***to*** *the fairground.*

attribute to[1] [B2 pass rel emph] (formal) explain by means of; give as the origin, cause or reason for. **O:** good, bad health, longevity; prosperity, misfortune, failure; success. **o:** hard work; regular habits; good, bad, luck □ *Mr Dolittle* ***attributes*** *his good health* ***to*** *careful living.*

□ ***To** his father can be **attributed** his intelligence, and **to** his mother his frivolous attitude to life.*

attribute to[2] [B2 pass rel] (formal) suggest as the author of. **S:** critic; musicologist. **O:** painting; sonnet; song, symphony. **o:** (minor) artist; poet; composer □ *Shakespeare's plays have often been **attributed to** others, and especially **to** Bacon.*

attune (to) [B2 pass rel] (formal) make appropriate to; bring into harmony (with) □ *T S Eliot successfully **attuned** his language **to** the times in which he lived.* □ *When a man is about to die, his mind may well be **attuned to** prayer.* □ *His mind is **attuned to** mine* (or: *Our minds are **attuned***).

auction off [B1i pass] sell (off) by auction. **S:** Army, Navy, Air Force; Civil Service; store, factory. **O:** surplus; unwanted goods, supplies, stocks, materials □ *From time to time the Army **auctions off** unwanted supplies of various kinds.* □ *The old machinery that was **auctioned off** turned out to be quite useless.*

augur ill/well for [A2] (formal) indicate that sth will probably develop badly/well. **S:** action, behaviour; (recent) events, (new) taxes; his coming to power. **o:** us etc; the future (of); our hopes of doing sth □ *John and Mary have started quarrelling already. That doesn't **augur well for** their future happiness.* □ *The arrival of our crack troops in the battle area **augurs ill for** the enemy.*

avail (against) [A2 emph rel] (formal) be of use (against), be effective (against) or superior (to). **S:** nothing; only a supreme effort; (his) courage, skill, energy, determination. **o:** (as for **S:**) □ *I'm afraid his courage will not **avail** (**against** his opponent's great strength).* □ ***Against** such an onslaught nothing could **avail**.*

avail oneself of [B2 rel] (formal) use; take advantage of[1] (q v). **o:** facilities (provided); chance, opportunity; offer, proposal; every means in one's power. **A:** always, fully, without hesitation, with pleasure □ *You should **avail yourself of** every opportunity to practise your English.* □ *The means **of** which he **availed himself** to achieve his ends were not beyond criticism.* □ note the form in letters and speeches: *May I **avail myself of** this opportunity to...; I should like to **avail myself of**....*

avenge oneself (on) (for) [B2 rel] (formal) act against sb in return for some injury one has suffered; take revenge (on) (for) (q v). **o:** (***on***) (my father's) murderer; the destroyer of my reputation, happiness; the author of (my) misfortunes, ruin, disgrace; (***for***) shame, ruin, misfortune, disgrace, loss □ *He swore to **avenge himself** (**on** his enemy) **for** the insult that had been offered to his name and reputation.* □ *The man **on** whom he **avenged himself** was quite innocent of the alleged offence.* □ also: *The young king **avenged** his father's murder **on/upon** the conspirators.*

average out (at) [A1 A3 rel B1i pass B3 pass rel] show an average (of); calculate the average (of). **S:** [A1 A3] **O:** [B1 B3] revenue, takings; salary, wages; cost; output; score, (number of) goals, runs; (hours of) sunshine, rainfall □ [A3] *The rainfall for the period under review **averaged out at** about three inches a month.* □ [B3] *The income tax authorities **averaged** his profit **out at** £3 000 a year for five years.* □ [A3] *Our speed **averaged out at** 40 miles an hour* (= *We **averaged** 40 miles an hour all the way*).

avert (from) [B2 pass rel] (formal) stop facing or contemplating; turn away (from)[1] (q v). **O:** eyes, gaze, mind, thoughts. **o:** problem; idea, thoughts, sight; consequences, results; (approaching) examination, trial, test; (his) predicament; poverty, misery, unhappiness □ *I did my best to **avert** my thoughts **from** the dying man.* □ *It's no use **averting** your eyes* (***from** the poverty and suffering which is all around you*). □ *His Finals were something **from** which he preferred to **avert** his mind.*

awake(n) (from) [A2 rel B2 pass rel] wake up (from); return to reality (from). **o:** (deep, light, profound) sleep; dream. **A:** [A2] suddenly, gradually, slowly; with a start; [B2] roughly, gently □ *He **awoke** (**from** a restless sleep) to find that all his fears were unfounded.* □ *He was roughly **awakened from** his dream of making a fortune when his partner decamped with £10 000.*

awake(n) to [A2 rel B2 pass rel] (formal) (make sb) realize, understand. **o:** realities, facts, possibilities, dangers, risks, urgency, potentialities, opportunities. **A:** painfully, slowly, gradually □ *It's time you **awoke to** the realities of the situation.* □ *We have at last **awoken** John **to** the fact that there's no easy way to success.* □ *During the 1930s Churchill tried to **awaken** the British people **to** the need for rearmament.*

award (to) [B2 pass emph rel] give, grant, officially (to). **S:** judge, committee, jury. **O:** prize; medal, cup, certificate; sum, amount; damages, compensation. **o:** winner, runner-up, loser; plaintiff, widow □ *The first prize was **awarded to** the youngest competitor.* □ *£12 000 was the amount that the court **awarded** (**to** the victim of the accident).*

B

back away (from) [A1 A3 emph rel] move back (from), retreat (from) (q v), out of fear or dislike. **S:** prisoner, suspect; child, animal. **o:** guard, policeman; noise, fire □ *As the men at the bar reached for their guns, the onlookers **backed away**.* □ *Even well-disposed people **back away from** Richard when they see that ingratiating smile.*

back down [A1] retreat, withdraw (charges, claims, accusations etc). **S:** critic, rival, opponent. **A:** completely, abjectly □ *After being confronted with our evidence, the other side had to **back down**.* □ *Even those who seemed to have good reason to criticize have **backed down**.*

back into [A2 pass B2 pass rel] drive (a vehicle) backwards into sth, esp through carelessness or inexperience. **S:** [A2] **O:** [B2] car, lorry, tractor. **S:** [A2 B2] driver, farmer. **o:**

(another) car; tree, gatepost □ *I don't exactly enjoy being* **backed into** *by learner drivers.* □ *He succeeded in* **backing** *a new car* **into** *the only lamp-post in the street.*

back off [A1] move (a vehicle) back from a position too close to sth else. **S:** driver; car, bus; line of traffic. **A:** a bit, a few yards □ *'Do you mind* **backing off** *a bit, Sir, while we clear this wreck out of the way?'* □ *'I don't like that car sitting on my tail. Wave to him to* **back off.**'

back on to [A3] have at its back, face at the back. **S:** house, shop; study, kitchen. **o:** courtyard; lane, alley □ *The burglar is unlikely to have got in through the dining-room window—it* **backs on to** *several other houses.*

back out/out of [A1 A2 pass] withdraw from an undertaking, promise. **o:** agreement, scheme, arrangement □ *Once you've given your word, don't try to* **back out.** □ *It's no good* **backing out of** *it now—with my own ears I heard your last words.* HSG

back up[1] [B1i nom pass adj] give moral, physical support to; supplement. **O:** subordinate, colleague, wife; attack, landing; course, programme. **A:** loyally, fully □ *Alexander* **backed** *me* **up** *wholeheartedly as he always did.* MFM □ *Ada's been complaining that there's nobody to* **back her up** *if anybody gets nasty.* HD □ **Back-up** *materials, in the form of records and textbooks, are a normal accompaniment of TV language courses.* □ *The lectures and seminars of the course are to be* **backed up** *by a heavy programme of field work.*

back up[2] [A1] (cricket) (of the non-striking batsman) move down the wicket as the ball is delivered, to support a possible attempt at a run by the striker □ *Jameson* **backed up,** *was sent back, struggled for a foothold, and was run out when a fielder hit the stumps.* G

bail out[1] [B1i pass adj] (legal) free until trial by payment of a cash guarantee. **S:** friend, well-wisher. **O:** prisoner, accused □ *An anonymous well-wisher* **bailed** *the prisoners* **out.**

bail out[2] [B1i pass adj] empty of water (with buckets etc). **S:** sailor, passenger. **O:** boat □ *The few survivors of the shipwreck* **bailed out** *their lifeboat.* □ alt spelling: **bale.**

balance out [A1 B1ii] match, be equal (to). **S:** debits and credits, weights, teams; advantages, faults. **O:** each other, one another □ *At the end of the financial year his accounts* **balanced out.** □ *The experience of our side and the youthful determination of the other* **balance** *each other* **out.**

bale out/out of [A1 A2] (aviation) jump by parachute (from a damaged aircraft). **S:** pilot, crew. **o:** plane, balloon; cockpit □ *Realizing he could do nothing to save his aircraft, the pilot* **baled out.** □ *You must practise your* **baling-out** *drill.* □ alt spelling: **bail.**

balk at [A2 pass adj] hesitate or refuse to face or accept; jib at (q v). **S:** horse, mount; customer, authorities. **o:** fence, wall; conditions, terms □ *His horse* **balked at** *the water jump.* □ *Our accountant* **balked at** *the high cost of the new proposals.* □ alt spelling: **baulk.**

balls up [B1i nom pass adj] (taboo) ruin, mishandle; mess up (q v). **O:** organization, work; game, outing □ *The public would laugh fit to burst if someone really* **ballsed up** *the Civil Service or the Cabinet.* JFTR □ *Don't let that firm handle your auditing: they made a complete* **balls-up** *of ours.*

band together [A1 B1ii] unite, form groups. **S:** workers, employers, townspeople. **O:** themselves, ourselves □ *The villagers* **banded** *(themselves)* **together** *to protect their homes and property from armed marauders.*

bandy about [B1ii pass adj] (informal) pass from person to person (idly or with disrespect). **O:** story, name, word □ *They are* **bandying** *his name* **about** *a good deal.* □ *Mr Charlton was not used to hearing the word virgin* **bandied about** *very much, especially in public.* DBM □ *Responsibility for the environment is a much* **bandied-about** *phrase in official circles nowadays.*

bandy words (with) [B2 emph rel] argue, dispute (with) (usu in an undignified way) □ *'I don't propose to waste my time* **bandying words with** *you!'* □ *Palmer's dignity did not allow her to* **bandy words with** *her social inferiors.* WDM

bang one's head against a brick wall [B2] (informal) continue trying to achieve sth after painful experience has shown that it cannot be achieved; run one's head against/into a brick wall (q v) □ *'Can't you see that he has no intention of paying you back? You're* **banging your head against a brick wall.**' □ *She hasn't a hope of getting him to change his mind. She's just* **banging her head against a brick wall.** □ continuous tenses only.

bank on[1] [A2 pass adj rel] (informal) confidently expect, reckon on/upon (q v). **o:** change, success, co-operation; being first, winning the fight □ *Stupidly, I had only* **banked on** *catching two or three animals, so had not brought a really large cage with me.* BB □ *The* **banked-on** *change of heart did not take place after all.*

bank on[2] [A2 pass] (informal) find reliable, depend on/upon[1] (q v). **o:** food, fabric, car; service, company □ *You can* **bank on** *this creamy-white wool.* H □ *Those brakes can't be* **banked on** *if we have to pull up suddenly.* □ usu with *can/could.*

bank up[1] [A1 B1i pass adj] form into a heap or ridge. **S:** [A1] **O:** [B1] earth, gravel, snow, sand □ *Seaweed* **banks up** *along the water's edge.* □ **Banked-up** *drifts of snow had made the roads impassable.*

bank up[2] [B1i pass adj] heap with fuel (to ensure that a fire burns slowly for a long time, e g overnight). **O:** fire, furnace, stove □ *'Don't forget to* **bank up** *the fire before coming up to bed.'*

bargain away [B1i pass adj] abandon in return for something of less value (often with an unworthy motive). **O:** rights, freedom, advantage □ *They've* **bargained away** *in a few minutes privileges which took us many years to secure.* □ *Our hard-won liberties should not be* **bargained away** *lightly.*

bargain for [A2 pass] (informal) expect, be willing or prepared to accept. **o:** change, reverse (of fortune); behaviour, treatment □ *We didn't exactly* **bargain for** *him turning up like that, out of the blue.* □ *When he married for a second time, Fred got more than he* **bargained for.** □ often preceded by *more than.*

barge in/into [A1 A2 pass] (informal) enter, interrupt, rudely or clumsily. **o:** house, room; discussion □ *Midge doesn't like strangers* **barg-**

ing in. AITC □ *'Why must you always come* ***barging into*** *the conversation?'*

bark up the wrong tree [A2] (informal) direct an inquiry or accusation at the wrong place or person □ *If the police think I was mixed up in the train robbery, they're* ***barking up the wrong tree***.

barter away [B1i pass adj] ⇨ bargain away.

base on/upon [B2 pass emph rel] use as a basis or foundation for. **O:** policy, strategy; appeal, argument. **o:** fear, prejudice; reason, evidence □ *His success in business is* ***based on*** *a shrewd assessment of what the customer wants.* □ *The Chancellor is* ***basing*** *his trading forecast* ***on*** *figures for the past five years.*

bat around [A1 nom] (informal) hasten here and there (often with the suggestion that one is tired as a result) □ *'Don't bother me now: I've been* ***batting around*** *all morning and I'm just about ready to collapse.'* □ *'Have a quick* ***bat around*** *and see what's in the shops.'* □ nom form is usu not hyphenated.

batten down the hatches [B1iii pass] (nautical) secure hatches firmly (with battens); prepare a ship generally for a storm at sea. **S:** sailor, crew □ *All hands were mustered to* ***batten down the hatches***.

batten on [A2 pass emph rel] exploit, grow fat on. **S:** unscrupulous trader, lazy colleague, parasite. **o:** work, generosity (of others) □ *He was warning fellow traders against the parasitical practices of companies who* ***batten on*** *the efforts of others.* T

battle it out [B1ii] (informal) fight to a conclusion. **S:** armies, ships; boxers, rivals □ *That's just like you — try to* ***battle it out*** *on your own!* □ *This weekend, eight teams* ***battle it out*** *in the quarter-finals of the League Cup.*

baulk at [A2 pass adj] ⇨ balk at.

bawl out [B1ii pass] (informal) scold severely. **S:** referee, sergeant, traffic cop. **O:** player, subordinate, law-breaker □ *The contender for the heavy-weight title was* ***bawled out*** *for punching low.* □ *John got a* ***bawling-out*** *for dangerous driving.* □ nom form is bawling-out.

be about[1] [A2] have begun work, be busy working. **S:** workpeople, shopkeepers. **o:** ⚠ one's affairs, business □ *It was eight o'clock and most of the townspeople* ***were*** *already* ***about*** *their business.* ⇨ go about[4].

be about[2] [A1] be present here and there (and likely to endanger health, safety etc). **S:** (a lot of) 'flu; fog, smog □ *'Be sure to wrap up well: there* ***is*** *a lot of 'flu* ***about***.*'* □ *'Drive home carefully: the weather report says there****'s*** *a lot of ice* ***about*** *on the roads.'* □ note the construction with *there*.

be about/around[1] [A1 A2] be present in a place (though the speaker is not sure exactly where). **o:** ⚠ the place, the house □ *'Where's Bill?' 'Oh, he****'s*** *somewhere* ***about***.*'* □ *'I haven't seen Nick all morning.' 'I have. He****'s around*** *the house somewhere.'* □ *somewhere* usu present.

be about/around[2] [A1] be available, be in circulation. **S:** (consumer) article, commodity; (rare) medal, coin; picture, antique □ *These sports saloons seem to be gaining in popularity. There* ***are*** *certainly plenty of them* ***about*** *on the roads.* □ *You'll be lucky to find any of this furniture in the antique shops; there* ***isn't*** *much of it* ***around***. □ note the construction with *there*.

be above[1] [A2] not be open or liable to. **S:** remarks, behaviour, character. **o:** ⚠ criticism, reproach, reproof, suspicion □ *His handling of Government money during his term of office* ***was*** *not entirely* ***above*** *reproach.*

be above[2] [A2] be too important, or morally superior, to undertake sth small or mean. **S:** Crown, judiciary, priest. **o:** party politics, mundane matters; taking bribes, influencing decisions □ *Don't worry: Father* ***is*** *quite* ***above*** *trying to influence your choice in this matter.* □ *Some of the staff* ***are*** *not* ***above*** *putting their hands in the cash-box.*

be above one/one's head [A2] (informal) be too difficult or obscure to understand. **S:** remarks, theory, lecture. **m:** miles, a long way □ *The last paper he gave, on the theory of flight,* ***was*** *way* ***above my head***.

be abreast of [A3] have fresh or current knowledge of. **S:** research worker, teacher, civil servant. **o:** trends, events, progress □ *He takes several learned journals and manages to* ***be abreast of*** *developments in his field.* ⇨ get abreast of.

be after[1] [A2] pursue, try to catch. **S:** authorities; police, warder. **o:** prisoner, suspect, runaway □ *'We're still* ***after*** *the man who broke into your shop yesterday.'* □ *'If you trespass on my land I'll* ***be after*** *you!'* ⇨ come after[2], go after[1].

be after[2] [A2] seek, try to obtain. **S:** employer; applicant, unemployed person. **o:** staff; post, job, vacancy □ *There* ***are*** *too many men* ***after*** *the same job.* □ *You may feel you are quite capable of handling the work you* ***are after***. H ⇨ go after[2].

be after[3] [A2] covet, wish to steal or take away. **S:** rival, thief. **o:** (another's) wife, job, valuables □ *He****'s*** *not* ***after*** *the pictures or the family silver.* OMIH

be against [A2] be contrary to, be in defiance of. **S:** conduct, step; joining the party, signing the petition. **o:** (one's) interests, wishes, will □ *Their joining the defensive pact would surely* ***be against*** *our interests.* ⇨ go against[1].

be ahead/ahead of [A1 A2] have progressed beyond sb else; have reached a stage where others cannot easily follow. **S:** artist, thinker; industry. **m:** some way, a long way. **o:** contemporary, colleague; competitor □ *America* ***is*** *way* ***ahead*** *in most important aspects of space technology.* □ *'You****'re*** *a long way* ***ahead of*** *me there. Do you mind going back over your argument?'* ⇨ get ahead/ahead of.

be along (to) [A1 A3] come from one place to another, often a short distance (e g within the same building). **o:** house; office, room; meeting, reunion □ *'Come along to my office when you have a free moment.' 'All right, I'll* ***be along*** *in about half an hour.'* □ *Will he* ***be along to*** *the meeting of the housing committee this evening?* ⇨ come along (to), bring along (to).

be around[1] [A1 A2] (informal) be active (and prominent) in a particular field or profession. **S:** actor, singer; politician. **o:** (movie) business, (pop music) scene; (political) arena □ *The Beatles are going to* ***be around***, *at least as individual performers, for a few years yet.* □ *Of course, he's* ***been around*** *the sports commentating scene for a good many years.*

be around[2] [A1] (informal) have acquired

worldly wisdom, and esp wide experience in sexual matters □ *You can tell from the confident, rather self-satisfied gleam in his eye that he's* **been around**. □ *Barbara — now there's a girl that's* **been around**. *Perhaps not quite the sort you should take home to meet your parents, though.* □ perfect tenses only.

be around[3] [A1 A2] be present in a place. ⇨ be about/around[1].

be around[4] [A1] be available, be in circulation. ⇨ be about/around[2].

be around/round (at) [A1 A3] come to, visit, sb or a place (usu within the same town); be with sb, at a place, having come on a visit. **o:** John's, one's grandmother's; club, pub □ *'What time shall we expect you?' 'Oh, I'll* **be around** *by nine at the latest.'* □ *You can't accuse him of breaking into the shop. He* **was round at** *my house all evening.* ⇨ bring around/round (to)[1], come around/round (to)[1], go around (to).

be at[1] [A2] (informal) try to persuade, in a carping, unpleasant way. **o:** husband, child. **Inf** to change, to improve, to return □ *'There you are, you see. She's* **at** *me again!'* □ *Hawkins* **was** *still* **at** *her to pick up the relationship where they had left off.* NM □ inf usu present. ⇨ get at[5].

be at[2] [A2] (informal) attack; handle sth which is not one's property; tamper with (q v). **S:** pest, intruder, child. **o:** corn, wine, (another's) belongings □ *The mice* **are at** *the cheese again: put it in a safer place.* □ *Geoffrey's* **been at** *my shaving things again.* ⇨ get at[1].

be at attention [A2] (military) be standing in an alert posture, with the feet together. **S:** soldier, airman; policeman; company, squad □ *The men* **were at attention** *as the inspecting officer passed through the ranks.* ⇨ bring/come to attention.

be at a dead end [A2] have reached a point where no further progress is possible. **S:** work, studies, research; inquiry, investigation □ *There came a point when his research* **was at a dead end** *— he couldn't see how to go forward.* ⇨ bring/come to a dead end.

be at an end [A2] have ended; have been used up or exhausted. **S:** dispute, argument; fighting, bloodshed; patience, tolerance □ *Leaders hope that serious differences on the issue among their followers* **are now at an end**. □ *I must warn you that my patience* **is** *almost* **at an end**. ⇨ bring/come to an end; put an end/a stop to.

be at a halt/standstill [A2] (of sth moving, or in progress) have stopped. **S:** work, production; factory, yard □ *Bus services in the city* **are** *practically* **at a halt**. □ *The docks have* **been at a** *complete* **standstill** *since Monday.* ⇨ come/bring to a halt/standstill.

be hard at it/work [A2] (informal) be very busy, be working hard. **S:** staff; team □ *Rescue gangs* **were** *already* **hard at it** *when we reached the scene of the crash.* □ *'Still* **hard at work**, *Peter? Now, don't stay up too late!'*

be at it [A2] (informal) behave mischievously, be a nuisance. **S:** rogue, scoundrel □ *The apples keep disappearing from the trees in my garden; I suppose those children* **are at it** *again.*

be at pains to do sth [A2] take great care to do sth. **S:** councillor, official, inspector. **adj:** great, considerable. **Inf** to explain, to justify, to seem fair □ *The Inland Revenue* **were at** *some* **pains to point out** *how we might benefit from the revised schedule.*

what be at [A2] (informal) what sb is trying to do or say □ *I can never understand* **what** *on earth he's* **at**. □ *'Do you mind telling me* **what** *exactly you're* **at**?' □ in direct and indirect questions. ⇨ get at[4].

be at grips with [A2] be tackling; be engaged in a struggle with. **o:** (**with**) problem, issue, question □ *I don't think the writer* **was** *ever* **at grips with** *any serious moral issue.* □ *At that time he* **was at grips with** *the disease which was later to kill him.* ⇨ bring/come/get to grips with.

be at one (with) [A2] have the same views or feelings (as); agree (with) (q v). **S:** meeting, audience, follower. **o:** speaker, leader □ *She* **is at one with** *her husband* (or: *They* **are at one**) *in believing that this is the best course to follow.* □ *They desire to enter, and* **be at one with**, *a vaguely conceived People, whose lives they could not even imagine.* HD

be away [A1] be in a drawer etc, because one has finished using it etc. **S:** paper, book; knitting; linen, woollens □ *I don't know that I can find the letters. They're* **away** *in old shoe boxes in the attic.* ⇨ put away[1].

be well away[1] [A1] (informal) make a good start, be in advance of opponents. **S:** horse, runner; businessman □ *The Queen's horse* **was well away** *at the start of the 3.15 race.* □ *With his father's name and his mother's money young Johnnie should* **be well away**.

be well away[2] [A1] (informal) enjoy oneself noisily (through having drunk too much); be drunk □ *By the time we arrived at the party, Dick* **was well away**.

be back[1] [A1] return; have returned. **A:** soon, shortly; by lunch-time, before supper □ *I'll* **be back** *in a minute with your tea.* DC □ *He'll* **be back** *in time to put them to bed.* DC ⇨ bring back[1], come back[1], get back[1], go back[1], take back[1].

be back[2] [A1] have been replaced. **S:** book, ornament, clock. **A:** where it belongs, in its rightful place, with its owner □ *The grandfather clock* **was back** *in its old place.* □ *'Make sure the dogs* **are back** *in their kennels before you go to bed.'* ⇨ get back[3], put back[1].

be before[1] [A2] be in front of sb else; (be going to) have or enjoy sth earlier than sb else. **m:** several places, some way □ *'Don't push! I* **was before** *you in the queue.'* □ *'Don't forget I'm* **before** *you with that newspaper.'* ⇨ come before[1].

be before[2] [A2] appear, be presented for a decision, the judgment of a court, etc. **S:** he etc; case; matter. **o:** court, magistrate; board, committee □ *This is the third time that the accused has* **been before** *this Court.* □ *The question* **is before** *a Select Committee of the House of Commons at this very moment.* ⇨ bring before, come before[2], go before[2], put before[2], take before.

be before sb's time [A2] (informal) happen, live, earlier than sb was in a certain place (e g school, university; regiment; club). **S:** it, that; change, event; he etc. **m:** way, long, considerably □ *This used to be the master bedroom before we did the alterations upstairs. That* **was before your time**, *of course.* DC □ *'Do you* *remember a French master with a squeaky voice? Or perhaps he* ***was before your time****?'*

be behind[1] [A1 A2] be late (later than), be in arrears. **S:** tenant; firm, country. **A:** with the rent, in meeting commitments, on delivery dates □ *Everybody seems to* ***be behind*** *this morning.* TGLY □ *John's often* ***behind*** *in making his payments.* ⇨ fall behind with, get behind (with).

be behind[2] [A1 A2] be inferior (to), be losing (to). **S:** country, competitor □ *They* ***were*** *well* ***behind*** *their nearest rivals in the production of fissile material.* □ *Jones* ***was behind*** *on points at the end of round three.* ⇨ fall behind.

be behind[3] [A2] be the explanation for, be the cause of. **S:** fear, greed, clash of interests; change of policy, bid for power, rise in costs □ *I wonder what* ***was behind*** *John's sudden interest in our welfare?* ⇨ lie behind[2].

be behind bars [A2] (informal) be in prison. **S:** bandit, confidence trickster, murderer □ *The last of the bank-robbers* ***is*** *now safely* ***behind bars****.* ⇨ put behind bars.

be behind the times [A2] not be modern, not be up to date (in ideas, methods etc). **S:** plan, strategy; idea, philosophy, morality □ *I found his thoughts on crime and punishment to* ***be*** *very much* ***behind the times****.* □ *His views on marriage* ***are*** *a bit* ***behind the times****.*

be below[1] [A2] be lower than, inferior to. **S:** performance; output, production; attendance, capacity; quality. **o:** normal, (former) level; expectations, what was forecast; standard □ *Figures for soft drinks sales* ***were below*** *what we are used to in the summer.* □ *Output* ***is*** *considerably* ***below*** *last year's level.* ⇨ fall below.

be below[2] [A2] be junior to, or lower than, sb in rank. **S:** lieutenant; corporal. **o:** captain; sergeant □ *A major* ***is*** *immediately* ***below*** *a lieutenant-colonel in rank.* □ *Jones* ***was below*** *Rogers when he joined the firm, but he was quickly promoted to a post of equal responsibility.*

be below[3] [A1] (nautical) be below deck-level, e g in a cabin or the hold. **S:** crew, passenger; cargo □ *Most of the timber* ***was below*** *in the hold, but some had to be stowed on the after-deck.* ⇨ go below (decks), take below.

be beneath [A2] seem too unimportant, vulgar etc to be considered. **S:** money matters, household affairs, business dealings. **o:** ⚠ (one's) attention, notice, regard □ *'Of course, the question of where the money for the next meal is coming from* ***is beneath*** *your attention!'*

be beneath contempt [A2] be utterly despicable. **S:** conduct, behaviour, remarks □ *I've lost all respect for him: I think his criticism of the monarchy* ***was beneath contempt****.* □ *To suggest that he was a petty agitator* ***was beneath contempt****.* UTN

be beneath one's dignity [A2] be sth which one feels one cannot do without some loss of dignity (usu implying that the person has a high opinion of himself). **S:** housework, manual work; (it...) to help his younger brother, (it...) to play party games □ *A little light weeding in the garden shouldn't* ***be*** *too much* ***beneath your dignity****.*

be beside the point [A2] be irrelevant, have nothing to do with the matter in question. **S:** that, this; who it was, whoever did it □ *Whether John or Patrick lost the tape-recorder* ***is beside the point****.* □ *The judicial argument over his interpretation of the Constitution* ***is beside the point****.* OBS

be beside oneself (with) [A2] be overwhelmed by strong feelings. **S:** widow, victim, survivor; candidate; prisoner. **o:** (**with**) grief, anxiety, rage, frustration □ *The headmaster* ***was beside himself with*** *alarm because raindrops were falling on the school prizes.* SPL □ *You can imagine how embarrassing it all is.* ***I'm*** *simply* ***beside myself****.* UTN

be between ourselves/you and me [A2] (of a secret) be shared by the speakers (and not with others). **S:** ⚠ this, that, it, this matter □ *'Now this* ***is*** *strictly* ***between ourselves****, but did you know that David is being promoted next month?'* □ *Eva has invited some friends up.* ***Between you and me****, it's for business reasons.* RATT □ without be, used as an adv phrase; note the extended form: between you, me and the gatepost.

be beyond[1] [A2 emph] have gone beyond a point where he/it can be saved, mended etc. **S:** patient, case; machine, meter; crew, passenger. **o:** help; remedy, cure; salvation, redemption; repair; rescue □ *One wing of the car* ***was beyond*** *repair — a rear mudguard half torn off.* HD □ *No one can ever be regarded as* ***(being) beyond*** *redemption.*

be beyond[2] [A2 emph] be more than one can calculate, expect, believe etc. **S:** cost, total; success, result; problem; claim, statement. **o:** reckoning, calculation; hope, (one's) expectations; understanding, comprehension; belief, credibility □ *So far, twenty-eight patients have been treated, and the improvement is said to* ***be beyond*** *all expectations.* NS □ *The intricacies of the law of libel* ***are beyond*** *my ken* (= knowledge). SD ⇨ go beyond.

be beyond a joke [A2] (informal) be too serious to joke about. **S:** behaviour, manners, dress; situation, incident □ *'This* ***is*** *quite* ***beyond a joke****! Open the door, and let me out at once!'* ⇨ go beyond a joke.

be beyond/past caring [A2] have reached a point where one no longer cares (about sth). **O:** (of **caring**) whether one lives or dies, how things will turn out, what to do in another crisis □ *'Don't you think we ought to find another music teacher for John?' 'Don't ask me, darling,* ***I'm*** *really* ***past caring****.'* □ *When an officer* ***is beyond caring*** *for the safety of his troops, he should be removed from his command.*

be beyond/past (one's) endurance [A2] be more than one is prepared to bear or tolerate. **S:** behaviour, conduct; insolence, slovenliness □ *His treatment of his mother* ***is past endurance****.* □ *This latest outburst of his —* ***it's*** *quite* ***beyond my endurance****.*

be down[1] [A1] (informal) lack, be deficient by (some amount). **S:** stock, account. **m:** ten pounds, a thousand pairs; quite a bit □ *I've checked the till and* ***we're*** *forty pounds* ***down****.* UTN □ *The bar* ***is*** *ten bottles of Scotch* ***down****.* □ modifier usu present.

be down[2] [A1] have fallen, been reduced. **S:** price, cost; (level of) demand, output □ *The level of demand* ***is down*** *since the new measures were introduced to reduce spending.* ⇨ bring down[5], come down[3], go down[5].

be down[3] [A1] be entered or written down. **S:** name, age; opinion, view. **A:** on paper, in a notebook; in black and white □ ***Is*** *the date of the next meeting* ***down*** *in your diary?* □ *'Don't try to deny that you said it. Your words* ***are down*** *here in black and white.'* ⇨ get down[4], go down[9], put down[8], set down[2], take down[3].

be down as [A3] (informal) have one's name entered or recorded as (sometimes with the suggestion that the entry is false). **S:** name; he etc. **o:** Smith, Brown etc □ *Her* ***name's down as*** *Smythe in the telephone book, but she's really just plain Smith.* ⇨ put down as[1].

be down at heel [A3] (informal) be badly worn down; be in a generally shabby state. **S:** shoe, boot; Smith, Brown, etc □ *He's always so* ***down at heel;*** *is he hard up or just slovenly?* □ *Our cases were collected by a* ***down-at-heel*** *hall porter.* □ adj form is down-at-heel.

be down by the bows/stern [A3] (nautical) be sinking; have the bows or stern under water. **S:** ship, boat □ *When the rescue craft arrived, the 'Discoverer'* ***was*** *already* ***down by the stern****, and sinking fast.*

be down for [A3] have one's name entered for admission to a school (esp a preparatory or public school). **S:** child; name. **o:** Eton, Shrewsbury □ *His name's* ***been down for*** *his father's school since birth: we wanted to be absolutely sure of getting him in.* ⇨ put down for[2].

be down for a count of... [A3] (boxing) be knocked to the floor and stay there while the referee counts (not long enough, however, to be counted out) □ *The British contender for the heavyweight title* ***was down for a count of*** *six in the fifth round.* ⇨ be out[9], count out[2].

be down (from) [A1 A3] have left a university (esp Oxford or Cambridge) □ *Their son* ***is*** *just* ***down from*** *Oxford after taking a degree in chemistry.* ⇨ come down (from), go down[8], send down.

be down in the dumps/mouth [A3] (informal) be, appear, miserable or dejected □ *Bill's* ***been*** *a bit* ***down in the mouth*** *ever since they put the tax up on beer.* ⇨ get down in the dumps/mouth.

be down on[1] [A3] (informal) be critical of; be prejudiced against □ *He can be a thoroughly bad writer. Some of the critics* ***are*** *terribly* ***down on*** *him.* PW □ note nom form in: *They have a* ***down on*** *him.*

be down on[2] [A3] (informal) quickly note and point out. **S:** supervisor, manager; teacher. **o:** slip, error. **A:** at once, immediately, like a ton of bricks □ *The examiners* ***were down on*** *his mistake in a flash.* ⇨ come down on[1].

be down on[3] [A3] (informal) demand money or redress from. **S:** creditor, victim (of an accident). **o:** (bankrupt) businessman, (negligent) workman □ *When the news got about that Smith's business was failing, his suppliers* ***were down on*** *him for payment of his debts.* ⇨ come down on[2].

be down on one's luck [A3] (informal) suffer a setback or misfortune □ *'Well, Lumley, I'm sorry* ***you're down on your luck****. I should have thought you could have got a better job than this, though.'* HD

be down and out [A1] (informal) be destitute (without work or means and dependent on public assistance). **S:** worker, farmer; class □ *After about ten years of casual work or none at all, they* ***are*** *practically* ***down and out****.* □ *A crowd of* ***down-and-outs*** *clustered around the soup-kitchen.* □ nom form is down-and-out(s).

be down to [A3] (informal) have nothing left except. **o:** our last farthing, my last pair of stockings □ *The garrison had held out for a month and* ***were*** *now* ***down to*** *their last cartridge.*

be down with [A3] (informal) be ill with. **o:** stomach upset, bad cold □ *They****'re*** *both* ***down with*** *a nasty bout of 'flu.* ⇨ go down with.

be (all) for [A2] (informal) (strongly) favour, support. **S:** minister, candidate, employer. **o:** increased pensions, reduced costs; sharing wealth, giving the young a chance □ *He****'s all for*** *getting what he can out of the firm; but he's not so keen on giving anything in return.*

be for it/the high jump [A2] (informal) (be going to) be punished or reprimanded. **S:** (naughty) child; scamp, rascal □ *'You'll* ***be for it*** *when your father comes home!'* □ *'If you mess about with my typewriter again, you'll* ***be for the high jump****.'* □ often with *shall/will*.

be in[1] [A1] be fashionable, be the fashion. **S:** red, black; silk, leather; foreign travel □ *Leather* ***is in*** *at the moment; plastic is out.* □ *This is very much an* ***in*** *style just now.* □ note attrib use of in in last example. ⇨ come in[1]; be in/bring into/come into fashion/vogue.

be in[2] [A1] be gathered, be harvested. **S:** harvest, crop; grapes, potatoes □ *The fruit crop, the best they had had for years,* ***was*** *now safely* ***in****.* ⇨ bring in[1], get in[1].

be in[3] [A1] be in the shops (because they have been gathered etc). **S:** strawberries, pheasant, trout □ *'Have you any peaches?' 'No, sir, I am afraid they****'re*** *not* ***in*** *yet.'* ⇨ come in[2]; be in season, come into season.

be in[4] [A1] (politics) be elected; be in office. **S:** party, representative □ *'Did you know our local MP* ***is in*** *again?'* □ *The Republicans have* ***been in*** *since the hand-over of power.* ⇨ come in[3], get in/into[3], put in[6].

be in[5] [A1] (cricket) be batting. **S:** side, team; player □ *The home side* ***is in*** *at the moment; but we shall be batting soon.* ⇨ go in[4], put in[7].

be in[6] [A1] remain alight. **S:** stove, furnace □ *The fire we lit last night* ***is*** *still* ***in*** *this morning.* ⇨ keep in[2].

be in[7] [A1] (of the sea) have reached the highest point on the shore. **S:** ⚠ the tide, water □ *'Be careful about swimming when the tide****'s in****; the beach shelves steeply here.'* ⇨ come in[7].

be in action [A2] (military) be active, be in a position where he or it can operate. **S:** force, troops; artillery, tanks □ *Our men* ***were in action*** *within an hour of arriving in the front line.* □ *At that moment, there* ***were*** *only two guns* ***in action****.* ⇨ bring/come/go into action.

be all in [A1] (informal) be exhausted, be tired out □ *After six weeks' training, the recruits* ***were*** *just about* ***all in****.*

be in being/existence [A2] have started its/their existence. **S:** body, organization; army; industry; university □ *The negotiating machinery which they had worked so hard to set up* ***was*** *at last* ***in being****.* □ *At that time there* ***was*** *no procedure* ***in existence*** *for handling this kind of case.* ⇨ bring/come into being/existence.

be in blossom/flower [A2] have blossomed,

flowered. **S:** tree, shrub; rose, azalea □ *On both sides of the road the cherry-trees* ***were in blossom.*** □ *The crocuses* ***are*** *now* ***in flower.*** ⇨ bring/come into blossom/flower.

be in bud/leaf [A2] (of a bud, leaf, on a tree or bush) have appeared or shown itself. **S:** tree, shrub; branch, twig □ *The roses* ***are in bud*** *early this year.* □ *The plane trees lining the main street* ***are*** *already* ***in leaf.*** ⇨ come into bud/leaf.

be in employment/work [A2] be employed, have a job □ *Those who* ***are in*** *part-time* ***employment*** *should leave this part of the form blank.* □ *The father****'s*** *still* ***in work,*** *but the two teenage boys are finding it hard to get jobs.*

be in fashion/vogue [A2] be fashionable. **S:** natural fabrics, plastic; maxicoat, miniskirt □ *Styles which are now the latest thing may often have* ***been in fashion*** *thirty years ago.* □ *The cult of violence in the cinema* ***is*** *now* ***in vogue:*** *let us hope it is a passing fashion.* ⇨ bring/come into fashion/vogue; be in[1], come in[1].

be in focus [A2] (of sth viewed through a microscope, telescope etc) be sharp and clear; (fig) be clearly visible, intelligible. **S:** microscope, specimen; question, problem, matter □ *All the details of the insect's wing* ***were in*** *sharp* ***focus.*** □ *Two important aspects of the question* ***are*** *now* ***in*** *clear* ***focus;*** *shall we discuss those before moving on?* ⇨ bring/come into focus.

be in force [A2] have begun to operate (and be in some way binding and enforceable). **S:** law, regulation, requirement □ *A new code of practice for hoteliers* ***is*** *now* ***in force.*** □ *There* ***was*** *nothing* ***in force*** *to stop travel-agents misleading bookers.* ⇨ bring/come/put into force.

be in hand [A2] have been started or undertaken. **S:** work; arrangements; checking, correction □ *The editing of the manuscript* ***is*** *now* ***in hand.*** □ *Work* ***is*** *already* ***in hand*** *on the proposed extension of the motorway.* ⇨ have/take in hand.

be in jeopardy [A2] be threatened, endangered. **S:** plan, scheme; chances, prospects; trade, employment; relations □ *There has been a fall in demand for their products, and thousands of jobs in the area* ***are in jeopardy.*** □ *Because of infringements of the cease-fire, the peace talks* ***are in*** *serious* ***jeopardy.*** ⇨ put in jeopardy.

one's luck be in [A1] (informal) (of sb) be fortunate, be lucky □ (horoscope) ***Your luck is in*** *and you should be able to look forward to one of your smoothest weeks for some time.* WI

be in the open [A2] be obvious, evident; have been made public. **S:** feelings; enmity, envy; dispute, differences (between people); matter, issue □ *It is far better that your quarrel should* ***be in the open;*** *you now know where you both stand.* □ *The real causes of grievance* ***are*** *now* ***in the open.*** ⇨ bring/come into the open.

be in the picture [A2] (informal) have been given up-to-date information, be fully informed (about sth). **S:** staff, colleagues □ *'All right, now that I****'m*** *fully* ***in the picture*** *what can I do to help you?'* □ *'I'm not sure that we****'re*** *quite* ***in the picture.*** *Can you tell us exactly what was said at that meeting?'* ⇨ put in the picture.

be in play [A2] be involved, be at work, have started to influence sth. **S:** force, factor, circumstance □ *Mighty forces* ***are in play*** *in the present round of negotiations.* ⇨ bring/come into play.

be in sb's possession [A2] be held, possessed by sb (usu temporarily or illegally). **S:** (stolen) vehicle, firearms, drugs □ *I don't know how the missing documents came to* ***be in his possession*** (or: *how he came to* ***be in possession of*** *the documents*). □ the second pattern in the example is used by the police in statements of evidence: *The accused* ***was in possession of*** *cannabis.* ⇨ come into sb's possession.

be in power [A2] have reached, attained, (political) control. **S:** party, group; clique, junta; class □ *A coalition government* ***was in power*** *in Britain during the Second World War.* ⇨ come/put into power.

be in season [A2] be seasonable or available (in shops). **S:** oysters, (fresh) salmon; strawberries, grapes □ *Don't buy imported strawberries; —they're so expensive. Wait till they****'re in season*** *here.* ⇨ come into season; be in[3], come in[2].

be in service/use [A2] have begun to serve the public, be used. **S:** bus, lorry; railway, road; bridge, tunnel □ *A new Cross-Channel link will* ***be in service*** *for the holiday traffic.* □ *The footbridge over the river* ***is*** *no longer* ***in use.*** ⇨ bring/come/go into service/use.

be in sight/view [A2] be visible, have appeared. **S:** coast; sea; train, car □ *From our position on the hillside, every detail of the landscape* ***was*** *clearly* ***in view.*** ⇨ bring/come into sight/view.

be well in hand [A2] have been controlled, be under control (q v). **S:** situation; crisis □ *He said there was no cause for alarm: the situation* ***was*** *now* ***well in hand.*** ⇨ have well in hand.

be in the wrong [A2] have acted wrongly; be made to feel that one has acted wrongly □ *'All right, I****'m in the wrong****—I shouldn't have lost my temper with him.'* □ *Why* ***am*** *I always* ***in the wrong****? Is it something about my face that sets people against me?* ⇨ put in the wrong.

be in at the finish/kill [A3] (informal) be present at the conclusion (usu unpleasant) of a conflict or chase. **S:** tracker, huntsman, soldier □ *That's a really bloodthirsty hound you've got there; he always loves to* ***be in at the kill.***

be in for[1] [A3] (sport) be going to compete in; enter for (q v). **S:** athlete, competitor. **o:** event, race □ *I****'m in for*** *the 100 metres and the high jump.* ⇨ go in for[1], put in for[1].

be in for[2] [A3] be an applicant for. **o:** job, post; vacancy □ *I understand he****'s in for*** *an administrative job in the Civil Service.* ⇨ put in (for).

be in for[3] [A3] (informal) be likely to experience. **o:** shock, hard times, far-reaching changes □ *It looked as if we might* ***be in for*** *a frosty spell.* TBC □ *Anyone who thinks that Kirkaldy's a dreadful industrial town* ***is in for*** *a very pleasant surprise.* SC

be in charge (of) [A2] direct, be responsible for, some process or organization. **S:** official, businessman, academic; office, department. **o:** (***of***) business; sales, recruitment; field, area □ *Jones* ***was in*** *complete* ***charge*** *while the manager was on holiday.* □ *We are looking for an experienced man to* ***be in charge of*** *research and development.* ⇨ take charge (of).

be in control (of) [A2] manage, regulate, the behaviour of sb, or the movement, progress, of sth. **S:** teacher, parent; pilot, driver; scientist. **o:** oneself; child, pupil; plane, car; experiment □

How can he take control of a class when he's not ***in control of*** *himself!* □ *The police were not satisfied that he* ***was in*** *complete* ***control of*** *the car.* ⇨ have control of/over, take control (of).

be in on [A3] have a share in, participate (in) (q v); be informed of. **o:** plan, scheme, venture; idea, suggestion □ *Most of the staff want to* ***be in on*** *the new pension scheme.* □ *The principal Trades Unions* ***were in on*** *the Minister's thinking from the start.* ⇨ bring/come/get/let in on.

be in on the ground floor [A3] (informal) have joined a venture etc at its outset. **S:** investor, shareholder; partner, associate □ *You're a lucky man. The business is bound to expand and prosper, and you****'re in on the ground floor****!* ⇨ come in on the ground floor²; get in³.

be in and out of [A2] (informal) be a frequent visitor to or inmate of. **o:** hospital, shop □ *He****'s in and out of*** *gaol all the time.* □ *You're an export delivery driver. You must* ***be in and out of*** *every principal dock in the country.* HD ⇨ go in and out (of).

be in accord/harmony/tune (with) [A2] match, agree (with) easily and smoothly. **S:** statement, declaration; move, action; decision. **o:** (***with***) (previous, earlier) statement etc; (others') wishes, desires □ *This document* ***is*** *hardly* ***in accord with*** *our earlier agreement.* □ *The Prime Minister's speech and that of his Deputy* ***were*** *not* ***in harmony*** (***with*** *each other*). □ *This step* ***is in tune with*** *our entire policy to date.*

be in collision (with) [A2] have struck, or collided (with). **S:** car, lorry; train; ship □ *A van* ***was in collision with*** *an articulated lorry* (or: *A van and a lorry* ***were in collision***) *on the M1.* ⇨ come into collision (with).

be in collusion (with) [A2] (legal) have made a secret agreement, contrary to law, for some purpose □ *The solicitor warned his client that he would not obtain a divorce if he was found to* ***be in collusion with*** *his wife* (or: *if he and his wife were found to* ***be in collusion***).

be in contact (with) [A2] have touched or met. **S:** (electrical) lead, wire; agent, businessman. **o:** (***with***) surface, plate; author, customer □ *Unless both the leads* ***are in contact with*** *the terminals, the current will not pass through* (or: *Unless the leads and the terminals* ***are in contact****, the current* etc). □ *I* ***am*** *already* ***in contact with*** *a London agent, who is trying to secure a booking.* ⇨ bring/come into contact (with).

be in line (with) [A2] follow, conform with, the rules or discipline of an organization. **S:** member, follower. **o:** (***with***) the majority; official doctrine □ *After several shifts of position he* ***is*** *now* ***in line with*** *the rest of the party.* ⇨ bring/come/fall into line (with).

be in touch (with) [A2] contact sb (face-to-face, or by letter etc); communicate (with). **o:** (***with***) relation, friend; customer, client □ *When* ***were*** *you last* ***in touch with*** *your wife's parents?* □ ***Are*** *you still* ***in touch with*** *the people you knew at college?* □ *I think that the next meeting of the Association should be in York. I shall* ***be in touch with*** *my colleagues about this.* ⇨ put in touch (with).

be (well) in with [A3] (informal) be on familiar terms with (and likely to profit from the connection). **o:** fashionable set, influential people □ *He* ***is in with*** *the bosses.* UL □ *He****'s well in with*** *all the theatre and television crowd.* ⇨ get in with.

be inside [A1] (police slang) be in prison. **S:** thief, murderer □ *'****Is*** *Pearson still* ***inside****?' 'No, he was let out early.'* ⇨ put inside.

be off¹ [A1 A2] have fallen, been thrown from. **o:** horse, pony; bicycle □ *'Can he manage to stay on? No, he****'s off****!'* ⇨ come off¹.

be off² [A1 A2] have become detached or separated. **S:** handle, knob; hook, plug. **o:** door, wall □ *'Half the buttons* ***are off*** *my shirt — can you sew them on?'* ⇨ come off², take off¹.

be off³ [A1] (informal) hurry away, leave at once □ *He glanced at his watch. 'And by the way, I must* ***be off****.'* DS □ *It's high time we* ***were off****.* ⇨ get off³, set off (on)¹.

be off⁴ [A1] be cancelled, not be going to take place. **S:** wedding, party, match □ *'There is not going to be any wedding,' I told him. 'It****'s off****.'* DIL □ *The threatened dock strike* ***is off****.*

be off⁵ [A1] be no longer available (on the menu). **S:** meat, pudding □ *'Steak pie****'s off****,' said the waitress.* ⇨ take off⁹.

be off⁶ [A1] be disconnected. **S:** water, gas, electricity (supplies) □ *The gas supply will* ***be off*** *while they repair the mains.* ⇨ go off⁷, turn off¹.

be off⁷ [A1] (informal) smell or be bad or rotten. **S:** cheese, beer, milk □ *'This fish you've given me* ***is*** *slightly* ***off****.'* ⇨ go off⁶.

be off⁸ [A2] (informal) lack interest in, lose appetite for. **o:** politics, golf, music, girls □ *I've* ***been off*** *cigarettes ever since I heard of the connection with lung cancer.* □ *The cat****'s off*** *his food.* ⇨ go off⁴, put off⁵, turn off².

be off⁹ [A2] (slang) be mad; be extremely foolish; be out of one's mind (q v). **o:** ⚠ one's head, rocker, chump, nut □ *'He must* ***be off*** *his nut to throw his money about like that.'* ⇨ go off⁸.

be off¹⁰ [A1] (horse racing) start. **S:** ⚠ they; the field, the horses □ *'The horses are under starter's orders. Now they're settling down. And* ***they're off****!'*

be off one's hands [A2] (informal) have taken away from one the expense and responsibility of looking after sb or sth. **S:** daughter, elderly relative; guest; house, car □ *'I hear Mary's just got engaged. Well, that****'s*** *the last of the girls* ***off your hands****!'* □ *We're finding it hard to get a buyer for the flat. We'll be relieved when it****'s off our hands****.* ⇨ take off sb's hands.

be (quick) off the mark [A2] (informal) be quick to grasp sth, seize an opportunity, etc. **S:** company, shop; manufacturer, inventor, salesman □ *Watch out for jealous colleagues: some of them* ***are*** *very* ***quick off the mark****.* □ *Ned* ***was off the mark*** *at once. His pottery seemed to become a vogue overnight.* CON

be well etc off (for) [A1 A3] (informal) be rich etc; be well etc supplied with sth. **m:** ⚠ (very, fairly) well, comfortably, badly. **o:** cash; beer, cigarettes □ *My family* ***aren't well off****.* EHOW □ *How* ***are*** *you* ***off for*** *money?* TC □ *He****'s*** *pretty* ***well off for*** *food and drink.* □ adj forms: well-off, comfortably-off, badly-off.

be off (on) [A1 A3] (informal) begin to speak, tiresomely and at length (about sth). **o:** favourite subject, pet theme, hobbyhorse □ *'Oh dear, he****'s off*** *again. Isn't there any way of stopping him?'* □ *She****'s off on*** *her pet subject, or rather obsession — sex and violence on TV.* ⇨ set off (on)², start off (on)[2].

be on[1] [A1] be going to take place. **S:** match; strike, ban □ *The shut-down threatened for this weekend* ***is** still **on**, but union leaders are trying to avert a stoppage.*

be on[2] [A2] (informal) be paid for by, be charged to. **S:** drink, lunch, party. **o:** the house, the management; me □ *'Now drink up and don't worry about expense: the beers **are on** me!'* □ *On Armistice Day, drinks **were on** the house.*

be on[3] [A1 A2] (racing) be staked or bet on sb or sth. **S:** money; his shirt; he etc. **o:** horse, dog; fighter; team □ *'I want five pounds each way on "Golden Lad" in the next race.' 'Right, sir, you're **on**!'* □ *My money **was on** an outsider in the last race, and I couldn't afford to lose.* ⇨ put on[8]; put one's shirt on.

be on[4] [A1] (cricket) (have begun to) bowl. **S:** (slow, fast) bowler □ *Snow **was on** for two more overs after lunch; then he was replaced by an off-spinner.* ⇨ bring on[4], come on[9], put on[10].

be on[5] [A1] be on stage (in a play, opera etc). **S:** actor; Hamlet; tenor, chorus □ *It's a very arduous part: he **is on** for most of the second act.* □ *'Hurry up, Peter, you**'re on**!'* (i e you should be on stage.) ⇨ come on[10].

be on[6] [A1] be being shown, performed. **S:** film, play, ballet □ *There**'s** a good film **on** at the Plaza this week.* □ *'King Lear' **was on** at the Playhouse last season.* ⇨ come on[11], put on[11].

be on[7] [A1] (legal) be being heard, considered (in court). **S:** ⚠ case, lawsuit, hearing □ *'Your case **is on** in Courtroom No 3, just along the corridor.'* ⇨ come on[12].

be on[8] [A1] be alight, be burning. **S:** light, lamp; (electric/gas) fire, radiator; radio □ *'The light**'s on** in the kitchen. Please turn it off.'* □ *'Did you know the television **was** still **on** when you came up to bed?'* ⇨ go on[15], put on[2], turn on[1].

be on the ball [A2] (informal) be alert, wide-awake (to opportunities etc). **S:** salesman, agent, negotiator □ *He**'s** not really **on the ball** — he lets so many chances slip by.*

be on one's feet [A2] have stood up; be standing. **S:** spectator; delegate, councillor; housewife, shop assistant □ *As soon as the guest speaker was announced, half the audience **was on its feet**, clapping and cheering.* □ *A busy housewife **is on her feet** for most of the day.* ⇨ bring to his feet, come to/get on one's feet.

be on one's honour [A2] be trusted to do sth on pain of breaking one's oath. **S:** child, pupil **Inf** to behave, not to cheat □ *'Now, don't forget, you**'re on your honour** to be absolutely quiet until Miss Jones gets back.'* □ usu followed by the inf. ⇨ put on his honour.

be on ice [A2] (informal) be shelved, be deferred (e g until more time or money is available to deal with it). **S:** idea, plan, project □ *The plan for the new book **is on ice** at the moment. I've been busy with too many other things.* ⇨ put on ice.

be on the map [A2] (informal) be prominent, be before the public's attention. **S:** town, village; festival; sport □ *Show-jumping as a spectator sport **is** increasingly **on the map** — largely because of TV coverage.* ⇨ put on the map.

not be on [A1] (informal) not be possible or allowed. **S:** ⚠ it, this, that □ *I told the Minister that we could not make proposals within the limits of £600 million — it **was** simply **not on**.* MFM

(the) pressure be on [A2] (of moral, political etc pressure) be firmly applied. **o:** government, leader; labour leader, employer □ *There **is** mounting **pressure on** the Government to resign.* □ ***The pressure is** now **on** the unions to reach a settlement.* ⇨ put pressure on/upon.

to be on the safe side [A2] (informal) in order to be sure (of arriving in time etc); to be safe, secure (from danger) □ *She looked at her watch. 'We'd better be going, **to be on the safe side**,' she said.* QA □ *He prefers to regard every animal as poisonous, just **to be on the safe side**.* BB □ a non-finite adv clause of purpose.

be on the scene [A2] have appeared, become involved in sth. **S:** police, ambulance; reporter, eye-witness □ *The fire brigade **were on the scene** within minutes of being called.* □ *Now that he**'s on the scene** we can expect nothing but disharmony.* ⇨ come on the scene.

be on trial [A2] (legal) be being tried in a court of law. **S:** accused, prisoner □ *'Let me remind the accused that he **is on trial** for his life.'* ⇨ bring to trial.

be on about [A3] (informal) speak with tiresome persistence about. **o:** illness, money, smart friends; how clever one is □ *I don't like the smart people your mother**'s** always **on about**.* □ *What **is** she **on about**?* RT ⇨ go on about.

be on one's guard (against) [A2] be wary of sth or sb (often given as a warning) □ *'I should **be on my guard** if I were you. He's not the sort of man I should trust.'* □ ***Be on your guard against** door-to-door salesmen with a smooth line of talk.* ⇨ put on his guard.

be on at [A3] (informal) nag persistently, try to persuade. **o:** him etc; husband, boyfriend. **Inf** to improve, to change □ *His wife**'s** forever **on at** him to do something about the fence.* □ *I've **been on at** her to change her hairstyle.* □ usu followed by the inf. ⇨ go on (at).

be well on in/into [A3] be late, be well advanced (in time); be old, be of advanced years. **S:** it; he etc. **o:** (***in***) the afternoon; years; (***into***) July; one's sixties □ *Although it **was well on in** the evening, we decided to try our luck at fishing again.* BM □ *By now, he must **be well on into** his seventies.*

be on to[1] [A3] (informal) be talking to, be in touch (with) (q v) (in order to inform or persuade). **o:** head office, headquarters; allies; aircraft, ships □ *'I've just **been on to** the accounts people about your expenses, Smith; I think they'll let you have them.'* □ *I've already **been on to** the spacecraft, telling it to go much slower.* TBC ⇨ get on to[1], put on to[1].

be on to[2] [A3] (informal) become aware of (and be following up that knowledge); make contact with (in the course of pursuit). **S:** customs, tax authorities, police; reporter. **o:** dodge, fraud, little game; gang; secret hideout □ *The CID **are on to** the men who were responsible for that break-in.* □ *The Inland Revenue **are on to** him for a currency deal he thought he'd got away with some years ago.* ⇨ get on to[2], put on to[2].

be on to a good thing [A3] (informal) find a pleasant or remunerative occupation or style of life □ *He**'s on to a good thing** in his new job: high wages, practically no income tax and a rent-free house.* ⇨ put on to[3].

be on/upon one [A2] have arrived (with the suggestion that the arrival may be sudden and unwelcome). **S:** dry season, winter, Christmas; election, Budget Day □ *The wet season* ***was on us****, and on the Adriatic coast it became cold and damp.* MFM □ *We'd hardly had time to get over a series of birthdays before Christmas* ***was upon us****.* ⇨ come on/upon one.

be out[1] [A1] (industry) have ceased work, be striking. **S:** workers, clerical staff. **A:** on strike; in sympathy, in protest against dismissals □ *The workers* ***are out*** *after last night's threat to stop overtime.* ⇨ bring out[1], come out[1].

be out[2] [A1] (informal) be released (from prison). **S:** prisoner, convict **A:** of gaol, on parole □ *'Stevens can't have cracked that safe, sergeant; he's not* ***out*** *until next week!'* ⇨ come out[2], let out/out of.

be out[3] [A1] (informal) (be sure to) be removed, ejected (e g from a club). **S:** drunk, trouble-maker □ *'Any more remarks like that and you****'re out*** *for good!'* □ *I knew that if I had too much to drink and started picking fights I'd* ***be out*** *on my ear.* ⇨ put out[2].

be out[4] [A1] flower, be in bloom. **S:** rose, almond blossom, bougainvillaea □ *If this fine weather keeps up, my hyacinths will* ***be out*** *in a day or two.* ⇨ bring out[4], come out[4].

be out[5] [A1] be visible (i e not covered by clouds, or not made invisible against bright sky). **S:** ⚠the sun, moon, stars □ *'The sun****'s out****; now I can get on with some gardening and you can sit out in a deck chair.'* ⇨ come out[5].

be out[6] [A1] be on sale, be published. **S:** book, article, report □ *A new magazine for the younger, smarter woman* ***is out*** *today.* ⇨ bring out[5], come out[6].

be out[7] [A1] be disclosed or revealed, leak out (q v). **S:** ⚠ secret, news □ *The secret they'd kept hidden from the press for so long* ***was*** *now* ***out****.* ⇨ come out[7], get out[1], let out[2].

be out[8] [A1] (cricket) be dismissed. **S:** batsman, side □ *Smith* ***was out*** *trying to turn a ball to leg.* □ *The Indian touring team* ***were*** *all* ***out*** *for 260.* ⇨ get out[4], give out[4].

be out[9] [A1] (slang) be fast asleep, be unconscious (after an exhausting day or knockout blow). **S:** boxer, soldier, worker. **m:** ⚠ right, dead. **A:** ⚠ for the count, like a light □ ASTON: *Sleep well?* DAVIES: *Yes. Dead* ***out****. Must have* ***been*** *dead* ***out****.* TC □ modifier or adjunct used, not both. ⇨ go out[2], put out[9].

be out[10] [A1] be no longer alight, be extinguished. **S:** fire, stove; candle, lamp, (electric) light □ *The lights* ***were*** *all* ***out*** *when we got home from the theatre: Mother must have gone to bed.* ⇨ go out[5], put out[10], turn out[10].

be out[11] [A1] (informal) be finished, be ended. **S:** night, week, month, winter □ *There'll be changes made in the school before the year****'s out****.* □ usu in a dependent clause after *before*.

be out[12] [A1] be inaccurate, be wrong. **S:** research worker, doctor; figures, forecast. **m:** (some) way, not far, five minutes, well, miles. **A:** by a long way, by miles; in one's calculations, when predicting recovery □ *Subsequent events show how well* ***out*** *he* ***is*** *in his diagnosis.* SC □ *His forecast of rapid growth in the public sector of industry* ***was*** *some way* ***out****.* □ modifier or adjunct used, not both. ⇨ put out[12].

be out[13] [A1] (informal) not be permissible (and therefore not be tolerable). **S:** cheating, kicking, stealing from the poor □ *'Now we'll have a good, hard game, but any hacking or barging from behind* ***is*** *strictly* ***out****.'*

be out[14] [A1] (informal) be no longer the fashion. **S:** jazz, short hair, long skirts □ *That style's* ***been out*** *for some months; you ought to study fashion more closely.* ⇨ go out[6]; be/go out of fashion.

be out[15] [A1] be announced, be declared. **S:** (examination) result, mark; class-list □ *'The results of the Bar exams* ***are out*** *— and you're through!'* ⇨ come out[13].

be out[16] [A1] (of the water level at the seaside) be low, have receded. **S:** ⚠ the tide, water □ *When the tide* ***is out****, you can walk across the sand to St Michael's Mount without getting your feet wet.* ⇨ go out[7].

be out to do sth [A1] (informal) aim, propose. **S:** government, firm. **Inf** to make changes, to improve exports, to reduce prices □ *Like so many others involved in the case, she* ***was out to make*** *money.* T

warrant be out [A1] (police) (of a written order to arrest sb) be issued. **A:** against sb, for the arrest of sb □ ***Warrants are out*** *for the arrest of two men wanted in connection with the murder.*

be out (at) [A1 A3] have left home (for an outing etc). **o:** the pictures, the theatre □ *'Mary****'s out*** *with her boyfriend.'* □ *I'm sorry to have missed you. I* ***was out at*** *the pictures when you called.* ⇨ come/go/take out (for/to).

be out for [A3] (informal) be determined to get; aim to further or serve. **S:** Government, industry; enemy, crook. **o:** better housing, good relations; their own ends, anything he can get; your blood □ *It is not money alone, but some hard thinking, which the campaign* ***is out for****.* TES ⇨ go (all) out (for).

be out from [A3] have left a port or airfield a stated time before; be a stated distance from. **S:** ship, boat, plane. **m:** ten hours, four days; fifty miles. **o:** London, Lagos, Orly Airport □ *Our aircraft* ***was*** *barely half-an-hour* ***out from*** *Newfoundland when it developed engine trouble.* □ *We* ***were*** *a good sixty miles* ***out from*** *base.* □ modifier usu present.

be out in [A3] be present in large numbers. **S:** police, troops, supporters, teenagers. **o:** ⚠ force, strength, large numbers □ *Loyal party men* ***were out in*** *strength at the rally held last night.*

be out/out of[1] [A1 A2] have left (an enclosed space). **S:** owner, occupant; (caged) bird, animal; car. **o:** his etc office, house; town; cage; garage □ *'I'm afraid you can't see the manager today: he****'s out of*** *town till Monday.'* □ *His car****'s out****, so he must have left home early.* □ *'How long has that parrot* ***been out of*** *its cage?'* ⇨ bring out/out of, come out/out of[1], get out/out of[1], take out/out of[1].

be out/out of[2] [A1 A2] have left the place where it was fixed. **S:** nail, screw; thorn; teeth; cork, stopper. **o:** plaster, wood; flesh; gum; bottle □ *'Well, the splinter****'s out of*** *your finger, now, so you can run along and have some iodine put on it.'* □ *We spent half a morning pulling carpet tacks out of the floor, so I think most of them* ***are out*** *now.* ⇨ come out/out of[2], get out/out of[2], take out/out of[2].

be out/out of[3] [A1 A2] have disappeared, been removed (with cleaning). **S:** mark, stain; colour, dye. **o:** jacket; carpet □ *'Well, the mark's* ***out****, but it certainly needed a lot of rubbing.'* ⇨ come out/out of[3].

be out of[1] [A2] be without (work), be unemployed. **S:** shipyard workers, half the town. **o:** ⚠ work, a job, employment □ *Nor did he give any reason why he himself came to* ***be out of*** *a job.* HD

be out of[2] [A2] be too far away (to hear, or be seen or be reached). **o:** ⚠ earshot, sight, view, range □ *The French coast* ***is out of*** *sight from here but at Dover it's clearly in view.* □ *The enemy positions* ***were out of*** *range to all but our heaviest guns.* ⇨ go out of sight/view.

be out of[3] [A2] (informal) have finished, exhausted, one's supply of. **o:** ideas, patience; breath; spare parts, soap, petrol, tea □ *'That was a stiff climb; I'm quite* ***out of*** *breath.'* □ *'We****'re out of*** *cigarettes; I'll go to the corner shop for some more.'* ⇨ run out[1], run out/out of.

be out of[4] [A2] be inappropriate, be unsuited to the occasion. **S:** remark, interruption, behaviour. **o:** ⚠ place, keeping with the occasion □ *His dress and manner* ***were out of*** *keeping with the solemnity of the occasion.* □ *Father believed that children's conversation* ***was out of*** *place at the meal table.*

be out of action [A2] (military) be no longer able to operate or function (esp because of enemy action). **S:** ship, tank; gun; radar □ *'Number 2 turret* ***is out of action****, Sir.'* □ *Because of accurate anit-aircraft fire, three of the raiders* ***were*** *already* ***out of action****.* ⇨ go/put out of action.

be out of the blue [A2] (informal) have appeared, been uttered, suddenly, unexpectedly. **S:** arrival, appearance; statement, comment, remark; find, discovery □ *His arrival was all the more pleasant for* ***being*** *completely* ***out of the blue****.* □ *The coins were lost for years, then they turned up one day, quite* ***out of the blue****.* ⇨ come out of the blue.

be out of one's depth [A2] (informal) be in company where the discussion, knowledge of the others etc is strange and difficult to understand □ *I was drinking with a group of car enthusiasts, and for much of the time* ***was*** *completely* ***out of my depth****.* □ *She****'s*** *always* ***out of her depth*** *in intellectual circles.* ⇨ get out of one's depth.

be out of fashion [A2] be no longer fashionable. ⇨ be out[14], go out[6]; go out of fashion.

be out of focus [A2] (of sth seen through a microscope etc) not be sharp and clear; (fig) not be clearly intelligible. **S:** slide; specimen; microbe; question, facts □ *The image is blurred; the slide* ***is*** *a little* ***out of focus****.* □ *'For me, the story* ***is*** *still a bit* ***out of focus****. Could you be more explicit?'* ⇨ go out of focus.

be out of hand [A2] be uncontrolled, become uncontrollable. **S:** wages, prices; child, pupil □ *The situation appears to* ***be*** *completely* ***out of hand****.* □ *'And have you seen their children? They****'re*** *quite* ***out of hand****.'* ⇨ get out of hand.

be out of line [A2] not behave in a normal or acceptable way. **S:** remark, comment, criticism □ *I must say I thought your behaviour at the meeting* ***was*** *a bit* ***out of line****.* □ *I felt you* ***were out of line*** *in suggesting that we expected to do a lot of business with them.*

be out of one's mind [A2] be mad; be extremely foolish □ *Some of the generals disregarded this latest order, which could only have come from a man who* ***was*** *already* ***out of his mind****.* □ *'You must* ***be out of your*** *tiny* ***minds*** *if you think I would do anything of the sort!'* ⇨ go out of one's mind.

be out of order[1] [A2] not be functioning properly **S:** system; stomach, bowels; telephone, lavatory □ *There's no point in ringing the bell. There's a notice saying it****'s out of order****.* □ *The lift****'s out of order****. Please use the stairs.*

be out of order[2] [A2] (legal, official) not be allowable by a court of law as a proper statement etc; be considered improper according to the rules of debate laid down for meetings. **S:** remark, comment, interruption; statement, question □ *The judge ruled that the prosecution* ***was out of order*** *in introducing details of the accused's private life.* □ *'You* ***are out of order****, Sir,' shouted the Chairman above the din. 'Kindly sit down.'*

be out of play [A2] (sport) (of the ball in football etc) have crossed the line marking the edge of the playing area □ *The linesman raised his flag to signal that the ball* ***was out of play****.* ⇨ go out of play.

be out of season [A2] not be available fresh (because they are not now being caught etc). **S:** salmon; grouse; peaches □ *There aren't any fresh strawberries: they****'re*** *just* ***out of season****.*

be out of service [A2] have ceased to be used. **S:** bus, train, aircraft □ *Most of the steam locomotives which once drew trains on this line* ***are*** *now* ***out of service****.* ⇨ go out of service.

be well out of it/that [A2] (informal) be lucky to avoid being involved in sth □ *'So you didn't take up that job abroad after all? Well, I think we can say you****'re well out of it****.'* □ *'Not married yet? You****'re well out of that****!'*

(be) out with it [A3] say what you want to say; say what is on your mind □ *'What's the matter boy? What? Come on, now.* ***Out with it****! What's the matter — can't you tell me?'* FFE □ *Reassured by her confusion, and really curious to know, Harold leaned back and said: 'Well,* ***out with it****.'* PW □ imper form only.

be outside [A2] not be sth which one is able to handle, understand etc. **S:** subject, topic, matter. **o:** (one's) province, competence; field, area (of interest); brief □ *I can't give you a decision on anything to do with housing. That****'s*** *quite* ***outside*** *my competence.* □ *Have a word with my colleague about that text; Old English* ***is*** *a bit* ***outside*** *my field.* ⇨ fall outside, stand outside.

be over[1] [A1] be ended, be finished. **S:** party, waiting, illness, winter □ *That was the last window he was going to do that morning. And as it was Saturday, that meant that work* ***was over*** *for the weekend.* HD ⇨ be over and done with, get over (and done with).

be over[2] [A1] remain, be left. **S:** meat, flour; sand, bricks □ *A small piece of flannel* ***was over*** *when the tailor had finished cutting out my suit.* □ *If there****'s*** *any cement* ***over*** *when you've finished, you might keep it for me.* ⇨ leave over[1].

be over[3] [A2] spend a long time doing (sth). **A:** ⚠ (too) long, along time, ages. **o:** lunch, breakfast, coffee □ *'Don't* ***be*** *long* ***over*** *breakfast; I want to get started as soon as possible.'* □ *'How* *long will they* ***be over*** *their tea-break?'* ⇨ take (over).

be over[4] [A1] (informal) come, have come, to visit sb (usu by travelling some distance). **S:** friend, relative, husband □ *'Will you* ***be over*** *on Saturday?' 'No, I can't manage it this weekend.'* □ *I wasn't in Leeds last week. I* ***was over*** *with my parents in Liverpool.* ⇨ bring over, come over[1].

be all over[1] [A2] (informal) be spread or passed from one person to another. **S:** news, scandal, rumour, report. **o:** office, factory, camp □ *'Haven't you heard about Peter and that new girl from the typing pool? It's* ***all over*** *the office!'*

be all over[2] [A2] (informal) greet effusively (with the suggestion that the effusiveness is rather unwelcome). **S:** dog; hostess, welcoming party □ *I'd hardly set foot inside the door when that great labrador of theirs* ***was all over*** *me.*

be all over[3] [A2] (informal) dominate completely (at sport). **S:** team, players; visitors, tourists □ *The visiting team* ***were all over*** *us for the first ten minutes of play.*

be all over the place [A2] (informal) be very untidy, be in a disorderly state; be scattered here and there; be badly controlled. **S:** calculations, accounts; clothes, books, toys; service (at tennis), putting (at golf) □ *Her hair* ***was all over the place****; you would think she'd not combed it for a week.* □ *Not a very good first over. His bowling* ***was all over the place****!*

be over and done with [A1] (informal) be completely ended, or forgotten (not likely to recur or be remembered). **S:** ⚠ that, it, everything □ *Their quarrels and misunderstandings* ***were*** *all* ***over and done with****: nothing could disturb their friendship now.* □ *That* ***was*** *a former life,* ***over and done with****, something he had forgotten about.* HD ⇨ be over[1], get over (and done with).

be past caring [A2] ⇨ be beyond/past caring.

be past (one's) endurance [A2] ⇨ be beyond/past (one's) endurance.

be past it [A2] (informal) lack the skill or vigour (esp sexual) that one once had □ *'He was a tremendous one for the girls as a young fellow, but he's a bit* ***past it*** *now, isn't he?'* □ *John used to be very good at making these fine drawings, but I suppose, with his eyesight going, that he's* ***past it*** *now.*

be round (at) [A1 A3] ⇨ be around/round (at).

be through [A1] (informal) reach the end of a relationship. **S:** couple, boy and girl □ *'I won't put up with any more broken promises from him: we're* ***through****.'*

be through the mill [A2] (informal) have received, as training, hard practical experience. **S:** son; manager, officer □ *The boss never believed in sending his sons to university. He'd* ***been through the mill*** *himself, and he thought it was the best possible training for management.* ⇨ go/put through the mill.

be through (to) [A1 A3] be put in contact by telephone (with). **o:** New York, one's home, the police □ *After a few minutes' wait in the call-box, I* ***was through****.* □ *'You're* ***through to*** *London, sir!'* ⇨ get through (to)[2], put through (to).

be through with [A3] (informal) be tired of, dissatisfied with (and therefore determined to abandon) sb or sth. **o:** husband, boyfriend; lies, deceit; smoking, gambling □ *'I'm* ***through with*** *hanging about all day, waiting for him to appear.'* □ *She* ***was through with*** *trying to pretend that she loved him.*

be to the fore [A2] be prominent, noticeable. **S:** speaker; delegate, deputy □ *If an argument develops, depend on it that he will* ***be to the fore****.* □ *A scramble for seats took place, with John well* ***to the fore****.* □ be omitted after *with.* ⇨ bring/come to the fore.

be under control [A2] have been tamed, mastered. **S:** fire; epidemic; riot, disturbance □ *The fire which threatened part of the business district this morning* ***is*** *now firmly* ***under control****.* □ *Teachers sometimes complain that their pupils* ***are*** *not properly* ***under*** *their parents'* ***control****.* ⇨ bring/get under control.

be up[1] [A1] have risen or increased (in price). **S:** tax, tariff; beer, petrol. **A:** (by) ten pence, five pounds □ *Cigarettes and whisky* ***are up*** *as a result of the last budget.* □ *Share dividends* ***were*** *£86 million* ***up*** *on the year.* SC ⇨ go up[2], put up[4], send up[1].

be up[2] [A1] have travelled to, be in, an important town (e g London); be in residence, be a student (esp at Oxford or Cambridge). **S:** don, undergraduate □ *'Is the family still* ***up*** *in Edinburgh?' 'No, they came back a couple of days ago.'* □ *My son will* ***be up*** *at Cambridge for the next few years.* ⇨ come up[2], go up (to).

be up[3] [A1] have finished or expired, have come to an end. **S:** time, leave, three weeks, term of office, period of tenure □ *His time* ***was up****: he'd have to hand over to a younger man.* □ *My annual leave* ***was up****.*

be up[4] [A1] remain out of bed. **A:** till all hours, all night □ *She* ***was up*** *half the night with a sick child.* □ *They* ***were up*** *until well into the small hours counting the votes.* ⇨ keep up[9], stay up[2].

be up[5] [A1] rise, get out of bed. **A:** late, at crack of dawn, early □ *He's always* ***up*** *with the lark.* BA ⇨ get up[1].

be up[6] [A1] arise, be raised, be considered. **S:** subject, matter, question. **A:** for debate; during the discussion □ *The housing policy of the Council* ***is up*** *for debate at the next meeting.* □ *Salaries* ***are up*** *for review at the next session of the teachers' panel.* ⇨ bring up[3], come up[4].

be up[7] [A1] (legal) be considered (by a court); be on trial (q v). **S:** case; accused. **A:** before the court, judge; for petty larceny, on an embezzlement charge □ *Two students* ***were up*** *in court for knocking off a policeman's helmet on Guy Fawkes' night.* ⇨ bring up[4], come up[5].

one's blood be up [A1] (informal) (of temper) be fully aroused □ *His tormentors had piled insult upon insult till now* ***his blood was*** *really* ***up****.* ⇨ get sb's blood up.

the game be up [A1] (informal) (of a pursuit, search) be ended successfully (with the suggestion that the search has been long and the quarry elusive). **A:** for the escaped convict, for the enemy leaders □ *And now his pursuers had caught up with him; for him, at any rate,* ***the game was up****.*

(one's) hand be up [A1] be raised to attract attention etc □ *'Why* ***is your hand up****, Jenkins? I said that nobody was to be allowed to leave the* *room.'* ⇨ put (one's) hand up.

be hard up [A1] (informal) be poor, be short of money. **S:** country, Exchequer; farmer □ *Our nation* ***is*** *very* ***hard up*** *and we cannot afford the waste which comes from adding together the demands of three services.* MFM □ *His father was a* ***hard-up*** *teacher.* □ adj form is hard-up.

something be up [A1] (informal) be about to happen, be impending, be in the air □ ***Something was up*** *all right. The hotel bars were seething with rumours of big changes ahead.*

the sun be up [A1] have risen □ *He's out working in the fields before* ***the sun's up.*** □ nom form is sun-up. ⇨ the sun come up.

be up and about [A1] (informal) be feeling better and able to get up. **S:** patient, invalid □ *Now don't you worry about your husband, Mrs Davis. He'll* ***be up and about*** *again in a few days.*

be up against [A3] be opposed by, be confronted by. **o:** (real) problem, difficulty; opponent, competitor □ *This meeting should do John some good — he's* ***up against*** *some real opposition at least.* ⇨ bring/come up against.

be up against it [A3] (informal) be faced with special difficulties or hardships □ *After the fall of France, Britain* ***was*** *really* ***up against it.***

be up (as far as/to) [A1 A3] have reached, stretched, extended (to). **S:** sea, tide; fog, gas; climber, procession. **o:** sea-wall, house; ceiling, roof; summit □ *The water* ***was up as far as*** *my shoulders.* □ *The sunflowers* ***are up to*** *the top of the kitchen window.* ⇨ bring/come up (as far as/to).

be up for [A3] be a candidate, applicant, for a post etc. **o:** re-election, admission, membership □ *I believe he's* ***up for*** *re-admission to the society at the next committee meeting.* ⇨ come up for, put up (for)[1].

be up for auction/sale [A3] be available or offered for purchase, be on the market. **S:** house; furniture, painting, silver □ *A rare collection of Chinese porcelain will* ***be up for sale*** *next week.* ⇨ come/put up for auction/sale.

be up in arms [A3] (informal) declare opposition or disapproval, protest □ *Kay* ***was up in arms*** *at once: her round, unmade-up face shone with high-minded intellectual disapproval.* ASA

be up in the clouds [A3] (informal) be out of touch with reality. **S:** thinking, ideas, all this. **mc** rather, somewhat, a bit □ *Of course, he's a bit* ***up in the clouds.*** *All this conservatism in religion makes him think we can put the clock back in everything.* ASA

be well up in [A3] (informal) be very knowledgeable about, be well versed in. **o:** science, languages, foreign affairs, literature □ *Not very* ***well up in*** *the law,* ***are*** *you? Otherwise you'd know that it isn't possible to get divorced until you've been married three years.* TC

be up (to) [A1 A3] have reached. ⇨ be up (as far as/to).

be up to[1] [A3] (informal) be doing, be engaged in (with the suggestion that the activity is mischievous or reprehensible). **o:** ⚠ mischief, something, no good; his tricks, pranks; what □ *A very strange fellow your friend Libby Dobson. What's he* ***been up to*** *all day?* UTN □ *I felt sure he* ***was up to*** *no good when I saw him hanging about the back door.* ⇨ get up to[2], put up to[2].

be up to[2] [A3] (informal) be well aware of sb's dishonest tricks (and be capable of handling them). **S:** police, officials. **o:** ⚠ all his fiddles, dodges, tricks □ *But, surely, all that's taken care of by the customs authorities and the dock police? They must* ***be up to*** *all the dodges.* HD

be up to[3] [A3] (informal) be sb's responsibility; rest with (q v). **S:** (it...) to help, whether to go, how to do it □ *It's* ***up to*** *you to find out who will lend you the money.* HD □ *Whether you learn or not* ***is*** *entirely* ***up to*** *you.* ⇨ leave up to.

be up to[4] [A3] (informal) be deep in, be overwhelmed by. **o:** ⚠ here; his etc ears, eyes, neck. **A:** ⚠ in debt, work □ *He's* ***up to*** *his eyes in card debts.* US □ *I* ***was up to*** *my ears in paper-work.*

be up to[5] [A3] (informal) be of an acceptable standard. **S:** work, performance, appearance. **o:** ⚠ standard, scratch, the mark; expectations; not... much □ *She had a boy who might or might not be her fiancé. He* ***wasn't up to*** *much, but he was her young man.* PW □ *It's such nonsense about his household not* ***being up to*** *scratch.* UTN □ often neg. ⇨ bring/come up to, get up to[1].

be up to date/the minute [A3] be fresh or recent or modern; reflect current fashion. **S:** ideas, thought; house, car. **mc** right, bang, really □ *Her clothes* ***were*** *bang* ***up to date.*** TGLY □ *His reports from Africa* ***are*** *really* ***up to the minute.*** □ adj forms are up-to-date and up-to-the-minute. ⇨ bring up to date, get up to date (with).

(not) be up to [A3] (informal) (not) be capable of doing, (not) be equal to. **o:** task, work, responsibility □ *I'm afraid he's* ***not up to*** *the job of President.* □ *None of us* ***were up to*** *going to town in that storm.* ⇨ feel up to, put up to[1].

be up (with) [A1 A3] (informal) be amiss or wrong, be the matter. **S:** ⚠ something, what. **o:** him etc □ *I knew something* ***was up*** *as soon as I saw the miserable look in his eyes.* □ *'What's* ***up with*** *you, now?'*

be upon one [A2] ⇨ be on/upon one.

be with[1] [A2] be employed by. **o:** company, corporation; ICI, Shell □ *'What have you been doing since you qualified?' 'I was in insurance for a bit, but now I'm* ***with*** *a shipping firm.'*

be with[2] [A2] (informal) follow, understand, what sb is saying. **S:** audience, class □ *'Did you follow that bit all right?* ***Are*** *you still* ***with*** *me — or shall I go over it again?'*

be with[3] [A2] (informal) support, back up[1] (q v). **A:** all the way, to the (bitter) end □ *If you do decide to oppose him, then we're* ***with*** *you all the way!*

be within[1] [A2] be near enough (to be heard, seen or reached). **o:** ⚠ earshot, sight, view, range □ *If we move forward we shall* ***be within*** *range of the enemy guns.* ⇨ bring/come/get within.

be within[2] [A2] be sth which one is able to discuss or handle knowledgeably. **S:** subject, topic, matter. **o:** (one's) competence, province; field, area (of interest); scope of the inquiry □ *Perhaps this is something which another body should consider. It* ***is*** *not* ***within*** *the terms of reference of this committee.* ⇨ fall within.

be within one's grasp [A2] be close enough to be attained soon. **S:** victory, success □ *With the junction of the allied armies, the overthrow of the enemy power* ***was*** *now* ***within*** *our* ***grasp.***

be within one's rights (to do sth) [A2] have legal or moral support for sth one wishes to do. **S:** citizen, consumer, parent. **Inf** to protest, to take the goods back, to remove one's child □ *You're perfectly* ***within your rights to demand*** *a choice of schools for the child.* □ *If you aren't satisfied with the service you're getting, you're quite* ***within your rights to cancel*** *the arrangement.*

bear down [B1i pass] (formal) overcome, conquer. **S:** forces, strength. **O:** enemy, opposition □ *Eventually, after much dogged fighting, our troops* ***bore down*** *all resistance.*

bear down on/upon [A3 pass] move swiftly and threateningly towards. **S:** ship, tank, horse; society hostess. **o:** victim; guest □ *The bird was* ***bearing down upon*** *us at a speed of twenty miles an hour.* DF □ *As he got to the doorway, Rose Lorimer* ***bore down on*** *him with Clarissa Crane in tow.* ASA

bear in mind [B2 pass] remain aware, conscious, of; keep in mind (q v). **O:** fact, truth; statement, admission; that he was not present □ *He urged MPs to* ***bear in mind*** *the serious offences committed nowadays by young persons.* T □ *Three factors must be* ***borne in mind***. T □ *Please* ***bear in mind*** *that we don't know any Mr Hawthorne.* OMIH

bear on/upon [A2] affect, relate to. **S:** action, remark, factor. **o:** matter at issue, question; what is at stake □ *These were vital decisions that* ***bore upon*** *the happiness of everybody.* □ *How does his story* ***bear on*** *what they are investigating?*

bear hard/severely on/upon [A2 emph rel] (formal) cause sb hardship or suffering. **S:** shortage, rationing; unemployment, short-time working; drought, flooding. **o:** townspeople; worker; farmer □ *The latest price increases* ***bear*** *most* ***severely on*** *people with fixed incomes.* □ *It is* ***upon*** *the small farmer that the changes will* ***bear hardest***.

bear out [B1i pass] support, confirm. **S:** evidence, facts, events; he etc. **O:** theory, supposition, hypothesis; him etc □ *Indeed, the facts* ***bear out*** *the hypothesis.* SNP □ *This expectation is not* ***borne out***. MFF

bear a resemblance to [B2 emph rel] be like, resemble. **adj:** some, a good deal of; no, (not) any/much, little, small; startling, uncanny. **o:** (one's) father, brother □ *Tennessee Williams' own character* ***bears no resemblance to*** *the people depicted in his plays.* TO □ *The French uniforms* ***bore a*** *superficial* ***resemblance to*** *those of Chinese regulars.* BM

bear witness to [B2 emph rel] (formal) provide evidence of, testify (to) (q v). **S:** garden, house, countryside. **adj:** eloquent, mute. **o:** work, efforts, skill □ *The village* ***bore*** *silent* ***witness to*** *the passage of the cyclone.*

bear up [A1] manage, cope; remain strong in face of hard conditions. **S:** patient, soldier; plant □ *How do they* ***bear up*** *against distress and shock?* AH

bear with [A2 pass] tolerate, put up with (q v); listen patiently to. **o:** him etc; mood, temper □ *She neither liked nor trusted Jack Corelli, but she* ***bore with*** *him when he came to the flat with his violent opinions and his bombastic talk.* AITC □ *If you will all* ***bear with*** *me for just a few minutes, I will explain.* AITC

beat about the bush [A2] (informal) go around a subject instead of coming directly to the point □ *'If you've got bad news, don't* ***beat about the bush****: come straight to the point.'* □ *'It's no use* ***beating about the bush****, Wormold, you are in trouble.'* OMIH

beat one's head against a brick wall [B2] ⇨ bang one's head against a brick wall.

beat down [B1i pass] make sb reduce the price he first asked. **O:** price, figure; him etc □ *He wanted eight hundred pounds for his car, but I managed to* ***beat*** *him* ***down*** *to six hundred.*

beat down (on) [A1 A3 rel] shine with intense heat (on). **S:** ⚠ the sun, sun's rays □ *The sun* ***beat down on*** *our necks and backs.*

beat off [B1i pass] repulse, throw back[3] (q v). **S:** defender, soldier. **O:** attack; attacker, enemy □ *All their attempts to break into our position were* ***beaten off***. □ *This policy is to provide a guard capable of* ***beating off*** *an attack, a guard that is armed, with firearms in reserve.* MFM

beat out [B1i pass] remove by striking with a hammer etc. **S:** mechanic, panel-beater. **O:** dent, mark □ *The dent on the wing of your car can be* ***beaten out*** *at the garage.*

beat one's brains out [B1ii] (informal) struggle with a frustratingly long and difficult task □ *Here am I* ***beating my brains out*** *on the accounts, and what thanks do I get?* □ *'How much longer are you going to* ***beat your brains out*** *over that letter? You're not writing a novel, you know.'*

beat one's/sb's brains out [B1ii pass] (informal) kill oneself, or sb, by being beaten, or beating him, severely about the head (though not necessarily by knocking out the brains) □ *There would be nothing to stop me from plunging down the well of the staircase and* ***beating my brains out*** *on the stone floor at the bottom.* CON

beat out (on) [B1i pass adj B3 pass rel] produce or play by drumming. **S:** drummer, musician. **O:** tune, rhythm; message. **o:** drum; desk, table □ *A small boy was* ***beating out*** *a tune* ***on*** *a tin can.*

beat to it [B2 pass] (informal) get somewhere, reach an objective, before sb else. **O:** opponent, rival □ *They had hoped to put their model on the market within the year, but a rival company* ***beat*** *them* ***to it***.

beat to his knees [B2 pass] force sb to submit, humble him. **S:** circumstances, environment; strain, competition □ *The stresses of business had* ***beaten*** *him* ***to his knees*** *in middle life.*

beat up [B1i pass adj] beat severely with fists, sticks etc. **S:** gang, thieves. **O:** guard, messenger, shopkeeper □ *The bank manager received a severe* ***beating-up*** *in last night's raid.* □ *Next year another three Britons were arrested for* ***beating up*** *a taxi-driver.* TO □ nom form is beating-up.

become of [A2] happen to, befall. **S:** ⚠ what, whatever. **o:** him etc; sister, wife; pet; property □ *Whatever* ***became of*** *that house they used as a weekend cottage?* □ *I don't know what will* ***become of*** *her now her husband has died.* □ occurs only in direct or indirect questions.

bed down[1] [A1 B1i pass] get, put, into a makeshift bed, e g of straw or sacks, in (usu) temporary quarters. **S:** [A1] **O:** [B1] scouts, hikers, soldiers □ *We settled round the fire, making quite sure that before we* ***bedded down*** *for the night* *there was an ample supply of wood at hand.* BM □ *The troops were* ***bedded down*** *in a barn.*

bed down[2] [B1i pass] provide with straw as bedding. **S:** groom, farmer. **O:** horse, cattle □ *The horses were watered, fed, and* ***bedded down*** *with clean straw.*

bed in [B1i pass adj] (military) lodge firmly in position in the ground in preparation for firing. **S:** gun crew. **O:** mortar, gun □ *After a few ranging shots, the guns were firmly* ***bedded in*** *and could begin accurate firing.*

bed out [B1i pass adj] (horticulture) transfer partly-grown plants from a greenhouse etc to beds in a garden. **S:** gardener, grower □ *This is the right weather for* ***bedding out*** *your tomatoes.* □ *'There'd better be no frost till I've got my stuff* (i e plants) ***bedded out.****'* TT

bed with [A2] (informal) have casual sexual intercourse with; sleep together/with (q v) □ *There aren't many girls in the office that he hasn't* ***bedded with*** *at some time or another.* □ *'Yes, I'm keen on him, but I haven't* ***bedded with*** *him, if that's what you're trying to suggest.'*

beetle off [A1] (informal) hurry, scurry, away □ *We all supposed you had* ***beetled off*** *to Africa as you always threatened.* □ *'Now, why don't you children* ***beetle off*** *into the garden and play?'*

beg off [A1 B1i pass] ask to be excused from attending a function or giving help; have someone excused or released □ *He promised to arrive early and lend a hand, but at the last moment he* ***begged off.*** □ *Those boys were to have been in detention last night, but the games captain* ***begged*** *them* ***off*** *to do nets practice.*

to begin with[1] [A2] at the beginning, initially; to start with[1] (q v) □ ***To begin with,*** *we had very little support, but later on people began to rally to us.* □ *They had few essential supplies* ***to begin with,*** *so they had to improvise.* □ to begin with is an adv phrase with no object; it may occur at the beginning or end of the sentence.

to begin with[2] [A2] in the first place, first and foremost; to start with[2] (q v) □ ***To begin with,*** *you must realize I have very little money.* □ to begin with is an adv phrase with no object; it usu occurs at the beginning of the sentence.

believe in[1] [A2] have confidence in, trust in (q v). **o:** adviser, friend; honesty, goodness □ *You can* ***believe in*** *him; he'll never let you down.* □ *Until now, I had always* ***believed*** *firmly* ***in*** *his good intentions.*

believe in[2] [A2] feel sure of the existence of. **o:** God; ghosts, fairies; an afterlife □ *Prissie gave an excited laugh. 'Oh! One doesn't really* ***believe in*** *ghosts, does one?'* DC □ *She was very pretty and so extraordinarily alive. She could almost make one* ***believe in*** *her world of fantasy.* DC

believe in[3] [A2] favour, support the idea of. **o:** not... giving too much freedom, taxing old people; boarding schools, penalties for motorists □ *She doesn't* ***believe in*** *staying at home when her parents go to a party.* W1 □ *He* ***believes*** *very strongly* ***in*** *female emancipation.*

believe of [B2 pass rel] believe that sb is capable of a particular (kind of) action. **O:** anything malicious, nasty, underhand; it, that □ *You say he's going to be a father again at forty-five? I wouldn't have* ***believed*** *it* ***of*** *him.* □ *After all the changes of policy we've had recently I'd* ***believe*** *absolutely anything* ***of*** *that man.* □ with *would*; often neg.

bent on [pass (B2)] (have) one's mind set on, (be) determined to. **o:** success, mischief; making trouble, getting on □ *He declined on the grounds that he was* ***bent on*** *an early start the next day.* OBS □ *These men are* ***bent on*** *undermining the power of union officials.* SC

bind over (to keep the peace) [B1i pass] (legal) give warning to the accused that he will appear in court if he fails to keep the peace etc. **S:** judge, magistrate. **O:** accused, prisoner □ *When his record had been considered, the accused was* ***bound over*** *for six months.*

bitch up [B1i pass] (slang) spoil, undo, sb's good work (usu through spiteful gossip). **O:** it, the whole thing; my arrangements □ *We had brought them together after their quarrel; then* he *had to come in and* ***bitch*** *the whole thing* ***up.***

bite back [B1i pass] quickly restrain oneself from saying sth embarrassing, confidential etc. **O:** remark; oath, exclamation; admission □ *He was about to say, 'But I know I've passed; my tutor's told me,' but he* ***bit back*** *the remark, remembering where he was.* □ *John nearly launched into one of his attacks on the Church, but it struck him that Marcelle's family were Catholics and he* ***bit*** *the offending words* ***back.***

bite sb's head off [B1ii pass] (informal) show ill temper towards sb (often without good reason); snap sb's head off (q v) □ *I must keep out of his way. I don't like having* ***my head bitten off*** *at the slightest provocation.* □ *It looks like I was on the right track that night, when you* ***bit my head off*** *in the Conservative Club.* CON

bite off more than one can chew [B1iii] (informal) attempt too much, undertake more than one can manage. **S:** manager, administrator □ *'You've* ***bitten off more than you can chew,****' said my brother, when he saw the trouble I was having with my new business.*

black out[1] [A1 nom] suffer temporary loss of consciousness or memory (esp during flight or after a severe blow). **S:** pilot, boxer □ *The pilot suffered a complete* ***blackout*** *when his aircraft broke the sound barrier.* □ *I had a fight with the Old Man, and after it I* ***blacked out.*** LLDR

black out[2] [B1i nom pass adj] make invisible from the air at night by covering windows, lights etc. **S:** householder, shopkeeper. **O:** house, factory; window, car headlights □ *During the war, we had to make sure windows were carefully* ***blacked out*** *at night.* □ *Wolverhampton was the first town in Britain to impose a nightly* ***blackout.*** TBC □ nom form (in current usage blackout — without a hyphen) refers both to the covering which blacks out windows etc and to the appearance of blacked-out streets etc.

black out[3] [B1i nom pass adj] bring television transmission to a halt by strike action. **S:** technician; union. **O:** programme; speaker, performer □ *Within seconds of going on the air, London Weekend Television was* ***blacked out.*** G □ *The possibility of further screen* ***blackouts*** *by television technicians was not ruled out.* G

black out[4] [B1i nom pass] not allow news etc to be released, suppress it. **S:** government, army, news agency. **O:** news, information □ *There was a complete* ***black-out*** *on information.* T □ *Their* *first decision was to draw a* ***black-out*** *over today's discussions.* G □ usu nom (in current usage **blackout** — without a hyphen).

blame (for) [B2 pass emph rel] attach to sb or sth the responsibility for sth (usu to escape blame oneself). **O:** partner, ally; staff; conditions, climate. **o:** failure, setback, disgrace; (poor) sales □ *The poor health of key players can fairly be* ***blamed for*** *the disastrous opening to the season.* ⇨ next entry.

blame on [B2 pass emph rel] fix, place, the responsibility for sth on sb or sth. **O:** disaster, setback; loss, disappearance. **o:** ally, colleague; youth, inexperience; time (of year), weather □ *It's not much use* ***blaming*** *our defeat* ***on*** *the weather!* □ *He was looking round for someone* ***on*** *whom to* ***blame*** *his own mishandling of things.* ⇨ previous entry.

blast off [A1 nom B1i pass] (space technology) (of a rocket-propelled space vehicle) be launched, launch. **S:** [A1] **O:** [B1] spacecraft; missile, rocket □ *The Apollo spacecraft will* ***blast off*** *at ten a m local time* (cf ***Blast-off*** *for the Apollo spacecraft will be* etc). □ *It's difficult to imagine the sensations of these three men being* ***blasted off*** *into space.*

blaze away [A1 B1i pass] (informal) fire at a rapid rate [A1]; exhaust one's ammunition [B1]. **S:** rifleman, gunner. **O:** cartridge, shell □ *The boys* ***blazed away*** *with their airguns until the tin can was full of holes.*

bleed to death [A2] die through loss of blood □ *A vein in his neck was severed and he* ***bled to death*** *among the wild lavender.* ASA

blend in (with) [A1 A3 emph rel B1i pass adj B3 pass emph rel] mix harmoniously (with), not (cause to) clash or jar (with). **S:** [A1 A3] **O:** [B1 B3] building, development; design, pattern; colour. **o:** background, surroundings, setting □ [A1] *'That purple doesn't* ***blend in*** *too well, does it?'* □ [A3] *The curtains* ***blend in*** *perfectly* ***with*** *the carpet.* □ [B1] *Various herbs are* ***blended in*** *to make a good soup.* □ [B3] *There has been no attempt to* ***blend in*** *the new office blocks* ***with*** *their Victorian surroundings.*

blink away/back (one's) tears [B1i] try to control or hide one's tears (by blinking) □ *Her voice rose higher and higher. She* ***blinked away the tears.*** THH □ *Brigit smiled, and* ***blinked back tears.*** DC

block in [B1i pass adj] fill sth so that it is a solid block. **O:** outline, drawing; fireplace; window, door □ *The previous owner* ***blocked in*** *most of the open fireplaces when central heating was installed.*

block off [B1i pass adj] separate one place from another by using a solid barrier etc. **O:** street, alley; pipe; trench □ *Police have* ***blocked off*** *all side-streets giving access to the main procession route.* □ *A landslide has* ***blocked off*** *traffic moving south towards the motorway.*

block out [B1i pass adj] (photography; printing) mask part of a negative, when printing or enlarging, so that light does not pass through it; cover part of a stencil etc so that paint does pass through it. **O:** negative; silk screen, stencil □ ***Block out*** *this unimportant detail at the top of your picture.*

blossom out [A1] mature, reach a developed or mature state. **S:** girl, pupil, athlete □ *I see my daughter is* ***blossoming out.*** *I see my Josephine is branching out on her own and breaking new ground.* THH

blot out [B1i pass] form a barrier between a person and an object, making the latter invisible, or difficult to recall to mind. **S:** cloud, smoke; confusion. **O:** sun, stars; scene; past memories □ *The summer night was* ***blotted out*** *by a driving rainstorm.* SD □ *But his image kept* ***blotting out*** *the pages: she couldn't think of him without seeing him.* PW

blow the cobwebs away [B1i pass] (informal) make the mind and spirits active and lively again. **S:** conversation; companionship; exercise, fresh air □ *You've been cooped up in that study far too long. What you need to* ***blow the cobwebs away*** *is a couple of weeks in the open air.*

blow down [A1 B1i pass] be knocked, knock, to the ground. **S:** [A1] **O:** [B1] tree; fence, gate; chimney, slate, tile. **S:** [B1] (strong) wind, gale □ *A flowering tree* ***blew down*** *and some small shrubs were flattened.* □ *The gale raged all night and* ***blew down*** *a TV aerial from the roof.*

blow in/into [A1 emph A2 emph] (informal) arrive, come in (esp in a lively or noisy way). **S:** politician, film-star, boss. **o:** town, New York; office □ *The Adjutant General* ***blew into*** *my office.* MFM □ *John* ***blew in*** *for a chat on his way home.*

blow off steam [B1iii] (informal) release pent-up energy, tension etc (e g in drinking, dancing, argument) □ *Dancing started on New Year's Day. This is a traditional time to* ***blow off steam.*** OBS ⇨ let off steam.

blow out[1] [A1 B1i pass] be extinguished, go out[5] (q v); extinguish, put out[10] (q v) (with a puff of air, draught etc). **S:** [A1] **O:** [B1] light; candle, lamp. **S:** [B1] he etc; wind □ *Someone opened the door and the lamp* ***blew out.*** □ *'****Blow*** *the candles* ***out*** *before you come to bed.'*

blow out[2] [A1 nom] (oil industry) (of petroleum vapour escaping from a well) emerge suddenly and violently at the surface. **S:** gas, vapour; well, drilling □ *Gas came up the outside of the bore pipe and* ***blew out,*** *as we say in the oil industry.* ITV □ *We have to launch a massive operation to repair the* ***blowout.*** ITV

blowout[1] [nom (A1)] bursting of a tyre on a motor vehicle □ *Coming over those rough mountain roads you have to be prepared for a few* ***blowouts.***

blowout[2] [nom (A1)] (slang) a feast, a good feed □ *Even when times were bad, there was always enough money for a good* ***blowout*** *at Christmas, or whenever someone got married.*

blow one's brains out [B1ii] kill oneself by shooting in the head □ *When finally his wife left him, Peter thought there was nothing left for him to do but* ***blow his brains out.***

blow itself out [B1ii] exhaust itself, dwindle to nothing. **S:** storm, wind, hurricane □ *The gale had not quite* ***blown itself out.*** *Even now a hard breeze whipped at the flowers.* US

blow over [A1] (informal) cease to excite feeling, no longer be thought important; die down (q v). **S:** scandal, controversy, trouble, business, affair □ *'You've really put the cat among the pigeons. But I shouldn't worry: the whole thing will have* ***blown over*** *in a few days.'*

blow to[1] [B2 pass] shatter to small pieces by

explosion. **S:** (explosive) charge; dynamite, gun-cotton. **O:** bridge, factory; dug-out, pillbox. **o:** ⚠ pieces, smithereens, atoms □ *The tanks were* ***blown to*** *pieces by high explosive.* ⇨ blow up⁴.

blow to² [B2 pass] kill sb by explosion. **S:** bomb, booby-trap. **O:** soldier, policeman. **o:** ⚠ blazes, glory, kingdom come □ *We were nearly* ***blown to*** *glory by the same flying-bomb.* AH

blow up¹ [A1] (informal) lose one's temper. **S:** associate, partner; wife, parent. **A:** over his decision, at him □ *I* ***blew*** *right* ***up****, saying that I disagreed completely with the conclusion of the report.* MFM □ *'I'm sorry I* ***blew up*** *at you this morning.'*

blow up² [B1i pass] (informal) lose one's temper with, reprimand severely. **S:** employer, parent. **O:** worker, child □ *That new teacher* ***blew*** *me* ***up*** *for not raising my cap to him in the street.* □ *I got quite a* ***blowing-up*** *for being late for practice.* □ nom form is blowing-up.

blow up³ [A1] arise, work towards a crescendo or crisis. **S:** storm, gale; political storm, crisis □ *It was one of those silly family rows that* ***blow up*** *over nothing and leave everyone shaking with rage.* CON

blow up⁴ [A1 B1i pass adj] (cause to) explode or smash to pieces. **S:** [A1] **O:** [B1] bomb, mine, shell; house, factory. **S:** [B1] enemy; raider, aircraft □ *The bomb* ***blew up*** *with an ear-splitting crash.* □ *Our other house was* ***blown up*** *by enemy action.* EHOW □ *We passed the wreckage of* ***blown-up*** *bridges.*

blow up⁵ [B1i pass adj] inflate, pump air or gas into; pump up² (q v). **S:** mechanic. **O:** tyre, rubber raft, balloon □ *I've got a flat tyre; I'll have to find a garage and get it mended and* ***blown up****.*

blow up⁶ [B1i nom pass adj] (photography) make bigger, enlarge. **O:** ⚠ negative, photograph, picture, snap □ *'Those photographs look promising. Why not get an expert to* ***blow*** *them* ***up*** *a bit bigger?'* □ *His study walls were covered with* ***blown-up*** *pictures of sailing-ships.* □ *In this* ***blow-up*** *of the negative, you can read the date on the newspaper that Wilson's carrying.*

blow up⁷ [B1i pass adj] (informal) inflate, exaggerate. **S:** press, critics. **O:** reputation, achievements; story, affair □ *His abilities as an actor have been greatly* ***blown up*** *by the weekend press; in fact, they are quite modest.* □ *It didn't really happen like that: the incident's been* ***blown up*** *out of all proportion.*

bluff it out [B1ii] survive a situation (e g in which one is pretending to be sb else) by deceit □ *When he was caught in the bank strong-room after hours, the cashier could tell the truth, and risk imprisonment, or try to* ***bluff it out****.*

bluff one's way out/out of [B1ii B2] escape from a difficult situation by pretence, by deceiving others. **S:** criminal, spy. **o:** tricky situation, tight corner □ *She turned to the officers. 'The man is trying to* ***bluff his way out of*** *the whole thing,' she said.* PP

blurt out [B1i pass adj] exclaim suddenly (often nervously); reveal something suddenly (through nervousness). **O:** apology, confused statement; secret, confidence □ *James was tongue-tied with embarrassment; then he* ***blurted out*** *to his guest, 'You needn't bother to come to this house again!'* □ *In his anxiety, the prisoner* ***blurted out*** *some of the information asked for.*

board out [A1 B1i pass adj] have meals outside the place where one sleeps; give sb food and lodging in a separate place from the school, college etc where he works. **S:** [A1] **O:** [B1] student, trainee, boy. **S:** [B1] school, bursar, authorities □ *Most students can still be accommodated in College, but increasing numbers are having to be* ***boarded out*** *in the town.* □ *Married men not living in camp receive a* ***boarding-out*** *allowance.*

board up [B1i pass adj] cover with boards (because a house is no longer occupied, is about to be pulled down etc). **O:** house, shop; window, door □ *The windows on the ground floor have been* ***boarded up****, chiefly to stop children climbing in and making nuisances of themselves.* □ *A row of* ***boarded-up*** *shops faced the sea-front.*

boast (about/of) [A2 pass emph rel] speak in praise of oneself, one's achievements etc. **o:** talent, (personal) quality; success, wealth; family □ *He was fond of* ***boasting about*** *his war record. In fact, as far as one could gather, he had spent the war years at Clacton-on-Sea.* □ *The Minister said that this Government had done more than any other to combat inflation. It was a record* ***of*** *which they could justifiably* ***boast****.*

bob up [A1 emph] (informal) (of an elusive or irrepressible person) reappear, re-emerge (though often discouraged from doing so) □ *The Scarlet Pimpernel kept* ***bobbing up*** *in the most unlikely places.* □ *You can't keep him down: he'll* ***bob up*** *when the police lose interest.*

bog down [A1 B1ii pass adj] (informal) (cause to) stick fast (in mud etc); (cause to) be heavily involved with sth. **S:** [A1] **O:** [B1] tank, car; speaker, overworked person, ambitious youth. **S:** [B1] driver; work, routine □ *Our transport* ***bogged down*** *in the thick mud.* □ *I hasten to reply before I get* ***bogged down*** *with other work.* □ *I like these people here only because I'm already on my way out. If I had to stay* ***bogged down*** *here, I'd hate them.* CON

bog up [B1i nom pass] (slang) confuse, muddle. **O:** procedure, drill, instructions; the whole thing □ *We carefully explained our very simple accounting system to her but in a few hours she'd got everything* ***bogged up****.* □ *They made a complete* ***bog-up*** *of the travel arrangements that we'd entrusted them with.*

boil down [B1i pass] (informal) state in outline, summarize. **O:** case, argument, proposal □ *I have tried to state briefly, to* ***boil down****, the most important area of conflict.*

boil down to [A3 B3 pass] (informal) (may) be summarized, or stated in outline, as; summarize, state in outline, as. **S:** [A3] **O:** [B3] case, dispute, issue; advice, story. **o:** essence, essentials □ [A3] *The good advice we gave him* ***boiled down to*** *this: that after tea he should stroll to the window.* SD □ [B3] *He* ***boiled*** *a boring rigmarole* ***down to*** *one or two brief sentences.* □ [B3] *The disagreements over nationalization can be* ***boiled down to*** *differences in their view of socialism.*

boil over¹ [A1] (of liquid in a pan) overflow the sides of the pan (when the liquid reaches the boil). **S:** milk, water; saucepan; potatoes, greens □ *'You'd better turn the gas down or else the vegetables will* ***boil over****.'*

boil over² [A1] reach a danger, or a crisis, point, explode. **S:** situation, quarrel. **A:** into violence, in an exchange of blows □ *The Palestine Police*

Force was fifty per cent below strength, and this at a time when the situation was clearly about to ***boil over***. MFM

boil over[3] [A1] (informal) be extremely angry, furious □ *John was* ***boiling over*** *and it was soon clear why; nobody had told him of our plans to move house.*

boil up [A1] (informal) develop, be about to occur. **S:** quarrel, first-class row, crisis □ *A dispute is* ***boiling up*** *over who should be the first to greet our royal visitors.*

bolster up [B1i pass] (informal) support, buttress. **S:** government, Treasury, armed forces. **O:** ally, system, rebellion □ *Our money has been used to* ***bolster up*** *unpopular regimes.* □ *Micky, trying to* ***bolster up*** *his own status, assumed an assurance that he did not feel.* PE

bolt down [B1i pass] swallow one's food quickly (through hunger or greed, or because one is in a hurry). **O:** meal, snack □ *You'll have violent indigestion if you* ***bolt down*** *your food like that.* □ *The surgeon on casualty duty just had time to* ***bolt down*** *a sandwich before the first case was wheeled in.*

bomb out [B1i pass adj] make homeless through bombing. **S:** enemy, aircraft. **O:** family; street, neighbourhood □ ***Bombed-out*** *families crowded into the public shelters.* □ *Our firm was* ***bombed out*** *but we soon managed to get on our feet again.* □ usu passive or adj.

bomb up [A1 B1i pass] (aviation) load with bombs. **S:** mechanic, ground-crew. **O:** aircraft, bomber □ *While the crews were briefed on the operation, their planes were* ***bombed up***.

bombard (with)[1] [B2 pass emph rel] send a heavy shower of missiles at sb. **O:** troops; trench, fortification; prisoner; orator, actor. **o:** shell, rocket; (rotten) fruit, vegetables □ *The allied positions were* ***bombarded with*** *shells of every calibre.* □ *The crowd expressed their dissatisfaction with the referee's decision by* ***bombarding*** *the pitch* ***with*** *beer cans.*

bombard (with)[2] [B2 pass emph rel] direct sth in a heavy, continuous stream at sb. **O:** office, headquarters; manager, secretary. **o:** question, inquiry, complaint □ *We've been* ***bombarded with*** *requests for the new model all week. Unfortunately, it will be some time before we can satisfy this level of demand.* □ *The invitations* ***with*** *which he was now* ***bombarded*** *he preferred to turn down, if he possibly could.*

bone up (on) [A1 A3 pass] (informal) make a close study (of) (usu for some special purpose). **o:** mathematics, French; wine and food, travel □ *I must* ***bone up on*** *my Italian if we are going abroad for a holiday.*

book in [A1 B1i pass] register, enter the name of (a guest on arrival at a hotel). **S:** [A1] **O:** [B1] guest, visitor. **S:** [B1] clerk, receptionist □ *'Carry these cases upstairs while I* ***book*** *the guests* ***in***.*'*

book up [A1] reserve accommodation (on a train or aircraft, in a hotel). **S:** traveller, holidaymaker □ *If you want to go to the Continent for your holiday, you ought to* ***book up*** *now.*

booked up [pass adj (B1)] have no seats or rooms left (for a traveller, theatregoer etc); have no free time left (through pressure of engagements etc). **S:** hotel; steamer; theatre, stadium □ *'I'm afraid we can't even offer you a seat in the balcony, sir; we're fully* ***booked up***.*'* □ *'I might go out if I had anybody to go with. Are you very* ***booked up*** *yourself?'* HD

bore to [B2 pass] (informal) be utterly dreary, tedious, to sb. **S:** story, joke; conversation, discussion; he etc. **O:** friend, audience. **o:** ⚠ death, distraction, tears □ *I don't want to* ***bore*** *myself* ***to*** *death reminiscing about those days.* JFTR □ *I couldn't decently leave my hosts, so I sat there, while their television* ***bored*** *me* ***to*** *distraction.*

borne in on [pass (B3)] (formal) (of the person affected) be made to realize. **S:** the idea of a new approach, the realization that he is right, the truth of what I had been told □ *The gravity of the situation was slowly* ***borne in on*** *him.* □ *It had been* ***borne in on*** *her how little she counted for him as a human being.* PW

botch up [B1i nom pass adj] (informal) spoil, mar, through inattention, carelessness etc. **S:** builder, plumber; manager, executive; minister, civil servant. **O:** it, the whole thing, things; job, repairs; arrangements; discussion, treaty □ *'Don't give the job to him: he'll only* ***botch*** *it* ***up*** (or: *make a* ***botch-up*** *of it).'* □ *The Minister said that negotiations were lengthy because he did not want a* ***botched-up*** *agreement.*

bother one's head about [B2] (informal) concern oneself in thinking about sth. **o:** poverty, hunger; problem, issue □ *Why* ***bother your heads about*** *what's happening on the other side of the world?* □ *'Now, don't* ***bother your*** *sweet little* ***head about*** *that.'* □ *This is something worth* ***bothering one's head about***. □ usu forms part of a suggestion or recommendation *not* to be concerned.

bottle up [B1i pass adj] (informal) suppress, not allow to show. **O:** emotion, desire, appetite; things, it all □ *It's better to express your anger now and then, rather than* ***bottle*** *it* ***up*** *and have an almighty explosion.* □ *She shows the strain of* ***bottled-up*** *emotion.*

bounce back [A1] (informal) recover jauntily from a setback. **S:** sportsman, entertainer; economy, sterling □ *He's had no end of bad luck, but he just seems to* ***bounce back*** *every time.* □ *In the City share prices* ***bounced*** *back this morning.* BBCR

bound up with [pass (B3)] be closely connected with or related to. **S:** position, life, future. **o:** his etc progress, science □ *She had her own existence now, even if that existence was* ***bound up with*** *an unfaithful husband.* PW □ *Their own political position is* ***bound up with*** *his.* SC

bow in/into [B1i pass B2 pass] welcome a visitor or customer with low bows. **S:** porter, doorman, shopwalker. **O:** guest, client □ *A crowd of flunkeys stood by the entrance waiting to* ***bow*** *the guests* ***in***. □ *She was* ***bowed into*** *a taxi.*

bow out [A1] (informal) give up a prominent position (e g in politics, on the stage). **S:** minister, director □ *So Sir Harold* ***bows out***, *at the end of a distinguished career in broadcasting.*

bow oneself out [B1ii] bow low to a superior (e g royalty) as one leaves his presence. **S:** retainer, courtier, servant □ *After the meeting of the Royal Council, the peers and officials* ***bowed*** *themselves* ***out***.

bow out/out of [B1i pass B2 pass] bow low to a visitor or customer as he leaves. **S:** waiter, manager. **O:** diner, guest □ *Then, collecting up our purchases, we were* ***bowed out of*** *the shop* *by the owner.* DF

bowl along [A1] drive swiftly and smoothly. **S:** carriage, car □ *His car* ***bowled along*** *at an even pace until it reached the village.*

bowl out [B1i pass] (cricket) dismiss sb by striking his wicket with the ball. **S:** pace-bowler; Jones etc. **O:** opening batsman, tail-ender; side □ *Half the side were* ***bowled out*** *before lunch.*

bowl over[1] [B1i pass] knock down (and roll over, spin around). **S:** car; shot, throw. **O:** pedestrian; barrel, tin can □ *He lent me his gun. I missed the first two, but then* ***bowled over*** *four rabbits in four shots.* RFW □ *The wing three-quarter was* ***bowled over*** *near the corner flag.*

bowl over[2] [B1i pass] (informal) overwhelm, impress deeply. **S:** beauty, charm, wit; sudden arrival, attack. **O:** admirer, audience; defender □ *The chef hadn't time to prepare the kind of speciality that would be likely to* ***bowl over*** *the taster.* ARG □ *You look devastating and I'm* ***bowled over***. EHOW

box in [B1i pass adj] prevent sb from going faster, manœuvring etc, by surrounding him on three sides at the edge of a racetrack. **S:** runner; car, horse. **O:** competitor, rival □ *The favourite was* ***boxed in*** *against the rails by rival jockeys.*

box up [B1i pass] confine or enclose in a small space. **S:** hunter, enemy; climate, geography. **O:** prey, inhabitant □ *These Islanders have been* ***boxed up*** *here for hundreds of years and they think they know everything.* RM □ usu passive.

branch off [A1 A2] turn from one road etc onto another usu smaller one. **S:** car, train. **o:** (main) road, line (of a railway) □ *'We've lost them — they must have* ***branched off*** *further back.'*

branch out [A1] expand or develop in a new direction. **S:** factory, enterprise; he etc □ *Hitherto we have only been concerned with heavy metal castings; now we are* ***branching out*** *into light alloys and plastics.* □ *I see my Josephine is* ***branching out*** *on her own and breaking new ground.* THH

brave it out [B1ii] (informal) confront and defy hostility, threats or suspicion. **S:** country, person □ *I don't want to see him, because I know he suspects me of disloyalty. But I suppose I'll just have to* ***brave it out***.

brazen it out [B1ii] (informal) behave, although one has done wrong, as if one has nothing to be ashamed of. **S:** thief, coward, naughty child □ *Everybody ignored his remark for what it was, the lowest form of wit, and contemptible into the bargain — but Miller just sat there and* ***brazened it out***. TT

break away (from)[1] [A1 A3 rel] leave or escape (from) suddenly. **S:** friend, acquaintance; prisoner. **o:** him etc; guard, captivity □ *Suddenly John spotted his bus pulling up opposite, and* ***broke away***. □ *The prisoner* ***broke away from*** *his guards while being taken to another gaol.*

break away (from)[2] [A1 nom A3 rel] cut one's ties or links (with). **o:** ideas, beliefs; family, tradition; the Old Guard, the Labour Party □ *He's* ***broken away from*** *his family and all they stand for and gone to live in Australia.* □ *He decided to* ***break away*** *from the Party and seek re-election as an Independent.* □ *This* ***break-away*** *group stands to the left of the Labour Party.*

break away (from)[3] [A1 nom A3 rel] end one's political dependence (on), become politically separate (from). **S:** province, region. **o:** state, country □ *One part of a federal state may attempt to* ***break away*** *to form an independent entity.* □ *Several major powers have now recognized the* ***break-away*** *state.* □ break-away is only used attrib, as here.

break back[1] [A1] (sport) suddenly reverse the direction in which one is moving (so as to upset the defence). **S:** fly-half, three-quarter (back); winger, striker □ *The scrum-half suddenly* ***broke back*** *behind his forwards and set off down the touch-line.*

break back[2] [A1 nom] (cricket) (of a ball striking the pitch) change its direction sharply □ *The second ball of the over* ***broke back*** *and took off a bail.* □ *That delivery had a vicious* ***break-back***.

break down[1] [B1i pass adj] knock or smash to the ground. **S:** fireman, demolition gang, police. **O:** wall, door, fence □ *Firemen had to* ***break down*** *a wall to get to families trapped on the ground floor.*

break down[2] [B1i pass] overcome, conquer. **S:** statesman; host, teacher. **O:** obstacle, barrier (to understanding); shyness, hostility, suspicion □ *We encountered a good deal of resistance to our pensions scheme, but by patient negotiation we* ***broke it down***. □ *The new ambassador regards as his first objective the* ***breaking-down*** *of suspicion and fear between the two countries.* □ *Another woman might be able to* ***break down*** *their reserve and give them the sense of an unfolding love.* PW

break down[3] [A1] give way completely to one's feelings, lose control □ *She appeared to be pretty calm, but at times she would* ***break down*** *and start weeping.* OBS □ *He felt he must cut this interview short if she was not to* ***break down*** *in public.* RFW

break down[4] [A1 nom] (mechanical) stop (through some mechanical or electrical failure). **S:** train, car, lorry, crane, lift □ *He and Ed had gone to another race-meeting. Ed's car had* ***broken down***. AITC □ *There was a* ***breakdown*** *on the main through-line to Edinburgh.* □ *A* ***breakdown*** *crew came to get the crane working again.* □ breakdown *crews (gangs, teams)* service or remove vehicles that have stopped *or* crashed.

break down[5] [A1 nom] cease, fail; be severed; collapse. **S:** communications, contact, relations; law and order, control; resistance □ *Telephone communication with all but a few outposts has* ***broken down***. □ *A coalition of Christian Democrats and Liberals* ***broke down***. □ *You can't imagine what it's like to feel that all your plans for the future have* ***broken down***. SPL □ *There has been a complete* ***breakdown*** *of law and order.*

break down[6] [A1 B1i nom pass] (may) be analysed or presented in detail; analyse, classify. **S:** [A1] **O:** [B1] results, totals; expenditure, outlay; budget. **S:** [B1] scientist; accountant, auditor □ *Expenditure on the project* ***breaks down*** *as follows: wages £10m, plant £4m, raw materials £5m.* □ *The accountant gave a* ***breakdown*** *of the expenses.* □ *The results of my test can be* ***broken down*** (or: ***break down***) *under four heads.*

break down[7] [B1i pass adj] (chemistry) change the chemical composition of. **S:** body, organ, secretions. **O:** starch, fat; molecule □ *The cow is* *an intermediary in our attempt to live off the land without having the bacteria which can* ***break down*** *cellulose in our stomachs.* NS

break down[8] [A1 nom] collapse (so that the person needs rest, special treatment etc). **S:** ⚠ health; sanity □ *His health had been affected, and might* ***break down*** *altogether if the strain continued.* □ *She suffered a* ***breakdown*** *(in health).* □ *He's heading for a nervous* ***breakdown****.* ⇨ break down[3], where the collapse is not lengthy or serious.

break in[1] [A1] interrupt. **S:** speaker, critic. **A:** sharply, abruptly, excitedly □ *'But what's going to happen to us?' one of the miners* ***broke in****.* □ normally precedes or follows direct speech.

break in[2] [B1i pass] accustom to new discipline, make docile; make soft and pliable. **S:** trainer, drill sergeant. **O:** horse, mount; recruit, novice; pair of boots □ *Petrucchio* ***broke in*** *a shrewish wife.* □ *New recruits are often* ***broken in*** *by repeated drilling on the barrack square.*

break in/into [A1 nom A2 pass adj] force an entry (into), force one's way in(to). **S:** burglar, intruder. **o:** shop, private house, warehouse □ *Tell them that those inside need protection against desperate characters who are trying to* ***break in*** *from outside.* TBC □ *There was a* ***break-in*** *at Smith's warehouse.* □ *Stores were* ***broken into*** *and looted during the riots.*

break in on/upon [A3 pass emph rel] interrupt, disturb. **S:** noise, voice. **o:** thinking, meditation, conversation □ *A sudden noise from outside* ***broke in upon*** *his day-dream.* □ *Their meeting was* ***broken in upon*** *by the arrival of a group of petitioners.*

break into[1] [A2] suddenly change from a slower to a faster pace. **S:** horse, elephant, herd. **o:** ⚠ a run, trot, canter, gallop □ *As soon as they scented water, the whole herd* ***broke into*** *a gallop.* □ *'I shall be late' — she was on the point of* ***breaking into*** *a run.* PW

break into[2] [A2] suddenly begin to laugh etc. **S:** audience, crowd. **o:** (loud) laughter, song, cheers □ *As the President's car appeared, the waiting crowds* ***broke into*** *loud cheers.*

break into[3] [A2 pass] take time from, encroach on/upon (q v). **S:** overtime, extra duties, nightwork. **o:** evenings, leisure time □ *'I can't take on any extra overtime: my weekends have been* ***broken into*** *far too much as it is.'*

break into[4] [A2 pass] use a high-value note or coin to buy an article costing less. **S:** customer, purchaser. **o:** pound note, ten-dollar bill □ *'I can't give you the forty pence I owe you without* ***breaking into*** *a five-pound note, so do you mind if I pay you back tomorrow?'*

break into[5] [A2 pass] open and consume (sth held in reserve for emergency use). **S:** garrison, beleaguered population, expedition. **o:** (reserve stocks of) water, food, ammunition; iron-rations □ *The stranded party* ***broke into*** *their emergency supplies of food and water.*

break into[6] [A2 pass adj] force an entry into. ⇨ break in/into.

break off[1] [A1 B1i pass adj] become separated, separate, from a larger object (by breaking). **S:** [A1] **O:** [B1] piece of brick, section of wall; mast, pole. **S:** [B1] workman; blow; sea, high wind □ *The mast had* ***broken off*** *at its base, and lay over the side of the boat.* □ *He* ***broke off*** *a piece of chocolate and offered it to me.*

break off[2] [B1i pass adj] end abruptly, discontinue. **S:** country, firm; army; friend, fiancé. **O:** relations, association, connection; battle; negotiations, conversation, engagement (= agreement to marry) □ *Napier* ***broke off*** *the pursuit.* BM □ *Our trading connection has been* ***broken off*** *owing to a disagreement over prices.* □ *No settlement of the dispute is in sight. The talks were* ***broken off*** *an hour ago and will not be resumed today.* □ *'Aren't they getting married then?' 'No, they've* ***broken it off****.'*

break off[3] [A1] (suddenly) stop talking, or interrupt one's remarks □ *George rose. 'As for me...,' he* ***broke off*** *as Christine came out of her room.* PE

break off[4] [A1] pause in one's work, take a break. **S:** workers, staff. **A:** for five minutes, at eleven o'clock. □ *The whole cast* ***broke off*** *for coffee in the middle of rehearsals.*

break out [A1] start suddenly and/or violently, flare up (q v). **S:** fire; epidemic, disease; rioting, violence, looting; quarrel; firing □ *Pandemonium* ***broke out*** *and there was a free-for-all fight.* DS □ *Rationing was not introduced till some time after the* ***outbreak*** *of war.* □ *The Plague* ***broke out*** *in London that Summer, and hundreds died.* W1 □ nom form is outbreak.

break out in[1] [A3] suddenly become covered in. **S:** patient; face, body. **o:** spots, pimples, sores; rash □ *His face had now* ***broken out in*** *a rash of red and purple blotches.* ⇨ break out on.

break out in[2] [A3] suddenly begin to express strong feelings. **S:** audience, person. **o:** tears, cries, curses □ *The soft music of the jazz quartet was like people who had been locked up,* ***breaking out in*** *tears and laughter.* THH □ *He suddenly* ***broke out in*** *a rage of sobs and curses.*

break out in a cold sweat [A3] (informal) be suddenly overcome with fear □ *He began to imagine he heard strange noises, and* ***broke out in a cold sweat****.*

break out/out of [A1 nom A2 pass] free oneself (from) (usu by forcibly removing barriers). **S:** prisoner; army; adolescent; writer, artist. **o:** cell, prison; trap, bridgehead, salient; bonds, strait-jacket □ *The armies encircled at Stalingrad were not able to* ***break out****.* □ *There has been a mass* ***break-out*** *of prisoners.* □ *The more interesting playwrights have* ***broken out of*** *the old conventional strait-jacket.*

break out on [A3 rel] appear suddenly upon. **S:** spots; rash. **o:** face, arm □ *A mass of sores had* ***broken out on*** *her leg.* ⇨ break out in[1].

break over[1] [A2] break upon, and sweep over, a floating or submerged object. **S:** sea, wave. **o:** ship, wreck; sea-wall □ *Heavy seas* ***broke over*** *the bows as we headed in towards the shelter of the coast.* □ *Large waves* ***broke over*** *him as he tried to gain a footing in the shingle.*

break over[2] [A2] sweep over sb in waves. **S:** (waves of) cheering, applause, abuse □ *He sat quietly in his place, apparently unaffected by the burst of cheering which* ***broke over*** *him.*

break through[1] [A1 nom A2 pass] penetrate. **S:** burglar, gang; army, tanks. **o:** wall, wire fence; front, defences □ *Thieves* ***broke through*** *a wall and a steel partition to get at the safe.* □ *There was a massive* ***breakthrough*** *by enemy armour on a narrow front.*

break through[2] [A1 A2] pierce, appear from behind. **S:** ⚠ the sun, moon. **o:** clouds, haze, mist □ *At half past eleven the sun **broke through**, beginning to dry at last the heavy dew on the grass.* DBM

break through[3] [A1 nom] make discoveries of a new and important kind. **S:** scientist, inventor, engineer □ *Chemists working on animal dye-stuffs have **broken through** in a number of directions.* □ *There was an exciting new **break-through** in cancer research.* □ usu nom.

break through[4] [A2 pass] penetrate, overcome. **S:** visitor, host. **o:** shyness, reserve, timidity; façade, front □ *No matter how hard one tries to bring him out, it's almost impossible to **break through** his reserve.*

break through the sound barrier [A2] (aviation) reach a speed above that of sound. **S:** aircraft, pilot □ *Residents have been complaining of the 'boom' which is heard whenever a jet **breaks through the sound barrier**.*

break up[1] [A1] disintegrate, shatter; crack up[2] (q v). **S:** ship, aircraft □ *The ship was caught in a south-easterly gale. She went aground and started to **break up**.*

break up[2] [A1] crumble, disintegrate (mentally or physically); crack up[1] (q v). **S:** patient, old man □ *I looked at his face again. If ever I saw a man on the point of **breaking up**, I saw one then.* CON □ *I know what he has to endure, but there is no sign of him **breaking up** under the strain yet.*

break up[3] [A1] (of individuals in a group) disperse, go their separate ways. **S:** party, meeting, gathering, reunion. **A:** in disorder, in disarray □ *We knew this before the party **broke up**, on that crucial first evening.* CON □ *Leicester stood up, stretched himself, and ambled out. The meeting **broke up**.* TBC ➪ next entry.

break up[4] [B1i pass] disperse, scatter (often by force). **S:** police, troops. **O:** crowd, demonstration, gathering, meeting □ *The meeting was threatening to get out of hand and the police were forced to **break it up**.* ➪ previous entry.

break up[5] [A1] disperse (at the end of a term). **S:** school; children □ *When do you **break up** for the Easter holidays?* SC

break up[6] [A1 nom] dissolve, come to an end (not necessarily through outside interference). **S:** relationship, friendship □ *Their marriage has virtually **broken up** — they are hardly ever in each other's company.* □ *The **break-up** of their partnership has been expected in the City for some time.* ➪ next entry.

break up[7] [B1i pass] bring to an end, destroy. **S:** rival, enemy; philanderer, adventuress. **O:** alliance, coalition; friendship □ *But she **broke up** his home life: he had been perfectly happy until she came along.* PW □ *Plenty of marriages have been successfully **broken up** that way.* AITC ➪ previous entry.

break up (into)[1] [B1i pass adj B3 pass emph rel] divide in pieces by cutting, smashing etc. **O:** beam, box; car, ship. **o:** length, firewood; piece, scrap □ *The ships were **broken up** and sold as scrap to dealers.* □ *The wood is **broken up into** short lengths.*

break up (into)[2] [B1i pass adj B3 pass emph rel] divide by analysis, administrative decision etc. **S:** scholar, scientist; grammarian; government, ministry. **O:** task, problem; word, sentence; farmland. **o:** section; syllable, phrase; plot □ *Sentences can be **broken up into** clauses, and clauses **into** phrases.* □ *The new regime is **breaking** the estates **up into** smallholdings.*

break with [A2 pass] end a friendship or association with, sever links with. **S:** son, elector, businessman. **o:** family; party; ally; associate □ *John has **broken with** his family; they can't agree over his choice of a wife.* □ *Several painters in the exhibition have **broken with** tradition.*

brew up [A1 nom] (informal) prepare a drink of tea (often in the open and by makeshift arrangements). **S:** workman, soldier □ *A group of men were **brewing up** in a sheltered corner of the building-site.* □ *'Eleven o'clock; time for a **brew-up**.'*

brick in/up [B1i pass adj] block or seal an opening, with bricks. **S:** builder, mason. **O:** window, doorway, fireplace □ *In former times people had some of their windows **bricked in** to avoid paying tax on them.*

brim over [A1] overflow, run over[1] (q v). **S:** cup, jug; barrel, sack; lorry □ *The boys had loaded on too much sand; the wheelbarrow was **brimming over**.*

brim over with [A3 rel] have an abundance of. **o:** confidence; high spirits, vitality; ideas □ *The new designer was **brimming over with** ideas.*

bring about[1] [B1i pass] cause to happen. **S:** time, circumstances, plan. **O:** change, death, failure □ *How should she present herself to him? As a lady of leisure, reading a book? Three minutes could **bring about** this transformation.* PW □ *The politicians don't seem to have **brought** any miraculous changes **about**.* ➪ come about[1].

bring about[2] [B1i pass] (nautical) change direction of movement. **S:** crew, helmsman. **O:** sailing-ship; yacht, dinghy □ *The helmsman **brought** us **about** and we went scudding off in a new direction.* ➪ come about[2], go about[5], put about[1].

bring a charge (against) [B2 pass emph rel] (legal) take steps that will lead to sb being accused of an offence in a court of law. **S:** private citizen; injured party □ *If you found someone loitering at the back of your house after dark, you might feel justified in **bringing charges against** him.* □ *'Of course, you could **bring a charge** of dangerous driving **against** him, but you might have some difficulty proving it in court.'*

bring along/on[1] [B1i pass] help, encourage, to develop. **S:** tutor, coach. **O:** pupil, trainee, (young) athlete □ *We're trying to **bring along** one or two promising young swimmers.* □ *That boy may get an Open Scholarship if we don't ruin everything by **bringing** him **on** too quickly.* ➪ come along/on[2], get along/on (with)[1].

bring along/on[2] [B1i pass] help to grow or flower more quickly. **S:** sun, fine weather, spell of rain. **O:** crop; vegetable, flower □ *The fine spell we've been having will **bring** the crops **along** very nicely.* ➪ come along/on[3].

bring along (to) [B1i pass B3 pass rel] conduct from one place to another, often a short way (e g within the same building). **O:** brother, friend. **o:** office; house; party, meeting □ *'I'm having a short staff meeting in my office at eleven. Oh, and would you **bring** Smith **along**, too?'* □ *You can **bring** a friend **along to** the party if you like.* ➪ be along (to), come along (to).

bring around/round (to)[1] [B1ii pass B3 pass rel] conduct, lead, sb to a place (usu within the same town etc). **O:** wife, children. **o:** my place, house; club □ *'Do **bring** your wife **around** one evening. We're longing to meet her.'* □ *'If you can't find room for these people you're welcome to **bring** them **around to** our place.'* ⇨ be around/round (at), come around/round (to)[1].

bring around/round (to)[2] [B1ii pass B3 pass rel] convert sb to one's own point of view. **O:** opponent; colleague, friend. **o:** ⚠ his (etc) way of thinking, point of view, assessment of the situation □ *Father wasn't keen to let us have the flat for our party, but we managed to **bring** him **round**.* ⇨ come around/round (to)[2].

bring away [B1iii] return home having formed a particular impression etc. **O:** (happy, pleasant) memories, (favourable, positive) impression □ *We **brought away** rather mixed impressions of our holiday in Spain.* ⇨ come away with.

bring back[1] [B1i pass] cause to return; restore borrowed property □ *He's gone away from home and nothing will **bring** him **back** again.* □ *'If you borrow my electric drill don't forget to **bring** it **back**.'* ⇨ be back[1], come back[1], get back[1], go back[1], take back[1].

bring back[2] [B1i pass] recall to mind, remind one of. **S:** scene, smell, conversation. **O:** memories; visit, travels; day □ *The river smell **brought back** a night some years before.* NM □ *How a few words can **bring** it all **back**!* ⇨ come back[3].

bring back[3] [B1iii pass] reintroduce, restore. **S:** Government, the authorities, 'they'. **O:** monarchy, one-party rule, corporal punishment □ *He's very much in favour of **bringing back** capital punishment.* □ *He feels that compulsory attendance at chapel should be **brought back**.* ⇨ come back[4].

bring back to health/life [B3 pass] restore sb to good health; revive him. **S:** doctor, expert care □ *And anyway he was dead. I couldn't **bring** him **back to life**.* DC

bring before [B2 pass] present for discussion, decision or judgement. **O:** him etc; case; matter, claim. **o:** committee, board; court, magistrate □ *We'd better have a word together now: the matter is being **brought before** the council tomorrow morning.* ⇨ be before[2], come before[2], go before[2], put before[2], take before.

bring down[1] [B1i pass] cause to fall from the sky by destroying, killing or wounding. **S:** fighter aircraft, anti-aircraft gun; hunter. **O:** hostile aircraft, balloon; partridge, duck □ *Several aircraft were intercepted and **brought down**.* ⇨ come down[2].

bring down[2] [B1i pass] cause to fall over and stop (by killing or wounding). **S:** shooting party, gamekeeper, poacher. **O:** rabbit, deer, antelope □ *We managed to **bring down** one or two of the herd, even though they were running fast.*

bring down[3] [B1i pass] (sport) tackle (Rugby football); cause to fall down (by tackling *or* fouling) (Assoc. football). **S:** full-back, wing-half. **O:** forward, wing-three-quarter □ *The attacking fly-half was **brought down** by a wing-forward before he had moved five yards.* □ *Our centre-forward was tripped and **brought down** inside their penalty area.*

bring down[4] [B1i pass] cause the defeat or fall of. **S:** measure, scandal, controversy. **O:** Government, administration, tyrant □ *The defection of a large number of back-benchers **brought down** the last Government.*

bring down[5] [B1i pass] reduce, lower. **S:** government measures, increased production; wholesalers, shopkeepers. **O:** prices, costs, expenditure □ *Grocers have agreed to **bring down** the cost of several basic commodities.* □ *Demand has been **brought down** by increases in imports.* ⇨ be down[2], come down[3], go down[5].

bring down[6] [B1i pass] (mathematics) transfer digits from one part of a calculation to another (usu in problems involving multiplication or division). **O:** next figure, next digit; eight, nine etc □ *To divide 7489 by 322 you first decide how many times 322 will go into 748. Having subtracted the product of this number (2) and 322 from 748, you **bring down** the next figure (9) and again divide by 322.* □ *When multiplying numbers ending in nought, **bring down** the noughts first.*

bring the house down [B1i] (informal) make an audience laugh, applaud etc, uproariously. **S:** joke, song; entertainer, clown □ *We had a real get-together at weekends. Everybody standing up and giving a song. I used to **bring the house down** with this one.* TOH

bring down to earth [B3 pass] make sb return to reality. **A:** ⚠ with a bump, with a bang □ *Losing a child like that **brought** them **down to earth** with a bump.* □ *The louder they both shouted the higher the moral plane they felt it necessary to ascend to, until only physical violence could have **brought** them **down to earth**.* HAA ⇨ come down to earth.

bring forth [B1iii pass] (formal or facetious) produce, yield. **S:** committee, conference, board, manager. **O:** idea, proposal, suggestion □ *I suppose Smith is unlikely to **bring forth** any sparkling new suggestions for improving our product.* ⇨ come forth.

bring forward[1] [B1i pass] raise, propose for discussion. **S:** councillor, chairman, member. **O:** issue, question, matter, proposal □ *At our next Council meeting, he is proposing to **bring forward** the question of developing the city centre.* ⇨ come forward[2].

bring forward[2] [B1i pass] transfer to an earlier date, advance. **S:** organizer, committee. **O:** meeting, party, fête; date; clock, watch □ *Because of the possibility of a clash with another event, the organizers have decided to **bring** the barbecue **forward** from the 12th to the 5th June.* □ *Clocks and watches should be **brought forward** one hour from midnight tonight.*

bring forward[3] [B1i pass] (accountancy) carry or transfer a total from the foot of one page (in a ledger) to the top of the next; or from the account for one period to the account for another. **S:** clerk, accountant, auditor. **O:** figure, total, amount □ *A credit balance of fifty pounds was **brought forward** from his September account.*

bring forward[4] [B1i pass] (commerce) in business practice, record that correspondence etc is to be produced for sb's attention at a future date; do this at the actual date. **S:** secretary, assistant. **O:** letter, file □ *Please **bring** this letter **forward** at the beginning of next month.* □ *I **brought** this*

***forward** yesterday, and you've done nothing about it.* □ often abbreviated to B/F or b/f.

bring home (to) [B1i pass B3 pass emph rel] make sth clear to sb, make him realize it. **O:** fact, truth; realization, understanding; it... that the end was near. **o:** public, audience; patient, sufferer □ *These programmes do much to **bring home to** people the serious risks of smoking.* □ *What he says **brings home** the fact that the gods of the running-track are human like the rest of us.* T □ *It was **brought home to** me that every day I had much to learn.* MFM ⇨ come/get home (to).

bring in¹ [B1i pass] gather, harvest. **S:** farmer, grower. **O:** harvest, crop □ *They could be sure of a few more days of fine weather in which to **bring in** the harvest.* ⇨ be in², get in¹.

bring in² [B1i pass] earn, produce, yield. **S:** property, farm; investment, stock; job, profession. **O:** return; dividend, profit; wage, salary, £100 a week □ *Moral indignation was as much out of place in business as the emotions were: it was all a question of what would **bring in** money.* PW □ *Personal appearances **bring him in** money.* PW □ note Indirect Object (*him*) in the last example. ⇨ come in⁵.

bring in³ [B1i pass] give sb a part to play in some scheme; give him a position of advantage. **S:** company, board; gang □ *They have **brought in** a public relations man to advise on press coverage.* □ *'Why **bring** Jones **in**? He'll do nothing to help.'* ⇨ come in⁶.

bring in⁴ [B1i pass] (police) arrest; bring to a police station for questioning. **S:** constable, detective. **O:** wanted man, suspect □ *'If you see anyone loitering near the bank, **bring him in**.'*

bring in⁵ [B1i pass] (Parliament) introduce. **S:** Government, private member. **O:** Bill; measure, reform □ *A back-bencher is **bringing in** a Bill designed to remove the present anomalies in the Purchase-Tax Schedule.* □ *Legislation is being **brought in** to revise the Homicide Act.*

bring in a verdict [B1iii pass] (legal) return, pronounce, a verdict on an accused person. **S:** jury, court □ *The jury **brought in a verdict** that Christine had died from falling off a cliff, but there was no evidence to show how she had come to fall off the cliff.* PE

bring in on [B3 pass] give sb a share in, let him participate in; inform sb of sth. **S:** government; leader, manager. **O:** public; (political) party, work force. **o:** plan, scheme; discussion, negotiation; idea, proposal □ *The Council greatly angered small shopkeepers by not **bringing** them **in on** the development of the city centre.* □ *People most likely to be affected must be **brought in on** our proposals from the beginning.* ⇨ be/come/get/let in on.

bring into action [B2 pass] (military) make active, put sth in a position where it can operate. **S:** (military) commander; (naval) captain. **O:** force; division, battalion; tank, gun □ *Because of the state of the ground, the artillery could not be **brought into action** at once.* ⇨ be in/come into/go into action.

bring into being/existence [B2 pass] create, establish, set up² (q v). **S:** government, committee, board. **O:** body, organization; machinery, procedure □ *A new army was **brought into being** as the result of moving divisions from another front.* □ *An information bureau was **brought into existence** to deal with inquiries.* ⇨ be in/come into being/existence.

bring into blossom/flower [B2 pass] cause blossom, flowers, to appear. **S:** fine spell, early Spring. **O:** bush, shrub; rose, daffodil □ *The mildness of the early Spring weather will have helped to **bring** the fruit trees **into blossom** quickly.* ⇨ be in/come into blossom/flower.

bring into disrepute [B2 pass] give people an unfavourable impression of sth, give sth a bad name or reputation. **S:** advocate, supporter; servant, agent. **O:** cause, ideology; industry, service □ *Unofficial strikes are so common, and shop stewards so often involved, that trade unionism is **brought into disrepute**.* SC □ *The inefficiency of one department can **bring** a whole industry **into disrepute**.* ⇨ fall into disrepute.

bring into fashion/vogue [B2 pass] make sth fashionable, make it the vogue. **S:** (dress) designer, model. **O:** leather, plastic; maxicoat, (the) midi-length □ *The growing prestige of British designers did a lot to **bring** the miniskirt **into fashion** all over Europe.* ⇨ be in/come into fashion/vogue; be in¹, come in¹.

bring into focus [B2 pass] adjust a microscope, telescope etc so that the object viewed through it is sharp and clear; (fig) bring clearly to sb's attention. **S:** scientist, technician; observer, commentator; event, development. **O:** microscope; specimen; matter, problem, issue □ *To **bring** the slide **into** sharp **focus**, turn this small wheel.* □ *Advances in space exploration have **brought into focus** one of the most dramatic questions in human history.* TO ⇨ be in/come into focus.

bring into force [B2 pass] make sth (which is in some way binding or enforceable) begin to operate. **S:** government, (local) council; Chamber of Commerce; Trades Union. **O:** law, Bill; regulation, requirement □ *If the present regulations are not effective, then others may have to be **brought into force**.* ⇨ be in/come into/put into force.

bring into the open [B2 pass] reveal, make evident; make public. **S:** newspaper, reporter; meeting, speech. **O:** attitude, feeling; dispute, quarrel; matter, question □ *If you had not allowed him to make that speech, this matter need never have been **brought into the open**.* ⇨ be in/come into the open.

bring into play [B2 pass] involve, cause to have an influence. **S:** statesman, negotiator; commander; artist. **O:** force, circumstance, factor □ *Old enmities have once more been **brought into play** in the struggle for the leadership.* ⇨ be in/come into play.

bring into prominence [B2 pass] cause to be well known, prominent. **S:** policy, view; resistance (to sth), refusal (to do sth); discovery, invention. **O:** member (of a party, of Parliament); scientist, artist □ *Liverpool was **brought into** new **prominence** by being the birthplace of several pop-groups.* □ *Expressing illiberal views may **bring** some politicians **into** temporary **prominence**.* ⇨ come into prominence.

bring into service/use [B2 pass] introduce sth to serve the public, open for use. **S:** council; railway board, bus company. **O:** railway line, air link; bus, taxi; bridge, tunnel □ *The Victoria*

*Line was **brought into service**, as part of the London Underground, to link important parts of the city.* □ *These canals were **brought** back **into use** for pleasure traffic.* ⇨ be in/come into/go into service/use.

bring into sight/view [B2 pass] cause to appear. **S:** movement; descent, turning. **O:** destination; coast, town □ *A sudden movement of the clouds **brought** the airfield **into view**.* ⇨ be in/come into sight/view.

bring into the world [B2 pass] cause sb to be born, be his parent(s) □ *'And now, Heaven forgive me, I'm **bringing** another child **into the world**.'* DC □ *What a dreadful **world** to **bring** children **into**!* ⇨ come into the world.

bring into contact (with) [B2 pass] help people to meet. **S:** friend, colleague; work, travel; (sheer) chance. **O:** author, artist; businessman; would-be suitor. **o:** (**with**) publisher, dealer; customer; his future wife □ *These visits **brought** me **into contact with** a large public outside the army.* MFM □ *He was **brought into contact with** her* (or: *They were **brought into contact***) *through an interest in music.* ⇨ be in/come into contact (with).

bring into line (with) [B2 pass] make sb conform with the rules etc of an organization or movement. **S:** leader; party. **O:** disciple, follower; dissident, heretic. **o:** (**with**) official doctrine, the majority view □ *It will take more than promises of a comfortable future to **bring** such an original mind (back) **into line**.* □ *It seems that nothing can **bring** him **into line with** his fellows.* ⇨ be in/come into/fall into line (with).

bring off[1] [B1i pass] rescue, carry to safety. **S:** lifeboat, rescue launch, helicopter. **O:** crew, passengers (of vessel) □ *The Yarmouth lifeboat **brought off** the crew of the stricken tanker.*

bring off[2] [B1i pass] (informal) succeed in sth. **S:** planner, leader, general, criminal. **O:** ⚠ it, a coup, the thing □ *If we had worked more closely together, between us we could have **brought off** a real coup.* DS □ *Now it seemed like a fine idea. He felt sure that he could **bring** it **off**.* AITC ⇨ come off[5].

bring on[1] [B1i pass] help, encourage, to develop. ⇨ bring along/on[1].

bring on[2] [B1i pass] help to grow or flower. ⇨ bring along/on[2].

bring on[3] [B1i pass] cause, produce, lead to. **S:** cold weather, overwork, over-eating. **O:** influenza, eye-strain, attack of indigestion □ *His heart hammered in a mad cadenza of exaltation that almost **brought on** an attack of nausea.* ARG □ *It was pneumonia **brought on** in winter.* AH ⇨ come on[6].

bring on[4] [B1i pass] (cricket) ask sb to bowl. **S:** captain, skipper. **O:** fast bowler, spinner □ *The fast bowlers were **brought on again after the tea interval**.* ⇨ be on[4], come on[9], put on[10].

bring out[1] [B1i pass] (industry) cause to strike, to withdraw labour. **S:** union official, shop-steward. **O:** workers, labour force □ *He has **brought** the engineering apprentices **out** on strike.* SC □ *It started as a strike in the foundry; then that **brought out** most of the assembly workers as well.* ⇨ be out[1], come out[1].

bring out[2] [B1i pass] help to lose shyness or reserve. **S:** husband, father, admirer. **O:** shy girl, diffident child, guest □ *She's a retiring sort of girl, but he's doing his best to **bring** her **out**.*

bring out[3] [B1i pass] introduce to society (as a debutante). **O:** daughter, girl □ *Mrs Fitzalan is **bringing out** her eldest daughter next season.* ⇨ be out[3], come out[3].

bring out[4] [B1i pass] cause to open or flower. **S:** fine weather, sunshine. **O:** rose, tulip □ *The hot weather has **brought out** all the blossom on the fruit trees.* ⇨ be out[4], come out[4].

bring out[5] [B1i pass] introduce onto the market; publish. **S:** manufacturer, makers; (name of) publisher. **O:** model, make; novel, biography □ *British Leyland are **bringing out** a new sports saloon next month.* ⇨ be out[6], come out[6].

bring out[6] [B1i pass adj] reveal, show up[1] (q v), clearly. **S:** sun, light; treatment, enlargement. **O:** detail, small mark, hidden feature □ *The low sun **brought out** the gold of the Cotswold masonry.* ARG □ *His photograph **brings out** the detail of the sculpture.* ⇨ come out[8].

bring out[7] [B1i pass] speak, utter. **O:** ⚠ word, declaration, statement □ *He didn't finish the sentence because if he had **brought out** the word it would probably have made him cry.* CON ⇨ come out[9].

bring out[8] [B1i pass adj] reveal, make clear or explicit. **S:** teacher, lecturer. **O:** truth, sense, meaning, point □ *The meaning of the poem was admirably **brought out**.* □ *That's a well **brought-out** point.* ⇨ come out[10].

bring out[9] [B1i pass] elicit, call forth (q v). **S:** adversity, need, danger. **O:** the (very) worst/best in him; (all) his cunning, his greed □ *The one person who never failed to **bring out** the spirit of competition in Robert was Ned Roper.* CON □ *Disaster **brought out** all that was best in the family.* AITC ⇨ come out[11].

bring out in [B3 pass] cause sb to be (partially) covered with. **S:** heat, humidity; diet. **O:** skin; face, chest. **o:** ⚠ a rash; spots, pimples □ *'Don't allow him to get excited: it **brings** him **out in** a nervous rash.'* ⇨ come out in.

bring out/out of [B1i pass B2 pass] cause to leave; carry from. **S:** fireman, police. **O:** owner, occupant; furniture. **o:** house, room □ *He rummaged about in the attic and **brought out** a pile of old documents.* □ *They gathered up the few belongings that they'd managed to **bring out of** the burning house.* ⇨ be out/out of[1], come out/out of[1], get out/out of[1], take out/out of[1].

bring out of his shell [B2 pass] (informal) help sb to overcome his shyness, or show a bolder side to his character. **O:** child, girl; pupil □ *It will take all of your patience and tact to **bring** John **out of his shell**.* □ *What **brought** him **out of his shell** was the invitation to talk about his only interest —astronomy.* ⇨ come out of one's shell.

bring over [B1i pass] cause sb to come from overseas; accompany sb travelling or settling overseas. **S:** immigrant, settler. **O:** wife, family □ *He's been teaching in this country for a year. Next summer he hopes to **bring** his family **over** from the States.* ⇨ be over[4], come over[1].

bring over (to) [B1i pass B3 pass] cause sb to change his allegiance. **O:** supporter, ally; general, scientist. **o:** us, our side □ *The rebel leader abruptly changed sides, **bringing** most of his fellow dissidents **over** with him.* □ *I don't think that many of the people in the centre can be **brought over to** the Government side.* ⇨ come over (to), go over to[1].

bring round[1] [B1i pass] (nautical) cause to face in the opposite direction. **S:** helmsman, coxwain. **O:** vessel, boat □ *They* ***brought*** *the ship* ***round*** *with a wash of water astern.* AH

bring round[2] [B1ii pass] cause to regain consciousness. **S:** doctor, nurse, first-aid man. **O:** spectator, patient □ *George fainted in the heat but was soon* ***brought round.*** ⇨ come round[2].

bring round (to)[1] [B1ii pass B3 pass rel] conduct, lead, sb to a place. ⇨ bring around/round (to)[1].

bring round (to)[2] [B1ii pass B3 pass rel] convert sb to one's point of view. ⇨ bring around/round (to)[2].

bring round to [B3 pass] direct or steer conversation so that one's own choice of topic is discussed. **O:** ⚠ conversation, discussion. **o:** one's own favourite subject; gambling, sport, cars □ *By talking about Scotland, Brown managed to* ***bring*** *the discussion* ***round*** *to salmon fishing — his favourite pastime.*

bring through [B1ii pass B2 pass] be responsible for sb's survival or recovery. **S:** skilled medical care, good doctors; sound leadership. **O:** patient; firm, business; country. **o:** illness; crisis, war □ *He was very badly injured; only the very finest treatment could have* ***brought*** *him* ***through.*** □ *Cool heads will* ***bring*** *us* ***through*** *this crisis.* ⇨ come through.

bring to[1] [B1ii pass] help to recover consciousness. ⇨ bring round[2].

bring to[2] [B1ii pass] (nautical) make sth stop. **S:** captain, mate. **O:** ship, boat □ *The unidentified ship was* ***brought to*** *by the firing of a warning shot across its bows.* ⇨ come to[2].

bring to[3] [B2 pass] make sth equal, reach, a certain sum. **S:** spending, purchase. **O:** bill, account; total. **o:** five pounds; ten dollars □ *If I buy the suit, it will* ***bring*** *my bill* ***to*** *rather more than I've budgeted for.* ⇨ come to[3].

bring to[4] [B2 pass emph rel] approach, tackle sth with a certain attitude etc. **S:** manager, planner; scholar, craftsman. **O:** wisdom, knowledge; fresh mind, lack of prejudice. **o:** task, work; job, post □ *The designer* ***brings*** *wide experience in this medium* ***to*** *his new task.* □ ***To*** *his new appointment the Minister* ***brought*** *knowledge gained at first hand.* ⇨ come to (with).

bring to sb's aid/assistance [B2 pass] direct, summon, assistance to sb in difficulties. **S:** shout, call, telephone message. **O:** (police) patrol car, breakdown van, fire brigade. **o:** (*of*) motorist, owner, occupant □ *A broadcast appeal* ***brought*** *rescue teams hurrying* ***to the aid of*** *the flood victims.* □ *Skilled mechanics can quickly be* ***brought to the assistance of*** *motorists.* ⇨ come to sb's aid/assistance/help.

bring to attention [B2 pass] (military) make soldiers etc adopt an alert position, with the feet together. **S:** sergeant, officer. **O:** troops; platoon, company □ *The sergeant* ***brought*** *the guard smartly* ***to attention*** *and saluted the inspecting officer.* ⇨ be at/come to attention.

bring to sb's attention/notice [B2 pass] make sb notice, be aware of, sth. **O:** it... that she was absent, that sth was amiss; fact, matter □ *An inspector first* ***brought*** *these deficiencies* ***to the attention of*** *the management.* □ *It has been* ***brought to my notice*** *that some senior boys are in the habit of visiting public houses in the town.* ⇨ come to sb's attention/notice.

bring to blows [B2 pass] make people start fighting. **S:** disagreement, difference (of opinion); rivalry, enmity. **O:** (two) sides, parties □ *The question of who should sit next to the guest of honour practically* ***brought*** *the two of them* ***to blows.*** ⇨ come to blows.

bring to the boil [B2 pass] cause to reach boiling point; (fig) bring to a point of crisis. **O:** pan, kettle; vegetables, rice; situation, the whole thing □ ***Bring*** *the water* ***to the boil,*** *put the rice in, and allow the pan to simmer until all the water has evaporated.* □ *What really* ***brought*** *things* ***to the boil*** *was a newspaper article alleging embezzlement.* ⇨ come to the boil.

bring to a climax [B2 pass] cause to reach a high level of intensity, drama etc. **S:** incident, interruption, fight. **O:** meeting, discussion, quarrel □ *The meeting was* ***brought to an*** *excited* ***climax*** *by the appearance on the platform of the rebel leader.* □ *Some brilliant writing for the brass instruments* ***brings*** *the passage* ***to a climax.*** ⇨ come to a climax.

bring to a dead end [B2 pass] make further progress impossible. **S:** interference, opposition; stubbornness; (lack of) clues, information. **O:** inquiry; research; discussion □ *The reluctance of the local people to talk had* ***brought*** *his investigation* ***to a dead end.*** ⇨ be at/come to a dead end.

bring to an end [B2 pass] end sth (often unpleasant or unsatisfactory). **O:** quarrel, hostility, misunderstanding; arrangement, treaty □ *Leaders were anxious to* ***bring to an end*** *the dissensions of the last few months.* T □ *I hope we have* ***brought*** *our arguments on fundamentals* ***to an end.*** OBS ⇨ be at/come to an end, put an end/a stop to.

bring to his feet [B2 pass] make sb stand up quickly. **S:** shock, blow; shout, cry; enthusiasm, excitement. **O:** onlooker, spectator □ *It was finally a remark of Edith's that* ***brought*** *him* ***to his feet*** *in a rush of anger.* HD □ *A jolt nearly threw me from the bed, and a second jolt* ***brought*** *me* ***to my feet.*** SD ⇨ be on/come to/get on one's feet.

bring to the fore [B2 pass] make prominent, give an active part to. **S:** situation; crisis, war; depression, revival. **O:** (able) leader, statesman; (dishonest) dealer, criminal □ *The conditions of the postwar years* ***brought*** *many enterprising men* ***to the fore.*** ⇨ be/come to the fore.

bring to fruition [B2 pass] cause sth to be fulfilled or realized. **S:** struggle, conflict; work, study; prayer. **O:** hope, dream; ambition; plan □ *Years of patient work had at last* ***brought*** *all his plans* ***to fruition.*** □ *The scheme was locally conceived, and* ***brought to fruition*** *with help from overseas.* ⇨ come to fruition.

bring to the ground [B2 pass] make sth fall to the ground or collapse. **S:** explosion, earth tremor; revolution, upheaval. **O:** tower, mast; regime □ *The gales* ***brought*** *trees and telegraph poles* ***to the ground.*** □ *They wanted to launch a general strike which would* ***bring*** *the State* ***to the ground.*** OBS ⇨ come to the ground.

bring to a halt/standstill [B2 pass] stop, arrest, the forward movement, or progress, of sth. **S:** driver; operator; striker. **O:** car, lorry;

machine, production-line; factory □ *He* ***brought*** *the car* ***to a halt****.* HD □ *A strike in the paint-shop* ***brought*** *production* ***to a standstill*** *this morning.* ⇨ be at/come to a halt/standstill.

bring to a head [B2 pass] cause to reach a point where a decision, change etc is necessary. **S:** arrival, intervention; failure, success. **O:** ⚠ matters, things, it □ *The arrival of a fourth child* ***brought*** *things* ***to a head*** *between husband and wife. He would have to get a job with more money.* □ *Matters were* ***brought to a head*** *when the boss tried to force still more work onto him. He resigned.* ⇨ come to a head.

bring to heel [B2 pass] subdue, bring under control (q v). **S:** government, regime. **O:** (rebellious) subject, province □ *It is no simple matter to* ***bring*** *a break-away region of several millions* ***to heel****.* □ *'I* ***brought*** *them* ***to heel****,' said Robert, gaily. 'I extracted some money from them, too, so drink up.'* CON ⇨ come to heel.

bring to himself [B2 pass] make sb conscious, aware, of what is happening. **S:** bang, explosion; light; door opening; (cold) air, water □ *The mention of a name* ***brought*** *him* ***to himself****. Had he heard it before?* ⇨ come to oneself.

bring to life [B2 pass] make sth live, give it vitality. **S:** actor, story-teller. **O:** story, poem; literature, history □ *She couldn't act very well, but for me she* ***brought*** *the whole silly play* ***to life****.* RATT ⇨ come to life.

bring to light [B2 pass] reveal sth which has been hidden. **S:** researcher, investigator, detective. **O:** fact, (piece of) evidence, detail □ *One newspaper claims to have* ***brought to light*** *some important new evidence.* □ *Some little-known details of his early life have been* ***brought to light****.* ⇨ come to light.

bring to a pretty pass/such a pass [B2 pass] allow, cause, things to reach a sad or sorry state. **S:** father; manager, director; government. **O:** things, affairs; us etc □ *'And who* ***brought*** *us* ***to such a pass****? You did, by sheer mismanagement.'* ⇨ come to a pretty pass etc.

bring to rest [B2 pass] control sth so that it stops, reaches a final position. **S:** driver, pilot. **O:** car, train, plane □ *Wrestling desperately with the controls, the pilot finally managed to* ***bring*** *his aircraft* ***to rest*** *in a cornfield.* ⇨ come to rest.

bring to his senses [B2 pass] make sb think and behave sensibly. **S:** experience, shock, disappointment. **O:** immature, irresponsible person □ *All I hope is that this recent accident will have* ***brought*** *him* ***to his senses****.* □ *Nothing but a strong letter from his bank manager will* ***bring*** *him* ***to his senses****.* ⇨ come to one's senses.

bring to a (successful) conclusion [B2 pass] end sth well which is moving in a positive direction. **S:** statesman, negotiator; commander. **O:** talks, discussion; campaign □ *Once a second front was opened in North-West Europe, we should be able to* ***bring*** *the war* ***to a successful conclusion*** *by the end of 1944.* MFM ⇨ come to a (successful) conclusion.

bring to trial [B2 pass] (legal) try in a court of law. **O:** suspect, accused; case □ *I sent the bomb which killed the postman. If* ***brought to trial*** *I should plead insanity.* ARG □ *Before we can* ***bring*** *our man* ***to trial****, we must catch him in the act.* ⇨ be on trial.

bring to grips with [B2 pass] make sb confront or tackle sth, make him struggle with it. **S:** experience; awareness, knowledge; travel, work. **O:** statesman; scientist, scholar. **o:** (***with***) issue, problem □ *Service in a developing country* ***brought*** *him* ***to grips with*** *the problems of poverty.* ⇨ be at/come to/get to grips with.

bring together [B1i pass] reconcile two parties who are in conflict. **O:** divorced, estranged couple; (warring, hostile) factions, parties, elements □ *I'm not sure that John and Margaret can be* ***brought together****.* □ *The Minister is trying to* ***bring*** *the two sides to the dispute* ***together*** *to discuss a new formula.* ⇨ come together.

bring under [B1ii pass] subdue, bring under control (q v). **S:** government, police. **O:** rebel, rioter □ *After some incidents that the police could not prevent, the rioters were* ***brought under*** *completely.*

bring under control [B2 pass] subdue, master; bring under (q v). **S:** fire brigade, health department; police, army. **O:** fire, epidemic; riot; crowd □ *Five fire engines* ***brought*** *the blaze* ***under control*** *in just over an hour.* OBS □ *Such bodies may sabotage the trade union movement if they are not* ***brought under control****.* SC ⇨ be/get under control.

bring up[1] [B1i pass adj] raise, rear, educate. **S:** parent, foster-parent, grandmother; nurse. **O:** child, family. **A:** properly, in style, in poverty □ *The nurse, suffering from conscience, adopted Prissie and* ***brought*** *her* ***up****.* DC □ *The fact of being* ***brought up*** *in a shabby and dirty town was another thing that helped us to be competitive.* CON □ compound adj forms: well-brought-up, badly-brought-up; nom form: upbringing.

bring up[2] [B1i pass] teach, persuade, sb in the course of his upbringing to do sth. **S:** parent, teacher, community. **O:** child, family. **Inf** to scorn convention, to respect his parents, to be courteous to strangers □ *He had been* ***brought up*** *to think that his parents always knew best.* □ *They had* ***brought up*** *their sons to stand on their own feet.* □ inf usu present.

bring up[3] [B1i pass] raise, call attention to. **S:** chairman, back-bencher, member of the board. **O:** question, matter, subject, proposal, point □ *I* ***bring*** *this story* ***up*** *now only to compare my experience with that of some unhappy fellow on the United States Energy Commission.* NS □ *'I think we're agreed on the main points. Does anyone want to* ***bring up*** *anything further?'* TBC ⇨ be up[6], come up[4].

bring up[4] [B1i pass] (legal) cause to appear for trial. **S:** police, CID. **O:** habitual offender, suspected thief. **A:** before the magistrates, before the beak; on a charge of drunken driving □ *They were* ***brought up*** *for causing a disturbance and obstructing the police.* ⇨ be up[7], come up[5].

bring up[5] [B1i pass] (military) convey or summon (to the front line). **S:** general; enemy; transport. **O:** armour, troops; supplies, ammunition □ *We would have to blast our way on shore and get a good lodgement before the enemy could* ***bring up*** *sufficient reserves to turn us out.* MFM ⇨ come up[6].

bring up[6] [B1i pass] (informal) vomit (up). **S:** child, patient. **O:** food, breakfast, everything □ *'I don't seem to take my meals well,' he said. 'I*

***bring up** most of what I've taken, if you'll pardon the phrase.'* ASA ⇨ come up[7].

bring up[7] [B1ii pass] (informal) make remarks or a movement stop suddenly. **S:** noise, blow, interruption, sight. **A:** ⚠ short, sharp, sharply, with a jerk □ *What **brought** me **up** short and made my irritation evaporate was the sight of two bulging sacks lying at his feet.* DF □ *We were **brought up** short by a sudden bellow from our friend.* BM

bring up the hard way [B1ii pass] (informal) give sb a severe upbringing (i e without special help or privileges). **S:** father, family □ *Father believed in **bringing** us **up the hard way**. He always said that a 'good' education would make us too soft for the harsh battles of life.* ⇨ come up the hard way; bring up[1].

bring up the rear [B1iii pass] come last (in a procession or column). **S:** heavy transport, cavalry, car □ *A short distance behind came a Peugeot, and **the rear** was **brought up** by a powerful dark-green Mercedes.* TO □ *Ned, who had just opened the door to me, **brought up the rear** with a portfolio of drawings.* CON

bring up against [B3 pass] make sb face or confront sb or sth. **S:** travel, experience; marriage, courtship; work. **o:** problem, difficulty; pressure, force; opponent □ *Working in a multi-racial community had **brought** him **up against** the realities of intolerance.* □ *He was **brought up against** his wife's fear and mistrust of strange people.* ⇨ be/come up against.

bring up (as far as/to) [B1ii pass B3 pass] lead, conduct, cause to rise, (to). **S:** road, path; bus; conditions. **O:** traveller; sea, tide. **o:** top, summit; sea-wall, houses □ *Strong winds **brought** the water swirling **up** the main street.* □ *'Did the guide **bring** you right **up to** the top?' 'No, only **as far as** that checkpoint.'* ⇨ be/come up (as far as/to).

bring up to [B3 pass] bring to an acceptable level or standard. **S:** authorities; teacher, coach. **O:** work, performance. **o:** ⚠ standard, scratch, the mark □ *His work in maths needs to be **brought up to** the standard of the others.* □ *After the recent inquiry, the electrical wiring in these houses has been **brought up to** scratch.* ⇨ be up to[5], come up to, get up to[1].

bring up to date [B3 pass] revise sth, adding current information, figures etc; give sb a report with current information. **O:** pamphlet, brochure; chart, map; ideas, thinking; employer, commander □ *Booklets published in the series 'Choice of Careers' are constantly **brought up to date**.* OBS □ *I have only a few additional facts to add to **bring** the report **up to date**.* EM □ ***Bring** me **up to date** quickly on the fuel crisis.* ⇨ be up to date/the minute; get up to date (with).

bring within [B2 pass] cause to come near enough (to be heard, seen or reached). **o:** ⚠ earshot, sight, view, range, striking distance □ *Five minutes would **bring** the aircraft **within** range of our warning and interception system.* ⇨ be within[1], come within, get within.

bristle with[1] [A2 rel] display a frightening or impressive array of; be fraught with. **S:** army, front; task, project, scheme; book, memoir. **o:** guns, bayonets; problems, snags; impressive titles, famous names □ *The first chapter, which **bristles with** names, is essentially a regimental history of the purely scientific side of the plutonium project.* NS

bristle with[2] [A2] show or display in an extreme form. **o:** rage, anger, indignation, displeasure □ *Just mention her name to him and he positively **bristles with** anger.*

broach (with) [B2 pass emph rel] raise, introduce, in conversation an important matter one wishes to discuss. **O:** matter, question, issue, subject. **o:** partner, employer; wife □ *I still had to **broach** (**with** her) the matter of her taking a job in America.* SPL □ *I **broached** the subject **with** Elspeth one evening.* SML

brood (on/over/upon) [A2 pass emph rel] think sombrely and at length (about). **o:** problem, difficulty; illness, disability; failure □ *The problem won't improve for being **brooded over**.* □ *'Yes, I know he's a sick man, but he will **brood on** it.'* □ *Then there was the much **brooded-upon** question of whether he'd made the right choice of career.*

brown off [B1ii pass adj] (informal) bore; annoy. **S:** routine, food; voice, manner □ *'Why must he talk like that? It really **browns** people **off**.'* □ *'You look **browned off**, Miss Traughton. Can I help?'* HAA

brush aside[1] [B1i pass] push to one side (as being lighter or weaker than oneself). **S:** army, force. **O:** defences □ *The enemy column **brushed aside** our defense and advanced south.*

brush aside[2] [B1i pass] disregard, treat as of little or no importance. **S:** organizer, director, manager. **O:** objections, difficulties, complaints □ *We had to learn to work with others, and many of our own ideas would be **brushed aside** for the good of the whole.* MFM

brush down[1] [B1ii nom pass] clean with brisk strokes of a brush. **O:** oneself; jacket, coat □ *Your jacket needs **brushing down**: it's covered with fluff.* □ *He always looks as if he could do with a good **brush(-)down**.* □ the hyphen is optional in the nom form (brush down or brush-down).

brush down[2] [B1ii pass] (informal) scold, reprove. **O:** child, pupil, employee □ *The games master gave him a good **brushing down*** (cf *He got a good **brushing down***) *for not turning out for training.* ⇨ the nom form in the previous entry.

brush off[1] [B1i pass B2 pass] remove with a brush. **S:** valet, cleaner. **O:** mud, dust, fluff □ *'I can't **brush** the dirt **off*** (or: *It won't **brush off**).'*

brush off[2] [B1i nom pass adj] (slang) reject, jilt, end a relationship with; avoid meeting or forming a relationship with. **S:** man, girlfriend; senior colleague, business associate. **O:** girlfriend, man; newcomer, junior □ *His girlfriend has just given him the **brush-off**.* □ *I've tried to make contact with the neighbours but they've always **brushed** me **off**.*

brush past [A1 A2] just touch sb as one passes him in a confined space □ *'Don't bother to move. I think I can just **brush past**.'* □ *Something that felt like a cat **brushed past** him in the darkness.*

brush up [B1iii pass adj] (informal) revise or practise a skill in order to be proficient in it once again. **S:** tourist, salesman, learner-driver. **O:** French, Spanish; knowledge of the law, Highway Code □ *You'll have to **brush up** your his-*

tory of art if you want a job in the museum. □ *His spoken Arabic was hurriedly* ***brushed up*** *before he took off on a sales tour of the Middle East.*

bubble over [A1] rise to a peak, reach a climax. **S:** enthusiasm, high spirits, good humour □ *Then excitement seemed to* ***bubble over*** *inside her. 'Life's so interesting, isn't it?' she said.* DC ⇨ next entry.

bubble over with [A3 rel] display a great deal of. **S:** child, holiday-maker. **o:** excitement, high spirits □ *With us travelled Rafael,* ***bubbling over with*** *enthusiasm for the whole trip.* DF ⇨ previous entry.

bubble up [A1] rise to the surface in bubbles and/or with the sound of bursting bubbles. **S:** gas, air; water, oil □ *The warm gases* ***bubbled up*** *through the water.*

buck up[1] [A1 B1i pass] (informal) become, make, more lively and cheerful; cheer up[1,2] (q v). **S:** [A1] **O:** [B1] patient, invalid. **S:** [B1] news; holiday, rest; meal, drink. **A:** no end, a great deal, a lot □ *He'd got depressed about his work, but he* ***bucked up*** *at the thought that he'd soon be on holiday.* □ *It was clear that Bennie's visit had* ***bucked*** *him* ***up*** *no end.* ILIH

buck up[2] [A1] (informal) make haste, hurry up (q v) □ *'****Buck up****, Peter, or you'll be late for school!'* □ *'He'll have to* ***buck up*** *if he wants to catch that train.'* □ often imper, or with *must, have to.*

buck one's ideas up [B1i pass] (informal) become more wideawake or alert □ *If he hopes to keep his job, he'll have to* ***buck his ideas up*** *a bit.* □ often with *have to, ought to, need to.*

buckle down to [A3 pass] (informal) begin (work) in earnest, set to (work) seriously. **o:** ⚠ job, task, work; it □ MICK: *But he won't* ***buckle down to*** *the job.* DAVIES: *He doesn't like work.* MICK: *Work shy.* TC □ *You can't play around with this assignment: it's something that needs to be* ***buckled down to*** *seriously.*

buckle to [A1] (informal) unite efforts in the face of common danger or hardship. **S:** family, country, partners □ *When their mother died, the children simply had to* ***buckle to*** *and run the house themselves.* □ *With Anna to lend a hand you'll be able to carry on until Laura gets here. It'll be a little adventure —* ***buckling to*** *and seeing it through.* TGLY

bugger about/around[1] [A1] (taboo) behave in a foolish or irresponsible way □ *'Now stop* ***buggering about****, Charlie. I've got work to do.'* □ *'If you carry on* ***buggering around*** *with that knife, you'll do yourself an injury.'*

bugger about/around[2] [B1ii pass] (taboo) treat sb in a foolish or casual way; behave as though one had a poor estimate of sb's worth etc. **S:** firm, dealer; clerk, official □ *'Look, all I want is a simple answer to a simple question. Now stop* ***buggering*** *me* ***about****!'* □ *'Don't try to be too clever with Fred. If he thinks you're* ***buggering*** *him* ***around****, he'll clobber you!'*

bugger off [A1] (taboo) leave, clear off[1] (q v) □ *He'd* ***buggered off*** *before I had a chance to get a word in.* □ *'Yah! Get away!* ***Bugger off****!'* PM □ often as imper.

bugger up [B1i pass] (taboo) spoil, ruin; make a hash/mess of (q v). **S:** workman, salesman; firm, agency. **o:** things, the whole thing, it; job, deal □ *'Don't go fiddling around with that spanner — you'll* ***bugger*** *the whole works* ***up****.'* □ *'Things can easily be* ***buggered up*** *by twits like you taking a hand.'*

build in/into[1] [B1i pass adj B2 pass emph rel] make as a permanent fixture in a house. **S:** builder, carpenter. **O:** cupboard, wardrobe, desk □ *Don't bother to buy cupboards: I'm arranging to have them* ***built in*** (i e ***built into*** *the walls).* □ *There was a* ***built-in*** *dresser in the kitchen.* □ usu [B1] passive and adj forms.

build in/into[2] [B1i pass adj B2 pass emph rel] make a firm and necessary part of sth. **S:** firm, solicitor, building-society, local authority. **O:** clause, proviso, requirement. **o:** lease, contract, agreement □ *The landlord has insisted on* ***building into*** *our agreement a clause forbidding us to sublet.* □ *The new contract with the employers includes a* ***built-in*** *agreement on wages.*

build into ⇨ build (up) into.

build on [A2 pass rel] use sth as a foundation for further progress. **S:** team, athlete; firm, factory. **o:** achievement, success, record □ *In their latest design, the company is clearly* ***building on*** *the success of previous years.*

build one's hopes on [B2 emph rel] choose sb or sth as the best means of achieving an objective. **S:** country; industry, agriculture; government, party. **o:** alliance, treaty; automation, mechanization; (new) leader, policy □ *It was* ***on*** *Mr Maudling that this group within the Conservative Party now* ***built its hopes****.*

build out [B1i pass] build as an extension to an existing structure. **O:** wing, extension; (extra) room; conservatory □ *Extra classrooms were* ***built out*** *from the main block.*

build over [A2 pass adj] cover with buildings. **o:** bomb-site, derelict land, marsh □ *The woods where he used to play as a child have all gone. They're* ***built over****, of course.* □ *This area to the left of the road is* ***built-over*** *farmland.*

build up[1] [A1 nom] accumulate, so as to form a block. **S:** traffic; queue, line □ *At Easter, traffic* ***builds up*** *along the roads to the coast.* □ *There is a serious* ***build-up*** *of cars on the A6 near Manchester.*

build up[2] [B1i pass adj] develop, cover with buildings. **O:** area, district, village □ *The whole district is being* ***built up****; soon you won't be able to see the fields for bricks and mortar.* □ *There is normally a speed-limit for traffic in* ***built-up*** *areas.* □ adj form built-up usu occurs with *area.*

build up[3] [B1ii pass] develop the strength or physique of. **S:** doctor, nurse, mother; exercise, diet □ *'Must go carefully all the same. Not too much excitement. You must* ***build*** *yourself* ***up*** *for the winter.'* PW □ *'Your brother has the nicest manners, but he needs* ***building up****; Vitamin B, I'd say.'* DC

build up[4] [B1ii nom pass] (informal) speak in glowing terms of (the praise may be exaggerated or undeserved). **S:** friend, colleague; former employer, chairman. **O:** performer, actor, promising beginner □ *Don't* ***build*** *me* ***up*** *too much: I'm really not that talented.* □ *He wasn't half the performer he was* ***built up*** *to be.* □ *The master of ceremony's* ***build-up*** *was effusive and largely insincere.*

build up (from) [B1i pass adj B3 pass emph rel] develop, extend, gradually and steadily (from a low level). **S:** leader, businessman, general, government. **O:** firm, practice; army; reputation, quality. **o:** scratch, zero, nothing □ *The rebels may well be planning to* ***build up*** *this kind of army with foreign assistance.* SC □ *We had to* ***build*** *the firm* ***up from*** *scratch after the devastation of the war.*

build (up) into [A2 A3 B2 pass B3 pass] (of parts) come, put, together to form a whole. **S:** [A2 A3] **O:** [B2 B3] piece, scrap; stamp, medal, book. **S:** [B2 B3] artist; collector □ [A3] *Eventually, these books will* ***build up into*** *a fine library.* □ [B2] *The sculptor has* ***built*** *these scraps of metal* ***into*** *a fine composition.*

build up (to)[1] [B1i nom pass adj B3 pass emph rel] increase, accumulate. **S:** bank, City; ally, enemy. **O:** reserves, capital; force, army. **o:** level; strength □ *The banks have* ***built up*** *sufficient reserves to cope with the crisis.* □ *The army has been* ***built up to*** *its wartime strength.* □ *A* ***build-up*** *of enemy forces has been reported.*

build up (to)[2] [A1 nom A3 emph rel B1iii pass adj B3 pass emph rel] develop, increase, intensify. **S:** [A1 A3] **O:** [B1 B3] pressure, tension; opposition, resistance. **S:** [B1 B3] overwork, stress; decision, attitude. **o:** pitch, intensity; climax □ [A1] *More tightness and pressure* ***build up*** *and your headache gets worse.* WI □ [A3] *Tension is* ***building up to*** *a climax in this troubled city.* □ [A1] *These measures will only lead to a* ***build-up*** *in communal strife.* □ [B1] *The tax laws* ***built up*** *resistance to the regime.*

bully off [A1 nom] (hockey) begin a game or period of play by striking sticks together. **S:** captain, player □ *There was a* ***bully-off*** *in one corner of the field following an infringement.*

bum around [A1] (slang) wander or hang about idly. **S:** scamp, wastrel, tramp □ *I think he proposes to* ***bum around*** *and get money from his parents whenever he runs short.*

bump into [A2] (informal) meet by chance (often after a long separation); run into[4] (q v) □ *You know, you remind me of a bloke I* ***bumped into*** *once, just the other side of the Guildford bypass.* TC

bump off [B1i pass] (slang) kill (usu by shooting). **S:** gangster, husband, brother. **O:** crony, rival, wife □ *'We'll all get* ***bumped off*** *when the balloon goes up,' he said.* RFW □ *'You* ***bumped*** *the old woman* ***off****, and you're going to pay or hang!'* PE

bump up [B1i pass] (informal) increase, raise. **S:** examiner, accountant; employer; shortage, scarcity, increased demand. **O:** mark, total; salary; value, shares □ *Towards the close of business prices were* ***bumped up*** *by news of changes in the tax laws affecting private incomes.*

bumped up [pass adj (B1)] (informal) (have) risen rather quickly to a high position from humble beginnings; (be) in a job which is made to sound more important than it is (by some special title). **S:** clerk, office boy, messenger □ *Mr Smythe wanted to speak to the real manager. He wasn't going to be satisfied with some* ***bumped-up*** *cashier.* □ *'We must have struck him as rather* ***bumped up****. You know, no proper social background.'* □ passive with *be, seem, appear.*

bung up [B1i pass adj] (slang) block, clog. **O:** drain, pipe; nose, bowels □ *'Don't throw tea leaves down the sink: you'll* ***bung*** *it* ***up****.'* □ *'I've been* ***bunged up*** (= constipated) *since I changed my diet.'*

buoy up[1] [B1i pass] keep afloat. **S:** life-jacket, 'mae-west'; driftwood. **O:** swimmer, survivor (of shipwreck) □ *He seized a piece of wreckage; this would* ***buoy*** *him* ***up*** *till rescue came.*

buoy up[2] [B1i pass] keep at a high or safe level. **S:** trading policy, improvement in the market. **O:** prices, share levels, trading figures □ *These hopes have been* ***buoying up*** *share prices.* OBS

buoy up[3] [B1i pass] keep cheerful or content. **S:** hope, thought; change of fortune □ *I was* ***buoyed up*** *by thinking I might manage to get married myself.* SML

buried under [pass (B2)] (be) overwhelmed by. **o:** (pile, mountain of) work, marking, correcting □ *'I can't get near him at the moment. He's* ***buried under*** *a pile of paperwork.'*

burn away[1] [A1] continue to burn. **S:** (coal-, gas-)fire □ *The fire was still* ***burning away*** *cheerfully in the grate.*

burn away[2] [A1 B1i pass] become, make less by burning; destroy by fire. **S:** [A1] **O:** [B1] fuel, oil; wick, fuse; tissue, flesh □ *Half the oil in the lamp had* ***burnt away****.* □ *When the pilot reached hospital, it was found that tissue had been* ***burnt away*** *from his face and hands.*

burn down [A1 B1i pass adj] be destroyed, destroy, to the foundations by fire. **S:** [A1] **O:** [B1] house, factory, farmhouse. **S:** [B1] mob, fire-raiser □ *The wood-shed* ***burnt down*** *in half an hour.*

burn for [A2 emph rel] (formal or facetious) wish ardently that one could have. **o:** her etc; (moment of) glory, triumph □ *These mercenary armies keep going because there's always some idiot* ***burning for*** *his moment of glory.*

burn off [B1i pass] remove, strip, by burning. **O:** paint, varnish □ ***Burn off*** *the old paint, fill any cracks in the woodwork, and rub down well with sandpaper.*

burn out[1] [A1 B1i pass adj] (technical) (cause to) damage and stop working (through electrical burning). **S:** [A1] **O:** [B1] motor, coil, armature □ *The high current taken by the armature when the motor is thus semi-stalled causes it to* ***burn out****.* WTR □ ***Burnt-out*** *armatures in most cases are rewound.* WTR

burn out[2] [A1] (space technology) use up its fuel. **S:** rocket, missile; motor □ *As the first rocket* ***burns out****, the second-stage motor ignites.*

burn out[3] [B1i pass adj] gut, reduce to a shell by fire. **O:** house, factory; car, tank □ ***Burned-out*** *lorries lined both sides of the road.* □ *The factory was completely* ***burnt out****.* □ usu passive or adj.

burn (itself) out [A1 B1ii] stop burning (because there is no more fuel). **S:** fire, flames; furnace, range □ *When we got back from the theatre we found that the fire had* ***burned itself out****.*

burn (oneself) out [B1ii pass] (informal) ruin one's health through overwork, dissipation etc □ *If you don't give up this evening work, you'll* ***burn yourself out****.* □ *The last time I saw him, he looked completely* ***burned out****.*

burn to [B2 pass] reduce sth by burning to ash etc. **O:** food; meal; fuel; (wooden) furniture, fitting. **o:** ⚠ (a) cinder(s), a crisp, ash □ *'Do I smell burning?' said Charmian. 'The pie and potatoes are* ***burned to*** *cinders.'* MM □ *'You've* ***burnt***

the bacon ***to*** *a crisp!'*

burn to death [B2 pass] kill by burning. **S:** fire, blaze. **O:** occupant; passenger □ *Three people were* ***burned to death*** *in a blazing van which overturned and burst into flames late last night.* DM

burn up[1] [A1] come to life, flare up (q v), as fuel is added. **S:** fire, stove □ *He threw a log on the fire, and it* ***burned up*** *with a crackle.*

burn up[2] [B1i pass adj] consume, get rid of, by burning. **O:** rubbish; leaf, twig □ *Throw the scraps in the incinerator and* ***burn them up****.*

burn up[3] [A1] catch fire and be destroyed as it enters the earth's atmosphere. **S:** meteorite; rocket □ *A meteorite leaves a long, brilliant trail as it* ***burns up*** *on entering the atmosphere.*

burn-up [nom (A1)] (slang) a race at high speed on a public road between young people riding motor-cycles □ *In between* ***burn-ups*** *on the by-pass, the gang meet for talk and coffee.*

burn with [A2] (formal) be filled with, or consumed by. **o:** passion, desire; ambition □ *She* ***burned with*** *longing for her absent lover.*

burst in/into [A1 A2] enter suddenly. **S:** messenger; stranger. **o:** room, hall □ *Suddenly Mr Lee* ***burst in****, in his shirtsleeves, and rushed across the living room into his bedroom.* OBS

burst in (upon) [A1 A3 pass] interrupt suddenly and excidedly. **o:** conversation, discussion □ *A staff officer* ***burst in upon*** *their discussion with the news that the enemy was only five miles away.* □ *'I don't see why I should be expected to help,' Peter* ***burst in*** *angrily.* □ burst in usu *follows* direct speech.

burst into[1] [A2] begin, suddenly and/or violently, to cry, laugh, sing etc. **S:** listener, viewer; child, old lady. **o:** ⚠ tears, sobs; laughter, a guffaw, song □ *Aunt Annabel, who has been nervous and jumpy lately, suddenly* ***burst into*** *tears.* DC □ *As the comic got into his stride, the audience* ***burst into*** *hoots of laughter.*

burst into[2] [A2] begin suddenly to flower. **S:** (flowering) tree, shrub; hedgerow. **o:** ⚠ bloom, blossom, flower □ *The orchards seemed to have* ***burst into*** *blossom overnight.*

burst into flames [A2] begin, suddenly and violently, to burn. **S:** car, van; petrol tank; oil fire □ *A child had knocked over an oil heater, which* ***burst*** *instantly* ***into flames****.* □ *The aircraft turned on its back and* ***burst into flames****.*

burst into sight/view [A2] (of a brilliant spectacle) suddenly appear. **S:** procession, cavalcade; demonstrators, marchers □ *The cavalry escort went by; then the royal coach with its outriders* ***burst into view****.*

burst out [A1] declare suddenly and with feeling, exclaim (without necessarily interrupting) □ *He angrily* ***burst out****, 'Why don't you stop pretending you know all the answers!'*

burst out crying/laughing [A1] suddenly begin to cry/laugh; burst into[1] (q v) □ *He looked about ready to* ***burst out crying****.* TC □ *I mentioned the incident later to a tailor friend and he* ***burst out laughing****.* TO

burst out/out of [A1 A2 emph rel] leave abruptly and/or violently, free oneself by violent efforts (from). **S:** crowd, mob; prisoner. **o:** gaol; cage □ *The gate suddenly gave way and an angry crowd* ***burst out of*** *the yard.*

burst out of [A2] grow too big or fat for. **S:** (growing) child, adolescent. **o:** clothes; trousers, shorts, jacket □ *All the children were* ***bursting out of*** *their school uniforms and there was no money to buy them new ones.*

burst through [A1 A2 emph rel] make an opening and come through it with sudden violence. **S:** army; infantry, tanks; raider, bandit. **o:** front, defences; door □ *Desperate efforts were made to seal off the gap* ***through*** *which the enemy divisions had* ***burst****.*

burst upon [A2] occur suddenly to, dawn on/upon (q v). **S:** truth, realization; wisdom of a course of action □ *The truth of what his wife had been saying suddenly* ***burst upon*** *him.*

burst with [A2] show an abundance of sth. **S:** child, youth; athlete. **o:** ⚠ health, vitality, energy, enthusiasm, go □ *Lady Emily and the Honourable Giles were* ***bursting with*** *health and good looks.* WDM

bury (oneself) (away) in [B2 pass B3 pass] move to, be situated in, a remote place. **o:** country; university, library; monastery □ *What made him go and* ***bury himself in*** *the country?* □ *We found the house at last. It was* ***buried away in*** *a remote part of the Yorkshire dales.*

bury one's face/head in [B2 pass] hide one's face as a sign of grief or pain, or so that others will not see one's expression or tears. **o:** ⚠ one's hands, handkerchief, the apron, bed-clothes □ *Suddenly the truth struck me, and I wanted to sit down and* ***bury my face in*** *my hands.* TC □ *Guy sat down and* ***buried his head in*** *the bed-clothes. He began to sob.* DC

bury (oneself) in [B2 pass rel] become deeply involved in. **o:** work; paper, book □ *Right after dinner, he would go into the study and* ***bury himself in*** *his paper-work.* □ *'Don't disturb your father: he's* ***buried in*** *the crossword.'*

buried under [pass (B2)] ⇨ entry after buoy up[3].

bust up [B1i nom pass adj] (informal) destroy, break up[7] (q v). **S:** rival, competitor; philanderer. **O:** partnership; marriage □ *Everything was fine between John and me until that woman stepped in and* ***bust us up****.* □ *Most of us could see the* ***bust-up*** *of their marriage coming.* ⇨ next entry.

bust-up [nom B1] (informal) violent quarrel □ *We could hear a tremendous* ***bust-up*** *going on in the next room — china being thrown all over the place.* ⇨ previous entry.

bustle about/around [A1 A2] move about briskly and busily. **o:** place, house □ *Mary* ***bustled about*** *in the kitchen getting a meal together while Peter found us something to drink.*

busy oneself (with) [B2 rel] occupy oneself, be busy, with a task. **o:** preparations, housework; cooking a meal, cleaning the kitchen; car, boat; carpentry, decorating □ *She always manages to find something to* ***busy herself with****.* □ *'I brought a thermos-flask with me.' He leant over and* ***busied himself with*** *a basket.* QA

butt in[1] [A1] (informal) interrupt (a conversation) rudely □ *I wish you wouldn't keep* ***butting in*** *when we are in the middle of a conversation.*

butt in[2] [A1] (informal) intervene, interfere, meddle □ *Of course, I don't want to* ***butt in*** *on the technical side.* RM □ *It's better that his affairs should be handled by one man. It makes confusion if someone else* ***butts in****.* PW

butter up [B1i pass] (informal) praise or flatter

insincerely (with a view to obtaining favours etc). **S:** employee, junior colleague. **O:** boss, employer, professor □ *'I wish he'd stop trying to* ***butter*** *me* ***up****. I hate hypocrisy.'*

butter up to [A3 pass] (informal) try to get close to sb by flattering him insincerely. **S:** junior boy; novice, recruit. **o:** prefect; boss, foreman □ *'Don't bother* ***buttering up to*** *me. I'm too old a hand to be won over by flattery.'*

button up [B1 pass adj] (informal) conclude or finalize (arrangements). **S:** committee, organizer, team. **O:** it all, the whole thing, all the details □ *I haven't said a word about it yet and I shan't, not till it's all* ***buttoned up****.* RFW □ usu passive.

buttoned up [pass adj (B1)] (informal) (be) secretive; (be) reserved, shy □ *He hasn't said a word about our part in the plan: he's terribly* ***buttoned up****.* □ *I've always found him an awkward,* ***buttoned-up*** *sort of fellow.* □ passive with *be, appear, seem.*

buy in [B1iii pass] buy a stock of sth (as a precaution in the event of a shortage). **O:** stock, supply; sugar, soap □ *People* ***bought in*** *stocks of tinned goods in anticipation of food rationing.*

buy oneself in/into [B1ii B2] obtain a share in (the control of) a business by buying stock. **o:** firm, business, company □ *A number of British companies are now* ***buying themselves into*** *European commerce and industry.*

buy off [B1i pass] (informal) persuade sb, by paying him money, not to act against one's interests. **S:** intending purchaser; superstitious fellow; victim of blackmail. **O:** competitor, business rival; god, demon; blackmailer □ *'If you're trying to* ***buy me off****, I'm afraid you've come to the wrong person.'* □ *Don't ignore his threats to report you: he'll have to be* ***bought off****.*

buy out[1] [B1ii pass] (military) obtain sb's release from the armed forces by a cash payment. **S:** soldier, sailor, airman; friend, relative. **O:** himself, themselves; son, brother □ *Those who find they don't like the life can* ***buy*** *themselves* ***out*** *for £20 between their eighth and twelfth week of training.* ST

buy out[2] [B1i pass] pay someone to give up a post, or a share in a business (often to secure a controlling interest oneself). **S:** partner, shareholder, chairman □ *New members can join by* ***buying out*** *an existing member at the current price of units.* H □ *Balzac's associates had persuaded him to* ***buy*** *them* ***out****, so that he was now sole proprietor.* PTLB

buy up [B1i pass] buy all, or as much as possible, of sth; obtain complete financial control over it. **S:** speculator, property tycoon, rival firm. **O:** land, property, office-space □ *A Manchester finance house is making a bid to* ***buy up*** *the entire company.* □ *All the land for miles around has been* ***bought up*** *by one speculator.*

buzz off [A1] (slang) leave, clear off[1] (q v) □ *He just* ***buzzed off*** *and left his wife to cope with the house and children.*

C

cage in [B1i pass adj] confine, limit sb's freedom of movement □ *This animal is dangerous and should be* ***caged in****.* □ *After being confined for so long he began to get a* ***caged-in*** *feeling.*

caked in/with [pass (B2)] thickly coated with, (be) encrusted with. **S:** hair, nails; clothes, shoes, boots. **o:** mud, grease, dirt, muck, soil, soap □ *When he arrived home from the match, he was* ***caked in*** *mud from head to foot.* □ *His ears were* ***caked with*** *shaving soap when he went for his interview.*

call (about) [A2] visit sb in his home, office etc (in order to discuss or investigate sth). **o:** the gas; sb's complaint, advertisement, inquiry □ *'Excuse me, madam, I've been asked by my Head Office to* ***call about*** *your outstanding debt on the cooker.'*

call (at) [A2] ⇨ call (in) (at).

call away [B1i pass] summon from one's surgery etc to attend on sb. **S:** doctor, midwife, nurse; police constable; priest. **A:** a few minutes ago; on business; to an urgent case, an accident □ *'I'm afraid the doctor isn't in. He was* ***called away*** *a few minutes ago.'* □ very often passive, with no agent mentioned.

call by [A1 A2] make a stop at (in the course of another, longer journey), often to collect sth or sb; call (in) (at) (q v) □ *'Will you be in at five o'clock this evening? If so, I'll* ***call by*** *and pick up my saw and other tools, if you don't mind.'*

call down [B1i pass] (military) order artillery, aircraft, to attack enemy targets. **S:** (field, infantry) commander. **O:** bombardment; mortar-fire; air strike □ *If the enemy advanced into the open, he would radio his field batteries and* ***call down*** *a pre-arranged bombardment.*

call down on sb's head [B3 pass] (formal or facetious) summon, invoke. **O:** ⚠ the wrath of God, curses, fire and brimstone, the vengeance of Heaven □ *It's no use* ***calling down*** *the wrath of God* ***on the heads of*** *your enemies; something more will be necessary to defeat them.*

call (for) [A2 pass rel] go to sb's house in order to take him somewhere; go to a house, shop, cinema etc in order to collect goods, tickets etc. □ *'What time shall I* ***call for*** *you tomorrow?'* □ *'Has the boy* ***called for*** *the laundry yet?'* □ *The goods will be* ***called for*** *by Mr White's son.*

call for [A2 pass] require, demand, need. **S:** the present conditions; the age (in which we live); his state of health; success, achievements, good luck, failure. **o:** skill, care; (careful, discrete, tactful, delicate), handling, examination; the exercise of judgement; a new approach, new thinking, immediate action; celebration, party; our gratitude, commiseration □ *The identification of blood groups and the analysis of ink in forged documents can* ***call for*** *considerable skill.* NS □ *'You've got the job? This* ***calls for*** *a drink!'*

call forth [B1iii pass] (formal) cause to appear, bring out[9] (q v). **S:** (difficult) situation, operation; performance, behaviour, action. **O:** courage, spirit; the will to fight or survive; criticism, protests □ *The dark days of 1940* ***called forth*** *the* *best in the character of the British people.*

call forward [B1i pass] invite or order sb to approach the speaker, to take some steps out of a group, row etc □ *The captain of the winning team was* ***called forward*** *to receive the cup.*

call in [B1i pass] request, order, the return of sth, because it is now unsuitable or no longer needed. **S:** ministry, department; library, store, bank; manufacturer. **O:** all unsold tickets; (out-of-date, surplus), equipment; defective cars; empty containers. **A:** immediately, at once, without delay, urgently □ *The Army is* ***calling in*** *all the unwanted ammunition.* □ *How many of the cars have been* ***called in****?*

call (in) (at) [A1 A2 rel A3 rel] stop at one place on the way to another. **S:** he etc; ship, boat. **o:** café, public house; (friend's, relation's) home; the hospital, the police station; the butcher's, the chemist's; Marseilles, Karachi □ *We* ***called (in) at*** *Joe's Bar on the way home from the cinema.* □ *The ship* ***calls at*** *several ports between Aden and London.* □ *'****Call in*** *this evening, if you can; I've something important to discuss.'*

call off[1] [B1i pass] stop or give the order to stop. **S:** military commander, police officer. **O:** pursuer; dog; chase, hunt; pursuit, attack □ *As we were getting too far from our base, I decided to* ***call*** *my men* ***off****.* □ *The pursuit was* ***called off*** *when it was clear that we had won the day.*

call off[2] [B1i pass] (informal) order dogs, pursuers, to stop searching, attacking or worrying sb. **O:** ⚠ the dogs, hounds, bloodhounds □ *'Why don't you mind your own business?' he said. 'There's been no harm done, and this lady here has* ***called off*** *the dogs....'* TT □ *'You can* ***call*** *your men* ***off****, Inspector. I give up.'*

call off[3] [B1i pass] cancel, abandon, drop. **O:** the whole thing; arrangement, deal; scheme, plan, proposal; strike; journey, expedition; picnic, excursion; engagement (between a man and a woman) □ *Why don't we* ***call off*** *this competition for her love?* QA □ *'I don't see any point in going on with our idea of a picnic, in weather like this. Let's* ***call*** *it* ***off****.'*

call (on) [A2 pass rel] visit (usu for business or official reasons). **S:** salesman, traveller, our representative; (health) inspector; doctor, vicar. **o:** customers; the sick; the aged and infirm; parishioners □ *Our representative will* ***call on*** *you in the course of the next week.* □ *Have you been* ***called on*** *by the new parson?*

call on/upon (to do sth)[1] [A2 pass rel] invite, request (sb to speak etc). **S:** Chairman; Best Man. **o:** speaker, lecturer; (distinguished) guest. **Inf** to deliver his lecture, to address us; to say a few words; to propose the health of the bride □ *'I will now* ***call on*** *Mr White* ***to propose*** *a vote of thanks to the Committee.'* □ *He was seldom* ***called upon to speak*** *at these gatherings.*

call on/upon (to do sth)[2] [A2 pass rel] urge, appeal to (sb to act in some way). **o:** organization, institution, nation; friend, relation, student, colleague. **Inf** to help, support, protest □ *We shall have to* ***call upon*** *our friends* ***to help*** *us.* □ *He* ***called on*** *other churches* ***to dissociate*** *themselves from the statement.*

call out[1] [A1] give a greeting, make a request etc, in a loud voice □ *'A lovely evening,' the man* ***called out*** *to me.* ARG □ *'If you want anything from the larder, just* ***call out*** *and I'll bring it.'*

call out[2] [B1i pass] state, declare, in a loud voice. **O:** (list of) names, prices, times, quantities; score, marks; results (of a competition) □ *'Please keep quiet while I* ***call out*** *the names of the successful competitors.'* □ *When Bill's name was* ***called out****, another boy said 'Present, sir!'*

call out[3] [A1] (of schoolchildren) try to attract the teacher's attention; speak in a loud voice, without permission □ *'How many times must I tell you not to* ***call out****, Jones?'*

call out[4] [A1] shout, try to attract attention; cry out (q v). **S:** drowning man; injured child. **A:** for help; in pain □ *The starving peasants* ***called out*** *for food, but the visitors had none to give.*

call out[5] [B1i pass] summon sb (to restore order etc). **S:** Government, Home Secretary. **O:** militia, Home Guard, special constabulary □ *A practical joker picked up the telephone and* ***called out*** *the fire-brigade.*

call out[6] [B1i pass] (industrial relations) order or authorize workers to go on strike. **S:** (Trades) Union, Executive Committee. **A:** on strike; in sympathy □ *Bus-drivers may be* ***called out*** *(on strike) in support of their recent wage-claim.*

call round (at) [A1 A3] pay a visit (to). **o:** John's place, house □ *'Do* ***call round*** *when you have the time. We're at home most evenings.'* □ *'I'll* ***call round at*** *my brother's this afternoon to pick up the book.'*

call to account [B2 pass] make sb explain an error, loss, failure etc. **S:** manager, boss. **O:** clerk, cashier □ *He may think that all this petty pilfering goes unnoticed, but one day he'll be* ***called to account****.* □ *The manager was* ***called to account*** *over some missing cash.*

call to mind [B2] recall, remember. **O:** him etc; the occasion; saying, promising that... □ *'I'm sure I've met the girl you're referring to, but I can't just* ***call*** *her* ***to mind****.'* □ *'Do you know her telephone number?' 'I ought to, but I can't quite* ***call*** *it* ***to mind****.'* □ *The accused said that he could not* ***call to mind*** *making any of the statements quoted by the police officer.*

call to order [B2 pass] formally request a meeting to be silent so that business may begin or continue. **S:** chairman; mayor, president. **O:** meeting, assembly, gathering □ *At two o'clock, the chairman* ***called*** *us* ***to order*** *and the afternoon session began.* □ *Despite attempts to* ***call*** *them* ***to order****, the audience continued to stamp.*

call up[1] [B1i pass] reach, communicate with, by telephone. **O:** shop, restaurant, bar; airport; ticket-office □ *'I tried to* ***call*** *you* ***up*** *last night, but no one answered the phone. Were you out?'*

call up[2] [B1i nom pass adj] (military) summon for military or national service. **S:** Government; Army. **O:** all able-bodied men, men between the ages of 18 and 25 □ *He was* ***called up*** *right at the beginning of the war.* □ *Have you received your* ***call(ing)-up*** *papers yet?* □ *The* ***call-up*** *of the 40-42 age-group was announced on the radio.*

call up[3] [B1i pass adj] (military) summon to one's aid. **S:** army, divisional commander. **O:** reserves, reinforcements; cavalry, armour □ *He saw that he would have to* ***call*** *his reserves* ***up*** *if defeat was to be avoided.*

call up[4] [B1i pass] recall to the memory, bring back[2] (q v). **S:** incident, smell, sound. **O:** memory, scene (from the past); past life, childhood □ *The sound of seagulls* ***called up*** *happy* *memories of his childhood holidays.*

call up the Devil [B1iii] (witchcraft) cause the Devil to appear, and obtain his assistance for some nefarious purpose □ *The local coven of witches were accused of regularly* ***calling up the Devil*** *to help them in their evil work.*

call upon[1] [A2 ass rel] invite, request (sb to speak etc). ⇨ call on/upon (to do sth)[1].

call upon[2] [A2 pass rel] urge, appeal to (sb to act in some way). ⇨ call on/upon (to do sth)[2].

calm down[1] [A1] become calm or quiet, recover one's temper □ *The sea* ***calmed down*** *as soon as the wind fell.* □ *'Here, Parkinson, have a cup of coffee and* ***calm down****!' 'To hell with a cup of coffee! Listen to this!'* TBC

calm down[2] [B1i pass] make or help sb to become quiet, or control his temper. □ *It was a real lesson in the power of a woman to* ***calm*** *a man* ***down****.* CON □ ***Calming*** *him* ***down*** *took longer than I had expected.*

camp out [A1] live in a tent (usu for a holiday) □ *'There is no possibility of accommodating any more visitors.' 'I see,' said the young man. 'But couldn't I* ***camp out****?'* RM

camp up [B1ii pass] (theatre) overact to an absurd degree, and in such a way as to please an unsophisticated audience. **O:** performance; show, play; it, the whole thing □ *'If the play is intrinsically bad, you will never turn it into a success by* ***camping*** *it* ***up*** *like that! It's best to let it die a natural death, and look for something better.'*

cancel out [B1i pass adj] reduce to nothing, wipe out[2] (q v). **S:** improvement, gain, success. **O:** failure, loss, deficit □ *A large inflow of investments has* ***cancelled out*** *their indebtedness.*

cancel (each other) out [A1 B1ii] (of similar or identical things) balance; make each other ineffective. **S:** factors, conditions, characteristics □ *'But hadn't they all been naughty, even Harold, even Irma naughty, and did not their naughtinesses* ***cancel each other out****?'* PW □ *In the long run the two sets of factors* ***cancel out****.*

care for[1] [A2] be pleased or attracted by; like to have or own. **o:** neighbour, colleague; cigarette, cup of tea □ *'You don't* ***care for*** *Helena, do you?' 'You didn't seem very keen yourself, once.'* LBA □ *I don't* ***care for*** *her new curtains.*

care for[2] [A2 pass adj] be responsible for, take care (of) (q v). **S:** family; the State; doctor, nurse. **o:** children; the sick, the wounded □ *If a man is asked to risk his life for his country, he must know that, should he be killed, his wife and children will be properly* ***cared for****.* □ *We were impressed by the well-****cared-for*** *gardens.*

carp (at) (about) [A2] (informal) continually complain to sb (about sth), refer insistently and irritatingly to sth. **o:** (***about***) conditions, terms; delay, inefficiency; cleanliness, service (in a hotel) □ *'It's no use* ***carping at*** *me* ***about*** *the rotten weather!'* □ *Don't waste time* ***carping about*** *their laziness — go and speak to them.*

carry about (with one) [B1ii B3] take from place to place, take everywhere (with one). **O:** briefcase, umbrella, stick □ *Why did you want to* ***carry*** *that document* ***about with you*** *all the time? You were bound to lose it sooner or later.* DC □ *Be sure to* ***carry*** *your passport* ***about with you*** *whenever you leave the hotel.*

carry along [B1ii pass] help to continue or complete a task, race etc; give encouragement or support to. **O:** runner, swimmer, competitor, team □ *The amateur football team was* ***carried along*** *by the enthusiasm of its supporters and finally defeated the more highly-rated professional club.* □ *Although he had spent years on his research, the scientist's conviction that he was on the threshold of a great discovery* ***carried*** *him* ***along****.*

carry away[1] [B1i pass] take, remove, usu by overwhelming force. **S:** river, sea; raging waters, torrent, flood, tidal wave; hurricane, whirlwind, tornado. **O:** everything in its path; structure, house, building □ *Several houses in the village were* ***carried away*** *when the swollen river suddenly changed its course.*

carry away[2] [B1i pass] move or fill sb with emotion so that he no longer has full control over his thoughts etc. **S:** speaker; occasion; feeling, sentiment □ *When he starts to sing, he just* ***carries*** *you* ***away****.* □ *'I should have thought before I spoke. I just get* ***carried away*** *with enthusiasm.'* DC □ *Isabel was* ***carried away*** *by the thought that almost for the first time she was having a serious conversation with her husband about books.* PW □ usu passive.

carry back (to) [B1ii pass B3 pass rel] recall to mind, cause to remember; take back (to) (q v). **S:** incident, smell, sound, voice. **o:** childhood, early days; first encounter, last reunion □ *The sound of seagulls* ***carried*** *me* ***back to*** *my childhood holidays at the seaside.* ⇨ bring back[2], call up[4].

carry all/everything before one [B2] advance irresistibly; sweep aside all opposition, capture all one's objectives. **S:** troops, army; team □ *With the overwhelming forces that he had managed to build up, Montgomery finally* ***carried everything before him*** *in Africa.* □ (humorously) *'She's a well-built woman, all right. She* ***carries everything before her****!'*

carry forward [B1i pass] (finance) take a sum of money etc from one page or column to the next, or from one week, one year, to the next. **O:** total; (outstanding) debt; deficit, surplus □ *It's no use* ***carrying*** *this debt* ***forward****; we might as well write it off.* □ often abbreviated to c/f.

carry off[1] [B1i pass] seize and bear away (as a captive). **S:** enemy, gypsies, witch; bird of prey. **O:** child; (defenceless) women, child; small animal □ *People used to be afraid that the gypsies might* ***carry*** *their children* ***off****.* □ *The eagle swooped and* ***carried off*** *a sleeping lizard.*

carry off[2] [B1iii pass] win. **S:** competitor; entry. **O:** award; trophy, cup, shield □ *The visiting team of athletes* ***carried off*** *most of the medals.*

carry it off [B1ii] (informal) manage, handle, a difficult or embarrassing situation successfully □ *If Mary's former husband had come in a little earlier, the guests would have been able to* ***carry it off*** *all right, but he had caught them off balance.* CON □ *My remark had obviously annoyed her. I tried feebly to* ***carry it off****.* SPL

carry on[1] [A1] continue □ *'Please* ***carry on*** *as usual while I listen to the class.'* □ *Other dogs would growl at me — but not Bruce — he just wags his lovely thick tail and* ***carries on*** *playing.* WI □ often followed by *-ing* form of a v.

carry on[2] [A1 nom] (informal) quarrel, argue, fuss, behave, noisily □ *Old Mr Khnopff was* ***carrying on*** *about his pen; he made such a fuss you'd think it was his head.* US □ *'Did you ever* *hear such a* ***carry-on*** *about nothing at all?'* □ (i) in substandard English: carry on *something awful, something dreadful* (= in an awful or dreadful manner); (ii) the nom form carryings-on, used only in the plural: *I heard him complaining about the* ***carryings-on*** *of some town council in the paper that he was reading.* HAHA

carry on[3] [A1 B1iii pass] continue, maintain. **S:** [A1] **O:** [B1] life, existence; routine, pattern □ *'Life on earth is not going to be impossible, but it will have to be* ***carried on*** *in far less favourable circumstances.'* TBC

carry on[4] [B1iii pass] conduct, hold. **O:** conversation, talk, discussion □ *You shouldn't* ***carry on*** *long conversations with your friends when someone else is waiting to use the telephone.*

carry on[5] [B1iii pass] conduct, transact, pursue. **O:** business, occupation □ *A great many shady businesses are* ***carried on*** *through the small-ad columns of respectable newspapers.*

carry on (with) [A1 A3 rel] (informal) have an irregular affair (with) □ *'Isn't it shocking! Everyone knows that Mary's husband is* ***carrying on with*** *the woman next door.'* □ *They'd been* ***carrying on*** *for years, but his wife never knew.*

carry out[1] [B1iii pass adj] fulfil. **O:** (one's) obligations, promises, threats; plan, agreement; instructions, specifications. **A:** faithfully; punctually; to the letter □ *If this difficult phase of highways planning is to be* ***carried out*** *efficiently, the engineer has to have all the help that modern methods of survey can supply.* NS □ *This order was not popular with the armoured units, but I was determined to see that it was* ***carried out*** *to the letter.* MFM

carry out[2] [B1iii pass] perform, conduct. **O:** experiment, test □ *Before testing this method on patients, Dr Baronofsky* ***carried out*** *tests for two years on three hundred dogs.* NS

carry over [B1i pass] (finance, commerce) retain as an item to be dealt with at a later date □ *'I propose that some minor matters on the agenda should be* ***carried over*** *for consideration at the next meeting.'* □ *If you do not take the holidays at the appropriate time, you may find that you cannot* ***carry*** *them* ***over*** *to the next year.* ⇨ carry forward.

carry through[1] [B1i pass] complete, pursue to completion. **O:** aim, plan, scheme, enterprise. **A:** to the (bitter) end; in the face of/in spite of every obstacle □ *These aims will be* ***carried through*** *to the end.* MFM □ *Scheme after scheme, absolutely foolproof, has been spoilt from the beginning by my never having enough capital to* ***carry*** *it* ***through***. HAHA

carry through[2] [B1ii pass B2 pass] sustain; help to survive difficult period. **S:** God, trust in God, hope (for a better life); determination, courage, grit. **o:** crisis; war □ (hymn) *He* (i e God) *is willing to aid you; He will* ***carry*** *you* ***through***. □ *A growing confidence in the new leaders helped to* ***carry*** *the soldiers* ***through***.

carry with one[1] [B2] obtain or keep the support of; persuade sb to follow, agree with, one. **O:** majority; committee, jury; crowd, assembled company □ *Nixon's rival in the 1972 Presidential Election appeared at first to be* ***carrying*** *the whole youth of the country* ***with him***.

carry with one[2] [B2] retain, be always aware or reminded of. **O:** memory, impression; guilt; happy recollection □ *I shall always* ***carry with me*** *the memory of that child's tortured face.*

carve out a career for oneself [B3] make, build, a career as a result of great effort □ *He managed to* ***carve out a career for himself*** *as an actor, though at first he hardly earned enough to keep body and soul together.*

carve up [B1i nom pass] (informal) dismember. **S:** victors, (victorious) allies. **O:** country, territory, state □ *The victors mercilessly* ***carved up*** *the defeated country, each taking an equal share.* □ *The great powers stood by and watched the* ***carve-up*** *of this remote and seemingly unimportant country.*

cash in (on) [A1 A3 pass rel] (informal) exploit, get the benefit of. **S:** (trade) rival, competitor; colleague, associate. **o:** shortage, scarcity; boom, expansion; discovery, success □ *The great problem is to prevent others* ***cashing in*** *before we've had time to market the product.* □ *He* ***cashed in on*** *the sudden popularity of Victorian bric-a-brac by selling all his old unwanted ornaments at enormous prices.* □ *If I find some woman trying to* ***cash in on*** *my chivalry by lashing out with her frail little fists, I lash back at her.* LBA □ note casher-in: *He's a great* ***casher-in*** *on people's financial difficulties: he lends money at an exorbitant rate.*

cast about for [A3 rel] seek, try to find, usu hurriedly or in an emergency; cast round for (q v). **o:** solution, answer; expedient, device; means, method (of escape) □ *He* ***cast about*** *in his mind* ***for*** *some plausible excuse for not turning up at the meeting.* □ *The suspect* ***cast about for*** *some way of escaping from the police-car.*

cast aside [B1i pass] remove, throw off[1] (q v); discard. **O:** coat, gloves; cares, anxieties, inhibitions; prejudice; (best) friend, (former) ally □ *'Are those your glasses,* ***cast aside*** *in the heat of passion?'* TGLY □ *As soon as he inherited his father's fortune, he* ***cast*** *his old friends* ***aside***. □ usu facetious, as in the first example, or formal as in the second.

castaway/cast away [nom pass (B1)] (be) sb left (whether by accident or deliberately); (be) sb washed ashore, after a wreck. **A:** on a desert island; far from civilization; somewhere in the Pacific □ *'If you were* ***cast away*** *on a desert island, would you be able to fend for yourself?'* □ *Robinson Crusoe is perhaps the most famous* ***castaway*** *in English literature.*

cast down [pass adj (B1)] (be) depressed, unhappy □ *He was not easily* ***cast down***, *but circumstances had combined to depress him.* □ *I've never seen such a* ***cast-down*** (or: ***downcast***) *expression!* □ passive with *be, get, seem, look*; note alt and more usu adj form: downcast.

cast in one's lot with [B3 emph rel] (formal) join, take the side of, share the fortune of. **o:** poor, needy, dispossessed; regime, established order; opposition; enemy, invader □ *After much hesitation, he decided to* ***cast in his lot with*** *the rebels.* □ *'If you* ***cast your lot in with*** *that crowd of layabouts, you'll soon be in trouble.'*

cast off[1] [A1] (nautical) release the ropes or cables used to hold a boat or ship in position alongside a quay etc. **S:** sailor, crew; ship, boat □ *The order was given to* ***cast off*** *and soon the ship was moving away from the quay.*

cast off[2] [B1i nom pass adj] remove, temporarily or permanently; take off and throw aside carelessly. **O:** clothes; jacket, shoes □ *He **cast off** his clothes and dived in to the cool water of the lake.* □ *She gives her **cast-offs** to her maid.*

cast off[3] [B1i nom pass adj] abandon, reject. **O:** lover, mistress □ *When he grows tired of a woman, he just **casts** her **off** like an old coat.* □ *He did not enjoy the role of the **cast-off** lover.* □ *This is a tale of Christian hope brought to the **cast-offs** of the affluent society.* T

cast off (stitches) [A1 B1iii pass] remove stitches from the needles, in knitting □ *At last she reached the end of the sleeve, and **cast off** with a sigh of relief.* □ *At the end of each line she **cast off** two **stitches**.* ⇨ next entry.

cast on (stitches) [A1 B1iii pass] put the first line of stitches on a knitting needle. □ She had to ***cast on** extra **stitches** to make the pullover wide enough.* □ *How many **(stitches)** do you **cast on** — twenty or twenty-two?* ⇨ previous entry.

cast out [B1i pass] expel, drive away. **O:** animals; weaklings; wrongdoers, perverts □ *The old animals were **cast out** from the herd.* LWK □ ***Cast out** from the society of his fellow-men, he wandered aimlessly about the country.* □ nom form is outcast: *The poor fellow had to live like an **outcast** when his last penny had gone.*

cast an eye/one's eyes over [B2] study, but only superficially; examine quickly □ *'Would you mind **casting an eye over** these calculations to see if you can spot any obvious mistakes?'* □ *It isn't enough just to **cast your eyes over** a second-hand car that you're thinking of buying: you should get an expert's report on it.*

cast round for [A3 rel] try to find, seek, usu hurriedly or in an emergency; cast about for (q v). **o:** pretext, excuse; explanation, answer □ *I **cast round for** a reasonable excuse to leave my guests. In the end, I simply walked out.*

cast up (on) [B1i pass adj B3 pass emph rel] throw, deposit (upon). **S:** sea, wave, tide. **O:** flotsam and jetsam; dead fish; body; seaweed. **o:** shore, beach; reef, rock □ *The shipwrecked sailors were **cast up on** the shore of a desert island.* □ *The sea **casts up** the detritus of civilization on rocks and beaches all over Europe.*

catch at a straw [A2] try to grasp some slight means of rescue or escape □ (proverb) *A drowning man will **catch at a straw**.* □ *Our close questioning had him floundering about, **catching at straws**.* ⇨ grasp at a straw.

catch in the act [B2 pass] surprise sb while he is committing a crime, catch red-handed □ *The police **caught** the thieves **in the act**: they were just opening the factory safe.* □ *He was **caught in the act** of embezzling money.* □ often passive.

catch in (at the waist) [B1i pass B3 pass] draw a loose garment together with a belt etc. **O:** dress; robe □ *This dress is rather loose, but it only needs **catching in** a little **at the waist**.*

catch on [A1] (informal) understand, see the significance of sth □ *'He's not very quick at **catching on**, is he?'* □ *He followed the conversation rather blankly for a while, then his expression changed. He was **catching on**.*

catch on (with) [A1 A3] (informal) become popular or fashionable. **S:** (new) idea, method, suggestion, fashion. **o:** the public; young people; customers; colleagues □ *The President's idea of rapid-fire legislation has not **caught on** in Congress.* SC □ *We thought of opening a bar downstairs, but the suggestion never **caught on with** the older committee members.*

catch out[1] [B1ii pass] show that sb is ignorant or doing sth wrong; and often, do this in a mean-minded way □ *The little girl saw she had been **caught out**. She looked as if she were going to cry; but then her face brightened again.* PW □ *He wouldn't know a fraud if he saw one. I know, because I've **caught** him **out**.* ASA □ *He tried to **catch** me **out** with his smart questions.* HD

catch out[2] [B1i pass] (cricket) dismiss a batsman by catching the ball after he has touched it with his bat and before it touches the ground □ *Three of the batsmen were **caught out** by the wicket-keeper* (= caught behind the wicket).

catch up[1] [B1i] seize, gather to oneself, hastily □ *The woman **caught up** her basket and ran out of the shop before anyone could stop her.* □ *He **caught** the child **up** in his arms.*

catch up[2] [B1i pass B3 pass] raise and fasten sth hanging free or loose. **O:** hem, skirt (of a dress); hair □ *Her hair was **caught up** with a long pin.*

catch up (in) [B1i pass B3 pass] trap **O:** hair; clothing. **o:** machine, machinery; wheel, cogwheel; (overhanging) branches, undergrowth □ *The poor boy had **caught** his coat **up in** the chain of his bicycle, and this caused the accident.* □ *She disentangled the sleeve of her jumper, which had got **caught up in** a rose bush.*

caught up in ⇨ entries after cater to.

catch up (on)[1] [A1 A3 pass] (informal) (make special efforts to) do sth which has been left undone, or neglected. **o:** reading, studies; sorting, tidying, cleaning □ *The secretary had to work in the lunch hour to **catch up on** her neglected filing.* WI

catch up (on)[2] [A1 A3 pass] get up-to-date with, become 'au fait' with. **o:** recent developments; the latest fashions; new thinking in sth □ *These are clothes that you can make from fabulous American patterns — but if you don't sew you can still **catch up on** new fashion pointers from across the Atlantic.* WI

catch up on [A3] (informal) overtake; defeat; change (a person's outlook or way of life). **S:** old age; rheumatism; marriage; (misspent) youth, (dubious) past □ *Marriage has **caught up on** her, she explained after some hesitation and a little smile that made me think I ought to sympathize.* HAHA □ *'I think his past is beginning to **catch up on** him.'*

catch up (with) [A1 A3 pass rel B1ii pass] (informal) draw level (with), reach the same stage (as) (after lagging behind). **S:** runner; cyclist, driver; car; student, worker. **o:** [A3] **O:** [B1] pack, main body (of runners); (main) party, column; rest of the class □ [A1 A3] *'You go on ahead; I'll **catch up** (**with** you) later* (or: [B1] *I'll **catch** you **up** later*).*'* □ [A3] *He's working hard to **catch up with** the others* (or: [B1] ***catch** them **up***), *after missing a term.*

cater for [A2 pass rel] serve the public, by providing refreshments; aim to satisfy (the needs of) particular groups. **S:** hotel, public house; club, cinema, TV. **o:** class, type (of customer); teenager, married couple □ *The management regrets that coach-parties cannot be **catered for**.* □ *This play centre **caters for** children of all ages.* □

There are groups of viewers that television doesn't seriously attempt to ***cater for****: those interested in hunting, shooting or avant-garde music, for instance.* ⇨ next entry.

cater to [A2 pass rel] aim to satisfy a stated need or demand. **o:** sb's sick mind; depraved taste, base appetite; sb's whims □ *Producers of pornographic material often claim that they are* ***catering to*** *a psychological need.* ⇨ previous entry.

caught up in[1] [pass (B3)] (be) involved in, usu involuntarily and sometimes against one's will. **o:** crowd, circle, set (of people); intrigue, plotting; war, revolution; (mad) whirl, round (of activity) □ *For a time my father, with a young wife, was* ***caught up in*** *a circle which included many famous names.* SD □ *He knew that one day he would be* ***caught up in*** *the war, like all his friends.* ⇨ catch up (in).

caught up in[2] [pass (B3)] (be) lost in, completely absorbed in. **o:** speculation; day-dream, reverie □ *When one is adolescent, one often gets* (or: *is*) ***caught up in*** *one's thoughts and dreams.* HAHA

cave in[1] [A1 nom] collapse. **S:** roof, mine, dugout □ *The roof of the mine* ***caved in*** *as a result of the explosion.* □ *The* ***caved-in*** *part of the passage was immediately beneath a row of houses.* □ *This tunnel is liable to sudden* ***cave-ins.*** □ the adj form is unusual in this [A1] pattern.

cave in[2] [A1 nom] (informal) yield, collapse morally (under some kind of pressure). **S:** prisoner, suspect □ *Under close questioning, the wretched man* ***caved in*** *abjectly and confessed all his misdemeanours.* □ *We'd expected some firm resistance on the part of the employers to the workers' demands, not a complete* ***cave-in****!*

centre in/on/upon [A2 emph rel B2 pass emph rel] have as, give to sth as, its focal point, its main concern. **S:** [A2] **O:** [B2] study, research; survey; attention, interest. **o:** field, area; problem □ *For some time all my interests have* ***centred in*** *the people's methods of agriculture.* NDN □ *His current work is* ***centred upon*** *the activity of small rodents.* ⇨ focus (on).

centre on/round [A2 emph rel B2 pass emph rel] have, fix, as its centre; (cause to) revolve about/around (q v). **S:** [A2] **O:** [B2] movement, activity; commerce, industry. **o:** (key) figure, personality; port, capital city □ *She became involved in the whirlpool of activity which* ***centred round*** *Joe.* AITC □ *To give access to markets, the new industries had been* ***centred on*** *a motorway junction.* □ some purists object to the use of round with the v centre.

chain up [B1i pass adj] restrain movement by means of a chain, or chains. **O:** dog, hound, dangerous animal; prisoner, captive □ *That dog ought to be* ***chained up****; it's dangerous.*

chalk out [B1i pass adj] make, draw, (the outline of) sth in chalk. **O:** outline, plan; limit, edge; ring, square □ *Goalposts were roughly* ***chalked out*** *on the playground wall.* □ *To explain his design to the visitors, the architect* ***chalked out*** *a simple plan on the blackboard.*

chalk up[1] [B1i pass] (informal) add to the, or one's, record, or score. **O:** victory, achievement, another one □ *In the first six months of this year the hotel-owner will have* ***chalked up****, round the world, thirteen opening ceremonies.* OBS □ *A group of Britons have* ***chalked up*** *a British record by descending nearly 4 000 feet down a cave in France.* T

chalk up[2] [B1i pass] write on a board or slate; specifically, give credit to a customer in a public house for drinks consumed □ *'I see your name is* ***chalked up*** *on the messages board.' 'Oh, is it? Thanks very much for telling me.'* □ *'Two double whiskies, and... oh,* ***chalk*** *it* ***up****, please?'*

change back into [A3 B3 pass] return to one-'s/his etc former shape, character etc □ *Dr Jekyll took a potion and* ***changed back into*** *Mr Hyde.* □ *When the princess went to bed she found that the toad had been* ***changed back into*** *a handsome prince.* ⇨ change (from) (into)

change down [A1 nom] (in driving a car) move to a lower gear □ *I didn't* ***change down*** *quickly enough, and stalled the motor.* CON □ *'That was a sudden* ***change-down****. You nearly threw me through the windscreen!'* ⇨ change up.

change (from) (into) [A2 rel B2 pass rel] (of the appearance, constitution or character of sb or sth) alter; transform. **S:** [A2] **O:** [B2] pumpkin; white rabbit; patient, invalid. **S:** [B2] magician; drugs, alcohol; disease □ *As the fairy godmother waved her wand, the four mice* ***changed into*** *splendid white horses.* □ *His sickness* ***changed*** *him* ***into*** *a miserable, demanding old man.* □ *He suddenly* ***changed from*** *a well-behaved child* ***into*** *a loutish adolescent.* ⇨ change back into.

change (into)[1] [B2 pass rel] break a larger unit of money into smaller ones; give for the currency of one country the equivalent currency of another. **O:** pound; dollar; francs; lire. **o:** new pence; dimes, quarters; sterling; deutschmarks □ *'Could you* ***change*** *this fifty pence* ***into*** *five tens for me, please?'* □ *You can* ***change*** *your sterling* ***into*** *the local currency at the airport.*

change (into)[2] [A2 rel] put on a garment, or garments (having removed another, or others). **o:** (clean, fresh) clothes; (smart) suit; (casual, old) sweater □ *'Just a minute, I'll* ***change into*** *something smarter.'* ⇨ next entry.

change (out of) [A2 rel] remove a garment, or garments (in order to put on another, or others). **o:** (old, dirty) clothes; overalls; (smart) suit □ *'Let's go for a walk.' 'All right; I'll just* ***change out of*** *these old things.'* LBA ⇨ previous entry.

change over (from) (to) [A1 nom A3 emph rel] adopt something new or different; change one's activity or profession. **o:** (***from***) one system, diet, regime, scheme; (***to***) another, a new one □ *Britain recently adopted the decimal system for its money; it* ***changed over*** *relatively smoothly* (or: *the* ***change-over*** *was relatively smooth*). □ *He used to drink tea at breakfast, but he's* ***changed over to*** *coffee.* □ *My wife wants to* ***change over from*** *gas* ***to*** *electricity for her cooking; she says it's cleaner.* □ *He decided against the Church, became a law student, but finally* ***changed over to*** *medicine.* SNP

change over/round[1] [A1] (of two people) exchange places, positions or roles; change places (with) (q v) □ *'I think I'd better drive the car into Birmingham, so if you'll stop at the next parking-place, we'll* ***change over****.'* □ *'Perhaps you and Brown had better* ***change round****: you need more experience of office routine.'*

change over/round[2] [A1 nom] (sport) (of opponents) change positions, change ends. **S:** players, teams, competitors, bowlers □ *After a* *certain number of points, the players* ***changed round*** *so that neither could benefit unduly from the wind or the position of the sun.* ▫ *After the* ***change-over*** *at half time, the visiting team had the benefit of the wind and scored three goals in quick succession.*

change round (from) (to) [A1 A3] (of the direction of the wind) alter, shift ▫ *The wind suddenly* ***changed round from*** *westerly* ***to*** *northerly, bringing with it the threat of snow.*

change up [A1 nom] (in driving a car) move to a higher gear ▫ *'I grind the gears whenever I* ***change up*** *from second to third. Is there something wrong with the clutch?'* ▫ (a driving instructor is speaking) *'Now a nice, smooth* ***change-up*** *to third. That's fine. Now just take it quietly along this straight bit of road.'* ⇨ change down.

change places (with) [B2] (of two people or groups etc) make reciprocal changes in seats, places, positions; change over/round ⚠11 (q v) ▫ *'Let me* ***change places with*** *you* (or: *Let's* ***change places****) so that you can be nearer the fire—I can see you're very cold!'* ▫ *'I wouldn't* ***change places with*** *Joe for all the tea in China: working on a sewage farm must be hellish!'*

charge (at) [A2 pass emph rel] make a headlong attack (towards). **S:** bull, goat, horse; tank; footballer. **o:** door, barrier, fence; adversary; goalkeeper, defender ▫ *He* ***charged at*** *me with his head down and both fists flying.*

charge (for) [A2 pass B2 pass] ask in payment (for). **O:** (a heavy) price, fee; ten pounds; ten per cent commission. **o:** admission, seat; treatment, service; cleaning, repairing ▫ *'How much do they* ***charge for*** *washing a car?'* ▫ *The conductor tried to* ***charge*** *me fivepence* ***for*** *a fourpence journey.* ▫ often with an indirect object as in the second example.

charge (up) to [B2 pass emph rel B3 pass] put on sb's account for later payment; debit to (q v). **O:** goods, purchases; clothing, durables. **o:** him etc; his etc account ▫ *'Please* ***charge*** *these goods* ***to*** *my husband's account.'* ▫ *'Why were the expenses of the reception* ***charged up to*** *me?'*

charge (with)[1] [B2 pass emph rel] (legal) allege that sb is guilty of; accuse (of) (q v). **o:** crime, misdemeanour; murder, theft, unlawful possession; being an accessory after the fact ▫ *The policeman* ***charged*** *him* ***with*** *driving a car while under the influence of alcohol.* ▫ *The offence* ***with*** *which he is* ***charged*** *carries a heavy penalty.*

charge (with)[2] [B2 pass emph rel] fill, make heavy (with). **O:** atmosphere, air; situation; theatre. **o:** excitement, fear; tension, expectation ▫ *His entry on stage had once again* ***charged*** *the scene* ***with*** *dramatic tension.* ▫ *The atmosphere was tense and* ***charged with*** *fear.* ▫ *It was a stucco wall, blank but unforgettably beautiful, empty but* ***charged with*** *all the meaning and the mystery of existence.* DOP ▫ usu passive.

charge with [B2 pass rel] (formal) allot a duty (to sb). **o:** task, job; duty, responsibility ▫ *The young officer was* ***charged with*** *the task of taking 200 prisoners to the rear.* ▫ usu passive.

chase around/round (after) [A1 A3] (informal) pursue, occupy one's time and energy with or in pursuit of. **o:** girls, women, dollies, rich widows ▫ *If he didn't spend so much of his time* ***chasing around after*** *girls he might have some chance of getting through his finals.*

chase up [B1i pass] (informal) make an effort to find quickly. **O:** information, latest figures, title of the book ▫ *While John was busy working out the main plot of the story, Peter was* ***chasing up*** *some relevant facts about a murder that had been committed in the village fifty years before.*

chat up [B1i pass] (slang) talk to sb in such a way as to gain his or her confidence, usu for the purpose of having an affair ▫ *'Who was that girl I saw you* ***chatting up*** *in the café last night?'* ▫ *Mary was being* ***chatted up*** *by a bearded youth when I arrived on the scene.*

chatter away [A1] keep talking in an idle or foolish way ▫ *Despite the horrors and anxieties of the previous two months, she* ***chattered away*** *as if it had all been a gay adventure.*

cheat (at) [A2 rel] (esp in games of skill or games involving gambling) play unfairly (at). **o:** cards, bridge, dominoes ▫ *He was asked to resign from the club when he was discovered* ***cheating at*** *cards.*

cheat of [B2 pass emph rel] prevent from enjoying. **S:** (cruel) Fate, circumstances; war, (economic) slump. **o:** achievement (of sth), success; fortune, wealth ▫ *The cat was* ***cheated of*** *its prey by the warning cries of the parent birds.* ▫ *It was the lack of a proper education,* ***of*** *which he had been* ***cheated*** *by his parents' poverty, which he felt most keenly.*

cheat out of [B2 pass rel] prevent from having by unfair or illegal means. **S:** (business) partner, associate; (dishonest) trader; relations. **o:** rights, privileges; share, portion; legacy ▫ *The poor child was* ***cheated out of*** *his inheritance by a dishonest lawyer.* ▫ *'Be careful! He'll* ***cheat*** *you* ***out of*** *your entitlement if he possibly can.'*

check in (at) [A1 nom A3 rel] sign the register, on arriving at a hotel etc; report one's arrival (to sb in authority at a place designated for the purpose). **S:** guest, visitor ▫ *'What time did they* ***check in****?'* ▫ *They had an accident on the road and did not* ***check in at*** *their hotel until after midnight.* ▫ *'Don't forget we've got to produce our tickets at the* ***check-in*** *point.'* ▫ *Having got through the* ***check-in****, they began to feel more relaxed.*

check off [B1i pass adj] mark items on a list as correct or as having been dealt with. **S:** despatch clerk; storeman; receptionist. **O:** item, entry; spare part, tool, component; name, guest ▫ *Please* ***check off*** *these parcels before they are despatched.*

check on [A2 pass] verify; investigate. **o:** presence, absence; number, tally, score; whether/if sb is present etc ▫ *She wanted to find out whether the children had their coats or not; she looked in the cloakroom to* ***check on*** *that.*

check out [B1i pass] (esp US) make a systematic inspection of a number of (listed) things. **O:** instruments, various systems; tyre-pressures ▫ *When all the instruments had been* ***checked out*** *according to the established routine, the pilot signalled that he was ready for take-off.* ▫ *We'd better* ***check*** *the whole place* ***out*** *in case it's been bugged.*

check out/out of [A1 nom A2] go through the formalities (such as paying a bill) before leaving. **S:** guest, visitor. **o:** hotel, self-service store, supermarket □ *'Has Mr Jones left yet?' 'Yes, he* ***checked out*** *five minutes ago.'* □ *We reached the* ***check-out*** *(counter), then discovered that we hadn't got enough money for all the things we'd collected from the shelves.*

check over [B1i pass adj] examine sth to find out if it is correct. **O:** bill, statement; list, letter, page □ *The secretary always* ***checked over*** *the letters before putting them on the director's desk.* □ ***Check*** *the manuscript* ***over*** *carefully before passing it to the typist.*

check through [A2 pass B1ii pass] inspect; ensure that the objects that are supposed to be present are in fact present; read, and look for errors in, written or printed matter □ *'Please* ***check through*** *the laundry and then put it away.'* □ [B1] *'Have you* ***checked*** *these proofs* ***through*** (or: [A2] *Have you* ***checked through*** *these proofs)?'* □ *'This account is full of mistakes! Wasn't it ever* ***checked through****?'*

check-up [nom (A1)] medical examination (usu of sb who now feels anxious about his health) □ *You'd better go to the doctor for a* ***check-up;*** *that cough sounds serious to me.* □ *I got a thorough medical* ***check-up*** *before going abroad.*

check up (on) [A1 A3 pass adj] investigate the behaviour, background etc of sb; test the truth or soundness of sth. **o:** him etc; story, account; movements; trustworthiness, reliability; the situation □ *'You've decided not to go back to your country?' 'You've been* ***checking up****?'* QA □ *An experiment was carried out to* ***check up on*** *the reliability of certain criteria.* □ *A fully* ***checked-up(-on)*** *set of figures was presented.*

cheer on [B1i pass] encourage (to further efforts). **O:** competitor, athlete □ *The crowd* ***cheered*** *the runners* ***on*** *as they started on the last lap of the race.*

cheer up[1] [A1] (informal) become happier, more cheerful □ *When she heard that her mother was safe she immediately* ***cheered up.*** □ *'You must* ***cheer up,*** *Mrs Gaye. You'll soon be walking again....'* DC □ (wryly humorous) ***'Cheer up!*** *The worst is yet to come!'*

cheer up[2] [B1i pass] (informal) raise the spirits of, make more cheerful. **O:** patient, invalid. **A:** no end, enormously □ *They sent the invalid a 'Get Well' card to* ***cheer*** *him* ***up.*** WI □ *The news of your return to this country has* ***cheered*** *me* ***up*** *no end.* □ *I'm going to see my father; he needs* ***cheering up*** (or: *to be* ***cheered up***) *after my mother's death.*

cheese off [B1i pass adj] (slang) make heartily sick or tired (of sth), make despondent, fed up (with) (q v); brown off (q v) □ *He's fed up with army discipline; every time I see him he tells me how* ***cheesed off*** *he is.* □ *What finally* ***cheesed*** *me* ***off*** *was being passed over when the Director's job fell vacant.*

chew on [A2 pass] (informal) consider slowly and carefully. **o:** offer, proposal, suggestion □ *'I'll give you till tomorrow to* ***chew on*** *my offer; you can take it or leave it.'* ⇨ next entry.

chew over [B1i pass] (informal) consider slowly and carefully. **O:** offer, proposal, suggestion □ *'You've had long enough to* ***chew*** *the matter* ***over;*** *I want my answer now.'* ⇨ previous entry.

chicken out/out of [A1 A3] (informal) lose one's courage (in the face of an enemy, or in a dangerous situation) □ *They feared that their allies would* ***chicken out*** *at the last moment.* □ *'You've come so far; you're not thinking of* ***chickening out of*** *the holdup now, are you?'*

chime in (with) [A1 A3] (informal) contribute to a conversation, interrupt it □ *'Can you think of some ready way of stopping him from* ***chiming in****?'* □ *The rest of us* ***chimed in with*** *short accounts of various ways we had developed of annoying the poor old chap.* CON

chime in with [A3] (informal) fit, suit. **o:** mood, feelings, wishes, desires hopes, plans □ *What he had said* ***chimed in*** *perfectly* ***with*** *Isabel's own immediate reaction; she exclaimed: 'Well, I am glad!'* PW

chip in (with)[1] [A1 A3] (informal) interrupt (a conversation); comment □ *I* ***chipped in*** *and said that in the Army whenever the Pay Code was mentioned everyone began to curse.* □ *'Who asked* you *to* ***chip in with*** *your opinion?'*

chip in (with)[2] [A1 A3] (informal) contribute. **o:** loan, offer (of money) □ *As usual, George was broke, so he couldn't* ***chip in*** *towards Mr Goatly's retirement present.* □ *'When Dad offered* ***to chip in with*** *£50 toward our holiday, we realized that it might just be possible to buy an old car and do a tour of Europe.'*

chisel out of [B2 pass] (informal) obtain by a trick, or deceit; cheat out of (q v). **o:** his money, share of property; entitlement; free time, holiday, tea-break □ *The boys were in a surly mood having been, as they thought,* ***chiselled out of*** *their right to a half holiday.* □ *'Watch that chap. He'll* ***chisel*** *you* ***out of*** *every penny you've got if you're not careful!*

chivvy along [B1ii pass] (informal) urge sb (often in an irritating or officious manner) to do sth, esp work, and usu to complete it by a certain time □ *The men were getting tired of being* ***chivvied along*** *by the corporal, and though they made a show of busy activity, progress in fact became slower and slower.* ⇨ jolly along.

choke back [B1i pass] suppress, restrain. **O:** tears, sobs; anger, fury □ *When she saw the pitiful condition of the children, she could barely* ***choke back*** *her tears.*

choke off (for) [B1i pass B3 pass] (slang) interrupt somewhat rudely or abruptly; reprimand sb severely (for doing sth); tell off (for) (q v) □ *Gerald felt a revulsion from the whole subject and hoped he would hear no more about it; he decided that if Vin phoned he would* ***choke*** *him* ***off.*** ASA □ *He got a terrible* ***choking off*** *from his father* ***for*** *borrowing the car without permission.*

choke the life out of [B2] kill by strangling; (fig) force to stop trading or operating □ *He grasped her by the throat and started to* ***choke the life out of*** *her.* □ *The government has nearly* ***choked the life out of*** *privately-run schools.*

choke up [B1i pass] block. **S:** mud, dirt; leaves, sticks; rubbish. **O:** drain, pipe, grid □ *The drains are all* ***choked up*** *with leaves.*

choked up (about) [pass (B1 B3)] (informal) (be) angry or upset, usu unnecessarily or neurotically so □ *'For God's sake don't tell Bill I've been seeing you,' she said. 'You know how* ***choked up*** *he gets* ***about*** *that kind of thing.'* □ *'What's wrong with old Carstairs this morning?' 'Oh, he's all* ***choked up about*** *Gerald being*

promoted over him.' □ passive with *be, get, look.*
chop about [A1] (informal) keep changing from one thing to another, from one direction to another □ *'First you say you want to be a doctor; then you're going to be a teacher; then you think you'll join the Army; I wish you wouldn't* **chop about** *so much.'* □ the expression *chop and change* means much the same.
chop down [B1i pass] bring to the ground by cutting at the base. **O:** tree, bush; post, pole □ *I'm going to* **chop down** *some of the old apple trees; they've almost stopped producing fruit.*
chop off [B1i pass] remove by cutting (usu with an axe) □ *These branches are overhanging the road; we'd better* **chop** *them* **off**. □ *In some countries, the hands of a thief are* **chopped off**.
chop up [B1i pass adj] cut into small pieces (usu with a heavy knife, or axe). **O:** meat, fish; fruit; mint, parsley □ *This furniture is so old and useless that you might as well* **chop** *it* **up** *for firewood.* □ *You will need a few sprigs of* **chopped-up** *parsley for the sauce.*
chuck away [B1i pass] (informal) not use properly, fail to take advantage of; throw away[2] (q v). **O:** fortune, cash; chances, opportunities □ *There were plenty of people ready to help Paul* **chuck** *his money* **away**, *but few to stand by him when he ended up bankrupt.* □ *He* **chucked away** *his opportunity of making a career for himself in the Civil Service and played around with some obscure religion in California.*
chuck oneself away on [B3] (informal) marry, keep company with, squander one's time, energy or money on, sb who is unworthy of one (in the opinion of others) □ *He was a fool to* **chuck himself away on** *such a frivolous woman.*
chuck out/out of [B1i pass B2 pass] (slang) remove forcibly, force to go. **o:** bar, club, pub; college, university; association □ *He didn't leave of his own free will; he was* **chucked out**. □ *I met him shortly after he'd been* **chucked out of** *University for persistent idleness.* □ note chucker-out: *When he asked for a job at the night-club, the manager said: 'Well, you're a big strong chap, and it just happens that we need a* **chucker-out**.*'* HD
chuck under the chin [B2pass] (informal) touch or stroke affectionately or playfully under the chin □ *The father* **chucked** *his little daughter* **under the chin** *and said 'Have you been a good girl today?'*
chuck up [B1i pass] (informal) abandon, leave. **O:** ⚠ one's job, post, position; everything □ *John just* **chucked up** *his job at the factory and said he intended never to work again.* □ *The job at the sewage farm was so unpleasant that it was* **chucked up** *by everyone who tried it.*
chug along [A1] move along slowly (accompanied by a deep note from its engine). **S:** (old) ship, boat; steamer, tug, tramp(-steamer) □ *The old ship kept* **chugging along** *although it was almost falling to pieces with age.*
chum up (with) [A1 A3] (informal) get on friendly terms with □ *George wondered whether he would enjoy a holiday in a small fishing village; but he soon* **chummed up with** *the fishermen's sons* (or: *he and the fishermen's sons soon* **chummed up**) *and they all had a wonderful time.*
churn out [B1i pass adj] (informal) produce regularly and in large quantities (usu with the implication that quality is poor). **O:** book; news, information; power; car, refrigerator, newspaper □ *Some pulp writers* **churn out** *two or three thousand words a day.* □ *They've got factories working round the clock,* **churning out** *cheap cloth for the mass market.*
churn up [B1i pass adj] disturb or move violently. **O:** water, slush; mud, sand □ *The ship's propellors* **churned up** *the water as it increased speed.* □ *The wheels* **churned up** *the mud in the road as the driver tried desperately to extricate his car.* □ *The* **churned-up** *mud made the country lanes impassable.*
circle (round) (over) [A1 A2 A3] (in flying) move (more or less) in circles over. **S:** plane, helicopter, glider; vulture, bird □ [A2] *The reconnaissance plane* **circled over** *the enemy's position, reporting their strength and dispositions to the troops on the ground.* □ [A1 A3] *We knew from the number of vultures* **circling round** *(***over** *us) that some living creature — whether an animal or a human being — was nearing its end below.*
claim back (from) [B1i pass B3 pass rel] ask for the return of, or simply take, sth to which one is or feels entitled. **O:** tax; the cost of the ticket; one's camera. **o:** the Inland Revenue; British Rail; the lost property office □ *A lot of people do not understand why they cannot* **claim back** *the income-tax that has been paid on their interest by the Building Societies.* □ *Much distress was caused to the foster parents when, after six years, Susan's mother* **claimed** *her* **back**. □ *One day the seal, which had grown up as a family pet, simply swam away. The sea had* **claimed back** *its own.*
clam up [A1] (informal) become totally uncommunicative, through suspicion, fear, distrust etc. **S:** suspect, witness; patient □ *When Inspector Smart began to question the arrested man's girlfriend about his whereabouts at eight o'clock the previous evening, she immediately* **clammed up** *and refused to say anything.* □ *I did not dare to suggest that Paul should see a doctor — still less a psychiatrist — because from previous experience I knew that he would* **clam up** *for a month if I did.*
clamp down (on) [A1 nom A3 pass rel] (informal) use one's authority against sb, or to suppress or prevent sth. **S:** authorities; police, (law) court, magistrate; government; tax authorities; moral guardians (of society) □ *There has been much tax evasion through expense accounts, but the Government is going to* **clamp down** (or: *there's going to be a Government* **clamp-down**). □ *It's high time they* **clamped down on** *violence in television programmes.*
clap in/into [B2 pass] put swiftly in/into jail etc, often without trial. **o:** ⚠ jail, prison, solitary confinement, irons □ *The prisoners were* **clapped in** *prison and kept there for several months without trial.* □ *In the old days it was commonplace for a sailor to be* **clapped into** *irons for some minor offence.*
clap on [B1i pass B2 pass] put on hastily. **O:** hat, cap; hand. **o:** head; arm; handle, knob □ *He* **clapped** *his hat* **on** *and strode angrily from the room.* □ *He* **clapped** *his hand* **on** *the hilt of his sword to show that he was quite prepared to*

fight. □ *The detective* ***clapped*** *the handcuffs* ***on*** *the man before he could escape.*

not (ever) clap eyes on [B2] (informal) not see □ *I* ***haven't clapped eyes on*** *Bill for months. What's happened to him?* □ *How can I describe her? I'd* ***never clapped eyes on*** *her till five minutes ago.* □ usu in present and past perfect tenses, as shown.

clap on sail [B1iii] (nautical) (of a sailing ship) increase speed by increasing the amount of canvas □ *When the privateer sighted the enemy warship, she* ***clapped on*** *every inch of* ***sail.***

clap on/onto [B1i pass B2 pass] (informal) add sth to the price etc of sth (esp in an unwelcome way); slap on/onto[2] (q v). **S:** Chancellor, Treasury, County Council. **O:** tax, another five per cent, an extra ten pence; standstill order; preservation order. **o:** petrol, cigarettes; the rates; the building of any more universities; the oak tree in my garden □ *We shan't get much benefit from the removal of import duty from European goods, because the Government's going to* ***clap on*** *Value Added Tax.* □ *We had just decided to fly to the Canary Islands for a holiday when the air lines* ***clapped*** *twenty-five per cent* ***on*** (or: ***onto***) *the fare.* □ *I can't make any structural alterations to my house because it was built in the nineteenth century and a preservation order has been* ***clapped on*** *it.*

clapped out [pass adj (B1)] (slang) (be) completely worn out and apparently beyond recovery or repair. **S:** he etc; car, lorry, bus; camera, radio □ *Of course, they could drag Smithers out of retirement to make the speech of welcome, but he's pretty* ***clapped out****, poor old boy!* □ *A group of determined schoolboys, with the help of their even more determined teacher, managed to get a* ***clapped-out*** *minibus back into working order.*

clash (with)[1] [A2 emph rel] join in combat or rigorous argument (with). **S:** troops, police; Prime Minister. **o:** demonstrators; Leader of the Opposition □ *Mr Wilson* ***clashed with*** *Sir Alec* (or: *Mr Wilson and Sir Alec* ***clashed***) *in the debate on steel nationalization.*

clash (with)[2] [A2] not match or harmonize (with) because of colour, design, etc. **S:/o:** colour, shade; purple, pink; blouse, skirt (because of their colour) □ *The red of her scarf* ***clashes with*** *the purple of her hat.* □ *The cushion covers* ***clashed*** *violently* ***with*** *the carpet* (or: *The covers and the carpet* ***clashed*** etc).

clash (with)[3] [A2 emph rel] occur at the same time as sth else (thus causing inconvenience). **S:** time, hour; meeting, ceremony, party. **o:** that set aside, arranged (for sth else); his, ours, one previously arranged □ *'You can't arrange a meeting for Friday: it would* ***clash with*** *my afternoon golf!'* □ *'Make sure his appointment doesn't* ***clash with*** *mine* (or: *our appointments don't* ***clash***)*.'*

class (with) [B2 pass emph rel] put in the same class or category (as). **S:** registrar, examiner, librarian. **O:** trade, occupation; candidate, performer; document, journal. **o:** (similar) type, person □ *I object to being* ***classed with*** *unskilled labourers; I'm a tradesman.* □ *It's a mistake to judge his work by the standards of men* ***with*** *whom he should never have been* ***classed*** *in the first place.*

claw back [B1i nom pass] (finance) recover, by taxation, money paid to individuals who are not considered in need of government assistance — a situation which arises when the individuals concerned cannot be conveniently or economically identified *before* payment is made □ *Back in 1968 the Government increased the family allowance but it was intended that only those with lower incomes should benefit. As family allowances are paid to everyone (with children) the tax system was used to recover this increase from those paying tax at the standard rate. This '****clawback****', as it is unattractively called, has been achieved by reducing personal allowances by £42 for each allowance received.* OBS

clean down [B1i pass adj] clean thoroughly, from top to bottom. **O:** house, place; door, wall □ *My mother always insists on* ***cleaning*** *the whole house* ***down*** *at least once a month.*

clean out [B1i nom pass] clean, usu by carrying or brushing dirt away. **O:** farmyard, cowshed, barn; wash-house, latrine □ *The stables are in a filthy condition. When* ***were*** *they last* ***cleaned out****?* □ *The whole place needs a good* ***clean-out*** (or: ***cleaning-out***).

clean out/out of [B1i pass B2 pass] (informal) take all a person's money or stock. **O:** tradesman, shopkeeper. **o:** beer, spirits, tobacco; change, cash □ *I haven't a penny left; buying all those books has completely* ***cleaned*** *me* ***out****.* □ *The tobacconist was* ***cleaned out of*** *cigarettes by people who expected the price to go up.*

clean up[1] [A1 nom B1i nom pass] remove dirt, etc; make a place clean. **O:** rubbish, debris; room; work-bench, desk □ [A1] *Now that the party's over, shall we* ***clean up*** (or: *have a* ***clean-up***)*?* □ [B1] *I wish you'd* ***clean up*** *your mess after you've been repairing your bicycle.* □ [B1] *I think we might give the place a bit of a* ***clean-up****.* □ one cleans up a mess *or* a place. ⇨ clear up[1].

clean up[2] [B1i nom pass] (informal) suppress, get rid of sth; make a place free of sth. **S:** government, city council; vice squad. **O:** corruption, vice; racket, drug traffic; town, back streets □ *It's time that the police took some effective action to* ***clean up*** *this town.* □ *There's been a considerable* ***clean-up*** *in the vicinity of the docks: you hardly ever see a prostitute there now.*

clean up[3] [B1i pass] (military) suppress an enemy (usu small groups still resisting after a major advance); mop up [2] (q v). **O:** nest, outpost, pocket of resistance; rearguard □ *The Battle of Normandy ended on the 19th August: it was on this day that we finally* ***cleaned up*** *the remnants of the enemy trapped in the 'pocket' east of Mortain.* MFM

clean up[4] [A1 B1iii pass] (informal) make money. **O:** a (small) fortune, a packet, a (cool) thousand □ *Don't just stand idly by while more enterprising people* ***clean up****.* □ *His invention was immediately successful, and in less than a year he* ***cleaned up*** *ten thousand pounds.* □ *Many a fortune has been* ***cleaned up*** *by confidence tricksters working on the greed and gullibility of others.*

clean (oneself) up [A1 nom B1ii pass] (informal) get washed (and possibly change into cleaner clothes) □ *'I'm just going home to* ***clean***

up (or: *to have a* ***clean-up***). *I'll meet you in an hour outside the post-office.'* □ *'Just give me five minutes to* ***clean myself up****; I'm covered in oil.'* □ only the passive with *get* is possible: *How long will you take to get yourselves* ***cleaned up****?*

clear away [B1i pass] remove objects in order to leave a clear space. **O:** leaves; debris; dishes, tea things □ *'I'll* ***clear*** *these dishes* ***away****; then we'll be able to work at the table.'*

clear (of) [B2 pass emph rel] declare to be free (from); absolve from (q v). **O:** oneself; the accused (man); the prisoner. **o:** ⚠ guilt, suspicion, responsibility, the charge □ *The signalman was* ***cleared of*** *all responsibility for the railway accident.* □ *The accusations you are making relate to charges* ***of*** *which my client has been* ***cleared****.*

clear one's mind of [B2 pass emph rel] dismiss from one's mind. **o:** (all, any) prejudice, thought of..., desire to..., wish for... □ *The jury were told that in considering their verdict they must* ***clear their minds of*** *all feelings of repugnance for the behaviour of the accused during the trial.*

clear off[1] [A1] (informal) run away □ *When the man saw the policeman, he* ***cleared off*** *as fast as his legs could carry him.* □ *'You've got no right to be here.* ***Clear off****!'*

clear off[2] [B1i pass] pay, complete payment for. **O:** debts, mortgage (on a house), remaining payments, arrears □ *The first thing I would do if I won a big prize in the football pools would be to* ***clear off*** *all my hire purchase payments.*

clear out [A1] (informal) leave home □ *'I'm fed up with being told what I can do and what I can't do; I'm* ***clearing out****. Goodbye!'*

clear out/out of[1] [A1 A3] (informal) leave quickly □ *'If you've got any sense, you'll* ***clear out*** *before my father comes home from work. He'll be furious if he finds you here.'* □ *'You'd better* ***clear out of*** *here before you cause any more trouble.'* HD

clear out/out of[2] [B1i pass B2 pass] ⇨ clean out/out of.

clear up[1] [A1 nom B1i pass] remove rubbish etc, make things tidy or orderly. **O:** rubbish, mess; muddle □ *'Aren't we going to* ***clear up*** *(or: have a* ***clear-up****) before we go out?'* □ *'We can't go until all the litter has been* ***cleared up****.'* □ one clears up a mess, *not* a place. ⇨ clean up[1].

clear up[2] [B1i pass] remove doubt about, find the solution to. **O:** point, matter; mystery; difficulty, misunderstanding □ *So far no lunar magnetic field has been detected, but rocket experiments should be able to* ***clear*** *the matter* ***up****.* NS □ *I decided to go and see him and get the point* ***cleared up*** *quickly, before trouble arose.* MFM

clear up[3] [A1] become fine. **S:** ⚠ the weather, it □ *The weather was bad early this morning but it* ***cleared up*** *before ten o'clock.*

clear with [B2 pass] have inspected and approved by. **O:** passport, papers, documents; goods, luggage, personal effects. **o:** authorities, police, (the) Customs, Security, Immigration □ *'Have these cameras been* ***cleared with*** *Customs?'* □ *You'd better get the visitors* ***cleared with*** *Security before you take them to the Commandant's office.*

climb down[1] [A1 A2] descend; get down (from) □ *Cats often find it easier to climb up a tree than to* ***climb down*** *(it).*

climb down[2] [A1 nom] (informal) retract, withdraw; admit a mistake □ *When he was proved wrong by the new evidence he was forced to* ***climb down*** *and accept that he was mistaken.* □ *Admit that you're wrong now and you will avoid a humiliating* ***climb-down*** *later on.*

cling to[1] [A2 rel] keep a firm, desperate, hold on; not release one's grip on. **S:** shipwrecked sailor; mountaineer. **o:** raft, plank of wood; bush, projecting ledge □ *Some of the victims of the fire climbed out of the building,* ***clung to*** *the window ledges for a minute or two and then dropped to their death a hundred feet below.*

cling to[2] [A2 rel] not relinquish; be unwilling to abandon. **o:** superstitious beliefs; outmoded customs; hopes, aspirations □ *The refugees* ***clung to*** *the hope that one day they would all be able to return to their native land, though it was obvious to others that this could never happen.* □ *'She still* ***clings to*** *him in spite of all his affairs — a sign of her own insecurity, I suppose.'*

clip on/onto [B1i nom pass B2 pass emph rel] fasten with a clip. **O:** brooch, bangle, earring; watch; microphone; paper, notice. **o:** arm, ear; lapel; board □ *'Can you* ***clip*** *these ear-rings* ***on*** (or: *Do these ear-rings* ***clip on;*** or: *Are these ear-rings* ***clip-ons****)?'* □ *He produced a board,* ***onto*** *which his secretary had* ***clipped*** *all the important documents.*

clock in/out [A1 nom B1i pass] record the time of one's arrival or departure (usu at a place of work) □ *Workers are expected to* ***clock in*** *at 8.30 a m.* □ *They* ***clocked*** *the men* ***out*** *at five.* □ *The* ***clockings-in-and-out*** *irritate the factory workers, but they are necessary in the interests of fairness and efficiency.* □ *'What is* ***clock-in*** *time* (or: ***clocking-in*** *time) at your office?'* □ clock-in and clock-out are only used attrib.

clock on/off [A1 nom B1i pass] often used in place of clock in/out.

clog up [B1i pass adj] fill, in such a way as to prevent normal working. **S:** grease, dirt, oil, waste matter. **O:** works, machinery; pipes, drains, wheels; pores □ *If you put too much grease into delicate machinery, it may* ***clog up*** *the works.* □ *The outlet-pipe had become* ***clogged up*** *with kitchen waste.*

close down [A1 nom B1i pass adj] (of production or activity) end, cease (permnently or for a time); shut down (q v). **S:** [A1] **O:** [B1] school; plant, factory; theatre; broadcasting. **S:** [B1] governor; owner, management □ *The factory had to* ***close down*** *through lack of orders.* □ *Television* ***closed down*** *for the night just after eleven o'clock.* DBM □ *We're faced with inevitable* ***close-down*** *because of the losses of the past three years.* □ *The Medical Officer said that all schools must be* ***closed down*** *during the epidemic.*

the days close in [A1] grow shorter □ *As autumn advances* ***the days close in*** *and the hours of light become fewer and fewer.*

close in (on/upon)[1] [A1 A3 pass] draw nearer to, or around sb, so as to attack or seize him. **S:** enemy; gunfire; pursuer. **o:** (defensive) position, outpost; fugitive □ *The sound of mortar-fire seemed to be* ***closing in****.* QA □ *Before we could establish any strong defensive position the enemy*

***closed in on** us.* □ *When he realized that he was being **closed in upon**, the fugitive shot himself.*

close in (on/upon)[2] [A1 A3 pass] envelop in an unpleasant, threatening way. **S:** winter; night, darkness; jungle; city. **o:** traveller; stranger □ *The night **closed in** again as the little oasis of light receded.* BM □ *When winter **closed in on** us, with constant rain and appalling mud, I sent for a waterproof suit.* MFM

close up[1] [A1] shut (temporarily). **S:** ⚠ (a) flower; (a) petal □ *These flowers **close up** at night.* □ close-up /ˈkləʊs ʌp/ is derived not from the verb close /kləʊz/ but from the adverb close /kləʊs/; thus: *Take a **close-up** (photograph) of Mary.*

close up[2] [A1 B1i pass] shut (temporarily); shut up [1] [4](q v) **S:** trader, owner. **O:** shop, office, factory □ *The Manager **closes up**; he is always the last to leave.* □ *She **closes** the office **up** at five o'clock.* □ *Is the shop **closed up** by the owner or by his wife?*

close up[3] [A1] (military) draw (nearer) together (usu in ranks). **S:** soldiers, troops □ *The marching men had to **close up** to let the oncoming convoy go past.*

close with[1] [A2] (military) start fighting; join battle (with) (q v). **S:** (assault) troops, infantry. **o:** enemy □ *After a long period of shelling, the infantry surged forward and **closed with** the enemy in hand-to-hand fighting.*

close with[2] [A2] agree on a price with, strike a bargain with. **o:** dealer, agent, salesman □ *After a good deal of discussion over the value of the picture I finally **closed with** him at a reasonable figure.*

one's face cloud over [A1] lose (its) brightness; betray anxiety or worry □ *When he heard the news of his friend's accident, **his face clouded over**.*

the sky cloud over [A1] become covered with clouds □ *Just as we were beginning to enjoy the sunshine, **the sky clouded over** and a cold wind began to blow.*

club together [A1] make contributions of money so that the total sum can be used for a specific purpose. **S:** colleagues, pals, friends, patients, neighbours, fellow-students □ *All the members of the orchestra **clubbed together** to present a silver baton to their conductor on his sixtieth birthday.*

cluster around/round [A1 A2 rel] surround closely □ *Reporters **clustered around** the distinguished visitor.* □ *He admired the roses **clustering round** the cottage door.*

clutch at a straw [A2] = catch at a straw.

clutter up [B1i pass] (informal) occupy space, giving a room, house etc an untidy appearance; (of knowledge, information etc) exist copiously but in a muddled way in sb's mind. **S:** junk, bric-a-brac; china, silver; books; ill-digested facts. **O:** attic, study; head, mind □ *Objects of every kind **cluttered up** the entrance to the house, so that it was almost impossible to get in.* □ *The passage was **cluttered up** with stacks of old books and pictures.* □ *His head's **cluttered up** with all manner of useless information.*

coast along [A1] ride or drive without much effort or, in the case of a car, without using the engine □ *We **coasted along** on our bicycles with the wind behind us.* □ *As the fuel-gauge pointed to 'empty', he switched off the engine whenever he could and just **coasted along**.*

cock up[1] [B1i] raise. **S:** animal; horse, dog. **O:** ears, leg □ *The horse **cocked** its ears **up** several seconds before I could hear anything.* □ *The dog **cocked** its leg **up*** (i e in order to urinate) *against the lamp-post.*

cock up[2] [B1i nom pass] (taboo) spoil, ruin; mess up (q v). **S:** organizer, manager, agent. **O:** arrangements, planning; tour, holiday; ceremony □ *Don't let him organize your trip; he completely **cocked up** ours* (or: *he made a complete **cock-up** of ours*). □ *Trust Smith to **cock** the whole thing **up**!*

coil around/round [B2 pass emph rel] wind sth in a spiral; wind around/round (q v). **O:** rope; wire, thread. **o:** capstan, bollard; bobbin, spool □ *The wire was **coiled round** the cylinder, and then the current was turned on.*

coil (itself) around/round [A2 B2 pass emph rel] wind (itself) in a spiral around. **S:** snake; rope, cable □ *The constrictor **coiled round** its prey and crushed the life out of it.* □ *The rope slipped from my hands and **coiled itself*** (or: ***got itself coiled***) ***around** the pulley.*

coil up[1] [B1i pass adj] form into a coil. **O:** rope, hawser, cable. □ *The sailors **coiled** the ropes **up** neatly and left them on the deck.*

coil (oneself) up [A1 B1ii pass] form (itself) into a coil. **S:** snake, centipede; girl □ *The snake glided under a stone and **coiled up** there.* □ *She **coiled herself up** in the corner of the sofa with a book.*

colour up [A1] (informal) blush, go red in the face (as a result of shyness, feelings of guilt or embarrassment) □ *'You — what's your name?' called the angry headmistress. 'Me, Miss?' he said, startled, and beginning to **colour up**.* TT □ *She **coloured up** at the mention of the young man's name.*

comb out [B1i pass] remove knots or tangles in hair, fibre etc. **O:** hair; skein, hank; knot, tangle □ *The little girl hated having her hair **combed out** because her mother did it roughly, and hurt her.*

come aboard [A1] board, come on board (esp a ship or plane). **S:** crew, passenger □ *A relief crew **came aboard** at Beirut to fly the aircraft on to Singapore.* ⇨ go aboard, take aboard.

come about[1] [A1] happen. **S:** it... that he was there; the accident; death, defeat, disgrace, failure; success □ *Can you tell me how the accident **came about**?* □ *How does it **come about** that you did not report the theft until two days after it occurred?* □ *It **came about** in this way: one day I was....* □ *Thus it **came about** that, one bright May morning, I swallowed four-tenths of a gramme of mescalin.* DOP □ often used with *How does/did it....* ⇨ bring about[1].

come about[2] [A1] (nautical) change direction of movement. **S:** sailing-vessel; yacht, dinghy; motor-boat □ *We **came about** and went off on a new tack.* ⇨ bring about[2], go about[5], put about[1].

come across[1] [A2] find, meet (usu by accident). **o:** (interesting) piece of information; (beautiful) wild flower; his etc name; (old) friend □ *Did you **come across** any old photographs of the family when you were looking through the lumber-room?* □ *I **came across** an old friend in Oxford*

Street this morning.

come across[2] [A1] be communicated, understood, heard. **S:** (his) voice; message; words □ *The preacher spoke for a long time but I'm afraid his meaning did not* ***come across****.* ⇨ get across (to), put across[1].

come across (with) [A1 A3] (informal) give; hand over. **o:** money; information; keys □ *He owes me five pounds, but I'm afraid he'll never* ***come across****.* □ *The robber gave the old man's arm a twist, and he at once* ***came across with*** *all the money he had in his pocket.*

come after[1] [A2 emph rel] follow in sequence □ *B* ***comes after*** *A; C* ***comes after*** *B.* □ *Does the cheese* ***come after*** *the pudding in your country?* □ ***After*** *the banquet* ***came*** *a firework display in the gardens.*

come after[2] [A2] (informal) follow in pursuit of. **S:** dog; police; farmer. **o:** intruder; suspect; trespasser □ *As soon as we started across the field the farmer* ***came after*** *us waving a big stick.* ⇨ be after[1], go after[1].

come along [A1] arrive, present (himself etc); turn up[5] (q v). **S:** he etc; chance, opportunity □ *He went to London whenever the chance* ***came along****.* □ *Is your daughter married yet? No, she's still waiting for Mr Right to* ***come along****.*

come along/on[1] [A1] be quick; make an effort, try harder □ ***Come along*** *Arthur; we can't wait all day!* □ ***Come on****, boys! Surely one of you can tell me the name of the author of 'Oliver Twist'!* □ usu imper.

come along/on[2] [A1] make progress. **S:** pupil, student; work, painting. **A:** well; nicely, quickly; like a house on fire; like nobody's business □ *My son has begun to* ***come along*** *very well in French since the new teacher was appointed.* □ *The horse has* ***come on*** *a ton* (= a great deal) *since making his debut at Wolverhampton.* DM □ *John is* ***coming on*** *like a house on fire now that he is receiving the proper treatment.* ⇨ bring along/on[1]; get along/on (with)[1].

come along/on[3] [A1] grow, progress (esp in the early stages). **S:** plant; flower, vegetable □ *'Those seedlings are* ***coming along*** *well in the greenhouse; I'll plant them outside when the weather gets a little warmer.'* □ *I forgot to put the glass back on the cold frame last night, and the frost took the tops off some tomato plants I had* ***coming on****.* TT ⇨ bring along/on[2].

come along (to) [A1 A3] come from one place to another, often a short distance (e g within the same building). **o:** office; meeting, party □ *Why doesn't your brother* ***come along to*** *the services in chapel as he used to?* □ *'We're having a few people in for drinks tomorrow. Do* ***come along*** *if you're free.'* ⇨ be along (to), bring along (to).

come along (with) [A1 A3] (instruction or firm request to) move somewhere quickly (with sb) □ *'****Come along****, and please don't make a noise — you'll disturb your mother.'* DC □ *'You'd better* ***come along with*** *me to the bar and have a drink. That's what you need to cheer you up.'* □ usu imper.

come apart [A1] fall into pieces. **S:** dress; table; cup, vase □ *The camera just* ***came apart*** *the first time I used it.* □ *I swear I didn't drop the plate: it just* ***came apart*** *in my hands!*

come apart at the seams [A3] (informal) disintegrate, fail, become decrepit. **S:** he etc; scheme, project, idea □ *Poor old Smith isn't the man he used to be; he's* ***coming apart at the seams****.* □ *The Government's financial policy is* ***coming apart at the seams****.*

come around/round (to)[1] [A1 emph A3] come to, visit, sb or a place (usu within the same town etc). **o:** (my) place, house □ *'I'm ringing to report a burst pipe. How soon can a plumber* ***come round****?'* □ *We'd love to* ***come around to*** *your place tonight, but I'm afraid we're a bit tied up with work at the moment.* ⇨ be around/round (at), bring around/round (to)[1], go round (to).

come around/round (to)[2] [A1 A3 rel] agree (after disagreeing), change one's attitude (so that it matches sb else's). **o:** ⚠ his etc way of thinking, point of view, assessment of the situation □ *John's opposed to our ideas at present, but in time he'll* ***come around****.* □ *Mother* ***came around to*** *my way of thinking, thus making life a lot easier.* □ *A few boys don't like the experiment in mathematics teaching; but some have* ***come round*** *since we started.* T ⇨ bring around/round (to)[2].

come at[1] [A2] attack □ *The crazed man* ***came at*** *me with a meat-axe.*

come at[2] [A2] reach, ascertain. **o:** facts; truth; causes □ *The purpose of the official inquiry is to* ***come at*** *the true facts leading up to the loss of the ship at sea.* ⇨ get at[3].

come away [A1] (Scottish) an invitation to sb to enter a room. □ usu imper. ⇨ come in/into.

come away (from) [A1 A3 rel] part, become detached (from). **S:** fitting, lock, post. **o:** base, door, socket □ *I pulled the rotten wood and it* ***came away*** *without difficulty.* □ *If the chicken is properly cooked, the meat will* ***come away from*** *the bones very easily.*

come away with [A3] leave a place, the company of others etc, with. **o:** feeling, impression; memories □ *We* ***came away with*** *the uneasy feeling that all was not well with their marriage.* ⇨ bring away, go away with.

come back[1] [A1] return. **A:** soon, shortly; in a year's time □ *I'm going away and I may never* ***come back****.* ⇨ be back[1], bring back[1], get back[1], go back[1], take back[1].

come back[2] [A1 nom] become fashionable again. **S:** fashion; style, trend □ *Long skirts have been out of fashion for a long time, but they are* ***coming back*** (or: *making a* ***come-back***) *this year.*

come back[3] [A1] return (to the memory). **S:** it (all); former knowledge; sb's name; details □ *At first I could not remember why everything seemed so familiar; then it all* ***came back****.* □ *The language I used to speak at my prep school* ***came back*** *to me.* SML ⇨ bring back[2].

come back[4] [A1] be restored. **S:** (former) system, regime □ *There are some people who would be glad to see corporal punishment* ***come back*** *for certain offences.* ⇨ bring back[3].

come-back[1] [nom (A1)] a (successful) return (to a profession etc). **S:** boxer, film-star, politician. **Verb** make, stage; attempt, try □ *After many years of obscurity, the once-famous film-star made an unexpected* ***come-back****.*

come-back[2] [nom (A1)] an answer; a re-assertion of oneself □ *Harold was no longer the*

Harold of the conference-room, dapper and self-assured. He tried to make a ***come-back,*** *however.* PW

come-back[3] [nom (A1)] means of enforcing an agreement or invoking the law □ *If you don't give the necessary details (date, name, address etc) when you buy the machine, you may have no* ***come-back*** *if it breaks down.*

come before[1] [A2] precede □ *A* ***comes before*** *B; B* ***comes before*** *C, and so on.* ⇨ be before[1].

come before[2] [A2] be presented for consideration, decision, judgment. **S:** he etc; case; matter, claim. **o:** court, committee, magistrate □ *My claim* ***comes before*** *the court tomorrow morning.* ⇨ be before[2], bring before, go before[2], put before[2], take before.

come before[3] [A2 emph rel] have greater importance than sth else. **S:** (one's) country, city; interests, needs (of the community). **o:** self, all else, personal advancement □ *The building of homes and schools should* ***come before*** *the building of new office blocks.* □ ***Before*** *all else must* ***come*** *the development of the economy.* ⇨ put before[1].

come between [A2] interfere in the affairs of; cause the separation or estrangement of (two people) □ *The lovers swore to let nothing and nobody* ***come between*** *them.* □ *It is often dangerous and never wise to* ***come between*** *a man and his wife.*

come between sb and sth [A2] prevent sb doing or enjoying sth. **o:** me etc; (***and***) my work, studies; rest, recreation □ *I'm not going to let a small matter like that* ***come between me and my sleep.*** □ *He won't let anything* ***come between him and his daily walk.***

come by[1] [A1] pass, esp of sth or sb moving towards the speaker □ *I moved my car out of the way so that the heavy lorry could* ***come by.*** ⇨ get by[1].

come by[2] [A2] obtain, usu as a result of effort. **o:** money; job; medal, coin, stamp □ *Jobs were not so easy to* ***come by*** *when I was a boy as they are now.* □ *It's difficult to* ***come by*** *first editions of Pope's works.* □ *I hope you* ***came by*** *all that money honestly.*

come by[3] [A2] receive, by accident; happen to get □ *How did you* ***come by*** *that scratch on your cheek?* KLT

come down[1] [A1 emph] collapse, drop; fall. **S:** ceiling, wall; curtain, picture; rain, sleet □ *I took out just one screw and the whole thing* ***came down.*** □ *The snow* ***came down*** *thick and fast.* ⇨ take down[1].

come down[2] [A1] fall to the ground (esp because of enemy fire or engine failure). **S:** (enemy) aircraft □ *Two enemy intruders* ***came down*** *inside our lines.* □ *The second engine cut out and we were forced to* ***come down*** *in the sea.* ⇨ bring down[1].

come down[3] [A1 emph] fall, be reduced. **S:** prices, costs, expenditure □ *Prices are much more likely to go up than to* ***come down.*** ⇨ be down[2], bring down[5], go down[5].

come down[4] [A1] (informal) make a present of money, give money (to sb) □ *Just when I was at my wits' end wondering how to pay my bills, my old aunt* ***came down*** *handsomely; she sent me a cheque for £100.*

come down[5] [A1] reach a decision; decide to exert one's influence. **A:** (finally, after some hesitation) against or in favour of sb or sth; on sb's side □ *The Prime Minister* ***came down*** *heavily on my side, and the Colonial Secretary was routed.* MFM

come down[6] [A1] come to a (country) place, either from London or the North □ *There's a girl* ***come down*** *to live here — she's married to a painter.* ASA □ in contrast, one *goes up* to London (as the capital), or to Scotland (if travelling north).

come-down [nom (A1)] (informal) a loss of prestige, face, social position □ *After owning her own little shop for so many years, it was quite a* ***come-down*** *for her to have to work for someone else.* AITC □ commonly modified by *rather a, a bit of a; a terrible, awful, dreadful;* note also the exclamation: *What a* ***come-down!***

come down (from) [A1 A3] leave (a university, esp Oxford and Cambridge) □ *'So you were at Cambridge in 1964. When did you* ***come down?'*** □ *I have just* ***come down from*** *the University with a mediocre degree in History.* HD ⇨ be down (from); go down[8].

come down in the world [A3] (informal) suffer a change for the worse (in economic circumstances, standard of living or employment) □ *Poor old George has* ***come down in the world*** *since his business failed.*

come down on[1] [A3] (informal) rebuke sb; criticize severely, often with a threat of punishment, for some fault. **o:** him etc; error, slip. **A:** like a ton of bricks (= with great severity), in a flash, instantly □ *If any man was slow in obeying orders, the sergeant would* ***come down on*** *him like a ton of bricks.* ⇨ be down on[2].

come down on[2] [A3] (informal) demand money or redress from. **o:** (negligent) workman, motorists; (bankrupt) trader □ *He* ***came down on*** *the driver of the car for heavy damages.* □ *All his creditors* ***came down on*** *him for prompt payment of his bills when they heard of his financial difficulties.* ⇨ be down on[3].

come down to[1] [A3] (informal) mean in essence, (can) be reduced to; boil down to (q v). **S:** it; the accusation; his story □ *So what it* ***came down to,*** *in the end, is that he'd got me the offer of a show from one of the better galleries.* CON □ *It* ***comes down to*** *two choices: You can either stay here and obey me, or leave and never return.* TGLY

come down to[2] [A3] reach, be passed on to. **S:** stories, songs, myths, legends; traditions, customs. **o:** us, them; nations, groups, tribes □ *These stories* ***come down to*** *us from our forefathers.*

come down to[3] [A3] (informal) have one's standard of living, behaviour, self-confidence etc so reduced that one is forced to do things that would normally be beneath one; be reduced to (⇨ reduce to[4]). **o:** seeking help, asking for money, begging in the streets □ *I never thought she would* ***come down to*** *asking my advice about her affairs.*

come down to earth [A3] (informal) return to reality. **A:** ⚠ with a bang, with a bump □ *The lovers are living in a kind of dreamworld; but one day they'll* ***come down to earth.*** □ cf (i) *No matter how high you jump you always* ***return to***

earth. (ii) *Never lose sight of it, or you might* ***come down with a bump***. DBM ⇨ bring down to earth.

when it comes down to [A3] (informal) (when it) is a question of. **o:** cunning, guile, greed; generosity, courage □ ***When it comes down to*** *sheer strength, there is no animal that can match the elephant.*

come forth [A1] (formal or facetious) emerge, be produced. **S:** thought, idea; proposal, suggestion □ *I had very great hopes of Jenkins' speech last night, but nothing very new* ***came forth***. ⇨ bring forth.

come forward[1] [A1] present oneself; make oneself known; move to the fore □ *The police want any witnesses of the incident to* ***come forward*** *and help them with their inquiries.*

come forward[2] [A1] be raised for discussion (esp at a formal meeting). **S:** issue, question, matter □ *The matter was deferred at last evening's meeting, but will* ***come forward*** *at our next session.* ⇨ bring forward[1].

come from [A2 emph rel] be a native of; be a product of □ *He* ***comes from*** *London.* □ *These toys* ***come from*** *Hong Kong.* □ ***From*** *this area* ***come*** *most of our best potatoes.*

come from/of[1] [A2] be descended from. **o:** (good, famous, notorious) family; a long line of artists, politicians, statesmen, drunkards □ *He* ***comes from*** *a very good family.* □ (a popular joke) *He* ***comes of*** *a long line of bachelors.*

come from/of[2] [A2] be the result of. **S:** nothing, anything; (no) good, harm; (only) good, harm; that's what. **o:** one's work, endeavours, efforts; meddling, interfering □ *'I wonder if anything will* ***come of*** *our tea-party,' said Isabel.* PW □ *Carry on with your present research. Nothing but good can* ***come of*** *it.* □ *Joan is furious with me for cleaning her house while she was on holiday. That's what* ***comes from*** *trying to be a good neighbour.* □ object is often the *-ing* form of a v as in the last example.

come-hither [nom (A1)] (informal) a clear invitation by a girl or woman to a man to start a flirtation □ *Sonja gave me such an obvious* ***come-hither*** *look that I felt myself blushing to the roots of my hair.* □ used attrib, esp with *look, smile*; note that come hither, as a v + particle, is obsolete.

come home (to) [A1 A3 rel] become painfully clear (to). **S:** fact, truth; danger; it... that he was dying. **o:** patient, sufferer; public □ *It eventually* ***came home to*** *the people that the war would be long and bloody.* ⇨ bring/get home (to).

come in[1] [A1] become fashionable. **S:** long hair, whiskers; short skirts, full sleeves □ *'Do you know exactly when wigs first* ***came in***, *in this country?'* ⇨ be in[1]; be in/bring into/come into fashion/vogue.

come in[2] [A1] become seasonable or available. **S:** strawberries, trout, pheasant □ *'Fresh salmon doesn't* ***come in*** *before February, does it?'* □ *'We haven't any nylon net curtains in stock just at present; but they should* ***come in*** *any moment now.'* ⇨ be in[3]; be in/come into season.

come in[3] [A1] (politics) gain power. **S:** (present) government; Wilson, Heath etc □ *When the present government* ***came in*** *the country was in a difficult financial situation.* ⇨ be in[4], get in/into[3]; put in[6].

come in[4] [A1] (sport) finish a race. **S:** athlete; horse, dog; yacht, car. **A:** first, second, last □ *He led most of the way but suddenly lost his strength and* ***came in*** *last.* □ *Where did Peter* ***come in*** *— second or third?*

come in[5] [A1] be received as income. **S:** dividend, profit; wage, salary □ *He doesn't work; but he has at least a thousand a year* ***coming in*** *from investments.* □ *She has a tiny bit* ***coming in*** *from a few shares that were left to me.* LBA ⇨ bring in[2].

come in[6] [A1] get some advantage from, have a part to play in, some concerted action. **S:** colleague, partner, member (of a team) □ *'Yes. I understand the scheme perfectly; but I don't see where I* ***come in***.*'* □ *'This is where you* ***come in***, *Bill: while we are getting round to the enemy's rear, you will distract them by a few bursts of machine-gun fire.'* ⇨ bring in[3].

come in[7] [A1] move towards the land. **S:** ⚠ the tide, the water, the sea □ *Don't stay on the rocks too long; the tide is* ***coming in*** *fast and you might get cut off.* □ *The tide's out now, but it starts to* ***come in*** *at about six o'clock.* ⇨ be in[7].

come in[8] [A1] (broadcasting, journalism) be received; reach the office, editor's desk etc. **S:** ⚠ (the) news, details; a story, report □ *News is just* ***coming in*** *of an air-crash over the Atlantic. We will give further details as soon as they are received.*

come in[9] [A1] (broadcasting) continue with, or contribute to, a commentary, discussion etc. **S:** reporter, commentator; member of the panel, audience □ *'And now for his impressions of the first round of this heavyweight contest, I pass you over to J. Barrington Dolby.* ***Come in***, *Barry!'* □ *'I should like to* ***come in*** *here, as I happen to know a good deal about how people live in these high-rise flats.'*

come in[10] [A1] (radio communication, e g between police-cars and their control points) ask sb to speak, report his position, that he has heard a message etc □ *'****Come in***, *Victor.* ***Come in***, *Victor. Over!'*

come in handy/useful [A1] be found useful on some future (usu unforseeable) occasion □ *'Don't throw those old jars away; they may* ***come in useful*** (or: ***handy***) *one of these days.'*

come in pat [A1] say without hesitation and just at the right moment □ *'I wonder where Eileen lives?' said Mary; and her five-year-old sister* ***came in pat*** *with the answer: 'At 23 Rose Gardens.'*

when one's ship comes in [A1] when one has plenty of money to spend □ *Perhaps,* ***when their ship came in***, *they would be able to change some of their ugly chairs for some more beautiful ones.* PW

come in for [A3] attract, be the object of. **S:** work, conduct, idea. **o:** (some, a lot of) admiration, attention; criticism, blame □ *The young artist's pictures* ***came in for*** *a great deal of attention.* □ *The Government's foreign policy has* ***come in for*** *a storm of criticism from the newspapers.*

come in/into [A1 emph A2 emph] enter. **o:** house; room, hall □ *The door opened, and Bill* ***came in***. □ ***Into*** *the hall* ***came*** *a wet, bedraggled figure.*

come in on [A3] join, have a share or part in. **S:**

public; tradesman, worker. **o:** plan, scheme, venture □ *If you want to* ***come in on*** *the venture, you must decide quickly.* ⇨ be/bring/get/let in on.

come in on the ground floor [A3] (informal) join a venture etc at the start. **S:** investor, speculator; partner, associate □ *Those who* ***came in on the ground floor*** *have seen their capital doubled in under three years.* ⇨ be in on the ground floor; get in[3].

not have enough imagination/intelligence/sense to come in out of the rain [A3] (informal) be very stupid or foolish □ *You think he's a great scholar, just because he reads old manuscripts. How could he be a great scholar? He* ***hasn't enough imagination to come in out of the rain.*** ASA

come in with [A3] (informal) join sb in a venture. **o:** firm, partnership, group □ *You can* ***come in with*** *us if you can put up* (= contribute) *five hundred pounds.*

come into[1] [A2 emph] enter. ⇨ come in/into.

come into[2] [A2] inherit. **o:** fortune, legacy; one's share of sth □ *She* ***came into*** *a fortune when her uncle died.* □ *I don't* ***come into*** *my share of the legacy until I'm twenty-one.*

come into action [A2] (military) begin to act, operate. **S:** troops; guns □ *There was a lull of a few seconds before the oiled machinery of pursuit* ***came into action.*** HD ⇨ be in/bring into/go into action.

come into being/existence [A2] start, begin, to exist. **S:** body, formation; industry □ *Later, two more armies* ***came into being*** *— the First Canadian under Crerar and the Third American under Patton.* MFM □ *Do you know when Parliament first* ***came into existence****?* ⇨ be in/bring into being/existence.

come into blossom/flower [A2] (of blossom, flowers) open, show. **S:** bush, shrub; crocus, daffodil □ *The trees are late* ***coming into blossom*** *this year.* ⇨ be in/bring into blossom/flower.

come into bud/leaf [A2] (of a bud, leaf, on a tree or bush) appear, show itself. **S:** tree, shrub; branch, bough □ *The rose-bushes have* ***come into bud*** *much later than usual.* ⇨ be in bud/leaf.

come into effect [A2] begin to operate, take effect. **S:** regulation, provision; arrangement, schedule; timetable, programme □ *The new cuts in income-tax will not* ***come into effect*** *until the beginning of August.* □ *The revised work-schedule* ***comes into effect*** *next week.* ⇨ put into effect.

come into fashion/vogue [A2] become fashionable. **S:** leather, plastic; long hair, gaudy ties □ *Short hair and short skirts* ***came into fashion*** *at about the same time during the 1920s.* ⇨ be in/bring into fashion/vogue; be in[1], come in[1].

come into focus [A2] (of sth viewed through a microscope, telescope etc) become sharp and clear; (fig) become clearly visible, intelligible. **S:** microscope, specimen; question, problem, issue □ *Draw the eyepiece towards you and the object will* ***come into*** *sharp* ***focus.*** □ *Now that you've explained the important issues, everything* ***comes into*** *much clearer* ***focus.*** ⇨ be in/bring into focus.

come into force [A2] begin to operate (and be in some way binding or enforceable). **S:** law, regulation, requirement □ *New regulations will soon* ***come into force*** *for the drivers of heavy vehicles.* □ *The Industrial Relations Bill* ***came into force*** *gradually — over a period of months.* ⇨ be in/bring into/put into force.

come into the open [A2] be frank, speak frankly; become obvious; be made public. **S:** he etc; view, attitude; feelings; hostility, greed; quarrel, controversy □ *Why don't you* ***come into the open*** *and say exactly what's on your mind?* □ *His hatred of his brother would have* ***come into the open*** *long before if he had not left home at such an early age.* TST ⇨ be in/bring into the open.

come into one's own [A2] reach fulfilment (of one's personality, capabilities etc) □ *I am thinking of the woman in early-middle or middle age, when she has fully established herself as the mother of the family, when she* ***comes into her own.*** □ *The Lotus car* ***came into its own*** *when Jim Clark won the great American race at Indianapolis.*

come into play [A2] become involved, start to have an influence. **S:** force(s), circumstance(s), factor(s) □ *All kinds of forces* ***come into play*** *when a nation's vital interests are threatened.* □ *If we want to sell abroad, a new set of factors — different tastes, local competition, and so on —* ***come into play.*** ⇨ be in/bring into play.

come into sb's possession [A2] come to be held, possessed, by sb (often temporarily or illegally). **S:** money, jewels; firearms □ *The police asked the arrested man how the revolver had* ***come into his possession*** (or: *how he had* ***come into possession of*** *the revolver*). □ the second pattern is used by the police in statements of evidence: *On that date the accused was said to have* ***come into possession of*** *a stolen vehicle.* ⇨ be in sb's possession.

come into power [A2] (politics) reach, attain, (political) power. **S:** party; administration; clique, faction □ *The present government* ***came into power*** *a year ago.* ⇨ be in/put into power.

come into prominence [A2] become well known. **S:** politician, (party) member; industrialist, trades unionist □ *He suddenly* ***came into prominence*** *as a result of his refusal to obey the party-line on the nationalization of steel.* ⇨ bring into prominence.

come into season [A2] become seasonable or available (in shops). **S:** oysters, (fresh) salmon; raspberries, peaches □ *Tomatoes* ***come into season*** *much earlier in Italy than in Northern Europe.* ⇨ be in season; be in[3], come in[2].

come into service/use [A2] begin to serve the public, begin to be used, available. **S:** (railway, air) line; ferry, bridge, road □ *The new type of bus* ***comes into service*** *later this month.* □ *This stretch of motorway will not* ***come*** *back* ***into use*** *until extensive tests have been made.* ⇨ be in/bring into/go into service/use.

come into sight/view [A2] appear. **S:** traveller; car, train; coast; town □ *As the plane came down through the clouds, green fields and white houses* ***came into sight.*** □ *The church spire* ***came into view*** *as we rounded the next bend.* ⇨ be in/bring into sight/view.

come into the world [A2] be born. **S:** infant, child □ *One of the arguments in favour of birth control is that only those children* ***come into the world*** *who are genuinely wanted.*

come into collision (with) [A2] hit; collide (with). **S:** car, lorry; ship; train □ *His car* ***came into collision with*** *a bus at the crossroads.* □ *The two vehicles* ***came into collision*** *at great speed.* ⇨ be in collision (with).

come into contact (with) [A2] touch; meet. **S:** (electrical) lead, wire; agent, official □ *When this piece of metal* ***comes into contact with*** *the wires* (or: *When the metal and the wires* ***come into contact****) the circuit is complete.* □ *In his job as Public Relations Officer he* ***comes into contact with*** *all kinds of people.* ⇨ be in/bring into contact (with).

come into line (with) [A2] conform with the rules etc of a movement, party etc. **S:** disciple, follower, adherent. **o:** (***with***) (party, church) doctrine, the official view □ *He is not the sort of man to* ***come*** *easily* ***into line with*** *the rest of his colleagues.* □ *The prospect of a Cabinet post is a strong inducement for him to* ***come*** *back* ***into line****.* ⇨ be in/bring into/fall into line (with).

come of[1] [A2] be descended from. ⇨ come from/of[1].

come of[2] [A2] be the result of. ⇨ come from/of[2].

come of age [A2] reach the age of legal responsibility: reach (in England) the age of 18 (formerly 21); reach maturity □ *When she* ***comes of age****, she will be able to do what she likes with the money her father left her.* □ *The Hire Purchase system, which recently* ***came of age****, now faces the problems of maturity.* OBS

come off[1] [A1 emph A2] fall from. **o:** horse, pony; bicycle □ *The horse refused at the first fence, and that's when I* ***came off****.* □ *He* ***came off*** *his horse when it refused to take* (= jump over) *a fence.* ⇨ be off[1].

come off[2] [A1 emph A2] become detached. **S:** handle, knob; paint. **o:** door; wall □ *When I lifted the jug up, the handle* ***came off****.* □ *The first time the baby played with the toy, a lot of the paint* ***came off****.* ⇨ be off[2], take off[1].

come off[3] [A1] be removable. **S:** handle; cover, lid; paint, varnish; glue □ *'Do these knobs* ***come off****?' 'No, they're fixed on permanently.'* □ *'The lid of this tin won't* ***come off*** *for me; can you move it?'*

come off[4] [A1] (informal) take place. **S:** marriage; race, hunt, moon-shot; royal visit □ *When does the next American moon-shot* ***come off****?* □ *My friend's marriage didn't* ***come off****; his fiancée broke off the engagement at the last minute.*

come off[5] [A1] (informal) be successful. **S:** trick, scheme; effort, attempt, manœuvre, experiment □ *It was a good scheme and it nearly* ***came off****.* DS □ *Their attempt to rob the mail-train didn't* ***come off****.* ⇨ bring off[2].

come off[6] [A1] (informal) fare. **S:** competitor, rival, opponent. **A:** well, badly; second best □ (horoscope) *Don't argue with a superior if you can avoid it. This is a week when you are likely to* ***come off*** *second best.* WI □ *How did Mary* ***come off*** *in the affair?*

come off[7] [A2] have finished doing sth, no longer be involved in sth. **S:** salesman, executive; detective. **o:** job, assignment; case □ *The journalist had just* ***come off*** *an assignment which had taken him half way round the world.* □ *'I want you to* ***come off*** *that fraud case,' said the inspector. 'I've got some more urgent work for you to do.'* ⇨ take off[6].

come off[8] [A2] be removed from (so that an overall price etc is less). **S:** fifty pence, £5; tax, surcharge, tariff. **o:** price; petrol, refrigerator; medical supplies □ *I'm waiting until Budget Day to see if something will* ***come off*** *the price of cars.* □ *Under the new trade agreement, the import tariff* ***comes off*** *certain kinds of goods.* ⇨ take off[8].

come off the gold standard [A2] abandon the system by which the value of a currency is based on that of gold □ *When Britain* ***came off the gold standard****, in 1931, the economy of many other countries was affected also.*

come off it [A2] (informal) not say things which one knows can't be true; stop trying to mislead others □ *'Oh,* ***come off it****! You can't expect me to believe that nonsense!'* □ *'We know you're just pretending to be concerned — now* ***come off it****!'* □ usu imper.

come on[1] [A1] be quick, make an effort. ⇨ come along/on[1].

come on[2] [A1] make progress. ⇨ come along/on[2].

come on[3] [A1] grow, progress. ⇨ come along on[3].

come on[4] [A1] leave a place in order to arrive at a destination later than sb else □ *'You had better go to the station now; I'll* ***come on*** *later.'*

come on[5] [A1] be cheerful or strong; pull oneself together (q v) □ *The woman had been weeping for more than an hour. At last her husband said gently: '****Come on****, now, my dear! Bear up! It isn't the end of the world, you know.'* □ imper only.

come on[6] [A1] start. **S:** fever, cold; headache, migraine; attack of hay fever □ *'My throat's dry and a bit sore; perhaps I've got a cold* ***coming on****.'* ⇨ bring on[3].

come on[7] [A1] begin to arrive. **S:** ⚠ night; winter □ *The travellers wanted to reach the inn before night* ***came on****.* □ *Winter is* ***coming on****: you can feel it in the air.*

come on[8] [A1] begin. **S:** ⚠ (the) rain, snow □ *Just as we were beginning to enjoy ourselves, the rain* ***came on*** *and spoilt everything* □ cf *It* ***came on*** *to rain/snow,* in which *rain* and *snow* are verbs.

come on[9] [A1] (cricket) begin to bowl. **S:** pace bowler, leg-spinner □ *A new bowler* ***came on*** *and soon succeeded in reducing the batsmen's rate of scoring.* □ *Trueman* ***came on*** *(to bowl) after the tea interval.* ⇨ be on[4], bring on[4], put on[10].

come on[10] [A1] (theatre) appear on, walk on to (the stage in a play, concert, opera etc); (sport) join a team (football etc) in the course of a match. **S:** actor; player □ *When Laurence Olivier* ***came on*** *for the first time, the audience applauded.* □ *Marsh* ***came on*** *as a substitute for Cooper only ten minutes before the end of the game.* ⇨ be on[5].

come on[11] [A1] be shown, performed. **S:** film, play, opera □ *'The big film doesn't* ***come on*** *until nine o'clock, so there's plenty of time for us to get to the cinema.'* □ *There's a very good play*

coming on *at The Lyric next week.* ⇨ be on[6], put on[11].

come on[12] [A1] (legal) be considered (by a court). **S:** ⚠ the case, lawsuit, hearing, action □ *They have been waiting a long time for their case to* ***come on***. ⇨ be on[7].

come-on [nom (A1)] (informal) gesture, tone of voice etc, which indicates that sb (esp a woman) is trying to make amorous advances □ *She had very large dark eyes. But she didn't look like a pick-up and there was no trace of* ***come-on*** *in her voice.* TLG

come on the scene [A2] appear; become a participant in some activity. **S:** police, fire-brigade, ambulance; (new) child, (second) wife □ *When their first child* ***came on the scene****, they had to change their way of life completely.* □ *I* ***came on the scene*** *long after the treasure had been largely plundered, but I am still enchanted by the glimpses I get, from time to time, of the riches that remain.* LWK ⇨ be on the scene.

come on down/in/out/round/up [A3] a more persuasive invitation than 'come in' (⇨ come in/into) □ *'****Come on in*** *and have a chat.'* □ *'****Come on up****. The front door's open.'* □ imper only.

come on in, the water's fine [A3] (informal) an invitation to sb to bathe in the sea, a river, a lake, a swimming pool; (fig) an invitation to sb to join an enjoyable or profitable activity □ *'If you're thinking of becoming a journalist like me, I'd be the last to discourage you.* ***Come on in, the water's fine****!'*

come on top of [A2] follow (often as a complicating or aggravating factor). **S:** additional burden, extra expense, family illness □ *This embarrassment,* ***coming on top of*** *a row with Berthe and Nicholas, was more than she could stand.* HAA

come on/upon [A2] encounter; find. **o:** traveller, stranger; book; antique; coin, medal □ *As we turned the corner we* ***came on*** *a group of men who were waiting for the public house to open.* □ *I* ***came on*** *this old edition of Pope's works while I was going through some trunks in the attic of my grandfather's house.*

come on/upon one [A2] (of sth unwelcome) arrive; affect, strike, one. **S:** winter, chilly spell, the rains; crisis, catastrophe □ *Many misfortunes* ***came upon us*** *during that harsh winter.* ⇨ be on/upon one.

come out[1] [A1] (industry) stop work, strike. **S:** workers (of any organized group). **A:** on strike; in support, in sympathy □ *The dockers have* ***come out*** *to a man.* CSWB ⇨ be out[1], bring out[1].

come out[2] [A1] leave, be released from, prison. **S:** prisoner, convict; detainee. **A:** of gaol, on parole, early □ *Jones got a three-year sentence, but he may* ***come out*** *early for good conduct.* ⇨ be out[2], let out/out of.

come out[3] [A1] formally enter society (of a debutante) □ *My eldest daughter* ***comes out*** *next season.* □ restricted to 'high' society; note coming-out as a modifier in: *She met a charming young man at her* ***coming-out*** *ball.* ⇨ be out[3], bring out[3].

come out[4] [A1] flower, blossom. **S:** tulip, rose; bud □ *The crocuses have* ***come out*** *early this year because of the mild winter.* ⇨ be out[4], bring out[4].

come out[5] [A1] appear, become visible. **S:** ⚠ the sun, moon, stars □ *The child loved to watch the stars* ***come out*** *at night.* □ *During the morning the sky was overcast, but in the afternoon the sun* ***came out****.* ⇨ be out[5].

come out[6] [A1] appear in the shops; be published. **S:** model, brand; book; novel, article □ *We have several additions to our very successful 'Primula' range* ***coming out*** *this month.* □ *'Have you found a title for the book?' 'No, not yet.' 'When will it* ***come out****?' asked Isabel.* PW ⇨ be out[6], bring out[5].

come out[7] [A1] be told; be disclosed, revealed. **S:** ⚠ the (real) truth; the news, the (whole) story, all the facts □ *The news has just* ***come out*** *that the Princess is going to have a baby next March.* □ *When Puchert was killed in 1959 by a bomb placed in his car in Frankfurt, the story of the Red Hand murders* ***came*** *right* ***out*** *into the open.* TO ⇨ be out[7], let out[2].

come out[8] [A1] be revealed or shown up clearly. **S:** detail; spot, work; curve, moulding; letter, engraving; face, feature; subject, sitter (of portrait painter) □ *The detail of the carving* ***comes out*** *very sharply in this oblique light.* □ *Everyone* ***came out*** *well in the wedding photograph except the bride, unfortunately.* ⇨ bring out[6].

come out[9] [A1] be spoken. **S:** ⚠ a/the word(s); a declaration, statement □ *No sooner had the words* ***come out*** *than I regretted my indiscretion in speaking them.* □ *The things she had prepared to say fled from her, and instead words* ***came out*** *which had no origin in her conscious mind.* PW ⇨ bring out[7].

come out[10] [A1] become clear or explicit, be revealed. **S:** truth, sense, meaning □ *I think the inner meaning of the composition* ***comes out*** *very clearly in his interpretation.* ⇨ bring out[8].

come out[11] [A1] emerge, be elicited. **S:** the best/worst in sb; strength, dependability, steadiness; weakness, shiftiness □ *At such testing times, only the good in him* ***came out****, and none of the bad.* □ *His eyes glinted and you could see the low cunning* ***coming out*** *in him as he sang the praises of the clapped-out car he was trying to sell.* ⇨ bring out[9].

come out[12] [A1] produce a satisfactory answer. **S:** sum, calculation, problem □ *'Can you help me with this sum, please? It won't* ***come out****.'* ⇨ get out[5], work out[2].

come out[13] [A1] be announced, be declared. **S:** (examination) result, mark, class-list; election results □ *When do the psychology results* ***come out****?* □ *I hope my A-level marks* ***come out*** *before I go on holiday.* ⇨ be out[15].

come out[14] [A1] be placed (in an examination, test etc). **A:** top, bottom; second, fifth □ *They were very disappointed when their son* ***came out*** *bottom in the examination.*

come out against [A3] show that one is opposed to sth, speak against it. **o:** proposal, suggested change; legislation, reform □ *In his speech to the House, the Minister* ***came out*** *clearly* ***against*** *any change to the existing law.*

come out at [A3] cost, be calculated at; work out at (q v). **S:** total; party; excursion, move □ *If you pay a pound for a hundred, they* ***come out at*** *1p each.* □ *What is the cost of putting your car back on the road going to* ***come out at****?*

come out (for/to) [A1 A3] leave home (with a friend) for an excursion, etc. **o:** (***for***) drive, walk, picnic; (***to***) the pictures, the theatre □ *Would you like to* ***come out for*** *a drive in the country?* □ (old song) *'Boys and girls,* ***come out to*** *play, the moon is shining bright as day.'* □ *Will you* ***come out to*** *dinner with me on Friday?* ⇨ be out (at), go out[1], go/take out (for/to).

come out in [A3] become (partially) covered with. **S:** skin; face, chest, arms. **o:** ⚠ pimples, hives, a rash, spots □ *Shortly after I had eaten the lobster I* ***came out in*** *spots.* ⇨ bring out in.

come out in the wash [A3] (informal) be set right, right itself/themselves (in the end); be made clear. **S:** it; things; everything □ *The modern tendency is to avoid taking decisions, and to procrastinate in the hope that things will* ***come out*** *all right* ***in the wash***. MFM

come out in favour (of) [A3] make a decision for, support. **o:** change, reform; law, Bill □ *The Liberals, who held the balance of power in Parliament,* ***came out in favour of*** *the Government.*

come out/out of[1] [A1 emph A2] leave, emerge from. **o:** house, school, cinema □ *We were caught up in a rush of people* ***coming out of*** *the football ground.* □ *Police went into the house to try to persuade the man to* ***come out***. ⇨ be out-/out of[1], bring out/out of.

come out/out of[2] [A1 emph A2] leave the place where it has been fixed. **S:** peg, nail, bolt. **o:** ground, wall, metal □ *The little girl's front tooth* ***came out*** *when she bit the apple.* □ *'Can you help me to open this bottle? The cork won't* ***come out***.*'* □ *The screw was rusty and wouldn't* ***come out of*** *the wall.* ⇨ be out/out of[2], take out/out of.

come out/out of[3] [A1 emph A2] disappear (with cleaning). **S:** mark, stain, spot; colour, dye □ *Do you think these ink-marks will* ***come out of*** *my dress if I boil it?* □ *The colours in these materials are guaranteed not to* ***come out***. ⇨ be out/out of[3].

come out/out of badly/well [A1] (informal) be revealed (as behaving or as having behaved in a good or bad way). **S:** nobody, everyone □ *In the scandal caused by the Minister's foolish behaviour, nobody* ***came out well***. □ *In the comparisons that were made between the two women, Isabel seldom* ***came out best***. PW

come out of the blue [A2] (informal) happen, appear, be said, suddenly, unexpectedly. **S:** he etc; arrival, return; comment, statement; discovery, success □ *She had* ***come out of the blue*** *just when she was wanted but, like so many others involved in the case, she was out to make money.* T □ *Those remarks of his tend to* ***come*** *right* ***out of the blue***, *and anyone not knowing him is invariably shocked.* ⇨ be out of the blue.

come out of one's shell [A2] (informal) overcome one's shyness; show a bolder, perhaps unexpected, side of one's character □ *I think she was rather pleased with me and the way I was* ***coming out of my shell***. HAHA □ *He has to know you for a long time before he really begins to* ***come out of his shell***. ⇨ bring out of his shell.

come out on the right/wrong side [A3] (informal) (not) lose money. **S:** dealer, trader, salesman □ *He sold his goods at very low prices but he always managed to* ***come out on the right side***.

come out on top [A3] (informal) win, overcome difficulties, prove oneself superior to others □ *He had a long struggle in his early days as a manufacturer, but he* ***came out on top*** *in the end.*

come out (to) [A1 A3] ⇨ come out (for/to).

come out with [A3] (informal) speak, say (perhaps after some hesitation). **o:** the truth, facts; shocking, filthy language; some strange remarks, statements; the (astonishing) theory, statement that... □ *When Steve dropped his nonsense and* ***came out with*** *the truth, he was at his most engaging.* SPL □ *He* ***came out with*** *a string of four-letter words that brought blushes to quite a few of the elderly ladies present.*

come (over) [A2] (informal) try to impress, persuade etc, by assuming a false manner or behaving in an insincere way. **noun complement:** it; the high and mighty, the barrack-room lawyer, the wronged wife □ *Of course, she tries to win sympathy by* ***coming*** *the badly-used little woman* ***over*** *everybody.* □ *Just let him try* ***coming*** *the big boss* ***over*** *me!* □ *It gives me a pain in the neck watching that fool* ***coming*** *it* ***over*** *people who are ten times better at the job than he is.*

come over[1] [A1] visit sb (usu after crossing the sea or making a journey by air or land) □ *If you can get leave, please* ***come over*** *this weekend.* RFW □ *My French pen-friend is* ***coming over*** *for a holiday this summer.* ⇨ be over[4], bring over.

come over[2] [A1] reach (England, America) as a migrant □ *My ancestors* ***came over*** *with the Normans (the Pilgrim Fathers).*

come over[3] [A2] (informal) overtake, seize, affect. **S:** (sudden) feeling, sense, wave, fit of; attack of hopelessness, futility; dizziness, nausea, fear; what ever...? □ *A fit of stubbornness* ***came over*** *him and he refused to have anything further to do with the scheme.* □ *'I've never seen him looking so cheerful! What has* ***come over*** *him?'*

come over[4] [A1] (suddenly) feel or become. **adj: complement** (all, quite, rather) tired, sick, faint, dizzy; nasty, bad-tempered; canny, crafty □ *I thought of this, and thought of that, and altogether I* ***came over*** *quite absent-minded.* TC □ somewhat sub-standard esp when *all* precedes the adj.

come over (to) [A1 A3] change sides, one's allegiance etc. **S:** country; power; agent, general, scientist. **o:** us, our side, the allies □ *At a crucial point in the war, one of the enemy's most powerful allies* ***came over to*** *our side.* □ *How would you like to* ***come over to*** *us? You could double your salary within a year.* ⇨ bring over (to), go over to[1].

come round[1] [A1] arrive (of a periodical event or occasion). **S:** Christmas, Easter; pay-day, my birthday; the annual Conference □ *The Commonwealth Prime Ministers' Conference* ***comes round*** *next month.* SC

come round[2] [A1] regain consciousness □ *'Thank goodness, dear, you're* ***coming round***. *You fainted you know.'* DC ⇨ bring round[2].

come round[3] [A1] (informal) recover one's good humour □ *He's sulking because his parents* *wouldn't let him go to the pictures; but he'll soon **come round**.*

come round (to)[1] [A1 emph A3] come to, visit, sb or a place (usu within the the same town etc). ⇨ come around/round (to)[1].

come round (to)[2] [A1 A3 rel] agree (after disagreeing), change one's attitude. ⇨ come around/round (to)[2].

come round to [A3] (informal) reach the point of doing sth after procrastination or unavoidable delay □ *When he finally **came round to** writing the letter, he found his feelings were easier to express than he had expected.* ⇨ get around/round to.

come through [A1 A2] recover from a serious illness (mental or physical); survive. **S:** patient; business, enterprise; country. **o:** illness; crisis, war □ *I knew there was something that I ought to say, something that would reassure my doctor that I had **come through**, only I did not know what it was.* □ *He considered himself fortunate to have **come through** two world wars unscathed.* ⇨ bring through.

come through (on) [A1 A3] make communication with sb (by means of); be received (by); (of a message) arrive. **S:** he etc; message, communication; news, results; order. **o:** telephone, line; wireless, radio □ *I was just leaving the office when Robert **came through on** the phone from London.* CON □ *A message was **coming through** from Brazil when the signal went completely.* TBC ⇨ be through (to), get through (to)[2], put through (to).

come to[1] [A1] recover consciousness □ *When he **came to**, he could not, for a moment, recognize his surroundings.* ⇨ come round[2].

come to[2] [A1] (nautical) stop; heave to (q v). **S:** ship, boat □ *The boat **came to** with a few feet of clear water to port.* □ *A police patrol boat hailed to us to **come to**.* ⇨ bring to[2].

come to[3] [A2] be equal to, reach, a total; amount to[1] (q v). **S:** bill, account; shopping, purchases, goods □ *The bill **came to** five pounds, fifty pence.* □ *I didn't expect those few items to **come to** so much.* ⇨ bring to[3].

come to sb's aid/assistance/help [A2] give aid etc to sb. **S:** rescue team, fire brigade, police. **o:** (*of*) climber, swimmer; occupant, owner □ *Firemen **came to the aid of** a man trapped on the top floor of a burning house.* □ *The motorist was asked to give his position, so that the breakdown truck could **come to his assistance**.* ⇨ bring to sb's aid/assistance.

come to attention [A2] (military) adopt an alert straight-backed posture, with the feet together. **S:** soldier; company, platoon □ *'When the officer speaks to you, **come** smartly **to attention**, and stand still!'* ⇨ be at/bring to attention.

come to sb's attention/notice [A2] be noticed, remarked. **S:** it… that he was there; fact, matter, circumstances □ *It **came to his attention** that his wife was often seen in the company of another man.* □ *It has **come to my notice** that you have not been working as well as you used to.* ⇨ bring to sb's attention/notice.

come to blows [A2] start fighting. **S:** (two) sides, parties, teams; rivals, opponents □ *We didn't actually **come to blows**, but we spent the rest of the day staring out of opposite windows.* DIL ⇨ bring to blows.

come to the boil [A2] reach boiling-point; (fig) reach crisis point. **S:** water, milk; situation, discussion □ *The kettle was **coming to the boil**, and he made quite certain that its spout was directed out of harm's way.* TT □ *Just as the rather heated exchange was about to **come to the boil**, the Chairman called the speakers to order.* ⇨ bring to the boil.

come to a climax [A2] reach a high level of intensity, drama etc. **S:** noise, din; disturbance, rioting; quarrel, disagreement □ *Their discussions **came to a** noisy **climax** late in the evening.* □ *Their argument **came to a climax** when she threw a plate at him.* ⇨ bring to a climax.

come to a bad etc end [A2] (informal) meet an unpleasant fate. **adj:** ⚠ bad, no good; sticky (= unpleasant), nasty □ *Give my regards to Carlo; tell him George **came to no good end**.* US □ *I always knew that chap would **come to a sticky end**.*

come to a dead end [A2] (informal) reach a point beyond which no progress can be made. **S:** inquiry, investigation; survey, research; conversation □ *It was puzzling; we seemed to have **come to a dead end**. 'Have you any idea why she did it?' 'None at all', he replied.* ⇨ be at/bring to a dead end.

come to an end [A2] end, finish; be exhausted. **S:** campaign, war; trouble, turmoil; patience, forbearance □ *We are all relieved that the month-old strike seems to be **coming to an end**.* □ *The good relationship which existed between managers and men has **come to an end**.* ⇨ be at/bring to an end, put an end/a stop to.

come to one's feet [A2] stand up quickly. **S:** audience, crowd (at a match) □ *Several members (of Parliament) **came to their feet** at once to answer the accusation.* □ *The audience **came to their feet** as the National Anthem was played.* ⇨ be on one's feet, bring to his feet.

come to the fore [A2] become prominent. **S:** member (of a group); politician, industrialist; scholar, writer □ *Past memories, which are overlaid during the waking state by our sensory impressions, **come to the fore** during sleep in the form of dreams.* SNP □ *He first **came to the fore** in a rather lean time for British politics.* ⇨ be/bring to the fore.

come to fruition [A2] be realized, fulfilled. **S:** hope, dream, ambition; plan, scheme □ *Their hopes of a happy life together never **came to fruition**.* WDM □ *After years of work, he had the pleasure of seeing all his plans **come to fruition**.* ⇨ bring to fruition.

come to grief [A2] be destroyed; be a failure. **S:** car, plane; scheme, plan; business □ *The ship **came to grief** on a hidden rock.* □ *The cocktail party nearly **came to grief**, for the chief guest did not arrive until it was well under way.*

come to the ground [A2] fall down. **S:** pole, tent; chimney, tower □ *The chimney **came** crashing **to the ground** in a cloud of dust.* ⇨ bring to the ground.

come to a halt/standstill [A2] (of the movement or progress of sth) stop, be unable to progress further. **S:** car, convoy; production, factory □ *Don't open the door until the car **comes to a** complete **halt**.* □ *Production has **come to a standstill** owing to the lack of raw materials.* ⇨ be at/bring to a halt/standstill.

come to harm [A2] be hurt, harmed; fall under a bad influence. **adj:** (no) great, (no) real, (no) serious □ *I shall really have to accompany you, if only in order to see that you* ***come to*** *no* ***harm****.* US □ *Most parents think that their children will* ***come to*** *no great* ***harm*** *if they go to a discotheque now and then.*

come to a head [A2] reach a critical or culminating stage. **S:** matter, argument, quarrel, crisis; (our) fears, doubts □ *The matter may* ***come to a head*** *at an early meeting of the Parliamentary Labour Party.* DM ⇨ bring to a head.

come to heel [A2] obey; accept an obedient role; fall into line (q v) □ *He had only to speak one word and his dog would* ***come to heel*** *at once.* □ *As I walked I threatened the universe. If it did not* ***come to heel*** *soon, my reprisals would begin and they would be terrible.* CON ⇨ bring to heel.

(if it) come to that [A2] (informal) if it is, were, a question of that (= 'now that (I) think about it'; 'since you mention it' etc) □ *He hated taking favours from her family.* ***If it came to that****, it was her family who was to blame for the whole thing.* DC □ *She went on to confess that she had never been to a cocktail party, and Pop said: '****Come to that****, neither have I!'* DBM

if/when it comes to the crunch/push [A2] (informal) if or when it becomes unavoidable; if the need is great enough □ *It was easy enough to visualize him blowing up the bridge* ***if it came to the push*** *and given the right company.* ILIH □ ***If it comes to the crunch*** *and we have to sell up I can always go back to my old job.*

come to it [A2] (informal) reach a state (usu unpleasant) as a result of a change in age, strength, ability, wealth, etc □ *'I hear that poor old Smith has had to resign from the Board because of ill-health.' 'Ah, well; I suppose we all have to* ***come to it*** *in the end.'* □ *'So John has got to start earning his living? We all have to* ***come to it****,' he said with a smile.*

come to life [A2] become lively, interested, animated; arouse oneself from a passive state □ *You're very awkward with Anne and Johnny. But with Alice you really* ***come to life****.* RATT □ *Only when I have a high temperature do my mental images* ***come to*** *independent* ***life****.* DOP ⇨ bring to life.

come to light [A2] be revealed or discovered. **S:** fact, evidence; truth □ *So far no case has* ***come to light*** *where false confessions have been produced because of the psychological effect of the instrument.* SNP □ *The accountant's part in the fraud* ***came to light*** *when a customer asked for an up-to-date statement of payments and withdrawals.* ⇨ bring to light.

(never/not) come to anything/come to nothing [A2] have no useful or interesting result; be a complete failure. **S:** inquiries; plans, scheme; hopes, work, agreement, deliberations, negotiations; love affair; he etc □ *No one had mentioned the security inquiries, which I assumed had* ***come to nothing****.* NM □ *The two men had brave schemes for making big money quickly. They* ***never came to anything****.* AITC □ *He* ***never came to anything*** *in the end.* ⇨ next entry.

(never/not) come to much [A2] (informal) (never, not) be, or do anything of any importance or consequence. **S:** he etc; scheme, plan, plot, conspiracy □ *As an artist, he'll* ***never come to much****: he lacks the creative fire.* □ *I doubt whether John's new venture will* ***come to much****; he hasn't got enough capital to make a success of it.* ⇨ previous entry.

come to oneself [A2] return to one's normal state; recover (full) consciousness □ *I didn't realize how ill I had been, how not myself, till I* ***came to myself*** *in that pretty, sunny sitting-room of yours.* PW ⇨ bring to himself.

come to the point [A2] deal directly with what is of chief importance (in a speech, letter, book etc). **A:** straight, straight away, directly, immediately; after some hesitation □ *The Home Secretary was both brusque and tactfully subtle at the same time. He* ***came to the point*** *straight away* (or: ***came*** *straight* ***to the point***). TBC

come to a pretty pass/such a pass [A2] (informal) reach (such) a sad or sorry state. **S:** things, events, affairs; they etc □ *Things have* ***come to a pretty pass*** *when she says she can't live on £25 a week.* □ *How did we* ***come to such a pass*** *that we could stand by while he took over control?* ⇨ bring to a pretty pass etc.

come to sb's/the rescue [A2] save sb from a difficult or dangerous situation. **S:** warden, gamekeeper; fireman; bank, insurance company □ *Let's not wait for somebody to* ***come to our rescue*** *— let's build a raft.* □ *The International Monetary Fund* ***came to the rescue*** *when Britain was in financial difficulties.* SC

come to rest [A2] stop, reach a final position. **S:** missile; spear; ball; train, plane □ *The car skidded off the road and* ***came to rest*** *a foot or two from somebody's front door.* ⇨ bring to rest.

come to one's senses [A2] behave, act, in a normal reasonable way, after having behaved unreasonably □ *Don't worry about John's obstinate refusal to collaborate; he'll* ***come to his senses*** *before long.* ⇨ bring to his senses.

come to something [A2] (informal) be surprising, strange. **S:** ⚠ it; (occasionally) we □ *'It's* ***coming to something*** *when I have to ask you for a kiss,' she said. 'Are you tired?'* DBM □ *We've* ***come to something*** *when workers turn down the offer of a fourteen per cent pay increase.* □ usu in the continuous and perfect tenses; often followed by a clause beginning with *when.*

come to a (successful) conclusion [A2] end well, successfully. **S:** meeting, negotiations; campaign, war □ *Talks aimed at settling the fisheries dispute have at last* ***come to a successful conclusion****.* ⇨ bring to a (successful) conclusion.

come to this [A2] (informal) reach a certain state or result. **S:** ⚠ it, things; he etc □ *This sudden clear view of his face, coupled with his fast, wild talking, suddenly made me realize that he was half-crazed. So* ***this*** *was what he had* ***come to****!* CON □ *I never thought things would* ***come to this****: you asking me for advice!*

come to the same thing (as) [A2] equal, be equivalent to, one another. **S:** it... if/whether you do A or B; (two, alternative) policies, plans, systems; answers, solutions □ *Whether you drink beer or whisky, it* ***comes to the same thing****; most of what you pay goes to the Government.* □ *Helen's elaborate speeches* ***came*** *in the end* ***to***

***the same thing as** Miss Small's brisk pronouncements.* AITC

come to (with) [A2] approach, tackle (with). **S:** scholar, scientist; planner, builder. **o:** (*to*) task, problem; post, position; marriage; (*with*) open mind, no preconceived ideas, complete lack of bias; unrealistic, romantic ideas □ *The young scientist **came to** the subject **with** a fresh, lively mind.* □ *The attitude **with** which you **come to** your new job is all-important.* ⇨ bring to[4].

come to grips with [A2] tackle; engage in a struggle with. **o:** (*with*) problem, question; disease; life □ *Man was really **coming to grips with** the question of how his newly acquired skills could help in the process of economic and social development.* T □ *This was a problem **with** which he never quite **came to grips**.* ⇨ be at/bring to/get to grips with.

come to terms with [A2] (learn to) manage or handle; reach a modus vivendi with. **o:** life, world, situation; (his) handicap, limitations; oneself □ *As Chris Kingsley says, 'Man will have to **come to terms with** his environment.'* TBC □ *'Every great artist has **come to terms with** life — think of Beethoven — how tortured he was in middle-age, and how serene at the end.'* PW

come together [A1] (of two parties in conflict) settle their differences, be reconciled. **S:** divorced couple; factions, sects □ *I doubt if they will **come together** again, even for the sake of the children.* ⇨ bring together.

come up[1] [A1] come upstairs □ *'Please don't wait down there; **come straight up**.'* ⇨ go up[1].

come up[2] [A1] travel to town (esp London) or towards the north; come into residence at a university (esp Oxford and Cambridge) □ *When you visit Britain next year, please **come up** to Edinburgh for a few days.* □ *He **came up** last year to read Modern History.* ⇨ be up[2], go up (to).

come up[3] [A1] appear above the soil; begin to grow. **S:** bean, pea, celery □ *I sowed some runner beans three weeks ago, but they haven't **come up** yet.*

come up[4] [A1] arise; be mentioned. **S:** question, problem, matter (of); (his) name. **A:** during, in, the discussion; in the course of conversation; for a decision, review □ *The question of drug-taking is bound to **come up** at the next Conference.* □ *His name **came up** whenever the matter of nuclear energy was discussed.* ⇨ be up[6], bring up[3].

come up[5] [A1] (legal) come to be considered (by a court); appear (in court). **S:** case; the accused, offender. **A:** for review; before the court; on a fresh charge; for attempted murder □ *The paper announced the cases that were to **come up** at the assizes the following day.* HD ⇨ be up[7], bring up[4].

come up[6] [A1] (military) move, be transported (to the front line). **S:** reserves; supplies; food, ammunition □ *All our supplies have to **come up** by this single railway.* □ *Roads and bridges were destroyed to prevent the enemy's reserves from **coming up**.* ⇨ bring up[5].

come up[7] [A1] (informal) be vomited. **S:** food; dinner □ *The child doesn't seem to be able to keep anything down. Everything it eats **comes up** again.* ⇨ bring up[6].

come up[8] [A1] rise through water to or above the surface. **S:** diver; fish, whale □ *He breathed like a diver **coming up** for air.* LWK □ note come up *for the third time* = have a last opportunity to be saved; be very close to death (the phrase refers to a belief that a drowning person rises three times to the surface of the water before being drowned).

come up[9] [A1] occur, arise. **S:** vacancy; opportunity □ I can't offer you a job now, but I'll let you know as soon as a vacancy ***comes up***. ASA

come up[10] [A1] appear (by chance); win (in a lottery). **S:** number, ticket, premium bond; he etc □ *One of my bonds **came up** in the last draw: I won a £25 prize.* □ *John's very lucky; he's always **coming up** on the (football) pools.*

come-uppance [nom (A1)] (one's) deserts, a punishment inflicted by Fate on sb richly deserving it □ *In the old melodramas the villain, often in the shape of the local squire-cum-capitalist, would inevitably get his **come-uppance** in the third act.* □ a humorous and unique nominalized form, not related to any common meaning of come up.

come up the hard way [A1] (informal) reach one's present position through hard work, without assistance or privileges etc □ *I **came up the hard way**: my father died before I was born, and I had to leave school when I was twelve.* ⇨ bring up the hard way; bring up[1].

come up smiling [A1] (informal) emerge bravely and cheerfully (from an unpleasant experience, defeat etc) □ *He's been disappointed in love three times already, but he always **comes up smiling**.* AITC

the sun come up [A1] rise □ *At this time of year **the sun comes up** at five and goes down at about eight-thirty in the evening.* ⇨ the sun be up.

come up against [A3] be faced with, be opposed by. **o:** problem, question (of); stubbornness, will; (fierce, strong, powerful) opposition; difficulty; enemy forces □ (horoscope) *Your carefree nature often **comes up against** the problem of money, for it just slips through your fingers.* WI □ *Not for the first time her will **came up against** her husband's.* NM ⇨ be/bring up against.

come up (as far as/to) [A1 A3] reach, extend to. **S:** town, houses; sea, fog; lawn, flowers □ *The tide never **comes up as far as** the road, even though the water is only a few feet away.* □ *The water in the swimming pool **came up to** my chin.* ⇨ be/bring up (as far as/to).

come up for [A3] be considered as an applicant, candidate etc, for. **S:** name; member (of a board). **o:** re-election, admission □ *Members of the faculty **come up for** election to the Board of Studies every two years.* ⇨ be up for, put up (for)[1].

come up for auction/sale [A3] come on the market, become available for purchase. **S:** house, farm; collection (of jewels, paintings) □ *An unusual collection of firearms dating from the 16th century **comes up for auction** next week.* □ *Is his house likely to **come up for sale** in the foreseeable future?* ⇨ be/put up for auction/sale.

come up (to)[1] [A1 A3] approach, move towards □ *The beggar **came up** (**to** me) with outstretched hand.*

come up (to)[2] [A1 A3] reach, extend (to). ⇨ come up (as far as/to).

come up to [A3] reach an acceptable level or standard. **S:** he etc; work, performance, result. **o:** ⚠ standard, scratch, the mark; sb's expectations, hopes □ *He didn't really* ***come up to*** *scratch in the end-of-year exams.* □ *For one reason or another their holiday in France didn't* ***come up to*** *expectations.* ⇨ be up to[5], bring up to, get up to[1].

come up to sb's chin/shoulder [A3] be (only) as tall as the height of another person's chin, shoulder; (***shoulder***—fig) be noticeably inferior to another person in accomplishment, ability □ *Mrs White only* ***comes up to her husband's chin*** *but there's no doubt who is the boss in* that *marriage!* □ *Some people would say that as a poet Wordsworth does not* ***come up to Browning's shoulder.*** □ often neg.

come up with[1] [A3] draw level with. **o:** convoy; car, lorry, traveller, stranger □ *The horseman* ***came up with*** *a group of people who were making the pilgrimage on foot.*

come up with[2] [A3] (informal) produce; find. **o:** suggestion, idea, information; (right) answer; solution; (plausible, convincing, reasonable) explanation □ *Scientists will have to* ***come up with*** *new methods of increasing the world's food supply.* □ *Some people apparently have an almost uncanny ability to* ***come up with*** *the right answer.*

come upon [A2] encounter. ⇨ come on/upon.

come upon one [A2] (of sth unwelcome) arrive. ⇨ come on/upon one.

come within [A2] come near enough (to be heard, seen or reached). **o:** ⚠ earshot, sight, view, range □ *At that moment a patrol* ***came within*** *view of our observation post.* □ *No aircraft* ***came within*** *range.* ⇨ be within[1], bring within, get within.

compare to [B2 pass rel] say, suggest, that one person or thing is like another. **O:** him etc; face, nose; house, machine. **o:** monster, angel; moon, turnip; rabbit-hutch □ *She was most offended when her husband* ***compared*** *her hat* ***to*** *a pudding basin.* □ *The sculpture of Rodin has been* ***compared*** *by some critics* ***to*** *that of Michelangelo.* ⇨ next entry.

compare (with) [B2 pass emph rel] set one person or thing beside another, examine them together, so as to find similarities or differences between them; do this in order to suggest similarities. **O:** figure, rate, output; machine, device; place, climate. **o:** another, others; that of... □ *If we* ***compare*** *the figure for crimes of violence* ***with*** *that of previous years, we see that there has been a great increase.* □ *The south of England is certainly beautiful, but it can't be* ***compared with*** (or: *it can't* ***compare with***) *the south of France for sunshine.* □ compare to (q v) may be used in the second of the senses given. ⇨ previous entry.

compensate (for) [A2 pass emph rel B2 pass emph rel] pay sb, offer him sth, because or a loss of injuries he has suffered; redeem some weakness. **S:** employer; insurer; nothing. **O:** worker; person insured, victim. **o:** loss, injury □ *Nothing will ever* ***compensate*** *(him)* ***for*** *the injuries he received in the accident.* □ *A firm which dismisses an employee on the grounds of redundancy is obliged to* ***compensate*** *him (****for*** *loss of employment).* □ *The car has a low top speed, but this is more than* ***compensated for*** *by superb road-holding.*

compete against [A2 pass emph rel] oppose, play against, sb in a contest etc. **S:** sportsman, athlete; business, trader □ *The young golfer has often* ***competed against*** *famous players, but so far he has always been beaten.*

compete (for) [A2 pass emph rel] rival others in trying to obtain sth. **S:** competitors, teams; trees, plants. **o:** cup, prize, medal; championship; sunshine □ *All the clubs in the Football Association are allowed to* ***compete for*** *the FA Cup.* □ *Where trees* ***compete for*** *space, air and light in the wild state, some are bound to fail to establish themselves.*

compete (with) [A2 emph rel] rival others (successfully). **o:** trade rival; industry, store; (fellow) student, pupil □ *Small suburban shops can't* ***compete with*** *the chain-stores in price, though they can do so in personal service.* □ *We are satisfied that we can* ***compete with*** *continental firms in an enlarged market.*

complain (about) [A2 pass rel] express an unfavourable opinion (about). **o:** wages, costs; work, employer; being neglected □ *If old Pearson isn't* ***complaining about*** *one thing he's* ***complaining about*** *another.* □ *The heating is so often* ***complained about*** *that I'm surprised it hasn't been improved.* ⇨ complain of[2].

complain of[1] [A2] mention some pain, discomfort etc; give as a symptom of illness. **o:** loss of weight, of appetite; fatigue; heartburn □ *The night before the woman had a heart attack she was* ***complaining of*** *indigestion.* □ *Several patients were admitted* ***complaining of*** *acute stomach pains.*

complain of[2] [A2] express dissatisfaction about. **o:** being ignored, not being consulted □ *You don't often hear a woman with two or three children* ***complaining of*** *not having enough to do.* □ object is usu the *-ing* form of a v. ⇨ complain (about).

compliment (on) [B2 pass rel] express one's admiration of. **o:** her hat, hair-style, new dress; his etc success, performance; promotion, appointment □ *Mrs Hunt was* ***complimented on*** *her choice of material for the bridesmaid's dresses.* □ *This is an achievement* ***on*** *which he should be* ***complimented.*** ⇨ congratulate (on/upon).

comply with [A2 pass emph rel] obey, abide by (q v); follow. **o:** direction, instruction, (club) rule; request, wish, desire □ *When you become a member of a club you generally agree to* ***comply with*** *the rules.* □ *Certain of their conditions are not easily* ***complied with.***

composed of [pass (B2)] (of a group) have as members, or parts, a certain number or kinds (of people, things) □ *The jury was* ***composed*** *entirely* ***of*** *men.* □ *The village was* ***composed of*** *two or three groups of thatched cottages, a church, a post-office and a small general store.* □ not often used in the present; never *be comprised of.*

compress (into) [B2 pass rel] reduce to a concentrated form; state concisely or briefly (in). **O:** wood chips, sawdust; story, facts. **o:** board, sheet; (small) space, compass □ *Wood cuttings* *and sawdust can be* ***compressed into*** *boards for furniture making.* □ *It is impossible to* ***compress*** *the story of the First World War* ***into*** *a few pages.*

compromise (with) (over) [A2 emph rel] reach agreement (with sb) (about sth), by abandoning part of one's demands. **o:** (***with***) trades union, work force; salesman, representative; (***over***) wages, conditions; contract, conditions □ *Nearly every strike is settled by employers* ***compromising with*** *their labour force.* □ ***Over*** *fishing rights in the North Sea the trawler-men are in no mood to* ***compromise****.*

compute at [B2 pass rel] (formal) calculate as; work out[2] (q v) at. **O:** cost, expenditure; loss. **o:** (a total of) £10 000, (a figure in excess of) £2 million □ *The public was astonished when Rolls Royce* ***computed*** *their debts* ***at*** *several hundred million pounds.*

conceal (from) [B2 pass emph rel] (formal) keep secret (from); hide (from). **O:** (true) facts, truth; house, building, fortifications. **o:** patient, dying man, (distraught) mother; view, road □ *The Doctor decided that he could not* ***conceal*** *the truth* ***from*** *the old man any longer.* □ ***From*** *a person as inquisitive as Janet it's hard to* ***conceal*** *anything.* □ *The house was* ***concealed from*** *the road by a small wood.*

concede (to) [B2 pass] (formal) acknowledge that one's opponent has won. **O:** election, victory. **o:** adversary, other side, opposing party □ *When three-quarters of the votes had been counted the Prime Minister* ***conceded*** *the election* ***to*** *his opponents.*

conceive of [A2 pass] (formal) imagine. **o:** situation, circumstances (in which...); period (when); reason (why) □ *The modern child finds it difficult to* ***conceive of*** *a time when there was no radio or TV.* □ *I can't* ***conceive of*** *anyone wanting to disturb the excellent relationship that has been built up with our allies.* □ often preceded by *difficult, not easy, hard,* (*scarcely*) *possible,* (*well nigh*) *impossible.*

concentrate (at) [A2 emph rel B2 pass emph rel] collect (at); bring together (at). **S:** [A2] **O:** [B2] troops, forces, men; tanks; fire-power, strength □ *The rioters* ***concentrated at*** *the main square in the town.* □ *An enormously powerful fleet was* ***concentrated at*** *Pearl Harbour.*

concentrate (on/upon) [A2 pass emph rel B2 pass emph rel] give one's full attention etc to; focus (on) (q v). **O:** ⚠ (one's) attention, thoughts; one's mind; one's efforts, energies. **o:** the job in hand; problem, work, plans; doing a good job; book, music □ *'I can't* ***concentrate on*** *what I'm doing while that noise is going on.'* □ *The girl* ***concentrated*** *her attention* ***on*** *the swinging watch and soon fell into a trance.* □ *If all one's efforts are* ***concentrated upon*** *reducing disharmony, there must be some improvement.*

concern (oneself) (about/over/with) [B2 pass] become occupied (about/over **concern (oneself) (about/over/with)** [B2 pass] become occupied (about/over sb or sth, showing some anxiety; with sb or sth, in a legitimate, straightforward, or sometimes interfering, way). **o:** loss, damage; sb's injuries; sb's movements, whereabouts □ *There is no need for you to* ***concern yourself about*** *where I was last night.* □ *He was much* ***concerned over*** *the plight of the refugees.* □ *'You would do better to* ***concern yourself with*** *your own business and not* ***with*** *mine!'* □ passive form with *be, become, get.*

concerned (in) [pass (B2)] (be) a party (to), (have) taken part (in). **o:** disturbance, riot; shouting, affray; demonstration □ *The police are anxious to interview everyone* ***concerned in*** *last night's incident* □ *He was only indirectly* ***concerned in*** *what took place.*

concur (with) [A2 emph rel] (formal) be of the same opinion as; agree (with) (q v). **o:** colleague, partner; opposing speaker, chairman □ *The Opposition* ***concurred with*** *the Government in their decision to grant asylum to the escaped political prisoners.* □ usu followed by a noun phrase introduced by *in,* as in the example, or by *in doing sth.*

condemn to [B2 pass emph rel] (legal; also fig) award the punishment of. **O:** prisoner, guilty man, the accused (person); traitor, slave, hostage. **o:** a month's, thirty years' imprisonment; life; hard labour; death; (a lifetime of) pain, misery, loneliness □ *The two men were found guilty of armed robbery, and* ***condemned to*** *four years' imprisonment.* □ *When the poor woman was widowed, she realized that she was* ***condemned to*** *a lonely old age.*

condition (to) [B2 pass emph rel] make a person or animal able to bear or endure. **S:** childhood, upbringing; training. **o:** hardship, poverty; strain □ *When a child has become* ***conditioned to*** *life in a city, he may feel quite at a loss in any other environment.* □ *The navy tries to* ***condition*** *its men* ***to*** *life in extreme climates.*

condole (with) (on) [A2] (formal) express sympathy (with sb) (for sth). **o:** (***with***) bereaved (woman etc), widow, distraught mother; (***on***) loss, death □ *It is natural to wish to* ***condole with*** *anyone who has lost a dear friend or relative.* □ *Peter wrote to* ***condole with*** *his friend* ***on*** *the death of his mother.*

conduce to [A2 emph rel] (formal) favour the development of, add sth to; contribute to[1] (q v). **S:** violence, anger, intolerance. **o:** good relations, racial harmony □ *Overcrowding in small houses hardly* ***conduces to*** *happy family relationships.*

conduct away (from) [B1i pass B3 pass rel] (formal) lead away, often with some show of force or compulsion. **S:** police, stewards, bodyguard. **O:** intruder, troublemaker, heckler. **o:** scene; meeting, platform □ *The hecklers were* ***conducted away from*** *the hall at the request of the Chairman.* □ *A steward took the man by the arm and* ***conducted*** *him firmly* ***away****.*

cone off [B1i pass] close one lane, carriageway etc of a (main) road (with cone-shaped markers) □ *Repairs are in progress on a two-mile stretch of the M1. Police have* ***coned off*** *the fast lane.* □ *Sections of the motorway have had to be* ***coned off****.* BBCTV

confer (on) [B2 pass emph rel] (formal) award, give, grant (to). **O:** title, peerage, knighthood; (honorary) degree □ *The title of Warden of the Cinque Ports was* ***conferred on*** *Winston Churchill.*

confer (with) [A2 pass emph rel] (formal) consult; discuss (with), in order to decide a course of action. **o:** solicitor; associates, board; director, manager □ *I shall have to* **confer with** *my Executive Committee before expressing an opinion on the possibility of the members of my Union returning to work.* □ *When everyone has been* **conferred with** *perhaps I can give you an answer* (cf *When we have all* **conferred**, *perhaps* etc).

confess to [A2 emph rel] acknowledge, admit to (q v). **o:** crime; stealing; killing, assaulting sb; (unreasonable) fear, dread; liking for, partiality to sth; being unable to appreciate modern art, literature etc; (a sneaking) admiration for sb; knowing nothing at all about sth □ *She* **confessed** *readily* **to** *what she described as an abysmal ignorance of politics and economics.* □ *Henderson would never have* **confessed to** *visiting strip clubs while he was in London, but...!*

confide in [A2 pass emph rel] tell one's secrets to sb (whom one trusts not to reveal them to sb else). **o:** sister, girlfriend, colleague □ *Modern girls seldom* **confide in** *their mothers.* □ *He is not the sort of man* **in** *whom I would readily* **confide**.

confine to[1] [B2 pass emph rel] limit, restrict, to. **O:** oneself; one's attention, remarks, criticism, observations. **o:** essentials, pertinent details, the matter in hand □ *I wish you would* **confine** *yourself* **to** *the matter under discussion.* □ *The jury were instructed to* **confine** *their attention* **to** *the facts, and to ignore anything that could be described as hearsay.*

confine to[2] [B2 pass emph rel] restrict sb's movements to a place, keep him within limits. **o:** one's room; the house; a certain area □ *As a result of the accident, the child was* **confined to** *the house for six weeks.* □ *As a punishment, the soldiers were* **confined to** *barracks for a week.* □ usu passive.

confirm in [B2 pass] (formal) reinforce (sb's opinions, habits etc). **S:** statement, revelation. **o:** suspicion, idea, belief; his tendency, habit; prejudice □ *What you have told me about Mr Bloggs* **confirms** *me* **in** *my suspicion that he beats his wife.*

conflict (with) [A2 emph rel] not match, be different. **S:** account, report, statement. **o:** evidence, facts, findings □ *The policeman's story* **conflicts with** *that of the accused* (or: *The policeman's story and that of the accused* **conflict**) *in several particulars.* □ *Your tale* **conflicts with** *what I have on the paper in front of me.*

conform (to/with) [A2 pass emph rel] be in accordance with; obey, observe, comply with (q v). **o:** specifications; rules, regulations; standards (of behaviour, manufacture etc) □ *Do these plans* **conform to** *the official specification for the building?* □ *If you are a member of a club, you must* **conform to** *the rules of that club.* □ *These are very simple requirements, but they must be* **conformed with**. □ *Joe's a born rebel: he just can't* **conform** (**to** *the ordinary rules of society*).

confront with [B2 pass emph rel] (formal) bring face to face with. **o:** facts; evidence, testimony □ *When the accused was* **confronted with** *the evidence of half a dozen witnesses, he broke down and confessed.*

confuse (with) [B2 pass emph rel] be unable to distinguish (between); mistake for (q v). **O:** geniune, authentic (article, product). **o:** fake, imitation (product) □ *I always* **confuse** *John Waite* **with** *John White* (cf: *I always* **confuse** *the two Johns; I always* **confuse** *John Waite* **and** *John White*). □ *This non-alcoholic cider must not be* **confused with** *the real stuff they drink in Somerset.*

congratulate (on/upon) [B2 pass] give one's good wishes, express pleasure and approval, to sb (in connection with some event or achievement). **o:** his etc engagement, marriage; the birth of a son, daughter; being awarded first prize, coming first; his good sense, sang froid, wise decision; promotion; appointment, nomination, election □ *I am writing to* **congratulate** *you most sincerely* **on** *your appointment as Headmaster of the Grammar School.* ⇨ compliment (on).

congratulate oneself (on/upon) [B2 emph rel] feel or express great satisfaction as a result of sth one has done or that has happened □ *You can* **congratulate yourselves on** *a very narrow escape; it's a miracle you weren't all burned alive.* □ *The bank-robbers were just* **congratulating themselves on** *the success of their raid when the police burst in on them.*

conjure up[1] [B1iii pass adj] evoke, suggest, a mental picture of. **O:** vision(s) of the past, of past glory, of days gone by; image, picture □ *The speaker's words* **conjured up** *a vision of a perfect world, where every man loved his neighbour.* □ *He tried to imagine the night-club proprietor and could only* **conjure up** *a picture of a fat, oily man.* PE □ *Hollywood's* **conjured-up** *visions of fabulous wealth suddenly assumed reality in Saudi Arabia.*

conjure up[2] [B1iii pass adj] cause to appear. **O:** spirits of the dead; the devil □ *Women practising witchcraft deceived their clients into believing that* **conk out** [A1] (slang) die; cease to function. **S:** he etc; car, lorry; radio, TV □ *It's hard for him to get to work and he pretty nearly* **conked out** *in November with that pleurisy.* □ *'You're quite welcome to have this old gramophone, but I'm afraid it's* **conked out**.*'*

connect up (to) [B1i pass adj B2 pass rel] join to a main supply or system; join together. **O:** telephone; wiring; electricity, gas, supply □ *There's a phone in our new flat, but it hasn't been* **connected up to** *the exchange yet.* □ *You won't get any current until you* **connect up** *the cells of the battery.*

connect with [A2] arrive in time for a traveller to catch some other convenient form of transport. **S:** bus, coach; plane □ *The early bus from the village* **connects with** *the 8.30 train.*

connected (with) [pass (B2)] (be) a member (of), have links (with) □ *'Excuse me. Are you* **connected with** *the visiting circus?' 'No, madam, this illuminated nose is merely to help me to see better.'* □ *Was Marie Antoinette* **connected with** *the Hapsburgs?* □ *This business is in no way* **connected with** *the shop next door* (or: *This business and the shop next door are in no way* **connected**). □ *The visit of the police was not* **connected with** *the lost child.*

connive at [A2 pass rel] give one's passive or moral support to. **S:** employer; local authorities; police. **o:** deceit, fraud; pilfering; immorality □ *The accountant refused to* **connive at** *his client's attempts to cheat the Income Tax authorities.* □ *A* *certain amount of petty thieving is* ***connived at*** *by the storekeepers.*

consecrate (to) [B2 pass] (formal) devote to some sacred or other specified purpose. **O:** oneself, one's life; cathedral, temple □ *The men solemnly* ***consecrated*** *their property and their lives* ***to*** *the liberation of their country.* □ *The new church was* ***consecrated*** *(****to*** *the glory and service of God) in the presence of a large congregation.*

consent (to) [A2 pass emph rel] not oppose, agree (to) (q v). **o:** engagement, attachment; (his) leaving home, going abroad; proposal, scheme, plan □ *The girl's parents reluctantly* ***consented to*** *her marriage, although she was only seventeen.* □ *The owner wouldn't* ***consent to*** *our making any structural changes in the flat.*

consign to [B2 pass emph rel] (formal) place in, deposit in (esp as a last resting place). **O:** coffin, body; prisoner; possessions. **o:** flames, waves; deepest dungeon; rubbish heap □ *In a simple ceremony the bodies of four sailors were* ***consigned to*** *the deep.* □ *He was* ***consigned to*** *a bleak prison in the old part of the city.*

consist in [A2] (formal) mean, be sth which is shown by; be equivalent to. **S:** happiness, serenity; loyalty, service. **o:** accepting one's limitations, making do with little; putting others before self □ *True patriotism* ***consists in*** *putting the interests of one's country above everything, including one's own life.* □ *Education does not* ***consist*** *simply* ***in*** *learning a lot of facts.*

consist of [A2] comprise, be composed of (q v). **S:** family, club; regiment, fleet; organism. **o:** members; tanks, ships; cells, nerves □ *The full set* ***consists of*** *72 glasses, that is one dozen of six different types.* □ *In Scotland, the jury* ***consists of*** *fifteen people, not twelve as in England.*

console oneself with [B2 rel] find comfort in. **o:** knowledge, knowing; reflection □ *You may have failed the examination, but you can at least* ***console yourself with*** *the thought that you did your best.*

consort with [A2 emph rel] (formal) keep company with, spend one's time or leisure in the company of. **o:** rogues, vagabonds, layabouts; prostitutes; professional gamblers □ *Mr Bloggs was distressed to discover that his daughter had been* ***consorting*** *for some time* ***with*** *drug addicts.*

conspire against [A2 rel] plot against, plan to overthrow. **S:** rebels, dissidents; underground army. **o:** state, regime, established order □ *A group of men were charged with* ***conspiring against*** *the duly elected government.*

conspire with [A2 emph rel] plot with, usu for an illegal purpose; (fig) join with, combine with. **o:** thief, crook; rebels, dissidents □ *A young policeman has been accused of* ***conspiring with*** *a gang of criminals.* □ *The bad weather* ***conspired with*** *a thoroughly disgusting hotel to make my holiday a resounding failure.* □ often followed by a *to*-inf as in the last example.

consult with[1] [A2] (esp US) seek the advice of. **o:** solicitor, attorney; bank; insurance company □ *You'd better* ***consult with*** *your doctor before you take on a job in such an extremely hot climate as that of the Congo.* □ American usage, where British English would normally have consult only.

consult with[2] [A2] (of equal participants) hold discussions, meet, in order to discuss matters of mutual interest □ *Senator Murphy, the Australian Attorney General, is to* ***consult with*** *the British Government on the ending of all residual powers over the Dominion* (= Australia) *held by Westminster and the Judicial Committee of the Privy Council.* T

(not) contain oneself (for) [B2] be unable to conceal or control a specified emotion. **o:** joy, anger, enthusiasm, delight □ *When the children were given a pony, they could hardly* ***contain themselves for*** *joy, but the novelty soon wore off.* □ with *can/could.*

contend (for) [A2 pass emph rel] (formal) struggle, compete, with others to win sth. **o:** prize, trophy; championship, leadership □ *How many teams are* ***contending for*** *the Cup this year?* □ *The boxer didn't consider such a small purse worth* ***contending for****.*

contend with [A2] handle, manage; bear, tolerate. **o:** much, a lot; family, mother-in-law; creditor, solicitor; problem, situation □ *I have enough to* ***contend with****, without bothering myself with your problems.* □ *If we've got to* ***contend with*** *your relatives for a week, we shall need a month's holiday afterwards.* □ *What with one thing and another, the poor chap has too much to* ***contend with****.* □ usu after *have (got) to.*

content (oneself) with [B2 pass emph rel] be satisfied with, not want more than. **o:** little money, a sufficiency; simple fare, basic necessities; what one has □ *We can't go abroad this year, so we'll have to* ***content ourselves with*** *a family holiday in London* (or: *we'll have to be* ***contented with*** etc).

continue (with) [A2 pass] not interrupt; go on doing sth, carry on[1] (q v) (with). **o:** work, study, task; hobby, pastime □ *The teacher told the class to* ***continue with*** *their work while he was out of the classroom.* □ *I don't propose to* ***continue with*** *chemistry beyond Form IV.*

contract out/out of [A1 A2 pass rel] withdraw (esp from a formal arrangement). **S:** country, ally; partner, associate. **o:** treaty, pact, alliance; undertaking, show, scheme □ *I've decided that after all I don't want to be associated with your scheme: I'm* ***contracting out****.* □ *We've had too many cases before of tenants* ***contracting out of*** *their obligations.*

contract (with) [B2 pass emph rel] (formal) form, enter into, a relationship (with). **O:** friendship, marriage; alliance, association □ *In her old age, my aunt had* ***contracted*** *a strong friendship* ***with*** *a retired sea-captain.* □ *And this is the country* ***with*** *which they now propose to* ***contract*** *a trade agreement!*

contract (with) (for) [A2 rel] make a formal agreement (with sb) to do sth. **o:** (***with***) builder, plumber, decorator, electrician; (***for***) repairs, extension, wiring □ *We* ***contracted with*** *a local carpenter* ***for*** *the woodwork* (or: *We* ***contracted with*** *him to do the woodwork) in our new boat.*

contrast (with) [A2 emph rel B2 pass emph rel] (of one thing) be sharply different from another; find, point out such differences. **S:** [A2] **O:** [B2] appearance, outward show, manner, voice. **o:** character, record, background □ [A2] *His wild threats* ***contrast*** *strangely* ***with*** *the mildness he displays when face to face with his* *rival.* □ [B2] *When the synthetic fabric is* ***contrasted with*** *the natural one, the difference is very apparent.*

contribute to[1] [A2] give, add, sth to. **S:** presence; wisdom; ideas, suggestions; speech, remarks. **o:** success; failure □ *The Queen's presence* ***contributed to*** *the success of what would otherwise have been a very ordinary affair.* □ *Bertrand Russell's speeches in Trafalgar Square* ***contributed*** *in an important way* ***to*** *the protest against nuclear proliferation.*

contribute to[2] [A2 pass emph rel B2 pass emph rel] give help towards. **O:** money, gifts, moral support. **o:** appeal, fund; resources, coffers □ *A great amount of money was* ***contributed to*** *the Bangladesh disaster fund by people from all walks of life.* □ *This is the kind of appeal* ***to*** *which most people will be glad to* ***contribute*** *(something).*

converge on [A2 emph rel] (all) move towards one point from two or more directions at once. **S:** forces; columns, patrols; assailants; shoppers. **o:** rendezvous, assembly-point, objective □ *Half-a-dozen groups of specially trained troops* ***converged*** *silently* ***on*** *the secret headquarters of the rebels.* □ *As the bulk of the German mobile reserves were located north of the Seine, they would have to approach our bridgehead from the east and would thus* ***converge on*** *Caen.* MFM

converse (with) [A2 emph rel] (formal) talk (to). **o:** guest, visitor, stranger; class, pupils □ *'If you want to* ***converse with*** *Japanese people, why don't you start learning Japanese?'* □ *The tutor will be expected to* ***converse with*** *the students on various aspects of British life.*

convert (from) (to)[1] [A2 emph rel] change from being, doing or using sth to sth else. **o:** (***from*** and ***to***) Catholicism, Judaism; gas, electricity; non-decimal system; fahrenheit scale □ *She* ***converted from*** *Christianity in order to marry a Muslim.* □ *We're thinking of* ***converting from*** *solid fuel* ***to*** *natural gas before the cold weather sets in.* □ *Britain* ***converted to*** *decimal currency on February 15th 1971.*

convert (from) (to)[2] [B2 pass emph rel] persuade sb, cause sth, to change from being, doing or using one thing to another. **O:** wife, fiancée; house, factory; car. **o:** faith, religion; solid fuel, electricity; diesel fuel □ *The preacher succeeded in* ***converting*** *a number of people* ***to*** *Unitarianism.* □ *The transmission on his car has been* ***converted from*** *manual* ***to*** *automatic — an expensive job.*

convert (into) [B2 pass rel] change, alter sth (into sth else). **O:** barn, attic, bakery; pounds, dollars. **o:** house, studio, workshop; francs, lire □ *They* ***converted*** *an old stable* ***into*** *a comfortable little house.* □ *'Do you think you could* ***convert*** *this candlestick* ***into*** *an electric lamp?'* □ *A lot of old people had difficulty in* ***converting*** *the old currency* ***into*** *the new.*

convict (of) [B2 pass rel] (legal) find or declare sb guilty (of sth). **o:** offence, crime; conspiracy; breaking and entering □ *The woman was* ***convicted of*** *murdering her old father, but she claimed that she had done so out of kindness.* □ *The offence* ***of*** *which he was* ***convicted*** *carries a stiff penalty.*

convince (of) [B2 pass emph rel] persuade sb of the truth (of sth); (in the passive) be sure (of sth). **o:** truth, validity; risk, peril; effectiveness, usefulness □ *'How can I* ***convince*** *you (****of*** *the dangers of drug-taking)?'* □ *Nothing that I could say had the slightest effect: my daughter was* ***convinced of*** *the young man's good intentions.* □ ***Of*** *this I am* ***convinced****: that Britain stands to gain by a close association with her neighbours.*

cook up [B1i pass adj] (informal) concoct, invent, often in haste. **O:** story, tale, plot; excuse, pretext □ *He arrived home at midnight with some* ***cooked-up*** *story of having been kept late at the office.* □ *If she meets a man who suits her, she'll soon* ***cook up*** *a resemblance to her ideal mate.* TC

cool down [A1 B1i pass] become or make cool or calm. **S:** [A1] **O:** [B1] it (= the weather); passion, temper; atmosphere; situation □ *'Thank heavens it's* ***cooled down*** *a little; I can't stand such hot weather for long.'* □ *'Keep these two men apart until they've* ***cooled down*** *a bit.'* □ *'Put them in a cell for an hour or two — that'll* ***cool*** *them* ***down****.'*

cool off [A1 B1i pass] become or make less warm, excited, ardent or interested □ *'I've got to* ***cool off****!' Mariette said, 'I'm going into the wood to* ***cool off****!'* DBM □ *After a while, these people* ***cool off*** *towards me and either answer in monosyllables or are plain rude.* WI □ *The Industrial Relations Act provided for a* ***cooling-off*** *period before a strike could take place.*

coop up (in) [B1i pass adj B3 pass rel] (informal) keep or confine sb/sth in a limited space. **o:** (this/that) place, room, house □ *She would implore me to come outside for a 'breather' when I felt like it, and not to stay all day '****cooped up in*** *that furnace'.* THH □ *I won't stay* ***cooped up*** *here for ten minutes longer even if your damned mother* ***is*** *lying in wait for me.* US □ *She refused to spend any more of her life* ***cooped up*** *like this (****in*** *such a tiny house).*

co-operate (with) [A2 pass emph rel] work together (with). **o:** authorities; local council; police, security forces; staff, management □ *If you will* ***co-operate with*** *us in organizing a fête, we will have a much more successful show than if we were each to organize our own.* □ *If John can* ***co-operate with*** *me, and I* ***with*** *him* (or: *If John and I can* ***co-operate****), everything should run smoothly.*

cope (with) [A2 pass adj emph rel] overcome some difficulty or personal crisis; deal effectively (with), manage adequately. **o:** crisis, situation; rush, pressure, numbers □ *Our collection of antiques reached such proportions that we were barely able to* ***cope with*** *it.* □ *The death of her parents is very sad, but it's something she will have to* ***cope with****.* □ *'A few extra people for the weekend? Well, that's something that's easily* ***coped with****.'*

copy down [B1i pass] write down sth which is spoken, or displayed on a large surface. **O:** speech, words; joke, saying; notice □ *The reporters* ***copied down*** *every word spoken by the Prime Minister.* □ *'When you've* ***copied down*** *the exercise that's on the blackboard, we'll go on with the next one.'*

copy out [B1i pass adj] write or type a copy of sth appearing in a book or document. **O:** chapter, paragraph; section, clause □ *This passage is well worth* ***copying out****.* □ *'Please* ***copy out*** *this let-*

ter and send the original to Mr Smith.'

cordon off [B1i pass adj] place a barrier across or round a place to prevent or check movement in and out. **S:** police, army, fire brigade. **O:** danger zone; street, house, beach □ *The whole area will remain* ***cordoned off*** *until the escaped lion is recaptured.*

cork up[1] [B1i pass] put a stopper (made of cork, plastic etc) in sth in order to keep out air. **O:** bottle, wine, beer, brew □ *'It's dangerous to* ***cork up*** *these bottles while the wine is still fermenting, you know!'*

cork up[2] [B1i pass adj] (informal) suppress. **O:** feelings, (natural) emotions, (healthy) reactions; hatred, love □ *It is very bad for you to* ***cork*** *your emotions* ***up*** *like that: you'd feel much better if you could 'let yourself go'.*

correlate (with) [A2 emph rel B2 pass emph rel] statistically, match sth closely; establish such a relationship. **S:** [A2] **O:** [B2] results, findings; figures; linguistic ability, intelligence; size, weight. **o:** each other; (other) sets, series (of figures etc) □ *The results of British research into the effects of smoking* ***correlate with*** *those of workers in other countries.* □ *We generally find that we cannot* ***correlate*** *performance in Mathematics* ***with*** *achievement in, say, English or History* (cf: *We cannot* ***correlate*** *performance in Mathematics and English* etc).

correspond to [A2 emph rel] be equivalent to. **S:** monarchy, Parliament, Foreign Office. **o:** presidency, Congress, State Department □ *An infantry company* ***corresponds*** *roughly* ***to*** *a cavalry squadron.* □ *In this engine the rotary section* ***corresponds to*** *the cylinders of a conventional model.*

correspond (to/with) [A2 emph rel] be equal or similar (to), match. **S:** story, report, version; figure, estimate. **o:** that given, the one made, what he had received □ *The witness's account* ***corresponded*** *fairly closely* ***to*** *the policeman's observations.* □ *I'm afraid your offer doesn't* ***correspond with*** *the figure I've heard mentioned.*

cotton on (to) [A1 A3] (informal) realize, fully understand, become fully aware of. **o:** fact, danger; implication, meaning, intention, what it all means □ *The man-in-the-street seems to be very slow in* ***cottoning on to*** *the significance of the new tax laws.* □ *'Don't you understand what she's trying to do to you? Haven't you* ***cottoned on*** *yet?'* □ *It was surprising how quickly the younger children* ***cottoned on*** *when they were taught English orally.*

couch (in) [B2 pass emph rel] express (in). **O:** protest, application, agreement; document, letter. **o:** strong, mild terms; legal, formal language □ *If his application for the job had been* ***couched in*** *more modest terms, he might have got it.* □ *You'll have to* ***couch*** *your statement to the court* ***in*** *rather more discreet language.*

cough up [A1 B1i pass] (slang) pay (usu reluctantly). **O:** money, cash □ *She asked a sum of money which was about the maximum that I would* ***cough up****, and then hastened to indicate a way in which I might recoup myself.* UTN □ *As you have no alternative, you might as well* ***cough up****.*

cough it up [B1ii] (slang) say something in the nature of a confession or that is in some way difficult to reveal □ *I can see that you've got something on your mind. I wish you'd* ***cough it up****, and stop trying to hide it.'*

count against [A2 B2 pass] be considered, consider, as a factor against, hold against (q v). **S:** [A2] **O:** [B2] failing, fault; mistake, slip; **O:** [B2] failing, fault; mistake, slip; background, origins □ *His inability to arrive at work on time* ***counted against*** *him when he asked for promotion.* □ *The family will* ***count*** *it* ***against*** *you that you weren't at the funeral.* □ *One careless mistake can hardly be* ***counted against*** *him.*

count among [A2 B2 pass] be or regard as one of; reckon among [1] (q v). **o:** friends, acquaintances □ *Mr Heffer no longer* ***counts among*** *my friends since he refused to lend me his lawnmower.* □ *There was a time when we were proud to* ***count*** *Mr Paterson* ***among*** *our supporters.*

count down [B1i nom pass] (esp space technology) count numbers in reverse order towards zero, as in launching a rocket, detonating an explosive charge etc □ *Millions of people saw Apollo 10 being* ***counted down****, on television.* □ *The* ***count-down*** *went perfectly until minus 13 minutes 47 seconds, when it was held for nearly three hours.*

count for [A2] be of (little etc) importance. **o:** ⚠ little, (not)... much, nothing □ *When it came to money, all his friendly promises* ***counted for*** *little: he was as mean as Scrooge.* □ *Surely all our hard work can't* ***count for*** *nothing! We deserve* some *reward, don't we?*

count (from) (up) to [A2 A3] (be able to) use or say numbers as far as. □ *Most children of five have no difficulty in learning to* ***count*** *(****from*** *one)* ***up to*** *a hundred.* □ *Each time you feel like having a violent quarrel with somebody,* ***count (up) to*** *ten before speaking.*

count in [B1i pass] include □ *If the cost of the trip is no more than five pounds, you can* ***count*** *me* ***in****.* □ *There are more than a hundred places of worship in the town, if we* ***count in*** *all the churches, mosques and synagogues.*

count on/upon [A2 pass emph rel] trust sb to help, give support etc; rely on/upon (q v). **o:** relative, friend; solicitor, bank manager □ *He* ***counted on*** *his sister for everything — the care of his children, the nursing of his sick wife, and even for a little pleasant company in the evenings.* □ *This house is the only thing in my life that has stayed in the same place. It's the only thing I can* ***count on****.* EHOW □ *You can always* ***count on*** *Bill for a pound or two when you're in difficulties.*

count out[1] [B1i pass] count things one by one, perhaps placing them on a surface. **O:** money, change; buttons, counters □ *The old lady laboriously* ***counted out*** *fifteen pence, snapped her purse shut and said 'There! Is that right?'*

count out[2] [B1i pass] (boxing) of a referee, count up to ten over a boxer who has been knocked down □ *The poor fellow was* ***counted out*** *in the first round.*

count out[3] [B1i pass] (informal) not include; discount as unimportant □ *If the coach is not going to return before midnight, you'd better* ***count*** *me* ***out****.* □ *He had never liked Alec as well as he did at that moment. As a rival he had* ***counted*** *Alec* ***out****.PW*

count the House out [B1ii pass] (Parliament)

adjourn a meeting of the House of Commons because too few members are present □ *It is many years since the House was* ***counted out*** *during discussions of an important piece of legislation.*

count to[A2] ⇨ count (from) (up) to.

count up [B1i pass] find the total of. **O:** times, occasions; marks; coupons, stamps □ *Now* ***count up*** *the points you've scored and compare them with the table. This will show you whether you are above or below average.* □ *Try* ***counting up*** *the number of people who come into the shop each day.*

count (up) to [A3] ⇨ count (from) (up) to.

count upon [A2 pass emph rel] ⇨ count on/upon.

counter (with) [A2 B2 pass] make, advance, sth in opposition; retaliate (with). **O:** threat, attack, thrust; rebellion; suggestion, proposal. **o:** more powerful weapons; uppercut to the jaw, sharp jab; punitive expedition; one's own proposal, (new) idea, argument □ *There was always the danger that if the enemy were too hard pushed on the ground they would* ***counter with*** *a heavy air strike.* □ *The ginger group that had been formed by the shareholders* ***countered*** *the Board's resolution* ***with*** *one of their own.*

couple on/onto [B1i pass B2 pass] link, attach (to); join on/onto (q v). **O:** (railway) wagon, coach; caravan, trailer. **o:** engine; car, van □ *Several coal-wagons were* ***coupled on*** *at Crewe.* □ *They covered a thousand miles with a heavy trailer* ***coupled onto*** *the back of their family saloon.*

couple up [B1i pass] join together (esp to form a railway train). **O:** wagon, coach □ *When all the coaches had been* ***coupled up****, they formed a train nearly three hundred metres long.*

couple (with) [B2 pass emph rel] join (to), esp in one's thoughts or remarks; associate with[2] (q v). **O:** name; place; occasion □ *It is natural that Stratford on Avon should always be* ***coupled with*** *the name of Shakespeare* (cf: *It is natural that the place and the name should always be* ***coupled***). □ *In his mind, the Normandy beaches will always be* ***coupled with*** *the allied landings in 1944.*

course through [A2 emph rel] (formal) rush, run, through. **S:** blood; sap; thoughts, ideas, fancies. **o:** veins, body; trunk; brain, mind □ *He felt the blood* ***coursing through*** *his veins as his excitement grew.* □ ***Through*** *his mind* ***coursed*** *all manner of confused thoughts.*

cover (against) [B2 pass rel] protect oneself etc by means of an insurance policy (against); insure against (q v). **O:** oneself, life; house, property; car. **o:** accident, incapacity, illness, death; fire, storm, flood, damage, burglary; theft □ *Insurance companies try to persuade young married men to* ***cover*** *themselves* ***against*** *illness or death.* □ *Are you* ***covered against*** *loss of earnings resulting from an accident?* □ *Does your car insurance* ***cover*** *you* ***against*** *damage to third parties?*

cover in [B1i pass adj] place a protective covering over. **O:** hall, driveway; yard, terrace □ *We decided to* ***cover in*** *the passage between the main building and the annex.* □ *The* ***covered-in*** *area gave shelter to the cattle during the winter.*

cover in/with [B2 pass rel] protect with, coat with; make dirt etc fly and fall on. **o:** paint, creosote; material, protective sheeting; soot, mud, lime □ *The walls had been* ***covered with*** *a dark-green paint.* □ *The room would look much brighter if we* ***covered*** *the sofa* ***with*** *a light-coloured material.* □ *A passing lorry ran through a puddle and* ***covered*** *us* ***in*** *mud from head to foot.*

cover in/with confusion/shame [B2 pass] embarrass, make confused or ashamed. **S:** remark, accusation, charge □ *Albert's young wife was* ***covered in confusion*** *when her in-laws called unexpectedly and found her still in bed at midday.* □ usu passive.

cover over/up [B1i pass] hide from view; protect with clothing etc □ *I'm glad to see that the police have* ***covered*** *the blood-stains* ***over.*** □ *'****Cover*** *the baby's feet* ***up****; he'll catch cold.'*

cover up (for) [A1 nom A3 pass B1i pass] (informal) hide the true state of affairs on one's own (or sb else's) behalf. **O:** blunder, error; inefficiency, inadequacy □ [A1] *The inefficient who successfully* ***cover up*** *are those who know how to put on a big display of efficiency when it will be noticed, and let the rest go hang.* OBS □ *'Don't try to convince me that nothing's been happening. I suspect that it's all a big* ***cover-up****!'* □ [A3] *If I'm late tomorrow you'll* ***cover up for*** *me, won't you.* □ [B1] *There are too many people in this office trying to* ***cover up*** *the mistakes of the past few years.* □ *President Nixon often wished that the Watergate* ***cover-up*** *affair would simply 'go away'.*

cover with ⇨ cover in/with.

cover with confusion/shame [B2 pass] ⇨ covered in/with confusion/shame.

cow into submission [B2 pass] make sb surrender through fear. **O:** occupied territory, conquered people □ *He is not the kind of man who is likely to* ***be cowed into submission.***

crack down (on) [A1 nom A3 pass] (informal) use one's authority (against), suppress, attack. **o:** rebels, dissidents; minority; vice, crime; prostitution, gambling □ *The police are always being urged to* ***crack down on*** *drug addicts.* □ *If the Inland Revenue officers had time they would* ***crack down on*** *tax evaders more quickly.* □ *What depresses some people here is that these* ***crack-downs*** (ie Khrushchev's attacks on abstract artists) *seem to be more or less regular occurrences.* OBS

crack up[1] [A1 nom] (informal) lose one's health or mental stability; break down[8] (q v) □ *If John goes on working and worrying as he has been doing he's bound to* ***crack up*** *sooner or later.* □ *'What's come over you? This isn't the time to* ***crack up****.'* YA □ *Then, one day at the office, the* ***crack-up*** *came and Joe was carted off to hospital. It was the end of his career.*

crack up[2] [A1 nom] (informal) disintegrate, shatter; break up[8] (q v). **S:** machine; organization □ *Suddenly, without warning, the plane seemed to* ***crack up*** *as it was about to take off.* □ *The* ***crack-up*** *of the Rolls-Royce company surprised and shocked everyone in Britain.*

crack up[3] [A1] (informal) praise highly. **O:** (new) fashion, fad, invention, pastime; town, country, area; comprehensive schools □ *Water ski-ing isn't all it's* ***cracked up*** *to be, in my opinion.* □ *I don't know why young Jones is* ***cracked up*** *as such a paragon: I find him rather dull, myself.* □ *Do you think the new aircraft is everything they*

***crack** it **up** to be?* □ usu followed by *to be*, or *as* and noun phrase.

cram into [B2 pass emph rel] push, force, into. **O:** (too much) food; (too many) people; everything, a lifetime's experience. **o:** one's mouth; bus, train; suitcase, bag; a few days □ *Children often **cram** too much **into** their mouths.* □ *It's dangerous for too many people to be **crammed into** a bus.* □ *The lovers tried to **cram** a lifetime **into** the six months they had together.* ⇨ next entry.

cram (with) [B2 pass rel] put, push, concentrate, a great deal or too much of sth into. **O:** drawer, room, house, desk; pocket, bag, purse; sb's head; book, encyclopedia. **o:** clothes, rubbish, furniture, letters, knick-knacks; odds and ends, scraps of paper; (useless) facts, nonsense; information, good advice □ *The Victorians **crammed** their houses **with** furniture and ornaments.* □ *It's no use **cramming** your head **with** a lot of unrelated facts: what you need is a system.* □ *This encyclopedia is **crammed with** information about everything under the sun.* ⇨ previous entry.

crane forward [A1] stretch one's neck forward in order to see better. **S:** onlooker, viewer, spectator □ *The audience **craned forward** as the conjuror came to the crucial part of his trick.*

crank up [A1 B1i pass] start an engine by means of a starting-handle □ *'The battery's flat! I'm afraid you'll have to **crank up**!'* □ *'Once the engine has been **cranked up**, she'll probably start easily on the battery.'*

crash about [A1] move about in a clumsy, noisy manner, knocking things over and so on □ *'I wish you wouldn't **crash about** like that as soon as you get home from school.'*

crash about one's ears [A2] collapse disastrously. **S:** his etc whole world; everything that he had achieved; his dreams, ambitions □ *When Bob's fiancée broke off their engagement, his whole world came **crashing abou? his ears**.* □ often in the form *come* crashing etc, as in the example.

crash across, along, away etc [A2] move across etc, causing noise and damage □ The tanks ***crashed** ruthlessly **through** the lines of infantry.* □ *The maid put the tray on an unsteady table, and everything **crashed to** the floor.* □ *The lorry went out of control and **crashed into** a group of people standing at a bus-stop.*

crash down [A1] fall noisily, heavily and often dangerously. **S:** tree, rock, house, waves □ *The rocks **crashed down** on to the road below.* □ *With gigantic waves **crashing down** upon her, the lifeboat made her way to the crippled ship.* □ *As the wind rose to eighty miles an hour, tree after tree **crashed down**.*

crave (for) [A2 pass emph rel] have a great desire or wish for; long (for) (q v). **o:** change; (new) role, environment □ *After a lifetime of work in the noisy city, Mr Stewart **craved (for)** a few years of peace in the country.* □ *He claimed to be a democrat, but secretly he **craved for** absolute authority.* AH □ *He had at last secured the position **for** which he **craved**.*

crawl across, along, away etc [A1 emph A2 emph rel] move slowly across etc (esp—of humans—on hands and knees) □ *Somehow the wounded animal managed to **crawl away** from its pursuers and **into** a hole.* □ *The traffic was so thick that we could only **crawl along** at about fifteen miles an hour.*

crawl (to) [A2 pass] (informal) act in a humble, submissive manner towards sb to obtain favours □ *The manager lost the respect of his staff when they saw him **crawling to** the Chairman.* □ *'Don't you come **crawling** (back) **to** me now that all your money's gone!'* □ *If there's anything he despises it's being **crawled to** by people wishing to curry favour.*

crawl with [A2] be full of, covered with, 'alive' with. **o:** small creatures, lice, maggots, vermin □ *The neglected child's clothes were found to be **crawling with** lice.* □ *The fields are **crawling with** mice and other pests.* □ usu continuous tenses.

credit to [B2 pass rel] ⇨ next entry.

credit with[1] [B2 pass rel] (finance, commerce) enter a sum of money, in sb's account, equal to the value of. **o:** the unsold goods, the damaged articles, the missing parts □ *We are returning the materials covered by your invoice number 108432 as they were not according to specification. Please **credit** our account **with*** (or: ***credit to** our account) the returned goods.* □ *We can't refund cash but we'll **credit** you **with** the value of the suit.* □ note credit *sb/sb's account.*

credit with[2] [B2 pass rel] believe sb to possess or be capable of. **o:** more intelligence, sense; being such a good tennis-player, long distance runner, footballer, cook, artist, mechanic □ *Who would have **credited** old Harold **with** being able to jump onto a moving bus at his age?* □ *'What on earth did you put your finger in the boiling sugar for? I **credited** you **with** more common sense than that!'*

creep across, along, away etc [A1 emph A2 emph rel] move across etc gradually, steadily. **S:** ivy, honeysuckle, vine; patrol, intruder; car, train □ *His particular dream was of a small country cottage, with rambler roses **creeping along** the fence.* □ ***Down** the path **crept** a long line of ants.*

creep in/into[1] [A1 emph A2 emph rel] enter very quietly □ *The erring husband, returning home at one a m, removed his shoes and **crept in** as silently as he could.* □ *She **crept into** the room and kissed the sleeping child.*

creep in/into[2] [A1 A2 emph rel] enter imperceptibly. **S:** sour, unpleasant, tone; unpleasantness □ *You should try to argue calmly and not allow any unpleasantness or bitterness to **creep in**.* □ *Once complications are allowed to **creep in**, the outcome is in danger.* MFM □ *A distinct note of acrimony had **crept into** their conversation.*

creep over [A2] affect gradually. **S:** feeling, (strange) sensation; the suspicion that □ *There **crept over** him, vaguely at first and then more strongly, the suspicion that he was being deliberately poisoned.*

creep up (on) [A1 A3 pass] approach silently or unobserved □ *We **crept up** (**on** them) and, peering through the brambles, saw they were having a picnic.* □ *'I dislike the feeling of being **crept up on**. Why don't you walk in boldly and say what you have to say?'*

creep up on [A3] approach imperceptibly. **S:** day of decision, time of parting, moment of truth

□ *The years went by and all the time the day for him to retire inexorably* ***crept up on*** *him.*

cringe away/back (from) [A1 A3 emph rel] (of animals and human beings in a state of fear or terror) retreat, draw back □ *The dogs would* ***cringe away from*** *a man with a whip in his hand.* □ *If we made any overtures of friendship she would* ***cringe back****, gazing at us with wide-eyed horror, her little hands trembling with fright.* DF ⇨ draw away/back (from).

cringe (before) [A2 emph rel] behave in a timid, cowardly or ingratiating way. **o:** father, schoolmaster, magistrate, policeman □ *The sight of a big strong man* ***cringing before*** *a member of the aristocracy would disgust most people.* □ ***Before*** *such emblems of authority as a police uniform, he would invariably* ***cringe****.*

crisp up [A1 B1i pass adj] of sth which has gone soft from a hard or crisp state, become or make crisp again; similarly, of things that were not previously hard (e g bacon) □ *These cornflakes have gone soft, but they'll be all right if you* ***crisp*** *them* ***up*** *in the oven.*

crock up [A1 B1i pass adj] (informal) become or make weak or useless. **S:** [B1] accident; fall, tumble; shock; exertion □ *A lot of people* ***crock up*** *suddenly these days — it's the effect of modern living, sedentary work and an over-rich diet.* □ *The news of his son's death finally* ***crocked*** *him* ***up****.*

crop up[1] [A1] (informal) be mentioned. **S:** topic, subject, theme □ *Wherever I went in Japan, the names of Harold Palmer and A S Hornby kept* ***cropping up****.* □ *If their daughter* ***crops up*** *in the conversation, remember you don't know anything about her affair with John!* □ *The pills must be good because the name was always* ***cropping up*** *in the Seattle papers.* RFW

crop up[2] [A1] (informal) happen, occur, appear. **S:** opportunity, job, chance; something □ *Things were always* ***cropping up*** *which forced Ned to demonstrate who was the boss.* CON □ *Things have* ***cropped up*** *that make my position here rather difficult, for myself and others.* HD □ *'Why don't you stay at home tomorrow? I can call you if anything* ***crops up*** *in the office.'*

cross (in) [B2 pass] obstruct, oppose sb (in sth he proposes to do). **o:** design, intention, ambition, objective □ *He is a friendly enough person, so long as you don't* ***cross*** *him (****in*** *his business plans).* □ *'What's the matter with Sally?' 'I would say she's been* ***crossed in*** *love!'*

cross off [B1i pass adj B2 pass] remove sth from a list etc by putting a line (or more rarely, a cross) through it; tick off [1] (q v). **O:** name; item; task, job, place. **o:** list; agenda □ *I found that my name had been* ***crossed off*** *the list of players, and somebody else's substituted.* □ *You can* ***cross*** *that job* ***off*** *— I've already mended the lamp.*

cross out [B1i pass adj] delete, put a line (or more rarely, a cross) through sth (usu because it is wrong). **O:** name, mistake, misspelt words, half the exercise □ *The teacher had* ***crossed out*** *much of what the boy had written.* □ *The envelope arrived with the old address* ***crossed out****, and the new one written alongside it.* □ *The exercise was made almost illegible by many* ***crossings-out****.* □ nom form: crossing(s)-out.

cross with [B2 pass] in breeding, mix one kind with another. **o:** breed, strain □ *This dog looks like the result of an alsatian being* ***crossed with*** *a spaniel.*

cross sb's hand/palm with silver [B2 pass] place a silver coin in sb's hand or palm (esp of a fortune-teller, gypsy etc) □ *'****Cross my palm with silver****, Sir, and I'll tell you what the future holds for you — and I can see you're a lucky gentleman by your face!'*

cross swords (with) [B2 emph rel] have a dispute (with), enter into (verbal) conflict (with). **o:** neighbour, colleague, (child's) teacher □ *When the Prime Minister* ***crossed swords with*** *the Leader of the Opposition* (or: *When they* ***crossed swords****) across the floor of the House, the former usually got the worst of it.*

crow one's head off [B1ii] (informal) talk in a boastful way □ *The Tories* ***crowed their heads off*** *when they won the 1970 General Election against the predictions of all the Opinion Polls.*

crow over [A2 pass] boast about a victory, taunt an enemy with his defeat. **o:** success, victory; wealth, strength; (another's) weakness, failure □ *It is unwise to* ***crow*** *too noisily* ***over*** *a defeated enemy, when you are in danger of suffering the same fate at the hands of another.*

crowd in (on/upon) [A1 A3 emph rel] thrust (themselves) forward, into the mind; press too closely around one. **S:** memories, thoughts, recollections; houses, traffic □ *Scenes of his past life came* ***crowding in upon*** *the drowning man.* □ *'Where we lived before, the scenery tended to* ***crowd in on*** *us.'* T

crowd in/into [A1 emph A2 emph B1i pass B2 emph] move in a crowd into a relatively small space. **S:** [A1 A2] **O:** [B1 B2] spectators, audience; passengers. **o:** room, ball; carriage, compartment □ [A2] *Hundreds of people* ***crowded into*** *the village hall to hear the local MP.* □ [B1] *I think we could manage to* ***crowd*** *a few more* ***in****.* □ [B2] ***Into*** *one small van the men* ***crowded*** *about twelve frightened sheep.*

crowd out/out of [B1i pass B2 pass] be the cause of keeping people out (of a place); because of one's own numbers, cause others to leave, or stay outside. **O:** newcomers, late arrivals, would-be spectators. **o:** hall, theatre, lecture-room □ *Pressure on study-space has* ***crowded out*** *new students from many university libraries* (or: *has* ***crowded*** *new students* ***out of*** *many* etc). □ *A fairly large proportion of expectant mothers are* ***crowded out of*** *Britain's maternity hospitals.* OBS

crowd round [A1 A2] form a large group round, press round. **S:** reporters, onlookers; students. **o:** celebrity; prisoner; teacher; platform, desk □ *Why do people* ***crowd round****, staring stupidly, whenever there's an accident?* □ *Passers-by* ***crowded round*** *the policeman as he made his arrest.*

crumble away [A1] fall in small pieces, disintegrate, gradually. **S:** rocks, walls, cliffs; ruins; opposition □ *The people living in the houses on the cliff-top grew more and more worried as it* ***crumbled away*** *into the sea.* □ *It is remarkable how completely the opposition to the nationalization of the railways* ***crumbled away****.*

crumple up[1] [A1 B1i pass adj] crease or break, and crush; (cause to) lose its former recognizable shape by compression, change of air pressure etc.

S: [A1] **O:** [B1] packet, tin; shell, crust; body-work (of car) □ *The small car just* ***crumpled up*** *on impact with the lorry.* □ *Eventually, I found the letter* ***crumpled up*** *into a ball in the baby's cot.*

crumple up[2] [A1] fail, collapse, give way. **S:** he etc; army, opposition, resistance □ *All organized resistance* ***crumpled up*** *when the tanks went in.* □ *One day Mr Moreton was a fine, healthy-looking man, the next he looked old and helpless: he had just* ***crumpled up.*** □ *In the face of the numbers, audacity, and precision of the attackers, the train's security, such as it was,* ***crumpled up.*** T

crusade (for) (against) [A2 emph rel] take part in a vigorous campaign (in support of, or against). **o:** changes (in the law, in society), reform; abolition, restoration (of sth) □ *In Britain there are groups constantly* ***crusading for*** *supposed improvements and* ***against*** *alleged evils.*

crush in/into [A1 A2 B1i pass B2 pass] (cause to) enter too small a space. **o:** theatre, cinema; compartment, bus □ [A1] *As soon as the train stopped, about two hundred people tried to* ***crush in*** (or: [A2] ***into*** *the few empty compartments).* □ [B1] *More than thirty head of cattle had been* ***crushed in*** (or: [B2] ***into*** *a lorry that was only big enough to take twenty).*

crush into [B2 pass] reduce, by the use of a heavy weight, or great pressure, to. **o:** pieces, dust, powder; an unrecognizable shape □ *The rocks were* ***crushed into*** *powder by a gigantic hammer.*

crush into submission [B2 pass] force to submit, by the exercise of superior force. **O:** occupied territory, subject people; opposition, hostile minority □ *The few remaining pockets of resistance were finally* ***crushed into submission*** *by the ruthless methods of the conquering army.*

crush out/out of [B1i pass adj B2 pass] extract, remove, by crushing. **O:** juice, moisture; spirit, life. **o:** sugar-cane, fruit, vegetable; people □ *The sugar-cane is taken to the factory where the juice is* ***crushed out.*** □ *When I last saw Mr Smith he looked like a man who had had the spirit* ***crushed out of*** *him.*

crush to death [B2 pass] kill by the weight of sth. **S:** rock-fall, avalanche □ *There is always the danger that someone will be* ***crushed to death*** *whenever great crowds of people panic.* □ usu passive.

crush up [B1i pass adj] press so as to soften, flatten or reduce to powder. **O:** stone, rock, rubble; chocolate, lump-sugar □ (instructions in a recipe) *The root-ginger should be* ***crushed up*** *before it is added to the boiling jam.*

cry down [B1i pass] (informal) belittle, give little importance to. **O:** attempt, initiative, move; achievement, success □ *The Opposition* ***cried down*** *every effort of the Government to improve the lot of working people.* □ *'Don't* ***cry down*** *the very real progress these people have made.'*

cry for [A2] cry or weep in an attempt to obtain sth. **o:** food, drink; attention, a cuddle; something, nothing □ *'That child is always* ***crying for*** *something. What does it want now?'* □ *'If you don't shut up,' shouted the angry mother, 'I'll damn well give you something to* ***cry for*** (= I'll beat you).' □ *'Don't take any notice of Johnny; he* ***cries for*** *nothing* (= *he* ***cries for*** *no good reason).'*

cry for the moon [A2] want the impossible □ *'They're always wishing they could afford a cottage in Sardinia, or take a cruise round the world, or something equally impossible. Just* ***crying for the moon.'***

cry off [A1 A2] withdraw from some previous arrangement or agreement. **o:** attending, visiting sb, going to the cinema □ *It was the only foggy night in November and Gerald was sorely tempted to* ***cry off*** *going to dinner but Leonie got him there somehow.* ASA □ *'I don't think I'll go swimming after all.' 'Oh, you're not going to* ***cry off*** *now are you, when I've persuaded everyone else to join us?'* □ in the [A2] pattern, the object is the *-ing* form of a v.

cry out [A1] exclaim, usu involuntarily (in pain or alarm); call out[4] (q v) □ *As the rocks thundered on down the mountain-side, the trapped men* ***cried out*** *in fear.* □ *As he drove, too fast, into the first of the bends, his passenger* ***cried out*** *to him to slow down.*

cry one's eyes/heart out [B1ii] (informal) weep in misery and for a long time □ *When the woman finally came down from the bedroom she looked as if she'd been* ***crying her eyes out.*** □ *The poor little girl* ***cried her heart out*** *when her father came home and told her that her dog had been run over.*

cry out for [A3 rel] plainly invite, be a natural subject for □ *Across the moors, the roads, winding, narrow, steep are perilous. If ever a stretch of country* ***cried out for*** *a swift, clean cut, this is it.* T □ *The coastline is full of possibilities, industrial, commercial, and residential: it's just* ***crying out for*** *development* (or: *it's just* ***crying out*** *to be developed*). □ note alt pattern with inf as in the second example.

cry over [A2 pass] lament, grieve, about. **o:** one's lost opportunities, misfortunes; injustice; the unfairness of sth; what's past □ *As usual I found Betty in her room,* ***crying over*** *her misfortunes — both real and imagined — and told her to pull herself together.* □ *These losses have been much* ***cried over,*** *and too seldom made good.*

it's no use crying over spilt milk [A2] (it's no use) complaining about something that cannot be rectified or changed. □ *'Look! The sooner you realize that your money has gone, the better it will be for you.* ***It's no use crying over spilt milk.'*** ⇨ previous entry.

cry oneself to sleep [B2] weep until one falls asleep □ *While the parents were laughing their heads off at some nonsense on television their unhappy son lay in bed and* ***cried himself to sleep.***

cuddle up (to) [A1 A3 pass] draw closer to another person (usu for warmth or comfort). **S:** child, pet □ *The twins* ***cuddled up*** *close together and fell asleep.* □ *The child* ***cuddled up to*** *her mother.* □ *Most mothers enjoy being* ***cuddled up to.***

cull from [B2 pass emph rel] (formal) collect from. **O:** flowers, gems; poems □ *General Wavell made a collection of poems '****culled from*** *other men's gardens'.*

culminate in [A2 rel] (formal) reach a climax in, end in. **S:** riots, disturbances; hopes, endeavours; search for; career. **o:** a lot of damage, many deaths, civil war; success, the discovery (of oil etc); his etc being made Managing Director □ *Everyone feared that the sectarian strife in Northern Ireland would* **culminate in** *civil war.* □ *The intensive search for gas and oil in the North Sea* **culminated in** *the discovery of several enormous finds.*

cure (of)[1] [B2 pass emph rel] restore to (health from sickness). **o:** malaria, yellow fever; stammer; shyness □ *Before the discovery of antibiotics it was extremely difficult to* **cure** *a person* **of** *tuberculosis.*

cure (of)[2] [B2 pass emph rel] cause to lose a harmful or unpleasant habit. **o:** nail-biting, snoring □ *Some people claim that they have been* **cured of** *smoking by hypnosis.* □ *That black eye that Joe got last night should* **cure him of** *minding other people's business.*

curl up[1] [A1] from being flat or straight, turn up into a curl or something like a curl; settle down to sleep (like a dog). **S:** paper, leaves, material □ *The pages of the book had* **curled up** *from the heat of the fire.* □ *She could only dream of the time when she could* **curl up** *between clean linen sheets again.*

curl up[2] [A1 B1ii] (informal) feel, make, nauseated □ *'His fawning manner whenever the boss is around just makes me* **curl up**. *I tell you — it* **curls** *me* **up**.*'*

curry favour (with) [B2] behave ingratiatingly towards sb for one's own advantage. **o:** superior; boss, manager; teacher, prefect □ *If I can't get what I want by earning it, I'll do without: I'm not going to* **curry favour with** *any man.*

cursed with [pass (B2)] (be) unfortunate in having. **o:** ill luck, (every) misfortune; stammer, limp □ *Mr Yates was* **cursed with** *a snore that shook the foundations of the house. His wife had to sleep in a separate room.* □ *Mr Fair seems to be* **cursed with** *the ability to see the other fellow's point of view, with the result that he has no firm opinions on anything.*

curtain off [B1i pass adj] separate by means of a curtain. **O:** recess, cupboard; part, extension (of a room) □ *A corner of the room had been* **curtained off** *as a kind of improvised wardrobe.* □ *He slept in a* **curtained-off** *alcove.*

cut across[1] [A2] take a short route (or a short cut) across. **o:** the field(s), playing-field, meadow, ice □ *Whenever the grass was dry the children would* **cut across** *the fields instead of keeping to the road.*

cut across[2] [A2] be contrary to, act in a manner contrary to. **o:** normal procedure; customary arrangements; beliefs, expectations □ *The voting on the laws relating to Sunday recreation* **cut across** *the traditional political border-line.* □ *Feeling on the Common Market* **cuts** *clean* **across** *normal party loyalties.*

cut at [A2 pass] attempt to sever, open, or wound with a knife. **o:** cord, rope; covering, wrapping; face, hand □ *He* **cut** *desperately* **at** *the rope in an attempt to free his foot.* □ *One of the men* **cut at** *her with a razor; the blade nicked the skin.*

cut away [B1i pass adj] remove by cutting. **O:** diseased tissue; undergrowth; dead wood, branches; torn sail, broken mast □ *The surgeon* **cut away** *the tumour with expert skill.* □ *You won't be able to make a good lawn here unless you* **cut away** *most of these overhanging branches.*

cut back[1] [B1i pass] (horticulture) cut or prune. **O:** tree, bush, shrub; branch □ *Some gardeners believe in* **cutting** *rose-bushes* **back** *very hard indeed — almost down to the ground.*

cut back[2] [B1i nom pass adj] reduce. **O:** production, investment, expansion □ *Owing to the unfavourable economic climate, the motor-car industry has* **cut back** *production by fifteen per cent.* □ *The* **cut-back** *(or:* **cutback***) in investment over the country as a whole is bound to increase unemployment.*

cut down[1] [B1i pass adj] fell. **O:** tree, bush □ *When I returned to my childhood home I was distressed to find that all the apple trees had been* **cut down**.

cut down[2] [B1i pass adj] (formal) kill. **A:** in his youth, prime; in a battle □ *Over the mantlepiece there was a portrait of their eldest son,* **cut down** *in the Second World War in the full vigour of his manhood.*

cut down[3] [A1 B1i pass] consume less; reduce. **O:** expenses, consumption, ration □ *'We must* **cut** *our expenses* **down** *somehow. I'll stop smoking and you had better spend less on beer.'* □ *'The doctor told me to* **cut down** *my consumption of carbohydrates.'* □ *'By the way, smoke if you want to — I'm trying to* **cut down**, *not with very much success as yet, I'm afraid.'* TT ⇨ cut down on.

cut down[4] [B1i pass adj] reduce the length of. **O:** clothes (usu implying that the *cutting down* is to make them fit a younger member of a family; otherwise 'shorten' is more frequently used); written article, report □ *The poor boy is terribly conscious of being the only one in the class who is wearing his father's* **cut-down** *trousers.* □ *If you can* **cut** *your article* **down** *to about 1 000 words, we will publish it in our next issue.*

cut down on [A3] reduce consumption of. **o:** (excessive) eating, drinking, spending, smoking □ *What with increased taxation and rising prices, I'm going to have to* **cut down on** *quite a lot of things — clothes, records and so on.* □ *When people* **cut down on** *tobacco, they often start eating too many sweets and put on weight.* ⇨ cut down[3].

cut down (to) [B1i pass B3 pass] in bargaining, persuade sb to reduce his price □ *At first he wanted £400 for his car, but I succeeded in* **cutting** *him* **down** *by £50.* □ *The tourist* **cut** *the hawker* **down to** *£4 for the vase and was very pleased with himself, little realizing that this still gave the man four hundred per cent profit.*

cut down to size [B3 pass] (informal) reduce the power or importance of sb or sth (whether real or imagined). **O:** problem; power of sth; groupings of nations □ *Will Mr Khrushchev try to make a deal with America, in order to* **cut** *the new Franco-German combination* **down to size**? OBS □ *It always pleases me to see some upstart 'financial genius'* **cut down to size** *and shown up as the charlatan he is.*

cut for [A2] (card games) lift a number of cards from the top of a pack and look at the card which is at the bottom of that 'slice' of the pack. The person who 'cuts' the card lowest (or highest) in value is entitled or obliged to do a specified thing. **o:** dealer; who makes the coffee, pays for the drinks □ *As there were five of us we* **cut for**

who would not play the first rubber (= round of games in bridge). □ *'The fire's going out. Let's* ***cut for*** *who gets the coal.'* □ in many card games, the first step is to cut for trumps, ie select the suit which is to be trumps by following the procedure already described.

cut the ground from under sb's feet [B2 pass] (informal) remove a cause of complaint, thus making it irrelevant; or, so change the circumstances that sb's action is pointless etc □ *For weeks we had pressed our demands, when suddenly the Government declared such deals to be illegal, so* ***cutting the ground from under our feet.*** □ *I was about to raise my offer for the farm when a neighbour* ***cut the ground from under my feet*** *by offering a sum that I couldn't possibly match.*

cut in[1] [A1] interrupt another person or a conversation between two other people □ *Edith's mouth had opened to yelp out the prepared condemnation, when Robert unexpectedly* ***cut in.*** HD □ *'The facts, Robert, the facts!' Ned* ***cut in.*** CON ⇨ cut into[2].

cut in[2] [A1] (of a driver) overtake a vehicle and turn dangerously into its path (to avoid oncoming traffic) □ *Impatient drivers who habitually* ***cut in*** *are bound to cause an accident sooner or later.*

cut in[3] [B1i pass] (informal) include sb, usu as a member of a group engaged in some profit-making activity and in return for an initial contribution of money, advice or service □ *Next time you form a syndicate, don't forget to* ***cut me in.*** □ *The gang decided they would have to* ***cut*** *the Weasel* ***in*** *if only to keep his mouth shut about their plans.*

cut in/into [B2 pass] divide by cutting. **o:** (a number of) pieces; halves, quarters; equal parts etc □ *The warship hit the submarine amidships and* ***cut*** *it* ***in*** *two.* □ ***Cut*** *this paper* ***into*** *one-inch strips, and then I'll explain how the game is played.*

cut into[1] [A2] make an incision in; start to divide up, carve or slice. **o:** flesh; meat; cake □ *As the little girl* ***cut into*** *her birthday-cake, everyone cheered and clapped their hands.*

cut into[2] [A2] interrupt. **o:** discussion, conversation; the silence □ *John's unwelcome voice* ***cut*** *gratingly* ***into*** *their quiet discussion.* ⇨ cut in[1].

cut off[1] [B1i pass] remove by cutting. **O:** piece, section; branch, leg □ *From the carcass roasting over the fire, the man* ***cut off*** *a succulent piece and handed it to me on a knife.* □ *The workman had a finger* ***cut off*** *by the machine he was operating — a moment of inattention, and it was too late.*

cut off[2] [B1i pass adj] interrupt, make unavailable. **O:** power; electricity, gas, water; supplies (of any commodity); sb's allowance of money, food, etc □ *The oil-producing countries threatened to* ***cut off*** *all supplies of petrol to Europe unless their terms were met.* □ *Final notice: Unless your outstanding account is paid within seven days of the date on this notice, we regret that we shall be obliged to* ***cut off*** *your supply of electricity.*

cut off[3] [B1i pass adj] prevent sb from leaving, or communicating outside, a place, by surrounding him. **S:** flood, avalanche; enemy, encircling movement. **O:** town, village; men, forces □ *The village was* ***cut off*** *by the snow for more than a month.* □ *Although the platoon was* ***cut off*** *by the enemy, they managed to hide until nightfall and regain their own lines under cover of darkness.* □ *The children were* ***cut off*** *by the tide and had to be carried up the cliff to safety.* □ usu passive.

cut off[4] [B1iii pass] occupy a position to prevent or block. **O:** ⚠ sb's retreat; every avenue of escape, sb's escape route □ *Although their retreat had been* ***cut off,*** *the men fought on to the bitter end.* □ *They will* ***cut off*** *all our escape routes except this one — which they can't know about.*

cut off[5] [B1i pass] interrupt a telephone conversation □ *Just when she had reached the most interesting part of the story we were* ***cut off.*** □ *'Operator! I've just been* ***cut off*** *while I was on the line to London. Could you reconnect me, please?'* □ *Somebody on the switchboard must have* ***cut*** *us* ***off*** *for a minute.*

cut-off[1] [nom (B1)] division, separation □ *There is no hard-and-fast* ***cut-off*** *between semi-skilled and unskilled workers.* □ (used attrib) *The* ***cut-off*** *point between 'great heat' and 'excessive heat' cannot easily be defined.*

cut-off[2] [nom (A1)] exit road from a motorway □ *'You've just passed an exit, but I think there's another* ***cut-off*** *about ten miles farther on.'*

cut off one's nose to spite one's face [B1iii] respond to a real or assumed offence in such a way as to harm oneself only, and not the offending person or agency □ *If the Trades Unions refuse to register under the Industrial Relations Act they will be* ***cutting off their noses to spite their faces.***

cut off (from) [B1ii pass adj B3 pass] prevent sb from having contact (with). **O:** oneself; him etc. **o:** friends; one's family; a circle of people, a kind of life; the outside world □ *It takes a very special kind of person to man a lighthouse — one who can stand being* ***cut off from*** *friends and society for weeks at a time.* □ *She's a strange person — very solitary — seems to* ***cut*** *herself* ***off*** *quite deliberately.*

cut off with a shilling [B3 pass] disinherit, except for a small amount that shows that the action is deliberate and that there has been no mistake □ *The old man's patience was finally exhausted and, in disgust at his eldest son's behaviour, he* ***cut*** *him* ***off with a shilling.***

cut out[1] [B1ii pass adj] take, by cutting from a piece of material, the shapes that are required for making something. **O:** dress, skirt, jacket □ *Before Mary could* ***cut*** *her dress* ***out,*** *she had to flatten the pieces of the pattern and pin them carefully to the material.* □ *The shoemaker carefully examined the leather before starting to* ***cut out*** *the uppers.*

cut out[2] [B1i pass adj] (informal) defeat; eliminate. **O:** his etc enemy, rival, competitor; best friend; (all) competition □ *Sam was getting on very well with Mavis until his best friend arrived with his new sports car and* ***cut*** *him* ***out.***

cut out[3] [B1i pass adj] delete, not include. **O:** word, phrase, expression, paragraph, section; (all, any) reference to, mention of, discussion of, allusion to, description of □ *Before we can print this book, you will have to* ***cut out*** *all the four-letter words and slighting references to the royal family.* □ *I think it's got the makings of a fairly good yarn, provided of course that you* ***cut out***

this verbal tomfoolery and make it clean cut. HD

cut out[4] [B1i pass adj] stop taking, eating, drinking or using; stop any harmful activity or bad habit. **O:** cigarettes, tobacco, alcohol, drugs; fat, meat, sugar, carbohydrates; game, sport; watching television, going to bed late □ *In a vain attempt to regain her youthful figure, she* ***cut out*** *carbohydrates completely — for about a week!* □ *I'm afraid the time has come when I shall have to* ***cut out*** *my weekly game of squash — I'm not as young as I was!* □ (words of a man on being arrested) *'You can* ***cut out*** *the rough stuff; I'm not armed.'* T

cut out[5] [A1] stop functioning; pack up[3] (q v). **S:** engine, motor □ *The investigation into the crash established that the two port engines had* ***cut out*** *shortly after take-off.* □ *As we were circling the field preparatory to landing, the engine* ***cut out***. MFM

cut out[6] [A1 nom] automatically stop providing heat, cool air. **S:** central heating (system); radiator, heater □ *When the temperature of the room reaches 70 degrees the convector heater* ***cuts out***. □ *The central heating system is fitted with an automatic* ***cut-out*** (i e an electrical device which causes the boiler to ***cut out*** when a given temperature is reached).

cut out (the) dead wood [B1iii pass] (informal) remove those parts which confuse or spoil a picture, description, test etc □ *The methods used have helped enormously in making questionnaires more reliable, in* ***cutting out dead wood***, *and generally in improving measurements along these lines.* SNP □ *Before we can hope to make this industry more efficient and competitive, there's a tremendous amount of* ***dead wood*** *to* ***cut out***.

cut it/that out [B1ii] (informal) stop doing or saying something that angers or irritates sb else □ *'Stop quarrelling, you two! Can't you see that I'm trying to concentrate. Just* ***cut it out****!'* □ *'I'm not going to be told what I must or must not do by you or anyone else, so you can* ***cut that out****!'* □ *'You blame me for everything that goes wrong and I wish you'd* ***cut it out***.*'*

cut out for [pass (B3)] (informal) (be) well matched, have the right abilities or qualities for. **o:** each other (esp of an engaged or married couple); particular job, kind of life □ *Peter and Susan seem to be* ***cut out for*** *each other.* □ *Something reasonable always turns up once you've abandoned the idea that one particular job is the only one you're* ***cut out for***. HD □ *'I don't know that I'm* ***cut out for*** *religion, but I'd like to know a good deal more about it. I can understand a lot of it, but this business of the Pope rather stands in the way.'* ASA

cut out/out of [B1i nom pass adj B2 pass] remove by cutting (from). **O:** picture, figure, coupon, article. **o:** newspaper, magazine, book □ *The children showed their teacher all the pictures of English towns that they had* ***cut out of*** *magazines.* □ *'I'm going to* ***cut*** *this advertisement* ***out*** *and send it to Alice; she may be interested in the job.'* □ *The table was covered with* ***cut-out*** *figures and shapes of animals, buildings, trees and people.*

cut through[1] [B1ii pass B2 pass rel] open a way by the removal of obstacles. **O:** one's way, passage, route. **o:** forest, jungle, defences; ice □ *The escaping prisoners managed to* ***cut*** *their way* ***through*** *the barbed wire round the camp.* □ *Only a powerful, specially equipped ship could* ***cut*** *a way* ***through*** *such tightly-packed ice.*

cut through[2] [A2] overcome or by-pass difficulties (esp bureaucratic). **o:** red tape, formalities □ *Every newly-elected Town Councillor swears that he will* ***cut through*** *the red tape of the local bureaucracy, but no one ever succeeds.* □ *If you have the patience to* ***cut through*** *all the verbiage you will find that there is much sense in the Committee's proposals.*

cut to [A2] (cinema, TV) change from one scene or aspect of a scene to another □ *'... so just as the escaped murderer is about to break into the farm, we'll* ***cut to*** *the tracker-dogs following the scent....'* □ *'While Peter and Arthur continue quarrelling,* ***cut to*** *Cynthia in close-up....'*

cut to pieces/ribbons/shreds [B2 pass] defeat utterly, inflicting great losses on; annihilate, decimate. **O:** defenders, attacking forces, armed raiders □ *The retreat turned into a rout and the would-be attackers were* ***cut to ribbons*** *by the enemy, who gave them no respite.* □ *The heavy cavalry caught the foot soldiers in line before they could form a square, and* ***cut them to pieces***.

cut (prices) to the bone [B2 pass] (informal) reduce prices to the lowest possible level □ *The competition between the supermarkets in the High Street was such that (the* ***prices*** *of) many products were* ***cut to the bone***, *leaving practically no profit-margin.*

cut to the quick [B2 pass] (informal) hurt sb's feelings deeply □ *Helen's sarcastic remarks about my efforts to help her and her family,* ***cut me to the quick***. □ *He was* ***cut to the quick*** *by such a display of callousness.*

cut up[1] [B1i pass adj] cut or chop into pieces. **O:** meat, vegetables, branches □ *The vegetables should be* ***cut up*** *into small pieces and dropped into the boiling water.* □ *You can* ***cut*** *this wood* ***up*** *very easily* (or: *This wood* ***cuts up*** *very easily) with an ordinary saw.*

cut up[2] [B1i pass] (informal) injure, damage with cuts, bruises etc □ *All the occupants of the two cars were badly* ***cut up*** *in the smash.* □ *Those fellows weren't too gentle with him. They* ***cut*** *him* ***up*** *very badly.*

cut up[3] [pass (B1)] (informal) (be) emotionally upset □ *Eve was very* ***cut up*** *when she heard that her friend had been sacked.* □ *The parents were naturally* ***cut up*** *at the news of their son's arrest on a charge of fraud.* □ *There's no need to be so* ***cut up*** *at not getting the job: it's only a matter of time before you fall on your feet* □ passive with *be, feel, seem.*

cut up[2] [B1i pass] (informal) injure, damage with cuts, bruises etc □ *All the occupants of the two cars were badly* ***cut up*** *in the smash.* □ *Those* **cut up rough** [A1] (informal) react violently; behave aggressively □ *If the left wing of the Labour Party continues to be ignored by the party leader, they are liable to start* ***cutting up rough***. □ *The potential clients were lining up, tumbling over themselves, only waiting for a word from Alec. Would that word be given, if Harold started to* ***cut up rough****?* PW

cut up (for) [A1 A3] (informal) be worth, or leave, a quantity of money at death □ *Old Amos* *is as mean as a miser but it wouldn't surprise me if he* ***cut up for*** *a million pounds.*

cut no ice (with) [B2 pass] (informal) not influence, not affect, carry no weight with. **S:** argument, defence, submission; evidence, so-called facts □ *All these statistics about increased wages* ***cut no ice with*** *me. What I want to know is how the government proposes to reduce unemployment.*

D

dab off [B1i pass adj] absorb, remove, with quick, light movements. **S:** housewife, cleaner. **O:** water, excess liquid; oil, dirt, mud □ *If you apply this cleaning fluid, you'll find you can simply* ***dab*** *the dirt* ***off.*** □ *Only allow a thin film of water to settle on the plates; any excess should be* ***dabbed off.***

dab on/onto [B1i pass adj B2 pass emph rel] apply, put on, lightly or gently. **S:** artist, painter; housewife, cleaner. **O:** paint, turpentine; polish, cleaning-fluid. **o:** canvas; furniture □ *The painter slowly built up his landscape,* ***dabbing on*** *small areas of green and yellow.* □ *The furniture cream should be* ***dabbed on*** *with a soft cloth.*

dabble (in) [A2 emph rel] study, give some attention to (without becoming seriously involved). **S:** businessman, gentleman of means/leisure. **o:** painting, the theatre; politics, law □ *Trevor* ***dabbled in*** *what he called art, until he was called up, when he got into the intelligence corps.* SPL □ *There were various pursuits* ***in*** *which he had* ***dabbled*** *from time to time — the piano was his latest.*

dally with[1] [A2 pass emph rel] consider, contemplate, idly in one's mind; play with[3] (q v), toy with[3] (q v). **S:** manager, developer, farmer, householder. **o:** scheme, project; idea, notion □ *The Electricity Board have been* ***dallying with*** *the idea of building a power station down here. But I doubt very much whether anything will come of it.* □ *We discussed a proposal* ***with*** *which he had been* ***dallying*** *for some time, but about which little had been done.*

dally with[2] [A2] appear to show an interest in sb (without intending a serious relationship); play with[2] (q v), toy with[2] (q v). **S:** philanderer, sponger. **o:** girl, woman □ *He* ***dallied with*** *her affections for a bit, but quickly moved on when she showed signs of wanting a more permanent relationship.*

dam up[1] [B1i pass adj] close by means of a dam; check, retain (waters) with a dam. **S:** government; (water, electricity) authorities; engineer. **O:** valley, gorge; river □ *When a river valley is* ***dammed up,*** *the waters contained by the barrage rise to form an artificial lake.*

dam up[2] [B1i pass adj] suppress, restrain; bottle up (q v). **O:** emotion, feeling; anger, resentment □ ***Dammed-up*** *feelings will burst out at some stage in a more violent form than if they had been expressed in the first place.*

damp down[1] [B1i pass adj] cause to burn more slowly (by adding ash or reducing the draught of air). **S:** stoker, caretaker, housewife. **O:** furnace, boiler, fire □ *The boilers are producing too much pressure: they'll have to be* ***damped down.***

damp down[2] [B1i pass adj] restrain, control. **S:** teacher, leader. **O:** enthusiasm, high spirits, ebullience □ *The party spirit was considerably* ***damped down*** *by the news that all leave had been stopped.* □ *Now he wanted to go back, but to* ***damp down*** *the urge he was sent to his brother's home in France.* RT

damp off [A1] (horticulture) rot and die through excessive damp. **S:** young plant, cactus □ *Don't give those plants too much water; they'll* ***damp off.***

dance across, along, away etc [A1 emph A2 emph rel] move across etc rhythmically, often to music □ ***Off*** *she* ***danced,*** *all thoughts of her examinations for the moment forgotten.* □ *The bridal procession* ***danced down*** *the street and* ***into*** *the groom's garden.*

dance attendance (on) [B2 emph rel] (formal) follow about attentively and/or slavishly (usu in the hope of obtaining favours). **S:** suitor; courtier, hanger-on (at court). **o:** young woman, pretty girl; prince, minister; rich relative □ *A swarm of would-be suitors* ***danced attendance on*** *the best-looking girls.* □ *He had for a long time* ***danced attendance on*** *the great, though without obtaining any special privileges in return.*

dangle before/in front of [B2 pass emph rel] offer prospects of wealth etc enticingly. **O:** promotion, advancement; profit, gain. **o:** employee, candidate; sb's eyes □ *The days may be past when graduates had prospects of dazzling careers in industry* ***dangled in front of*** *them.*

dart across, along, away etc [A1 emph A2 emph rel] move quickly, sharply, in a given direction. □ *Bill* ***darted back*** *into bed as his father's step was heard on the stairs.* □ *She opened the box and* ***out darted*** *a mouse.*

dart a glance/look at [B2 pass emph rel] look suddenly, sharply, at sb; shoot a glance (at) (q v). **adj:** furtive, anxious, hostile. **o:** stranger, visitor; watch, clock □ *She* ***darted an*** *interested* ***glance at*** *the handsome newcomer from under lowered eyelids.* □ *The villagers were guarded in their reception. So many suspicious* ***looks*** *were* ***darted at*** *him.*

dash against [A2 B2 pass] (cause to) crash violently against. **S:** [A2] **O:** [B2] boat, raft; body, skull. **S:** [B2] sea, wave; storm; (force of the) explosion, blast. **o:** rock, cliff; wall, pavement □ *The tanker* ***dashed against*** *the reef with a force which opened a great hole in her side.* □ *The force of the blast* ***dashed him against*** *the wall of the cave.*

dash (oneself) against [A2 B2] crash, hurl, oneself etc, against. **S:** heavy sea, big wave, breaker; assault troops, wave of attackers. **o:** shore, promenade; trenches, lines □ *Heavy seas* ***dashed against*** *the sea wall.* □ *Attacking waves of infantry* ***dashed themselves*** *in vain* ***against*** *a well-entrenched enemy.*

dash away a tear/one's tears [B1iii] brush

tears from one's eyes with a hand or handkerchief. **S:** girl, child □ *Brigit* ***dashed away her tears.*** DC

dash off [B1i pass adj] write, draw, very quickly; tear off [2] (q v). **S:** secretary, journalist; artist. **O:** article, letter, note; sketch, drawing □ *The thing had obviously been* ***dashed off*** *but it consisted of just the right number of lines.* CON □ *They would* ***dash off*** *one of these notes of credit as they stopped in some oak-dark room for port and steak.* OBS

dash one's/sb's brains out [B1i pass] kill oneself, or sb, by smashing the skull open. **S:** (violent) blow; bullet, stone, shell-splinter □ *He fell over the cliff-edge and* ***dashed out his brains*** *on the rocks below.* □ *One of the bodyguard* ***dashed his brains out*** *with a single blow from his club.*

dash over[1] [A2] crash, hurl itself, over. **S:** heavy sea, big wave. **o:** promenade, coast road, breakwater, promontory □ *As the storm built up, heavy seas* ***dashed over*** *a row of cottages built near the water's edge.*

dash over[2] [B2 pass] throw over in a stream. **S:** car, bicycle; clumsy fellow, comedian. **O:** water, mud; paint, whitewash. **o:** suit, trousers; floor, wall □ *A passing car* ***dashed*** *muddy water all* ***over*** *my clothes.* □ *The circus clowns* ***dashed*** *buckets of whitewash* ***over*** *each other.*

date from/back to [A2 emph rel A3 emph rel] have existed since, originate in. **S:** castle, church; custom, tradition; agreement, association, alliance; hostility, misunderstanding. **o:** Norman times, the Stone Age; the war, pre-war times □ *The connection with Hanover* ***dates back to*** *the 18th Century.* □ *The present harmony in the factory* ***dates from*** *a sensible agreement on wages and productivity.* □ ***From*** *what period do the ceremonies* ***date****?*

daub on/onto [B1i pass adj B2 pass emph rel] apply thickly and/or crudely (to). **S:** painter, sculptor; decorator. **O:** paint, clay, plaster. **o:** canvas, framework, wall □ *The children were encouraged to* ***daub*** *the colours* ***on*** *liberally.* □ *Modelling clay was* ***daubed*** *thickly* ***onto*** *a small metal framework and then worked into shape* (or: *A small metal framework was thickly* ***daubed with*** *clay* etc).

daub onto/over [B2 pass emph rel] smear sth thickly over a surface (staining it, or making it dirty). **S:** painter; mechanic; child. **O:** paint; oil, tar; jam, treacle. **o:** wall, woodwork; overalls; dress □ *Mary had* ***daubed*** *jam and chocolate all* ***over*** *her apron* (or: *had* ***daubed*** *her apron all* ***over with*** *jam* etc). □ *Oil and grease were* ***daubed onto*** *his shirt* (or: *His shirt was* ***daubed with*** *oil* etc).

daub with[1] [B2 pass rel] ⇨ daub on/onto.

daub with[2] [B2 pass rel] ⇨ daub onto/over.

dawn on/upon [A2] occur to sb, become clear to sb. **S:** sense, truth; the realization that...; it... that he might be dead, it... that she was seriously ill □ *The sense of all that he had been saying suddenly* ***dawned on*** *her.* □ *It* ***dawned on*** *them that they might be cut off by the tide.*

deal in[1] [B1ii pass] include sb in a game by dealing him a hand of cards etc. **S:** banker, croupier □ *Peter arrived late for our bridge party, but somebody quickly gave him a drink and then we* ***dealt*** *him* ***in****.*

deal in[2] [A2 pass rel] handle, do business in. **S:** shopkeeper; store, trading company. **o:** second-hand cars, stationery, stocks and shares □ *The small post-office on the corner* ***deals in*** *a lot else besides stamps and postal orders.* □ *Most foreign trading companies in West Africa* ***deal in*** *rubber, cocoa and vegetable oils.*

deal out [B1iii pass] administer; mete out (q v). **S:** father, boxer; magistrate. **O:** (good) hiding, thrashing; punishment, justice □ *The frontier town had set up a primitive court, which* ***dealt out*** *justice of a kind.* □ *The lighter boxer had a good deal of punishment* ***dealt out*** *to him by the end of the first round.*

deal with[1] [A2 rel] trade with, do business (with) (q v); talk with in order to reach a settlement etc. **o:** firm, company; supplier, wholesaler □ *We've* ***dealt with*** *the same firm for years and can thoroughly recommend them to you.* □ *They are bad people to* ***deal with****; always late on delivery dates.* □ *'Banda in jail was a myth, but Banda out of jail is a man, and one can* ***deal with*** *a man.'* SC

deal with[2] [A2 pass adj rel] handle, tackle, confront (so as to settle, remedy, reform etc). **S:** government, official; police, prison service; doctor, teacher. **o:** inquiry, complaint, grievance; crime wave, indiscipline; disease, learning problem □ *Any complaints about the quality of our goods will be quickly* ***dealt with*** *by local branches.* □ *The galloping increase of traffic in recent years must be* ***dealt with****.* SC □ *The problem of unemployment is the most serious of those* ***with*** *which the Government has to* ***deal****.*

deal with[3] [A2 pass] handle some offence (with the suggestion that the reckoning will be unpleasant). **S:** father, employer, superior officer □ *'I'll* ***deal with*** *you when I get home from the office!'* □ *'I'll get Father to* ***deal with*** *him later on.'* □ *In Cuba the police can* ***deal*** *as harshly as they like* ***with*** *émigrés from Latin America.* OMIH □ often used with *shall/will.*

deal with[4] [A2 pass rel] have as its subject, be concerned with; cover. **S:** article, lecture, book. **o:** Asia, the population problem, the English Romantics, coal □ *His first lecture* ***dealt with*** *relief and drainage; this week he's talking about rainfall.* □ *The subject isn't very well* ***dealt with*** *in his latest book.*

debar (from) [B2 pass emph rel] (formal) exclude by law or regulation from use or membership of. **S:** committee, Chamber of Commerce, trades union. **O:** member, associate. **o:** voting, using club premises; membership □ *Insane persons are* ***debarred from*** *voting at elections.* □ *New legislation may have to be introduced if clubs are to be prevented from* ***debarring*** *people* ***from*** *membership on grounds of race or colour.*

debit to [B2 pass emph rel] (commerce) subtract from the amount held in sb's account by a bank or commercial organization. **S:** bank, finance company; store. **O:** sum, amount; charge. **o:** customer; account; department □ *Would you kindly explain why this large sum has been* ***debited to*** *me* (or: *why I have been* ***debited with*** *this large sum*)*?*

debit with [B2 pass rel] ⇨ previous entry.

deceived in [pass (B2)] (formal) (have) come to realize that sb is not what one thought, (be) disappointed in. **S:** father, teacher, employer □ *I've been* **deceived in** *Smith: he has an impressive manner, but no real staying power or brains.*

deceive into [B2 pass] make sb believe sth which is untrue (esp for purposes of gain). **S:** enemy, rival; salesman, agent, confidence trickster. **O:** firm, purchaser, shopper. **o:** supposing, believing, thinking; buying, selling □ *The Prussians* **deceived** *Napoleon* **into** *thinking they had withdrawn away from the British.* □ *We were* **deceived into** *buying a house that was scheduled for demolition.* □ *-ing* form of a v as object of into.

decide against[1] [A2] (legal) deliver a verdict or judgment against; find against (q v). **S:** judge, magistrate, jury. **o:** plaintiff, accused, defendant, Crown □ *The Court* **decided against** *the Crown in the case of Regina* v *Carruthers.* ⇨ decide for/in favour of.

decide against[2] [A2 pass rel] resolve not to (have). **o:** continental holiday, boarding school, efficiency campaign; having guests, sending a letter, giving a party □ *We've* **decided against** *having a big family gathering this Christmas.* □ *They had* **decided against** *an expensive education for their children.* ⇨ decide on.

decide for/in favour of [A2] (legal) deliver a verdict or judgment in favour of; find for (q v). **S:** judge, magistrate. **o:** plaintiff, defendant □ *I doubt whether any court in the country would* **decide in his favour**. *His record must tell against him.* ⇨ decide against[1].

decide on [A2 pass rel] resolve to (have). **o:** sports car, saloon; bungalow, flat; expansion, reduction (of activity) □ *Finally, she* **decided on** *the white and yellow striped material.* □ *They need a new car, but the precise model is still to be* **decided on**. ⇨ decide against[2].

deck out/up (in) [B1ii pass B3 pass] (informal) put on as for a special occasion. **S:** girlfriend, young man, teenager, overblown matron. **O:** herself etc; child, wife. **o:** all her finery, his Sunday best, party frock □ *The female guests had* **decked** *themselves* **out in** *satin frocks and flowery hats.* □ *Sometimes she gets* **decked up in** *her black jeans and goes off to some sexy club.* FFE

deck with [B2 pass rel] decorate with; festoon with. **S:** council, townspeople, priest, child. **O:** street, wall; house, shop; Christmas tree. **o:** flag, bunting; garland, flower; paper-chain □ *The horns of the sacred cattle were* **decked with** *garlands.* □ *The authorities gave orders to* **deck** *the streets* **with** *flags and bunting.*

declare war (against/on) [B2 pass rel] announce officially that a state of war exists between two countries □ *Britain* **declared war on** *Germany on 3rd September, 1939.* □ *Hostilities were opened without* **war** *being* **declared**.

dedicate to[1] [B2 pass emph rel] (formal) give oneself to a purpose believed to be important; devote to (q v). **O:** oneself; one's life, career; energies. **o:** purpose, cause; helping the needy, caring for the sick □ *Members of religious communities have* **dedicated** *their whole lives* **to** *God's service.* □ *He felt that Socialism was the most important cause* **to** *which he could* **dedicate** *himself.*

dedicate to[2] [B2 pass emph rel] write one's name at the beginning of a work as a mark of gratitude, admiration etc. **S:** writer, composer. **O:** novel, poems; symphony, opera. **o:** parents, wife □ *Beethoven at first* **dedicated** *his 'Eroica' Symphony* **to** *Napoleon but afterwards tore out the fly-leaf in disgust.*

deduce (from) [B2 pass emph rel] (formal) arrive at a conclusion by examining and weighing evidence. **O:** knowledge, theory. **o:** facts, data; observations, measurements □ *You will notice water rising in the tube; now what do you* **deduce from** *that?* □ **From** *the presence of people of Asiatic stock in America we may possibly* **deduce** *that the two continents were at one time linked.*

deduct (from) [B2 pass emph rel] (formal) take one amount (esp a compulsory levy) from a larger. **S:** employer; bursar; tax office. **O:** contribution, insurance payment, income tax. **o:** wage, salary □ *Nowadays income tax is normally* **deducted from** *a person's wages before he receives them.* □ *Staff are requested to instruct the Bursar's Office to* **deduct** *common room subscriptions* **from** *their monthly salaries.*

defect (from) (to) [A2 emph rel] transfer one's allegiance from one country (or power bloc) to another, esp with the knowledge and encouragement of one's intending host or employer. **S:** (intelligence) agent, (military) expert, scientist □ *The year began with the bad news that two of our best agents had* **defected to** *the other side.* □ *'So you are the man who is going to make Semitsa* **defect from** *the Moscow Academy of Sciences and come to work in the west.'* L DEIGHTON: FUNERAL IN BERLIN

defend (against/from) [B2 pass emph rel] guard, protect, sb (from attack etc). **S:** dog; fence, barbed wire; law; ombudsman, trades union, professional body. **O:** house, factory; field, emplacement; (ordinary) citizen; worker, member. **o:** thief, trespasser; attack, invasion; invasion of rights, encroachment on privacy; discrimination □ *Here we are well* **defended against** *a surprise attack.* □ *The association exists to* **defend** *the consumer* **against** *unscrupulous traders.*

defer (to) [A2 pass emph rel] (formal) out of respect, treat as more important or authoritative. **S:** young man, pupil, newcomer. **o:** elder, senior; master, teacher; opinion, view □ *Generally the young should* **defer to** *the opinions of their elders, but such deference can be overdone.* □ *Grandfather ruled his family with a rod of iron; his views were invariably* **deferred to**. □ *There were some self-appointed experts* **to** *whom he was not prepared to* **defer**.

define (as) [B2 pass] state the characteristics peculiar to an object, quality etc. **O:** substance, element; acid, salt; virtue, vice. **o:** lacking flavour; something which corrodes; that which corrupts □ *A 'sentence' has been variously* **defined as** *'the expression of a complete thought', 'something beginning with a capital letter and ending with a full stop' and 'the largest unit of grammatical description'.* □ *How can one* **define** *visual beauty?* **As** *something which arouses pleasant sensations in the viewer?*

deflect (from) [B2 pass emph rel] cause to change course; turn aside (from). **S:** armour-plate, steel helmet; heckler, reporter; visitor; interruption. **O:** shell, bullet; speaker, lecturer;

attention. **o:** target; path, course; purpose, task; theme, topic □ *The steeply-sloped armour of the tank was designed to* ***deflect*** *anti-tank shells* ***from*** *their target.* □ *He was momentarily* ***deflected from*** *this train of argument by a knock on the door.*

delegate (to) [B2 pass emph rel] (formal) give a task etc to a trusted person (usu a subordinate). **S:** manager; commander; headmaster. **O:** duty, responsibility; task, work; organizing, planning. **o:** assistant, deputy; second-in-command □ *A mark of a good leader is his readiness to* ***delegate*** *a certain amount of decision-making* ***to*** *his assistants.* □ *The routine office work had all been* ***delegated to*** *his executive staff.*

delete (from) [B2 pass emph rel] (formal) remove, cross out (q v) (from). **S:** editor, censor. **O:** name; figure, amount; statement, remark; detail, reference. **o:** list, roll; report, accounts; record, transcript □ *When one dictator replaces another, a fresh set of names has often to be* ***deleted from*** *the history books.* □ *He turned to the end of the article;* ***from*** *the list of works consulted, all references to himself had been* ***deleted.***

delight in [A2] enjoy, take (unkind) pleasure in. **S:** elder brother, bigger pupil. **o:** teasing his small sister, ragging younger boys, pulling my leg, proving us wrong □ *Peter seems to* ***delight in*** *making other people suffer.* □ object of in is usu the *-ing* form of a v.

deliver oneself of [B2 rel] (formal) state, express (pompously, self-importantly). **o:** opinion, view; statement, claim, proposal □ *The judge* ***delivered himself of*** *the view that young people were treated far too leniently nowadays.* □ *A German General had* ***delivered himself of*** *an all-embracing classification about officers: the clever, the stupid, the industrious and the lazy.* MFM

deliver over/up (to) [B1i pass B3 pass rel] (formal) surrender, hand over[1] (q v) (to) (usu under duress). **S:** garrison, besieged army, gaoler. **O:** castle, town, prisoner, stores □ *The governor was ordered to* ***deliver over*** *the keys to the citadel.* □ *In an unpleasant moment he saw himself recaptured and* ***delivered up*** *again* ***to*** *his gaolers.*

delude (into) [B2 pass emph rel] (formal) deliberately mislead sb or oneself (into a particular state of mind). **S:** government, politician; press, radio. **O:** public; supporter, follower; oneself. **o:** belief, supposition; believing, supposing, expecting □ *For years we have been* ***deluded into*** *expecting a sudden economic recovery.* □ *They couldn't go on* ***deluding*** *themselves* ***into*** *thinking that in six months or a year their marriage would somehow right itself.*

delve into [A2 pass emph rel] search thoroughly (for facts, knowledge). **S:** scholar, archivist. **o:** manuscript, document; past, memory □ *He has been* ***delving into*** *accounts of daily life in the 16th Century.* □ *I had to* ***delve*** *pretty hard* ***into*** *my memory to recall where I had seen him before.*

demand (of) [B2 pass rel] require that sb should give or offer. **S:** work, task; office, job. **O:** sacrifice; persistence; a readiness, willingness (to do sth); that one should give up one's family life □ *Have you any idea what a full-time political career will* ***demand of*** *you?* □ *As director of these courses a great deal will be* ***demanded of*** *him.*

denude (of) [B2 pass rel] (formal) remove the covering from, strip bare of. **S:** wind and rain, storm; bad husbandry. **O:** tree; hillside, countryside. **o:** leaves, branches; soil □ *Intensive cultivation had* ***denuded*** *the hillsides* ***of*** *their covering of fertile soil.* □ *Trees were* ***denuded of*** *their leaves.*

depart from [A2 pass adj emph rel] (formal) do sth not in accordance with, make a break from. **o:** accepted practice, custom; established tradition, routine □ *The chairman* ***departed from*** *normal procedure by allowing reporters to be present during Council business.* □ *These were hallowed traditions* ***from*** *which he had no intention of* ***departing.*** □ *The rules were rigid in principle, sometimes* ***departed from*** *in practice.*

depend on/upon[1] [A2 pass rel] (be able to) believe that sb or sth will prove reliable; bank on[2] (q v). **o:** him etc; product, commodity; firm, service □ *You can't* ***depend on*** *this bus service — it's never punctual.* □ *He's a man who can be* ***depended upon*** *in a crisis.* □ *They could* ***depend on*** *John to support them.* □ usu with *can/could.*

depend on/upon[2] [A2 pass emph rel] be sure of, confidently expect, an event; reckon on/upon (q v). **o:** him/his turning up, him/his being on time, him/his supporting the motion; his support, co-operation, sympathy □ *You can* ***depend on*** *his support for your Bill.* □ *One could never* ***depend on*** *his arriving on time.* □ *He'll be there when he's needed;* ***on*** *that you can* ***depend.*** □ usu with *can/could.*

depend on/upon[3] [A2 emph rel] get income, material support or sustenance from. **S:** town, port, industry; family, child; painter, writer. **o:** manufacturers, trade, coal; father, parent; steady sales, rich patron. **A:** for its existence, for his livelihood; to survive; as a source of income □ *He* ***depends*** *for his livelihood* ***upon*** *a small income from investments.* □ *The town* ***depends*** *almost solely* ***on*** *the tourist trade.* □ *To remain in existence, the theatre must continue to* ***depend on*** *a state subsidy.*

depend on/upon[4] [A2 emph rel] follow directly or logically from; turn on[4] (q v). **S:** a great deal; whether we succeed, how we set about it. **o:** how they respond, the way it's tackled; the forces at our disposal □ *A great deal will* ***depend on*** *the way the Government responds.* SC □ *It all (= the answer)* ***depends on*** *what you mean by truth!* □ *How successful they were would* ***depend on*** *the speed with which the product could be distributed to the shops.*

depend on/upon it [A2] one may be sure or certain (of the fact); without any doubt □ *For* ***depend upon it,*** *my boy, the monster won't understand a word of this new-fangled language called English.* RM □ *He may* ***depend upon it*** *that we shall never surrender.* □ *'You can* ***depend on it.*** *I shall be there.'* □ depend on/upon it is often followed by a main clause or a *that*-clause; there is often no Subject.

deprive of [B2 pass emph rel] stop sb enjoying or using. **S:** gaoler, invader, tyrant; tall buildings, trees. **o:** freedom; luxuries, necessities;

sunshine, heat □ *The new laws threaten to* ***deprive*** *many people* ***of*** *the most elementary freedoms.* □ *Civilians were* ***deprived of*** *food and clothing in order to supply the growing armies.*

deputize (for) [A2 pass emph rel] act in the place of sb in authority during his absence. **S:** assistant-director, sub-manager, second-in-command □ *Mr Jones will be* ***deputizing for*** *me during my absence abroad.* □ *I dare say Stephens can be* ***deputized for*** *— we seem to have managed without his directing hand before.*

derive from[1] [B2 pass emph rel] (formal) get, obtain, from; draw from[2] (q v). **S:** patient, invalid; student, reader. **O:** relief, benefit; pleasure, instruction; income. **o:** course of treatment; studies, books; investments □ *Mary has* ***derived*** *a good deal of benefit* ***from*** *her tuition.* □ *Lonely people listening to the wireless can* ***derive*** *some comfort* ***from*** *the fact that every wireless in the street is linking the neighbours together.* UL

derive from[2] [A2 emph rel B2 pass emph rel] (formal) have, take, as its starting point or origin. **S:** [A2] **O:** [B2] product; word, name; ceremony, ritual. **o:** mineral; (Latin, Sanskrit) root, source; ancient custom □ *Margarine is* ***derived from*** *vegetable oils.* □ *The word* ***derives from*** *a Greek noun with a quite different meaning.* □ *The May-Day ceremonies are said to be* ***derived from*** *the fertility rites of the Ancient Britons.*

descend to [A2 pass emph rel] act in a mean or base way; stoop to (q v). **o:** (low) level, (such etc) depths; vulgar abuse, gossip; cheating, fraud; personalities □ *I never thought he would* ***descend to*** *abusing his former colleagues in public.* □ *There are no depths* ***to*** *which he will not* ***descend*** *in attempting to discredit his opponents.*

descend upon [A2] attack suddenly; swoop (down) (on) (q v). **S:** bandits, raiders; cavalry. **o:** encampment, village; column, stragglers □ *Bands of marauding horsemen would* ***descend upon*** *their isolated trading posts.*

describe as [B2 pass] say that sb is; claim that one is. **O:** him; oneself. **o:** clever, able; being very tall; an expert, an authority □ *His employer had* ***described*** *him* ***as*** *lacking in initiative and drive.* □ *He* ***describes*** *himself* ***as*** *a business executive; in fact, he is a clerk.*

deserve better/well of [A2] merit good or better treatment from. **o:** country, firm, employer □ *He* ***deserved*** *rather* ***better of*** *his employers than to be pensioned off at a few pounds a week.* □ *Lincoln* ***deserved well of*** *his country.*

despair of [A2 pass] be extremely doubtful of, sceptical about. **o:** ever seeing them again, ever succeeding; success, outcome, issue, recovery □ *After being cut off from the main party for two weeks they began to* ***despair of*** *rejoining their companions.* □ *Don't* ***despair of*** *being slim again until you know what this new, reducing idea can do for you.* DM

destine for [B2 pass emph rel] (formal) decide or ordain in advance that sb will be or do sth. **S:** family, schoolmaster. **O:** eldest son, brightest pupil. **o:** the church, law, medicine, army □ *From the beginning his father had* ***destined*** *him* ***for*** *a career at the Bar.* □ *By family tradition he was* ***destined for*** *Sandhurst and a career as a regular army officer.*

detach (from) [B2 pass emph rel] separate, remove (from). **S:** mechanic; railwayman; commander. **O:** engine, gearbox; tender, waggon; staff, personnel. **o:** car, chassis; train; regiment □ *Two carriages were* ***detached*** *(****from*** *the Edinburgh train) at York.* □ *Officers* ***detached from*** *their units may be given staff appointments.*

detail off [B1i pass] (usu military) assign, designate, appoint (usu to a specific task or for a particular purpose). **S:** sergeant-major, duty NCO; manager, foreman. **O:** fatigue party, squad; ten men; team, group □ *Half-a-dozen men were* ***detailed off*** *for guard duty.* □ *The best technique is to* ***detail off*** *known and stalwart supporters to enter into conversation with the other side before the meeting actually begins.* THH

detect (in) [B2 pass emph rel] find evidence of sth (in materials being examined, in sb's manner etc). **O:** sign, trace, mark; note, hint (of frivolity, seriousness, defiance). **o:** specimen, sample; voice, manner; suggestion □ *We* ***detected*** *minute quantities of copper* ***in*** *the rock samples.* □ *'Do I* ***detect*** *a certain lack of seriousness* ***in*** *what you're proposing?'* □ ***In*** *the way they talk about the job you can* ***detect*** *early signs of disillusionment.*

deter (from) [B2 pass emph rel] (formal) make sb lose the desire to do sth; discourage (from) (q v). **S:** industrial unrest, distance from markets. **O:** industry, investor. **o:** moving North, investing overseas, installing new machinery □ *Several factors* ***deter*** *new industry* ***from*** *coming to Cornwall.* OBS □ *Countries have not been* ***deterred from*** *waging conventional wars by their opponents' possession of nuclear weapons.* □ object is the *-ing* form.

detract from [A2 pass emph rel] (formal) lessen, diminish; weaken; take from[3] (q v). **S:** small size, power (of the engine), tiny cabin, awkward handling; length, difficulty, complexity. **o:** usefulness, appeal, attractiveness (to buyers); worth, value □ *Poor visibility forward and the bounciness of the suspension may* ***detract from*** *its appeal as a general-purpose farm vehicle.* □ *His high voice and unpleasing appearance* ***detracted from*** *his effectiveness as a speaker.*

develop (from) (into) [A2 rel B2 pass rel] (cause to) grow larger, become more powerful etc (from being small, weak etc). **S:** [A2] **O:** [B2] country, city; farm, factory; school, course. **S:** [B2] government, regional board; owner, proprietor; director, head. **o:** (***from***) principality, village; power, metropolis; estate, vast complex; the best, most advanced of its kind □ *The area to the south of the Maas has* ***developed into*** *Europoort, a complex of docks, refineries and warehouses.* □ *This great industry has* ***developed from*** *quite modest beginnings.* □ *The directors have plans to* ***develop*** *the club grounds* ***into*** *a stadium holding 40 000 people.*

deviate (from) [A2 pass emph rel B2 pass emph rel] (formal) (cause to) abandon, move away (from); diverge (from) (q v). **o:** chosen course, straight path; truth; policy, course of action □ *We shall not* ***deviate*** *by a hair's breadth* ***from*** *the mandate which the electorate has given us.* □ *They could not be* ***deviated from*** *what they believed to be their duty.*

devolve upon [A2 emph rel] (formal) be passed to, become the responsibility of. **S:** office, job, duties, function. **o:** second-in-command, Vice-Chairman, chief clerk □ *When the Ambassador is on leave, his duties* ***devolve upon*** *the First Secretary.* □ *It* ***devolved upon*** *his assistant to ensure that the guests were found hotels and entertained.*

devote to [B2 pass emph rel] give oneself to a purpose thought to be important; dedicate to[1] (q v); spend time, effort, doing sth. **O:** oneself; energies, thoughts; a lifetime, twenty years. **o:** golf, hunting; family, children; education; improving standards, curing disease, helping the poor □ *Ghandi* ***devoted*** *his whole life* ***to*** *the cause of peace.* □ *The centre pages of this issue will be* ***devoted to*** *an important feature on housing.* □ *Livestock breeders are* ***devoting*** *much thought and ingenuity* ***to*** *the improvement of this strain.*

dictate (to) [A2 rel B2 pass rel] say or read aloud sth which is to be written down (in shorthand or longhand). **S:** manager, executive; teacher. **O:** letter, draft; poem, problem. **o:** secretary; class □ *He* ***dictated to*** *his best books the passage which I've* ***dictated*** *(****to*** *you).'*

dictate to [A2 pass] give orders to, boss about. **S:** officious person, self-appointed authority. **o:** subordinate, wife, partner □ *I won't have him* ***dictating to*** *me.* □ *The shop stewards won't allow themselves to be* ***dictated to*** *by the official union leadership.*

die away [A1] recede, become fainter (or weaker) until eventually inaudible (or invisible); fade away (q v). **S:** voice; sobbing, shouting; commotion, din, tumult; anger, resentment □ (stage directions) *Sound of hooves walking on hard road. They* ***die*** *rapidly* ***away.*** E □ *Brigit's voice* ***died away*** *in stifled sobs.* DC □ *The thunder and lightning* ***died away*** *in heavy rain and her mind too faded away in vague confusion.* ASA

die back [A1] (horticulture) (of the shoots or stems of plants) die as far as the roots, which stay alive and send out new shoots the next year □ *The dahlias* ***died back*** *when we had that first cold spell.*

die down [A1] subside, become less intense (though without necessarily disappearing). **S:** flames, fire; storm; revolution, uprising, quarrel; anger, passion, tension, excitement □ *The feeling between them had* ***died/down affairs have died down*** *here, but they have added to the discomfort over the economic situation.* OBS

die for [A2] (informal) badly need or want. **o:** cigarette, pill, cup of tea; walk, bit of exercise, a sit down □ *'Go and see to that coffee. I'm* ***dying for*** *a hot drink.'* TOH □ *She was* ***dying for*** *a break, away from her family and household commitments* (cf *She was* ***dying*** *to have a break* etc). □ continuous tenses only.

die from/of [A2 emph rel] have as the cause of death. **o:** starvation, exposure; cancer, pneumonia □ *Climbing parties marooned in the open can easily* ***die of*** *exposure unless they know the proper precautions to take.* □ *The disease* ***from*** *which he* ***died*** *was at that time incurable.*

die of [A2] (informal) be in an extreme state of. **o:** hunger, thirst; boredom, curiosity □ *We're all* ***dying of*** *curiosity.* AITC □ *The cleverer children had been deliberately held back from advanced work. As a result they were* ***dying of*** *boredom.*

die off [A1] die one after the other. **S:** plant, tree; bird, animal; man, child □ *A water shortage had struck the area and the wild life was* ***dying off*** *alarmingly in the intense heat.* □ *They had to watch their young family* ***die off*** *through lack of food and proper medical attention.*

die out [A1] become extinct; disappear, no longer be practised. **S:** family, line, species, race; custom, practice □ *Only those species sufficiently adaptable to cope with changing conditions survived. The others* ***died out.*** □ *With the development of transport and the building of new factories many of the traditional crafts have* ***died out.***

differ (from) [A2 emph rel] be different (from); not be of the same opinion (as sb) about. **S:** private industry; civilian life; university teaching. **o:** nationalized concern; service life; schoolmastering □ *Russian* ***differs from*** *English in having a distinct alphabet and many inflected forms.* □ *Patrick* ***differs from*** *his brother in many ways* (or: *They* ***differ*** *(****from*** *each other) in many ways*). □ *The two parties* ***differ*** *very sharply* ***from*** *each other over the correct remedies to apply.*

dig in [B1i pass adj] (military) position sb or sth below ground level by digging an emplacement or trench. **S:** commander, crew. **O:** tank, gun, mortar; troops, company □ *The tanks were* ***dug in*** *so that only the gun turrets remained visible above the ground.* □ *Our officers had* ***dug*** *their platoons* ***in*** *along the reverse slope of a ridge.* ⇨ dig (oneself) in.

dig one's heels/toes in [B1ii] (informal) stubbornly refuse to give way (usu on a point of principle); stick one's heels in (q v) □ *But when it came separation, the wife* ***dug her heels in*** *firmly.* □ *I have stood a great deal from you without complaint, but after your last ridiculous and offensive letter I am going to* ***dig my toes in.*** US

dig (oneself) in [A1 B1ii pass] (military) dig a trench (for protection against enemy attack). **S:** company, platoon, troops □ *As soon as they had seized the enemy position, the infantry* ***dug (themselves) in.*** □ *'Get* ***yourselves dug in!****'* ⇨ dig in.

dig oneself in [B1ii pass] (informal) establish oneself firmly in a place or job (often with the suggestion that one is determined not to move or be moved). **S:** new neighbour, employee, member of staff □ *Smith seems to be ground floor.* □ *'Do you work here or something? We all thought you would* ***dig yourself in*** *at Oxford.'* THH

dig in the ribs [B2 pass] (informal) poke an elbow into sb's ribs (to draw attention to sth) □ *Jones is tiresome. Throughout the play he kept* ***digging*** *me* ***in the ribs*** *whenever anyone said anything remotely funny.* □ *Ma* ***dug*** *him sharply* ***in the ribs*** *and started laughing like a jelly.* DBM

dig in/into[1] [B1i pass B2 pass] (horticulture) sow, mix with soil, by digging. **S:** gardener, nurseryman. **O:** vegetable, plant, tree; compost, manure. **o:** field, soil □ *You'll need to* ***dig*** *those young trees* ***in*** *a bit deeper, unless you want the wind to blow them over.* □ *Manure should be well* ***dug into*** *the soil.*

dig in/into[2] [A1 nom A2] (informal) attack food hungrily; dive in (q v), tuck in/into[2] (q v). **o:** pie, cake; pile of bread and butter □ *'Don't stand on* *ceremony — **dig in**!'* (cf *have a good **dig-in**!*) □ *An enormous first course of turkey did not prevent them from **digging into** the Christmas pudding.*

dig out/out of[1] [B1i pass B2 pass] remove soil etc by digging; by so doing, form or construct sth. **S:** navvy, miner; soldier. **O:** sand, coal; tunnel, emplacement. **o:** quarry, mine □ *Ore **dug out of** these open-cast workings is tunnels underground.*

dig out/out of[2] [B1i pass B2 pass] rescue by digging. **S:** rescue-party, civil defence worker, fireman. **O:** victim, survivor, body. **o:** avalanche, fallen tunnel; wreckage, debris □ *A whole family was **dug out** from underneath a tangle of fallen beams and masonry.* □ *In the severe winter of 1947, farmers had to **dig** their livestock **out of** huge snowdrifts.*

dig out/out of[3] [B1i pass B2 pass] catch or capture by digging. **S:** farmer, poacher, rat-catcher. **O:** rabbit, fox, rat. **o:** burrow, lair, hole □ ***out**.*

dig out/out of[4] [B1i pass B2 pass] (informal) obtain by diligent searching or research. **S:** student, researcher. **O:** facts, information, details, figures. **o:** library, archives □ *'Where did he get hold of that information?' 'He managed to **dig** it **out of** some private library.'*

dug-out [adj (B1)] ⇨ entries after **duck out/out of**.

dig up[1] [B1i pass adj] break and turn over by digging (often to bring under cultivation land used for other purposes, e g pasture). **O:** potato patch, field; meadow, lawn □ *They were using machinery to **dig up** the front garden.* □ *When food was in short supply we **dug up** the tennis-court in order to grow more vegetables.*

dig up[2] [B1i pass adj] remove from the ground by digging. **O:** plant, bulb, tree □ *We must **dig up** those bushes; they're blocking our view of the garden.*

dig up[3] [B1i pass adj] reveal and remove from the ground, by digging (sth that has been deliberately hidden and/or has remained hidden for some time). **S:** dog; police; collector, explorer. **O:** bone, skeleton; firearms; coins, sculpture, pottery, human remains □ *Police have **dug up** the body of his first wife.* □ *A remarkable collection of terracotta heads has been **dug up** by archaeologists.*

dig up[4] [B1i pass] (informal) discover, reveal, by careful searching, sth which has remained hidden. **S:** reporter, detective. **O:** information; story; scandal □ *Jeffries is said to have been living in Bristol between 1965 and to have **dug up** some awful story about John being mixed up in a currency* **digress (from)** [A2 pass emph rel] (formal) wander away from a topic (when speaking or writing). **S:** speaker, lecturer, teacher. **o:** (main) theme, subject, central issue □ *As boys we had various ways of making the history master **digress from** the subject of a lesson.*

din in sb's ears [A2] sound, echo, in sb's ears. **S:** cry, shout; noise, tumult □ *The noise of the traffic was still **dinning in his ears** after he had shut the doors and windows.*

din in/into [B1i pass B2 pass emph rel] repeatedly urge sb to remember or be guided by; drum in/into (q v). **S:** teacher, parent, leader. **O:** lesson, precept, moral; need to work, necessity of honouring obligations. **o:** class, pupil, child, follower □ *'Of course I remember the code numbers. I've had them **dinned in** enough, haven't I?'* □ *The importance of exports had been **dinned into** manufacturers by successive governments, but to little effect.*

dine in [A1] have dinner at home □ *'My meeting has been cancelled, Marion. I shall be **dining in** after all.'*

dine off [A2] make one's dinner of, have as one's dinner. **o:** soup, melon, fish, asparagus □ *When he could afford it, he used to **dine off** half a chicken and salad, washed down with white wine.*

dine out [A1] dine either in a restaurant, or at a friend's house □ *'Don't prepare anything for me tonight, I shall be **dining out**.'*

dine out on [A3] (informal) have dinner at another's expense because of one's achievements or reputation. **S:** actor, musician, novelist, painter, popular entertainer. **o:** one West End appearance, his ability to tell funny stories, the growing popularity of her work □ *He would go back to town and **dine out on** the story of how he had freely ventured into the very heart of the industrial provinces and rubbed shoulders with the aborigines.* CON

dip into[1] [A2 pass] (informal) take money from. **S:** government, bank, industry. **o:** gold reserves, savings, party funds, account □ *The bank had to **dip into** its investments overseas to meet a financial crisis at home.* □ *Mother had to **dip into** her holiday money to pay the butcher.*

dip into[2] [A2 pass] (informal) make a brief study of. **o:** author; subject; book, article □ *I can't say that I know a great deal about modern painting — I've just **dipped into** one or two books on the subject.*

direct to [B2 pass emph rel] (formal) send to, address to (orally or in writing). **O:** remarks, comments, complaints, thanks. **o:** manager, officer, bursar □ *If you have any complaints to make concerning your food or accommodation, please **direct** them **to** the house manager.* □ *Inquiries about grants or scholarships should be **directed to** the College Bursar.*

direct one's/sb's attention to [B2 pass emph rel] (formal) (cause to) think carefully about or look closely at; draw (sb's) attention to (q v). **o:** problem, question, issue, matter □ *The shortage has been ignored for some months, but I am glad to say that the new minister is **directing his attention to** it.* □ *A policeman **directed the driver's attention to** a notice which read 'No Entry'.*

direct to/towards [B2 pass emph rel] (formal) spend time and effort doing sth. **S:** statesman, research worker, manager. **O:** efforts, energies, endeavours, resources. **o:** improvement of trade, betterment of the poor; building up defences, finding a new treatment □ *While in office he **directed** all his energies **to** finding a new solution to the race problem.* □ *Considerable thought had been **directed towards** improving the quality of the product.*

disabuse of [B2 pass emph rel] (formal) free, rid, sb or oneself of. **O:** him etc; oneself; the mind. **o:** idea, notion; prejudice; opinion, attitude □ *Once we can **disabuse** ourselves **of** the word, all sorts of arguments go by the board.*

MFM □ *His new followers held many strange views,* ***of*** *which he sought in various ways to* ***disabuse*** *them.*

disagree (with) [A2 emph rel] not match, not agree (with). **S:** statement, account, record; figure, sum. **o:** earlier, official, more reliable report, story; previous total. **A:** totally, in all respects, at all points □ *I'm afraid that the total I've arrived at* ***disagrees with*** *the one on your bill.* □ *Simon's estimate of the time it will take* ***disagrees with*** *mine* (or: *His estimate and mine* ***disagree***).

disagree with [A2 rel] (informal) have a bad effect on one's health etc. **S:** food, meal; fish, wine; heat, humidity □ *He's not feeling well: something he ate must have* ***disagreed with*** *him.* □ *Hot climates* ***disagree with*** *her.*

disagree (with) (about/over) [A2 emph rel] not be of the same opinion (as sb) (about sth); express such a difference of view. **S:** wife, brother; colleague, friend. **o:** (***about/over***) method, means, procedure; how to do sth, whether to take part. **A:** heartily, strongly, emphatically □ *The landlord* ***disagreed with*** *his tenants* (or: *He and they* ***disagreed***) ***over*** *where the new cottages should be built.* □ *I know you* ***disagreed with*** *me yesterday* ***about*** *the terms of a settlement; can we agree today?*

disappear (from sight/view) [A2] no longer be visible. **S:** ship, aircraft; column, procession □ *As we rounded the next bend, we found that the lorry had* ***disappeared*** *completely* ***from view.*** □ *For a while Mick* ***disappeared from sight*** *—reportedly to work for his Finals.*

disapprove (of) [A2 pass adj emph rel] (formal) have, express, a low opinion of, not think highly of. **S:** father; principal, head-teacher; employer. **o:** (son's) friend; pastime, habit; smoking, keeping late hours; perfume, lipstick; long hair □ *Tony shaved off his beard before the interview: he knew of employers who strongly* ***disapproved of*** *facial hair.* □ *Father is remarkably tolerant: there are few teenage tastes* ***of*** *which he actively* ***disapproves.***

discharge (from) [B2 pass emph rel] (formal) allow sb to leave; make sb leave. **S:** doctor, surgeon; army authorities, medical board; employer. **O:** patient, casualty; recruit; servant □ *She was* ***discharged from*** *the intensive care unit last week and transferred to a general ward.* □ *Rather than punish men regularly as habitual offenders, the Army may decide to* ***discharge*** *them* ***from*** *service altogether.*

discharge (from) (into) [B2 pass emph rel] pass, transfer, from one place to another. **O:** cargo, freight; oil, coal; corn, rice; gas, electricity. **o:** (***from***) ship, hold; container, wagon; gasholder, battery; (***into***) lighter, barge; lorry; tub, bin □ *Firmer action will be taken against companies* ***discharging*** *industrial waste* ***into*** *rivers.* □ *Grain is* ***discharged from*** *giant holders* ***into*** *long lines of trucks.*

disconnect (from) [B2 pass emph rel] separate one thing from another. **O:** condenser, loudspeaker; engine, coil. **o:** circuit, (source of) power; wheels, battery □ *If you push down the clutch pedal, the engine is* ***disconnected from*** *the transmission.* □ *Make sure you* ***disconnect*** *the television (****from*** *the mains supply) before you open up the back.*

discourage (from) [B2 pass] try to persuade sb not to do sth; make sb lose interest (in doing sth). **O:** motorist; climber, explorer; student, pupil. **o:** driving too fast; venturing too far; doing one's best, achieving all one might □ *Try to* ***discourage*** *him* ***from*** *driving back to London tonight.* □ *We were effectively* ***discouraged from*** *having anything further to do with mathematics by his inept teaching.* □ the object is the *-ing* form of a v.

discriminate (against) [A2 pass emph rel] treat sb differently (and usu less favourably) because of his race, religion etc. **S:** system, regime; law; police. **o:** Catholic, Jew; (coloured) immigrant, migrant worker; drug addict; woman □ *There is evidence that some employers* ***discriminate against*** *women applicants.* □ *We're not* ***discriminated against,*** *we're patronized—which is far worse.*

discriminate between [A2 emph rel] (formal) because of training, sensitivity etc, be able to judge which of two things is better etc. **o:** (two) performances, recordings; editions; wines; tobaccos; good and bad; ordinary and superior □ *You don't need to be a professional musician to* ***discriminate between*** *two performances of the same work* (or: *to* ***discriminate*** *one performance* ***from*** *the other*). □ ***Between*** *two such obviously fine instruments I find it hard to* ***discriminate.***

discriminate from [B2 pass emph rel] ⇨ previous entry.

disembark (from) [A2 emph rel B2 pass emph rel] go, put sb, ashore (from). **S:** [A2] **O:** [B2] crew, passenger. **S:** [B2] captain, master. **o:** ship; liner, tanker □ *Troops can be* ***disembarked from*** *ships lying off shore and carried in shore in flat-bottomed craft.*

disengage (from) [A2 emph rel B2 pass emph rel] (formal) (cause to) separate, detach (from an involvement). **S:** [A2] **O:** [B2] country, political party; business, firm; army, soldier. **o:** alliance, pact; association, enterprise; struggle, battle □ *De Gaulle was anxious that France should* ***disengage from*** *military dependence on the United States.* □ *Stephen's parents tended to* ***disengage*** *him* ***from*** *any relationship that would help his growing-up.*

disentangle (from) [B2 pass emph rel] separate, free (from a complicated state). **O:** truth; essential fact, central thread, main point. **o:** falsehood; garbled tale, complicated account □ *Trollope discussed the difficulty that arises in novel-writing of* ***disentangling*** *men and women* ***from*** *their surroundings.* SPL □ ***From*** *this complex pattern of events we can* ***disentangle*** *two important trends.*

dish out [B1i pass] (informal) distribute, give out² (q v). **S:** storekeeper, quartermaster; employer, commander; government. **O:** tool, weapon, map, clothing; praise, commendation, thanks; medal, 'gong' □ *New overalls and helmets were* ***dished out*** *before the party went underground.* □ *The boss is delighted, he's been all over the works* ***dishing out*** *bonuses and handshakes.*

dish it out [B1ii] (informal) inflict punishment; cause pain or distress; hand it/(the) punishment out (q v) □ *There he was in the thick of the fight,* ***dishing it out*** *with the best of them.* □ *I can damage people too. I can* ***dish it out*** *just like* *everybody else.* FFE

dish up[1] [A1 B1i pass adj] (informal) put into plates, serve. **O:** meal, supper; stew, vegetables □ *I was just about ready to* ***dish up****.* TGLY □ *Mother* ***dished*** *the food* ***up*** *straight out of the saucepan.*

dish up[2] [B1i pass] (informal) offer, present. **S:** newspaper, editor; producer, playwright, author. **O:** concoction, mixture; brand (of humour, entertainment) □ *In his latest article Smith* ***dishes up*** *a familiar mixture of reactionary opinions and thinly-disguised personal abuse.*

disinclined (for) [pass (B2)] (formal) not (be) in the mood (for), (be) unwilling to undertake. **o:** real effort, hard work, serious conversation □ *Having just eaten a heavy meal, he felt* ***disinclined for*** *any serious work.* □ *I had been talking all morning; I was* ***disinclined for*** *further argument* (or: ***disinclined*** *to argue any further*). □ passive with *be, feel, seem.*

dislodge (from) [B2 pass emph rel] move sth or sb from a place where it or he is fixed. **S:** gale, gust; attack, thrust. **O:** slate, tile; enemy. **o:** roof; position, nest □ *A careless movement can* ***dislodge*** *sharp pieces of stone* ***from*** *the rock-face.* □ *Artillery will not* ***dislodge*** *the enemy* ***from*** *his well-entrenched positions.*

dismiss (from) [B2 pass emph rel] take away sb's employment. **O:** official, servant. **o:** office, post; employment, service □ *No lecturer may be* ***dismissed from*** *his post for misconduct without a proper inquiry being held.* □ *He'd had teaching jobs abroad;* ***from*** *each of them he was* ***dismissed****.*

dismiss (from one's mind/thoughts) [B2 pass] not think any further about sth. **O:** problem, difficulty; matter, question; doubt, anxiety □ *'I'm sure I hurt their feelings.' 'Nonsense. Don't let it bother you,* ***dismiss*** *it* ***from*** *your mind.'* □ *These suspicions weren't easily* ***dismissed from*** *his thoughts. After all, Janet had been seen out with Carter on two occasions.*

dispense with[1] [A2 pass] (manage to) exist, function, without; do without[1] (q v). **S:** country, industry. **o:** assistance, aid, co-operation, services □ *You may dislike having to depend upon him, but it will be some time before you can* ***dispense with*** *his support altogether.* □ *The patient's recovery has reached a point where the doctor's services can be* ***dispensed with****.* □ usu with *can/could.*

dispense with[2] [A2 pass] suspend, set aside[3] (q v). **o:** formality, protocol, procedural rules □ *I suggest we* ***dispense with*** *formality and proceed with our discussions on an informal basis.*

dispose of[1] [A2 pass] settle, resolve. **o:** objection, argument, criticism; difficulty, problem □ *The problem of who to select as his successor was quickly* ***disposed of****.* □ *The statement does not, however,* ***dispose of*** *the doubts about the Government's earlier posture.* OBS

dispose of[2] [A2 pass] get rid of, destroy. **o:** political opponent, rival contender; wife; dead body, incriminating evidence; rubbish □ *Most of the opposition had been* ***disposed of****; only a few remained alive and out of prison.*

dispose of[3] [A2 pass] sell. **o:** house, boat, land, possessions □ *When the crash came, the family was forced to* ***dispose of*** *all its possessions.* □ *The silver was* ***disposed of*** *to an antique dealer.*

dispose of[4] [A2] possess, have at one's disposal. **S:** army, commander; industry, economy. **o:** forces, reserves; guns, men; resources □ *Between them Rokossovski and Vatutin* (two Russian generals) ***disposed of*** *enough strength to hold off the German attack.* B □ *The Russian artillery* ***disposed of*** *over 20 000 pieces, of which over 6 000 were 76-mm anti-tank guns.* B

well etc disposed towards [pass (B2)] (feel) sympathetic etc towards, (be) inclined to speak well etc of. **A:** ⚠ well, kindly, favourably; ill, unkindly, unfavourably. **o:** regime; policy, idea; change, innovation □ *Students seem* ***well disposed towards*** *the idea of moving their accommodation nearer the University site.* □ *The middle classes are* ***favourably disposed towards*** *the new military junta.* □ passive with *be, feel, seem*; an adv is present.

dispossess (of) [B2 pass emph rel] (formal) take away property etc from sb (often in order to distribute it to others). **S:** workers' government, popular regime. **O:** landowner, industrialist, foreign investor. **o:** property; land, factory □ *The upper classes may be* ***dispossessed of*** *their special powers and privileges by a slow process of evolution.*

dissociate from [B2 emph rel] (formal) say that one (or sb) opposes or is in disagreement with. **O:** oneself; board, panel, committee. **o:** opinion, view; remark, statement □ *The chairman* ***dissociated*** *himself and his colleagues* ***from*** *the views expressed in the report.* □ *The Archbishop called on other churches to* ***dissociate*** *themselves* ***from*** *the Dutch Reformed Church.* SC

dissuade (from) [B2 pass emph rel] (formal) persuade sb not to follow a course of action. **O:** child, pupil; follower, member. **o:** course, undertaking; fighting, rebelling; leaving, resigning □ *The police finally* ***dissuaded*** *the marchers* ***from*** *entering Whitehall.* □ *John allowed himself to be* ***dissuaded from*** *taking up a post overseas.*

distinguish between [A2 emph rel] (be able to) tell the difference between. **o:** good and evil, truth and falsehood, one species and another □ *He can't* ***distinguish between*** *a genuine antique and a reproduction* (or: ***distinguish*** *one* ***from*** *the other*). □ *He could never* ***distinguish*** *with certainty* ***between*** *the Scandinavian colours.* OMIH □ with *can/could.*

distinguish from[1] [B2 pass] ⇨ previous entry.

distinguish from[2] [B2 pass emph rel] be a mark of the difference between persons or things. **S:** language, higher intelligence; organizing ability, urban culture. **O:** species, mankind; race, community. **o:** non-human animals; most others, any other □ *Superior intelligence and the use of language* ***distinguish*** *man* ***from*** *the other primates.* □ *He was not easily* ***distinguished from*** *the general run of people we get here — until he began to talk.*

distract (from) [B2 pass emph rel] draw sb's attention etc away from. **S:** noise; explosion, report; visitor, caller; telephone, television. **O:** ⚠ sb's thoughts, mind; sb's attention. **o:** work, reading; what one is saying; anxieties, fears □ *His thoughts were* ***distracted from*** *this painful topic by the sudden arrival of a neighbour.* □ *He needs to concentrate. Don't* ***distract*** *his mind* *from his studies.*

distribute (among/to) [B2 pass emph rel] give, hand out[1] (q v), sth among/to a number of people. **O:** leaflets, brochures; tools, weapons; food, warm clothing. **o:** crowd, audience; workers, soldiers; refugees □ *Duplicated notes were **distributed to** the class at the end of each lecture.* □ *Rice was **distributed among** the children thronging around the lorry.*

dive in [A1] (informal) begin eating hungrily, attack one's food; dig in/into[2] (q v), tuck in/into[2] (q v) □ *'Don't wait for us to join you at the table: just **dive in**.'* □ *'Find a seat, then you can **dive in**. You want milk, don't you?'* YA

dive in/into [A1 emph A2 emph rel] plunge headfirst into water □ *'You **dive in** first and test the temperature of the water!'* □ ***In** he **dived** and emerged spluttering half-way across the pool.*

dive (one's hand) into [A2 B2] (informal) thrust one's hand quickly into. **o:** pocket, purse, handbag □ *He **dived into** his jacket pocket to make sure his wallet was still there.* □ *Someone **dived his hand into** my handbag and made off with my purse.*

diverge (from) [A2 emph rel] (formal) move away (from), become more and more separate (from); deviate (from) (q v). **S:** path, course; views, policy; development, growth, career. **o:** that/those of one's colleagues, associates □ *I find that his thinking **diverges** increasingly **from** what is officially taught and recognized.* □ *From that point onwards his career **diverged from** Philip's* (or: *his career and Philip's **diverged***).

divert (from) [B2 pass emph rel] turn aside from one course or purpose to another. **O:** traffic, shipping; cargo, produce; worker, scholar. **o:** route, destination; use, purpose; aim, objective □ *The country's leaders were not prepared to allow such large stocks of timber to be **diverted from** military uses.* □ *Police have **diverted** all south-bound traffic **from** the motorway for a ten-mile stretch near Nottingham.* □ *He had fixed on his target for the next six months. **From** this nobody and nothing would **divert** him.*

divest of [B2 pass emph rel] (formal) remove sth (as one would a garment) from sb or sth; take away from sb, as a mark of disgrace, sth granted or conferred earlier. **O:** himself; scene, building; officer, public servant. **o:** mark, sign, trace; charm, mystery; honour, title □ *George Orwell could never fully **divest** himself, as he tried to do while living amongst working-class people, **of** his upper-class identity.* □ *She was beautiful by candlelight. In the cold light of day she was **divested of** the unusual attractiveness which had made him choose her rather than any of the others.* □ *At a formal ceremony the officers were **divested of** their badges of rank, medals and decorations. This was the visible sign that the right to command had been taken from them.*

divide among/between [B2 pass emph rel] share sth among/between people. **S:** brothers, associates, criminals. **O:** inheritance, booty, proceeds, profits. **o:** themselves; family, shareholders □ *How many children has the legacy to be **divided between**?* □ *The members of the investment club **divide** their profits equally **among** themselves.*

divide between [B2 pass] give, allow, about the same length of time to. **O:** time; day, afternoon; holiday. **o:** golf and gardening, swimming and sunbathing, reading and writing □ *He usually **divides** his holidays **between** the beach and the casino.* □ *His day is evenly **divided between** work and relaxation.*

divide from[1] [B2 pass emph rel] keep separate from, form a barrier between. **S:** railway, Maginot Line, fence, path. **O:** poorer area, Germany, his land, airfield. **o:** fashionable district, France, my farm, surrounding ploughland □ *His study is **divided from** the living-room by a thin wooden partition.* □ *The Red Sea **divides** Africa **from** Asia.*

divide from[2] [B2 pass rel] make separate from, (actively) set apart from. **S:** law, policy; resettlement, migration. **O:** mother, husband; tribe. **o:** children, wife; land □ *God **divided** the sea **from** the land.* □ *This test will **divide** the sheep **from** the goats.*

do (as/for) [A2] serve in place of, as a substitute for. **S:** plank, stick, saucer, blanket. **o:** shelf, weapon, ashtray, tent □ *'Don't throw those bricks away. They'll **do as** supports for my bookshelves.'* □ *These pieces of scrap timber will **do** perfectly well **for** the frame of the bed, but we'll need a proper spring mattress.* □ *'What about this bale of straw — that'll **do as** a pillow, won't it?'*

do away with[1] [A3 pass adj] (informal) abolish, get rid of. **S:** government, ministry, board. **o:** restriction, rule; institution; tax, surcharge, penalty □ *The death penalty has been **done away with** in many European countries.* □ *You can't **do away with** the House of Lords.*

do away with[2] [A3 pass] (informal) kill, destroy. **o:** oneself; cat, horse □ *Hymns of the sort that made you want to **do away with** yourself had been sung.* TGLY □ *The horse broke a leg at the first jump and had to be **done away with**.*

do well by [A2] (informal) treat sb kindly or generously. **S:** guardian, benefactor; employer, industry. **o:** dependant; employee □ *A humane society always **does well by** its old people.* □ *She **did** very **well by** me at first, just like you, mam, but then she grew tired of it all.* LLDR ⇨ entry after doll (oneself) up.

do down [B1i pass] (informal) try to make sb or sth appear small, mean, unimportant etc. **O:** parent, class, country □ *They're all so incredibly catty and dishonest, all trying to impress each other or **do** each other **down** the whole time.* ILIH □ *'I hope I'm not **doing down** the national Exchequer,' I said anxiously.* DIL

do (for) ⇨ do (as/for).

do for[1] [A2] (informal) keep house for, clean and keep a house tidy for □ *They can't afford domestic help, so they have to **do for** themselves.* □ *Mrs Bloggs has **done for** us for over twenty years.*

do for[2] [A2] (informal) manage to obtain. **o:** supplies, fresh meat, water □ *How will the crews **do for** drinking water when they're afloat in an open raft?* □ *What shall we **do for** fresh fruit while the dock strike is on?* □ only in questions and after *what* and *how*. ⇨ do badly/well for.

do for[3] [A2 pass] (informal) act in such a way that sb is ruined, killed etc. **S:** (incompetent) doctor, surgeon; general; minister, government. **o:** patient, case; troops; industry, agriculture □ *There were heavy casualties on the first day. The* *general nearly* **did for** *the lot of us with his plan of attack.* □ *The bank won't come to the rescue for ever — we'll be* **done for** *in six months.* □ usu passive; no continuous tenses.

do badly/well for [A2] (informal) have a bad/good supply of, obtain a small/large number of. **o:** tips, gratuities, luxuries; duty-free cigarettes, cheap drink; awards, scholarships □ *The staff at that hotel* **did** *very* **well for** *tips and presents.* □ *The independent schools* **do well for** *open scholarships at the older universities.* □ *We didn't* **do** *too* **badly for** *coal during the miners' strike; we'd managed to stock up.* ⇨ do for [2].

do well for oneself [A2] (informal) become prosperous; improve one's social position. **S:** tradesman, salesman; doctor, solicitor □ *Now's the time when accountants can* **do well for themselves**. RATT □ *Frank was* **doing** *very* **well for himself**. *Import-export was booming.* TO

do in [B1i pass] (slang) kill sb or oneself □ *These were professional killers who* **'did in'** *John Regan, and they knew more about fingerprints and ballistics than I did.* CON □ *I was feeling black and ready to* **do** *myself* **in**. LLDR

done in [pass (B1)] ⇨ entry before doomed to.

do out[1] [B1i pass] (informal) make clean by scrubbing, sweeping etc; clean out (q v). **S:** cleaner, charwoman, housewife; groom. **O:** hall, room; yard, stable □ *She* **did out** *the bathroom with lots of soap and hot water.* □ *The yard needs to be* **done out** *thoroughly* (or: *needs a thorough* **doing-out**) *with a stiff broom.*

do out[2] [B1i pass] (informal) make tidy or orderly (by removing scrap paper, unwanted clothes etc). **S:** clerk, student, child, housewife. **O:** desk, cupboard, wardrobe, drawer □ *'You must* **do out** *your desk drawer: it's full of waste paper and unanswered letters.'* □ *It's time the children's toy cupboard was* **done out**. *It looks a mess and they can never find anything they want.*

do out of [B2 pass] (informal) prevent sb from having sth (often by trickery or neglect). **S:** employer, landlord; colleague, rival. **o:** pension, paid holiday; grant, allowance; job, promotion □ *Of course I'm furious. He just* **did** *me* **out of** *a trip to the West Indies this summer.* □ *But I was not to be* **done out of** *the truth so easily. 'Are these illnesses curable?' I persisted.* THH

do over[1] [B1ii pass] clean or redecorate (all the surfaces of). **O:** house, place; bathroom; cooker □ *'Haven't you noticed how the paintwork is chipped and flaking? It really needs* **doing over** (or: *to be* **done over**)*.'* □ *'The kitchen's always so messy after we've had guests. Give me a hand to* **do** *it* **over**, *will you?'*

do over[2] [B1ii pass] (slang) give sb a severe and thorough beating; beat up (q v). **S:** gang; raider, bandit. **O:** shopkeeper, bank clerk; (innocent) bystander □ *Poor old Mike, he got* **done over** *by a gang of roughs after a football match.*

do (ample/full) justice to [B2 pass emph rel] give to sb or sth the care, attention, fair treatment etc, that he or it deserves. **S:** report, account; observer, critic; guest, diner. **o:** achievement, character; performance; meal □ *She felt that her brother's works did not* **do justice to** *the depth and courage of his humanity.* HAA □ *The fact that we had eaten an hour earlier prevented us from* **doing full justice to** *her cooking.*

do to death [B2 pass] kill. **O:** prisoner, hostage □ *The few guards soon lost their nerve and simply* **did** *their charges* **to death** *in some wood or quarry.* B

do something to [B2] (informal) excite, stir sb's feelings; concern, disturb. **S:** expression, voice, figure; song, performer □ (popular song) *You* **do something to** *me!* □ *But I can hear her coughing. That little cough* **does something to** *me.* AITC

do up[1] [B1i pass adj] renovate, modernize, (by making repairs, installing modern amenities); redecorate. **S:** property developer, owner, tenant; decorator, builder. **O:** derelict cottage, old farmhouse, mews; kitchen, bathroom, front of house □ *I did all this* (indicating the cottage) *for Mr Harrington. A very clever boy I was recommended to,* **did** *it* **up** *for us.* FFE □ *We're getting a professional decorator to* **do** *the boys' bedroom* **up**.

do up[2] [B1i pass] make into a bundle or parcel. **O:** washing, books, magazines, presents, firewood □ *I must* **do up** *some old clothes for the church jumble sale.* □ *She* **did** *her hair* **up** *in a bun to keep it out of her eyes.* □ *Under her arm was what looked like a framed picture* **done up** *in brown paper.* TGLY

do up[3] [B1i pass] fasten. **O:** zip(-fastener), shoelaces, buttons, hooks and eyes; dress, coat □ '**Do** *your flies* **up**.' CSWB □ *He was in his trousers and shirt,* **doing up** *his braces.* TC

do up[4] [A1] be fastened, may be fastened. **S:** suit, coat, dress, skirt □ *The skirt* **does up** *at the back.* □ *'How does this jacket* **do up**?' □ usu with simple tenses.

do with [A2] (informal) need, want. **o:** drink, meal, cigarette; break, holiday □ *'I could* **do with** *two weeks away from the children and the washing-up.'* □ *'You can both stop leaning against the wall: I can* **do with** *a helping hand.'* □ *This car could* **do with** *a good polish.* □ occurs only with *can/could.*

do business (with) [B2 emph rel] trade (with), deal with [1] (q v). **o:** manufacturer, supplier; store, shop □ *One likes to* **do business with** *a British firm. One knows where one is.* OMIH □ *They aren't good people to* **do business with**. *They keep you waiting for deliveries.*

what do with[1] [B2] where did you etc put, lose, hide, sth. **o:** handbag, keys, papers □ *'Miss Smith,* **what** *have you* **done with** *the United Cement Holdings file?'* □ '**What** *did the porter* **do with** *our luggage?'* □ usu perfect and simple past tenses.

what do with[2] [B2 pass] how shall we etc handle, treat, use. **o:** complaint, inquiry; delegation, visitor; prisoner, delinquent □ **What** *on earth are we going to* **do with** *all these young people drifting in from the countryside?* □ **What** *do the Government propose to* **do with** *all the surplus stores left over after the war?* □ **What's** *to be* **done with** *all this stuff in the attic?* □ usu with *shall, will, be going to* etc.

what (to) do with oneself [B2] how should one occupy one's time, give meaning to one's existence □ '**What** *do the children* **do with themselves** *during the holidays?'* □ *Now that her husband's dead, she doesn't know* **what to do with herself**. □ what do with etc may form the Object of a larger sentence (as in the second example).

do without[1] [A1 A2 pass] exist, function, manage, without: go without (q v), dispense with[1](q v). **o:** services, help; food, warmth □ *Most householders seemed to have decided to* ***do without*** *professional care for their windows.* HD □ *You must buy sweets with your own pocket-money or* ***do without.***

do without[2] [A2] (informal) not require, and resent having. **o:** interference, unkind comment, criticism, innuendo □ *We can certainly* ***do without*** *John poking his nose in every five minutes.* □ *'I can* ***do without*** *that kind of advice, thank you.'* □ with *can/could* only.

dole out [B1i pass adj] distribute, serve (sometimes with the suggestion that the portions are small and grudgingly given). **O:** soup, bread; money □ *Receipts from the mails go straight to the US Treasury, which then* ***doles out*** *only whatever sum is authorized by the purse-holders on Capitol Hill.* OBS □ *If this is the kind of thing you and your pals* ***dole out*** *for the proletariat and its poor, grubby artists, you had better think again.* EGD

doll (oneself) up [B1ii pass adj] (informal) dress smartly, as for a special occasion (sometimes with the suggestion that the dressing-up is extreme or vulgar) □ *She could put on her Number Ones* (= best uniform) *and* ***doll herself up*** *smartly to go home and cut a dash.* RFW □ *She was* ***dolled up*** *without being over-dressed.* CON □ *'P'raps you think I'm not good enough to meet your bleedin'* ***dolled-up*** *friends.'* PE

hard done by [pass (A2)] (informal) (be) unfairly treated. **S:** employee, son, wife □ *He always claimed to be* ***hard done by****. In fact, he'd always been very generously treated by his employers.* □ *If he's not getting more than the minimum gratuity after so many years in their service he's being* ***hard done by.*** ⇨ do well by.

done in [pass (B1)] (informal) (be) exhausted, (be) dog tired. **A:** thoroughly, completely, a bit, rather □ *'What's the matter, Simmonds? You look all* ***done in.****'* ITAJ □ ASTON: *Any time you want to... get into bed, just get in.* DAVIES: *I think I will. I'm a bit... a bit* ***done in.*** TC □ passive with *be, feel, look, seem.*

doomed to [pass (B2)] (be) bound to meet or suffer. **S:** scheme, plan, enterprise. **o:** disappointment, failure, frustration, inefficacy □ *His plan to drive a trunk-road across the central desert was* ***doomed to*** *failure.* □ *This species was* ***doomed to*** *extinction* (or: ***doomed*** *to become extinct).* □ *Every embodied spirit is* ***doomed to*** *suffering* (or: ***doomed*** *to suffer).* DOP

doss down [A1 nom] (slang) get into a makeshift bed (e g of straw or sacking, and often on the ground); get into a rough or simple bed in a doss-house. **S:** tramp, down-and-out □ *In Paris tramps often* ***doss down*** *under the bridges or on the gratings of ventilator shafts.* □ *The vicar gives them a cup of soup and lets them* ***doss down*** *in the crypt.* □ *I was annoyed to find somebody having a* ***doss-down*** *(or: a* ***doss down****) on my favourite park bench.*

dote on/upon [A2 pass adj emph rel] show much, or too much, affection for; centre one's affections on. **S:** mother, husband. **o:** children, wife □ *They* ***dote on*** *the younger child, and the older one's naturally very envious.* □ *I'm afraid he* ***dotes upon*** *his wife and she's not above abusing his affection.* □ *Conversation centred on a much* ***doted-upon*** *first baby.*

double back[1] [A1] quickly turn around and retrace one's footsteps (to elude pursuers). **S:** fox, wolf; bandit, escaped convict □ *Half-way through the wood we lost the fox; it must have* ***doubled back*** *on its tracks.*

double back[2] [B1i pass adj] fold back (so as to form a double thickness or layer). **O:** sheet, blanket, coverlet; paper □ *When making a bed you* ***double*** *the top edge of the sheet* ***back*** *over the blankets.*

double up[1] [A1] bend, fold up; be convulsed (with). **S:** body; he etc. **A:** in agony, with pain, with laughter □ *This made him* ***double up*** *with laughter.* BB □ *Funny thing is that when you say it on the stage half the audience* ***double up*** *just like Fred Zombie himself.* JFTR

double up[2] [B1ii pass] cause to bend in the middle. **S:** pain, attack, blow; comedian, joke, performance. **O:** body; audience, onlooker □ *Someone struck him hard in the stomach; the pain* ***doubled*** *him* ***up.*** □ *The bystanders were* ***doubled up*** *with mirth.*

double up (on) [A1 A3] (informal) form pairs in order to share sth. **o:** space; room, bed; food, ration □ *There's enough corned beef to go round, but you'll have to* ***double up on*** *the baked beans.* □ *'We haven't any single rooms left. Do you mind* ***doubling up****?'*

doubt of [A2 pass] (formal) have doubts about, be pessimistic about. **o:** success, outcome, result □ *The enterprise had begun badly and we* ***doubted of*** *its further progress.*

dovetail (into) [A2 rel] fit snugly (into); conform harmoniously (with). **S:** panel, cross-piece; idea, proposal. **o:** frame, upright; scheme, design □ *The sides of the cigar-box* ***dovetail*** *beautifully (****into*** *each other).* □ *'They're interesting suggestions but they don't quite* ***dovetail into*** *the rest of the plan, do they?'*

doze off [A1] fall into a light sleep; drop off[2] (q v), nod off (q v) □ *After a substantial lunch, he* ***dozed off*** *in his armchair.* □ *He waited, hoping desperately that he would not* ***doze off.*** T

drag down [B1i pass] bring to a low physical or moral level. **S:** illness; influenza, malaria; dissolute life; drudgery, routine □ *She can't stand the intense heat — it really* ***drags*** *her* ***down.***

drag in/into[1] [B1i pass B2 pass] (informal) make sb take part in an activity or be the subject of discussion etc against his will, or against the will of other interested persons. **O:** him etc; (his) wife, family; name. **o:** helping, working; argument, debate, discussion; controversy □ *'No, John, I won't be* ***dragged into*** *making polite conversation with the wives while you have one of your interminable meetings with the men.'* □ *'You're free to write what you like about me. But you mustn't* ***drag*** *my wife's name* ***in.*** *Keep her out of it.'*

drag in/into[2] [B1i pass B2 pass] (informal) constantly (and tiresomely) introduce a particular topic into the conversation etc. **O:** pet topic, favourite theory; sport, money. **o:** discussion, debate, argument □ *Why must he keep* ***dragging in*** *references to his medals? We know he's a war hero, but must he keep reminding us?* □ *There* *are some people about with only one thought in their heads: they must* ***drag*** *sex* ***into*** *every conversation.*

drag off (to) [B1ii pass B3 pass] (informal) lead sb against his will (to). **o:** concert, film, play; meeting, service □ *He will* ***drag*** *her* ***off to*** *parties, and she spends the whole evening trying to look inconspicuous in some corner.*

drag on [A1 emph] continue endlessly and tediously. **S:** quarrel, war, unhappy marriage; speech, concert □ *We could take no chances; if we failed in Normandy the war might* ***drag on*** *for years.* MFM □ *The partnership might have* ***dragged on*** *indefinitely if Peter hadn't decided on a clean break.*

drag out [B1i pass adj] make sth longer than it need be, thus causing tedium. **O:** meeting; discussion, debate; performance □ *'Do you think we might end the discussion there? I see no point in* ***dragging*** *it* ***out*** *any further.'*

drag through the mire/mud [B2 pass] disgrace sb or sth by shameful behaviour. **O:** name; family, school; reputation □ *The wretched boy was solemnly accused of* ***dragging*** *the honoured name of the school* ***through the mud****, when what he needed (and probably expected) was a good hiding.*

drag up[1] [B1i pass adj] (informal) allow a child to grow up without proper discipline or training. **O:** child, ward □ *Their children are allowed to roam the streets and come and go as they please—they're simply being* ***dragged up*** *any old how.* □ usu passive.

drag up[2] [B1i pass] (informal) deliberately recall or revive an event (usu unpleasant) from the past which is generally forgotten (and should perhaps have remained forgotten); rake up (q v). **S:** reporter, gossip columnist. **O:** event, episode, incident □ *What made you* ***drag up*** *that particular episode in my murky past?* □ *Some newspapers haven't anything better to do than to* ***drag up*** *the past indiscretions of well-known public figures.*

dragoon into [B2 pass rel] force, bully, into doing sth. **S:** father, schoolmaster, sergeant, salesman. **o:** taking up the law, doing Latin, accepting promotion, buying a second car □ *He was* ***dragooned into*** *joining the police by his father. Left free to choose for himself he would have worked in a bank.* □ *Voices from loudspeakers* ***dragoon*** *housewives* ***into*** *buying unwanted soap powders.* □ the object is the *-ing* form of a v.

drain away[1] [A1 B1i pass] (cause to) flow away down a waste-pipe, or drain. **S:** [A1] **O:** [B1] (dirty) water, slops, dregs □ *The bath is fitted with double filters through which the waste could* ***drain away****.* WI

drain away[2] [A1] decrease, disappear, gradually. **S:** fear, anxiety; anger, fury; energy □ *Robert yawned. His tension seemed to have* ***drained away****, leaving him, if anything, rather bored with the discussion.* CON

drain from [B2 pass emph rel] gradually reduce the volume or strength of. **S:** demand, pressure; (economic) expansion, development; exertion, effort. **O:** resources, talent; strength, energy. **o:** country, area; body □ *You'd be moving into a department* ***from*** *which the liveliest minds have been* ***drained*** (or: *a department which has been* ***drained of*** *its liveliest minds*). □ *The very will to survive had been* ***drained from*** *him* (or: *He had been* ***drained of*** *the very will* etc).

drain of [B2 pass] ⇨ previous entry.

drain off [B1i pass] draw liquid from sth until it is empty. **O:** water; petrol, oil; reservoir, tank □ *A nurse lanced the boil to* ***drain off*** *the pus.* □ *The main cylinder will have to be* ***drained off*** *before I can change the fittings.*

drape over [B2 pass emph rel] hang a cloth etc in folds over sth. **O:** bedspread, counterpane; flag, bunting. **o:** bed, couch, table; monument □ *The Union Jack was* ***draped over*** *the bier* (or: *The bier was* ***draped with*** *the Union Jack*).

drape with [B2 pass rel] ⇨ previous entry.

draw ahead/ahead of [A1 A2] move forward or in front; progress beyond, get ahead/ahead of (q v). **S:** car, bicycle, runner; competitor, trading concern. **o:** rest of the field, nearest rival □ *A policeman on a motor-cycle came alongside to give us a message. Then he* ***drew ahead.*** □ *We have* ***drawn ahead of*** *our nearest continental competitors in this field.*

draw alongside [A1 A2] (of sb approaching from behind) stop, or move along, at the side of. **S:** car, motor-cycle □ *A police patrol car* ***drew***

draw apart (from) [A1 A3 emph rel] move away (from); become emotionally separate (from). **S:** ship, vehicle; (political) group, movement; lover, friend □ *A small group was seen to* ***draw apart from*** *the others and move off into the forest.* □ *There are signs that he is* ***drawing apart*** *in his political sympathies.* □ *I don't share your pessimism about Peter and Hilary. Far from* ***drawing apart****, I think they're coming closer together.*

draw aside[1] [B1i pass] pull to one side. **O:** curtain, blanket, covering □ *An inquisitive neighbour* ***drew*** *the lace curtain* ***aside*** *to see what was going on.* □ *The sheet was* ***drawn aside*** *to reveal the patient's ribs.*

draw aside[2] [B1i pass] take sb on one side (to talk to him quietly or confidentially). **S:** chairman, colleague; umpire, referee □ *The visiting captain* ***drew*** *the fast bowler* ***aside*** *to warn him about throwing.* □ *The manager* ***drew*** *me* ***aside*** *and muttered something about a proposed merger.*

draw the line (at) [B2 pass emph rel] not go beyond a certain limit in one's conduct. **o:** dishonesty, deceit; backbiting, malicious gossip; cheating one's friends, being unfaithful to one's wife □ *I may be an attractive woman, but I* ***draw the line at*** *cradle snatching.* DBM □ *Stephens liked to think that he was a tolerant man, but he wouldn't have that couple in his house again.* ***The line*** *had to be* ***drawn*** *somewhere* (or: ***at*** *some point*).

draw away/back (from) [A1 A3 emph rel] withdraw, move away (from). **A:** in distaste, in horror; shyly, suspiciously □ *'Why don't you kiss me? Come.' Prissie's body stiffened. She tried to* ***draw away from*** *his embrace.* DC □ *It seemed that he* ***drew back*** *for a moment, alarmed, as if the scrappy, grubby piece of paper frightened him.* DC

drawback [nom (A1 B1)] disadvantage, snag, pitfall. **adj:** serious, considerable, unfortunate, irritating □ *I don't see any serious* ***drawbacks*** *in* *the plan as you've outlined it.* □ *Your design has two important* ***drawbacks****: the wheel-base is too narrow and too much of the car's weight is forward of the front wheels.*

draw down [B1i pass] lower, pull down[1] (q v). **O:** blind, curtain; hat, veil, peak □ *He* ***drew*** *the blinds* ***down*** *to keep out the direct rays of the sun.* □ *The peak was well* ***drawn down*** *over the batsman's eyes.*

draw down (upon one's head) [B1iii pass B3 pass] by one's conduct, attract sb's anger etc. **S:** remark, comment; action, step. **O:** ⚠ sb's anger, fury; the wrath of God, scorn, opprobrium □ *'Don't prop your feet on the Old Man's desk. You'll* ***draw down*** *the wrath of God* ***upon your head****.'*

draw from[1] [B2 pass rel] ⇨ draw out/out of[4].

draw from[2] [B2 pass emph rel] obtain from, derive from[1] (q v). **O:** comfort, consolation, relief. **o:** thought, realization, knowledge □ *I don't see why I should* ***draw*** *comfort* ***from*** *the fact that I'm paid in ten days' time. How do I manage for food in the meantime?*

draw in [A1] (of the hours of daylight as summer changes to autumn) become shorter. **S:** ⚠ the days, the evenings □ ***The days*** *are beginning to* ***draw in****: I shan't get so much gardening done in the evenings.*

draw one's horns in [B1i pass] become defensive or cautious. **S:** trader, investor; spending public, customer □ *The building societies have* ***drawn in their horns*** *following the increase in Bank Rate. You won't be able to get your mortgage now.* □ *If Malouel was going to* ***draw in his horns*** *he would need every penny he could lay his hands on.* US

draw in/into[1] [A1 A2] arrive (at); pull in/into[1] (q v). **S:** train; express, Pullman, Inter City. **o:** station; platform □ *As I reached the ticket barrier the London train was just* ***drawing in****.* □ *The 'Cornish Riviera'* ***drew into*** *Plymouth a few minutes ahead of schedule.*

draw in/into[2] [B1i pass B2 pass emph rel] lead sb gradually but firmly to take part in sth. **o:** involvement; struggle, battle; debate, discussion; fighting, arguing □ *Originally, the dispute was confined to the paint shop, but little by little other groups of workers were* ***drawn in****.* □ *The armoured spearheads were not to be* ***drawn into*** *battle with the men they surrounded: the task of mopping up was to be left to the infantry.* □ *The argument* ***into*** *which he had allowed himself to be* ***drawn*** *followed the usual irritating pattern.*

draw off[1] [A1] withdraw, retreat. **S:** enemy; troops, forces □ *The enemy* ***drew off*** *as soon as we made a show of superior strength.*

draw off[2] [B1i pass adj] remove liquid from. **S:** publican, wine-merchant; doctor, nurse. **O:** wine, beer; pint, litre; fluid, matter, blood □ *The pressure inside one of the casks was building up and some liquid had to be* ***drawn off****.* □ *Doctors were able to* ***draw off*** *the matter which had collected near the wound.*

draw off[3] [B1i pass adj] remove, pull off[1] (q v). **O:** sock, stocking, glove (and other close fitting garments) □ *John* ***drew*** *his socks* ***off*** *and bathed his sore feet.*

draw on[1] [B1i pass adj] don (clothing), pull on[2] (q v). **O:** sock, stocking, glove (and other close-fitting garments) □ *He* ***drew on*** *his gloves, picked up his umbrella and went out.*

draw on[2] [B1ii pass] make sb continue steadily forward on his course. **S:** thought, prospect; greed, curiosity, ambition □ *He was* ***drawn on*** *by the hope of improving his own social position and that of his family.* □ *The feeling that he was near his destination* ***drew him on****.*

draw on[3] [A1] approach, come near; come on[7] (q v). **S:** ⚠ night, winter □ *As winter* ***drew on*** *we felt the lack of an efficient way of heating the house.*

draw on/upon [A2 pass emph rel] use, exploit. **o:** experience, knowledge, wisdom, skill □ *Your expert knowledge will be* ***drawn upon*** *increasingly as negotiations proceed.* □ *He* ***draws on*** *his childhood memories for the material of most of his stories.* □ *It is* ***on*** *these skills that the Weizmann Institute has* ***drawn****.* NS

draw out[1] [B1ii pass] help to feel less shy or reserved; bring out[2] (q v) □ *From his mother, Eric had learnt the wonderful gift of* ***drawing*** *people* ***out****.* HAA □ *He had chattered away to her in German; he had* ***drawn her out****, he had made her laugh.* PW

draw out[2] [A1] (of the hours of daylight as summer approaches) become longer. **S:** ⚠ the days, the evenings □ *Thank goodness the days are* ***drawing out*** *again, though. I'm so sick of the winter.* EGD

long drawn out [pass adj (B1)] (be) unduly or tiresomely prolonged or protracted. **S:** fight, argument, debate, discussion □ *The debate over the residual powers of the States has been* ***long drawn out****.* □ *There followed a* ***long-drawn-out*** *legal tussle over the compensation to be paid to the bereaved families.* □ adj form has two hyphens.

draw out/out of[1] [B1i pass B2 pass rel] produce (from an inner space). **O:** pistol, knife, wallet, handkerchief, pipe. **o:** holster, belt; pocket, handbag □ *He opened his safe and* ***drew out*** *a petty-cash box.*

draw out/out of[2] [B1i pass B2 pass rel] remove, extract (from); pull out[1] (q v). **O:** cork, thorn, nail, stump (of a tooth). **o:** bottle, toe, plank, gum □ *He tore his hand trying to* ***draw*** *a nail* ***out of*** *a piece of wood.* □ *The stump was* ***drawn out*** *quite painlessly.*

draw out/out of[3] [B1i pass B2 pass rel] (banking) withdraw (from). **O:** sum, amount, balance, savings. **o:** bank, post-office; current account □ *He was wondering how much of his fifty pounds Robert had* ***drawn out*** *to squander on wine, women and drugs.* CON

draw out/out of[4] [B1i pass B2 pass rel] elicit, persuade sb to tell or offer. **O:** information, story, episode; confession, admission □ *They managed to* ***draw out of*** *him* (or: ***from*** *him) a full account of his escape from captivity.* □ *The story was* ***drawn out*** *by slow degrees.*

draw out/out of[5] [A1 A2] leave, depart (from); pull out/out of[1] (q v). **S:** train; the 5.30, the night express. **o:** station; King's Cross, Waterloo □ *The last train to Leeds was* ***drawing out*** *as I ran into the station.*

draw a veil over [B2 pass emph rel] conceal unpleasant etc events when telling a story, so as not to offend or upset the hearer or reader. **S:** narrator, author; history. **o:** events, proceedings; (undignified) scene, (angry) exchange □ *Under-*

standably, ***a veil*** *was* ***drawn over*** *the reactions of the villagers as they returned to their devastated houses.* □ ***Over*** *the events taking place in the bedroom the censor* ***drew a*** *discreet* ***veil****.*

draw (sb's) attention to [B2 pass emph rel] make sb notice, or be aware of. **o:** oneself; case, situation; discrepancy, anomaly □ *'You talk about this bird Reilly* ***drawing attention to*** *himself — but weren't you captain of the team?'* HD □ *A headline on the front page* ***draws attention to*** *the fuller story inside.* CON □ ***Mr Woodburn's attention*** *was* ***drawn to*** *this question by visiting French MPs.* SC

draw to a close [A2] finish, reach its end. **S:** evening, weekend; holiday, visit; (period of) service, office; life □ *My stay in Bafut eventually* ***drew to a close****.* BB □ *The long day of work which had been their lives was* ***drawing to a close****.* UL

draw to/towards [B2 pass] by force of personality etc, attract people to oneself. **S:** charm, warmth (of manner); beauty, good looks □ *He had a rather austere manner which kept some people at a distance. Yet many were* ***drawn to*** *him by his lack of artifice and his fondness for plain speaking.* □ *Those eyes of hers* ***draw*** *many poor victims* ***towards*** *their doom!*

draw up[1] [A1] stop, come to a halt. **S:** car, taxi, carriage □ *One day we* ***drew up*** *on the quay-side at Dunkirk.* BM □ *A taxi* ***drew up*** *in front of the house.*

draw up[2] [B1i pass] bring near to, place close against. **O:** chair, sofa, table □ *The table was* ***drawn up*** *against the wall.* □ *Irma made her sit down in the easy chair and* ***drew up*** *the other.* PW

draw up[3] [B1i pass] place or arrange (close together in lines). **S:** officer, NCO. **O:** soldier, competitor, vehicle. **A:** in three ranks, in revue order; on the square □ *10 000 men or more were* ***drawn up*** *in a hollow square and I first spoke individually to the unit commanders.* MFM □ *The cars had to be* ***drawn up*** *close together in a dead straight line to facilitate loading.* HD □ often passive.

draw up[4] [B1i pass adj] prepare, draft, compose. **S:** committee, board; solicitor, attorney. **O:** agreement, treaty, report, contract □ *A new arrangement was* ***drawn up****.* NM □ *The society have* ***drawn up*** *a similar list of six conditions.* T □ *He instructed a new will to be* ***drawn up****.* □ *You'll find it's a carefully* ***drawn-up*** *document.*

draw oneself up [B1ii] straighten oneself (often in a solemn, formal or pompous way) □ *When I apologized for the mess in his car, he* ***drew himself up****, looked me in the face, and said: 'Sir, it's an honour.'* MFM □ *Robert's manner changed in an instant. He* ***drew himself up*** *portentously, walked stiff-legged over to the table, and sat down.* DC

draw up sharp/sharply [B1ii pass] make sb stop abruptly; cause to pause and consider or reflect. **S:** remark, comment, reflection □ *A noisy interruption from the back of the hall* ***drew*** *the speaker* ***up sharp****.* □ ***Drawn up sharply*** *by the second mention of the word milord that day, Angela Snow had no time to make any sort of comment.* BFA □ *The absence of all the familiar landmarks* ***drew*** *me* ***up sharp****.*

draw oneself up to one's full height [B3] strike a dignified or important attitude □ *The teacher had put up with quite enough indiscipline. He* ***drew himself up to his full height*** *and thundered at the class.* □ ***Drawing herself up to her full height****, she swept from the room.*

long drawn out [pass adj (B1)] ⇨entry after draw out[2].

not dream of [A2 pass] (informal) not, on any account, do sth, not conceive of doing sth. **o:** interfering, intervening; arguing, opposing; permitting □ *At this age* (fifteen) ***no*** *self-respecting middle-class parent would* ***dream of*** *allowing his own children to leave school.* OBS □ *I would****n't dream of*** *insisting on your taking a picture against your will.* MFM □ with *could/would*; the object is the *-ing* form of a v.

dream up [B1i pass] (informal) devise; create (esp sth wildly fanciful, foolish etc). **O:** scheme, project; character, plot, situation □ *Everything has worked out wonderfully. This is better than anything we ever* ***dreamed up*** *in Earls Court Road.* UTN □ *For his first play, Charles Hamblett has* ***dreamed up*** *a seedy bunch of riff-raff — drunks, lay-abouts, morons.* DM □ *Trust you to* ***dream up*** *a script in which the hero — that's me — gets shot in the first act.*

dredge up[1] [B1i pass adj] raise from the bottom of the sea, or the bed of a river, by dredging. **O:** silt, sand, mud; rubbish □ *The wreckage of a wooden ship was* ***dredged up*** *from the harbour bottom.*

dredge up[2] [B1i pass adj] recall to the conscious mind some event, not necessarily unpleasant, which has been long forgotten. **O:** story, incident; moment □ *His grandfather was a fine raconteur,* ***dredging up*** *quite effortlessly, and with a great wealth of detail, scenes and incidents from his early life.*

dress down [B1ii pass] (informal) reprimand, admonish; tell off (for) (q v). **S:** father, foreman, officer □ *He got up and stood over him, arms akimbo like a caricaturist's washerwoman* ***dressing*** *someone* ***down****.* ASA □ *The force of his personality was so blasting that for a moment he had me feeling that I was in for a* ***dressing-down*** *myself.* CON □ often occurs in the nom form **dressing-down**.

dress up[1] [A1 B1i pass adj] put on formal clothes, as for a party, ceremony etc; (esp of children) put on clothes normally worn by another person, or at another period □ *There's an official reception at the High Commissioner's next week. It will mean* ***dressing up****.* □ *Children often enjoy* ***dressing up*** *in their parents' clothes.* □ *Mary* ***dressed up*** *in Elizabethan costume for the annual Fancy-Dress Ball.*

dress up[2] [B1i pass adj] (try to) make one's thoughts seem more impressive by adding details, using special language etc. **O:** argument, statement, evidence □ *It's perfectly simple and understandable. You needn't* ***dress it up*** *with all this nonsense.* RATT

drift along [A1] go through life without aim or purpose □ *His upbringing seems to have left him incapable of sustained effort; he just* ***drifts along****.*

drift apart [A1] become gradually estranged, slowly lose interest in each other. **S:** friends, husband and wife, brothers □ *He and his wife have never had a serious quarrel. Through* *mutual indifference they've just* ***drifted apart***. □ *Having been close friends in the war Viola was genuinely worried to find that they had* ***drifted*** *so far* ***apart*** *that she had lost all touch with her.* RFW

drift away/off [A1] move slowly, casually, away. **S:** crowd, audience; smoke, cloud, mist □ *He thought of a pleasure-garden where entertainment would vary with the weather and couples could* ***drift off*** *into the dark between a meal and a show.* OBS □ *The smoke pall* ***drifted away*** *to reveal the blackened shell of the building.*

drill in/into [B1i pass adj B2 pass emph rel] teach by persistent exercise, repetition. **S:** teacher, instructor. **O:** rule, multiplication table, procedure. **o:** class, pupil □ *The language patterns were thoroughly* ***drilled in***. □ *I simply don't believe that spoken skills can be* ***drilled into*** *learners in a language laboratory.*

drink down/off [B1i pass] drink until nothing remains (often at one draught). **O:** milk, medicine, beer □ *I* ***drank*** *the stuff* ***off*** *in one gulp. It burned my throat.* □ suggests faster drinking than drink up (q v), but is less likely to occur in commands.

drink in[1] [B1i pass] (informal) listen with eager attention to. **S:** pupil, disciple, follower, party member. **O:** ⚠ his words, every word, his remarks; it all □ *A packed audience* ***drank in*** *every word he uttered.* □ *A quiet little man sat in a corner of the hall,* ***drinking*** *it all* ***in***.

drink in[2] [B1i pass] (informal) absorb by eager attention. **S:** traveller, visitor. **O:** atmosphere; calm, tranquillity; beauty, picturesqueness □ *They sat outside on the terrace,* ***drinking in*** *the particular quality of the light at that time of day.*

drink oneself to death [B2] kill oneself by excessive drinking □ *It would be very easy, cheap and pleasant to* ***drink oneself to death*** *in Portugal.* ILIH □ *If Finn was* ***drinking himself to death*** *somewhere, it would be my last sad act of friendship to leave him to it.* UTN

drink under the table [B2] (informal) drink more alcohol than sb else while remaining more sober than he. **O:** everyone, most people □ *This time, if he met Tillie, she wouldn't* ***drink*** *him* ***under the table***. PE □ *You pride yourselves on your capacity, but he can* ***drink*** *you all* ***under the table***!

drink up [A1 B1i pass] drink until nothing remains in a cup or glass (often in one draught), finish one's drink (up). **O:** milk, medicine, beer □ *'I brought them to heel,' said Robert gaily, tapping his inside pocket. 'I extracted some money out of them, so* ***drink up***, *lads.'* CON □ *'****Drink*** *your milk* ***up***, *Johnnie, or you won't go out and play!'* □ very often in commands. ⇨ drink down/off.

what be driving at [A2] (informal) (what) is he etc trying to do or achieve; (what) is he etc trying to say or explain □ *'****What*** *on earth are you* ***driving at***? *Can't you come to the point?'* □ *'You can see* ***what*** *I'm* ***driving at***, *can't you? It would surely be easy for you to get me in on your visits to the docks.'* HD □ continuous tenses only. ⇨ what be at; get at[4].

drive back [B1i pass] force to withdraw. **S:** police; troops, planes. **O:** crowd, rioters; enemy □ *The attacking force was* ***driven back*** *to its starting point.* □ *The police* ***drove*** *the spectators* ***back*** *behind the crash barriers.*

drive back on [B3 pass] oblige, force, sb (as a last resort) to use sth he would rather avoid. **o:** one's own resources; subterfuge, deceit; cruder methods; local food, cheaper petrol □ *I had finished all my cigarettes and couldn't find any of Robert's Gauloises lying about, so I was* ***driven back on*** *my pipe.* CON □ *This last retort of Peter's had* ***driven*** *him* ***back on*** *methods he seldom used. He turned to personal abuse.*

drive a wedge between [B2 pass] separate, cause disharmony between, sets of people. **S:** issue, question; movement, change (of home, of job). **o:** two wings (of a party); colleagues, partners; married couple □ *Differences of outlook may* ***drive a wedge between*** *the various national groups which make up the team.*

drive in [B1i pass] (military) force to withdraw towards the main body of one's unit. **O:** sentry, piquet (picket), outpost □ *Our piquets were* ***driven in*** *as a prelude to the main enemy attack.*

drive-in [nom (A1)] (US) (public facility, esp a bank, cinema, church or restaurant) into which one drives and where one is served, entertained etc, while remaining seated in one's car □ *Because of their greater dependence on the motor car, Americans have a greater range of* ***drive-in*** *facilities than the British, though* ***drive-in*** *banks are found in some large cities in Britain.* □ usu attrib, as in: ***drive-in*** *(movie) theater.*

drive in/into [B1i pass adj B2 pass emph rel] force to enter by striking with a hammer etc. **O:** stake, peg, nail. **o:** ground, wall, plank □ *A wooden stake was* ***driven*** *firmly* ***into*** *the ground.*

drive into a corner [B2 pass] (during an argument) force sb into a position from which it will be difficult to reply □ *Quoting facts and figures quickly* ***drove*** *him* ***into a corner***. □ *When he's* ***driven into a corner*** *he invariably loses his temper.*

drive off[1] [A1 B1ii pass] (of a car etc) leave, go away; (of a passenger) leave, be taken away □ *The first of the starters in the Monte Carlo Rally were already* ***driving off*** *in a flurry of powdered snow.* □ *Teresa's movements were designed to produce the greatest effect. For example, she arrived and was* ***driven off*** *in a yellow vintage Rolls.*

drive off[2] [A1] (golf) drive the ball from the tee at the start of a game or 'hole' □ *TV cameras were set up near the first tee, where competitors were soon to* ***drive off*** *in the first round of the championship.*

drive off[3] [B1i pass] (military) repel, defeat. **O:** enemy; attack, assault □ *The counter-attacks by mixed forces of tanks and infantry were* ***driven off*** *with heavy loss.*

drive out/out of [B1i pass B2 pass rel] expel, force to leave (an enclosed space); make sb forget, overlook sth. **S:** government, police, soldier; anxiety, preoccupation. **O:** alien, intruder, invader; thought, memory. **o:** country, position; mind, head □ *Russian emissaries were* ***driven out of*** *Afghanistan at pistol point.* TBC □ *The prosaic question* ***drove out*** *all others.* NM □ *Any misgivings they might have felt were* ***driven out*** *by the sight of his cheerful face.*

drive out of his mind/wits [B2 pass] make

mad, drive insane; reduce to a very nervous or anxious state. **S:** noise, tension, strain, conflict □ *'You're asking for a bloody good hiding, lady, just be careful. Oh! She'd* ***drive*** *you* ***out of your mind.'*** TOH □ *Everyone seems completely tired out — as if he had been* ***driving*** *them right* ***out of their wits.*** HSG □ *She was* ***driven*** *almost* ***out of her mind*** *with anxiety.*

drive round the bend/up the wall [B2 pass] (informal) drive sb mad; infuriate sb, annoy him unbearably; send up the wall (q v) □ *You two will* ***drive*** *me* ***round the bend*** *soon. I know you're going to drive me mad.* LBA □ *I'm fed up to the back teeth with all this caper. It's* ***driving*** *me* ***up the wall.*** TT

drive to despair/desperation [B2 pass] cause to give up all hope, make desperate. **S:** state of trade, collapse of one's business; laziness, deceitfulness, bad manners □ *Tim's casual attitude to work had* ***driven*** *his serious-minded father* ***to despair.*** □ *The condition of the market at present almost* ***drives*** *one* ***to desperation.***

drive to drink [B2 pass] (informal) make sb so desperate that he seeks forgetfulness, or relief, in drinking. **S:** failure, neglect, unkindness, insensitivity □ *It is understandable that certain situations might* ***drive*** *anyone* ***to drink.*** UL

drive up the wall [B2 pass] ⇨ drive round the bend/up the wall.

drone on [A1 emph] speak tediously and at length. **S:** parson, politician, boring acquaintance □ *Is there an easy way to stop him* ***droning on*** *about the internal combustion engine?* □ ***On*** *he* ***droned*** *interminably until we felt our nerves could stand no more.*

drool over [A2 pass] (informal) give foolish or slavish attention to. **S:** collector (of antiques, etc), connoisseur (of food etc); parent, proprietor. **o:** wine, food; child, new car □ ***Drool over*** *a favourite meal, then start a cook-book of magazine and newspaper recipes.* WI □ *He* ***drools over*** *his hoard of bric-a-brac like a doting parent.*

drop back [A1] be left behind; move back (deliberately). **S:** runner, member of party, car □ *We found that one of the three escort trucks had* ***dropped back*** *in the dust with a mechanical defect.* SD □ *The sergeant had* ***dropped back*** *to pick up any stragglers.*

drop behind [A1 A2] be left behind, fall behind (q v); (deliberately) allow others to move ahead. **S:** runner, car; country, industry. **o:** main party, rest of field; rival, competitor □ *Britain has* ***dropped behind*** *Japan as a producer of cheap cotton fabrics.* □ *Jones had* ***dropped behind*** *on the back straight and Morley went on to win the race by a clear twenty metres.* □ *John and Mary had* ***dropped behind*** *in order to be alone.*

drop by/in/in on [A1 A3 pass] (informal) call on casually, pay a casual visit to □ *She should say to the parents, 'Come to tea on Friday,' rather than ask them just to* ***drop in*** *at any time.* WI □ *They would just* ***drop in on*** *us for a chat at any odd moment.*

drop in/into [A1 A2] (informal) enter casually, pay a casual visit to (a place). **o:** church, club, pub □ *In the evening we would* ***drop into*** *a roadside pub for a beer and sandwich.* □ *They hear the single melancholy church bell, and* ***drop in*** *and sit peacefully in some richly carved old stall.* PW

drop off[1] [A1] (informal) diminish, decrease, slacken; fall off[1] (q v). **S:** attendance, production, business □ *Our sales of ice-cream and soft drinks start to* ***drop off*** *at the beginning of September.* □ *Takings at the pier have* ***dropped off*** *this season.*

drop off[2] [A1] (informal) fall into a light sleep or doze; doze off (q v), nod off (q v) □ *I felt myself* ***dropping off*** *in the middle of the second act.* □ *Just as he was* ***dropping off,*** *there was a loud bang from downstairs.*

drop off[3] [A1 B1i pass] (informal) alight; allow to alight, set down[1] (q v) □ *I* ***dropped off*** *at the corner of Bouverie Street.* □ *Get the driver to* ***drop*** *you* ***off*** *at the Central Station.*

drop out [A1 nom] leave school prematurely (before the end of a secondary or high-school course) □ *I* ***dropped out,*** *right at the beginning, and said that Higher Cert. was good enough for me and they could keep Oxford and Cambridge.* CON □ *The* ***drop-out*** *rate is highest in the poorest urban areas.* □ *There is a close connection between early* ***drop-out*** *and delinquency.*

drop out/out of [A1 A2] withdraw (from), leave; abandon. **S:** minister; player, competitor; runner, horse, pursuer. **o:** government; team, match; race, contest, struggle □ *He has* ***dropped out of*** *politics.* EHOW □ *Peter* ***dropped out*** *before completing one circuit of the track.* □ *Jack was joining our party for the theatre, but he's had to* ***drop out.***

the bottom drop out of the market/price [A2] (informal) (of prices) fall to a very low level □ *This was Cornwall's closest brush with disaster since* ***the bottom dropped out of the*** *world* ***price*** *of tin in the nineteenth century.* OBS □ *Are you prepared to hang on to your shares until* ***the bottom drops out of the market****?*

drown out B1i pass adj make sth impossible to hear by covering it with a louder noise. **S:** (noise of) traffic, music, thunder; heckler. **O:** speaker, conversation □ *I started shouting, but Mike* ***drowned*** *me* ***out.*** JFTR □ *A gang of rowdies tried to* ***drown out*** *any speaker who tried to present a quietly reasoned case.*

drum in/into [B1i pass B2 pass] make sb bear in mind or remember, by frequent repetition; din in/into (q v). **S:** teacher, parent. **O:** rule, table, formula; need to be tidy, virtue of hard work. **o:** pupil, son □ *He'd had the fear of the Lord* ***drummed into*** *him from an early age.*

drum on [A2] beat against, pound on (continuously). **S:** finger, foot; rain, hail. **o:** table, piano, floor; window, roof □ *The rain* ***drumming on*** *the corrugated iron roof kept me awake last night.*

drum out of [B2 pass] expel publicly to the sound of the drum; expel in a solemn or formal manner. **O:** officer, soldier; member, official. **o:** regiment, army; club, association □ *His behaviour is so awful that he ought to be* ***drummed out of*** *decent society.* □ first sense military (and now archaic).

drum up [B1iii pass] summon by beating on a drum; obtain by canvassing or solicitation. **O:** troops, reinforcements; support, backing, extra votes □ *Fresh soldiers were* ***drummed up*** *from a nearby wood.* □ *The minister has managed to* ***drum up*** *some support for the idea.* □ first sense military (and now archaic).

dry out [A1 B1i pass] become, make, quite free of water. **S:** [A1] **O:** [B1] land, soil; corn, hay, rick; clothing. **S:** [B1] sun, wind □ *The flood-waters subsided and the hot sun* ***dried out*** *the wooden buildings.* □ *We waited for our wet clothes to* ***dry out.***

dry up[1] [A1 B1i pass adj] evaporate, turn into water vapour. **S:** [A1] **O:** [B1] stream, well, reservoir, pond. **S:** [B1] drought, heat □ *The smaller rivers and streams* ***dry up*** *in the summer.* □ *I was walking over the* ***dried-up*** *bed of a Breckland mere recently.* G

dry up[2] [A1 B1i pass adj] make dry by wiping with a cloth; wipe up[2] (q v). **O:** cups and saucers, tea-things □ *'Help me* ***dry up*** *after lunch.'* □ *I gave Mother a hand with the* ***drying-up.*** □ nom form (the) drying-up commonly occurs.

dry up[3] [A1] be exhausted, come to an end. **S:** savings, capital; wit, humour, resourcefulness □ *He was very glad of Betty's allowance! This was £2.10s. a week, and it seemed never to* ***dry up.*** HD □ *They feared a* ***drying-up*** *of their inventiveness.* AH

dry up[4] [A1] become unable to speak (through shyness or nervousness). **S:** actor, speaker, broadcaster □ *He paused, and John, knowledgeable in such things, feared that he was about to* ***dry up.*** ASA □ *I* ***dried up*** *after a bit and presently he got me talking about myself.* RFW

dry up[5] [A1] (informal) stop talking, be quiet, shut up[2] (q v) (the speaker has said too much and further remarks will be unwelcome) □ *'Now I'm going to* ***dry up*** *and let someone else have his say.'* □ JIMMY: *I will tell you the simple truth about her. She is a cow.* CLIFF: *You've gone too far, Jimmy. Now* ***dry up!*** LBA □ often imper.

duck out/out of [A1 A2 pass] (informal) avoid, shirk, escape. **o:** duty, obligation, responsibility, chore □ *When I saw it coming I* ***ducked out:*** *I didn't want to be there when it was presented.* CON □ *He's* ***ducked out of*** *producing the school play this year.*

dug-out[1] [adj (B1)] (military) shelter hollowed out of the ground, esp at the back of an open trench, and covered with material affording protection against enemy fire □ *Chuikov's own command post was in a* ***dug-out*** *sunk into the side of the river-bed.* B □ *While the bombardment continues, the men huddle in their* ***dug-outs.*** □ an adj form, but used as a noun. ⇨ dig out/out of[1].

dug-out[2] [adj (B1)] (boat) made by hollowing out the trunk of a tree □ *In the general area of the Niger Delta,* ***dug-out*** *canoes* (or: ***dug-outs***) *are an important means of transport: they are used for fishing, carrying goods to market, or simply ferrying people about.* □ an adj form, which may also be used as a noun. ⇨ dig out/out of[1].

dug-out[3] [adj (B1)] (slang) retired officer, civil servant etc, brought back into employment (e g in an emergency) □ ***Dug-outs,*** *convalescents and boys without battle experience are not likely to stand up to continuous bombardment.* □ *It was hard to find young men to fill teaching posts during the war, so the schools employed a number of* ***dug-outs.*** □ an adj form, but used as a noun.

dust down [B1i pass] remove dust etc from sth by brushing or flicking; brush down[1] (q v) □ *Peter was coated in cement and sand, but we picked him up and* ***dusted*** *him* ***down.*** □ ***Dust*** *yourself* ***down*** *— you're covered in plaster from the ceiling.*

dwell on/upon [A2 pass adj emph rel] think, speak, write, often at tedious length, about. **o:** past glories, achievement; failing, weakness, disability □ *It doesn't do to* ***dwell*** *over much* ***on*** *one's shortcomings.* □ *He was repeating criticisms that had been made of him,* ***dwelling on*** *them, sometimes agreeing with them.* NM □ *These were objects by which she could* ***dwell*** *a little sadly* ***on*** *the lost hopes of the past.* HAA

E

earmark (for) [B2 pass emph rel] intend sth to be used for a (special) purpose (sometimes by using an identifying mark). **O:** supplies, stores; money, funds. **o:** customer; purpose, use □ *Your article on tropical diseases has been* ***earmarked for*** *future publication.* □ *The antique dealer's wife always* ***earmarked*** *the best pieces* ***for*** *her own collection.*

earth up [B1i pass] (horticulture) cover or partially cover with soil. **O:** roots, asparagus, celery □ *The gardener conscientiously* ***earthed up*** *the young plants.* □ *The* ***earthing up*** *should be done in the winter, to protect the asparagus from frost.*

ease back (on) [A1 A3 B1i pass] pull gently towards one. **o:** [A3] **O:** [B1] joystick, controls, throttle □ (in gliding) *'We're flying too fast, so I'll* ***ease back (on)*** *the stick and gain a little height.'* □ (in powered flight) *'You can* ***ease*** *(the throttle)* ***back*** *now that we have climbed high enough.'* □ may be used also of the throttle in cars, motor-boats.

ease across, along, away etc [B1i pass B2 pass] move sth across etc by the use of gentle pressure, careful judgement etc □ *The men skilfully* ***eased*** *the pillar* ***down*** *until it stood exactly where it was required.* □ *My foot was rather sore, but I managed to* ***ease*** *it* ***into*** *a large slipper.*

ease down [A1] reduce speed □ *There's a narrow bridge ahead, so you'd better* ***ease down.***

ease of [B2 pass] remove, to lighten sb's burden; relieve of [1] (q v); take away from, by means of deception, cheating; relieve of [3] (q v). **o:** pain, burden; anxiety, worry, feelings of guilt; money □ *The doctor promised that the medicine he had prescribed would* ***ease*** *the poor man* ***of*** *his suffering.* □ *In London, as in all large cities, there are plenty of people ready to* ***ease*** *you* ***of*** *a few pounds if they see that you are a stranger.*

ease off [A1] (informal) become less severe; do sth with less severity or intensity; slacken off (q v). **S:** pressure, intensity; work, business; worker, athlete □ *The tension between the two countries has* ***eased off.*** □ *'You're working too hard; you'd better* ***ease off.'*** □ He looked casu-

*ally to left and right and, when the flow of traffic had **eased off**, crossed the road.* LLDR □ *For four days and nights the curve continued to decline but on the fifth day the decline **eased off**.* TBC

ease up[1] [A1] move along, usu to make space for sb □ *'I wonder if you could **ease up** a little, as there are several people without seats.'*

ease up[2] [A1] (informal) become less pressing; do sth with less intensity □ *I'm very busy just now, but when things have **eased up** a little, I'll come and see you.* □ *'Don't take life so seriously! **Ease up**!'*

eat away (at) [A3 B1i pass] erode. **S:** sea, river. **o:** [A3] **O:** [B1] support, base; rock, cliff □ *The sea has been **eating away at** the coast for years, and now the houses on the cliff-top are in danger.* □ *You can see from here how the river bank is slowly being **eaten away**.*

eat into[1] [A2 pass] dissolve, consume. **S:** acid, caustic; rust. **o:** metal, steel; plate, pipe, superstructure □ *The sulphuric acid **eats into** those parts of the metal that remain exposed after the wax coating has been applied.*

eat into[2] [A2 pass] consume; use unwillingly. **o:** savings, reserves, nest-egg, capital □ *The costs of the legal action **ate** deep **into** my savings.* □ *He's only been able to keep up appearances by **eating into** his capital.*

eat one's head off [B1ii] (informal) eat excessively □ *The children came in an hour ago from their long walk, and now they're in the dining-room **eating their heads off**.*

eat out [A1] have a meal at a restaurant etc, rather than at home □ *It's a good idea to **eat out** once in a while: a change of scene and cooking is good for you. Not to mention the fact that somebody else has to do all the work!*

eat one's heart out [B1ii] grieve bitterly □ *Ever since her boyfriend walked out, the poor girl has been **eating her heart out**. She doesn't sleep, and she's lost interest in life.*

eat out of sb's hand [A2] be completely docile or compliant to another person's wishes (as of a wild animal that has been tamed) □ *Owing to the importance of Paula's position she had everyone, including the local constabulary, **eating out of her hand**.* DF □ usu **have (got) sb eating** etc.

eat out of house and home [B2 pass] (informal) ruin by eating □ *'These friends of yours are **eating us out of house and home**! When are they going to leave?'* □ *There isn't a thing left in the larder. I was **eaten out of house and home** during the school holidays.* □ usu humorous or semi-humorous.

eat up[1] [A1 B1i pass] eat heartily; finish the food served □ *'There's plenty for everyone, so **eat up**!'* □ *'You're not going out to play until you've **eaten** all your carrots **up**.'*

eat up[2] [B1ii pass] consume; bother, worry. **S:** ⚠ curiosity; envy, jealousy □ *'I can tell that there's something wrong by the way you've been behaving. What's **eating** you **up**?'* □ *Curiosity was simply **eating** her **up*** (or: *She was simply **eaten up** with curiosity) — she had to know who had given me such an expensive present.* □ usu passive.

eavesdrop (on) [A2 rel] listen secretly to sb's conversation □ *'How do you know that Mrs Hill is going to have a baby? You must have been **eavesdropping on** our conversation.'*

ebb away [A1] recede slowly; fade. **S:** tide, daylight; life □ *As daylight **ebbed away**, the lights of the village came on one by one.* □ *Life, Mr Charlton felt, was **ebbing away** from him.* DBM □ *The old sense of being subservient to those mysterious Powers which had to be appeased and humoured was gone. Perhaps it had **ebbed away** during those lonely nights in bed....* CON

economize (on) [A2 pass emph rel] reduce one's spending (on). **o:** housekeeping; clothes; entertainment; travel; holidays □ *It was typical of Augustus to spend pounds on the meal and then try to **economize on** the wine — spoiling the ship for a ha'porth of tar.* □ *If you have an expensive car, it's foolish to try to **economize on** servicing it.*

edge (one's way) across, along, back etc [A1 A2 B1ii B2] move slowly and with great care across etc □ *The climber **edged** warily **along** the narrow shelf* (cf ***around** the protruding rock*), *with a fall of 2 000 feet below him.* □ *The policeman **edged his way forward**, towards the distraught woman who was threatening to throw herself and her child from the roof to the street below.*

edge with [B2 pass] put around the edge of □ *My old Grannie always used to **edge** her tablecloths **with** lace.* □ *The plates were all **edged with** a rich border of gold.*

edit out/out of [B1i pass B2 pass] remove words, phrases etc, from the draft of a book or article in the process of editing it □ *The four-letter words were always **edited out of** radio scripts until quite recently.*

eff off [A1] (taboo) leave, go away (a euphemism for fuck off (q v)) □ *The leader of the gang walked up to one of the bystanders and told him to **eff off**, if he didn't want to get hurt.*

egg on [B1i pass] encourage to do sth (usu of a foolish, adventurous or criminal nature) □ *A certain curiosity **egged** me **on**, a quite un-morbid desire to explore the magnitude of my loss.* SD □ *The older children were **egging** the younger ones **on** to steal money from their parents.*

eject (from)[1] [B2 pass] remove sb forcibly (from a place) because of his bad behaviour. **O:** drunk, undesirable □ *Henry has been **ejected from** more pubs than you've had hot dinners.*

eject (from)[2] [A2 B2 pass] (aviation) cause (oneself) to be thrown clear of (a plane). **S:** [A2] **O:** [B2] pilot, navigator; crew □ *The pilot saw that his plane was out of control and **ejected from** it while it was still possible to do so.*

eke out [B1iii pass] find some way, however meagre, to live; broaden, enlarge, sth. **O:** a living; miserable existence; book, article □ *His last reading of Byron had been aimed at **eking out** his review of a new biography....* ILIH □ *In some countries thousands of graduates are forced to **eke out** a living by doing work of a menial nature.*

elbow one's way across, along, back etc [B1ii B2] progress, advance, using one's elbows to move people aside. **o:** crowd, spectators, bystanders, row □ *The ambulance-men had to **elbow their way through** the huge crowd standing round the crashed cars.*

elect to [B2 pass emph rel] give a sufficient number of votes to sb to give him a place in. **o:**

Council, Parliament, Senate; Presidency □ *Eisenhower was* ***elected to*** *the Presidency for a second term of office.*

elevate to [B2 pass] (formal) increase a person's status by promoting him to. **o:** the peerage, House of Lords, position of President of the company □ *'When a politician becomes an embarrassment to his party in the Commons, he may be 'kicked upstairs', i e* ***elevated to*** *the peerage.*

eliminate (from) [B2 pass] extract, remove from. **O:** waste matter; poison; lead; possibility of suicide; candidate; competitor. **o:** body; liquid; paint; our considerations; election; race □ *Once you have* ***eliminated*** *the obvious causes of death* ***from*** *your list you must, I am afraid, consider the possibility of foul play.* □ *In the first round of the FA Cup most of the amateur teams were* ***eliminated*** *(****from*** *the competition).*

elope (with) [A2 rel] leave home (with) in order to marry; run away (with) (q v) □ *My mother* ***eloped with*** *my father when she was seventeen, and got married at Gretna Green.*

emanate from [A2 emph rel] (formal) come, proceed, issue, from. **S:** light; smell; influence, power. **o:** a hidden source; a vase of gardenias; a group of high ranking officers □ *The strength of the Trades Union Congress* ***emanates from*** *the support of millions of individual workers.*

emancipate (from) [B2 pass emph rel] make free (from); release (from). **O:** women; working class, minority groups, black people. **o:** drudgery, tyranny of the home, child-rearing; slavery, inferior status, inequality, exploitation, ignorance, prejudice □ *The Women's Liberation Movement is by no means the beginning of their struggle to* ***emancipate*** *themselves* ***from*** *what they consider to be the injustices of a world run by and for men.* □ *The aim of Black Power is to* ***emancipate*** *(****from*** *an inferior status) those whose skin is not white.*

embark on/upon [A2 pass rel] make a start on, begin. **o:** project, scheme, campaign; journey, voyage □ *Whatever made John* ***embark on*** *such a hair-brained scheme? He'll be ruined!*

embed (itself) in [B2 pass rel] stick or secure (itself) in. **S:** arrow, bullet, splinter. **o:** tree; leg, finger □ *A shell splinter* ***embedded itself in*** *the wall above his head.* □ *The sword was so deeply* ***embedded in*** *the rock that no one could move it.*

embodied in [pass (B2)] (be) contained in, represented by. **S:** rights, law, principles. **o:** constitution, rules, treaty □ *The rights and obligations of all the member countries of the Common Market are* ***embodied in*** *the Treaty of Rome.*

embroiled in [pass (B2)] (formal) (be) engaged or involved in (possibly unwillingly or through lack of foresight etc). **o:** argument, row; futile discussion, somebody else's fight □ *The independent member for Wigan said that he did not intend to get* ***embroiled in*** *the inter-party strife over the Royal family.* □ passive with *be, get.*

emerge (from) [A2 emph rel] (formal) be the result (of,) become apparent (from). **o:** discussion, correspondence, negotiations, exchanges □ *It was clear from the communiqué that no agreement was likely to* ***emerge from*** *the week-long talks between the foreign ministers of the two countries.* □ *It* ***emerged from*** *John's letter to his wife that he had already made up his mind to leave her for good.*

emigrate (from) (to) [A2 emph rel] leave, go away (from one country in order to live in another) □ *The tendency for young people to* ***emigrate from*** *Scotland* ***to*** *England shows no sign of being reversed.* □ *The family decided to uproot themselves en bloc and* ***emigrate to*** *Australia.*

empty (itself) into [A2 B2] take out all the contents of, and put, pour etc, into another. **S:** river, stream; Indus. **o:** sea, ocean, lake □ *The river Ganges* ***empties (itself) into*** *the Bay of Bengal.*

empty out [B1i pass] remove all the contents of; allow to fall out. **O:** room, attic, barn; bag, pockets □ *The boys who were suspected of stealing were made to* ***empty out*** *their pockets in the headmaster's study.* □ *The bag had broken and* ***emptied*** *its contents* ***out*** *along the road.*

enamoured of [pass (B2)] (formal) (be) greatly attracted by, in love with □ *I must confess that I am not greatly* ***enamoured of*** *life in the tropics: the heat is too great for my northern blood!* □ *The young man became* ***enamoured of*** *an attractive widow — a* femme fatale *who left him after a few weeks of high living.* □ passive with *be, become.*

encase in [B2 pass rel] cover completely with, enclose in. **O:** coffin; baked chicken; packet. **o:** sarcophagus; clay; waterproof covering □ *The old wooden chest was richly* ***encased in*** *leather, protected at the corners with ornamental metalwork.* □ *Medieval knights,* ***encased in*** *armour from head to foot, had to be lowered into their saddles on ropes.*

encroach on/upon [A2 pass] (formal) erode; take a part of, occupy. **S:** sea; visitors; neighbours; legislation. **o:** land, coast; his time; civil rights □ *If the sea* ***encroaches*** *any further* ***on*** *the cliff, the houses at the top will be in great danger.* □ *I apologize for* ***encroaching upon*** *your valuable time, but I should appreciate your advice in an important matter.*

encumber (with) [B2 pass rel] (formal) assume, or give to sb the burden or liability of; pile or load upon. **O:** oneself; troops; room. **o:** responsibilities, obligations; family, debts, large mortgage; excessive baggage, useless equipment; old-fashioned furniture □ *One should not* ***encumber*** *oneself* ***with*** *hire purchase repayments at the beginning of a marriage.* □ *The army was* ***encumbered with*** *tanks that could move at only half the speed of the enemy's.* □ *The estate was so* ***encumbered with*** *debts that it was not worth inheriting.* □ often passive.

end in¹ [A2] have as its extremity, tip or termination □ *The tube* ***ended in*** *a large bulb, where the gas condensed into a colourless liquid.* □ *The scorpion's tail* ***ended in*** *a menacing point, and the child sensibly decided to leave it alone!* □ *Not all English words which* ***end in*** *-ly are advrebs.*

end in² [A2] reach, come to, an end in. **S:** path, road; marriage. **o:** field, farmyard; divorce-court □ *The track became less and less distinct,* ***ending*** *finally* ***in*** *an impassable marsh.* □ *It was obvious to everyone that the marriage would sooner or later* ***end in*** *separation if not divorce.*

end in³ [A2] have as its result or culmination. **S:** long struggle; battle; trial, jury's deliberations; argument, discussion, debate. **o:** failure, success;

victory, defeat, chaos, the capture of a thousand prisoners, the route of the enemy; a verdict of guilty (not guilty); uproar, confusion, pandemonium □ *The Liberals were disappointed when all their attempts to improve their position in Parliament* ***ended in*** *a gain of only two seats.* *The long-drawn-out struggle between the drug company and the Government over prices finally* ***ended in*** *a satisfactory settlement.* □ *The argument between the two drunks* ***ended in*** *a free-for-all in which about twenty people became involved.*

end up [A1] finally be or do sth; finish (as). **A:** Prime Minister; dead, bankrupt, in jail; like everyone else, the same as his father □ *The nuts are pressed for their vegetable oil, which* ***ends up*** *as margarine.* NS □ *If we take her too seriously, we'll all* ***end up*** *in a mental home.* YA □ *'Carry that box of explosives carefully or we'll* ***end up*** *dead ourselves!'* □ JIMMY: *That's how you'll* ***end up****, my boy — black-hearted, evil-minded and vicious.* LBA □ *Every time she tried to argue with her husband she* ***ended up*** *crying her eyes out.*

end up (with) [A1 A3 B1i B3] finish by doing or having; finish off/up with (q v). **S:** [A1] **O:** [B1] concert, meal, party □ *The party* ***ended up with*** *the singing of Auld Lang Syne.* □ *We* ***ended*** *the dinner* ***up with*** *fruit and coffee.*

endear to [B2] cause to be liked. **S:** habit, practice; character, temper. **O:** him, himself; child, guest, lodger □ *His habit of interrupting the speakers* ***endeared*** *him* ***to*** *nobody, and he found himself excluded from one activity after another.* □ *The little girl's unselfishness* ***endeared*** *her* ***to*** *the old lady, who gave her a ruby ring as a birthday present.*

endowed with [pass (B2)] (be) the possessor of, (be) fortunate enough to have. **o:** second sight, a sixth sense; the gift of beauty, eloquence □ *Few men are* ***endowed with*** *the brain of an Einstein.* □ *She was* ***endowed with*** *the beauty of Helen of Troy, and the tongue of a fishwife.*

enfold in one's arms [B2 pass] hold close and protectively. **O:** baby, child, woman □ *When she found the abandoned child on her doorstep, she lifted it up and* ***enfolded*** *it* ***in her arms****.*

engage in [A2] be a participant in, a party to. **o:** hostilities, warfare; politics; backbiting □ *If you* ***engage in*** *local politics, you cannot expect to have much time for your family.* □ *I have no time to* ***engage in*** *gossip, so please don't come to me with your rumours and complaints.*

engaged in [pass (B2)] (be) busy doing sth, occupied with. **o:** petty theft; preparing for the party, building a garage □ *John and his brother are* ***engaged in*** *some plan for acquiring land and starting in business as market gardeners.* □ *'Those men are behaving very suspiciously. They're* ***engaged in*** *some fishy business, I'll be bound.'*

engage with [A2] make effective contact with; begin fighting sb, join battle (with) (q v) □ *If the big cogwheel does not* ***engage with*** *the small one, the clock stops.* □ *We decided to* ***engage with*** *the enemy at dawn, unless he had retreated during the night.*

engrave on [B2 pass emph rel] cut a mark or series of marks on; establish firmly on or in. **O:** name; face, incident, place. **o:** presentation cup, plate; memory, mind □ ***On*** *one side of the cup were* ***engraved*** *the names of all the teams who had won the championship.!* □ *The old man's words were* ***engraved on*** *my memory: I could never forget them.*

engrossed (in) [pass (B2)] (formal) (have one's mind) completely occupied (with). **o:** work, problem; book, story; one's thoughts □ *Alfred was so* ***engrossed in*** *his own problems that he did not notice that the cakes were burning.*

engulfed in [pass (B2)] (be) so covered as to be obliterated by; (be) overwhelmed by. **S:** town, city, village; coast; fields, crops. **o:** lava, water, mud □ *The countryside was* ***engulfed in*** *a sea of mud left by the receding flood-water.* □ *The country was* ***engulfed in*** *an economic crisis of the utmost severity.*

enlarge on/upon [A2 pass emph rel] expand, add details to. **o:** statement, original version, theory, proposal □ *I should be grateful if you could* ***enlarge*** *a little* ***on*** *your recent suggestions for improving the club's premises.* □ *The Chairman thought that it would be in everybody's interests if the unfortunate incident in which two of the members had come to blows* ***was*** *not* ***enlarged upon****.*

enlighten (about/on) [B2 pass] (formal) give the important facts (about). **o:** what happened; the subject of nuclear fission; their private relations □ *Nobody seemed to be anxious to* ***enlighten*** *me* ***about*** *the events that had led up to the dispute.* □ *When I walked into the room it was obvious that Helen had been* ***enlightening*** *my wife* ***about*** *why I was so often 'delayed at the office'.*

enlist in [A2 B2 pass] (military) (cause to) join, become a member of. **o:** army, navy, air force; his father's regiment □ *Some young men* ***enlist in*** *the army while they are still at University. By doing so, they receive an immediate income a good deal higher than their normal grant as a student.* □ *A boy can't be* ***enlisted in*** *the Army without his parents' consent.*

enmeshed in [pass (B2)] (formal) (be) inextricably caught or trapped in. **S:** youths; debaters; litigants. **o:** crime; argument; the toils of the law □ *Before we become too* ***enmeshed in*** *legal niceties, may I suggest that we bear in mind the need for a quick decision in the interests of the children?*

enquire ⇨ inquire.

enroll in [A2 rel B2 pass rel] enter one's name (or another person's name) in. **o:** evening class, Mr Jones's Art class □ *Have you* ***enrolled in*** *the car maintenance class this year?* □ *Mrs Jones has* ***enrolled*** *her daughter* ***in*** *the Ballet class.*

ensconce (onself) in [B2 pass rel] settle, install, oneself well and comfortably in □ *The old man had, as usual,* ***ensconced himself in*** *his favourite corner of the bar, a pint of mild ale on the table in front of him.* □ *Bloggs is too comfortably* ***ensconced in*** *his modest, undemanding, job ever to consider making a change.*

enshrined in [pass (B2)] (formal) (be) stated, described, formally and solemnly in □ *The rights of all men are* ***enshrined in*** *the Charter of the United Nations.* □ *The glorious history of the regiment is* ***enshrined in*** *the official records.*

ensnare (in) [B2 pass rel] (formal) catch (in), generally by the use of deception, trickery etc. **O:**

bird, rabbit; the beardless youth; the unwary. **o:** net, trap; her toils; wild scheme □ *A whole flock of Icelandic geese was attracted by the decoys and* ***ensnared in*** *the cleverly contrived tunnel of nets.* □ *The confidence trickster has little difficulty in* ***ensnaring*** *the greedy* ***in*** *his clever plots.*

entangle in [B2 pass rel] (cause to) become intertwined in such a way as to make separation difficult or impossible; catch up (in) (q v). **O:** itself, himself; clothes, hair. **o:** bushes, branches □ *'How did Alice manage to* ***entangle*** *her hair so badly* ***in*** *the brambles?' 'She was playing hide-and-seek with her brother.'*

entangled (with) [pass (B2)] (be) intertwined or connected (with sth) so that the two cannot easily be separated; (be) involved (with), in such a way that one cannot easily free oneself. **S:** fishing line; legitimate business; husband, secretary. **o:** weeds; criminal operations; woman next door, boss □ *The weeds were so* ***entangled with*** *the plants* (or: *The weeds and plants were so* ***entangled***) *that it was impossible to remove them without spoiling the flowers.* □ *His private expenditure was so* ***entangled with*** *his business expenses that his accountants despaired of ever sorting out his affairs to the satisfaction of the Income Tax authorities.* □ *I hear that young Woodley is* ***entangled with*** *some woman old enough to be his mother.*

enter for [A2 B2 pass] officially present oneself or another person as a competitor in; put in for[1] (q v). **o:** race, contest, competition □ *I'd like to know what joker* ***entered*** *me* ***for*** *the cake-making competition!* □ *It is incredible what plain-looking women will* ***enter for*** *beauty contests.*

enter in/into [B2 pass] make a record of sth in, by writing it. **O:** note, transaction, name. **o:** diary, ledger, register □ *Every night before she went to sleep, Mary* ***entered*** *the events of the day* ***in*** (or: ***into***) *her diary.* □ *When the last item had been duly* ***entered in*** *the ledger, the clerk closed it and put it in its usual place before locking up and going home.*

enter into[1] [A2 pass] begin, start. **o:** conversation, negotiations, relations □ *Susan could see that the man in the opposite seat was dying to* ***enter into*** *conversation with her, and as she found him quite attractive she helped him by asking 'Do you happen to know what time this train is due at Euston?'* □ *The two governments* ***entered into*** *preliminary discussions in the hope of reaching complete agreement at a full conference.*

enter into[2] [A2] give, provide, mention. **o:** details, particulars; a long account □ *'There's no need to* ***enter into*** *a lot of unnecessary detail: just tell the court the main facts of the case.'*

enter into[3] [A2] be considered as a (necessary, vital) part of. **o:** calculations, considerations; plan, scheme; it □ *The possibility of an air-attack from the west did not* ***enter into*** *the calculations of the General Staff. So they were entirely unprepared when the apparently impossible actually happened.* □ *'If you had any charity at all, you'd forgive him for what he did.' 'Charity doesn't* ***enter into*** *it. It's a matter of sticking to one's principles.'*

enter into the spirit (of) [A2] act, behave, with a spirit, an attitude, which suits the occasion □ *Scrooge found it impossible to* ***enter into the spirit of*** *Christmas until he had learnt to appreciate its true meaning.* □ *When George arrived home and found a party in progress, he soon* ***entered into the spirit of*** *it.*

enter up [B1i pass] record (in a book etc, provided for the purpose). **S:** nurse; warden; chemist. **O:** temperature, blood pressure, pulse rate of a patient; names of visitors; drugs, poisons sold □ *It is very important that every sale of a dangerous poison should be* ***entered up*** *at the time of sale.*

enter upon [A2 pass rel] (formal) begin, commence. **o:** career, duties, term of office; a period of peace, calm, prosperity □ *When the President* ***entered upon*** *his second term of office, everyone hoped that he would show more wisdom than in his first.*

entice away [B1i pass] cause sb to leave another person (or his/her home) by means of promises, often unfulfilled. **O:** daughter, wife, servant, youth □ *The girl was so innocent and unsuspecting that she was* ***enticed away*** *by the first man who offered her some pretty dresses and a few pieces of jewellery.* □ *Mrs Brown is not speaking to Mrs Green any more. She reckons that Mrs Green* ***enticed*** *her gardener* ***away****.*

entitle to [B2 pass emph rel] give sb the right to enjoy sth. **S:** rank, position. **o:** privileges; a fair hearing □ *I don't know that his rank* ***entitles*** *him* ***to*** *special treatment from the court* (cf *that he is* ***entitled to*** *special treatment because of his rank*). □ *His position as a friend of the family doesn't* ***entitle*** *him automatically* ***to*** *a share of the inheritance.*

entrap into [B2 pass rel] (formal) make sb do or say sth by a trick; trap into (q v). **S:** interrogator, police; wife; girl. **O:** suspect, thief, prisoner; husband, young man. **o:** giving himself away, confessing to the crime; marriage, eloping with her □ *Experienced guerrilla fighters are not easily* ***entrapped into*** *revealing their positions.*

entrust to [B2 pass rel] give to sb for safe keeping. **O:** money, documents; children. **o:** (the care of) a solicitor; friend □ *I wouldn't advise you to* ***entrust*** *anything of value* ***to*** *Kingsley-Smith.* ⇨ next entry.

entrust with [B2 pass rel] make sb responsible for the safety, custody etc, of. **O:** messenger; pilot; inexperienced maid. **o:** a large quantity of money; one's life; children □ *I'm sorry to say that Kingsley-Smith is not the kind of man who can be* ***entrusted with*** *either money or secret information. The first he will try to keep, the other he will try to sell.* ⇨ previous entry.

enveloped in [pass (B2)] (be) surrounded by, wrapped in (q v). **S:** countryside, lake; house; affair, subject. **o:** mist, fog; flames, smoke; mystery, obscurity, confusion □ *'And now, ladies and gentlemen,' shouted the diver, 'I shall perform the most dangerous dive of all! I shall set fire to myself and plunge into the sea,* ***enveloped in*** *flames!'* □ *The whole business of the Director General's appointment has been* ***enveloped in*** *mystery from start to finish.*

equate (to/with) [B2 pass rel] state that two things are equal or compatible; liken to (q v) □ *In his speech he* ***equated*** *the Government's attitude on pensioners* ***with*** *the practice of ancient tribes who used to abandon their old people once they* *were of no more use.*

equip (for) [B2 pass rel] give to sb the necessary equipment for. **o:** task, work; climb; campaign, attack □ *Can the Council really claim that they had* ***equipped*** *their road-workers adequately* ***for*** *such dangerous conditions* (or: *to face such conditions*) *as they experienced in last week's storms?* □ *John turned up for the ten-mile walk* ***equipped for*** *something more like an assault on Everest.*

equip (with) [B2 pass rel] provide with, fit up (with) (q v). **O:** expedition; hospital; school; every normal child. **o:** many tons of supplies; latest apparatus, devices, kidney machine; every luxury, splendid laboratories, bright classrooms; what is necessary for his survival □ *Nature had* ***equipped*** *the boy* ***with*** *two hands, but not, apparently,* ***with*** *the brains to use them properly.* □ *The Russian trawler was* ***equipped with*** *masses of electronic devices.*

escape (from) [A2 emph rel] break free (from); be released involuntarily (from). **S:** prisoner; lion, pet hamster; cry of pain. **o:** captors, jail, captivity; cage; lips □ *Within a period of only three weeks, five prisoners succeeded in* ***escaping from*** *the 'top security' prison.* □ *An involuntary exclamation of joy* ***escaped from*** *her lips. 'Oh, John! Is that for me?'*

escort (from) [B2 pass rel] accompany, lead, away (from). **S:** police; guard. **O:** arrested man; distinguished visitor. **o:** magistrates' court; platform □ *Several policeman had to* ***escort*** *the referee* ***from*** *the football field to protect him from the angry spectators.* □ *The young woman was* ***escorted from*** *the court by her solicitor.* ⇨ next entry.

escort (to) [B2 pass rel] accompany as a partner, guard or protector (to). **O:** prisoner; young lady; ambassador □ *At the eleventh hour an attractive young man was found to* ***escort*** *Laetitia* ***to*** *the ball.* □ *The ambassador was* ***escorted to*** *the plane by the Foreign Secretary.* ⇨ previous entry.

estimate at [B2 pass] roughly guess, assess, calculate, to be. **O:** attendance, crowd; profit; size, scale farm □ *The police* ***estimated*** *the number of demonstrators* ***at*** *about 2 000 though the organizers* ***estimated*** *it* ***at*** *5 000.* □ *The tax inspector* ***estimated*** *Sir Joseph's income* ***at*** *£25 000 for the current year.*

estranged (from) [pass (B2)] (formal) (be) no longer on friendly terms (with) □ *I didn't realize that Arthur was* ***estranged from*** *his wife* (or: *that Arthur and his wife were* ***estranged***). *They seemed to be a perfect match. What went wrong?*

etch in [B1i pass adj] draw in, with a pen, pencil etc. **O:** background, details, horizon, trees □ *'Your drawing would look better,' he said, 'if you were to* ***etch*** *something* ***in*** *over on the left, to give the composition more balance.'*

evacuate (from) (to) [B2 pass rel] remove (from a dangerous building, or area) (to a safer one). **O:** troops, women and children, non-combatants, inhabitants □ *During the war hundreds of thousands of children were* ***evacuated from*** *the industrial* ***to*** *rural areas.*

even out [B1i pass] spread evenly over a period or among people. **O:** payments, load, work, responsibility □ *Not everyone likes to pay large sums for electricity or gas. It is much better if payments can be* ***evened out*** *on a monthly or perhaps weekly basis.*

even up [B1i pass] obtain, restore, a balance; make equal. **O:** things, matters; sides, teams □ *We gave the Smiths a bottle of gin last Christmas, so this year they gave us a bottle of scotch to* ***even*** *things* ***up*** *a bit.* □ *When the German relay team dropped their baton, we were lucky to be able to* ***even*** *the score* ***up****, so that everything depended on the result of the marathon.*

evict (from) [B2 pass rel] compel, force, sb to leave. **O:** farmer; tenant, occupier; squatter. **o:** farm; house, flat; office block, building □ *All the tenants on the estate marched in protest when the Council* ***evicted*** *an old man* (***from*** *his home*) *because he had neglected the garden.*

evolve (out of) [A2 B2 pass] grow, develop, slowly (from); produce, elaborate (from). **S:** [A2] **O:** [B2] machine, process, fruit. **S:** [A2] mammal, all life □ *This method of manufacture* ***evolved out of*** *a long process of trial and error* (cf *This method was* ***evolved*** *by a long process* etc). □ *The inventor* ***evolved*** *his complex machine* ***out of*** *a relatively simple device.* □ *Life on this planet earth* ***evolved out of*** *some very minute unicellular creatures.*

exact (from) [B2 pass] (formal) require or force sb to give. **O:** money, taxes; an apology, homage, obedience □ *If the government goes on* ***exacting*** *so much* ***from*** *the taxpayer, it will not last long.* □ *The old woman* ***exacted*** *an apology* ***from*** *the tradesman for having questioned her honesty.*

examine in [B2 pass rel] test sb's knowledge about a stated subject. **o:** physics, chemistry; business management, accountancy □ *My son was* ***examined in*** *First Aid last week. He's got about six Scout badges now.*

examine on [B2 pass] test sb's knowledge of a specific point. **o:** detail, point, aspect □ *Each student was* ***examined on*** *a different aspect of the nervous system.*

excel at [A2 emph rel] perform outstandingly well in some activity. **o:** games; cricket, archery, gymnastics □ *John did not make much of a mark at school in his studies, but he* ***excelled at*** *playing the fool!*

excel in [A2 emph rel] reach a high standard in an academic subject etc. **o:** French, Latin; music, painting □ *Churchill, who had such a distinguished career as a statesman and writer,* ***excelled in*** *nothing at all at school.*

exchange (with)[1] [B2] give sth in exchange for sth similar that another person has. **O:** badges, souvenirs; seats, places □ *Bill amused the children in the car by* ***exchanging*** *his hat* ***with*** *Mary's.* □ *'Would you like to* ***exchange*** *places* ***with*** *me? I don't think you're very comfortable in that seat, are you?'* □ *After the final whistle blew, the England captain* ***exchanged*** *shirts* ***with*** *his opposite number* (cf *the two captains* ***exchanged*** *shirts*).

exchange (with)[2] [B2 rel] have some form of communication with. **O:** (a few) words; ideas, views □ *I usually* ***exchange*** *a few words of greeting* ***with*** *my neighbour after breakfast.* □ *'I found it very refreshing to* ***exchange*** *ideas* ***with*** *your father. He has some very original views on how to deal with modern industrial pollution.'*

exchange words with [B2] have a disagreement or argument with; bandy words (with) (q v) □ *'Come on home, George! It's ridiculous to waste your time* ***exchanging words with*** *such an ignorant hypocrite!'*

(not) exchange more than a few/half a dozen words (with) [B2] (not) have much communication (with), (not) have any real acquaintance (with) □ *A lot of people in England don't know their neighbours. I'm ashamed to say that I have****n't exchanged more than half a dozen words with*** *the chap who lives next door since last Christmas!* □ usu in the perfect tenses. exchange (with) [2].

excuse (for) [B2 pass emph rel] forgive (for). **o:** his offensive remarks, behaviour; failing to recognize you, arriving late □ *'Please* ***excuse*** *me* ***for*** *using your telephone without asking permission: I thought you wouldn't mind.'* □ *Nothing can possibly* ***excuse*** *him* ***for*** *such rude behaviour in the presence of a lady.*

excuse (from) [B2 pass emph rel] allow sb not to fulfil some duty, obligation □ *As you were kept working so late today, you will be* ***excused from*** *attending the early meeting tomorrow morning.* □ *I'd like to be* ***excused from*** *any further participation in this scheme: it takes up too much of my time.*

exempt (from) [B2 pass emph rel] officially, legally, free sb from the obligation or duty to do sth. **o:** military service; preliminary examinations; any further jury service □ *Bill was* ***exempted from*** *national service because he was in a 'reserved occupation'.* □ also be exempt from: *Nobody should* ***be exempt from*** *doing some of the unpleasant jobs in the running of the camp.*

exercise in [B2 pass rel] give practice in. **O:** horse; team; students. **o:** jumping over ditches; new tactics; giving ready responses to questions □ *The recruits are* ***exercised*** *every day* ***in*** *the art of self-defence.*

exercise over [B2 pass rel] use, in dealing with sb. **O:** influence, authority, power □ *People with strong personalities should be very careful how they* ***exercise*** *their influence* ***over*** *weaker people.* □ *Rasputin* ***exercised*** *some strange hypnotic power* ***over*** *the Tsar and his wife.*

exile (from) (to) [B2 pass rel] send away (from) (to), as a punishment or precaution. **o:** (***from***) Court, Moscow, his native land; (***to***) the country, Siberia, France □ *Many a political rebel has ended his days* ***exiled from*** *the land that was dear to him.*

exonerate (from) [B2 pass emph rel] (formal) pronounce free from, not guilty of. **o:** (all) blame, responsibility; charge □ *After a long inquiry, the Manager was* ***exonerated from*** *the charge of neglect and from any responsibility for the fire that destroyed the factory.*

expand into [A2 B2 pass] become, make larger. **S:** [A2] **O:** [B2] short story; small town. **o:** full-length novel; large industrial centre □ *The BBC has decided to* ***expand*** *the programme on the Common Market* ***into*** *an open-ended discussion.* □ *This once small family business has* ***expanded into*** *a public company employing many thousands.*

expatiate upon [A2 emph rel] (formal) talk at length and with (sometimes boring) authority or enthusiasm about, hold forth (q v) upon. **o:** the delights of the English countryside; the virtue of moderation in all things; his latest discovery □ *'There goes James again! What is he* ***expatiating upon*** *this time?' 'How the Romans made glass, I believe. I haven't been listening really!'*

expect (of) [B2 pass] hope that sb will do sth or behave in a certain way; ask (of) (q v). **O:** too much, a great deal; great things □ *The boy's parents* ***expected*** *too much* ***of*** *him, with the inevitable result that they were disappointed, and he left home at the earliest opportunity.*

expel (from) [B2 pass emph rel] force to leave, send away (from). **O:** air; enemy; boy, girl; member. **o:** tube; occupied territory; school; club. □ *In such a small house it is important to have some method of* ***expelling*** *the smell of cooking* ***from*** *the kitchen.* □ *Two boys were* ***expelled from*** *the Grammar School for smoking marijuana and offering it to others.*

expend energy (on) [B2 pass emph rel] use, consume, energy on. **o:** task, work; building, reorganizing □ *It isn't worth* ***expending*** *too much* ***energy on*** *redecorating the house if you're going to move out of it next year.*

experiment on/upon [A2 pass rel] test the effectiveness of techniques, (q v), drugs etc, on. **o:** criminals, human beings, guinea-pigs □ *Anti-vivisectionists are opposed to research which involves* ***experimenting on*** *live animals.* □ *My wife* ***experiments on*** *me before she serves a new dish to our guests. She calls it 'trying it out on the dog'!*

experiment with [A2 pass] adopt, use, to test the effectiveness of or discover the effect of. **o:** new methods, form of government, traffic control, drugs □ *The children were warned not to* ***experiment with*** *such dangerous drugs as LSD and amphetamine.* □ *Uruguay was at one time famous for its readiness to* ***experiment with*** *new forms of government.*

explain away [B1i pass] give a satisfactory reason for; remove objections to sth by means of a convincing argument. **O:** behaviour, slip of the tongue, attitude; difficulty, apparent inconsistencies □, *We left John trying to* ***explain away*** *the lipstick mark on his collar to his angry, tearful wife.* □ *Mr McCrea advances a theory to* ***explain away*** *some of the difficulties connected with this process* (of the aggregation of matter in the Universe). NS

explain (to) [A2 pass rel] make clear (to); tell (sb) the facts (about). **O:** the workings, plan, situation, meaning □ *'Would you be kind enough to* ***explain*** *the meaning of this expression* ***to*** *me?'* □ *The teacher* ***explained*** *the principles of nuclear fission (****to*** *the class), but only a few of them seemed to understand.* □ not * ***explain*** *me the meaning of this expression.*

explode with [A2] exclaim loudly as a result of. **o:** anger, fury, rage; frustration □ *When I arrived home at midnight I found my father purple in the face and about to* ***explode with*** *rage at his guests' failure to leave at a reasonable hour.*

expose to [B2 pass rel] put in a vulnerable position in respect of. **O:** child; population; country. **o:** danger, corruption, vice; the cold of winter, disease, starvation; invasion □ *In 1971 the people of East Bengal (now known as Bangladesh) were* ***exposed to*** *every kind of danger — flood, famine, disease and war.*

expunge (from) [B2 pass rel] (formal) remove (from) and thus treat as never having been stated or recorded; delete (from) (q v). **O:** name, words; conviction. **o:** record(s), minutes □ *Following the prosecution on a charge of perjury of the main witness at the youth's trial, his conviction and sentence were ordered to be* ***expunged from*** *the record.* □ *Time had* ***expunged from*** *his memory all recollections of the terrible events he had witnessed.*

extort from [B2 pass emph rel] (formal) obtain from, by means of threats or violence. **O:** money; confession, admission of guilt □ *The gang specialized in* ***extorting*** *large sums of money* ***from*** *men in important positions, by threatening to expose certain connections or activities which they wanted to keep secret.*

extract (from) [B2 pass rel] obtain (from), by means of a mechanical or chemical process. **O:** oil; dyes; juice; essence. **o:** earth; coal; orange; flowers □ *It is one thing to locate oil, but it is quite another to* ***extract*** *it (****from*** *the earth) and transport it to the centres of industry.*

extract from [B2 pass] obtain from, by any means ranging from physical violence to gentle persuasion. **O:** money; information, confession; new dress, hat, washing-machine; promise □ *Mrs Smith* ***extracted*** *a new refrigerator* ***from*** *her husband when he told her about his Christmas bonus.* □ *When he has* ***extracted*** *everything he can* ***from*** *a new acquaintance, he drops him like a hot brick.*

extricate (from) [B2 pass emph rel] (formal) free, remove (from). **O:** himself, friend, colleague; lorry; lump of meat. **o:** difficulties, an embarrassing situation, predicament; mud, quagmire; child's throat □ *Mr Mason had a good lunch at the restaurant and then discovered that he had no money in his pocket to pay for it. He was wondering how to* ***extricate*** *himself* ***from*** *this difficulty when he saw an old friend sitting at another table. 'Saved!' he exclaimed to himself.*

exult at [A2 rel] (formal) feel overjoyed, triumphant, because of. **o:** the prospect of winning a fortune, the thought of completing the task, one's new-found freedom □ *Few people would not* ***exult at*** *the overthrow of the ruling junta.*

exult in [A2 pass rel] (formal) take pride in, derive pleasure from. **o:** the defeat, humiliation, of his enemy; one's own strength, one's ability to overcome difficulties □ *Mr Smeeth, with the drudgery of the office a thing of the past,* ***exulted in*** *the sense of freedom that came from his longed-for release.* □ *It is not pleasant to see a triumphant politician* ***exulting in*** *the downfall and discomfiture of his opponent.* ⇨ next entry.

exult over [A2 pass rel] (formal) meanly enjoy the sight or thought of. **o:** his disgrace, downfall, misfortune, defeat; defeated enemy, team, champion □ *I left the scene quickly, not wishing to witness the crowd* ***exulting over*** *the capture and lynching of the unfortunate bandits, however cruel they themselves had been.* ⇨ previous entry.

F

face away (from) [A1 A3] (turn, so as to) look or point in the opposite direction (from). **S:** listener, spectator; building. **o:** platform, speaker; street, traffic □ *Sarah was overcome with embarrassment. She* ***faced away*** *to hide her blushes.* □ *The estate is so designed that the front of each house* ***faces away from*** *busy roads.*

face up to [A3 pass adj] accept honestly and courageously. **S:** parent, teacher; government, local council. **o:** responsibility, burden, task; prospect, possibility (of loss, failure) □ *He had to* ***face up to*** *the depressing possibility of the creature's death.* RM □ *There's no running away from the facts; the truth just has to be* ***faced up to.***

fade away [A1] gradually become weaker; become less audible, die away (q v). **S:** strength, vitality; inventiveness, inspiration; music, cheering □ *Old soldiers never die, they only* ***fade away.*** □ *The clip-clop of the horse's hooves* ***faded away*** *into the distance.*

fade out [A1 nom B1i pass adj] gradually become or make invisible or inaudible (esp on radio, TV etc). **S:** [A1] **O:** [B1] voice, music, sound effects; image, picture; speaker, performer. **S:** [B1] broadcasting company, studio; producer □ *When you turn on a transistorized radio the sound comes on immediately; when you turn off, it* ***fades out*** *gradually.* □ *I hope that during his television appearance, there will be no* ***fade-outs*** *or blackouts!* □ ***Fade out*** *the storm effect here, and turn up the music.*

fade up [B1i pass] gradually make louder (esp in a radio or TV studio). **S:** technician, sound effects man. **O:** music, voice; announcer □ *As the signature tune was faded out, the voices of a group talking around a table were* ***faded up.***

fag out [B1ii pass adj] (informal) make quite tired, exhaust; tire out (q v). **S:** exercise; game, race; entertaining, being sociable □ *Standing on your feet all day really* ***fags you out.*** □ *After ten minutes of his conversation I feel quite* ***fagged out.*** □ usu passive or adj.

fall about one's ears [A2] collapse utterly; crash about one's ears (q v). **S:** his (whole) world; their achievements □ *Soon the secure, enclosed life he had built up for himself would* ***fall about his ears.***

fall about (laughing/with laughter) [A1] (informal) laugh uproariously, uncontrollably. **S:** audience; listener, viewer □ *Nick's a born clown. Just the sight of him is enough to make you* ***fall about laughing.*** □ *People* ***fell about*** *when he told them he was doing 'O' Level woodwork and music.* BBCR

fall apart [A1] disintegrate, fall to pieces (q v). **S:** car, house; alliance, coalition; defence, case; marriage, partnership □ *I don't know how Mick managed to keep the car on the road for so long. At the end, it was practically* ***falling apart.*** □ *Ann did what she could to keep the marriage from* ***falling apart.*** *If she and Robert broke up, she decided, it wouldn't be her fault.*

fall away (to)[1] [A1 A3] slope steeply (towards). **S:** field, meadow; garden, orchard. **o:** river, road □ *Beyond the garden, an area of woodland* ***fell*** *sharply* ***away to*** *the river bank.*

fall away (to)[2] [A1 A3] sink, drop (to a lower level). **S:** demand, supply; production, output. **o:** level; zero, nothing □ *As demand for funds slackened off, the rate* ***fell away to*** *the clearing banks' basic level of 3.3/8 per cent.* T □ *Output from the power stations* ***fell away*** *steeply as restrictions on the movement of coal took effect.*

fall back [A1] (military) withdraw, retreat. **S:** troops; army, division □ *The Russians were finding an offensive war of movement very different from the fluid fighting of 1941 and 1942, when they had been* ***falling back*** *towards their dumps and railheads.* B

fall back on [A3 rel] approach, consult for support or comfort (in difficult times); use sth as a last resort if other things fail. **o:** mother, family; religion; pension, savings; simpler plan, more straightforward approach, threat of dismissal □ *He grasps at things greedily, like a child, just because he hasn't any inner certainty to* ***fall back on.*** PW □ *And if the scheme didn't work there was always the Home Secretary's plan to* ***fall back on.*** TBC □ *If the men didn't respond to a reasoned approach there were other methods we could* ***fall back on.*** □ fall back on usu occurs as inf immediately following n; less often as a main (finite) v.

fall behind [A1 A2] move back behind others; be overtaken by them; drop behind (q v). **S:** runner, horse; company, industry. **o:** rest of the field; competitor, rival □ *This country has* ***fallen behind*** *several of its competitors in the manufacture of cheap cotton goods.* □ *Fears of* ***falling behind*** *in the arms race lead eventually to more of the expansion which first prompted the fears.* ⇨ be behind[2].

fall behind with [A3] fail to pay sth for some time. **o:** payment, instalment; deliveries, quota □ *Teenagers were more likely to* ***fall behind with*** *the rent.* H □ *He'd stopped deliveries, because I* ***fell behind with*** *the bill.* CON ⇨ be behind[1], get behind (with).

fall below [A2 emph rel] drop lower than a permitted or desired level etc. **S:** oil, water; wage, earnings; intake, recruitment; production, demand. **o:** point, level; figure, percentage; standard □ *This group of workers is determined that its earnings will not* ***fall below*** *the average for the whole industry.* □ *Output for the current year will* ***fall below*** *that for last year.* ⇨ be below[1].

fall between two stools [A2] fail to be either of two satisfactory alternatives. **S:** policy, scheme, plan; show, performance; speech, statement □ *The display* ***falls between the two stools*** *of an historical exhibition and a survey of the visual arts of the period — it is not wholly satisfactory as either.* T

fall by the wayside [A2] (euphemism for) fail to make progress in life; slip into dishonest ways □ *In Mr Robert Hollis's play 'June Fall' on BBC television, the discards are the people who* ***fall by the wayside*** *and stop developing, the world's rejected guests.* T □ *'It's a funny thing, but even the best of us can* ***fall by the wayside*** *and yours truly* (= the speaker) *is no exception.'* OBS

fall down[1] [A1 emph] collapse, fall to the ground. **S:** building, tent, scaffolding; old man, cripple □ *The steel scaffolding* ***fell down*** *and narrowly missed a couple of bystanders.* □ *The old lady* ***fell down*** *in the street and broke her leg.*

fall down[2] [A1] collapse, be shown to be false or inadequate; fall to the ground (q v). **S:** argument, case; policy, approach □ *The Council's answer to the population expansion is to build high blocks of flats, but that's where the plan* ***falls down*** *— who wants to live in them?*

fall down on it/the job [A3] (informal) fail to make a success of sth, not be able to handle it. **S:** employee, workman, contractor □ *I don't want Jeremy to be Prime Minister or anything of that sort. He'd only* ***fall down on it.*** PW □ *Don't put him in charge of planning: he's sure to* ***fall down on the job.***

fall for (in a big way) [A2 rel] (informal) be (strongly) attracted to; fall in love (with) (q v) (madly) □ *A man who's on the way up is continually raising the standard of the women he can* ***fall for.*** CON □ *I* ***fell for*** *Irma* ***in a big way,*** *Harold.* PW

fall for (hook, line and sinker) [A2 rel] (informal) allow oneself to be persuaded by. **o:** line of talk, argument, propaganda □ *I never take my wife to the market. She* ***falls for*** *all that sales talk much too easily.* □ *The garage said the car had been driven carefully by one previous owner, and of course I* ***fell for*** *it* ***hook, line and sinker.*** □ *If you* ***fall for*** *that, you'll* ***fall for*** *anything!*

fall from grace [A2] lose one's position as a trusted favourite of those in power; lapse from grace (q v). **S:** minister, adviser, courtier, favourite □ *Becket* ***fell from grace*** *because of his supposed interference in the temporal realm.*

fall from power [A2] lose a position of power, relinquish office. **S:** Government, party □ *This administration* ***fell from power*** *over its handling of the economic crisis.*

fall from/out of favour (with) [A2] (formal) lose a favoured or privileged position; fall from grace (q v). **S:** minister, courtier □ *Jones has* ***fallen out of favour with*** *the party leadership.* □ *I had* ***fallen from favour*** *and would be lucky to pass out of the College at all.* MFM

fall in[1] [A1] collapse, give way. **S:** roof, ceiling, wall; sides of a trench □ *The roof of the new tunnel hasn't been properly supported: it shows signs of* ***falling in.***

fall in[2] [A1 B1i pass] (military) form into ranks (as when on parade). **S:** [A1] **O:** [B1] soldier, troops; platoon, battalion. **S:** [B1] sergeant-major, officer □ *The company* ***fell in*** *and took up their dressing from the right.* □ *Platoon sergeants* ***fell*** *their men* ***in*** *on the barrack square.*

fall in[3] [A1] (legal) expire. **S:** ⚠ the lease, leasehold □ *As the leases of these old properties* ***fall in,*** *they are being pulled down to make way for office blocks.*

fall in alongside/beside [A3] join a person or group that is already walking or marching along □ *I* ***fell in beside*** *him and the three of us, with the kid sitting aloft, walked over the line.* CON □ *Onlookers left the pavement and* ***fell in alongside*** *the marching demonstrators.*

fall in/into [A1 emph A2 emph rel] drop accidentally into sth (e g by tripping over an obstacle). **A:** head over heels, head first, headlong. **o:** river, swimming-pool □ *He thrust the hands forward, tore at the water and **fell** flat **in** the pool.* PM □ *This reminded me of a rather fat boy who had once **fallen** head foremost **into** a muddy puddle.* SNP

fall in with[1] [A3 pass rel] encounter, meet; join or rejoin (after an absence) □ *We **fell in with** a party of nomads encamped by a water-hole.* □ *I crossed into Assam and **fell in with** our forces in Imphal.* ARG

fall in with[2] [A3 pass rel] show support for. **o:** scheme, arrangement; proposal, suggestion □ *He believed he had been looking forward to **falling in with** Alec's request.* PW □ *For if Isobel had fallen in love with Alec, would she have **fallen in with** his scheme for getting hold of Irma?* PW

fall in love (with) [A2] feel a sudden, strong attraction etc for sb of the opposite sex. **A:** madly, head over heels. **o:** (one's) pupil, neighbour, secretary □ *But if Guy were **falling in love with** her, was she genuinely returning Guy's affection?* DC □ *You're still crazy about Fergus. What are you going to do if he **falls in love with** another woman?* DC

fall into[1] [A2 emph rel] (may) be divided into; have as components. **S:** lecture, article, subject. **o:** three sections, two parts □ *The present talk **falls into** three parts.* □ *The three sections **into** which my argument may be said to **fall** are these.*

fall into[2] [A2 emph rel] become comatose; fall fast asleep; move into a hypnotic state; pass into [3] (q v). **o:** ⚠ a coma; a deep sleep; a trance □ *The patient was given an injection and afterwards **fell into** a deep sleep.* ⇨ go into[4].

fall into[3] [A2] acquire, develop. **o:** ⚠ bad, undesirable habits, ways; the habit of doing sth □ *It was to be expected that a young man with easy-going parents and considerable private means should keep bad company and **fall into** undesirable habits.* □ *Paul had **fallen into** the habit of calling at his brother's flat on Thursday evenings.*

fall into[4] [A2 emph rel] drop accidentally into sth. ⇨ fall in/into.

fall into decay [A2] gradually become rotten or decayed (physically or morally). **S:** house, boat, factory, installation; monarchy, parliament, university □ *During the long period of the Depression, the sheds and warehouses were allowed to **fall into decay**.* □ *The laws and institutions of the republic had long **fallen into decay**.*

fall into a decline [A2 rel] begin to sink to a low level. **S:** country, economy; morals, arts □ *The intense competition from overseas has caused the cotton industry to **fall into a decline**.* □ *Without government help, these local theatres will not recover from the serious **decline into** which they have **fallen**.*

fall into a (deep) depression [A2 rel] become dispirited, morally depressed □ *After the loss of her second child, she **fell into a depression** from which it was difficult to rouse her.*

fall into disfavour [A2] = fall from/out of favour.

fall into disgrace [A2] reach a state where one is no longer respected or well regarded. **S:** courtier, official; schoolboy □ *A little indiscreet gossip isn't enough to make you **fall into disgrace** with all your friends.* □ *From a level of easy success I suppose it's a simple matter to **fall into disgrace**.*

fall into disrepair [A2] through neglect, reach a state where repairs are needed. **S:** building; church, palace; machinery, mechanism □ *The stonework of the tower was crumbling, and the great clock had **fallen into disrepair**.*

fall into disrepute [A2] lose one's good name or reputation. **S:** press, television; police, civil service □ *The company has **fallen into disrepute** in recent years.* □ *An examination system which cannot provide an objective measurement of aptitude must **fall into disrepute**.* ⇨ bring into disrepute.

fall into disuse [A2] reach the state of no longer being used. **S:** expression, phrase; practice, custom; ceremony □ *Words which **fall into disuse** may sometimes be revived with a new meaning.* □ *The practice of wearing gowns to attend lectures has now **fallen into disuse**.*

fall into place [A2] (begin to) form an orderly, intelligible pattern. **S:** (scraps of) evidence, (parts of) the story, (pieces of) the puzzle □ *'Of course, now that you tell me about the man's relationship with his wife, the whole picture **falls into place**. It explains, for instance, why he was always desperately short of money.'*

fall into sb's/the right etc hands [A2 emph rel] be seized by sb, pass into sb's possession, care etc. **S:** document, map; evidence; refugee, escapee. **adj:** (the) right, wrong; enemy, foreign; friendly, allied □ *Old Mother Curry's always there to help. It's a good thing you've **fallen into the right hands**.* HAA □ *But what if our distinguished guest **fell into the wrong hands**? What if the other side got hold of him?*

fall into line (with) [A2] accept, conform to, what others do or propose. **A:** tamely, abjectly; reluctantly. **o:** (***with***) the others, the majority, public opinion, the general view □ *When the Chairman proposed a tightening-up of credit facilities, most of the Board **fell into line**.* □ *After a period in the political wildnerness, he has **fallen** back **into line with** the rest of his party.* ⇨ be in/bring into/come into line (with).

fall into step (with) [A2] begin to walk in step with sb; (fig) start to accept or follow rules, procedures etc laid down by others. **o:** (***with***) companion; marchers, procession; committee, political masters □ *Charles followed him into the street, and **fell into step** as they trudged along.* HD □ *The militants on the executive are unlikely to **fall into step with** leaders they regard as over-conciliatory.*

fall off[1] [A1] become smaller or fewer; lessen, decrease; drop off[1] (q v). **S:** orders, exports, takings, income □ *Attendances at our matinees have **fallen off** this season.* □ *There has been a marked **falling-off** in admissions to the advanced course.* □ nom form is falling-off.

fall off[2] [A1] worsen, deteriorate. **S:** standard, quality; service, catering □ *The cooking **fell off** remarkably; I remember I several times had to go out to a restaurant to quell my hunger.* CON □ *Our customers complain of a distinct **falling-off** in quality.* □ nom form is falling-off.

fall on [A2] occur on, take place on. **S:** Easter, New Year's Day, Bank Holiday; his birthday, their anniversary. **o:** Monday, weekday □ *His birthday **falls on** a Sunday this year.* □ *What day* *does Christmas* ***fall on****?*

fall on deaf ears [A2] not be heard or noted (because others are not present, or not wishing to listen). **S:** cry, shout (for help); appeal, plea; request, application □ *His suggestion for a three-Power world-wide Western directorate* ***fell on deaf ears****.* SC □ *Claims for a twenty per cent salary increase are likely to* ***fall on deaf ears****.*

fall on one's feet [A2] (informal) make a quick recovery after difficult times (often through good luck) □ *'He came back from the war penniless and landed a good job right away.' 'Yes, he has the knack of* ***falling on his feet****, hasn't he?'* □ *'You got extra* (in prison) *because you looked so clean and Nordic. Oh yes, you always* ***fell on your feet****.'* RATT

fall flat on one's face[1] [A2] (informal) fall to the ground suddenly and in an undignified way □ *With a mighty heave, he succeeded in lifting both feet from the ground, and promptly* ***fell flat on his face****.* DF □ *He had not gone many steps before he stumbled on the uneven ground and* ***fell flat on his face****.* BM

fall flat on one's face[2] [A2] (informal) suffer an undignified setback or defeat (esp after attempting sth which is beyond one's powers). **S:** (young, inexperienced) politician, negotiator, salesman □ *Don't imagine that you can get the better of him in argument. More experienced debaters than you have* ***fallen flat on their faces*** *before now.* □ *If he tries to tackle that kind of market before he's made a thorough study he'll* ***fall flat on his face****.*

fall on/to one's knees [A2] kneel down (to beg for favours or mercy). **S:** slave, suppliant, subject □ *The prisoners* ***fell on their knees*** *to beg for clemency.*

fall on/upon[1] [A2] attack fiercely; seize greedily. **S:** soldier; bandit, thief; hungry child. **o:** convoy, column; booty, plunder; food □ *The 2nd Cavalry roamed the marshy length of the river Teberev,* ***falling upon*** *isolated units of German infantry.* B

fall on/upon[2] [A2 emph rel] be borne by, be incurred by. **S:** expense, cost; blame; burden, work; attack, fighting □ *When anything goes wrong, the blame usually* ***falls on*** *his younger brother.* □ *The full cost of the wedding* ***fell on*** *me.* □ ***On*** *this part of the front* ***fell*** *the main weight of the attack.*

fall on/upon[3] [A2 rel] (formal) (of sb) catch sight of, see. **S:** ⚠ his etc eye, gaze □ *His gaze* ***fell upon*** *a small party of men moving up the hill-side.* □ *His eyes* ***fell on*** *the looking-glass.* EHOW

fall on/upon sb's ears [A2 emph] (formal) be heard, become audible. **S:** sound, noise; cry, shriek □ *As we entered the temple, a curious chanting* ***fell upon our ears****.* □ ***Upon their ears fell*** *a low, humming sound.*

fall on/upon evil days/hard times [A2] (formal) suffer hardship, misfortune. **S:** country; industry, farming; class, family □ *During the reign of Henry VI the country* ***fell on evil days****.* □ *It was a nobleman's house, though* ***fallen upon evil days****.* WDM

it fall on/upon sb to do sth [A2] (formal) be, become one's responsibility to do sth □ ***It fell upon me to open*** *the exhibition in the mayor's absence* (or: *The responsibility for opening etc* ***fell upon me****).* ⇨ fall on/upon[2].

fall out[1] [A1] happen, occur. **S:** ⚠ things, events, everything. **A:** thus, in this way; as arranged, as we had anticipated □ *I was pleased with the way things had* ***fallen out****.* UTN □ *Everything* ***fell out*** *as we had planned.* □ an adv phrase or clause is usu present.

fall out[2] [A1 B1i pass] (military) dismiss, (cause to) go off parade. **S:** [A1] **O:** [B1] soldier, platoon. **S:** [B1] sergeant, officer □ *At the end of the drill parade, the battalion* ***fell out****.* □ *The troops had been* ***fallen out*** *by the roadside.*

fall-out [nom (A1)] radioactive dust (resulting from a nuclear explosion) □ *The claim made for the shelters is that they will protect people from radioactive* ***fall-out****.* OBS □ *'Dirty' bombs produce a higher level of* ***fall-out*** *than 'clean' ones.*

it fall out that [A1] (formal) happen, come about[1] (q v), that □ *Thus* ***it fell out,*** *to Muriel's delight,* ***that*** *she was able to cross to Little Today without arousing any possible suspicion.* RM □ *How did* ***it fall out that*** *the two men arrived to address the same meeting at the same time?* ⇨ fall out[1].

fall out/out of [A1 A2] fall from an enclosed space at a high level to a lower level. **S:** bird; baby, spectator. **o:** nest; cot, window □ *'I'm so glad you didn't hurt yourself when you* ***fell out of*** *bed, Mrs Baye.'* DC □ *'Hold on to the side of the boat. You'll* ***fall out****!'*

fall out (with) [A1 A3 rel] (informal) get on bad terms (with); quarrel (with) (about/over) (q v) □ *He has a knack of* ***falling out with*** *everyone.* PP □ *'Did you and mother* ***fall out****?'* R

fall out of favour (with) [A2] ⇨ fall from/out of favour (with).

fall out of love (with) [A2] no longer be strongly attracted to, convinced by etc. **o:** wife, witness; politician, party □ *Sarah's not particularly fickle. She's just of an age when girls* ***fall*** *in and* ***out of love*** *all the time.* □ *How would the leader's morale stand up if there are to be repeated demonstrations that the voters are* ***falling out of love with*** *him?* OBS

fall outside [A2] not be sth which one can handle, understand etc; stand outside (q v). **S:** matter, question; finance, housing. **o:** (one's) province, competence; field, area (of interest) □ *The future expansion of secondary school building* ***falls outside*** *the scope of the present inquiry.* ⇨ be outside.

fall over[1] [A1] fall forward and to the ground (usu after slipping or tripping). **S:** old lady, small boy, footballer □ *Johnny slipped on a banana skin and* ***fell over****.* □ *Mrs Jenkins missed her footing and* ***fell over****.*

fall over[2] [A1] (of a stationary object) fall from an upright to a horizontal position. **S:** vase, lamp-standard, monument □ *A suit of armour* ***fell over*** *with a loud crash.*

fall over backwards to do sth [A1] (informal) take special care, go to great pains (esp to please sb). **Inf** to appease, to placate; to meet objections □ *But I think everybody* ***falls over backwards to be*** *fair to female doctors.* DIL □ *They* ***fall over backwards to lay on*** *gracious service on a few favoured express trains.* T

fall over oneself to do sth [A2] (informal) strive anxiously or eagerly (esp to achieve or obtain sth). **S:** host, salesman, employer. **Inf:** to buy, to win, to acquire; to retain, to protect □ *The oil firms were* ***falling over themselves to obtain*** *concessions from the Government.* □ *These people are* ***falling over themselves to keep*** *the British space effort confined to small satellites.* NS

fall overboard [A1] (nautical) fall from the deck of a ship etc into the water □ *The spaces between the rails on the promenade deck are so wide that it would be easy for a child to slip through and* ***fall overboard.*** ⇨ go overboard.

fall through [A1] (informal) fail, miscarry. **S:** scheme, plan, project □ *The scheme* ***fell through*** *because of some big business deal Ned had to stay and attend to.* CON □ *We're not going to Spain after all — the whole thing's* ***fallen through.***

fall to[1] [A1] begin (to eat, fight, work). **S:** guest, diner; contestants, team. **A:** with gusto, with enthusiasm □ *A meal had been prepared. I* ***fell to*** *with ravenous appetite.* DOP

fall to[2] [A2] start, begin. **o:** asking, thinking, considering, quarrelling □ *I* ***fell to*** *brooding.* PP □ *And she* ***fell to*** *wondering again who her enemy might be.* MM □ the object is the *-ing* form of a v.

fall to the ground [A2] collapse, crumble (for want of proof or evidence); fall down [2] (q v). **S:** theory; argument, case, contention □ *This hypothesis* ***falls to the ground*** *because intelligence correlates only to a slight extent with 'good taste'.* SNP

fall to one's knees [A2] ⇨ fall on/to one's knees.

it fall to sb/sb's lot to do sth [A2] (formal) become sb's task or responsibility. **Inf** to arrange, to organize; to design, to devise; to welcome, to receive □ ***It fell to my lot to form*** *an administration.* EM □ ***It fell to Mr Johnson-Smith****, a former TV broadcaster,* ***to interrupt*** *Mr Heath at the end of the programme.* G

fall to pieces [A2] be broken, shattered, utterly; fall apart (q v). **S:** jug, cup; car, van; defence, argument, case □ *No wonder the car's* ***falling to pieces.*** *Have you seen how he drives it?* □ *He was the coward whose cloak of broadminded, humane conduct had* ***fallen to pieces*** *in one moment.* HAA

fall under [A2] be classified as, be placed within a certain category. **S:** matter, question; item. **o:** heading, head; (the heading of) petty cash, foreign trade □ *Does the entertainment of visitors* ***fall under*** *the heading of miscellaneous expenditure?* □ *'No, we're not discussing the Christmas appeal just yet. That* ***falls under*** *"any other business".'*

fall under sb's/the spell [A2 rel] be charmed, captivated, by. **S:** woman; pupil, patient □ *The young candidate addressed the women's branch: the entire audience* ***fell under his spell.*** □ *His fellow-townsmen* ***fell under the*** *same* ***spell,*** *but finally it was broken and he had to carry out his great plans in actual fact.* SNP

fall upon[1] [A2] attack fiercely. ⇨ fall on/upon[1].

fall upon[2] [A2 emph rel] be borne by. ⇨ fall on/upon[2].

fall upon[3] [A2 rel] catch sight of. ⇨ fall on/upon[3].

fall upon sb's ears [A2 emph] ⇨ fall on/upon sb's ears.

fall upon evil days/hard times [A2] ⇨ fall on/upon evil days/hard times.

it fall upon sb to do sth [A2] ⇨ it fall on/upon sb to do sth.

fall within [A2] be sth which one is able to discuss or handle. **S:** question, matter. **o:** (one's) competence, province; field, area (of interest) □ *The allocation of funds for research projects does not* ***fall within*** *the competence of this committee.* ⇨ be within[2].

fan out [A1] move away from each other, while advancing; spread out[2] (q v). **S:** troops, search party, hunters □ *The Army was* ***fanning out*** *north of Naples.* SD □ *Police with tracker dogs were* ***fanning out*** *over the moor.*

fancy oneself as [B2] (informal) consider that one is well suited to a certain role, or that one does a particular job well, even though one may have little aptitude, training etc. **o:** lover, father; actor, painter; driver, handyman □ *He was a clerk at the works.* ***Fancied himself as*** *a writer.* RATT □ *If you* ***fancy yourself as*** *a nurse then go down to Aldgate, we've got a first-aid post there.* CSWB

farm out [B1i pass] give sb or sth to others to be responsible for or manage. **S:** mother; firm. **O:** child; work, responsibilities □ *You are* ***farming*** *your baby* ***out*** *on that unspeakable woman.* AITC □ *The work of producing the many electrical components has been* ***farmed out*** *to small manufacturers.*

fasten on/upon [A2 pass emph rel] choose, in a keen, alert way, for special comment or criticism; seize on/upon (q v). **o:** idea, suggestion, proposal; weakness, □ *Defence counsel* ***fastened on*** *this flaw in his line of reasoning.* □ *One of his points was* ***fastened upon*** *by the treasurer. 'Have you considered the likely cost of another sales campaign?' he asked.*

father on/upon [B2 pass emph rel] claim that sb is the father, author or originator of. **O:** child, offspring; manuscript, book; device, gadget □ *'Don't pin the blame on me: I had nothing to do with the idea. Try* ***fathering*** *it* ***on*** *someone else.'*

fathom out [B1i] (informal) (try to) discover, or devise, an explanation for sth. **O:** it, things; why he had done it, where they had gone □ *I could have sworn I left my keys on the desk. I can't* ***fathom out*** *where they've got to.* □ *Don't tell me the answer; let me try to* ***fathom*** *it* ***out*** *for myself.*

fatten on/upon [A2 emph rel] grow fat, rich etc at the expense of sb else. **S:** idler, parasite, sponger. **o:** efforts, toil, sweat (of others, of the poor) □ *It is now a distortion to represent the owners of industry in western countries as a small and indolent class* ***fattening on*** *the labours of others.*

fatten up [B1i pass adj] give a person or animal plenty to eat, causing him or it to gain weight. **O:** underweight child; livestock □ *I'm trying to* ***fatten him up*** *as fast as I can.* BFA □ *The pigs are being* ***fattened up*** *for market.*

fawn (on) [A2 pass] attempt to win sb's favour by servile behaviour. **o:** employer, teacher; the rich, the powerful □ *He* ***fawns on*** *anyone in an influential position.* □ *Don't try to win his support in that way — he hates to be* ***fawned on.***

fear for [A2] feel anxious about the health etc of

sb, or the future development of events. **o:** sb's health, life, survival; the future, the development (of sth) □ *The miners' families* ***fear for*** *the lives of the men trapped underground.* □ *'Don't attempt to climb on that very difficult rock-face. I should* ***fear for*** *your safety.'* □ *There is no need to* ***fear for*** *the future of the economy. It is now on a sound course.*

fed up (with) [pass adj (B1)] (informal) (be) depressed or irritated (by); have had enough (of); (be) tired of (q v). **o:** manner, attitude; climate, place, job; wife, husband. **A:** thoroughly, utterly; to the back teeth □ *They were getting a bit* ***fed up with*** *her by that time, so they wrote her rather a sharp letter.* RFW □ *I'm* ***fed up with*** *being wholesome. I long to be seductive and tempting.* RATT □ *'Why the long face, Frank? I've never seen you look so* ***fed up****.'* □ passive with *be, feel, get, look.*

feed back (into/to)[1] [B1i nom pass B3 pass] (radio, electronics) return part of the output of a circuit as an input to the preceding stage of that circuit. **O:** signal, oscillation; information. **o:** stage; circuit; appliance, device □ *Part of the output of an amplifier can be* ***fed back*** *to get rid of sound distortion* (cf *Amplifier* ***feedback*** *can get rid of sound distortion*). □ usu nom or passive as here.

feed back (into/to)[2] [A1 nom A3] (of a hearer's unconscious gestures or expressions, or conscious comments) indicate to a speaker, teacher etc how well he is being received, so enabling him to adapt to his audience; (of ideas etc) return in an altered or extended form to their point of origin, so making possible still more progress. **S:** response, reaction; experience, knowledge; ideas, techniques. **o:** research, industry □ *The teachers complain that nothing is* ***feeding back to*** *them from the classroom* (cf *that there is no* ***feedback*** *from the classroom*). □ *A lot of ideas are* ***feeding back*** *from the applied sciences (such as agriculture or metallurgy)* ***into*** *the pure sciences (such as botany or chemistry)* (cf *There is a lot of* ***feedback*** *from the applied to the pure sciences*).

feed off[1] [A2 pass rel] use as a source or supplier of food, materials, energy etc. **S:** outpost, station; factory, machine; newspaper, radio station; author, teacher. **o:** base, depot; power-station, generator; news agency; idea, thought □ *When fresh food and water are not available, the camel can* ***feed off*** *its hump.* □ *The central services of the BBC to some extent* ***feed off*** *the regional stations.* ⇨ feed on.

feed off[2] [A2 rel] take food from a flat, open utensil. **o:** plate, platter, dish □ *The guests sat cross-legged around a low table and* ***fed off*** *silver dishes.*

feed on [A2 emph rel B2 pass emph rel] have, give to sb, as food or sustenance. **S:** [A2] **O:** [B2] cattle, chickens; dog, goldfish; child; public, electorate; student. **S:** [B2] farmer; owner; parent; dictator, propaganda machine; teacher. **o:** cake, corn; scraps; milk, meat; lies, pap □ *Of course the children look undernourished. Their mothers can't afford to* ***feed*** *them* ***on*** *meat and fish every day.* □ *I'm not surprised that his classes never express an original thought when the stuff they're* ***fed on*** *is second and even third hand.* ⇨ feed off[1].

feed up [B1ii pass] bring a person to his proper weight by giving him nourishing food. **O:** patient, convalescent; orphan, refugee □ *'I think he looks half-starved. Wants* ***feeding up****. I'll find him a good fat kipper.'* DBM

feel for[1] [A2 rel] search for sth (with the hands). **o:** light-switch, door-knob; wallet, purse; wall, door □ *Prissie's fingers pressed the catch of the locket and from habit* ***felt for*** *the folded paper within.* DC □ *In the fog he* ***felt for*** *the kerb with his walking-stick.*

feel for[2] [A2] feel sympathy for, sympathize with. **o:** unhappy, distressed (person); the bereaved, the homeless; orphan, refugee □ *It's easy to* ***feel for*** *people in need; it's harder to bring yourself to do something practical about it.*

feel in one's bones (that) [B2 emph] (informal) sense, suspect (instinctively or intuitively) that sth is the case. **O:** it; that he is untrustworthy, that something was amiss, that trouble was afoot □ *I* ***felt in my bones that*** *Archer didn't do him justice and I wanted to make sure.* HAA □ *I knew that something of the sort would happen. I* ***felt*** *it* ***in my bones****.*

feel like [A2] fancy, feel in the mood for. **o:** party, night out, drive in the country; walking, drinking, dancing □ *He didn't* ***feel like*** *anything to eat.* TO □ *Those who* ***felt like*** *hearing the story again came over and added themselves to the audience.* HD

feel on top of the world [A2] (informal) feel very light-hearted, in good spirits □ *'You look depressed, Peter.' 'I'm not depressed. I'm* ***feeling on top of the world****.' 'Are you? You don't sound very convincing.'* □ *'He's got every reason to* ***feel on top of the world*** *— a beautiful wife, talented children, no financial worries.' 'It all sounds marvellous. Where's the catch?'*

feel out of it/things [A2] (informal) feel that one is not fully sharing in an occasion, either because of shyness, or because one is unused to the company, conversation etc □ *Not that she* ***felt out of it****; her nature was a silent one and she could sit quietly while people talked without* ***feeling out of things*** *herself or making other people feel embarrassed.* WDM

feel out of place [A2] not feel at home, comfortable, at one's ease (because the place, or one's companions, are foreign, of a different social class etc) □ *Many of us would* ***feel out of place*** *in a duke's drawing room or a bishop's palace.* □ *I want to work here, where I know what people are like. Not in another country, where I would* ***feel out of place****.* AITC

feel up to [A3] (informal) feel able to (make), feel capable of (undertaking). **o:** much; sustained effort, long journey; meeting, working; it □ *I don't know whether George* ***feels up to*** *opening presents.* EGD □ *When I suggested that I should walk part of the way, he said: 'Of course, if you* ***feel up to*** *it.'* NM ⇨ (not) be up to; put up to[1].

fence in[1] [B1i pass adj] enclose a space, or animals, with a fence. **O:** garden, orchard; field, meadow; stock, cattle □ *Thousands of acres of open range were* ***fenced in*** *to prevent cattlemen trespassing on what had become private property.* □ *It was some two acres in extent, neatly* ***fenced in*** *with tall palms.* DF

fence in[2] [B1i pass adj] restrict a person's freedom. **S:** regulation; rule; manners, custom;

requirement, duty □ *He felt* ***fenced in*** *by domesticity, by his nine-to-five daily routine, by the social demands of suburban living.* □ *'Don't* ***fence*** *me* ***in****, Mary, don't make me feel trapped.'*

fence off (from) [B1i pass adj B3 pass emph rel] separate one area (from another) by means of a fence. **O:** playground, flower-garden; private land; rubbish tip □ *The children can't play in the front garden until it's been* ***fenced off from*** *the main road.*

fend for oneself [A2] keep house, feed oneself etc, without outside assistance □ *The old couple have no one to do the washing and heavy cleaning: they have to* ***fend for themselves****.* □ *The rations issued to the patrols would last for two days; after that they would* ***fend for themselves****.*

fend off [B1i pass adj] deflect, turn aside; prevent from coming near, keep at a distance. **O:** blow, thrust; visitor, envoy, acquaintance □ *He neatly* ***fended off*** *a jab at his chest.* □ *Instead of bothering to* ***fend off*** *the sneer, I just said simply, 'Yes.'* CON

ferret out [B1i pass] (informal) find, discover, by diligent searching. **O:** letter, document; reference, detail; information, fact □ *He* ***ferreted out*** *my address from somewhere, and wrote to ask how I was doing.* CON □ *They have overlooked another aspect, one that's more difficult to* ***ferret out****.* HD

festoon with [B2 pass rel] decorate with chains (of flowers etc) which hang in loops; deck with (q v). **O:** street, house; wall, door; curtain; book. **o:** flowers, leaves; ivy; paper-chains, ribbons; squiggles, notes □ *The children had* ***festooned*** *the Christmas tree* ***with*** *tinsel and fairy lights.* □ *The margins of his notebook were* ***festooned with*** *doodles.*

fetch up [A1] (informal) eventually arrive (in a place) □ *We all* ***fetched up*** *simultaneously at the same spot.* SPL □ *She left him a little time before she* ***fetched up*** *in Forfar and came to you.* RFW

fight (one's way) back (to) [A1 A3 emph rel B1ii B3 emph rel] return, by struggling hard (to a position previously held). **S:** country, firm; politician; patient. **o:** position, place; the top; health □ [A1] *Still he* ***fought back****, and there were even moments when he felt, fleetingly, the old symptoms of vitality and spiritual health.* HD □ [B3] *After several reverses, they* ***fought their way back to*** *their old seats on the Board.*

fight down [B1i pass] suppress, control, hold in check. **O:** anger, rage, disappointment □ *He told me what the trouble was. He* ***fought*** *it* ***down*** *and as the minutes passed I thought he was going to win out.* TBC

fight off [B1i pass adj] repel, drive off [3] (q v); not allow to approach. **O:** attack, aircraft; suitor, salesman; insect, pest; cold, depression □ *All the bombing attacks were* ***fought off*** *with heavy loss.* □ *He's been* ***fighting*** *Monica* ***off*** *for years but she'll catch him in the end.*

fight it out [B1ii] (informal) fight until a conclusion is reached. **S:** lawyers, accountants; troops, armies □ *Don't interfere in a matrimonial squabble — let husband and wife* ***fight it out*** *among themselves.* □ *Mixed groups of tanks and infantry* ***fought it out*** *with the enemy in sub-zero temperatures.*

figure in [A2 emph rel] appear as a character in; have a (prominent) part in. **o:** play, novel; account, report; list, programme; talks, negotiation □ *Many characters in Balzac's 'Human Comedy'* ***figure in*** *more than one novel or story.* □ ***In*** *the discussions leading to Britain's accession to the European Community Mr Rippon* ***figured*** *prominently.*

figure out [B1i pass] (informal) understand sth by thinking about it; work out [3] (q v); reckon, calculate. **O:** problem, snag, difficulty; it (all); cost, expenses □ *We can't* ***figure out*** *why he's been behaving so oddly.* □ *The cost of the operation will need to be* ***figured out*** *very precisely.*

file across, along, away etc [A1 emph A2 emph rel] go across etc in a single line □ *The men* ***filed across*** *a narrow foot bridge.* □ *The staff* ***filed into*** *the canteen for their mid-morning break.*

file away [B1i pass] put away in an (office) file. **S:** secretary, clerk. **O:** letter, circular; report, record □ *'Just* ***file*** *this correspondence* ***away*** *under 'Forecasts of Sales', will you, Miss Brown?'* □ *Heaven knows what the Ministry does with our production figures.* ***Files*** *them* ***away*** *somewhere, I suppose.*

fill in[1] [B1i pass] enter in writing, write in/into[1] (q v). **O:** particulars, details; name, occupation □ *There were many details to be* ***filled in*** *and a detailed plan to be drawn up.* MFM □ ***Fill in*** *your address at the bottom of the application form.*

fill in[2] [B1i pass adj] make a hole etc level with the surrounding surface by filling it. **O:** hole, trench, fireplace □ *If we* ***fill in*** *that old fireplace, we'll have a wall free for bookshelves.* □ *The ruts must be* ***filled in*** *so that traffic can pass.*

fill in time [B1iii] (informal) spend the interval between two stages in one's career in a temporary job □ *Girls who are not so much in demand often* ***fill in time*** *working in department stores and coffee bars.* H □ *She's not really interested in nursing — just* ***filling in time*** *until she gets married.*

fill in (on) [B1i pass B3 pass] (informal) give sb up-to-date information (on), bring up to date (q v) (on). **o:** latest exploit, recent move, future plan, actual situation □ *She always* ***fills*** *us* ***in on*** *what her programme is.* TGLY □ *As we drove off, I was* ***filled in on*** *the latest developments at the London office.*

fill in/out/up [B1i pass adj] complete sth in writing (by supplying the information required). **O:** form, application, tax-return □ *What's a doctor for? Not to sit all day* ***filling out*** *forms for the National Health.* AITC □ *We asked Mr Charlton if he had yet* ***filled up*** *the forms.* BFA □ *'I'm afraid your application for benefit is incorrectly* ***filled in****.'*

fill out[1] [A1] gain in weight; grow rounder or fatter. **S:** face, cheeks □ *He's* ***filled out*** *a lot with all the good food and regular exercise.*

fill out[2] [B1i pass adj] make fuller, more substantial (by adding material). **O:** story, account; treatment □ *The manuscript might be usable, the editor wrote, if the author could* ***fill*** *it* ***out*** *a little.* ARG □ *As a series of episodes, I find this book entertaining; it would be even more successful if the story-line were* ***filled out****.*

fill up[1] [A1 B1i pass] become, make, completely full. **S:** [A1] **O:** [B1] gutter, channel; reservoir; stadium, theatre □ *Following the heavy rains, the* *storage tanks were **filling up** again.* □ *All parts of the theatre were quickly **filling up**.* □ *'I've **filled up** all the buckets I can lay my hands on.'* □ *'Please **fill up** (the hall) from the front — the speaker's voice won't carry to the back.'*

fill up[2] [B1i nom pass] make completely full (esp with drink or fuel). **O:** glass, jug; (petrol-)tank □ (request to a barman to refill glasses) ***'Fill 'em up** again!'* □ (request to a garage attendant to fill one's tank) ***'Fill her up!'*** □ *'Stop at the next garage for a **fill-up**.'* □ *'Here's a glass that needs **filling up** (or: a **fill-up**).'*

find against [A2] (legal) find sb guilty in a court of law; decide against [1] (q v). **S:** court; magistrate, jury. **o:** plaintiff, defendant □ *We **find against** the defendant and order him to pay costs in the sum of £100.* ⇨ next entry.

find for [A2] (legal) reach a verdict in favour of; decide for/in favour of (q v). **S:** court, jury. **o:** plaintiff, defendant □ *When the case was retried, the jury **found for** the defendant.* ⇨ previous entry.

(not) find it in oneself/one's heart to do sth [B2] be unable (through kindheartedness or delicacy of feeling) to do sth. **O:** it... to criticize, to blame, to punish, to kill □ *I **cannot find it in myself to condemn** a mother who steals food for a hungry child.* □ *He nearly **found it in his heart to apologize**.* OMIH

find out[1] [A1 B1iii pass] learn by study, calculation, or inquiry. **O:** answer, cost, size; when we leave, whether to go; that the disease is curable, that resistance is futile □ *When you can't account for money, do you feel a need to **find out** what you have done with it?* WI □ *I know nothing about this job, but **finding out** will be enjoyable.* □ *It was **found out** that some evacuees progressed faster at school than children who had not left the home environment.*

find out[2] [A1 B1iii] discover a mistake, a loss, sb's dishonesty etc. **O:** where the money went, what has been happening, how the loss occurred □ *You'd better send on another fifty pounds to stop their **finding out**.* DC □ *One day someone will start asking questions and **find out** precisely why we've been losing so much money.*

one's sin(s) will find one out [B1ii] (formal or facetious) (one's) wrongdoing will be discovered □ *Mark my words: **his sins will find him out!*** □ ***Your sin will find you out.*** □ the latter is a text from the Bible.

find an answer/a solution (to) [B2 pass emph rel] be able to solve. **S:** science, technology; religion, philosophy; government, industry. **o:** question; riddle, puzzle; dilemma, quandary □ ***A solution** has not yet been **found to** the fundamental problems of industrial relations.* SC □ *These are questions **to** which we shall not **find** easy **answers**.*

find favour with [B2 emph rel] (formal) appear favourable to sb (and so be well received by him). **S:** petitioner, suitor; scheme, project; proposal, idea. **o:** king, court; committee, board; public, electorate □ *This was obviously a reasonable suggestion; it didn't, however, **find favour with** the men.* ARG

finish off [B1i pass] end rapidly; kill, destroy. **O:** discussion, dispute; victim, prey □ *I finally said we must **finish off** the war in Italy quickly.* MFM □ *This last unhappy warrior had been **finished off** by a cut on the head.* SD □ *That last climb nearly **finished** me **off**.*

finish off/up [B1i pass] eat or drink every bit or drop of □ *Old Smith came round for a chat and **finished off** the remains of my whisky.* □ *'Do **finish up** the fruit salad — it'll only go to waste if you don't'.*

finish off/up (with) [A1 A3 emph rel] end, conclude, a festive occasion, performance etc, by having or doing sth; end up (with) (q v). **o:** cigar, brandy, port; loyal toast, rousing speech, Old Lang Syne □ *The Male Voice Choir **finished off with** a rousing chorus (or: **finished off** by singing etc).* □ *We had Madeira and nuts to **finish up with**.*

finish with[1] [A2] end a relationship or connection with. **o:** girlfriend, husband; firm, business; academic life □ *I've **finished with** our grocer for good: that's the third time he's tried to give me short change.* □ *He's **finished with** gadding about — it's the quiet life for him now.*

finish with[2] [A2] finish using, consulting etc; have no further need of. **o:** newspaper, book □ *'Have you **finished with** our lawn-mower yet? We shall be needing it this weekend.'* □ *Scobie stood up. 'May I go, Sir, if these gentlemen have **finished with** me?'* HOM □ usu with perfect tenses.

finish with[3] [A2] finish chastising or punishing □ *'Before I've **finished with** you, you'll regret the day you were born!'* □ *'No, he can't go. I haven't **finished with** him yet!'* □ usu with perfect tenses.

fire ahead/away [A1] (informal) start questioning □ *'I want to ask you something.' 'Ask on', Pop said. '**Fire away**'.* BFA

fire off [B1i pass] expend, use up, esp by shooting. **O:** ammunition; magazine, belt (of cartridges); bullets, rockets; questions, curses □ *With this machine gun you could never **fire off** more than two magazines without a break. The barrel would get too hot, and would need to be changed or allowed to cool down.* □ *'Now then, ladies and gentlemen, if you've **fired off** all your questions I think we might let the speaker have a rest.'*

fish for [A2 pass adj] (informal) try to obtain (by indirect methods); angle for (q v). **o:** compliments, applause; story, information □ *Don't be taken in by his charm: he's **fishing for** an invitation to the big party.* □ *She was a vain but constantly sought-after young woman: the **fished-for** compliments were never slow in coming.*

fish out/out of [B1i pass B2 pass] (informal) extract, raise (from). **O:** coin, handkerchief; tin can, dead body. **o:** pocket, drawer; river, canal □ (stage direction) *Mrs Bryant leaves washing up to **fish out** some curtains.* R □ *Several derelict cars are **fished out of** the canal every month.*

fit in/into[1] [B1i pass B2 pass emph rel] find space or room for. **O:** table, bed; case, box. **o:** room, office; boot (of a car), chest, trunk □ *'I don't see how we can **fit in** any more chairs'.* □ *'Try to **fit** the record-player **into** the space beside the bookcase'.*

fit in/into[2] [B1i pass B2 pass emph rel] find a time for. **O:** patient, customer. **o:** programme, list (of appointments), schedule □ *'Sorry, I can't **fit in** any more callers this morning.'* □ *Mrs Smith will have to be **fitted in** next week.* □ ***Into***

*one hour on Monday afternoon I have to **fit** about five appointments.*

fit in (with) [A1 A3 rel] live in harmony (with one's companions), adjust well to one's surroundings. **S:** newcomer, immigrant. **o:** neighbour, native □ *How would they **fit in**, in this new land?* WI □ *The new boy **fitted in** well **with** his room-mates.*

fit in with [A3] match, suit, not clash (with). **S:** statement, claim; behaviour; arrangement, plan. **o:** facts, appearance, declared aim; yours □ *The answer disappoints you or doesn't appear to **fit in with** your temperament.* WI □ *At least my ideas work. Because they **fit in with** the way life's lived.* TGLY □ *Our holidays must be timed to **fit in with** yours.*

fit out [B1i pass adj] supply to sb or sth new equipment, stores, or clothes. **O:** ship, garrison; house; children, recruit □ *The 'Discoverer' is being **fitted out** for a new expedition to the Arctic.* □ *I went to a large clothes shop where they could **fit** you **out** for anything.* DIL □ a shop that fits people out with a wide range of clothes (complete outfits) is an outfitters.

fit up [B1i pass] install, mount. **O:** lamp, wash-basin, desk □ *There's room at the end of the garage to **fit up** a work-bench.* □ *The most up-to-date appliances have been **fitted up** in the new flats.*

fit up (with) [B1i pass B3 pass rel] give as equipment to sb; equip (with) (q v). **O:** patient, handicapped person; house, workshop. **o:** artificial limb, hearing aid; appliance, gadget □ *If you speak to your oculist he'll see that you're **fitted up with** new spectacles.* □ *He's had the new place **fitted up with** every labour-saving device.*

fix on/onto [B1i pass adj B2 pass emph rel] attach, fasten (to). **O:** button, clip; switch, dial. **o:** jacket, dress; radio, motor □ *I want the garage to **fix** a rev-counter **onto** the dashboard — a sports car should look sporty.* □ *'**Fix on** a new zip for me — the old one's broken'.*

fix on/upon [B2 pass emph rel] (formal) look intently at; gaze at (q v). **O:** ⚠ one's gaze; one's eyes, attention. **o:** scene, spectacle □ *Throughout the display his gaze was **fixed on** the horsemen in the foreground.* □ ***On** this golden prospect all his attention was now **fixed**.*

fix up [B1i pass] arrange, organize. **O:** meeting, talks; lunch; trip, tour □ *'I haven't done anything about my visit to Madrid yet.' 'Why not get a travel agent to **fix** it **up** for you?'* □ *'Try to **fix** me **up** an appointment for eleven tomorrow morning.'* □ the second example has an Indirect Object after the v.

fix up (with) [B1i pass B3 pass] (informal) arrange for sb to have. **O:** friend, relative; oneself. **o:** room, job, meal, girlfriend □ *He's **fixed** himself **up with** a very smart flat on the sea-front.* □ *'You can sleep here if you like.... Till you... get yourself **fixed up**.* TC

fix it/things up (with) [B1ii pass B3 pass] (informal) arrange the matter (often by getting sb to make special concessions) □ *'You won't go to gaol. I've **fixed it up**.'* AITC □ *They can leave school early today to play football. John's **fixed it up with** the Headmaster.*

fix with [B2] (formal) look intently at (esp in an unfriendly or hostile way). **o:** ⚠ a (cold, fishy) stare, an intent, angry) look; (terrifying) glare □ *Small boys should not burst into a master's study unannounced. The housemaster **fixed** Jenkins **with** a decidedly hostile look.*

fizzle out [A1] (informal) end in a feeble and unsatisfactory way. **S:** scheme, attack, argument, enthusiasm □ *His protest **fizzled out**.* NM □ *The first and only attempt to tax the British gambler **fizzled out**.* SC

flag down [B1i pass adj] stop by waving with a flag or the hand. **S:** traffic police, hitchhiker. **O:** passing car, taxi □ *A student hitchhiking to London **flagged** me **down** on the Great North Road.*

flake away/off [A1] separate, detach itself, in flakes. **S:** paint, stucco, pebbledash, rust □ *We scraped at the woodwork, and the paint just **flaked away**.*

flake out [A1] (slang) collapse from exhaustion; faint □ *After the guests had gone and the dishes were cleared away, we simply **flaked out** in a couple of armchairs.* □ *Some poor old dear had **flaked out** in the waiting-room.*

flare up [A1 nom] suddenly begin to burn more brightly or fiercely; burst into a sudden rage; reach a more violent state. **S:** fire, candle; boss, husband; fighting, battle □ *Robert looked as if he were about to **flare up** and tell me to mind my own business.* CON □ *The war will all **flare up** again and everyone says it will be much worse than before.* RFW □ *The Southern Area commander reported a sudden **flare-up** of fighting on his front.*

flash across [A1 A2 emph] cross (a surface etc) like a sudden, bright light. **S:** lightning, meteor, rocket; expression, smile. **o:** sky, horizon; face □ *A flight of aircraft **flashed** low **across** the field.* □ *A sudden smile of recognition **flashed across** his face.*

flash (at) [B2 emph rel] send a sudden bright look etc at sb. **O:** ⚠ a look, glance; a smile □ *Mother **flashed** a reassuring smile **at** the child.* □ *She **flashed** a discreet glance **at** the young man seated in the corner of the compartment* (or: *She **flashed** the young man in the corner a discreet glance.*

flashback [nom (A1)] (cinema) a return during a film either to events that have already been shown, or to events that occurred before the main action of the film began □ *The main action of the film portrayed the hero's adult life; scenes from his boyhood were shown in **flashback**.*

flash into [A2 emph] enter, like a sudden bright light. **S:** aeroplane, train; thought, idea; recollection. **o:** sight, view; sb's mind □ *A small, brilliantly coloured bird **flashed into** view.*

flash on [A1] be lit, with sudden brightness. **S:** light, illuminations □ *Someone pressed a switch and all the lights on the Christmas tree **flashed on** together.*

flash out [A1] appear like a sudden bright light; speak in a sudden outburst of passion. **S:** brilliance, radiance; anger, temper; he etc □ *She **flashed out** at Martin: 'Do you really believe that no one has any idea what's in the wind?'* NM □ *The sheer exuberance of the man **flashes out** even in what we would call a normal conversation.*

flecked with [pass (B2)] (be) marked with small patches of. **S:** sky; ground. **o:** small clouds; flowers, leaves □ *The grass underneath the trees* *was **flecked with** patches of sunlight.*

flick from/off [B2 pass] remove with a sharp tap or brushing movement of the finger(s). **O:** dust, fluff; fly, wasp; ash. **o:** sleeve; cheek; cigar □ *The waitress **flicked** the bread crumbs **from** the table cloth and brought plates and glasses.*

flick out [A1 B1i pass] (cause to) emerge, come forward, in a sudden, sharp, light movement. **S:** [A1] **O:** [B1] tongue, tail, paw □ *The lizard's tongue **flicked out** and trapped an insect.* □ *The cat **flicked out** a paw and drew the ball of wool towards it.*

flick through [A2 nom pass] (informal) scan a book etc, turning the pages with a quick movement of the thumb; thumb through (q v). **o:** magazine, review; (pile of) photographs, exam scripts □ *Patients in the waiting room idly **flicked through** magazines as they waited for their names to be called.* □ *'Have you read the report yet?' 'I've hardly had time to do more than **flick through** it* or: *give it a **flick(-)through**).'*

flicker out [A1] (of a naked light) gradually go out with small spurts of flame; (fig) be extinguished little by little. **S:** flame; match; candle, lamp; fighting, resistance □ *The candles **flickered out** one by one and the room was plunged in darkness.* □ *The flame of resistance never entirely **flickered out** in occupied Europe.*

flinch from [A2 pass emph rel] try to avoid (through fear, moral cowardice etc). **o:** truth; unpleasant task, responsibility □ *Don't **flinch from** the facts!* □ *It is an unpleasant decision to take, but it should not be **flinched from**.*

fling (at) [B2 pass emph rel] express (to sb) in a sudden, violent way. **O:** accusation, charge; taunt, jibe; insult, curse. **o:** prisoner, accused; servant, menial □ *Perhaps you should check your facts before **flinging** charges of corruption **at** half the Board of Directors.* □ *You'd think that all the criticism that had been **flung at** him might have dented his self-esteem — but nothing of the kind!*

fling one's head back [B1i pass] stand generally erect, with the head pressed back (from feelings of pride, arrogance etc) □ *'That story you told about your royal blood isn't true, is it?' Prissie **flung back her head** and seemed momentarily to gain height.* DC

fling down a challenge [B1iii pass] challenge dramatically. **S:** politician; boxer, promoter; newspaper □ *The Party has **flung down a challenge** to its political rivals to debate the issue on television.*

fling out/out of [A1 A2] leave in an angry and dramatic manner. **o:** room, meeting □ *Following an angry exchange with the Chairman, Jones gathered up his papers and **flung out of** the room.*

fling one's arms up in horror [B3] express surprise and shock (on hearing news) □ *Smith **flung his arms up*** (or: ***flung up his arms***) ***in horror** at the news that his son was living on the Riviera with a rich divorcee.*

flip over [A1 B1i pass] turn over with a sharp, sudden movement. **S:** [A1] **O:** [B1] plane, glider; screen; card. **S:** [B1] (gust of) wind, breeze; player □ *The plane stalled, **flipped over** onto its back and crashed near the perimeter fence.* □ *He **flipped over** the thin piece of pasteboard and read the address scribbled on the back.*

flip through [A2 nom pass] = flick through.

flirt (with) [A2 pass emph rel] (usu of a woman) talk, behave, in an attractive, enticing way, without intending a serious involvement; run risks. **o:** sb else's boyfriend; danger □ *Don't take her too seriously, she's only **flirting with** you.* □ *Deal gently with the poor boy — he's not used to being **flirted with**.*

flock in/into [A1 emph A2 emph rel] enter in a flock. **S:** audience, spectators; fans; students. **o:** theatre, cinema; stadium, ground; lecture-hall □ *Munich hotels were unable to cope with the huge numbers **flocking in** for the Olympic Games.* □ *Thousands of Scots **flocked into** Barcelona for the European Cup tie.*

flock together [A1] (esp of people with common interests or loyalties) gather, come together, in a crowd. **S:** scientists, teachers; trade unionists, (political) party members □ *Brighton was full of Conservative Party stalwarts, **flocking together** for their annual conference.* □ (proverb) *Birds of a feather **flock together**.*

flog to death [B2 pass] (informal) try to persuade sb of the worth or desirability of sth so persistently that he loses interest in it. **S:** advertiser, salesman; politician; inventor. **O:** product; scheme; idea □ *The need to 'export or perish' has been dinned into manufacturers so fervently that this worthy cause may have been **flogged to death**.*

flood in/into [A1 A2 emph rel] arrive in great quantities (at). **S:** letters, entries, applications, offers of help. **o:** office, bank, college □ *Donations have been **flooding in** since the appeal made for help over the radio* (or: *We have been **flooded with** donations* etc). □ *If oil pollution does eat into that £50 million **flooding into** Cornwall each year, everyone in the county will feel it in his pocket.* OBS

flood out [B1i pass adj] (of flood waters) force sb to leave his home. **O:** villager, farmer □ *Hundreds were **flooded out** when the canal burst its banks.* □ usu passive.

flood with [B2 pass emph rel] ⇨ flood in/into.

flop about/around [A1] make a dull, flapping sound as one moves about (usu because one is wearing loose shoes) □ *Grandmother **flopped around** comfortably in a pair of old carpet slippers.*

flop down [A1 emph] fall heavily or clumsily (e g through tiredness) □ *At the end of a working day all he feels like doing is **flopping down** in an armchair to watch television.*

flounder about/around [A1] move about clumsily (and often helplessly, as in mud); (fig) react in a clumsy, helpless way (as when faced with a difficult problem). **S:** walrus, seal; prisoner, accused □ *A heavy lorry was **floundering around** in thick mud at the entrance to the building site.* □ *The next question from counsel left the witness **floundering about** for an answer.*

flow across, along, away etc [A1 emph A2 emph rel] move across etc in a steady stream. **S:** water, oil, lava; pedestrians, traffic; reinforcements, supplies □ *Requests for blankets, tents and medical supplies are **flowing into** the offices of the relief organizations.* □ *Fresh material and drafts of infantry continued to **flow up** to the front.* B

flow from [A2 emph rel] follow logically from, result from (q v). **S:** improvement, benefit; wealth, prosperity; conclusion, result. **o:** change, decision; development; argument □ *This is an important technical innovation* ***from*** *which will* ***flow*** *many benefits to industry.* □ ***From*** *the court's decision these consequences must surely* ***flow.***

flow over [A2] (of noisy or disturbing events) take place all around sb without greatly affecting him; wash over (q v). **S:** noise, hubbub, din; tensions, jealousies; rebukes, reprimands □ *He doesn't allow himself to be excited by the children's squabbles. The bickering and fisticuffs simply* ***flow over*** *him.*

fluff out/up [B1i pass adj] shake into a soft mass like fluff. **S:** bird, animal; housewife, maid. **O:** feather, fur; pillow, cushion □ *Birds* ***fluff out*** *their feathers as a protection against the cold.* □ *A nurse smoothed out the sheets and* ***fluffed up*** *the pillows.*

flutter about [A1 A2] move here and there in a nervous, restless way. **S:** woman, girl □ *Our hostess* ***fluttered about****, taking quick nervous puffs at her cigarette.* □ *'Stop* ***fluttering about*** *the place. Sit down, and I'll buy you a drink.'*

flutter down [A1 emph] descend, come down, with sharp irregular flapping movements. **S:** bird, leaf, petal; letter, paper □ *Tons of ticker-tape* ***fluttered down*** *into Fifth Avenue from office windows.*

fly in the face of [A2] oppose sth which is customary, reasonable etc. **S:** he etc; action, step; decision. **o:** (***of***) tradition, custom; reason, logic; fact, evidence; unity, comradeship □ *Revolutionization of long distance road haulage would* ***fly in the face of*** *all commonsense.* SC □ *Being more hard-headed than Dr Heck, they will avoid attempting to* ***fly in the face of*** *international unity.* TES

fly in/into[1] [B1i pass B2 pass] cause to land (at an airfield). **S:** pilot, co-pilot. **O:** aircraft, plane, jet; passenger, cargo. **o:** London Airport; Madrid, Kano □ *The pilot* ***flew*** *the badly crippled bomber* ***in*** *on one engine.* □ *Tons of freight are* ***flown into*** *this airport every day.* ⇨ next entry.

fly in/into[2] [A1 A2] (of a pilot) cause to land; (of a passenger) arrive aboard an aircraft; (of an aircraft) come in to land. **S:** pilot; tourist, visitor; jet, cargo-plane. **o:** Rome □ *My partner has just* ***flown in*** *from London; we can begin discussions at once.* □ *Aircraft arriving later today will have to* ***fly into*** *Gatwick through heavy fog.* ⇨ previous entry.

fly into [A2] suddenly become very angry. **o:** ⚠ a (fit of) temper, rage, passion; an angry fit □ *The child* ***flew into*** *a rage and began scattering its toys about.* □ *He'll* ***fly into*** *a temper and tell me the contract for the murals is off.* CON

fly off the handle [A2] (informal) lose one's temper. **S:** wife, husband, school-teacher □ *She's always* ***flying off the handle*** *at the children.* □ *Don't* ***fly off the handle*** *every time you run up against a small problem.*

flyover [nom (A1)] bridge carrying one (main) road over another at an important junction □ ***Flyovers*** *or underpasses will be built wherever the motorway cuts across existing trunk-roads.*

fly past [A1 nom] fly in formation as part of a ceremonial parade (often over the route of the parade on the ground). **S:** fighter, bomber □ *The crowd looked up as a squadron of jet-fighters* ***flew past.*** □ *The ceremony ended with a* ***flypast*** *of new aircraft.* □ usu nom.

foam at the mouth[1] [A2] send out foam from the mouth (as during an epileptic fit). **S:** epileptic, rabid dog □ *A symptom of rabies is* ***foaming at the mouth.***

foam at the mouth[2] [A2] (informal) show extreme anger (without literally foaming at the mouth) □ *When Smith was told that children had been trampling on his prize vegetables, he practically* ***foamed at the mouth.***

fob off onto [B3 pass] trick or deceive into buying or accepting; palm off (on) (q v). **S:** dishonest trader, door-to-door salesman, confidence trickster. **O:** inferior goods, shoddy article. **o:** gullible customer, innocent shopper □ *Unscrupulous firms are* ***fobbing*** *these goods* ***off onto*** *the unsuspecting housewife.* □ *Last year's model was* ***fobbed off onto*** *us.* ⇨ next entry.

fob off (with) [B1ii pass B3 emph rel] trick or deceive into buying or accepting; stop sb achieving his aim or purpose by trickery or delaying tactics; palm off (with) (q v). **S:** dishonest trader, confidence trickster. **O:** gullible customer. **o:** inferior goods; half-truth, yarn, tale □ *We were entitled to be treated as equals and we would not be* ***fobbed off with*** *Skybolt.* T □ *Let me make my point, and I am not to be* ***fobbed off*** *this time.* TBC □ *He might* ***fob*** *Madame La Botte* ***off with*** *50 francs, if he happened to be in the mood.* US ⇨ previous entry.

focus (on) [A2 emph rel B2 pass emph rel] think of one thing to the exclusion of others; concentrate (on/upon) q v). **O:** ⚠ (one's) attention, thoughts; one's mind; one's efforts, energies. **o:** problem; question, matter; speaker, lecturer; process □ *He finds it hard to* ***focus*** *his thoughts* ***on*** *one thing for longer than five minutes.* □ *Public attention at the moment is* ***focused on*** *the problems of industrial relations.*

foist (off) on [B2 pass emph rel B3 pass emph rel] trick or deceive into buying or accepting; pass an unpleasant responsibility on to. **S:** dishonest trader etc; superior. **O:** inferior goods etc; problems, difficulties. **o:** gullible customer etc; subordinate □ *He* ***foisted off*** *a few cases of inferior scotch* ***on*** *a too eager customer.* □ *I'm sorry all this has been* ***foisted on*** *you.* EHOW ⇨ fob off onto.

fold back [B1i pass adj] turn one (part of a) thing back over itself. **O:** page, sheet (of paper); canopy, hood (of a vehicle); cover, sheet (on a bed) □ *They drove in bright sunshine, with the hood of the car* ***folded back.***

fold in/into [B1i pass B2 pass emph rel] (cooking) mix with (existing ingredients). **S:** chef, cook. **O:** eggs, sugar. **o:** flour, mixture □ (recipe) *Then* ***fold in*** *the rest of the sugar and flavouring.*

fold up[1] [B1i pass adj] make a neat (and perhaps portable) package etc of sth by turning parts of it back upon themselves. **O:** newspaper; sheet, tablecloth; deck-chair, camp bed, tent □ *The table linen was neatly* ***folded up*** *and put away.* □ *'Would you* ***fold up*** *the garden chairs and put them in the conservatory?'*

fold up[2] [A1] (informal) collapse with mirth or pain. **S:** audience, spectator; boxer, patient □

From the moment he appeared on stage, the audience ***folded up*** *in their seats.* □ *He jabbed me just once in the solar plexus and I* ***folded up****.*

fold up[3] [A1] (informal) suffer moral or spiritual collapse; finish trading. **S:** country, enemy, industry, □ *They felt that if she didn't* ***fold up*** *when her boy died, she wouldn't* ***fold up*** *when the balloon went up* (= when war began). RFW □ *Several national newspapers have* ***folded up*** *in the past ten years.*

follow in sb's footsteps [A2] continue a tradition or process established by a predecessor; adopt the same trade or profession as one's father □ *We shall not recount the many experiments carried out by Rhine and by others who have* ***followed in his footsteps*** *over the years.* SNP □ *One of my passes was in Maths, so my old lady decided that I should* ***follow in*** *my poor* ***father's footsteps****.* JFTR

follow on [A1 nom] (cricket) (of the second side to bat in a match) bat again, having failed in the first innings to come close enough to one's opponent's score □ *Australia were all out for 120 in their first innings and had to* ***follow on****.* □ *He defended his decision not to enforce the* ***follow-on*** *against India at Edgbaston.* G

follow through[1] [B1ii pass] continue doing sth until a conclusion is reached. **S:** thinker, scientist; designer, builder. **O:** argument, experiment; project, development □ *'Don't keep breaking off. I'd like to hear you* ***follow*** *the argument* ***through*** *to a conclusion.'* □ *He takes several schemes in hand, but lacks the persistence to* ***follow*** *them* ***through****.*

follow through[2] [A1 nom] (sport) continue a stroke to the full extent of one's arm after hitting the ball. **S:** batsman, tennis player, golfer □ *To hit the ball clean and hard you must develop a smooth* ***follow-through****.*

follow up[1] [B1i nom pass adj] continue, develop, by doing sth better or more ambitious; extend, exploit. **O:** process, series; campaign; achievement, success, victory □ *This production team have had one successful television series; how will they* ***follow*** *it* ***up*** (or: *what will they do for a* ***follow-up****)?* □ *Don't rest on your laurels:* ***follow up*** *your success and start looking for new markets now.*

follow up[2] [B1i pass] investigate closely; follow where something leads. **O:** story, rumour; lead, clue □ *I decided to* ***follow up*** *one or two hints that had been dropped at her cocktail party.* □ *The night editor decides which of the stories that are phoned in should be* ***followed up****.*

fool about/around [A1] behave in a casual and silly way; play about/around (with) (q v). **A:** with a revolver, in a sports car, on a golf course □ *He should know that you don't* ***fool around*** *on a rifle range.* □ *'What the blazes are you* ***fooling about*** *at, Joe?'* CON □ *Everyone knows he's been* ***fooling around*** *with some girl at the office.*

forbear (from) [A2 emph rel] (formal) not begin to do, stop doing, sth (esp sth which offends or irritates others); refrain (from) (q v). **o:** interference (in sth), over-attention (to sth), indulgence (in sth); comment, criticism; being drawn in, giving an opinion □ *This was a warning to* ***forbear from*** *being too deeply involved in the company's affairs.*

force down sb's throat [B2 pass] (informal) compel an unwilling listener etc to accept sth; ram/stuff down sb's throat (q v). **S:** regime, (political) party; radio, TV; advertiser, public relations man. **O:** dogma, doctrine; slogan, catchphrase; product, merchandise □ *We would have to walk delicately and not* ***force*** *our ways* ***down the throats of*** *all and sundry.* MFM □ *You're not obliged to sit in front of a television set and have that rubbish* ***forced down your throat****.*

force on/upon [B2 pass] compel to accept. **S:** shopkeeper, salesman; victorious power, strong neighbour. **O:** goods; terms, conditions; war. **o:** housewife; small country □ *This country didn't want the war. It was* ***forced upon*** *us by powers that needed our coal and iron.* □ *Madge had* ***forced*** *a crisis* ***on*** *me.* UTN

force up [B1i pass adj] cause to rise (by applying strong pressure). **S:** shortage; bad harvest; strike; wage increase. **O:** price, cost □ *Increasing the wages of the bus crews will* ***force up*** *fares.* □ *The gloomiest forecast was that Britain's entry into Europe would* ***force*** *the cost of living* ***up*** *very considerably.*

foredoomed to failure [pass (B2)] (be) destined to fail before it starts. **S:** scheme, development, venture □ *Since the bigger firms were not prepared to give it their backing, the project was* ***foredoomed to failure****.*

forget about [A2] lose remembrance of; fail to keep in the memory; not think further about, dismiss (from one's mind/thoughts) (q v). **o:** the past; experience, event; visit, arrangement, appointment; (unpleasant) experience, (nasty) shock □ *Helping his son with his physics homework reminded him of things he'd long* ***forgotten about****.* □ *'Thanks for reminding me — you know, I'd* ***forgotten*** *all* ***about*** *him coming this afternoon.'* □ *'Don't worry,' she said soothingly, 'just go away and* ***forget about*** *all this.'* DC

fork out [A1 B1iii pass] (informal) pay, usu unwillingly. **S:** public, tax-payer. **O:** cash, money □ *'That will be another half-crown.' Brownsworth* ***forked out****.* RM □ *It would be laughable if we weren't always having to* ***fork out*** *money for the police which ought to be spent on roads.* RM

form from [B2 pass emph rel] make a whole from parts; (passive) have as its components. **O:** rock, stone; cloud; lake, sea; company, association. **o:** liquid; drop, particle; pool; (smaller) unit □ *These substances are* ***formed from*** *a mixture of liquids solidifying under great pressure.* □ *There is a proposal to* ***form*** *a new political party* ***from*** *those breaking away from the major groups.* ⇨ next entry.

form into [A2 rel B2 pass rel] assemble to make a group etc. **S:** [A2] **O:** [B2] followers, young people. **o:** committee, club, brotherhood; company, brigade □ *The children were* ***formed into*** *small groups, which went from door to door collecting money and old clothes.* □ *On the word of command, the company* ***formed*** *smartly* ***into*** *three ranks.* ⇨ previous entry.

form (a) part of [B2 emph rel] be a part of, an element in. **S:** episode, incident; chapter, section; limb, organ; company, regiment. **o:** story, film; book, article; trunk, abdomen; army □ *There is discussion over whether the new Department should* ***form part of*** *the Faculty of Arts.* □ *There is a complex rehousing plan* ***of***

*which this development **forms** only **a** small **part**.*

form up [A1 B1i pass] (military) (cause to) assume parade order or formation. **S:** [A1] **O:** [B1] troops, company, battalion; vehicles. **S:** [B1] officer, sergeant □ *The battalion **formed up** by companies on the barrack square.* □ *The troops had been **formed up** in review order.*

fortify (against) [B2 pass emph rel] make stronger, more resistant (against). **O:** town, position, emplacement; oneself. **o:** attack, invasion; cold, flu □ *The forward positions were strongly **fortified against** artillery bombardment.* □ *There were more difficult times ahead, **against** which his natural resources would do little to **fortify** him.*

foul up [B1i nom pass adj] (informal) spoil, mess up (q v); make unpleasant, sour. **O:** things; arrangements, organization; relationship, marriage □ *When everything is running smoothly, why must he step in and **foul** things **up**?* □ *His easy-going ways with other women have **fouled up** a good working partnership.* □ *We'll finish the building on time provided there are no **foul-ups** in supplying materials.*

frame up [B1i nom pass adj] (informal) arrange (by falsifying evidence, corrupting witnesses etc) to make an innocent person appear guilty. **S:** enemy, rival; police, official □ *It's hard to **frame** you **up**.* BBCTV □ *In most cases in which a person is **framed up** by the police, the victim is too surprised, or ignorant, to help himself.* BBCTV □ *We have been expecting a **frame-up** for a long time. But this time we have got witnesses.* G

freak out [A1 nom] (slang) move into a heightened or depressed state of mind (esp now, after taking drugs); behave in a lively, fanciful or abandoned way (e g during a party or celebration) □ *He took a lot of acid* (LSD) *and really **freaked out**.* □ *John's party last weekend was wild — a real **freak-out**.*

free from [B2 pass emph rel] make free, independent, of. **O:** oneself; country, people; client; patient. **o:** slavery, dependence; obligation, undertaking; anxiety □ *A local authority grant **freed** John **from** financial dependence on his parents.* □ *Are we **freed from** anxieties about the future by taking out another insurance policy?*

freeze off [B1i nom pass] (informal) keep at a distance by being too unfriendly or remote; drive away **O:** suitor, visitor, customer □ *If this were all, outsiders could hardly succeed with working-class people; they would be likely to impress them but also to **freeze** them **off**.* UL □ *Before he had got half-way through his sentence she was giving him the Siberian **freeze-off**, a routine she must have known all about.* CON

freeze out [B1i pass] (informal) prevent from doing business by boycotting goods etc; exclude from society by unfriendly behaviour. **S:** rival, competitor; neighbour, club member □ *Some of the smaller traders are being **frozen out** by the big combines.*

freeze over [A1] become covered with ice. **S:** lake, river, sea □ *During the severe winter of 1947 even the sea **froze over**.* ⇨ frozen over.

freeze to death [A2] die through exposure to extreme cold. **S:** men, livestock □ *Flocks and herds were cut off by deep snowdrifts and **froze to death** in the open.*

freeze-up [nom (A1)] period of extreme cold, with ice and snow □ *During last year's **freeze-up**, traffic was brought to a halt along the full length of the motorway.* □ *I must do something about protecting the water-pipes in case we have another bad **freeze-up**.*

freshen up [A1 nom] (informal) wash, shave etc, so as to feel fresh after a journey etc □ *I shall have time for a quick **freshen-up** at the hotel before the meeting begins.*

frighten away/off [B1i pass] frighten, thus causing to stay away or go away. **S:** dog, guard; loud noise. **O:** intruder, thief; stranger □ *Of course the job won't **frighten** her **away**. She likes babies, otherwise she wouldn't be here.* DC □ *The sound of us moving about upstairs must have **frightened** the burglar **off**.*

frighten into [B2 pass] cause sb to do sth by means of threats, terrorization. **O:** population; child; victim. **o:** submission, obedience; stealing; handing over his money □ *The villagers were **frightened into** surrendering nearly all their grain by the drunken soldiers.* □ *The older boys **frightened** the younger ones **into** stealing money from their mothers' purses.*

frighten to death [B2 pass] frighten very severely. **S:** crowd, traffic; air travel; animal, bird □ *The baby monkeys would get stricken with all sorts of complaints and **frighten** us **to death**.* BB □ *His wife is **frightened to death** on the few occasions when she has to travel by air.*

fritter away [B1i pass] (informal) waste money etc by spending it in a number of separate and unimportant ventures. **O:** money, time, energies □ *I do hope that all you've got to give the world won't be **frittered away** in side-tracks and bypaths.* HAA □ *I didn't want us to **fritter** it **away** on things we don't really need.* AITC

frost over [A1] become covered with frost. **S:** window(-pane), gate, pavement □ *The windows had **frosted over** in the night; Mary breathed on them and scraped with her finger nails.* ⇨ next entry.

frosted over [pass adj (B1)] (be) covered with frost. **S:** window, glass □ *After the severe cold of last night, the windows were **frosted over**.* ⇨ previous entry.

frozen over [pass adj (B1)] (be) covered with ice. **S:** pond, lake, river □ *Farmers broke the ice on the drinking troughs that were **frozen over**.* □ *Even heavy lorries could cross the **frozen-over** rivers.* ⇨ freeze over.

fuck about/around[1] [A1] (taboo) behave in a foolish or irresponsible way; bugger about/around[1] (q v) □ *'When's he going to stop **fucking about** and do an honest day's work?'* □ *'Is it you that's been **fucking around** with my camera?'*

fuck about/around[2] [B1ii pass] (taboo) treat sb in a foolish or thoughtless way; behave as though one has a poor estimate of sb's worth etc; bugger about/around[2] (q v). **S:** boss, sergeant, teacher □ *'Now don't **fuck** me **about**. I came here looking for proper service, not to be palmed off with dud equipment.'* □ *'Don't **fuck** me **around**, Harry. Give me the money and let's get out of here.'*

fuck off [A1] (taboo) leave, go away; bugger off (q v) □ *'If he comes here bothering you, tell him to **fuck off**.'* □ *'We wanted to have a word with Geoff, but he'd **fucked off** home.'*

fuck up [B1i nom pass] (taboo) mismanage, spoil, ruin; bugger up (q v). **O:** things, the whole works; engine, suspension; scheme, project □ *He said he didn't want his motor* ***fucked up*** *by some kid with oil on his hands.* □ *'The meeting was a complete* ***fuck-up*** *from start to finish.'*

fulminate (against) [A2 emph rel] (formal) criticize, condemn, fiercely; thunder against (q v). **o:** luxury, idleness, vice □ *From every pulpit, clergymen* ***fulminate against*** *sin.*

fume (at) [A2 rel] show irritation (without fully expressing it) in response to sth. **S:** motorist; shopper, consumer. **o:** delay, hold-up; incompetence, rudeness □ *We* ***fumed at*** *the casualness of waitresses who could keep us waiting for half-an-hour and then serve half-cold soup.*

fur up [A1] become coated with a white crust (the result of e g boiling water which contains lime). **S:** kettle, saucepan □ *In areas where the water is 'hard' pots and kettles quickly* ***fur up.***

furnish (to) [B2 pass emph rel] give, hand, to sb for his use or exploitation; supply (to) (q v). **O:** supplies, stocks; equipment; excuse, pretext, justification. **o:** customer; store, factory; rival, opponent □ *The firm won a contract for* ***furnishing*** *boots* ***to*** *the army* (or: ***furnishing*** *the army* ***with*** *boots*). □ *Don't go out of your way to* ***furnish*** *opportunities* ***to*** *your rivals* (or: ***furnish*** *them* ***with*** *opportunities*). □ sentences like: *They were well* ***furnished with*** *the basic necessities* have no corresponding passive using furnish to.

furnish with [B2 pass emph rel] ⇨ previous entry.

fuss about[1] [A1] (informal) move about, behave, in a nervous, excited way □ *'Stop* ***fussing about****: the taxi will arrive on time, and we shan't miss the train.'*

fuss about[2] [B1ii pass] (informal) unsettle, irritate sb by giving too much attention to him. **S:** wife, mother; teacher □ *She does* ***fuss*** *the children* ***about*** *so* (or: *She does* ***fuss over*** *the children so*) *— making sure they're well wrapped up, and worrying about minor illnesses.*

fuss over [A2 pass] ⇨ previous entry.

G

gabble away [A1] (informal) talk rapidly and possibly indistinctly, insensitive to the reactions of bystanders or listeners □ *The two women* ***gabbled away*** *twenty to the dozen while the waitress noisily cleared the table — cloth and all.*

gad about [A1 nom] (informal) go from place to place, usu for pleasure; gallivant about (q v) □ *The way Tom* ***gads about****, I can't see how he will ever pass his finals.* □ *Unless one exercises some self-control, it is only too easy to become a* ***gadabout*** *— going from one party to another, from one friend's house to another, and never doing anything useful.*

gain in[1] [A2] become heavier, taller etc. **S:** child; company, firm; army. **o:** weight, size, girth; height; strength, power □ *You seem to have* ***gained*** *a lot* ***in*** *weight since I last saw you.* □ *The army has* ***gained*** *greatly* ***in*** *striking power with the acquisition of five hundred of the latest tanks.*

gain in[2] [A2] acquire more of a particular moral or intellectual quality; grow in (q v). **S:** parent; manager; politician. **o:** experience; knowledge, wisdom, understanding; cunning, astuteness; (moral) stature, authority □ *Alfred is a person who never seems to* ***gain in*** *wisdom, no matter how painful the results of his actions may be.* □ *The Leader of the Opposition* ***gained*** *significantly* ***in*** *stature as a result of his speech on Northern Ireland.*

gain on[1] [A2] draw closer to sb or sth pursued. **S:** our car, ship; runner; Labour; police. **o:** the car, the ship, ahead; leaders in the race; the Conservatives; thieves □ *The police-launch was* ***gaining on*** *the boat when suddenly a shot was fired from it. Then the police were sure that they were after the right man.*

gain on[2] [A2] move further ahead of sb or sth. **S:** car, ship; runner; Labour. **o:** others; the enemy; the rest of the field; the Conservatives □ *The leading group of three continued to* ***gain on*** *the rest of the runners and were soon half a mile clear of them.*

gain on/upon [A2] (formal) consume part of, erode. **S:** sea, river, floods. **o:** land, cliffs, bank □ *Year by year the ocean* ***gained upon*** *the shore, and finally took toll of the houses that had once been the pride of the town.*

gallivant about [A1] (informal) go from place to place, usu for pleasure; gad about (q v) □ *Coffee-parties in the morning, theatre in the evening, car-rides every day — if she spent more time looking after her family and less time* ***gallivanting about****, everyone would be a lot happier.*

galvanize into action/activity [B2 pass] cause to act instantly □ *A shot rang out and* ***galvanized*** *the patrol* ***into action****. They rushed for cover and began to move in the direction from which the firing had come.*

gamble away [B1i pass] lose by gambling. **O:** fortune, inheritance; week's wages □ *Having* ***gambled away*** *half his salary at cards and spent the rest on drink, Bottomley had to borrow from his friends to pay the rent and buy some food.* □ *Many a family fortune has been* ***gambled away*** *on the Stock Exchange.*

gamble on [A2 B2 pass] make bets on; make plans in the hope that certain unpredictable things will happen that will assist their fulfilment. **O:** money, savings; everything, one's future. **o:** horses, dogs, the Stock Exchange; the outcome; the occupants of the house being asleep, the weather being favourable, the train being on time □ *Only a fool would* ***gamble*** *his life's savings* ***on*** *the Stock Exchange in the hope of making easy money.* □ *'I wouldn't* ***gamble on*** *James's footing the bill, if I were you.'* □ *'We must allow plenty of time to get to the airport — we can't* ***gamble on*** *the road being clear.'*

gang up against/on [A3 pass] (informal) organize or form groups, alliances, against □ *It isn't pleasant to see a lot of young men* ***ganging up against*** *their distinguished, if aging, seniors.* □ *The spokesman said that Australia, Canada* *and New Zealand would not* ***gang up against*** *Britain's joining the Common Market.* BBCTV □ *If ever the two boys tried to tease their sister, all her friends used to* ***gang up on*** *them.*

gape (at) [A2 pass rel] look open-mouthed (at); goggle (at) (q v) □ *'Don't just stand there* ***gaping at*** *the poor man, help him to his feet!'* □ *The villagers were so astonished at the appearance of a Rolls Royce in their midst that they could only* ***gape at*** *it.* □ also gawk (at), gawp (at).

garner up [B1i pass] (formal) harvest and store; gather in (q v). **O:** crop, grain □ *When the potatoes had been* ***garnered up****, the ground was ploughed over for sowing.*

garnish with [B2 pass] add as a trimming to food, decorate with. **O:** dish; roast chicken, lamb, sole meunière □ *The salmon was brought to the table whole, and was* ***garnished with*** *parsley and slices of tomato and cucumber.*

gasp (at) [A2 pass rel] show great surprise, horror etc, by a sudden involuntary release of one's breath. **o:** news; his nerve; risk; the intensity of the bombing, the pictures of the starving people □ *When theatre audiences first saw 'Oh Calcutta!' they* ***gasped at*** *the audacity of some of the scenes.* □ *People have seen so many horrible things on television that scenes they would have* ***gasped at*** *ten years ago they now view with apparent indifference.*

gasp for breath [A2] have great difficulty in breathing; be very surprised by sb's remarks, behaviour etc □ *The low punch made him* ***gasp for breath****.* □ *The sheer insensitivity of his remarks leaves one* ***gasping for breath****.*

gasp out [B1i pass] say, while struggling for breath. **O:** message, warning, last request □ *The dying man* ***gasped out*** *a few incomprehensible words and then collapsed in his wife's arms.*

gather (from) [B2 pass emph rel] learn, understand (by or from). **O:** nothing, very little; how much, what; that he means to attend. **o:** remark, statement □ *Did you* ***gather from*** *what the man said that he intended to make a bid for the house or not?* □ ***From*** *what John said I* ***gather*** *he'll be giving up his job in the summer.*

gather in [B1i pass] harvest, collect a crop; garner up (q v). **O:** crop; oats, barley □ *There was a week of rain which ruined the wheat crop before it could be safely* ***gathered in****.*

gather round[1] [A1 A2 emph rel B1i pass B2 pass emph rel] (cause to) assemble round. **S:** [A1 A2] **O:** [B1 B2] crowd, group, spectators. **o:** accident; entrance to the palace, newly-arrived ship □ [B2] *The barker managed to* ***gather*** *a small group of curious passers-by* ***round*** *the platform.* □ [A1] ***'Gather round****, folks, and see some of the biggest bargains you ever set your eyes on!'*

gather round[2] [A1 A2] come to sb's side and give him moral, physical or material support. **S:** the family; friends, comrades, companions; Masons, Rotarians □ *As soon as one of their number was threatened by the law, the Mafia closed ranks and* ***gathered round*** *him.* □ *'A man ought to be given a chance to be born at home, and he certainly ought to have a chance to die there. The family* ***gathers round****, you know, and it's only right he should feel the event is something of an occasion.'* DIL

gathered to one's fathers [pass (B2)] (euphemism) die □ *I write to tell you that my dear old friend Jonathan, who suffered so uncomplainingly for so many years, has at last been* ***gathered to his fathers****.* □ usu with *has/have been.*

gather together [B1i pass] collect, assemble. **O:** tools, books, toys; things □ *'Please tell the children to* ***gather*** *all their games* ***together*** *so that we can take our visitors into the lounge for a cup of tea.'*

gawk/gawp (at) [A2 pass rel] = gape (at).

gaze around/round [A1 A2] look round in surprise, amazement etc □ *Unable to believe his good fortune, he* ***gazed round*** *at the gifts that his friends had showered upon him.*

gaze at [A2 pass rel] look at, in a steady, concentrated way □ *When we found Joe, he was sitting on a rock,* ***gazing at*** *the sea.* □ *She dropped the sheet of paper as if she had been stung. She* ***gazed at*** *it in complete horror, as if it were some horrible insect.* DC

gaze on/upon [A2 pass rel] (formal) let one's eyes remain on. **o:** such beauty, perfection; such a sight, view, prospect □ *Never in his life had he* ***gazed upon*** *such splendour. The haughty ladies of his provincial home-town were like washerwomen besides these eastern beauties in their splendid palaces.*

gaze round [A1 A2] ⇨ gaze around/round.

gear down [A1 B1i pass] change into a lower gear in order to lose speed, or to increase speed effectively, or to keep better control of a car or machine; reduce in force or intensity. **O:** machine; activity, production, output □ *He* ***geared down*** *as he came into the corner, but was already accelerating before he came out of it.* □ *The dosage was* ***geared down*** *to a level which would work on the infected cells but not upset their normal metabolism.* □ in the first example change down (q v) is more common.

gear up [A1 B1i pass] increase in operational efficiency. **S:** [A1] **O:** [B1] industry, economy; administration; army □ *The party organization is ready to be* ***geared up*** *to the election, whenever it takes place.* □ *The Department is* ***gearing up*** *for an increased intake of students.*

gee up [A1] an order traditionally used (or thought by others to be used) by a person to a horse = move faster!, start moving! □ ***'Gee up*** *there, Neddy,' shouted the little boy, and Tom obediently set off at a smart trot with the child clinging to his neck.*

gen up (about/on) [A1 A3 B1i pass B3 pass] (informal) learn or teach (about), obtain or give sb the essential facts (about) □ [A3] *To my surprise, the visitors had* ***genned up about*** *the project very thoroughly and there was little I could tell them that they didn't already know.* □ [B3] *I went in to see MacGilvery, and he was all* ***genned up about*** *my genius and how Braithwaite was going to turn my book into a best-seller.* JFTR □ [B3] *One of the second-form children had* ***genned*** *his older brother* ***up on*** *where the headmaster kept his cane, and during prayers he had nipped into the headmaster's study and stolen it.* □ probably derived from 'obtain or give general information about, on'.

get about[1] [A1] move from place to place, often with the implication of overcoming difficulty to do so □ *Considering his age, the old man* ***gets***

about *a great deal.* □ *Now that the traffic has been restricted in the centre of the city, it's easier to* ***get about.*** □ *My father isn't able to* ***get about*** *since he had his stroke last year.*

get about[2] [A1] circulate, spread; get abroad (q v). **S:** news, rumour, story; it □ *It* ***got about*** *that the British Centre was recruiting more teachers.* □ *I don't know how such a rumour* ***got about.*** *There's absolutely no truth in it.* ⇨ go about[2], put about[2].

get above oneself [A2] have too high an opinion of oneself, have ideas above one's station □ *That young man is* ***getting above himself.*** *He's only been in the firm two weeks and he's already telling his seniors how to do their work.*

get abreast of [A3 B3] draw or bring level with. **S:** [A3] **o:** [B3] ship, boat; latest thinking, discoveries □ *As soon as the lifeboat* ***got abreast of*** *the foundering ship, the captain got a line aboard her and started to take the crew off.* □ *It did not take China long to* ***get abreast of*** *Russian and American technology in guided missiles.* ⇨ be abreast of.

get abroad [A1] spread, circulate; get about[2] (q v). **S:** news, rumour, report □ *The news* ***got abroad*** *that the Chancellor had decided to make cuts in the VAT on some goods.*

get across[1] [A1 A2 B1ii pass B2 pass] (cause, help, to) cross, usu implying some difficulty or obstacle. **o:** bridge, river, street; border, frontier □ [A2] *Only half the company* ***got across*** *the bridge before it was blown up.* □ [B2] *The young officer was congratulated for* ***getting*** *all his men* ***across*** *the river.* □ [A1] *The frontier is so well guarded that no one can* ***get across.*** ⇨ go/send/take across (to).

get across[2] [A2] (informal) annoy, offend, irritate; form a bad relationship with; get on the wrong side of (q v) □ *Those two men are so different in temperament that they were bound to* ***get across*** *each other.* □ *Be careful how you talk to Mr Swann. He's an unpleasant man to* ***get across.***

get across (to) [A1 A3 B1ii pass B3 pass] communicate, transmit, make clear (to); get over (to) (q v). **S:** [A1 A3] **O:** [B1 B3] message, joke, information □ [B1] *So if this Cloud contains separate individuals, the individuals must be able to communicate on a vastly more detailed scale than we can. What we can* ***get across*** *in an hour of talk they might* ***get across*** *in a hundredth of a second.* TBC □ [B3] *The comedian didn't seem to be able to* ***get*** *his jokes* ***across to*** *his audience — they all fell flat!* □ [A3] *The class was so stupid that it seemed impossible to* ***get across to*** *them by mere language.* ⇨ come across[2], put across[1].

get ahead/ahead of [A1 A2] progress (beyond) □ *As soon as he settled down to the routine of his new job, Alex* ***got ahead*** *splendidly.* □ *By doing just a little extra homework each day, the girl* ***got*** *well* ***ahead of*** *the rest of the class.* ⇨ be ahead/ahead of.

get along [A1] succeed in doing sth; manage; get by[3] (q v). □ *'How are you managing to do your work without an assistant?' 'Oh, I* ***get along*** *somehow.'* □ *John's* ***getting along*** *in France better than he expected, considering he could hardly speak a word of French when he arrived.*

get along/away with you! [A3] an exclamation of mild rebuke or disbelief; go along with you! (q v) □ *'I'm going to see 'West of Suez' with Arthur this evening.'* ***'Get along with you!*** *Arthur wouldn't be seen dead at a play by Osborne!'* ⇨ get on![5], go on![14].

get along/on (with)[1] [A1 A3] make progress (with a task etc). **o:** work, studies; German; new novel, painting □ *'How is Tim* ***getting along with*** *the old car he bought? Has he got it into working order yet?'* □ *I'm not* ***getting on*** *very fast* ***with*** *this pile of marking.* ⇨ come along/on[2], bring along/on[1].

get along/on (with)[2] [A1 A3 rel] have a harmonious relationship (with); live or work together (well etc). **S:** child, schoolboy, employee. **o:** parents, classmates, colleagues. **A:** (not) very well; splendidly, badly; like a house on fire; like nobody's business, like one o'clock □ *My mother and I don't always* ***get on*** *very well, but I believe in the saying, 'Home is where the heart is.'* H □ *In my view, the fact that Bevin and Morrison never* ***got on*** *was due to Ernie's* (= Bevin's) *distrust of Herbert as 'a slick wire-puller'.* OBS □ *You two have so much in common that you should* ***get along*** *like a house on fire.* □ *If only 'them' and 'us' had the same ideas we'd* ***get on*** *like a house on fire, but they don't see eye to eye with us and we don't see eye to eye with them, so that's how it stands and how it will always stand.* LLDR □ (reading from a letter:) *'We're* ***getting on*** *like a house on fire.' How peculiar, she thought, similes are: why should* ***getting on*** *like a house on fire mean that everything was going well? And again, 'The children are* ***getting on*** *like one o'clock, especially Janice.'* PW □ *Her mother was quiet and good-natured — the easiest person in the world to* ***get along with.*** □ *She* ***got on*** *well* ***with*** *Aunt Ellen* (or: *She and Aunt Ellen* ***got on*** *well*)*, but found her rather a sick woman with mysterious internal pains.* RFW

get along without [A3] succeed reasonably well, manage to live or work, without sth or sb. **o:** (any) help, assistance; apparatus, equipment, spare parts; (regular) water supply; friends, other people □ *I don't know how Mrs Briggs* ***gets along without*** *domestic help in that large house.* □ *I have to* ***get along without*** *even proper equipment and work in a damned shack like this.* HD

get around/round[1] [A2 pass] (informal) gain the confidence, trust, favour of sb, usually for a special purpose □ *The girl told her boyfriend that she would try and* ***get round*** *her father to lend them the car for the day.* □ *'You seem to have* ***got round*** *Mrs Williams all right. Tea in bed every morning! It's unheard-of.'*

get around/round[2] [A2] tackle successfully, overcome. **o:** problem, obstacle, difficulty; incompatibility (of two things) □ *When the prisoners had burrowed their way twenty yards towards the perimeter of the camp they came up against a concrete wall sunk deep into the ground. There didn't seem to be any way of* ***getting around*** *that.* □ *There seems to be no way of* ***getting round*** *the difficulty of keeping prices down when the cost of imports goes on rising.*

get around/round to [A3 pass] find the necessary time for; reach the point of tackling sth after settling other matters that must take priority (sometimes implying procrastination). **o:** thinking about our holidays; taking out an insurance policy; digging the garden over; writing to my parents □ *He had long had the idea of starting a market-garden, but it was only last year that he* ***got round to*** *looking at possible pieces of land.* □ *When I finally* ***got round to*** *buying the Christmas cards it was too late. The shops were all sold out.* □ *I did plenty of designs he hasn't* ***got around to*** *using yet.* CON □ *The so-called 'weekly letter' from boarding-school was often not* ***got around to*** *by several of my friends.* □ the object is usu the *-ing* form of a v.

get at[1] [A2 pass] reach, gain access to (and take, eat etc). **S:** curious eyes; thieving hands; children; mice. **o:** private papers, books; jewellery, deeds of the house, family silver, housekeeping money; jam, honey; dangerous medicines; flour, cheese □ *A sensible man keeps his savings in the bank — not in the house where some thief can* ***get at them.*** □ *I'm afraid that rabbits have been* ***getting at*** *your chrysanthemums again.* □ note the unusual adj forms **get`atable** and **unget`atable** (= can/cannot be got at). ⇨ be at[2].

get at[2] [A2] tackle, start to work on. **o:** job, roof; serious business □ *I wish the snow would thaw so that I could* ***get at*** *the garden.*

get at[3] [A2 pass] learn, ascertain, discover. **o:** truth, facts; real wishes, intentions; the root of the trouble; the cause of the disturbances □ *The members of the official board of inquiry had great difficulty in* ***getting at*** *the truth of the matter: there seemed to be a conspiracy of silence.* □ *What I'm trying to* ***get at*** *is whether you want to marry the girl for her money or because you love her.* ⇨ come at[2].

get at[4] [A2] suggest, in an indirect way □ *'I don't know what you're* ***getting at*** *exactly, but if you're suggesting that my brother is dishonest you'd better think again.'* □ *'Don't you see what I'm* ***getting at****? If we shared a flat we could each live much more cheaply.'* □ nearly always in a clause introduced by *what.* ⇨ what be at.

get at[5] [A2 pass] (informal) criticize; nag □ *Olive is always* ***getting at*** *her husband because he doesn't keep the garden tidy.* □ *Whenever his mother-in-law started talking about men who drink too much, he had a feeling he was being* ***got at.*** ⇨ be at[1].

get at[6] [A2 pass] (informal) (try to) influence, esp by improper means. **o:** witness, jury □ *'You didn't use to be so anti-religious. Who's been* ***getting at*** *you?'* □ *The judge said it was obvious from the man's behaviour in the witness-box that he had been* ***got at.***

get away (from)[1] [A1 nom A3 rel] manage to leave the place one is in; escape (from) (q v) □ *It was nice of you to invite me to tea tomorrow, but I'm afraid I can't* ***get away*** *(****from*** *the office).* □ *There's so much still to be done before we go on holiday that I can't see us* ***getting away*** *on time.* □ *Nobody knows how more than a hundred Tupamaros* ***got away*** *(****from*** *prison) without being noticed.* □ *Their* ***get-away*** *was very well planned, obviously.* □ *The gang's* ***get-away*** *car was found abandoned in a cul-de-sac not far from the scene of the robbery.* □ note also the expression *to make one's* **get-away** *(in a fast car, under cover of night* etc).

get away (from)[2] [B1ii pass B3 pass] assist sb to leave a place, esp for his own good; remove sth unwanted (from). **O:** women and children; spectators; ivy; net. **o:** the fighting, the danger; the fire; the wall; the propeller □ *The nail had gone rusty in the wood and I couldn't* ***get*** *it* ***away.*** □ *The poor woman must be* ***got away from*** *her children for a while and allowed to have a good rest.* □ *'****Get*** *all these dirty dishes* ***away****! The place is like a pigsty!'*

get away from [B3 pass] win, secure, sth or sb in a struggle from; attract sb back from. **O:** bone, stick; children. **o:** dog; estranged husband □ *'How are we going to* ***get*** *the ball* ***away from*** *the dog?'* □ *'You'll never* ***get*** *Doris* ***away from*** *Madrid now. She's fallen in love with the place.'* ⇨ take away (from)[2].

get away from it all [A3] (informal) go away in order to gain relief from one's worries, responsibilities, excessive work etc □ *He just couldn't wait for the day when he could pack up his bags and* ***get away from it all.*** *The rat race had finally got him down.* □ *It's no use* ***getting away from it all*** *if the cause of all your troubles lies within yourself.*

get away with[1] [A3] steal and escape with. **S:** thieves, burglars, bandits, confidence tricksters, con-man, (armed) gang, smash-and-grab raiders. **o:** property; jewellery, antiques, pictures, gold to the value of £10 000; the contents of the safe; £2 000 in notes and money-orders; one of the biggest hauls this year □ *Bandits wearing stockings over their faces raided the Midland Bank in Beckenham this morning and* ***got away with*** *over £20 000.*

get away with[2] [A3] (informal) go unpunished (even if caught); not suffer for. **o:** anything; outrageous behaviour, slander; impudence, indiscipline; it □ *What was amusing him was the thought that he, forty years old and weighing twelve stone, had punched a fourteen-stone international footballer of twenty-eight in the mouth and* ***got away with*** *it.* PE □ *'Don't side with him, David, because if you side with him he knows he can* ***get away with*** *it.'* ITAJ □ *'You can't write to Head Office over your manager's head! You'll never* ***get away with*** *a breach of the rules such as that.'* □ *Other men knocked off early and* ***got away with*** *it. Joe was always the one who got pulled up....* AITC ⇨ next entry.

get away with[3] [A3] receive the relatively light or negligible punishment of; get off[6] (q v). **o:** a reprimand, mild rebuke, warning; a fine of five pounds; seven days in gaol; suspension for a month □ *'As it's a first offence,' the solicitor said, 'I think she'll* ***get away with*** *a fine. It'll be a heavy one, though; the magistrate'll aim at frightening her.'* ASA ⇨ previous entry.

get away with murder [A3] (informal) (be able to) do anything, however outrageous, and not be punished for it, or be thought the less of because of it □ *With that innocent, smiling face of his, he could* ***get away with murder.*** □ *'You have no real sense of justice, James. People you don't happen to like never get a bloody chance, and the others can* ***get away with murder.****'* ILIH

get away with you! [A3] ⇨ get along/away with you!

get back[1] [A1] return to one's starting point □ *'When Tom* ***gets back,*** *please tell him that Jill* *phoned.'* □ *'Good heavens! It's nearly midnight! I must be* **getting back**. *My wife will be wondering what's happened to me!'* □ *Johnny's mother told him that he was to* **get back** *home before dark.* □ *When did Jarvis* **get back** *from India?* □ *The nurse was annoyed to find the patient wandering round the ward and told him to* **get back** *into bed at once.* ⇨ be back[1], bring back[1], come back[1], go back[1], take back[1].

get back[2] [A1] go to a reasonable, sensible distance; stand away □ *The police had great difficulty in making the curious crowd* **get back** *and let the ambulance through.* □ *'***Get back***! There's a bomb in this building!'* □ usu in direct or indirect commands.

get back[3] [B1ii pass] return sth or sb to its, his, place □ *He took the spring out of the clock, but now he can't* **get** *it* **back**. □ *If you take Mary out for a drive you must promise to* **get** *her* **back** *for her music lesson.* □ *'I'm afraid we are very busy and can't* **get** *your TV set* **back** *for this evening; but we can lend you one.'* ⇨ be back[2], put back[1].

get back[4] [B1i] recover possession of □ *'Don't lend Bill your umbrella! If you do, you'll never* **get** *it* **back**.*'* ⇨ give back (to)[1], have back[1].

get one's own back [B1ii] (informal) retaliate, get revenge, give tit for tat □ *Margaret had a habit of snubbing her lover in public; perhaps it was her way of* **getting her own back** *for the way he completely dominated her in private.* □ *If Kate ever smacked her little brother she knew that somehow he would* **get his own back***—perhaps by scribbling all over one of her drawings or breaking one of her china dogs.*

get back at [A3 pass] (informal) retaliate, give tit for tat. **o:** his critics, boss; shopkeeper, supplier; bully, know-all □ *The shopkeeper refused to change the faulty radio, maintaining that it was all right when I bought it, so I decided to* **get back at** *him by writing to the local paper about it.* □ *Civil servants have no way of* **getting back at** *individuals who criticize them, so they sometimes take it out of the public in general.*

get back into circulation [A3] (informal) return to normal life, mix once more with one's friends and colleagues □ *You could have a few things done to your face by a surgeon and* **get back into circulation** *again, but even false passports have to be renewed from time to time, and the whole business is pretty tricky.* DS □ *It's about time you* **got back into circulation**, *isn't it? After all, you can't spend your whole life here sitting against that wall,...* THH

get back into harness [A3] (informal) return to work □ *'I'm glad to say,' the doctor told him, 'that if you continue to make such good progress, you'll be able to* **get back into harness** *within a month.'*

get back to [A3] resume; return to. **o:** work, one's studies, the job in hand; the main point in the argument; what you were saying (about...) □ *The student was glad to* **get back to** *his books after a vacation that had seemed too long.* □ *'But to* **get back to** *the question of your immediate plans... What are you doing next week?'*

get back to the grindstone [A3] return to one's job, with the implication that the job is uninteresting, difficult or tiring. □ *To think that in three days' time our holiday will be over and we'll have to* **get back to the grindstone**. □ sometimes simply 'Back to the grindstone!' ⇨ keep one's nose to the grindstone.

get behind (with) [A1 A3] not progress at the necessary rate, in business, studies etc; fall into arrears □ *Owing to his illness, Peter couldn't keep up with the rest of the class and* **got** *badly* **behind**. □ *Mr Jones* **got behind with** *the payments on his car and had to surrender it to the garage.* ⇨ be behind[1], fall behind with.

get by[1] [A1 A2] pass (an obstacle) □ *There was such a crowd outside the shop window that the young woman with the pram couldn't* **get by**. □ *The traffic had come to a halt. Nothing could* **get by** *the accident.* ⇨ come by[1].

get by[2] [A1] be accepted; pass scrutiny, inspection □ *Ramsbottom didn't possess a dinner-jacket, but he was told that he would* **get by** *in a dark suit.* □ *Mike thought that he could* **get by** *with the minimum of work. His tutor quickly disabused him!*

get by[3] [A1] be successful in life or in a situation, survive; get along (q v) □ *'Don't worry, Johnnie,' she said, 'I'm not prophesying ruin. You'll* **get by***—indeed, you'll probably drift from strength to strength, but I don't want to go with you.'* ASA □ *The old lady never seemed to have much money, but somehow she managed to* **get by***—though I don't know how.* ⇨ next entry.

get by on/upon [A3 emph rel] survive by means of, by recourse to. **o:** small income, pension, allowance, grant; a handful of rice; native intelligence, wit □ *Without the breakdown she would have* **got by upon** *her native wit, and with her competence she would have made her way in peace time.* RFW □ *'You've got a job, haven't you, on that fancy magazine? We can* **get by on** *that for a start.'* AITC ⇨ previous entry.

get down[1] [A1 emph A2] descend □ *The cat climbed to the top of the tree and then became afraid to* **get down**. □ *A man escaped from the burning building by* **getting down** *a ladder.*

get down[2] [A1 emph] of children, leave the table at mealtimes □ *The children sat through the meal in complete silence and spoke only to ask permission to* **get down**. □ *'Now,* **down** *you* **get**!*'*

get down[3] [A1 emph] assume a stooping or kneeling position. **A:** on all fours; on one's knees □ *Her back was aching from having to* **get down** *in order to put things in and out of the bottom drawer.* □ *I thought I heard a mouse under the bed, and* **got down** *on all fours to have a look.* □ *She* **got down** *on her knees and prayed that her husband would survive the storm.* ⇨ go down on one's knees?(to).

get down[4] [B1i pass] write, record, note, sth, usu implying speed or difficulty. **O:** everything, the main points, the gist of what he said; lecture, message, confession, the number of the car, address □ *I didn't* **get down** *every word, but I certainly* **got** *a good deal of the conversation* **down**. □ *'Make sure you* **get** *his confession* **down**, *and his signature at the bottom of it.'* ⇨ be down[3], go down[9], put down[8], set down[2], take down[3].

get down[5] [B1i pass] swallow, usu with difficulty. **O:** medicine, pill; wine, whisky; meat, rice □ *The little boy* **got** *his medicine* **down** *with the* *help of a spoonful of jam.* □ *I could hardly* **get** *the last of the cous-cous* **down**. *It was delicious, but my hostess had given me too much.* ⇨ go down[3].

get down[6] [B1ii pass] (informal) depress, demoralize. **S:** weather; things in general, life, work; sb's attitude, behaviour; disease, drink □ *He wished he had the courage to inflict on her the pain of being told the ways she* **got him down**. ILIH □ *Going straight* (= being honest) *was* **getting** *Vin* **down** *a little.* ASA □ *Don't let your work* **get** *you* **down**. *You must try to forget about it when you leave the office.* □ *It's a terrible state of affairs when you let drink* **get** *you* **down** *like that.* DBM □ *Considering what Barbara has had to put up with, she doesn't seem in the least* **got down**.

get down[7] [B1i pass B2 pass] cause to fall or descend □ *Several nurses tackled the intruder and* **got him down**. *Then three of them sat on him while the others fetched the police.* □ *'Will you give me a hand to* **get** *this trunk* **down** *(the stairs)?'* ⇨ go down[4].

get down (from) [A1 emph A3] dismount (from). **o:** horse, pony □ *The drunken rider did not exactly* **get down** *(***from** *his horse); it would be truer to say that he fell off (it) into his friends' arms.*

get down in the dumps/mouth [A3] (informal) become depressed, miserable □ *He's one of those people who can't stand his own company. As soon as he finds himself alone he* **gets down in the dumps**. ⇨ be down in the dumps/mouth.

get down to [A3 pass] (informal) tackle, take steps to manage or settle. **o:** work, job; his writing; things, it; thinking about sth □ *From the day our schooldays began, we were taught, implicitly, that every other boy was a potential rival and that we must all* **get down to** *the sacred task of outdoing one another.* CON □ *Their eldest son is returning from Britain to Australia for good, to* **get down to** *managing the estate.* □ *'Look! You'll never finish that job unless you forget everything else and* **get down to** *it.'*

get down to brass tacks [A3] (informal) discuss, talk about, sth in practical, businesslike terms □ *'It's time George stopped all this theorizing and* **got down to brass tacks**. *What we want to know is how much the job will cost, not how scientific the method is going to be.'*

get down to business [A3] start serious discussion about sth, perhaps after some time has been spent on irrelevant or social talk □ *The two men had a couple of drinks together, talked about their families and their holidays for a while, and finally* **got down to business**. □ *'I hope you don't mind if we* **get down to business** *straight away, as I've got to catch the four o'clock train.'*

get down to a fine art [B3 pass] (informal) learn to do sth with perfection. **O:** carving the joint; catching rats; getting money out of his father; making beer □ *Betty always manages to have something urgent to do — homework, music practice, feeding her pets — when it's time to wash the dishes. She's* **got** *it* **down to a fine art**. □ usu in the perfect tense, as in the example.

get home[1] [A1 B1ii pass] arrive at one's house; bring or take sb to his house □ *'What time did you* **get home** *last night?'* □ *'If you'll come round for coffee, I'll promise to* **get** *you* **home** *before ten o'clock.'* □ *This package is not intended to mend a puncture perfectly. It is more in the nature of a* **'get-you-home'** *kit.*

get home[2] [A1] (racing, athletics) reach the winning-post, target etc, first. **S:** favourite, team, record-holder □ *My horse* **got home** *by a nose!* □ *The hundred metres champion managed to* **get home** *by a tenth of a second.*

get home (to) [A1 A3 B1ii pass B3 pass] (cause to) be understood, hit the target. **S:** [A1 A3] **O:** [B1 B3] point; criticism, barb, satire □ [A1] *The TV programme* **got home** *all right. The next morning, the papers were full of it.* □ [B1] *Politicians are adept at* **getting** *their point* **home**, *even in the face of constant interruption from their opponents.* □ [B3] *We left the meeting confident that we had at last* **got** *the essential part of our proposal* **home to** *the more conservative members of the Council.* ⇨ bring/come home (to).

get in[1] [B1i pass] collect, harvest; bring back (e g nets to a boat); bring indoors. **O:** debts, rent, rates, taxes; crops, fruit; nets, lines; washing; children □ *The farmers were delighted to* **get** *the hay* **in** *so early in the year.* □ *The fishermen went to* **get** *the lobster pots* **in** *and were delighted to find one in each pot.* □ *'***Get** *the washing* **in** *quick! It's raining.'* □ *The firm went bankrupt because their bad debts couldn't be* **got in**. ⇨ be in[2], bring in[1].

get in[2] [B1i pass] send a message to, obtain the services or advice of. **O:** specialist, another doctor; plumber, electrician; management consultants □ *When he saw how ill his mother was he told the doctor he would like to* **get** *a specialist* **in**. □ *When the pipe burst, a plumber had to be* **got in** *as no one knew where the stopcock was, and water was pouring through the ceiling.* ⇨ have in.

get in[3] [A1] (informal) gain an advantage by being the first or one of the first to do sth. **A:** ⚠ first; early; on the ground floor; at the start □ *The charter firm* **got in** *first with a £50 return fare to the Caribbean.* □ *It was obvious, when I came to give my account of how the quarrel had started, that Beryl had* **got in** *first and prejudiced her friend against me.* □ *Reg had* **got in** *on the ground floor, and as the firm had progressed, so had he.* ⇨ be/come in on the ground floor.

get a blow/punch in [B1i pass] (boxing) succeed in hitting one's opponent; (informal) attack or retaliate verbally □ *The challenger was so outclassed that he couldn't* **get a** *single* **blow in**. □ *He* **got** *several good* **punches in** *with his left.* □ *When his wife dragged up his infidelities, he was not slow in* **getting a blow in** *about her flirtations.*

get one's eye/hand in [B1ii] develop the ability to judge distances etc in games, especially ball-games, and consequently play well and easily; develop skill with one's hands □ *If Sobers can* **get his eye in**, *he'll score a century off this bowling.* □ *Once the girl* **got her hand in**, *she was soon getting through as much work as the more experienced machinists.* ⇨ keep one's eye/hand in.

get a word in (edgeways) [B1ii] (informal) succeed in saying something, where many people are talking or where another will not stop talking

□ *The scorn, ridicule, slander and threats poured over him in a remorseless stream that flowed so steadily he had no chance to **get a word in**.* DF □ *The three old friends had so much to talk about that I couldn't **get a word in edgeways**.* □ usu neg.

get in/into[1] [A1 emph A2] enter □ *The thieves **got in** through the floor by means of a tunnel.* □ *They **got into** the strongroom through the floor.* □ *'Don't stand there dithering! **Get in**! The water's not all that cold.'* □ *I believe in **getting into** the water as quickly as possible.* ⇨ come in/into, let in/into.

get in/into[2] [A1 A2 B1ii pass B2 pass] (cause to) enter, arrive (at). **S:** train; ferry; bus. **o:** station, Dublin, town. **A:** on time; late, early, punctually □ [A1] *'What time does the 2.05 from Euston **get in**, please?'* □ [A2] *The coach **gets into** Carlisle at about 6.15.* □ [B2] *In spite of the heavy seas the Captain **got** his ship **into** Liverpool on time.*

get in/into[3] [A1 A2 B1ii pass B2 pass] (politics) (cause to) be elected (to). **S:** [A1 A2] **O:** [B1 B2] government; the Tories, Labour, the Liberals. **S:** [B1 B2] the floating vote; the defence issue, the Common Market issue □ [A1] *The Conservatives **got in** with a small majority.* □ [A2] *The independent candidate **got into** Parliament with a thumping majority.* □ [B1] *The Prime Minister's support **got** the official party man **in**.* ⇨ be in[4], come in[3], put in[6].

get in on [A3 B3 pass] (informal) join an activity, with the implication that joining is desirable but possibly difficult. **o:** new organization; grants for restoring old property; the play; trip to Italy; the act □ *It's important that you should **get in on** the discussion about the property that the firm is considering acquiring.* □ *Don't let Matthew know we are thinking of forming a new society — he would try to **get** his wife **in on** it and they would try to run it.* □ *When the children started to kick the ball about the dog tried to **get in on** the act as usual.* ⇨ be/bring/come/let in on.

get in with [A3] (informal) (try to) form a relationship with, often with the implication that one has an ulterior motive in doing so □ *'If you want to drink — drink with others. Everyone likes a drink. You come over to the Golf Club with me, you'll soon find that out. I'll make you a member. You'll **get in with** them in a jiffy if you'll only try.'* FFE □ *I tried hard to **get in with** a pretty girl who was sitting by herself, but she wouldn't have anything to do with me.* □ *He managed to **get** well **in with** some of the local nobs by joining the golf club.* □ note the occasionally used expression: get in bad with: *The new man was unfortunate enough to **get in bad with** the foreman on the first day.* ⇨ be (well) in with.

get in contact/touch (with) [A2 B2 pass] (help to) meet or make contact (with) □ *I've been intending to **get in contact** (**with** you) about a plan I have for opening a small shop as a side-line.* □ *Bill and Sally miss each other badly. Somebody ought to **get** them **in touch with** each other again.* ⇨ be in/bring into/come into contact (with); be/put in touch (with).

get into[1] [A2 B2 pass] get dressed in, put on[1] (q v); force sb or sth into. **O:** himself, feet; baby; actor. **o:** suit, shoes; clothes; mask □ *At the end of the six-hour flight, I couldn't **get** my feet **into** my shoes as they had swollen so much.* □ *At the dress rehearsal the hero couldn't be **got into** the armour he was supposed to wear.*

get into[2] [A2] penetrate. **S:** sand, dust; flies, wasps; smell, stink, gas, fumes. **o:** hair, eyes, nose, mouth, ears; everything; jam, honey, room; every corner of the house, the hall □ *The molten lava **got into** every nook and cranny on its downward path.* □ *Spiders seem to **get into** every corner of the woodwork. They're everywhere.*

get into[3] [A2 B2 pass] (cause to) suffer, become a victim of. **o:** trouble, hopeless mess, tangle; debt □ *It's easier to **get into** debt than to get out of it again!* □ *'Please don't make so much noise. You'll **get** me **into** trouble.'* □ *How on earth did Sally **get** herself **into** such a ridiculous situation?* □ get (sb) into trouble sometimes means become or make pregnant.

get into[4] [A2 B2 pass] (cause to) acquire, develop, learn, become familiar with. **o:** ⚠ (the way, hang, of) it; the habit (of doing sth) □ *The children **got into** the bad habit of switching on the television as soon as they came in from school.* □ *You'll find changing gear difficult at first, but you'll soon **get into** the way of it.* □ *Painting is a fascinating hobby once you **get into** it.* □ *'Who or what **got** you **into** the habit of taking drugs?'* ⇨ get out of[2].

get into[5] [A2 B2 pass] enter involuntarily, cause sb to enter, a certain emotional state. **S:** [A2] **O:** [B2] father, teacher. **o:** rage, fury, temper; tizzy, stew, paddy □ *When Johnson found that his wife had gone out without waiting for him he **got into** a blind fury and smashed the furniture up.* □ *'Try not to **get** your father **into** a temper tonight. I want a bit of peace and quiet.'* □ *'You shouldn't let yourself **get into** a stew about nothing. It's bad for your blood pressure!'*

get into[6] [A2] seize, possess, a person's emotions, thoughts. **S:** ⚠ something, the Devil, I don't know what □ *We could not understand why the child was being so deliberately contrary and unco-operative. Something must have **got into** him.* □ *I don't know what **got into** me to say a thing like that to Mollie. I had absolutely no intention of offending her, but it just came out.*

get into[7] [A2] enter. ⇨ get in/into[1].

get into[8] [A2 B2 pass] (cause to) enter, arrive at. ⇨ get in/into[2].

get into[9] [A2 B2 pass] (politics) (cause to) be elected to. ⇨ get in/into[3].

get into the act [A2] (informal) figure in some activity □ *Whenever there was a birthday-party in the family and they sang 'Happy Birthday to you!' the dog tried to **get into the act** by barking in support.* ⇨ get in on.

get into sb's black books [A2] (informal) incur sb's strong disapproval □ *I **got into Lady Whatsit's black books** as soon as I mentioned that I was a Labour supporter.*

get into deep water [A2] become involved in matters that are too difficult, beyond one's capacity or ability to handle □ *'We'd better not talk about starting up a new company before the first one is operating successfully, or we'll be **getting into deep water**.'*

get into a fix [A2 B2 pass] (informal) cause sb/oneself to be in a difficulty of some kind □ *George has **got** (himself) **into a fix** by arrang-*

ing absent-mindedly to take two girls out on the same evening. □ *Trust him to* **get into a fix** *with his landlord; he never has been able to organize his finances.*

get into one's head [B2] (informal) understand fully, appreciate the significance of sth; imagine. **O:** these facts; it... that I'm not God □ *'I wish you would* **get** *it* **into your head**, *once and for all, that I'm not made of money.'* □ *How did Tom* **get** *it* **into his head** *that Medicine is an easy profession?* □ *Mollie* **got** *it* **into her head** *that her problems would cease to exist if she went to Australia.*

get one's hooks into/on [B2] (informal) win sb's attention or affections; exercise power over. **o:** man; boss, tutor □ *The secretary was so busy* **getting her hooks on** *the new manager, that she hardly noticed that everyone in the office was laughing at her.* □ Subject is usu feminine and object is usu masculine.

get into hot water [A2 B2 pass] (informal) find oneself in serious trouble, do sth that results in trouble for oneself or others □ *The young clerk* **got into hot water** *for handing over the documents without obtaining a receipt.* □ *'You'll be* **getting** *yourself and me* **into hot water** *if you take the car out again. The insurance doesn't cover a second driver.'*

get into a rut [A2] (informal) be trapped in one's routine, a set pattern of life; become fixed in one's ways, no longer have any ambition or initiative □ *By the time Harold was forty, he realized that he had* **got into a rut** *and that there was nothing he could do about it.*

get into one's stride [A2] reach the stage when one is performing an action at one's best, speaking fluently and enthusiastically etc □ *When the preacher* **got into his stride** *it became obvious that we were in for a very long sermon.* □ CLIVE: *Let us therefore not gasp too excitedly at the loftiness of Mother's family tree. Unbeknownst to Father it has, as you see, roots of clay (Clive pours himself some coffee. Walter stares at him in silence, as he* **gets into his stride**). FFE

get one's teeth into [B2] grip firmly with the teeth; eat; (informal) tackle with determination, work with concentration on. **S:** dog; hungry boys; new manager. **o:** rat; dinner; job, problem □ *It was obvious that being put in complete charge of the office gave her something to* **get her teeth into**. □ *I don't like my new job at all. There doesn't seem to be anything that I can* **get my teeth into**. □ *'Sally is in her father's business. She's* **got her teeth into** *poor John's neck feathers.'* HAHA □ often preceded by *have something to.*

get the better of [B2 pass(o)] master, defeat, overcome; get one's own way in opposition to, or after argument with. **S:** he etc; events, fears, curiosity. **o:** wife; them □ *It was natural for Tom not to let pass an opportunity for* **getting the better of** *me.* SPL □ *Don't always try and* **get the better of** *her over every stupid incident.* H □ *He was* **got the better of** *by an older hand at the investment game.*

get the hang of [B2] (informal) understand, appreciate; see how to do sth. **o:** him, what he said; this type of art, architecture; driving this car, riding a horse □ *'I can't exactly make him out. Just can't* **get the hang of** *him, that's all.'* TC □ *That lecture was beyond me. I couldn't* **get the hang of** *what he was saying at all.* □ *Not many people seem to have* **got the hang of** *this new kind of music: it's just a lot of squeaks, crashes and groans without any apparent meaning.*

get hold of [B2 pass(o)] (informal) obtain; reach, contact □ *'How did you* **get hold of** *her address?' 'Easy! I looked it up in the telephone directory.'* □ *At that time travel permits were not easily* **got hold of**. □ *If it is very urgent, I may be able to* **get hold of** *the doctor for you during the lunch-hour.*

get hold of the wrong end of the stick [B2] (informal) completely misunderstand the situation or something said □ *'If you owe John five pounds, why don't you stop arguing and pay him?' 'Me pay him! You've* **got hold of the wrong end of the stick**, *my dear! It's John who owes me five pounds!'* □ *'Mother thinks that Sally has been unfaithful to Bill. Trust her to* **get hold of the wrong end of the stick**!'

get wind of [B2 pass(o)] hear news of, usu in an indirect or roundabout way □ *Whenever we* **got wind of** *a fat parcel of diamonds on its way out of Africa towards Monsieur Diamant or his friends, we tipped off London.* DS □ *If your brother* **gets wind of** *our plans to go to Iceland for a holiday, he'll want to come with us.* □ *It was amazing that preparations for the landing were not* **got wind of** *by the enemy.*

get the worst of [B2] be defeated, be overcome. **o:** it, things; argument, fight □ *The young man up till then had been adopting a non-belligerent attitude, and he had, I felt, been* **getting the worst of** *things; the women, I decided, were taking an unfair advantage of him.* □ *When two armies come to blows, it is usually the ordinary people who* **get the worst of** *it.* ⇨ get the better of; have the best/worst of.

get off[1] [A1 emph A2] dismount, alight (from). **o:** horse, bicycle; train, bus □ *The policeman told the child to* **get off** *the pony.* □ *The absent-minded professor forgot to* **get off** *at Newcastle and was taken on to Edinburgh.* □ *'***Off** *you* **get** *and let me have a ride!'* ⇨ let off[1], put off[6].

get off[2] [A2] not sit, stand, walk, sail, drive etc on. **o:** father's chair; your behind; ladder, wall, roof; grass, flowerbeds, tennis-courts □ *'We'd better* **get off** *the lake before the storm breaks, or we'll get soaked.'* □ *The children were told to* **get off** *the scaffolding round the building.* ⇨ keep off[2].

get off[3] [A1 B1i pass] (cause to) leave, start a journey □ *'What time are you leaving tomorrow?' 'We hope to* **get off** *before seven o'clock.'* □ *The children had to* **get** *themselves* **off** *to school as both their parents went out to work at eight o'clock.* ⇨ be off[3], set off (on)[1].

get off[4] [B1i pass B2 pass] (manage to) remove (from). **O:** feet; clothes; paint; hands; boots. **o:** the mantelpiece; the floor; the door; my property; feet □ *Her finger had swollen so much that she couldn't* **get** *her ring* **off**. □ *'***Get** *that stinking animal* **off** *the table and back into its cage.'* ⇨ take off[2].

get off[5] [A1 B1i pass] go, dispatch, by post, radio etc; supervise the sending of. **S:** [A1] **O:** [B1] message, cable, wire, letter □ *Our man in Sydney is the obvious person to make the neces-*

sary contacts in Papua. We ought to ***get*** *a cable* ***off*** *to him immediately.* □ *'Please make sure these letters* ***get off*** *by the five o'clock post.'* ⇨ send off[1].

get off[6] [A1 B1ii pass] escape or nearly escape punishment; save sb from punishment; get away with[3] (q v). **A:** lightly; with a suspended sentence, with a warning, with a caution, with a fine; scot-free □ *Considering his record, he was lucky to* ***get off*** *with a six-month sentence.* □ *The lawyer* ***got*** *his client* ***off*** *with a fine of five pounds.* □ *It was her youth that* ***got*** *her* ***off****, not her innocence.* ⇨ let off[2], let off with.

get off[7] [A1] escape or nearly escape injury in an accident. **A:** lightly, unscathed; with only a few scratches and bruises, with a broken rib or two, with minor injuries □ *Fortunately the two cars did not crash head on, so Bill* ***got off*** *with nothing worse than a bad fright.* □ *The advance party was ambushed but* ***got off*** *relatively lightly. They suffered only one killed and four wounded.*

tell sb where he gets off/where to get off [A1] (informal) reproach, reprove, admonish □ *That bully has been throwing his weight around for too long. It's high time somebody* ***told him where he got off****.* □ *The old lady* ***told the policeman where he got off*** *in no uncertain terms.*

get off one's chest [B2 pass] (informal) say something which one has long wanted to say and thus relieve one's feelings; not suppress one's opinions. **O:** it; home truths; load □ *'Don't just sit there brooding! If you've got something you want to tell me, for heaven's sake* ***get*** *it* ***off your chest*** *and let's discuss it.'* □ *When her husband arrived two hours late for dinner she* ***got*** *a few home truths* ***off her chest*** *and felt all the better for it.*

get the weight off one's feet/legs [B2] (informal) sit or lie down (often said to a pregnant woman, or anyone who has some weakness or who has been standing for a long time) □ *'Come on, sit down, Kathy.* ***Get that weight off your legs****.'* LLDR □ *'You're looking a bit tired. Why don't you* ***get the weight off your feet****?'* ⇨ take the weight off one's feet.

get off on the right/wrong foot [A3 B3 pass] (cause to) make a good/bad start; start off on the right etc (q v) □ *Stalin was deliberate in making the best of his disadvantages and often he liked to* ***get*** *his interlocutor* ***off on the wrong foot****.* OBS □ *The professor seemed to have a gift for* ***getting off on the wrong foot*** *with a new colleague.* □ *The marketing director took pains to* ***get*** *the campaign* ***off on the right foot****.* □ the expression is perhaps derived from marching, where it is important that all the men should start with the same (i e the correct) foot.

get off to a good etc start [A3 B3 pass] begin (sth) well etc. **S:** [A3] **O:** [B3] competitor, horse; enterprise, campaign. **S:** [B3] steward, official; manager. **adj:** good, bad, poor, slow, splendid, flying □ *The runners* ***got off to a flying start*** *and looked like beating the record.* □ *The widespread publicity failed to* ***get*** *the fund* ***off to a good start****. People were just not interested in Victorian Gothic architecture.*

get off (to sleep) [A1 A3 B1ii pass B3 pass] fall asleep; send to sleep □ [A3] *Although I was absolutely exhausted from the long journey, I simply could not* ***get off to sleep****. That's what happens to me when I'm overtired. At other times I can drop off with the greatest of ease!* □ [B3] *It took the girl half an hour to* ***get*** *the baby* ***off to sleep****.*

get off with [A3 B3 pass] (informal) become friendly with, or deliberately attract, a person of the opposite sex; arrange such a relationship for sb □ *We never thought our Gertie would* ***get off with*** *anyone, let alone a chap with a Jaguar.* □ *He* ***got off with*** *my secretary, a thing he no doubt imagined I was secretly burning to do myself.* □ *'It's time Sam had a girlfriend. Can't you* ***get*** *him* ***off with*** *that nice girl you keep talking about?'*

get on[1] [B1i] get dressed in; put into position. **O:** things (= hat and coat); something warm, bathing costume, swim-suit; lid, cover □ *'I'll just* ***get*** *my things* ***on*** *and we'll go for a short walk.'* □ *He took the top off the jar but couldn't* ***get*** *it* ***on*** *again.* ⇨ have on[1], put on[1].

get on[2] [A1 B1ii] (cause to) make progress in general; advance. **A:** nicely; at work, in business, in life, in the world □ *'Well, Mrs Jones, you're* ***getting on*** *very nicely. Keep taking your pills, and come and see me again in a month's time.'* □ *When the brain runs out of sugar, the undernourished ego grows weak, can't be bothered to undertake the necessary chores, and loses all interest in those spatial and temporal relationships which mean so much to an organism bent on* ***getting on*** *in the world.* DOP □ *He looked upon his new car as a symbol of his success, the proof that he was* ***getting on*** *in the world.* □ *Most people find that if they want to* ***get on****, they must conform to the conventions of the society in which they live.* □ *The instructor* ***got*** *his students* ***on*** *so well that they had covered the course three weeks before the allotted time.*

get on[3] [A1] fare, perform, in a particular situation; make out[6] (q v) □ *'How did you* ***get on*** *in your oral examination?' 'Not too badly. I don't think I failed, anyway!'* □ *I didn't* ***get on*** *too well in France. My school French was quite useless; nobody could understand a word I said.* □ *'Hello, Simon! Haven't seen you for ages. How are you* ***getting on*** *these days?' 'Can't complain. And you?'*

get on[4] [A1] (of time) become late; (of people) advance in age or grow old. **S:** it, year; father □ *'Time's* ***getting on****, so will you all start getting ready, please? The bus will be here for you in twenty minutes.'* □ *The year is* ***getting on****. There was a touch of frost last night.* □ *'The headmaster is* ***getting on*** *a bit, isn't he? He'll have to retire soon, I should think.'* □ *When a woman's* ***getting on*** *in years, and not very well, it's a great comfort to have a girl about the place who's sensible and responsible.* RFW □ usu in continuous tenses. ⇨ get on for, go on (for).

get on![5] [A1] (informal) used as an exclamation of disbelief, surprise etc; go on![14] (q v) □ *'Guess how far I walked yesterday?' 'Ten miles?' 'No, thirty-two miles!'* ***'Get on!'*** ⇨ get along/away with you!, go along with you!

get on sb's back [A2] (informal) harass, bother, sb □ *'You were late arriving at work today, Jones.' 'Oh, Lord, are you going to* ***get on my back****, too? I had two hours of complaints from my wife last night, and a load of bills by this* *morning's post!'* ◻ FLINT: *Look, George — nobody else has seen these reports, especially Grace, thank God. Far as I'm concerned they were never written, but man, what's happened to you?* DIXON: *Don't* **get on my back**, *Sarge* (= Sergeant) — *I've had enough.* BBCTV

get on one's feet [A2] stand up for a special purpose, e g to speak in a debate ◻ *When the member for Sefton* **gets on his feet** *in the Commons, there's no knowing when he will sit down again.* ⇨ be on/come to one's feet, bring to his feet.

get on one's/his feet [A2 B2 pass] (cause or help to) recover. **S:** [A2] **O:** [B2] firm, company, party; the wounded, injured; patient ◻ *After the recent unrest the car industry will need time to* **get on its feet** *again.* ◻ *A quick way of* **getting** *a malingerer* **on his feet** *is to cut down his unemployment allowance.*

get a grip on [B2] gain or regain full control of. **o:** oneself; things, affairs, events ◻ *'I could see years ago that you hadn't* **got a grip on** *things. But I didn't think you would have come down to this.'* HD ◻ *'Look here, Bill! You really must* **get a grip on** *yourself. You can't let your wife see you in this state.'*

get one's hands on[1] [B2 rel] obtain sth, often as a fulfilment of one's desires or as an essential part of a long-cherished plan; lay one's hands on[1] (q v). **o:** money, an electric drill, her private diary, a nice plot of land, a cottage in the country ◻ *He's a second-hand dealer. It doesn't matter what it is: anything he can* **get his hands on**, *he sells.* ◻ *If only I could* **get my hands on** *a couple of hundred pounds, I'd be able to get married.*

get one's hands on[2] [B2] (informal) get near enough to sb or sth to seize or hit him, it etc; lay one's hands on[3] (q v) ◻ *'That woman's got a nerve. Just let me* **get my hands on** *her!'* ◻ *'Those cats kept me awake again all last night. If I could* **get my hands on** *them, I'd kill them.'*

get one's hooks on [B2] ⇨ get one's hooks into/on.

get a move on [B1ii] (informal) be quick; take urgent steps to do sth ◻ *'If you don't* **get a move on**, *you'll miss the last bus.'* ◻ *That student is going to have to* **get a move on** *if he wants to pass his finals.*

get on the move [A2 B2 pass] (cause to) start moving. **S:** [A2] **O:** [B2] army; family; holiday-makers; animals; swallows; traffic ◻ *After the terrible crashes in the fog, it was several hours before the traffic could* **get on the move** *again.* ◻ *It was dawn before the men could be* **got on the move** *over the difficult, unfamiliar terrain.*

get on sb's nerves [A2] annoy, irritate, sb ◻ *Tony and Bill discussed the idea of sharing a flat but sensibly decided that, in view of their differing tastes and habits, they would soon* **get on each other's nerves.** ◻ *She* **gets on my nerves,** *the way she never stops talking about her brilliant son.* ◻ *The constant noise of aircraft flying overhead* **gets on everyone's nerves.**

get one's skates on [B1ii] (informal) be quick, make haste ◻ *If you're going to meet your friends at the station, you'll have to* **get your skates on,** *because the train is due in five minutes!*

get on sb's wick [A2] (slang) annoy, irritate, sb; get on sb's nerves (q v) ◻ *'The boss* **gets on my wick** *with his everlasting complaints about timekeeping. And he thinks nothing of rolling up to the office at ten o'clock himself.'*

get on the wrong side of [A2] form a bad relationship with; get across[2] (q v) ◻ *The unfortunate girl* **got on the wrong side of** *her mother-in-law from the start by refusing her offer of some old curtains.* ◻ *I would advise you not to* **get on the wrong side of** *Smith. He can be very awkward and is capable of making life very uncomfortable for you.*

get on for [A3] approach, draw near to, a stated time or age. **S:** it (of time); old Bloggs ◻ *'What time is it?' 'I don't know exactly, but it must be* **getting on for** *midnight.'* ◻ *'I've got to go. It's* **getting on for** *five and I promised to meet my wife at the bowling-club.'* ◻ *The old woman continued to look after herself in her own little house although she was* **getting on for** *a hundred.* ⇨ get on[4], go on (for).

get on/onto [A1 A2 B1ii pass B2 pass] (cause, help, to) mount, board. **o:** horse, bicycle; bus, tram, train; boat, ship, hovercraft, hydrofoil; plane ◻ *The bus was full when it stopped at the school, so the children couldn't* **get on.** ◻ *Before you can learn to ride a horse you have to be able to* **get on** (or: **onto**) *it.* ◻ *The plane wasn't large enough to take all the people, and the travel agent couldn't* **get** *them all* **on.** ◻ *Will you help me to* **get** *these sheep* **onto** *the cart?* ◻ *The ticket-inspector asked me whether I'd* **got on** *at Edinburgh or Newcastle.*

get on to[1] [A3 pass] contact, often by telephone but also by letter etc. **o:** electricians, suppliers; emergency service, police, fire-station; HQ, our man in Bristol ◻ *I was told that the garage did not carry the necessary spare parts, but that they would* **get on to** *the makers and order them straight away.* ◻ *If the fire-station had been* **got on to** *at once, the hotel might have been saved.* ⇨ be on to[1], put on to[1].

get on to[2] [A3] trace, find, detect; become aware of sb's presence or activity. **o:** the scent, trail; his movements, whereabouts ◻ *The murder squad followed every bit of information and eventually* **got on to** *the wanted man's trail in a remote area of Scotland.* ◻ *The secret service* **got on to** *the enemy agent shortly after he arrived in the country and watched his every move.* ⇨ be on to[2], put on to[2].

get on to[3] [A3 pass] realize, become aware of. **o:** his double life; the girl's real intentions; his dishonesty, deceit; the fact that... ◻ *When Maureen* **got on to** *the real reason for her husband being 'kept late at the office', it was not long before the whole affair was out in the open.*

get on to[4] [A3] move from one activity, or phase, to another; pass on (to)[3] (q v). **o:** more important matters; something more interesting; the next item on the agenda ◻ *'Now that we've cleared up those necessary routine matters we can* **get on to** *what we've all been looking forward to: Mr Cowley's report on his visit to Thailand.'* ◻ *'I hate all this theory. When do you think we're going to* **get on to** *something useful?'* ◻ *We don't* **get on to** *anatomy until next year.*

get on (with)[1] [A1 A3] make progress (with). ⇨ get along/on (with)[1].

get on (with)[2] [A1 A3 rel] have a harmonious relationship (with). ⇨ get along/on (with)[2].

get on with [A3] continue to do. **o:** work, job; homework, the gardening, housework □ *'Put that novel away and* ***get on with*** *your work!'* □ *'Excuse me if I* ***get on with*** *this letter, but the post goes in twenty minutes. Then we'll have a cup of tea and a chat.'* □ *'I wish you'd* ***get on with*** *your dinner and go out! I want to clear up and have a rest.'* ⇨ go on[5], go on with.

let sb get on with it [A3] (informal) an expression of exclamatory force, implying that sb is intent on doing sth and should be allowed to do it, regardless of the consequences, and the speaker's disapproval □ *'If Ethel and Mavis think they can run the boutique without any help, well, all I can say is,* ***let them get on with it****.'*

get on without [A3] manage, survive, keep going, without □ *How will Mr Andrews* ***get on without*** *a housekeeper? He's never had to look after himself before.*

get out[1] [A1] become known, leak. **S:** news, secret, information, date of the invasion □ *Somehow the news* ***got out*** *that Cassius Clay was in the hotel, and a crowd gathered outside in the hope of seeing him.* □ *'If it ever* ***gets out*** *that you were behind the raid on Barclay's Bank today, you'll be in real trouble, because a man was killed by the gang.'* ⇨ be out[7], come out[7], let out[2].

get out[2] [B1ii] receive, draw, be given. **O:** (not) a lot, much; nothing □ *In most walks of life you only* ***get out*** *what you put in. Only the lucky few strike it rich and get big rewards for little effort.* ⇨ get out of[3].

get out[3] [B1i] speak, utter. **O:** a word, the words, the message; it □ *The woman was in such a state of shock after the accident that she couldn't* ***get*** *a word* ***out****.* □ *When John finally plucked up enough courage to ask for an increase in wages, he had quite a job to* ***get*** *the words* ***out****.* □ *Although the old man was deeply moved, he nevertheless managed to* ***get out*** *a short speech in which he thanked everyone for his retirement present.*

get out[4] [A1 B1ii pass] (cricket) (cause to) lose one's wicket; be dismissed, dismiss □ *'How did Edrich* ***get out****?' 'He was caught behind the wicket.'* □ *When England* ***got*** *Sobers* ***out****, there seemed to be a faint chance that they would win the match.* ⇨ be out[8], give out[4].

get out[5] [B1ii pass] succeed in solving, or finding the correct answer to; work out[3] (q v). **O:** calculation, sum; puzzle, problem □ *Not a single boy in the class could* ***get*** *the problem* ***out****.* ⇨ come out[12].

get one's rag out [B1ii] (slang) become angry □ *'Now keep your hair on, Bill! There's no need to* ***get your rag out*** *every time Doris comes home a bit late. She's a good girl and you must trust her.'*

get out/out of[1] [A1 emph A2] go away, usu from a building, room etc; escape from danger □ *It's easy to get into a good seat at the theatre, but not so easy to* ***get out*** *if you want to leave early.* □ *'The police are coming. We'd better* ***get out****, and quick!'* □ *'I advise you to* ***get out*** *while the getting is good (*= while it is still possible to do so*).'* AITC □ *'Anyone with poor nerves should not stay in the motor manufacturing business. He should* ***get*** *the hell* ***out****!'* ⇨ be out/out of[1], bring out/out of, come out/out of[1], take out/out of[1].

get out/out of[2] [B1ii pass B2 pass] cause to leave a room, building; extract (from). **O:** children; armed man; rabbit; screw; splinter. **o:** room; house; burrow; wood; finger □ *We had to find some way of* ***getting*** *the nurse* ***out*** *(****of*** *the house) for a few minutes so that we could talk freely.* □ *Our car couldn't be* ***got out*** *(****of*** *the garage) because there were several other locked cars around it.* ⇨ be out/out of[2], come out/out of[2], take out/out of[2].

get out/out of[3] [A1 A2] leak, escape (from). **S:** gas, water, acid; tiger, snake; prisoner; patient. **o:** pipe, tank, container; cage, basket; jail, cell; bed □ *'I don't know how the acid* ***got out****. The battery isn't broken, and it hasn't been moved.'* □ *The villagers were terrified when they heard that the lion had* ***got out of*** *its cage.*

get out of[1] [A2 pass] avoid; not do what one ought to do. **o:** all the dirty work, night duty, obligations, war; going to school □ *Her sons were experts at* ***getting out of*** *hard work.* □ *I wish I could* ***get out of*** *going to the party this evening; I don't feel like standing round and talking for three hours.* □ *Some men would do anything to* ***get out of*** *the war. It was not unknown for a recruit to shoot himself in the leg 'accidentally'.* □ *Going to the dentist is something which can't always be* ***got out of****.*

get out of[2] [A2 B2 pass] (cause to) lose, abandon. **o:** ⚠ (the way, hang, of) it; the habit (of doing sth) □ *After living for two years in a hotel, I had completely* ***got out of*** *the way of doing things for myself.* □ *'If only you could* ***get out of*** *the habit of smoking, you would soon feel better.'* □ *'Can't you* ***get*** *this child* ***out of*** *the habit of repeating everything I say?'* □ *Since her family grew up and left home, she's quite* ***got out of*** *the way of cooking and baking. It seems pretty pointless now.*

get out of[3] [B2 pass] obtain, gain, from. **O:** something, (next to, practically) nothing; ten per cent; a good profit □ *Too many people spend their time wondering what they can* ***get out of*** *others, instead of what they can give to others.* □ *'Don't imagine that I'm going to* ***get*** *a huge profit* ***out of*** *this deal. I'm probably going to lose money on it.'* □ *There's nothing to be* ***got out of*** *this book: it's years out of date.* ⇨ get out[2].

get out of[4] [B2 pass] make sb yield sth, sometimes by dubious means. **O:** truth; admission, confession; the whole story □ *The interrogators finally* ***got*** *a statement* ***out of*** *the prisoner, but it was not a true one. He was simply too exhausted to resist their pressure any longer.* □ *Nothing could be* ***got out of*** *the Minister. All he would say was that the talks with the Union would continue in the morning.* □ *I held my breath. I had to step carefully now if I was to* ***get out of*** *him the full confession for which I thirsted; and as I inhaled slowly I could smell Hugo's thoughts.* UTN

get out of bed (on) the wrong side [A2] (informal) be in a bad mood or temper from the moment one gets up □ *'What's the matter with Percy? He's cursing at everyone this morning.' 'I don't know. He must have* ***got out of bed on the wrong side****, or something.'* □ an alt construction is get out of the wrong side of the bed.

get the best/most/utmost out of [B2 pass] use to the best advantage, employ most effectively. **o:** him, employee; car, horse; Parker pen; life, holiday □ *You don't* ***get the best out of*** *men by treating them as a bunch of idiots.* □ *To* ***get the best out of*** *your Kenwood mixer, follow the directions carefully.* □ *The doctors have told him that he has only six months to live, so he's trying to* ***get the most out of*** *them.*

get blood out of a stone [B2 pass] (informal) extract something (esp money) from a 'source' which does not contain it or which does not easily yield it □ *Persuading John to part with his annual subscription to the Liberal Party is like* ***getting blood out of a stone.*** □ *It's no use asking your father for a loan. You can't* ***get blood out of a stone*** (or: ***Blood*** *can't be* ***got out of a stone***).

get out of one's depth [A2] (of a non-swimmer) be in water in which one cannot stand or walk, and thus be in danger of drowning; be in a situation which one cannot manage, which one cannot understand □ *Peter managed quite well in chemistry at school, but when he went to the university he soon* ***got out of his depth.*** ⇨ be out of one's depth.

get out of the groove/rut [A2] abandon one's boring, unadventurous mode of life □ *'I don't suppose I'll like America, but it's time I* ***got out of the groove*** *here.'* RFW □ *'Why don't you do something to* ***get out of the rut*** *if you're so dissatisfied with your job?'*

get out of hand [A2] become uncontrollable. **S:** children, horse; business, organization □ *I could see that the children were* ***getting out of hand*** *because of my presence, so I said goodbye and left.* □ *He tried to expand the firm too quickly. His staff did not have enough experience, production* ***got out of hand,*** *and he went bankrupt.* ⇨ be out of hand.

get out of one's head/mind [B2] stop thinking about, forget if only for a short time. **O:** it, idea (...that); picture, fear, prospect, thought (of...) □ *I wish I could* ***get*** *the picture of that awful accident* ***out of my head.*** □ *You must try to* ***get*** *your work* ***out of your mind.*** *You ought to take up a hobby!* □ *Try as he might, he could not* ***get*** *the idea* ***out of his head*** *that there was a conspiracy to cheat him of his entitlement under his father's will.* □ *'If you think I'm going to pay all your debts, you can* ***get*** *the idea* ***out of your head*** *now, because I'm not.'*

get out of it! [A2] (slang) do not exaggerate, do not say things that nobody can believe □ *'I'm going to give Harry a piece of my mind next time I see him.'* ***'Get out of it!*** *You couldn't give a sick mouse a piece of your mind!'* □ imper only.

get a kick out of [B2 pass] (informal) enjoy, find great etc pleasure in. **adj:** no, not much of a; terrific, tremendous □ (song) *'I get no kick from champagne, But I* ***get a kick out of*** *you.'* □ *'I'm no good,' said Bill, 'no good at all and, as you well know, I don't even* ***get a kick out of*** *admitting it any more.'* HAA □ *'Selling brushes from door to door — you wouldn't think that* ***a kick*** *could be* ***got out of*** *that sort of life, would you?'*

get no change out of [B2 pass] (informal) be unsuccessful in one's attempts to persuade, manipulate, seduce or exploit sb. **adj:** not any/much, (very, precious) little □ *'He was a critic who tried to take liberties with all the lady novelists... You'll remember him, I daresay.' 'Vaguely,' said Lettie. 'He* ***never got much change out of*** *me.'* MM □ *'If that man is a Jehovah's Witness he* ***won't get any change out of*** *your father!'* □ *'I suppose several people have been inquiring about him since he died?' 'A lot from the newspapers did, but they* ***got no change out of*** *me. I keep meself to meself.'* PP □ *'I can see there's* ***not much change*** *to be* ***got out of*** *him!'*

get out of sb's sight [A2 B2 pass] remove oneself or sb from another person's presence □ ***'Get out of my sight,*** *you wretch! I never want to set eyes on you again.'* □ *I'm going to* ***get out of your sight*** *as soon as I can get a bit of money in my pocket.* TOH □ *'I wish you would* ***get*** *these quarrelling kids* ***out of my sight*** *for an hour or two.'*

get out of one's system [B2 pass] (informal) stop wishing that one had; no longer be attracted to or fascinated by; satisfy a desire in order to make oneself free of it □ *'Do you think you'll want to go back and live in England?' he asked. 'I don't think so,' I said. 'I think I've* ***got*** *that much* ***out of my system.'*** RFW □ *'You look so miserable! I suppose it's that man again. Why don't you try and* ***get him out of your system?'*** □ *A religious upbringing — now that's something that can't easily be* ***got out of one's system.*** RFW

get out of sb's/the way [A2 B2 pass] remove oneself, sb or sth from the scene; step aside from the path of sb or sth; complete of a job, task etc □ *'If you don't* ***get out of the way,*** *you're liable to be knocked down by a bicycle or something.'* □ *'If your father comes home drunk,* ***get*** *the little children* ***out of the way*** *before he starts hitting them.'* □ *'Once I've* ***got*** *this pile of marking* ***out of the way,*** *I'll come for a walk with you.'*

get over[1] [A2 pass B2 pass] (cause to) climb, cross. **S:** [A2] **O:** [B2] sheep, horse; children, troops. **o:** wall, fence; stream, bridge □ *'How did the cattle manage to* ***get over*** *the road?'* □ *We* ***got*** *the children safely* ***over*** *the fence and ran across the field towards the house.*

get over[2] [A2 pass] surmount. **o:** obstacle, difficulty, problem □ *Three scientists at Stanford University think they can* ***get over*** *the barrier by exploiting the properties of macrophages.* NS □ *The negotiators had considerable difficulty in* ***getting over*** *the linguistic problems in the drawing-up of an agreed statement.*

get over[3] [A2 pass] become calm, healthy etc, again; recover (from)[1] (q v). **o:** shock, disappointment, surprise; handicap, illness; effort; being made redundant, being disinherited; the loss of his wife; it □ *I can't* ***get over*** *a thing like that happening to him.* QA □ *She never quite* ***got over*** *being jilted by Geoffrey.* □ *Being held up at gun-point and robbed isn't an experience that is easily* ***got over.*** □ *John was disappointed that he didn't get the job, but he'll* ***get over*** *it.*

get over[4] [A2] (not) fully believe, appreciate or understand. **o:** the wonders of modern science; the ease with which they robbed the bank; sb's impudence, madness, bad behaviour □ *'I can't* ***get over*** *that woman's cheek. Coming in here and complaining about a dress she bought six months ago!'* □ *The astronaut couldn't* ***get over*** *the fact that in spite of the accident to the space-*

vehicle he had returned safely to Earth. □ usu neg in statements.

get over[5] [A2 pass] overcome, master, suppress. **o:** one's embarrassment, confusion, shyness, inhibitions; stutter; disinclination to work □ *When I last saw Marie she had almost completely* ***got over*** *her nervousness in the presence of strangers.*

get over[6] [A2] travel over, cover. **o:** a lot of ground, the distance □ *These new tractors* ***get over*** *twice the acreage that the old ones used to cover.* □ *The athlete failed to* ***get over*** *the distance in the minimum time to qualify for the final.*

get over (to) [B1ii pass B3 pass] make clear, convey (to); impress sb with; get across (to) (q v). **O:** oneself; one's personality, sincerity; anger, distress □ *Dressed in deepest black, possessing more personal force than anyone else in court, and more ability to* ***get*** *it* ***over****, she made a great impression.* PW □ *The lecturer, though he knew his subject inside out, was quite incapable of* ***getting*** *anything useful* ***over to*** *the students.* ⇨ put over (to).

get over with [B3 pass] (informal) do sth necessary but unpleasant (finally, once and for all). **O:** it; work; formalities □ *'If we must visit your parents today let's go early and* ***get*** *it* ***over with****.'* □ *He looked upon the marriage ceremony as a mere formality — something to be* ***got over with*** *as quickly as possible.* □ *'Let's* ***get*** *the goodbyes* ***over with*** *and go!'* □ in this expression, with has no object of its own. ⇨ next entry.

get over (and done with) [B1ii pass] (informal) do sth necessary but unpleasant (finally, once and for all). **O:** work; formalities, the serious business □ *'I'll be glad when we've* ***got*** *this job* ***over****. It's so boring!'* □ *When the usual form-filling and signing had been* ***got over****, he was at last free to look for the friends he knew would be there to welcome him.* □ *If your tooth is aching you should go to the dentist, and soon! You might as well* ***get*** *it* ***over and done with****.* □ in the complete expression, with has no object of its own. ⇨ be over[1], be over and done with; previous entry.

get round[1] [A1 A2 pass] (sport) succeed in completing a course, a test etc for a stated score or in a given time. **o:** course, track, circuit, speedway; dartboard □ *Jack Nicklaus* ***got round*** *the course in 67 — five under par.* □ *The runners* ***got round*** *the first lap in just under sixty-one seconds.* □ *The champion* ***got round*** *the board with 25 throws.*

get round[2] [A2 pass] avoid, legally if not honourably. **o:** law, regulations, rules □ *The lawyer was well known for his skill at* ***getting round*** *the law, usually on technical points. So that many of his clients, while obviously guilty of traffic offences, got off scot-free.* □ *He believed that there were no tax-laws that couldn't be* ***got round*** *somehow or other.*

get round[3] [A2 pass] gain the confidence of. ⇨ get around/round[1].

get round[4] [A2] tackle successfully. ⇨ get around/round[2].

get round the table [A2 B2 pass] (of two or more groups in dispute) (cause to) sit down together in order to discuss a problem and find a solution to it. **S:** [A2] **O:** [B2] workers and employers; the government and the unions; the management and the cleaners □ *What the strikers want is that the dismissed men should be reinstated. Until they are, they say they won't* ***get round the table*** *with anybody — employers or arbitrators.* □ *'Surely what we all want is to* ***get*** *the two sides* ***round the table*** *and talking?'*

get one's tongue round [B2 pass] pronounce, articulate. **o:** word, name □ *Chinese students of English have great difficulty in* ***getting their tongues round*** *some English words — especially those containing the sounds of r and l. 'Rival librarians' is for them an almost unpronounceable expression.* □ *English* ***tongues*** *simply can't be* ***got round*** *the sounds of some African languages.*

get round to [A3 pass] ⇨ get around/round to.

get through[1] [A1 A2] manage to pass through. **o:** hole, gap, aperture, eye of a needle, crack □ *You would wonder how such a large animal could* ***get through*** *such a small hole.* ⇨ go through[1].

get through[2] [A1 A2 B1ii pass B2 pass] (help to) be successful in; (help to) pass. **o:** (the first round); driving-test □ [A2] *I* ***got through*** *the written papers but failed in the oral examination.* □ [B1 B2] *I wouldn't expect that instructor to* ***get*** *anyone* ***through*** *(the driving-test).*

get through[3] [A1 A2 B1ii pass B2 pass] of a Bill, (cause to) be approved by Parliament and so become an Act of Parliament. **S:** [A1 A2] **O:** [B1 B2] the Industrial Relations Bill; new law on capital punishment; reform of the law on divorce □ [B2] *The Government rarely has any difficulty in* ***getting*** *its annual Finance Bill* ***through*** *Parliament.* □ [A1] *People began to doubt whether the Bill would ever* ***get through****.* ⇨ go through[6], put through[2].

get through[4] [A2 pass] consume, drink, eat, spend. **o:** ten aspirins a day; a bottle of gin a week; enough for two people; a fortune, a lot of money □ *They say that the old man* ***got through*** *a fortune when he was young, and lived in poverty for the rest of his life.* □ *You would wonder how so much food could be* ***got through*** *by such a small child.* ⇨ go through[2].

get through[5] [A2 pass] manage to do, read, write etc. **o:** homework; all these files; fifty letters a day; a lot of reading □ *My new secretary is very quick; she* ***gets through*** *a lot of work in a morning.* □ *'I've brought you a very interesting book on the Sudan.' 'Thanks, but I haven't* ***got through*** *the one you brought yesterday yet!'* □ *When I've* ***got through*** *the 'get through' entries I'll get on with the 'get to' ones!*

get through (to)[1] [A1 A3 pass B1ii pass B3 pass] reach, or bring to, its/one's destination, after overcoming difficulties. **S:** [A1 A3] **O:** [B1 B3] message; survivor; supplies, reinforcements □ [A1] *If more supplies do not* ***get through****, thousands of refugees will die.* □ [B3] *The ammunition could not be* ***got through to*** *the men, and they had to surrender.*

get through (to)[2] [A1 A3 B1ii B3] (help to) make contact, by radio etc (with). **o:** police, London □ [A1 A3] *'The telephone operator told me that all the lines were engaged. That's why I couldn't* ***get through*** *(****to*** *you).'* □ [B1 B3] *At the fifth attempt the operator* ***got me through*** *(****to*** *New York).* □ [A1] *At midday a messenger* *arrived from the radio station, to say that the American had* **got through** *to inform them that there was a lull in the fighting in Asunción.* DF ⇨ be/put through (to).

get through to[1] [A3 B3 pass] (sport) (help to) reach, get as far as. **o:** the final (stage), the semi-final(s) □ *Colchester were lucky to* **get through to** *the fifth round of the Cup.* □ *How many times did Laver* **get through to** *the final of the men's singles at Wimbledon?* □ *The new manager* **got** *the team* **through to** *Wembley in his first season.*

get through to[2] [A3] make sb understand the meaning of what one is saying; communicate with sb □ *The boy is just stupid: I can't* **get through to** *him at all, even when I explain things in words of one syllable.* □ *The police were told that the injured man was still in a dazed state and that it would be impossible to* **get through to** *him.* ⇨ get through (to)[2].

get through with[1] [A3 pass] finish, complete. **o:** job; housework; selling the house □ *By the time we had* **got through with** *all the formalities, all we wanted to do was go to the hotel and rest.* □ *No sooner had the tedious job of decorating the house been* **got through with** *than a pipe burst in the attic and ruined everything.*

get through with[2] [A3 pass] (informal) finish dealing with sb, implying physical attack or verbal correction □ *'When I've* **got through with** *that bastard even his own mother won't recognize him.'* □ *When the Matron had* **got through with** *the grumbling patients, they felt thoroughly ashamed of themselves.*

get to[1] [A2] reach, arrive at (q v). **o:** village, hotel, destination; coffee; the most interesting part □ *We didn't* **get to** *the hotel until midnight.* □ *An unpleasant grin spread over the boy's face as he* **got to** *the juicy part of the novel.* □ note the expression *Cut the cackle and* **get to** *the horses* (or: *'osses*), often reduced simply to *Cut the cackle,* meaning 'Cut out the unnecessary preliminaries, and tell us the important news or facts.'

get to[2] [A2] begin to do sth, reach the point of doing sth. **o:** wondering, asking himself; the point where..., the stage of thinking... □ *In his disturbed state, he* **got to** *screaming obscenities at anyone who troubled him in any way.* □ *Lying in bed, unable to sleep, I* **got to** *thinking how nice it would be to go away and start a new life somewhere else.*

get access to [B2 pass rel] (formal) reach, sometimes by overcoming some obstacle. **o:** attic, roof, secret room; the White House; classified information, state secrets; rival's plans □ *The police are still not sure how the thieves* **got access to** *the safe. No damage seemed to have been caused to the building.* □ *We realized too late that* **access** *could easily be* **got to** *our stronghold by means of a long-forgotten tunnel.* ⇨ have access to.

get to the bottom of [A2 pass(o)] find the cause of, solve (a problem), fathom. **o:** mystery, affair, goings-on; it □ *'I'm determined to* **get to the bottom of** *this outrageous rumour.'* □ *Sherlock Holmes had a reputation for* **getting to the bottom of** *any crime, however baffling it might seem to others.* □ *'I shan't be satisfied till this whole business is* **got to the bottom of**!'

get to the top (of the ladder/tree) [A2] reach the highest position in one's chosen career □ *This is a go-ahead organization, where every girl has every chance to* **get to the top**. H □ *From the earliest age, you could see that he would* **get to the top of the tree** *— no matter what profession he chose.*

get to work (on) [A2] start working, operating, studying etc; tackle, begin, sth □ *The men piled out of the coach, rushed into the restaurant and immediately* **got to work on** *the meal that had been prepared for them.* □ (book review) *I wish that she would chuck her tape-recorder off Brighton pier and* **get to work on** *a real book again.* OBS

get to first base with [A2] (esp US informal) make significant progress towards achieving an objective, esp of a man making amorous advances to a woman □ *Sam was crazy about Helen, but he never even* **got to first base with** *her.* □ *We ran out of money before we could* **get to first base with** *our project to open an antique shop in the village.* □ from the game of baseball; usu neg or with neg implications.

get to grips with [A2 pass(o)] tackle in earnest. **o:** problem, work; opponent, enemy □ *It's time you stopped tinkering about with those trifling repairs on your car, and* **got to grips with** *the basic trouble by decarbonizing the engine.* □ *When Alex* **gets to grips with** *a problem, he doesn't leave it alone until he's found the solution.* □ *The question of where our energy is coming from in the next decade needs to be* **got to grips with** *in a serious way.* ⇨ be at/come to/bring to grips with.

get together[1] [A1 nom] meet socially; discuss sth with a view to forming a common front □ *'Hello, Bill! Haven't seen you for ages!' 'That's a fact. Look! Let's* **get together** *later and have a long chat about old times.'* □ *The younger members of the staff decided to* **get together** *over the question of weekend duty. They didn't see why the older men shouldn't do their fair share.* □ *The firm had its annual* **get-together** *at the Anchor Inn. A good time was had by all.*

get together[2] [B1i pass] assemble, collect. **O:** body, party, group, army of men; papers, documents; impressive amount of information □ *Enough volunteers were* **got together** *to keep the beaches clean all through the summer.* □ *'I want you to* **get** *your things* **together**, *so that we can leave at a moment's notice.'*

get it together [B1ii] (informal) (be able to) manage, organize, sth satisfactorily □ (Jean Shrimpton in an interview) *'I didn't seem to get on at all well during my session with Cecil Beaton* (the photographer). *Perhaps I was too young to see what he wanted. I couldn't* **get it together**.*'* BBCTV □ *'People don't dance like that these days, Dad! Why don't you go and see some real dancing? Try and* **get it together**!*'*

get under [A2 B2 pass] (cause to) pass beneath; shelter, hide under. **o:** barbed wire, rope, hedge; tree, tarpaulin, stairs □ *The rabbits couldn't* **get under** *the wire netting, so for once we were able to grow a few vegetables.* □ *The dog had the sense to* **get under** *some old boxes to shelter from the storm.* □ *The children had to be* **got under** *the stairs whenever there was an air-raid.*

get under control [B2 pass] subdue, master. **O:**

fire, floods; people, mob, crowd; children; riot, uprising, rebellion, mutiny, revolt □ *The fire-brigade arrived within minutes of the alarm and quickly* ***got*** *the conflagration* ***under control.*** □ *The government hasn't got enough troops to* ***get*** *the rebellious province* ***under control.*** □ *When the mob had been* ***got under control,*** *several of the ring-leaders were arrested.* ⇨ be/bring under control.

get under sb's skin [A2] be a constant source of irritation to sb □ *I don't know what it is about that fellow Fotheringay, but he always manages to* ***get under my skin.*** □ note that the words *I've got you under my skin,* the title of a song, mean 'I can't stop thinking about you' — where the *irritation* is of a pleasant nature! Note also that the expression here is *have/have got sb under one's skin,* which has a transitive construction and is grammatically different from the headphrase.

get up[1] [A1 emph B1ii pass] rise from one's bed; call or awaken sb, and possibly lift him out of bed. **S:** [A1] **O:** [B1] baby; father; boys. **A:** early, late; at the crack of dawn, in time for □ (old song) *'Oh, it's nice to* ***get up*** *in the morning, But it's nicer to lie in bed!'* □ *'Isn't it time you* ***got*** *the baby* ***up*** *for its bottle* (= for its milk)*?'* □ *'If I'd been* ***got up*** *earlier I wouldn't have missed my train.' 'It's high time you were able to* ***get*** *yourself* ***up,*** *my boy!'* ⇨ be up[5].

get up[2] [A1 emph] rise to one's feet from a chair, the ground; stand (up) (q v) □ *When the Chairman asked if there were any questions, about four people* ***got up*** *at once.* □ *The man fell to the floor with a crash and couldn't* ***get up*** *again. He was hopelessly drunk.* □ *I* ***got up*** *from the table and left the room as quickly as possible.*

get up[3] [A1 A2 B1ii pass B2 pass] (help to) climb; carry up. **S:** [A1 A2] **O:** [B1 B2] old man, car, lorry; load, furniture. **o:** hill, mountain, incline, cliff; stairs, steps, ladder □ [A2] *Your car will never* ***get up*** *that hill...* □ [A1] *...but mine will* ***get up*** *in second gear!* □ [B2] *'How do you expect to* ***get*** *this filing-cabinet* ***up*** *all those stairs?'* □ [B1] *'I don't know. All I know is that it has got to be* ***got up****! And it's your job to* ***get*** *it* ***up****!'* ⇨ go up[1].

get up[4] [A1 B1ii pass] (cause, help to) mount a horse, bicycle etc □ *'Can you* ***get up*** *by yourself, or shall I help you?' 'Thank you. I can manage to* ***get up*** *by myself.'* □ *'Quick!* ***Get*** *the girl* ***up*** *behind me and let's start before her father arrives!'*

get up[5] [A1] rise, increase in force, become violent. **S:** ⚠ the wind, storm, sea □ *Although the wind was obviously* ***getting up,*** *and with it the sea, the foolish couple left harbour in their flimsy catamaran.* □ get the wind up (q v) has an entirely different meaning.

get up[6] [B1i pass] organize, arrange. **O:** party, concert, exhibition; appeal, petition (against/on behalf of/for) □ *What a miserable way to earn a living!* ***Getting up*** *dreary leg-shows in the provinces.* □ *The prisoners-of-war kept their spirits up by* ***getting up*** *bingo sessions, art classes, sing-songs and so on.* □ *The students* ***got up*** *a country-wide campaign in support of nuclear disarmament.*

get up[7] [B1ii nom pass adj] dress in a special way, dress up[1] (q v); make beautiful or attractive **O:** daughter, child; oneself; book, present, room □ *She may not be very beautiful but she certainly knows how to* ***get*** *herself* ***up*** *effectively.* □ *'Do you like my* ***get-up****? 'I do! The colour suits you perfectly.'* □ *The girl's mother had* ***got*** *her* ***up*** *as Marie Antoinette — not very successfully, however!* □ *'I envy you the village,' Gerald said; 'it's charming.' 'Is it?' Dollie asked. 'It always seems to be a bit* ***got-up*** *for tourists.'* ASA

get up[8] [B1i pass] prepare, study; memorize. **O:** German, chemistry; part, role □ *When we went to see John he was busy* ***getting*** *the Law of Torts* ***up*** *for his exam.* □ *'What are you going to do next, after you've* ***got up*** *your Hamlet?'*

get up a(n)/one's appetite/thirst [B1i pass] develop an appetite or thirst, do sth which produces an appetite; work up[3] (q v) □ *Mariette has gone for a ride now to* ***get her appetite up.*** DBM

get sb's back up [B1ii pass] (informal) annoy, antagonize, sb □ *No, Borstal* (a kind of prison for young offenders) *didn't* ***get my back up,*** *because it's always been up, right from when I was born.* LLDR □ *'Why should a simple request* ***get your back up****? I only asked you if you would like to wash the dishes.' 'But I* always *bloody-well wash the dishes! That's what's so annoying.'* □ *When he came in and threw his coat on a chair it was obvious that* ***his back*** *had been* ***got up*** *by something or other.* ⇨ put sb's back up.

get sb's blood up [B1ii pass] enrage, anger, make sb feel aggressive □ *His insolent manner really* ***got my blood up*** *and for two pins I would have punched him on the nose.* ⇨ one's blood be up.

get one's/sb's monkey up [B1ii] (slang) become or make angry, work oneself or sb up into a temper □ *The class* ***got the teacher's monkey up*** *by deliberately asking a lot of irrelevant questions.*

get up steam [B1iii] develop enough pressure of steam to drive sth; (informal) (of persons) prepare oneself to make an effort. **S:** ship; ferry, tug; he etc; □ *We saw the boat in the harbour* ***getting up steam*** *for the daily crossing to the island.* □ *'Do you think you could* ***get up*** *enough* ***steam*** *to take these letters along to the post-office for me?'*

get the wind up [B1ii] (informal) become frightened, alarmed □ *When somebody knocked at the door and asked if Mr Philpotts was in, Jo* ***got the wind up.*** *He thought it was the police!* □ *Every time I hear about more redundancies in the electronics industry, I* ***get the wind up.*** *The factory I work at produces only radar equipment.* □ *With the approach of the General Election, the Government* ***got the wind up*** *and cut taxes by about fifteen per cent.* ⇨ [6]; get up have/put the wind up.

get up against[1] [A3 B3 pass] stand, sit, huddle very close to; place very near to. **O:** piano, sacks, ladder. **o:** wall, partition □ *The child* ***got up against*** *the radiator in his efforts to keep warm.* □ *'Can you help me to* ***get*** *this load of sand* ***up against*** *the tree, where it will stay dry?'*

get up against[2] [A3] form a bad relationship with; find oneself in conflict with. **S:** new shop-steward; French assistant; students. **o:** manager, management; headmaster, head of the French department; authorities, Vice-Chancellor □ *I had only been working in the hotel for a week when I*

***got up against** the head waiter, and he began to make life unbearable for me.* □ *She's hopelessly headstrong; she always **gets up against** people in authority.*

get up on one's hind legs [A3] (informal) rise to one's feet in order to speak to a group of people □ *Mr Clark had been in the House of Commons for nine months before he found the courage to **get up on his hind legs** and make his maiden speech.* ⇨ get up².

get up to¹ [A3 B3 pass] (cause to) reach; raise to. **o:** standard, required level □ *The boy despaired of ever **getting up to** the high standard required for entry to the University.* □ *It is inadvisable to pay too much attention to advertisements that promise to **get** you **up to** managerial status in one or two years.* ⇨ be up to⁵, bring up to, come up to.

get up to² [A2] be occupied in, be busy with (q v) (usu with the implication that the activity is undesirable, foolish or surprising). **o:** what; mischief; his old tricks □ *What on earth will Mike be **getting up to** next? First he bought antiques, then it was old houses, and now it's old ships. He'll soon be trying to buy Tower Bridge and take it to the States.* □ *Old Juppers has been **getting up to** his dirty tricks with young children again; he's back in gaol for a couple of years.* ⇨ be up to¹, put up to².

get up to date (with) [A3 B3 pass] do sth which is due or overdue; inform (oneself) about. **o:** the latest developments, news □ *The teacher spent five hours on Sunday **getting** his marking **up to date*** (or: [A3] ***getting up to date with** his marking*). □ *'What's been going on in the world while I've been ill? I really must **get** myself **up to date**!'* ⇨ be up to date/the minute, bring up to date.

get with child [B2 pass] (formal) make pregnant. **O:** girl; fiancée, wife, mistress □ *'Sin' is **getting** a girl **with child** before marriage and then not marrying her.* UL □ *She couldn't name the father; all that emerged was that she had been **got with child** while she was under the influence of alcohol.*

get within [A2] reach a position where one can hit or be hit, see or be seen etc. **o:** ⚠ striking distance, earshot, range, sight □ *It was obvious that they would never **get within** striking distance of the guest of honour, so they just sat on the stairs and enjoyed the free drinks.* □ *We were now **getting within** range of the enemy batteries* (i e we could hit or, more likely, be hit by, them). ⇨ be within¹, bring within, come within.

gibe (at) [A2 pass] mock, scorn, jeer (at) (q v). **o:** sb's modest attempts, efforts; misfortunes, poverty; mistakes □ *Children can be very cruel; they often **gibe at** the feeble efforts of their younger brothers and sisters to do what the older members of the family can do with ease.*

ginger up [B1i pass] (informal) put more life, energy, enthusiasm, into sb or some activity. **O:** him, the Party; fund-raising campaign, movement for equal pay for women □ *'It's obvious that the Liberal Party needs **gingering up**; it's dying on its feet.'* □ *He asked me to '**ginger up**' the evacuation of the* (Nile) *Delta cities.* MFM

gird on [B1iii pass] (formal, dated) fix or fasten on. **O:** sword, armour, suit of mail □ *The young knight **girded on** his father's sword and went forth to avenge him.*

gird up one's loins [B1iii] (formal, dated) prepare for action, esp for battle □ *He **girded up his loins** and called upon his enemy to come forward and meet him in single combat.* □ *It was becoming clear from its actions that the Government was **girding up its loins** for another confrontation with the Unions.*

girdle about/around [B1ii pass] (formal) surround (in a picturesque way). **O:** island, lake, castle □ *A thick forest **girdled** the castle **about**.* □ *The loch was pleasantly **girdled about** with beech, fir and aspen.* □ *The tiny tropical island was **girdled round** with a coral reef.* □ usu passive.

give away¹ [B1i nom pass adj] give, free of charge; sell at a very low price. **O:** money, possessions, old clothes; everything; samples, free packets □ *The young man **gave** his entire fortune **away**, and went to live on a small island.* □ (letter) *Why do politicians, and newspapers, give the impression that a Chancellor has money to **give away**?* T □ *'Four pounds for that book! It isn't exactly **given away**, is it?'* □ *'Please don't bring any more of those plastic **give-away** tulips into the house.'* □ *'Have you seen the latest **give-away**? A packet of bird-seed with every jar of coffee. Grow your own hemp, I suppose!'*

give away² [B1i pass] distribute, present. **O:** prizes, medals, diplomas, certificates □ *'Do you really think it necessary to drag the Mayor in, just to **give away** a few certificates to kids who have passed their first swimming test?'*

give away³ [B1i nom pass adj] betray, reveal, voluntarily or involuntarily. **O:** secret; someone, something, nothing; oneself, itself □ *He had invented secrets, he hadn't **given** them **away**.* OMIH □ *Love is its own torturer; and, like cruder tortures, it makes its victim want to tell the truth — the truth about itself. It is by nature self-betraying; if nothing else, the eyes **give** it **away**.* PW □ *He was aware as he spoke that the tremble in his voice was the **give-away** that the police had been waiting for.*

give away⁴ [B1i pass] fail to take or use, through foolishness or neglect; throw away² (q v). **O:** opportunity, the chance of a lifetime; game, match □ *Whether from laziness or ineptitude Sam **gave away** his last chance to make his reputation as an actor.* □ *If you **give** your chances **away** like that, how can you expect to win the game?*

give away⁵ [B1i pass] in a marriage ceremony, lead the bride to the groom's side and 'give' her to him. **S:** Mr Jones; the bride's father, brother, uncle, guardian. **O:** bride; daughter, sister, niece, ward □ *As her father was too ill to be present, the bride was **given away** by her uncle.*

give away⁶ [A1] yield, give way. **S:** wall, floor, roof; ground, river bank □ *It was no use to say that the floor of the wardrobe was rotten and had **given away** with Nurse Ellen's heavy body.* DC □ the form give way is found much more often than give away in this meaning.

give the game/the show away [B1ii] (informal) betray sb's plan, intentions, voluntarily or involuntarily □ *Hour after hour we lay in silence, waiting for some movement from the enemy. If only they would open fire and **give the show away**.* SD □ *We wanted to go out without telling* *the children, but my wife asked me about the times of the buses and* ***gave the*** *whole* ***game away.*** ⇨ give away[3].

give back (to)[1] [B1i pass B3 pass] return to its/sb's owner; hand back (to) (q v). **O:** confiscated goods; catapult; pen, book, suitcase □ *The teacher said he would* ***give*** *the boy's white mouse* ***back to*** *him at the end of the school-day.* □ *'Isn't it time you* ***gave*** *Mary her ear-rings* ***back****? She may want to wear them herself!'* □ *The photographic equipment was* ***given back to*** *the tourist when he proved that it belonged to him.* ⇨ get back[4], have back[1].

give back (to)[2] [B1i pass B3 pass] allow to enjoy again. **O:** sight; freedom, liberty; dead son □ *There was nothing the doctors could do to* ***give*** *me* ***back*** *the use of my legs. The paralysis was complete and irreversible.* □ *'****Give*** *me* ***back*** *my husband!' the woman screamed at the President. 'Don't leave him to rot in gaol'* (cf *'****Give*** *my husband* ***back to*** *me!'*).

give back (to) with interest [B1i pass B3 pass] repay with interest; reply to (an insult, offence, attack etc) but with greater force or effectiveness; pay back (for) (q v) □ *Morris borrowed heavily from his brother when he started his business, but eventually* ***gave*** *it all* ***back to*** *him* ***with interest.*** □ *Whatever slanders she had suffered from the tongues of her neighbours she* ***gave back with interest*** *in the fullness of time.* □ usu in the fig rather than in the lit meaning.

give for [B2] sacrifice, exchange, for. **O:** ⚠ one's eyes, eye-teeth, back teeth, right arm; one's life, one's all □ *Sarah would have* ***given*** *her eyes* ***for*** *a ballet dress.* DC □ *'What a very romantic story! And now of course he would* ***give*** *his life* ***for*** *you.'* OMIH □ *She missed the company of children so much that she would have* ***given*** *her right arm* ***for*** *the slightest sound from the tiniest throat.* HSG □ *As they stumbled across the dusty plain, John said, 'I'd* ***give*** *my back teeth* ***for*** *a pint of cold beer.'* □ with the words *life, all,* the expression usu indicates the literal sacrifice of one's life: *He* ***gave*** *his life* ***for*** *his country.*

give cause for [B2 pass] arouse, be the reason for. **o:** alarm, anger, concern □ *...the state of the Defence Services of Britain* ***gave cause for*** *'grave concern' and unless steps were taken to put the matter right we could look forward only to great disasters if we became involved in war.* MFM □ *During the night the old lady took a turn for the worse and today her condition* ***gives*** *us* ***cause for*** *deep anxiety.* □ the second example has a Direct Object (cause) and an Indirect Object (*us*); note the passive transform: *We are* ***given cause for*** *deep anxiety.*

give credit for [B2 pass emph rel] believe that sb possesses; credit with[2] (q v). **o:** him etc; pupil, soldier; (***for***) intelligence, common sense, ability, determination, initiative, performance □ *Harry's actions gave evidence of a will stronger than I would have* ***given*** *him* ***credit for.*** □ *I wouldn't have* ***given*** *him* ***credit for*** *such fine feelings. I always thought he was rather a coarse fellow. But I was wrong.* □ the second example has a Direct Object (credit) and an Indirect Object (*him*) followed by the prep phrase with for; cf the active and passive patterns in: *We can't* ***give*** *him* ***credit for*** *much sense.* □ *He can't be* ***given credit for*** *much sense.* ⇨ give credit (to) (for), take credit for.

give scope for [B2 pass emph rel] allow, encourage, the use of. **o:** imagination, expansion, his talents □ *...the search for a neat code of rules of civilized behaviour, though it would* ***give scope for*** *ingenuity, would be largely a waste of time.* SC □ *It is ironic that only war has seemed to* ***give*** *young men* ***scope for*** *their spirit of adventure.* □ the second example contains a Direct Object (scope) and an Indirect Object (*young men*) followed by the prep phrase with for; note the passive transform: *Young men seemed to be* ***given*** *no* ***scope for*** *the spirit of adventure.*

give forth [B1iii pass] (formal, jocular) emit, produce. **O:** cry, yell; smell, stench □ *The strange animal did not run away, but stood its ground* ***giving forth*** *a mooing sound.* □ *On summer evenings the flowers* ***gave forth*** *an almost intoxicating scent.* □ *The engine* ***gave forth*** *a horrible grinding noise, and stopped.*

give in [B1i pass] give sth to a person who is authorized to receive it; hand in (q v). **O:** script, exercise; kit □ *All papers should be* ***given in*** *before 12.30. Candidates disobeying this rule may be disqualified.* □ *'Who* ***gave*** *my name* ***in*** *for the cross-country run on Saturday? I certainly didn't!'*

give in (to) [A1 A3 pass] allow oneself to be overcome by; give way to[2] (q v), yield (to) (q v). **o:** pressure, force; persuasion, argument; self-pity □ *All sorts of other things I've had — tempers, scenes, reconciliations,* ***giving in*** *sometimes, sometimes holding out,....* PW □ *The rebels were obliged to* ***give in to*** *the superior strength of the loyalists.* □ *Since she took up Women's Lib she has stopped* ***giving in to*** *her husband on every point of difference between them: she sticks to her guns.* □ *It would have been easy to* ***give in to*** *sentimental melancholy.* ILIH □ *Blackmail is something that should never be* ***given in to****; but that is easier said than done.*

give of one's best [A2] work or perform as well as one possibly can □ *When a man is not properly nourished, you can hardly expect him to* ***give of his best*** *whether at work or play.* □ *The general* ***gave of his best*** *in order that the army should be well prepared for all eventualities.* MFM □ *'If every one of you* ***gives of his best*** *today, I'm sure you can win the Cup.'*

give evidence of[1] [B2 pass] produce witnesses or other proof in support of. **o:** court, magistrate; (***of***) identification, negligence □ *The prosecution* ***gave*** *the court* ***evidence of*** *identification before proceeding with the case against the accused.* □ the example has a Direct Object (evidence) and an Indirect Object (*the court*) followed by the prep phrase with of.

give evidence of[2] [B2] show signs of. **S:** room, clothes, objects, antique furniture. **o:** having been searched, worn, damaged, touched up □ *The packing-cases which were examined by the foreman* ***gave evidence of*** *having been tampered with; that is why he sent for the police.*

give off [B1iii pass] emit, release, produce. **O:** smoke, vapour; fumes, odour, scent, aroma; radiation, gamma rays □ *The Daimler* (a car) *stood patiently in the sun outside, its leather* ***giving off*** *a hot smell.* HD □ *The acid* ***gives off*** *a characteristically pungent odour.* □ *So much smoke was*

***given off** by the lignite that the air soon became unbreathable.*

give on to [A3] overlook; allow access to. **S:** entrance, door; window, french window. **o:** garden, street, stream, park, courtyard □ *The front of the house **gave on to** the street, and the back **on to** a long, narrow garden, with a gate opening on a rough sandy path.* CON □ *The lounge window **gave** immediately **on to** an immaculately-kept rockery.*

give out[1] [A1] become exhausted. **S:** supplies, strength; the road, track; patience; memory, ingenuity □ *The engine spluttered ominously. We exchanged anxious glances. Our worst fears were about to be realized. The petrol was **giving out**.* □ *Conversation ground slowly but surely to a halt as reminiscence and invention both **gave out**. An embarrassed silence fell on the company.* □ *The hunted animal's strength finally **gave out**, and the hounds were upon it like lightning.*

give out[2] [B1i pass] distribute; hand out[1] (q v). **O:** pencils, examination papers, books; leaflets, handbills, brochures; free cigars □ *When the papers had been **given out** the supervisor rang a bell and the students began to read them.* □ *Several people have been arrested in Red Square for **giving out** leaflets without permission.*

give out[3] [B1i pass] announce, make known. **O:** news, figures; it… that the Minister had resigned □ *He **gave out** that he would come to my headquarters and investigate the matter.* MFM □ *'Whatever made you **give** such a terrible piece of news **out** on the morning of the girl's wedding? It was sheer cruelty.'* □ *It was **given out** that casualties from the air-raid had been very light. This was intended to deceive the enemy, but of course it did nothing of the kind.* □ *The accused man had **given** himself **out** to be a qualified doctor.*

give out[4] [B1ii pass] of an umpire, say that a batsman (cricket) or striker (baseball) is dismissed, has failed, and that his innings (cricket) or inning (baseball) is at an end □ *The umpire raised his hand without hesitation. The white hope of the England side had been **given out**.* ⇨ be out[8], get out[4].

give over [A1] (substandard) stop (doing sth), be quiet □ *'We want boiled eggs, too!' the twins said, as in one voice. 'Can we have boiled eggs?' '**Give over**. Can't you see I'm cutting the pineapple?' Ma said.* DBM □ *'**Give over** pushing me, Maisie! You'll have me off the chair altogether in a minute.'*

give over to [B3 pass] abandon to. **O:** oneself; village, defeated population □ *He seemed to **give** himself **over** entirely **to** the gratification of his senses. All thought for others had been pushed out of his mind.* □ *The ruthless officers **gave** the city **over to** their men, who raped and pillaged without mercy.*

given over to [pass (B3)] (be) used for, have as its particular end or purpose □ *A large part of our productive capacity has been **given over to** the new model as a result of its enormous popularity.* □ *We have to make a translation of the electrical activity in our brains. To do this, quite a bit of the brain is **given over to** the control of the lip muscles and of the vocal chords.* TBC

given to [pass (B2)] (be) prone to, (be) in the habit of, have a tendency to □ *Old Baker is much **given to** boasting about his wartime exploits.* □ *'I'm not **given to** (making) predictions, so don't ask me what's going to happen in the next general election.'* □ the object is usu the *-ing* form of a v, as in the examples.

give birth to [B2] produce, be delivered of. **S:** woman, wife; ewe, cow, mare. **O:** baby, bouncing boy, lovely little girl, twins; lamb, calf, foal □ *When the father was told that, as a result of a fertility drug, his wife had **given birth to** sextuplets, he said 'That is too much of a good thing!'* □ (song) *'The South Lands **gave birth to** the blues.'*

give credence to [B2 pass emph rel] (formal) believe, support, sth, perhaps in spite of certain factors that may make this difficult. **S:** we; evidence, corroboration. **adj:** no; some, little. **o:** tale, story, account, claims □ *It was impossible to **give credence to** his story of hair-breadth escapes and heroic feats on the battlefield.* □ *The corroboration of four out of five of the witnesses **gave** some **credence to** the man's alibi.* □ *Little **credence** should be **given to** such wild rumours.* □ not recommended as a substitute for *believe* in informal contexts.

give currency to [B2 pass emph rel] be responsible for circulating. **o:** rumour, story, accusations; ideas, theories, proposals □ *Any newspaper that **gives currency to** such inflammatory reports should be brought before the Press Council.*

give an ear/eye to [B2] watch, listen to (while mainly occupied in some other way); pay attention (to) (q v). **o:** (***ear to***) door, bell; baby, children; (***eye to***) oven, joint; baby □ *'**Give an eye to** the fire while I'm out, won't you? There's plenty of coal in the scuttle.'* □ *'I can't go out unless there's someone to **give an ear to** the telephone.'*

give the lie (direct) to [B2 pass emph rel] show to be untrue. **o:** rumour, story, statement □ *There were discussions of how to counteract this rumour and **give the lie to** it.* HAA □ *The wonderful response of the young people to the call for help for the old members of the community **gave the lie direct to** the idea that they were entirely self-centred and thoughtless.* □ *With the Government's measures to reduce unemployment **the lie** has finally been **given to** the Opposition's allegations.*

give place to [B2] be replaced or succeeded by; give way to[1] (q v). **S:** sunshine; laughter; sorrow; joy. **o:** rain; tears; happiness; sadness (and vice-versa) □ *With the announcement of the cease-fire, despair at last **gave place to** hope, albeit restrained hope.*

give rise to [B2 rel] be the cause of. **S:** inflation; greed; floods. **o:** alarm, panic spending; corruption in industry and government; disease, cholera, starvation, homelessness □ *The government's economic policy **gave rise to** increased unemployment, though it is true that it produced a favourable balance of payments in the country's international trade.* □ *The problems to which these developments **give rise** are capable of solution if we keep our original purpose in mind.*

give teeth (to) [B2 pass] (informal) make truly effective, enforceable. **o:** rules, regulations, law, emergency measures □ *The Press Council, as a self-disciplinary body, would be more useful if it had more power. Some new measures are needed to* ***give teeth to*** *it* (or: ***give*** *it* ***teeth***).

give thought (to) [B2 pass emph rel] consider, think (about). **adj:** some, any, much; careful, serious. **o:** where one will spend one's holidays; future career; getting ready for our guests; Christmas, Tom's birthday-present □ *Have you* ***given*** *any* ***thought to*** *which university you would like to go to when you leave school?* □ *I was just* ***giving thought to*** *the problem of next term's timetable when my brother arrived out of the blue.* □ *It's high time that Millie* ***gave*** *serious* ***thought to*** *whether she is ever going to get married or not.* □ *'I haven't* ***given*** *much* ***thought to*** *the problem'* (cf *'I haven't* ***given*** *the problem much* ***thought***').

give tongue to [B2] say aloud. **o:** one's suspicions; words that had been better left unsaid □ *'Soho' they tell us, was once a hunting call. I felt like* ***giving tongue to*** *it.* CON □ *If I had* ***given tongue to*** *my doubts about the plan, we might all have been saved a lot of trouble.*

give voice to [B2 pass emph rel] utter, express, not necessarily aloud. **o:** feeling, annoyance, anger, anguish; objection, suspicion, doubts □ ***To*** *their feelings of frustration and dissatisfaction with the government, the public were at last able to* ***give voice*** *when a general election was called.* □ *If the Professor had any objections to some 'new-fangled' scheme he could always be relied upon to* ***give voice to*** *it, and vehemently too!*

give way to[1] [B2] be replaced or succeeded by; give place to (q v) □ *The grey clouds gradually broke up and* ***gave way to*** *a blue sky.* □ *As we left the house, the grey streets gradually* ***gave way to*** *open spaces until we were at last in the open country.* □ *Everywhere small family businesses are* ***giving way to*** *large and more impersonal corporations.*

give way to[2] [B2] allow oneself to be overcome by; give in (to) (q v), yield (to) (q v). **o:** emotion; anger, fear, hysterics; pressure, argument, persuasion □ *It was no use. She didn't shout, but she* ***gave way to*** *a low controlled anger.* DC

give weight to [B2 pass emph rel] strengthen, provide strong(er) evidence for. **adj:** more, some; added, further, extra. **o:** theory, statement, movement, warning, probability □ *The facts that he had not been seen in his usual haunts and that he had answered the phone at ten o'clock* ***gave weight to*** *his claim that he had not been out on the evening in question.* □ *Added* ***weight*** *was* ***given*** *last year* ***to*** *the possibility that there is vegetation on Mars by the American astronaut, William Sinton.* TO □ ***To*** *this speculation recent discoveries* ***give*** *further* ***weight***.

give credit (to) (for) [B2 pass] ensure that sb's effort is properly recognized. **adj:** all (of) the, some (of the); (not) enough, insufficient □ *'Will you be famous?' 'I doubt it. Unlike most writers I shall* ***give*** *all the* ***credit to*** *my ghosts.' 'Ghosts?' 'That's what they call those who do the real work while the author takes the pay.'* OMIH □ *The* ***credit for*** *the success of the concert should be* ***given to*** *the teacher who organized it.* □ *The police haven't been* ***given*** *sufficient* ***credit for*** *keeping essential services running.* ⇨ give credit for, take credit for.

give up[1] [B1i pass] surrender, allow to be taken. **O:** disputed territory, island; advanced positions □ *The general was content to* ***give up*** *a few miles of desert and retreat to a stronger, fortified line.*

give up[2] [B1i] leave, abandon; resign (from) (q v). **O:** job, appointment, career □ *For no apparent reason Matthew* ***gave up*** *his lucrative job in the City and emigrated to Canada.*

give up[3] [B1i pass] relinquish, sell; dispose of[3] (q v). **O:** car, boat; house, home □ *'I'm afraid that business is so bad that we'll have to* ***give*** *something* ***up***. *We'd better sell the horses.'* □ *Nothing could persuade her to* ***give up*** *her home: it was much too big for her, but it was where she had always lived.*

give up[4] [B1i] reveal, disclose; yield up[2] (q v). **O:** information, jealously guarded secret, treasure □ *It was not until the twentieth century that Tutankhamun's tomb* ***gave*** *its secrets* ***up*** *to the world.* □ *'Harold,' commanded Isabel, 'I insist on knowing the exact sum.' 'One thousand three hundred and forty-nine pounds six shillings, if you want to know,' said Harold, with the air of a stone* ***giving up*** *its blood* (a reference to the expression get blood out of a stone (q v)). PW

give up[5] [B1i pass] hand over custody of; abandon one's claim to. **O:** child(ren), ward, foster-child(ren) □ *When she realized that she would have to* ***give up*** *her children, she dropped the idea of getting a divorce.* □ *If the natural mother of a child claims custody, it is often very hard for the foster-parent to* ***give*** *it* ***up***.

give up[6] [B1i pass] no longer seek to avoid, or protect sb from, capture. **O:** oneself; escaped prisoner; spy, agent □ *The desperate man forced his hostages to drive on through the night. He was afraid, hungry and thirsty, but he had no intention of* ***giving*** *himself* ***up***. □ *The young girl became infatuated with the enemy agent and promised that she would conceal him in the attic of her home and never* ***give*** *him* ***up*** *to the police.*

give up[7] [B1ii pass] no longer expect, or hope for, the arrival of □ *Although she had waited up until midnight, Alice was actually surprised when she heard the key turn in the lock and Charles walked in. She had almost* ***given*** *him* ***up***. □ *'I suppose you thought we had decided not to come?' 'Well, you were very nearly* ***given up***, *it's true!'*

give up[8] [B1ii pass] have no hope of a person's recovery □ *Everyone — the doctors, the nurses, his own family — had* ***given*** *him* ***up***, *when he surprised them all by suddenly taking a turn for the better.*

give up[9] [B1iii pass] stop eating, drinking, using or indulging in; cut out[4] (q v). **O:** starchy foods, meat, alcohol; wine, beer; smoking, cigarettes; trips to London, daily swim; gambling, cards, roulette □ *'You had better* ***give up*** *wearing your new suit to work or it will soon look as shabby as all your other clothes.'* □ *He couldn't resist trying to make money on the Stock Exchange. He always lost, but he couldn't* ***give*** *it* ***up***. □ *It's easy to say that dairy products are bad for the heart, but the eating habits of a lifetime are not so easily* ***given up***.

give up[10] [B1i pass] renounce, no longer hold. **O:** religion; belief(s), convictions, principles □ *Just because the man she's going to marry is an* *atheist, there's no need for Elizabeth to* ***give up*** *her own beliefs.*

give up[11] [B1iii pass] abandon, no longer pursue (one's efforts etc). **O:** all thought of, all attempt to, any pretence of, the search for; trying to please sb, trying to understand what he was talking about; it □ *The income-tax officer was so beguiled by the young lady's charms that he* ***gave up*** *all thought of extracting further information from her — other than her telephone number.* □ *With the advancing years Aunt Florence was gradually forced to* ***give up*** *her gay social life.* □ *Mr Charlton, soporific as well as fearful, made no hint of a move and Ma* ***gave*** *it all* ***up****, at last, in disgust* (*it* = her attempt at match-making between Mr Charlton and her daughter). DBM

give up[12] [A1] admit defeat or one's inability to do sth (e g in a guessing game, or in an attempt to convince sb of something) □ *'Look! I've mentioned every possible kind of seat I can think of. I don't know any other kinds. I* ***give up****. What's the answer?' 'A chaise-longue.'* □ *'I've explained the situation to John a hundred times if I've explained it once. He does not or will not understand. I* ***give up****!'* □ *'You* ***give up*** *too easily. You could do it if you really set your mind to it.'*

give up (all) hope [B1iii pass] abandon hope, lose hope □ *After three days of continuous flights over the Atlantic,* ***all hope*** *of finding the missing aircraft was* ***given up*** *and the search abandoned.* □ *Even though the woman had been missing for three years, her mother refused to* ***give up hope*** *that one day she wold walk into her home again.*

give up the fight/the (unequal) struggle [B1iii] abandon the fight etc; be defeated □ *I tried a variety of materials as leads, and the one that took him* (= a captured animal) *longest to get through was a thong of rawhide, but even this* ***gave up the unequal struggle*** (i e was eaten through) *eventually.* DF □ *After years of trying to wrest a living from the infertile acres he had inherited, Timothy finally* ***gave up the fight*** *and turned to catering for tourists.*

give up for dead/lost [B3 pass] assume that sb is dead, has been lost; consider sb to be 'past redemption', ineducable, past help etc □ *When the climbers were three days overdue at the rendezvous, they were* ***given up for lost*** (or: ***dead***). *It was thought that no one could survive for so long without food on the north face of the mountain.* □ *When Sue's father — a pillar of the Church — heard that she had been living with an avowed atheist, he* ***gave her up for lost****.* ⇨ give up[7].

glam up [B1i pass] (slang) give a glamorous, or superficially attractive, appearance, to. **S:** she, they. **O:** herself; town, factory, dance-hall □ *'Why are you all* ***glammed up*** *this evening, Mother?' 'Don't be cheeky!'* □ *The management insisted on* ***glamming up*** *the factory for Princess Anne's visit.*

glance at [A2 pass adj rel] look quickly at. **o:** book, article; clock □ *I* ***glanced at*** *my watch and was surprised to see that it was nearly midnight.*

glance off [A1 A2] hit, at an angle, without penetrating. **S:** arrow, bullet, shell, stone; her barbed remarks. **o:** armour, wall, tank; head; his thick skin □ *The bullet* ***glanced off*** *the soldier's badge and buried itself in a nearby tree.* □ *It was impossible to insult Roger. Every remark, however barbed, just seemed to* ***glance off*** *his incredibly tough hide.*

glance over/through [A2 nom pass adj rel] scan quickly. **o:** book, article, newspaper, report, letter; poem, short story, script □ *'Do you think you could* ***glance over*** *the minutes that I've drafted of our last meeting, before I have them typed out?'* □ *As a conscientious parent, she always* ***glanced through*** *her daughter's homework and signed it.* □ *'You might give the article a quick* ***glance-through****.'*

glance round [A1 A2] look quickly round □ *He walked into the room,* ***glanced round****, saw nobody that he knew, and left again at once.* □ *The actor* ***glanced round*** *the audience and spotted his wife in the third row.*

glare (at) [A2 pass] look, with an intense expression of enmity, hostility, (at). **S:** teacher; sergeant-major; husband; thief. **o:** child; the offending soldier; his wife; the policeman □ *The two men stood* ***glaring*** *drunkenly* ***at*** *each other, while the crowd looked on with amusement.*

glare contempt/defiance/hate (at) [B2] look with an intense expression of contempt etc at □ *The youth* ***glared defiance at*** *the magistrate as he received a sentence of fifteen days in prison.*

the sun glare down [A1] pour light and heat down □ ***The sun glared down*** *with merciless intensity on the six men adrift in the lifeboat.*

glass in [B1i pass adj] enclose with glass. **O:** verandah, porch, entrance, patio □ *If we were to* ***glass in*** *the back entrance, the kitchen would not be so cold.* □ *Although they lived in the north of Scotland, they were often able to sit in their* ***glassed-in*** *verandah even in the middle of winter.*

glaze in [B1i pass adj] = glass in.

glaze over [A1] (formal) assume a fixed, trance-like, sightless appearance as though mere objects of glass, perhaps revealing lack of interest in sth. **S:** ⚠ one's eyes, expression □ *The dying man's eyes* ***glazed over*** *as he sank deeper into unconsciousness.* □ *She observed her guests' expressions* ***glazing over*** *with boredom at the insipidity of the conversation.*

glean (from) [B2 pass emph rel] obtain (from), search and find (in). **O:** information, details, facts, knowledge. **o:** old books; newspapers; overheard conversation, passing remarks □ *Old Smith always pretends that he gets his information straight from the highest authority, whereas he merely* ***gleans*** *what facts he can* ***from*** *junior clerks, and puts his own interpretation on them.*

glide across, along, away etc [A1 A2 B1ii B2] move very smoothly across etc □ [A1 B1] *The pilot managed to* ***glide*** (*the plane*) ***down*** *to a safe landing.* □ [A2] *The apparition* ***glided out of*** *the library,* ***down*** *the passage,* ***up*** *the stairs and* ***through*** *the wall at the top!*

glisten in/on [A2 emph rel] ⇨ next entry.

glisten with [A2] be covered, or filled, or specked, with drops or particles that reflect light. **S:** eyes; grass; trees. **o:** tears; dew, raindrops; frost □ *The poor child's eyes* ***glistened with*** *tears* (or: *Tears* ***glistened in*** *her eyes*) *as she read the letter telling her that her pet rabbit had died.* □ note the fig use, as in: *The young man's* *eyes* ***glistened with*** *amusement as he heard the story of his friend's accident in the dinghy.*

glitter in/on [A2 emph rel] ⇨ next entry.

glitter with [A2] give out or reflect light; shine with. **S:** sky; Christmas tree; tiara, diadem, crown, dress; neck □ *The sky* ***glittered with*** *a myriad stars* (or: *A myriad stars* ***glittered in*** *the sky*). □ *The film-star's neck* ***glittered with*** *a million pounds' worth of diamonds* (or: *A million pounds' worth of diamonds* ***glittered on*** *her neck*).

gloat over[1] [A2 pass rel] look at one's possessions with greedy, selfish, miserly delight □ *The old miser took his bag of gold coins out of the safe and* ***gloated over*** *them every night.* □ *The thieves* ***gloated over*** *their haul from the jeweller's shop, little realizing that the 'treasure' was all made of worthless paste.*

gloat over[2] [A2 pass rel] derive sadistic pleasure from. **o:** his rival's downfall; the ruin of his neighbour; the Prime Minister's embarrassment; James's misfortunes □ *'I can't understand why you should* ***gloat over*** *John's losing his job. You could easily be next on the list of "redundant workers".'*

glory in[1] [A2] be proud of; be pleased by, derive great pleasure from. **o:** his ability to speak five languages; his attractiveness to the fair sex; devoting his life to others □ *St Francis of Assisi* ***gloried in*** *his love for all God's creatures.* □ *For a few brief years, the actor* ***gloried in*** *his success with London audiences. Then, suddenly, he faded from the limelight.*

glory in[2] [A2] (jocular) possess, by accident, some 'glorious' or amusing attribute (especially one's name); rejoice in (q v) □ *Sarah Smith went to Spain and fell in love with a young man who* ***gloried in*** *the name of Juan Luis Velásquez de Albornoz y Madariaga.* □ *One of the characters in The Mikado* ***glories in*** *the title of The Lord High Executioner.*

gloss over [A2 pass adj] ignore; try to conceal or lessen. **o:** faults, mistakes, errors, inconsistencies; humble origins; unsuitability for the job; murky past □ *It is important that a politician's vices should be known and if necessary exposed. They should not be* ***glossed over***. □ *I deplore the modern tendency to* ***gloss over*** *the low standards in some of our schools.*

glow with [A2] show, throw out, reflect or be filled with. **S:** face, whole body, eyes; forest, trees. **o:** health, pride, joy, pleasure, enthusiasm; colour □ *The children ran into the house from the beach, their faces* ***glowing with*** *health and vigour.* □ *The whole countryside* ***glowed with*** *the russet tints of autumn.*

glower (at) [A2 pass] stare in a threatening or defiant way (at) □ *The child would not go, but stood by the door* ***glowering at*** *his father.*

glue to [B2 pass] join to by means of glue. **O:** poster, stamp, photograph; (table) leg; toupee, false beard. **o:** wall, envelope, passport; table; head, chin □ *When you've* ***glued*** *the spindles* ***to*** *the chair, put a couple of screws in as well to hold them firmly.*

glued to [pass (B2)] (appear to be) attached to sth as though with glue. **S:** maid, child, young man. **o:** keyhole, television □ *Half the nation was* ***glued to*** *television, watching the Miss World competition, while civil war was threatening to break out at any moment.* □ the expression *with/have one's eyes* glued to (*the keyhole* etc) is frequently used.

glut with [B2 pass] fill to excess with. **O:** market; oneself. **o:** produce; maize, apples, meat, cheap goods; food, sweets, chocolates □ *The market was* ***glutted with*** *potatoes, and thousands of tons were left to rot in the fields.* □ *The children* ***glutted*** *themselves* ***with*** *strawberries stolen from their neighbours' gardens.*

gnaw away [B1i pass] destroy, as by the teeth of a rodent. **O:** wood(work); floorboards □ *Parts of the wooden support of the house had been dangerously* ***gnawed away***. *Immediate repair was essential.*

gnaw (away) at[1] [A2 pass A3 pass] bite at (continuously), in the manner of a rodent. **S:** rat, mouse, rabbit, lion. **o:** wood; bone □ *It was obvious from their appearance that the young trees had been* ***gnawed at*** *by some small creature.* □ *The tiger in the cage* ***gnawed*** *listlessly* ***at*** *an old bone.*

gnaw (away) at[2] [A2 A3] hurt or trouble without respite. **S:** sense of guilt, remorse, injustice; hatred, sorrow, despair. **o:** conscience, heart, mind □ *Day in, day out, the feeling that he had been misjudged and punished for another man's crime* ***gnawed at*** *him until he became obsessed with ideas of revenge on society.*

go aboard [A1] board, get on a ship, plane (and in US, occasionally: train) □ *'The ship's leaving in half an hour, so we'd better* ***go aboard*** *and make ourselves comfortable.'* □ *'All aboard that's* ***going aboard***!*'* ⇨ come/take aboard.

go about[1] [A1] go, walk, travel from place to place; move in society, among friends etc; go around/round[1] (q v). **A:** in shabby clothes; in an old rattle-trap, on a bicycle □ *Is it dangerous to* ***go about*** *bareheaded when it's raining?* □ *I would advise you not to* ***go about*** *criticizing your superiors.* □ cp the second example with go about *doing sth* as in go about[3].

go about[2] [A1] circulate, be current; go around/round[2] (q v). **S:** story, rumour □ *The rumour is* ***going about*** *that John and Mary are getting married.* ⇨ get about[2], put about[2].

go about[3] [A2] approach, tackle, make a start at. **o:** it; repairing the car; problem, job, matter □ *I've got a big brown mole on my cheek. It's not very flattering and I want to get rid of it. How should I* ***go about*** *it?* H □ *She'll do anything for you if you* ***go about*** *it in the right way.* □ *Peter hasn't the faintest idea of how to* ***go about*** *finding a better job.* □ cp the second example with go about *-ing* in go about[1]. ⇨ set about[1].

go about[4] [A2] be, keep, busy with. **o:** work, affairs, business, everyday jobs □ *While the bombs were exploding daily in Belfast, the housewives* ***went about*** *their everyday tasks of keeping their homes going.* ⇨ be about[1].

go about[5] [A1] (nautical) change direction, move onto a fresh tack. **S:** ship; captain □ *As soon as the captain heard the cry 'Man overboard' he ordered the ship to* ***go about*** *and search for the missing man.* ⇨ bring about[2], come about[2], put about[1].

go about one's business [A2] mind one's own business, occupy oneself with one's own affairs; stop interfering with the affairs of other people □ *'If your brother comes here with any more criti-*

cism mbout how we bring the children up, I'll tell him to ***go about his business****.'* ⇨ send about his business.

go about (with) [A1 A3] keep company (with); court with a view to marriage; go around/round (with) (q v) □ *I'm afraid your daughter is* ***going about with*** *a man who is old enough to be her father.* □ *How long have Eric and Hilda been* ***going about*** *(****with*** *each other)?*

go abroad [A1] leave one's own country to visit or live in another □ *The young widow felt that she wanted to get away for a while, so she decided to* ***go abroad*** *for a long holiday.* ⇨ take abroad (with).

go across (to) [A1 A2 A3] pass from one side to the other (of); go over (to) (q v). **o:** (***across***) road, bridge; river; Channel; (***to***) shop; other bank; France □ [A2] *Planks were laid so that the villagers could* ***go across*** *the marshy area.* □ [A3] *'I'm just* ***going across to*** *the pub for half an hour.'* ⇨ get across[1]; send across (to), take across (to).

go after[1] [A2] pursue, try to catch. **o:** suspect, runaway, wanted man □ *The police warned the public not to* ***go after*** *the escaped prisoner, as he was armed and dangerous.* ⇨ be after[1], come after[2].

go after[2] [A2] pursue; try to get. **o:** job, position, championship; girl. **A:** with a will, with determination; as though his life depended on it □ *Once Sam decided what he wanted, he* ***went after*** *it with a single-mindedness that reminded me of his father.* ⇨ be after[2].

go against[1] [A2] be contrary to; be out of harmony with. **S:** scheme, plan, idea; his way of life. **o:** my principles, philosophy, religion, beliefs □ *The idea of trying to cheat the income tax authorities* ***went against*** *his principles — he had a strong sense of civic responsibility.* □ *That a man could be saved from disease by means of the injection of a serum seemed to* ***go against*** *logic.* ⇨ be against.

go against[2] [A2] be lost by; be unfavourable to. **S:** war; fight; election; (legal) case, action □ *The thought that the battle could* ***go against*** *them never for a moment entered into the generals' calculations.*

go against the grain [A2] be contrary to one's wishes or natural inclinations. **S:** it; giving money away, paying high prices; doing as one is told □ *The children finally went and changed their wet clothes, though it obviously* ***went against the grain*** *(with them).* □ *Staying in bed may* ***go against the grain*** *but that's what you must do if you want to get better.* □ sometimes found in the form go against sb's grain as in: *It* ***went against my grain*** *to spend ten pounds on a meal.*

go aground (on) [A1 A3 emph rel] (nautical) become stuck on mud, sand or rocks. **S:** ship, boat; tanker, liner, dinghy, launch □ *The coaster, on its first trip up the estuary, missed the narrow channel and* ***went aground on*** *a mud-bank.* ⇨ run aground (on).

go ahead[1] [A1 nom] proceed, do what one wants to do. **A:** with one's plans; without further delay □ *Now that you've had the all-clear from your doctor you can* ***go ahead*** *and start up your new shop.* □ *The government has decided to* ***go ahead*** *with its plans to develop the North-East.* □ *We can't do anything about your proposal until we get the* ***go-ahead*** *from the local Council.*

go ahead[2] [A1 nom] proceed, make progress; go forward (with) (q v). **S:** we, firm; scheme, building; work. **A:** like a house on fire, (very) fast; at a good speed, vigorously □ *Once our policy is formulated we intend to* ***go ahead*** *full steam* (or: ***go*** *full steam* ***ahead***). TBC □ *With the strike settled, work on the new bridge* ***went ahead*** *like wildfire.* □ *The best way to get ahead yourself is to join a* ***go-ahead*** *company.* □ nom form usu attrib, as in the last example.

go ahead/ahead of [A1 A2 emph] continue a journey in advance of others; go on[3] (q v). **o:** main party, the others □ *A few carefully chosen men* ***went ahead*** *while the main body remained concealed in the valley.* □ *The scouts* ***went ahead of*** *the main force and reported back the strength of the enemy.* □ ***Ahead of*** *the main group* ***went*** *an advance party to test the new route to the South Col.* ⇨ send ahead/ahead of.

go along [A1] proceed with any sustained activity, including travelling □ *They kept up their spirits by singing one song after another as they* ***went along****.* □ *They* ***went along*** *whistling to keep up their courage in the dark.* □ *You'll get more skilful at this job as you* ***go along****.*

go along (with) [A1 A3] accompany sb to a certain place □ *As everyone else was going to the pub, I decided to* ***go along*** *too.* □ *'I have to go to the dentist this morning.' 'Would you like me to* ***go along with*** *you?'*

go along with[1] [A3] be part of. **S:** the furniture, shrubs; a free supply of detergents. **o:** the flat, house; the washing-machine □ *A splendid bookcase* ***goes along with*** *the complete Encyclopaedia if you pay cash.*

go along with[2] [A3 pass] share sb's opinion; act in agreement with. **o:** him etc; policy, scheme, proposal □ *I don't necessarily* ***go along with*** *all you say about politics. I don't quite like the idea of everything getting outside our control.* □ *If we decide to* ***go along with*** *your party on the question of improving the street-lighting, we shall expect your party to* ***go along with*** *us on the provision of more funds for the library.*

go along with you! [A3] a mild rebuke or expression of disbelief; get along/away with you! (q v) □ *'Two thousand pounds a year?* ***Go along with you!*** *The job isn't worth fifteen hundred!'* □ *'Now, children,* ***go along with you!*** *You've been indoors all morning — go and get some fresh air!'* ⇨ get on[5], go on[14].

go around/round[1] [A1] go from place to place or from person to person; go about[1] (q v). **A:** doing, saying, that kind of thing; pretending that sex doesn't exist; looking as though butter wouldn't melt in one's mouth; with one's head in the clouds, with a face like thunder □ *You can't* ***go around*** *making up things about being assaulted by people who don't exist.* DC □ *Mrs Hatchett is* ***going round*** *like Macbeth muttering 'Doomed for a thousand years to walk this earth'.* DC ⇨ go about[1].

go around/round[2] [A1] circulate, pass from person to person; go about[2] (q v). **S:** news, word; story, rumour □ *Word* ***went round*** *that something important was in the offing, so the meeting was well attended.* TBC

go around/round (with) [A1 A3] keep company (with); go about (with) (q v). **o:** him/her; the wrong sort of people □ *I see that John has been* **going around with** *the same girl for three months now. It must be serious!* □ *Though they have been* **going around** *for two years now, they still haven't decided whether to marry or not.* ⇨ take around/round (with).

go aside [A1] move away from other people □ *The two lawyers* **went aside** *and discussed their clients' proposals for a settlement of the action.* ⇨ take aside/to one side.

go astray [A1] get lost; be mislaid; behave illegally or immorally. □ *A good sheepdog never lets any sheep* **go astray** *from the flock.* □ *I'm sorry that I haven't answered your letter. Unfortunately, it has* **gone astray** *and I don't remember exactly what you said in it.* □ *It is only too easy for a young girl to* **go astray** *in London, especially if she is a stranger without friends.* ⇨ lead astray.

go at[1] [A2] attack physically; argue, discuss sth heatedly. **o:** ⚠ it; each other. **A:** ⚠ hammer and tongs, hell for leather, tooth and nail □ *The two women lost their tempers and* **went at** *each other tooth and nail.* □ *The Committee has been in session for three hours on the question of the proposed increase in membership fees, and they're still* **going at** *it hammer and tongs.*

go at[2] [A2] tackle; make great efforts to do sth. **o:** job, work, task; it. **A:** with a will, with determination, with renewed vigour; for all he was worth, as though his life depended on it □ *The villagers* **went at** *the building of a dam with a will, once they had seen that the rising water could be stemmed.* □ *Once John decided to do something, he* **went at** *it for all he was worth.* □ *'I know you want to help me, but there's no need to* **go at** *it like a madman!'*

go away[1] [A1 emph] depart, leave a place or sb's presence; go off[1] (q v) □ *'I'm tired of your constant complaints:* **go away** *and leave me in peace!'* □ (nonsense rhyme) *I met a man upon the stair, A little man who wasn't there. He wasn't there again today! My God, I wish he'd* **go away**! ⇨ send away.

go away[2] [A1] (specifically, of a bride with her bridegroom) leave the wedding-guests and go on one's honeymoon □ *Mary bought a very smart outfit to* **go away** *in.* □ (rhyme) *This is the most beautiful blue, it's* **going-away** *blue.* □ going-away used attrib with *dress, hat, shoes* etc.

go back[1] [A1 emph] return. **S:** children; books; one, you. **A:** to school; to the library; to one's childhood home; to the scene of the accident □ *'This machine is* **going back** *to the shop where I bought it. It's no good!'* □ *You should never* **go back**, *they say, to the scene of your past romance.* □ *'Why didn't you turn round and* **go back**, *if you thought you'd hit somebody with your car?'* ⇨ be back[1], bring back[1], come back[1], get back[1], take back[1].

go back[2] [A1] return to an earlier point in space, time, a discussion etc □ *'Now that you've done a year in Medicine, you can't very well* **go back** *and starts an Arts course.'* □ *Once we decide to emigrate, there will be no* **going back**. *Our decision will be final and irrevocable.* □ *With the collapse of Piaget's theory about the development of a child's reasoning, we must* **go back** *to square one* (i e the starting-point). □ *'But to* **go back** *to what I was saying about life in the country....'*

go back[3] [A1] (of clocks and watches) be set to an earlier time in order to allow for changing hours of daylight (esp in UK for the winter) □ *'What date do the clocks* **go back** *this year?'* □ *'I'm looking forward to the clocks* **going back** *next Sunday: it means an extra hour in bed!'* ⇨ put back[2].

go back on [A3 pass] retract, fail to fulfil. **o:** one's word, promise, solemn undertaking, pledge; previous choice □ *'I promised you that I'd help you, didn't I? Well, I'm not* **going back on** *that.'* □ *If you witness a drunkard signing the pledge* (i e that he will stop drinking), *you feel personally responsible when he* **goes back on** *it.* CON □ *Promises are made to be kept, and not lightly to be* **gone back on**.

go back (to) [A1 A3] have its origin in; date from/back to (q v). **S:** our family; the company; custom, belief, practice; devotion, attachment to sth; taste, liking for sth; hatred of sth □ *'The fifteenth century! Good gracious, I didn't realize that his title* **went back** *that far.'* □ *We have to* **go back to** *the early years of industrial revolution if we want to trace the history of mass production.* □ *Ann's love of horses* **goes back** *as far as she can remember.* H

go before[1] [A1 A2] precede in time; live (and die) before one's own time (esp of pioneers). **S:** those who; many; our ancestors □ *We have endeavoured to live up to the standards of those who have* **gone before** (or: **gone before** *us*). MFM

go before[2] [A2] appear before, in order to explain one's actions or to receive punishment; be presented for discussion, approval etc □ *In my day, a boy who was caught smoking in school* **went before** *the headmaster and was probably beaten.* □ *My application to add a room to my house* **goes before** *the planning committee next week.* ⇨ be before[2], bring before, come before[2], put before[2], take before.

pride goes before a fall [A2] (proverb) used to indicate or warn against, the fact that a boastful or proud statement (action etc) is often quickly followed by some event which disproves it and appears to be a form of retribution □ *Last week Jimmy was boasting about his large salary. This week he is without a job.* ***Pride goes before a fall.***

go behind sb's back [A2] act unfairly, unethically, deceitfully □ *'I know that you and I don't agree about everything, but I thought I could trust you to discuss our problems frankly, and not to* **go behind my back** *complaining to the manager.'*

go below (decks) [A1 A2] (nautical) on a ship, leave the deck and go down to the living quarters etc □ *A seaman* **went below** *to fetch the mate a cup of cocoa.* ⇨ be below[3], take below.

go between [A2] fit well into a position between; pass between □ *This picture* **goes** *nicely* **between** *the portraits of your father and mother.* □ *Trying to avoid the jealousy of Mary while keeping on good terms with Jane was like* **going between** *Scylla and Charybdis.*

go-between [nom (A2)] an intermediary or messenger, esp between lovers □ *The little girl* *was quite unaware that she was being used as a **go-between** by her elder sister and the married man next door.*

go beyond [A2] exceed, surpass. **o:** one's brief, instructions; expectations, intentions; all reason □ *We expected Mr Graham to be displeased with our decision, but his anger **went beyond** all reason.* □ *A prize of £100 would have been marvellous, but the announcement that I had won £10 000 **went beyond** my wildest dreams.* ⇨ be beyond[2].

go beyond one's duty [A2] exceed one's obligations *either* officiously *or* out of courage, determination etc □ *It was clear that the Town Clerk had **gone beyond his duty** in ordering the new (and very expensive) street-lighting without authority.* □ *If soldiers did not occasionally **go beyond their duty** and act on their own initiative, the Army would function too rigidly to be effective.* □ a soldier is often 'decorated' for actions that go beyond the call of duty.

go beyond a joke [A2] become a serious matter, no longer funny □ *Your teasing of the new typist has **gone beyond a joke** and I advise you to stop it.* ⇨ be beyond a joke.

go by[1] [A1 A2] pass (before, in front of, near to, sb). **S:** procession, cavalcade, parade; band □ *As each contingent **went by**, there was a burst of applause from the watching crowd.* □ *The parade **went by** us, and soon silence descended once more on the square.*

go by[2] [A1] pass, elapse; go on[7] (q v). **S:** time; days, weeks, months; seconds, minutes; an age, an eternity □ *As the months **went by**, the villagers gradually got accustomed to the stranger in their midst.* □ *In days **gone by*** (or: *In **bygone** days) it was hardly safe to travel anywhere by night.* □ note the form bygones in: *Let **bygones** be **bygones*** (i e Let us forget past quarrels or disagreements and make a fresh start).

go by[3] [A1] pass without being used or grasped. **S:** opportunity, chance, opening □ *Mr Simpson hesitated just a little too long over the offer of a partnership in the firm; and when he finally made up his mind to accept, the opportunity had **gone by**.*

go by[4] [A2] be guided by, take one's course, direction, from. **o:** star; map, compass □ *We had no compass, and only the distant gunfire to **go by*** (i e to judge our position).

go by[5] [A2] judge according to. **o:** advice, recommendation; past experience; what John says; appearances □ *If the FAO experts' report is anything to **go by**, there's going to be another terrible famine in Bengal.* □ *'Please don't **go by** what I say! My taste in films is not very reliable.'* □ *It's often a mistake to **go by** appearances: that poor-looking individual is anything but poor. In fact, he's a millionaire.*

go-by [nom (A1)] the act of ignoring, disregarding, not selecting sb (e g for promotion) □ *Gilbert accepted me in his rather pompous way, even when my own family had given me the **go-by**.* ASA □ only in the phrase *give sb the* go-by.

go by the book/rules [A2] act in a rigid, strictly correct, or bureaucratic manner □ *'If you **go by the book** you shouldn't have any trouble with the authorities.'*

go by the name of [A2] be known as, be called □ *This wild flower **goes by the name of** Old Man's Beard.*

go down[1] [A1] set, disappear below the horizon. **S:** ⚠ the sun, moon, stars □ *As the sun **went down** the whole sky became suffused with a red glow.*

go down[2] [A1 emph] (nautical) sink, disappear below the surface of the sea; (of men) drown. **S:** ship, boat, vessel; captain, crew, yachtsman, fisherman □ *We watched amazed as the destroyer keeled over and **went down**.* □ *The ship struck a hidden reef and **went down** with all hands.* □ *In the tradition of the sea, the captain stayed on board until all the passengers and crew had left; but he himself **went down** with his ship.*

go down[3] [A1] be swallowed. **S:** soup, fish, dinner; wine, cocktail, drink; pill, medicine. **A:** very well, famously; badly; the wrong way □ *John was delighted that his wife's cooking should **go down** so well. The main guest was his boss!* □ *Either from the sherry **going down** the wrong way or from pure rage, Tom's face turned purple.* SPL □ *It was Portuguese champagne and **went down** like mother's milk.* ILIH ⇨ get down[5].

go down[4] [A1 emph] fall, collapse □ *The policeman hit the man once with his truncheon, and he **went down** like a felled ox.* ⇨ get down[7].

go down[5] [A1] be reduced in amount. **S:** prices, charges, fees, subscriptions; taxes, rates □ *It's a strange thing, but prices always seem to be going up. They never **go down**!* ⇨ be down[2], bring down[5], come down[3].

go down[6] [A1] be lowered (in level). **S:** wine, whisky; sugar, flour; reserves, trading balance □ *Now and then Pop decided that the punch was **going down** rather too fast and added another harmless dash of rum, a little Kirsch, or a glass of brandy.* BFA □ *If our stocks of food **go down** much further, we shall have a hard winter.*

go down[7] [A1] be reduced in force or degree. **S:** wind; temperature, the glass (= barometer), the mercury □ *If the wind doesn't **go down** before three o'clock, we won't be able to take off today.* □ *The glass is **going down**, so we must expect a change in the weather.*

go down[8] [A1] leave university at the end of a term or finally □ *...he was trying to remember, first, who this was, and secondly, whether he was one of the present generation of undergraduates or had **gone down**.* HD ⇨ be/come down (from), send down.

go down[9] [A1] be written down, recorded. **S:** statement, speech, evidence, complaint □ *Every word uttered in court **went down** for future reference.* ⇨ be down[3], get down[4], put down[8], set down[2], take down[3].

go down on one's knees (to) [A3] adopt a kneeling position in order to do sth; abase oneself (before) □ *The little girl **went down on her knees** and put her doll to bed.* □ *If you wanted something to eat after nine o'clock in that restaurant you almost had to **go down on your knees** and beg for it.* ⇨ get down[3].

go down to[1] [A3] be defeated by. **S:** champion, record-holder, challenger; batsman. **o:** newcomer, younger man; fast ball □ *The reigning champion **went down to** a hammer-blow in the twelfth round.* □ *The Roman Empire finally **went down to** the barbarians.*

go down to[2] [A3] approach, esp a river or the sea □ (children's rhyme) *Adam and Eve and Pinch-me-tight* ***went down to*** *the river to bathe. Adam and Eve were drowned. Who do you think was saved?* □ *Men who* ***go down to*** *the sea in ships...* (= earn their living on the sea).

go down to[3] [A3] reach, get as far as. **S:** book, volume, article. **o:** the sixteenth century; 1945 □ *This book is no use to me; it only* ***goes down to*** *the General Election of 1951.*

go down to history/posterity [A3] be remembered for many years to come □ *Winston Churchill will* ***go down to history*** *as the man who rallied the British people when they seemed to be defeated.*

go down (with) [A1 A3] be accepted (by). **S:** he etc; suggestion, proposal; scheme, plan; offer; explanation, story, account; my divorce, decision to emigrate □ *'How do you think Gigi will* ***go down****?' 'Well, I think she'll* ***go down*** *all right* ***with*** *father, but I'm not so sure about mother.'* □ *I gave my name as Jessie Proctor. It* ***went down*** *all right, and it matches the initials on my case.* RFW □ *Joe's explanation for his lateness didn't* ***go down*** *at all well. His wife saw through it immediately.*

go down with [A3] become ill with. **o:** measles, flu, mumps, severe chill, cholera, malaria, typhoid □ *Mr Armstrong was unable to go into the office on Monday because he had* ***gone down with*** *influenza.* □ usu restricted to illnesses that strike quickly. ⇨ be down with.

go for[1] [A2] leave one's home or place of work to take exercise etc. **o:** walk, stroll, run, drive in the country; a sail □ *'My husband has just* ***gone for*** *a constitutional* (= a regular walk for one's health), *but he'll be back in half an hour.'*

go for[2] [A2] go somewhere to obtain or fetch sb or sth. **o:** newspaper, milk; drink; doctor, police □ *When she found that the baby still had a high temperature after twelve hours, the young mother decided to* ***go for*** *the doctor.* □ *After lunch, Bill* ***went for*** *a quick one to the local pub.* HAA ⇨ send for[1].

go for[3] [A2 pass] attack, physically or verbally. **S:** dog, youth; journalist; wife. **o:** intruder, old man; Prime Minister; husband. **A:** with a razor, a two-handed sword; with venom □ *When Charlie arrived home drunk once again, his wife* ***went for*** *him with the rolling pin.* □ *Just as the man was about to push his way into the house, the girl called out 'Come on, Fido!* ***Go for*** *him!', and the intruder fled.* □ *I didn't mean to kill Micky; he* ***went for*** *me with a razor.* PE □ *...she had already been twice* ***gone for*** *by Mrs Thompson for trying to make herself useful.* TGLY

go for[4] [A2] be true for, include. **S:** this, that; what I say □ *'Tell the men that they can knock off for an hour.' 'Does that* ***go for*** *me, too?'* □ *'Your sister is a selfish girl — and that* ***goes for*** *you, too.'*

go for[5] [A2] like, be attracted by. **o:** him etc; pop music, modern art; every new gadget □ *I don't* ***go for*** *horror films, and I can't understand why anyone likes them.* □ *'There's a peach of a girl sitting by herself over there. Why don't you go and chat her up?' 'I don't* ***go for*** *blondes, thank you!'* □ *He* ***goes for*** *its full, delicious flavour. I* ***go for*** *its economy.* WI □ often neg.

go for[6] [A2] be sold for. **S:** house, land, second-hand car, antique. **o:** far more/less than we expected, a mere twenty pounds, a price I couldn't possibly afford □ *The old cottage, dilapidated as it was,* ***went for*** *over £5 000.* □ *'How much do you think these Chinese vases will* ***go for****?'* □ note esp go for a song = go for very little money, be sold very cheaply.

go for a Burton [A2] (slang) be killed (originally an RAF expression meaning that a companion had not returned from a flying mission) □ *There was gloom in the bar when it was realized how many of our friends had* ***gone for a Burton*** *during the night's raids.*

go for nothing/very little [A2] be in vain, have no/little importance; count for (q v) nothing etc. **S:** (all one's) work, effort, endeavour, sacrifice, devotion; influence, position, money □ *When the company was taken over by Giant Containers Ltd, a lot of people lost their jobs. Their loyalty and hard work* ***went for nothing.*** □ *We realized that all the care we had taken to bring up and educate our daughter had* ***gone for nothing*** *when she ran away with her French teacher.*

go for a song [A2] ⇨ go for[6].

go forth [A1] (Biblical, formal) issue, be created, emerge. **S:** order, command, edict; an army, a fleet □ *From Herod's palace the command* ***went forth*** *that all young children were to be slain.* □ *We must call the whole people to our help, as partners in the battle; only from an inspired Nation can* ***go forth****, under these conditions, an inspired Army.* MFM

go forward (with) [A1 A3] proceed, make progress (with); go ahead[1] (q v). **S:** [A1] **o:** [A3] work, plans, reorganization, rationalization of production methods □ *Work on the new hospital is* ***going forward*** *at a satisfactory pace.* □ *The Committee decided to* ***go forward with*** *its plans for the compulsory purchase of land, so that the road could be widened.*

go from bad to worse [A2] continue to deteriorate. **S:** matters, things, situation; behaviour; the condition of the homeless □ *As 1955 sped on, things* ***went from bad to worse*** *in the territory, though various means of tightening up security at the mines began to take effect.* DS □ *With inflation and rising unemployment, the situation is* ***going from bad to worse*** *for millions of people.*

go home[1] [A1] go to one's place of residence, return to one's country □ *'It's terribly late! I must* ***go home****! My father gets furious if I'm out after midnight.'* □ (slogan on a wall) *Yanquis* (= Americans), ***go home!***

go home[2] [A1] (euphemism) die; go to heaven □ *'Poor old Joe's* ***going home*** *at last. It's a pity he couldn't have lived to a hundred.'* □ *I'm afraid those old rose bushes are* ***going home;*** *but they've been marvellous for the last twenty years.*

go home[3] [A1] hit the target, have the intended effect. **S:** barb, taunt; reply □ *Rufford was a skilful debater, and his calculated sarcasm* ***went home****. His opponent flushed under the attack.*

go in[1] [A1 emph] enter a house, school, shed etc □ *'We can't discuss your problems standing here in the rain. Let's* ***go in*** *and make ourselves comfortable.'* □ *I* ***went in*** *by the back door and found myself in the kitchen.* ⇨ get in/into[1], go into[1].

go in[2] [A1 emph] disappear behind a cloud. **S:**

⚠ the sun, moon, stars □ *Just as we were ready to be photographed, and all saying 'cheese' to produce those fake smiles, the sun* ***went in****!*

go in[3] [A1 emph A2] fit. **S:** cork; key; foot; plug; suit. **o:** bottle; lock; shoe; socket; bag □ *'The piano's too big; it won't* ***go in*** (*this room*)*.'* ⇨ put in[4].

go in[4] [A1 emph] (cricket) take one's turn to bat etc. **S:** batsman; side; team □ *My uncle used to* ***go in*** *number four for Beckenham* (i e he was the fourth batsman). □ *Then* ***in went*** *the skipper at six wickets down to try and prevent a total collapse.* ⇨ be in[5], put in[7].

go in[5] [A1] be understood or assimilated. **S:** facts, information, news □ *'It's no use. I've read and re-read the chapter on the life-cycle of the river fluke, but it won't* ***go in****!'* ⇨ take in[6].

go in and win [A1] (informal) a standard form of encouragement to sb who is about to take part in a competition, sit an examination etc □ *'Remember that we're all on your side! So* ***go in and win****!'*

go in sb's favour [A2] (legal) be decided in sb's favour. **S:** case, action, suit □ *After many anxious days when things looked very black, the case finally* ***went in my friend's favour****.*

go in fear of one's life [A2] be afraid that one may be killed, esp by assassination or murder □ *As her husband became more and more violent every time he had too much to drink, the poor woman* ***went in fear of her life****.*

go in (at) one ear and out (at/of) the other [A2 A3] be unheeded or unlearnt, of sth said to an inattentive, uninterested or unintelligent person □ *It's no use asking Tim to deliver any messages for you. Everything* I *say to him* ***goes in at one ear and out at the other****.*

go in for[1] [A3] enter as a candidate or contestant. **o:** competition, examination; tournament, event; the 5 000 metres □ *He* ***went in for*** *too many events, and so won none.* ⇨ be in for[1], put in for[1].

go in for[2] [A3] have as one's chosen career. **o:** teaching, medicine, architecture, politics, the law □ *My son is* ***going in for*** *catering, and part of his course takes place in France.*

go in for[3] [A3] play, have as a sport; have as a hobby, pastime etc. **o:** cricket, golf, tennis, swimming; keeping rabbits, breeding dogs, collecting stamps; bird-watching □ *'Why don't you* ***go in for*** *collecting antiques or something? You need something to take your mind off your work.'*

go in for[4] [A3] regularly practise, make a habit/practice of (q v); use. **o:** smoking; exercise; that sort of thing; scandal-mongering, gossip; flag-waving, name-dropping □ *I'm not one of those people who* ***go in for*** *dieting — I'm much too fond of eating!* □ *Mr Brown* ***goes in for*** *a strange kind of phraseology in his letters, a would-be literary style that doesn't quite come off.*

go in and out [A1] shine intermittently. **S:** light, lamp, sign □ *The neon lights* ***went in and out****, at one moment turning the square into day and the next plunging it back into darkness.*

go in and out (of) [A1 A2] move about from one place to another, usu entering and leaving premises, or cover of some kind □ *I wish that child would keep still for a while, and stop* ***going in and out*** *like a dog at a fair.* □ *The visitors* ***went in and out of*** *the various pavilions so fast that they could not have appreciated everything they saw at the Exhibition.* ⇨ be in and out of.

go into[1] [A2] enter; insert a part of oneself (esp one's hand). **o:** room, corner, den; drawer, desk, cupboard □ *The old lady* ***went into*** *a room at the back of the shop and returned with a beautiful Meissen figure which she placed carefully on a table before us.* □ *Somebody keeps* ***going into*** *my desk and pinching my pencils.* □ *The dog used to* ***go into*** *a corner of the room as soon as its master left the house, and stay there till he returned.* ⇨ go in[1].

go into[2] [A2] hit, make (violent) contact with. **o:** wall, tree, barrier; crowd, oncoming traffic □ *The car must have* ***gone into*** *the side of the house at a tremendous speed. The car was unrecognizable and one side of the house was destroyed.*

go into[3] [A2] be admitted to (usu temporarily); go to live in. **o:** hospital, mental home, convalescent home; lodgings, digs □ *I hear that old Mrs Smith has had to* ***go into*** *hospital again; evidently she wasn't completely cured last time.* □ *Most University students have to* ***go into*** *digs for at least one or two years.*

go into[4] [A2] enter a certain mental or physical state, begin a pattern of behaviour, usu involuntarily. **o:** a trance, coma; hysterics, fit, convulsions; a decline; peals, shrieks, fits of laughter □ *At this point a hypnotist will remind us that, if he can be induced to stare intently at a shiny object, a patient may* ***go into*** *a trance.* HAH □ *When old Martha died, her husband immediately* ***went into*** *a decline and followed her to the grave within a month.* ⇨ fall into[2], go off into.

go into[5] [A2] join, adopt as a career; start, organize. **o:** the Army, Navy, Air Force, Merchant Navy; the Church; politics, family business; business (for oneself) □ *A good many Army officers* ***go into*** *the Church when they retire.* □ *Nothing would induce me to* ***go into*** *the family business!* □ *...on the other hand, I would not be averse to* ***going into*** *business on my own account.*

go into[6] [A2] adopt a (different) kind of dress. **o:** mourning; long trousers; lighter clothes □ *People don't* ***go into*** *mourning these days. It's all part of our wanting to forget about death.* □ *The boy felt a fool when he had to* ***go into*** *short trousers while all his friends at day-schools were allowed to wear what they liked.*

go into[7] [A2 pass adj] examine, consider, discuss. **o:** details, particulars; the why and the wherefore of...; question, problem, evidence; accusations, allegations; the cost, usefulness of a scheme; it □ *'Please don't spend too much time* ***going into*** *details of your case. Just let me know the main points.'* □ *'I know you want to tell me about your father's illness; but please don't let's* ***go into*** *it now.'* □ *We've been* ***going into*** *the how and how much of flat-sharing, with the help of a number of girls who are doing it very successfully.* H □ *The chancellor said that these proposals would have to be* ***gone into*** *very carefully.*

go into[8] [A2 emph] be capable of dividing (another, given figure) so that the result is greater than one □ *Six* ***goes into*** *twelve, twice. But thirteen* ***into*** *twelve doesn't* ***go*** (or: *won't* ***go***).

go into abeyance [A2] be suspended, shelved or postponed indefinitely. **S:** laws, draft legislation, the citizen's right to a quick trial, the government's plans to expand the economy □ *I'm afraid that our new pension scheme will have to* ***go into abeyance*** *until the present depression is over.* □ *'No imprisonment without trial' is a principle that* ***goes into abeyance*** *when the nation's security is in danger from terrorists.*

go into one's act/routine [A2] (informal) start one's (well-known) pattern of behaviour □ *Whenever the village centenarians, Alf and Jo, were asked by some innocent visitor how old they were, they would* ***go into their act*** *of 'I'm older than him', 'He isn't, I'm the oldest', and so on.*

go into action [A2] begin an attack, start a planned operation □ *The commandos* ***went into action*** *at night with their faces blackened for better concealment.* □ *Every night she would put on her war-paint and* ***go into action*** *along the Bayswater Road, where she knew there would be plenty of eager customers.* ⇨ be in/bring into/come into action.

go into a (flat) spin [A2] (of an aircraft) get out of control in this way; (of a person) lose one's former self-control or balanced way of life □ *The first time the young pilot flew solo he* ***went into a spin*** *and only just succeeded in getting the aircraft under control 500 feet above the ground.* □ *When Mary broke off the engagement, John seemed to* ***go into a flat spin****. He was hardly ever sober for three months.*

go into a huddle [A2] informal) confer, consider what action to take □ *The professors* ***went into a huddle*** *and decided that the students' breach of the rules could not be overlooked.*

go into service/use [A2] begin to be used. **S:** new model, gun, machine □ *The 747s could not* ***go into service*** *before the crews agreed on a new salary structure.* ⇨ be in/bring into/come into service/use.

go near (to) [A1 A2 A3] approach close to. **o:** the edge of the cliff; bull; nettles; (also in [A3]) solving the problem, meeting sb's wishes, requirements □ *'Don't* ***go near*** *that dog; it's very savage.'* □ *'I told you not to* ***go near*** *your father's study while he's working.'* □ *The yacht* ***went*** *too* ***near to*** *te rocks and was soon swept on to them.* □ *His suggestion* ***went*** *very* ***near to*** *resolving our dilemma.* □ usu neg or with some modifying word like *too, very* (near); (near) *enough.*

go off[1] [A1 emph] leave a place, room, building, country; go away[1] (q v); exit from the stage. **A:** to look for his friends; for a short holiday; in high dudgeon □ *They sold up their house and* ***went off*** *to live in Canada with their married daughter.* □ (stage directions) *John* ***goes off*** *L.* (= left) *as a face appears at the window C.* (= centre). □ *'This* (discussion) *is unbearably scientific,' said Ann Halsey. 'I'm* ***going off*** *to make tea.'* TBC ⇨ take off (to).

go off[2] [A1] be good, bad etc in the event. **S:** match; conference, meeting, visit; interview. **A:** well, as expected, without a hitch □ *'How did the meeting* ***go off****? Did the expected row take place or was it quite peaceful?'* □ *Aunt Ellen had the operation this morning and it all* ***went off*** *quite well.* RFW

go off[3] [A1] fall asleep □ *He didn't seem to be able to* ***go off****, so he went into the kitchen and made himself a cup of tea.* □ *'As soon as the baby's* ***gone off*** *we'll be able to relax and watch television.'* ⇨ put off[8].

go off[4] [A2] lose one's liking for. **o:** coffee, beer, cheese; the Irish; the cinema, pop music; painting as a hobby □ *The children seem to have* ***gone off*** *cornflakes for breakfast.* □ *I've* ***gone off*** *the south of France since it became so overcrowded.* □ *He* ***went off*** *driving altogether after his accident.* ⇨ be off[8], put off[5], turn off[2].

go off[5] [A1] make a (sudden) ringing noise; fire, detonate, explode. **S:** alarm, alarm-clock; gun, pistol; bomb, device, booby-trap, fireworks. **A:** by accident; with a bang □ *Just as the burglar thought he was safely inside the house, the alarm* ***went off****.* □ *My alarm-clock doesn't wake me any more. When it* ***goes off*** *I just stop it in my sleep.* □ *The bomb-disposal squad worked feverishly to defuse the bomb before it could* ***go off****.* ⇨ let off[4], set off[1].

go off[6] [A1] turn sour,, become unfit to eat or drink, go bad. **S:** yesterday's meat; milk; wine □ *'This milk was fresh this morning, but it's* ***gone off****. It must be the weather.' 'Yes, there's thunder in the air, I'm sure.'* ⇨ be off[7].

go off[7] [A1 emph] become unavailable. **S:** water, gas, electricity, power □ *Just as the weather turned cold, the electricity supply* ***went off****.* ⇨ be off[6], turn off[1].

go off[8] [A2] (slang) go mad, behave in a crazy manner. **o:** ⚠ one's head, rocker, nut, chump □ *Poor old Tom* ***went off*** *his head, spent all his money in six months and ended up begging in the streets.* □ *What with all those children and a shiftless husband, it's no wonder Mrs Hapless finally* ***went off*** *her rocker and rushed down the street in her nightgown.* ⇨ be off[9].

go off the boil [A2] stop boiling; (informal) pass the point of maximum enthusiasm, excitement, sexual stimulation etc □ *'Don't let the potatoes* ***go off the boil****, will you dear?'* □ *Just when the workers were about to go on strike, the wives began to point out that they would have no money for Christmas, and the movement* ***went off the boil****.* □ (of a woman expecting a child who, after feeling the first pains of childbirth, has stopped experiencing them) *'She's just* ***gone off the boil****, as they say in the midwifery trade.'* DIL

go off the deep end [A2] (informal) show extreme anger; rant and rave □ PETER: *You should have heard her the other night. You know what happened? Her wandering boy returned. He hadn't been home for two weeks. And she* ***went off the deep end****.* TOH □ *When Angela found out that her husband had spent the weekend with her best friend in a Brighton hotel she* ***went off the deep end****.*

go off the rails [A2] (informal) (begin to) behave in an antisocial, immoral, dishonest or criminal way □ *It was odd how Harold, who had never since his marriage taken a step along the primrose path, never* ***gone off the rails*** *in any way or wished to, proved himself a past-master of intrigue.* PW ⇨ run off the rails.

go off at half-cock [A3] (informal) start sth before preparations are complete, thus endangering or spoiling the result □ *The publicity for the new car* ***went off at half-cock*** *following a leak of information about all the novel features that it incorporated.* ⇨ go off[2].

go off at a tangent [A3] abruptly change the subject under discussion; take up a minor point, losing track of the main argument; act unpredictably and somewhat irrelevantly □ *We were talking about the cost of tomatoes when John* ***went off at a tangent*** *and started talking about the revival of wine-making in England.*

go off into [A3] suddenly enter a certain mental etc state. **o:** hysterics; fits of laughter; a dead faint □ *Every time the baby started throwing his food about, his sisters* ***went off into*** *shrieks of laughter.* ⇨ go into[4].

go off with [A3] leave (illicitly) in sb's company, run away (with) (q v); steal and carry away, run away with[1] (q v). **o:** his best friend's wife; his employer's collection of gold medals □ *'The fat's in the fire! Myra's* ***gone off with*** *Ted!'* □ *After twenty years of honest service, the cashier suddenly* ***went off with*** *£10 000 of the company's money.*

go on[1] [A2] depart for the purpose of. **o:** holiday, vacation, safari; a trip, excursion, course □ *Only the rich can afford to* ***go on*** *safari these days.* □ *It's time I* ***went on*** *a refresher course — I'm getting out of touch with modern techniques.* ⇨ send on[1].

go on[2] [A1] continue one's journey □ *The party of explorers decided that they could not* ***go on*** *with darkness closing in.* □ *We all voted to* ***go on****, despite the signs of a thunderstorm on the horizon.*

go on[3] [A1] continue a journey ahead of others; go ahead/ahead of (q v) □ *Mr Hood said that he would have to* ***go on****, as he was due at a meeting at eleven o'clock. The others could follow at their leisure.* ⇨ send on[2].

go on[4] [A2] mount and travel on, esp as a treat. **o:** donkey, horse, elephant, camel; speed-boat, yacht; roundabout, slide; the Big Dipper, the Ghost Train □ *The children* ***went on*** *everything at the Fair, and then found they hadn't enough money to get the bus home.*

go on[5] [A1] continue an activity, or relationship; carry on[1] (q v). **A:** walking, working, talking; as before, like that, as though... □ *I want to* ***go on*** *being a teenager, because I am enjoying every minute of it.* H □ *Like some infernal monster, still venomous in death, a war can* ***go on*** *killing people for a long time after it's all over.* RFW □ *'We can't* ***go on*** *as though nothing has happened. It has happened. You've broken your promise.'* □ *What I like about Mr Kaplan is that in spite of everything, he* ***goes on*** *trying.* ⇨ get/go on with.

go on[6] [A1] of a state of affairs, continue without change. **S:** rivalry, jealousy, backbiting; cold war, state of suspended hostility □ *She felt that she could not keep up the pretence much longer. How long, she wondered, could it* ***go on****?* □ *The cold war between the two countries seemed to* ***go on*** *and* ***on****.* □ *After Mr Appleby left the firm everything* ***went on*** *as usual.*

go on[7] [A1] pass (by), go by[2] (q v). **S:** time; months, days, weeks, years □ *As the years* ***go on****, we grow both wiser and sadder.*

go on[8] [A1] continue speaking, after a short pause □ *'If it's your inheritance, I don't see why you shouldn't like it.' When Brigit didn't answer at once, she* ***went on*** *almost belligerently, 'Anyway, I adore it all.'* DC

go on[9] [A1] add some new point to what has previously been said or written. **Inf** to say, to explain, to observe □ *After criticizing our proposal in every detail, the director* ***went on*** *to reassure us that there was nothing personal in his comments.* □ Inf always present.

go on[10] [A1] happen, take place. **S:** what; something very strange, fishy, interesting, important; not much □ *Something wasn't right there, and she wanted to know what was* ***going on****.* WI □ *Young people are leaving the country for the cities. There's more* ***going on*** *there.* □ *The major problem of colour television is still the unsolved one of what* ***goes on*** *in the retina.* □ *'If you never read the newspapers, you'll never know what's* ***going on*** *in the world.'* □ *'What's* ***going on*** *between that couple over there? There's something very odd about their behaviour.'* □ note the unusual use of the simple present tense in the following: *'There's something not quite straightforward about the way you're all behaving. Come on now! What* ***goes on****?'*

go on[11] [A2] act according to; be guided by. **o:** hearsay, rumour, gossip; what you read in the papers □ *It's a mistake to* ***go on*** *the Government's account of the talks with Russia. It's incomplete, at best.* □ *The detectives admitted that after questioning several dozen people they still had no real evidence to* ***go on****.* □ *I suddenly saw that the belief I had been* ***going on*** *all my life was quite without foundation.*

go on[12] [A2] be spent on. **S:** money, income; half of what he earns; pension; proceeds of a sale. **o:** the car, the house, food, heating, clothes; luxuries, (non-)essentials; records □ *'A lot of my grant* ***goes on*** *books; but I think it's money well spent. Don't you?'*

go on[13] [A2] begin to receive; get help from. **o:** national assistance, relief; half pay; the dole, the parish □ *A lot of people who never expected to be unemployed have had to* ***go on*** *the dole.*

go on![14] [A1] (informal) used as an exclamation in various meanings, depending on the situation and reflected by the intonation of the speaker etc (e g 'I don't believe you!', 'Don't exaggerate'; 'I dare you to (do sth)'; 'Please do it!'; 'Stop hesitating! Do it!'); get on![5] (q v) □ *'How old are you?' 'I'm forty.'* ***'Go on!*** *You don't look a day over thirty!'* □ *'I don't know whether to write to Mary or not.'* ***'Go on!*** *What harm could it do?'* □ often preceded by *'Oh....'* ⇨ get along/away with you!, go along with you!

go on[15] [A1] be lit. **S:** light, lamp □ *What time do the illuminations* ***go on*** *tonight?* □ *We had been sitting for a couple of hours in candlelight when to our relief the lights* ***went on*** *again.* ⇨ be on[8], put on[2], turn on[1].

goings-on [nom (A1)] ⇨ second entry after goggle (at).

gone on [A2] ⇨ third entry after goggle (at).

go on the stage [A2] earn one's living as an actor □ *To her parents' dismay, Brigit decided to* ***go on the stage****.*

go on the streets [A2] earn one's living as a street prostitute □ *Before changes were made in the law, some prostitutes literally* ***went on the streets****. Now, they operate more discreetly from bars and clubs.*

go on tour [A2] travel from place to place to entertain or do business. **S:** opera company, the

National Ballet, circus; play; pop group; director, publicity manager □ *The Royal Shakespeare Company* **goes on tour** *for several weeks every year.* □ *'I'm afraid you can't see the Manager until next week; he's* **gone on tour** *to Europe.'*

go on about [A3] talk endlessly about (usu in an unreasonable or complaining way) □ *'Yes, yes! I admit I was wrong in not keeping you informed of my plans. But please don't* **go on about** *it!'* □ *'That woman bores me stiff! The way she* **goes on about** *her paragon of a son!'* ⇨ be on about.

go on (at) [A1 A3] nag, criticize, complain (to sb) about his work, behaviour etc □ *'Why do you* **go on at** *that poor girl all the time? She does her best.'* ⇨ be on at.

go on before [A1] precede; lead □ (hymn) *'Onward Christian soldiers, Marching as to war, With the cross of Jesus,* **Going on before***.'* □ *Sometimes one feels that the standards of the more responsible people in the community are not exactly* **going on before**! □ usu in the continuous tenses as in the examples.

go on (for) [A1 A3] be approaching a certain age □ *'I am sixteen,* **going on** *seventeen'.* □ *'You wouldn't think so to look at him, but that man is* **going on for** *seventy.'* □ usu in the continuous tenses as in the examples. ⇨ get on[4], get on for.

go on for [A3] of time, get near, approach □ *'Good Lord! It's* **going on for** *one o'clock and I promised to see George at half past twelve!'* □ usu in the continuous tenses as in the example.

go on (to)[1] [A1 A3] pass from one subject or item to the next, in an agenda etc □ *'If nobody has any objection then, we'll* **go on***.'* □ *The Chairman said that as time was short, we should* **go on to** *the next item.* □ *'I don't want any pudding, thank you. I'd like to* **go** *straight* **on to** *the coffee.'*

go on (to)[2] [A2 A3] adopt (as a new or temporary habit). **o:** ⚠ a diet; the wagon; the pill (i e contraceptive) □ *The doctor told me that I would have to* **go on to** *a strict diet.* □ *Mr Allen decided to* **go on** *the wagon* (= stop drinking alcohol) *after he had smashed up his second car.* □ *Many women* **go on to** *the pill after they have had two children.*

go on to [A3] change working arrangements to. **S:** factory; half the employees; steel industry. **o:** overtime, short time, full production; four-day week □ *The National Coal Board says that if consumption continues to fall, several big mines will have to* **go on to** *short time or stop production altogether.*

go on with [A3] continue doing. **o:** your work, what you were doing □ *The teacher told the class to* **go on with** *the exercise quietly while he was out of the room.* ⇨ get on with, go on[5].

enough/something to go on with [A3] (sth that is) sufficient for the time being, with the suggestion that more is to follow □ *'I can't let you have the whole amount now, but I can give you* **something to be going on with***. Will five pounds do?'* □ *'Have you got plenty of reading material?'* **'Enough to go on with***, thank you.'* □ *'Here's a cup of tea* **to be going on with***. I'll give you something to eat shortly.'*

go on with you [A3] (informal) a remark made to tease or rebuke sb □ *I laid the flat of my hand sharply between her breasts, as though swatting a mosquito. Sticking strictly to clinical terms, I admitted loftily, 'I certainly feel a distinct thrill.'* **'Go on with you***, Doctor,' she said, giving me a wink and a poke in the ribs.* DIL

go out[1] [A1] absent oneself (from home etc) for some purpose □ *'What a pity you didn't arrive half an hour ago. Mary's* **gone out** *riding and won't be back until six o'clock.'* □ *'If you* **go out** *drinking every night you'll never pass your exams or save any money.'* □ followed by *-ing* form of a v. ⇨ go out (for/to).

go out[2] [A1] become unconscious. **A:** like a light; within a minute; for the count □ *After the sustained effort of the day I lay down on the bed and* **went out** *like a light.* □ *One blow to the chin and the challenger* **went out** *for the count* (= was knocked out). ⇨ be out[9], put out[9].

go out[3] [A1] (euphemism) die □ *He said, knowing there was no hope of recovery for him, 'It's the one thing that will make me* **go out** *with an easy mind, Sarah, the knowledge that you and Terry and Pauline will not suffer financially.'* WI □ *'I wish I had led a more relaxed existence. As it is, I shall* **go out** *thinking of all the fun I've missed.'*

go out[4] [A1] end, depart. **S:** the year; September □ *1970* **went out** *with the news of a major earthquake in Peru.* □ *When March comes in like a lamb, it* **goes out** *like a lion.* □ GEOFF: *Has anybody ever tried?* JO: *What?* GEOFF: *Taking you in hand.* JO: *Yes.* GEOFF: *What happened to him?* JO: *He came in with Christmas and* **went out** *with the New Year.* TOH

go out[5] [A1] stop burning, shining. **S:** fire, light □ *We were looking forward to getting back to a warm house, but when we arrived the fire had* **gone out***.* □ *I had just begun to go upstairs when the lights* **went out***.* ⇨ be out[10], put out[10], turn out[1].

go out[6] [A1] cease to be fashionable. **S:** miniskirts, woollen underwear, liberty bodices; that theory; wearing black, dressing up on Sundays; chaperones □ *'You can't wear that to the party! Miniskirts* **went out** *years ago.'* □ *The idea that women can't do the same work as men* **went out** *with the dodo.* □ *Great train robberies were thought to have* **gone out** *with the silent films.* OBS ⇨ be out[14]; be/go out of fashion.

go out[7] [A1] ebb. **S:** ⚠ the tide, sea, water □ *The sea, at certain parts of the coast,* **goes out** *so far that it can no longer be seen.* ⇨ be out[16].

go out and about [A1] leave one's house, visit friends, go shopping etc (usu after a period of confinement) □ *I'm glad to hear that your mother can* **go out and about** *once more. She's made a wonderful recovery from her illness.*

go (all) out (for) [A1 A3] make a great, concentrated, effort (to obtain). **o:** what he wants; success. **A:** to finish the job; to win the war □ *He* **went all out for** *a job that would not disappear at the first signs of a depression.* □ *Don't trust that man. He just* **goes out for** *anything he can get.* □ *If you want to beat the other competitors you'll have to* **go all out***.* ⇨ be out for.

go out (for/to) [A1 A3] leave a building, go into the open air. **o:** (*for*) ride, trip, run; (*to*) beach, park; pictures □ *'Please* **go out** *and tell the children to make less noise.'* □ *'I'm just* **going out to** *the post. If anyone calls, ask them to wait.'* □

'I think you should ***go out for*** *some fresh air instead of watching television all day.'* ⇨ be out (at); come/take out (for/to), go out[1].

go out of[1] [A2] disappear from. **S:** ⚠ the sting, venom, fury; the (sour, harsh) note, tone. **o:** correspondence, remarks, attack □ *As time went by and the old man became mellow, the fury* ***went out of*** *his parliamentary speeches.*

go out of[2] [A2] become reduced, less marked. **S:** ⚠ the heat, passion, tension. **o:** argument, debate, discussion □ *When it was clear that nobody was particularly interested in the matter, apart from the protagonists, the heat* ***went out of*** *the argument.*

go out of action [A2] cease to operate. **S:** submarine, gun, fighter; pump □ *The enemy's fighters seem to have* ***gone out of action****: perhaps they have been subjected to overheating in the recent battles.* ⇨ be/put out of action.

go out of business [A2] fail in business, or simply stop trading or operating □ *A lot of small grocers have* ***gone out of business*** *since the advent of the supermarkets.* □ *Some people believe that it would be a good thing if certain manufacturers were to* ***go out of business****.* ⇨ put out of business.

go out of fashion [A2] be no longer, cease to be, fashionable. **S:** miniskirts; that theory □ *Morality has* ***gone out of fashion****. Permissiveness is all.* ⇨ be out of fashion; be out[14], go out[6].

go out of focus [A2] cease to be sharply focused □ *Just as we were about to take a photograph of the diseased cell, the microscope* ***went out of focus****.* ⇨ be out of focus.

go out of one's mind [A2] become mad □ *When the young woman heard the dreadful news she* ***went*** *clean* ***out of her mind****.* ⇨ be out of one's mind.

go out of sb's mind [A2] be forgotten. **S:** appointment, meeting, promise to do sth, message □ *I'm so sorry I forgot to turn up at the meeting. I fully intended to, but it* ***went*** *right* ***out of my mind****.*

go out of play [A2] (sport) of the ball in football, tennis etc, go over the lines marking the pitch or court □ *Channon took a quick shot at goal but the ball* ***went*** *harmlessly* ***out of play****.* ⇨ be out of play.

go out of service [A2] cease to be used. **S:** old models, equipment □ *The 'slow' jets of the 1960s* ***went out of service*** *as they were replaced by more modern machines.* ⇨ be out of service.

go out of sight/view [A2] disappear from sight. **S:** land, competitors, hunted animal □ *The fog came down like a curtain and in a few moments the coastline had* ***gone out of sight****.* ⇨ be out of[2].

go out of one's way to do sth [A2] take particular trouble. **Inf** to be helpful; to be as pleasant, unpleasant, as possible; to look one's best; to make a success of sth □ *Most specimens are fairly straightforward and are not much trouble once they are used to the routine, but occasionally we would get a creature which appeared to* ***go out of its way to cause*** *extra work.* DF □ *He wouldn't* ***go out of his way to help*** *his own mother, even if she were starving.*

go out (to)[1] [A1 A3] leave a building, go into the open air. ⇨ go out (for/to).

go out (to)[2] [A1 A3] go overseas (esp to some distant place) □ *My son* ***went out to*** *Australia ten years ago.* □ *'Are you* ***going out*** *by plane or by ship?'* □ *Beryl has decided to* ***go out to*** *South America as an English teacher.*

go out to [A3] be extended to, be offered to. **S:** ⚠ one's sympathy, heart(s) □ *Our hearts* ***go out to*** *all the victims of the earthquake in Yugoslavia.*

go over[1] [A2 pass] check, examine, inspect; look over[2] (q v). **o:** accounts, inventory; contents of a house; claim, appeal □ *I've* ***gone over*** *the statement, and it seems to be in order.* □ *You'll have to* ***go over*** *the figures again; they don't balance out.*

go over[2] [A2] survey, inspect, with a view to renting or buying; look over[1] (q v). **o:** house, flat, castle; boat □ *The prospective tenants* ***went over*** *the accommodation, but made no comment except to thank the old lady for her trouble.* □ *The surveyor gave the house a thorough* ***going-over*** *and advised us not to buy.*

go over[3] [A2 pass] clean; inspect and repair. **o:** room, kitchen; car, boat; gutters □ *The girl* ***went over*** *the room quickly with a duster.* □ *Would you mind giving the engine of my car a good* ***going-over****? It's producing a very strange noise.*

go over[4] [A2 pass] ponder, consider; examine or re-examine. **o:** the facts; the same ground; his story, account, allegation □ *We* ***went over*** *every detail of his story in an effort to discover whether it was true or not.* □ *'Please don't mention Aubrey to me. I'm not* ***going over*** *all that ground again. I'm finished with him; do you understand?'* □ *The detective* ***went over*** *the facts in his mind for the twentieth time, but still the vital clue eluded him.*

go over[5] [A2 pass] search. **S:** police, detective; custom's officer. **o:** suspect, prisoner; baggage □ *A woman police-officer* ***went over*** *the girl from head to toe, but would not say what she was looking for.*

go over[6] [A2 pass] rehearse, test one's knowledge of sth learned or studied; go through[5] (q v). **o:** lines, part; scene two; French homework □ *The boys' mother used to* ***go over*** *their sums with them every evening.* □ *I can't come out this evening. I'm in the college play and must* ***go over*** *my lines again.*

go over[7] [A1] be received. **S:** (maiden) speech; performance; proposal, plan. **A:** (extremely) well; rather badly; a bomb □ *How did John's talk to the Women's Institute* ***go over****?* □ *Your idea for a sweepstake on the yacht race* ***went over*** *big! Everyone was enthusiastic.*

going-over [nom (A2)] ⇨ entry after goggle (at).

go over the wall [A2] leave or escape from a life of confinement, whether physical or spiritual. **S:** prisoner, nun □ *The world is always more interested in the one nun who* ***goes over the wall*** *than the thousands who don't.*

go over (to) [A1 A3] cross a river, lake, the sea etc (so as to reach); go across (to) (q v). **o:** mainland, island, the other bank □ *A boat* ***goes over to*** *the island once a week with mail and provisions.* ⇨ take over (to).

go over to[1] [A3] transfer one's allegiance to; defect (from) (to) (q v). **S:** rebel MP, Communist; spy, agent; brigade, regiment, army; priest, bishop. **o:** other side, the Labour Party; enemy, allies; Rome (= Roman Catholicism), Methodism □ *Mr Blake, after years of dissatisfaction with Labour,* ***went over to*** *the Conservatives.* □ *The chief of intelligence has* ***gone over to*** *the Russians.* □ *Italy* ***went over to*** *the Allies in 1944.* □ *'It's the first time I've ever joined a couple in Holy Matrimony according to the rites of the Anglican Church,' the Canon persisted, 'and heard the bridegroom say, barely an hour later, that he's thinking of* ***going over to*** *Rome.'* CON ⇨ bring/come over (to).

go over to[2] [A3] abandon one thing or practice and adopt another. **o:** violin; pop art; vegetarian diet; bicycle □ *Sarah's given up the piano and* ***gone over to*** *the flute.* □ *We thought Jim was going to be another Sutherland, but he's* ***gone over to*** *pop art.* □ *I'm afraid you'll have to* ***go over to*** *a vegetarian diet if the price of meat goes on rising!*

go over to[3] [A3] (broadcasting) transfer to. **o:** our reporter on the spot, news desk; New York, Tokyo; Westminster, Wembley □ *'We're interrupting the programme to* ***go over to*** *our news desk for an important bulletin.'* □ *'Let's* ***go over to*** *Lords to hear the latest on the Test Match from Brian Johnstone.'*

go overboard [A1] (nautical) fall or be thrown from a ship □ *During the storm a lot of the deck cargo* ***went overboard.*** □ *'Why has the ship stopped?' 'I think somebody must have* ***gone overboard.****'* ⇨ fall overboard.

go overboard about/for [A3] be enthusiastic about, commit oneself totally to. **o:** the new play; Australia; modern architecture □ *It would be very foolish of the Government to* ***go overboard about*** *nuclear energy to the extent of running the coal industry down to nothing.* □ *Mavis has* ***gone overboard for*** *some new Eastern religion.*

go round[1] [A1 A2] make a detour, walk, drive etc, along the outside perimeter of. **o:** centre of the city; park, prison; island; military installations □ *The front gate was shut, so we had to* ***go round.*** □ *'Don't sound your horn while you're* ***going round*** *the hospital.'*

go round[2] [A1 A2] walk inside a building etc in order to inspect it or its contents; look around/round[2] (q v). **o:** museum, castle, Westminster Abbey, Hyde Park; Flower Show, exhibition; school, hospital, prison □ *'While you're here, would you like to* ***go round****?'* □ *So many distinguished visitors* ***went round*** *the school, that the children hardly looked up from their work when a stranger was brought into the classroom.* ⇨ take round.

go round[3] [A1] spin, or seem to spin; be dizzy or confused. **S:** the world; the room, everything; my head □ *It's love that makes the world* ***go round.*** □ *After a couple of glasses of whisky, the bar began to* ***go round.*** *He had forgotten that he was drinking on an empty stomach.* □ *His head seemed to* ***go round,*** *and he clutched at the nearest passer-by.*

go round[4] [A1 A2] be sufficient (for). **o:** the guests; starving children; all these people □ *'Don't worry! There's enough coffee to* ***go round.****'* □ *The hostess didn't know what to do, as she hadn't got enough food to* ***go round*** *so many people.* □ *How can India possibly find enough rice to* ***go round*** *these millions of refugees?*

go round[5] [A1] go from place to place or person to person. ⇨ go around/round[1].

go round[6] [A1] circulate. ⇨ go around/round[2].

go round (to) [A1 A3] visit □ *'Let's* ***go round*** *and see Mary. She's always ready for a chat.'* □ *The police* ***went round to*** *the woman's house as soon as they received her call.* ⇨ be around/round (at), bring around/round (to)[1], come around/round (to)[1].

go round (with) [A1 A3] ⇨ go around/round (with).

go through[1] [A1 A2] pass from one side of an object to the other, sometimes implying the exercise of force. **S:** thread; piano; lorry; ship; motor-cyclist. **o:** needle; door; gate; canal; shop-window □ *This rope is too thick to* ***go through*** *the hole.* □ *The piano* ***went through*** *the door easily, but the sideboard wouldn't* ***go through*** *at all.* □ *The bus ran down the hill out of control, and* ***went through*** *the wall of a house at the bottom.* ⇨ get through[1].

go through[2] [A2 pass] use, consume. **o:** stock, store; food, beer; fortune □ *'Do you mean to say that we've* ***gone through*** *all those envelopes I bought last week?'* □ *It didn't take Albert very long to* ***go through*** *his inheritance.* ⇨ get through[4].

go through[3] [A2 pass] examine, explore, search. **o:** every room; all my pockets; his papers □ *The woman* ***went through*** *every drawer and cupboard in the house, but she could not find the missing silver.* □ *The police* ***went through*** *the building with a fine tooth-comb, but they found no evidence that would help them to catch the thief.* □ *It was obvious that the room had been* ***gone through*** *by an intruder.*

go through[4] [A2 pass] perform, enact. **o:** marriage, initiation, matriculation, degree (ceremony) □ *Tom and Sarah had been living together for years, but finally* ***went through*** *the marriage ceremony for the sake of their children.* □ *I hate the idea of attending the funeral but I suppose it'll have to be* ***gone through.*** ⇨ go through with.

go through[5] [A2 pass] review, rehearse; go over[6] (q v). **o:** facts, arguments, pros and cons; scene, text □ *They* ***went through*** *the details of the plan over and over again to make sure that there was no possibility of failure.* □ *'Let's* ***go through*** *the last scene in Act Two again. We haven't got it right yet.'* ⇨ take through.

go through[6] [A1] be completed, concluded (usu successfully). **S:** appointment, application; Bill (the form of legislation before it becomes an Act of Parliament); scheme, deal, agreement; divorce □ *As soon as Jo's divorce has* ***gone through,*** *he's going to marry Alice.* □ *If this deal doesn't* ***go through,*** *we're ruined.* □ *Surely my application for a visa has* ***gone through*** *by now? I can't understand the delay.* ⇨ get through[3], put through[2].

go through[7] [A2] be published in. **S:** book, title; article. **o:** three printings; ten editions □ *His book was an immediate success and* ***went through*** *ten editions in a year.*

go through[8] [A2 pass] suffer, endure, experience. **o:** operation; years of pain; ordeal; fire; boring performance □ *Before the days of* *anaesthetics people had to* ***go through*** *dreadful pain when they were operated on.* □ *He would have* ***gone through*** *fire for the girl he loved.* □ *'Well, I'm glad we don't have to* ***go through*** *that again for another year! Speech Day bores me to tears.'* □ *'After what he* ***went through*** *with his first wife, you'd think he would have steered clear of marriage for the rest of his life.'*

go through sb's hands [A2] be handled by, be the responsibility of sb. **S:** thousands of pounds; jewellery, diamonds; (secret, confidential) papers, documents; patients, cases □ *...more than a million pounds' worth of diamonds* ***went through his hands****, and around forty thousand of them stuck to his fingers.* DS □ *'I hope that new man is trustworthy if you're going to let these documents* ***go through his hands****.'*

go through the mill [A2] (informal) serve an apprenticeship; do humble, difficult and menial tasks before attaining high or senior status □ *The best men at running industry are those who have had to* ***go through the mill*** *themselves.* ⇨ be/put through the mill.

go through the motions [A2] pretend to do sth; do sth but without sincerity or serious intent □ *Her husband* ***went through the motions*** *of welcoming her guests, but left the room at the first opportunity.*

go through (the) proper channels [A2] follow the correct, prescribed steps. **S:** application, complaint, letter □ *It is no use your asking me for promotion. You'll have to* ***go through the proper channels****.* □ *Applications for leave must* ***go through proper channels****.*

go through with [A3 pass] complete, take to a conclusion, not leave unfinished. **o:** arrangements, plan; robbery, execution; it □ *As the time approached for the guests to arrive, Mrs Winthrop wished she had never invited them; but she realized that she would have to* ***go through with*** *it.* □ *A month before the wedding was due to take place, Mr Puddy received a letter from his fiancée saying that she couldn't* ***go through with*** *it, as she'd fallen in love with someone else.* ⇨ go through[4].

go to[1] [A2] visit, attend. **o:** school, university; market □ *The old woman* ***went to*** *market every week without fail, to sell her eggs and butter.* □ *Does your son* ***go to*** *university?* ⇨ send to.

go to[2] [A2 pass] take, put oneself to (⇨ put to[4]). **o:** (a lot of, no end of, endless, infinite) trouble; great pains to do sth; ridiculous lengths □ *The British Council* ***went to*** *no end of trouble to arrange a programme for the eminent visitor to Britain.* □ *She* ***went to*** *absurd lengths to please her new boss; but he sacked her within a month.*

go to[3] [A2] be given to, be awarded to; be inherited by. **S:** special prize, gold medal; my uncle's fortune; honour, privilege □ *The first prize for Biology* ***went to*** *the youngest child in the class.* □ *The distinction of being the first to split the atom* ***went to*** *Rutherford.* □ *The family was furious when the old man's entire possessions* ***went to*** *his housekeeper.*

go to[4] [A2 pass] spend (much money); incur. **o:** (extra, great, unnecessary) expense □ *'Why don't you hire a caravan for a couple of weeks each year instead of* ***going to*** *the expense of buying one?'*

go to bed [A2] retire to bed for a rest, sleep or because one is ill □ *'I don't feel well; I'm* ***going to bed****.'* ⇨ send to bed.

go to bits [A2] ⇨ go to pieces.

go to the country [A2] (politics) call a general election □ *The Prime Minister said that if Parliament went against him on the crucial issue of our joining the Common Market, he would be forced to* ***go to the country****.*

go to the dogs [A2] (informal) decline in power, efficiency etc; change for the worse. **S:** the country, old school, family life □ *From the way some people talk, you'd think that the country had been* ***going to the dogs*** *for the last fifty years.* □ *I had to resign my membership because the club was* ***going to the dogs****.*

go to earth/ground [A2] (of animals) take refuge underground, in a burrow, lair etc; (of people) hide oneself away. **S:** fox, quarry, hunted animal; escaped criminal, wanted man, refugee □ *When the master of the hounds realized that the quarry had* ***gone to earth*** *and the dogs had lost the scent, he called off the hunt.* □ *The police believe that the murderer has* ***gone to earth*** *somewhere in London.* ⇨ run to earth/ground.

go to extremes [A2] be immoderate in one's actions □ *He is the kind of man who cannot do anything in moderation. If he drinks, he drinks too much; if he drives a car, he drives too fast; if he goes out for a meal, he goes to the most expensive hotel. He always* ***goes to extremes****.* ⇨ next entry.

go to the other extreme/go from one extreme to another/the other [A2] pass from one exaggerated view or action to its opposite □ *Before we* ***go to the other extreme*** *of assuming that Mr Khruschev's power was absolute, there is one important difference to remember between him and Stalin.* BM □ *'Last week you wanted to marry him as soon as you could; now you wouldn't marry him if he was the last man on earth. You do* ***go from one extreme to the other****, don't you?'* ⇨ previous entry.

go to sb's head [A2] affect a person's balance or judgement. **S:** strong drink, beer, champagne; success, praise, money; sudden fame, notoriety □ *The wine* ***went to Susan's head****. What with that and the heat, she simply passed out at the table.* □ *Don't let the manager's congratulations* ***go to your head****. Next week he's just as likely to bite your head off.* □ (song) *'You* ***go to my head****, And you linger like a haunting refrain.'*

go to the heart of [A2] hit, reach the central point of. **o:** ⚠ the matter, question, problem □ *'You're getting married?' 'Yes.' 'To whom?' asked Donna Rachele, who liked to* ***go to the heart of*** *a question.* ARG □ *Providing a few clinics for drug addicts may help, but it doesn't* ***go to the heart of*** *the problem.*

go to hell etc [A2] (informal) an offensive expression dismissing or rejecting a person or his ideas, wishes etc. **o:** ⚠ hell, blazes, Hades, the Devil, Jericho □ *'As far as I am concerned, if you aren't willing to work for a living, you can* ***go to hell****'!* □ *'I'm fed up with this office. I'm going out!' 'But what shall I tell Mr James if he wants to see you?' 'Tell him to* ***go to hell****!'*

go to it [A2] give energy and time to doing sth, make a special effort to do sth (often used to urge sb on) □ *'****Go to it****, John! You could beat the* *record this time!'* □ *After dinner we* ***went to it*** *again, carting paints and easels about.* CON

go to pieces [A2] lose one's self-control, health, integrity □ *When Sam heard of his son's death he* ***went to pieces****; but as time passed he gradually returned to something like his old cheerful self.* □ *Following their defeat in the election the Labour Party seemed to* ***go to pieces*** *for a time.* □ also occasionally go to bits.

go to the police [A2] inform the police □ *The blackmailer warned his victim that if he* ***went to the police*** *he would regret it.*

go to the polls [A2] (politics) cast one's vote at an election □ *The number of people who actually* ***go to the polls*** *seems to depend on the weather. That, in a democracy, is surely absurd!* □ *The country was in no mood to* ***go to the polls*** *for a second time in less than six months.*

go to pot [A2] (informal) be spoilt, ruined □ MYRA: *It would take you six months to study for that examination.* TONY: *A year, after my brain's* ***gone to pot*** *in the army.* EHOW □ the expression existed long before the word *pot* took on the meaning of *cannabis*.

go to press [A2] (publishing) (be sent to) be printed. **S:** paper, book; last edition; the Times □ *It's too late to include the announcement in tomorrow's paper. It's* ***gone to press****.*

go to rack and ruin [A2] reach a state of disrepair, decay, through neglect; become disorganized □ *Now the house was* ***going to rack and ruin****. Aunt Annabel patiently inquired how it could be expected to do anything else, with only a cook-housekeeper, one maid, and a daily.* DC

go to sea [A2] earn one's living on a ship □ *The boy was tired of looking for a job near his home and eventually decided to* ***go to sea****.*

go to seed [A2] (of vegetables etc) go beyond the edible stage and produce seeds; (of people) become unattractive ('seedy-looking') through self-neglect, over-indulgence, or unhealthy living □ *'What a pity you let all those cabbages* ***go to seed****. They're no use now.'* □ *An aging Romeo stepped out of the car, grey, pale and* ***gone to seed****.*

go to town [A2] (informal) do sth with enthusiasm, vigour, thoroughness and relish □ *When the Leader of the Opposition turned to consider the Government's secret negotiations with Ruritania, he fairly* ***went to town****. His supporters cheered him as he called for the resignation of the Foreign Secretary.* □ *She's really* ***going to town*** *over Alan's room. First of all she said it needed new curtains....* RFW

go to trial [A2] (legal) be tried in a court of law □ *'If I'm caught, I have my own plan. You can be sure that I shall never* ***go to trial****.'*

go to the wall [A2] be defeated; fail, become bankrupt. **S:** company, firm; weaker competitors □ *When the new toy cars with 'hot' wheels* (i e producing less friction and therefore making the cars faster) *appeared on the British market, several manufacturers of the old types* ***went to the wall****.* □ (Conservative Party election broadcast) *If prices and incomes were uncontrolled, it would be the old-age pensioners, the lowly paid, the people without powerful trade unions — it is these people who would* ***go to the wall****.* BBCTV

go to war [A2] start, engage in, a war □ *No sane leader would ever* ***go to war*** *if he knew that he must lose it. But then... not every leader is sane!* □ usu of nations rather than individuals.

go to waste [A2] be wasted, unused. **S:** food; effort; natural resources; man, girl □ *'How can you let all this food* ***go to waste*** *when there are so many starving people in the world?'* □ *'I wouldn't like to see any daughter of mine* ***going to waste*** *as a chorus-girl in a provincial theatre.'*

go to work (on) [A2] start operating; tackle (a job); set to[1] (q v) □ *Intelligence* (i e secret service) *agents* ***went to work*** *and soon found the reason for the leak of information to the enemy.* □ *The young architect* ***went to work*** *with a will* ***on*** *his first commission.* □ a famous advertisement, ***'Go to work on*** *an egg'*, had two meanings: (a) have an egg (for breakfast) before you leave for the office, factory etc; (b) tackle, i e eat, an egg.

go together[1] [A1] match; be good, right, agreeable when worn, consumed etc, at the same time. **S:** red and green; oysters and champagne; coffee and liqueur □ *'Do you think this hat and coat* ***go*** *well* ***together****? Or do they clash?'* □ *Potatoes and rice don't* ***go together****. They make a stodgy meal.* ⇨ go with[4].

go together[2] [A1] of two or more things, states, qualities etc, be found in one person, place, environment etc. **S:** poverty and disease; sunshine and health; wealth and selfishness □ *Bullying and cowardice often* ***go together****.* □ *Chastity and charity do not necessarily* ***go together****.* ⇨ go with[3].

go together[3] [A1] keep each other company, often with a view to marriage. **S:** Paul and Pamela; those two □ *While he had been away on this last trip to America, she had had a chance to take stock of herself, and it had come as a shock when she realized they had been* ***'going together'*** *for over a year.* WI ⇨ go with[2].

go under[1] [A1] sink below the surface of the sea, river etc. **S:** helpless child; boat □ *Just as the would-be rescuer reached the drowning man, he* ***went under*** *for the third time and was never seen again.*

go under[2] [A1] fail, become bankrupt. **S:** he etc; company, business, firm, organization, aircraft industry □ *Poor Donaldson had no head for business, and it was not long before he* ***went under****.*

go under[3] [A2] be known as; hide one's identity behind; pass by/under the name of (q v). **S:** flower, criminal, writer. **o:** name, title; sobriquet, nom de plume, guise □ *Willow Herb also* ***goes under*** *the name of Old Man's Beard.* □ *One of the robbers* ***went under*** *the guise of a respectable dealer in antiques.*

go under the hammer [A2] be sold at auction. **S:** his home, pictures, collection of antiques, all his worldly possessions □ *Everything that Joss possessed* ***went under the hammer*** *to pay his debts.* □ *We must do everything we can to prevent the old homestead from* ***going under the hammer****.*

go under (to) [A1 A3] be overcome (by). **o:** a stronger man; their powerful neighbour; a new predator □ *The greater part of the rabbit population of Britain* ***went under to*** *the disease of myxomatosis.* □ *Unless the textile industry reorganizes itself quickly, it will* ***go under*** (***to*** *foreign competition*).

go up[1] [A1 emph A2 emph] climb; pass upwards, on or through. **o:** stairs, ladder; hill, cliff; wall; tree; side of a ship, rigging; chimney, pipe, funnel □ *Since the old lady fell, she's been unable to* ***go up*** *steps.* □ *The squirrel* ***went up*** *the tree like greased lightning.* □ *The brush was too big to* ***go up*** *the flu.* ⇨ get up[3].

go up[2] [A1 emph] rise, increase. **S:** prices, expenses, the cost of living □ *Everything seems to be* ***going up*** *these days: coal, groceries, busfares, rents... Why doesn't the Government do something about it?* □ *'Have you seen the paper today?* ***Up go*** *the prices again!'* ⇨ be up[1], put up[4], send up[1].

go up[3] [A1] rise, reach a higher level; be raised. **S:** pressure, barometer, glass; temperature, mercury □ *I see the mercury is* ***going up****. Perhaps we're going to get a spell of good weather at last.*

go up[4] [A1] be constructed. **S:** buildings, skyscrapers; new schools, hospitals etc □ *'Everywhere you look, you can see glass and concrete monstrosities* ***going up****.'* □ *New universities* ***went up*** *at a fantastic rate in the 1960s.* ⇨ put up[3].

go up[5] [A1 emph] be destroyed, be blown up (⇨ blow up[4]). **S:** building, bridge, ship, ammunition dump; all our hopes, plans. **A:** in flames, in smoke, with a bang, with a roar □ *The gelignite store received a direct hit and* ***went up*** *in a huge spectacular explosion that was heard for miles around.* □ *With the outbreak of renewed hostilities on the border all our hopes for peace have* ***gone up*** *in flames.* □ *I could see the commission for the murals* ***going up*** *in smoke.* CON ⇨ send up[2].

go up[6] [A1 emph] (theatre) be raised; be lit. **S:** ⚠ the curtain, lights □ (stage directions) *In the first act the curtain* ***goes up*** *on a typical sitting-room of a small English semi-detached house.*

the balloon go up [A1] (of a war, a major offensive) begin □ *I shamelessly snatched an extra twenty-four hours from my office on Sunday in order that I might see Bill before 'Overlord'* (= the invasion of Europe)*, before* ***the balloon went up****.* RFW

go up the wall [A2] (informal) go nearly mad from frustration, overwork, annoyance □ *When I arrived home, I found mother* ***going up the wall****. The fire was out, the baby was crying, Johnny had just cut his knee and our visitors were due to arrive at any moment.* ⇨ send up the wall.

go up in the world [A3] reach a higher position in society, in one's profession etc □ *When Tony married the millionaire's daughter, he certainly* ***went up in the world****.* □ *Arnold's* ***gone up in the world****, hasn't he? It's quite something to start as an apprentice and end up running an industry with 50 000 employees.* □ *Three women in my life, but the one I want doesn't want me. Who cares? That's the way it goes. I'm* ***going up in the world*** *before the world goes up before me.* DBM

go up (to) [A1 A3] go to a university, or to London ('town') from the provinces, or towards the north □ *At New College, Gaitskill* (who ***went up*** a year earlier than X) *became passionately interested in politics, ballroom dancing and social life.* OBS □ *I'm* ***going up to*** *town for a few days. Is there anything I can do for you while I'm there?* □ *My parents have* ***gone up to*** *Scotland for a short holiday.* ⇨ be up[2], come up[2].

go with[1] [A2] accompany □ *The younger children stayed with their uncle while the older ones* ***went with*** *their parents to Spain.*

go with[2] [A2] keep company with, perhaps with a view to marriage □ *How long has Alice been* ***going with*** *Steven? I thought Adam was her boyfriend.* ⇨ go together[3].

go with[3] [A2] be part of; be included with. **S:** fields, paddock, two acres; scarf; disease; crime. **o:** house; dress; poor hygiene; poverty □ *We were delighted to find that a large rock garden* ***went with*** *the house.* □ *Crime does not necessarily* ***go with*** *poverty; some rich men are criminals.* ⇨ go together[2].

go with[4] [A2] match; suit; combine well with. **S:** hat; lipstick, powder; his voice. **o:** dress; shoes; complexion; his distinguished appearance □ *Her behaviour when under the influence of alcohol hardly* ***goes with*** *her high standards when sober.* ⇨ go together[1].

go with a bang/swing [A2] (informal) be very successful, enjoyable. **S:** party, concert, pop festival □ *The pop festival on the Isle of Wight* ***went with a bang****.* □ *When we arrived at 9 o'clock the party was well under way and* ***going with a swing****.*

go with the tide [A2] follow others, take the line of least resistance □ *Max hasn't got a mind of his own on any matter of importance; he just* ***goes with the tide****.*

go without [A1 A2] not have; suffer the absence of; do without[1] (q v). **o:** food; shoes, clothes; shelter □ *The doctor willingly* ***went without*** *his dinner if by attending a patient quickly he could relieve his suffering.* □ *Millions of the refugees were given food, but thousands had to* ***go without*** *and died of starvation.*

it/that goes without saying [A2] it is so obvious that it is not (or is hardly) necessary to say it □ *When you visit England* ***it goes without saying*** *that you will be my guest.*

goad into [B2 pass rel] provoke sb to do sth or into a certain state. **S:** jeers, mockery, complaining tone; hunger, need, despair. **o:** a fury; losing my temper, retaliating, striking out; stealing a loaf of bread, breaking into a shop □ *The soldiers were well trained and refused to be* ***goaded into*** *attacking the crowd of jeering, stone-throwing youths and girls.*

goad on [B1i pass] tempt, force or provoke sb to do sth foolish, antisocial, illegal etc. **O:** starving men, prisoners, rebels □ *The older children* ***goaded*** *the youngsters* ***on*** *to break all the windows of the deserted house.* □ *The accused girls said that they were* ***goaded on*** *by their need to buy more and more drugs.*

gobble up [B1i pass] eat quickly, consume; devour; assimilate. **S:** geese, dogs; children; large countries; companies; computer. **O:** grain, meat; dinner; small neighbours; family businesses; facts □ *Imperial powers throughout history have always tended to* ***gobble up*** *their weaker neighbours.* □ *The fourth-generation machine could* ***gobble up*** *work at a quite fantastic rate.*

goggle (at) [A2 pass] (informal) stare wide-eyed (at); gape (at) (q v) □ *The boys stood on the beach* ***goggling at*** *the girls as they ran down to* *the water.* ◻ *Instead of doing something useful, the crowd just stood there* ***goggling*** *(****at*** *the victims of the accident).*

going-over [nom (A2)] the questioning of sb; (sometimes) a physical attack on sb ◻ *The police gave the suspected murderer a long* ***going-over****, but could get no admission from him.* ◻ *When the old man was found unconscious in the street, it was obvious that he had been given a savage* ***going-over*** *by several people.* ◻ usu in the patterns *give sb/get a* going-over. ⇨ go over[5].

goings-on [nom (A1)] behaviour, usu of an extraordinary or reprehensible kind. **adj:** (such) odd, frightful, peculiar, disgusting, strange, queer, inexplicable ◻ *Fred's father became so disgusted by his* ***goings-on*** *that he stopped his allowance.* ◻ *There have been some peculiar* ***goings-on*** *in the village recently, I can tell you!* ⇨ go on[10].

gone on [A2] (be) infatuated with, (be) very much in love with; (be) obsessed by. **o:** girl; the Rolling Stones, Beethoven; Chinese food ◻ *John* ***is*** *quite* ***gone on*** *that girl he met when he was on holiday in Paris.* ◻ *'Jo's still* ***gone on*** *Elvis Presley. How square can you get!'* ◻ not strictly a passive construction.

goose up [B1i pass adj] (informal) make more intense, lurid, daring, racy, or sensational ◻ *The author not only built up his characters through a series of distasteful episodes, but also* ***goosed up*** *the language — sprinkling each page with the now famous four-letter words.*

gore to death [B2 pass] of a horned animal, kill a person or other animal with its horns ◻ *The bullfighter had escaped with his life many times, but finally, on the day he had planned to retire, he was* ***gored to death****.*

gorge (oneself) on [A2 B2] eat voraciously. **S:** vultures; rats; children. **o:** rotting carcases; grain; ice-cream and chocolate ◻ *We came across a crocodile scarcely able to move after* ***gorging on*** *some dead animal.* ◻ *The boys* ***gorged themselves on*** *the cakes, and left the bread and butter uneaten.*

gorged with [pass (B2)] (be) sated with, (have) eaten sth to excess ◻ *The guards,* ***gorged with*** *meat and wine, were easily overcome and the castle quickly captured.*

gouge out [B1i pass] force out, with one's fingers or an instrument. **O:** eyes; channel, groove ◻ *King Lear's daughters stood by while his eyes were* ***gouged out****.* ◻ *Some vandal had* ***gouged out*** *his initials on the newly finished altar.* ◻ *The monster machine* ***gouged out*** *a deep trench across the field, revealing a rich layer of coal.*

grab at [A2 pass] attempt to seize; grasp at (q v). **o:** falling child; branch of a tree; chance, opportunity ◻ *A passer-by* ***grabbed at*** *the falling child, and was just quick enough to draw him out of the path of a lorry.* ◻ *He recognized the offer of a job in the factory as a chance to be* ***grabbed at*** *without hesitation.*

graduate (in) (from) [A2 rel] complete a degree-course (in a subject) (at a university etc) ◻ *He* ***graduated in*** *metallurgy* ***from*** *Birmingham in 1973.* ◻ *The boy* ***graduated in*** *crime* ***from*** *the slums of Glasgow.*

graft in/on (to) [B1i pass B3 pass] of living tissue and plants, attach to another for purposes of cure or propagation. **O:** skin, piece of bone; cutting ◻ *The tendon had been so skilfully* ***grafted in*** *that the boy was able to flex his finger quite normally after 4 weeks.* ◻ *The gardener could* ***graft*** *as many as twenty cuttings an hour* ***on to*** *briar stems.*

graph out [B1i pass] display in the form of a graph ◻ *When the results of the previous six months' trading had been* ***graphed out****, it was clear that the firm was rapidly heading for bankruptcy.*

grapple with [A2 pass rel] tackle, come to grips with (q v). **o:** thief, intruder; invaders, enemy; problem ◻ *The police warned the public that it would be dangerous to* ***grapple with*** *the wanted man, as he was armed and dangerous.* ◻ *It is high time that the government* ***grappled with*** *the ever-growing unemployment in the country.*

grasp at [A2 pass] try to seize; grab at (q v). **o:** opportunity, chance, offer ◻ *When my daughter was offered a trip to Hong Kong by her employers, she* ***grasped at*** *it with both hands.*

grasp at a straw [A2] attempt to save oneself from certain disaster by any means, however unlikely to succeed; catch at a straw (q v) ◻ *Like a drowning man* ***grasping at straws****, the thief tried to enlist the sympathy of the crowd even as the police were pushing him into the Black Maria.*

grass (on) [A2 pass] (criminal slang) give information to the police about a companion's crime, plans etc ◻ *'I don't want it to be said I* ***grassed on*** *my mates', the accused man said.* ◻ *'It's obvious that Joe the Knife has been* ***grassed on*** *by somebody. I wouldn't like to be that somebody when he gets out of jail!'*

grate on [A2 pass] produce a grinding or grating sound which is hard to tolerate; irritate. **S:** gate; chalk, lead; his manners, behaviour. **o:** hinge; blackboard, slate; my nerves; everybody present, his wife ◻ *The sound of the owlets screeching in the tree all night* ***grated on*** *his nerves and prevented him from sleeping.* ◻ *The new man's loud, coarse voice* ***grated on*** *everyone in the office.*

gravitate to/towards [A2 rel] move towards, as though drawn by some natural force ◻ *You could be sure that if Norman and his pals were in the hotel, they would have* ***gravitated*** *quite inevitably* ***to*** *the bar.* ◻ *She was so attractive that all the men in the room* ***gravitated towards*** *her, leaving their wives fuming.*

greet with [B2 pass rel] offer, in the form of a 'welcome'. **o:** a smile, a warm welcome; jeers and catcalls, enthusiasm; a burst of applause; a barrage of stones ◻ *When the distinguished visitor entered the hall he was* ***greeted with*** *ironic cheers by the noisy students.*

grieve for/over [A2 pass] feel sorrow on recalling sb or sth. **o:** dead friend; the passing of one's youth ◻ *'It's no use* ***grieving over*** *"the good old days", you know. They've gone for ever, and anyway... were they really so good?'* ◻ *For a little while the girl* ***grieved for*** *her dead hamster, but she got over it after a few days.*

grin from ear to ear [A2] smile broadly, showing great pleasure or amusement ◻ *'Would you mind telling me what's amusing you? You've been sitting there,* ***grinning from ear to ear****, for the past ten minutes!'*

grind away (at) [A1 A3] work with grim determination (at) □ *'I see James's light is still on, although it's nearly two a m.' 'Yes, he has a biology exam on Friday, and he's* ***grinding away*** *(****at*** *it) to make up for lost time.'*

grind down [B1i pass] oppress. **S:** tyranny, government, military forces; poverty, taxation □ *In the sixteenth century the European invaders ruthlessly* ***ground down*** *and exploited the Indians of South America.* □ *The peasants were* ***ground down*** *by a tyrannical squirearchy, and were unable to help themselves.* □ *The small force of resistance fighters was* ***ground down*** *by the sheer weight of the occupying army.*

grind into [B2 pass] press with great force into. **O:** cigarette; fist; heel. **o:** saucer, ashtray; the defenceless man's face; ground □ *He dropped the photograph and* ***ground*** *his foot* ***into*** *it to show his hatred of his wife's lover.*

grind into/to [B2 pass] reduce to, by grinding. **O:** corn; stone. **o:** flour; powder, pieces □ *When the stone had been* ***ground to*** *a fine powder it was used as the base for certain cosmetics.*

grind on [A1] move inexorably forwards. **S:** machine, juggernaut; bureaucratic procedures; process of law □ *The situation was out of our hands and the war machine* ***ground*** *slowly* ***on*** *towards disaster.*

grind out[1] [B1i pass] play heavily, drearily. **S:** band; gramophone, nickelodeon, jukebox. **O:** tune, song, number, the latest hit □ *In the dreary smoke-laden atmosphere of the dock-side café, an ancient record-player* ***ground out*** *some tune of long ago.*

grind out[2] [B1i pass] speak, say sth, in a grating voice □ *For the tenth time that day, the sergeant* ***ground out*** *the names of the parts of the machine-gun. Would these damned recruits never learn?* □ *'I'll get you for this!' the man* ***ground out*** *between clenched teeth as he was led away by the police.*

grind to [B2 pass] ⇨ grind into/to.

grind to a halt [A2] come slowly, inevitably and perhaps noisily to a stop. **S:** car, lorry, machine; motorized forces; invasion, army □ *As the supplies of petrol gave out, the retreating columns* ***ground to a halt*** *one after the other, leaving the troops at the mercy of the enemy's airforce.* □ *The procession* ***ground to a halt*** *as it approached Trafalgar Square: there was no room for any more demonstrators.*

gripe (at) [A2 pass] (informal) complain about, usu unreasonably. **o:** treatment, proposal, the way the matter was handled □ *'No matter how generous the terms of the settlement may be, you'll always find somebody ready to* ***gripe at*** *them—the professional grousers, you might call them!'* □ *'What's old Bloggins* ***griping at*** *now? Last week it was women being taken on as mechanics....'*

groan out [B1i pass] utter with a groan. **O:** sad news; story; last wishes □ *The wounded messenger collapsed and* ***groaned out*** *the news of the surrender.*

groan (with) [A2] produce a long, low sound from the throat, deliberately or involuntarily; (of inanimate objects) be afflicted in a way that would cause a human being to make such a sound. **S:** injured man; audience; table, festive board. **o:** dismay, misery, pain; mock dismay; food, sweetmeats of every kind; luxuries □ *The dying man* ***groaned with*** *agony as the rescuers tried to move him.* □ *The audience* ***groaned with*** *mock pain at the comedian's ancient jokes.* □ *The children could hardly believe their eyes when they saw the banquet laid out—the tables* ***groaning with*** *good things to eat.*

grope after/for [A2] try to find, in a blind, fumbling way. **o:** switch; right word, expression; formula; name; the truth □ *I* ***groped*** *in the dark* ***for*** *the torch which I knew must be somewhere in the room.* □ *The lecturer paused,* ***groping for*** *the most effective word to express his meaning.* □ *Throughout the ages men have* ***groped after*** *the meaning of the Universe and their own role in it.*

well etc grounded in [pass (B2)] having a deep knowledge of. **A:** well, solidly, thoroughly. **o:** logic, the law, politics, comparative religion □ *Every educated man of the nineteenth century was* ***well grounded in*** *Latin and Greek.*

ground on [B2 pass emph rel] give, provide, as a basis. **O:** theory, belief, policy □ *The government claimed that its policies were* ***grounded on*** *the realities of the situation and not on wishful thinking.* □ *They* ***grounded*** *their religion* ***on*** *Nature—or what they could observe of Nature.*

group around/round [A2 B2 pass] (cause to) surround as a group. **S:** [A2] **O:** [B2] class, men; tanks, divisions. **S:** [B2] teacher; commander. **o:** blackboard, desk; village, forest □ *We* ***grouped*** *ourselves* ***round*** *the leader in order to hear his last instructions before we set out.* □ *The class was* ***grouped around*** *the teacher, watching him demonstrate a chemical reaction, when a stone shattered one of the windows.*

group together [B1i pass] place in the same category, or in one place. **O:** mental illnesses; insects; books □ *It is absurd to* ***group*** *all murderers* ***together****, as though they were all equally wicked or antisocial.* □ *It would be better if these books were* ***grouped together*** *under 'author' rather than under 'subject'.*

grouse (about) [A2 pass] complain about, usu with little justification. **o:** food, conditions, lodgings, beds; weather; poor fishing; the BBC □ *He's the kind of chap who will always find something to* ***grouse about****, no matter how perfect the arrangements are.*

grovel before [A2] humble oneself, abase oneself, abandon one's dignity, before □ *'I'm damned if I'm going to* ***grovel before*** *the foreman and ask to be let off just because for once I arrived an hour late for work.'*

grow away from [A3] cease to have a comfortable, loving, easy relationship or rapport with. **o:** parents, former friends, the gang □ *It often happens that a girl who in her early teens has been very close to her mother suddenly* ***grows away from*** *her as she makes new friends and her horizons widen.* □ *After only one term at the university, David was conscious that he had* ***grown away from*** *his old school friends and that things would never be the same again.*

grow from[1] [A2 B2 pass] (cause to) germinate and reach fruition. **S:** [A2] **O:** [B2] flowers, fruit, vegetables, plants. **o:** seed; a cutting □ (proverb) *Great oaks* ***from*** *little acorns* ***grow****.* □ *'How do you like my tomatoes? I* ***grew*** *them* ***from*** *seed.'* □ *Were these roses* ***grown from*** *seed or from* *cuttings?* ⇨ grow into.

grow from[2] [A2 emph rel] have as its origin; arise from (q v), grow out of[3] (q v). **S:** interest; fear; admiration; desire. **o:** reading sth, meeting sb; an unpleasant experience as a child; what he had heard about...; ambition to... □ *His interest in ships* **grew from** *talking to his father, who had always longed to go to sea, and from reading the innumerable books about them that he found on his father's shelves.*

grow in [A2] become wiser, more worthy to lead, more important etc; gain in[2] (q v). **o:** wisdom, stature, importance, authority □ *John has certainly* **grown in** *strength, but not, unfortunately,* **in** *wisdom. He's just as foolish as ever with his money.* □ *The Prime Minister was not an impressive figure when he took office, but he has* **grown** *greatly* **in** *stature over the past three years.*

grow into [A2] become, with the passage of time. **S:** he, she; actor; politician; corner shop; sapling. **o:** strapping girl, handsome young man; polished performer; clever statesman; flourishing business; sturdy tree □ *We did not meet again for ten years. By then, the rather puny boy had* **grown into** *a six-footer weighing 220 pounds.* □ *The small family business* **grew into** *a company of international importance.* ⇨ grow from[1].

grow on [A2] become gradually more attractive, interesting, likeable to. **S:** John, Liverpool; style of painting, writing, speaking, acting; country life □ *When I first went to live in Glasgow I found it rather a dreary place, but after a while it began to* **grow on** *me.* □ *The Portuguese 'fados' sound strange at first, but they quickly* **grow on** *you.*

(money) doesn't grow on trees [A2] (a saying) it is not easy to obtain money, it has to be worked for □ *'I can't give you ten pounds for a trip to London, Jill.* **Money doesn't grow on trees***, you know!'* □ (a mother, exasperated at her sons' excessive consumption of expensive apples): *'Apples* **don't grow on trees***, you know!'*

grow out of[1] [A2] become too big for. **o:** clothes, suit, dress, shoes □ *'It's terrible the way Sheila's* **growing out of** *her shoes; she needs a bigger size every three months!'* □ outgrow is used in the same meaning: *She's* **outgrown** *all her clothes.* But note: *She's* **outgrown** *all her friends* can mean 'She's grown taller than all her friends' or 'She's become more mature than them' (and consequently does not associate with them). ⇨ next entry.

grow out of[2] [A2 pass] abandon, lose with the passage of time or with maturity. **o:** bad habits; dependence on his mother; need for excitement □ *'Don't worry about Johnny's tantrums. He'll* **grow out of** *them. Children always do.'* □ outgrow is used in the same meaning: *He's* **outgrown** *his habit of wetting the bed.* ⇨ previous entry.

grow out of[3] [A2] have as its origin or cause; arise from (q v), grow from[2] (q v). **S:** war between A and B; financial troubles; love affair. **o:** unresolved dispute over their borders, persecution of the minority populations in each country; improvident spending; daily contact in the shop □ *The plot to kill the President* **grew out of** *the inordinate ambition of a few colonels.* □ *Joe's present unfortunate position — six months in jail —* **grew out of** *his uncontrollable temper.*

grow over [A2 B1ii pass B2 pass] (cause to) cover, spread over[1] (q v). **S:** [A2] **O:** [B1] ivy, weeds; climbing plants; mould, fungus; hair. **o:** tree, flower-bed, side of the house, wall; food; scar □ [A2] *Bracken, brambles, ivy and a variety of clinging plants had* **grown over** *the garden and given it the appearance of an impenetrable jungle* (or: *The garden had become* **overgrown/grown over with** *bracken* etc, *giving it the appearance* etc). □ [A2] *Mould had* **grown** *all* **over** *the food in the larder while they were away on holiday.* □ [B2] *To avoid recognition he had* **grown** *his hair longer and* **over** *the scar on his forehead.* □ note the passive transform **grown over with** and the alt form **overgrown with**, both with *be/become*; the latter is more usual in horticultural contexts.

grown over with [pass (B2)] ⇨ previous entry.

grow up[1] [A1] become adult; go through one's formative years □ *'What are you going to be when you* **grow up***, Anne?' 'I'm going to be a nurse.'* □ *Children are unpredictable: half the time they want to be with the* **grown-ups***, the other half they can't get far enough away from them.* □ *Sarah is only fifteen, but her opinions and reactions are surprisingly* **grown-up***.* □ *'How is it that you are so fond of South America?' 'I* **grew up** *in Uruguay!'* □ grown up resembles the passive and **grown-up** the adj of a [B1] pattern; grown-up(s) is also used as a noun.

grow up[2] [A1] behave or think as an adult ought to, face the realities of life as it *is*, not as a child might imagine it to be □ *'You don't mean to say that there are still prostitutes in Soho?' 'Oh, really! When are you going to* **grow up***!'* □ *'It's no good, George. There's only one thing you can do about it, and that's* **grow up***. Stop being the kind of person that people play practical jokes on.'* HD

grow up into [A3] become, as one grows older. **o:** thief, nice person, scrounger □ *'I punished Tim for not telling the truth. I'm not going to let him* **grow up into** *a liar if I can help it.'*

grub about [A1] busy oneself in some obscure way, perhaps in search of sth or to organize things, and getting dirty in the process. **A:** under the bushes; among old books; in the cellar □ *'I don't know where your mother is. Probably* **grubbing about** *in the vegetable garden or somewhere.'* □ *A fat sow was* **grubbing about** *near the gate and refused to move out of our way.*

grub up [B1i pass adj] pull out of the ground, and get dirty in doing it. **O:** weeds, potatoes, tree stump □ *The last time the old man was seen alive he was* **grubbing up** *some roots of heather on the mountainside.*

grumble (at) (about/over) [A2 pass rel] complain (to sb), perhaps in a surly, ill-tempered way (about sth). **o:** (**about/over**) food, lodging; treatment, low pay; weather □ *Old Scrooge was for ever* **grumbling at** *Bob Cratchit* **about** *his work.* □ *'It's no good* **grumbling at** *me* **about** *your treatment in hospital. Write to the Board of Management.'*

guard against [A2 pass rel] be careful to avoid, take precautions against. **o:** illness; colds, infection; scandal, suspicion; developing bad habits; invasion of one's privacy, prying eyes □ *A doctor* *must always* ***guard against*** *passing on disease to his family.* □ *You must* ***guard against*** *any tendency to take your privileges for granted.* □ *Hasty reactions to provocation should be* ***guarded against****.*

guess at [A2 pass] estimate, try to imagine. **o:** her age; likely effects of; his probable reaction; the cause of the explosion □ *If you want me to* ***guess at*** *John's reaction to your suggestion, I think he would welcome it.* □ *It's a mistake to* ***guess at*** *a woman's appearance from the sound of her voice!* □ *His origins can only be* ***guessed at****.*

guide across, along, away etc [B1i pass B2 pass] of a specially trained dog or experienced person, lead across etc. **O:** search-party, police, climbers □ *The police-dog* ***guided*** *its handler* ***to*** *the hidden drugs.* □ *The rescuers were* ***guided to*** *the trapped miners by their courageous singing.*

gull out of [B2 pass] obtain by trickery from. **O:** drunken man, young boy, innocent peasant. **o:** money, horse; everything he had □ *The con-man* ***gulled*** *the unsuspecting traveller* ***out of*** *every penny he had with him.*

gulp down [B1i pass] swallow quickly. **O:** cup of tea; dinner, food, medicine □ *The firemen paused for a couple of minutes,* ***gulped down*** *a cup of hot soup and returned to the job of fighting the fire.*

gum down [B1i pass adj] secure with gum. **S:** envelope; stamp, label □ *The stamp had not been properly* ***gummed down*** *and had come off the parcel, so we had to pay the postage again.*

gum up the works [B1iii pass] (slang) make progress impossible, spoil everything □ *Just when some stability seemed to have been introduced into industry, the Civil Service* ***gummed up the works*** *by going on strike for more pay.*

gun down [B1i pass] (informal) shoot unmercifully, often with the implication that the victims are defenceless. **o:** women and children, villagers; prisoners, suspects; rival (gangster, politician); presidential candidate □ *Nobody will ever know how many innocent peasants were* ***gunned down*** *in Vietnam.* □ *As the Colonel emerged from the meeting, the guerrillas, concealed behind the grill of an air-shaft,* ***gunned*** *him* ***down****.*

gun for [A2 pass] (informal) seek an opportunity to expose sb as inefficient, unconscientious, careless, or otherwise a vulnerable member of an organization, class etc □ *'I advise you to be very careful over the next few weeks; old Sanders is* ***gunning for*** *you, so he'll be looking out for any excuse to report you to the boss.'* □ *Poor Harry! He had no idea that he was being* ***gunned for*** *until the blow fell!*

gush from/out of [A2] flow freely and with some force from. **S:** blood; water; oil. **o:** severed vein, wound; broken pipe; newly-drilled well □ *Suddenly there was a shout from the men on the rig and the next thing we knew was that water was* ***gushing from*** *the well to a height of fifty feet.*

gush over [A2 pass] be excessively demonstrative towards or about sb. **o:** new baby; son's fiancée; visiting celebrity □ *'I wish Mummy wouldn't* ***gush over*** *Peter's little successes at school: it makes him feel a fool in front of his friends.'*

H

habituate to [B2 pass emph rel] (formal) make sb learn to accept or expect; get sb used to (q v). **S:** he etc; experience, event; war, famine, drought; achievement, success. **O:** oneself; population, citizens. **o:** hardship, deprivation, shortage; flattery, applause □ *He had* ***habituated*** *himself* (cf *He was* ***habituated***) ***to*** *the solitary life.* □ *The responsibility of command had* ***habituated*** *him* ***to*** *making quick decisions.*

hack down [B1i pass adj] cut to the ground with rough blows; chop down (q v). **O:** tree, branch □ *Men were* ***hacking down*** *an old privet hedge to make way for an ugly modern fence.*

hack off [B1i pass adj] remove with rough chopping blows; chop off (q v). **O:** branch; limb; length, section (of rope, piping) □ *The cook* ***hacked off*** *a piece of the roasted carcass and handed it to me in his fingers.*

haggle (over) [A2 pass rel] attempt, by making proposals and counter-proposals, to settle the price of goods, the terms of an agreement etc, in one's favour. **S:** traders, merchants; negotiators. **o:** price; wage, conditions □ *Let's not* ***haggle over*** *the odd few pounds in the price. Shall we settle at a round figure of £250?* □ *The trade union side did not consider it a waste of time to* ***haggle over*** *the finer points of the package deal.*

hail from [A2 rel] have as a place of origin. **S:** visitor, tourist; ship. **o:** abroad, the North; foreign port □ *Judging from his speech, I should say he* ***hails from*** *North of the Border* (= Scotland). □ usu informal when referring to persons.

ham up [B1i pass adj] (informal) act on the stage in a crude or exaggerated way (either through inexperience or for deliberate effect). **S:** actor, performer. **O:** it, the (whole) thing; part, passage □ *Why must every comedy show on TV contain a* ***hammed-up*** *extract from Shakespeare?* □ *'Don't on any account* ***ham*** *this scene* ***up****. If anything, underplay it — play it down.'*

hammer down [B1i pass] secure, fasten, sth by striking it (or driving in nails). **O:** lid, top, cover □ *The cover, which had already been roughly fitted into position, was now* ***hammered down****.*

hammer in/into[1] [B1i pass B2 pass] force, drive, in by striking. **O:** post, stake; nail, rivet □ *First the pegs were* ***hammered into*** *the ground in a large circle, then the tent was raised and the ropes fastened.*

hammer in/into[2] [B1i pass B2 pass] force sb to learn sth (by tiresome repetition). **S:** teacher, preacher, pedant. **O:** lesson; moral, point; French, grammar. **o:** flock, class; head □ *Please don't advise me not to marry John; my parents have been* ***hammering*** *the lesson* ***in*** *long enough.* □ *We had Latin* ***hammered into*** *our heads for five years. How much of it do we still* *remember?*

hammer on/onto [B1i pass B2 pass] fasten in position by beating or striking. **S:** blacksmith, carpenter. **O:** lid, top, metal cap □ *A protective copper strip was* **hammered onto** *the end of the post.* □ *When you've packed the box,* **hammer** *the lid* **on**.

hammer out[1] [B1i pass] make flat or smooth by beating; remove an irregularity by beating. **S:** panel-beater, coach-builder. **O:** metal sheet, panel, wing; bump, dent □ *That dent is not big enough to be worth* **hammering out**; *we can fill it in.*

hammer out[2] [B1i pass] evolve, agree, sth through hard work or discussion. **S:** conference, negotiators. **O:** new proposals, compromise solution, final draft □ *After prolonged discussion, the delegates* **hammered out** *a form of words that was acceptable to everyone.*

hand back (to) [B1i pass B3 pass] return sth (to its owner); give back (to)[1] (q v). **S:** official, policeman; teacher. **O:** passport, driving licence; exercise-book, examination script □ *Please remember to* **hand back** *your room key before leaving the hotel.* □ *'I haven't managed to mark your essays yet. I'll* **hand** *you them* **back** (or: *I'll* **hand** *them* **back to** *you) on Thursday.'* □ the second example shows the Indirect Object construction.

hand down[1] [B1i pass adj] pass on to a child below one in age or size. **O:** clothes, shoes; book, toy □ *In poor families, clothes may be* **handed down** *from one child to the next.* □ *Peter was dressed in a pair of his brother's* **hand-me-downs** (**handed-down** *trousers* etc). □ *The kids had to wear* **hand-me-down** *jackets.* □ nom form is hand-me-down(s).

hand down[2] [B1i pass adj] transmit, usu over several generations. **O:** custom, tradition; enmity, prejudice □ *Adam and Eve were repairing the skins* **handed down** *to them from generations of their forbears.* US □ *These ceremonies have been* **handed down** *through the centuries, and remain practically unchanged.* □ usu passive.

hand down[3] [B1i pass] (legal) pass sentence on sb convicted of a crime. **S:** court; judge, magistrate. **O:** judgment; sentence (of thirty years) □ *After the jury had returned its verdict the judge* **handed down** *very heavy sentences ranging from fifteen to twenty-five years on all the accused.*

hand in [B1i pass adj] submit; tender; surrender (because completed, worn out, or no longer required); give in (q v). **O:** exam script, form; resignation, protest; uniform, equipment □ *The Minister* **handed in** *his resignation in protest against the Cabinet's European policy.* □ *Unserviceable kit should be* **handed in** *at the quartermaster's stores after muster parade.*

hand off [B1i nom pass] (rugby football) push away a would-be tackler with straightened forearm and spread fingers □ *Smith* **handed off** *the full-back and raced for the corner-flag.* □ *Jones was penalized for a too vigorously administered* **hand-off**.

hand on [B1i pass adj] pass sth to the generation following one's own. **O:** burden, trust, responsibility; knowledge, skill □ *Each new generation coming into the Sixth will have this body of experience* **handed on**, *and they'll be able to make their own contribution.* CON □ *Everyone was choking with their experience of life and wanted to* **hand it on**. ITAJ

hand out[1] [B1i nom pass] distribute, circulate; give out [2] (q v). **S:** lecturer, salesman. **O:** duplicated sheet, summary, sales brochure □ *Duplicated material illustrating the lecture was* **handed out** *to the students* (cf *Illustrative* **hand-outs** *were given to the students*). □ **Hand-outs** *were pushed through our letter-boxes as the first stage in this new trade war.* □ the hand-out is the written or printed material itself.

hand out[2] [B1i nom pass] offer as charity (to the unemployed, earthquake victims etc). **O:** soup, bread; clothing, blankets; gift parcels □ *The President* **handed out** *gifts of food and clothing to the survivors of the shipwreck.* □ *During the slump, many thousands of workers survived on* **hand-outs**. □ the hand-out is the food, clothing etc itself.

hand it/(the) punishment out [B1i pass] (informal) give a severe beating to, thrash soundly; dish it out (q v) □ *Smith was really going for his opponent,* **handing it out** *with both fists.* □ *This new class of ship is built to* **hand out (the) punishment**.

hand over[1] [B1i pass] surrender. **S:** breadwinner; captor, enemy; intruder, assailant. **O:** money, pay-packet; prisoner, hostage; gun, knife □ *This was the day of the week that Uncle Saunders was expected to* **hand over** *the house-keeping money.* CON □ *Having expelled the student, the authorities almost literally* **handed** *him* **over** *to the secular arm.* OBS

hand over[2] [A1 nom B1i nom pass] transfer a position of authority or power; make, complete, checks on cash, equipment etc as part of this transfer. **S:** government, administration; governor, minister; storekeeper. **O:** territory, colony; office, post; stores, plant □ *The time had now come for* **handing over** *power* (or: *a* **hand-over** *of power) to a local, elected government.* □ *I shall be glad to* **hand** *this job* **over**. □ *The stores were properly* **handed over** *to the new man — even the nuts and bolts were checked.*

hand it to [B2] (informal) (one must) give credit or praise to □ *'They're a clever lot, you've got to* **hand it to** *them.'* ILIH □ *'She's been wonderfully cheerful, and interested in everything — you've really got to* **hand it to** *her.'* ILIH □ always occurs with *must* or *have (got) to*.

hang about/around [A1 A2] (informal) wait idly (e g for sth to happen); wait about/around (q v). **S:** (would-be) customer, spectator. **o:** door, entrance □ *Cai* (an animal) *only saw that I had put something in her cage which was alive, and she was not going to* **hang about** *and see what it was.* DF □ *Desmond had spent several weeks* **hanging around** *the garage making friends with the rest of the ring* (i e gang of diamond smugglers). DS

hang back (from) [A1 A3 emph rel] hesitate, through timidity or fear, to do sth; hold back [2] (q v). **o:** fight; discussion; saying anything, taking part □ *When the police came around asking questions, Peter* **hung back from** *giving information.* □ *He's a solitary child — always* **hangs back from** *any group activities.*

hang behind [A1] linger in a place after others

have left. **S:** spectator, student □ *One or two of the audience* ***hung behind*** *after the lecture to have a word with the speaker.*

hang in the balance [A2] (of events) have reached a critical point, where the result may go either way. **S:** future; result, outcome, issue; life, career □ *If your heart begins to fail when the issue* ***hangs in the balance****, your opponent will probably win.* MFM

hang on[1] [A1] (informal) wait, pause; hold on [1] (q v). **A:** a second, a jiffy □ *Mrs Roth said she'd* ***hang on*** *a bit.* TT □ *'Got a match, Bob?' he asked.* ***'Hang on,'*** *Bob replied.* BM □ often imper.

hang on[2] [A1] (informal) grip sth firmly, hold tight; survive a crisis, hold fast; hold on [2] (q v) □ ***'Hang on*** *with your knees. Don't let go.* ***Hang on*** *tight. Like grim death.'* DBM □ *The most we can hope for is that by staying put, by digging our caves, we shall be able to* ***hang on.*** TBC

hang on[3] [A2 emph rel] require that some condition should first be met; hinge on/upon (q v). **S:** future; career; result, outcome. **o:** vote, election; decision, resolution; support, backing; whether one is supported, what happens later □ *The survival of the government* ***hangs on*** *tonight's crucial vote.* □ ***On*** *our ability to compete in difficult markets* ***hangs*** *our future as a trading nation.*

hang on to [A3 pass] (informal) keep, retain; not give or sell to sb else; hold on to [2] (q v). **o:** (one's) lead, advantage; shares, profits; what one has □ *Was Wouvermans keeping his word to* ***hang on to*** *the picture?* US □ *I'm* ***hanging on to*** *those shares — I think they'll show a sizeable gain after the Budget.*

hang out[1] [B1i pass] spread damp washing on a clothes line, so that it can dry. **O:** washing, clothes □ *'I've just got one or two shirts to* ***hang out*** *— then we can go shopping.'*

hang out[2] [A1 nom] (informal) live, reside; visit a place frequently □ *'What did you say you were doing? And where are you* ***hanging out****?'* THH □ *'If I were you I'd look for him at the jazz club. It's a favourite* ***hang-out*** *for students.'*

hang over[1] [A2 emph] envelop (sth); possess (sb). **S:** (cloud, atmosphere, spirit, of) gloom, depression. **o:** proceedings; gathering, meeting; company □ *Robert tried with a few good-humoured remarks to break through the cloud of gloom* ***hanging over*** *his colleagues, but his words struck no response from them.*

hang over[2] [A2 emph] seem likely to occur soon, be imminent. **S:** (prospect, possibility, of) ruin, disaster, failure; (threat of) dismissal, expulsion; examination, interview. **o:** army, industry; employee, member; student □ *With the prospect* ***hanging over*** *them of expulsion from their holdings, the smaller farmers were forced to seek work in the growing industrial towns.* □ *Now that my Bar exams are* ***hanging over*** *me I don't want to take on any new outside commitments.*

hang over[3] [B2 pass emph rel] suspend things from a surface so that they may cover it. **O:** carpet, tapestry; picture, drawing, poster; medal, cross. **o:** wall, ceiling; chest; uniform □ ***Over*** *one wall of the study he had* ***hung*** *a set of framed prints.* □ *Trophies were* ***hung*** *all* ***over*** *the walls* (or: *The walls were* ***hung with*** *trophies*). RATT

hangover/hung over [nom pass (B1)] (informal) (suffer) the consequences of drinking heavily the evening before □ *He's feeling terribly* ***hung over*** *after last night's party.* □ *I woke up with a dreadful* ***hangover*** *this morning.*

hang together[1] [A1] co-operate, support one another □ *It was better to* ***hang together*** *than separately* (i e *than be* ***hanged*** *separately*). DS □ *We can come through any crisis if we* ***hang together.***

hang together[2] [A1] form an intelligible whole, a coherent pattern. **S:** evidence, clues; story, picture; everything, it all □ *'The two parts of his statement don't quite* ***hang together****, do they?' said the inspector. 'We'll have to question him again.'*

hang-up/hung up [nom pass (B1)] (informal) (suffer) inconvenience; or some kind of emotional or nervous upset or inhibition □ *We've been badly* ***hung up*** *through the inefficiency of the dispatch department.* □ *Another* ***hang-up*** *students complain of is too little personal contact with the teaching staff.* □ *She's strangely* ***hung up*** (or: *has a strange* ***hang-up***) *about meeting new people.*

hang up (on) [A1 A3 pass] end a telephone conversation (with sb) by replacing the receiver □ *She's incorrigible on the telephone. You literally have to* ***hang up*** *in her ear.* DC □ *I didn't have a chance to apologize: she* ***hung up on*** *me.*

hang upon [A2 pass] listen with devoted attention to. **S:** audience; follower, supporter; admirer, lover. **o:** ⚠ (sb's) every word, words, reply; sb's lips □ *They* ***hung upon*** *their leader's words.* EM □ *Certainly he knew how to captivate Irma: she seemed to* ***hang upon*** *his lips.* PW

hanker after/for [A2 pass emph rel] have a strong desire for. **o:** fame, wealth □ *She got rid of nearly all the raw fish without* ***hankering*** *much* ***after*** *a gravy dinner and cider.* TGLY □ *It was quite an important journal of its kind, but he was ambitious and* ***hankering for*** *Fleet Street.* HD

happen along [A1] (informal) appear by chance, happen to arrive □ *He was obviously annoyed that the child had* ***happened along.*** CON □ *He had to* ***happen along*** *just as we were about to settle the whole thing amicably.*

happen on/upon [A2] meet, discover, by chance. **o:** old friend, acquaintance; rare commodity, congenial job □ *'Where did you pick up those uncut stones?' 'I just* ***happened on*** *them in a small jeweller's in Zanzibar.'*

hark at [A2] (informal) (just you) listen to X (implying that what X says is untrue, conceited, or otherwise not worth listening to) □ *'Just* ***hark at*** *him — anyone would think he owned the place!'* □ imper.

hark back (to) [A1 A3 pass emph rel] mention again, recall. **o:** past event, earlier tradition, former achievement □ *To understand this entails* ***harking back to*** *a revelation I made earlier on.* SPL □ *But the tradition is not entirely dead. It is* ***harked back to****, leaned upon as a fixed and still largely trustworthy field of reference.* UL

harmonize (with) [A2 emph rel B2 pass emph rel] (cause to) blend or fit in pleasingly (with). **S:** [A2] **O:** [B2] colour, shade, tone; note; mood, feelings; behaviour. **o:** one another; the other; background, surroundings □ *These notes don't* ***harmonize*** (***with*** *each other*). □ *His tem-*

perament does not **harmonize with** *a slow, even pace of life.* □ *Find a pattern that can be* **harmonized with** *the one on the curtains.*

harness (to) [B2 pass emph rel] connect a source of energy to sth so that the latter is driven. **O:** horse, ox; energy, power. **o:** cart, wagon; economy, industry □ *The farmer* **harnessed** *a pair of oxen* **to** *the heavy wagon.* □ *The productive energies of a whole people were* **harnessed to** *the war effort.*

harp on [A2 pass adj] talk persistently and tiresomely of. **o:** grievance, suffering, lack of money □ *She's always* **harping on** *the family's neglect of her. In fact everyone goes to visit her once a week.* □ *That's a string that's been* **harped on** *many times before.*

hatch out[1] [A1] (of shells) break open; (of a young bird etc) break through the egg shell. **S:** egg; batch; chick, grub, caterpillar, snake □ *The eggs* **hatch out** *in the warm mud of the river-bank.*

hatch out[2] [B1i pass] cause or help a shell to break open, or a young bird to break through the shell. **S:** chicken farmer; mother bird. **O:** egg; batch; chick, grub □ *The mother hen* **hatches out** *her young by covering the eggs with her warm feathers.* □ *Several batches a day can be* **hatched out** *with the new incubator.*

haul over the coals [B2 pass] (informal) reproach or reprimand severely. **S:** father, employer; chief, boss □ *He* (the Minister) *said it was a new experience to be* **hauled over the coals** *in the Cabinet room.* MFM □ *'What was all the fuss about?' 'Oh, just the Old Man* **hauling** *me* **over the coals** *for borrowing his car again.'*

haul up (before) [B1i pass B3 pass] (informal) bring for trial in a court of law. **O:** thief, bigamist; defaulter; truant. **o:** judge, magistrate, 'beak'; commanding officer; headmaster □ *This is the second time that Matthew has been* **hauled up** *on a dangerous driving charge.* □ *The least that can happen is that you'll be* **hauled up before** *the company commander and given a severe reprimand.*

have about [B2 emph rel] be checked, restrained, by moral uncertainty or principles, from doing or believing sth. **O:** ⚠ (some, serious, certain) misgivings, reservations, qualms, scruples. **o:** accepting, receiving; taking, removing; advising, proposing □ *I wouldn't* **have** *any qualms* **about** *taking his money.* DC □ *We* **had** *few serious misgivings* **about** *recommending him for promotion.*

have doubts about [B2 emph rel] be uncertain, unsure, about. **adj:** some, no, one's; grave, serious. **o:** integrity, truthfulness, reliability; (sb's) work, research; how things will develop, whether to continue □ *We may* **have** *serious* **doubts about** *the quality of working-class life today.* UL □ *They had always* **had** *their* **doubts about** *George; others refused to believe in his guilt.* PE

have about one [B2] be carrying somewhere on one's person. **O:** letter, form; watch, lighter □ *'Do you want a cigarette? I should* **have** *one* **about me** *somewhere.'* ⇨ have on one/one's person.

have a/this thing about[1] [B2] (informal) feel especially attracted to, fond of or interested in sb or sth. **o:** dark girls, tall men; wine, rich food; sea, desert; astronomy, antiques □ *Of course he* **has a thing about** *her. He always* **has a thing about** *petite brunettes who need looking after.* □ *David's always* **had this** *terrific* **thing about** *the army - ever since his grandfather gave him his first set of model soldiers.*

have a/this thing about[2] [B2] (informal) feel a particular (and often irrational) fear or dislike of sb or sth. **o:** strangers, foreigners; snakes, spiders; travelling, being left alone □ *She* **has this** *silly* **thing about** *men with beards. Won't let one anywhere near her.* □ *It's the particular one* (i e girl) *he doesn't like at the time that he calls Clementine. It's just* **a thing** *he* **has about** *that name.* DC

have one's wits about one [B2] be alert and shrewd, be sharp-witted. **S:** salesman, dealer; sailor, airman □ *You need to* **have your wits about you** *in the market. The last time I bought from a market trader I was given rotten fruit from the back of the pile.* □ *'He's an awful fellow, Alec is, a real smart-alec, when he* **has his wits about him.**' PW

have feelings about/on [B2 emph rel] feel a certain way, adapt a particular attitude, about. **adj:** (any, no) decided, particular, strong. **o:** divorce, abortion; capital punishment; disarmament; drugs, drink, smoking □ *I* **have** *no* **feelings** *one way or the other* **about** *what you are suggesting.* □ *It* (the aristocracy) *was not a matter* **on** *which he* **had any strong feelings**. US

have a grudge against [B2 emph rel] feel ill-will towards sb (for no good reason, or because of sth he has done). **S:** teacher, prefect; police, magistrate, traffic warden; boss, foreman. **o:** pupil, class; motorist; student, hippie; workman □ *John's been put into detention so many times that he's beginning to feel his form master must* **have a grudge against** *him.* □ *Mary never forgot that she* **had a grudge against** *Africans in general, and she used to pick on any strange ones that came to camp.* BB

have around/over/round [B1ii] entertain at one's house (usu for a short time, e g for a meal or drinks) □ *'I'll be* **having** *a few people* **round** *for a beer one of these evenings,' said the man.* HD

have at [B2] (informal) try to achieve or do sth different and challenging. **O:** ⚠ a bash, crack, shot, stab, go, try. **o:** title, championship; trophy, cup; exam; persuading, convincing, converting, sb □ *At the next meeting, he's going to* **have** *a stab* **at** *the 5 000 metres record.* □ *As things stand, I don't mind* **having** *a go* **at** *doing up the place.* TC

have it away/off (with) [B1ii B3] (slang) make love to (implying that the love-making is illicit, or at least furtive) □ *While Smith was in the North on business, Jones was* **having it away with** *his wife.* □ *How does he know she's not* **having it off** *whenever his back's turned?*

have back[1] [B1i] have sth returned which has been borrowed. **O:** book, paper; car, lawnmower □ *You can make use of my typewriter, but I must* **have** *it* **back** *by the weekend.* □ *When can you let me* **have back** *the money that I lent you?* □ often used with *let*; not in continuous tenses. ⇨ get back[4], give back (to)[1].

have back[2] [B1ii] allow a spouse or lover from whom one is separated to return. **O:** wife, husband; boyfriend; fiancée □ *She wouldn't* ***have*** *him* ***back*** *if he was the last man on earth.* ⇨ take back[2].

have by [B2 emph rel] have a child by X = X is the father of the child □ *She* ***had*** *a daughter* ***by*** *her first husband and two sons* ***by*** *her second.* □ *Bess* ***had*** *a boy* ***by*** *the fellow who's walking around the Court today.* WI

have down [B1ii] have sb to stay at one's (country) house as a guest, either from London or the north. **A:** for a few days, at Christmas □ *They're planning to* ***have*** *their grandchildren* ***down*** *for the weekend.* ⇨ come down[6].

have their tails down/up [B1ii] (informal) be dispirited, depressed; be confident, elated □ *The troops* ***had their tails down*** *and there was no confidence in the higher command.* MFM □ *Having won the President's Cup, the team* ***had their tails up*** *for the final of the league championship.*

have for [B2 emph rel] be interesting, attractive to sb. **S:** book, music, play; writer, composer; woman; face, figure. **O:** (certain, great, tremendous) appeal, attraction, fascination, interest □ *The topic seemed to* ***have*** *a fascination* ***for*** *her.* TST □ ***For*** *me, the poetry of Keats has always* ***had*** *an enormous appeal.*

have an ear/eye/a nose for [B2 emph rel] be able to detect, or appreciate sth, because one's senses are alert or well trained. **adj:** no; good, sensitive; discerning, sharp. **o:** music, opera; colour, design; scandal, gossip □ *He* ***has no ear for*** *music.* □ *I've not* ***got*** *much of* ***an eye for*** *dresses.* OI □ *The writer* ***had a*** *keen* ***eye for*** *evidences of superstition.* NDN □ *A good reporter* ***has a nose for*** *news.*

have a flair/gift for [B2 emph rel] be naturally gifted in some respect. **adj:** no, (not) any; special, remarkable. **o:** languages, mimicry; making things, handling machinery; foolery, saying the wrong thing □ *'Did you have any difficulty in learning to shoot?' 'No, sir.' She* ***had a flair for*** *it.* RFW □ *He* ***had no gift for*** *making polite conversation at parties.*

have no fears/terrors for [B2 emph rel] not alarm or frighten sb. **S:** mathematics, science; flying, motoring; tests, exams; speaking in public, meeting new people. **adj:** no, (not) any, few □ *Unknown hazards must* ***have no terrors for*** *us.* MFM □ *Rowdy meetings should* ***have no fears for*** *an old professional like you.* ⇨ have of.

have no time/use for [B2 emph rel] think very little etc of, have a poor etc opinion of. **adj:** some, a lot of; (not) much, little. **o:** shirker, coward; bigot, show-off; (upper, lower) class; boss, trade unionist; democracy, the monarchy □ *The colonel never* ***had any time for*** *officers who had risen from the ranks.* □ *He* ***had no use for*** *girls who did not know their way around.* AITC

have a soft/weak spot for [B2 emph rel] (informal) feel a special fondness for. **o:** (one's) youngest child, baby, orphan; vagrant, down-and-out □ *Valerie sends her regards. She has always* ***had a weak spot for*** *you.* US □ *People* ***have a soft spot*** *in their hearts* ***for*** *alcoholics.* OMIH

have in [B1ii] have sb working in one's house. **O:** decorator, builder, plumber, carpenter □ *I'm afraid we can't have you to stay after all: we****'ve (got)*** *the decorators* ***in*** *all this week.* ⇨ get in[2].

have confidence in [B2 emph rel] be sure in one's mind that sb is capable, or that things will turn out well. **adj:** a lot of; (not) any/much; considerable. **o:** manager, officer; parent, teacher; sb's ability, capabilities; future □ *His personal authority would need to be great enough for the public to* ***have confidence in*** *him.* SC □ *He* ***has*** *very little* ***confidence in*** *himself.* □ *The vote indicates that the House* ***has*** *no* ***confidence in*** *the Government.*

have faith (in) [B2 emph rel] believe in the power, effectiveness etc, of. **adj:** no, (not) any/much, little; absolute, minimal. **o:** God; leader; promise, word □ *Such men must* ***have faith in*** *God and they must think rightly on the moral issues involved.* MFM □ *After so many disappointments, he finds it hard to* ***have faith in*** *doctors.*

have in hand [B2] have started or undertaken. **S:** contractor; agent, organizer; editor, examiner. **O:** work; alterations; arrangements; checking □ *There's no need to worry about the electrical fittings. We'll* ***have*** *the work* ***in hand*** *by the end of July.* ⇨ be/take in hand.

have a hand/part in [B2 emph rel] be partly responsible for, be involved in, sth which happens. **adj:** no, (not) any. **o:** decision; move, step; development, enterprise; forming opinion, changing conditions □ *Sir Roy says that his government* ***had no hand in*** *the decision.* OBS □ *The man* ***had a hand in*** *shaping my ideas.* ITAJ □ *The rehousing programme was something* ***in*** *which the minister was proud to have* ***had a part.***

have it in one (to do sth) [B2] be capable (of doing sth), have the ability (to do sth). **Inf** to succeed, to go far, to hold sb's attention for long □ *You'll find you can make good if you* ***have it in you.*** HD □ *She never had the certainty that she* ***had it in her to draw*** *the love she coveted.* MM

have it in mind to do sth [B2] ⇨ next entry.

have in mind [B2] be considering, contemplating; propose, intend. **O:** idea, proposal; remedy, answer; it... to warn sb, to increase spending □ *Don't give your confidence to others regarding a plan you* ***have in mind.*** WI □ *It was this weapon that the Minister of Defence* ***had in mind.*** NS □ *He* ***had*** *it* ***in mind*** *to initiate staff talks with the Americans.* MFM

have a place in [B2 emph rel] appear in, figure in (q v). **S:** parent, child; upbringing, schooling; accident, disaster. **adj:** some, no, little; important, significant, special, minor. **o:** affections; biography, novel; report, record □ *The working-class mother* ***has an*** *honoured* ***place in*** *most accounts of working-class childhoods.* UL □ ***In*** *the Report now published, the establishment of new universities* ***has a*** *prominent* ***place.***

have a say/voice in [B2 emph rel] be involved in deciding future events. **S:** general public, ordinary person; consumer, user (of public services). **adj:** some; (not) any/much, little; considerable. **o:** (future) developments; what should happen, how things should develop; deciding, shaping, controlling, planning (sth) □ *They will* ***have a*** *determining* ***say in*** *their own future.* SC □ *The ordinary MP may feel he* ***has no*** *effective* ***voice in*** *determining policy.*

have in one's spell [B2] exert a magic power or control over. **S:** lover; actor, orator; sportsman.

O: girl; audience, onlookers; opponent □ *Well, well, Bessie girl, Solly's* ***got*** *you* ***in his spell.*** HSG □ *For twenty minutes of the first half, the Brazilian forwards* ***had*** *a packed stadium* ***in their spell.***

have a stake in [B2 emph rel] have invested money, effort etc in sth (and therefore stand to lose or gain). **S:** businessman, industrialist; inventor, designer, craftsman; investor; public, taxpayer. **adj:** some; no, not much of a; considerable, sizeable. **o:** region; economy; industry, business; venture, enterprise □ *He'd invested in local property. Unlike other European traders, he* ***had a*** *genuine* ***stake in*** *the country.* DS □ *Involving workers in management may help them feel they* ***have a*** *bigger* ***stake in*** *the success of their company.*

have well in hand [B2] be easily able to control sth. **O:** situation; crisis □ *Hopalong was trying to give the impression that he* ***had*** *the situation* ***well in hand*** *really and was just about to do what his friends had merely saved him the trouble of doing.* TT ⇨ be well in hand.

have it in for [B3] (informal) intend to make trouble for (often through sheer ill-will) □ *They* (the police) ***have got it in for*** *your blue-eyed Larrie.* ASA □ *The prefects* ***have it in for*** *this form. They must have taken a dislike to us on sight.*

have of [B2 emph rel] fear, be frightened of. **O:** ⚠ a dread, fear, horror, terror. **o:** isolation, the dark, open spaces; snakes, spiders □ *I might sleep and wake again before the night had really started. I* ***had*** *a horror* ***of*** *this.* UTN □ *She* ***has*** *this inexplicable fear* ***of*** *the empty house next door.* ⇨ have no fears/terrors for.

have the best/worst of [B2 emph rel] profit, benefit, most from sth; suffer most from sth. **S:** country; army; industry, business; contestant. **o:** it, things; struggle, conflict, argument; deal, arrangement □ *You can depend on it that when we come to divide the spoils Philip will* ***have the best of*** *the share-out.* □ *Most of these forces had serious problems on their hands, but of those plagued by the latter, Sierra Leone* ***had*** *easily* ***the worst of*** *it.* DS ⇨ get the worst of.

have the courage of [B2] be courageous enough to act according to one's feelings etc. **o:** ⚠ one's convictions, desires, feelings, instincts, inclinations □ *He was a sensualist who never* ***had the courage of*** *his desires.* ASA □ *I should have* ***had the courage of*** *my instincts, cancelled the old plan, and started again from scratch.* LWK

have control of/over [B2 emph rel] direct, control, command. **S:** civil power, army, church, ordinary people. **adj:** some; no, (not) any/much; absolute, total. **o:** city, district, area; (people's) lives, movements □ *The Constitution must give citizens confidence that they will* ***have control of*** *their own destinies.* □ *She* ***has*** *very little* ***control over*** *the children; they seem to decide how they will behave.* ⇨ be in/take control (of).

have it off (with) [B2 B3] ⇨ have it away/off (with).

have on[1] [B1i] be wearing. **O:** clean shirt, bow tie; nothing □ *She may* ***have on*** *a fur coat.* AITC □ *Fergus* ***had*** *his light-hearted face* ***on*** *again.* DC □ *'You shouldn't feel hot. You've nothing* ***on.***' RATT ⇨ get on[1], put on[1].

have on[2] [B1ii] have sth arranged, have sth on one's programme or as a commitment. **O:** meeting, appointment, engagement; anything, nothing □ ***'Have*** *you* ***(got)*** *anything* ***on*** *this evening?' 'Yes, one or two short meetings.'*

have on[3] [B1ii pass] (informal) deceive, trick □ *He was doing what he'd been paid for, but half the time I reckoned that he was* ***having me on.*** JFTR □ *I suspected we were being* ***had on*** *by the greengrocer, so we weighed the vegetables when we got back.*

have on[4] [B2] (informal) have (no) reason or evidence to suggest that sb is responsible, etc. **S:** police; rival organization, firm. **O:** ⚠ (not) anything, nothing, something; what, how much □ *'Belfounder* ***hasn't*** *anything* ***on*** *us legally; and if he starts making complaints I can make plenty of counter-complaints about the way I was treated.'* UTN □ *Joe couldn't be sure how much the police* ***had on*** *him, but the suspicion that they might have something was enough to make him leave town.*

have on the brain [B2] (informal) be greatly preoccupied, or obsessed, with sth. **O:** power, money, sex □ *'Some boy?' Terence echoed scornfully. 'You've* ***got*** *sex* ***on the brain.'*** HAA

have compassion/pity on [B2 emph rel] have kind and tender feelings for sb in distress. **adj:** no, (not) any/much; little, great. **o:** poor, homeless, hungry (people) □ MYRA (breaking down and crying): *Tony,* ***have pity on*** *me sometimes.* EHOW □ *The Church* ***has compassion on*** *those whose conduct falls short of its moral teachings.*

have a crush/pash on [B2 rel] (informal) love (in an immature way); be infatuated with. (q v) **S:** schoolgirl, girl student, young parishioner. **adj:** big, serious, terrific, tremendous. **o:** teacher, lecturer, vicar □ *It was the story of a schoolgirl who'd* ***had a crush on*** *an old man.* PP □ *You might choose somebody more suitable to* ***have a pash on*** *— he's married, with five children.* □ pash is rather dated.

have designs on [B2 rel] (informal) plan, propose to take, win, control etc. **adj:** no, (not) any; serious. **o:** girl, woman; man; top position, controlling interest □ *I can assure you that I* ***have*** *no* ***designs on*** *Peter's job.* □ *Darling, I want to go unattached. Maybe the devil's* ***got designs on*** *me.* DPM

have one's eye on [B2 rel] (informal) have chosen sb or sth as a desirable conquest, acquisition etc. **o:** girl, man; house, business; job, vacancy □ *I looked around, wondering which young starlet the Baron* ***had his eye on.*** PP □ *There was this nice little corner shop he'd* ***had his eye on*** *for some time.*

have one eye on [B2] give part of one's attention to one thing (while the rest is engaged somewhere else). **o:** clock, time; saucepan, kettle; baby, toddler □ *It was a tricky experiment — he had to* ***have one eye on*** *the thermometer all the time.* □ *He had a double motive, he* ***had one eye on*** *his own future.* NM ⇨ keep one eye on.

have feelings on [B2 emph rel] ⇨ have feelings about/on.

have on one's hands [B2] have goods that one does not need and would like to sell; have a responsibility that one finds irksome. **O:** (spare, surplus) stores, supplies; elderly relative, maiden aunt, (sb else's) children □ *'I've an extra gas cooker* ***on my hands.*** *Do you want to take it off* *me?'* □ *I now* ***have*** *a ghost* ***on my hands — another father would have the decency to die and stay dead.*** HSG

have on one's mind [B2] be thinking about, and worried or concerned by, some problem. **O:** something, nothing; a lot, a great deal; arrangements, organization; party, wedding □ *'You've* ***got*** *something* ***on your mind****. You aren't still worrying, are you?'* OMIH □ *'Don't bother your father now — he* ***has*** *too much* ***on his mind****.'*

have on one/one's person [B2] be carrying (esp in a pocket or handbag). **O:** money, change; passport, ticket; comb, nail-file □ *'I suppose you wouldn't* ***have*** *the price of a drink* ***on you****?'* □ *'****Have*** *you* ***got*** *the key of the sideboard* ***on you****?'* MM ⇨ have about one.

have time on one's hands [B2] (informal) have little (work) to do, not be under pressure of work □ *'Still here then, I see,' he said conversationally. 'You must* ***have*** *plenty of* ***time on your hands****.'* TGLY □ *'Now that Father's retired he'll* ***have*** *more* ***time on his hands****.' 'That's what worries me. He'll feel miserable with so little to do.'*

have a bearing on/upon [B2 emph rel] be related to; affect, influence; bear on/upon (q v). **S:** (sb's) presence, participation, involvement; belief, feeling. **adj:** (not) any/much, little; direct, important. **o:** outcome, result; case, affair, issue □ *The points you are raising* ***have some bearing on*** *the case now being tried.* □ *Whether you love him* ***has no bearing on*** *whether he's good or bad.* AITC

have an effect/impact (on/upon) [B2 emph rel] affect, influence in some way. **adj:** some; (not) any/much, little; slight, marginal; strong, favourable; adverse, contrary. **o:** production, demand, sales; (foreign) relations, policy; strategy, planning □ *The measures which the Chancellor has taken should* ***have a*** *favourable* ***impact upon*** *the balance of payments.* SC □ *These provisions have* ***had no*** *marked* ***effect on*** *the unemployment figures.*

have out [B1ii] cause to be removed by a surgeon or dentist. **O:** tooth, appendix □ *He was* ***having*** *his tonsils* ***out****, which is a severe operation for an aging man.* HD

have out (with) [B1ii B3] (informal) discuss a matter frankly, often angrily, (with sb) until understanding is reached. **O:** it; the thing, the question, the whole issue □ *'I'm going round to Ned's. We've got to* ***have*** *this thing* ***out****.'* CON □ *Their determination to* ***have*** *the apartheid issue* ***out*** *has not been changed in any degree.* SC □ *'I* ***had*** *it* ***out with*** *her about the pilchard tins,' said Frank petulantly.* ASA

have over/round [B1ii] ⇨ have around/over/round.

have control over [B2 emph rel] ⇨ have control of/over.

have an/the edge over [B2 emph rel] (informal) be in a position of advantage compared with sb else. **adj:** (a) distinct, noticeable, considerable. **o:** neighbour, rival, competitor □ *As far as having influence among those top half-dozen men, Sir Harold Johnson* ***had the edge over*** *Annette's father.* SML □ (with reference to the US investment drive abroad) *Germany* ***has a*** *comfortable* ***edge over*** *France.* SC

have a hold over [B2 emph rel] be able to restrict a person's freedom, decide how he will act etc, because of some special advantage one has (e g information which could be used to damage him). **adj:** no, (not) any, (not) much of a; slight, considerable. **o:** enemy, rival, competitor □ *'He* ***has a hold over*** *you, you realize that?' 'I don't see how.' 'His family own the land adjoining yours, and in time you will need that land to expand your workshops.'*

have access to [B2 emph rel] be able to reach or use. **adj:** some; no, not any/much; free, open, direct, restricted. **o:** garden, garage; shop, bank; paper, document, book; evidence, facts □ *The café was a large room opening out on to the street, and the public* ***had access to*** *it.* T □ *Thanks to the owner of a private library, I now* ***have access to*** *personal correspondence from that period.* □ *From the flat, we* ***have*** *easy* ***access to*** *shops and schools.* ⇨ get access to.

have recourse to [B2 emph rel] use, adopt, a particular means (usu unpleasant) to achieve one's ends; resort to (q v). **o:** device, ruse, trick; argument, excuse, pretext; lawyer, solicitor, agent; the law □ *He held the attention of the company round the bar without* ***having recourse to*** *any tricks to make guests listen.* RM □ *He hoped the affair could be settled without either of them* ***having recourse to*** *legal proceedings.*

have a right to sth/to do sth [B2 rel] be entitled to possess or enjoy. **adj:** some; no, (not) any; a perfect, an undeniable. **o:** share, part (of property); money; assistance, help □ *'You had so many beautiful things, and Clementine...'* ***'Had a right to*** *some,' said Fergus softly.* DC □ *France* ***has*** *as* ***much right to*** (or: ***to have***) *nuclear weapons as Britain.* SC

have their tails up [B1ii] ⇨ have their tails down/up.

have the wind up [B1ii] (informal) be frightened □ *I don't mind actual flying, but every time the plane takes off or lands I* ***have the wind up****.* ⇨ get/put the wind up.

have up (for) [B1ii pass B3 pass rel] (informal) cause to appear in court (charged with an offence). **o:** armed robbery, petty larceny □ *'If I see you hanging about these shops again, I'll* ***have*** *you* ***up for*** *loitering with intent.'* □ *That's the second time he's been* ***had up for*** *dangerous driving.*

have a bearing upon ⇨ have a bearing on/upon.

have an effect/impact upon ⇨ have an effect/impact on/upon.

have an affair (with) [B2 rel] have a sexual relationship with sb to whom one is not married (the implication is that the couple are emotionally involved, but that the relationship is impermanent: at least one of the partners may already be married; ⇨ live with). **S:/o:** (married) man, woman; boss, assistant □ *'I'm glad you are being married. In Havana I thought you were just* ***having an affair****.'* OMIH □ *Paul's first reaction to the discovery that his wife was* ***having an affair with*** *an old family friend was one of bewilderment rather than shock.*

have no truck with [B2 rel] (informal) not (be prepared to) deal with, recognize, or accept. **adj:** no, (not) any, little. **o:** vagrant, slacker; brutality, insensitivity, thoughtlessness, bad manners □ *The lighthouse men* ***had no truck with*** *the* *islanders and in no sense 'belonged'.* SD □ *He'll* ***have no truck with*** *art or religion; for him everything that cannot be weighed or measured is suspect.*

have a way with one [B2] (informal) be able, through charm or force of personality, to lead or captivate others □ *Even as a small boy he* ***had a way with him*** *— he charmed every elderly lady in sight.* □ *She was the sort of woman who* ***had a way with her*** *— which meant that she usually got what she wanted.* LLDR

have a word with [B2 rel] speak to sb (esp to make inquiries, seek advice, or reprimand). **adj:** quick, quiet, private. **o:** bank manager, house agent, solicitor; child, pupil □ *'I wonder whether I could* ***have a word*** *or two* ***with*** *you, sir.'* EM □ *'John's left his room in a mess again. You promised to* ***have a word with*** *him about it, darling.'*

have words (with) [B2] (informal) talk angrily (with), esp to reproach or reprimand. **o:** child, pupil; employee, subordinate □ *'If you fiddle with my camera again you and I are going to* ***have words****, young man* (cf *I am going to* ***have words with*** *you)!'*

haze over [A1] become covered with a thin mist or cloud; lose sharpness or focus. **S:** sky, sun, landscape; eyes □ *Whenever anyone mentions his name, her eyes* ***haze over****.*

head for [A2] (informal) move towards, be on a course that leads to. **o:** London, Spain; trouble, disaster; show-down, clash □ *We* ***headed for*** *Turkey.* BM □ *'If you go on with him, Jinny, you're* ***heading for*** *disaster.'* AITC □ *You're* ***heading for*** *serious trouble.* TGLY □ in American English: *We were* ***headed for*** *Turkey/ You're* ***headed for*** *trouble* etc.

head off[1] [B1i pass] (informal) reach an important place before sb else, thus giving him important news, preventing him from escaping etc. **O:** enemy, thieves, bandits; stampeding herd, runaway car □ *The first thing to be done was to* ***head off*** *the enemy from the tender spots and vital places.* MFM □ *'If you take the next turning to the right, you'll be able to* ***head*** *them* ***off*** *at the big crossroads.'*

head off[2] [B1i pass] (informal) prevent sb from moving to a topic that is boring, or embarrassing, by getting him to think about sth else □ *This grandfather was slightly easier to deal with, because it was sometimes possible to* ***head*** *him* ***off****; he did have one other topic that interested him — the career of Stanley Matthews.* CON

heal over [A1 B1i pass] (cause to) close or be sealed (with the growth of scar tissue); (of quarrels etc) (cause to) end, be mended. **S:** [A1] **O:** [B1] cut, wound; rift, breach □ *The deep gash in his arm would take weeks to* ***heal over****.* □ *With the passage of time the divisions between the two countries have* ***healed over****.*

heal up [A1 B1i pass adj] get, make, completely better. **S:** [A1] **O:** [B1] wound, sore, cut; leg, arm □ *Within a few weeks their feet had* ***healed up*** *nicely, and we had no recurrence of the trouble.* DF □ *I had no more bother with the rash. The swims in salt water must have* ***healed it up****.*

heap on/upon[1] [B2 pass emph rel] place in heaps on. **O:** food; rice, meat; earth, sand, rock. **o:** tray, plate; bank, slag-tip □ *They* ***heaped*** *more food* ***on*** *my plate* (or: ***heaped*** *my plate* ***with*** *more food) than I could eat.*

heap on/upon[2] [B2 pass emph rel] award to, address to, in abundance. **O:** honours, praise; curses, opprobrium. **o:** guest, explorer; disgraced leader □ *His popular following was fickle: honours were* ***heaped upon*** *him one moment and curses the next.*

heap with [B2 pass rel] ⇨ heap on/upon[1].

hear from [A2 pass rel] receive news (esp a letter) from □ *Mother hasn't* ***heard from*** *you for quite some time. She's beginning to think you must be ill.* □ *Until we* ***hear from*** *head office we can't give you your permit.* □ *Let's* ***hear from*** *you soon.*

hear of[1] [A2 pass] come to know (of the existence) of. **o:** country, firm; product, commodity □ *'Have you* ***heard of*** *nylon?' 'Yes, it's some kind of synthetic fibre.'* □ *'Do you know Patterson?' 'No, I've never* ***heard of*** *him.'* □ *I first* ***heard of*** *the firm, and had dealings with them, three years ago.*

hear of[2] [A2 pass] have news of, have reports of the (continuing) existence of □ *He disappeared from Europe about a year ago, but the police have been* ***hearing of*** *him in South America.* □ *They started out to cross the Sahara in a saloon car, and have not been* ***heard of*** *since.*

not hear of [A2] refuse to consider or allow. **o:** any such thing, such a thing; his paying, your resigning □ *'Smith leave our service after all these years? I wo****n't hear of*** *such a thing!'* □ *She would****n't hear of*** *his sharing in the expenses.* □ neg, with *will/would/could.*

hear out [B1ii pass] listen until sb has finished his remarks. **A:** attentively, silently □ *The rest of the company* ***heard*** *the Astronomer Royal* ***out*** *with interest.* TBC □ *The questioner was* ***heard out*** *in complete silence.*

heat up [B1i pass adj] re-heat, for serving, food which has been cooked and allowed to get cold. **O:** pie, pasty; stew, goulash □ *I like a freshly-cooked meal — I don't want a dish of* ***heated-up*** *meat and vegetables.* □ *Many foods now on the market are pre-cooked and only require* ***heating up****.*

heave in sight [A2] (nautical) appear above the horizon, become visible. **S:** ship, vessel □ *A fourmasted schooner* ***hove in sight****.*

heave to [A1] (nautical) (cause to) come to a standstill (without anchoring or mooring). **S:** skipper, master; (sailing-)ship, clipper, barque □ *The frigate fired a warning shot across the privateer's bows to make her* ***heave to****.*

heave (one's heart) up [A1 B1ii] (informal) be violently sick □ *John must have been mixing his drinks. I found him* ***heaving his heart up*** *in the kitchen.* □ *Some politicians make you want to* ***heave up****.*

hedge in[1] [B1i pass adj] put a hedge around; fence in[1] (q v). **O:** garden, field, plot □ *She began to climb the hill to Tilecotes, between the* ***hedged-in*** *gardens.* WI □ *These fields were* ***hedged in*** *during my grandfather's time.*

hedge in[2] [B1i pass adj] restrict one's freedom of action; fence in[2] (q v). **S:** regulation, protocol; fear, inhibition □ *Custom* ***hedged*** *her* ***in*** *and made her helpless.* WI □ *He felt* ***hedged in*** *on financial matters.* SC □ *We were being increasingly* ***hedged in*** *by controls and restrictions.*

heel over [A1] (nautical) lean to one side. **S:**

ship, vessel; steamer, ferry □ *The boat* ***heeled over*** *in a strong wind blowing up the channel.*

help along/forward [B1ii pass] assist the progress of. **O:** process, development, reaction; things, matters □ *The experiment was not* ***helped forward*** *by Smith opening a door at the crucial moment.* □ *Then, to* ***help*** *matters* ***along****, his wife's father offered to pay the deposit on a new house for them.*

help off with [B3 pass] help sb to remove. **S:** doorman, valet, flunkey. **O:** guest, visitor. **o:** overcoat, jacket □ *'Let me* ***help*** *you* ***off with*** *your coat.'*

help on with [B3 pass] help sb to put on. **S:** footman, valet. **O:** guest, visitor. **o:** coat, cloak □ *He quickly selected the least tatty-looking raincoat, which was Ned's, and began to* ***help*** *me* ***on with*** *it.* CON □ *The ladies were* ***helped on with*** *their coats and wraps.*

help out [A1 B1i pass] (informal) help sb to face and overcome a difficulty. **O:** friend, wife, ally. **A:** with the harvest; during the vacation, over Christmas □ *Thank you again for the way you pitched in to* ***help out*** *during the German thrust.* MFM □ *Janet finished her work and crossed to* ***help*** *May* ***out*** *with hers.* RFW

help to [B2 pass] serve sb with. **O:** guest, diner; oneself. **o:** fish, meat, pudding □ *They were* ***helped to*** *some more vegetables.* □ *The fair-haired sergeant* ***helped*** *himself* ***to*** *one of his own cigarettes.* RFW

hem about/around/round [B1ii pass] surround, beset. **S:** obstacle, problem, difficulty □ *His position was precisely the same as it had been before his attempt to face the problems that* ***hemmed*** *him* ***around.*** HD □ *He felt* ***hemmed about*** *by forces that he was powerless to overcome.*

hem in [B1i pass adj] confine, restrict the movements of. **S:** enemy; fire, forest, snowdrifts; financial commitments, unhappy relationship □ *The man looked round him with the desperate, hunted eyes of an animal* ***hemmed in*** *by a ring of fire.* PW □ *His marriage had* ***hemmed*** *him* ***in.*** NM

herd together [A1 B1i pass] gather together as, or like, a herd of animals. **S:** [A1] **O:** [B1] cattle; prisoners, refugees; guests □ *Try to stop the men* ***herding together*** *around the bar.* □ *The school party was* ***herded together*** *and shepherded on board the ship.*

het up [pass (B1)] (informal) (be) irritated, excited; bothered, annoyed. **A:** all, quite, so, very □ *Father seemed terribly* ***het up*** *over something last Saturday. What was bothering him?* □ *We needn't have got so* ***het up*** *about it. He* ***did*** *say he would like to come and stay with us again.* PW □ passive with *be, seem, look, sound, get.*

hew down [B1i pass adj] cut down with rough chopping blows; hack down (q v). **O:** tree, branch □ *A line of poplars was* ***hewn down*** *to make way for an ugly parade of shops.*

hide away (in) [A1 nom A3 emph rel] take cover or shelter (in), conceal (oneself) (in). **S:** guerrilla, partisan, bandit; escaped convict; deposed ruler. **o:** the mountains, the jungle □ *Rather than be taken into captivity, the bulk of the army* ***hid away in*** *the mountains and forests.* □ *The gang returned to their secret* ***hideaway in*** *shanty-town.*

hinge on/upon [A2 emph rel] require that some condition should first be met; hang on[3] (q v). **S:** result, success, outcome; everything. **o:** co-operation, response, reaction □ *The success of the conference* ***hinges upon*** *the Cabinet decision which is expected at any moment.* □ *Everything* ***hinged on*** *the speed with which the armour could complete its flanking movement.*

hint at [A2 pass rel] indicate, mention (in a slight or indirect way). **S:** minister, manager, headmaster. **o:** tax reduction, wage standstill, further expansion, far-reaching changes □ *In his annual address to the employers' federation, the Minister* ***hinted at*** *an increase in the capital grants for new factories.* □ *The possibility of an early election was inadvertently* ***hinted at.***

hire out [B1i pass adj] allow temporary use of sth in return for payment. **S:** sailors; council, parks department. **O:** rowing-boats, canoes; deck chairs, umbrellas □ *Punts are usually* ***hired out*** *by the hour.* □ *Hotel owners* ***hire out*** *changing-cabins and umbrellas by the season.*

hiss off (the stage) [B1i pass B2 pass] force to leave the stage by hissing in disapproval. **S:** audience, claque. **O:** actor, singer, dancer □ *At his first appearance in a starring role he was* ***hissed off*** *by an unsympathetic audience.*

hit back (at) [A1 A3] (informal) counter-attack vigorously; reply with vigour to verbal attacks (e g in the press or on TV). **S:** bomber; tank, gun; government; trades unionist. **o:** airfield; emplacement; critic, opposition; employer □ *As soon as an enemy battery opens fire fighter-bombers can be ordered into the air to* ***hit back.*** □ *In a rousing speech to party loyalists the Prime Minister* ***hit back at*** *those who 'sought to undermine the Government's incomes policy'.*

hit it off (with) [B1ii B3 emph rel] (informal) enjoy good relations (with); get along/on (with)[2] (q v) □ *How well do he and his boss* ***hit it off*** *(or: does he* ***hit it off with*** *his boss)?* □ *I don't think they* ***hit it off****, doctor. They're at daggers drawn the whole time.* ART

hit the nail on the head [B2 pass] (informal) make a point, interpret a remark, precisely □ *The report spoke of a period of unfulfilled promise. That* ***hit the nail*** *squarely* ***on the head.*** T □ *'Not that Ibsen doesn't* ***hit the*** *moral* ***nail on the head****, every time.'* HAA

hit on/upon [A2 pass] (informal) suddenly devise or discover. **o:** scheme, idea, solution □ *The committee eventually* ***hit upon*** *a formula that would be acceptable to all.* □ *Then an idea was* ***hit upon*** *that seemed the answer to all our problems.*

hit out (at)[1] [A1 A3] (cricket) attack the bowling vigorously. **o:** pace bowling, spin attack □ *The opening batsmen seemed reluctant to* ***hit out at*** *the seam bowlers.*

hit out (at)[2] [A1 A3] (informal) make a vigorous attack (in the press, on TV etc) (against sb or sth). **S:** minister, church leader, trade unionist. **o:** restrictive practices, industrial sabotage; moral laxity; government policy □ (headline) *Bishop* ***hits out at*** *hippie culture.*

hitch up [B1i pass adj] pull up at the knees (before sitting) so as to preserve the crease. **O:** trousers, slacks, pants □ *He sat down on a kitchen chair,* ***hitching up*** *his trousers, carefully, as if afraid of destroying a knife-edged crease.*

CON

hive off [A1 B1i pass adj] (cause to) detach itself, form a separate body. **S:** [A1] **O:** [B1] swarm, colony; department, branch, section. **S:** [B1] beekeeper, farmer; management, planners □ *There were discussions about* ***hiving off*** *profitable BOAC routes to a private airline.* OBS □ *Next year, the biochemistry section will* ***hive off*** *to form an independent department.*

hold against [B2 pass] (informal) allow sth to affect one's judgement of sb; allow to count against (q v). **O:** past failings, criminal record; it... that he's taught abroad; the fact that he's worked for a rival firm □ *I don't* ***hold*** *it* ***against*** *him that he's spent three years in gaol.* □ *The fact that he's let you down once before shouldn't be* ***held against*** *him.*

hold back[1] [B1i pass] check, restrain; prevent from advancing. **S:** dam; barrier, fence; police, troops. **O:** river, flood-waters; crowd, mob □ *Millions of tons of water are* ***held back*** *by a complex system of dykes.* □ *The thin cordon of police could do nothing to* ***hold back*** *the crowd; they flooded on to the pitch.*

hold back[2] [A1] hesitate to act through caution or fear; hang back (from) (q v) □ *Because of the uncertain state of the market, buyers are* ***holding back.*** □ *She* ***held back,*** *not knowing what to do or say.*

hold back[3] [B1i pass] prevent from making progress. **S:** poor education, unpleasant manner, unsuitable background. **O:** candidate, ambitious youth □ *John felt that he was* ***held back*** *from further promotion because of his working-class background.* □ *Now that the end's in sight, nothing can* ***hold*** *him* ***back.***

hold back[4] [B1i pass] withhold, delay, the release or granting of. **S:** government, ministry; state corporation, employer. **O:** information, report; result; increase (in salary), wage award □ *The laboratory has been advised to* ***hold back*** *any announcement of its findings.* □ *There will be sharp resentment if they have their salaries* ***held back*** *for too long.* BBCTV

hold down[1] [B1i pass] restrain, keep at a low level; keep down[3] (q v). **S:** firm, department, school. **O:** costs, prices; numbers; pressure □ *They were blamed for their failure to* ***hold down*** *expenditure.* SC □ *Last year we had to* ***hold down*** *student intake because of the cuts in the grants.* OBS

hold down[2] [B1i pass] suppress, hold in submission; keep down[4] (q v). **S:** tyrant, dictator; police, army. **O:** country, district; people □ *How long can a small force of mercenaries* ***hold down*** *an entire people?.*

hold a/the job down [B1i] (informal) (manage to) remain in one job for some length of time. **S:** ex-convict, vagrant □ *Many Borstal boys have been unable to* ***hold down a job.*** T □ *Father fixed him up with work when he came out of prison, but he couldn't* ***hold the job down.*** □ sentence often neg; with *can/could.*

hold (good/true) (for) [A2] apply (in the case of), be valid (for). **S:** remark, statement; promise, guarantee, undertaking; warning □ *The same requirement* ***holds good for*** *any applicant wishing to study natural sciences.* □ *'What I have said* ***holds*** *as much* ***for*** *houses to rent as* ***for*** *houses to buy.'*

hold no brief for [B2 emph rel] not support, feel no sympathy for. **adj:** no, (not) any, little. **o:** system, government; violence, disruption; anarchist, pacifist □ *'You* ***don't hold any brief for*** *him?' 'I don't know. Maybe he was sincere.'* PP □ *'Don't look surprised. You know I* ***hold no brief for*** *people with extreme views.'*

hold no fears/terrors for [B2 emph rel] = have no fears/terrors for.

hold forth [A1] speak pompously, as if one's hearers were an audience, and at some length. **S:** commentator, pundit, critic, teacher. **A:** at (great, considerable, some) length □ *Robert was still* ***holding forth,*** *in the middle of a knot of satellites.* CON □ *Paula introduced the carpenter, and* ***held forth*** *at great length on his prowess, personality, and intelligence.* DF

hold in [B1i pass adj] restrain, check; keep in[4] (q v). **O:** emotions; resentment, frustration □ *Eventually these feelings could be* ***held in*** *no longer; there were outbreaks of violence everywhere.*

hold in high/low regard [B2 pass emph rel] feel considerable, little, respect for. **O:** president, official; office, post; degree, diploma; skill, craftsmanship □ *Not that the Land Dayaks resent European authority. They* ***hold*** *it* ***in the highest regard.*** NDN □ ***In*** *such* ***high regard*** *is the University* ***held*** *that the number of applicants far exceeds the available places.*

hold off[1] [A1] be delayed, not occur; delay, restrain oneself. **S:** rain, storm, winter; enemy □ *The monsoon* ***held off*** *for a month; then the rain fell in torrents.* □ *The Nationalists had* ***held off*** *while their troops rested and reinforcements arrived.*

hold off[2] [B1i pass] prevent sb from overwhelming oneself; keep at bay (q v). **S:** beleaguered garrison; goalkeeper; celebrity, hero; government. **O:** attackers; forwards; press, fans; inflation, unemployment □ *For several days a small force* ***held off*** *the attacks of a numerically superior enemy.* □ *He's been* ***holding*** *her* ***off*** *for years, but sooner or later he'll have to give in.*

hold on[1] [A1] (informal) wait, pause; hang on[1] (q v). **A:** a second, a minute □ *'Just* ***hold on*** *a second while I get my breath back.'* □ *'Tell him to* ***hold on*** *a minute: I haven't written down a word he's said.'* □ often imper.

hold on[2] [A1] stay in an exposed or dangerous position; stand firm in the face of danger; hang on[2] (q v). **S:** surrounded troops, shipwrecked sailors; government □ *The party cut off by the tide were told to* ***hold on;*** *help would soon reach them.* □ *At the height of the financial crisis, all they could do was* ***hold on*** *and hope that conditions would improve.*

hold on[3] [B1i pass] fasten; keep in position. **S:** glue; pin, bar; clasp, buckle. **O:** knob; medal, brooch; strap □ *The soles of his shoes were just* ***held on*** *by a few stitches.* □ *Use special adhesive for this job: ordinary glue won't* ***hold*** *the handle* ***on.***

hold on to[1] [A3 pass] keep grasping sth, not let it go. **o:** rope; branch, root □ *'Don't panic; just* ***hold on to*** *that rock and I'll come and fetch you down.'* □ *He was* ***holding on to*** *a window-ledge for dear life when the fireman got to him.*

hold on to[2] [A3 pass] (informal) keep, retain;

not give or sell to sb else; hang on to (q v). **o:** advantage, lead; property, shares □ *It's not enough to take over the lead; we must* ***hold on to*** *it!* □ *I should* ***hold on to*** *those bonds: they'll appreciate considerably.*

hold out[1] [A1] resist, hold firm, stand fast. **S:** force, defence □ *From a purely military point of view, the* ***holding out*** *in North Africa once the Mareth Line had been broken through could never be justified.* MFM □ *That so small a force was able to* ***hold out*** *against such odds is certainly proof of bravery.* BM

hold out[2] [A1] last, remain. **S:** stocks, supplies, rations □ *We can stay here for as long as our supplies of food and water* ***hold out.***

hold out[3] [B1iii pass] offer, afford. **O:** ⚠ (the) hope, prospect, possibility □ *The prospect was* ***held out*** *of growing prosperity in the years to come.* □ *Radio astronomy investigations seem to* ***hold out*** *the best hopes of obtaining such proof.* NS

hold out for [A3 rel] (informal) deliberately delay reaching an agreement in the hope that one can get more; stand out for (q v), stick out for (q v). **S:** politician, trades union leader, negotiating team. **o:** greater concessions, full amount; granting of one's demands □ *Mr Smith rejected one splendid deal and is now* ***holding out for*** *the lot.* G □ *Having won the first round, the unions are likely to* ***hold out for*** *more than their original demand.* ⇨ hold out[1].

hold out (on) [A1 A3 pass] (informal) refuse to yield or surrender (to). **S:** dealer, seller, owner; girl. **o:** customer, buyer; boyfriend □ *'He's an obstinate old fool; he insisted in* ***holding out****, partly from sentiment, and partly from conceit. So we've busted him.'* ASA □ *'The little minx, she's been* ***holding out on*** *me. She with her delusions of grandeur.'* DC ⇨ hold out[1].

hold over [B1ii pass adj] defer; postpone; stand over[2] (q v) **S:** committee, council. **O:** question, matter; decision, vote □ *The final item on the agenda will be* ***held over*** *until our next meeting.*

hold to[1] [A2 pass adj rel] not abandon or change; stick to[2] (q v). **o:** choice, decision; course of action; principles, beliefs □ *We shall* ***hold*** *firmly* ***to*** *what has already been agreed.* □ *One obstacle to a settlement is the strongly* ***held-to*** *conviction that the employers have already decided to close the factory.*

hold to[2] [B2 pass rel] make sb keep or be faithful to. **o:** promise, guarantee, assurance; offer, proposal □ *'You can have the car when I go abroad.' 'I'll* ***hold*** *you* ***to*** *that.'* □ *One promise* ***to*** *which they must be* ***held*** *is that there will be no more redundancies.*

not hold a candle to [B2] (informal) not (be able to) match, emulate, sb, sb's achievements. **S:** industry, transport; organization, set-up; method, process. **o:** rival, competitor □ *In speed and efficiency of delivery we* ***can't hold a candle to*** *our European competitors.* □ *'What about Arsenal's chances for the Cup?' 'They* ***can't hold a candle to*** *Leeds.'* □ with can/could.

hold together [A1 B1i pass] remain united; unite. **S:** [A1] **O:** [B1] country, political party; membership, followers □ *The Party has* ***held together*** *wonderfully during the current crisis.* □ *What has* ***held*** *the Christian Democrats* ***together****?* SC

hold under [B1ii pass] suppress, hold in submission; keep under[3] (q v). **S:** regime, dictatorship; police, troops. **O:** (subject, colonial) people, race □ *The country is* ***held under*** *by appeals to patriotism, some economic inducement, and, where necessary, force.*

hold up[1] [B1i nom pass adj] delay; halt. **S:** strike, working to rule; flooding, landslide; narrow road, pressure of traffic. **O:** production, delivery; traffic, travellers □ (picture caption) *Ships* ***held up*** *by the strike of dockers at Liverpool.* G □ (headline) *Industry hit by docks* ***holdup****.* G □ *'What's the* ***holdup****? We're usually on our way by now.'* BBCTV □ *The worst road* ***hold-ups*** *were on the A74 Glasgow to Carlisle road.* SC □ in current usage nom is holdup — without a hyphen.

hold up[2] [B1i nom pass] force by the threat of violence to hand over money or valuables. **S:** gang, bandit. **O:** bank, post-office; coach, train □ *Masked men* ***held up*** *a wages van in South London.* □ *After the* ***holdup****, the gang got away in a fast car.* □ in current usage nom is holdup — without a hyphen.

hold up as an example [B3 pass] offer as a model (of conduct, success etc) to be imitated □ *I wish he'd stop* ***holding up*** *the elder brother* ***as an example*** *to emulate: it's bad for the young one's confidence.*

hold up to ridicule/scorn [B2 pass] mock, scorn, sb or sth, and try to make others do the same. **O:** colleague, associate; values, standards; work, achievement □ *It's a common thing to hear democratic socialism* ***held up to ridicule****, rather less common to hear serious alternatives proposed.*

(not) hold with [A2] (informal) (not) support, feel sympathy for; (not) approve of[2] (q v). **o:** plan, scheme, idea; blood sports; socialism; religion □ *I* ***don't hold with*** *all this revolutionary talk.* □ *'Why did you enter* (for the contest) *if you* ***don't hold with*** *it?'* CON □ hardly ever positive except when used in questions.

hold one's own (with) [B2 emph rel] be able to compete successfully or on equal terms (with). **S:** industry, factory; worker, designer; athlete, footballer; soldier. **o:** anyone, everybody; opposition, competition □ *Scottish teams cannot* ***hold their own with*** *the best in Europe.* SC □ *Those who liked champagne were able to* ***hold their own with*** *those who preferred whisky.* RM

hole out [A1] (golf) sink the ball in the hole □ *A young man sees no reason why he should not* ***hole out*** *and, in his ignorance, he does so more often than most. If he retains his faith in his ability to* ***hole out*** *then he remains a good putter.* OBS

hole up [A1] (slang) hide, seek refuge □ *The gang has* ***holed up*** *somewhere in the mountains.* □ *He'd holed up at a local motel.* BBCTV

home onto [A2 rel] move or be directed towards. **S:** aircraft, spacecraft. **o:** (radar) beam; signal, impulse □ *Especially in fog, or at night, an approaching aircraft will* ***home onto*** *a radar beam and in this way be guided to its destination.*

hook up [B1i pass] fasten (a garment) by means of 'hooks and eyes'. **O:** dress; girl □ *Her evening dress had to be* ***hooked up*** *at the back — a much slower process than zipping it up* (q v). □ *'Do you mind* ***hooking*** *me* ***up****?' she said.*

hook-up [nom (B1)] linking of radio or TV stations to transmit the same programme □ *There was a nation-wide **hook-up** to carry the President's state of the Union message.*

hoot off [B1ii pass B2 pass] force to leave, stop speaking, with hoots of disapproval. **S:** audience, public. **O:** actor, speaker. **o:** the stage, the platform □ *Whenever the Minister tries to explain his policies in public he's **hooted off**.*

hop off [A1] (slang) leave, go away □ *'**Hop off** before you get a thick ear.'* □ *'If you see anyone hanging around here tell them to **hop off**.'* □ usu imper.

hope (for) [A2 pass adj rel] hope that sth will take place, be granted etc. **o:** change, improvements; success, victory; reduction, easing (of tension, strife) □ *The travelling public is **hoping for** an early settlement of the rail dispute.* □ *Where is the **hoped-for** takeover by a moderate administration?* G

hope for the best [A2] hope that all will end well □ *I don't know how the negotiations will go. All we can do is sit back and **hope for the best**.* □ *Virginia knew that Ella came to see Joe; but there was nothing she could do about it, except **hope for the best**.* AITC

horn in (on) [A1 A3 pass] (informal) by cunning or force get oneself into a situation which seems profitable; muscle in (on) (q v). **S:** (get-rich-quick) trader, publisher, writer. **o:** deal, racket, market □ *They had come up for the day with no other motive than to **horn in on** Myra's second wedding* (= gatecrash the party). CON □ *Mike started planning my campaign like a Desert General who hasn't yet **horned in on** the memoir racket* (= made money from writing war memoirs). JFTR

horse about/around [A1] (informal) play about in a noisy, clumsy way; engage in horseplay □ *There was a certain amount of **horsing about** in the dressing-room after the game was over.*

hose down [B1i nom pass] wash from top to bottom with water from a hose. **O:** car, shop-front, window □ *I give the car a good **hose down** every Sunday morning.* □ no hyphen in nom form.

hot up [A1] (informal) intensify, increase. **S:** struggle, contest; trade, business □ *Competition in the British sea cruise market is **hotting up** visibly after the successful launching of the Travel Savings Association.* T

hound out/out of [B1ii pass B2 pass] (informal) force sb to leave (often by a conspiracy to damage his good name etc). **S:** envious colleague, political rival. **o:** job, Cabinet post □ *Do you want to get me **hounded out of** the Civil Service altogether?* SML □ *By digging up a few unsavoury details about his past they managed to have him **hounded out**.*

howl down [B1ii pass] prevent sb from being heard by shouting scornfully. **S:** crowd, audience. **O:** speaker □ *The guest speaker was **howled down**, and it was some time before the chairman could restore order.*

huddle together [A1] move, press, close, together for warmth or protection. **S:** sheep, cattle; children, refugees □ *The children **huddled together** on a pile of old sacks.*

hum with [A2] be in a state of intense activity. **S:** factory, classroom, kitchen. **o:** life, activity □ *The mill is very streamlined, scientific, and it fairly **hums with** wheels.* WI

hung over [pass (B1)] ⇨ hangover/hung over.

hung up [pass (B1)] ⇨ hang-up/hung up.

hung with [pass (B2)] ⇨ hang over³.

hunger for [A2 emph rel] long to have sth (which one may have lacked). **o:** news, information; (new) experience, change; excitement, sensation □ *He **hungered for** some contact outside his own circumscribed world.* □ *The letters **for** which she **hungered** grew fewer, then stopped altogether.*

hunt down [B1i pass] pursue and find. **S:** police, guard, tracker dog. **O:** escaped prisoner, criminal □ *Small detachments left hiding out in the forest were **hunted down** by our men.*

hunt out [B1i pass] search for, and find, sth that was previously used and has been put away. **S:** housewife. **O:** old clothes, family photographs □ *I'll have to **hunt out** the children's old clothes to give to the rag and bone man when he calls.* □ *I've got the picture for you somewhere, but it'll need some **hunting out**.*

hunt up (in) [B1i pass B3 pass rel] search for sth (in). **S:** scholar, research worker. **O:** reference, quotation, detail. **o:** library, archives; dictionary, atlas □ *He's **hunting up** details of Elizabethan household expenditure **in** a document of the time.*

hurl (at) [B2 pass emph rel] throw violently (at); fling (at) (q v). **O:** spear, stone; abuse, taunt, insult; oneself. **o:** troops, police; speaker □ *The streets were littered with stones and bottles **hurled at** the soldiers.* □ *The full-back **hurled** himself full length **at** the man's legs.*

hurry up [A1 B1ii pass] (informal) (cause to) make haste □ *'I wish the bus would **hurry up** and come; I've been waiting here for hours.'* □ *'**Hurry** those children **up**!'* □ *The estate agent seems helpful enough, but he needs **hurrying up**.*

hush up [B1i pass] prevent sth from becoming known. **O:** matter, thing; it (all); loss, theft □ *You can't **hush** a thing like this **up**.* EM □ *It'd all be **hushed up**.* NM □ *They tried to **hush up** the small matter of ten thousand being missing from the till.*

I

ice over [A1] become covered with ice; freeze over (q v). **S:** lake, pond, pool, river; road □ *When a road **ices over** it can be extremely dangerous, because drivers may mistake the coating of ice for dampness.* □ *The children were delighted to find that the pond had **iced over** during the night; perhaps, after all, they would be able to try out their new skates.*

ice up [A1 B1i pass] be covered, cover, with ice and be made, make, unworkable or unusable because of it. **S:** [A1] **O:** [B1] wings, machinery, rigging □ *The superstructure of the boat had* ***iced up*** *dangerously during the night, putting it in peril of capsizing.* □ *In the days before the introduction of de-icing control systems, a pilot had to be careful about flying at high altitudes as the plane's wings might get* ***iced up****.* □ *The flying spray had* ***iced up*** *every inch of the deck and everything on it.*

identify with[1] [A2 emph rel] find one's own feelings reflected in or in some way represented by; take as a model. **o:** character (in a play); father, teacher □ *I found the play unsatisfactory: there wasn't a single character — hero or anti-hero —* ***with*** *whom I could* ***identify****.*

identify with[2] [B2 pass emph rel] accept as representing one's ideas, intentions etc. **O:** army, military commander; central government, party, movement, revolution; oneself. **o:** progress, the forces of reaction □ *As the Army closed in on the beleaguered town, the Governor announced that he could no longer* ***identify*** *himself* ***with*** *the policies of the Central Government.* □ *The university authorities are* ***identified*** *in the minds of the students' leaders* ***with*** *the forces of reaction.*

idle about [A1] be inactive, not bestir oneself. **S:** young man, lazy fellow, unoccupied soldiers □ *John was a very active sort of person and could not bear to see others* ***idling about*** *when they might have been working or at least occupying themselves healthily.*

idle one's/the time away [B1i] pass the time in an idle or wasteful way, whether voluntarily or not. **S:** soldier, pupil □ *The troops had nothing to do but* ***idle the time away*** *while waiting for a ship to come and take them off the beaches.* □ *When you find yourself sitting in front of an examination paper you'll regret* ***idling your time away*** *in empty conversation.*

imbued with [pass (B2)] (formal) (be) filled with. **o:** a desire to do good; a driving ambition; patriotism; hatred of ignorance and superstition □ *The true scientist is* ***imbued with*** *the urge to discover something new about man and his environment.*

immerse in [B2 pass emph rel] plunge below the surface of; become totally absorbed in, interested by. **O:** himself; his head. **o:** water; pleasure, work; book, the morning paper □ *When a body is* ***immersed in*** *a fluid it apparently loses weight* (Archimedes' Principle). □ *When Alfred inherited his father's estate he* ***immersed*** *himself* ***in*** *pleasure. Before long, he found that there was little money left.* □ *I walked into the study and found Mr Johnson* ***immersed in*** *his writing, as usual.*

immure in [B2 pass emph rel] (formal) confine to (part of) a building; imprison in. **O:** himself; his daughter, wife. **o:** attic, study; convent, the house □ *Old Silas went out of his mind and* ***immured*** *himself* ***in*** *the attic. He never went out from one year's end to another.* □ *It used to be the custom for erring daughters to be* ***immured in*** *a convent, and sometimes forced to remain there till the end of their days.*

impale on [B2 pass emph rel] stick on the end of. **O:** victim; tyrant; child. **o:** pole, spear, spiked shaft □ *After the Restoration of the Monarchy, Cromwell's head was* ***impaled on*** *a pole and displayed to the public.* □ *In 'Lord of the Flies', the children* ***impaled*** *a pig's head* ***on*** *a spear.*

impart to [B2 pass emph rel] (formal) give to; communicate to. **O:** movement; news, secret; an aura of authenticity □ *The batsman completely failed to realize that strong leg-spin had been* ***imparted to*** *the ball by the bowler.* □ *The presence of an establishment figure in the person of Lady Mildew* ***imparted*** *some semblance of 'respectability'* ***to*** *what was otherwise a pretty rebellious crowd.*

impel to [B2 pass emph rel] (formal) drive sb to do sth, sometimes against his desire or inclination. **o:** firm measures, drastic steps, greater efforts; crime □ *Their feeling that the moment was ripe for action* ***impelled*** *the Party* ***to*** *still greater efforts.* □ *The extreme measures* ***to*** *which the Cabinet was* ***impelled*** *by the ever-increasing inflation made the government extremely unpopular in the country.*

impinge on/upon [A2 emph rel] (formal) affect in some way; strike, touch □ *The so-called revolution scarcely seemed to have* ***impinged upon*** *the habits and standard of living of the wealthy.* □ *In his sleepy state the sound of a car driving up to the door scarcely* ***impinged on*** *his consciousness.*

implant (in) [B2 pass emph rel] put (in), establish (in), in such a way as to be not easily removed or eradicated. **O:** idea, notion; desire, terror, fear. **o:** mind; them □ *Milton* ***implanted in*** *his daughters a great fear of, if not respect for, their father.* □ *The young revolutionary* ***implanted in*** *the peasants a burning desire to take and own the land on which they had for so long slaved.*

implicate (in) [B2 pass emph rel] (formal) cause to be a party (to); (passive only) share the guilt or responsibility (for). **O:** others; colleague, workmate. **o:** crime; murder, fraud; plot, scandal □ *'Your own part in this crime is despicable enough, but your attempt to* ***implicate*** *an innocent person* ***in*** *it passes description.'* □ *It came as a great shock to the old lady to find that her sons had been* ***implicated in*** *the plot to kidnap a child.*

import (from) (into) [B2 pass emph rel] bring (from one country, culture, language etc) (to another). **O:** transistors, cotton goods, motor-cars; drugs, cannabis; cholera; fashions □ *The police caught a young couple trying to* ***import*** *a huge quantity of heroin* ***from*** *somewhere in the Mediterranean.* □ *In every country there are people who would like to prevent foreign words being* ***imported into*** *their language.*

impose (on) [B2 pass emph rel] place (on), put on[6] (q v). **O:** tax, levy, duty; purchase tax, value added tax (VAT); task, burden, obligation □ *The government would not dare to* ***impose*** *taxes* ***on*** *such necessities as bread or milk.* □ *I am sorry to* ***impose*** *a new burden* ***on*** *you so soon after your illness, but there is no one else who is capable of doing this work.*

impose on/upon [A2 pass] obtain a favour from sb, esp by using undue pressure. **o:** generous, kind person; his generosity, kindness, good nature □ *'Really, Mary! You must not be so generous towards everyone who comes asking you for money. Don't allow yourself to be*

imposed upon!' □ *'Could I **impose on** you for a little help with this letter? I don't quite know the best way to phrase it without causing offence.'*

impose oneself/one's company on/upon [B2 rel] inconvenience sb by one's presence □ *As there was no train until the evening he was forced to **impose himself on** his hosts for longer than he had intended. He was aware that he had outstayed his welcome.* □ *The outing was ruined for everyone by a drunken tramp who **imposed his company on** the party and could not be shaken off.*

impress on/upon [B2 pass emph rel] in saying or writing something to sb, try to stress or fix some aspect of it in his mind. **O:** the importance of..., the need to..., the desirability of...; his parting words; itself, themselves □ *They **impressed on** their children the virtue of always telling the truth.* □ *The dying man's words were **impressed on** my memory, though I could not understand them; 'Look beyond the sunset... beyond the sunset...,' he said* (cf *His words **impressed** themselves **on** my memory* etc). □ ***On** all the witnesses the judge **impressed** the necessity of telling everything they knew about the movements of the accused.*⇨impress with.

impress (with) [B2 pass] produce a positive or favourable 'impression' on. **o:** her strong character; beauty, intelligence, learning, gaiety, ingenuity, resilience □ *The girl **impressed** her fiancé's relations **with** her vivacity and sense of humour.* □ *The spectators were greatly **impressed with*** (or: ***by***) *the jockey's skill in bringing his difficult mount first past the winning post.*

impress with [B2 pass] fix sth in sb's mind. **o:** the need for secrecy; urgency, importance (of the task) □ *The office manager **impressed** the new bookkeeper **with** the importance* (or: ***impressed upon** the new book-keeper the importance*) *of keeping the accounts balanced day by day.* ⇨ impress on/upon.

improve on [A2 pass] do better than, produce sth of a better standard or quality than. **S:** athlete; candidate; artist; beautician. **o:** previous best time, performance; earlier attempt; early work; nature □ *The girl **improved on** her previous performance by swimming the distance in less than a minute.* □ *The art of hair stylists is to **improve on** nature, though some of the so-called improvements leave one in doubt about their ability!*

impute to [B2 pass emph rel] (formal) hold responsible for, attribute to[1] (q v). **O:** failure, accident, débâcle □ *Never one to see his own weaknesses, he had no hesitation in **imputing** the failure of his marriage **to** his wife's shortcomings.* □ *At the inquest, the accident was **imputed to** a mechanical failure of the signalling system.*

incarcerate (in) [B2 pass emph rel] (formal) imprison (in). **o:** dungeon, cell; convent, house in the country □ *The young bride complained that she was **incarcerated in** a Victorian mansion, far from her relatives and friends.* □ *Many people think that it is wrong to **incarcerate** criminals **in** confined quarters for as long as thirty years.*

inch (one's way) across, along, back, etc [A1 A2 B1ii B2] move carefully across etc inch by inch. 5⇨ edge (one's way) across etc.

incite to [B2 pass] encourage or urge to participate in. **o:** crime; murder, mutiny, rebellion □ *In all countries any person who **incites** others **to** insurrection is guilty of treason.* □ *The boy's punishment was made more severe because he had **incited** other normally well-behaved pupils **to** open defiance of the school authorities.*

incline forward [A1] lean towards sth or sb □ *As the old lady's voice grew weaker, the solicitor **inclined forward** in an attempt to catch her last words.*

incline to [A2 B2 pass] (formal) tend to support or accept; tend to develop. **S:** [A2] **O:** [B2] court, jury; assessor, examiner. **S:** [B2] evidence, observation. **o:** view, opinion □ *'I've listened to all your arguments in favour of releasing the prisoner, but I'm afraid that in spite of all you have said I **incline to*** (or: *am **inclined to***) *the opposite opinion. He will go to prison for three months.'* □ *She would be beautiful if she didn't **incline to** obesity.*

incline towards [A2] bend, lean, in the direction of. **o:** speaker; the Left, the Right □ *As the noise outside the hall increased we all **inclined towards** the speaker, straining to hear him.* □ *More and more people are **inclining towards** the Liberal Party as they become disenchanted with the two main parties that have governed the country for half a century.*

include among [B2 pass emph rel] give as part of, as one of. **O:** name; uncle; film-star, pop-singer; Greek; playing the tuba. **o:** the missing; guests, acquaintances; his talents □ *The names of two of my friends were **included among** those listed as missing after the raid behind the enemy's lines.* □ ***Among** John's talents was **included** the unusual one of being able to tell you the name of any semi-precious stone you showed him.*

include (in) [B2 pass emph rel] make, or consider as, part (of). **O:** tools, supply of spare parts; latest composition; difficult questions; me. **o:** purchase price; concert; examination; list of contributors □ *Are the books **included in** the sale of the bookcase, or are they a separate lot?* □ Sam Goldwyn, a Hollywood film magnate, when invited to take part in something of which he did not approve, exclaimed *'Include me out!'*

incorporate (in/into) [B2 pass emph rel] make a part or feature (of). **O:** new ideas, theories, proposals; methods, processes; subsidiary companies. **o:** article, book, plan, thesis; main organization □ *The Government has **incorporated in** the Bill many of the suggestions put forward by the Opposition* (cf *The Bill **incorporates** many of the suggestions* etc). □ *Many new safety features have been **incorporated in** the new version of this popular car.*

inculcate (in) [B2 pass emph rel] (formal) establish, fix by example, precept and repetition; instil in (q v). **O:** duty, respect, principles. **o:** him, his mind □ *The priest **inculcated in** his parishioners the need to live pure, honest lives, 'in the service of God'.* □ ***In** all of their followers the party leaders **inculcated** the need to lead pure, honest lives, 'in the service of the community'.*

indent (for) [A2 pass rel] apply formally (for), according to a set procedure. **o:** supply of stationery; equipment □ *As it takes some time for an application to be approved, you should always* ***indent for*** *your office requirements well in advance.*

indoctrinate (with) [B2 pass emph rel] (formal) deliberately teach sb to hold certain views, attitudes etc, possibly using methods that leave the person unable to resist, or to maintain opposite ideas. **o:** Catholicism; Communism, Socialism □ *It was clear that our guests had been* ***indoctrinated with*** *some strange notion that the end of the world would come in 1984.* □ *It is against the Geneva Convention for prisoners to be* ***indoctrinated with*** *ideas alien to their culture and cherished beliefs.*

induce (in) [B2 pass emph rel] (physics; formal) cause to enter. **O:** current, magnetism; certain attitudes. **o:** wire, filings; the mind □ *it is a simple matter to* ***induce*** *magnetism* ***in*** *an iron bar, given the necessary equipment.* □ *The sweet music and dim lights* ***induced in*** *the couple a feeling of euphoria that was enhanced by liberal draughts of gin and whisky.*

indulge in [A2] allow oneself to have. **o:** an occasional glass of wine, a Mediterranean cruise, the luxury of a sauna bath; criticism of others □ *We were surprised when Mr Silas offered us an interest-free loan: it was so unlike him to* ***indulge in*** *such philanthropy.* □ *On Sunday afternoons, a lot of working men* ***indulge in*** *a short sleep in front of the fire.*

infatuated (with) [pass (B2)] (be) strongly attracted (to); (be) foolishly affected (by). **o:** young woman, married man; self-esteem □ *After thirty years of happy married life, Alfred suddenly became* ***infatuated with*** *a girl of nineteen and left his family to live with her.* □ *It is impossible to reason with anyone so* ***infatuated with*** *his own importance as your brother.*

infect (with) [B2 pass rel] give, pass (a disease) (to); cause to behave, or feel, in a similar way (to). **O:** water; air; him, others. **o:** disease, cholera; germs; good humour, enthusiasm; need, desire □ *Some of the refugees were suffering from cholera and it was not long before they had* ***infected*** *the drinking-water* ***with*** *the disease.* □ *During an epidemic of influenza the air in trains and buses quickly becomes* ***infected with*** *germs.* □ *The whole class was* ***infected with*** *the teacher's own enthusiasm for the subject.* □ *It was the desire* ***with*** *which numerous investors were* ***infected*** *to get in on the boom at any price that led to the astronomical rises in Australian mining shares.*

infer from [B2 pass emph rel] (formal) draw a conclusion from; deduce (from) (q v). **O:** that something had happened. **o:** his behaviour; your comments; the reports I have heard □ ***From*** *his demeanour on entering the room I* ***inferred*** *that the interview had not gone well for him.* □ *The judge* ***inferred from*** *the answers of the witness that he was trying to conceal something.*

infiltrate into [A2 emph rel B2 pass emph rel] (cause to) enter, penetrate, in a surreptitious way; pass into, in small numbers or quantities. **S:** [A2] **O:** [B2] troops, spies, agents; ideas □ *The company managed to* ***infiltrate*** *two or three men* ***into*** *their rival's Research and Development unit, and so were kept informed of everything that they were doing.* □ *If only a handful of commandos could* ***infiltrate into*** *(or: be* ***infiltrated into****) the enemy's defensive positions, the attack would have a good chance of success.*

inflict on/upon [B2 pass emph rel] cause sb to suffer or undergo. **O:** wound; irreparable damage; defeat; death penalty; a long recital, oneself. **o:** him etc; country, city; enemy; murderer; captive audience □ *It is many years since the death penalty was last* ***inflicted on*** *anyone in Britain.* □ *Montgomery believed in assembling an overwhelming force and then* ***inflicting*** *a crushing blow* ***on*** *his opponent.* □ *'I won't* ***inflict*** *myself* ***on*** *you today. I can see you're too busy to listen to my complaints!'*

inform against/on [A2 pass] betray sb to one's enemies, the police etc. **o:** one's friends, comrades, fellow-conspirators □ *The IRA* (Irish Republican Army) *deals ruthlessly with anyone who* ***informs against*** *one of its members.*

infuse into [B2 pass emph rel] by means of oratory, exhortation etc, fill with; inspire (in) (q v). **O:** renewed interest, curiosity; enthusiasm, spirit. **o:** men, followers, army, class □ *The leader had the gift of being able to* ***infuse*** *enthusiasm* ***into*** *the most sceptical member of the group* (or: *being able to* ***infuse*** *the most sceptical member of the group* ***with*** *enthusiasm*).

infuse with [B2 pass emph rel] ⇨ previous entry.

ingratiate oneself (with) [B2 emph rel] seek to obtain the favour of, even at the expense of one's dignity, principles etc □ *It was sickening to watch young Stevenson trying to* ***ingratiate himself with*** *the professor, knowing as we did how much the old man detested and despised him.*

inhibit (from) [B2 pass] make sb hesitate, or be reluctant, to do sth. **S:** upbringing; (previous) failures, rebuffs. **o:** talking to women; expressing his opinion, saying what he feels, fulfilling his desires; evil impulses □ *His strict upbringing* ***inhibited*** *him* ***from*** *asking questions, with the result that he tended to get left out of any serious discussion.*

initiate (into) [B2 pass emph rel] make sb familiar (with), make sb a member (of), esp in a ceremonial way. **o:** mysteries of antique-collecting; the art of fencing; the family circle; club, society, masonic order □ *The poet Laurie Lee was* ***initiated into*** *the mystery of love by a young girl called Rosie.* □ *The youths were* ***initiated into*** *manhood by the most frightful ordeals imaginable.*

inject into[1] [B2 pass rel] make sth enter the body, by means of a hypodermic needle etc. **O:** drug, serum, solution. **o:** arm, finger; vein, bloodstream; child □ *A nurse has to take care not to* ***inject*** *air* ***into*** *the bloodstream of her patients.* □ *It was pitiful to see the young addicts* ***injecting*** *drugs* ***into*** *their veins for a few hours of relief from their craving.* □ *Be careful not to* ***inject*** *this strong solution* ***into*** *a young child* (or: *not to* ***inject*** *a young child* ***with*** *this strong solution*).

inject into[2] [B2 pass] (formal) change the tone of, by the addition of some positive, usu brighter, element. **O:** some life; a little gaiety, enthusiasm. **o:** proceedings, performance, meeting □ *The whole business was as dull as ditch-water until old Mrs Appleby got to her feet and started to* ***inject*** *a little life* ***into*** *the discussion.*

inject with [B2 pass rel] ⇨ inject into[1].

ink in [B1i pass adj] use ink to write words on a map, fill an empty space in a drawing etc; go over with ink anything already drawn or written in pencil. **O:** place-names, background □ *'Your drawing would look better if you were to* ***ink in*** *the area to the left of the mill, perhaps with some bushes or distant mountains.'*

inlay with [B2 pass rel] set in the surface of. **O:** tray, table, cigarette-box. **o:** gold, silver; ivory, bone □ *Chiniot, in the Punjab, is famous for its trays* ***inlaid with*** *metal.* □ *The tomb of Jehangir Khan was* ***inlaid with*** *semi-precious stones.* □ usu passive.

inoculate (against) [B2 pass rel] (medicine) protect against a disease, by means of an injection. **O:** population, refugees, inhabitants. **o:** smallpox, cholera, yellow fever □ *The Red Cross nurses worked eighteen hours a day,* ***inoculating*** *tens of thousands of people* ***against*** *the dreaded cholera.* □ *'Have you been* ***inoculated against*** *typhoid fever?'*

inquire (about) [A2 rel] seek information (about). **o:** times of trains, package holidays to Greece, the possibility of getting a job □ *'There was a lady in here a few minutes ago* ***inquiring about*** *domestic help. I told her that we weren't an employment agency.'* □ *Where ought I to go to* ***inquire about*** *London bus-tours?*

inquire after [A2 pass] ask about the welfare, state of health, of; ask after (q v) □ *I met your old friend Joshua the other day. He was* ***inquiring after*** *you, and sent his kind regards.* □ *It's reassuring to be* ***inquired after*** *when you're ill. It shows your friends haven't stopped being concerned about you.*

inquire for [A2] ask to see, ask if sth is available. **o:** boss, manager; you □ *'While you were out, a young man rang up* ***inquiring for*** *you. He said he would ring again later.'* □ *'If you're passing the optician's this morning, would you mind dropping in and* ***inquiring for*** *my new specs?'*

inquire into [B2 pass] investigate, look into[2] (q v). **S:** police; headmaster; assistant manager. **o:** attack on a girl, robbery; leak of the examination questions; complaint; the matter □ *I told the policeman that I was worried by the noises from the empty house next door, and he said he would* ***inquire into*** *it.*

inquire of [A2 B2] put questions to sb. **O:** reason; why the train is late, whether he will attend **o:** me; maid, telephonist, gardener, clerk. □ *If you want to know about getting a visa for Thailand it's not much use* ***inquiring of*** *your Icelandic friends! Write to the Consul or the Ambassador—someone in authority.* □ *The old lady* ***inquired of*** *a bystander the reason for the delay in the Queen's arrival.* □ when the Object in the [B2] pattern is a clause, it follows the prep phrase.

inscribe in/on [B2 pass rel] make letters, marks etc in or on. **O:** name, year, record, account of a battle. **o:** tomb, stone, tablet, wall; silver cup, plate, cigarette-box, watch □ *When Mr Fotheringay retired he was presented with a gold watch* ***in*** *which his name and the dates of his service (1924–1974) were* ***inscribed.*** □ *The story of Adam and Eve was* ***inscribed on*** *the door of the Cathedral* (or: *The door was* ***inscribed with*** *the story* etc).

inscribe with [B2 pass rel] ⇨ previous entry.

insert between [B2 pass emph rel] push, place, between. **O:** comma; wad of cotton, paper, cloth; piece of rubber. **o:** two words; teeth; wires □ *These plugs would be safer if you could* ***insert*** *some kind of insulating material* ***between*** *the wires.*

insert in/into [B2 pass emph rel] push, place, in/into. **O:** plug; key; hand; advertisement; extra paragraph; coin. **o:** socket; lock; bag; magazine; article; slot □ (instructions on a vending machine) ***Insert*** *a 5p piece* ***into*** *the slot and pull the drawer.* □ *As soon as the burglar* ***inserted*** *his jemmy* ***into*** *the window the hidden detectives leapt out and arrested him.*

insinuate oneself into [B2] gradually enter by stealth or deceit **o:** the meeting; boss's favour, confidence □ *The cat somehow* ***insinuated itself into*** *the larder, and feasted off a large joint of meat.* □ *The office-staff watched the new typist trying to* ***insinuate herself into*** *the manager's favour and were much amused. They had seen it all before!*

insist on/upon [A2] do sth, require sth, maintain sth, in spite of objections from others. **o:** going for a walk, helping me with my work; a replacement for the broken part; an answer; his innocence; absolute secrecy □ *They lived together as man and wife, but she* ***insisted on*** *paying the rent out of her own salary.* □ *She didn't really want tea, but Nurse Ellen* ***insisted on*** *making it.* DC □ *I was perfectly well five minutes after my fall, but my hostess* ***insisted on*** *sending for a doctor.* □ *The only thing that worried the detective about the case was that Willie* ***insisted on*** *his innocence, and somehow he sounded convincing.*

inspire (in) [B2 pass emph rel] produce (in sb), as a result of one's behaviour, example etc; infuse into (q v). **S:** he etc; example; courage, spirit; authority, assured manner. **O:** confidence, enthusiasm, hope, the desire to emulate (him) □ *It was my father's courage and devotion that* ***inspired in*** *his men the determination* (or: ***inspired*** *his men* ***with*** *the determination) to hold out against what seemed like overwhelming odds.* □ *The doctor's clumsy handling of the syringe did not* ***inspire*** *confidence* (***in*** *his nervous patient*) (or: *did not* ***inspire*** *his nervous patient* ***with*** *confidence*).

inspire (with) [B2 pass emph rel] ⇨ previous entry.

install (in) [B2 pass emph rel] place, establish, fix, in. **O:** oneself; visitor, newcomer; new bookcase; television. **o:** the easy chair; back room, new home; library, lounge; corner of the room □ *The mistress of the house reluctantly* ***installed*** *the two refugees* ***in*** *a spare room.* □ *'Don't forget that the men are coming to* ***install*** *the refrigerator (****in*** *the kitchen) this morning.'* □ *visitor, newcomer* etc can function as Subject where Object is the reflexive pronoun: *The newcomer* ***installed*** *himself* ***in*** *the large leather chair....*

instil in [B2 pass emph rel] establish, fix firmly by teaching and repetition; inculcate (in) (q v). **O:** the fear of God, a healthy respect for the law, obedience. **o:** him, his mind □ *My parents were very puritanical and* ***instilled in*** *me the value of a God-fearing, self-denying sort of existence.* □ *The idea was gradually* ***instilled in*** *the mind of* *the young prince* (or: *The mind of the young prince was gradually* ***instilled with*** *the idea*) *that he was of almost god-like importance and far above other men.*

instil (with) [B2 pass] ⇨ previous entry.

instruct in [B2 pass emph rel] give sb lessons in. **O:** children; soldiers; students. **o:** hygiene; the use of weapons; computer technology □ *When the visitor entered the classroom, the group of handicapped men were being* ***instructed in*** *weaving.*

insulate (from) (with) [B2 pass emph rel] keep separate from, prevent contact with. **O:** (power) drill, radio; experimental laboratory, space vehicle. **o:** (***from***) the main current; the surroundings; (***with***) fuse, pvc (polyvinyl chloride); heat shield □ *It is important to* ***insulate*** *the furnace* ***from*** *any neighbouring woodwork* ***with*** *brick and asbestos.* □ *The recording studio should be well* ***insulated from*** *any source of noise.* □ *If the wires are not well* ***insulated with*** *rubber or some other non-conductor, there will be a grave risk of fire.*

insure against [A2 pass B2 pass] protect oneself etc by means of an insurance policy (a contract which guarantees the payment of money in certain circumstances); cover (against) (q v); take measures against. **O:** oneself; possessions; car, house, yacht. **o:** death, loss of a limb; theft, fire, total loss, damage (by flood or storm) □ *Every father should* ***insure*** *himself* ***against*** *premature death or prolonged illness for the sake of his wife and children.* □ *Take care that all eventualities are* ***insured against.*** □ *The general tried to* ***insure against*** *defeat by building up an overwhelming force of artillery and tanks.*

integrate (with) [B2 pass rel] (formal) make an essential part (of); cause to form a whole (with). **O:** building; river; college. **o:** setting; canal system; university □ *The new residential blocks were skilfully* ***integrated with*** *the rest of the College to form a pleasing, self-contained whole.* □ *One of the attractive features of the course was the way the practical work had been* ***integrated with*** *the theoretical aspects of the subject* (or: *the way the practical work and the theoretical aspects had been* ***integrated***).

intend for [B2 pass rel] wish sb to have or receive sth; propose that sb should enter or join sth □ *In the nineteenth century younger sons were often* ***intended for*** *the Church, the Army or the colonies.* □ *'I* ***intended*** *these flowers* ***for*** *your mother, but as she is away I'd be glad if you would accept them.'* □ *The parcel of explosive did not reach the man* ***for*** *whom it was* ***intended.***

inter (in) [B2 pass emph rel] (formal) bury (in). **O:** body, mortal remains, ashes; victims of the air disaster □ *The old man said that he wished to be* ***interred in*** *the family grave.*

intercede (with) [A2] (formal) approach sb in authority on behalf of sb else. **o:** Home Secretary; girl's father; men's leader; Governor □ *A group of MPs promised to* ***intercede with*** *the Home Office on behalf of the girl who, though in prison, was said to be mentally ill.* □ *We approached a friend, hoping that he would* ***intercede*** (***with*** *the headmaster*) *to prevent John's expulsion, but he refused to do anything about it.*

interest in [B2 rel] help, lead, sb to study sth with interest. **O:** oneself; one's pupils; customer; visitor; the public. **o:** local history; new car; buildings; environment □ *Mr James was a gifted teacher of economics, who managed to* ***interest*** *his students* ***in*** *every aspect of the subject.* □ *Astronomy was one of the subjects* ***in*** *which he had* ***interested*** *himself while in the Sixth Form.*

interfere in [A2 rel] show an undue interest in sth which is not one's concern, meddle in (q v). **o:** his affairs; things that don't concern you; their marriage □ *I advise you not to* ***interfere in*** *matters that you don't fully understand and which are in any case none of your business.* □ *There are certain aspects of nature* ***in*** *which it is, to say the least, unwise for men to* ***interfere.***

interfere with[1] [A2 pass] disturb, mishandle, sth without sb's permission; meddle with (q v). **o:** my bicycle; these papers; the manager's private correspondence □ *'Who's been* ***interfering with*** *my wine? Somebody's been trying to syphon it off, and now it's all over the floor!'*

interfere with[2] [A2 pass] (euphemism) attack, assault, usu sexually, and possibly violently. **o:** girl, woman; boy, child □ *Medical evidence was called to prove that the murdered girl had been brutally* ***interfered with.***

interfere with[3] [A2] be an obstacle to, hinder. **o:** business, duty; important matters, progress; his research □ *Some people say that if your business* ***interferes with*** *your leisure you should cut out some of your business!* □ *'Nothing must be allowed to* ***interfere with*** *our search for the truth!'*

interlard with [B2 pass rel] (formal or jocular) make part of a text, with the aim, or effect, of impressing, shocking, etc. **O:** book, poem, speech, writings. **o:** purple passages, biblical allusions, foreign phrases, slang expressions □ *It is extraordinary how readily the modern newspaper editor will* ***interlard*** *his leading articles* ***with*** *expressions that would have been quite unacceptable forty years ago. How times change!* □ *The Chairman* ***interlarded*** *his speech* ***with*** *patently insincere praise for all and sundry.*

interleave with [B2 pass rel] place between the leaves of a book □ *Meg enjoyed my gift more than I would have thought possible: a little drawing book* ***interleaved with*** *transparent paper for tracing.*

intermarry (with) [A2 rel] make or allow marriages (with) □ *Many a tribe and ruling house has survived by* ***intermarrying with*** *its rivals, rather than waging war on them.* □ *The priestly caste does not normally* ***intermarry with*** *the warrior caste* (or: *The priestly and the warrior castes do not normally* ***intermarry***).

intermingle (with) [A2 rel] mix (with), in such a manner as to be no longer or not easily identifiable; move about freely together, not avoiding others. **S:** detectives, pickpockets, agents. **o:** crowd, football supporters, holiday-makers, audience □ *Several policewomen, glamorously clothed for the occasion,* ***intermingled with*** *the gamblers, looking out for the drug-pushers who were said to operate in the club.* □ *People from a hundred countries* ***intermingled*** *freely* (***with*** *each other*) *at the Olympic Games.*

intern (in) [B2 pass emph rel] imprison, confine (in) (often as a preventive measure and without trial). **O:** aliens, suspected members of an illegal army, anarchists. **o:** camp, prison □ *The number of persons* ***interned in*** *special camps in Northern Ireland was over six hundred at the beginning of 1972.*

intersperse among/between [B2 pass emph rel] ⇨ next entry.

intersperse with [B2 pass emph rel] (formal) put in, insert, here and there; interrupt from time to time. **O:** trees; speech; report; book. **o:** evergreen shrubs; jokes directed at the Duke; amusing comment; biographical notes and references □ *The trees were* ***interspersed with*** *evergreen shrubs* (or: *Evergreen shrubs were* ***interspersed among*** *the trees*). □ *I could never have completed the work if it had not been* ***interspersed with*** *regular visits to the pub for a chat with my friends.* □ *The poor fellow arrived home soaked to the skin, and his account of how he had fallen into the river was liberally* ***interspersed with*** *fits of sneezing.* □ often passive.

intervene (between) [A2] place oneself between, adopt a mediating role (between). **S:** policeman, bystander; boy; referee. **o:** two drunken men; mother and father; contestants □ *The woman tried to* ***intervene between*** *her husband and son, but she was roughly pushed aside.* □ *'I would advise you not to* ***intervene*** *(****between*** *those two drunks). You might get hurt.'*

intervene (in) [A2 emph rel] enter, whether by invitation or not, and whether in a conciliatory role or not. **o:** quarrel, dispute; debate, discussion; the affairs of another country □ *Kennedy's attempt to* ***intervene in*** *the affairs of Cuba met with a severe rebuff at the Bay of Pigs.* □ *The Prime Minister decided that it was unnecessary for him to* ***intervene*** *personally* ***in*** *the debate on the future of Concorde.* □ *Anyone who* ***intervenes*** *(****in*** *the quarrel) may find that it is not easy to avoid deep involvement.*

intimidate (into) [B2 pass emph rel] (formal) cause to act in a particular way, through fear or by means of threats; frighten into (q v). **O:** small boy; servant; witness. **o:** giving away his sweets; leaving a window open; keeping quiet □ *'My Lord, it is obvious that the witness is being* ***intimidated*** *(****into*** *remaining silent). In the circumstances, I would request that he be given police protection and a warning of the penalty for perjury or for concealing knowledge of a crime.'* □ *This child cannot be blamed for performing illegal acts* ***into*** *which he was* ***intimidated*** *by his father.*

intoxicated by/with [pass (B2)] (be) very excited by; (be) carried away (⇨ **carry away**[2]) with. **o:** success, good news, freedom, joy; fresh air, the Christmas spirit □ *The crowd were* ***intoxicated by*** *the news of the relief of Mafeking and filled the streets of London in celebration.* □ *Tom was* ***intoxicated with*** *the joy of knowing that at last he had gained his degree and would from now on be financially independent.*

intrigue against [A2 pass rel] (formal) plan secretly to remove etc, plot against □ *A small group of dissatisfied officers* ***intrigued against*** *the government. On the appointed day they arrested the President and seized power.* □ *The Director of the firm was aware that he was being* ***intrigued against****, but he had no means of finding out exactly how and by whom.*

introduce (into) [B2 pass rel] make available (in), perhaps for the first time. **O:** potatoes, tobacco; disease; cannabis. **o:** Britain; school; the community □ *Sir Walter Raleigh has the doubtful honour of having* ***introduced*** *tobacco (****into*** *England) from America.* □ *It is not known precisely how myxomatosis was* ***introduced into*** *Britain.* □ *The police have a good idea how most of the cannabis that is* ***introduced into*** *the country gets past the customs.*

introduce into[1] [B2 pass] push sth thin or fine into. **O:** tube, catheter; key, wire. **o:** wound, artery; lock, hole □ *A thin, hollow needle was carefully* ***introduced into*** *the patient's abdomen, and some fluid was drawn off.*

introduce into[2] [B2 pass emph rel] make a part of, an element in. **O:** topic, subject; a new factor, fresh ideas; his name. **o:** the conversation, argument □ *You had no right to* ***introduce*** *my name* ***into*** *the discussion. You know very well that I wanted to be kept out of your quarrel with your father.* □ ***Into*** *the curriculum for the sixth form a number of new, non-examinable subjects were* ***introduced****.*

introduce (to) [B2 pass rel] make known by name (to). **O:** girlfriend; new officer; teacher; lecturer. **o:** parents; the mess; class; audience □ *'Well, John,' said Mary, who had been listening to the conversation for a minute or more, 'Aren't you going to* ***introduce*** *me* ***to*** *your friend?'* □ *The chairman* ***introduced*** *the speaker* ***to*** *the audience in a few, well-chosen words.* □ *'I don't think we've been* ***introduced*** *(****to*** *each other),' said my neighbour at dinner. 'My name's Stephen Black.'*

introduce to [B2 pass] make known to sb for the first time. **O:** students; children; listeners. **o:** the latest theories on the origin of the universe; the mysteries of the laser-beam; the intricacies of international trade; the song-birds of the region □ *When I visited Japan I was quickly* ***introduced to*** *the etiquette of the tea-ceremony.* □ *Who* ***introduced*** *you* ***to*** *the distinctions between the accents of Lancashire and Yorkshire people?*

intrude (oneself) into [A2 B2 rel] (formal) enter uninvited, often in a rude manner. **o:** meeting, king's presence, confidential discussion □ *He* ***intruded (himself) into*** *the conversation without a word of apology.*

intrude upon[1] [A2] (formal) enter sb's presence etc, without invitation. **o:** his privacy, time; a private celebration □ *I am very sorry to* ***intrude upon*** *your grief, but this is a matter which requires your personal attention.*

intrude upon[2] [B2 pass] (formal) enter, advance into, force a way into (the presence of). **O:** itself, oneself; views, opinions □ *The idea* ***intruded*** *itself* ***upon*** *my mind that I knew just as much about the matter as my teacher.* □ *He is always* ***intruding*** *his opinions* ***upon*** *others, and well deserves his reputation as a bore.*

inundate (with) [B2 pass rel] (formal) cover as with a flood of water, overwhelm. **O:** staff; Post Office; BBC; Leader of the Party. **o:** work; Christmas mail; complaints; telegrams of congratulation □ *When Charlie Brown won £50 000 on the pools, he was* ***inundated with*** *begging-letters.* □ *The public* ***inundated*** *the Foreign Office* ***with*** *requests for information about relations who had been unable to leave Dacca before* *the fighting began.* □ *'Have you had many replies to your advertisement?' 'I've been* **inundated** *(***with** *them)!'*

inure (oneself) to [B2 pass emph rel] (formal) make oneself hard, resilient, so that one can withstand. **o:** living on a pittance; the cold climate; the hardships that go with old age □ *Once old Joe had* **inured himself to** *the solitary life of a widower, he began to improve in health and spirit.* □ **To** *physical pain he could* **inure** *himself;* **to** *mental suffering never!* □ *The Bengalis are to some extent* **inured to** *disasters of every kind, but their suffering must never be minimized or glossed over.*

invalid home [B1ii pass] send home from abroad, because of ill-health or wounds. **O:** soldier, representative, company servant, diplomat □ *The ambassador decided that he must* **invalid** *his sick radio-officer* **home**. □ *'Smith was* **invalided home** *last year.' 'Some tropical disease?' 'Alcohol, old boy. The demon drink!'*

invalid out/out of [B1ii B2 pass] relieve or remove sb from his job etc on account of illness. **O:** soldier, airman; civil servant □ *When Brown was told that he was being* **invalided out of** *the army, he was very distressed: he could not imagine life without his friends and comrades.* □ *'Did Brown resign from the British Council?' 'No; he was* **invalided out**.*'*

inveigh against [A2 pass] (formal) attack violently, in speech or writing. **o:** corruption; the permissive society; the ruling class; the police □ *There are many people who lose no opportunity of* **inveighing against** *what they describe as declining morals, slovenliness in dress, carelessness in the use of language, pornography, the spinelessness of the younger generation and so on and so forth.*

inveigle into [B2 pass] (formal) persuade or trick sb by flattery or deception into doing sth. **O:** her husband; his inexperienced partner; my young brother; the old lady. **o:** giving her a mink coat; raising an unnecessarily large loan; stealing sweets; parting with her life's savings □ *It was clear that the older of the two accused men had* **inveigled** *his companion* **into** *helping him to rob the post office.* □ the object is the *-ing* form of a v.

invest in[1] [A2 rel B2 pass rel] put money in, with a view to earning interest or increasing one's capital; use one's time or energy in some activity in the hope that profit (of some kind) will result. **O:** savings, weekly sum, inheritance; time, energy. **o:** stocks, shares, property, small shop; studying for a degree, learning Esperanto, building an extension to his house □ *What you* **invest in** *depends entirely on your needs — basically whether you want to increase your income or your capital.* □ *The widow was persuaded by an unscrupulous rogue to* **'invest'** *all her money* **in** *a spurious company. Needless to say, both rogue and money disappeared for ever.* □ *He* **invested** *every spare minute* **in** *trying to 'improve his mind'.*

invest in[2] [A2] (informal) buy, acquire. **o:** new clothes; record-player; sports-car □ *The student decided to* **invest** *his entire fortune (£50!)* **in** *an old car.* □ *I've decided to* **invest in** *a pearl necklace for my wife. It will probably pay dividends for a couple of months at least!*

invest with[1] [B2 pass rel] (formal) formally declare that sb possesses; give to sb as an award. **O:** governor, viceroy; consul-general, ambassador. **o:** (full) powers (to do sth); authority; order (of chivalry) □ *When the Commander of the army was wounded, his second-in-command was automatically* **invested with** *his authority.* □ *The Queen* **invested** *the celebrated author* **with** *the Order of Merit.*

invest with[2] [B2 pass rel] (formal) cover, surround, with. **O:** history; alliance. **o:** romance; an aura of respectability □ *The presence of the Vice-Chancellor* **invested** *the proceedings* **with** *an importance that they might otherwise have lacked.*

invite in/over/round [B1ii pass] ask sb to come into a house, study, office etc □ *'Don't stand talking at the gate, Mary!* **Invite** *your friend* **in**!*'* □ *Our parents have* **invited** *us* **round** *for a meal on Sunday.*

involve in [B2 pass rel] get sb or sth into a difficult situation or condition; cause to be mixed up in (q v). **O:** himself; his parents; them. **o:** trouble, robbery, conspiracy; other people's affairs; expense; debt □ *Somehow he managed to* **involve** *several of his friends* **in** *his matrimonial troubles.* □ *George is so* **involved in** *debt that he is afraid to appear in the pub in case he meets half a dozen of his creditors!* □ *An accident* **in** *which more than fifty vehicles were* **involved** *caused the death of six people on the M1 last night.* □ *The accountant's errors* **involved** *everyone* **in** *a great deal of extra work.*

iron out [B1i pass] remove by means of a hot iron; (fig) remove by means of discussion, compromise, or other appropriate action. **O:** creases, wrinkles; trousers, dress; problem, differences of opinion, misunderstandings □ *'Would you mind* **ironing** *the collar of this shirt* **out** *for me?'* □ *There are no difficulties that cannot be* **ironed out** *if both parties are determined to reach an agreement.* □ *If you want your article to be understood by the average reader you'd better* **iron out** *some of the subtleties in your argument.*

isolate (from) [B2 pass rel] make separate (from), prevent from coming into contact with others, or another thing. **O:** patient; case of typhoid; dangerous criminals; significant facts. **o:** others; the rest of the hospital; harmless petty thieves; the mass of data □ *After enduring the rat-race in London for many years he then went and* **isolated** *himself (***from** *his fellow-men) by going to live on a small uninhabited island off the west coast of Scotland.* □ *It is wrong to try to* **isolate** *drug-taking* **from** *the general condition of our society; cure the ills of that society and you will cure drug-taking.*

issue from [A2 emph rel] come from in a stream. **S:** smoke; blood; stream of pure water; stream of abuse. **o:** chimney, every window in the building; his wounds; the side of the mountain, rock; the press □ **From** *the upstairs windows of the house there* **issued** *a dense cloud of black smoke.* □ *As John put his coat on and got ready for work, the usual barrage of complaints and instructions* **issued from** *the bedroom.*

itch for [A2] (informal) wait impatiently for; long (for) (q v). **S:** children; clerk; young couple; soldiers. **o:** Christmas Day; five o'clock; a house of their own; the order to go into the attack □ *It was* *obvious that Milly had been* ***itching for*** *an opportunity to get Pat by herself, so that she could give her the length of her tongue.* □ *He stood by the window,* ***itching for*** *the arrival of the postman and, he hoped, a reply to his proposal of marriage.*

J

jab at [A2 pass B2 pass] aim a strong blow at sb; direct sth sharp towards sb. **O:** fist, elbow; umbrella. **o:** opponent; face, stomach, solar plexus, ribs □ (boxing instructor) *'Keep* ***jabbing at*** *him with your left. With your reach you're bound to get under his guard.'* □ *'Don't* ***jab*** *your finger* ***at*** *me: I'm not on trial and you're not the prosecutor!'*

jab out [B1i pass] remove with a sharp blow. **O:** stone, nail; eye □ *If you get a thorn stuck in your finger don't try to* ***jab*** *it* ***out*** *with a needle.* □ *'Don't wave that stick about. You'll* ***jab out*** *somebody's eye.'*

jack in [B1i pass] (slang) leave, abandon; pack in [1] (q v). **O:** job; business; course (of study) □ *I can't take any more of this night-work. I'll have to* ***jack*** *it* ***in.***

jack up[1] [B1i pass adj] lift (one side of) using a (screw-)jack. **S:** mechanic, driver. **O:** car, lorry □ *A* ***jacked-up*** *car stood at the kerb-side; the driver was changing a wheel.* □ *'****Jack*** *her* ***up*** *a bit more. The wheels are still touching the ground.'*

jack up[2] [B1i pass adj] (informal) raise, increase. **O:** salary, wage; allowance; payment □ *'We know you're not happy about the money you're getting. We think it could be* ***jacked up*** *a bit.'* □ *If they* ***jack up*** *the wage rates they'll have to cut down on expenditure somewhere else.*

jack up[3] [B1i pass] (informal) arrange, organize, properly. **O:** things, the (whole) thing; tour, trip □ *What about your holiday? Have you got everything properly* ***jacked up****?* □ *We didn't need to worry about tickets or reservations. Travel Section* ***jacked*** *the whole thing* ***up*** *for us.*

jam in/into [B1i pass B2 pass] press sb or sth tightly into a small space. **O:** audience; passengers; belongings, clothes. **o:** hall; car, bus, (railway) compartment; box, case □ *'Don't* ***jam in*** *too much clothing; you won't be able to close the lid.'* □ *'Give the papers to me; I can* ***jam*** *a few more* ***into*** *my briefcase.'*

jam the brakes on [B1i pass] (informal) apply the brakes suddenly and forcefully; slam the brakes on (q v) □ *I had to* ***jam on the brakes*** *sharply to avoid hitting two schoolchildren.*

jangle on/upon [A2] seem very discordant or unpleasant to the ear. **S:** screech, whine; bell, fiddle. **o:** ⚠ sb's ears, nerves □ *The sound of that drill* ***jangles*** *horribly* ***on*** *the nerves.* □ *I can't stand the woman. I can still hear that high-pitched voice* ***jangling on*** *my ears!* ⇨ next entry.

jar on/upon [A2] be unpleasant to, seem discordant to. **S:** sound, music; voice, accent. **o:** him etc; sb's ears, nerves □ *'Turn the radio off! That music* ***jars on*** *my nerves.'* ⇨ previous entry.

jar (with) [A2 emph rel] not match, not be in harmony (with). **S:** colour, pattern; arrangement; view, opinion □ *The stripes on his tie* ***jarred with*** *the checks on his jacket* (or: *The stripes and checks* ***jarred***). □ *Everything he said seemed to* ***jar with*** *our most firmly held convictions.*

jazz up [B1i pass adj] (informal) put more energy or colour into, brighten, enliven. **O:** music, tune; party, celebration; room, decorations □ *'Go out and get some more to drink: this party needs* ***jazzing up*** *a bit.'* □ *The room decorations appeared to have been* ***jazzed up.*** *The overall effect was loud and restless.*

jeer (at) [A2 pass] mock, taunt; gibe (at) (q v). **S:** spectators, audience. **o:** prisoner, victim; speaker, performer □ *The accused was* ***jeered (at)*** *by the crowd as the police bundled him into a car.*

jib at [A2 pass rel] refuse or be reluctant to go forward, or accept sth; balk at (q v). **S:** horse, mount; car, tank; employee. **o:** fence, obstacle; extra work, wage freeze; working overtime, losing wages □ *The staff don't mind the new work schedule, but they'd* ***jib at*** *taking a cut in wages.*

jibe with [A2] match, be in accord with **S:** account, story; behaviour, manners; appearance; position, status. **o:** record, transcript; pretensions, claims (for oneself); merits, deserts □ *'His account of what happens* ***jibes*** *pretty closely* ***with*** *what I've got written here.'* □ *The optimistic picture painted by the chairman doesn't* ***jibe with*** *the company's actual trading record.*

jockey for [A2 rel] move about, manœuvre, pushing others aside in order to improve one's position. **S:** rider, runner; politician, courtier. **o:** position, place; privilege, advantage □ *There was a certain amount of barging on the first bend as the runners* ***jockeyed for*** *the inside position.* □ *Since even minor appointments were in the gift of the Prince, the court was thronged with young men* ***jockeying for*** *favours.*

jog along/on [A1] (informal) make steady but unexciting progress. **S:** factory, business; worker, employee □ *He just* ***jogs along*** *contentedly from year to year without any thought of promotion.* □ *The industry is happy to* ***jog along*** *in the old way.*

join in [A1 A2 emph rel] add oneself, or one's support, to sth taking place. **S:** audience, crowd. **o:** race, entertainment; applause, conversation □ *A group of bystanders was invited to* ***join in*** *the game.* □ *'Who said you could* ***join in****?'* □ *This is an exciting game* ***in*** *which the whole family can* ***join.***

join on/onto [A1 A2 B1i pass B2 pass emph rel] (esp of a smaller thing in relation to a larger) be fixed, attached, to; fix, attach, to. **S:** [A1 A2] **O:** [B1 B2] part, component; waggon, carriage; caravan, trailer. **o:** body; train; lorry □ [A1] *'Where does this bit of the model* ***join on****? Is it part of the chassis or part of the engine?'* □ [B1 B2] *Two extra carriages were* ***joined on*** (i e ***onto*** *the train) at Doncaster.* □ [A2 B2] *The dress pattern doesn't really explain how the cuff* *__joins onto__* (or: *is __joined onto__*) *the sleeve.*

join together/to [B1i pass B2 pass emph rel] bring (two things) together, attach one thing to another (so as to form a continuous whole). **O:/o:** rail, rod, pipe, wire □ *The welding is so smooth that you can hardly see where the sections of pipe are __joined together__* (or: *where one section of pipe is __joined to__ another*). □ *One rail is __joined to__ the next by means of a metal plate; space is left between them to allow for expansion.*

join up [A1] (military) join the armed forces □ *He __joined up__ as a private in a county regiment.* DS □ *Why should I hope for a big war so that I could __join up__ and get killed?* LLDR

join up (with) [A1 A3 emph rel] meet and unite (with sb or sth), esp with a common aim or purpose; link up (with) (q v). **S:** force, body (of men); company, firm; road, branch line. **o:** army; neighbour, competitor; motorway, main line □ *The commando force __joined up with__ the airborne troops near the captured bridges.* □ *Grants the boiler makers __joined up with a__ small transport firm in order to save on delivery costs.* □ *The M62 __joins up with__ the M1* (or: *The M62 and the M1 __join up__*) *a few miles south of Leeds.*

join battle (with) [B2 pass rel] begin fighting sb; begin a serious struggle or argument (with). **o:** enemy; infantry, armour; neighbours, in-laws; employer, trades union □ *__Battle__ was __joined__, shortly after ten o'clock, __with__ advance elements of two enemy divisions.* □ *As for my instinct in __joining battle with__ Sammy and Sadie, it has been a sound enough instinct.* UTN

join forces (with) [B2 emph rel] meet sb and unite one's men and resources with his; come together (with sb) in a common enterprise; join up (with) (q v). **S:** army; division, regiment; manufacturer, tradesman. **o:** garrison, defenders; neighbour, competitor □ *A force sent round on a flanking march __joined forces__ again __with__ the main body two days later.* □ *I never thought seriously about __joining forces with__ Wales — I've been boss of my own works too long to relish being a co-director.* RATT

join hands (with) [B2 rel] come together, be united, esp in friendship. **S:** nation, people; army, force. **o:** neighbour, (old) enemy □ *The leading troops of the English Army __joined hands with__ the right flank of the Fifth U.S. Army.* MFM □ *The vision was held out to us of one great nation __joining hands with__ another across the sea* (cf *of two great nations __joining hands__* etc).

joke about [A2 pass] talk about, treat, in a light hearted way (perhaps when seriousness is called for). **o:** matter, things; loss, misfortune, hardship, infirmity □ *'If John's just been kicked out of a job I don't see that it's anything to __joke about__. Show a little sympathy instead.'* □ *It's not unusual for young people to __joke about__ notions and institutions that their parents regard as sacred.*

jolly along [B1ii pass] (informal) keep sb in a good humour so that he will continue to collaborate, agree to work etc. **O:** parent; wife; employee □ *The job won't be finished on time unless you __jolly__ the men __along__ with an occasional bonus.*

jot down [B1i pass adj] make a quick written note of. **S:** policeman, reporter. **O:** address, particulars, details □ *He had __jotted down__ the licence number: FAX 160.* TO □ *'I'll just __jot__ that time __down__ before I forget it.'*

judge by/from[1] [A2] take sth as evidence, form one's opinion according to. **o:** testimony, press report; what has come down to us, what has emerged □ *To __judge from__ the evidence of the experts, the deceased was still alive at three o'clock.* □ *__Judging by__ the look on his face, he doesn't think much of our local wine.* □ *'Thirty years ago,' he said. 'That's a lot of years __judged by__ anybody's standards.'* PP □ judge is in a non-finite form (*to*-inf pp or *-ing* form).

judge by/from[2] [B2 pass emph rel] form one's estimate or view (of sb or sth) according to; conclude that sth is the case. **O:** age, quality, freshness; truth, reliability; that he is telling the truth; whether he can be trusted. **o:** appearance, smell, taste; statement, testimony □ *People still __judge__ a man __by__ the company he keeps.* FFE □ *'I __judge__ trees __by__ their fruit,' Louie said.* HAA □ *__From__ the finger marks high on the cupboard we can __judge__ that he was a tall man.*

juggle (with) [A2] (as a kind of music-hall or circus act) pass objects skilfully from one hand to the other so that at least one is in the air at any time; hold or balance several things insecurely **o:** hoop, ball; china; plate, cup □ *The older brother rode round the stage on a bicycle while the younger sat on his shoulders __juggling (with)__ four silver hoops.* □ *'Help your mother carry the things into the dining-room. She's in the kitchen __juggling with__ a pile of hot dishes.'*

juggle with [A2 pass] (informal) handle, manipulate sth skilfully (for pleasure, or in order to deceive etc). **S:** (public) speaker, writer; (dishonest) accountant, salesman. **o:** words; figures, accounts; facts □ *Peter loves __juggling with__ language, so much so that one often loses the thread of his story or argument.* □ *He's been __juggling with__ the accounts so as to defraud the Inland Revenue.* □ *Anyone running his eye down these columns could see that the cash entries have been __juggled with__.*

jumble up (with) [B1i pass adj B3 pass rel] throw together in confusion; muddle up (with) (q v). **O:** papers, documents; clothes; ideas □ *'Don't __jumble up__ your ties and socks now that I've sorted them out!'* □ *Recent happenings were __jumbled up__ in her mind __with__ events recalled from early childhood.*

jump at [A2 pass adj] (informal) seize eagerly; leap at (q v). **o:** ⚠ the opportunity, the chance, the offer □ *If he offered me a job sweeping out the theatre I'd __jump at__ the chance.* □ *This looks like a genuine offer of international inspection. Russia should __jump at__ it.* SC

jump down sb's throat [A2] (informal) address or answer sb sharply or irritably □ *'Stop pitying yourself.' 'Don't __jump down my throat__.'* TOH □ *'Guy — now don't __jump down my throat__ — you're not in debt, are you?'* DC

jump off[1] [A1 nom] (military) begin, be launched. **S:** campaign, battle; attack, advance □ *The attacks __jumped off__ without the usual preliminary bombardment.* □ *The __jumping-off__ point for the next phase of the advance was a line of hills.* □ *The general had ordered an early __jump-off__* (i e time of *__jumping off__*).

jump off[2] [A1 nom] (show-jumping) compete in an additional round of jumping when two or more horses have tied in the first round. **S:** horse; rider

□ *Four competitors had a clear first round and will be* ***jumping off*** *later this evening.* □ *In the* ***jump-off*** *the winner had a lead of two seconds over his nearest rival.*

jump on [A2 pass] (informal) turn one's attention sharply to sb so as to challenge or reprove him. **S:** teacher, drill-sergeant, coach. **o:** inattentive pupil, recruit □ *The children sat quaking in their seats while the master,* ***jumping on*** *individuals at random, would set them impossible problems.* □ *His wife* ***jumped on*** *him if he seemed to be taking Virginia's side.* AITC

jump to conclusions/the conclusion [A2 pass] be over-hasty in judging a person or event □ *'I know I was standing near the till when you came back into the shop, but don't* ***jump to conclusions.'*** □ *You seem to have* ***jumped to the conclusion*** *that because of what happened to this young man there must have been foul play.* EM

jump to it [A2] (informal, military) move quickly, look sharp; get a move on (q v) □ *'I want you in three ranks by that wall. Come on —* ***jump to it****!'* □ *'Shun, stand at ease!' The thought of her* ***jumping to it*** *gave him a delicious thrill.* PW □ usu imper.

jump up [A1 emph] spring to one's feet, stand up suddenly □ *Then suddenly Fergus* ***jumped up****. 'I have the answer!'* DC □ ***Up jumped*** *Peter with an angry look on his face.*

justify (to) [B2 pass emph rel] (formal) explain one's actions etc (to sb) so that they seem reasonable. **O:** oneself; (one's) behaviour, conduct. **o:** colleague; audience; critic □ *I don't see that I need to* ***justify*** *my conduct* ***to*** *you.* □ ***To*** *these people he could not expect to* ***justify*** *the course of action he had followed.*

jut out [A1] project, protrude; stick out[1] (q v). **S:** balcony, roof; rifle, cannon □ *The stern of the ship* ***juts out*** *over the water.* □ *His chin* ***juts out*** *rather a lot.*

K

keel over[1] [A1] overturn completely or partially, capsize. **S:** boat, ship, lifeboat □ *The old Queen Elizabeth liner burnt out and* ***keeled over*** *while anchored off Hong Kong in January 1972.*

keel over[2] [A1] lose one's balance and fall □ *John walked into the room unsteadily, fixed me with a glazed stare, uttered the words 'I think I'm going to...',* ***keeled over*** *and fell unconscious at my feet.*

keep one's head above water [B2] not sink or drown; (fig) remain solvent, just manage to cope with one's duties etc □ *Though I could not swim, I just managed to* ***keep my head above water*** *by kicking my legs about until somebody reached me and dragged me to the river bank.* □ *Mr Chester has had a great deal of extra work recently, but he just manages to* ***keep his head above water.*** □ *The dock strike made things very difficult for our firm, what with shortages of raw materials, non-shipment of our goods and so on, but we* ***kept our heads above water*** *thanks to our good stocks, and sales to the home market.* □ *Virginia's life was a whirlpool which centred round Joe, but she struggled to* ***keep her head above water****, and to appear as if she had nothing on her mind.* AITC

keep abreast (of) [A1 A3 B1ii pass B3 pass] (cause to) stay level (with), be overtaken by; inform oneself or sb (about). **o:** rival, competitor; events, the news, the times; fashion □ [A3] *In the strong breeze the catamaran skimmed over the water,* ***keeping abreast of*** *the motor-launch.* □ [A1 A3] *So much is happening in the world of science that it's difficult to* ***keep abreast*** *(****of*** *all the latest developments).* □ [B3] *Is the opera company's first duty to make available the acknowledged operatic masterpieces... or should it concentrate on* ***keeping*** *the public* ***abreast of*** *current developments?* T ⇨ stay abreast (of).

keep after [A2 pass] not abandon the pursuit of; chivvy. **o:** escaping prisoner; pupils, servants □ *The police* ***kept after*** *the bandits until they finally trapped them in a cul-de-sac.* □ *'If you want to get any essays out of that crowd of layabouts, they have to be* ***kept after.'*** □ *'Don't* ***keep after*** *the nurses all day long or they'll all resign!'*

keep ahead/ahead of [A1 A2] not lose one's position in front of others. **S:** favourite; newspaper; designer; bank robbers. **o:** other race-horses, newspapers, designers; pursuers □ *Barrier Reef led the field from the start and* ***kept ahead of*** *it right to the winning-post.* □ *If you want to* ***keep ahead of*** *your rivals, you'll have to work very hard.* □ *Don't try to* ***keep ahead*** *in the rat race — it isn't worth it!* ⇨ stay ahead/ahead of.

keep one step ahead/ahead of [A1 A2] retain one's position in front of others by a small margin □ *Gibbs* ***kept one step ahead of*** *the police for years, but they finally tracked him down in Australia.* □ *Not knowing much Italian, it was all the teacher could do to* ***keep one step ahead*** *(****of*** *the class).* □ one step is an adv phrase of degree.

keep at[1] [A2] continue persistently in one's efforts, not abandon. **o:** it; the job; your studies □ *The only way to get a dictionary written is to* ***keep at*** *it, day after day.*

keep at[2] [B2 pass] make sb work, force sb to make a prolonged effort. **O:** students, workers, troops □ *The old professor was a martinet. He* ***kept*** *his students* ***at*** *their studies when they would have preferred to be at the discotheque. But in the end they all thanked him for it.*

keep at[3] [A2] worry, pester. ⇨ keep (on) at.

keep at arm's length/a distance [B2 pass] not allow to come near or close to one. **O:** neighbour; danger, disease; temptation □ *If you're wise, you'll* ***keep*** *Mrs Jones* ***at a distance****. She's the worst gossip in the village.* □ *I had none of the frustration that Luke felt and perhaps Martin also, because they were being* ***kept at arm's length*** *from a piece of scientific truth.* NM

keep at bay [B2 pass] cause to remain at some

distance; hold off[2] (q v). **O:** attackers; rats, mosquitoes; hunger, poverty; inflation; unemployment □ *When fiddling about with lens and exposure meters I found it essential to have someone stand over me with a hat, to **keep** at least some of the insects **at bay**, otherwise it was impossible to concentrate and my temper frayed rapidly.* DF □ *Industry as a whole is trying to **keep** rising costs **at bay**.*

keep away (from) [A1 A3 B1ii pass B3 pass] not go near; prevent from going near, touching, using etc. **S:** [A1 A3] **O:** [B1 B3] children; poison; crowd; weed-killer; paraffin oil. **o:** fire; baby; distinguished visitor; flowers; food □ [B1 B3] *It's the job of the police to **keep** the spectators **away** (**from** the players).* □ [B3] *Children should be **kept away from** the river.* □ [A1 A3] *The spectators have to **keep away** (**from** the players).* □ [B1] *'What's been **keeping** you **away**? You haven't been round to see us for ages.'* □ [A3] *If Jo doesn't **keep away from** that woman, he's going to regret it. Her husband is a jealous and violent man.* ⇨ stay away (from)[1,2].

keep back (from)[1] [A1 A3 B1i pass B3 pass] stay at a distance (from); prevent from getting too close (to). **S:** [A1 A3] **O:** [B1 B3] crowd; enemy; small craft. **o:** the Prime Minister; our positions, the river; the round-the-world yacht □ [B1] *The crowd was so great that the organizers of the demonstration could not **keep** them **back** when they reached the barriers.* □ [A1] *'**Keep back**!' the doctor shouted, as the onlookers crowded round. 'Give the man some air!'* □ [A3] *The conjuror liked to **keep** well **back from** the front of the stage so that the audience could not follow all his movements.* □ [B3 A3] *The President's security men did their best to **keep** the crowds **back from** him, but they despaired when he refused to **keep back from** the crowds!*

keep back (from)[2] [B1i pass B3 pass] not tell (to), not let sb know. **S:** husband; doctor; witness. **O:** the news; information, vital details; the truth. **o:** wife; patient; police, court □ *The President decided not to **keep back** the facts concerning the secret negotiations any longer, and announced them on January 25th.* □ *The specialist recommended that the exact nature of the woman's illness should be **kept back from** her.* □ *The news of the army's defeat was **kept back from** the people for several days.* ⇨ keep from[1].

keep back (from)[3] [B1i pass B3 pass] not pay (to), retain (from). **O:** a certain percentage; 50p a week □ *It is quite normal to **keep back** ten per cent of the cost of a building for a period of six months or so, in case faults are found in it.* □ *We agreed to let our employer **keep back** twenty pence a week **from** our wages to go into a special fund for welfare purposes.*

keep down[1] [A1] not reveal one's position; lie low; not raise oneself □ *'There's somebody coming! **Keep down** and don't make a sound!'* □ *'When we reach the footbridge over the canal, **keep down** or you'll bang your head on it!'* (i e 'we' are on a boat).

keep down[2] [B1ii pass] not raise. **O:** head; voice; arms □ *My father's parting words as I left to join my unit were '**Keep** your head **down** and your eyeballs moving!'* □ *'I wish you two would **keep** your voices **down**. I can hardly hear myself think!'* □ *'**Keep** your arms **down** by your side and take a deep breath,' the radiographer said as she retreated behind her protective screen.*

keep down[3] [B1i pass] not increase, prevent from increasing; hold down[1] (q v). **O:** prices, taxes, rates, the cost of living; one's weight □ *The government seems to be making little effort to **keep** the cost of living **down**. Prices have gone up by fifteen per cent in the last year.* □ *The doctor, who played a good deal of golf as a pretence of getting exercise and **keeping** his weight **down**, though in reality preferring the comforts of the clubhouse, remarked that it was warmish.* DBM

keep down[4] [B1ii pass] repress, hold down[2] (q v). **O:** population, conquered country, occupied territory; a good man □ *The peasants were **kept down** ruthlessly by the occupying power, which formed an unholy alliance with the landowning class.* □ *'I hear that Monica is competing in the skiing competition again in spite of breaking her leg last year.' 'You can't **keep** a good man **down**!'* □ the second example shows the expression in a sentence which has become a saying or generalized comment; it can be used with reference to men, women or children.

keep down[5] [B1i pass] control, restrain. **O:** anger, fury □ *It was all I could do to **keep** my anger **down** when I heard how the visitor had been treated in my absence.*

keep down[6] [B1ii pass] remove, kill, not allow to multiply or grow. **O:** flies, mosquitoes; rabbits, foxes; weeds □ *There is no absolutely foolproof way of **keeping** the flies **down** during the summer.* □ *If you want good crops of flowers and vegetables you must **keep** the weeds **down**.*

keep down[7] [B1ii] retain in the stomach. **S:** baby, invalid, dying man. **O:** milk, food, (not) anything, solids; medicine □ *Unless we can find a way of making the baby **keep** its food **down**, it is simply going to starve to death.* □ *'Can you prescribe something else for me, doctor? I can't **keep** these powders **down** at all.'* ⇨ stay down[2].

keep from[1] [B2 pass] not let sb know, not tell; keep back (from)[2] (q v). **O:** it; the news, the truth □ *However bad the situation is, the facts should not be **kept from** the people who are most concerned — the public at large.* □ *Mercifully, we managed to **keep** the news of Tom's imprisonment **from** his father. It would have killed him.*

keep from[2] [A2 B2 pass] avoid; stop, prevent, sb doing sth. **o:** overworking, taking on too much responsibility; quarrelling □ *While you're recovering from influenza you should try to **keep from** getting wet or going back to work too soon.* □ *'Please **keep** the children **from** swimming in the sea. There are some dangerous currents just off the shore.'* □ *He seemed to have forgotten who it was whose name he wanted to know, and also how to **keep** his head **from** nodding.* CON □ the object is the *-ing* form of a v.

keep the wolf from the door [B2 pass] (informal) be, earn or obtain, enough to feed oneself and one's family. **S:** wages, food □ *George did not care for the job he was offered nor the salary that went with it, but at least it would **keep the wolf from the door** until he* *could find something more to his liking.* □ *During the Depression of the 1920s and 1930s many men found it almost impossible to* ***keep the wolf from the door****.*

keep in[1] [A1 A2] remain inside, not emerge (from). **S:** old lady; rabbit, mouse □ *It's best to* ***keep in*** *while the temperature is so far below freezing point, unless you have to go out to earn your living.* □ *The rabbits* ***kept in*** *their burrows most of the day, and only came out to eat as darkness fell.* ⇨ keep indoors; stay in/indoors.

keep in[2] [A1 B1ii pass] stay alight, continue to burn; maintain, not allow to be extinguished. **S:** [A1] **O:** [B1] lamp, fire; furnace. **S:** [B1] maid, servant; stoker, caretaker □ *The stove will* ***keep in*** *all night if you put enough anthracite on in the evening.* □ *'Whose job is it to* ***keep*** *the fires* ***in****?'* ⇨ be in[6].

keep in[3] [B1i pass] detain after normal school hours, as a punishment. **O:** pupils, class, culprits □ *'Our teacher was in a bad temper today. She* ***kept*** *us all* ***in*** *for half an hour.'* ⇨ stay in[1].

keep in[4] [B1i pass] restrain, not give vent to; hold in (q v). **O:** anger, annoyance, feelings of indignation □ *The policeman was provoked by the hostile crowd but he managed to* ***keep*** *his anger* ***in****, and dealt with the situation coolly and competently.*

keep in[5] [B2 pass] maintain in a state of. **o:** ⚠ luxury, style □ *The pop-singer took pride in the fact that he* ***kept*** *his mother and sister* ***in*** *luxury.* □ *In a voice that was supposed to be that of a Victorian mill-owner the old fool said, 'Will you be able to* ***keep*** *my daughter* ***in*** *the style to which she is accustomed?' To which Susan replied, 'Oh, Dad, don't talk daft!'*

keep in[6] [B2 pass] (informal) give, allow, sb a regular supply of. **o:** cigarettes, beer, nylons, chocolates □ *Such jobs as he had from time to time barely* ***kept*** *him* ***in*** *drink and cigarettes.* AITC □ *He won first prize in a lottery — enough to* ***keep*** *him* ***in*** *beer for a year.*

keep in check[1] [B2 pass] control, avoid an excess of. **O:** expenditure, inflation, wage demands; consumption of carbohydrates; drinking □ *Unless imports are* ***kept in check*** *we are in danger of losing our favourable balance of trade.* □ *If I hadn't* ***kept*** *myself* ***in check****, I might have said something that I would have regretted later.*

keep in check[2] [B2 pass] prevent any further advance by. **O:** enemy; process of erosion; cholera □ *By prompt action the Indian authorities managed to* ***keep*** *the threatened epidemic of typhus* ***in check****.* □ *The enemy was* ***kept in check*** *by the floodwater, which made the terrain impossible for armoured vehicles.*

keep in the dark [B2 pass] (informal) deliberately not inform; keep in ignorance (q v) □ *'Let me tell you that I don't like being* ***kept in the dark*** *about matters that affect me as closely as my daughter's future life.'* □ *He must* ***keep*** *Bunder absolutely and permanently* ***in the dark*** *about Dogson and his mission to reveal the secrets of the drug traffic.* HD

keep one's eye/hand in [B1ii] retain one's skill by using it from time to time, though not as frequently as before □ *I don't find much time to play squash these days, but I do try to* ***keep my hand in*** *at the weekends.* □ *Peter* ***keeps his eye in*** *by joining in the occasional game of darts at the pub.* ⇨ get one's eye/hand in.

keep in ignorance [B1i pass] withhold information or education from. **O:** population; child, wife □ *In medieval times it was the policy of the Church to* ***keep*** *the people* ***in ignorance****. Education represented the greatest danger to their entrenched position.* □ *You can't* ***keep*** *children* ***in ignorance*** *of the facts of life indefinitely.*

keep in line [A2 B2 pass] (cause to) stay in one's allotted position; (cause to) observe the 'rules' of any group □ *If everyone* ***keeps in line****, we'll get through the Customs more quickly!* □ *The girls are the firmest of friends, and woe betide any of the men in the cast who doesn't* ***keep in line****.* RT □ *The Chief Whip* ***kept*** *the recalcitrant members of the Labour Party* ***in line****.*

keep in mind [B2 pass] not forget, constantly remember; bear in mind (q v). **O:** me; dangers, possibilities, difficulties; what you told me about, why you're here □ *'We've got to* ***keep in mind*** *how very small a disturbance — small from the astronomical point of view — could still wipe us out of existence.'* TBC □ *'You'll* ***keep*** *my son* ***in mind****, won't you — just in case a vacancy should occur in your firm?'*

keep in order[1] [B2 pass] discipline; not allow to behave in an uncontrolled way. **O:** troops, class, group, children □ *The headmaster was astounded to see how well this notoriously difficult class was being* ***kept in order*** *by his new teacher — a mere slip of a girl, in his eyes.*

keep in order[2] [B2 pass] maintain neatly, correctly, efficiently. **O:** books, one's affairs, estate; household □ (advertisement) *A Lloyd's Bank cheque book enables you to* ***keep*** *your money affairs* ***in*** *good* ***order*** *and to pay your bills in the safest and most convenient way.*

keep in his place [B2 pass] not allow sb to forget his position, his (inferior) status □ *They're good technicians, but they have to be* ***kept in their place****.* □ *Mrs Curry would have enjoyed discomfiting Hubert with Ron's presence, but she conceded the priority to* ***keeping*** *Ron* ***in his place****. 'I shan't want the car until five, Ron,' she said; 'you'd better go to the cinema.'* HAA

keep in sight[1] [B2 pass] stay in a position from where one can see; not allow sth to remain unobserved or to disappear from view. **O:** land, ship; enemy □ *He wasn't a good navigator, so he* ***kept*** *the coastline well* ***in sight*** *as he moved from one harbour to the next.*

keep in sight[2] [B2 pass] not forget about. **O:** goal, objective, purpose □ *So long as you* ***keep*** *your main objective* ***in sight****, there's no reason why you shouldn't have a little variety in your life!*

keep in sight of [A2] remain where one can see, or be seen by. **o:** the coast, the lifeguards □ *The children had been warned to* ***keep in sight of*** *the land in case they were caught in a storm.*

keep in (a state of) suspense [B2 pass] cause to be in a continual state of fear, worry, expectation etc □ *'Don't* ***keep*** *me* ***in a state of suspense****, please! If you know the results of my examination, tell me!'* □ *While the astronauts passed through the earth's atmosphere there was a temporary blackout in communications, and the whole world was* ***kept in suspense****, wond-*

ering whether they would land safely.

keep in training [A2 B2 pass] maintain oneself, or others, in a state of fitness for physical or intellectual competition or activity □ *The girl* ***kept in training*** *all the year round in the hope of swimming the English Channel in the summer.* □ *'What's the best way of* ***keeping*** *a team of footballers* ***in training****?'* □ *'I cannot recollect at the moment….' 'You should* ***keep*** *your memory* ***in training****,' she said.*

keep in with [A3 pass] (informal) remain on good terms with sb, either to gain some advantage from him or to avoid being victimized by him; keep on the right side of (q v). **S:** pupil; customer; prostitute; actress; lodger. **o:** teacher; grocer, coal-merchant; police; theatrical agent; landlady □ *We'll have to* ***keep in with*** *her in case we can't ever pay the rent….* AITC □ *In wartime people who before were always ready to accuse the butcher of giving short weight went to great lengths to* ***keep in with*** *him.*

keep in step (with) [A2] move forward together, like soldiers on the march. **S:** pay, wages, salary; flow of raw materials; supply of experts; country. **o:** cost of living, other forms of income; rate of production, expanding industry; needs of society; allies, rivals, competitors □ *There have been a number of movements in the constable's pay which have* ***kept*** *broadly* ***in step with*** *average industrial earnings.* DM □ *By this means I hoped to get orderly government working in the British Zone as quickly as possible and at the same time to* ***keep in step with*** *the Americans.* MFM

keep in touch (with) [A2] maintain communications (with); (of two or more persons) obtain regular information about one another □ *If Anna and Sadie were friends, then to consort with Sadie was one way of* ***keeping in touch with*** *Anna.* UTN □ *Montgomery provided himself with a very small operations staff for* ***keeping in touch with*** *the battle situation.* □ *It's a pity you're going to Australia. But, anyway, let's* ***keep in touch****, shall we?'* □ *As they were both amateur radio enthusiasts they were able to* ***keep in*** *daily* ***touch*** *(****with*** *each other) over the air.*

keep indoors [A1 B1ii pass] not (allow to) leave the house □ *On a day like this, with the rain pouring down and the temperature near freezing point, it's best to* ***keep indoors****.* □ *We always* ***keep*** *our children* ***indoors*** *after dark, since that horrible murder last year.* ⇨ keep in[1]; stay in/indoors.

keep track of [B2 pass (o)] follow the course of; carry in one's mind; remember the whereabouts of. **o:** the satellite; everybody's movements; one's friends □ *There are so many pieces of hardware circling the earth that only a computer could possibly* ***keep track of*** *them all.* □ *The drug squad successfully* ***kept track of*** *the suspected smugglers and arrested them all in an apartment in New York.* □ *He's working on so many projects that it's a wonder they're all* ***kept track of****.* □ *'You can't expect me to* ***keep track of*** *all the children and do the housework too.'*

keep off[1] [A1] not begin. **S:** ⚠ the rain, snow □ *The thick clouds passed overhead, but fortunately the rain* ***kept off*** *the whole day.* □ *The thunderstorm, which had been brewing all evening,* ***kept off*** *until we were safely indoors.*

keep off[2] [A1 A2] stay at a distance from; not walk on □ *Two large signs, with the words* ***KEEP OFF*** *painted on them, had been attached to the sides of the boat.* □ (notice) ***Keep off*** *the grass.* ⇨ get off[2].

keep off[3] [B1i pass B2 pass] cause to stay at a distance. **O:** wild animals; marauding tribes. **o:** farm; territory □ *One of the problems faced by the road-builders in some parts of the Amazon jungle was how to* ***keep off*** *the fierce people whose land they were crossing.* □ *'****Keep*** *those blasted squatters* ***off*** *my land!'* □ *'How can I* ***keep*** *the flies* ***off*** *this jam?'*

keep off[4] [A2 B2 pass] not eat or drink; prevent from eating, drinking or drug-taking. **o:** carbohydrates, sweets and chocolates; whisky □ *The only way to get your weight down is to* ***keep off*** *fattening foods, and cut out alcohol altogether.* □ *The doctor ordered the woman to be* ***kept off*** *all solid food for at least twenty-four hours.* □ *A lot of people see no reason for* ***keeping off*** *cannabis, in spite of the laws against its use.* ⇨ stay off.

keep off[5] [A2 B2 pass] not mention, avoid. **o:** topic; tricky subject; question of who pays □ *By mutual consent, the negotiators* ***kept off*** *the religious issue, and concentrated on economic and political differences.* □ *Everyone knew that the conversation should be* ***kept off*** *the subject of Mr Smith's bankruptcy. It was a source of embarrassment to the whole family.*

keep one's eyes off [B2] not covet, not look at with desire or longing; (in the neg, esp with *not be able to*) be fascinated by. **o:** that girl; my new picture; her jewellery □ *'You'd better* ***keep your eyes off*** *Carmen,' said James. 'She's spoken for!' 'Oh, yes? And who's spoken for her?' 'I have!'* □ *The young soldier could not* ***keep his eyes off*** *the hands of the woman sitting opposite him in the train. She had about a thousand pounds' worth of rings on her fingers!*

keep one's hands off [B2] not touch, not take. **o:** him etc; that machine; other people's money □ *'You* ***keep your*** *dirty* ***hands off*** *me!' the girl shouted, as Johnny tried to stroke her hair.* □ *The trouble with Marigold is that she can't* ***keep her hands off*** *her sister's clothes or her money or her books, or indeed anything at all that belongs to her.*

keep on[1] [A1] continue one's journey □ *The climbers had a long discussion about their position. Some were for returning to their base-camp, others were for* ***keeping on*** *in the hope of reaching the top with one last effort.* □ *'Is this the way to Willersey?' 'Yes. Just* ***keep on*** *till you reach Broadway; then you'll see the signpost to Willersey.'*

keep on[2] [B1ii pass] continue to wear. **O:** best clothes; wet swim-suit; hat; boots; dark glasses □ *In a church men take their hats off; in a synagogue, they* ***keep*** *them* ***on****.* □ *'I've told you before not to* ***keep*** *your socks* ***on*** *if they get wet.' 'Do you think I should change my dress for dinner?' 'No.* ***Keep*** *that one* ***on****. You look fine in it.'*

keep on[3] [B1i pass] continue to employ. **O:** servants, employees; old retainer, farm-hand □ *When Lord Lamont gave up his country seat he* ***kept on*** *only two of his numerous servants.* □ *Some of the men who were under notice were*

kept on *by the firm at the insistence of the Union.*

keep on[4] [A1] persist in the face of difficulties. **A:** through thick and thin; in the face of great odds; despite all setbacks □ *Helen Keller, born with the most appalling physical handicaps,* ***kept on*** *in spite of every difficulty until she became a well-educated, useful member of society.*

keep on doing sth [A1] not stop doing sth □ *'Saunders* ***keeps on insisting*** *that he is ruined; but he's taking a holiday in the South of France as usual!'* DC □ (one child talking to another) *'I've told you over and over again, and I* ***keep on telling*** *you, they wouldn't want to marry you, you aren't old enough to marry, is she Mummy?'* PW □ *I* ***keep on forgetting*** *to post my wife's letters!* □ *'Do be quiet, Sally, and don't* ***keep on asking*** *such silly questions.'*

keep a close watch on [B2 pass] observe carefully and constantly. **o:** the prisoners; the movements of the general; the children □ *The authorities* ***kept a close watch on*** *every airport and seaport following the escape of the prisoners from jail.* □ ***A close watch*** *is* ***kept on*** *the activities of all known anarchists.*

keep an/one's eye on [B2 pass] observe and if necessary take appropriate action; watch over (q v). **adj:** ⚠ (a) careful, professional, sharp, watchful, weather. **o:** old people; children; house; things; what others are doing □ *I asked him why he didn't come back home; at least he had friends there who could* ***keep an eye on*** *him.* CON □ *I don't know what would happen if we weren't here to* ***keep an eye on*** *you.* US □ *An agent provocateur, or police spy, might join an extremist party in order to* ***keep an eye on*** *it: you could not expect him to share its views and attitudes.* SNP □ *I'd be failing in my duty if I didn't* ***keep a*** *weather* ***eye on*** *your welfare.* □ ***A*** *careful* ***eye*** *will have to be* ***kept on*** *the younger brother — he's the dangerous one.*

keep one eye on [B2] give part of one's attention to. **o:** the time, the clock; the kettle; the baby □ *It isn't easy to concentrate on one's work when you've got to* ***keep one eye on*** *a baby that's crawling all over the place.* ⇨ have one eye on.

keep on its feet [B2 pass] (informal) preserve; prevent from collapsing; maintain in a healthy financial state. **O:** firm, school, country; project □ *A press baron bought the ailing newspaper and promised to* ***keep*** *it* ***on its feet*** *for at least two years.* □ *The Prime Minister of the island fought a long battle to* ***keep*** *his country* ***on its feet.***

keep on one's feet [A2] (boxing) not be knocked out; not collapse □ *The young challenger was not in the same class as the champion, and the wonder was how he managed to* ***keep on his feet*** *for three rounds.* □ *I don't know how she* ***keeps on her feet*** *after slaving all day, first in the office and then at home in the kitchen.*

keep one's finger on the pulse of [B2] be fully aware of, have up-to-date knowledge of. **o:** the country's mood; public opinion; the Stock Exchange □ *A commander must always* ***keep his finger on the*** *spiritual* ***pulse of*** *his armies.* MFM □ *A successful politician is one who* ***keeps his finger on the pulse of*** *the electorate.*

keep a firm/tight grip/hold on [B2 pass pass(o)] exercise close, careful, strong control over. **o:** the purse-strings, household expenditure; the youngsters □ *Unless* ***a tight hold*** *is* ***kept on*** *the purse-strings, a man can soon find that his family is spending more than he is earning.* □ *Those boys are pretty wild — they need* ***a firm hold keeping on*** *them* (or: ***a firm hold*** *needs to be* ***kept on*** *them*).

keep one's hair/shirt on [B1ii] (informal) not lose one's temper or composure □ *'That's my record-player! What are you doing with it?'* ***'Keep your hair on****. I'm only seeing how it works.'* □ *'If this is the way you treat my bicycle, I won't ever lend it to you again.'* ***'Keep your shirt on****! I'll get it fixed for you.'* □ *Now if we all* ***keep our hair on*** *and stop flinging accusations about, perhaps we can find a way out of the difficulty.* □ usu imper.

keep one's mind on [B2] not let one's attention wander from, concentrate on/upon (q v). **o:** the business, matter in hand; one's work; what one is doing □ *I found it hard to* ***keep my mind on*** *what the colonel was saying.* QA □ *'You mustn't keep worrying about your health. Try to* ***keep your mind on*** *other things — going away for a holiday, for example. Or you could read more books.'*

keep on the rails [A2 B2 pass] (informal) (cause to) observe the laws and conventions of society □ *We have all* ***kept on the rails****. There have been no scandals in the family; none of us have appeared in the police-courts or gone to prison; none of us have been in the divorce courts.* MFM □ *By taking a constant interest in his son's progress, he helped to* ***keep him on the rails*** *when so many other young men were falling foul of the law.*

keep on the right side of [A2] (informal) avoid offending sb, often in the hope of being rewarded or favoured by him; keep in with (q v) □ *We must* ***keep on the right side of*** *the captain. He could make things very uncomfortable for us if we were to annoy him in any way. A captain of a ship has a lot of power!* □ *He believed in* ***keeping on the right side of*** *his wealthier relations!*

keep on the right side of the law [A2] act legally, not break the law □ *'Look! I don't mind how you get this information, so long as you* ***keep on the right side of the law****.'*

keep a tab/tabs/a tag on [B2] (informal) follow closely the movements, activity, development of. **o:** known criminals, suspects □ *'Alec seems to be* ***keeping a tab on*** *his wife these days. Does he think she's got a lover?'* □ *...I've* ***kept a*** *pretty close* ***tab on*** *most of what he's said these last twenty years.* PP □ *'You* ***keep tabs on*** *'um, Ginger. See wot 'e does, where 'e goes. Don't let 'im see you if you can 'elp it.'*

keep on one's/his toes [A2 B2 pass] continue to be, make sb remain, alert, observant, ready for action □ *The old lady's horoscope read: 'Go all out for what you want today. Plenty of variety to* ***keep*** *you* ***on your toes****!'* □ *The sergeant-major* ***kept*** *the cadets* ***on their toes****. They never knew what they were going to have to do next.* □ *'The Chairman's visiting the warehouse today, so* ***keep on your toes*** *and be ready to answer any questions.'*

keep on (about) [A1 A3] continue talking about or referring to (in an irritating manner) □ *'Bill and his girl! He's a nice chap, but oh dear, he* *does* **keep on**, *doesn't he?'* □ *'I wish you wouldn't* **keep on about** *that dress you want to buy. We can't afford it and that's that!'* □ *Baker* **keeps on about** *El Alamain so that you'd think he won the bloody battle single-handed.* ⇨ be/go on about.

keep (on) at [A2 A3] worry, pester, harrass (continuously) with suggestions, requests, complaints. **o:** their father; elder brother; friend; teacher □ *The children* **kept (on) at** *their mother to take them to the fair, but she was always too tired.* □ *'Don't* **keep (on) at** *me about Johnny Smith getting a bicycle for his birthday.* You're *not getting one and that's final.'*

keep on (at/in) [B1ii pass B3 pass] not remove (from); continue to employ (at/in). **O:** child; caretaker □ *I'm thinking of* **keeping** *my boys* **on** (**at** *school) until they've taken their A-level exams.* □ *Although the duke had to economize, he* **kept** *about twenty servants* **on at** *his main residence and several others* **in** *the stables.* ⇨ keep on³; stay on (at).

keep on top (of) [A1 A2] maintain a position of superiority. **o:** opponent, opposition; job □ *The Prime Minister* **kept on top of** *the Opposition more by their ineptitude than by his own skill.* □ *'Old Charlie's looking a bit worn out, isn't he? How much longer do you think he'll be able to* **keep on top of** *his job?'* □ *No matter what happens to everyone else, Slick Freddie will* **keep on top**. ⇨ stay on top (of).

keep out/out of [A1 A2 B1i pass B2 pass] (cause to) remain outside. **S:** [A1 A2] **O:** [B1 B2] the public; crowds; undesirables; rabbits □ [A1] *There was a notice on the railings round the power-house bearing the words '***Keep out***! 20 000 volts'.* □ [B1] *The landlord of the pub said that he had no intention of* **keeping** *the hippies* **out** *so long as they behaved themselves.* □ [B2] *We've tried everything to* **keep** *the moles* **out of** *the garden, but without success.* □ [A2] *The public must* **keep out of** *the private rooms in Blenheim Palace.*

keep out of¹ [A2 B2 pass] not expose oneself or others to. **O:** the children; the men, troops; one's, sb's name. **o:** harm's way; the sun, the cold; the papers □ *During periods of civil strife, parents usually try to* **keep** *their children* **out of** *harm's way.* □ *I didn't come to Spain for my holidays to* **keep out of** *the sun. Just the contrary, in fact.* □ *The drunken driver turned out to be a well-known preacher, and he begged the police to* **keep** *his name* **out of** *the papers.* ⇨ stay out of.

keep out of² [A2 B2 pass] avoid or ensure that others avoid. **S:** [A2] **O:** [B2] your brother; the men. **o:** trouble, mischief; the way, my way, your father's way; other people's quarrels □ *Half of all morality is negative and consists in* **keeping out of** *mischief.* DOP □ *He learnt early in life that it was best to* **keep out of** *other people's quarrels.* □ *'I wish you would* **keep** *those screaming kids* **out of** *my way. They're giving me a headache.'*

keep one's nose out of [B2] (informal) not take an unwelcome part in. **o:** my business; other people's affairs; matters that don't concern one □ *'It happens to be nothing to do with Ed, but you* **keep your nose out of** *it, anyway.'* AITC □ *She could never learn to* **keep her nose out of** *her son's private life, though she was always made unhappy by what she discovered.*

keep to¹ [A2 pass B2 pass] not (allow to) leave or wander from. **o:** the main road, route; the point (at issue) □ *We did our best to* **keep** *the rally drivers* **to** *the official route, but a few of them strayed off it.* □ *If you would* **keep to** *the point, Mrs Bagwash, we should all be very grateful to you.* □ *The author gives a lively airing to one or two of the bees in his bonnet but on the whole his Olympic Diary* **keeps to** *the point with admirable discipline.* T

keep to² [A2 pass B2 pass] (cause to) follow, observe. **A:** firmly, closely. **o:** prearranged plan, schedule □ *The success of our enterprise depended on everyone* **keeping** *faithfully* **to** *the plan.* □ *Try to ensure that this timetable is strictly* **kept to**.

keep to³ [A2 B2 pass] (cause to) remain in, not leave. **o:** one's bed; the house □ *My friend was obliged to* **keep to** *his bed because of a fever.* □ *During the winter a lot of old people are forced to* **keep to** *the house, the weather being so cold and treacherous.*

keep an ear/one's ear(s) (close) to the ground [B2] (informal) notice signs of coming events or tendencies (as an American Indian used to detect the approach of others by placing an ear against the ground) □ *When we want to know what the students are thinking about the authorities, we only have to consult Fraser, who effectively* **keeps an ear to the ground**. □ *'What's the gossip of the market, Tom? You fellows certainly do* **keep your ears to the ground**.' QA

keep to a/the minimum [B2 pass] maintain at the lowest possible level; minimize. **O:** expenditure, outlay; demands, requirements □ *There has to be some verbal guidance to the action, but descriptive comment is* **kept to a minimum**. UL □ *If we* **keep** *the illustrations* **to a minimum**, *the cost of the book will not be excessive.* □ *The chairman asked the speakers to* **keep** *their remarks* **to the minimum** *in order to give everyone a chance to air their views.*

keep one's nose to the grindstone [B2 pass] (cause to) work persistently and hard, with the implication that the work is difficult, monotonous, or disliked □ *Only by* **keeping one's nose to the grindstone** *can one hope to improve one's standard of living.* □ *Miss Pennington was one of those teachers who enjoyed seeing that children's* **noses** *were* **kept** *firmly* **to the grindstone**. ⇨ get back to the grindstone.

keep to oneself [B2 pass] not tell others about, not let others know. **O:** information, news; intentions, plans □ *...later in the day, he thought of introducing a few private harmless jokes of his own. What these were he was* **keeping to himself**. DBM □ *One's sins and consequent feelings of guilt are often best* **kept to oneself**. □ *London suffered much less than a number of other European cities, and I will* **keep** *my bomb stories* **to myself**, *except to say that I made the acquaintance of more than one 'near miss'.* AH

keep (oneself) to oneself [A2 B2] not concern oneself with other people's business, not meet or join other people socially, maintain a veil of secrecy around oneself □ *'I suppose several people have been enquiring about him since he died?' 'A lot from the newspapers did, but they* *got no change out of me. I* ***keep meself to meself*** (substandard = myself).*'* PP □ *Nobody knows much about old Smout. He* ***keeps to himself*** *most of the time.*

keep to the straight and narrow (path) [A2 B2 pass] (cause to) live a blameless though perhaps unexciting life □ *I was surprised to hear that Johnson had been divorced by his wife on the grounds of adultery. I thought he always* ***kept to the straight and narrow***. □ *The chaplain tried hard, but unsuccessfully, to* ***keep*** *the boys* ***to the straight and narrow path***.

keep together[1] [A1 B1ii pass] not (allow to) become dispersed, scattered. **O:** stamp collection; books, papers, files; toys □ *'Bobby, I do wish you would learn to* ***keep*** *your things* ***together*** *and not leave them all over the house.'* □ *It is incredible how these old records have been* ***kept together*** *through the centuries.* □ *If all the cars* ***keep together*** *when we drive through the tribal territory we shall be quite safe.*

keep together[2] [A1 B1ii pass] (cause to) maintain a co-ordinated action. **S:** [A1] **O:** [B1] oarsmen, orchestra, choir □ *The eight men* ***kept together*** *throughout the boat race as though they were one.* □ *The bad-tempered conductor found it more and more difficult to* ***keep*** *the players* ***together****: perhaps they were getting back at him!*

keep body and soul together [B1ii pass] (informal) stay alive, but with some difficulty; scrape a living □ *Somehow the millions of unemployed of the 1930s managed to* ***keep body and soul together****, though on the meanest possible diet.* □ *'So you got that contract for the million-pound office block? Well that should help you to* ***keep body and soul together*** *for a while!'*

keep under[1] [A1 A2 B1ii pass B2 pass] remain or hold below the surface □ [A1] *The escaping prisoners, swimming across the river, managed to* ***keep under*** *as the searchlight raked the surface.* □ [B2] *The crocodile killed its prey by* ***keeping*** *it* ***under*** *the water and drowning it.*

keep under[2] [B1ii pass B2 pass] maintain in a state of unconsciousness or strong sedation □ *The poor man's pain was so intense that he was* ***kept under*** *by means of regular injections of morphine.*

keep under[3] [B1ii pass] maintain control over, suppress; hold under (q v). **O:** the population; his sons; fire □ *The army managed to* ***keep*** *the population of the occupied country* ***under*** *for a few months, and then trouble began to break out.* □ *The flamboyant character in the check suit and the loud tie surprised everyone by admitting that he could be* ***kept under*** *— by a strong enough hand!* □ *The local volunteers managed to* ***keep*** *the outbreak* ***under*** *and prevent it reaching a nearby petrol-station.* ⇨ keep under control.

keep under[4] [B2 pass rel] keep observing, maintain a constant watch etc over. **O:** suspect; patient; premises. **o:** ⚠ observation, surveillance, scrutiny □ *The plain-clothes officers were told to* ***keep*** *the suspected man* ***under*** *constant observation.* □ *The bookshop displaying the near-pornographic photographs was* ***kept under*** *police surveillance for two weeks.*

keep under control [B2 pass] not allow to spread. **O:** fire, epidemic, outbreak; locusts □ *The threatened epidemic of smallpox was* ***kept under control*** *by the authorities' vigorous action.* ⇨ keep under[3].

keep under sb's feet [A2] get in sb's way, inconvenience sb by one's presence □ *'Damn the cat! I've trodden on it again! But it will* ***keep under my feet*** *all day...!'* □ *'Don't* ***keep under your father's feet*** *while he's trying to mend the sink.'*

keep under one's hat [B2 pass] (informal) remain secret about, not tell anyone about. **O:** it; the terms of the agreement; the news, plan; our intentions □ *'Mary and I are going to be married; but please* ***keep*** *it* ***under your hat*** *until we've told her parents.'* □ *'It's almost certain that you will get the manager's job when he leaves: but* ***keep*** *it* ***under your hat*** *— I'm not supposed to tell you!'* □ often imper.

keep up[1] [A1 B1i pass] not fall or sink, prevent from falling or sinking. **S:** [A1] **O:** [B1] swimmer; construction, house □ *The surviving sailors managed to* ***keep up*** *for several hours and were eventually picked up by a lifeboat.* □ *The children use waterwings to* ***keep*** *themselves* ***up*** *in the water whilst they're learning to swim.* □ *Those houses are so badly built that one wonders how they* ***keep up*** *in a strong wind.* □ *Some schoolboys wear a belt to* ***keep*** *their trousers* ***up***. ⇨ stay up[1].

keep up[2] [A1 B1i pass] remain, maintain, at a high level. **S:** [A1] **O:** [B1] costs, wages, prices; production □ *In spite of strikes, the national output managed to* ***keep up****. It even increased a little beyond the previous year's.* □ *So long as the cost of raw materials* ***keeps up****, prices of consumer goods will* ***keep up****, too.*

keep up[3] [A1 B1i pass] maintain, not allow to decline. **S:** [A1] **O:** [B1] spirits, courage, morale, determination, strength □ *Women patients in hospitals are encouraged to use their make-up to* ***keep up*** *their morale.* □ *'Do drink this soup I've made, dear. You must* ***keep*** *your strength* ***up****, you know!'* □ *The troops' spirits were* ***kept up*** *by the occasional visit of well-known entertainers to their camps.* □ *I tried to* ***keep*** *my courage* ***up*** *by telling myself that the war would be over within a few weeks and then I could return to my family.* □ *The men's spirits* ***kept up*** *in spite of their desperate situation.*

keep up[4] [B1i pass] maintain, by expenditure of money and energy. **O:** two establishments; (such) a large estate, big house; extensive gardens □ *Glass of beer in hand, he found a companion some moments later in Sir George Bluff-Gore, who owned a large red-brick Georgian mansion that was too expensive to* ***keep up***. DBM □ *He can't afford to* ***keep up*** *a house in the country* (or: *afford the* ***upkeep*** *of a house in the country*). □ nom form is upkeep (sing only).

keep up[5] [A1] continue unchanged, unabated. **S:** storm, hurricane; weather, sunshine, rain □ *If this rain* ***keeps up****, all the crops will be ruined.* □ *Everybody hoped that the weather would* ***keep up*** (= continue fair) *for the annual sports.* □ *The hurricane* ***kept up*** *for several days and left a swathe of destruction across the country.*

keep up[6] [A1 B1iii pass] continue at a high level of intensity. **S:** [A1] **O:** [B1] attack, onslaught, bombardment; propaganda; interruptions, heckling, catcalls, insults; constant flow of information, criticism, questions □ *There wasn't much traffic, and they crowded the narrow streets, calling across to one another,* **keeping up** *an endless flow of sharp little fragments of repartee.* CON □ *All the time he was doing this, he'd* **keep up** *a long, snarling monologue, usually about Baxter.* CON □ *Bomber Command ordered that attacks on the industrial centres be* **kept up** *relentlessly.*

keep up[7] [B1iii pass] maintain, continue, produce with regularity. **O:** effort(s), the good work; hire-purchase (HP) payments, rent □ *'I see your sales figures for the last quarter were well up on the previous one. Splendid!* **Keep up** *the good work!'* □ *'If we don't* **keep up** *the payments on the car, I'm afraid the HP Company will take possession of it.'* □ *I regret that I can no longer* **keep up** *my annual subscription to the golf-club, so I am tendering my resignation.*

keep up[8] [B1iii pass] continue to practise, observe; not allow to lapse or be neglected. **O:** the old customs, tradition; the annual reunion; correspondence; friendship; my French □ *Although the children knew all about the myth of Father Christmas, they still liked to* **keep up** *the old Christmas customs.* □ *Quite a lot of people* **keep up** *the tradition of making pancakes on Shrove Tuesday.* □ *The two families, who had got on so well together on the Costa Brava, promised each other that they would* **keep up** *the friendship in Britain.* □ *If only I'd* **kept up** *my German, I might have got that job in Berlin.*

keep up[9] [B1ii pass] prevent from going to bed at the usual time. **S:** (sick) child; noise, celebrations. **O:** parents; guests, visitors □ *'Good heavens! It's nearly half past midnight. I must go and I do hope I haven't* **kept** *you* **up**!' □ *'You shouldn't* **keep** *your guests* **up** *talking until the small hours. They may be dying to go to bed!'* □ *...she knew about having to be gay and lively for him and always ready to listen when he wanted to talk, and being sometimes* **kept up** *half the night if he felt like a party.* AITC ⇨ be up[4], stay up[2].

keep up appearances [B1iii pass] continue to observe the conventions; present an unchanged front or appearance in public, esp following some loss of status, prestige or fortune □ *She would rather go hungry and* **keep up appearances** *than eat properly and wear last year's fashions.* □ *When I was a girl everyone was pure, today virgins are as rare as unicorns — still, I'll give white clothes* (as a wedding present) *to* **keep up appearances.** DPM

keep one's chin/pecker up [B1ii] (informal) not lose one's courage, hope, determination, optimism □ *'I don't think I'll ever be able to pass my exams.' 'You've got nothing to worry about. You've done all the work you were asked to do. So* **keep your pecker up**. *It'll be all right.'* □ *'Bill's just been sacked; what are we going to do?' 'Something will turn up. Just* **keep your chin up** *— for the sake of the children, at least.'* □ usu imper.

keep one's end up [B1i] (informal) 'perform' well, appear cheerful (esp in a difficult situation); defend oneself against attack, implied criticism, or rivalry □ *He* **kept his end up** *as host, even when Goodrich was retailing the diverting and fantastic adventures which had made him miss his train.* PW □ *Charles* **kept his end up** *fairly well. The invaluable 'News of the World' provided them with topics.* HD □ *He laughed, if he remembered to, whenever Alec's name was mentioned, and sometimes in Alec's face, and called him 'poor old Alec', just to* **keep up his end** *with him, and drown his sense of inferiority — which was strengthened by the benefits Alec had conferred on him.* PW

keep it up [B1ii] not relax one's efforts, maintain a high standard of achievement □ *The leading runner had covered the first three laps in very fast time. If only he could* **keep it up** *he would break the world record.* □ *Robert's father studied the report and looked up. 'This is excellent, Bob. I hope you'll* **keep it up**.'

keep up to the mark [B3 pass] ensure that sb works or behaves as well as he is able to. **S:** coach; general; director; headmaster. **O:** team; officers; actors; staff and pupils □ *You can trust the Matron of this hospital to* **keep** *her nurses* **up to the mark**. □ *A strong Prime Minister can be relied upon to* **keep** *his Ministers* **up to the mark** *in every way.*

keep up (with)[1] [A1 A3] work, play, walk, dance etc with the same vigour, speed, skill or expenditure of energy as. **o:** the youngsters; the experts; my cousin □ *Middle-aged people look ridiculous trying to dance to pop music; they simply can't* **keep up with** *the younger folk.* □ *Even when Josh was in his sixties he took part in swimming competitions, and a lot of younger people couldn't* **keep up with** *him.* □ *Please don't walk quite so fast. Your legs are longer than mine and I can't* **keep up** (**with** *you*)! □ *Johnny finds it difficult to* **keep up with** *the rest of the class in mathematics.*

keep up (with)[2] [A1 A3] progress, rise, at the same rate as. **S:** wages; small firms. **o:** prices; multiple stores □ *The main cause of industrial unrest is that the workers' incomes are not* **keeping up** (**with** *rising prices*). □ *The government said they would try to ensure that old age pensions* **kept up with** *the ever-increasing cost of living.*

keep up with[1] [A3] maintain the same social and material standards as. **o:** one's neighbours, friends □ *Most people, in this competitive society, think they must* **keep up with** *their neighbours.* □ *'It's no use asking me for a fur coat just because Mavis has got a new fur coat. My salary is only about half of her husband's, and we just can't* **keep up with** *them, that's all.'* ⇨ keep up with the Joneses.

keep up with[2] [A3] inform oneself about, learn about, be 'au fait' with. **o:** the news; latest developments; public opinion □ *Julie is one of those women who always* **keep up with** *the latest fashions.* □ *There is so much going on in the London theatrical world that I just can't find time to* **keep up with** *it.* ⇨ keep up with the times.

keep up with[3] [A3] maintain contact with, through visits, correspondence etc. **o:** their friends in Venezuela, one's schoolfriends, old acquaintances, their friends in Venezuela; former colleagues □ *Between whiles — for Alec was writing hard — she visited her old friends. She had scarcely* **kept up with** *them at all, so alien had been the mere thought of them to the life she led at Marshport.* PW □ *For some years after his retirement he* **kept up with** *a number of his old* *workmates, but as time went by he dropped them one by one.*

keep up with the Joneses [A3] (informal) try to maintain the same material and social standards as one's (richer) neighbours; keep up with[1] (q v) □ *It's one thing to be able to* ***keep up with the Joneses****, but quite another to try to* ***keep up with the Armstrong-Joneses*** (i e Lord Snowdon and Princess Margaret). UL □ *He was a pathetic, self-deluded man who, on two thousand pounds a year, tried to* ***keep up with the James Bonds*** *of this world.* □ in contrast, Tommy Atkins was the humble, obscure, anti-hero type of the First World War. The following gives an interesting twist to the expression: *Certainly working-class people have a strong sense of being members of a group.... The group does not like to be shocked or attacked from within. There may be little of the competitive urge to* ***keep up with the Joneses*** *but just as powerful can be the pressure to* ***keep down with the Atkinses****.* UL □ it is now common for the name Jones to be replaced by that of any other persons who are in the public eye on account of their luxurious mode of living or other enviable attributes.

keep up with the times [A3] adapt oneself in order not to become out of date, old-fashioned □ *It's no use hoping that you can go on without changing your business methods. If you don't* ***keep up with the times****, you'll get left behind.* □ *'I see you've introduced self-service in your restaurant.' 'Yes; you've got to* ***keep up with the times****.'* ⇨ keep up with[2].

keep faith with [B2] not break one's promises to. **S:** government; company. **o:** the electorate; workers □ *We* ***kept faith with*** *our allies by going to their help when they were invaded.* □ *The management has failed to* ***keep faith with*** *the employees by withholding the promised bonus.*

keep pace with [B2 pass(o) emph rel] be produced, progress, at the same rate as. not fall behind (q v). **S:** sales; supply; building. **o:** production; demand; requirements □ *Design must* ***keep pace with*** *technological innovation; it should neither lag behind it nor try to anticipate it.* □ *The provision of accommodation for students has not* ***kept pace with*** *the increase in places at universities and technical colleges.* □ *The tremendous demand for the new model just couldn't be* ***kept pace with****.*

keep within bounds [B2 pass] not allow to become excessive or unreasonable. **O:** claims; enthusiasm, excitement; celebrations; consumption of alcohol, tobacco; expenditure □ *The government says that it is doing its best to* ***keep*** *increases in prices* ***within bounds****.* □ *If your claims for expenses are* ***kept within*** *reasonable* ***bounds****, the Insurance Company will probably meet them in full.*

keyed up [pass (B2)] (be) extremely tense □ *When my brother left the house this morning he* ***was all keyed up****. The examination had been on his mind for weeks.* □ passive with *be, appear, look, get.*

kick against [A2 pass] defy, protest about; resist, usu in vain. **o:** authority, the law, the rules; fate, nature □ *It's no use trying to* ***kick against*** *the rules; you'll be the sufferer in the end.* □ *'Don't* ***kick against*** *fate. What will be, will be.'*

kick against the pricks [A2] protest about the inevitable, possibly in such a way as to inflict pain on oneself □ *'I'm not going back to that school. I hate it! I hate it!' 'Look, dear! It's no use* ***kicking against the pricks****. Everyone has to stay at school to the age of sixteen. You'll just have to grin and bear it.'*

kick around [A1 A2] (informal) be present, alive; be in existence. **S:** Joe, old Jolyon; idea □ *'Good Lord! It's Dick! How long have you been* ***kicking around*** *(these parts)? I thought you were in the States!'* □ *'You don't mean to say that old Thompson is still* ***kicking around****! He must be a hundred if he's a day.'* □ *The idea of flight had been* ***kicking around*** *for centuries before man actually achieved it.* □ in continuous tenses only.

kick around/round [B1ii pass] (informal) discuss in a tentative, informal way. **O:** idea, notion, suggestion □ *After the clinical examination, the consultant invited his students to put forward any suggestions they had about the nature of the disease, so that they could* ***kick*** *them* ***around*** *for a while.*

kick-back [nom (A1)] (slang) perquisite, backhander □ *'Every job has its* ***kick-backs****,' the leader of the gang told the newcomer. 'In our job we help ourselves to little things from the passengers' luggage between the aircraft and the Customs. If you want us to cut you in, it'll cost you a fiver.'* □ originally, the reaction of a car or motor-cycle engine when the starter-handle or 'kick-start' pedal is used; the pressure produced in the engine may kick back.

kick back (at) [B1ii A3] kick sb in retaliation; counter-attack □ *'Dad! Billy's kicking me!' 'Then* ***kick*** *him* ***back****!'* □ *We ought to* ***kick back at*** *all these unfair allegations of corruption in our organization.*

kick downstairs [B1ii pass] push, propel, sb downstairs, with a kick; demote □ *The irate husband seized his wife's lover and* ***kicked*** *him* ***downstairs****.* □ *Poor old Fleming was* ***kicked downstairs*** *to a job in Accounts.* ⇨ kick upstairs.

kick in [B1i pass] break (open), damage; dislodge with a kick. **O:** door; face, teeth □ *As the door was locked, and I could hear someone screaming for help, I* ***kicked*** *it* ***in*** *and rushed into the house.* □ *Some muggers are quite capable of* ***kicking*** *a person's teeth* ***in*** *if he tries to resist.*

kick in the teeth [B2 pass] (informal) treat with a brutal lack of consideration □ *The old lady complained that the Association of Professional Tennis Players had* ***kicked*** *the public* ***in the teeth*** *by refusing to play at Wimbledon.* ⇨ previous entry.

kick off[1] [B1i pass] remove with a kick. **O:** shoes, slippers □ *He* ***kicked*** *his slippers* ***off*** *and dropped on to the bed.*

kick off[2] [A1 nom] (sport) start. **S:** match, game, final; the Mayor, Miss Great Britain □ *The match is due to* ***kick off*** *at 2.15.* □ *A television personality was invited to* ***kick off*** *at the final.* □ *We were delayed by the traffic and missed the* ***kick-off****.* □ for a kick-off = for a start, as the first point or argument of many: *'Why don't you believe what Tom says?' 'Well, I know for a fact that he wasn't anywhere near the place,* ***for a***

kick-off. And besides, everyone knows he's a liar!'

kick out/out of [B1i pass B2 pass] (informal) expel, send out forcibly; disown. **O:** employee; interloper, intruder, unwanted guest □ *'You're only allowed one mistake in this firm. If you slip up a second time they* ***kick*** *you* ***out*** *without any hesitation.'* □ *A group of directors tried to* ***kick*** *the young tycoon* ***out of*** *his position as Chairman, but he turned the tables on them.* □ *Tony was asked to help* ***kick out*** *the gatecrashers at the party; for his pains he was rewarded with a broken bottle thrust into his face. He was lucky not to lose his eyesight.* □ *The film-star's son went around boasting that he had been* ***kicked out*** *by his father for refusing to toe the line.*

kick over the traces [A2] be ill-disciplined, disobey people in authority, especially one's parents □ *I couldn't see eye to eye with the old man* (= my father). *I* ***kicked over the traces****, and I've lived my life in the entertainment business.* HD □ *Maybe I was too confident, and showed it. But I had received many rebuffs and there is no doubt they were good for me; they kept me from* ***kicking over the traces*** *too often and saved me from becoming too overbearing.* MFM

kick round [B1ii pass] ⇨ kick around/round.

kick up[1] [B1i pass] disturb, make uneven. **O:** carpet; layer of dust, sand, gravel □ *The maid was forever straightening the fringes of the carpet, but five minutes later the children had inevitably* ***kicked*** *it* ***up*** *again.* □ *A man sat at a table in a corner of the saloon idly* ***kicking up*** *the sawdust at his feet.*

kick up[2] [B1iii] create, produce. **O:** ⚠ a row, fuss, dust, shindy □ (of a baby) *She* ***kicked up*** *a terrible fuss, which was all it was, because as soon as I went into her room she stopped, and started giving me flirtatious smiles, so it couldn't have been wind or anything.* WI □ *The prisoners, at a pre-arranged signal, began to* ***kick up*** *a hell of a row with the aim of attracting the attention of people passing the prison.*

kick up its heels [B1iii] of a horse, kick into the air with its heels and run about, enjoying its freedom □ *As soon as Ned was released into the field he* ***kicked up his heels*** *and ran off to join the other horses near the stream.*

kick upstairs [B1ii pass] (informal) promote to a position which carries greater prestige or financial reward, but which carries less power (esp from the House of Commons to the House of Lords). **O:** manager, former Minister of Defence □ *The only way for us to get rid of old Smith is to* ***kick*** *him* ***upstairs****; then we'll be able to appoint Brown, and get some life into the business.* ⇨ kick downstairs.

kid (on/up) [B1ii] (informal) tease, tell sb sth in jest but with a serious expression on one's face. **O:** me; the poor child; his brother's friends □ *'If he tells you that you've won first prize in the competition, don't believe him. He's probably* ***kidding*** *you* ***(on)****.'* □ BOY: *And you really will marry me?* JO: *I said so, didn't I? You shouldn't have asked me if you were only* ***kidding*** *me* ***up****.* TOH □ kid up is regional (Northern).

kill off [B1i pass] destroy, get rid of. **O:** prisoners, all the children; the weak; insects, pests, mosquitoes, locusts; buds, early shoots □ *People in the village wondered what went on behind the high walls of the mental home. Did they sometimes* ***kill off*** *the more dangerous patients?* □ *A late frost* ***killed off*** *nearly all the apple-blossom, with the result that we had a very poor crop this year.* □ *Since the mosquitoes were* ***killed off****, the island has become a far pleasanter place to live in.*

kill with kindness [B2 pass] treat too well, be so indulgent towards sb as to cause him great harm □ *Her idea of being a good wife and mother was to heap the table with food. But as it was mostly starch and fat she was literally* ***killing*** *her family* ***with kindness****.*

kill two birds with one stone [B2] do two things, achieve two objectives, by means of a single action □ *'Why don't you come and discuss your idea when you're next in Edinburgh?' 'Well, I have to see my solicitor there next week, so perhaps I could drop in and have a chat with you while I'm there.' 'That's right.* ***Kill two birds with one stone****.'*

kindle with [A2] become alive with. **S:** eyes, heart. **o:** excitement, amusement, interest, avarice; joy, love, desire □ *As the young lady read her lover's letter, the colour came to her cheeks and her eyes* ***kindled with*** *excitement.*

kip down [A1 nom] (slang) lie down and go to sleep. **S:** tramp, hippy, student; team □ *We all piled out of the hot coach and* ***kipped down*** *for a couple of hours* (or: *had a* ***kip-down*** *for a couple of hours*) *in the shade of some trees at the side of the road.* □ *The hippies were tough. They could* ***kip down*** *anywhere — on grass or on concrete — and sleep through the night like babes.*

kip out [A1] (slang) sleep in the open air □ *Every night during the summer thousands of young people* ***'kip out'*** *on the beaches. It costs nothing and it makes them feel adventurous.*

kiss away [B1i pass] remove, as a result of kissing. **O:** tears, frown; jealousy, anger □ *Alfred walked into the house with a thousand worries written across his face. His wife helped him off with his coat and tried to* ***kiss*** *the anxiety* ***away****.*

kiss off [B1i pass] remove by kissing. **O:** make-up; lipstick, powder □ *'Now look what you've done! I was all ready to go out and you've* ***kissed*** *my lipstick* ***off****! What's more, you've got it all over your face!'*

kit out [B1i pass] equip. **O:** oneself; expedition, troops □ *Before they left for their new post, they* ***kitted*** *themselves* ***out*** *at Gieves, the specialists in tropical clothes.* □ *The men were* ***kitted out*** *with the latest gear for high-altitude climbing.*

kit up [B1ii pass adj] dress; equip. **O:** oneself; child; Hell's Angels □ *'Look at that trendy couple —* ***kitted up*** *in all the latest gear!'* □ *Some of the would-be skiers had* ***kitted*** *themselves* ***up*** *absurdly in the most expensive equipment you can imagine.*

kneel down [A1] get on to one's knees; (continuous tenses) be or remain on one's knees. **S:** child; congregation, worshippers; maid, charlady □ *Mary* ***knelt down*** *at the side of the bath and supported the baby's head in one hand as she gently washed it with the other.* □ *When the young man entered the church he saw that the congregation was* ***kneeling down*** *in prayer.*

knit together [A1 B1i pass] join, unite. **S:** [A1] **O:** [B1] bones; thread, strand (of a story). **O:** [B1] brows; members of a family, of society □ *The surgeon said that it would be six months before the two parts of the broken femur* **knitted together** *firmly.* □ *My father* **knitted** *his brows* **together** *in a thunderous frown and ordered me to go to my room.* □ *War, more than anything else, seems to* **knit** *the various strata of society* **together**. *When peace returns, the old divisions return with it.*

knit up [B1i pass] make by knitting; use completely by knitting. **O:** a pair of socks; wool; a few odd ounces (of wool, nylon etc) □ *Susan was amazingly quick with her needles. She could* **knit up** *a baby's coatee in an afternoon.* □ *The old lady spent several hours a day* **knitting up** *old scraps of wool into little squares, which she would later join together to make a blanket for her grandchild.*

knock about[1] [A2] (informal) move, travel, have one's haunts in □ *When he was a child, he used to* **knock about** *the market, trying to find a little work to earn a few coppers.* □ *There are always a few old men* **knocking about** *the Grassmarket in Edinburgh; it's a sort of open-air club for tramps and down-and-outs.* □ *'Our elder son has been* **knocking about** *the Continent for several months. We don't know exactly where he is or what he's doing.'* □ *'Why don't you get on one of those tramp steamers that* **knock about** *South East Asia? That's the way to relax for a few weeks.'*

knock about[2] [B1ii nom pass] (informal) beat, treat in a brutal manner; pretend to do this, esp in early, silent films □ *The young woman tried to conceal her damaged eye behind dark glasses, but it was obvious to everyone in the office that her husband had been* **knocking** *her* **about** *again.* □ *'I don't care for the old* **knock-about** *comedies* (ię ones in which the characters are **knocked about**) *of the early film-makers. I prefer more subtle forms of humour.'* □ knock-about is used attrib in the second example.

knock about together/with [A1 A3] (informal) be often in each other's company, keep the company of. **o:** the same old crowd, bunch; his old cronies; some undesirable characters; that girl □ *'You ought to be more careful who you're seen* **knocking about with**. *Remember that a man is judged by the company he keeps.'* □ *'It's amazing! Julie is still* **knocking about with** *that good-for-nothing Dave. What on earth does she see in him?'* □ *'Are Julie and Dave still* **knocking about together**?' □ *'I think I should tell you that your daughter's* **knocking about with** *some pretty unsavoury people in London.'*

knock one's head against a brick wall [B2] = bang one's head etc.

knock against/on [B2] (cause to) hit, strike, often causing damage or pain. **O:** head, shin; jug, bucket □ *Tom* **knocked** *his head* **on** *the protruding iron bar and had to have six stitches in it.* □ *I carelessly* **knocked** *the jug* **against** *the tap and broke it.*

knock at/on [A2] strike, rap, at/on. **o:** door, window, entrance □ (children's rhyme) *One, two, buckle my shoe; Three, four,* **knock at** *the door; Five, six, pick up sticks* etc. □ *'I'm sure I heard someone* **knocking on** *the window just now!'*

knock back[1] [B1i pass] (informal) drink quickly, (esp alcohol). **O:** whisky, beer, pint □ *The stranger ordered a double rum and* **knocked** *it* **back** *in three seconds flat. 'That's better,' he said, as he rubbed his hands together. 'Same again, please!'* □ *...he mixed two Ma Chéries, double strength, adding an extra dash of brandy to hold the feeble things together. 'There you are.* **Knock** *that* **back**!' DBM

knock back[2] [B1ii pass] (informal) cost, set back[2] (q v). **S:** new car; court case; daughter's wedding; dress, suit □ *'I like your new stereo equipment. It must have* **knocked** *you* **back** *a couple of hundred pounds.' 'No, it didn't. I put it together myself.'* □ *'How much did your wife's new hat* **knock** *you* **back**?'

knock down[1] [B1i pass] cause to fall. **O:** opponent, challenger, champion; fence, obstacle □ *Only two or three boxers have ever succeeded in* **knocking** *Mohammed Ali* **down**. □ *The horse hesitated at the last moment and instead of taking the fence in its stride crashed into it and* **knocked** *it* **down**.

knock down[2] [B1i pass] hit with a vehicle and cause to fall, often inflicting injuries or causing death □ *I think she must have been hurrying over to Harrods and been* **knocked down**. *Probably she's still unconscious.* DC □ *Last night a hit-and-run driver* **knocked** *a man* **down** *in the village and killed him.* □ *The child was* **knocked down** *by a lorry as he ran across the road.*

knock down[3] [B1i pass] demolish. **O:** building, house, fort □ *When the slum property has been evacuated it will be* **knocked down** *and replaced by modern blocks of flats.*

knock down[4] [B1i nom pass adj] (auctioneering) sell. **O:** lot number thirty-four; the old bicycle, car, picture; farm, homestead □ *'For the last time, thirty pounds. I am offered thirty pounds for this antique chamber-pot. Any advance on thirty pounds? Thirty pounds. Going, going --- sold to the gentleman in the dark spectacles at the back', and the auctioneer brought his hammer down on the table. 'Things like that used to be* **knocked down** *at five shillings!' said Alison.* □ *...in the depression of the thirties, when everyone was going broke and all the properties were coming under the hammer at a* **knocked down** (cf **knock-down**) *price* (i e at a low price), *the McConchies were prudently buying land.* RFW □ nom form is attrib, as in the second example.

knock down[5] [B1i nom pass adj] dismantle for ease of transport. **O:** machine, car, apparatus □ *In many Asian countries there are assembly plants for the construction of cars which are imported in* **knocked-down** (cf **knock-down**) *form from Europe, America and Japan.* □ **Knock-down** *furniture from Sweden has become very popular in recent years.* □ nom form is used attrib as in these examples.

knock down[6] [B1i pass] cause to reduce; beat down (q v). **O:** price, cost, charge; second-hand car dealer □ *She is never happy unless she succeeds in* **knocking** *the bill* **down** *by a few pence. So tradesmen always add a little to their prices in anticipation of this.* □ *'I managed to* **knock** *the landlady* **down** *a pound, so I got the bedsitter for four pounds a week,' he boasted.*

knock for six [B2 pass] (cricket) (of a batsman) score the maximum points (six runs) from a single stroke; (informal) deal a severe blow to; affect deeply or devastatingly □ *When the bowler had been* **knocked for six** *off three successive balls, the captain decided that a change was overdue.* □ *'Didn't you get to know of the Hampden Cross housing estate? The Council are putting one up all the way round here. (It will)* **knock** *the value of the property* **for six**, *of course.'* DIL □ (advertisement) *'***Knock** *him* **for six** *with a Helena Rubinstein Heart of Coral smile....'* H □ *Montgomery urged his troops to* **knock** *Rommel* **for six** *out of Africa.*

knock them in the aisles [B2] (theatre) score a great success with 'them' (i e the audience, the public), usu by a humorous performance, play etc □ *When the mass did the right thing, they were the 'public'; when they did not react satisfactorily they were simply 'them' ('just can't get them moving tonight', 'if this doesn't* **knock them in the aisles**, *well, blast 'em').* HD

knock in/into [B1i pass B2 pass] drive in (into) by means of a hammer etc. **O:** nail; board, piece of wood, bung. **o:** wood; place; hole □ *The child tried hard, but couldn't* **knock** *the nail* **in**. □ *The pieces had been so accurately made that it was easy to* **knock** *them* **into** *position.*

knock (some) sense into [B2 pass] (informal) force sb to behave in a sensible way. **adj:** some, any, a little, a bit of □ *I've been trying for years to* **knock some sense into** *my youngest daughter, but she insists on going her own way.*

knock off[1] [B1i pass B2 pass] remove, with a blow (from). **O:** cup; man; insect. **o:** table; horse, deck; wall, coat □ (traditional song) *'Every time that I go out, The monkey's on the table. Get a stick and* **knock** *it* **off**. *Pop goes the weasel!'* □ *A low branch of the tree, stretching across the path,* **knocked** *the unwary rider* **off** *his mount.*

knock off[2] [A1 A2] (informal) stop work. **S:** men, workers, factory. **o:** work; what you're doing □ *'I'll meet you at the factory gate after work.' 'O.K. What time do you* **knock off**?' □ *'We always* **knock off** *early on Christmas Eve. Nobody's in the mood to do any work, and we usually have a drink and a bit of an office party before we go home.'* □ *The whistle went, the machines stopped and the men* **knocked off** *for lunch.* □ *'Isn't it time you* **knocked off** *that tedious job for a while?'*

knock off[3] [B1i pass B2 pass] reduce the price of sth by a stated amount. **O:** ten per cent, a few pence, a copper or two. **o:** the price, estimate, bill □ *The greengrocer always* **knocked** *a little* **off** *the price of his fruit for the old age pensioners.* □ *'Did you pay the full price for this book?' 'No. The girl* **knocked** *twenty-five pence* **off** *because it was shop-soiled.'* □ *'You overcharged me ten pence last week.' 'Oh, did I? Sorry. I'll* **knock** *it* **off** *your next bill.'*

knock off[4] [B1i pass] (informal) write, compose rapidly or easily; throw off [4] (q v), toss off [2] (q v). **O:** a song, couple of verses, short story, article □ *Edward Lear had an extraordinary imagination. He seemed to be able to* **knock off** *a limerick with the greatest of ease in a few minutes.* □ *This script shows every sign of having been* **knocked off** *in great haste. It is very badly written.*

knock off[5] [B1i pass] (slang) kill. **O:** policeman, guard, 'copper', watchman □ *'Nowadays, thieves seem to think nothing of* **knocking off** *an old watchman in the course of their crimes. Bring back capital punishment, I say!'*

knock off[6] [B1i pass] (slang) steal (from). **O:** a lorry-load of whisky, gold watch; bank □ *'I like your new transistor radio. Where did you get it?' 'Oh, I* **knocked** *it* **off** *in a shop in Tottenham Court Road while no one was looking.'* □ *The two men got drunk and boasted that they had* **knocked off** *a bank in London the previous day.* □ *'I like the fancy ring you're wearing. Where did you* **knock** *that* **off**?'

knock sb's block/head off [B1ii] (slang) (threaten to) strike sb, usu by way of punishment or retaliation □ *'If I see that kid in my orchard again I'll ruddy well* (= bloody well) **knock his block off**.' □ usu with *shall/will.*

knock it off [B1ii] (slang) (order to) stop doing sth which displeases, irritates; pack it in (q v), pack it up (q v), turn it in (q v) □ *'Do me a favour, Art! You've been whistling that same tune all morning.* **Knock it off**, *will you?'* □ usu imper.

knock spots off [B2] (informal) surpass, be far better than, excel □ *This restaurant is very expensive, but Mother's cooking would* **knock spots off** *it.* □ *Manchester decided to put on a firework display that would* **knock spots off** *anything that Liverpool might have planned for the royal visit.* □ *When it comes to foreign languages, the girls can usually* **knock spots off** *the boys.*

knock on[1] [A2] strike, rap, at/on. ⇨ knock at/on.

knock on[2] [B2] strike, often causing damage. ⇨ knock against/on.

knock on[3] [A1 nom B1ii pass] (rugby football) knock the ball forward with the hands (not permitted by the rules of the game) □ *Although Jerry thought he had scored a try, the referee had in fact blown his whistle for a* **knock-on** *some seconds earlier.*

knock-on [nom (B1)] domino (effect); the inevitable consequence of some initiating action □ *The increase in interest rates is bound to have a* **knock-on** *effect throughout the financial world.* □ usu attrib, as in the example.

knock on the head [B2 pass] (informal) effectively prevent the realization of; dismiss as absurd. **O:** idea, scheme, plan; superstition, belief □ *The increase in the price of cars has* **knocked** *our hopes for a new one this year* **on the head**. □ *'It's high time this myth about eighteenth-century design was* **knocked on the head**.' HAA

knock on wood [A2] (US) expression used to fend off bad luck (= British English: *touch wood*) □ *'I hear that Jo and Phyllis are getting married on Friday the 13th.' 'Yes!* **Knock on wood**!'

knock out[1] [B1i nom pass] make unconscious by means of a blow, very strong drink etc. **O:** boxer; challenger, opponent; passenger, passer-by; guest □ *Joe Frazier* **knocked** *his inexperienced opponent* **out** *in the first round of the contest.* □ *The fight ended in a* **knock-out** *victory for the challenger.* □ *The driver of the car was* **knocked out** *at the moment of impact, and could remember nothing of the circumstances of the accident.* □ *After two glasses of the home-made wine, I had to lie down. It had* **knocked** *me* **out**.

knock out[2] [B1i nom pass] (informal) astound, stop as with a blow □ *Mary's new outfit* **knocked** *me* **out**. *I'd never seen anything so beautiful (or expensive!) in my life.* □ *She's beautiful, anyway, but in that hat she's a* **knock-out**. □ *'The new musical at the Drury Lane Theatre is a* **knock-out**. *You must see it.'*

knock out[3] [B1i pass] (informal) overwhelm; render speechless, incapable of action or thought. **S:** news, warning, results of the test □ *For a moment I was completely* **knocked out** *by the news of my friend's death. It was some time before I could convince myself that it had really happened.* □ *The letter informing the manager that his services would no longer be required* **knocked** *him right* **out**. *He refused to see anyone all day.*

knock one's pipe out [B1i] empty the ashes from one's pipe □ *The old man leaned forward and* **knocked his pipe out** *against the grate.*

knock out/out of[1] [B1i pass B2 pass] remove by means of a blow or repeated blows. **O:** contents, ashes; tooth □ *Several of the child's teeth were* **knocked out** *in the accident.* □ *'***Knock** *the powder* **out** *(***of** *the tin) gently. We don't want it all over the room.'*

knock out/out of[2] [B1i nom pass B2 pass] eliminate, esp in competitions □ *Ipswich* **knocked** *Fulham* **out** *(***of** *the League Cup) in the third round, and then were* **knocked out** *themselves in the fourth.* □ *'It's a* **Knockout**!*'* (a European obstacle game of this name shown on BBC television, also known as Jeux sans Frontières).

knock the bottom out of [B2 pass] (informal) suddenly remove the basis of. **o:** one's case, argument, confidence; her world; the market □ *The unexpected evidence of a passer-by* **knocked the bottom out of** *the youth's statement that he was nowhere near the scene of the crime.* □ *'You always think that you're immune, and that things like this only happen to other people. Then, when they happen to you, it* **knocks the bottom out of** *your confidence.* AITC □ *When John's wife left him for another man,* **the bottom** *seemed to have been* **knocked out of** *his world.* □ *The news of renewed bombing in Vietnam* **knocked the bottom out of** *the stock market.*

knock hell/the living daylights out of [B2 pass] (slang) give sb a severe, brutal, thrashing; beat unmercifully □ *'I'll kill her. I'll* **knock the living daylights out of** *her.'* TOH □ *Old George used to arrive home drunk every Saturday night and* **knock hell out of** *his wife. Nobody could ever understand why she never left him.*

knock the spirit/the stuffing out of [B2 pass] (informal) demoralize by physical attack or psychological shock □ *No amount of bombardment seemed to* **knock the spirit out of** *the guerrillas. They always reappeared, ready to strike at their enemy in the most unexpected places.* □ *Four days of continuous bombardment had* **knocked the stuffing out of** *the defenders, who eventually surrendered to the greatly superior forces surrounding them.* □ *I released his shoulder, letting my hand fall helplessly to my side as if his words had* **knocked** *all* **the spirit out of** *me.* CON

knock through [A1] remove a wall, partition etc, in order to enlarge the area of a room, usu by combining two, or in order to make a new door, serving-hatch etc □ *The apartment was occupied by a designer, who had* **knocked through** *between the two small bedrooms, and ripped out the simple plumbing, installing in its place an elegant décor of white tiles and chromium.* OBS □ *The middle interior wall has gone, and one can see through into the back garden with its breakfast patio. The* **knockers-through** *are here.* L

knock together [B1i pass] prepare, construct rapidly and without finesse; knock up[3] (q v). **O:** meal, snack; some kind of shelter; a sledge for the children; a few bookshelves; crude bed □ *I don't pretend to be much of a handyman, but if need be I could* **knock** *a rough table* **together**. □ *The hut looked as if it had been* **knocked together** *by someone in a great hurry.*

knock their heads together [B1ii pass] (informal) force two quarrelling people behave sensibly by this or similar violent action □ *When the woman could bear the children's squabbling no longer she grabbed them both by the hair and* **knocked their heads together**. □ *Sometimes one feels that the leaders of the political parties should have* **their heads knocked together**.

one's knees knock together [A1] feel, or show, great fear □ *As I went into the boss's office I could feel* **my knees knocking together**. *Had he been told about my terrible mistake in putting the letters in the wrong envelopes?*

knock up[1] [B1i pass] drive or hit upwards with a blow. **O:** fist, arm, weapon; latch, bar □ *As the intruder rushed at me with a knife, I* **knocked** *his arm* **up**, *and hit him in the stomach with the poker.*

knock up[2] [B1i pass] awaken by knocking on a door (or window). **O:** us; mill-workers; travellers; visitor □ *'Would you mind* **knocking** *me* **up** *at about 7 o'clock tomorrow, as I must catch an early train to London?'* □ *In some Lancashire towns the mill-owners employed their own* **knockers-up** *who went round banging on the windows of the workers every morning to wake them up.*

knock up[3] [B1i pass] prepare, make, quickly and without much planning; knock together (q v). **O:** snack, meal, dinner; shelter, hen-house, kennel, rabbit-hutch □ *My mother was a marvel at* **knocking up** *a meal for an unexpected guest. There always seemed to be something in the larder.* □ *'Have you seen the garage that George has built? It looks more like a shack* **knocked up** *out of driftwood by a gang of four-year-old boys.'*

knock up[4] [B1iii pass] (cricket) make, score. **O:** a good score; twenty runs, a century (= a hundred runs) □ *At last the captain of the side found his form and* **knocked up** *his best score of the season — a faultless 70.*

knock up[5] [B1ii pass] make tired, exhausted or ill. **S:** climb, effort; the struggle to swim to the shore; experience, shock; overwork □ *'Please don't try to dig up the whole garden in one day: you'll* **knock** *yourself* **up**.*'* □ *Tom was completely* **knocked up** *as a result of his prolonged effort to qualify for the Olympics team.*

knock up[6] [B1ii pass] (slang) make a woman pregnant □ *'Why ever did she let him* **knock** *her* **up**? *You'd have thought she'd never heard of the*

Pill! Now I suppose she'll have to have an abortion.'

knock-up [nom (A1)] (tennis) a short period of practice before starting to play a game □ *While the players were having a* ***knock-up****, the crowd settled down in their seats in expectation of a first-class match.*

knot together [B1i pass] join by means of a knot. **O:** two pieces of rope, string; laces □ *We escaped from the burning hotel by* ***knotting*** *several sheets* ***together*** *and using them as a rope.*

know about [A2 pass B2 pass emph rel] have knowledge of, be aware of. **O:** anything, nothing; a lot, a good deal □ *'Did you* ***know about*** *your son's shocking behaviour at the club last night?' 'Yes, thank you. I* ***know*** *all* ***about*** *it.'* □ *'You can't park your car here, sir! There's a double yellow line near the pavement.' 'Oh, I didn't* ***know about*** *that.' 'Ignorance of the law is no defence, I'm afraid. I'll have to book you.'* □ *'Why weren't you at the committee meeting yesterday?' 'I didn't* ***know*** *anything* ***about*** *any committee meeting.'* □ *Not much is* ***known about*** *some of the tribes in Papua.*

not know about [A2] not recognize or accept the truth or admissibility of sth. **o:** that; (any words used by a previous speaker) □ *'Joan's a pretty girl, isn't she?' 'I do****n't know about*** *pretty. She's certainly got plenty of money—which makes her attractive, anyway!'* □ *'The Common Market should be good for world trade.' 'I do****n't know about*** *that. It looks more like an exclusive club, to me.'* □ usu first person, neg, simple present tense.

know by sight [B2 pass] know, without being an acquaintance of. **O:** her; film-star; your friend; the Vice-Chancellor □ *'Have you ever met Professor James?' 'No, But I* ***know*** *him well enough* ***by sight****, of course.'*

(not) know from [B2] (not) be able to distinguish, separate or recognize the difference between. **O:** him etc; one brother, twin; goldfinch. **o:** Adam, a crow; another; yellowhammer □ *'You remember Mrs Fortescue, don't you?' 'Mrs Fortescue? I seem to recall the name, but I would****n't know*** *her* ***from*** *Adam (or: I would****n't know*** *her* ***from*** *a crow).'* □ *That nurse's head is always in the clouds. She never seems to* ***know*** *one patient* ***from*** *another.*

not know one's arse from one's elbow [B2] (taboo) be ignorant, inefficient, stupid □ *'Don't ask Algernon for any advice over your financial affairs—he doesn't* ***know his arse from his elbow****.'*

know of [A2] have knowledge or experience concerning; be slightly acquainted with. **o:** a nice, quiet spot for a holiday; a good way to make money; an interesting restaurant □ *There is only one way that I* ***know of*** *to pass examinations, and that is to work hard and be fully prepared.* □ *'Excuse me. Do you by any chance* ***know of*** *a short cut to the Vicarage?'* □ *'Is anyone going to visit Uncle Tom in hospital this evening?' 'Not that I* ***know of****.'* □ *'Do you know Sir Ralph Thomas?' 'No. I* ***know of*** *him, but I've never met him.'* □ where know of is contrasted with know, the word of is pronounced in its strong form, /ov/, as in the last example.

know through and through [B1ii] know and understand perfectly. **O:** him etc; her husband; the boss; men □ *She had only been with him once, for a weekend—but her thoughts had been so constantly with him—and never more than when they were forbidden access to him—that she felt she* ***knew*** *him* ***through and through****.* PW □ *Mary* ***knew*** *children* ***through and through****. After all, she had brought up six of her own.*

known to [pass (B2)] (be) on the records of. **S:** tramp, suspect; applicant; tenant; client. **o:** the police, authorities; the Home Office; estate agent; department store □ *People who are* ***known to*** *the police naturally tend to be suspected if they were near the scene of a crime and unable to explain what they were doing there.* □ cp the more straightforward passive of know sb: *Mr Jones has been* ***known to*** *me for several years, and I can write with confidence about his suitability for the vacancy in your office.*

knuckle under (to) [A1 A3 pass] (informal) give way in the face of pressure, accept orders (from). **o:** (the likes of) him; authority; injustice □ *The British Government had* ***knuckled under to*** *threats of violence, which had created unsurmountable obstacles to progress.* SC □ *In spite of every argument, the recalcitrant students refused to* ***knuckle under****, and continued their occupation of the Vice-Chancellor's room.*

kowtow (to) [A2 pass] make oneself subservient to; seek one's objectives through undignified behaviour □ *The British miners are not the kind of men who will* ***kowtow to*** *people in authority. They have pride in their work and pride in themselves.* □ *He may have made a lot of money as a shipowner, but that doesn't mean he has to be kowtowed to.*

L

labour over [A2 pass rel] work hard and continuously at some difficult task; toil over (q v). **o:** paper, document; draft, communiqué; marking, corrections □ *The editor* ***laboured over*** *the manuscript till early morning.* □ *Some kinds of writing are all the better for being* ***laboured over****.*

labour under[1] [A2 emph rel] (formal) have as a disadvantage or handicap. **o:** disability, infirmity □ *The new regime removed many of the injustices* ***under*** *which the population had* ***laboured****.*

labour under[2] [A2 emph rel] (formal) be misled or blinded by. **o:** (mistaken, false) idea, supposition; misapprehension □ *Our political opponents* ***labour under*** *the delusion that support for our policies is dwindling.*

lace up [B1i nom pass] fasten, close up, with laces. **O:** shoe, jacket; football □ *His swimming-trunks are* ***laced up*** *(or:* ***lace up****) at the side.* □ *Her new boots can be* ***laced up*** *(or: are* ***lace-***

ups). □ the form lace-up(s) refers only to footwear.

lace (with) [B2 pass] add spirits to a (hot) beverage. **O:** tea, coffee. **o:** rum, whisky □ *On night watch, the sailors drank hot tea* ***laced with*** *rum.*

laden with [pass (B2)] bearing heavy loads or burdens; (be) loaded with, burdened with. **S:** table, tree; businessman, official. **o:** food, fruit; care, responsibility □ *The traditional picture of an English Christmas includes a table* ***laden with*** *food and drink.* □ *One doesn't normally think of Stephen as a man* ***laden with*** *anxieties.* ⇨ load down (with).

lag (behind) [A1 A2] fail to keep level (with), hang to the rear (of). **S:** runner, car; industry, factory. **o:** leader, pack; competitor □ *In steel production, we* ***lag behind*** *the rest of Europe.* □ *Our figure* ***lags behind*** *the national average.* SC

lam into [A2 pass] (slang) attack violently (with the fists, or verbally); lay into (q v). **S:** boxer; listener, critic □ *In the last round, Smith fairly* ***lammed into*** *his opponent.* □ *What did the poor man say that made you* ***lam into*** *him like that?*

land (in) [B2 pass rel] (informal) make things end unhappily, badly, for sb. **O:** firm; colleague, friend; oneself. **o:** mess, muddle; (bankruptcy) court, the gutter □ *Just look at the mess you've* ***landed*** *us* ***in!*** □ *You know where he'll* ***land*** *us all next time?* ***In*** *gaol.*

land onto [B2 pass] ⇨ land with.

land up [A1] (informal) reach a final point (after a journey, career etc). **S:** (lost) parcel, letter; wanderer, vagabond; petty thief, bigamist □ *His hat blew off in a strong wind and* ***landed up*** *on top of a lorry.* □ *After knocking about the world for a few years Michael* ***landed up*** *teaching in his home town.* □ *The probation officer had a warning for Bill: 'One more appearance in court and you could* ***land up*** *in prison.'*

land with [B2 pass] (informal) oblige sb to accept a burden. **S:** boss, colleague. **o:** task; arrangement, organization; child, invalid □ *I've been* ***landed with*** *an extra set of papers to mark.* □ *Someone has* ***landed*** *me* ***with*** *the job of fixing hotel rooms for the visitors* (or: ***landed onto*** *me the job of fixing hotel rooms* etc). □ *The family were* ***landed with*** *mother-in-law* (or: *Mother-in-law was* ***landed onto*** *the family*) *for the entire weekend.*

lap up[1] [B1i pass adj] drink, by taking up liquid on the tongue. **S:** cat, dog. **O:** milk, water □ *The milk you put out in the saucer was quickly* ***lapped up.***

lap up[2] [B1i pass adj] (informal) absorb, learn, greedily or eagerly. **S:** spoilt child, favourite; student. **O:** flattery, praise, compliment; facts, knowledge □ *Irma could call him the silliest things — 'treasure', 'little sparrow' — and he would* ***lap*** *them* ***up.*** PW □ *He will take all the instruction you can give him — he just* ***laps*** *it* ***up.***

lapse (from) [A2 emph rel] (formal) fall short of a high standard, esp in one's moral life. **o:** (high) standard, level, position □ *If you will adopt such a lofty moral stance you shouldn't be surprised when occasionally you* ***lapse from*** *it.*

lapse from grace [A2] fall from a position in which one is highly regarded, favoured etc; fall from grace (q v). **S:** adviser, associate; favourite □ *Gunning spoiled his chances for quick promotion by writing newspaper articles that were overcritical of his party chiefs. And once having* ***lapsed from grace*** *he found it hard to climb back into favour again.*

lard with [B2 pass emph rel] (formal) add sth pompous, flowery etc to one's words. **O:** speech, address. **o:** compliment, praise; anecdote, quotation □ *He* ***larded*** *his remarks* ***with*** *references to his importance in local affairs.* □ *The sailors' language was richly* ***larded with*** *oaths.*

lash down [B1i pass adj] tie firmly in position with ropes etc. **O:** sail, canvas; tarpaulin, awning; hatch; load; box, bale □ *A tarpaulin was spread over the hay-rick and firmly* ***lashed down*** *to prevent it blowing off in a high wind.* □ *The crew* ***lashed down*** *the cargo of timber stowed on the foredeck.*

lash out (at) [A1 nom A3 emph rel] make a sudden and violent attack (physical or verbal) (upon). **S:** horse, mule; speaker, politician; husband, teacher. **o:** rider, stranger; tax-evader, slacker; child □ *It seemed that he was going to* ***lash out at*** *her, but he controlled himself.* DC □ *He treated the television interview as an opportunity to have a* ***lash-out at*** *the opposition party.*

lash out (on) [A1 A3] (informal) spend freely or lavishly (on sth); pay a lot (and more than one is willing to pay) (for sth). **o:** food, wine; perfume, cigars; luxuries, fripperies □ *When David goes on one of his European trips he* ***lashes out on*** *presents for the whole family.* □ *Many parents resent having to* ***lash out on*** *unnecessary items of school uniform which their children will in any case grow out of in a year.*

last out[1] [A1] not be consumed, expended or exhausted. **S:** supply, store; money; food, water, fuel □ *We can hold this position for as long as the ammunition* ***lasts out.*** □ *The petrol should just about* ***last out*** *till we get to the next village.*

last out[2] [A1] (be able to) complete some difficult task without collapsing etc; remain alive, survive. **S:** climber, explorer; sick, elderly, person □ *'We shall have to call a halt soon. Some of the youngsters haven't enough puff* (= breath) *in them to* ***last out*** *till the end of the climb.'* □ *The group round the bed could see that the old man was sinking fast: he would probably not* ***last out*** *the afternoon.*

latch on (to) [A1 A3 pass] (informal) get into sb's company, become a member (of); listen carefully (to). **o:** girl; party, group; remarks □ *When a man is rejected, he may for a time* ***latch on to*** *some less attractive girl.* □ *As the mists cleared from my brain, I* ***latched on to*** *their conversation.* CON

laugh (at)[1] [A2 pass emph rel] show amusement (at sb or sth). **o:** comedian; joke, story □ *He* ***laughed at*** *the way the clowns kept falling over their big feet.*

laugh (at)[2] [A2 pass emph rel] mock, ridicule; make fun of (q v). **o:** misfortune, impediment; speech, dress □ *Thoughtless children sometimes* ***laugh at*** *beggars and tramps.* □ *It's that sanctimonious air that people can't stand — small wonder he's* ***laughed at.***

laugh (at)[3] [A2 pass emph rel] disregard, scorn. **o:** danger, risk; problem □ *He* ***laughs at*** *the difficulties — they just spur him on to further effort.* □ *His mother's pleas to be careful were just* ***laughed at.***

laugh away [B1i pass] dispel, drive away, by

laughing, some unpleasant feeling or sensation in oneself or others. **O:** anxiety, fear, misgivings; depression, tears □ *'I know you're very brave, but you can't just* **laugh** *a toothache* **away**. *You'll have to see a dentist.'* □ *Jane had this tremendous fear of the dark, and her husband would try to* **laugh** *it* **away**, *saying it was just her overdeveloped imagination.*

laugh in sb's face [A2] (informal) reject with cruel mockery. **S:** captor; boss; (cruel) lover □ *When I asked him for longer time to pay back the loan, he just* **laughed in my face**.

laugh off [B1i pass adj] (informal) try, by laughing, to pretend that sth for which one is responsible has not happened or does not exist. **O:** blunder, faux pas; neglect, responsibility □ *This is a mistake that can't easily be* **laughed off**. □ *'Don't worry,' he said, trying to* **laugh off** *his resentment at the intrusion.* AITC □ *'Well, I've something to tell you. Your bungling has set the project back a month. Now try* **laughing** that **off**!'

laugh one's head off [B1ii] (informal) laugh noisily and cheerfully (often at sb else's expense). **S:** onlooker, listener □ *As he picked himself up from the floor, he saw a couple of boys* **laughing their heads off**.

laugh on the other side of one's face [A2] (informal) be made to appear ridiculous because one's supposed reason for being pleased with oneself etc is shown to have no real basis □ *'Laugh as much as you like. I've got some news here that will make you* **laugh on the other side of your face**!' □ *If Robert thinks he has outwitted the chemistry master, he is due for a surprise. Mr Prescott will make him* **laugh on the other side of his face**. □ often with *will/would* (*make*), as in the examples; note the plural: *'This'll make them* **laugh on the other side of their faces**.'

laugh out of [B2 pass] (try to) make sb forget his unhappiness by laughing. **o:** depression, misery □ *He could tell she was in a bad mood, and tried to* **laugh** *her* **out of** *it.*

laugh out of court [B2 pass] (informal) dismiss sth scornfully as false, ridiculous etc. **O:** charge, accusation; claim, statement □ *The story was untrue — the villagers had* **laughed** *it* **out of court**. HAA □ *Any attempt to charge us with some legal offence would be* **laughed out of court**. TBC

laugh up one's sleeve [A2] (informal) be secretly amused at sb else's failure etc □ *He could sense that his former colleagues were* **laughing up their sleeves** *over his dismissal.* □ *She felt that the waiter was* **laughing up his sleeve** *at her inability to pay.*

launch into [A2 pass] begin a long and involved speech etc (often in a vigorous or violent way). **S:** orator, critic. **o:** tale, account; rigmarole; (verbal) tirade, onslaught □ *Mr Blearney* **launched into** *another of his stories.* HD □ *Before she could speak he had* **launched into** *a long and circumstantial narrative.* HD

launch out (into) [A1 A3 pass rel] (informal) change to sth involving challenge and risk. **S:** firm, businessman; producer, writer. **o:** manufacture, politics; journalism □ *Why must a dancer* **launch out** *as choreographer as well?* OBS □ *You'll want to* **launch out into** *something with a proper salary.* THH

lay about [A2] (informal) fight, struggle (physically or verbally). **o:** one (= oneself); opponent, assailant □ *With his free arm he proceeded to* **lay about** *him.* SD □ *Aren't you* **laying about** *them for your discharge from hospital?* THH

layabout [nom (A1)] (informal) sb who habitually avoids work (and may be a petty criminal) □ *He's a wretched, idle* **layabout** — *never done a day's work in his life.*

lay aside[1] [B1i pass] put down, place to one side. **O:** reading, needlework □ *She* **laid aside** *her knitting to rest her eyes for a moment.*

lay aside[2] [B1i pass] relinquish, abandon. **O:** burden, responsibility, cares of office □ *Now that his sons are growing up, certain of his responsibilities can be safely* **laid aside**.

lay aside/by [B1i pass] save for future needs. **S:** parent, young couple. **O:** money, cash □ *They've a little money* **laid by** *for emergencies.* □ *We must* **lay** *something* **aside** *for the boy's education.*

lay at sb's door [B2 pass emph rel] say that sb is responsible for sth; attach to[2] (q v). **O:** ⚠ the blame, the responsibility, the guilt □ *The blame for these accidents should be* **laid at the door of** *careless drivers.* □ *With so many reports to mislead one, it is hard to say* **at whose door** *the responsibility should be* **laid**. ⇨ lie at sb's door.

lay before [B2 pass] present sth to an official body for discussion, passing into law etc. **O:** plan, proposal; Bill. **o:** committee, council; Parliament, the House □ *His proposals were* **laid before** *a select committee of members.* □ *Here is a draft of the legislation he intends to* **lay before** *Parliament.*

lay by [B1i pass] ⇨ lay aside/by.

layby [nom (B1)] recess at the side of a main road where vehicles may be parked □ *We parked the car in a* **layby** *and had a picnic lunch.*

lay down[1] [B1i pass adj] prescribe, indicate. **O:** rule, principle; what action to follow □ *We had to* **lay down** *the general direction in which the answer lay.* MFM □ *Follow the procedure* **laid down** *in our booklet.*

lay down[2] [B1i pass] store in a cellar to mature. **O:** claret, burgundy, port □ *Father* **laid down** *a few good bottles before the war.*

lay down[3] [B1i pass] (begin to) build. **O:** ship, vessel; railway □ *Several of the new-type tankers are being* **laid down** *on Tyneside.*

lay down one's arms [B1iii] (military) surrender. **S:** army, regiment; troops □ *The majority of their soldiers simply* **laid down their arms**. B

lay down the law [B1i] (informal) talk with authority (real or assumed) about sth; hold forth (q v). **S:** (so-called) expert, specialist; critic, rebel. **A:** on pollution, on law and order; about cricket, about football □ *It is not right for the soldier to* **lay down the law** *in political matters.* MFM □ *A man in the saloon bar was* **laying the law down** *on fly fishing.*

lay down one's life (for) [B1iii B3 emph rel] (formal) sacrifice one's life (on behalf of). **S:** patriot, fanatic. **o:** country, king; cause, convictions □ *Young men flocked to the recruiting offices, willing to fight, and if need be to* **lay down their lives**. □ *This is a cause* **for** *which he is prepared to* **lay down his life**.

lay down to [B3 pass] convert into pasture (i e for cattle or sheep). **O:** field, big acreage. **o:** ⚠

grass, clover □ *The farmer decided to* ***lay*** *ten acres* ***down to*** *grass.*

lay the blame (for) (on) [B2 pass emph rel] regard as the one responsible (for an error, evil etc); put the blame (on) (q v). **o:** (***for***) loss, setback; mistake, blunder; decision, plan, policy; (***on***) wife; partner; government □ *There was no one person* ***on*** *whom all* ***the blame*** *could be* ***laid****; responsibility for the failure was evenly shared.* □ *The Churches are united and vocal in opposing apartheid and* ***laying the blame for*** *the recent tragic events where it belongs.* SC

lay in [B1i pass adj] provide oneself with a stock of; stock up (with) (for) (q v). **O:** winter fuel, food supplies, provisions □ *They* ***laid in*** *a good supply of coal in the summer, when prices were low.*

lay into [A2 pass] (informal) attack violently (with one's fists or verbally), lam into (q v) □ *I saw Jones* ***lay into*** *a man twice his size.*

lay hold of [B2 pass(o)] seize, grasp; obtain, acquire. **S:** porter, gaoler; speculator, developer. **o:** bundle, case; prisoner, victim; property, land □ *We* ***laid hold of*** *the rope and pulled lustily.* BB □ *Michael was firmly* ***laid hold of*** *by the collar and shaken till his teeth rattled.* □ *He was lucky to* ***lay hold of*** *a block of shares before the price went up.*

lay off[1] [A1 A2] (informal) stop doing sth harmful etc; stop doing sth unpleasant, irritating etc. **o:** it; drink, cigarettes, drugs; all-night parties; bullying, shouting □ *So long as I can make good my threat they'll* ***lay off*** *the use of force.* TBC □ *I was told that I should* ***lay off*** *these visits.* MFM □ *A prefect came in. 'There's far too much noise in here', he said. '****Lay off****, or I'll put the lot of you in detention.'*

lay off[2] [A2] (informal) stop troubling, molesting, sb, his property etc, leave sb or sth alone. **o:** family, girlfriend; chickens, sheep □ *'Take it easy, then he'll soon* ***lay off*** *you.'* AITC □ *'****Lay off*** *my tie and give me a kiss.'* SC

lay off[3] [B1i nom pass adj] dismiss from work (usu temporarily, while trade is bad). **S:** firm, management. **O:** worker, staff □ *The factory was* ***laying*** *people* ***off****.* AITC □ *He is a skilled worker* ***laid off*** *from his job in a Belfast shipyard.* T □ *Other* ***lay-offs*** *have been at the Austin works* (cf *Other men have been* ***laid off*** *at* etc). OBS

lay off[4] [A1 nom] aim to one side of a target to allow for wind or movement of the target. **S:** gunner, hunter □ *I bowled over four rabbits by* ***laying off*** *enough ahead of them.* RFW □ *It came straight at us. One couldn't miss: no* ***lay-off*** *at all sideways.* RFW

lay on[1] [B1i pass adj] supply, provide, furnish. **S:** landlord, council; firm, host. **O:** water, electricity, gas; car, transport; driver, escort □ *We had electricity* ***laid on****.* H □ *'I'll* ***lay on*** *a car tomorrow and have you run down to London.'* DIL

lay on[2] [B1i pass adj] organize, make arrangements for. **O:** concert, display, outing □ *It's his birthday. That's why I* ***laid on*** *a party.* QA □ *The reception at the Town Hall was well* ***laid on****.*

lay on[3] [B1i pass adj] (informal) exaggerate, make sth seem bigger, worse etc, than it really is. **O:** it; pathos, sorrow, regret; pleasure, gratitude. **A:** (rather, a bit) thick, with a trowel □ *The only sin he ever had to confess was the sin of Pride: and he* ***laid*** *it* ***on*** *thick.* US □ *That's how we like our humour —* ***laid on*** *with a trowel.* OBS □ *He was* ***laying*** *it* ***on*** *a bit, with all this talk of wanting to help the poor.*

lay the blame (on) [B2 pass emph rel] ⇨ lay the blame (for) (on).

lay one's cards on the table [B2 pass] (informal) declare openly one's assets, intentions etc; put one's cards on the table (q v) □ *How did Alec know that Harold wouldn't take advantage of these confidences? How foolish to* ***lay*** *all* ***his cards on*** *the table!* PW □ *The negotiators felt they had nothing to lose by* ***laying*** *some of* ***their cards on the table*** *at the beginning of the talks.*

lay emphasis/stress on [B2 pass emph rel] treat as specially important, give special attention to. **S:** government, council; planner, developer; report, survey. **adj:** much, little; great, special, particular. **o:** wishes, consent (of the governed); cost, profit; lack, absence (of amenities) □ *The White Paper* ***lays*** *special* ***emphasis on*** *the development of nursery schools in the 'educational priority' areas.* □ *Too little* ***stress*** *has been* ***laid on*** *preserving an existing sense of community in the planning of new estates.*

lay eyes on [B2] perceive, sight sb; set eyes on (q v). **A:** never; first, next. **o:** his etc wife, brother; prisoner, accused man □ *'Do you deny having spoken to the witness on the day in question?' 'Yes, sir, I do. In fact I've never* ***laid eyes on*** *him before.'* □ *'He's a hooligan. When I first* ***laid eyes on*** *him, I thought he's certainly not the type for my Cairy. Too damn rough.'* YAA

lay one's hands on[1] [B2 rel] take, obtain (in order to use as one's property); get one's hands on[1] (q v). **o:** extra capital, spare cash; office space, building land □ *His primary concern was to catch, kill, stuff and describe as many kinds of beasts as he could* ***lay his hands on****.* HAH □ *The Russians were removing and sending eastwards all machinery and stocks* ***on*** *which they could* ***lay their hands****.* MFM

lay one's hands on[2] [B2 rel] find sth one is looking for. **o:** book, paper, reference □ *I arranged these shelves, and I could* ***lay my hands on*** *anything.* EM □ *I was never able to* ***lay my hands*** *quickly and accurately* ***on*** *quotations.* SML

lay one's hands on[3] [B2] (informal) seize, arrest, in order to punish or hurt; get one's hands on[2] (q v). **o:** criminal, mischief-maker □ *The place is swarming with policemen just waiting to* ***lay their hands on*** *some of us.* CSWB □ *Heaven help that boy if I ever* ***lay my hands on*** *him.*

never/not lay a finger/hand on [B2] (informal) not harm or molest at all. **o:** child; wife, daughter □ *We have firm discipline, but the staff* ***never lay a finger on*** *the boys.* □ *'Nobody has* ***laid a hand on*** *me. Yet.'* TOH

lay out[1] [B1i pass] spend. **O:** cash, a lot (of money) □ *He had to* ***lay out*** *all he had on the airline tickets.* ILIH □ *Last year there was a considerable* ***outlay*** (= expenditure) *on school uniforms.* □ nom form is **outlay**.

lay out[2] [B1i pass] (informal) make unconscious by striking; knock out[1] (q v) □ *I* ***laid*** *one of them* ***out*** *and I had another one round the throat.* TC □ *If you slap my face — by God, I'll* ***lay*** *you* ***out****!* LBA

lay out[3] [B1i nom pass adj] arrange parts in relation to each other and to the whole in a convenient and pleasing manner. **S:** editor, printer; architect, landscape-gardener, planner; shopkeeper, window-dresser. **O:** front page, contents; suburb, street, park; wares, stock, goods □ *The empty ashtrays were **laid out** neatly on the little tables* TC □ *Oswald took an unskilled job doing photo **lay-out** work.* OBS □ *We admired the neatly **laid-out** flower-beds.*

lay out[4] [B1i pass adj] spread out ready for use. **S:** valet, chambermaid. **O:** clean underclothes, evening dress, shoes □ *The drill is to **lay out** the clothes that he'll be wearing in the evening.* RFW □ *His dinner jacket was already **laid out** on the bed.*

lay out[5] [B1i pass adj] prepare for burial. **S:** undertaker, family. **O:** deceased, corpse □ *The family passed one by one through the small parlour where the father's body was **laid out**.*

lay claim to[1] [B2 pass(o) emph rel] (legal) maintain that in law one is entitled to sth. **S:** relative, associate. **o:** estate, fortune; title (of nobility) □ *There was little doubt that Gray's will would be contested: his former wife would surely **lay claim to** the large sum he had left to his housekeeper.* □ *'If the property was ever **laid claim to** by a surviving relative you might have difficulty proving your title to it.'*

lay claim to[2] [B2 emph rel] maintain, assert, that one knows, understands etc, sth. **o:** knowledge, understanding, expertise; familiarity (with); being a connoisseur, having some competence □ *'Of course, I **lay** no **claim to** expert knowledge of the stock market, but it strikes me that these companies have an excellent record of growth.'* □ *'Have I ever **laid claim to** being a good mother?'* TOH

lay to rest[1] [B2 pass] (formal) bury. **O:** body, remains □ *In a simple ceremony, the victims of the disaster were **laid to rest** in the village churchyard.*

lay to rest[2] [B2 pass] finally remove or allay. **S:** explanation; statement, communiqué. **O:** story, tale; rumour, scandal; doubt, uncertainty □ *An official statement **laid to rest** the remaining fears about possible redundancies in the industry.* □ *'That affair was finally **laid to rest** years ago. Don't go and resurrect it again.'*

lay up[1] [B1i pass adj] store, stock. **O:** foodstuffs, fodder, provisions, fuel □ *We'll need to **lay up** a good supply of feed if this winter's going to be like the last.*

lay up[2] [B1i pass adj] take off the road; put out of commission. **O:** motor vehicle, ship □ *He's had to **lay** his **car up**: he can't afford the insurance premiums.* □ *For thirteen years the flying boat has been **laid up** on the Isle of Wight.* BBCTV

lay up[3] [B1i pass adj] make inactive, confine to one's bed. **S:** chronic illness, serious injury, broken limb □ *A bout of malaria had **laid** me **up** for a few weeks.* □ *Furthermore, he was **laid up** with a bad knee.* MFM

lay up for oneself [B3] ensure by one's present conduct, or neglect, that trouble will follow. **O:** trouble, difficulty, problems, bother □ *You are **laying up for yourselves** the most appalling economic problems.* BBCTV □ *He's **laid up** no end of trouble **for himself**.*

lead astray [B1i pass] tempt sb to do wrong. **S:** criminal, corrupt man. **O:** young people, innocent girls □ *He **led** many girls **astray** with his easy, superficial charm.* ⇨ go astray.

lead in [A1 nom] introduce, open (one's remarks, speech, performance etc) □ *The chairman **led in** with some flattering references to the visiting speaker's record in the industry.* □ *There was a long **lead-in** on the piano; then the strings and woodwind came in together.*

lead off [A1] begin, start □ *Ned, the General Editor, **led off** with a general survey of the objectives to be aimed at.* CON □ *The town band **led off** by playing the National Anthem.*

lead on [B1ii pass] (informal) (try to) persuade sb to do, believe etc, sth by making false promises. **S:** advertiser, salesman; poster, brochure; playboy □ *Travel brochures do **lead** you **on** with their promises of five-star treatment in luxury hotels.* □ *'Haven't you noticed the predatory gleam in his eye? He's probably **leading** you **on**.'*

lead up the garden path [B2 pass] (informal) mislead, deceive. **S:** rogue, imposter; politician, expert. **O:** police; electorate; consumer □ *We have been **led up the garden path** before with such promises* (i e of magnificent cricket). SC □ *Someone posing as a television reporter has been **leading** us **up the garden path**.*

lead up to [A3 pass] occur, one after the other, before sth; prepare, have as a consequence. **S:** incident, occurrence; discussion, argument. **o:** conflict, war; agreement □ *The report describes the negotiations which **led up to** the settlement.* □ *Every event in Oswald's life **led up to** that moment.* OBS

leaf through [A2 pass] read in a brief, inattentive way, turning the pages quickly; flick through (q v). **o:** book, magazine □ *I can't claim that I've read the article at all carefully: I've just **leafed through** it.* □ *Mary **leafed** idly **through** some old magazines as she waited for her taxi to arrive.*

leak out [A1] (informal) become known despite efforts to keep it secret. **S:** news, information; secret □ *The news **leaked out**.* WDM □ *Stringent precautions were taken to prevent the details of the wedding **leaking out**.*

lean on [A2 pass] (criminal slang) make sb act as one wishes by the threat or use of force, by blackmail etc. **S:** gangster, racketeer. **o:** bookmaker, small-time crook □ *'It's a protection racket. All his thugs need to do is **lean on** the small shopkeepers and they'll cough up* (q v) *soon enough.'* □ *'Joe's soft. He'll co-operate. He just needs **leaning on** a little.'*

lean on/upon [A2 pass emph rel] choose especially for support; (as likely to prove reliable). **o:** parent, teacher; counsel, advice □ *In a crisis, the headmaster tends to **lean** overmuch **on** senior members of staff.* □ *It was reassuring to have someone **upon** whom he could **lean** for a while.*

lean out/out of [A1 A2] (of the head and shoulders) be thrust out of, project from. **o:** window, porthole □ *The window of our hotel bedroom was not well placed. If you **leant** a long way **out** you could just glimpse a small triangle of blue sea.* □ *Passengers are requested not to **lean out of** the carriage windows.*

lean over [A1 A2 pass] slant, incline, one's

head and shoulders (so that one can more easily hear sb, see what he is doing etc) ▫ *Peter* ***leant*** (or: ***leaned***) ***over*** *and whispered something in Felicity's ear.* ▫ *I do so hate people* ***leaning over*** *me when I am trying to read the paper.*

lean over backwards [A1] (informal) try one's hardest to help, understand, co-operate etc. **S:** assessor, examiner; court, jury ▫ *The examiners* ***leant over backwards*** *to find some saving merit in the candidate's literature paper.* ▫ *People were* ***leaning over backwards*** *to be pleasant to this odious little man.* ▫ followed by *-ing* form or *to*-inf.

lean-to [nom (A1)] small outbuilding partly supported by the walls of a larger one ▫ *He stores his garden tools in a small* ***lean-to***. ▫ *There was a* ***lean-to*** *greenhouse against the brick wall of the garage.*

leap at [A2 pass adj] seize eagerly, jump at (q v). **o:** ⚠ the opportunity, the chance, the offer ▫ *If he offered me a small part in his new production, I'd* ***leap at*** *the chance.* ▫ *The opportunity was laid before him and eagerly* ***leaped at***.

learn from [A2] by studying one's mistakes etc, and those of others, ensure that they are not repeated. **o:** experience(s); mistake, blunder ▫ *'At my age,' Milly said, 'one has to* ***learn from*** *other people's experiences.'* OMIH ▫ (Helen has just learnt that her teenage daughter is pregnant) *'Oh, Jo, you're only a kid. Why don't you* ***learn from*** *my mistakes?'* TOH

learn off (by heart/rote) [B1i pass B3 pass] memorize perfectly. **O:** part, lines (in a play); formula, theorem ▫ ***'Learn*** *these words* ***off by heart.'*** BFA ▫ *'Can you* ***learn off*** *the part by the end of the week?'*

lease back [B1i nom pass] (commerce) sell the freehold (or sometimes the long lease) of a property and obtain in return temporary possession on a lease (i e in order to free the capital tied up in the property). **O:** property, office block ▫ *The Managing Director suggested to the Board that the best way of obtaining capital for the expansion programme would be to sell the company's headquarters to a finance house and then* ***lease*** *them* ***back***. ▫ *In recent years there has been a spate of* ***leaseback*** *deals as more and more firms cash in on the value of the properties they own.*

leave about/around [B1ii pass B2 pass] fail to put away carefully and tidily. **O:** clothes; book, paper. **o:** place; room, house ▫ *'Don't* ***leave*** *your toy soldiers* ***around*** *the house: I walk on them all the time.'* ▫ *The nurse took pride in her work: she wouldn't have* ***left*** *things* ***about***. DC

leave aside [B1i pass] not consider, not calculate. **O:** matter, question; cost, inconvenience ▫ ***Leaving*** *the matter of cost* ***aside***, *we still have to find time off from other work.* ▫ *I don't see how you can* ***leave aside*** *his neglect of his family.*

leave it at that [B2 pass] (informal) say or do nothing further, let matters rest there ▫ *The insurers weren't prepared to compensate him for loss of earnings, so he had to* ***leave it at that***. ▫ *'It isn't like that,' I said wearily. 'I did love you, but I can't now. Let's* ***leave it at that***.*'* RATT

leave behind[1] [B1i pass] fail or forget to bring or take; abandon (as in a retreat). **O:** raincoat, umbrella; wallet, key; wounded, dying ▫ *'It's a fine day: you can* ***leave*** *your mac* ***behind!'*** ▫ *In their withdrawal, much of the heavy equipment had to be* ***left behind***.

leave behind[2] [B1i pass B2 pass emph] (formal) leave as a sign or record that sb has acted or sth has occurred. **S:** government, regime; invader; typhoon, storm. **O:** record, legacy; devastation, damage ▫ *Some rulers have* ***left behind*** *no lasting memorial.* ▫ *The cyclone* ***left behind*** *it a trail of destruction.*

leave down [B1ii pass] allow to remain in a lowered position. **O:** handle, lever, switch ▫ *All switches should be* ***left down*** *during the experiment.* ⇨ stay down[1].

leave (for)[1] [A2 B2] depart, to travel to another place. **O:** home; London. **o:** office, work; New York ▫ *We* ***leave for*** *Madrid by the next plane.* ▫ *He* ***left*** *home* ***for*** *the station a few minutes ago.*

leave (for)[2] [B2 pass rel] abandon, in order to follow sb or sth new. **O:** army, law; wife, family. **o:** Church, politics; another woman ▫ *He* ***left*** *business* ***for*** *a new career as a social worker.* ▫ *At forty-five, she'd been* ***left for*** *some new girlfriend.*

leave for dead [B2 pass] abandon sb in the belief that he is dead ▫ *He'd been* ***left for dead*** *on the battlefield, but later on he turned up at the base hospital.*

leave in [B1i pass] allow to remain where it is. **O:** damper, plunger; application, proposal, bid; passage, reference ▫ *The damper was* ***left in*** *overnight to prevent the fire from burning out.* ▫ *I shouldn't* ***leave in*** *that reference to your employer: I should take it out.* ⇨ stay in[2].

leave off[1] [B1i pass] no longer wear or put on. **O:** jumper, winter woollens, overcoat ▫ *Cardigans and sweaters can be* ***left off*** *when the warmer weather comes.*

leave off[2] [A1 A2] stop, cease. **o:** work; arguing, interrupting ▫ *The rain hadn't* ***left off*** (or: *It hadn't* ***left off*** *raining*). PW ▫ *Ned* ***left off*** *talking about the firm.* CON ▫ object is usu the *-ing* form of the a v.

leave on[1] [B1i pass B2 pass emph rel] allow to stay in position. **O:** lid, cover; kettle, pot; cloth. **o:** saucepan; gas, stove; table ▫ *'Where did you* ***leave*** *the keys?' '****On*** *the desk'.* ▫ *'****Leave*** *the cloth* ***on***. *I want to lay the table for supper.'* ⇨ stay on[1].

leave on[2] [B1i pass adj] allow to stay alight or keep burning. **O:** light, lamp; fire; television ▫ *The electric fire had been* ***left on*** *overnight.* ▫ *'You can* ***leave*** *the hall-light* ***on***.*'* ⇨ stay on[2].

leave out [B1ii pass] leave in the open (e g through forgetfulness). **O:** toy, pram; washing ▫ *If you* ***leave*** *your bicycle* ***out*** *at night, you'll soon have trouble with rust.* ⇨ stay out[2].

leave out/out of [B1i pass adj B2 pass] not include or mention (in); omit (from) (q v). **o:** guest-list; party, group; arrangements ▫ *My name can be* ***left out of*** *this: I don't want to be involved.* ▫ *When you wrote the invitations, did you* ***leave*** *anyone* ***out?*** ▫ *His was one of the* ***left-out*** *names.*

leave out of [B2 pass] not consider, not take account of (q v). **O:** (possible) reaction, consequences; what sb will do. **o:** ⚠ account, consideration; the reckoning ▫ *Make sure that nothing is* ***left out of*** *account.* ▫ *He had* ***left out of*** *consideration the resentment of his former col-*

leagues.

leave over[1] [B1i pass adj] leave as a remainder (the best part having been consumed). **O:** oddment, scrap; bone, crumb □ *The force must have all it needed. Other armies would do their best with what was* **left over**. MFM □ *The older children had the lion's share; the small ones had to make do with* **left-overs**. □ left-overs (always pl) is the adj form used as a noun. ⇨ be over[2].

leave over[2] [B1ii pass adj] reserve for attention at a later date. **S:** council, committee. **O:** business; item, question □ *I regret that these matters will have to be* **left over** *until our next meeting.* ⇨ lie over.

leave to [B2 pass emph rel] leave sb in charge of sth. **O:** arrangements, organization, staffing; everything, things, it (all) □ *'Now just you* **leave** *it* **to** *me.'* □ *The catering can be* **left to** *mother.* □ *It is* **left to** *the new Parliament to make a European electoral law.* OBS □ note construction with *it* in the last example.

leave to chance [B2 pass] not take too much care over the details of a task, so allowing sth to happen by chance. **O:** issue, outcome, result; something, (not) anything □ *Nelson prepared against every contingency, but recognized that something must be* **left to chance**. MFM □ *In the experiment, we* **leave** *nothing* **to chance***: weights are checked twice over.*

leave to it [B2 pass] (informal) let sb proceed with a task, without help or interference □ *He gave the new crew their instructions and then went off,* **leaving** *them* **to it**. □ *I suppose we could have gone out and* **left** *her* **to it**, *but neither Jimmy nor I would have enjoyed the party if we had.* WI

leave to his own devices [B2 pass] allow sb to solve a difficult problem unaided; leave sb alone (to do as he wishes). **O:** staff; assistant, trainee; pupil, guest □ *He* **left** *us* **to our own devices***; he didn't mind how the work was done as long as it was finished when we'd promised.* RATT □ *Unmarried officers posted to the War Office were* **left to their own devices** *to find accommodation.* MFM □ *Altogether I was not in the most jovial of moods, and Jacquie had long since* **left me to my own devices**. DF ⇨ next entry.

leave to his own resources [B2 pass] leave sb to solve a difficult problem unaided. **O:** employee, student, soldier □ **Left** *entirely* **to his own resources** *I doubt whether Jeffries would last a week in this job.* □ *Don't organize the children's play all the time:* **leave** *them* **to their own resources** *once in a while.* ⇨ previous entry.

leave up [B1ii pass] allow to remain in a raised position. **O:** picture, notice; flag, curtain; switch, lever □ *The decorations can be* **left up** *for another day.* ⇨ stay up[3].

leave up to [B3 pass] let some important decision, choice etc be made by sb. **O:** organization, distribution; it... how to divide the money, it... whether to go or stay □ *'How shall I raise the money?' 'I don't know. I'll* **leave** *that entirely* **up to** *you.'* ⇨ be up to[3].

leave word (with) [B2 pass emph rel] leave a message (with sb) □ *I was looking for the secretary* **with** *whom John had* **left word** *of his departure.* □ **Word** *was* **left with** *a neighbour that we would be back soon.*

lecture at [A2 pass adj] (informal) address in a formal, pompous manner (esp to scold or reproach). **o:** wife, child; employee □ *His poor wife is always being* **lectured at** *on her spending habits.* □ *'He doesn't talk to me, he* **lectures at** *me!'*

lecture (to) [A2 pass emph rel] give a formal talk to a group of students □ *He* **lectures to** *undergraduates on the Elizabethan theatre.*

leech onto [A2 pass] (informal) attach oneself firmly and persistently (like a leech) to sb. **S:** child, pupil; neurotic. **o:** teacher; doctor □ *The girl's really* **leeched onto** *Philip. He can't shake her off. I suppose it goes to show you can take too close an interest in problem children.*

leer (at) [A2 pass rel] look at in a crude, unpleasant way suggesting desire or ill-will. **o:** pretty woman; victim □ *She was tired of feeling* **leered at** *all the time.* □ *A face* **leered at** *him through a grating in the door.*

lend (to)[1] [B2 pass emph rel] let sb have the temporary use of sth; let sb borrow money at interest. **S:** friend, neighbour; bank, building society. **O:** lawn-mower, bicycle; money □ *I don't mind* **lending** *these papers* **to** *you* (or: **lending** *you these papers*)*, but do be sure to return them.* □ *Building societies attract deposits at one rate of interest and* **lend** *the funds thus accumulated* **to** *house buyers at a higher rate of interest.*

lend (to)[2] [B2 pass emph rel] (formal) assist, support, materially or morally. **S:** government; industry; scholar, scientist. **O:** his etc backing, support; authority, name; prestige; oneself. **o:** venture, scheme, project; speculation, swindle; theory □ *There are proposals to develop new industries away from the existing major centres.* **To** *this kind of trend the government will* **lend** *its full support.* □ *He refused to* **lend** *himself or his organization* **to** *such blatant profiteering.*

lend (to)[3] [B2 pass emph rel] (formal) make (more) significant, believable etc. **S:** event, development. **O:** meaning, significance; credibility, genuineness. **o:** view, interpretation, analysis □ *It is these considerations that* **lend** *particular significance* **to** *the annual congress opening in Perth today.* SC □ *What* **lends** *some plausibility* **to** *this historian's view of events* (or: **lends** *his view some plausibility*) *is that trade links with Britain were well developed at this time.*

lend itself to[1] [B2 emph rel] (formal) be suitable for, be well suited to. **S:** garden; room, attic; subject, theme, topic. **o:** solitary walks; conversion, extension; treatment □ *The cellars* **lend themselves to** *conversion into a workroom and store.* □ *The play* **lent itself** *admirably* **to** *presentation on an open stage.*

lend itself to[2] [B2 emph rel] (formal) because of inherent weaknesses etc, be liable or subject to ill use. **S:** democracy, free enterprise, universal education. **o:** abuse, misuse □ *Any system of taxation* **lends itself to** *manipulation by clever or unscrupulous men.* □ *The various malpractices* **to** *which the election arrangements could* **lend themselves** *were pointed out by neutral observers.*

let down[1] [B1i pass adj] lower, drop, let fall. **O:** bucket; rope, ladder; dress; hair; standard □ *The hem of your dress needs to be* **let down** *an inch.*

□ *Her parents had maintained their standards of value. She had **let** hers **down**.* PW

let down[2] [B1i nom pass adj] (informal) fail sb who believes that one is reliable, disappoint his hopes. **O:** friend, brother, wife □ *'You won't go to gaol. I fixed it up. I didn't **let** you **down**.'* AITC □ *He's been **let down** so much* (or: *had so many **let-downs**) in the past that he trusts no one.*

let down[3] [B1i pass adj] release the air from, deflate. **O:** tyre, balloon □ *'Some joker has **let down** the back tyres of my car!'* ⇨ let out/out of.

let down[4] [B1i nom pass adj] (informal) make sb's spirits sink, depress them □ *He felt at once relieved and **let down**.* PW □ *A feeling of **let-down** had followed years of boisterous vigour.* OBS □ *It was a tremendous **let-down** to be told we had failed.* □ usu passive and nom.

let down[5] [A1] lose height (so as to land). **S:** aircraft; pilot □ *Eleven hours out of Paris, the Air France plane **let down** into Rio de Janeiro.* T

let one's (back) hair down [B1ii] (informal) relax and enjoy oneself (e g at a party) □ *'Go on,' he said, '**let your hair down** — go gay.'* TT □ *This is the night that the Cricket Club really **lets its back hair down**.*

let the side down [B1ii] (informal) disappoint or fail one's friends, colleagues etc; behave in a way regarded as unacceptable by one's family, social class etc □ *He will always do his part — he never **let the side down**.* MFM □ *If you take a job as a window-cleaner, you're just **letting the side down**.* HD

let in [B1i pass] allow sth to enter or penetrate. **S:** window; roof, wall; leather, shoe. **O:** light; cold, rain; water □ *My kitchen wall **lets in** the damp.* □ *Air is **let in** through vents at the side of the car.*

let the clutch in [B1i pass] (motoring) release the clutch pedal of a motor vehicle, so connecting the engine and transmission □ *Pop **let in the clutch** and began to steer a course of slow elegance.* DBM

let in for [B3 pass] (informal) make sb assume responsibility for. **O:** firm, colleague; oneself. **o:** (extra) work, expense, trouble □ *'I hope you realize what you're **letting** yourself **in for**!'* □ *He's been **let in for** a lot of extra duty.*

let in/into [B1i pass B2 pass rel] allow sb to enter, admit. **O:** guest, spectator; oneself. **o:** club, theatre; house □ *He **let** himself **into** the study with a spare key.* □ *If they try to buy tickets don't **let** them **in**.* ⇨ come in/into, get in/into[1].

let in on [B3 pass emph rel] (informal) allow sb to know about or take part in sth that was previously hidden from him. **O:** stranger, new partner. **o:** scheme, enterprise; the act □ *That would have involved **letting** a third person **in on** the act: my mother.* CON □ *He was **let in on** the arrangements without our consent.* ⇨ be/bring/come/get in on.

let into [B2 pass emph rel] set in a hollowed-out place in sth. **O:** cupboard, lighting; tube, pipe. **o:** wall, ceiling; body (of patient) □ *The figure stood on a shelf **let into** the study wall.* □ *A tube is **let into** his leg to carry off fluid.*

let into a/the secret [B2 pass] (informal) share one's secret with sb □ *Don't **let** Peter **into the secret**: it won't remain a secret for long.* □ *I'll **let** you **into a secret**: I'm being sent abroad.*

let off[1] [B1i pass B2 pass] allow to disembark or alight (from). **S:** skipper, crew; conductor. **O:** passenger. **o:** boat, plane; bus □ *I asked the captain to **let** me **off** at the next port of call.* □ *The guard won't **let** anyone **off** the train between stations.* ⇨ get off[1], put off[6].

let off[2] [B1i pass] (informal) release without punishing. **S:** court, judge. **O:** prisoner, accused □ *He was charged with petty larceny, but the court **let** him **off**.* □ *'I'll be lenient this time, but you won't get **let off** again.'* ⇨ get off[6], let off with.

let off[3] [B1i pass B2 pass] (informal) allow sb not to do some unpleasant task. **O:** prisoner, defaulter. **o:** chore, fatigue; peeling potatoes □ *'Is he on guard duty tonight?' 'No, he's been **let off**.'* □ *'What's he been **let off** doing this time?'*

let off[4] [B1i pass] fire; explode. **S:** soldier; engineer. **O:** rifle, gun; charge, explosives □ *A brass cannon was **let off** dangerously with real gunpowder.* SD □ *Small boys **let** a few fireworks **off**.* ⇨ go off[5], set off[1].

let off[5] [A1 B1i pass] (taboo) break wind, fart. **O:** ⚠ a fart; one □ *If I **let off** in the parlour she'd have me shipped off to the hospital to be disembowelled.* JFTR

let off[6] [B1iii pass] allow others to rent a building in portions. **O:** flat; room, office □ *The three floors of this large Victorian house were **let off** as separate flats.* □ *The agent isn't keen to **let** the offices **off** in penny packets; he wants to find one tenant for the whole building.*

let off the hook [B2 pass] (informal) free sb from an unpleasant task, an embarrassing situation etc □ *I thought I'd have to talk to old Mrs Jenks all evening, until Penny came along and **let** me **off the hook**.* □ *'Don't think, because you've been **let off the hook** once, that you can always slide out of the dirty jobs!'*

let off steam [B1iii] (informal) release tension, feelings that have been restrained etc; blow off steam (q v) □ *Still fuming with frustration, I sat down and applied for the vacancy, rather as a means of **letting off steam**.* SD □ *I **let off steam** by mimicking and muttering silently.* OBS

let off with [B3 pass] give to sb a lighter sentence than the law allows. **S:** court, judge. **O:** offender, prisoner. **o:** a caution, a fine, six months (in prison) □ *My pal Mike got **let off with** probation because it was his first offence.* LLDR ⇨ get off[6], let off[2].

let on (about) [A1 A3 pass B1iii] (informal) reveal, disclose; give away[3] (q v). **O:** that he knew, that we are friends. **o:** plan, scheme; how we did it □ [A1] *It doesn't do to **let on** too much.* MFM □ [A3] *We didn't **let on about** how rich we were.* LLDR □ [B1] *Do not **let on** that I have given away his secret ingredient.* ARG

let sb get on with it [A3] ⇨ entry after get on with.

let out[1] [B1iii pass] utter. **O:** cry, yell, scream □ *He **let out** a spontaneous cry.* NM □ *She **let out** a yelp of pain.*

let out[2] [B1i pass] reveal, disclose. **O:** news, information; secret; (it)... that John was leaving □ *Who **let out** the details of the reshuffle in the department? It was confidential news.* □ *Keep this to yourselves — don't **let** it **out** to the press.* ⇨ be out[7], come out[7], get out[1].

let out[3] [B1i nom pass] (informal) release sb from an unpleasant obligation □ *He appeared just in time to propose the vote of thanks, which* ***let*** *me* ***out*** *nicely* (cf *gave me a welcome* ***let-out***).

let out[4] [B1i pass adj] make wider or looser. **S:** tailor. **O:** dress, trousers □ *I've got so fat that I'll have to* ***let*** *the waistband* ***out*** *several inches.*

let out[5] [B1i pass adj] make available for hire; hire out (q v). **O:** horse, donkey; boat □ *Farm machinery is* ***let out*** *by the week.*

let out/out of [B1i pass B2 pass] allow to leave, release (from). **O:** gas, water; animal, prisoner. **o:** tyre, tank; cage, gaol □ *'Who* ***let*** *the air* ***out of*** *my tyres?'* □ *'****Let*** *me* ***out of*** *here!* ***Let*** *me* ***out****!'* ⇨ be out[2], come out[2].

let the cat out of the bag [B2 pass] (informal) reveal, disclose, a secret through carelessness □ *'I wanted Mother's present to be a surprise; now you've gone and* ***let the cat out of the bag****!'*

let through [B1i pass B2 pass] allow to pass. **O:** goods; visitor; car; errors, defective goods. **o:** customs; immigration; control-point □ *Most of their party were* ***let through*** *customs without an examination.* □ *A number of mistakes in the proofs were* ***let through****.*

let up [A1 nom] (informal) relax (one's alertness or efforts); ease, slacken. **S:** worker, team; (bad) weather, storm; pressure, volume (of work) □ *Petrie's mind never* ***let up*** *for an instant.* SD □ *We will never stop, or* ***let up*** (cf *there will be no* ***let-up****), till Tunis has been captured.* MFM

level down [A1 B1i pass adj] lower, reduce, the high standards of a few to the level of the many (esp to achieve equality). **S:** government, firm, school. **O:** wage, benefit; mark, standard □ *Does the country as a whole benefit from* ***levelling down*** *the rewards and privileges of the rich?* □ *Some believe that the extension of higher education has* ***levelled down*** *university standards.* ⇨ level up.

level off [A1 B1i pass adj] make level sth which is uneven, rough etc. **O:** board; surface, top □ *Rub with sandpaper to get a smooth,* ***levelled-off*** *surface.*

level off/out [A1] move horizontally (after climbing); remain steady (after a rise). **S:** aircraft; price, wage □ *We climbed steeply after take-off, and* ***levelled out*** *at 25 000 feet.* □ *After the recent big increases, wages are now tending to* ***level off****.*

level up [A1 B1i pass adj] raise the standards of the poorest, least able etc, to the level of the few (esp to promote equality). **O:** standard, mark; salary, benefit □ *To achieve excellence with equality, we must* ***level up*** *the modern schools —not level down the grammar schools.* ⇨ level down.

lick into shape [B2 pass] (informal) raise to the proper standard of discipline, efficiency, organization etc. **S:** instructor; coach; sergeant; organizer. **O:** trainee; runner, footballer; recruit; project, scheme □ *They're not a very promising bunch but we'll soon* ***lick*** *them* ***into shape****.* □ *If Ann and Yvette will make another brew of coffee, perhaps we can do something towards* ***licking*** *this business* ***into shape****.* TBC

lick off [B1i pass adj B2 pass] remove by licking. **O:** jam, sugar □ *The chocolate coating had all been* ***licked off*** *the cream buns.*

lick up [B1i pass] take up into the mouth by licking. **S:** cat, dog. **O:** milk, water □ *'Don't mop up the spilt milk; the cat will* ***lick it up****.'*

lie ahead/ahead of/before [A1 emph A2 emph rel] (formal) be going to confront or happen to one in the future. **S:** difficulty; hazard, danger; death □ *He thought of the disease that might* ***lie ahead of*** *him.* NM □ ***Before*** *him* ***lay*** *the prospect of continuing hardship.*

lie at anchor/its moorings [A2 emph] (nautical) be anchored or moored (usu offshore). **S:** ship, boat □ *The fleet* ***lay at anchor*** *half a mile off the headland.*

lie at death's door [A2] be at the point of death, be close to dying □ *For weeks father* ***lay at death's door****.*

lie at sb's door [A2 emph rel] is borne by. **S:** ⚠ the blame, the responsibility, the guilt □ *The responsibility for the present crisis* ***lies*** *squarely* ***at the door of*** *the government.* □ ***At whose door*** *does the blame* ***lie****?* ⇨ lay at sb's door.

lie back [A1] move back so that one is supported on a bed, or by the back of a chair □ *She had* ***lain back*** *in the easy chair.* DC □ *She was so weak and exhausted she had to* ***lie back****.* DC

lie before [A1 emph A2 emph rel] ⇨ lie ahead/ahead of/before.

lie behind[1] [A1 emph A2 emph] (formal) have happened to one, be in the past. **S:** achievement, exploit; hardship, suffering □ *And* ***behind*** *them* ***lay*** *bitter memories of what midwinter was like.* B □ ***Behind lay*** *nothing but defeat; ahead lay the certainty of victory.*

lie behind[2] [A2] be the explanation for, be the cause of. **S:** ambition, desire for power; necessity, expediency; incompetence, mismanagement. **o:** move, event; retreat; failure, price-rise □ *What* ***lies behind*** *the recent Cabinet changes is the need to get rid of certain unpopular Ministers.* □ *I'm not sure what* ***lay behind*** *his remarks, but it wasn't good will.* ⇨ be behind[3].

lie down [A1 nom] be, move into, a horizontal position on a bed (to rest or sleep) □ *'You're going to* ***lie down*** *for a bit.'* PE □ *He was* ***lying down*** *on the sofa when we came in.* □ *She likes to have a* ***lie-down*** *after lunch.*

lie down on the job [A3] (informal) neglect to do a job properly, not put all one's effort into a job □ *These men are hardly* ***lying down on the job*** *— they're working all hours to finish it.*

lie down (under) [A1 A3] (informal) accept without protest or resistance. **o:** tyranny, oppression; abuse, insult □ *We have no intention of* ***lying down under*** *these accusations* (cf *We have no intention of taking these accusations* ***lying down***). □ note the equivalent patterns: lie down under sth = *take sth* lying down.

lie in[1] [A1 nom] (informal) stay in bed after the normal time for getting up □ *They let us* ***lie in****, but I got up for breakfast.* RFW □ *Sally will be bound to sleep late and give us a nice Sunday* ***lie-in****.* WI

lie in[2] [A1] stay in bed to await the birth of a child. **S:** woman, expectant mother □ *Normally, a woman will* ***lie in*** *a few hours before the birth of her child* (cf *Her* ***lying-in*** *(period) begins a few hours before the birth*).

lie in ruins [A2] be completely destroyed. **S:** city; factory, house; policy, programme □ *Much of the industrial North of France* ***lay in ruins****.* □ *By this time, the Government's policy for the* *statutory control of incomes **lay in** complete **ruins**.*

lie in store (for) [A2] be going to happen (to sb) □ *No one knew what **lay in store for** us round the next bend in the river.*

lie over [A1] await attention at a later date. **S:** business, matter, item □ *There are several important matters **lying over** from last week.* ⇨ leave over².

lie to [A1] (nautical) have halted, be anchored; halt, anchor. **S:** ship; cruiser, launch, dinghy □ *The yacht was **lying to** in about six fathoms.* □ *They reached the other side at about midnight and **lay to** about four miles off shore.* RFW

lie up¹ [A1] go into hiding (e g to escape pursuers, to attack enemies). **S:** bandit; soldier, guerrilla □ *Nobody saw him all through the war. I think he **lay up** in the mountains.* RM □ *The partisans **lay up** by day, and by night sallied out to attack convoys.*

lie up² [A1] stay in bed to rest during an illness. **S:** patient, sick child □ *John must **lie up** for a few weeks until his leg mends.*

lift down (from) [B1i pass B3 pass emph rel] move (usu with the hands) from a higher to a lower level. **O:** crate, box, drum, bale. **o:** shelf, lorry □ *'That looks a heavy case: let me **lift** it **down** for you.'*

lift off [A1 nom] (space technology) rise vertically from the launching-pad. **S:** rocket, missile □ *Twenty minutes to go before the rocket **lifts off**.* □ *The space vehicle made a perfect **lift-off**.*

lift up¹ [B1i nom pass] raise (physically). **O:** child; arm, leg; box □ *'If you **lift** me **up** (or: give me a **lift(-)up**) I can just get a leg over the wall.'* □ *'**Lift** your foot **up**: you're standing on the hem of my dress.'*

lift up² [B1i pass adj] stimulate or inspire spiritually. **S:** preacher, statesman; sermon, address; presence. **O:** congregation, audience □ *His very presence **lifted** us all **up*** (cf *We all found his very presence **uplifting***). □ *Talking to her gave me a tremendous **uplift**.* □ nom form is uplift.

light on/upon [A2 pass emph rel] discover by chance, happen to find. **o:** treasure, manuscript; (secret) passage, tunnel □ *He had **lighted*** (or: ***lit***) ***upon** a new method of refining the metal.* □ *He showed us a rare edition **on** which he'd **lighted** in Rome.*

light out/out of [A1 A2] (informal) leave (esp hurriedly, and to escape from sb). **S:** bandit, raider; police, cavalry □ *The gang didn't waste any time over farewells. Just packed their bags and **lit out of** town.*

light up¹ [A1 B1i pass adj] apply a flame to tobacco (in order to smoke). **O:** cigar, pipe □ *He settled comfortably in an armchair and **lit up**.* □ *Pop had **lit up** one of his best Havanas.* BFA

light up² [B1i pass adj] illuminate, provide with lights. **S:** council; trader. **O:** building; shop □ *Public buildings were **lit up** for the Victory celebrations.* □ *Not many shop windows were **lit up** last Christmas because of the Government restrictions on the use of electricity.*

light up³ [A1] switch on the head-(or side-)lights of a motor-vehicle at dusk; switch on the street lighting. **S:** motorist, lorry-driver □ *It's seven o'clock, and still one or two cars haven't **lit up**.* □ *At this time of the year, official **lighting-up** time is six-thirty.*

light up⁴ [A1 B1i pass adj] become, make, bright or flushed with emotion. **S:** [A1] **O:** [B1] face, eyes. **S:** [B1] anger, passion □ *His eyes were still able to **light up** under the influence of curiosity or greed.* RM □ *His face was **lit up** with sudden excitement.*

lit up [pass adj (B1)] ⇨ entry after listen in (to).

light upon [A2 pass emph rel] ⇨ light on/upon.

liken to [B2 pass emph rel] (formal) say that one thing is like another □ *Someone **likened** his voice **to** the croaking of a bull-frog.* □ *The nervous system can be **likened to** a telephone exchange.*

limber up¹ [A1 nom] (sport) make one's muscles loose through exercise (e g before a race); loosen up¹ (q v). **S:** athlete, footballer □ *He always **limbered up*** (or: *had a **limber-up***) *before his afternoon match.*

limber up² [A1 B1i pass adj] (military) fasten a gun to a limber (ammunition box on wheels). **S:** battery, troop, gunner. **O:** 6-pounder □ *He ordered the troop to **limber up** and move out.* □ *A brigade of field artillery was waiting, **limbered up**.* SD

limit (to) [B2 pass emph rel] keep numbers or quantity at a low level; restrict (to)¹ (q v). **O:** number; entry, participant; application. **o:** a few; 100, a dozen □ *The numbers granted passes have had to be **limited to** ten for security reasons.*

line-out [nom (A1)] (Rugby football) parallel lines of forwards formed at right angles to the touch line, to receive a ball which has just gone out of play □ *The wing three-quarter throws the ball in at **line-outs**.*

line up¹ [A1 B1i pass adj] (cause to) form into lines or ranks. **S:** [A1] **O:** [B1] soldiers; vehicles. **S:** [B1] officer; steward, attendant □ *The sergeant **lined** his platoon **up** on the parade-square.* □ *The lorries were **lined up**, ready to move off.*

line up² [A1] form a queue, to get transport, buy food etc; queue (up) (for) (q v). **S:** passenger, shopper, spectator □ *Fans began **lining up** early in the morning to buy their cup-tie tickets.*

line up³ [B1i nom pass] (informal) assemble, bring together; organize, arrange. **S:** impresario, producer. **O:** performer, artist; item, number, turn □ *They've **lined up** some excellent entertainers for our show.* □ *There was a good **line-up** of musical and comedy acts on television tonight.*

line up (against) [B1i pass B3 pass] place in line for execution by a firing-squad. **S:** invader, soldier. **O:** hostage, prisoner. **o:** wall, barn □ *They pulled out the first five civilians, **lined** them **up** on the lawn, and shot them.* SD □ *Old men and women were **lined up against** a wall and shot.*

line up alongside/with [A3] (informal) become the ally of, associate with¹ (q v). **S:** deputy, delegate, member. **o:** majority, minority; extremist, moderate □ *He's **lining up alongside** the most reactionary people in his party.* □ *They're not the sort of folk I'd expect a confessed liberal to **line up with**.*

line up behind [A3 rel B3 pass rel] (informal) (cause to) follow sb, to take him as their leader. **S:** [A3] **O:** [B3] group, party; conference, meeting; rebel, dissident. **S:** [B3] leader, chairman □

The majority of rank-and-file members are happy to ***line up behind*** *the new leadership.* □ *Have you noticed the kind of support he has got* ***lined up behind*** *him?*

line up in one's sights [B3 pass] point a rifle etc directly at a target. **S:** marksman, hunter. **O:** target, prey □ *For a moment, he had the deer* ***lined up in his sights*** *— then it vanished.*

line up with [A3] ⇨ line up alongside/with.

linger on [A1] stay, remain (after others have gone); stick, persist (in the mind etc). **S:** guest, visitor; smell, scent; tradition □ *Harold* ***lingered on and on****, and even treated himself to a third half-pint.* PW □ *Today these practices are no more, but their memory* ***lingers on****.*

linger (over) [A2 pass emph rel] take more time than is normal or desirable (esp when completing a task or describing events). **o:** meal; ceremony, speech; (gory, unsavoury) details, facts □ *'You've* ***lingered*** *long enough* ***over*** *breakfast. Eat up. We're leaving in five minutes.'* □ *'Don't you feel that newspaper accounts of these disasters tend to* ***linger*** *rather nastily* ***over*** *the details?'*

link together/with [B1i pass B2 pass rel] say, suggest, that two persons or events are connected. **S:** newspaper; report, rumour. **O:** name, celebrity, public figure. **o:** girl, pop star; creation, institution (of sth) □ *At various times the popular press have* ***linked*** *this amiable but idle young man* ***with*** *models, starlets and even the occasional heiress.* □ *We should not conclude that her death was necessarily* ***linked with*** *the reported outbreak of smallpox* (cf *that the two events were necessarily* ***linked together***). □ *More than anything, perhaps, Aneurin Bevan is* ***linked*** *in the public mind* ***with*** *the establishment of the National Health Service* (cf *the name and the event are* ***linked together*** *in the public mind*).

link up (with) [A1 nom A3 emph rel B1i nom pass adj B3 pass emph rel] (cause to) form one whole (with), connect (with); join up (with) (q v). **S:** [A1 A3] **O:** [B1 B3] town, village; force, army; business, firm. **o:** another, a neighbour, (chief) competitor □ [A3] *12 Army Group would* ***link up with*** *the Dragoon force* (cf [A1] *The two units would* ***link up****; or: do a* ***link-up***). MFM [B1] ***Link up*** *the islands as far as possible.* SC □ [A1 B1] *This American leader announces a first major* ***link-up*** *of supermarkets in this country.* T □ [B3] *Arrangements were well advanced for* ***linking up*** *this newly opened length* (of motorway) ***with*** *the Lancaster by-pass.* T

listen in (to) [A1 nom A3 pass rel] listen to a radio programme or performer. **o:** talk, play; music □ *He likes to* ***listen in*** (or: *have a* ***listen-in***) *late at night.* □ *I just don't find such programmes worth* ***listening in to****.*

lit up [pass adj (B1)] (informal) (be) merry on alcohol, (be) drunk □ (popular song) *We're going to get* ***lit up*** *when the lights go on in London.* □ *A couple of* ***lit-up*** *revellers went past.* ⇨ also light up[1, 2, 3, 4].

litter about/around [B1i pass B2 pass emph] scatter here and there untidily. **O:** book, paper, clothes □ *He just* ***litters*** *his stuff* ***around*** *— no wonder he can never find anything!* □ *Papers were* ***littered about*** *the study in the utmost confusion.*

live above/beyond one's income/means [A2] spend more than one can afford □ *With the cost of everything rising as it is, we find we're constantly* ***living beyond our means****.*

live apart (from) [A1 A3] (of a married couple) live in separate houses, though without obtaining a divorce □ *After leading a cat and dog existence for about five years Philip and Mary decided it might be better if they* ***lived apart****.* □ *Since Jane's been* ***living apart from*** *her husband* (cf *Since they've been* ***living apart***)*, she finds she can manage for most things perfectly well on her own.*

live down [B1i pass] behave in such a way that one's failings etc are forgotten. **O:** one's past; shame, disgrace; a lot, too much □ *He seems determined to prove that his fateful decision in 1956, which gave him so much to* ***live down****, was an honourable one.* □ *We can never hope to* ***live down*** *these shortcomings.* FFE

live for [A2] have as one's main reason for living. **o:** work, sport, one's family □ *He* ***lives for*** *the day when he can retire and grow roses.* □ *They* ***live for*** *nothing but pleasure.*

live (in) [A2 emph rel] have as one's home or dwelling. **o:** flat, digs; caravan, tent; area, district □ *He* ***lives in*** *an expensive part of town.* □ *The houses* ***in*** *which they are forced to* ***live*** *are rat-infested.*

live in [A1] reside in the building etc where one works. **S:** cook, housemaid, chauffeur, caretaker □ *They've had a cook-housekeeper* ***living in*** *for the last six months.* □ *'What's against us having a servant to* ***live in****? There's room for one.'* PW ⇨ live out.

lived in [pass adj (A2)] (informal) have the comfortable, settled look of a home □ *Their place really looks* ***lived in*** *— nothing expensive or modish just to impress people.* □ *It takes time for a house to acquire that* ***lived-in*** *appearance.*

live in hope (of) [A2] look optimistically for an improvement. **o:** (*of*) early election; radical change, some reform; fresh trial □ *The prisoner* ***lives in hope of*** *an early release.* □ *The exam results haven't come through yet, but I* ***live in hope****.*

live in the past [A2] behave as though events, values etc have not changed from what they were earlier. **S:** (retired) politician, army officer, official; philosopher, theorist, artist □ *'Time passes. You are* ***living in the past****, Taylor.'* MM □ *How could I* ***live in the past*** *when you and Bernie are so good to me?* HAA

live in the present [A2] accept, order one's life according to, conditions now □ *He seems incapable of* ***living in the present****: always hankering after a glorious past which in fact existed only for a privileged few.* □ *He's a robust, down-to-earth fellow,* ***living*** *very much* ***in the present****.*

live in sin [A2] (usu jocular) live together without being married □ *These days the Government are making it so much cheaper for people to* ***live in sin****.* DIL □ *Do I detect a growing, satanic glint in her eyes? Do you think it's* ***living in sin*** *with me that does it?* LBA

live off the country [A2] support oneself by obtaining food from the country one is staying in or passing through. **S:** traveller, explorer; soldier, partisan □ *Why take so much tinned food* *with you to France? Buy local fruit and vegetables — **live off the country**.* □ *In their zone the Russian armies were **living off the country**, which they had systematically sacked.* MFM

live off/on [A2 rel] have as one's diet, survive by eating. **o:** raw fish, root vegetable □ *Do these people **live off** human flesh?* LWK □ *Some of the cattlemen of Africa **live** entirely **off** the produce of their herds.* □ *'I can't **live on** air!'*

live off/on the fat of the land [A2] (informal) enjoy the best food, drink, lodging, entertainment etc □ *The poor people starved, while a few **lived off the fat of the land**.* □ *He could get out of London, **living on the fat of the land** in George's house.* PE

live on[1] [A1] survive, endure. **S:** family; work, reputation, name □ *He will die, but his fame will **live on** after him.*

live on[2] [A2 emph rel] feed and support oneself on a stated amount, or from a certain source. **o:** income, salary; profit, rent; charity, hand-outs □ *I can't **live on** that wage.* □ *Do you know how little they manage to **live on**?*

live on one's own [A2] live alone. **S:** old person; widow, invalid □ *I don't think I'd have the courage to **live on my own** again.* LBA □ ***Living on your own** is certainly better than life with a man you can't stand.*

live out [A1] reside away from the place where one works (though it might be possible to live in (q v)). **S:** servant, student, soldier □ *All married students are allowed to **live out** after the first two terms in College.* BM □ *Workers who don't use company accommodation are given a **living-out** allowance.*

live out one's days/life [B1iii] spend one's whole life. **A:** in one's native town, as an ordinary worker, in humble circumstances □ *These two old men had **lived out their lives** as industrial labourers.* CON □ *No doubt he would **live out his days** in the same Welsh valley.*

live out of [A2] not have a settled life, or fixed address, so that one's belongings are kept in suitcases. **o:** suitcase, trunk, box □ *That's all we do, **live out of** a travelling-bag.* TOH

live out of cans/tins [A2] (informal) subsist on tinned foods — which are easily prepared — usu because other foods are hard to buy or cook. **S:** camper, explorer; (front-line) soldier; homeless person; vagrant □ *Their home was a shack on a piece of waste land, and they **lived out of tins**.* □ *I shall be glad when we get a proper cooker and can stop **living out of tins**.*

live over again [B1ii pass] relive; experience again in the imagination. **O:** life, career; experience; it all □ *If I had to **live** my life **over again** I wouldn't choose to spend it in a cold climate.* □ *Hearing these old soldiers talk Father was **living over again** his experiences as a young recruit.*

live through [A2] experience and survive. **o:** famine, war, revolution □ *He had **lived through** the worst years of the depression.*

live to a/the ripe old age (of) [A2] (informal) live to be very old □ *Grandfather **lived to the ripe old age of** ninety.* □ *I can't see him **living to a ripe old age**: he smokes too much.*

live together/with [A1 A2 emph rel] live in the same house, as husband and wife, but without being married □ *This isn't the provinces, you know. I'm **living with** Celia, as you can see* (or: *We are **living together*** etc.) CON □ *The girl **with** whom he had been **living** for two years suddenly packed her bags and left.*

live under [A2] experience the rule of. **S:** citizen, subject. **o:** system, regime, government; king, emperor, dictator □ *The country is now **living under** a military dictatorship.* □ *He's **lived under** three monarchs, and survived them all.*

live under the same roof (as) [A2] reside in the same house (as sb) □ *We had **lived** on terms of close friendship **under the same roof**. It was not an easy parting.* AH

live it up [B1ii] (informal) lead an easy, pleasure-filled life □ *He was in London, **living it up** on his winnings from the football pools.* □ *The advertisements invite one to **live it up** in the rich playgrounds of Jamaica.*

live up to [A3 pass adj] reach a standard that one has set oneself, or that is expected of one. **S:** he etc; machine, device. **o:** standard, claim (made for sth), expectations, position (in life) □ *We cannot **live up to** our moral pretensions.* NM □ *The beast had **lived up to** his reputation for stupidity.* DF □ *He is not satisfied by a too easily **lived-up-to** standard of achievement.*

live with[1] [A2 rel] (learn to) accept. **o:** fact, situation; disability, disease; shortcomings, failings □ *You've lost all your money; now you must learn to **live with** the situation.* □ *You must **live with** the fact that you're no longer as active as you were.* □ usu after *have to, must.*

live with[2] [A2 emph rel] ⇨ live together/with.

liven up [A1 B1i pass adj] (informal) become or make more cheerful or lively. **S:** [A1] **O:** [B1] things; proceedings, party, evening; guest; audience, class □ *How he likes to **liven** things **up**!* DC □ *Another drive and the evening would have **livened up** no end.* ILIH

load down (with) [B1i pass adj B3 pass rel] place many heavy burdens on sb or sth; overburden sb, making him strained, depressed etc. **O:** lorry, cart; staff, colleague; wife. **o:** parcel, box; care, worry, responsibility □ *The van moved off, **loaded down** to the springs **with** every stick of furniture they possessed.* □ *He seemed **loaded down with** the burdens of office.*

load up (with) [A1 A3 rel B1i pass adj B3 pass rel] fill to the top, place a full load upon. **S:** warehouseman, driver, (freight) handler; removal man, packer. **O:** lorry, truck, goods van, hold (of an aircraft); oneself. **o:** cargo, merchandise; cloth, whisky, butter □ [A1] *'Lower the tailboard and start **loading up**'.* □ [A3 B3] *The Nepalese porters **loaded** (themselves) **up with** food, medical supplies and oxygen equipment.* □ [B1] *The van seems pretty fully **loaded up**.*

load with [B2 pass rel] award honours etc to sb in abundance. **S:** government, country. **O:** public servant, general. **o:** medal, decoration □ ***Loaded with** every honour that his country could bestow, Cathcart would now retire from active political life.*

loaf about/around [A1 A2] (informal) stand or wander idly here and there; hang about/around (q v). **S:** crowd, gang; teenager; vagrant; petty criminal. **o:** the place; town, the streets □ *Parents seem to get particularly irritated when their teenage sons **loaf around** with their hands in their pockets.* □ *As there wasn't anything to do in the* *place but work, they were uncomfortably conspicuous* ***loafing about*** *the streets.* CON

lock away/up (in) [B1i pass B3 pass emph rel] put for safe keeping in a drawer etc, which is then locked. **O:** jewels, silver. **o:** bank; safe, vault, strong-room □ *Take good care to* ***lock away*** *your jewellery before going away on holiday.* □ *'You're old enough to take a drink if you want one. I don't keep it* ***locked up****.'* PFE

lock in[1] [B1ii pass B2 pass emph rel] deliberately put sb in a room etc, and then lock the door from the outside. **O:** prisoner, escapee; wayward child. **o:** cell, guardroom; bedroom □ *The prisoners-of-war were* ***locked in*** *their huts at night to discourage further attempts at escape.*

lock in[2] [B1ii pass B2 pass] prevent sb from leaving a room etc, by mistakenly locking the door, losing the key etc. **O:** him etc; oneself. **o:** flat; cellar, lavatory □ *'Open the door, you idiot! You've* ***locked*** *me* ***in****.'* □ *The cashier spent an uncomfortable night* ***locked in*** *the basement. The porter had turned the key in the door.*

lock out [B1i nom pass adj] (industrial relations) prevent workers from entering a factory (e g in response to a threat of strike action). **S:** owner, employer. **O:** work force, worker □ *Workmen have been* ***locked out*** *until they agree to the employers' terms.* □ *There has been a* ***lock-out*** *at the Liverpool firm of Smith and Weston.* G

lock out/out of[1] [B1ii pass adj B2 pass] deliberately prevent sb from entering a place by locking the door etc on the inside. **S:** parent, warden (of a hostel etc), porter. **O:** child, student. **o:** house, college, hall of residence □ *Father threatened to* ***lock*** *us* ***out*** *if we didn't get back from the party before midnight.* □ *In some university towns, landladies are requested to* ***lock*** *students* ***out*** *if they do not return to their lodgings by a certain time.*

lock out/out of[2] [B1ii pass B2 pass] (accidentally or mistakenly) prevent sb or oneself from entering a place, e g by losing the key. **O:** him etc; oneself. **o:** flat, office, bedroom □ *He'd* ***locked*** *himself* ***out*** *of the house and had to get in by breaking a window.*

lock up [A1 B1i pass adj] make a house etc secure by locking doors and windows. **O:** house, garage; shop, store; car □ *He always* ***locks up*** *last thing at night.* □ ***Lock*** *everything* ***up*** *securely before going away on holiday.*

lock-up[1] [nom (B1)] place where prisoners may be kept temporarily; prison □ *The suspects were kept in the station* ***lock-up*** *overnight.*

lock-up[2] [nom (B1)] shop or garage usu at some distance from the house of the tradesman or owner □ *Her father has a small* ***lock-up*** *tobacconist's in the old part of town.* □ *I pay a pound a week for the rent of a* ***lock-up*** *garage.* □ a lock-up (no second noun) is a lock-up *shop.*

lock up (in)[1] [B1i pass B3 pass emph rel] put in a drawer etc. ⇨ lock away/up (in).

lock up (in)[2] [B1i pass B3 pass emph rel] imprison. **O:** felon, criminal. **o:** gaol, prison; cell, dungeon □ *He was* ***locked up*** *for trying to break the Official Secrets Act.* NM □ *'Where is he now,* ***locked up****?' 'No, he's dead.'* TOH

lock up (in)[3] [B1i pass B3 pass emph rel] enclose, be contained (in). **S:** mechanism; process. **O:** power, energy □ *Our new process* ***locks up*** *pounds of energy* ***in*** *every grain of the breakfast food.* □ *Many ignore the beauty* ***locked up in*** *every minute speck of material around us.* HAH

lock up (in)[4] [B1i pass adj B3 pass rel] invest money in such a way that it cannot easily be changed into cash. **S:** firm, company; investor. **O:** capital; estate, fortune; savings. **o:** business; plant, machinery; shares □ *He had most of the money from the profitable years* ***locked up in*** *the building and expansion programme. For working capital he had to borrow from the bank.*

lodge (against) (with) [B2 pass emph rel] (formal) place a statement (usu of protest or complaint) with the authorities so that they can take action. **S:** committee, action group; citizen, consumer. **O:** complaint, protest; petition. **o:** (***against***) intimidation, brutality; plan; (proposed) extension, development; (***with***) local council; police; solicitor □ *Police action in controlling the crowd was unnecessarily severe. A formal complaint is being* ***lodged with*** *the Chief Constable.* □ *Following the recent explosion, statements have been* ***lodged against*** *the Gas Board accusing them of negligence.*

lodge (in) [A2 emph rel] enter and become stuck fast (in). **S:** bullet, shell fragment. **o:** skull, bone; foot, chest □ *A piece of shrapnel had* ***lodged in*** *the brain, causing damage to the centres controlling movement.*

log up [B1iii pass] travel for a specified time or distance; have the times and distances one travels recorded (i e in a log-book). **S:** pilot, driver. **O:** flight, run, journey; hours, miles □ *The pilot of the crashed aircraft had* ***logged up*** *several hundred hours' flying time on jets.* □ *'I see you've* ***logged up*** *a thousand miles on this truck since the last service. You'd better bring it into the garage straight away.'*

loiter about/around [A1 A2] stand or walk about casually, often with the intention of doing mischief. **o:** the place; door, entrance-way □ *Small boys would* ***loiter about*** *in the entrances of smart hotels, hoping to pick up a few tips.* □ *'Who's that shifty-looking character* ***loitering around*** *outside?'*

loll about/around [A1 A2] sit, lie or lean on sth lazily; lounge about/around (q v). **o:** the place; room, bar □ *There are too many of these people* ***lolling about*** *with nothing to do but plan trouble.* □ *He* ***lolls around*** *in an armchair; she does the washing-up.*

long (for) [A2 pass adj emph rel] desire (to have) sth strongly. **o:** success, money, fame; horse, car; wife, family □ *One* ***longs for*** *the South of France.* NM □ *This* ***longed-for*** *change was slow in coming.* □ *He never found the peace* ***for*** *which he* ***longed****.*

look after [A2 pass adj] be responsible for, care for [2] (q v); take responsibility for paying bills, etc, take care (of) (q v). **S:** nurse, doctor, mother; trustee, agent. **o:** patient, old person, sick child; affairs, finances □ *I thought the nurse was* ***looking after*** *you.* DC □ *He seemed well* ***looked after****.* □ *'I'll* ***look after the*** *bill.'* □ *The Council are* ***looking after*** *that side of the arrangements.* □ *He knows how to* ***look after*** *himself* (= protect himself, his interests).

look ahead (to) [A1 A3 rel] project oneself into the future. **o:** nineteen-eighties, end of the century □ *You can expect to find a multi-storey building on this site. Of course, I'm* ***looking ahead*** *five years when I tell you this.*

look around/round[1] [A1 nom A2] examine what is around one (usu while standing still). **o:** one; room, hall; gathering, assembly □ *You* ***looked round*** *you as you stood waiting for the bus to take you to school* (cf *You had a* ***look round*** *as you stood* etc) TC □ *I* ***looked around*** *the crowded amphitheatre, hoping to find an empty seat.*

look around/round[2] [A1 nom A2] inspect or survey (moving about while doing so), go round [2] (q v); examine goods for sale; survey prospects or possibilities. **o:** office, study; town, castle; store, department □ *'Was there anything you particularly wanted, sir?' 'No, I'm just* ***looking around.****'* □ *'Have you got a job yet?' 'No, I'm having a good* ***look round*** *before committing myself.'* □ nom form not usu hyphenated.

look at[1] [A2 pass] examine sth closely (to establish its genuineness or value). **S:** valuer, expert. **o:** porcelain, silver, painting; collection □ *I can't tell you what it's worth, you must get an expert to* ***look at*** *it.* □ *Ask a museum to* ***look at*** *the figure.*

look at[2] [A2 pass] examine (for possible disease, damage or faults). **S:** doctor, dentist; plumber, mechanic. **o:** shoulder, tooth; tap, engine □ *You must get that gum* ***looked at.*** □ *Get a carpenter to* ***look at*** *those floorboards.*

not look at [A2] not consider or entertain. **o:** proposal, suggestion, offer □ *They would****n't*** *even* ***look at*** *our bid.* □ *I will* ***not look at*** *any price under £3 000.* □ usu after *will/would.*

to look at [A2] (informal) to outward appearances, on the surface □ ***To look at*** *him, you wouldn't think he'd just suffered a major setback.* □ *He's not much* ***to look at.*** □ inf only.

look away [A1] turn one's eyes away, avert one's gaze □ *The sunlight on the water was so dazzling that one had to* ***look away.*** □ *She* ***looked away*** *in embarrassment.*

never/not look back [A1] (informal) make continuous progress. **S:** actor, writer; businessman □ *Once you make an appearance on television you'll* ***never look back.*** □ *The public realized that a new star had arrived, and since then Ann has****n't looked back.*** H

look back (on/upon) [A1 A3 pass emph rel] return (to) in one's thoughts, cast one's mind back (to). **o:** event, time, change □ ***Looking back,*** *I don't remember any inward struggle at all.* CON □ *The people would soon begin to* ***look back*** *with longing* ***on*** *the old regime.* MFM

look beyond [A2 pass rel] place oneself imaginatively in the future. **o:** the present, the here and now, actual circumstances □ *Try to* ***look beyond*** *your present hardships to future happiness.*

look down [A1] lower one's eyes, one's gaze. **S:** child, girl. **A:** shyly, modestly; with a blush □ *Sarah* ***looked down*** *in embarrassment. When would this terribly intense young man stop talking to her?* □ *John* ***looked down*** *to hide his confusion. He hadn't realized the door led to the ladies' changing-room.*

look down one's nose (at) [A2] (informal) regard sb or sth in a superior, condescending way. **o:** (***at***) poorer people, the 'lower orders'; speech, remarks, habits (of others) □ *The English neighbours would say 'Mrs Middleton's quite mad', and* ***look down their noses.*** ASA □ *'Don't* ***look down your nose at*** *a fat woman, Flo.'* RM

look down on/upon [A3 pass adj] (informal) despise, consider as inferior. **o:** one's father; working people; the poor, the illiterate □ *Parents scrape and save and sacrifice themselves, and then their children* ***look down on*** *them.* PW □ *The really unskilled class are* ***looked down on*** *by everyone.*

look (for) [A2 pass adj emph rel] seek, try to find. **o:** new job, house by the sea, business; lost cat, handkerchief □ *'What are you* ***looking for?****' 'A little sympathy.'* □ *The chance which he had* ***looked for*** *was now freely offered to him.* □ *Traditional Japan needs* ***looking for.*** BBCTV

look for trouble [A2] (informal) behave in a way which suggests that one seeks unpleasantness, a violent response etc □ *You could see from his face that he was* ***looking for trouble.*** □ *There's no sense coming into a new place just* ***looking for trouble.***

look forward to [A3 pass adj] anticipate with pleasure. **o:** holiday, meeting, evening out; going abroad, returning home □ *She had been* ***looking forward to*** *leaving the hospital wards for a holiday in the Orkneys.* WI □ *The third baby, Brigit had almost* ***looked forward to*** *with a timorous pleasure.* DC □ *His retirement is very much* ***looked forward to*** *by the office staff.*

look-in [nom (A1)] (informal) a chance to take part or be involved □ *I wanted to talk to her, but with all those fellows around I didn't get a* ***look-in.*** □ *John would like to race, but the club won't give him a* ***look-in.*** □ usu in the patterns *get, give sb, have, a* look in.

(not) look in the eye/face [B2] (informal) (not) look at sb fearlessly and without shame. **O:** boss, father; questioner, challenger □ *'The sure sign of a liar — you can****'t look*** *me* ***in the eye,*** *can you?'* E □ *When I had signed the contract, I felt I could hardly* ***look*** *Hugo* ***in the face*** *any more.* UTN □ often with (*not*) *be able to/dare to.*

(not) look a gift-horse in the mouth [B2] (informal) (not) look too critically at sth offered to one as a free gift □ *It was one of mother's maxims* ***never*** *to* ***look a gift-horse in the mouth.*** HAHA □ *'Why did you let Nora stay on after I'd gone?' 'Why* ***look a gift-horse in the mouth****?'* AITC

look in (on) [A1 A3 pass] (informal) call (on) briefly, pay a short visit (to) □ *We* ***looked in*** *at Burlington House.* AH □ *I ought to visit the Mediterranean countries where British troops were stationed, and also* ***look in on*** *Trans-Jordan.* MFM □ *I suppose the doctor will* ***look in*** *when he gets a chance?* HOM ⇨ next entry.

look into[1] [A2] (informal) make a brief call or visit to. **o:** office, surgery; mother's (house); club □ *I must* ***look into*** *the garage on the way home to book a service for the car.* ⇨ previous entry.

look into[2] [A2 pass] investigate, inquire into (q v). **o:** case, matter, question □ *Police are* ***looking into*** *the disappearance of a quantity of uncut gems.* □ *Perhaps you wouldn't mind* ***looking into*** *it for me?* TT

look on [A1] be a spectator □ *Most people aren't good enough to take part in first-class matches; they have to be content to* ***look on*** (or: *to be*

lookers-on, *to be* ***onlookers***). □ *I was merely* ***looking on***. AH

look on/upon (as) [A2 pass] regard, consider (as). **o:** (***as***) an enemy of the state, popular hero □ *I* ***look upon*** *him* ***as*** *the betrayer of his country in its darkest hour.* □ *He is* ***looked upon as*** *something of an authority on rare books.* ⇨ next entry.

look on/upon (with) [A2 pass] regard, consider (with). **o:** (***with***) disfavour, mistrust, suspicion □ *He has always been* ***looked upon with*** *disapproval by his wife's mother.* □ *'Tell me, how do people* ***look upon*** *him in general?'* ⇨ previous entry.

look onto/out on [A2 A3] give or command a view of. **S:** bedroom, dining-room. **o:** alley, wall, garden □ *The long low windows* ***looked out on*** *a driveway at the side of the house.* OBS

look out[1] [A1] take care, beware; mind out (q v), watch out (q v) □ *'****Look out****, Peter, that step's not safe!'* □ *'Tell them to* ***look out****, the ceiling's threatening to fall in.'* □ usu in imper sentences.

look out[2] [B1i pass] search for and produce. **O:** old clothes, books, photographs, stamps □ *I must* ***look out*** *some bits and pieces for the church jumble sale.* □ *Perhaps he'll* ***look out*** *one of his old girl friends.* LBA

look-out[1] [nom (A1)] sentry, one who keeps watch; place from which a watch is kept □ ***Look-outs*** *were posted at night in our forward positions.* □ *They manned a* ***look-out*** *post in the front line.* ⇨ look out (for).

look-out[2] [nom (A1)] (informal) prospect, outlook. **adj:** poor, grim; bright □ *It's a bleak* ***look-out*** *for anyone hoping for quick profits.* □ *It's not a very bright* ***look-out*** *if you're thinking of a career in the coal industry.*

(be) sb's look-out [nom (A1)] (informal) (be) sb's (own) concern or responsibility □ ***It's your*** *own* ***look-out*** *whether you pass or fail.* □ *If he can't be bothered to write, and misses his opportunities,* ***that's his look-out****.*

look out (for) [A1 nom A3 pass] watch or search carefully (for); watch out (for) (q v). **o:** new car, second-hand radio; talent, capable player; criminal, fugitive □ *The policemen are* ***looking out for*** *burglars.* CON □ *Jeremy will soon be old enough to go to boarding school. We must be* ***looking out for*** *one.* PW □ *Keep a sharp* ***look-out for*** *Peter.* □ *Mother is always on the* ***look-out for*** *bargains.*

look out/out of [A1 A2] direct one's gaze through. **o:** window, door, arch □ *He drew back the curtains and* ***looked out of*** *the window.*

look out on [A2 A3] ⇨ look onto/out on.

look over[1] [A2 nom pass] survey, inspect, do a tour of inspection of; go over[2] (q v). **o:** house, garden; estate, farm; factory □ *We were allowed to* ***look over*** *their new plant near Coventry.* □ *The surveyor will come back later to do a full inspection. He just had time to give the place a quick* ***look-over*** *before lunch.*

look over[2] [B1i pass] examine closely, scrutinize; go over[1] (q v), look through[3] (q v). **O:** document, letter; claim, appeal; arm, heart □ *Her green eyes* ***looked*** *them* ***over*** *indifferently from under her dusty lashes.* ARG □ *The Medical Board gave the applicants a thorough* ***looking-over****.*

look round[1] [A1 nom A2] examine what is round one. ⇨ look around/round[1].

look round[2] [A1 nom A2] inspect or survey. ⇨ look around/round[2].

look round[3] [A1 A2] observe cautiously around an obstacle. **o:** screen, door, pillar, newspaper □ *The door was half open and I* ***looked*** *carefully* ***round*** *it.* □ *With a periscope you can* ***look round*** *corners without being seen.*

look round[4] [A1] turn to look at sth behind one □ *I made a rustling sound and the lady in front* ***looked round*** *angrily.* □ *'Don't* ***look round*** *now but there's a police car following us.'*

look through[1] [A1 A2 pass emph rel] direct one's gaze through. **o:** window, telescope □ *He* ***looked through*** *the living-room window at a rain-soaked garden.* □ *The skylight* ***through*** *which he was now* ***looking*** *was directly above the staircase.*

look through[2] [A2 nom pass] survey or scan (often briefly or summarily). **o:** book, paper; stamp-collection, notes □ *He gave his notes a quick* ***look-through*** *before giving his lecture.* □ *He* ***looks through*** *several newspapers before breakfast* (or: *He gives them a* ***look-through***).

look through[3] [B1ii pass] inspect carefully, part by part, go over[1] (q v), look over[2] (q v). **o:** application, proposal, recommendation; document, letter □ *I've given your prospectus a very careful* ***looking-through****.* □ *'Have you read the man's references?' 'I haven't finished* ***looking*** *them* ***through*** *yet.'*

look through[4] [A2] not see sb or sth that is clearly visible; deliberately ignore sb whom one can plainly see. **o:** friend, acquaintance □ *'You must be as blind as a bat. I was standing ten yards away, and you* ***looked*** *straight* ***through*** *me.'* □ *'In that icily superior way of his, he* ***looked*** *right* ***through*** *us.'*

look to [A2 pass rel] choose especially (for support, help etc). **o:** government, private industry; personal enterprise, individual courage. **A:** to help us, for assistance □ *Let this be a warning against* ***looking to*** *personal diplomacy to settle issues.* SC □ *Don't* ***look to*** *him for help!* □ *He's not the sort of man* ***to*** *whom one* ***looks*** *for reassurance.*

look to one's laurels [A2] beware of losing one's reputation. **S:** athlete, sportsman; industrialist, inventor □ *One or two younger scientists are challenging him in this field, so he must* ***look to his laurels****.*

look towards [A2] face. **S:** house, entrance. **o:** river, golf course, open country □ *The front of the house* ***looks towards*** *the open sea.*

look up[1] [A1] raise one's eyes □ *He didn't* ***look up*** *from his newspaper when I entered the room.*

look up[2] [A1] (informal) improve, get better. **S:** trade, business; turnover, figures; things □ *Prospects for the small builder are* ***looking up****.* □ *Things should start to* ***look up*** *for the motor trade this Spring.*

look up[3] [B1i pass] try to find (usu in a work of reference); seek information about. **O:** detail, account; quotation, expression; train, bus, plane; him etc □ *He comes back with an enormous dictionary, sits down and* ***looks up*** *the word.* KLT □ *All I can do is* ***look up*** *the figures and find that we were the richest country in the world.* CON □ *I* ***looked*** *him* ***up*** *in 'Who's Who'.* □ *Evidently he'd* ***looked up*** *the train; it wasn't all a matter* *of wild impulse.* CON

look up[4] [B1i pass] (informal) search for sb's house so as to visit him. **O:** old friend, acquaintance □ *I've promised that the next time I go to London I'll* ***look*** *him* ***up****.* □ *Mine was not the kind of life where you 'ran into old friends', or were* ***'looked up'*** *by them.* THH

look up and down [B1ii pass] (informal) examine in an admiring, sexually calculating, or contemptuous, way □ *Standing with her hands on her hips, she* ***looked*** *George* ***up and down*** *in mock admiration.* PE □ *I was staring out of the driver's seat, taking in every word she said. She* ***looked*** *me* ***up and down****.* THH

look up to [A3 pass adj] admire, regard, with respect. **o:** leader, teacher, father □ *He was still a leading member of the local organization, much* ***looked up to*** *for his maritime war experience.* RFW □ *People you can* ***look up to****, with no frills, no snob-stuff, are pretty rare.* PW

look upon [A2 pass] ⇨ look on/upon (as), look on/upon (with).

loom ahead [A1 emph] await one menacingly in the future. **S:** adult responsibilities, matrimony, military service □ *I had just attained the glory of the sixth form at school, with scholarships* ***looming ahead****.* SD □ *The Second Front in Europe, the invasion across the Channel, was* ***looming ahead****.* MFM

loom up [A1] appear suddenly and menacingly. **S:** ship; rock, iceberg □ *Another rock* ***loomed up*** *and they only missed it by a fraction.* PW

loosen up[1] [A1 B1i pass] make oneself or sb more physically relaxed or supple; limber up[1] (q v) □ *He* ***loosened up*** *with a few exercises before the big match.* □ *I got to* ***loosen*** *myself* ***up****, you see what I mean? I could have got done in* (= killed) *down there.* TC

loosen up[2] [A1 B1i pass] (cause to) relax, become less stiff, formal or solemn □ *When I told her that I was his brother from Australia she* ***loosened up*** *and invited me into the parlour.* RFW □ *'Perhaps I'm beginning to* ***loosen up****,' Pyle said. 'Your influence. I guess you're good for me, Thomas.'* QA

lop off [B1i pass adj] cut off cleanly with a bill-hook or sword. **O:** branch; arm □ *The ground was littered with* ***lopped-off*** *branches.* □ *His arm was* ***lopped off*** *at the elbow.*

lord it over [B2] (informal) behave in a superior way towards. **S:** butler; matron; prefect. **o:** lesser servant; nurse; junior boy □ *She'd be Queen and* ***lord it over*** *all the other servants, and live in luxury.* RFW ⇨ queen it over.

(not) lose any sleep about/over [B2 emph rel] (informal) (not) be greatly worried or concerned over sth. **o:** news, announcement; proposal, suggestion; change, occurrence; him/his being appointed □ *There's* ***no*** *need to* ***lose any sleep over*** *the aircraft. I think it was probably trying to land.* RFW □ *'I should have thought you might wish it hadn't happened?' 'Oh, I have****n't*** ***lost any sleep about*** *it.* NM

lose by [A2 B2 pass] suffer financially or personally through. **O:** nothing; not… anything, not… much □ *Why not join us? I promise you that you won't* ***lose by*** *it* (i e it will be to your advantage). □ *How much do they stand to* ***lose by*** *this merger?* □ *I suppose there's nothing to be* ***lost by*** *sending a small patrol to the other side of the island.* □ usu in neg/interr sentences.

lose (in) [B2 pass emph rel] no longer trust, have faith in etc. **O:** trust, confidence, faith, interest. **o:** leader, management; enterprise □ *Customers are* ***losing*** *confidence* ***in*** *our ability to meet delivery dates.* □ *All belief has now been* ***lost in*** *their promises.*

lose (oneself in [B2 pass emph rel] become absorbed in. **o:** game, sport; story, book □ *I soon* ***lost myself in*** *the rediscovered pleasures of the game.* □ *Mick was* ***lost in*** *the intricacies of a new electric motor.*

lost in [pass (B2)] ⇨ entry after lose contact/touch (with).

lose (all) trace of [B2 pass emph rel] have no clues as to the whereabouts of. **S:** family; police; search-party; secretary. **o:** (missing) child; escapee, suspect; climber, explorer; record-card, letter □ ***All trace*** *has been* ***lost of*** *the climbing party missing since last weekend.*

lose count (of) [B2 pass(o) emph rel] be faced with such large numbers of people etc, that one cannot count them all. **o:** (number of) times, occasions (sth has happened); (his) cars, yachts; wives, mistresses □ *I've* ***lost count of*** *the times he's bored us with that particular story.*

lose sight of[1] [B2 pass(o) emph rel] no longer be able to see. **o:** land, ship, quarry □ *We* ***lost sight of*** *the enemy in some thick scrub about half a mile to our front.* □ *The fugitive was* ***lost sight of*** *in the crowd.*

lose sight of[2] [B2 pass(o) emph rel] forget about; not keep fresh in one's mind. **o:** objective, aim, goal; advantage, merit □ *The reasons for which they went to war were soon* ***lost sight of****.* □ *My mind could take such decisions without* ***losing sight of*** *the main question.* QA

lose track of [B2 pass(o) rel] no longer be able to trace or follow sb or sth whose progress one is interested in. **o:** him etc; movements, progress; aircraft, ship □ *I can follow his career up to 1958, then quite abruptly I* ***lose track of*** *him.* □ *His plane was* ***lost track of*** *about two hours out from London Airport.*

lose the use of [B2] be unable, through illness or injury, to use. **o:** hand, arm, leg □ *The doctors did what they could, but he* ***lost the use of*** *both legs.*

lose on [A2 emph rel B2 pass emph rel] lose money as a result of some activity. **O:** a fortune, a packet, one's shirt; investments, savings. **o:** gamble, venture; deal, transaction □ *He* ***lost*** *heavily* ***on*** *the deal.* □ *It's a project* ***on*** *which we stand to* ***lose*** *a large sum of money.* □ *You can* ***lose*** *a packet* ***on*** *horse racing whether you study the horses or not.*

lost on [pass (B2)] ⇨ second entry after lose contact/touch (with).

lose one's hold on/over [B2] no longer control; not master or dominate any longer. **S:** teacher, leader; scholar, craftsman. **o:** class, (political) party; subject-matter, material □ *Some parents hate to relinquish control: the more they* ***lose their hold on*** *their children, the more they seek to retain it by unfair means.*

lose out (to) [A1 A3 emph rel] (informal) be overcome and replaced (by). **S:** live theatre, music hall; tradition, family; small trade, private initiative. **o:** television; the new morality; big combines □ *In face of competition from the mul-*

tiples the small neighbourhood shop is bound to ***lose out****.* □ *The hard way, the grind, the moral lesson, duty, all were* ***losing out to*** *the easy way, money, charm, a well-known name.* ASA

lose one's hold over [B2] ⇨ lose one's hold on/over.

(not) lose any sleep over [B2 emph rel] ⇨ (not) lose any sleep about/over.

lose ground (to) [B2 pass emph rel] retreat, give way, in face of pressure from. **S:** trade, industry; product, commodity; army. **o:** (overseas) pressure, competition; invader □ *We have been* ***losing ground*** *fast* ***to*** *foreign producers and we must do something to stop the rot.* T □ ***To*** *popular developments in music and the visual arts 'tradition' as represented by academies has everywhere* ***lost ground****.*

lose contact/touch (with) [B2 pass emph rel] no longer be closely connected (with), or in a close relationship (with). **S:** ship, aircraft; actor, writer; politician; teacher, parent. **o:** shore, base; audience, public; the masses, his origins; class, child □ *Radio* ***contact with*** *the lightship has been* ***lost*** *but will soon be restored.* □ *No one whom Dave has taught seems ever to* ***lose touch with*** *him.* UTN

lost in [pass (B2)] (be) filled with, (be) overwhelmed with. **o:** ⚠ thought; admiration, wonder □ *We were* ***lost in*** *admiration for his achievements.* □ passive with *be, feel, seem.*

lost on [pass (B2)] (be) wasted on sb, (be) unnoticed by sb. **S:** remark, comment, observation; charm, attentiveness; finesse, subtlety (of manner) □ *'It's like having a television set you never look at.' The illustration was* ***lost on*** *Sir George, who had no television set.* DBM □ *This impressive display of western air power was not* ***lost on*** *the Russians.* MFM

lost without [pass (B2)] (informal) (be) unable to live happily, work efficiently etc, without sth. **o:** daily paper, sporting news, television; tobacco, whisky; conversation, companionship □ *Anna's life worked to schedule; like a nun, she would have been* ***lost without*** *her watch.* UTN □ *Oh, don't try and take his suffering away from him — he'd be* ***lost without*** *it.* LBA □ passive with *be, feel, seem.*

lounge about/around [A1 A2] (informal) lie or sit in a casual, lazy manner; loll about/around (q v). **o:** the place; sitting-room, bar □ *'Do you think that instead of* ***lounging about*** *you could give a hand with the dishes?'* □ *If my son wants to* ***lounge around*** *at home, he doesn't have to choose my favourite armchair.*

louse up [B1i pass] (slang) spoil, ruin. **S:** (clumsy, inconsiderate) fool, oaf. **O:** chance, prospects (of success); party, celebration; things, the whole thing □ *We'd just got Monica settled with a few reassuring words when you had to* ***louse*** *everything* ***up*** *by opening your big mouth!*

lull to sleep [B2 pass] send to sleep by rocking. **S:** (movement of) train, aircraft; mother. **O:** passenger; infant □ *The swaying motion of the train must have* ***lulled*** *me* ***to sleep****. The next thing I knew was waking with a jerk at King's Cross.*

lumber (with) [B2 pass] (informal) pass to sb else an awkward or inconvenient person, object or task. **o:** relative, pet animal; ugly furniture, unusable china; organizing, arrangements □ *Every Summer we get* ***lumbered with*** *Aunt Mabel for a fortnight.* □ *'Why* ***lumber*** *me* ***with*** *all this paperwork?'*

lump together [B1i pass] (informal) join together, treat as one. **O:** items, belongings; towns, states; accounts, bills □ *Their incomes are* ***lumped together*** *for tax purposes.* □ *They've* ***lumped*** *the two districts* ***together*** *under one administrator.*

lunch in [A1] have one's midday meal at home, at the hotel where one is staying etc. **S:** guest, resident □ *Non-resident students who wish to* ***lunch in*** *should inform the Domestic Bursar before ten o'clock.*

lunch out [A1] have one's midday meal away from home etc □ *The management will be glad to provide a packed meal for residents wishing to* ***lunch out****.*

lunge at [A2 rel] throw oneself forward at a target, as when thrusting with a sword. **S:** adversary, assailant □ *The intruder* ***lunged at*** *Stevens with a knife; Stevens snatched up a briefcase to ward off the blow.*

lure away (from) [B1i pass B3 pass emph rel] persuade sb to leave a place or person by false or genuine promises. **S:** manufacturer, publisher, director of research. **O:** executive, author, scientist □ *I've heard too many tales of bright young research workers being* ***lured away*** *only to find their position changed for the worse.* □ *You will need to be very seductive or very devious to* ***lure*** *her* ***away from*** *someone she is so clearly attached to.*

lust after [A2 pass] strongly desire; covet. **o:** woman; money; fame, glory □ *In particular, he* ***lusted after*** *those things which people born to money took for granted and didn't greatly desire.*

M

make no bones about [B2] not hesitate to say or do sth, act or speak about sth frankly and vigorously. **o:** blaming sb, accusing sb, coming to sb's defence □ *Mr Justice Dankwerts* ***made no bones about*** *stigmatizing its use as dishonest trading.* T □ *He* ***made no bones about*** *describing her in 'The Times' as an absolutely incomparable singer.* T □ object is usu the *-ing* form of a v.

make a fuss (about/over) [B2 pass emph rel] become (extremely) excited or worried about sth, for no good reason. **adj:** much, a deal of, a lot of, no end of (a) □ *Jean Pierre was* ***making a fuss about*** *one of the translations.* UTN □ *The unexpected rise in British factory investment,* ***about*** *which so* ***much fuss*** *has been* ***made****, should be greatly welcomed.* OBS □ *They are* ***making a lot of fuss over*** *nothing!* ⇨ next entry.

make a song and dance (about/over) [B2 pass] (informal) become unreasonably (and absurdly) excited or worried about sth □ *Kay's* *parents* ***made a*** *dreadful* ***song and dance about*** *her being out after midnight.* ▫ ***A*** *tremendous* ***song and dance*** *was being* ***made over*** *the change in the licensing laws.* ⇨ previous entry.

make one's way across, along, back etc [B1ii B2 emph rel] move, proceed, across, along, back etc. **o:** road; river, sea; room, corridor ▫ *It was an hour and a half or so later that the company* ***made its way back*** *to the transmitting station.* TBC ▫ *Armed with lengths of string and fish-hooks, we would* ***make our way down*** *to the river-bank in the morning.* DF

make after [A2] chase, pursue. **o:** quarry, prey, thief ▫ *The rabbit shot from its burrow and two dogs* ***made after*** *it at top speed.*

make at [A2] attack; move towards sb as if to attack him ▫ *He* ***made at*** *the man with a heavy ruler snatched from the table.* ▫ *The dog* ***made at*** *the postman with his teeth bared.*

make eyes at [B2] (informal) look at flirtatiously or coquettishly. **o:** older boy, good-looking man ▫ *'Stop* ***making eyes at*** *the waiter, Mary. We shan't get our meal any quicker!'* ▫ (music hall song) *Come and* ***make eyes at*** *me down at the old 'Bull & Bush'!* ▫ *There's nothing for the French boys to do but* ***make eyes at*** *Mariette.* BFA

make a grab (at) [B2 rel] (informal) suddenly stretch out a hand and try to grasp sth. **adj:** quick, sharp, sudden. **o:** rope, handle; hand, sleeve ▫ *I could do nothing more than* ***make a*** *wild* ***grab at*** *him with my arms.* BB

make a pass (at) [B2] (informal) suggest by word or gesture that one would like to make love to sb (esp used of cases where one or both persons have other commitments) ▫ *'If he ever* ***makes a pass at*** *you I'll wring his neck.'* AITC ▫ *'I was quite shameless, wasn't I? The owner's wife* ***making a*** *big* ***pass at*** *one of the salesmen.'* PE ▫ pass may be pl, as in: *Men don't* ***make passes at*** *girls in glasses.*

make away/off (with) [A1 A3 pass] steal and hurry away with. **o:** cash, valuables, luggage ▫ *While we were having coffee two small boys* ***made off with*** *our suitcases.*

make away with oneself [A3] take one's own life, commit suicide; do away with[2] (q v) ▫ *'You don't think she had any motive for* ***making away with*** *herself, Mother?'* RFW

make for[1] [A2 pass] move towards (e g to escape). **S:** audience, crowd; vehicle; ship. **o:** exit, gate; sea ▫ *'I can't listen to any more of this rubbish!' he said, and* ***made for*** *the door.* EM ▫ *The bar was instantly* ***made for*** *by the thirsty audience.* ▫ *The convoy* ***made for*** *the open sea.*

make for[2] [A2 pass] rush towards (so as to attack). **S:** aircraft, tank; elephant, bull ▫ *Two sentries* ***made*** *straight* ***for*** *him with drawn swords.*

make for[3] [A2 pass] help to make possible, to ensure. **S:** good management; improved motorways; enlightened teaching. **o:** better labour relations; safer driving; sound education ▫ *International football matches do not always* ***make for*** *better understanding between countries.* ▫ *A big family's a wonderful interest. It* ***makes for*** *the stability of marriage.* QA

make allowances (for) [B2 pass emph rel] consider, allow for (q v), certain factors (when measuring, assessing or judging sth or sb). **adj:** some, no, (not) any, few; certain, due. **o:** growth, shrinkage; wind, tide; age, inexperience ▫ *The financing of road improvements is just as much of a burden to one place as another when* ***allowances*** *are* ***made for*** *size and revenue.* SC ▫ *The jury were asked to* ***make*** *all* ***allowances for*** *the age of the accused.* ▫ *Now that I had seen this attitude abroad, I was even less ready to* ***make allowances for*** *it.* AH ▫ allowances occasionally sing, as in: *When every* ***allowance*** *has been* ***made for*** *his inexperience....*

make amends (for) [B2 pass emph rel] ⇨ make amends (to) (for).

make a beeline for [B2 pass emph rel] (informal) hurry directly towards. **o:** door, exit, bar ▫ *He was now* ***making a beeline for*** *indoors to discover what Steve was doing.* SPL ▫ ***A beeline*** *was* ***made for*** *the best seats.*

make a bolt/dash for [B2] (informal) hurry (to catch a train etc, keep an appointment); suddenly escape from captivity. **o:** bus, train; freedom, open door; it ▫ *I became oblivious of the passage of time and had to* ***make a bolt for*** *it to get the bus.* WDM ▫ *The prisoners* ***made a dash for*** *the open window while their guards' attention was distracted.*

make a break for it [B2] (informal) escape from captivity while one's captors' attention is elsewhere ▫ *He was looking at her frequently, perhaps to make sure of catching her if she decided to* ***make a break for it.*** TGLY ▫ *I'm not so daft as to* ***make a break for it*** *on my long-distance running.* LLDR

make a long arm for [B2] (informal) stretch out to reach ▫ *'Would you* ***make a long arm for*** *my pipe? It's on the shelf behind you.'*

make a name for oneself [B2] (informal) earn oneself a reputation (in a particular field) ▫ *The Prime Minister favoured Gott, who had* ***made a*** *great* ***name for himself*** *in the desert.* MFM ▫ *He's* ***made*** *quite* ***a name for himself*** *as an after-dinner speaker.*

make a/one's play for [B2] (informal) try by some special action to secure or capture sth, or win sb's interest. **o:** job, vacancy; sb's attention; pretty girl ▫ *'Stephens has been with the company for a year now. How long do you think it'll be before he* ***makes a play for*** *the top job?'* ▫ *'Did you notice how Bill's eye lighted on the girl in the yellow dress? He'll be* ***making his play for*** *her in just a minute.'*

make room (for) [B2 pass pass(o) emph rel] make space, or time, into which sb or sth can be fitted. **o:** furniture, junk; passenger; activities, speaker ▫ *Somehow the extra children will have to be* ***made room for.*** ▫ *'I suppose the cells are full of my spies.' 'We can always* ***make room for*** *another by having a few executions.'* OMIH ▫ *More* ***room*** *will have to be* ***made*** *on the programme* ***for*** *these performers.*

make tracks (for home) [B2] (informal) leave sb's company, or house, to return home ▫ *'It's really time we were* ***making tracks for home.*** *Thank you for a delightful evening.'* ▫ *'Come on,' said Finn, 'let you and I be* ***making tracks.'*** *We had been there nearly three-quarters of an hour.* UTN

make (from)[1] [B2 pass emph rel] shape, fashion (raw material). ⇨ make (up) (from) [1].

make (from)[2] [B2 pass emph rel] fashion,

tailor (a garment). ⇨ make (up) (from) ².

make a dent in [B2 pass rel] (informal) make less, reduce; damage, weaken. **o:** savings, bank balance; reputation, credibility, authority □ *'All these bills for repairs to the house have* ***made a*** *big* ***dent in*** *our holiday money.'* □ *Stories of official corruption have* ***made a*** *serious* ***dent in*** *the government's high-minded campaign against lawlessness.*

make one's way in the world [B2] progress in one's career, make a success of one's working life □ *He hasn't the determination to* ***make his way in the world.*** □ *If he hasn't* ***made his way in the world*** *by now, he never will.* MM

make (into)¹ [B2 pass] shape, fashion (raw material). ⇨ make (up) into ¹.

make (into)² [B2 pass rel] shape, fashion (cloth). ⇨ make (up) (into) ².

make into [B2 pass emph rel] cause to become; transform (into) (q v). **O:** boy, trainee, recruit; mild person; loft, barn. **o:** man, manager, leader; tiger, bully; flat, studio □ *He wasn't always a bully. You* ***made*** *him* ***into*** *one.* FFE □ *Many of the cinemas have been* ***made into*** *bowling alleys and bingo halls.*

make inroads (into) [B2 pass emph rel] absorb or consume a considerable part (of). **adj:** grave, extensive. **o:** savings, reserves, capital □ *Our recent economic difficulties have caused serious* ***inroads*** *to be* ***made into*** *our gold and currency reserves.*

make of [B2 pass emph rel] (not) understand (at all); understand, interpret, to a stated extent. **O:** nothing; very little, hardly anything; something. **o:** behaviour, character; work, art; writing, sound □ *He tired very quickly, as his predecessor had prophesied, of the popular records and could* ***make*** *nothing* ***of*** *the others.* TST □ *Nothing much could be* ***made of*** *the scribble in his notebooks.* □ *'What did you* ***make of*** *the old lady?'* PP

make the best of [B2] do one's best in difficult conditions, or with limited means. **o:** situation; confinement, isolation; resources, gifts □ *He was sorry his talents were not greater, but he was ready to* ***make the best of*** *them.* □ *We must* ***make the best*** *we can* ***of*** *the few natural resources we have.*

make the best of a bad job [B2] (informal) do the best one can in unfavourable circumstances □ *Aubrey Clover, resigned to* ***making the best of a bad job,*** *said, 'We'll have to rehearse on the day itself.'* WDM □ *They were unhappily married, but each had determined to* ***make the best of a bad job.***

make the best of both worlds [B2] combine the best aspects of different ways of life, philosophies etc □ *Some have tried to* ***make the best of both worlds*** *— the best of Indianism, the best of Christianity.* DOP □ *This device is really an invitation to* ***make the best of both worlds,*** *the telescopic and the microscopic, at a single glance.* HAH

make capital of [B2 pass rel] ⇨ make capital (out) of (entry after how make that out).

make a clean breast of it/the whole thing [B2] make a full confession of sth □ *'If you don't* ***make a clean breast of it*** *to the police I shall have to give them the information.'* EM

make effective/good use of [B2 pass pass(o) emph rel] use well; put to effective/good use (q v). **o:** superior strength, reserve troops; spare capital, new machines □ ***Effective use*** *was* ***made of*** *aid sent from overseas.* □ *The composer* ***makes good use*** *of the augmented brass section.* □ *How can an underdeveloped country* ***make the best use of*** *science?* NS

make an evening/a night/weekend of it [B2] (informal) devote a whole evening etc to a party, outing, pleasurable pursuit □ *Tharkles, released from supervision by Edith's absence, had suggested that they should* ***make a weekend of it*** (i e spend the weekend together). HD □ *'Say you'll be back by one — unless you decide to* ***make a night of it.'*** OMIH

make an example of [B2 pass pass(o) emph rel] punish sb for an offence in order to deter others from committing similar offences. **S:** magistrate, court; headmaster. **o:** offender, culprit □ *'Wasn't it high time,' said one letter, 'for* ***an example*** *to be* ***made of*** *these juvenile thugs?'* □ *Those responsible for the disturbance in the main block of the prison were* ***made an example of*** (or: ***made examples of***) *by the governor.*

make an exhibition of oneself [B2] draw attention to oneself through loud, vulgar behaviour. **adj:** disgusting, dreadful, fearful □ *'Did you have to* ***make*** *such* ***a*** *vulgar* ***exhibition of yourself*** *at the party? Why must you always be the centre of attention?'* □ *'Do try to stop the children* ***making exhibitions*** (or: ***an exhibition***) ***of*** *themselves in front of their grandparents!'*

make a fool of [B2 pass(o)] make sb feel foolish by leading him to expect sth which is not forthcoming □ *We were all* ***made fools of*** *by some door-to-door salesman.* □ *That girl has* ***made a fool of*** *more than one man.* □ *I wanted to laugh now: what* ***fools*** *we had both* ***made of*** *each other!* QA

make a fool of oneself [B2] make oneself appear ridiculous through clumsy or thoughtless behaviour □ *Aisgill had a watchful coldness about him which almost frightened me; he looked utterly incapable of* ***making a fool of himself.*** RATT □ *There was the sort of tug-of-war between rival organizations. The result was that we both* ***made fools of ourselves.*** DS

make a friend of [B2] put oneself on close and friendly terms with sb one already knows (e g a pupil) □ *He never bothered to* ***make a friend of*** *his son.* □ *A probation officer best succeeds if he tries to* ***make friends of*** *the young people in his care.*

make fun of [B2 pass(o)] mock, ridicule; laugh (at)² (q v). **o:** sister, wife; speech, gestures; ambition, aspiration □ *We all* ***make fun of*** *him behind his back, of course.* OBS □ *'You're* ***making fun of*** *me,' she said in a low voice. 'I'm quite serious.'* RATT □ *His efforts to improve himself are constantly* ***made fun of.***

make a fuss of [B2 pass pass(o)] give much (perhaps too much) attention, hospitality etc to sb. **adj:** much, a lot of; (not) any. **o:** guest, visitor; son □ *We were* ***made*** *so* ***much fuss of*** *by the welcoming committee.* □ *Too* ***much fuss*** *can be* ***made of*** *very young children.* □ *We* ***made*** *such* ***a fuss of*** *them. Gave them cigarettes and mugs of tea.* CSWB

make a go of [B2 pass(o)] (informal) make sth (esp a relationship) succeed. **o:** it; marriage, partnership, life together; business, venture □ *Why didn't we **make a go of** it? Where did our love go to?* HSG □ *I think Helena and Tony will **make a go of** it.* NM

make a good etc job of [B2 pass pass(o) rel] (informal) perform a task well, ill etc (esp make repairs or decorations to sth well, badly etc). **adj:** good, excellent, satisfactory; poor, dreadful. **o:** car, cooker; bathroom, kitchen □ *Many machines wash, rinse, spin-dry — but the new Acme Twin-Speed Combination **makes a better job of** all three.* DM □ ***A first-class job** was **made of** the new extension to their kitchen.*

make a habit/practice of [B2 pass pass(o) emph rel] form, develop the habit of. **o:** it, this; turning up in time, greeting one's colleagues □ *'Use my telephone by all means, but don't **make a habit of** it.'* □ *He **made a practice of** doing his exercises in front of an open window.* □ *He **made a habit of** taking a nap after lunch* (cf *He **made** it **his habit** to take a nap* etc).

make a hash/mess of [B2 pass pass(o) rel] (informal) mismanage, mishandle; mess up (q v). **adj:** dreadful, absolute. **o:** arrangements; finance, account; booking, reservation □ *The travel agents **made a** complete **hash of** our bookings.* □ ***A** perfect **mess** had been **made of** the seating plan.*

make hay of [B2 pass(o) rel] (informal) demolish, destroy; throw into confusion (⇨ throw into). **o:** argument, case; opposition, rival □ *He **made hay of** the careful arguments of opposition speakers.* □ *All your plans for a continental holiday will be **made hay of** if the bank won't advance the money.*

make head or tail of [B2 pass(o)] (informal) (not) understand at all. **o:** report, lecture, note □ *He was for some time completely unable to **make head or tail of** the blotted scrawl.* EM □ *She'd taken some notes, which she subsequently could not **make head or tail of**.* WDM □ with *can/could + not/hardly*.

make heavy weather of [B2 pass pass(o)] (informal) make a task seem more difficult than it really is. **o:** problem, sum; packing, removals; painting, repairs □ *He picked up the briefcase and began to **make heavy weather of** the straps to have something to do.* TT □ *You're **making** terribly **heavy weather of** a perfectly simple calculation.*

make an honest woman of [B2 pass pass(o)] (informal) marry a woman with whom one has been having an affair □ *Come on down to the church and I'll **make an honest woman of** you.* TOH □ *Even the silliest little shopgirl has the sense to try and get **an honest woman made of** herself.* ASA

make light of [B2 pass(o)] treat as slight or unimportant. **o:** discomfort, pain, inconvenience □ *The privations he must have suffered during his imprisonment were **made light of** in his talks with reporters.* □ *This he put forward as a youthful folly. In fact, he **made light of** the whole episode.* ASA

make a man of [B2 pass(o)] help to grow up, to reach manhood. **S:** travel, danger, adventure □ *Two years at sea will help to **make a man of** him.* □ *He was **made a man of** by having to take responsibility for others.* □ *The Navy intends to **make men of** you* (*recruits*). ⇨ make into.

make a meal of it [B2] (informal) overdo sth, do sth to excess □ *'I don't mind you bringing a few friends in to play, Phil, but let's not **make a meal of it**.'* □ *He wasn't satisfied with saying a few words in reply. He had to **make a meal of it**!*

make a mental note (of) [B2 pass pass(o) rel] resolve especially not to forget. **o:** remark, saying; number, time □ *I **made a mental note of** the phrase.* RATT □ *Here is another point that ought to be **made a mental note of**.* ⇨ make a note (of).

make mention of [B2 pass pass(o) emph rel] (formal) mention, speak of; refer to [1] (q v). **adj:** some; no, (not) any □ ***Mention** has already been **made of** the other surviving members of the family.* □ *I was sitting on one of the walls of the partially excavated bath-building **of** which I have **made mention**.* SD

make mincemeat of [B2 pass pass(o)] (informal) maul severely, demolish utterly. **o:** attack, opposition □ *The infantry were **made mincemeat of** by the artillery.* □ *A good lawyer would **make mincemeat of** your case.* □ *Yorkshire **made mincemeat of** the Surrey attack in piling up a score of 434 for 4 declared.* DM

make a mockery of [B2 pass pass(o) emph rel] bring to a low level, be a travesty of. **S:** behaviour; treatment, handling; trial. **adj:** complete, total. **o:** democracy, justice, free speech □ *The conduct of the elections **made an** absolute **mockery of** democratic processes.* □ *The judge's frequent interventions **made a mockery of** justice.*

make the most of [B2 pass pass(o) rel] get as much from experience etc as one can, exploit it to the full. **o:** opportunity, chance; freedom, youth □ ***Make the most of** your life — because life is a holiday from the dark.* HSG □ *'I never met a girl like you, so I might as well **make the most of** having you here.'* AITC

make much of [B2 pass pass(o) emph rel] stress, emphasize. **o:** factor, element; family background, old school tie □ *In conversation he **makes much of** his aristocratic connections.* □ *One further criticism must be mentioned because **much** has been **made of** this.* SNP □ *Running has always been **made much of** in our family, especially running away from the police.* LLDR

make nonsense of [B2 pass pass(o)] render worthless. **S:** facts, evidence. **adj:** complete, absolute. **o:** pretensions; story, account, version □ *His extravagant style of life **makes nonsense of** his claim to be a simple man of the people.* □ *The official statements were **made nonsense of** by on-the-spot reports.*

make a note (of) [B2 pass pass(o) emph rel] record in one's mind or on paper. **o:** size, shape, position (of a place); time, destination (of a train etc) □ *Still Charles hung back, **making a note of** the obviously complex traditions of the place.* HD □ ***A** careful **note** should be **made of** the exact dimensions of the emplacement.* ⇨ make a mental note (of).

make nothing of [B2 pass(o)] overcome with ease some apparently difficult obstacle. **S:** athlete; boxer; student, scientist, inventor. **o:** obstacle, jump; opposition; problem, difficulty □ (commentary on a horse and rider jumping obstacles) *'She comes round again to take that* *fence and of course **makes nothing of** it.'* BBCTV ⇨ make of.

make a nuisance of oneself [B2] irritate others by making a noise, interrupting etc; risk unpopularity by criticizing authority etc □ *The children are **making** confounded **nuisances of themselves**.* □ *If the Council continues with its plans to demolish this neighbourhood there are people who are prepared to **make a nuisance of themselves** by organizing protest meetings, lobbying their MP and even withholding their rents and rates.*

make a point of [B2 pass] be careful to, take particular care to. **o:** being punctual, greeting people by name; it, this □ *Do you **make a point of** being on time for work and social appointments?* WI □ *She **makes a point of** having someone around to sort things out for her.* EHOW

make a secret of [B2 pass emph rel] try to hide. **adj:** no, (not) any, little. **o:** plans, intentions, designs; wishes, feelings □ *Uncle Saunders had **made no secret of** his disapproval and disappointment.* DC □ *You knew I was doing that at the club. I never **made a secret of** it.* AITC

make sense of [B2 pass pass(o) emph rel] understand, interpret. **adj:** some, no, (not) any, little; perfect. **o:** conversation, message, language □ *I can never **make sense of** a word he says.* □ *The code couldn't be **made sense of** by our experts.*

make a success of [B2 pass pass(o) emph rel] be successful in some activity. **adj:** considerable, remarkable. **o:** job, task, project □ *He was given the job last year and has since **made a** great **success of** it.* □ *I rather doubt if such an ambitious scheme could be **made a success of**.*

make use of [B2 pass pass(o) emph rel] employ, use. **adj:** some; wide, extensive, frequent. **o:** techniques, processes; foreign labour, woman worker □ *The chapels had ministers who were not Oxford-trained, and **made** wide **use of** lay preachers.* UL □ *The machine **makes use of** the principle of digital sorting.* NS

make a virtue of necessity [B2] pretend that sth which one is obliged to do or accept is good for one's character, moral development etc □ *The Churches enjoined fasting partly to allow the faithful to **make a virtue of necessity** and partly, too, so that the wealthy might have a taste of what their poorer brothers and sisters had to put up with.* OBS

make the worst of [B2] fail, refuse, to make any effort when faced with difficulties. **o:** situation, crisis, setback □ *Some element in her character forced her to **make the worst of** a bad day.* AITC □ *Dave was now changing over from **making the worst of** the affair to making the best of it.* UTN

make the worst of both worlds [B2] combine the worst features of two ways of life, philosophies etc □ *You want to **make the worst of both worlds**. You want to marry an older woman who hasn't any money.* RATT □ *Working overtime and paying extra tax on one's earnings seems very much like **making the worst of both worlds**.*

make demands (of/on) [B2 pass emph rel] ask for help, thus placing a burden on sb or sth. **adj:** excessive, heavy, repeated. **o:** staff, helpers, supporters; resources, funds □ *Dave is an old friend but he has no money. I felt perhaps I oughtn't to **make demands on** Dave.* UTN □ *Excessive **demands** have been **made of** the spares department: our stocks are down to rock-bottom.*

make off [A1] leave in a hurry (esp to escape from other people) □ *Suddenly Myrtle slid down from the gate and quietly **made off** beside the hedgerow.* SPL □ *The priest struggled up the cliff alone and **made off**.* RFW

make off (with) [A1 A3 pass] ⇨ make away/off (with).

make (on) [B2 pass emph rel] make a certain profit as the result of a business transaction. **O:** nothing; profit, return; pile, packet (of money). **o:** deal, transaction; investment, sale □ *John was prepared to sell me his car for what he paid for it: he wouldn't **make** a penny **on** the deal.* □ *There wasn't very much money to be **made on** property transactions in the London area in the years immediately following the war, as redevelopment was strictly controlled till 1954.*

make an attempt on [B2 pass] try to break or exceed. **o:** record; time, speed, distance (set up by sb) □ ***A** fresh **attempt** is being **made on** the land speed record later this year.* □ *The Kenyan runner **made** two further **attempts on** the 5 000 metres record that summer.*

make an attempt on sb's life [B2 pass] try to assassinate (a prominent person) □ *Last night **a** fresh **attempt** was **made on the life of** the Crown Prince.* □ *That was the palace where the President had never slept since **the** last **attempt** was **made on his life**.* OMIH □ also pl: *Further **attempts** have since been **made on his life**.*

make demands (on) [B2 pass emph rel] ⇨make demands (of/on).

make an impression (on)[1] [B2 pass emph rel] affect in a particular way by one's appearance or behaviour. **adj:** favourable, good; bad, unfortunate. **o:** jury, selection board, prospective buyer □ *The Russians were clearly anxious to **make a** good **impression** (i e **on** the British).* MFM □ ***The** right kind of **impression** was **made on** the visiting delegation.*

make an impression (on)[2] [B2 emph rel] get people to notice one, impress them. **o:** newcomer, visitor □ *'He does like to **make an impression** (**on** people), doesn't he? Notice the way he always sweeps into a room.'* □ *Tom's stock method of **making an impression on** anyone was to indicate that he understood them perfectly.* SPL

make a start (on) [B2 pass emph rel] begin, start (to do sth). **adj:** no, (not) any; fresh, new; early, belated. **o:** task, job; notes, corrections; writing a report, repairing a machine □ *There was work to do, awaiting him in his room. He had better **make a start on** it now.* EM □ ***A start** has yet to be **made on** building a much-needed relief road to the south of the city centre.*

make out[1] [B1i pass adj] write; complete. **O:** cheque, application, claim □ *He won't know I've gone except when he comes to **make out** the pay cheques.* TC □ *Applications have to be **made out** in triplicate.* □ *He picked up a laundry list **made out** on the back of an envelope.*

make out[2] [B1iii pass] claim, assert, maintain. **O:** that one is overworked, that one can cure all ills; themselves... to be badly treated, him... to be cleverer than he is □ *I'd just tell them to **make out** that they were taking the risk themselves.* CON □ *It was not the cure everyone **made** it **out** to be.* TGLY □ *They **make** themselves **out** to be poorer than they really are.* □ *It was **made out** that he had no business being there.*

make out[3] [B1i pass] manage to see, read. **O:** figure, face, building. **A:** just, barely, scarcely; in the mist, half-light, gloom □ *I could **make out** the expression on his face.* NM □ *The outline of the house could just be **made out**.* □ usu with *can/could.*

make out[4] [B1ii] understand the nature or character of sb; work out [4] (q v) □ *I really can't **make** him **out**. Why does he offend the very people who try to help him?* □ usu with *can/could + not.*

make out[5] [B1iii] understand. **O:** it; what he was after; how he came to be there, why he always disagreed □ *I could never **make out** if they wanted our help or not.* □ *I can't **make** it **out**: why doesn't he spend some of his money on a car that won't break down?* □ usu with *can/could + not.*

make out[6] [A1] (informal) progress, prosper; get on[3] (q v). **S:** business, firm; family, son; things □ *I wonder how John is **making out** in his new practice?* □ *How are you **making out** with Mary?* (i e How is your love-affair progressing?) □ usu in direct and indirect questions after *how.*

make out a case [B1iii pass] argue, plead (in favour of or against) □ *I can't agree with you, but I grant that you've **made out** a very good **case**.* □ ***A case** could be **made out** that it's more humane to kill off these wild animals.* TES □ *He has **made out a** strong **case** for the repeal of the law.* □ case may be followed by a *that*-clause, *in favour of, for* or *against.*

how make that out [B1ii] how (does/did one) arrive at a particular conclusion or statement □ *'You say that we shall be making a loss for the next three years. Well, **how** do you **make that out**?'* □ *Someone from the floor asked the speaker **how** he **made that out**.* □ direct or indirect question.

make capital (out) of [B2 pass rel] use to one's own advantage, exploit (often unscrupulously). **S:** press, critic, opponent. **adj:** much, a lot of, no end of. **o:** confession, remark; resignation, move □ *The newspapers have **made capital out of** his indiscreet statement on television.* □ *A good deal of **capital** will be **made of** their unwillingness to testify before the Committee*

make a mountain out of a molehill [B2 pass] greatly exaggerate a difficulty, problem etc □ *He said the Government were frightened of nothing. The real trouble was we were **making a mountain out of a molehill**.* MFM □ note pl: *'Don't **make mountains out of molehills**.'*

make over [B1i pass adj] convert; change, transform. **O:** house, room, garden; face, manner, appearance □ *The basement has been **made over** into a workshop.* □ *Though you say you've **made over** your outside in a week, no one can do that with the inside* (i e the personality). PTTP

make a fuss (over) [B2 pass emph rel] ⇨make a fuss (about/over).

make a song and dance (over) [B2 pass] ⇨make a song and dance (about/over).

make over (to) [B1i pass adj B3 pass emph rel] transfer the ownership of sth (to). **O:** income, property, business, house □ *The best farming land was **made over to** the younger son.* □ *To avoid death duty, grandfather **made over** the greater part of his property as soon as he retired.* □ ***To** which of his partners is he **making over** the residue of his estate?*

make advances (to) [B2 pass emph rel] approach sb (esp a woman) in the hope of making a conquest. **adj:** cautious, timid, bold. **o:** girl, woman; smaller firm, shareholders (of a business one wishes to control) □ *'I'd be glad if you'd stop **making advances to** my daughter.'* □ *Tentative **advances** have already been **made to** our shareholders by a multinational company.*

make application (to) [B2 pass emph rel] (formal, official) write, apply, asking for information, a form, an allowance etc. **o:** office, department; Registrar, Town Clerk □ *To obtain a new birth certificate for your son, **make application to** the Adopted Children's Register.* TO □ ***Application** should be **made** in the first instance **to** the local office of the Ministry.*

make a difference (to) [B2 pass emph rel] affect, influence; alter, change (things). **adj:** no, (not) any, (not) much; serious, considerable. **o:** me etc; feelings, attitude; prospects, future □ *My secret activity had **made no difference** at all **to** my friendship with Hugo.* UTN □ *He was brought up in a fashionable district. That didn't **make any difference to** me.* CON □ ***A** big **difference** was **made to** our trading position by devaluation.*

make love to [B2 pass(o) rel] kiss and caress; have sexual intercourse with. **adj:** ardent, passionate □ *I never wished to **make love to** Mrs Thompson, though I certainly wouldn't have thrown her out of my bed.* RATT

make amends (to) (for) [B2 pass emph rel] repay or compensate sb for sth one has failed to do in the past; make up for[2] (q v). **adj:** generous, handsome. **o:** (***to***) him etc; (***for***) failure, sin, crime □ *There was the College putting forth all its beauty as if to **make amends to** him **for** all it had denied.* HD □ *Whatever disappointment he had been in life, he was certainly beginning to **make** some **amends** (**for** it) in death.* PP

make up[1] [B1i pass] replace, make good. **O:** loss, deficiency, wastage; leeway □ *Our losses will have to be **made up** with fresh drafts* (i e of troops). □ *There is a tremendous amount of leeway to **make up** if he wants to have a chance of winning this race.*

make up[2] [B1i pass adj] provide a road with a hard surface of bitumen etc to make it suitable for fast motor traffic. **O:** road, street, drive, carriageway □ *Half the roads in the estate are still to be **made up**.* □ *There's a good **made-up** road from the capital to the main port.*

make up[3] [B1i pass adj] compose, invent (possibly to deceive). **O:** words, tune, story; the whole thing, things, it □ *These entertainers **make** their stories **up** as they go along.* □ *You can't go around **making up** things about being assaulted by people who don't exist.* DC □ *There isn't any little girl called Clementine. He's just **made** her **up**.* DC

make up[4] [B1i nom pass adj] arrange type, illustrations etc, in columns or pages for printing.

O: page, column □ *The way the front page is* ***made up*** *may need to be altered several times* (or: *The* ***make-up*** *of the front page may need* etc).

make up[5] [B1iii nom pass] form, compose, constitute. **S:** cell, tissue, sinew; man, individual; island, atoll. **O:** body; tribe, nation; chain, group □ *What are the qualities that ideally should* ***make up*** *a man's character?* □ *Society is* ***made up*** *of people with widely differing abilities.* □ *There are plans to change the* ***make-up*** (= composition) *of the Board.* □ *There is something in his* ***make-up*** (= nature, character) *that repels people.*

make up[6] [B1i pass adj] add more fuel to a fire etc. **O:** fire, stove, boiler □ *The fire needs* ***making up***. □ *If the stove isn't* ***made up****, it'll go out.*

make up[7] [A1 nom B1i nom pass adj] prepare one's face, body for a performance in the theatre, or on film or television; apply cosmetics to the face to make it more attractive. **S:** actor, cast; woman. **O:** himself; face, nose, eyes □ *It took Laurence Olivier more than an hour to* ***make up*** (or: *do his* ***make-up****) for the part of 'Othello'.* □ *The actor applies several kinds of* ***make-up*** *to his face* (e g cream, greasepaint, powder). □ *Her hair is dyed platinum blonde and she is heavily* ***made up***. DPM

make up[8] [B1i pass] prepare by mixing together various ingredients. **S:** chemist, druggist (US). **O:** medicine; tonic, cough cure; prescription □ *The doctor writes out a prescription and you get it* ***made up*** *at the chemist's.* □ *He* ***made up*** *a medicine from the juice of berries and applied it to the wound.*

make up[9] [B1i pass] prepare a bed which is not at present in use (e g for a patient); prepare a makeshift bed (e g for an unexpected guest). **O:** bed, cot, campbed □ *Sister sat down on the wire-works of the bed. I had not had time to* ***make*** *it* ***up*** *yet.* DC □ *I had a bed* ***made up*** *for me on the sofa.*

make up[10] [B1i pass] prepare a basket etc of food, esp for a journey or outing. **O:** (picnic-)basket, hamper; sandwich lunch □ *The hotel will* ***make*** *you* ***up*** *a packet of sandwiches for the journey.*

make up[11] [B1i pass] (make) complete. **O:** (full) strength, numbers, complement; (required, total) sum, amount □ *Our benefactor* ***made up*** *the total with a cheque for £1 000* (cf *A cheque for £1 000* ***made up*** *the total*). □ *We recruited locally to* ***make up*** *our full complement of labourers* (cf *Local recruits* ***made up*** *our full complement* etc). ⇨ make up to[1].

make up a four (at bridge) [B1iii] (cards) make a game of bridge possible by offering or agreeing to be the fourth player □ *Ask old Mr Smith if he'd mind* ***making up a four***.

make one's/sb's mind up [B1i pass] (cause to) decide, reach a decision □ *'Look, I've* ***made up my mind****. I want to have the party here.'* TOH □ *He had been pondering the great decision. Now* ***his mind*** *was* ***made up***. TO □ *He wants somebody to* ***make up his mind*** *for him.* □ make one's mind up may be followed by clauses introduced by *that, what, whether, how* etc.

make up for[1] [A3 pass] outweigh; compensate (for) (q v). **S:** strong personality; hard work; inventiveness. **o:** unattractive appearance; lack of intelligence; shortage of natural resources □ *My face is a bit thinner, but the rest of me is rapidly* ***making up for*** *that.* AITC □ *Pay increases will not always* ***make up for*** *poor working conditions.* NS

make up for[2] [A3 pass adj emph rel] redress; repay sb for one's past failures etc; make amends (to) (for) (q v). **S:** kindness, considerate treatment. **o:** neglect, rudeness; what sb has undergone □ *How could he* ***make up for*** *all that she had suffered because of him?* □ *His display of bad manners was scarcely* ***made up for*** *by his subsequent behaviour.*

make up for lost time [A3] make a special effort to do sth after starting late □ *So, now that we are practically neighbours, we must* ***make up for lost time****. Do look us up!* □ *We came into this field late, so we must work hard to* ***make up for lost time***.

make (up) (from)[1] [B1i pass B2 pass emph rel B3 pass emph rel] shape, fashion, manufacture (a finished article) from (raw material). **O:** brick, block; batten, joist; bracelet, locket. **o:** rubble, slag; timber, scrap; coin, chain □ [B2] *We're* ***making*** *a bed* ***from*** *scrap timber.* □ [B3] *She wore a necklace* ***made up from*** *silver coins.* ⇨ make (up) (into)[1].

make (up) (from)[2] [B1i pass adj B2 pass emph rel B3 pass emph rel] fashion, tailor (a garment) from (cloth). **O:** suit, trousers, skirt. **o:** material, stuff; piece, length, roll □ [B3] *Two full-length dresses can be* ***made up from*** *this piece.* □ [B2] *I'm having a suit* ***made from*** *the worsted you gave me.* ⇨ make (up) (into)[2].

make (up) (into)[1] [B1i pass B2 pass B3 pass] shape, fashion (raw material) into (a finished article). **O:** cement; powder; dough; pulp. **o:** block; pudding; bread; paper □ [B3] *You can get these pieces of old gold* ***made up into*** *a brooch.* □ [B2] *In this one factory, trees are cut into pieces and pulped, and the pulp is* ***made into*** *paper.* ⇨ make (up) (from)[1].

make (up) (into)[2] [B1i pass adj B2 pass rel B3 pass] fashion (cloth) into (a garment). **O:** cloth; worsted; piece, length. **o:** coat, jacket, dress □ [B1] *A friend is* ***making up*** *the dress-length Mary bought on her holiday.* □ [B1] (notice outside tailor's shop) *Customers' own materials* ***made up***. ⇨ make (up) (from)[2].

make up to[1] [B3 pass] raise to, increase to (a particular level). **O:** mixture, liquid; sum, amount. **o:** consistency, concentration; figure, level □ *You can* ***make*** *the lemonade* ***up to*** *full strength if you add more juice.* □ *If you contribute a few pounds, I'll* ***make*** *the collection* (of money) ***up to*** *the total required.* ⇨ make up[11].

make up to[2] [A3 pass] (informal) make oneself pleasant to sb in order to win favours. **o:** pretty girl; employer, officer, prefect □ *He's not the sort of man who likes being* ***made up to***. □ *On his first day at the office, he started* ***making up to*** *the prettiest secretary.*

make it/this up to [B3 pass] (informal) give to sb in compensation for sth he has missed or suffered □ *I am sorry you missed the outing.* ***It*** *will be* ***made up to*** *you at Christmas.* □ *When I get you home safely in the country I'll* ***make*** *all* ***this up to you***. DC

make it up (with) [B1ii B3] settle a quarrel,

one's differences, (with); make one's peace (with) (q v). □ *I don't know if Philip and Rosemary have **made it up** or not* (cf *I don't know if Philip has **made it up with** Rosemary or not*). EHOW

make with [A2] (slang) deliver; produce, create. **o:** money; food; music, jokes □ *'Can't you see our tongues are hanging out? **Make with** the drinks!'* □ *'We need some slogans for the promotion of the new hairspray, so start **making with** the ideas.'*

make a deal (with) [B2 pass emph rel] agree to terms for doing business. **o:** client, trading partner; enemy □ *'I'll **make a deal with** you. You can have the plans if you split the profit with us.'* DM □ *United Copper **made a deal with** a European consortium to share the mineral rights* (cf *United Copper and the consortium **made a deal** to share* etc).

make friends (with) [B2 rel] get on pleasant, intimate terms (with) □ *'You'll find us all wanting to **make friends with** you. Do you like the idea?'* PW □ *John **made friends with** Bill* (or: *John and Bill **made friends***). □ *The letter was probably from one of the patients **with** whom she had **made friends** in the hospital.* DC

make great etc play with [B2 pass pass(o) emph rel] (in a dramatic way, and esp in argument or debate) stress, emphasize; handle, play with[1] (q v), for dramatic effect. **adj:** ⚠ great, much, a good deal of. **o:** one's achievements, privations, sufferings; figures, estimates; gold watch and chain, documents □ *She **made great play with** the years of work she had given to Mrs Portway.* ASA □ *She took off and put on (her spectacles) a hundred times a day, **making as much play with** them as a barrister in court.* AITC □ *The Prime Minister **made a good deal of play with** the contrast between the backward-looking Opposition and the new thinking amongst Conservatives.* OBS

make a hit (with) [B2 emph rel] (informal) impress favourably; make an impression (on)[1] (q v). **S:** speaker, actor, politician. **o:** audience, public □ *My daughter Janice asks me to send you her love — you **made a** big **hit with** her.*

make (a) peace (with) [B2 pass emph rel] end hostilities with another state, power group etc. **o:** neighbour; aggressor □ *The elected government gave way to a caretaker regime that was prepared to **make peace with** the invaders at almost any cost to the nation.* □ *A more lasting **peace** could be **made with** the Unions if the restrictions on wage settlements were relaxed.*

make one's peace with [B2 emph rel] settle a quarrel, one's differences, with sb (by apologizing, agreeing to co-operate etc); make it up (with) (q v). **o:** church, political party; leader, father, wife □ *Johnson had no intention of **making his peace with** his superiors simply to give an impression of harmony within the department.* □ *'Have you **made your peace with** your wife yet?' 'I've certainly tried, but she refuses to talk to me.'*

make shift (with) [B2 pass(o) rel] use for lack of sth better, make do (with). **o:** inferior materials, poor tools □ *We can't get fresh supplies so we'll have to **make shift with** local substitutes.* □ *He can't afford copper, but aluminium will do as a **makeshift*** (= substitute). □ nom form is makeshift(s).

map out [B1i pass adj] arrange, organize (in one's mind or on paper). **O:** journey, route; programme, plan (of events) □ *We must get the whole expedition clearly **mapped out** on paper before we start to order equipment.* □ *It was a well **mapped-out** itinerary, taking in all the places of interest in the area.*

march on [A1] (military) enter a parade-ground formally at the start of a parade. **S:** battalion, company □ *At the beginning of a ceremonial parade, the Regimental Sergeant Major gives the order to **march on**.*

march past [A1 nom A2] (military) move ceremonially past a senior officer, who 'takes the salute'. **S:** troops, column, contingent, parade. **o:** sovereign, inspecting officer; saluting base □ *The battalion **marched past** their commanding officer.* □ *After the inspection, there is a **march-past** of all troops on parade.*

mark down[1] [B1i pass adj] note, choose, especially (as deserving punishment, or as suitable for use) □ *He was certain the man had **marked** him **down**, was out to wring his neck.* LLDR □ *I drove on to the Aosta Palace, which I had **marked down** for my brigade headquarters.* SD

mark down[2] [B1i pass adj] indicate that the price of an article has been reduced. **O:** dress, suit; linen, china □ *Many household articles are **marked down** during summer sales at the big London stores.* ⇨ mark up[2].

mark down[3] [B1i pass] reduce the marks awarded to a student, class etc. **O:** boy, pupil, form □ *The boys at the top of the form were **marked down**, as the gap between them and the rest did not reflect their true merits.*

mark for life [B2 pass] wound or injure sb so badly that he is permanently scarred. **S:** enemy, rival; experience, ordeal □ *'If I see you near my sister again, I'll **mark** you **for life**!'* □ *His experiences as a prisoner of war have left him **marked for life**.*

mark in [B1i pass adj] add (small) details to a map, picture etc. **O:** road, track, conventional sign; leaf, twig □ *The district boundaries are **marked in** with a fine mapping pen.*

mark off [B1i pass adj] separate one thing from another with a line or boundary. **O:** place, space; enclosure, car-park; period, stage □ *An area at the end of the site was **marked off** as a future playground.* □ *This phase in his life was **marked off** from the rest by the death of his father.*

mark out [B1i pass adj] draw the internal dividing lines within a space (e g places where windows are to go on a drawing of a wall). **O:** tennis-court, football pitch, gymnasium floor; elevation, plan □ *The sports field is **marked out** for an athletics meeting by the ground staff.*

mark out (for) [B1i pass B3 pass rel] decide in advance that sb will succeed. **S:** firm, employer. **O:** trainee, recruit, entrant. **o:** early promotion, special treatment, management training □ *He's the bosses' blue-eyed boy: you can tell he's been **marked out for** quick promotion.* □ *One or two of the graduate entry have been **marked out** as 'likely to succeed'.*

mark up[1] [B1i nom pass adj] (in retail trading) decide the selling price of sth after taking into account all the costs to oneself (charged by the manufacturer, wholesaler etc); (in overseas trade) decide such a price in relation to the cost of importing. **O:** price, figure; goods, books □ *Poultry farmers have recently been complaining that wholesalers and butchers have been* ***marking up*** *the farmers' prices for Christmas turkeys by up to one hundred per cent.* □ *The* ***mark-up*** *price of British books abroad has been fluctuating considerably in recent months as the value of the pound strengthens or weakens.*

mark up[2] [B1i nom pass adj] increase the existing price of sth (in order to absorb higher costs, to earn more profit etc). **O:** food, clothes, soft furnishings □ *Spirits have been* ***marked up*** *following price increases announced in the Budget.* □ *Housewives are complaining of a* ***mark-up*** *of ten per cent on some household goods.* ⇨ mark down[2].

mark up[3] [B1i pass] increase the marks awarded to a student etc. **O:** pupil, form; script, paper □ *If we* ***mark up*** *Jones on two or three papers he will just scrape a pass.*

mark up[4] [B1i pass adj] (publishing) prepare a manuscript for the printer by making corrections, inserting new material etc. **O:** manuscript (ms); book, article □ *When a manuscript has been accepted for publication, it is passed to an editor for detailed scrutiny. The editor's subsequent* ***marking up*** *of the manuscript consists of deletions or additions to the author's text, together with instructions to the printer on the typefaces to be used.*

marry above [A2] marry sb in a higher social class than one's own. **o:** him etc; himself etc; one's (proper) station (in life) □ *People who* ***marry above*** *themselves in the social scale have the same kinds of problem as those who marry outside their religion or nationality.*

marry beneath [A2] marry sb in a lower social class than one's own. **o:** him etc; himself etc; one's (own) station, class □ *John's father threatened to disinherit him if he* ***married beneath*** *himself.*

marry in/into [A1 A2 rel] become a member of a particular group through marriage (can suggest calculation on the part of the person marrying in). **o:** aristocracy, landed gentry; (religious) community, faith □ *She wasn't born into the nobility, she* ***married in.*** □ *He* ***married into*** *a rich farming family.*

marry off [B1i pass] find husband(s) for one's daughter(s) □ *When his last daughter is happily* ***married off,*** *he can afford to relax.*

marry out/out of [A1 A2] leave the religious community into which one was born by marrying a member of another church etc. **o:** faith, church □ *On the strictest interpretation, a Catholic is only* ***marrying out of*** *the faith if his partner is a non-Catholic* and *refuses to be married according to the rites of the Catholic Church.*

marry up [A1 nom B1i nom pass adj] join together, unite. **S:** [A1] **O:** [B1] components, parts; halves of the train; forces. **S:** [B1] fitter, assembly worker; railwayman; military commander □ *The regular troops* ***married up*** *with partisans pressing down from the hills.* □ *The two parts of the project are not well* ***married up.*** □ *They achieved the first* ***marry-up*** *of our separate television networks.*

marvel (at) [A2 pass adj emph rel] find wonderful or impressive. **S:** spectator, layman. **o:** speed, efficiency, ingenuity, fluency □ *Ninety-eight per cent will* ***marvel at*** *the accuracy with which we have been able to diagnose their handwriting.* SNP □ *We* ***marvel at*** *man's skill and inventiveness in putting complex pieces of machinery into space.*

mask out [B1i pass adj] (photography) when printing or enlarging, cover part of the negative, so that light does not pass through it. **O:** portion, part (of a negative, photograph) □ *We can get rid of the unwanted detail in the foreground by* ***masking out*** *the bottom of the negative during processing.*

match against/with [B2 pass emph rel] set sb or sth in competition against or with; pit against (q v). **O:** boxer, wrestler; fighting cock; strength, wits, brains, cunning □ *He's prepared to* ***match*** *his skill and strength* ***against*** *all comers.* □ *You've been* ***matched with*** *one of the best amateur fighters.*

match up [A1 B1i pass adj] fit together to form a pleasing ensemble, or a complete and intelligible whole. **S:** [A1] **O:** [B1] garments, furnishings, curtains; gems, ornaments; parts, aspects (of a story, of the evidence) □ *'Have you noticed how well the blouse goes with my long skirt? The whole outfit* ***matches up*** *beautifully.'* □ *'I can't* ***match up*** *the two halves of the photograph. A bit is missing from the middle.'* □ *The police had some difficulty in* ***matching up*** *the statements taken from the two witnesses.*

measure off [B1i pass adj] measure, mark the end of, and cut away a portion of a larger piece. **O:** half, three-quarters; 2 feet, 3 inches, six and a half metres; piece, length (of cloth, wallpaper etc) □ *The assistant* ***measured off*** *a dress-length from the roll.* □ *He had a 12-foot length* ***measured off*** *from a piece of oak.* □ *'How much shall I* ***measure*** *you* ***off****?'* □ note the Indirect Object (*you*) in the last example.

measure up (to) [A1 A3 pass rel] be of the same size, standard, quality etc (as). **S:** place, food, service; appearance, character. **o:** reports, expectations, hopes; him etc □ *Visually the fellow* ***measured up****: he was tall, slightly stooping.* ILIH □ *Differentiate between the genuine private detectives and others who do not* ***measure up to*** *our standards.* T □ *The reputation which had preceded him would take a good deal of* ***measuring up to.***

meddle in [A2 pass rel] show undue interest in sth which is not one's concern; interfere in (q v). **o:** (sb else's) business, affairs, concerns □ *I'm furious with him for* ***meddling in*** *our family disputes.* □ *Our affairs are constantly being* ***meddled in*** *by outsiders.*

meddle with [A2 pass rel] handle sth which does not concern one, and of which one has little knowledge (so disturbing or disarranging it); interfere with[1] (q v). **o:** papers, documents, collection; fitting, circuit, machine □ *Somebody's been* ***meddling with*** *the photographs I laid out so carefully.* □ *The filing system I worked out has been* ***meddled with*** *by some busybody.*

mediate (between) [A2] (formal) try to help two parties holding conflicting views to reach a settlement. **o:** husband and wife, employer and trades unionist; rival firms, hostile powers □ *When the two sides in an important industrial dispute reach deadlock the Secretary of State* *may attempt to* ***mediate between*** *them.* □ *It would take someone with the wisdom of Solomon to* ***mediate between*** *these two: each is so utterly convinced he's in the right.*

meet up (with) [A1 A3 pass] encounter, make contact (with), esp by chance □ *By 1954, when we* ***met up with*** *him, he had six German clerks working for him.* DS □ *It was some years before we* ***met up*** *(****with*** *each other) again.*

meet with[1] [A2 pass] experience, encounter. **o:** kindness, generosity; good reception; hostility, opposition □ *They* ***met with*** *stubborn resistance.* BM □ *We* ***met with*** *nothing but understanding from the doctors.*

meet with[2] [A2 pass] suffer, be overcome by. **o:** accident, misfortune, disaster □ *'Mrs Portway is very ill,' she said. 'She* ***met with*** *an accident.'* ASA □ *Every attempt to rescue the marooned party* ***met with*** *further misfortune.*

melt away [A1] disappear, vanish. **S:** fog, mist; crowd, throng; fear, anxiety □ *As the sun rose the early mist* ***melted away****.* □ *Her suspicion* ***melted away*** *as he began to talk.*

melt down [B1i pass adj] melt articles of gold or silver to use the metal as raw material; melt (stolen) bullion etc so that it is no longer recognizable to the owners. **O:** jewellery, ring, old gold; gold bar, plate □ *The bars are stamped with distinguishing marks and will have to be* ***melted down*** *before the thieves can hope to dispose of them.* T

melt in sb's/the mouth [A2] (informal) be so light or soft that it dissolves readily in the mouth; be delicious. **S:** cake, pastry; fudge, caramel □ *This birthday cake simply* ***melts in the mouth****.*

mess about [A1] (informal) behave in a foolish, boisterous way; work in a pleasant, casual, disorganized way □ *'Tell the boys to stop* ***messing about*** *upstairs: I'm trying to work.'* □ *He spends the weekends* ***messing about*** *with his car.*

mess about (with) [B1ii pass A3 pass emph rel] (informal) handle sb roughly or inconsiderately; handle sth clumsily or incompetently. **O:** wife, girlfriend; patient. **o:** girl; engine, car; tooth, injury □ *If he was your lover why couldn't you have been kinder to him? You can't* ***mess about with*** *people like Guy.* DC □ *'Stop* ***messing*** *my daughter* ***about*** (i e trying to seduce her in a clumsy way).' □ *He's been* ***messed about (with)*** *by the doctors for the past two years.*

mess together/with [A1 A2] (military) come together in one place for meals and a common social life. **S:** officers; sergeants, warrant officers □ *In barracks all the officers of a battalion* ***mess together*** (i e in the 'Officers' Mess'). *In the field, parts of a battalion may be widely separated and a platoon commander* ***messes with*** *the other officers in his company.*

mess up [B1i nom pass adj] (informal) mishandle, mismanage; confuse, disarrange. **O:** bookings, travel arrangements, flight schedules, seating plan □ *Don't ask them to organize your itinerary: they made a complete* ***mess-up*** *of ours.* □ *I've sorted the list out; now don't* ***mess*** *it* ***up*** *again.*

mete out [B1i pass] (formal) administer, deal out (q v). **O:** punishment, hard blows, harsh treatment; justice; rewards □ *The judgement* ***meted out*** *to the accused did not satisfy the public.* □ *The king and his court moved about the country,* ***meting out*** *justice at the assizes.*

mill about/around [A1] move about in a disorderly or confused way. **S:** children, crowd, spectators; thoughts, ideas, impressions □ *The first of the girls were* ***milling about*** *in the corridor.* TT □ *Conflicting fancies* ***milled around*** *in his mind.*

mind out [A1] (informal) take care to avoid danger etc; look out[1] (q v), watch out (q v) □ ***'Mind out****, the dish is hot!'* □ *'You'll trip over the cat if you don't* ***mind out****!'* □ usu imper.

miss out [B1i pass adj] forget, fail, to include. **S:** printer, compositor; hostess; singer. **O:** comma, word; name, title; verse, line □ *Through an oversight his name was* ***missed out*** *from the list of guests.* □ *He* ***missed out*** *the 't' from 'often'.* □ *No one is to be neglected or made to feel* ***missed out****.*

miss out (on) [A1 A3 pass rel] (informal) not be present at, not experience; fail to notice, and thus to enjoy or profit from. **S:** visitor; businessman; editor. **o:** celebration, reception, welcome; bonanza, oil-strike; scoop, story □ *Only a distinguished visitor can hope for such a reception and even he may* ***miss out*** *if the people find him too grand.* NDN □ *If he finds that his own paper has* ***missed out on*** *some important fact, his day is soured to begin with.* L

mist over [A1] become covered with mist, tears, or a thin film of water; become darkened or obscured. **S:** landscape, view; eyes; spectacles, looking-glass, windscreen; mind □ *His glasses kept* ***misting over*** *in the steam from the boiler.* □ *His brain* ***misted over*** *for a moment, then cleared suddenly.* HD

mist up [A1] become obscured by a film of water (usu resulting from condensation). **S:** windscreen, window; goggles, spectacles □ *A fan directs a stream of warm air over the car's windscreen to prevent it from* ***misting up****.* □ *'I'm as blind as a bat: my glasses have* ***misted up****!'*

mistake for [B2 pass emph rel] wrongly suppose that sth or sb is sth or sb else □ *People are always* ***mistaking*** *him* ***for*** *his twin brother.* □ *He was* ***mistaken for*** *an enemy scout and badly wounded.*

mixed up [pass adj (B1)] (informal) (be) muddled, confused in one's thoughts or feelings □ *I think that she's been very* ***mixed up*** *and she feels as if she's had to fight the whole world.* DC □ *He discussed personal problems with a group of very* ***mixed-up*** *teenagers.* □ passive with *be, feel, seem.*

mixed up in [pass (B3)] (informal) (be) a party to, or member of (esp sth secret or illegal). **o:** robbery, conspiracy, plot, intrigue; organization, spy ring □ *He was* ***mixed up in*** *that horse-doping case.* □ *What a business to get (yourself)* ***mixed up in****!*

mix up (with)[1] [B1i pass adj B3 pass rel] be unable to tell one thing or person from another. **O:** colour, twin, name □ *He's forever* ***mixing*** *me* ***up with*** *my brother.* □ *One fault with his reading is that he still* ***mixes up*** *'b' and 'd' (or* ***mixes up*** *'b'* ***with*** *'d').*

mix up (with)[2] [B1i nom pass adj B3 pass rel] mix two or more things together so that one does not know which is which; muddle up (with) (q v). **S:** organizer, agency, official. **O:** ticket, luggage, children, papers □ *The office* ***mixed up*** *our flight* *documents* (or: *made a* ***mix-up*** *of our flight documents*)*: John got mine and I got his.* □ *The porter got our bags* ***mixed up****: I nearly walked off with someone else's.*

mixed up with [pass (B3)] (informal) (be) involved with (esp for an immoral or illegal purpose). **o:** woman, (sb else's) wife; gang, crowd □ *The Colonel got worried about that woman Hector was getting* ***mixed up with*** *in Tallulagahabad.* RM □ *His parents disapproved of the people he was* ***mixed up with****.*

mock-up [nom (B1)] full-size model of an aircraft etc, made of wood and cardboard (or other materials that are ready to hand) □ *The* ***mock-up*** *is particularly useful in the development of the flight compartment.* IJA □ *I want to propose a vote of thanks to Sergeant Wilson for an excellent* ***mock-up*** *of a boat.* BBCR

monkey about/around [A1] (informal) play mischievously □ *It's dangerous to* ***monkey around*** *in a workshop.* □ *'Stop* ***monkeying about*** *with those matches!'*

moon about/around/round [A1 A2] (informal) wander about listlessly, aimlessly. **o:** house, place □ *He's no longer* ***mooning round*** *at Kenspeckle, thank goodness.* RM □ *I wish that girl would stop* ***mooning about*** *the house.*

mop up[1] [B1i pass adj] absorb liquid using an absorbent sponge, mop, or rag. **O:** (spilt) coffee, milk, orange juice □ *She* ***mopped up*** *the pools that had formed under the leak in the ceiling.*

mop up[2] [B1i pass adj] (military) clear 'pockets' of enemy troops left behind in the general advance; clean up[3] (q v). **O:** isolated pockets of resistance □ *There are still some enemy remaining and they are being* ***mopped up****.* MFM □ *There were still some* ***mopping up*** *operations to be undertaken.* MFM

mope about/around/round [A1 A2] wander here and there in a dispirited, dejected way. **o:** house, place □ *'Can't you get Jennifer's mind off that young man? She's been* ***moping about*** *the place all weekend.'*

motion aside/away [B1i pass] direct sb to move away or to one side, with a motion or gesture. **S:** steward, flunkey, doorkeeper, attendant □ *The official* ***motioned*** *us* ***aside*** *with a superior sweep of his arm.* □ *The taxis were* ***motioned away*** *by the policeman on duty.*

mount up [A1] form a bigger and bigger amount, accumulate. **S:** expenses, costs; savings, pounds □ *The small loss of weight from her day's production wouldn't be noticed, but the stolen carats would* ***mount up*** *fast.* DS □ *Put aside a pound a week and you'll be surprised to find how quickly your savings* ***mount up****.*

move about/around [A1 B1ii pass] go, be sent, from one place to another (esp because of one's work) □ *Salesmen are constantly* ***moving around*** *from one town to another.* □ *The families of servicemen are* ***moved about*** *a good deal.*

move along [A1 B1ii pass] (police) (cause to) disperse, go away (said of, or to, onlookers who have gathered near the scene of an accident etc) □ *'Now,* ***move along*** *there, please,' said the policeman.* □ *A screen of police kept would-be spectators* ***moving along****.*

move right down [A1 A2] (request from a conductor to passengers) move away from the doorway towards the front of a bus or tram; pass along/down (q v) □ *'****Move right down*** *inside please!* ***Move right down*** *the car!'*

move in [A1 B1i pass] (cause to) occupy, take possession of, a house etc. **S:** [A1] **O:** [B1] family, couple. **S:** [B1] council, church □ *The family are* ***moving in*** *on the first of the month.* □ *'Won't the agricultural people have something to say if they're shot out* (= made to leave) *and we're* ***moved in****?'* TBC ⇨ move (into).

move in (on) [A1 A3] move closer to sb or sth so as to handle, tackle or treat him or it. **S:** demolition team, bulldozer; riot squad, police; (film, television) camera. **o:** building, rubble; demonstrators; actors □ *The camera* ***moved in on*** *the sofa for a close-up sequence.* □ *The tanks* ***moved in*** *to flush the snipers from their nests.* □ *Important changes are* ***moving in on*** *the industry* (i e are about to affect it). OBS

move (into) [A2 emph rel B2 pass emph rel] (cause to) occupy, take possession (of). **S:** [A2] **O:** [B2] family, homeless people. **S:** [B2] local authority, housing trust □ *'Where are the Council* ***moving*** *you?' '****Into*** *a new flat.'* □ ***Into*** *that one council house have* ***moved*** *father, mother and seven children.* ⇨ move in.

move on[1] [B1ii pass] (police) tell sb to move from where he is causing an obstruction, unlawfully parked etc; tell sb to move along (q v). **S:** police, traffic warden. **O:** motorist, onlooker, loiterer □ *We wanted to park in front of the bank, but the traffic warden* ***moved*** *us* ***on****.* □ *Before the crowd could get big enough to pose a threat to law and order, the police* ***moved*** *the people* ***on****.*

move on[2] [A1] progress, move to a better job, house, style of life □ *I've been in this job for five years now; it's time I was* ***moving on****.* □ *He's* ***moved on*** *to higher and better things.*

move out [A1 B1i pass] (cause to) move from, vacate, a house, flat, camp etc. **S:** [A1] **O:** [B1] tenant, occupant, owner; troops. **S:** [B1] council, health authorities; officer □ *The tenants of the condemned houses are being* ***moved out*** *and into new council flats.* □ *'Tell the men to pack their kit: we're* ***moving out*** (= leaving camp or barracks)*.'*

move over [A1] move away so as to leave more room for another occupant of a bed, bench etc □ *'****Move over****: you're taking up more than half the bed!'*

move towards [A2 rel] approach, move nearer to. **S:** powers, contending states, negotiators. **o:** settlement, agreement □ *The statesmen have* ***moved*** *away from their opposed positions and* ***towards*** *a compromise settlement.* □ *We are* ***moving towards*** *a better understanding between our two countries.*

move up[1] [A1 A2 rel] progress in one's work, rise socially. **o:** the social scale, pyramid, ladder, hierarchy □ *He'll* ***move up*** *a rung or two when his qualifications are confirmed.* □ *He's* ***moved*** *very rapidly* ***up*** *the promotion ladder.* □ *She's* ***moving up*** *in the world.*

move up[2] [A1] (finance) rise; improve its position. **S:** price, rate, cost; share, stock, copper, rubber □ *The exchange rate of the pound* ***moved up*** *sharply to well over 2·91 dollars.* SC □ *Mining shares* ***moved up*** *to a new level.*

move up[3] [A1 B1i pass] (military) move into the battle area. **S:** [A1] **O:** [B1] division, battalion;

armour, guns. **A:** into the (front) line, to the front □ *Two companies were **moved up** under cover of darkness to reinforce the front line.* □ *As they **moved up**, they tangled with troops coming out of the line.* RFW

mow down [B1i pass] (military) cut down as if they were grass being mown with a scythe. **S:** machine-gun (fire), (rapid) rifle fire. **O:** assault troops, attackers □ *The first wave of assault troops was **mown down** before it had passed through its own wire.*

muck about/around [A1] (informal) occupy oneself in a sloppy, idle, foolish way; mess about (q v) □ *I wish he'd stop **mucking about** and get down to some serious work.* □ *Many accidents are caused by children **mucking about** on railway lines.*

muck about (with) [B1ii pass A3 pass] (informal) handle sb or sth roughly, clumsily, incompetently etc; mess about (with) (q v). **O:** girl; patient; customer. **o:** girl; car, motor, radio; wound □ *That dealer has been **mucking** me **about** for days: I despair of getting a satisfactory answer out of him.* □ *'Stop **mucking about with** that stereo: I've just paid £20 to get it fixed.'*

muck in (with) [A1 A3] (informal) put oneself on close, friendly terms with workmates etc, sharing their work and pleasures □ *He's a lone wolf: never **mucks in with** the others.* □ *They should have **mucked in** together, the whole crowd of them, and settled their disputes in bed.* PW

muck out [B1i pass] clean dung from stables etc; clean out (q v). **O:** cowshed, pigsty, farmyard; pig, cow □ *He has to **muck out** the horses* (i e the stables) *every morning at six.* □ *Give the yard a thorough **mucking-out**.*

muck up [B1i nom pass adj] (informal) spoil, ruin; mess up (q v). **O:** garden, study; layout, arrangement; holiday, outing □ *While I considered that the Allies could win the war by the end of 1944, I was fairly certain we would **muck** it **up**, and would not do so.* MFM □ *The weather really **mucked up*** (or: *made a real **muck-up** of) our weekend.*

muddle through [A1] (informal) reach one's goal despite inefficiency, the lack of a plan or programme etc □ *The Labour Party had a theory fifty years ago, but it's no use for them now. They're just hoping to **muddle through** without it.* SML

muddle up (with) [B1i pass adj B3 pass emph rel] (informal) mix two or more things together so that one does not know which is which; mix up (with)[2] (q v). **S:** official, porter, agency. **O:** tickets, reservations □ *My personal letters got **muddled up with** a batch of circulars.* □ *The stamps were found **muddled up** in a drawer.*

mug up [B1i pass adj] (slang) learn by intensive study, esp before an exam; swot up (q v). **O:** chemistry, law; formulae, figures (the kind of information that is usually memorized) □ *I'm **mugging up** my medicine, too.* DIL □ *All the candidate could offer were a few facts hastily **mugged up** before the examination.*

mull over [B1i pass] consider slowly and carefully; ponder on/over (q v). **O:** remark, statement, proposal □ *He wanted the chance of **mulling over** his conclusions about the old boy.* ILIH □ *Arguments for and against had been thoroughly **mulled over**.*

muscle in (on) [A1 A3 pass] (informal) use force or guile to get a share of, or participate in, sth important or profitable. **S:** gang, hoodlum; rival, colleague. **o:** market, racket, money; project, scheme □ *I see red when I think anyone is trying to **muscle in on** my property.* AITC □ *The Association has been trying to **muscle in** for years now, but we have always rejected their applications to be affiliated.* RM

muse on/over/upon [A2 pass adj rel] think about, ponder, in an absorbed, dreamy way. **o:** past adventures, pleasant events □ *He **mused upon** the flattering comments made by the young woman.* □ *Their offer to lend us their seaside cottage was pleasant to **muse on**.*

muss up [B1i pass] (informal) make untidy, disarrange. **O:** hair, clothes □ *'I'm not crawling about in that dusty attic and **mussing up** my new dress.'* □ *'Keep your hands to yourself. You're **mussing** my hair **up**!'*

N

nag (at) [A2 pass adj] criticize, find fault (with) continuously; press sb irritatingly to do sth. **S:** wife. **o:** husband □ *He feels constantly **nagged at**.* □ *She's been **nagging at** him to mow the lawn.* □ *She never stops **nagging** (**at** her husband and children)!*

nail back [B1i pass adj] fasten sth back with nails. **O:** door, shutter, flap □ *The shutter kept banging to and fro in the wind, so we **nailed** it **back** against the wall.* □ ***Nail** the edges **back** at right angles to the cover.*

nail down[1] [B1i pass adj] fasten sth flat onto another surface with nails. **O:** carpet; lid, cover □ *If the corner of the carpet curls up, **nail** it **down**.*

nail down[2] [B1ii pass] get sb to say precisely what he believes or wants to do □ *John's very difficult to **nail down**: you can never get him to speak his mind on anything.* □ *Try to **nail** him **down** on the subject of religious education.*

nail down[3] [B1ii pass] specify more exactly, define the character of sb or sth precisely. **O:** him etc, character; problem, subject □ *Harold had **nailed** him **down**, robbed him of his mystery. His secret was out.* PW □ *Can we **nail** it* (the concept) ***down** a little more precisely?* SNP

nail on/onto [B1i pass adj B2 pass] fasten one thing to another with nails. **O:** shelf, cupboard, box. **o:** wall, door □ *Don't **nail** the uprights **onto** the wall; screw them on.*

nail one's colours to the mast [B2 pass] make one's views known on a subject, and abide firmly by them □ *The Home Secretary **nailed his colours** firmly **to the mast** on the question of arming the police.*

nail up[1] [B1i pass adj] secure sth with nails so

that it cannot easily be opened. **O:** door, window, shutter; box, trunk □ *Doors of derelict houses may be boarded and **nailed up** to prevent children getting in.* □ *Mr Fiske sat down on a **nailed-up** crate and beat his hands gently upon his knees.* AITC

nail up[2] [B1i pass adj] fasten sth to a surface so that it hangs from that surface. **O:** painting, tapestry, awning □ *He **nailed up** a sign over the door which said: 'No Admission'.*

name (after) [B2 pass] give a child the same first name as. **o:** father, grandparent □ *They **named** the girl Mary — **after** her mother.*

narrow down (to) [B1i pass B3 pass] reduce the number of people or places being investigated by clearing certain suspects etc. **S:** detective, search party. **O:** investigation, inquiries, search. **o:** farm, street; small number of suspects □ *They **narrowed** the search for the missing boy **down to** a few streets near the school.*

negotiate (with) [B2 pass emph rel] (formal) arrange, conclude, settle, sth through formal discussion. **O:** contract, deal; treaty, settlement; release, transfer. **o:** firm, labour force; (foreign) power, government □ *It was announced that Tyneside shipyards had **negotiated** deals worth £30m **with** a major oil company.* □ *The British **negotiated** satisfactory terms **with** the French* (or: *The British and the French **negotiated** satisfactory terms*).

nest (in) [A2 emph rel] build a nest (in); have its nest (in). **S:** bird; mouse, rat. **o:** tree, creeper; attic, wainscoting □ *Clearing the attic we had unearthed a family of mice **nesting in** a pile of old newspapers.*

nestle down [A1] settle oneself comfortably under bedclothes, a rug etc □ *Robin had **nestled down** in his father's sleeping-bag on the floor of the dinghy.*

nestle up (against/to) [A1 A3 pass] press close to another person for warmth or comfort. **o:** husband, lover; mother □ *The children **nestled up** close together and fell fast asleep.* □ *Liza **nestled up against** her mother and dozed fitfully.*

nibble (at) [A2 pass] take small bites (from); eat sparingly and without appetite. **o:** biscuit, sausage; bait □ *The cheese left out on the kitchen table had been **nibbled at**. Mice again.* □ *Father never had much for breakfast. He would drink a cup of black coffee and **nibble at** a piece of dry toast.*

niggle (over) [A2 pass] (informal) be fussy, behave in a petty way (about sth). **o:** terms, conditions; price □ *'I don't see why they should **niggle over** paying a few pounds into the fund. They're rich enough, Heaven knows.'* □ *'We had tremendous difficulty getting the agreement signed. Every little clause was **niggled over**.'*

nip across, along, away etc [A1 A2] (informal) move sharply, hurry, across etc □ *'I must just **nip out** to the shops before the children come home from school.'* □ *'**Nip across** to Mrs Jones and borrow a pound of sugar.'*

nip in the bud [B2 pass] stop sth or sb from going any further (because the event, or his actions, may become dangerous, unpleasant etc). **S:** authority; parent, teacher. **O:** revolt, escapade, adventure; scheme, development □ *He sat down with the air of having **nipped** some possibly dangerous nonsense **in the bud**.* ASA □ *His new-found intimacy with his son had been **nipped in the bud**.* ASA

nip off [B1i pass adj] (horticulture) remove with a sharp cutting or pinching action. **S:** gardener. **O:** shoots, growth □ *He **nipped off** the side shoots from his geraniums.*

nod off [A1] (informal) fall asleep (esp in one's chair), letting one's head fall forward at the same time; doze off (q v), drop off[2] (q v) □ *I must have **nodded off**, I sometimes do, on a Sunday, over my paper.* HD □ *I managed to make my mind a blank, even **nodding off** for a moment at one point.* CON

noise abroad [B1i pass] (formal) announce, make known. **O:** reputation, fame; result, outcome; announcement; it... that he was retiring □ *Rumours of his dismissal were **noised abroad** in the department.* □ *It was **noised abroad** that he was taking up a new appointment.* □ *'Who **noised it abroad** that I had spoken to him?'*

nose about/around [A1 nom] (informal) go about searching or prying (often into matters which are not one's concern); poke about/around (q v) □ *I wish I could stop him **nosing about** — he's not wanted here.* □ *The children had a good **nose-around*** (or: ***nose around***) *in the attic.*

nose out [B1i pass adj] discover by smell, or by persistent searching. **O:** rat, ferret, rabbit; scandal, sensation □ *The dog **nosed** a rat **out** from behind a pile of old newspapers.* □ *Trust him to **nose out** some choice piece of scandal.*

notch up [B1i pass adj] (informal) record a score (formerly by cutting notches in a stick); achieve, attain. **S:** hunter, marksman; player, performer. **O:** bullseye, hit; pheasant, grouse; big score, several victories □ *We **notched up** one or two rabbits in a day's shooting.* □ *Our teams have **notched up** a number of wins in matches against visiting sides.*

note down [B1i pass adj] record in writing, write down (q v). **O:** detail, particulars; recipe, formula □ *He **noted down** every word I said.* □ *The date of the meeting was carefully **noted down**.*

number off [A1 B1i pass adj] (military) (cause to) call out the number of the place one occupies in a rank of soldiers. **S:** [A1] **O:** [B1] soldiers, men. **S:** [B1] sergeant, NCO □ *The platoon **numbered off** from the right.* □ *The company was **numbered off** by the sergeant major.*

O

object (to) [A2 pass adj emph rel] oppose, express one's displeasure (at). **o:** noise, disturbance; being contradicted, having to stay on at school □ *He's always **objecting**, but never **to** anything in particular.* □ *I **object to** being woken* *up early.* □ *The new transport plan is much* ***objected to.***

oblige (by) [B2] it would be less of a nuisance or irritation (if); you will please (do sth), be so good as to (do sth). **o:** asking your children to make less noise, parking your car elsewhere □ *You'd* ***oblige*** *me* ***by*** *keeping your thoughts on the subject to yourself.* □ *You would* ***oblige*** *me* ***by*** *giving more time to your work* (or: ***oblige*** *me if you gave more time to your work*). □ an apparently polite request which is in fact threatening or sarcastic; with *would.*

oblige (with) [B2] (kindly) lend or give sth to sb. **o:** match, light; lift in one's car □ *'Could you* ***oblige*** *me* ***with*** *5p for the gas meter?'* □ *I asked him if he could* ***oblige*** *us* ***with*** *a lift to the nearest garage.* □ with *can/could.*

obtrude (upon) [A2 emph rel B2 emph rel] (formal) force or push (itself etc) forward, esp in an unwelcome way. **S:** [A2] **O:** [B2] ideas, thoughts, opinions; presence, personality □ *His vulgar presence* ***obtruded*** *(itself)* ***upon*** *the company when it was least welcome.* □ *Painful memories* ***obtruded upon*** *his attempts to reflect calmly.*

occur to [A2 emph rel] come into one's mind, enter one's head. **S:** thought, idea, plan; (it...) that he should know; (it...) to ask why □ *The possibility of a way out of the impasse had never* ***occurred to*** *anyone.* □ *It had never* ***occurred to*** *her to ask herself why she was so unpopular.* □ *That he should have some deep personal objection had never* ***occurred to*** *me.*

offend (against) [A2 pass adj emph rel] break, contravene; behave in a way that is at variance with. **o:** code (of behaviour), conventions, manners, proprieties □ *He seems to take pleasure in* ***offending against*** *the codes accepted by most people.*

offer up [B1i pass adj] (religious worship) present (to God). **S:** congregation, worshippers. **O:** prayers, sacrifices □ *The priest* ***offered up*** *a slaughtered chicken.* □ *Thanks were* ***offered up*** *for mercies received.*

officiate (at) [A2 emph rel] (formal) conduct a ceremony (esp religious). **S:** priest, minister, rabbi. **o:** wedding, funeral; dedication, unveiling □ *The bride's father, the Reverend Peter Masters,* ***officiated*** *yesterday* ***at*** *the wedding of Miss Cynthia Masters to Mr Stephen Drew.*

ogle (at) [A2 pass adj] look intently, and with love or longing, (at); make eyes at (q v). **o:** (pretty) nurse, student □ *He* ***ogles at*** (or: *He* ***ogles***) *all the attractive secretaries in the office.* □ *She was embarrassed at being* ***ogled at*** *so persistently.*

omit (from) [B2 pass emph rel] (formal) not mention or state; leave out/out of (q v). **S:** author, speaker. **O:** reference, mention; statement, claim; charge, accusation. **o:** book, report, speech □ *The finance minister was careful to* ***omit from*** *his remarks any mention of the critical fall in the gold reserves.* □ ***From*** *the most recent edition of Maitland's book the chapter dealing with his arrest and imprisonment by the regime has had to be* ***omitted.***

ooze out/out of [A1 A2] (of a thick fluid) come out, emerge, slowly. **S:** blood; oil. **o:** wound, cut; flaw □ *Black oil was* ***oozing out of*** *a crack in the engine casing.*

open fire (on) [B2 pass pass(o) rel] begin firing (at). **S:** enemy; infantry, sniper; gun; ship. **o:** position; trench, strongpoint □ *It would not have surprised me if someone had* ***opened fire on*** *us from an upstairs window.* UTN □ *A searchlight picked her* (the ship) *up, and* ***fire*** *was* ***opened on*** *her from the shore.* RFW

open onto [A2] allow one to reach; lead to, give access to. **S:** door, french-window, gate. **o:** backyard, garden □ *The back gate* ***opens onto*** *a private road.* □ *The door of the cottage* ***opens onto*** *an uninterrupted stretch of countryside.*

open out[1] [A1] widen, broaden. **S:** river, valley □ *The river* ***opens out*** *suddenly into a broad estuary.* □ *At that point, the road* ***opens out*** *and becomes a dual carriageway.*

open out[2] [B1i pass adj] unfold. **O:** map, blueprint, chart □ *He* ***opened*** *the road-map* ***out,*** *and laid it on his knee.*

open out[3] [A1] unfold, blossom; develop. **S:** flower, bloom; character, personality □ *In the warmth of the room, the roses* ***opened out*** *in a few days.* □ *She* ***opened out*** *a good deal while she was with us.* PW

open up[1] [A1] open the front door; let police officers enter a building to arrest suspects etc □ *Mother!* ***Open up!*** *Let me in, I'm home.* DPM □ *'****Open up*** *in the name of the law!'* □ *We told them to* ***open up*** *or we'd break the door down.* □ direct or indirect command only.

open up[2] [B1i pass adj] unwrap, undo (a parcel etc); unfasten, unlock (a box etc); bring (a room etc) back into use by unlocking it. **O:** packet, package; suitcase, trunk; wing, room □ *'****Open up*** *the boot of the car, and let me look inside.'* □ *Some of the smaller state rooms in the palace have not been* ***opened up*** *for years.*

open up[3] [B1i pass adj] form, cause to appear, by cutting etc. **O:** gap, breach, passageway □ *The infantry* ***opened up*** *a corridor across the minefield for the armour to pass through.* □ *They* ***open up*** *a chink in the defensive armour of the Exchequer.* SC

open up[4] [B1i pass adj] reveal, lay bare (esp for subsequent development, exploitation). **O:** territory, land, the West (US); coal-fields, oil-fields; prospect, horizon □ *The Government is* ***opening up*** *a new area for settlement by peasant farmers.* □ *His stories* ***open up*** *new worlds of the imagination.* AH

open up[5] [A1 B1i pass adj] (sport) (of play in a game) become, make, more lively and mobile. **S:** [A1] **O:** [B1] play, game, match □ *In the second half the game* ***opened up*** *and several attractive passing movements began.*

open up[6] [A1] (informal) talk freely and openly □ *She hoped that he would* ***open up*** *at once about his visit, but he didn't.* PW □ *It was only after he had had a few drinks that he could* ***open up.***

open up[7] [A1] (military) begin to fire. **S:** gun, battery, artillery □ *His battery of rockets* ***opened up*** *over their heads.* BM □ *A machine gun* ***opened up*** *from a concealed position.*

operate (on) [A2 pass rel] (medicine) perform surgery (upon). **S:** surgeon; heart specialist, obstetrician. **o:** patient □ *Mr Smith was* ***operated on*** *for a constriction of the intestine.* □ *'Has Mr Cutler* ***operated*** *yet? Yes, but not* ***on*** *Mrs Jones.'*

opposed to [pass (B2)] (be) against, not support. **o:** change; plan, scheme; treaty, agreement; his going, my being there □ *He is totally* ***opposed to*** *any change in the existing law.* □ *The Church of England is on record as being* ***opposed to*** *apartheid.* SC □ passive with *be, seem, remain.*

opt in favour of/for [A2 pass] choose, select (from among a number of alternatives). **o:** fuller participation, better schools, alternative plan □ *The Council* ***opted for*** *a by-pass to carry heavy commercial traffic away from the town centre.*

opt out/out of [A1 A2 pass adj] refuse to take part, to be concerned, to make decisions etc. **o:** commitment, responsibility □ *To* ***opt out*** *at this critical moment would be quite indefensible.* ASA □ *He'd simply* ***opted out of*** *every situation of trust he'd been placed in.*

order about/around [B1ii pass adj B2 pass] keep telling sb to do this and that in a bossy way □ *'I mean, he's got no right to* ***order*** *me* ***about*** *the place.'* TC □ *A military mood came over him and he longed to* ***order*** *her* ***about****: 'Shun! Stand at ease!'* PW

order off (the field) [B1i pass B2 pass] (sport) order to leave the field of play; send off (the field) (q v). **S:** referee. **O:** player □ *Jones was* ***ordered off*** *in the second half after repeated fouls on the opposing winger.*

order out [B1i pass adj] order police or troops to parade (usu to control a demonstration, civil disturbance etc). **S:** government, council. **O:** riot police, soldiers □ *As a dangerous situation was developing in the city, security forces were* ***ordered out*** *to control it.*

order out/out of [B1ii pass B2 pass] order to leave. **o:** hall, room; presence □ *The children were* ***ordered out of*** *the kitchen while their mother was working.*

order up [B1i pass] (military) order to move from a position in the rear to the front line. **S:** general, commander. **O:** division, brigade; tanks, infantry □ *Two battalions were* ***ordered up*** *to strengthen a weak point in the line.*

oust (from) [B2 pass] remove abruptly (from), drive out/out of (q v). **O:** intruder, interloper; ruler, minister. **o:** seat, place; position, office, power □ *Smith was* ***ousted from*** *his Cabinet post as the result of manœuverings on the part of his rivals.*

owe to [B2 pass emph rel] give, name, sb or sth as the reason for some achievement; attribute an achievement to sb or sth. **O:** success, pre-eminence; discovery, invention; it... that we are now happier. **o:** colleague, friend; hard work, ingenuity □ *We* ***owe*** *the increase in exports* ***to*** *the energy of our sales force.* □ ***To*** *what qualities of character do they* ***owe*** *this remarkable recovery?*

owe it to [B2] be, feel, obliged to do sth for sb; be bound to do sth, because it is in one's interests to do so. **O:** it... to set an example, to work hard; to buy insurance, to get a house; to wear a hat, to buy our shoes. **o:** family, employer; oneself □ *I* ***owed it to*** *my parents to come home, for they were getting tired and old.* RFW □ *You're lucky to be fair — you* ***owe it to*** *yourself to use 'Stablond' shampoo always.* H

own up (to) [A1 A3 pass adj] admit or confess that one is to blame. **o:** being in the wrong, having stolen □ *Sometimes the mistakes are much more important than that. What is important is that we* ***own up****, and say we are sorry.* TT □ *All this will have to be* ***owned up to****.*

P

pace off [B1i pass] measure in paces part of a total distance or length. **O:** part, half; twenty feet, fifty metres □ *'****Pace off*** *about four feet along the side of the marquee and knock in a peg. Then* ***pace*** *the same distance* ***off*** *again, and so on all the way round.'*

pace out [B1i pass] measure the full extent of sth in paces or steps. **O:** room, field; distance, dimensions □ *He* ***paced out*** *the length and width of the room, and decided it would do for his purposes.*

pace up and down [A1 emph A2 emph] walk backwards and forwards (esp out of impatience, restlessness etc). **S:** prisoner; exam candidate, interviewee. **o:** cell; waiting-room, corridor □ *'Stop* ***pacing up and down*** *like a caged tiger, David. The train will be here in a minute.'*

pack away [B1i pass] put sth in a box, cupboard etc, because it is no longer needed, for safe keeping etc; put away[1] (q v). **O:** toy, book; shirt, dress; machine, rifle □ *'****Pack away*** *your books, children. It's time for break.'* □ *All the glass and china was carefully* ***packed away*** *in cases and stored in the attic.*

pack down [A1] (rugby football) (of opposing packs of forwards) form a scrum □ (TV commentary) *'The referee's bringing the forwards back five yards, and they're* ***packing down*** *just inside the England half.'*

pack in[1] [B1i pass] (informal) abandon, renounce; jack in (q v). **O:** job, work; smoking, gambling; racing, football □ *I've* ***packed in*** *this telephone-answering service so anyone can get me personally any time of day or night.* JFTR □ *Smoking's no good for your health: it's time you* ***packed*** *it* ***in****.*

pack in[2] [B1i] (informal) leave sb's employment; end a relationship with sb. **O:** boss, boyfriend □ *The girl had only worked for Mr Touchitt for a week when she* ***packed*** *him* ***in****. It was the same old story: he couldn't keep his hands to himself.*

pack in[3] [B1ii] (informal) draw people in large numbers to a theatre etc. **S:** comedian, singer. **O:** ⚠ the crowds; them □ (one performer to another) *'Do you remember the way we used to* ***pack*** *them* ***in*** *at the old Alhambra?'*

pack it in [B1ii] (informal) stop doing or saying sth noisy, destructive etc; knock it off (q v), pack it up (q v), turn it in (q v) □ *'You're bringing the house down with your caterwauling; why don't you* ***pack it in****?'* □ ***Pack it in*** *old son, Mister what's-his-name'll be here soon to have a look at this chair of his.* ITAJ

pack off (to) [B1i pass B3 pass rel] send away, dispatch, briskly or urgently (to). **O:** refugee, patient. **o:** quiet spot, safe retreat □ *I **packed** them **off** with notes **to** the appropriate hospitals.* DIL □ *He **packed off** his wife with Mrs Paine and left a few days later.* OBS □ *When the children knocked on Mr Ransby's door and asked for a penny, he **packed** them **off** with a flea in their ear.*

pack out[1] [B1i pass adj] fill or pad (with material, paper etc) to capacity; pad out[1] (q v). **O:** jacket (e g of a boiler), casing; coat, sleeve □ *The men **packed out** the trousers of their overalls with newspaper to keep out the bitter cold.*

pack out[2] [B1i pass adj] fill to capacity. **O:** concert hall, theatre, stadium □ *The Festival Hall was **packed out** for Menuhin's first concert.* □ *A great throng **packed out** the lecture theatre and overflowed into the corridors.* □ *The company played to **packed-out** houses for more than a year.*

pack up[1] [A1 B1i pass] put one's belongings into cases etc, before leaving home etc. **O:** books, goods; stall; home □ *Several dealers found the business left over inadequate to pay their overheads, and they **packed up** and left.* DS □ *He **packed up** the few possessions he had and moved out.*

pack up[2] [A1] (informal) abandon everything one is doing (and not try to start again); give up[12] (q v) □ *I shall tell him straight out that if he doesn't take this on, he may as well **pack up**.* ASA □ *If you don't know where you're going you might just as well **pack up**.* FFE □ usu with *may-/might (just) as well.*

pack up[3] [A1] (informal) stop, fail; cut out[5] (q v). **S:** motor, engine □ *Fifty miles out from land our port engine **packed up** on us.*

pack it up [B1ii] (informal) stop an activity (esp one causing an unpleasant noise or disturbance); knock it off (q v), pack it in (q v) turn it it (q v) □ *The children were making an awful din and I told them to **pack it up**.*

pad out[1] [B1i pass adj] pack material into part of a garment etc; pack out[1] (q v). **O:** shoulder, sleeve □ *The shoulders of his jacket were **padded out** to make them look square.* □ *The bedhead was covered with fabric and the surface then **padded out** with cotton wool.*

pad out[2] [B1i pass adj] make fuller by adding (unnecessary) material. **S:** novelist, journalist. **O:** book, paper, report □ *The passage was tiresomely **padded out** with references to the author's fashionable friends.*

paint in [B1i pass adj] add or insert in paint. **O:** detail, figure □ *The standing figure to the right was **painted in** after the rest of the picture was completed.* □ *They give a form to the world, **painting** it **in** excitingly and often amusingly.* NDN

paint on/onto [B1i pass adj B2 pass rel] apply to a surface, using paint. **O:** title, name; moustache, eyebrow; stripe, square □ *Windows and doors had been **painted onto** an end wall of the house.* □ *Groucho Marx's moustache was **painted on**.*

paint out [B1i pass adj] cover sth by applying paint over the top of it. **O:** name, detail □ *Parts of old paintings which appear unpleasing to later artists are sometimes **painted out**.*

pair off (with) [A1 A3 rel B1i pass adj B3 pass rel] (cause to) form pairs □ [A1] *The scouts **paired off** and began to patrol the area.* □ [A3] *Angela **paired off with** Douglas and Jane **with** Stephen.* □ [B3] *Each girl in the party was **paired off with** a boy.*

pal up (with) [A1 A3] (informal) become friends; become the friend of □ *Two or three of us who'd **palled up** went off at weekends to the sea.* □ *In the first form he **palled up with** a boy from the same village.*

pale at [A2 emph rel] become pale or white at, show signs of fear at. **o:** the (very) thought (of), the mention (of), the sight (of) □ *The poor fellow, though no coward, **paled at** the mention of an injection.* □ *Meeting his mother-in-law for the first time was a prospect **at** which he **paled**.*

pall (on/upon) [A2 emph rel] (formal) become dreary or uninteresting because used, spoken etc, too long. **S:** voice, manner, conversation □ *His funny stories begin to **pall** (**on** his listeners) after the second time of telling.* □ *His glib manner **palls on** one within a short time of first meeting him.*

palm off (on) [B1i pass adj B3 pass emph rel] (informal) persuade sb to accept sth or sb by underhand means; fob off onto (q v). **O:** shoddy goods, surplus stock; unwelcome guest. **o:** unsuspecting public, gullible customer; friend □ *Export rejects may be **palmed off** in the street markets.* □ *We **palmed off** the unimportant Carter **on** somebody else.* OMIH □ *He's the kind of dealer **on** whom anything can be **palmed off**.* ⇨ next entry.

palm off (with) [B1i pass B3 pass emph rel] (informal) persuade sb to accept sth or sb by deceit, misrepresentation etc; quieten or pacify sb with; fob off (with) (q v). **O:** gullible consumer, customer. **o:** inferior produce; half-truth □ *The salesman tried to **palm** us **off with** some shop-soiled sheets.* □ *We couldn't have our Superstore just yet and we were **palmed off with** promises.* DPM ⇨ previous entry.

pan off/out [B1i pass adj] (mining) wash gold-bearing gravel in a pan, separating off the gravel □ *The prospector **panned off** bits of sand and gravel scooped from the bed of a stream.*

pan out[1] [A1] (mining) yield gold. **S:** area, strike, river □ *We had been working the stream for ten days, but it hadn't **panned out**.*

pan out[2] [A1] (informal) develop well/badly; work out[5] (q v). **S:** events, the future; it, things □ *Nobody knows how the economy will **pan out** over the next few years.* □ *Don't spend too much time worrying how things are going to **pan out**.*

pander to [A2 pass adj emph rel] feed, promote; cater to (q v). **S:** newspapers, television, pulp literature. **o:** taste for violence, interest in crime □ *The Sunday press **panders to** the public interest in the seamy and sensational.* □ *This is the kind of depraved appetite **to** which television often **panders**.*

pant for [A2 rel] show by one's rapid breathing that one needs to drink; show strong desire for. **o:** water; opening, chance, break □ *'Of course I'm thirsty. If you'd spent the day working in the fields you'd be **panting for** a cool drink!'* □ *'Can't you see how desperate she is to get into films? She's just **panting for** a screen test.'*

pant out [B1iii pass] deliver in short quick

breaths. **S:** messenger, envoy. **O:** statement, message □ *The messenger sat down to rest and* ***panted out*** *his sad story.* □ *The dying man* ***panted out*** *his last wishes.*

paper over[1] [B1iii pass adj] cover over with (wall-)paper. **O:** door, ceiling; crack, opening □ *A number of stains on the wall were* ***papered over****.*

paper over[2] [B1iii pass adj] cover or hide thinly and imperfectly. **S:** statement, agreement. **O:** divisions, differences of viewpoint □ *The split had only been* ***papered over*** *by declarations that could hardly be reconciled.* OBS □ *Some vague formula may be found to* ***paper over*** *the disagreements.* SC □ *The* ***papered-over*** *cracks in front-bench unity were now beginning to show through.*

parcel out [B1i pass adj] divide into small plots. **O:** estate, land □ *Some landowners voluntarily* ***parcelled*** *some of their land* ***out*** *among the local peasants.* □ *An extensive tract of land was* ***parcelled out*** *into small holdings.*

parcel up [B1i pass adj] make a parcel of. **O:** old clothes, rags, toys □ *We* ***parcelled up*** *some games and toys to take to the Children's Home at Christmas.* □ *She wore so many bulky sweaters and scarves that she always presented a* ***parcelled-up*** *appearance.*

pardon (for) [B2 pass emph rel] forgive (for). **o:** mistake, omission, laziness; being late □ *'Please* ***pardon*** *me* ***for*** *not arriving sooner.'* □ *There were so many faults he had to be* ***pardoned for****.*

pare down[1] [B1i pass adj] make smaller by removing thin strips. **O:** stick, panel, (carved) figure □ *The neck of the figure was* ***pared*** *right* ***down*** *with chisel and mallet to make it appear lean and withered.* □ *The hungry-looking man at the next table* ***pared*** *his chop right* ***down*** *to the bone.*

pare down[2] [B1i pass adj] reduce considerably. **O:** budget, allowance, finances □ *The committee have* ***pared*** *his travelling allowance* ***down*** *to the bare minimum.* □ *Expenditure on new building is* ***pared*** *right* ***down****.* □ *Even with a* ***pared-down*** *budget, we shall have trouble to make both ends meet this year.*

pare off [B1i pass adj B2 pass] remove in thin strips (usu with a knife). **O:** skin, peel; bark □ *To get at the fruit, you* ***pare off*** *the rather thick peel with a sharp knife.* □ *Plastic surgeons have perfected the technique of* ***paring*** *strips of skin* ***off*** *one part of the body and grafting them on elsewhere.*

parley (with) [A2 pass emph rel] (military) discuss the possibility of a truce, an exchange of prisoners etc (with). **o:** enemy, opposing forces □ *An officer came forward with a white flag to* ***parley*** *(****with*** *our general).* □ *The encircled forces were in no mood to* ***parley*** *or be* ***parleyed with****.*

part from [B2 pass] (informal) persuade to spend or give away[1] (q v). **o:** money, cash; pet □ *He's not easily* ***parted from*** *his money.* □ *He's a difficult man to* ***part from*** *his cash.* □ *Have you tried* ***parting*** *him* ***from*** *his brass* (= money)*?* □ *The little boy wouldn't be* ***parted from*** *his pet rabbit.* ⇨ next entry.

part with [A2 pass rel] spend, give away[1] (q v); relinquish. **o:** money, cash; pet; furniture, ornament □ *She made them listen and even on occasion* ***part with*** *money for her objects of charity.* ASA □ *He's not the sort who's happy to* ***part with*** *hard-earned cash.* □ *In order to raise money Aunt Martha had to* ***part with*** *some of her most treasured possessions.* ⇨ previous entry.

part company (with) [B2 pass(o) emph rel] leave sb, separate oneself from sb; not hold the same beliefs, opinions etc as sb, differ (from) (q v). **o:** expedition, convoy; employer, firm; colleague, associate; speaker □ *I regretfully* ***parted company with*** *my fellow-climbers at the end of the first stage of the ascent.* □ *I* ***part company with*** *him* (or: *He and I* ***part company***) *over the question of Britain's entry into Europe.*

partake of[1] [A2 pass emph rel] (formal) share; be partly responsible for, have a hand/part in (q v). **o:** meal, feast; success, triumph, joy; charge, responsibility □ *They invited us to* ***partake of*** *their simple fare.* □ *He spoke uncomplainingly of the arduous duties* ***of*** *which he had* ***partaken****.*

partake of[2] [A2] (formal) resemble in part, contain sth of the nature of. **S:** conduct, behaviour, action; appearance, manner. **o:** arrogance, presumption, conceit □ *I can't help thinking that his generosity* ***partakes*** *somewhat* ***of*** *patronage.*

participate (in) [A2 emph rel] (formal) be involved (in), take part (in) (q v). **o:** activity; demonstration, match; show, display; enterprise, undertaking, venture □ *The Town Council decided not to* ***participate in*** *the financing of the new swimming pool, but to leave the fund-raising entirely to private enterprise.* □ *The reorganization of the school system was a complex operation,* ***in*** *which officials, teachers and parents all* ***participated****.*

partition off [B1i pass adj] divide or separate by means of a partition. **O:** room; office, kitchen; corner, bay □ *The main rooms have been* ***partitioned off****.* □ *A small bathroom has been* ***partitioned off*** *from the original kitchen.*

partner off (with) [A1 A3 rel B1i pass adj B3 pass rel] make a pair, a couple; form people into couples; pair off (with) (q v). **S:** master of ceremonies, hostess □ [B1] *Our hostess* ***partnered*** *everyone* ***off*** *for the next dance.* □ [A3] *Most of our group had* ***partnered off with*** *somebody before the weekend.* □ [B1] *When Mavis arrived at the party she found nothing but* ***partnered-off*** *couples, and nobody left to take an interest in her.*

pass along/down [A1] (instruction from bus conductor to passengers) move to the front of the bus, and don't block the entrance; move right down (q v) □ *Now,* ***pass*** *right* ***along*** *inside, please.*

pass away [B1i pass] occupy time in a pleasant, easy way. **S:** he etc; cards, outdoor sports, conversation. **O:** ⚠ the time, the evening □ *He* ***passed*** *the evening* ***away*** *looking at his collection of stamps.* □ *A hand of cards* ***passes*** *an evening* ***away*** *pleasantly enough.*

pass away/on/over [A1] (euphemism) die □ *'You'll be sorry to hear that Mr Barker's* ***passed over****,' she said.* ASA

pass between [A2] be exchanged by. **S:** angry words, heated arguments; secret, confidence □ *I never heard a kindly word* ***pass between*** *them.*

□ *They'll never speak together again after what's* ***passed between*** *them.* □ *'Remember! No one must ever know what has* ***passed between*** *us.'*

pass by[1] [A1 A2] go past. **S:** pedestrian, vehicle. **o:** door, house □ *The procession* ***passed*** *right* ***by*** *my door.* □ *Somebody* ***passing by*** (= *A* ***passer-by***) *asked me the way to the Town Hall.*

pass by[2] [B1ii pass] not touch or affect, leave alone. **S:** great event, excitement, disturbance □ *She feared commitment, and hoped that the great challenges of life would* ***pass*** *her* ***by*** (or: ***by-pass*** *her*). □ *Life's colourful pageant would best oblige him by continuing to* ***pass*** *him* ***by***. ILIH

pass by[3] [B1ii pass adj] not consider; avoid (because too difficult). **O:** area, field; passage, episode; problem, difficulty □ *We cannot neglect whole areas of aesthetic appreciation, but we must* ***pass*** *them* ***by*** *in our attempt to isolate one aspect of aesthetics.* SNP □ *If you try to* ***pass*** *the problems* ***by*** (or: ***by-pass*** *them*), *they'll remain to dog you.*

pass by[4] [B1ii pass] avoid, shun. **S:** friend, colleague, girl □ *John made quite a noise when one or other of his girl friends* ***by-passed*** *him* (or: ***passed*** *him* ***by***). □ *He had a feeling that his friends were* ***passing*** *him* ***by***.

life pass by [B1ii] (informal) (of the various opportunities and pleasures of life) go by without one having gained from them, or enjoyed them □ *You seem to be afraid that* ***life*** *might* ***pass*** *you* ***by*** *without giving you time to enjoy it to the full.* WI □ *He may have been more pessimistic than unfortunate, but he couldn't help feeling that* ***life*** *had* ***passed*** *him* ***by***.

pass by on the other side [A1] fail, refuse, to go to the aid of people in need □ *People in the poorer countries will die needlessly if the richer countries* ***pass by on the other side***.

pass by/under the name of [A2] be known by a particular name (though it is not, in fact, one's own); go under[3] (q v) □ *At that stage in his criminal career, he* ***passed by*** *the* ***name*** *of Bloggs.* □ *What* ***name*** *is he* ***passing under*** *at the moment?*

pass down[1] [B1i pass adj] transmit, through the generations; hand down[2] (q v). **O:** tradition (of service, of scholarship), craft; myth, tale, saga; jewelry, silver. **A:** from father to son, by oral tradition, by word of mouth □ *The skill has been* ***passed down*** *over four generations.* □ *The accumulated knowledge which has been* ***passed down*** *on this subject is well presented in this volume.*

pass down[2] [A1] move to the front of the bus. ⇨ pass along/down.

pass for [A2 rel] be accepted as having certain qualities (though one, or it, may not possess them in fact). **o:** scholar, gentleman, native-speaker; gold, silver □ *He looked at the collection of odds and ends that* ***passed for*** *china.* TT □ *Among the people of that small town he* ***passed for*** *a man of considerable means.* □ *He was unable to maintain the image of the perfect gentleman* ***for*** *which he had succeeded in* ***passing*** *at first.*

pass (the ball) forward [A1 B1ii pass] (rugby football) when throwing the ball to another member of one's team, make it move forward (rather than back, as the rules require). **S:** scrum half, three-quarter □ *If* ***the ball*** *is* ***passed forward*** (or: *If there is a* ***forward pass***) *the referee orders a set scrum.*

pass in review [B2 pass] survey, consider one by one. **O:** events, developments; successes, achievements; setbacks □ *In his address to the Board, the Chairman* ***passed in review*** *the principal events of the trading year.*

pass into[1] [A2] gain admission to (by passing an examination). **o:** college, school; military academy □ *He* ***passed into*** *Sandhurst by the narrowest possible margin.*

pass into[2] [A2] become a part of, because of its importance, notoriety, etc. **o:** ⚠ history, legend, folklore □ *William Howard Russell's words 'the thin red streak', used of the 93rd Regiment at Balaklava, have* ***passed into*** *history as 'the thin red line'.*

pass into[3] [A2] move from a conscious state into an unconscious one; fall into[2] (q v). **S:** patient; injured, wounded man. **o:** ⚠ a deep sleep; a coma; a trance □ *Patients under hypnosis* ***pass into*** *a trance-like state.*

pass off[1] [A1] lift, recede, be felt no more. **S:** pain, irritation; anger, depression □ *This bout* ***passes off***. NM □ *Mescalin is completely innocuous, and its effects will* ***pass off*** *after eight or ten hours.* DOP

pass off[2] [A1] take place, be carried through. **S:** meeting, discussion, debate; party, celebration. **A:** quietly, well; in orderly fashion, without fuss □ *'How did the demonstration* ***pass off****?' 'Without incident.'* □ *The Soviet leaders are clearly very anxious that the year should* ***pass off*** *smoothly.* OBS □ adv or adv phrase usu present.

pass off[3] [B1i pass] turn attention away from, so as to avoid embarrassment. **O:** incident, moment; reference, allusion □ *Even if someone else raised the subject of the lecture, he would* ***pass*** *it* ***off*** *as easily as he could.* ASA

pass off (as) [B1ii pass B3 pass] represent sb falsely (as). **O:** oneself; wife, friend. **o:** tourist, millionaire, VIP □ *He has been* ***passing*** *himself* ***off as*** *a deaf mute.* T □ *He* ***passed*** *his wife* ***off as*** *an official member of the party.*

pass on [A1] ⇨ pass away/on/over.

pass an opinion (on) [B2 pass emph rel] state one's views (on a subject). **S:** expert, specialist; auctioneer, valuer. **o:** subject, matter; purchase, requisition □ *The research student asked his supervisor to* ***pass an opinion on*** *the material he had collected.* □ *There are few matters* ***on*** *which our friend will not* ***pass an*** *unsolicited* ***opinion***.

pass sentence (on) [B2 pass emph rel] (legal) say what a convicted person's punishment is to be. **S:** court; judge, magistrate. **o:** accused, defendant □ *'Have you anything further to say before I* ***pass sentence on*** *you?'*

pass on (to)[1] [B1i pass adj B3 pass] hand sth to the next person, or another person; get rid of sth, by giving it to another person. **O:** note, memorandum, file; job, task □ ***Pass*** *the letter* ***on to*** *whoever's next on the distribution card.* □ *If you can't do the job yourself,* ***pass*** *it* ***on to*** *someone who can.* □ schoolchildren sometimes pass messages in a whisper like this: *'Miss Brown's got a tear in her dress.* ***Pass*** *it* ***on****!'*

pass on (to)[2] [B1i pass adj B3 pass] enable sb (esp the ordinary person) to benefit from a decrease in costs etc; oblige him to pay, or share, an increase. **O:** saving, economy; increase (in price, cost); tax. **o:** general public; consumer; taxpayer □ *There would be a saving to the airlines of about £70 million a year, some of which could be* ***passed on to*** *the public in lower fares.* OBS □ *The retailer can absorb some of the increase in costs, but he is certain to* ***pass on*** *a percentage* ***to*** *the customer.*

pass on (to)[3] [A1 A3 pass] move from one activity, or stage, to another; get on to[4] (q v). **o:** (another) point, matter; post, stage (in a career); object, point of interest □ *'If there's no further discussion, perhaps we can* ***pass on.****'* □ *He had found time to* ***pass on to*** *her later.* TGLY □ *It seemed the most natural thing in the world for her to* ***pass on to*** *television from the theatre.*

pass out[1] [B1i pass] distribute (generously, as a gift). **O:** drink, cigarette; ticket (for a show, or football match); sample (of merchandise) □ *He's a generous spender: when he wins money at the races, he starts* ***passing out*** *the beer and cigarettes.* □ *The exhibitors at the trade fair* ***pass out*** *free samples to stimulate interest.*

pass out[2] [A1 B1i pass] (military) successfully complete a course of training at a military academy etc; post to a unit after such completion; appear in the ceremonial parade to mark the completion of the course. **S:** [A1] **O:** [B1] cadet, recruit, trainee □ *A number of selected cadets of my batch were to be* ***passed out*** *in December, 1907.* MFM □ *I decided to get back to England in time to take the* ***Passing Out*** *Parade myself, so that I could fasten the Belt of Honour on my son.* MFM □ nom form, used attrib with *parade, ceremony,* is passing(-)out.

pass out[3] [A1] (informal) faint, lose consciousness □ *'My, fancy that being a real burglar last night. I'd have* ***passed out*** *if I'd known.'* DC □ *'I'd only have to point a gun at him and say bang, bang, and the little twerp would* ***pass out*** *cold from fright.'* AITC ⇨ be out[9].

pass over[1] [B1i pass adj] omit, fail to include; fail to notice. **O:** fact, detail, particular □ *If there's something here I must see, then rest assured I shan't* ***pass*** *it* ***over.*** □ *I would ask every person who came along to tell me where Chesterfield Mews was. I wouldn't* ***pass over*** *anyone.* CON

pass over[2] [B1iii pass] avoid, not face, sth (because it is painful or embarrassing). **O:** feeling; disturbance, conflict; subject, topic □ *Emotion was something to be covered up, or* ***passed over*** *with a few short words.* PW □ *You can't* ***pass over*** *these painful sources of conflict, and hope they'll disappear.* □ *Sex is something that the Victorians preferred to* ***pass over*** *— in public at least.*

pass over[3] [B1ii pass adj] not consider for promotion (sb who is, or might suppose himself to be, eligible) □ *When the senior appointments were made, Jones was* ***passed over*** *in favour of a younger man.* □ *Bill is going around with that gloomy look of the* ***passed-over*** *executive.*

pass over[4] [B1i pass adj] fail to grasp, let slip; pass up[2] (q v). **O:** chance, opportunity, opening □ *The halt gave an opportunity for further speech which Patrick, being Patrick, felt he could not afford to* ***pass over.*** TGLY

pass over[5] [A2 pass adj] review, scan; run through[3] (q v). **o:** paragraph, section, sentence; (sequence of) events, happenings □ *I will* ***pass*** *briefly* ***over*** *the events of last evening to refresh your memories.* □ *The Chairman* ***passed*** *quickly* ***over*** *the first few items to leave more time for the main business of the meeting.*

pass over[6] [A1] (euphemism) die. ⇨ pass away/on/over.

pass one's eye over [B2 rel] scan, survey, briefly; look through[2] (q v). **o:** letter, form; essay, exercise □ *I can't say I've examined the document closely; I just had time to* ***pass my eye over*** *it.*

pass the hat round [B1i pass] (informal) collect money (usu for a workmate who is sick, retiring etc); take the hat round (q v) □ *When George died, they* ***passed the hat round*** *to pay for the wreath.*

pass through[1] [A1 A2 pass] go through a town etc, perhaps making a brief halt, but not staying □ *'Why don't you stay the night?' 'No, thank you: we're just* ***passing through.****'*

pass through[2] [A2] undergo, and complete, a course of training at. **o:** officer cadet school, staff college; medical school; university □ *His brother had* ***passed through*** *police college to qualify for promotion to Inspector.*

pass through[3] [A2 pass rel] experience, suffer. **o:** (difficult, testing) period, time; adverse circumstances □ *John* ***passed through*** *a difficult period shortly after his marriage broke down, but after a year or so his health and spirits picked up.* □ *The astronauts* ***passed through*** *an anxious hour when the onboard computer started to malfunction.*

pass under the name of [A2] ⇨ pass by/under the name of.

pass up[1] [B1i pass] hand to sb positioned above oneself. **O:** hammer, nails, ladder, bucket □ *'****Pass up*** *the paint pot and brush, and I'll put another coat on the ceiling.'* □ *The top section of the derrick had to be* ***passed up****, piece by piece.*

pass up[2] [B1i pass adj] (informal) fail to grasp, allow to slip by; pass over[4] (q v). **O:** chance, opportunity, occasion; deal, contract, sale □ *It doesn't do to be too modest. You can* ***pass*** *a lot of business* ***up*** *that way.* ASA □ *You can't afford to* ***pass up*** *too many openings like that.* □ *If all his* ***passed-up*** *chances were placed end to end they'd stretch to the moon.*

paste up[1] [B1i pass] attach to a surface (usu at or above eye-level) with paste. **O:** poster, notice; wallpaper □ *There were posters advertising the bullfight* ***pasted up*** *all over town.*

paste up[2] [B1i nom pass] (publishing) arrange typeset matter, and possibly illustrations, by pasting them onto pages for photographic reproduction and printing (e g by offset) or as a rough guide for the printer to arrange the pages himself; paste already printed pages onto larger sheets to enable an author or editor to insert corrections etc (e g for a new edition) □ *'Has the Art Department* ***pasted up*** *the captions to the illustrations yet? I want them to go to the printer tomorrow.'* □ *The underground press produces its magazines by the cheapest method possible — typing the text on ordinary typewriters, using photographs from many printed sources and* ***pasting*** *the lot* ***up*** *together to make camera-ready copy for cheap offset litho printing.* □ *The publisher agreed to provide the author with a* ***paste-up*** *of the pages of the dictionary that he wanted to make correc-*

tions to.

pat down [B1i pass] flatten, settle, or replace with a pat. **O:** hair; turf, wicket □ *She* ***patted down*** *one or two unruly wisps of hair.* □ *The batsman walked out to* ***pat down*** *some bumps in the pitch.*

patch up[1] [B1i pass adj] repair roughly or temporarily. **O:** wall, floor; car, plane □ *He was little use at emergency* ***patching up*** *of electrical equipment.* HD □ *A few squares of glass had been* ***patched up*** *with treacle-brown paper.* BFA □ *I do not want to be saved, but the damned doctors might* ***patch*** *me* (i e my body) ***up***. ARG

patch up[2] [B1i pass adj] settle, resolve. **O:** quarrel, argument, difference □ *The matter was* ***patched up*** *without resort to the police.* ARG □ *We managed to* ***patch up*** *the dispute before any heads were broken.*

patter about/around/round [A1 A2] move about etc with quick, light, tapping footsteps. **S:** mouse, rat, kitten; child □ *We could hear mice* ***pattering about*** *in the attic above our heads.* □ *'Sarah, is that you* ***pattering around*** *downstairs?'*

pave (with) [B2 pass emph rel] cover a road etc with paving-stones. **O:** road, drive, path. **o:** flag, cobble □ *The road was* ***paved with*** *cobblestones.* □ *The road to Hell is* ***paved with*** *good intentions.* □ the second example is a proverb: cf *'The road to Fleet Street,'* (i e success in journalism) *said Charles with mock solemnity, 'is* ***paved with*** *disappointments.'* HD

paw about/around [B1ii pass] (informal) handle sth or sb in a clumsy, insensitive way. **O:** fruit, vegetables; girl □ *'I don't want to buy tomatoes that have already been* ***pawed around*** *by other customers!'* □ *Helen had firm views on how her young men should behave. Decisive kissing was one thing; irresolute* ***pawing about*** *was quite another.*

pay back (for) [B1i pass B3 pass] punish sb in return for some injury one has suffered; pay out (for) (q v). **o:** neglect, humiliation, hurt □ *You may think you can get away with neglecting your responsibilities, but events will* ***pay*** *you* ***back***. HD □ *She* ***paid*** *him* ***back for*** *his casual infidelities.* □ *'I shouldn't try anything on with him, if I were you. He would* ***pay*** *you* ***back*** *with interest.'*

pay back (to) [B1i pass adj B3 pass rel] repay, return, money (to). **O:** loan, what is owing. **o:** relative, bank □ *'I'll have some luck and* ***pay*** *you* ***back***,*' he promised.* DC □ *It's high time he* ***paid*** *me* ***back*** *the £100 he owes me.* □ *The sum was* ***paid back to*** *the bank with interest.* □ note the position of the Indirect Object in the first two examples.

pay (for) [A2 pass adj rel B2 pass rel] give money in exchange (for) □ *Before he pays he likes to know what he's* ***paying for***. □ *'I* ***paid*** *good money* ***for*** *that bicycle: now take care of it.'* □ *'Have those articles been* ***paid for***, *Madam?'* □ *'How much did you* ***pay*** *him* ***for*** *the watch?'*

pay for [A2] suffer for, be punished for. **o:** blunder, omission, failure. **A:** ⚠ dearly, heavily □ *Sometimes you have had to* ***pay*** *dearly* ***for*** *mistakes.* WI □ *If we fail to act now, we shall find ourselves* ***paying for*** *inaction later on.*

pay in/into [B1i pass B2 pass emph rel] hand money to a cashier for lodging in an account. **O:** cash, banknote, cheque. **o:** current account, savings account; bank, post office, building society □ *His monthly salary is* ***paid into*** *the bank by his employers.* □ *When you deposit money with the bank, you enter the amount on a* ***paying-in*** *slip.* □ nom form, used attrib with *slip, form,* is **paying-in**.

pay off[1] [B1i pass adj] pay in full and discharge from service. **O:** worker; gang; crew □ *The crew of the merchant ship were* ***paid off*** *at the end of the trip and a fresh one engaged.* □ *It's all most regrettable but it looks as though I'm compelled to* ***pay*** *you* ***off*** *for your caretaking work.* TC

pay off[2] [B1i pass adj] settle, clear, by matching what one owes with the same amount. **O:** debt, overdraft (at a bank) □ *You'll have to* ***pay off*** *your old loan before being allowed a new one.* □ *All his outstanding debts have been* ***paid off***.

pay off[3] [B1i nom pass] (slang) give money to sb to prevent him from carrying out a threat. **O:** protection gang, blackmailer □ *Publicans are known to have* ***paid off*** *one gang of terrorists to stop their pubs being blown up by another.* □ *A girl was sent out to collect the* ***pay-off*** *— a parcel of notes thrown onto the pavement from a passing car.*

pay off[4] [A1 nom] (informal) succeed, work. **S:** scheme, idea, device □ *Occasionally the checking* ***pays off*** *and there is the excitement of a chase or an arrest.* T □ *Sinatra fought like a tiger for the part of Maggio in the film — a gamble which* ***paid off*** *with an Oscar.* H □ *He worked like a slave for years; but the* ***pay-off*** *came when he was offered a partnership in the firm.*

pay out[1] [B1i pass adj] pass, release, through the hands. **O:** rope, cord, cable □ *He placed the gelignite carefully on the seat and* ***paid out*** *the wire.* TO □ *Knotting the rope round a projecting stone cornice, he* ***paid*** *it* ***out*** *into the darkness.* ARG

pay out[2] [A1 B1i pass adj] hand accumulated payments to a member of a savings club etc. **S:** club, association; treasurer □ *You can save up for toys by paying into a Christmas Club over the year; the club* ***pays out*** *in December.* □ *We can't* ***pay out*** *more than we receive.*

pay out[3] [A1 B1i pass adj] (informal) hand money to sb for his use, in exchange for sth (the suggestion is that one is made to pay too much and too often) □ *An awful lot of money gets* ***paid out*** *to these people.* DBM □ *Mr Charlton had already* ***paid out*** *millions to this swindle in weekly contributions.* DBM □ *He's tired of* ***paying out*** *on school fees and uniforms.*

pay out (for) [B1i pass B3 pass] (informal) punish sb in return for some injury one has suffered; pay back (for) (q v). **o:** thoughtlessness, unkindness □ *Someone will try to* ***pay*** *you* ***out*** *if you trample too much on the feelings of others.* □ *He felt that he had been more than* ***paid out for*** *a few indiscretions.*

pay attention (to) [B2 pass emph rel] look (at); listen (to); consider, attend (to) (q v). **S:** host; audience; fashion model, actress; manager, student. **adj:** some, no; little, scant; close, careful. **o:** stranger, guest; remark, speech; appearance, dress; event, development □ *'Please* ***pay*** *no* ***attention to*** *her, my lady,' Briggs interrupted, obviously distressed.* EM □ *A creative moment had arrived and he* ***paid*** *no* ***attention to*** *the world beyond it.* OMIH □ *Close* ***attention***

is being ***paid to*** *present movements in the money market.*

pay court (to) [B2 pass emph rel] treat sb with the respect, admiration etc, usu shown to a prince. **o:** minister, tycoon; actor, artist □ *He represented the power of money as Jack did: he was another king. As I watched them all* ***paying court to*** *him, I wondered how on earth he came to marry Alice.* RATT

pay heed (to) [B2 pass emph rel] heed, attend to, sth which it is important not to ignore. **adj:** no; little, small; careful, great. **o:** warning; portent, sign; safety, well-being □ *It is all to the good that the Conservative Party is to* ***pay*** *greater* ***heed to*** *the voice of youth.* SC □ *Auchinleck appeared to be* ***paying*** *little* ***heed to*** *the welfare of the British soldiers in India.* MFM

pay lip service to [B2 pass emph rel] declare that one regards sth as important while not treating it as important in fact. **o:** need (for); desirability, usefulness (of); idea, notion (of); expansion, development; friendship, brotherhood □ *Trades unionists* ***pay*** *only* ***lip service to*** *the need for research.* SC □ *The authorities must cease to* ***pay lip service to*** *Allied co-operation and must instead embark on a policy of unselfish solidarity.* MFM

pay tribute to [B2 pass emph rel] express one's admiration for sb, one's recognition of his qualities etc. **S:** employer, commander; successor, opponent. **adj:** his etc, this; generous, handsome, warm. **o:** staff; ally, partner; wisdom, vision □ *I want to take this opportunity to* ***pay*** *a public* ***tribute to*** *him.* MFM □ *Mr Macleod has* ***paid tribute to*** *Dr Banda's desire that the tension should be lowered.* SC □ *Among the many* ***tributes paid to*** *the outgoing President was a simple message from his personal chauffeur.*

pay up [A1] (informal) hand money to sb (usu one is under some obligation or pressure to pay) □ *I must* ***pay up****, and without argument or comment.* UTN □ *My goods have vanished and the insurance company will have to* ***pay up****.* DC □ *You might as well smile and* ***pay up****.*

peal out [A1] (of bells) resound one after the other; have the resonant sound of bells. **S:** bells; voice, laughter □ *The church bells* ***pealed out*** *to mark the final expulsion of Axis forces from Egypt.* □ *Miss Maxwell's voice* ***pealed out*** *over the cocktail party chatter.*

peck at [A2 pass adj] take small mouthfuls of; eat only part of (from lack of appetite); pick at[1] (q v). **o:** food; breakfast, dinner □ *She* ***pecked*** *daintily* ***at*** *a salad.* □ *He* ***pecked*** *listlessly* ***at*** *his breakfast of egg and bacon.*

peek (at) [A2 pass adj rel] look quickly (at), peep (at)[1] (q v) □ *Halfway through the sitting she asked if she could* ***peek at*** *the portrait he was doing of her.* □ *We didn't see much, because we only had a chance to* ***peek at*** *what was happening).*

peel off[1] [A1 B1i pass adj] remove the peel of a fruit; remove the outer coverings of sth, clothing etc. **O:** skin; (wrapping-)paper; jacket, pullover □ *'I don't need a knife, I can* ***peel*** *the skin* ***off*** *with my fingers.'* □ *'It's hot in here: I think I'll* ***peel off*** *(my jacket).'*

peel off[2] [A1 nom] (aviation) move independently out of formation (e g when attacking enemy aircraft). **S:** fighter, interceptor (aircraft) □ *As soon as an enemy bomber formation was sighted, the squadron leader gave the order to* ***peel off****.*

peep (at)[1] [A2 pass adj rel] look quickly (at), peek (at) (q v) □ *She* ***peeped*** *quickly* ***at*** *the sleeping child.*

peep (at)[2] [A2 pass adj] look slyly and inquisitively (at). **o:** neighbour, lover □ *Strangers to the area had the feeling that they were being* ***peeped at*** *from behind lace curtains.* □ *I wish she'd stop* ***peeping*** *(****at*** *me).*

peep out [A1] come partly and suddenly into view. **S:** ⚠ the stars, moon, sun □ *The sun* ***peeped out*** *through a gap in the clouds.*

peer (at) [A2 pass adj] look closely (at), as if unable to see well or recognize, or out of curiosity □ *She* ***peered at*** *him closely, as if not believing it could really be he.* □ *They were used to being* ***peered at*** *on arriving in a strange town.*

peg away (at) [A1 A3 pass] (informal) work or struggle persistently (at); plug away (at) (q v). **o:** writing, research; training, exercise □ *Between fights the boxer* ***pegged away at*** *roadwork and exercises in the gym.* □ *'You're bound to find the answer in the end: just keep* ***pegging away****.'*

peg down [B1i pass adj] fasten in position on the ground with pegs. **O:** flap, fly-sheet; tent □ *In the rain and wind it was hard to* ***peg down*** *the walls of the tent.* □ *A plastic sheet was* ***pegged down*** *over the compost heap to hasten decomposition.*

peg (down) (at) [B1i pass B2 pass B3 pass] hold, fix, prices etc at a relatively low level. **S:** government; dealer, supplier; industry. **O:** price, cost; wage, salary. **o:** level; percentage □ *The Government agreed to* ***peg down*** *the retail price of certain basic foodstuffs.* □ *As an anti-inflationary measure, permitted wage increases would be* ***pegged at*** *6 per cent above the 1972 level.*

peg down (to) [B1i pass B3 pass] (informal) make sb follow, or commit himself to, a particular course of action. **o:** definite undertaking; deadline; exact figure, clear estimate □ *It's proving very difficult to* ***peg*** *him* ***down to*** *a definite date for completion.* □ *When it's a matter of getting a clear promise, he's hard to* ***peg down****.*

peg out [A1] (informal) faint or collapse from exhaustion; die □ *Several of the runners* ***pegged out*** *at the end of the course.* □ *At this height, a climber can* ***peg out*** *from lack of oxygen.*

peg out a claim [B1iii pass] mark with pegs the boundaries of a piece of land of which one claims ownership □ *The settlers* ***pegged out claims*** *in the new lands they were opening up to the West.* □ *We must gain space rapidly and* ***peg out claims*** (i e seize territory) *well inland.* MFM

pelt (with) [B2 pass rel] throw (objects etc) at sb in a continuous shower. **o:** bricks, stones, mud; eggs, tomatoes; questions □ *The crowd lost patience with the speaker and started to* ***pelt*** *him* ***with*** *rotten eggs.* □ *The prisoner in the stocks was* ***pelted with*** *anything they could lay their hands on.* □ *Reporters surrounded the Minister and* ***pelted*** *him* ***with*** *questions on the progress of the talks but he refused to comment.*

pen in [B1i pass adj] confine, enclose in a pen; restrict the movements or freedom of. **O:** sheep, goats, cattle; child, employee □ *The flocks were* ***penned in*** *for the night as a protection against* *marauding wolves.* □ *She feels* ***penned in*** *by her life. She can never get away from the kitchen stove or the children.*

pension off [B1i pass adj] discharge sb from service (esp at the end of his career and with a pension); discontinue using sth because it is old and worn. **S:** government; company; army. **O:** civil servant; employee; officer; machine, weapon □ *'I know Pollard is past his best, and he'll certainly never be promoted, but it's a bit soon to* ***pension*** *him* ***off****.'* □ *A number of* ***pensioned-off*** *teachers were brought back into the schools to fill the places of younger men called up for military service.* □ *Half the destroyers in the fleet were ready to be* ***pensioned off****. They were kept on because nothing new was coming from the shipyards.*

pent up [pass adj (B1)] (be) restrained, repressed. **S:** emotion; resentment, frustration; energy □ *Her impulses were carefully controlled, her feelings closely* ***pent up****.* □ *'Were you blazing with* ***pent-up*** *desire like people in books?'* RATT

people with [B2 pass emph rel] (formal) fill with people etc. **S:** migration; author; travel, time. **O:** area, region; tale, narrative; mind, imagination. **o:** fisherman, trader; character; fancies □ *The westward expansion of the nineteenth century had* ***peopled*** *the Middle West* ***with*** *farming communities.* □ *His dreams were* ***peopled with*** *strange, terrifying fantasies.*

pep up [B1i pass adj] (informal) make more interesting, lively or powerful. **O:** food, drink; conversation, entertainment; proceedings □ *Seems they're pickled gherkins — just what they want to* ***pep up*** *their diet with.* BFA □ *I would consider drastically curtailing the number of* (radio) *series and taking steps to* ***pep up*** *those that were left.* L

pepper with [B2 pass rel] (informal) strike sb with a stinging shower of. **o:** shot, stones; questions, insults □ *The dog went off to fetch in the dead rabbit. It was* ***peppered with*** *shot all down one side.*

perch (on) [A2 emph rel] alight or rest (on). **S:** bird; parrot, sparrow; child. **o:** bar, branch, gate □ *The pigeons are quite tame. If you stand perfectly still they'll* ***perch on*** *your shoulder.*

perk up [A1 B1i pass adj] (informal) (cause to) become more lively and interested. **S:** [B1] news, change, event □ *She was very huffy, so I suggested she could use some of the money. She* ***perked up*** *at that.* JFTR □ *I felt liberated. And so life had* ***perked up*** *again.* SML □ *'I need a stiff drink to* ***perk me up****!'*

permit of [A2] (formal) allow, leave, room for. **S:** situation, circumstances; moment, time. **o:** delay, hesitation; compromise, makeshift □ *The times we are living through do not* ***permit of*** *weakness or indecision.* □ usu neg.

persist (in) [A2 pass adj] (formal) continue stubbornly to do sth, or to follow a course of action. **o:** interrupting, behaving unpleasantly; habit, conduct, line of action □ *'If you* ***persist in*** *heckling every time that someone tries to speak, I shall have you removed.'* □ *This line of conduct, if* ***persisted in****, could only get him deeper into debt.*

persuade (of) [B2 pass] convince sb that sth is the case. **o:** sincerity, truth; practicality, futility □ *He managed to* ***persuade*** us ***of*** *the workability of the scheme; now we had to* ***persuade*** *the boss.* □ *You don't have to* ***persuade*** *me* ***of*** *the likelihood of an outbreak* (or: *that an outbreak is likely*).

pertain to [A2] (formal) belong to; form a proper or appropriate part of. **S:** farm, land; wildness, enthusiasm, freedom. **o:** manor, mansion; age, time, season □ *Individual farmers must respect grazing rights* ***pertaining to*** *the community.* □ *The fire and dash* ***pertaining to*** *youth are not much in evidence among these people.*

pester the life out of [B2 pass] (informal) bother, trouble, sb unbearably (esp to obtain some gift or service from him). **S:** child, pupil; salesman, newspaperman □ *Players leaving the stadium had* ***the life pestered out of*** *them by small boys looking for autographs.* □ *Never again would a journalist* ***pester the life out of*** *the mother of a week-dead son.* PP □ note the passive with *have.*

peter out [A1] dwindle to nothing, gradually lose its force or momentum. **S:** stream, path; talk, chat, story; attack, offensive □ *The boom of the 1920s* ***petered out*** *at about the same time.* OBS □ *My search for Janet Prentice seemed to have* ***petered out****.* RFW □ *The Victorian age seemed to be* ***petering out*** *at about the end of 1918.* AH

petition (for) [A2 pass emph rel B2 pass emph rel] appeal (for) by submitting a written document signed by many people. **O:** MP, Parliament. **o:** release of detainees, change in the law, pensions for the disabled □ *Several organizations* ***petitioned*** *the Government* ***for*** *the release of the political prisoners.* □ *They* ***petitioned for*** *an early end to the fighting.*

phase out [B1i pass adj] gradually stop making or supplying sth. **O:** manufacture, provision (of); (model of a) car, aircraft; organization, set-up □ *The anti-tank company was armed mainly with the 75 mm, although production of this gun was being* ***phased out*** *in 1942.* B □ *There are proposals to* ***phase out*** *the hitherto separate Department of Economic Geography.*

phone in [B1i nom pass adj] address, submit, by telephone, esp to a radio or TV programme. **O:** question, inquiry, problem; news item, story, report □ *Listeners are invited to* ***phone in*** *their questions to the Shadow Foreign Secretary from six o'clock this evening.* □ *The new* ***phone-in*** *formula for Radio 3's request programme 'Your Concert Choice' has been widely criticized.* □ nom form used attrib.

pick at[1] [A2 pass adj] take small, or a few, mouthfuls of sth (either from fastidiousness or lack of appetite); peck at (q v). **o:** lunch, supper; meat, pudding □ *'Did she finish her rice pudding?' 'No, she just* ***picked at*** *it.'* □ *She* ***picked at*** *the shellfish for a few moments, then pushed the plate away.*

pick at[2] [A2 pass adj] criticize, find fault with; nag (at) (q v). **o:** wife, child, employee □ *'Leave the child alone: you're always* ***picking at*** *her!'* □ *She'd been* ***picked at*** *so often by parents and teachers that she didn't know how to behave.*

pick holes in [B2 pass] (informal) criticize, comment adversely on. **o:** scheme, plan; speech, report; book, film □ *It's easy for an outsider to* ***pick holes in*** *our programme. What you don't* *understand is the technical difficulties we face.* □ ***Holes** can be **picked in** any scales of pay.* TES

pick off [B1i pass adj] shoot (persons or animals) one by one with deliberate aim. **S:** sniper, marksman. **O:** officer, specialist □ *They had probably been **picked off** by American snipers at the head of our advance.* SD □ *They **pick off** the officers first, so as to throw the attack into confusion.*

pick on [A2 pass adj] (informal) choose (repeatedly) for criticism, blame, punishment, or an unpleasant task. **A:** always, forever. **o:** smaller brother, weaker person □ *He ignored his wife's plea to stop **picking on** his daughter and lifted his hand to settle her with a blow.* LLDR □ *He's constantly being **picked on** to do the dirty jobs.* □ *'Why **pick on** me every time?'*

pick out[1] [B1i pass] choose from a number of similar objects. **O:** (largest, least expensive) fruit, vegetables; dress, suit □ *Cyril had a lot of azaleas in pots. I **picked out** a big red one just coming into bloom.* RFW

pick out[2] [B1i pass] separate, distinguish, from surrounding persons or objects □ *I tried to **pick out** her face in the crowd pressing through the door.* □ *His house is easily **picked out** from the rest: it has a large blue door.*

pick out[3] [B1i pass] (of a person who plays by ear) find the notes of a tune by trial and error. **A:** on the piano, on the guitar □ *He tried to **pick out** the tune of a song he had heard on the radio.*

pick out[4] [B1i pass adj] relieve, complement the main colour (e g of a room) with touches of another colour □ *The colour scheme was brown, with the mouldings **picked out** in orange.*

pick over [B1i pass adj] lift and turn over so as to examine and make a choice from. **O:** fruit, vegetables; clothing □ *The housewives **pick** the fruit **over** carefully before making their minds up which to buy.* □ *You won't find any good tomatoes in that basket; they've been well **picked over**.*

pick up[1] [B1i pass] take hold of and raise □ *She **picked up** the half-finished letter and put it on the mantelpiece.* DC □ *'You dropped the plate on the floor; now you can **pick it up**.'*

pick up[2] [B1i pass adj] collect; take on board. **O:** groceries, newspaper; load, cargo □ *'Don't forget to **pick up** the ice-cream on the way home.'* □ *We **picked up** a consignment of cigarettes at the warehouse.*

pick up[3] [B1iii nom pass] (informal) collect as wages, earn □ *There are men in that factory **picking up** sixty pounds a week.* □ *'He earns good money, he does. He **picks up** a packet.'* PW □ *'A ten-pound Christmas bonus for pensioners. Now that's not a bad **pick-up**.'*

pick up[4] [B1i pass] collect; take on board; stop to give a lift to. **O:** passenger, crew member; hitchhiker □ *You can walk or ride the mile or two to the crossroads where the school bus will **pick you up**.* WI □ *The giant tankers have to start slowing down some 15 miles before they reach a rendezvous point to **pick up** a pilot.* OBS □ *He **picked up** two students outside Doncaster and dropped them off in Central London.*

pick up[5] [B1i pass adj] rescue from the sea. **S:** lifeboat, helicopter. **O:** shipwrecked sailor, aircrew; survivor □ *Air-Sea Rescue **picked up** the downed airman after receiving an SOS message.* □ *Survivors of the air disaster were **picked up** by small boats.*

pick up[6] [B1i nom pass] (informal) make sb's acquaintance, usu with a view to having sexual relations □ *He went home with a girl he'd **picked up** at the party.* □ *He made a smooth **pick-up*** (i e conquest). □ *'I'd be grateful if you'd keep your street **pick-ups*** (i e the girls you ***pick up*** on the street) *out of my wife's house,' he said in a whisper of rage.* ASA

pick up[7] [B1i nom pass] find, and arrest or return to custody. **S:** police, prison authorities. **O:** suspect, escaped prisoner □ *He was implicated in a murder, and sooner or later they would **pick** him **up**.* HD □ *The prisoners missing from the working party were **picked up** within forty-eight hours.* □ *They complain that the **pick-up** operation netted only small fry* (= rank-and-file terrorists). BBCTV

pick up[8] [B1i pass] receive, intercept. **S:** radar, radio receiver. **O:** signal, message; plane, ship □ *'Point all our aerials upwards. Then we'll **pick up** reflections of our own transmissions.'* TBC □ *It should have been possible to **pick up** signals telling us more about the moon itself.* NS

pick up[9] [B1i pass] hear, gather. **O:** story, rumour, (scrap of) information □ *He'd **picked up** some tale that we were to have a cut in wages.* □ *She's always on the prowl, **picking up** scraps of gossip.* □ *'I hear that Buckingham Palace is to be turned into a museum.' 'Where did you **pick** that **up**?'*

pick up[10] [B1i pass] acquire a knowledge of or skill in (usu casually, without special study). **O:** some knowledge of politics, the law; painting, carpentry; (a smattering of) a language □ *I **picked up** scraps of knowledge from a variety of sources.* SD □ *Branson seems to have **picked up** his philosophy of food during his career with the Indian Civil Service.* OBS □ *She isn't very quick at **picking up** the language.* PW

pick up[11] [B1i pass] acquire, buy (usu as a bargain). **O:** bargain, snip; antique, objet d'art, furniture □ *There are still some charming things to be **picked up** in Bruges itself, for a mere song* (i e for very little money). US □ *Bric-a-brac **picked up** on his many journeys to the continent filled the room.*

pick up[12] [A1] improve; recover. **S:** patient, sick person; health, condition □ *You'll soon **pick up** after a day or two in bed.* □ *His health and spirits **picked up** after a week at the seaside.* □ *Another draught of alcohol injected fire into his body. 'My God, this is a perfect **pick-me-up**,' Pop said* (i e a perfect way to make him ***pick up***). BFA □ note unusual nom form.

pick up[13] [A1] improve; recover. **S:** sales, exports; the market; sterling □ *The shares **picked up** after an early spate of panic selling.* □ *Consumption of wines and spirits **picked up** again before the New Year.*

pick up[14] [A1] start to function again. **S:** motor, engine □ *The port engine spluttered and seemed about to cut out; then it **picked up** again.*

pick up[15] [B1i pass] continue telling a story etc after an interruption (e g at the end of one episode in a series); take up[7] (q v); manage to continue following a story etc after an interruption. **O:** story, tale; (thread of the) argument □ *We **pick up** the story again at the point where John has* *lost his job at the newspaper office.* □ *Because of the disturbance outside the window I lost the thread of the discussion and had some difficulty in* ***picking*** *it* ***up*** *again.*

pick-me-up [nom (B1)] ⇨ pick up[12].

pick oneself up [B1ii] raise oneself after a fall □ *He was knocked down in the scramble, but he quickly* ***picked himself up*** *and dusted himself down.*

pick up speed [B1iii] accelerate, gather speed. **S:** train, ship □ *The train moved slowly from the station, but* ***picked up speed*** *as it reached the open country.*

pick up the threads [B1iii] (informal) readjust to a job, a mode of life, a relationship, after a period of absence, separation □ *'You must realize that I've been away from the job for five years. It'll take me a little time to* ***pick up the threads*** *again.'* □ *With some lingering mistrust on both sides Bill and Jane set about* ***picking up the threads*** *of their marriage again.*

pick-up (truck) [nom (B1)] small commercial vehicle with, at the back, an open top and low sides and tail-board □ *Plumbers, electricians and jobbing builders often use* ***pick-up trucks*** *to transport their tools and materials.* □ *A young man in a top hat plays jazz on a piano wedged into the back of a parked* ***pick-up truck.*** OBS ⇨ pick up[2].

pick up with [A3 pass] (informal) meet, make the acquaintance of. **o:** curious fellow, odd creature, shady character □ *He's liable to bring home any odd character that he* ***picks up with*** *in a pub.*

pick (with) [B2 pass] seek, look for, a reason or excuse for quarrelling or fighting (with sb). **O:** ⚠ a quarrel, an argument; a fight □ *'We've got our chance at last. Why do you have to spoil it by* ***picking*** *quarrels* ***with*** *me about nothing?'* AITC □ *'Peter's going through a tiresome stage. Always* ***picking*** *fights* ***with*** *his brother for no reason at all.'*

picture to oneself [B2] imagine sth, summon a picture of it into the mind. **O:** effect, result; scene; devastation, congestion □ *Readers can* ***picture to themselves*** *the utter confusion that would result if the procession were routed through these narrow streets.*

piece out [B1i pass adj] complete, by adding pieces or parts. **O:** story, account; picture, design □ *You must* ***piece out*** *the full story from your own imaginations.*

piece together [B1i pass adj] assemble, fit together; form (a whole) by fitting (parts) together. **O:** patches, scraps (of material); rug, blankets; facts, evidence □ *Bits of wood and metal were* ***pieced together*** *to form a roof.* □ *She* ***pieced together*** *a blanket from odds and ends of wool.* □ *A defence had somehow to be* ***pieced together*** *from a few fragments of evidence.*

pile in/into[1] [A1 A2 B1i pass B2 pass] (cause a group etc to) press into a space too small to take the group in comfort. **o:** car, boat, flat □ [A2] *All five of us* ***piled into*** *Peter's car and headed back to the flat.* □ [A1] *'****Pile in****! There's room for a few more on the floor.'* □ [B1] *We* ***piled*** *all the luggage* ***in*** *and drove off.*

pile in/into[2] [A1 A2 pass] (informal) attack sb violently; attack food with appetite; pitch in/into (q v). **o:** enemy, opponent; feast, meal □ *John* ***piled into*** *the man opposite, almost knocking him down at the first assault.* □ *'The food's ready.* ***Pile in****!'*

pile on the agony [B1iii] (informal) make the description of an event more painful than it need be □ *She* will ***pile on the agony*** *when she describes her visits to the dentist: she makes a filling sound like a major operation.*

pile it on [B1ii] (informal) exaggerate, make sth seem more important or dramatic than it is □ *John* does ***pile it on****: anyone would thænk that he's the only one with domestic problems.* □ *'Stop* ***piling it on****: it's not half as bad as you make it appear.'*

pile the pressure on [B1i pass] cause sb to work or struggle harder by giving him more tasks etc. **S:** employer, teacher; opposing team □ *The tutors* ***piled on the pressure*** *from the very beginning of the course.* □ *The French forwards really* ***piled the pressure on*** *in the second half of the match.*

pile on runs [B1iii pass] (cricket) add quickly to one's total of runs. **S:** batsman, (batting) side □ *There was no fall in the scoring rate when the new ball was taken: Sobers and Kanhai continued to* ***pile on runs.***

pile on/onto [B1i pass B2 pass] place sth in heaps upon sb or sth; burden sb with an undue amount of sth. **O:** coal, wood; work, responsibilities. **o:** fire, stove; staff, subordinate □ *Wood was* ***piled onto*** *the bonfire until the flames roared* (cf *The bonfire was* ***piled with*** *wood*). □ *Why is it that all the extra work gets* ***piled onto*** *me at Christmas time?*

pile out/out of [A1 A2] emerge in a mass or crowd, usu from a confined space. **o:** room, car, aeroplane □ *We* ***piled out of*** *the back of the car and stretched our cramped limbs.*

pile up[1] [A1 nom] accumulate, usu because of a stoppage of work. **S:** goods, exports, mail. **A:** at the docks, in warehouses □ *Perishable goods are* ***piling up*** *at the docks because of the strike of tally-clerks.* □ *Posting at peak times often leads to a* ***pile-up*** *of mail at the Post Office.*

pile up[2] [A1 nom] (of cars travelling close behind each other) crash into each other. **S:** car, lorry □ *Several cars* ***piled up*** *after ignoring the fog warning on the motorway.* □ *There was a* ***pile-up*** *involving a van and several private cars.*

pile with [B2 pass] ⇨ pile on/onto.

pilot through [B1ii pass B2 pass] cause to pass through various legislative etc stages; put through[2] (q v). **S:** minister, back-bencher; councillor. **O:** Act, measure; scheme, project. **o:** second reading, committee stage □ *Mr Ashley has successfully* ***piloted*** *his private member's Bill* ***through*** *its various stages.*

pin against [B2 pass rel] trap sb between oneself and a tree etc, and prevent him from moving away. **o:** tree, wall, door □ *He was* ***pinned against*** *the fence by a boy twice his size; he could hardly breathe.* □ *A stout customer* ***pinned*** *the hapless assistant* ***against*** *the counter, and demanded to see the manager.*

pin down[1] [B1i pass] trap; prevent sb from moving from cover or showing himself. **S:** beam, tree, girder; rubble, masonry; machine-gun fire, shelling □ *They seemed to have* ***pinned*** *his legs* ***down*** *under a heavy weight.* HD □ *Troops were* ***pinned down*** *in their trenches by accurate* *mortar fire.*

pin down[2] [B1i pass adj] define exactly. **O:** essence, character, tone □ *And — this is the part I can't **pin down** in words — he had conveyed, to the right onlooker, that he knew what he was doing.* CON □ *It was difficult to **pin down** exactly what it was in her that pleased him so much.* □ often neg.

pin down[3] [B1ii pass] persuade sb to define his position, state his intentions. **O:** official, politician; expert, pundit □ *He's a very difficult man to **pin down**: he seems to enjoy being all things to all men.* □ *Have you tried **pinning** him **down** on the question of capital punishment?*

pin one's faith on/to [B2 pass emph rel] trust or depend on sb or sth to help one. **o:** religion, socialism; leadership, political movement □ *Some **pinned their faith on** the emergence of a new national leader, others **on** a religious revival.* □ *'But we objectors over here in this corner are **pinning our faith to** Yvette's question. It seems to me a very good one.'* TBC

pin up [B1i nom pass adj] attach to a surface with pins. **O:** drawing, photograph, map; hanging, curtain □ *Pictures of pop-stars were **pinned up** over Katherine's bed.* □ *Sarah's favourite **pin-ups** were the cowboy heroes of television Westerns.* □ nom form used esp of pictures of attractive girls (or men) which are pinned up; also of the persons represented in the pictures.

pine away [A1] grow pale and thin through sorrow or illness □ *Mary has **pined away** dreadfully since her young man broke things off.*

pine (for) [A2 pass adj emph rel] desire strongly to return to or recover. **o:** former times, the good old days, lost freedom; peace, seclusion □ *Working-class people do not much **pine for** their lost freedom; they never regarded it as more than temporary.* UL □ *Emigrants are often **pining for** home (or: **pining** to return home) within weeks of arriving in their new country.*

pipe down [A1] (informal) be quiet (e g stop talking, making a noise) □ *Ashore, '**Pipe down**' means silence. Afloat it means several things: men working aloft to return on deck, washed clothes or hammocks to be removed, or simply 'hands turn in'.* RFW □ *'Have you come to see Mariette?' 'No, **pipe down**, you loony. Nobody knows anything about that.'* DBM □ usu imper.

pipe up [A1] begin to speak (usu in a thin, high voice) □ *The still small voice **piped up**.* PP □ *Suddenly Irma **piped up** and said: 'Please, what is a harpy?'* PW

piss about/around [A1] (taboo) behave in a foolish, boisterous way; work in a casual disorganized way; mess about (q v) □ *'Look, just stop **pissing about** for five minutes. I've got work to do.'* □ *'Smith and Murray have been **pissing around** with that order since January. Tell them, if they don't bloody well get a move on we'll take our business somewhere else.'*

piss off[1] [A1] (taboo) go away □ *He told me to **piss off**, or he'd clobber me.* □ *'I've had about as much of you as I can stand. Now, **piss off**!'*

piss off[2] [B1ii pass adj] (taboo) bore; annoy; brown off (q v). **S:** work, routine; voice, music □ *By this time Bill was really **pissed off** with the job and was looking for a way out — any way out.* □ *'It really **pisses** you **off**, doesn't it, the way he thinks we've got to jump like trained monkeys every time he snaps his fingers!'*

pit against [B2 pass emph rel] (formal) set sb or sth in competition against; match against/with (q v). **O:** strength, wits, skill, courage; oneself □ *When he had slain the king's champion, there was no one left to **pit** his skill and courage **against**.* □ *'Don't **pit** your puny wit **against** my massive intelligence.'*

pitch in/into [A1 A2 pass] (informal) attack violently; begin working vigorously, attack food with appetite; pile in/into[2] (q v). **o:** rival, opponent; task, job; meal □ *Thank you again for the way you **pitched in** to help out during the German thrust.* MFM □ *After a day in the fields, they **pitched into** the food with a rare appetite.*

pitch in (with) [A1 A3] (informal) give, offer, one's help or support. **S:** colleague, neighbour, ally. **o:** story, report; figures, statistics; donation, subscription □ *'If the talks start going badly for us, **pitch in with** the results of the consumer survey. They may make all the difference.'* □ *Local businessmen **pitched in with** an offer to meet advertising costs.*

pitch up [B1ii pass adj] (cricket) when bowling, make the ball strike the pitch near(er) the batsman. **O:** ball, delivery □ *'You're dropping 'em short, Geoff. **Pitch** 'em **up** a bit.'* □ *Boycott shapes early to drive a well-**pitched-up** ball.*

place above □ (in this and all of the following place entries, the grammatical patterns, definitions, collocates etc, are the same as for the corresponding put entries (to which cross-reference is made.) ⇨ put above.

place at a premium ⇨ put at a premium.

place before ⇨ put before[2].

place sb in an awkward etc position ⇨ put sb in an awkward etc position.

place in inverted commas ⇨ put in inverted commas.

place in jeopardy ⇨ put in jeopardy.

place one's trust in ⇨ put one's trust in.

place one's cards on the table ⇨ put one's cards on the table.

place a construction on ⇨ put a construction on.

place on one side ⇨ put on one side[1].

place a premium on ⇨ put a premium on.

place pressure on/upon ⇨ put pressure on/upon.

place a strain on/upon ⇨ put a strain on/upon.

place a/one's finger to one's lips ⇨ put a/one's finger to one's lips.

place a match to ⇨ put a match to.

plague with [B2 pass emph rel] address, direct, so many questions etc, at sb that they burden and irritate him. **O:** office, department; employer, teacher. **o:** questions, inquiries; suggestions; fears, doubts □ *At this time of year university admissions offices are **plagued with** inquiries from anxious applicants.* □ *'Don't **plague** me **with** your problems. Take them to someone else.'*

plan ahead [A1] arrange things in advance □ *A general may have to **plan** months **ahead**, a platoon officer only a few hours.* □ *You should **plan ahead** for really good cold-meat-and-salad eating.* TO

plane away/off [B1i pass adj] remove with a woodworker's plane. **S:** carpenter, cabinet-maker. **O:** irregularity, rough patch □ *The cuts and scratches that the packers made on the desk can be* ***planed away****.*

plane down [B1i pass adj] lower, reduce, make thinner, with a woodworker's plane. **O:** surface, edge; board, beam □ *You need to* ***plane down*** *the edges until all the roughness disappears.* □ ***Plane*** *one side of the panel* ***down*** *until it fits snugly into place.*

plaster one's hair down [B1i pass adj] (informal) make hair lie flat by coating it with brilliantine etc □ *The gang wore leather jackets and had long* ***hair plastered down*** *over their ears.*

plaster over/up [B1i pass adj] cover, seal, with plaster. **O:** crack, blemish, hole □ *The cracks in the ceiling have to be* ***plastered up*** *before you can start painting.*

play about/around (with) [A1 A3 pass] handle, treat, in a casual and irresponsible way; fool about/around q v. **o:** young girl, sb else's wife; other people's money, property; dangerous drugs, explosives □ *It's time he stopped* ***playing around*** *and began to take life seriously.* □ *He's* ***playing around with*** *a girl young enough to be his daughter.* □ *This is not a substance that can be* ***played about with*** *by anybody.*

play along (with) [A1 A3 pass] (informal) act in accordance (with); go along with² (q v). **o:** leader, majority; scheme, system, arrangement □ *But he did have the sense to* ***play along with*** *the school system to the extent of going into the Sixth.* CON □ *The minority parties will have to be persuaded to* ***play along****.*

play at¹ [A2] pretend for fun to be sb or do sth. **o:** mothers and fathers, cops and robbers, pirates, cowboys; keeping a shop, camping out □ *Small boys usually like* ***playing at*** *soldiers, and small girls* ***at*** *nurses or mothers.*

play at² [A2 pass] engage in casually or half-heartedly. **o:** being king, being a businessman □ *Office routine is just something he* ***plays at****; the one thing that really interests him is golf.* □ *This is a job that needs to be tackled whole-heartedly — not* ***played at****.*

what be playing at [A2] (informal) (rhetorical question) expression of anger at sb who is behaving foolishly and/or dangerously □ (mother finds small boy playing with matches) *'And* ***what*** *do you think* ***you're playing at****, young man?'* □ *I asked them* ***what*** *on earth they* ***were playing at****.* □ direct or indirect question construction.

play back¹ [B1i nom pass adj] run the tape forward through a tape-recorder again, so that the material recorded on it can be heard. **O:** tape, recording; conversation, discussion □ *I am going to* ***play back*** *part of the statement you made to the police.* □ *Let's have a* ***play-back*** *of the first half of Act One.*

play back² [A1] (cricket) step back (transfer weight to the back foot) in order to play a stroke. **S:** batsman, cricketer □ *He* ***played back*** *to a short ball outside the off stump.* □ *When you get a good-length ball, it's hard to know whether to* ***play back*** *or forward.* ⇨ play forward.

play back³ [B1i pass adj] (sport) return, send back. **O:** ball, shot; volley, lob □ *He* ***played*** *a good-length ball* ***back*** *to the bowler.* □ *There is always the danger of being caught by the bowler from a* ***played-back*** *ball.*

play down [B1i pass adj] try to make sth appear less important than it is. **O:** success, contribution; danger, crisis, defeat □ (headline) *Wilson* ***plays down*** *Greater London Council defeat.* ST □ *She tried to* ***play down*** *his part in the affair and play up her own.*

play for time [A2] try to delay defeat, an embarrassing admission etc, by keeping one's opponent or questioner at a distance. **S:** boxer, cricketer; commander, army; politician, government □ *'I can't hear a word,' said Madge. This was untrue. She was* ***playing for time****.* UTN □ *I* ***played for time*** *a bit more, but finally he got me to admit that I could come, and that I didn't have to return till the next day.* CON

play forward [A1] (cricket) step forward (transfer weight to the front foot) in order to play a stroke. **S:** batsman □ *Amiss* ***plays forward*** *to a well-pitched ball outside the off stump.* ⇨ play back².

play the New Year in [B1i pass] play to celebrate and announce the start of a New Year. **S:** band, orchestra, Scots piper □ *Veteran of* ***playing in the New Year****, Jimmy Shand, along with his band, will be playing for dancers at Perth.* RT □ *They* ***played*** *the Old Year out with Auld Lang Syne and* ***the New Year in*** *with Roll Out the Barrel.*

play oneself in [B1ii] (cricket) lay a secure foundation for an innings by playing slowly and cautiously at the start □ *After* ***playing himself in*** *carefully, Smith began to hit out at the looser balls.*

play a part/role (in) [B2 pass emph rel] be an element in; figure in (q v). **S:** colleague, partner; idea, feeling; luck; belief, faith. **adj:** some; no, (not) any; small; large, considerable; important, significant. **o:** success, recovery; book, play; thought, philosophy □ *During the first few years of marriage the couple are likely to maintain the frequent picture-going which* ***played*** *such* ***a*** *large* ***part in*** *their courtship.* UL □ ***The*** *active* ***part*** *which the Trades Unions have* ***played*** *has certainly served to make Scotland's economic needs much better understood.* SC □ ***In*** *bringing about such a change the Churches have* ***a*** *very important* ***role*** *to* ***play****.* SC □ ***The part played*** *by religion* (i e ***in*** the opening up of Africa) *was very great.* BN

play into sb's hands [A2] act to sb's advantage, usu by doing sth hoped for or planned for by that person. **o:** (*of*) rival, enemy; authorities □ *By taking the harder road through the mountains we avoided* ***playing into the enemy's hands****.* □ *The thieves* ***played into the hands of*** *the police by using a conspicuous get-away car.*

play off [A1 nom] (of teams or competitors that have secured the same number of points, won the same number of matches, in a championship) play the deciding match □ *There will be a* ***play-off*** *between Smith and Peters next week* (or: *Smith and Peters will* ***play off*** *next week*).

play off against [B3 pass] oppose one person to another, for one's own advantage. **O:** competitor, firm, country □ *One way of securing the new market would be to* ***play*** *our principal trade rivals* ***off against*** *each other.* □ *It is a favourite occupation of some countries to* ***play*** *Britain and America* ***off against*** *each other.*

play on [A1] (sport) continue to play, resume play □ *A linesman signalled 'off-side', but the* *referee overruled him and ordered '**play on**'.*

play on/onto [A1 B1ii pass B2 pass] (cricket) knock the ball onto one's own wicket. **O:** ball, delivery. **o:** stumps, wicket □ *'How was he out?' 'He **played on**.'* □ *Smith **played** a turning ball **onto** the stumps.*

play on/upon[1] [A2 pass] make use of words and expressions with a similar form but different meaning for humorous effect etc. **o:** ⚠ words, language □ *The language of much advertising consists of **playing** elaborately **on** words.* □ *The writer **plays upon** the similarities between ordinary and technical language.*

play on/upon[2] [A2 pass] exploit, develop (usu to harm sb). **o:** fear, suspicion; credulity, superstition □ *The Empire **played upon** its neighbours' fears of military expansion to obtain trade concessions from them.* □ *Their memories of past injustices were cleverly **played upon**.*

play out [B1i pass adj] enact, perform. **O:** episode, interlude, scene, drama □ *He was conducted past the dingy form rooms where the pitiful farce of his childhood had been **played out**, act after endless act.* HD □ *Their love affair was **played out** against the unromantic background of an English seaside town.*

played out [pass adj (B1)] have lost one's talent, vitality etc. **S:** footballer, athlete; businessman; painter □ *He's not the writer he was. People are beginning to say he's **played out**.* □ *She drifted from one affair to another, finally setting up house with a **played-out** opera singer.* □ passive with *be, seem, look.*

play the Old Year out [B1i pass] play to celebrate the end of an old year. ⇨ play the New Year in.

play out time [B1iii] (sport) (of a team on the defensive) survive to the end of a game without conceding a goal (or try), or losing a wicket □ *Defending his wicket watchfully, the last man in **played out time**.*

play up[1] [A1] (schoolboy slang) play with vigour and enthusiasm □ *'**Play up**, the School!'* □ usu imper.

play up[2] [A1 B1ii pass] (informal) be a nuisance, annoy; deliberately antagonize, torment; physically hurt. **S:** wife, husband, pupil; back, leg; rheumatism, arthritis □ *My shoulder's **playing up** horribly.* □ *Don't you see how unhappy he must be with this woman? That's why he had this breakdown — because she **played** him **up**.* PW □ *The children did their best to **play up**.* TST

play up[3] [B1i pass adj] stress, emphasize. **O:** contribution, role, part □ *Depend on him to **play up** to the full his own part in reaching the settlement.*

play up to [A3 pass] (informal) flatter, encourage (to win advantage for oneself). **o:** employer, boss; pretty woman □ *'**Play up to** her, won't you? Be the husband who's taking a holiday — playing while the cat's away.'* PW □ *He's the sort of man who dislikes being **played up to**. He prefers a more straightforward approach.*

play upon[1] [A2 pass] ⇨ play on/upon[1].

play upon[2] [A2 pass] ⇨ play on/upon[2].

play with[1] [A2 pass] amuse oneself by handling; handle in a casual, absent-minded way, toy with[1] (q v). **o:** (toy) soldier, farm, zoo; necklace, bangle □ *'Where's Stephen?' 'Up in the attic **playing with** his toy railway, I expect.'* □ *While we spoke, the manager **played with** a carved paper knife.*

play with[2] [A2 pass] treat lightly, dally with[2] (q v), toy with[2] (q v). **o:** him etc; feelings, affections; sensitivities, susceptibilities □ *She's not a woman to tolerate being **played with**.* □ *You can **play with** a woman's affections once too often.*

play with[3] [A2 pass] consider, but not very seriously; dally with[1] (q v), toy with[3] (q v). **o:** notion, idea, scheme □ *He's often **played with** the idea of emigrating to Canada, but that's as far as it's gone.*

play the devil/hell (with) [B2] (informal) seriously disturb or upset sth or sb; severely reproach sb. **S:** climate; altitude, pressure; food, water; father, boss. **o:** experiment, test; digestion; child, employee □ *I've had enough dope to **play hell with** my nervous system.* TST □ *'Dad'll **play** merry **hell with** you when he finds out you've broken his favourite record.'* □ *Alice would accept these things* (i e self-pity and class-consciousness), *though she'd **play the devil with** me for my stupidity.* RATT

play with fire [A2] court danger, do things that might lead to trouble □ *She's inviting trouble if she gets involved with that circle; but some people like **playing with fire**.*

plead (with) (for) [A2 pass emph rel] earnestly request, beg, sb to help, forgive etc. **o:** (***with***) guard, captor; (***for***) one's life; mercy, forgiveness; release, freedom □ ***With** that kind of man you will **plead** in vain.* □ *'You can try **pleading with** the landlord **for** more time to pay the arrears, but I doubt whether you'll succeed.'*

plod away (at) [A1 A3 pass] (informal) work in a slow, dull, laborious way (at). **o:** studies; French, maths; job; banking □ *He's not the kind to make sharp leaps forward. Just keeps **plodding away**.* □ *Mike's not content to **plod away at** a desk job for ever.*

plonk down [B1i pass] (informal) place sth roughly or heavily on a surface. **O:** dish, bag, box; money □ *The postman was able to compel any citizen to assist him to carry the mail bags just for one mile. After that the citizen could **plonk** them **down** on the road.* WI □ *'Come on the trip if you like, but you'll have to share in the expenses. So **plonk down** your money!'*

plough back (into) [B1i pass adj] reinvest profits etc (in a business). **O:** takings, earnings, profits. **o:** business; development, research; retooling (the plant) □ *We must increase the rate of **ploughing back** new money **into** re-equipment and expansion.* OBS □ *My father had been **ploughing back** much of the profits **into** the land and saving the rest for death duties.* RFW

plough in [B1i pass adj] cover, bury, with earth from the plough. **O:** crop, stubble, manure □ *That year the farmers couldn't get the right price for their cabbages and had to **plough** them **in**.*

plough through [A2 pass] (informal) read, study, sth with difficulty. **o:** book, essay, thesis; legislation □ *'We've **ploughed through** all the documents that can possibly have a bearing on your case.'*

plough up [B1i pass adj] uncover with the plough. **O:** potato, root vegetable; metal objects □ *In parts of Northern France, farmers still*

plough up *shell fragments, weapons and equipment.*

pluck out/out of [B1i pass adj B2 pass] withdraw, draw out/out of[2] (q v), sharply or quickly. **O:** nail, thorn, needle. **o:** flesh, limb □ *He bent over and* ***plucked*** *the thorn* ***out*** *with his teeth.* □ *He* ***plucked*** *the box* ***out of*** *the fire before the flames caught it.*

pluck up courage [B1iii] overcome one's fears, summon up (q v) one's courage □ *At last Gerald* ***plucked up courage*** *to say, 'Well, for me, Miss Dollie hasn't changed at all, Mrs Salad.'* ASA □ STANLEY: *You told him you thought the furniture we make was shoddy and vulgar?* CLIVE: *(****plucking up*** *a little* ***courage****) Well, those terrible oak cupboards.* FFE

plug away (at) [A1 A3 pass] (informal) work persistently (at); peg away (at) (q v). **o:** homework, housework, accounts □ *'How is the French coming on?' 'Oh, I keep* ***plugging away****.'* □ *'Don't you want to be read?' Mrs Jones demanded. 'Can't think why you* ***plug away at*** *your book if you don't.'* US

plug in [B1i pass adj] connect sth with the power supply by means of a plug. **O:** (electric) cooker, fire, kettle; radio □ *She* ***plugged in*** *the radio and switched on, and there was the familiar hum.* TT

plug up [B1i pass adj] fill with a plug (of wood, plaster, etc). **O:** hole, gap, crack □ ***Plug up*** *any cracks in the panel with plastic wood.*

plump down[1] [A1] (informal) sink quickly and heavily. **A:** into an armchair, onto the floor □ *She glanced quickly around the crowded room and* ***plumped down*** *on the only available chair.*

plump down[2] [B1i pass] (informal) place down quickly and decisively. **O:** baby; shopping bag; (playing-)card, entrance fee, membership card □ *The child was* ***plumped down*** *on the counter while she rummaged in her bag.* □ *He* ***plumped*** *his money* ***down*** *to secure one of the few remaining tickets.*

plump for [A2 pass adj] (informal) choose with decision and confidence □ *I wanted the red car, but Mary* ***plumped for*** *the blue one with grey seats.* □ *The selection committee* ***plumped for*** *the safe, conservatively inclined candidate.*

plump up [B1i pass adj] pat with the hands to make round and fat. **O:** cushion, pillow □ *She smoothed out the sheets and* ***plumped up*** *the pillows.*

plunge in/into [A1 emph A2 emph rel] throw oneself headfirst into water; dive in/into (q v). **o:** water; sea, river □ *Without pausing for thought, Robin dashed from the cabin, clambered onto the handrail, and* ***plunged in****.* □ *The van broke through the parapet and* ***plunged into*** *twenty feet of water.*

plunge into[1] [B2 pass rel] cause sth suddenly to go dark or sb to become depressed etc. **O:** room, hall; audience, listener. **o:** darkness; (deep) gloom, depression □ *A power failure* ***plunged*** *the whole house* ***into*** *sudden darkness.* □ *I thought this kind of happiness must be unstable—just as suddenly as it had come it would collapse and* ***plunge*** *her* ***into*** *deeper despair.* SPL

plunge into[2] [A2 rel B2 pass rel] suddenly (cause to) enter, be involved in. **S:** [A2] **O:** [B2] continent, country, people. **o:** war, conflict, strife □ *The country had* ***plunged*** *swiftly* ***into*** *open conflict with its neighbours.* □ *We were* ***plunged into*** *civil war by the attempted secession of the eastern provinces.*

plunge into[3] [A2 rel B2 pass rel] suddenly (cause to) incur, be overwhelmed by. **S:** [A2] **O:** [B2] country, firm. **o:** debt, (financial) crisis □ *The company* ***plunged*** *deeper* ***into*** *debt.* □ *There had seemed no way of staving off the economic crisis* ***into*** *which we were now* ***plunged****.*

ply between [A2] (nautical) travel regularly, provide a regular service, between one place and another. **S:** steamer, ferry. **o:** the island and the mainland; Dover and Calais □ *Ferries carrying passengers and commercial lorries* ***ply*** *daily* ***between*** *Hull and Rotterdam.*

ply with [B2 pass rel] keep constantly supplied with; direct constantly at. **o:** food, cigarettes, comforts; questions, inquiries □ *He was* ***plied with*** *everything that would make his stay in hospital more comfortable.* □ *Relatives beseiged the shipping offices and* ***plied*** *the staff* ***with*** *anxious inquiries.*

point out[1] [B1i pass] show, indicate. **O:** beauty spot, place of interest □ *The guide* ***pointed out*** *the best known paintings in the gallery.*

point out[2] [B1i pass] make clear, explain. **O:** fact, truth; aspect, side (of a question) □ *Not that he wasn't quick to see his own advantage, when it was* ***pointed out*** *to him.* PW □ *The Mortonstowe transmitters were capable of handling an enormous quantity of information, as Kingsley was not slow to* ***point out****.* TBC

point to[1] [A2 pass] indicate, when making a case, defending one's position etc. **o:** growth, increase; figure, amount □ *In defence of his policy, the Minister* ***pointed to*** *the sharp decrease in road deaths.*

point to[2] [A2] suggest, be evidence of. **S:** sign, evidence; statement, report. **o:** guilt, involvement; quick election, early withdrawal □ *All the signs at the moment* ***point to*** *an early resumption of the fighting.*

point up [B1i pass] emphasize, underline. **O:** contrast, difference, change □ *The recent wage increases* ***point up*** *still further the difference between this government and the last.* □ *This admission only serves to* ***point up*** *an aspect of police work that the public fails to understand.* L

poke about/around [A1 nom] (informal) search, pry, inquisitively; nose about/around (q v). **A:** among papers, possessions; in one's study, spare room □ *'What are you doing* ***poking about*** *among my private papers?'* □ *I only left them alone for a couple of minutes and when I came back they were having a* ***poke(-)around*** *in my writing-desk.*

poke fun at [B2 pass(o) emph rel] ridicule, mock. **o:** appearance, manner, speech □ *He was often* ***poked fun at*** *at school because of his shabby clothes.* □ *Loyalty, patriotism, the old school tie—these were all things* ***at*** *which we loved, in our superior way, to* ***poke fun****.*

poke one's nose in/into [B1ii B2] (informal) take an unwelcome interest in the concerns of others; pry (into) (q v). **o:** ⚠ (sb else's) affairs, business, concerns □ *I wish he'd stop* ***poking his*** *long* ***nose into*** *my affairs.* □ *If you'd stop* ***poking your nose in*** *where it's not wanted, we could get some work done.*

poke up [B1i pass] jab at a fire with a poker so that it burns more brightly □ *He* ***poked*** *the coals*

up *into a blaze.*

polish off[1] [B1i pass adj] (informal) finish eating, writing etc, sth quickly; finish off/up (q v). **O:** dish, course; scrap, left-overs; work □ *I can* ***polish off*** *the rest of the typing in no time.* □ *The rest of the Christmas pudding was* ***polished off*** *by the children.*

polish off[2] [B1i pass adj] (informal) defeat, eliminate, finish off (q v). **O:** opposition, contender □ *His opponents in the eliminating rounds were quickly* ***polished off.*** □ *Having disposed of the main opposition, he could* ***polish off*** *the remainder at his leisure.*

polish up[1] [A1 B1i pass adj] become clean and bright and clean with polishing; rub sth with polish until it becomes bright. **S:** [A1] **O:** [B1] (metal) ornament; weapon, accoutrement; (varnished) table, chair □ *These old pieces of brass have* ***polished up*** *beautifully.* □ *The silver will need to be* ***polished up*** *for the dinner party.* □ *The furniture could do with a good* ***polishing-up.***

polish up[2] [B1i pass adj] (informal) work at sth to improve its quality or effectiveness. **O:** French, German; (knowledge of) administration, business methods □ *I'll have to* ***polish up*** *my Italian: it's getting a bit rusty.* □ *Our sales techniques need* ***polishing up.***

ponder (on/over) [A2 pass adj emph rel] consider slowly and thoughtfully; reflect on/upon[1] (q v). **o:** past error, event; (future) outcome, result □ *Brigit did not* ***ponder on*** *these things too long. The morning was too lovely for problems or gloom.* DC □ *I* ***pondered on*** *William, stranded perhaps in Mesopotamian wastes, a lonely speck in that desert.* BM □ *These are minor problems* ***over*** *which you needn't* ***ponder*** *too long.*

pop across, along, away etc [B1i pass B2 pass] (informal) bring, take sth across etc quickly. **O:** book, parcel, letter □ *'I'll just* ***pop*** *this letter* ***into*** *the post.'* □ *John* ***popped*** *his head* ***round*** *the door.* □ *'I'll* ***pop*** *the results* ***over*** *when I get a minute.'*

pop along, around, down, in, over, round [A1] (informal) make a brief, casual visit to sb □ *'There's a meeting tonight, and I was thinking of* ***popping along*** *for half an hour or so.'* □ *'I just* ***popped in*** *to say hullo.'* EHOW □ ***'Pop round*** *when you get time. It's always nice to see you.'* □ pop in this sense combines esp with the particles shown. ⇨ **come along (to), come around/round (to)**[1] etc.

pop off[1] [A1] (informal) die □ *'Now you can all stop talking about my money: I've no intention of* ***popping off*** *yet.'*

pop off[2] [A1 B1i pass] (informal) be fired, fire, with a sharp explosion. **S:** [A1] **O:** [B1] firework; rifle, gun; (champagne) bottle, cork □ *A brilliant flare* ***popped off*** *right over our heads.* □ *There were children running all over the place,* ***popping off*** *toy guns.*

pop out/out of [A1 emph A2] come out (of) with a pop (a sharp, explosive sound). **S:** cork, stopper. **o:** bottle, tube □ *The cork* ***popped out*** *and the champagne gushed from the bottle.*

pop up[1] [A1 emph] (informal) appear (esp in unlikely places, when unexpected etc) □ *Rogers disappeared for a whole year, then* ***popped up*** *in Bolivia, of all places.* □ *'Then when finally we've given him up for lost,* ***up*** *he* ***pops!'***

pop up[2] [A1 nom] (esp of illustrated pages in a book) rise into three-dimensional form as the book is opened □ *'There you are, you see. You just press the pages flat and all the animals* ***pop up.'*** □ nom form is used attrib, as in: *a* ***pop-up*** *book.*

pore over [A2 pass adj] study with close attention. **o:** book, document; figure, table; painting, sketch □ *He* ***pored over*** *drawings.* BB □ *We* ***pored over*** *the sketches for a long time.* BB

portion out [B1i pass adj] divide in portions (among a number of people). **O:** food, rations; land; work. **A:** evenly, fairly, justly □ *The standard ration pack had to be* ***portioned out*** *among fourteen men.* □ ***Portioning*** *land* ***out*** *equally among one's children leads to the proliferation of uneconomic holdings.*

post away [B1i pass] send (away) to another place of duty. **O:** officer, soldier □ *I'm afraid Captain Jones is no longer here: he's been* ***posted away.***

post (to) [B2 pass emph rel] appoint to a post, or place of duty. **O:** soldier, Government official □ *'Where's he being* ***posted (to)?'*** *'Oh,* ***(to)*** *somewhere in the Far East.'* □ *I hope you will be* ***posted to*** *my battalion.*

potter about/around [A1 nom] (informal) move in a leisurely, unorganized way from one little job to another. **A:** in the garden, in one's study □ *I imagine that he enjoys life.* ***Pottering about*** *and buying his drawings.* ASA □ *I'll take it easy today; perhaps have a* ***potter-about*** *in the garden.*

pounce (on/upon)[1] [A2 pass emph rel] make a sudden attack on (often from above). **S:** eagle, hawk; tiger; aircraft; raider, bandit □ *The big cats wait for the right moment, then* ***pounce*** *swiftly (****on*** *their prey).* □ *Guerrillas* ***pounced on*** *the convoy from both sides of a narrow ravine.*

pounce (on/upon)[2] [A2 pass emph rel] choose in a keen, alert way for criticism etc. **o:** (every) error, slip, mistake □ *The teacher would* ***pounce on*** *every slip the child made, however insignificant, and hold her up to ridicule before the whole class.* □ *This is the kind of careless mistake* ***on*** *which examiners love to* ***pounce.***

pound at/on [A2 pass] strike heavily and repeatedly (at). **o:** door, table; drum, piano □ *Must he always* ***pound on*** *the table to make his point?* □ *'My ears have been* ***pounded at*** *for the past hour; when is he going to switch off that damned drill?'*

pound (away) (at) [A1 A2 pass A3 pass] (military) bombard heavily (and continuously). **S:** artillery; bomber. **o:** line, position; fortification □ *Heavy artillery* ***pounded away*** *in the distance.* □ *Waves of rocket-carrying aircraft* ***pounded (at)*** *the enemy columns.*

pour across, along, away etc[1] [A1 A2 emph rel] move in a continuous stream across etc. **S:** crowd, refugees, city workers; ants, termites □ *Tourists* ***pour into*** *London during the summer.* □ *The spectators* ***poured out of*** *the stadium.*

pour across, along, away etc[2] [B1i pass B2 pass emph rel] cause to move across etc in a stream. **O:** water, oil; grain, sand □ *Molten metal is* ***poured into*** *moulds.* □ *Any unused sugar can be* ***poured back*** *into the tin.*

pour down [A1] fall in a continuous stream, in torrents. **S:** ⚠ the rain; it □ *The rain* ***poured down*** *steadily* (or: *There was a steady* ***downpour****) all afternoon* (cf *It* ***poured with*** *rain all afternoon*). □ *It was* ***pouring down*** *non-stop* (cf *It was* ***pouring with*** *rain non-stop*). □ nom form is downpour.

pour forth/out [A1 B1i pass] (cause to) emerge in a stream. **S:** [A1] **O:** [B1] speech, music; propaganda, lies. **S:** [B1] orator, choir; radio-station, loud-speaker □ *We let the wretched man* ***pour out*** *his tale of woe.* □ *The loud-speakers in the square* ***poured forth*** *a continuous programme of martial music.* □ *Strong feelings were* ***poured out*** (or: *There was an* ***outpouring*** *of strong feelings*).

pour in/into [A1 A2 emph rel] arrive in a stream (at). **S:** application, inquiry; donation, gift □ *Thousands of pounds* ***poured into*** *our London office in response to the broadcast appeal.* □ *The switchboards were jammed as angry protests* ***poured in*** *from all over the country.*

pour off [A2] flow freely from the pores of the skin. **S:** ⚠ (the) sweat, perspiration □ *After a few laps of the track, the sweat was* ***pouring off*** *the runners.*

pour on [B2 pass emph rel] express strongly adverse feelings towards sth; ridicule, scorn sth. **S:** commentator, critic; expert. **O:** ⚠ contempt, ridicule, scorn. **O:** effort, attempt; achievement □ *Now that mobility is the keynote in defence thinking, it is easy to* ***pour*** *scorn* ***on*** *those who planned fixed-site missiles like Blue Streak.* SC □ *Despite all the ridicule that has been* ***poured on*** *the more extreme advocates of Women's Lib, the movement certainly has a serious case, which deserves serious attention.*

pour out[1] [A1 B1i pass adj] serve a beverage from a pot, bottle etc. **S:** hostess, waitress. **O:** (cup of) tea, coffee □ *'Let me* ***pour out*** *the tea at least.'* TGLY □ *'Tea? Do sit down and I'll* ***pour*** *you some* ***out****.'* □ *'Shall I* ***pour out*** (i e Shall I serve the tea)*?'* □ note the position of the Indirect Object in the second example.

pour out[2] [A1 B1i pass] (cause to) emerge in a stream. ⇨ pour forth/out.

pour with [A 2] ⇨ pour down.

prance about/around [A1 A2] (informal) dance about in a light-hearted or foolish way □ *There was a certain amount of* ***prancing about*** *in the corridors when the exam results were posted.* □ *'Tell those children to stop* ***prancing around*** *on the landing and get into bed.'*

pray (to God) (for) [A2 pass emph rel] make a request to God for sth or on behalf of sb. **o:** food, water; help, forgiveness; sick people, the dying □ *The farmers are* ***praying for*** *rain.* □ *He's past* ***praying for*** (i e he can no longer be helped). □ *They* ***prayed to God for*** *guidance in difficult times.*

preach (at) [A2 pass] give moral advice in an aloof, superior way □ *'Please don't* ***preach at*** *me,' Virginia said. 'I came home to get some help.'* AITC □ *We were tired of being* ***preached at*** *by sanctimonious ushers with no knowledge of life outside the school gates.* CON

preclude from [B2 pass] (formal) prevent from doing sth, make impossible one's doing sth. **o:** participation, attendance; having a share, standing for office □ *The sudden change in events* ***precluded him from*** *a share in the Government.* □ *Retiring members of the Board were* ***precluded from*** *seeking re-election for three years.*

predispose to/towards [B2 pass] (formal) (of an earlier event) make sb likely or inclined to do or accept sth at a later time. **S:** upbringing, training, indoctrination. **o:** acceptance, refusal; scholarship, music, the law, medicine □ *His father's harsh treatment of him* ***predisposed*** *him* ***to*** *a rejection of authority in later life.* □ *He was* ***predisposed towards*** *literary studies by the bookish environment of his early years.*

preface with [B2 pass emph rel] (formal) place before the main body of a speech, text etc. **S:** speaker; chairman; editor. **O:** address, speech; chapter. **o:** (short) reference (to), (brief) mention (of) □ *'If I may, I should like to* ***preface*** *my remarks* ***with*** *a short tribute to my predecessor in the chair.'*

prepare (for) [A2 pass adj emph rel B2 pass emph rel] (cause to) get ready (for). **O:** oneself; pupil, class; follower, subject; article, book; room. **o:** exam; ordeal, hardship; the press; guest □ ***'Prepare*** *(yourselves)* ***for*** *a shock!'* □ *These long-****prepared-for*** *discussions open in Brussels on Monday.* □ *He's* ***preparing*** *a paper* ***for*** *the next meeting of the Association.* □ ***'Prepare*** *the children* ***for*** *the big news.'*

present to [B2 pass emph rel] ⇨ next entry.

present with [B2 pass rel] give, offer, sth as a present or reward. **o:** medal, scroll (of honour), sum of money □ *He was* ***presented with*** *the keys of the city* (or: *He had the keys of the city* ***presented to*** *him*). □ *The company* ***presented*** *him* ***with*** *a gold watch on the day he retired* (or: ***presented*** *a gold watch* ***to*** *him* etc).

preside (over) [A2 pass emph rel] be the chairman (at); sit at the head of the table (at a formal meal). **o:** meeting, rally; dinner □ *He was a brilliant industrial diplomat, who* ***presided over*** *banquets and regally entertained foreign potentates.* OBS

preside over [A2] witness, from an important position, events over which one has little control. **S:** government, administration; minister, director. **o:** decline, collapse, break-up □ *Successive post-war governments have* ***presided over*** *the gradual dissolution of the British Empire.* □ *The directors were not content to* ***preside*** *inertly* ***over*** *the liquidation of their most valuable subsidiary.*

press across, along, away etc[1] [A1 A2] move with a steady pressure across etc. **S:** spectator, demonstrator; crowd, mob □ *The advance guard* ***pressed forward*** *to maintain contact with the enemy.* □ *The fans* ***pressed through*** *the tunnels and* ***onto*** *the terraces of the stadium.* □ *A mass of new sights and sounds* ***pressed in*** *upon them.*

press across, along, away etc[2] [B1i pass adj B2 pass] using firm pressure, cause to move across etc steadily. **O:** crowd; demonstrators, troops; assault □ *The police* ***pressed*** *the students* ***back*** *behind the barriers.* □ *The movement of wheeled vehicles was impossible. The attack, however, had to be* ***pressed forward*** *under all circumstances.* B

press ahead/forward/on (with) [A1 A3] continue steadily and with determination (to carry sth out); push ahead/forward/on (with) (q v). **o:** proposals, plans; efforts, endeavours □ *We must **press ahead with** our efforts to reach an agreement.*

press (for) [A2 pass emph rel B2 pass emph rel] make repeated and urgent requests (for); push (for) (q v). **O:** ministers, Government. **o:** debate, discussion, inquiry □ *We are **pressing** (the Government) hard **for** a renewal of talks.* □ *Reporters **pressed** him **for** an explanation* (or: ***pressed** him to give an explanation*). □ *The engineers' representatives have won all the concessions **for** which they were **pressing**.*

press home [B1i pass] make, apply, forcefully; push home (q v). **O:** attack, assault; accusation □ *This particular charge was **pressed home**.* LWK □ *The attacks were **pressed home** despite determined resistance.*

press home an/one's advantage [B1iii pass] use well, exploit, an opportunity or advantage □ *She was rather more concerned with her appearance than with the strong-room key, so he **pressed home his advantage** and took the key.* TO □ *The employers were prepared to discuss wages, and they **pressed home the advantage** this gave them by raising the matter of productivity.*

press on/upon [B2 pass] offer sth insistently (out of gratitude, or in hope of gain); insist that sb accepts sth (against his will). **O:** attentions, favours; money, gifts; opinions, beliefs □ *The crowds **pressed** food and wine **upon** the liberating troops.* □ *I wish he'd stop trying to **press** his political views **upon** his students.*

press out/out of [B1i pass adj B2 pass] force to leave, separate, by applying pressure. **O:** oil, juice; part, component. **o:** seed, fruit; (sheet of) metal, card □ *This machine **presses** the oil **out of** palm kernels.* □ *The parts of the model have been printed on cardboard; all you have to do is **press** them **out** and assemble them.*

presume on/upon [A2 pass] (formal) test, strain, too much the goodwill etc of another person. **o:** patience, indulgence; kindness, good nature; hospitality □ *It would be unwise to **presume** over much **upon** the tolerance of these people.* □ *I think we have already **presumed** too much **on** your generosity.*

pretend to [A2 pass emph rel] (formal) claim (somewhat vainly) to possess. **o:** wit, understanding, knowledge; talent, gift □ *He doesn't **pretend to** a detailed knowledge of the system.* □ *She **pretends to** various abilities she doesn't, in fact, possess.*

pretty up [B1i pass adj] (informal) make (falsely) pretty or charming. **O:** child; street, house; story □ *Here was a row of simple cottages, **prettied up** for sale to commuting stockbrokers.* □ *The script will have to be **prettied up** to give it box-office appeal.*

prevail on/upon [A2 pass emph rel] (formal) persuade (to do sth) □ *The judge was **prevailed upon** to show clemency.* □ *At dinner he **prevailed on** her to take some wine. It wasn't easy.* PW □ *He allowed himself to be **prevailed on**.* □ object is usu followed by the inf.

prey on/upon[1] [A2 pass adj] pursue and kill as one's normal food; select as victims for one's attacks. **S:** hawk, eagle; tiger, lion; pirate, bandit. **o:** small bird; antelope; merchant shipping □ *Owls **prey on** small rodents, especially mice.* □ *Aircraft **preyed upon** the columns of refugees.* □ *Bullion ships plying out of the Carribean were **preyed upon** by pirates.*

prey on/upon[2] [A2 pass] assail, beset, deeply trouble. **S:** doubt, fear, anxiety. **o:** ⚠ him etc; sb's mind, thoughts □ *Was it the accident with the car and the blackmailing letters that were **preying on** his mind?* DC □ *It would appear that his impending trial **preyed on** his mind* (or: ***on** him*). T

price out of the market [B2 pass] set one's prices so high that no one buys one's goods. **O:** oneself; product, goods □ *If you don't accept a lower profit, you'll **price** yourself right **out of the market**.*

prick out [B1i pass] (horticulture) plant in the earth, in holes pricked with a pointed stick. **O:** seedling, young plant □ *'I'm just going to **prick out** some young cabbage plants.'*

prick one's ears up [B1i pass] (of a dog, horse) raise the ears (a sign that it is listening closely); (of a person) pay careful attention □ *The horse seemed so interested in what was going on that after being led away some paces she turned, **pricked up her ears**, and looked around.* DBM □ *'I've been thinking about Myrtle for some time, Joe.' 'Oh?' I **pricked up my ears**.* SPL

pride oneself on/upon [B2 emph rel] regard as a special reason for pride or satisfaction. **o:** skill, craft; sensitivity, finesse □ *He had always **prided himself on** his tact in handling such crises.* □ *He **prided himself** justly **on** his skill in negotiation.* □ ***On** this ability to learn new languages he had always **prided himself**.*

prink up [B1i pass adj] (informal) make smarter, more attractive. **O:** oneself; one's face, clothes □ *She's in the women's room. **Prinking** herself **up** a bit extra, not that she needs it.* TC

print off[1] [B1i nom pass adj] (photography) make prints or enlargements on sensitive paper from a negative film or plate □ *How many copies of the wedding group do you want **printed off**?* □ *I want to do a **print-off** from that negative* (or: ***print off** photographs from that negative*).

print off[2] [B1i nom pass adj] (printing) print copies of a book etc (with the implication that another printing is to be made from the same plates) □ *We **printed off** 10000 copies* (cf *did a **print-off** of 10000*) *from the existing plates.* □ note the special nom form offprint = an extra printing of (usu) a single article from a journal, in a small number of copies for the author's own use.

print out [B1i nom pass adj] (of a computer) provide printed information from the data stored in a computer 'bank' in accordance with a programme specification □ *At the end of the working day the computer is programmed to **print out** an analysis of the orders received and invoiced and the resulting stock levels.* □ *The texts were fed into the computer and several **print-outs** were obtained, showing, among other things, word-frequency distribution and sentence lengths.* □ nom form more frequent in current usage.

prize off [B1i pass adj B2 pass] remove, raise (usu by force applied to a lever). **O:** lid, cover, top. **o:** tin, box, cask □ *We **prized** the lids **off** the packing cases with a tyre lever.* □ ***Prize off** the cover with your thumbs.* □ alt spelling: prise.

prize out/out of [B1i pass adj B2 pass]

remove, extract (from) (usu by force applied to a lever); obtain with difficulty (by applying moral pressure etc). **O:** stone, nail; secret, confession. **o:** (animal's) hoof, tyre; suspect, prisoner □ *Sharp pieces of grit were* ***prized out of*** *the tyre treads.* □ *Foreign espionage would do its utmost to* ***prize out*** *these secrets.* TBC □ *She* ***prized*** *the story* ***out of*** *him by threatening to inform his employers.* □ alt spelling: prise.

proceed against [A2] (legal) take steps to bring sb to trial. **S:** police; (solicitor's) client, plaintiff. **o:** suspect, prisoner □ *'But before we go to the trouble and expense of* ***proceeding against*** *this man I must be satisfied that your charges are well founded.'*

proceed from [A2 emph rel] (formal) have as a cause or starting-point. **S:** event; agreement, treaty. **o:** decision, plan; meeting, discussion □ ***From*** *this small error many unfortunate misunderstandings have* ***proceeded.*** □ *The plans were then made* ***from*** *which the momentous events of 1944* ***proceeded.***

proceed to[1] [A2] (formal) take the next item etc in succession. **o:** next item (on the agenda); vote, election □ *'May we* ***proceed,*** *then,* ***to*** *the election of a committee?'* □ *'Let us* ***proceed to*** *nominations for President.'*

proceed to[2] [A2] (formal) go forward from a lower university degree to a higher one. **o:** the (degree of) MA, PhD □ *Graduates wishing to* ***proceed to*** *the MA may do so on payment of the necessary fees and dues.*

profit by [A2] by studying one's mistakes etc, ensure they are not repeated. **o:** ⚠ one's mistake, experience; sb's advice, counsel □ *We ought to* ***profit by*** *our mistakes.* □ *He's been married twice, but doesn't seem to have* ***profited*** *much* ***by*** *the experience.* ⇨ next entry.

profit (from) [A2 pass emph rel] get some benefit (from), be helped (by). **o:** course, training, instruction; trip, stay □ *He* ***profited*** *greatly* ***from*** *his three years at university.* □ *These young volunteer teachers* ***profit*** *personally and professionally* ***from*** *their year overseas.* ⇨ previous entry.

prohibit from [B2 pass] (formal) forbid sb to do sth. **o:** smoking, walking on the grass, using public transport □ *We are* ***prohibited from*** *selling cigarettes to young children.* □ *The school* ***prohibits*** *the younger boarders* ***from*** *going to the cinema.* □ object is the *-ing* form of a v.

pronounce (on/upon) [A2 pass emph rel] (formal) give a considered opinion or verdict on some matter. **S:** expert, adviser, consultant. **o:** health, safety; efficiency, viability □ *The air is heavy with the voices of experts,* ***pronouncing on*** *everything from the effect of fluoride on drinking water to the future of motor traffic in cities.*

prop up[1] [B1i pass adj] raise, and keep in a raised position, by means of supports. **S:** nurse, mother; farmer, building. **O:** patient, child; fence, outhouse □ *Nurse Ellen had tucked her up and left her to sleep, but she* ***propped*** *herself* ***up*** (on the pillows). DC □ *The gardener* ***propped up*** *the apple tree with a stout plank.*

prop up[2] [B1i pass] support sth which would otherwise collapse. **O:** (failing) company, business; uneconomic enterprise; badly-run organization. **A:** with public money, government support □ *The Minister said that it was not the duty of any government to* ***prop up*** *a failing company, no matter how prestigious its name.*

prospect for [A2] (mining) search for minerals. **o:** diamonds, gold; copper, bauxite □ *Where in the nineteenth century amateur fortune hunters* ***prospected for*** *gold, today professional geologists* ***prospect for*** *oil, uranium and industrial metals.*

protect (against/from) [B2 pass emph rel] serve as a shield or defence (against). **S:** armour plate, barricade; law, regulation; police. **O:** passenger, crew; customer, retailer; citizen. **o:** shell-fire, explosion; unfair trading; violence □ *An armoured shield will* ***protect*** *the driver* ***against*** *all but a direct hit.* □ *Is the tenant adequately* ***protected from*** *exploitation?* □ *Pensions tied to the cost-of-living index can* ***protect*** *retired people* ***from*** *the effects of inflation.*

protest (against) [A2 pass emph rel] express objections (to); do this in the form of an organized demonstration. **o:** intrusion, rudeness; rent increase, atomic weapons, racial discrimination □ *Crowds of young demonstrators* ***protested against*** *the increase in students' fees.* □ *Small groups of dissidents* ***protested*** *courageously* ***against*** (or: *made a courageous* ***protest against***) *this armed intervention.* □ cf US usage: *Demonstrators* ***protested*** *the increase in fees.*

provide for[1] [A2 pass adj emph rel] ensure, by earning enough and by careful spending, that one's family etc has enough to live on (now, and/or in the event of future separation or death). **o:** wife, children, parent; widow □ *If you decide to divorce, you must see to it that your wife is properly* ***provided for.*** □ *The children are* ***provided for.*** OMIH □ *He's always* ***provided*** *well* ***for*** *his family* (cf *He's always been a good* ***provider***).

provide for[2] [A2 pass] make such efficient arrangements that all possible difficulties can be overcome. **o:** every eventuality, all contingencies □ *Every possible failure of the electrical system has been* ***provided for,*** *generally by duplicating the circuits.*

provide for[3] [A2 pass] (parliament, legal) establish the legal basis or authority for the later actions or conduct of Government or individuals. **S:** Act (of Parliament), Bill. **o:** the hand-over of power, confiscation of property; easier divorce, a higher school-leaving age □ *The Bill* ***provides for*** *the eventual self-government of the territory.* □ *A clause in the agreement* ***provides for*** *the arbitration of all disputes by an independent body* (or: ***provides*** *that all disputes shall be arbitrated* etc). □ *Equal pay for women is* ***provided for*** *in the party manifesto.*

provoke (into) [B2 pass rel] goad, vex, sb so much that he reacts angrily, behaves violently etc. **o:** temper, rage, outburst; slapping, beating □ *Jibes about his low salary always* ***provoked*** *him* ***into*** *violent displays of temper.* □ *The continual noise in the classroom* ***provoked*** *him* ***into*** *slapping one or two hands* (or: ***provoked*** *him to slap* etc).

prowl about/around [A1] go about carefully looking for food or an opportunity to steal. **S:** lion, tiger; thief, layabout □ *The big cats* ***prowl about*** *in the savannah grass, looking for an incautious prey.* □ *'What's going on down there?*

*Who's **prowling about** downstairs?'* DC

pry (into) [A2 pass adj emph rel] show too much interest in (other people's affairs); poke one's nose in/into (q v). **o:** others' affairs, matters that don't concern one □ *She **pries** too closely **into** the private life of her friends.* □ *'This is something I said you weren't to **pry into**.'*

pucker up [A1 B1i pass adj] come or draw together into small folds or wrinkles. **S:** [A1] **O:** [B1] brow, eyes, lips; skin □ *His eyes were **puckered up** against the strong sunlight.* □ *She had the little **puckered-up** face of a seal, very worried-looking.* CON

puff across, along, away etc[1] [A1 A2] go across etc, sending out smoke etc and/or panting noisily. **S:** engine, train; runner, messenger □ *Our train **puffed into** the station ten minutes late.* □ *Steam **puffed up** from a crack in the metal.* □ *A few weekend athletes **puffed along**, unhappy at the unaccustomed exercise.*

puff across, along, away etc[2] [B1i pass B2 pass] send, drive, across etc, in short, sudden gusts. **S:** pipe, tube, chimney; smoker. **O:** smoke, fumes, smog, gas □ *The factory chimneys **puff** dense smoke **into** the air.* □ *'Don't **puff** your tobacco smoke **into** my eyes.'* □ *Air is **puffed up** through the liquid.*

puff (at/on) [A2] draw smoke from a pipe etc, usu in short gusts. **o:** pipe, cigar, cigarette □ *He was **puffing** nervously **at** a cigarette.* □ *'Stop **puffing** (**on** that pipe) for a moment, and listen to me.'*

puff out[1] [B1i pass adj] (informal) make sb short of breath. **S:** exercise, exertion; race, climb □ *Climbing up the long staircase to his office quite **puffed** me **out**.* □ *We were completely **puffed out**: we had to sit down for a few minutes to get our breath back.*

puff out[2] [B1i pass] cause to go out, extinguish, with a sharp gust of air. **O:** light, flame; lamp, candle □ *A sudden gust of wind from the open window **puffed** the candle **out**.*

puff one's chest out [B1i pass adj] cause one's chest to expand with air (from pride, or in order to appear smart on parade) □ ***His chest** was **puffed out** with pride on the day that they gave him his medal.* □ *Little boys marched up and down with **puffed-out chests**.*

puff up [B1i pass adj] fill sb with conceit, with too great a sense of his importance. **S:** money, success, status □ *Uncle Saunders is only a noisy pompous ass, **puffed up** by too much money.* DC □ *They're a couple of **puffed-up** idiots — very much in need of deflating.*

pull about/around [B1ii pass adj] handle roughly, mistreat. **O:** wife, child; furniture □ *'If you don't stop **pulling** me **about**, I'll scream the place down.'* □ *'I wish the dogs would leave the cushions alone: they're looking terribly **pulled-about**.'*

pull ahead/ahead of [A1 A2] move in front (of); progress beyond; draw ahead/ahead of (q v). **S:** car; runner; business firm, economy. **o:** opposition, rival □ *'That driver's trying to overtake. Slow down a bit and let him **pull ahead**.'* □ *Liverpool has **pulled ahead of** Arsenal in the race for the League leadership.*

pull alongside [A1 A2] stop, or move along, at the side of; draw alongside (q v). **S:** car; tug, launch. **o:** lorry; steamer □ *A motor-cyclist **pulled alongside** and signalled that my off-side door wasn't properly shut.* □ *'We'll **pull alongside** her and put a salvage crew aboard.'*

pull apart[1] [B1ii pass] use force to separate the parts of sth; pull to pieces[1] (q v). **O:** box, cupboard; garment; flower □ *The table is so made that you can easily **pull** it **apart** (or: that it easily **pulls apart**).*

pull apart[2] [B1ii pass] criticize severely; pull to pieces[2] (q v). **S:** tutor, foreman. **O:** idea; plan, scheme; work, achievement □ *There's nothing more dispiriting than having your essays **pulled apart** in front of other students.*

pull around [B1iii pass adj] ⇨ pull about/around.

pull aside [B1i pass] move sth to one side (esp to reveal what is behind it); draw aside[1] (q v). **O:** curtain, hanging; mask, veil (of secrecy, deceit) □ *We **pulled aside** a dingy curtain to reveal a flight of steps running downwards.* □ *The cloak of secrecy was **pulled aside** by a newspaper photographer who spotted a prototype of the car while on an assignment in Austria.*

pull at/on [A2] draw smoke steadily from a pipe etc. **o:** pipe, cigar □ *The old man **pulled** thoughtfully **at** his pipe before replying.*

pull away (from) [B1ii pass B3 pass] use force to move sth or sb away (esp from danger). **O:** bomb; pilot, passenger. **o:** house; wreckage, ruins; fire □ *With great presence of mind a fireman **pulled** the driver **away from** the burning cab.*

pull back [A1 B1i pass] (military) (cause to) retreat, withdraw. **S:** [A1] **O:** [B1] tanks, infantry. **S:** [B1] commander □ *The battalion **pulled back** two miles during the night and took up prepared positions.* □ *The bad condition of the roads made relief impossible without **pulling** the division **back** to Orel, so the 4th Panzer had struggled on.* B

pull down[1] [B1i pass adj] lower, draw down (q v). **O:** blind, shade; hat □ *His hat was **pulled** well **down** over his eyes so that nobody should guess his true identity.*

pull down[2] [B1i pass adj] demolish, destroy. **O:** theatre, monument, house □ *A row of back-to-back houses is being **pulled down** to make way for new flats.* □ *Many people are opposed to the **pulling-down** of buildings of historical interest.*

pull down[3] [B1ii pass adj] (informal) weaken, leave in a poor condition. **S:** malaria, influenza; poor diet, feeding □ *'Bit thinner, aren't you? You look a bit **pulled down**, you know.'* PW □ *That long spell in hospital **pulled** him **down** a lot.*

pull down[4] [B1ii pass] (informal) cause to fall to a lower position (e g in a class or form). **S:** mark, score; written test, oral □ *He seemed all set to win a gold medal, but his performance in the third round **pulled** him **down**.* □ *It was the written paper that **pulled** me **down**.*

pull in[1] [B1i pass] (informal) earn, draw. **O:** good wage; two thousand a year □ *He's **pulling in** a regular salary.* NM □ *They're **pulling in** a lot of overtime* (money paid for working extra hours) *on that job.*

pull in[2] [B1i pass] (informal) attract, draw, to a place of entertainment, an opportunity of investment etc. **O:** crowd, audience; investment, savings □ *'We used to* ***pull in*** *a good Saturday crowd at the Palace Theatre.'* □ *They need to have a high rate of interest in order to* ***pull in*** *money from investors.* BBCTV

pull in[3] [B1i pass] (informal) fetch to the police station (for questioning). **O:** suspect, loiterer, habitual offender □ *Two youths loitering near a supermarket were* ***pulled in*** *on suspicion.*

pull in/into[1] [A1 A2] enter, arrive (at); draw in/into[1] (q v). **S:** train. **o:** station, terminus □ *Our train* ***pulled into*** *Paddington dead on time.* □ *As we* ***pulled in****, an hour late, our connection to Rome was pulling out.*

pull in/into[2] [A1 nom A2] move towards, draw closer to, the side of the road, bank etc. **S:** boat; car, lorry. **o:** shore, quay; kerb, lorry-park □ *The steamer* ***pulled in*** *towards the quay-side.* □ *'Find a good place to* ***pull into*** *for some tea on the way to London* (or: *Find a good* ***pull-in*** *on the way to London*).*'* □ the café where you pull in for refreshments is a pull-in. □ pull up[1].

pull off[1] [B1i pass adj B2 pass] remove (with some force). **O:** shoe, jumper; leaf, bud □ *'Here, help me* ***pull*** *these boots* ***off****.'* □ *'See if you can* ***pull*** *the cloth* ***off*** *the table without disturbing these glasses.'*

pull off[2] [B1i pass] (informal) succeed in sth, make a success of sth. **O:** it; coup, deal, speculation; scoop □ *Every time he* ***pulled off*** *a big deal it made a paragraph in the 'Sentry'.* CON □ *'We did it, we've* ***pulled*** *it* ***off****, we've won.'* BBCTV

pull on[1] [A2] draw smoke steadily from a pipe etc. ⇨ pull at/on.

pull on[2] [B1i pass] don (clothing), draw on[1] (q v). **O:** boot, sock, shirt □ *He* ***pulled*** *a sweater* ***on*** *over his woollen shirt.*

pull out[1] [B1i pass] extract, draw out/out of[2] (q v). **S:** dentist; carpenter. **O:** tooth; nail, tack □ *I was afraid he was going to* ***pull out*** *one of those big molars.*

pull out[2] [B1i nom pass] remove, detach. **O:** supplement, (comic-, magazine-)section □ *The map is at the back of the book, and may be* ***pulled out*** (or: ***pulls out***) *for easy reference.* □ *In this week's issue there is a special section you can* ***pull out*** (or: *a special* ***pull-out*** *section*) *on French wines.*

pull out all the stops [B1iii] (informal) use all one's power, resources etc, to achieve an objective □ *The Government* ***pulled out all the stops*** *to get the Industrial Relations Bill through Parliament in a single session.* □ *Helen, desperately afraid that Archie would leave her,* ***pulled out all the stops*** *to keep her hold over him.*

pull one's finger out [B1ii] (informal) stop behaving in a lazy, inefficient way. **S:** firm; manager, accountant, storekeeper □ *'He's got till the end of the month to get his research project written up and typed, so he'd better* ***pull his finger out****.'* □ *'That's twice I've been let down by the garage over spare parts. If they don't* ***pull their finger(s) out*** *I'll take my custom elsewhere.'*

pull out/out of[1] [A1 A2] leave, depart from; draw out/out of[5] (q v). **S:** train, bus, coach. **o:** station □ *Then the train* ***pulled out****.* TC □ *The three-thirty was* ***pulling out of*** *platform five as I ran into the station.*

pull out/out of[2] [A1 A2] move out of a line of traffic, in order to overtake the vehicle in front, enter a faster traffic lane. **S:** driver, motorist; car, lorry □ *The car in front* ***pulled out*** *to overtake just as I was about to overtake* it. □ *Don't* ***pull out of*** *a line of stationary vehicles unless the road behind you is clear.*

pull out/out of[3] [A1 A2 pass] force oneself to emerge, recover, (from). **o:** illness; mood, depression □ *He's been dogged by failure for years; now he's working strenuously to* ***pull out****.* □ *'But he'll* ***pull out of*** *it. He has these spells, you know. He's never been strong.'* AITC

pull out/out of[4] [A1 nom A2 pass B1i nom pass adj B2 pass] (cause to) withdraw, retire (from). **S:** [A1] **O:** [B1] troops, force; trade mission; diplomatic representative. **o:** colony, base, occupied territory □ [A1] *I had lain in the grass and impotently watched the enemy* ***pulling out*** *below me.* SD □ [A1] *If he agrees, Britain will be failing to make the clean* ***pull-out*** (or: *to* ***pull out*** *cleanly*) *which is essential to the Government's strategy.* OBS □ [A2] *I want to state — as I* ***pull out of*** *active employment — how I think the land should be made to lie.* MFM □ [B1] *The 'withdrawal' now talked about in Britain is the far more radical one of* ***pulling out*** *British troops.* ST

pull over [A1 B1ii pass] move towards the roadside, either to stop or to allow other vehicles to overtake. **S:** [A1] **O:** [B1] car, lorry. **S:** [A1 B1] driver, motorist □ *I shouted to the driver of the tractor to* ***pull over*** *and let me through.* □ *Having stopped the driver, the traffic policeman asked if he would kindly* ***pull*** *his car* ***over*** *to the side of the road.*

pull the wool over sb's eyes [B2 pass] (informal) conceal one's true actions or intentions from sb by a display of virtue. **o:** (*of*) employer, teacher, husband □ *'I'm afraid you can't* ***pull the wool over the eyes of*** *the Tax Inspectors. They have ways of finding out.'* □ *'She's had* ***the wool pulled over her eyes*** *for years. You don't imagine he always travels to London on business, do you?'*

pull round[1] [B1ii pass] force sb or sth to face another way (esp in the opposite direction). **O:** nose, tail (of an aircraft); bow, stern (of a boat) □ *A tug* ***pulled*** *the bow of the ship* ***round****.* □ *A hand descended on his shoulder, and he was* ***pulled round*** *to face a pair of glaring eyes.*

pull round[2] [A1 B1ii pass] (informal) (help to) regain consciousness □ *'How long will she take to* ***pull round*** *after her operation?'* □ (of a person injured in an accident) *'Loosen his clothes and give him a little brandy: that'll soon* ***pull*** *him* ***round****.'*

pull through[1] [A1 A2 pass B1ii pass B2 pass] (help to) recover (from an illness); (help to) survive a period of danger or crisis. **S:** [A1] **O:** [B1] patient; country, firm. **o:** sickness; time of trial, emergency □ [A1] *The patient has an excellent chance of* ***pulling through****.* □ [B2] *It was this spirit which* ***pulled*** *them* ***through*** *the darkest moments of the war.*

pull through[2] [B1i nom pass adj] (military) clean the bore of a rifle by drawing through it an oily rag attached to a cord. **O:** rifle, revolver □ *Rifles should be regularly* ***pulled through*** *with a piece of flannelette.* □ the pull-through is the weighted cord to which the rag is fastened.

pull to pieces[1] [B2 pass] separate the parts of

sth by force; pull apart[1] (q v). **O:** model, construction; garment, cloth; prey □ *The rags are washed and **pulled to pieces** by machine.* □ *A tiger can **pull** a roebuck to **pieces** in a matter of minutes.*

pull to pieces[2] [B2 pass] criticize severely, find serious faults in; pull apart[2] (q v). **O:** persons; theory, argument, case; evidence □ *The new theory of the origin of the universe was **pulled to pieces** by many of the world's leading astronomers.* □ *The poor woman was **pulled to pieces** by her neighbours. Her hair-style, her clothes, her make-up, her accent, her political opinions: nothing escaped criticism.*

pull together[1] [A2] act in concert, combine efforts □ *If we all **pull together**, we should be able to get the country out of the mess it's in.* □ *The old habit of looking well after the wage earners* (i e in working-class families) *is still alive; so is the stress on the need for all to **pull together**.* UL

pull together[2] [B1i pass] draw the parts of sth closer to each other, restore its wholeness or unity. **O:** assembly, party, regiment, (industrial) company, country □ *There is the NATO alliance, which will soon disintegrate unless we do something to **pull** it **together**.* MFM □ *It was he more than anybody who **pulled** the Party **together** after our defeat in the last election.*

pull oneself together [B1ii] (informal) take command of oneself, take firm control of one's feelings and impulses and begin to behave purposefully □ *She had her ups and downs, but she had always managed to **pull herself together** and have a good time.* H □ *Under their patronizing and hostile stares he **pulled himself together**, walked into the kitchen, and sat down on a chair.* HD

pull under [B1ii pass] drag below the surface (of a river, the sea). **S:** ⚠ the current, undertow □ *The currents were deceptively strong at this point, and nobody would swim for fear of being **pulled under**.*

pull up[1] [A1 nom B1i pass] stop, halt. **S:** [A1] **O:** [B1] car, lorry. **S:** [A1 B1] driver, motorist □ *More slowly than usual he drove towards his office. At last he **pulled up**.* PW □ *He **pulled** his car **up** within a few yards of the wreckage.* □ *His pursuer **pulled up** short to greet us with an affable little bow.* BM □ a pull-up is a café where drivers (usu of commercial vehicles) can stop for refreshments. ⇨ pull in/into[2].

pull up[2] [B1ii pass] (stop in order to) check or reprimand □ ALISON: *I'm sorry. I'll go now.* (*She starts to move upstage. But his voice **pulls her up**.*) JIMMY: *You never even sent any flowers to the funeral.* LBA □ *Even his wife had to **pull him up** over his wrong-headed notions this afternoon.* RM

pull up[3] [A1 B1ii pass] improve one's position (in a race, contest etc). **S:** [A1] **O:** [B1] pupil, competitor. **S:** [B1] marks, points; performance, effort □ *His mark in the geography paper **pulled him up** several places.* □ *He **pulled up** to within a few yards of the leaders.*

pull one's socks up [B1i] (informal) take command of oneself, become more purposeful and alert □ PENNY: *Please Peter, pull yourself together.* PETER: *Leave me alone.* ALEX: ***Pull up your socks**, son.* DPM □ *If he wants to be considered for promotion next year, he'd better **pull his socks up**.*

pull oneself up by one's own bootlaces/bootstraps [B1ii] (informal) try to improve one's position by one's own unaided efforts □ *We can't expect countries with problems of bad feeding and disease to **pull themselves up by their own bootstraps**.* □ *Unable to borrow capital to repair and modernize its plant, the company was forced to **pull itself up by its own bootlaces**.*

pump in/into[1] [B1i pass adj B2 pass emph rel] cause sth to flow in by using a pump. **O:** gas, air; oil, water. **o:** tank, reservoir □ *Millions of gallons of liquid oxygen were **pumped into** the fuel tanks.* □ *Too much oil had been **pumped in**, and it overflowed everywhere.*

pump in/into[2] [B1i pass B2 pass] (informal) cause sb to learn or acquire by force or persuasion. **O:** facts, information. **o:** head, brain □ *It's a hard job **pumping** facts and figures **into** unwilling pupils.* □ ***Pump** enough propaganda **in**, and they'll believe anything.*

pump in/into[3] [B1i pass B2 pass] put money in, with a view to giving support, earning interest etc. **O:** money, capital. **o:** industry, company □ *There may be strong social reasons why the Government should **pump** money **into** industries which, economically, seem no longer viable.* □ *Nigeria's economy is booming and foreign companies are confidently **pumping in** capital.*

pump out/out of [B1i pass adj B2 pass] cause sth to flow out by using a pump. **O:** gas, air; oil, water. **o:** balloon; tank, sump, hold □ *They pursued two ideas: the first was to **pump** the oil **out**; the second was to refloat the ship.* OBS □ *The petrol is **pumped out of** the spare tank and into the main tank.*

pump out of [B2 pass] (informal) cause sb to reveal sth by applying pressure. **O:** information, story □ *We **pumped** the full story **out of** him little by little.*

pump up[1] [B1i pass adj] cause sth to rise by using a pump. **O:** (crude) oil, water □ *The oil is **pumped up** from deep underground reservoirs.*

pump up[2] [B1i pass adj] inflate, fill with air etc, using a pump; blow up[5] (q v). **O:** tyre, balloon, (air-)mattress □ ***Pump** the tyres **up** hard before going out on the road.* □ *The newly **pumped-up** balloons suddenly began to burst as the heat increased.*

punch down/in [B1i pass adj] drive below the surface of a plank etc, using a (nail) punch. **O:** nail, tack □ *You should **punch down** any old nails or screws before attempting to lay a carpet or linoleum.* □ ***Punch in** the nails and then fill the holes flush with putty.*

punch out/out of [B1i pass adj B2 pass] cut from wood, metal etc, using a sharp tool called a 'punch'; stamp out/out of (q v). **O:** disc, strip; coin, button □ *The figures are **punched out of** a continuous strip of cardboard.* □ *The machine **punches out** hundreds of coins in an hour.*

punch up[1] [B1i pass] cause a machine to register a certain amount (esp of money) by striking a key sharply. **O:** £2·25, ten dollars fifty □ *She **punched up** the cost of our groceries on the cash register.*

punch up[2] [A1 nom] (informal) have a (fist) fight, exchange punches □ *If there is any **punching up** between the two (sides), it's going to be* here. BBCTV □ *He was involved in some* ***punch-up*** *after an all-night party.* □ usu nom.

urge (of) [B2 pass] (formal) free, cleanse, rom. **o:** ⚠ guilt, shame, sin □ *After making a full confession, he felt* ***purged of*** *any sense of sin.*

urse up [A1 B1i pass adj] (of the lips) draw together in tight folds (usu as a sign of disapproval or displeasure). **S:** [A1] **O:** [B1] lips, mouth □ *While he told his mildly shocking stories, she would sit with* ***pursed-up*** *lips.*

ush about/around [B1ii pass] (informal) order sb to do this and that in a bullying tone; order about/around (q v) □ *'I won't be* ***pushed around*** *by him any longer!'* □ *'I wish he'd stop* ***pushing*** *people* ***about*** *as though they were children.'* □ *'You may be able to* ***push*** *your brother* ***around****, but you'd better not try it on with me.'*

ush ahead/forward/on [A1] advance in a steady, determined way; press ahead/forward/on (q v). **S:** team, expedition, army □ *I was asked to* ***push on*** *and help the Fifth Army.* MFM □ *We* ***pushed on*** *and now there was no doubt about the right direction: we came in sight of the walls of Pekin.* BM

ush ahead/forward/on (with) [A1 A3 pass] continue in a determined way (to carry sth out). **o:** proposals, plans, scheme □ *Now that problem is solved, there is nothing to stop us* ***pushing ahead.*** □ *We are* ***pushing forward with*** *our plan to complete an inner ring road.* □ *Redevelopment must be* ***pushed on with*** *as fast as money permits.*

ush along [A1] (informal) (of a guest) leave one's host □ *'I'm afraid I really ought to be* ***pushing along*** *now.'* □ *'It's time I was* ***pushing along.'*** □ used by a guest as a polite, though informal formula when taking leave; also, even more informally, push off[2] (q v).

ush around [B1ii pass] ⇨ push about/around.

ush aside [B1i pass] push sb firmly (or roughly) to one side. **S:** steward, guard. **O:** spectator, bystander □ *The order came to clear the hall. People standing in the aisles were roughly* ***pushed aside.*** □ *When the government took office, the inexperienced young hopefuls were* ***pushed aside*** *in the scramble for places.*

ush back[1] [B1i pass] move sb back under firm pressure, cause to retreat. **S:** police; army. **O:** crowd; enemy □ *The demonstrators were* ***pushed back*** *behind the crush barriers.* □ *The invaders were* ***pushed back*** *beyond their own frontiers.*

ush back[2] [B1i pass adj] move sth back that has slipped forward out of its usual place. **O:** glasses, hair, hat □ (radio review of a play) *'And then, the little habit he had of* ***pushing*** *his spectacles* ***back*** *on his nose.'* BBCR □ *She kept* ***pushing back*** *wisps of hair that fell over her eyes.*

ush by/past [A1 A2] move past sb, pressing against him, or pushing him to one side □ *A number of latecomers* ***pushed past*** *us to reach their seats* (e g at the cinema). □ *A waiter* ***pushed by*** *me, almost knocking the glass from my hand.* □ *'The next time he tries to* ***push by****, trip him up! That way, he may learn some good manners!'*

ush (for) [A2 pass B2 pass] make repeated and urgent requests (for); press (for) (q v). **O:** chairman; debtor. **o:** debate, adjournment; payment □ *A small faction is* ***pushing*** *hard* ***for*** *new talks* (or: ***pushing*** *hard to get new talks).* □ *Don't* ***push*** *him too hard* ***for*** *a settlement.*

push forward[1] [A1] advance in a steady way. ⇨ push ahead/forward/on.

push forward[2] [B1i pass] force sb or sth upon the attention of others, so as to obtain their assent, favours, custom. **O:** oneself; child, relative; claim, case; product, ware □ *He's never been one to* ***push*** *himself* ***forward.*** □ *He* ***pushed forward*** *his claim to be considered the rightful heir.*

push forward (with) [A1 A3 pass] ⇨ push ahead/forward/on (with).

push home [B1i pass] make, administer, forcefully; press home (q v). **O:** attack; charge, accusation □ *Resistance had been obstinate and the attack was* ***pushed home*** *with every sort of savagery.* SD □ *He had now found the weakness in his adversary's case, and he* ***pushed home*** *his points with vigour.*

push off[1] [A1 B1i nom pass] move out into the stream by pushing against the bank with a pole or oar; shove off[1] (q v); set in motion, start. **S:** [A1 B1] boatman, sailor. **O:** punt, dinghy □ *Bill* ***pushed us off*** (or: *gave us a* ***push-off****) and we went skimming away from the shore.* □ ***'Push off*** *as soon as you're ready!'* □ *Listen to the excellent symphony orchestra that Malcolm Sargeant has* ***pushed off*** *in Palestine.* SD

push off[2] [A1] (informal) leave, go away; push along (q v) □ *'Well, I'll* ***push off,'*** *the girl said. 'See you later, Charlie.'* DBM □ *He comes into town periodically, looks up a few friends, and then* ***pushes off*** *again.* □ even more informally, shove off[2] (q v).

push on [A1] ⇨ push ahead/forward/on.

push on (with) [A1 A3 pass] ⇨ push ahead/forward/on (with).

push the boat out [B1ii] (informal) hold a cheerful, boisterous party (with drink, singing, dancing etc). **S:** club, society, college □ *Do you remember how we* ***pushed the boat out*** *the night that we won back the championship?*

push over [B1i pass] make sb or sth overturn or fall to the ground by pushing him or it. **O:** him etc; vase, ornament; bucket, jug □ *I was nearly* ***pushed over*** *by a crowd of boys suddenly pouring out of the school gates.* □ *One or two tables were* ***pushed over*** *in the scramble.*

push-over [nom (B1)] (informal) an easy triumph or victory (over sb) □ *Saturday's match should be a* ***push-over*** *for Leeds: they're playing a fourth division team.*

push past [A1 A2] ⇨ push by/past.

push through [B1i pass B2 pass] make a (legislative etc) body pass or enact sth by applying steady pressure. **O:** measure, reform; Bill. **o:** parliament, committee □ *We're trying to* ***push*** *legislation* ***through*** *before the Christmas recess.* □ *You can't* ***push*** *proposals on this sort of scale* ***through*** *the Finance Committee.*

push up [B1i pass] increase at a steady rate. **O:** temperature, pressure; price, wage □ *Wage increases have* ***pushed up*** *the price of electricity.* □ *The usual drinking parties at New Year will* ***push*** *the road death figures* ***up.*** BBCTV

push up daisies [B1iii] (informal) be dead and in one's grave □ *I'm not worried about twenty* *years from now: in twenty years' time I shall be* ***pushing up daisies****.* □ *And where are all these brave fellows who were going to change the world? —* ***Pushing up daisies****!*

put about[1] [A1 B1ii pass] (nautical) (cause to) change direction. **S:** [A1] **O:** [B1] boat, ship □ *The skipper* ***put us about*** *to avoid submarines that had been reported in that area.* ⇨ bring about[2], come about[2], go about[5].

put about[2] [B1i pass] circulate, pass from one person to another. **O:** tale, rumour; it... that he was being dismissed, it... that wages were going up □ *Somebody has* ***put*** *the story* ***about*** *that the Department is being closed down.* □ *It was* ***put about*** *that he was seeing a great deal of a certain young lady.* ⇨ get about[2], go about[2].

put above [B2 pass emph rel] regard, treat, as more important than; put before[1] (q v). **O:** (national) survival, recovery; honour, integrity. **o:** all else; safety, self-interest □ ***Above*** *such considerations of cost we should* ***put*** *the welfare of the men who work the machines.* □ *The investigations reveal that few men were determined to* ***put*** *the integrity of the Administration* ***above*** *its survival.*

put across[1] [B1i pass] communicate, convey; persuade others to like or accept; put over (to) (q v). **O:** idea, thought; scheme, plan; oneself □ *He may be a very clever research worker, but he's very poor at* ***putting*** *the stuff* ***across*** *to a class.* □ *He finds it hard to* ***put*** *himself* ***across*** *to a selection board.* ⇨ come across[2], get across (to).

put across[2] [B2 pass] (informal) trick sb into accepting or believing sth; put over (on) (q v). **O:** ⚠ it; this, one; anything, something. **o:** teacher, employer, judge □ *You'd better not try to* ***put*** *anything* ***across*** *him.* □ *He* ***put*** *one* ***across*** *the police once, but they're not likely to be caught a second time.*

put the cat among the canaries/pigeons [B2 pass] (informal) excite strong emotions, esp shock, dismay, anger □ *I then said that I had never known the Services reduced to such a parlous condition. This fairly* ***put the cat among the canaries****.* MFM □ *'By jove, if the monster started rutting next October that would* ***put the cat among the pigeons****, what?'* RM

put aside[1] [B1i pass] place to one side, abandon; set aside[1] (q v) (to free oneself for another activity). **O:** book, knitting; study, subject □ *She* ***put*** *her needlework* ***aside****, and we had a talk.* □ *He* ***put aside*** *his textbooks when he left school and never reopened them.* □ *They* ***put aside*** *their rifles and packs and resumed a peaceful life.*

put aside[2] [B1i pass] save for spending later; save, reserve, an article for a customer who cannot afford to pay for it now; put on one side[1] (q v). **O:** money, cash; suit, dress □ *I've a nice little sum of money* ***put aside*** *for a rainy day.* □ *'If you'd like to pay me a small deposit, I'll* ***put*** *the suit* ***aside*** *for you, sir.'*

put aside[3] [B1i pass] forget, disregard; put on one side[2] (q v). **O:** grievance, difference; bitterness, hatred □ *At such a time of crisis, we must try to* ***put aside*** *all differences of party or class.* □ ***Put aside*** *all that has happened and try to start again.*

put at [B2 pass] calculate, estimate, to be. **O:** age, size, height, capacity. **o:** fifty, 12 by 10 metres, thirty feet, ten gallons □ *'What wou you* ***put*** *the outer radius* ***at****?'* TBC □ *I'd* ***put t*** *weight* ***at*** *about fourteen pounds.*

put at his ease [B2 pass] make sb feel free fro anxiety or embarrassment. **S:** ruler, commande manager; distinguished guest. **O:** subordinat member of staff □ *Being well aware that those c the civil side were apprehensive of what I mig do, I took great trouble to* ***put*** *them* ***at the ease****.* MFM □ *They were seated in armchair offered cigarettes, and generally* ***put at the ease****.*

put at a premium [B2 pass] make especial important, set a special value upon; put a pre mium on (q v). **S:** situation, circumstances; cr sis, emergency. **O:** skill, intelligence; cunnin deception □ *Our dependence on overseas tra* ***puts*** *drive and resourcefulness in the expo industries* ***at a premium****.* □ *In these communiti loyalty to the family is* ***put at a premium****.*

put away[1] [B1i pass] put sth in a box, draw etc, because one has finished using it, to make room tidy etc. **O:** paper, book; doll, toy. □ *Th correspondence was all* ***put away*** *in number files.* □ *The other day I found an old doll. I had* ***put*** *it* ***away*** *again because he wouldn't touch* DC ⇨ be away.

put away[2] [B1i pass] save, put by (q v). **O:** good amount, a tidy sum, a fortune □ *She's got pound or two* ***put away*** *in National Savings. I'll have to* ***put*** *something* ***away*** *for my retir ment.*

put away[3] [B1i pass] (informal) confine, esp a mental home. **O:** mental patient, psychotic □ *was like those nightmares in which the dream sees himself* ***put away*** *for lunacy.* HD □ *He w* ***put away*** *for attacking young children.*

put away[4] [B1i pass] (informal) consume co siderable quantities of food and drink; tuc away[1] (q v) □ *I don't know how he manages* ***put*** *it all* ***away****.* □ *He* ***put away*** *half a doze cakes while my back was turned.*

put away[5] [B1i pass] (informal) destroy, kil usu because of old age or illness; put dow (q v). **S:** veterinary surgeon. **O:** dog, cat □ *Th dog Billy was dying, and in September he had be* ***put away****.* RFW

put back[1] [B1i pass] replace, return. **O:** book record □ *'Kindly* ***put*** *the book* ***back*** *in its prop place.'* □ *I recaptured (the animal) and* ***put*** *hi* ***back*** *in the tin without much opposition.* DF □ be back[2], get back[3].

put back[2] [B1i pass] move the hands of a cloc back to conform with the end of official Summe Time, or to give the correct time. **O:** clock, watc □ *All the clocks should have been* ***put back*** *o hour last night.* □ *' Your watch is fast;* ***put back*** *ten minutes.'* ⇨ go back[3]; put forward[3].

put back[3] [B1i pass] move to a later time c date. **O:** party, wedding; programme, exercise date, time □ *The invasion was* ***put back*** *twent four hours while the chiefs waited for bett weather reports.* □ *The date had been* ***put bac*** *from March to April.* NM

put back[4] [B1i pass] slow, delay, retard. **C** programme; production, output □ *Drought h* ***put*** *our agricultural programme* ***back*** *to wher we started from.* □ *The strike of drivers has* ***pu*** *our deliveries* ***back*** *one month.*

put the clock back [B1i pass] return to th

past, restore the institutions and values of the past □ *All this Anglo-Catholicism* (a form of Christianity which revived certain medieval features of Christian worship) *makes him think we can* **put the clock back**, *but there's a tough core of common sense there, all the same.* ASA □ (radio programme 'Today') *The 'Mirror' says nobody can* **put back the clock** *and get rid of decimal currency.* BBCR ⇨ put back[2].

put before[1] [B2 pass emph] treat, regard, sth as more important than sth else; put above (q v). **O:** country, national interest; economic revival, military strength. **o:** self; all else, all other aims □ ***Before*** *everything else we must* **put** *the rebuilding of our damaged cities.* □ *The determination of the Six is to* **put** *the development of the community* **before** *all other considerations.* SC ⇨ come before[3].

put before[2] [B2 pass emph] present for sb's consideration. **O:** plan, proposal, scheme. **o:** committee, board □ *Proposals for sweeping reform were* **put before** *the ministers.* □ ***Before*** *a startled meeting he* **put** *his latest demands.* ⇨ be before[2], bring before, come before[2], go before[2], take before.

put the cart before the horse [B2 pass] (informal) reverse the proper order of events, cause and effect etc □ *To speak of one language for the world as leading to one purpose is to* **put the cart before the horse**. SC □ *Emotion comes first, the physiological concomitants come second. James and Lange maintain that this is* **putting the cart before the horse**. SNP

put one foot before/in front of the other [B2] (informal) (not) be able to walk. **S:** elderly person, invalid □ *She was hardly able to* **put one foot before the other** *because of the tightness of the skirt above the ankles.* AH □ *He'd had so much to drink that he couldn't* **put one foot in front of the other**. □ with *can/could + not, hardly, scarcely.*

put behind bars [B2 pass] (informal) put in gaol, imprison. **S:** authorities; magistrate, court. **O:** bank-robber, gunman □ *We shall sleep more soundly in our beds when this violent criminal has been* **put behind bars**. ⇨ be behind bars.

put behind one [B2 pass] not allow sth that has happened in the past to affect one in the present. **O:** (past) disappointments, failures; disagreements, differences □ *'His 'O' level results were disappointing, but of course he's* **put** *all that* **behind him** *now.'* □ *'I know the way we were snubbed still rankles, but it's got to be* **put behind us** *now. We must co-operate with these people.'*

put by [B1i pass] save, put away[2] (q v). **O:** a few pounds, a small nest egg □ *'It's all right, love. I've got a bit of money* **put by**.*'* TOH □ *Have a bit* **put by** *for a rainy day.*

put down[1] [B1i pass] place on a table, shelf etc; set down sth which is a danger or nuisance to oneself or others □ *She had* **put** *the sewing needle* **down** *on the chair by the window.* DC □ ***'Put down*** *that knife before you hurt somebody!'*

put down[2] [A1 B1ii] land, settle. **S:** [A1] **O:** [B1] plane, helicopter □ *He* **put** *the glider* **down** *in a corn-field.* □ *The helicopter hovered over us looking for a place to* **put down**.

put down[3] [B1i pass] allow to alight. **S:** driver, pilot; bus, plane. **O:** passenger, crew □ *The bus stopped at the station to* **put down** *one or two passengers.* ⇨ set down[1].

put down[4] [B1i pass] place in a cellar to mature. **O:** wine, port, brandy □ *When you see what they're charging for French wines now I'm glad I* **put down** *a couple of cases of claret and three dozen chablis last year.*

put down[5] [B1i pass] suppress, silence. **O:** opponent, critic, rebel □ *If Tvardovsky* (an editor and critic) *annoys the old-fashioned writers, then Tvardovsky must be cautioned, but not* **put down** *completely.* OBS

put down[6] [B1iii pass] suppress, abolish. **O:** organized crime, vice; gambling, prostitution □ *They introduced measures aimed at* **putting down**, *or at least restricting, organized gambling.* □ *Off-course betting ought to be* **put down**!

put down[7] [B1i pass] destroy, kill, because it is old or sick; put away[5] (q v); destroy because it is a nuisance or danger. **O:** pest, vermin; rat, rabbit □ *They have become pests and have to be* **put down**. OBS □ *We tried* **putting down** *mice and other small vermin with poison.*

put down[8] [B1i pass] enter, record; write down (q v). **O:** name, address; thought, impression □ *When the lists were first drawn up, you* **put** *your name* **down** *mechanically.* CON □ *One feels almost ashamed of* **putting** *it* (this view) **down** *in black and white again.* SNP □ **Put** *the date* **down** *in your diary so that you don't forget it.* ⇨ be down[3], get down[4], go down[9], set down[2], take down[3].

put down[9] [B1iii pass] (Parliament) table, include in the agenda, for a meeting or debate. **O:** motion, resolution □ *Some MPs are in favour of* **putting down** *a resolution which would come before the Parliamentary Labour Party.* OBS □ *The Conservatives may* **put down** *a censure motion on the Government's handling of the Torrey Canyon affair.* OBS

put one's foot down[1] [B1ii] (informal) press down the accelerator, causing the vehicle to travel faster □ *Don't think, when you reach the motorway, that you can just* **put your foot down** *and relax.* □ *He* **put his foot** *right* **down** *on the accelerator and felt the car surge forward.*

put one's foot down[2] [B1ii] (informal) assert one's authority, adopt a strong position against some course of action □ *Isobel was longing to be called up for service. But here her father unexpectedly* **put his foot down** (and forbade her to join up). PW □ *'Robin doesn't seem to see that there has to be some hierarchy in the place!' 'Then you must* **put your foot down**, *darling.'* ASA

put down roots [B1iii] adopt a settled way of life (e g by buying a house, starting a family) □ *Once I took a wife I should have to* **put down roots** *and settle for a definite way of life.* CON

put down as[1] [B3 pass] write, enter, sb or sth in a record, or on a form (often with a view to misleading or deceiving sb else). **O:** private spending, holiday trip; oneself; girlfriend. **o:** business expenses, necessary journey; self-employed; wife □ *When travelling abroad, Smith often* **puts down** *the cost of entertainment* **as** *business expenses.* □ *She was* **put down** *in the hotel register* **as** *Mrs Jones.* □ *He* **put** *himself*

***down** on the Income Tax Returns **as** 'unemployed'.* ⇨ be down as.

put down as[2] [B3 pass] consider to be, take to be. **o:** commercial traveller, retired officer □ *Noticing his military bearing, I **put** him **down as** a retired major.* □ *He was **put down as** an ordinary waiter and passed almost unnoticed among the others.*

put down for[1] [B3 pass] record that sb is willing to contribute to charity, buy sth at sale etc. **o:** a dozen raffle tickets; fifty pounds; two suits □ *'How many tickets shall I **put** you **down for**?' 'Half a dozen.'* □ *You can **put** me **down for** fifty Preference Shares.*

put down for[2] [B3 pass] enter a child's name for admission to a school (esp a fee-paying boarding-school). **O:** son, name. **o:** Westminster, St. Paul's □ *Inflation does not seem to have affected the demand for places at public schools. Children's names are still **put down** at birth **for** those with the best academic records (or those conferring the greatest social cachet).* ⇨ be down for.

put down to[1] [B3 pass] enter an amount in a particular account. **o:** expenses, petty cash □ *You can **put** the lunch **down to** my account.* □ *Expenditure on Christmas decorations was **put down to** petty cash.*

put down to[2] [B3 pass] regard as being due to, give as the explanation for. **O:** outburst, scene; behaviour, conduct; epidemic, famine. **o:** temper, ignorance, poor breeding; inadequate precautions, bad transport □ *I did notice that you were depressed, but I **put** it **down to** drink.* ASA □ *I know he'd got a bit pompous, but I **put** that **down to** Marie Helene* (his wife). ASA □ *The shortage can be **put down to** bad planning.*

put forth[1] [B1iii pass] (formal) sprout; display, put out[3] (q v). **O:** shoot, bud, (young) leaf □ *In the Spring, the hedgerows **put forth** new buds.*

put forth[2] [B1iii pass] (formal) exert, display; put out[8] (q v). **O:** vigour, strength, energy □ *The day was superb, and here was the College **putting forth** all its beauty.* HD

put forward[1] [B1i pass] advance, propose, suggest. **O:** argument, theory; proposal, suggestion; plan, scheme □ *A German member **put forward** a code of legal conduct for astronauts approaching a new planet.* TO □ *It's an explanation often **put forward** by our friend: he's convinced that economics is at the bottom of everything.*

put forward[2] [B1i pass] propose, recommend. **O:** oneself; colleague, employee. **A:** as a candidate; for promotion; for an award, honour, title □ *His name was **put forward** for inclusion in the Honours List.* □ *He was **put forward** as the man most likely to win the ear of the conference.*

put forward[3] [B1i pass] move the hands of a clock forward (clockwise), advance the hands. **O:** clock, watch □ *Clocks should be **put forward** one hour tonight at the beginning of official Summer Time.* □ *'**Put** your watch **forward**: you're five minutes slow.'* ⇨ put back[2].

put one's best foot forward [B1ii] (informal) make haste, hurry □ *If you want to get home by nightfall, you'll have to **put your best foot forward**.* □ *The work force **put its best foot forward** to meet the promised delivery date.*

put in[1] [A1] interrupt another speaker (to say sth), interpose, interject □ *'It's the firm's time,' Baxter insisted. 'He's carrying out an experiment,' I **put in**.* CON □ *'I'm sure you saw the monster.' 'It was more like a spout,' the stalker **put in**.* RM

put in[2] [B1i pass] include, insert (in a narrative, account etc). **O:** comma, full stop; detail, episode □ ***Put in** the proper punctuation marks.* □ *'Don't forget to **put in** the bit about Jim falling into the river!'* □ *'And you can **put in** that I was prepared to be helpful.'*

put in[3] [B1i pass] devote, spend. **O:** two weeks, some time □ *Harold consciously tried to **put in** a quarter of an hour each day improving his putting* (i e at golf). PW □ ***Put in** a few hours of careful weeding and he'll be pleased!* WI □ ***Put in** some time asking yourself why.* EHOW □ often followed by the *-ing* form of a v.

put in[4] [B1i pass] fit, install. **O:** cork, plug; central heating, new plumbing □ *'**Put** the cork back **in** the bottle.'* □ *We're **putting in** a completely new system of wiring and switches.* □ *We've pulled out the old pipes and **put in** copper ones.* ⇨ go in[3].

put in[5] [B1i pass] give duties to (usu in a building, office block etc). **O:** guard, night-watchman □ *They've **put in** a caretaker to keep an eye on people coming in and out of the building.* □ *A security man was **put in** to check on doors and windows.*

put in[6] [B1i pass] (politics) elect (to office). **O:** Labour, the Conservatives □ *Labour was **put in** with an increased majority at the last General Election.* ⇨ be in[4], come in[3], get in/into[3].

put in[7] [B1i pass] (cricket) ask the opposing team to bat (e g after winning the toss); tell a member of one's own side to bat. **S:** captain, skipper. **O:** side, team; (fast-scoring) batsman □ *The home side **put** the visitors **in** to bat on a fast wicket, and had half of them out before tea.* ⇨ be in[5], go in[4].

put (all) one's eggs in one basket [B2 pass] (informal) give all one's attention to a single end (e g by loving one person to the exclusion of all others); risk all that one has in a single venture (e g by using all one's troops in one attack) □ *He can't reconcile himself to living with one woman for ever — to **putting all his** emotional **eggs in one basket**.* □ *Office development in the City — now that's **one basket** you shouldn't **put all your eggs in**.* □ ***His eggs** have been **put in** too many **baskets**.* □ note the pl forms: *several, too many* baskets, suggesting the spreading of interests or resources.

put in an/one's appearance [B1iii] (informal) appear (often briefly) at a function, parade etc from a sense of obligation or good form (not for pleasure or out of interest). **S:** VIP, minister, director □ *Jeremy **put in a** brief **appearance** towards the end of our party, and was then wafted off somewhere more important.* □ *'Wait five minutes — just to show you've **put in an appearance** — and then go for a drink.'* □ *He waited for the right moment to **put in his appearance** — just as supper was about to be served.*

put in an awkward etc position [B2 pass rel] make things awkward etc for sb. **adj:** awkward, difficult, embarrassing, impossible □ *The support given to the rebels by local officials **put** the government **in a difficult position**.* □ *This then* *is* ***the difficult position in*** *which we are* ***put*** *by their refusal to co-operate.* □ *Is that all you can say? 'I'm sorry'? Such* ***an awkward position*** *I* ***put*** *you* ***in****, don't I?* FFE

put one's foot in it [B2] (informal) say sth embarrassing or hurtful, out of thoughtlessness or insensitivity, thus making oneself appear foolish □ *I just said what came into my head, and there I go,* ***putting my foot in it*** *as usual.* AITC □ *There is a dazzling reward for allowing your best friend to make advances to your young woman in your presence — that of seeing him* ***put his foot in it****.* SPL

put a (good) word in [B1i pass] (informal) speak or testify on sb's behalf. **A:** for me, on my behalf, in his defence, in support of her □ *'Here, Lumley,' he called, as the policeman marched him away, 'you* ***put in a word*** *for me, will you?'* HD □ *The Head was always prepared to* ***put a good word in*** *for his former pupils.*

put in inverted commas [B2 pass] place a word or phrase between quotation marks to indicate that one is specially conscious of it (e g because it is foreign or a slang term); in speech, pronounce a word etc with special intonation (for the same reasons as above). □ *He was so ashamed and suspicious of the word 'love' that he had to* ***put it in inverted commas****.* PW □ *Until borrowed words are fully assimilated into the language they are often* ***put in inverted commas****.*

put in jeopardy [B2 pass] threaten, menace, endanger. **O:** trade, communications; security, vital interests. **adj:** grave, serious □ *The chances of an important representative match at Twickenham are* ***put in jeopardy*** *by the weather.* T □ *The hold-up in the supply of fuel* ***puts*** *our whole advance* ***in jeopardy****.* ⇨ be in jeopardy.

put in mind of [B2 pass] remind of, call to mind; suggest a similarity to □ *Sudden and grateful immersion in country air and country silence* ***puts*** *me* ***in mind of*** *an observation by Norman Douglas.* AH □ *She made love strenuously; I was* ***put in mind of*** *a hard set of mixed tennis.* RATT

put in a nutshell [B2 pass] state in a few words, succinctly. **O:** ⚠ it, the whole thing; the matter, problem, question □ *Alexis* ***puts*** *it* ***in a nutshell****: losing power is the most dreadful prospect that a politician can think of.* TBC □ *The whole position was* ***put in a nutshell*** *by none other than Daniel Defoe.* SNP

put in order [B2 pass] arrange tidily, according to a pattern. **O:** papers, books; study, office; affairs, business □ *His study is a chaos: his housekeeper has long since given up trying to* ***put*** *his papers* ***in order****.* □ *Congress has suggested that the union should* ***put*** *its affairs* ***in order****.*

put one's (own) house in order [B2 pass] organize one's (own) affairs efficiently. **S:** government; management, administration; military command □ *At present* (1958) *NATO is in the doldrums. It needs to* ***put its house in order*** *while the going is good.* MFM □ *Britain must not abandon for ever the idea of joining the Common Market. The immediate task is to* ***put her own house in order****.* T □ *These companies must first* ***put their own houses in order****; then they may qualify for development grants.*

put in the picture [B2 pass] (informal) give sb up-to-date information about sth. **O:** staff, colleagues; one's family □ *Details of the campaign were kept secret until the last moment; then the men were* ***put in the picture****.* □ *You've got to* ***put me in the picture****. What's this business with your Philip?* EHOW ⇨ be in the picture.

put in his place [B2 pass] by exerting one's authority, remind sb of his junior status □ *Any junior boy who tried to address a prefect would be* ***put*** *very firmly* ***in his place****.* □ *His manner indicated that the subject was closed, and I'd been* ***put in my place****.* RATT □ note pl form: *We were* ***put*** *firmly* ***in our places****.*

put oneself in sb's place/shoes [B2] try, by an effort of sympathy, to share the feelings of another person □ *Try to* ***put yourself in his shoes****. Would you have behaved any differently in the circumstances?* □ *Remembering our own bereavements and humiliations, we can condole with others, we can* ***put ourselves in their places****.* DOP

put in the shade [B2 pass] (informal) by one's own success, eminence etc, make that of others appear of small account. **O:** achievement, effort □ *You can do a big dash* (= sprint) *later that* ***puts*** *everybody else's hurry* ***in the shade****.* LLDR □ *The first part of the programme was* ***put in the shade*** *by the appearance of the star attraction.*

put a sock in it [B2] (slang) behave in a more lively and energetic way □ *You'll need to* ***put a sock in it*** *if you want to attract an audience to your show.* □ *'****Put a sock in it****! I want this stuff moved before the end of the morning.'* □ usu direct or indirect command.

put a spoke in sb's wheel [B2 pass] (informal) stop or hinder sb's activities (which may be unpleasant or dishonest) □ *'No, you can't get out of it as easily as all that, Miss Richards — it's about time that someone* ***put a spoke in your*** *little* ***wheel****.'* TT □ *She did not spare him, and if he lost his flicker of self-assurance, she welcomed it. She had* ***put a spoke in that wheel****, anyway.* PW

put that in one's pipe and smoke it [B2] (informal) tell an opponent (when taking an independent and defiant stand) to accept and digest an upleasant fact □ *I'm not going to become a Catholic so they can* ***put that in their pipe and smoke it****.* HAA □ *We weren't going to shift our ground one bit, and he could* ***put that in his pipe and smoke it****.* □ usu with the imper, or *can/could.* Note pl form: *'You can* ***put that in your pipes and smoke it****'* and compare the first example.

put one's trust in [B2 emph rel] trust, regard as reliable or dependable. **adj:** one's; no, (not) any/much, (not) a lot of. **o:** God, Church; friend, ally; sb's story, account □ *They did not* ***put their trust in*** *the information they received from the well-tried and veteran staff of the Eighth Army.* MFM □ *He was still* ***putting his trust in*** *material efficiency, in 'getting on'.* CON □ *There was no-one around him* ***in*** *whom he felt he could* ***put*** *very much* ***trust****.*

put in the wrong [B2 pass] make it seem, perhaps unjustly, that sb else is to blame for sth; act wrongly, thus losing any moral advantage. **O:** colleague, wife; oneself □ *He's always trying to* ***put me in the wrong****; in this way he hopes to* *spoil my relationship with my students.* □ *If I hadn't* **put** *myself* **in the wrong** *by doing that, I might have taken a high moral line about the typescript.* UTN ⇨ be in the wrong.

put in (for) [A1 A3 pass B1i pass B3 pass] submit, make, enter, sth (for). **O:** application, claim, request, demand. **o:** job, promotion; leave; expenses □ [A3] *I'd like to* **put in for** *a posting up north or somewhere, but they'd never let me go.* RFW □ [B3] *A claim has been* **put in for** *higher wages.* □ [A1 B1] *He's due for some leave and is thinking of* **putting in** *(an application).* ⇨ be in for[2].

put in for[1] [B3 pass] (sport) enter sb's name as a competitor, enter for (q v). **S:** coach, club. **O:** athlete; runner, long-jumper. **o:** event, race □ *We're thinking of* **putting** *young Peter* **in for** *the 100 metres and the discus.* ⇨ be in for[1], go in for[1].

put in for[2] [B3 pass] recommend, propose sb as deserving, as being a suitable applicant for. **S:** superior officer, employer. **o:** award, decoration; post, job, transfer □ *His commanding officer is* **putting** *him* **in for** *the Victoria Cross.* □ *He's being* **put in for** *something on the administrative side.*

put in touch (with) [B2 pass] cause persons to meet; bring into contact (with) (q v), put on to[1] (q v) □ *I got put on to the idea of Alcoholics Anonymous. They* **put** *me* **in touch with** *a marvellous woman.* ASA □ *He* **put** *Father* **in touch with** *another collector* (or: **put** *Father and another collector* **in touch**). □ *They were* **put in touch** *by a church organization.* ⇨ be in touch (with).

put one foot in front of the other [B2] ⇨ put one foot before/in front of the other.

put in/into[1] [A1 A2] (nautical) call, dock, moor (at). **S:** ship, boat. **o:** harbour, port. **A:** at a port, at Singapore; for a refit, for supplies □ *We'll* **put in** *at the next port for refuelling.* □ *The yachts* **put in** *to shelter from the storm.* □ *The 'Norfolk Yeoman'* **put into** *Newlyn yesterday with a catch of gleaming fresh mackerel.* OBS

put in/into[2] [B1i pass B2 pass] devote, expend (in doing sth). **O:** effort, work, thought, planning. **o:** arranging, finishing □ *He's the boy who goes over the stack of battered old recordings. I call my memory and* **put in** *some work with a sapphire needle.* TC □ *A lot of careful planning was* **put into** *making the day a success.*

put the fear of death/God in/into/up [B2 pass] (informal) thoroughly frighten sb; force sb to submit or obey by the strength of one's authority. **S:** explosion, accident; boss, schoolmaster, sergeant-major, mother-in-law □ *'The question is,' said Rose, 'who's the fellow that's trying to* **put the fear of God in** *us?'* MM □ *The drill sergeant begins by* **putting the fear of death into** *every new recruit.* □ *He'd had* **the fear of God put up** *him by a domineering mother. It seemed a natural transition to marry a shrewish wife.*

put inside [B1ii pass] (police slang) put in prison. **O:** criminal; burglar, shoplifter □ *One of your scientists has been giving us away. They're going to* **put** *him* **inside** *soon.* NM □ *He's been* **put inside** *for breaking and entering.* ⇨ be inside.

put into effect [B2 pass] implement sth, make sth a reality; carry out[1] (q v). **S:** administrator, engineer. **O:** plan, programme; phase, stage (of an operation) □ *'It's a first-rate scheme, and he's just the man to* **put** *it* **into effect**.*'* □ *Your proposal looks good on paper, but I'm not convinced it can be* **put into effect**. ⇨ come into effect.

put into force [B2 pass] cause to operate, to have the force of the law. **O:** law, regulation; speed limit □ *There is pressure on the Government to* **put** *new currency regulations* **into force**. □ *A new upper limit on price increases has been* **put into force**. ⇨ be in/bring into/come into force.

put one's heart and soul into [B2 pass] undertake, engage in, sth with total dedication. **o:** profession, business; building a home, bringing up a family □ *If each one of us* **puts his** *whole* **heart and soul into** *this next contest, then nothing can stop us.* MFM □ **Into** *the work of rebuilding their cities after the devastation of war, the peoples of Europe* **put their heart and soul**.

put the idea/thought into sb's head [B2 pass] make sb think or believe □ *'She says I've fallen in love with Alec? What could have* **put that idea into her head**?*'* PW □ *It was a question about the price of houses in York that first* **put into my head the thought** *that he had applied for another job.*

put ideas into sb's head [B2 pass] (informal) make sb think, without justification, that he is specially important, or entitled to some benefit; or that he is being badly served, or is in some danger. **adj:** (such) absurd, odd, strange □ *He goes about* **putting ideas into people's heads** *that Utopia is just around the corner.* □ *I hope this fellow doesn't go* **putting ideas into the heads of** *these islanders that the monster is going to pay them a visit.* RM □ *Some strange* **ideas** *are being* **put into** *ignorant* **heads** *by this self-styled prophet.*

put into power [B2 pass] give political control to sb (esp through an election). **S:** voter, votes. **O:** party, administration □ *An electoral landslide* **put** *the Labour Party* **into power** *in 1945.* □ *Before de Gaulle was* **put into power** *in 1958, France was often governed by unstable coalitions.* ⇨ be in/come into power.

put into words [B2 pass] express in words. **O:** emotion; fear, love, hatred, anxiety; thought, idea □ *He could not now* **put into words** *his intense fear of the witch doll in the cupboard.* DC □ *Though they could not have* **put** *it* **into words**, *their objection to him was that he did not wear uniform.* HD

put words into sb's mouth [B2] suggest that sb has said, or implied, sth when in fact he has not □ *'I'll understand if you haven't a place for me,' she said. 'Who said I hadn't? Don't* **put words into my mouth**, *Virginia.'* AITC □ *'Now you're* **putting words into my mouth**. *When did I say anything about moving?'* □ note pl form: *'Don't go* **putting words into people's mouths**!*'*

put off[1] [B1i pass adj] postpone, delay, defer. **O:** decision; party, appointment □ *I've been* **putting** *it* **off** *and not thinking about it, hoping that something would turn up.* RFW □ *Their translation into reality is* **put off** *until the Greek Calends.* SNP □ *It's no good trying to* **put off** *the* *evil day* (the time when sth unpleasant has to be done).

put off[2] [B1i pass] discourage, prevent, from: seeing one, making contact, collecting a debt, discussing an important matter etc. **O:** wife, boyfriend; landlord, tradesman; visitor. **A:** with a promise, an excuse; by pretending to be ill, busy □ *Maybe he had* **put** *her* **off** *too often when she had wanted to talk.* TO □ *They went out eight or ten times and then she started* **putting** *him* **off**, *just a little: he was getting possessive.* H □ *The grocer won't be* **put off** *with airy promises any longer; he wants his money.*

put off[3] [B1i pass] displease, repel. **S:** appearance, language; manners, breath □ *He could be a good salesman, but his manner* **puts** *customers* **off**. □ *Many people are* **put off** *by his surly behaviour* (or: *find his surly behaviour* **off-putting**). □ *Don't be* **put off** *by her sharp tongue.* □ *Harold realized to his surprise that instead of being* **put off** *by Irma's lack of English he rather enjoyed teaching her.* PW □ note unusual adj form **off-putting**.

put off[4] [B1i pass] distract (from doing sth), disturb (while doing sth). **S:** noise, interruption; heat; insect □ *He was trying to write, but the continuous noise outside his window* **put** *him* **off**. □ *His opponent's delaying tactics are designed to annoy him and* **put** *him* **off**.

put off[5] [B2 pass] cause to lose interest in, or appetite for. **S:** experience, incident; teacher, instructor. **o:** food, drink; French, maths; driving, smoking □ *My drill sergeant* **put** *me* **off** *the army for good.* □ *She was* **put off** *learning languages by incompetent teaching.* ⇨ be off[8], go off[4], turn off[2].

put off[6] [B1i pass B2 pass] allow to alight or disembark; compel to alight etc. **S:** captain, pilot. **O:** passenger, stowaway. **o:** bus, boat, aircraft □ *I asked the conductor to* **put** *me* **off** *at the cinema.* □ *The stowaways were* **put off** *the ship at the next port of call.* □ *If he makes trouble he'll be* **put off** *the plane.* ⇨ get off[1], let off[1].

put off[7] [B1i pass] (formal) discard, lay aside. **O:** uniform, regalia; care, worry, responsibility □ *The war was over but Harold was still in khaki; he never looked so nearly a gentleman again when he* **put** *it* **off**. PW □ *He had* **put off** *all personal cares.* RFW

put off[8] [B1ii pass] send to sleep; anaesthetize. **S:** hot drink; injection, pill; exhaustion □ *'What about a nice cup of tea to* **put** *you* **off** *to sleep again?'* DC □ *A whiff of gas'll soon* **put** *you* **off**. ⇨ go off[3].

put off the scent/track/trail [B2 pass] prevent sb from following a suspect etc by giving false clues. **O:** policeman, detective □ *Nothing would* **put** *Mr Blearney* **off the scent**. HD □ *We managed to* **put** *our pursuers* **off the track** *by walking our horses up river for a few hundred yards.*

put off his stride/stroke [B2 pass] (informal) disturb the rhythm or steady progress of sb's work; spoil sb's composure. **S:** noise, disturbance, interruption □ *These telephone calls* **put** *him completely* **off his stroke** *and ruined a morning's work.* □ *She coloured faintly, and seemed* **put off her stride**. US ⇨ put off[4].

put on[1] [B1i pass] get dressed in, don. **O:** coat, hat; suit, trousers □ **Put on** *some clothes.* EHOW □ *I don't know what dress to* **put on**. ⇨ get on[1], have on[1].

put on[2] [B1i pass] light, switch on. **O:** light, lamp; (electric/gas) fire, radiator □ *'Half a tick and I'll* **put on** *the light.'* PW □ *I'll* **put** *the light* **on**. TOH ⇨ be on[8], go on[5], turn on[1].

put on[3] [B1i pass] grow heavier, fatter, by a certain amount. **O:** (a lot of) weight; ten pounds, two kilos; two inches (round the waist) □ *In the month she had been with them she hadn't* **put on** *any weight.* DC □ *How much (weight) did you* **put on** *over Christmas?*

put on[4] [B1i pass] (cricket) add runs to the score for an innings. **O:** fifty, one hundred (runs) □ *The tail-end batsmen* **put on** *48 between them.* □ *Ninety was* **put on** *for the first wicket.*

put on[5] [B1i pass B2 pass] add some amount to the price, cost, of. **S:** Government, company; budget, legislation. **O:** several pounds, two pence in the pound. **o:** price, total, bill; cost of living □ *Their latest measures will* **put** *several pence* **on** *the weekly food bill.* □ *The bill came to two pounds but the waiter* **put on** *a few extra pence.* □ *This'll* **put** *pounds* **on** *the cost of living.*

put on[6] [B1i pass B2 pass] place (on); impose (on) (q v). **O:** tax, duty. **o:** wine, tobacco □ *What'll they be* **putting** *a tax* **on** *next?* □ *The Government is proposing to* **put on** *a new range of taxes to pay for social services.*

put on[7] [B1i pass] add to existing services. **O:** extra train, holiday flight, ten coaches □ *Southern Region are* **putting on** *ten extra trains to cope with the holiday traffic.*

put on[8] [B1i pass B2 pass] (racing) place money with a bookmaker, as a wager; stake on[1] (q v), wager (on) (q v). **O:** money, fortune. **o:** horse, dog □ *I've* **put** *a couple of pounds* **on** *Mountain King in the three-thirty.* □ **Put** *a pound to win* **on** *Running Wild.* □ *'Are you a betting man?' 'Oh, I* **put** *a few pounds* **on** *in the course of a year.'* ⇨ be on[3]; put one's shirt on.

put on[9] [B1i pass B2 pass] (informal) apply physical or moral pressure (to be unpleasant, exact favours, promises etc). **O:** ⚠ the screw(s), the squeeze, the heat □ *He could live off the fat of the land in George's house, and see just exactly what George was worth, and* **put** *the screws* **on** *him good and proper.* PE □ *'I take it you have your fighting boots on this morning? Has the Old Man been* **putting** *the screw* **on**?' TT

put on[10] [B1i pass] (cricket) give a spell of bowling to sb, bring (a bowler) into action. **O:** pace bowler, spinner □ *He* **put** *Gibbs* **on** *to bowl from the Kirkstall Lane end.* □ *Sobers took the new ball after tea, and* **put** *the fast bowlers back* **on**. ⇨ be on[4], bring on[4], come on[9].

put on[11] [B1i pass] produce, present, mount. **O:** show, display; play, pantomime; exhibition □ *Here is Claudian's description of the show* **put on** *by Manlius Theodorus in* AD *399.* HAH □ *It was all agreed that this gallery was to* **put on** *a one-man show* (exhibition of paintings). CON ⇨ be on[6], come on[11].

put on[12] [B1iii pass adj] (informal) assume a manner, a pose (in order to impress, deceive). **O:** it; act, façade; airs; voice, accent; anger, annoyance □ *She was obviously very good for Bill. He didn't have to* **put on** *an act for her.* RFW □ *He had his pipe at the ready in case it should be necessary to* **put on** *his don's act at* *short notice.* HD □ *'He does* **put** *it* **on**, *doesn't he?'* □ *'The expensive voice and manner are all* **put on**, *you know.'*

put the blame (on) [B2 pass emph rel] hold responsible (for); lay the blame (for) (on) (q v). **o:** leader, government; poor communications, bad weather □ *Calamity after calamity descended upon the village, and the highly superstitious people* **put** *all* **the blame on** *Anak Agung Nura.* TO □ *Some of* **the blame** *must be* **put on** *the manager for not anticipating the shortage.* □ *They looked for someone* **on** *whom they could* **put the blame** *for this latest reverse.*

put a bold/brave/good face on [B2 pass] appear brave and cheerful on the surface, even though one is disappointed, defeated etc. **o:** ⚠ it, things; events, proceedings □ *After the election shock, he turned to address his supporters, determined to* **put** *as* **brave a face on** *it as he could manage.* □ *He wouldn't have been pleased, of course, but he would have shrugged his shoulders and for Isobel's sake* **put a good face on** *it.* PW □ *There is not much optimism in the air, but at least both sides are* **putting a brave face on** *proceedings.* DAILY TELEGRAPH

put a/the brake on [B1ii pass B2 pass] (informal) reduce the speed or activity of sth. **S:** government; employee; general. **o:** development; investment; advance □ *The troops for the landing were taken from Alexander's force in Italy and that* **put a brake on** *his operations.* MFM □ *Mr Wilson's assertion that it is because the Government cannot restrain the City that they have to* **put the brake on** *the economy as a whole, shows how well out he is in his diagnosis.* SC

put one's cards on the table [B2 pass] (informal) declare openly one's assets, intentions, proposals etc; lay one's cards on the table (q v) □ *'I think I ought to* **put** *all* **my cards on the table**. *I'm not rich. But when my father dies I'll have about fifty thousand dollars.'* QA □ *She didn't seem excited, but this was a business deal, and he couldn't expect her to* **put** *all* **her cards** *down* **on the table**. PW

put a construction on [B2 pass emph rel] interpret in one's own individual way. **adj:** one's own, this, what; certain, particular; special, different. **o:** event, occurrence; crisis, drama □ *The same drama may be played out before two spectators each of whom will* **put his own construction on it**. MFF □ **On** *the same collection of evidence each of the witnesses had* **put a** *different* **construction**. □ *'You say that you borrowed the car, believing it to belong to a friend. Now* **what construction** *am I to* **put on** *that?'*

put on his/its feet [B2 pass] restore to health, prosperity; set on his/its feet (q v). **S:** treatment, rest; loan, capital. **O:** patient; country, economy □ *They were not sympathetic to a viewpoint which might* **put** *Germany* **on its feet**, *merely to provide a market for Britain or to save the British taxpayer.* MFM □ *The factory was* **put** *back* **on its feet** *through the joint efforts of management and workers.*

put one's finger on [B2 rel] (informal) indicate precisely, specify exactly. **o:** trouble, source of danger; anomaly, fallacy □ *I thought there was a contradiction somewhere, as there was in most of Tom's counsels, but I could not* **put my finger on** *it.* SPL □ *Both are in normal American khaki, just a little different, in ways it's difficult to* **put your finger on**, *from what they wear today.* OI

put the finger on [B2 pass] (slang) accuse, point an accusing finger at. **o:** accomplice, associate □ *Questioned by the special investigators, Ulrich* **put the finger on** *the Attorney-General.* TO □ *He turned pale as it became clear that* **the finger** *would next be* **put on** *him.*

put on his guard [B2 pass] warn sb of a danger □ *His words* **put** *me* **on my guard** *against speaking too freely over the telephone.* □ *He was* **put on his guard** *by reports of missing drugs that had been appearing in the paper.* ⇨ be on one's guard.

put on his honour [B2 pass] bind sb solemnly to do sth, trust sb to do sth on pain of breaking his oath. **O:** pupil; employee; prisoner □ *'Your teacher is not feeling very well, and so I am going to* **put** *you* **on your honour** *to go on with your work.'* TT □ *A prisoner on parole is* **put on his honour** *to return to custody by a certain date.* □ often followed, as here, by an inf. ⇨ be on one's honour.

put on ice [B2 pass] (informal) suspend, shelve, sth, possibly with the intention of reviving it later. **O:** proposal, scheme, plan □ *The Prime Minister is speaking in a way that suggests* **putting** *the famous Peace Treaty* **on ice**. OBS □ *His designs will be* **put on ice** *until money is available to implement them.* ⇨ be on ice.

put on the map [B2 pass] (informal) make prominent, bring to the notice of the public. **O:** resort, festival, fair; sport, pastime □ *Now a society wife, Barbara Goalen* **put** *modelling* (the profession of mannequin) **on the map**. H □ *'This will hit the world's press. You've* **put** *General Thé* **on the map** *all right, Pyle.'* QA ⇨ be on the map.

put one's money on [B2] (informal) confidently expect sb or sth to succeed. **o:** contender, candidate; plan, idea □ *A lot of experts, when they talk about the next Sinatra, are* **putting their money** *on Johnny Mathis.* H □ *I'm* **putting my money on** *Smith to win the next by-election.* ⇨ put on[8].

not to put too fine a point on it [B2] (informal) to speak bluntly, to speak the plain truth □ ***Not to put too fine a point on it****, we're finished, all washed-up — it's the end of the road.* □ ***To put not too fine a point on it****, Querini lives by a now diminishing talent (he is nearly fifty-two) and by his wits.* US □ a subordinate (adv) clause.

put on one side[1] [B2 pass] save for use or spending later; reserve an article for a customer who cannot afford to pay for it now; put aside[2] (q v). **O:** product, part, component; money, cash; (new) suit □ *The outside skin, or husk, George said, is* **put on one side** *to make bran.* WI □ *He tries to* **put** *a few pounds* **on one side** *for his old age.* □ *'Would you like me to* **put** *the jacket* **on one side** *for you, sir?'*

put on one side[2] [B2 pass] forget, disregard; put aside[3] (q v). **O:** jealousy, suspicion, strife, dissension □ *The detailed arguments which have been tearing the party in two could be* **put on one side**. T □ *Let us* **put on one side** *the fears which have divided us in the past.*

put a premium on [B2 pass] make sb or sth

seem more important or worthwhile, set a special value upon; put at a premioum (q v). **S:** climate, soil; danger, uncertainty. **o:** careful husbandry, skill; courage, endurance □ *The immediate and present nature of working-class life* **puts a premium on** *the taking of pleasures now, discourages planning for the future.* UL □ *The sort of weather we have been having alters the character of rugby,* **putting a premium on** *forwards, with backs at a disadvantage.* T

put one's shirt on [B2] (informal) gamble all the money one has on a particular horse etc; be confident that sb or sth will succeed □ *'I'm* **putting my shirt on** *Devil's Disciple to win the next race.'* □ *You may not think that our toothpaste will corner the market, but I'd* **put my shirt on** *it.* □ *The scheme must have some merits: the committee are* **putting their shirts on** *it.* ⇨ put on[8].

put one's thinking cap on [B1i] (informal) think carefully about a problem □ *Before I can give you an answer I'll have to* **put my thinking cap on.** □ *It's time they* **put on their thinking caps** *and sorted out the problems.*

put the (tin) lid on it/things [B2] (informal) be the final event that provokes an outburst, be the last straw □ *'After the distance I've covered today all I want is to go to bed.' That* **put the lid on it:** *he was in a bad temper.* ARG □ *On the way back, I had a flat tyre. And I found the spare was flat, too. That pretty well* **put the tin lid on things.** TGLY

put years on [B2 pass] make sb feel or appear older; say sth which makes sb appear older than he is or would like to feel. **adj:** several; ten, twenty □ *The terrible events of those few months* **put years on** *him.* □ GEOFF: *It's your grandchild.* HELEN: *Oh, shut up, you* **put years on** *me.* TOH

put pressure on/upon [B2 pass emph rel] persuade by constant argument, the threat of force etc (to do sth). **adj:** a lot of, some; no, (not) any/much. **o:** trades union, employer; leader, governing body; neighbour, dependent □ *Does any Government care about the protests of nice-minded humanitarians? They care about having* **pressure put on** *them.* EHOW □ *It was* **on** *the weak border states that the greatest* **pressure** *was* **put.** □ *They* **put pressure on** *the council to change its housing policy.* ⇨ (the) pressure be on; put on [9].

put a strain on/upon [B2 pass emph rel] place sb or sth under force or pressure so that he or it is tested and stretched. **adj:** a lot of, some; no, (not) any/much. **o:** resources, capacity; industry, agriculture; forces, nerves □ *A sudden and severe* **strain** *was* **put upon** *us by the cutting off of these supplies.* □ **On** *these troops the switch in the enemy's attack* **put an** *unexpected* **strain.**

put on to[1] [B3 pass] help people to meet or speak; put in touch (with) (q v). **S:** receptionist, inquiry desk, telephone operator. **O:** caller, visitor. **o:** manager, secretary □ *All I had to do was ring him up and he would* **put** *me* **on to** *his private secretary and she would read out a specially prepared 'release'.* CON □ *He insisted on being* **put on to** *the man in charge.* ⇨ be on to[1], get on to[1].

put on to[2] [B3 pass] inform sb of a person's whereabouts or activities so that he can be caught. **S:** enemy, police informer. **O:** police, law. **o:** escapee, fugitive; sb's track, trail □ *Sooner or later he will be spotted in the street, and the police will be* **put on to** *him.* □ *He can't go on defrauding the Inland Revenue for ever: somebody some day will* **put** *the tax man* **on to** *him.* ⇨ be on to[2], get on to[2].

put on to[3] [B3 pass] inform sb of the existence of sth interesting or advantageous. **S:** agent, broker; friend, colleague. **o:** a good thing; bargain, snip; opening in industry, vacant post; club, holiday resort □ *It was Randall who had* **put** *Stocker* **on to** *this afternoon drinking club.* CON □ *I was* **put on to** *this cheap line in printed cotton by a friend in the trade.* ⇨ be on to a good thing.

put out[1] [A1] (nautical) move towards the open sea, away from the shore. **S:** captain, crew; boat, ship. **A:** to sea; from harbour, from the shore □ *We* **put out** *to sea on the early morning tide.*

put out[2] [B1ii pass] remove by force, eject. **S:** doorman, bouncer. **O:** troublemaker, gatecrasher, drunk □ *The next time he brings his noisy friends to the club we'll have them* **put out.** ⇨ be out[3].

put out[3] [B1iii] sprout; display. **S:** tree, shrub. **O:** leaf, bud, shoot □ *The plants* **put out** *early shoots.* AH

put out[4] [B1i pass] issue, publish, usu for a special purpose, e g to explain one's policy, apologize for delays etc. **S:** government department, official news agency, public relations firm. **O:** pamphlet, document; report, statement □ *The Department of Social Security have* **put out** *a pamphlet explaining the new rates of pension for retired people.* □ *Head Office has* **put out** *an official statement denying press reports of a possible take-over.*

put out[5] [B1i pass] issue, circulate. **S:** police, army. **O:** general call, SOS; description □ *A detailed description of the wanted man has been* **put out** *to all mobile patrols.*

put out[6] [B1i pass] broadcast, transmit, by radio or television. **S:** BBC, Granada Television; studio, station. **O:** news bulletin, sports report, talk; play, concert □ *They clustered around the radio, listening to the news of the invasion* **put out** *by the BBC.* RFW

put out[7] [B1iii pass] produce, generate. **S:** power station, generator; motor, engine; battery. **O:** 100 kilowatts, 15 horse power □ *The engine of a wartime fighter aircraft* **put out** *more than one thousand horsepower* (or: *had an* **output** *of more than one thousand* etc). □ nom form is output.

put out[8] [B1i pass] exert, display. **O:** strength, vigour, energy, enthusiasm □ *The speech ended in an appeal to party workers to* **put out** *all their energy and enthusiasm during the electoral campaign.* □ *Never had our supporters* **put out** *so much effort* (or: *Never had there been such an* **output** *of effort from our supporters*). □ nom form is output.

put out[9] [B1i pass] make unconscious (by striking with the fists, with an anaesthetic etc). **S:** boxer, assailant; doctor, anaesthetist. **O:** opponent; patient □ *A whiff of ether will* **put** *you* **out** *in a few seconds.* □ *The champion* **put** *his opponent* **out** *in the fifth round — and he stayed* *out.* ⇨ be out[9], go out[2].

put out[10] [B1i pass] extinguish; switch off[1] (q v), blow out[1] (q v). **O:** light, lamp; (gas, electric) fire; flame, candle □ *Nurse Ellen, in Brigit's room, drew the curtains and* ***put out*** *the lights.* DC □ *The fire brigade were still* ***putting out*** *small fires started by the plane crash.* ⇨ be out[10], go out[5], turn out[1].

put out[11] [B1i pass adj] dislocate. **S:** accident, fall, blow. **O:** shoulder, knee, ankle □ *He* ***put*** *his back* ***out*** *badly, falling down the stairs like that.*

put out[12] [B1i pass] cause an inaccuracy in sth; throw out[6] (q v). **S:** movement, shock; temperature, pressure. **O:** instrument, dial; figure, calculation, reading. **A:** (by) a long way, (by) ten seconds □ *Inaccuracies in the measuring vessels must have* ***put*** *his results* ***out*** *by a mile.* □ *The final totals can have been* ***put out*** *by as much as five per cent.* ⇨ be out[12].

put out[13] [B1ii pass adj] inconvenience sb; spoil or complicate sb's arrangements. **S:** his sudden arrival; extra guests; a change in the programme □ *'I hope it hasn't* ***put*** *your housekeeper* ***out****, Mr Alexander, having three extra suddenly thrust upon her.'* WI □ *The hotel was seriously* ***put out*** *by the sudden cancellation of holiday bookings.*

put out[14] [B1ii pass adj] upset, dismay, worry. **S:** rudeness, insensitivity, tactlessness □ *'Come and lunch with me,'* (said Marie-Helene). *He pleaded an urgent engagement. She looked so* ***put out*** *that he felt he had been rude.* ASA □ *She was wearing her* ***put-out*** *expression, as she so easily can when my boorish friends are around.*

put out feelers [B1i pass] (informal) take exploratory steps to see if conditions are right for trade, a peace settlement etc □ *Their government is* ***putting out feelers*** *through a neutral delegation; they are clearly anxious for a rapprochement.*

put out of action [B2 pass] (military) cause to stop working, firing etc. **S:** (enemy) fire, bombardment; artillery, aircraft. **O:** installation, emplacement; gun; radio □ *Accurate gunnery had already* ***put*** *three of the leading tanks* ***out of action****.* ⇨ be/go out of action.

put out of business [B2 pass] (commerce) force sb to stop trading, lead to sb's commercial failure. **S:** economic slump, decline in efficiency, labour troubles, rising prices. **O:** company, firm; store, shop; artisan □ *If a major manufacturer is in serious difficulties, the suppliers and contractors dependent on him may be* ***put out of business****.* ⇨ go out of business.

put sb's nose out of joint [B2 pass] (informal) ruffle or upset an overconfident or interfering person □ *The next time he comes around cadging, I'll remind him of the five pounds he owes us: that'll* ***put his nose out of joint****.* □ *She didn't expect you to stand up to her as you did;* ***her nose*** *was* ***put*** *badly* ***out of joint****.* □ note pl form: *'If they step in where they're not wanted, they'll get* ***their noses put out of joint****.'*

put out (to)[1] [B1i pass B3 pass emph rel] pass all or part of a job to a manufacturer or worker who is not one's employee, and who will do the work off one's premises. **S:** (large) manufacturer, factory. **O:** work, job; fitting, finishing; (making of a) part, fitting, component. **o:** subcontractor, small artisan □ *The manufacture of belts and buckles is* ***put out to*** *subcontractors.* □ *Already contractors are queuing outside Crook's door and about fifty per cent of the work will be* ***put out****.* ST

put out (to)[2] [B1i pass B3 pass emph rel] lend at interest (to). **S:** government, bank, insurance company. **o:** public; borrower, mortgagor □ *The building societies attract deposits from investors and then* ***put out*** *this money, at a higher rate of interest,* ***to*** *those wishing to buy houses.*

put over (on) [B1i pass B3 pass] (informal) get sb to accept a story, statement, claim etc that is untrue or worthless; put across[2] (q v). **S:** confidence trickster, (dishonest) salesman. **O:** ⚠ one, a fast one, something. **o:** uncritical public, gullible housewife □ *He's not the sort of man you can* ***put*** *something* ***over on****.* □ *You get these door-to-door salesmen coming round, trying to* ***put over*** *a fast one* ***on*** *the honest citizen.*

put over (to) [B1i pass adj B3 pass] convey, communicate effectively (to); put across[1] (q v). **S:** speaker, critic, narrator. **O:** point, case, argument; story, tale; sincerity, conviction. **o:** listener, viewer □ *This evening he was not* ***putting over*** *a story* ***to*** *an untried audience.* ASA □ *John was waving across the room and smiling with all the charm he already* ***put over*** *at twelve years old.* ASA ⇨ get over (to).

not put it past [B2] (informal) consider sb quite capable of doing sth malicious, illegal etc. **O:** it... to cause trouble, it... to upset people's feelings □ *I would****n't put it past*** *him to steal money from his own grandmother.* □ *'She thinks you may be the culprit.' 'I doubt it,' he said. 'Well,' she said, 'I would****n't*** *have* ***put it past*** *you.'* MN □ used with *would.*

put through[1] [B1i pass] conclude, complete; carry through[1] (q v). **S:** department, firm. **O:** programme, plan; change, reorganization □ *At the moment we are trying to* ***put through*** *a mass literacy programme.* □ *The harbour redevelopment was* ***put through*** *in record time.* ⇨ go through[6].

put through[2] [B1i pass B2 pass] cause to pass through various legislative or administrative stages. **O:** Bill, Act, measure; scheme, idea. **o:** stage, phase, process □ *These proposals have to be* ***put through*** *several committees before they become part of the constitution.* □ *Jones'll* ***put*** *it* ***through*** *the Faculty Board, if anybody will.* ⇨ get through[3], go through[6].

put through[3] [B2 pass] provide for sb so that he or she can complete (part of) his or her education. **o:** school, college, university □ *He managed to* ***put*** *each of his four children* ***through*** *boarding school.* □ *He was* ***put through*** *university with money left by his grandfather.*

put through the mill [B2 pass] (informal) give to sb the severe training of practical experience. **O:** child, trainee, aspirant to leadership □ *Most of his present officers were* ***put through the mill****;* *he considers battle experience more valuable than college training.* □ *I'd been through a Remand Home* (institution for young offenders) *before; and Mike was* ***put through the same mill****, because all the local cops knew he was my best pal.* LLDR ⇨ be/go through the mill.

put through (to) [B1i pass B3 pass] connect (with) (by telephone). **S:** operator, switchboard. **O:** caller; call □ *'An outside call, Mr Murdoch*

*'Oh, **put** him **through**.'* BBCTV □ *'When Mr Parkinson comes on the line, you will **put** the call **through to** me.'* TBC ⇨ be through (to), get through (to)[2].

put a call through (to) [B1i pass B3 pass] make a telephone call (to). **o:** London, Paris; office, shop □ *'Shan't keep you waiting long: there are one or two **calls** I've got to **put through**.'* □ *Marlowe next **put through a call to** Bill Barnett of Caltech.* TBC

put to[1] [B2 pass rel] convey, express, communicate, to. **O:** point, suggestion, proposal; situation; it... that there were better times coming. **o:** meeting, audience; board, committee □ *Let me **put** the situation **to** you as I saw it in January and February. In February I planned to take over control.* TBC □ *The proposals were **put to** us very briefly and forcibly.* □ *The Prime Minister can **put** it **to** his supporters that there will almost certainly be a considerable swing back to the Government.* OBS □ *It might be **put to** the delegates that any* reasonable *demands would be heeded.*

put to[2] [B2 pass emph rel] submit, pose. **O:** question, query, inquiry. **o:** panel, chairman; tribunal, board of inquiry □ *'The audience is now invited to **put** its questions **to** our visiting speaker.'* □ *'**To** which of our experts do you wish to **put** that question?'*

put to[3] [B2 pass] ask a meeting etc to vote on a particular proposal. **O:** matter, question; proposal, resolution. **o:** ⚠ the vote; the assembly, meeting □ *'I propose that the matter be **put to** the vote, Mr Chairman.'* □ *The secretary rose to **put** the motion **to** the assembly for its approval.*

put to[4] [B2 pass rel] make sb suffer or undergo. **o:** extra expense; unnecessary bother, some inconvenience, endless trouble □ *She is ready to oblige anyone provided this doesn't **put** her **to** any trouble.* UTN □ *You can't imagine the trouble I've been **put to** by the Council.* □ *He's been **put to** no end of expense by subsidence under the front of his new house.* ⇨ go to[2].

put to[5] [B2] (legal) suggest, submit to, a witness etc. **O:** it... that you were in Brighton on that date; it... that the door was in fact open. **o:** ⚠ you; the witness, the accused □ *The counsel for the defence harries her: 'I **put** it **to** you that you acted out of spite?'* PW □ *'I **put** it **to** the witness, My Lord, that my client was nowhere near York at the time.'*

put to bed [B2 pass] send a newspaper in its final edited form to be printed. **O:** paper, late (extra) edition; 'Guardian', 'Mirror' □ *'I suppose you've been **putting** the "Independent Socialist" **to bed**,' said Dave.* UTN

put to death [B2 pass] execute (by order of civil or military authorities). **O:** prisoner, hostage; rebel, critic □ *On a scaffold in Tyburn the first English monks were **put to death** by order of the King.* WI □ *They **put to death** anyone appearing in the streets after curfew.*

put to effective/good use [B2 pass] use well, profitably; make effective/good use of (q v). **O:** time, interval, pause; forces, labour; money, savings □ *The 3rd Division certainly **put** that first winter **to good use** and trained hard.* MFM □ *I felt they could have **put** their savings **to better use** by buying a small car.*

put an end/a stop to [B2 pass pass(o)] end, stop. **o:** quarrel, unpleasantness; war, riot, disturbance □ *It's high time this leakage of information was **put a stop to**.* □ *This appeared to **put an end to** one of the most disturbing intervals in recent British politics.* OBS □ *Is there any hope of **putting a stop to** this mad triple arms race?* OBS ⇨ be at/bring to/come to an end.

put the final/finishing touches to [B2 pass emph rel] complete the final details of. **o:** arrangements; meal, food; account, story □ *Heinz Wolf was **putting the finishing touches to** his report.* TO □ *While **the finishing touches** are **put to** the dinner, we'll stroll round the garden.* CON □ *The centre piece was to be a massive cake, **to** which the caterers were now **putting the final touches**.*

put a/one's finger to one's lips [B2 pass] signal to sb to be quiet by raising a finger to one's lips □ *Hugo followed, making a noise like a bear. I turned back and **put my finger to my lips**.* UTN

put to flight/rout [B2 pass] cause to flee in disorder. **O:** enemy, invader □ *Our men in a sharp counter-attack had **put** the enemy **to flight**.* □ *The twentieth century, vulgar, discordant and disquieting, had invaded the stronghold of the eighteenth and **put** it **to rout**.* EM □ *All their fears were **put to flight** by the news that help was on the way.*

put a match to [B2 pass] ignite, set fire/light to (q v). **o:** fire; wood, coal; paper, document, record □ *I've laid the fire in the hearth; all you have to do is **put a match to** it.*

put one's mind to [B2 pass] give one's full attention to; set one's mind to (q v). **o:** task, job; studies □ *I'm sure we can get it all sorted out if we **put our minds to** it.* ILIH □ *He'd do well in the exams if only **his mind** was **put to** his studies.*

put a name to [B2 rel] (informal) identify by name. **adj:** definite, exact, precise. **o:** noise, smell; foodstuff, liquid □ *The silence became full of sound: noises you couldn't **put a name to** — a crack, a creak, a rustle.* QA □ *He was somebody you read of every other day in the newspaper, yet we couldn't **put a name to** him.* □ usu with *can/could + not.*

put paid to [B2 pass(o) emph rel] finish, destroy. **o:** hope, plan, prospect □ *One blow and you'd be dead, which would **put paid to** any thoughts of Australia.* LLDR □ *Our tour was finally **put paid to** by a series of arguments with theatre managers.* □ *The programme **to** which the timidity of our backers had **put paid** might still be mounted the next year.*

put pen to paper [B2] begin to write □ *His Newark pupils just wouldn't **put pen to paper**.* OBS □ *All the evidence would have to be assembled before he could **put pen to paper**.*

put to rights [B2 pass] settle, arrange properly, restore to a proper state. **O:** matter, question; grievance, wrong, injustice □ *It will be some time before the wrongs suffered over many years are **put to rights**.* □ *One of her worries was that the conjugal bedroom had not yet been **put to rights*** (i e tidied up). AH

put to shame [B2 pass] make sb or sth seem slight or insignificant by comparison. **O:** him etc; efforts, achievement; resistance, resilience □ *This little man with his variety of games and* *complex music* **puts** *many other so-called 'superior' cultures* **to shame**. LWK □ *Our recovery was* **put to shame** *by their display of sustained energy.* □ *The face was dominated by a pair of tremendous eyes that would have* **put** *any self-respecting owl* **to shame**. BB

put to sleep [B2 pass] (euphemism) destroy an animal (generally a household pet) painlessly by using gas; put away[5] (q v), put down[7] (q v). **O:** dog, cat □ *The head-waiter poisoned his own dog. That's not the way to* **put** *a dog* **to sleep**. OMIH □ *Their cat was growing old and blind, and would have to be* **put to sleep**.

put to the test [B2 pass] try, test, the strength of. **O:** readiness, preparedness; defence, army; theory, idea. **adj:** final, ultimate □ *The radar interception system was fully* **put to the test** *by the air battles of 1940.* □ *Soon it is likely that all suppositions about extra-terrestrial life will be* **put to the test**. TO

put together [B1i pass] fit together pieces to make a whole, assemble. **O:** part, component, fragment; scrap of evidence; model, puzzle; case □ (nursery rhyme) *All the King's horses and all the King's men/Couldn't* **put** *Humpty* **together** *again.* □ *'You took the thing apart; now* **put** *it* **together**.*'* □ *He had managed to* **put together** *a convincing case from the accounts of eye-witnesses.*

put our/your/their heads together [B1ii] (informal) combine our (etc) thinking, think together, so as to solve a problem more quickly □ *We shall have to sit down sometime and* **put our heads together** *and think about ways and means.* THH □ *If only the leaders would* **put their heads together** *we might find a way out of our difficulties.*

put two and two together [B1ii] (informal) make the simple connection between related facts and draw the obvious conclusion □ *The police can* **put two and two together**, *you know; they'll be on his track in no time.* □ *There was a theft from the safe just before he went on an expensive holiday: it's only a matter of time before somebody* **puts two and two together**.

put towards [B2 pass] give money as a contribution to a particular fund. **O:** fifty pounds; (part, a fraction of) one's income. **o:** cost, expense; holiday, education (of children); trousseau, dowry □ *'You'd think he could have* **put** *something* **towards** *the outing, wouldn't you?'* □ *'You take care of the household expenses and I'll* **put** *half my salary* **towards** *the cost of the holiday.'*

put up[1] [B1i pass] raise, hoist. **O:** flag, banner; picture, curtain □ *'It's time we* **put up** *the Christmas decorations in the living-room.'* □ *On the other wall was a blanket,* **put up** *to hide a hole in the plaster.*

put up[2] [B1i pass] fasten in a place where it will be seen; display. **O:** notice, announcement; banns; result; team, name (of winner etc) □ *The names of the successful candidates will be* **put up** *on the College notice board.*

put up[3] [B1i pass] build, erect. **O:** house, factory; tent, marquee; statue, column □ *These were buildings* **put up** *in Czarist days.* AH □ *They're having a memorial to him* **put up** *by public subscription.* ⇨ go up[4], set up[1].

put up[4] [B1i pass] raise, increase. **O:** cost, price, rent, tax, premium □ *Every time a new tenan[t] moves into that flat, he* **puts up** *the rent a bi[t] more* (or: *he* **ups** *the rent* etc). □ *The rate o[f] interest was* **put up** *in the last Budget.* □ up (as a v) is sometimes used, informally, for put up in this sense. ⇨ be up[1], go up[2], send up[1].

put up[5] [B1iii pass] pretend to be, feel, or have done, sth in order to hide one's true origins, activities etc. **O:** ⚠ a front, façade, show, smoke-screen □ *Royal blood, indeed! Her grandfathe[r] had more likely been a poverty-stricken actor. But one had to admire the girl for the façade sh[e]* **puts up**. DC □ *The fundamental secret of covering up inefficiency is the art of* **putting up** *a front.* OBS □ *Tom gave loud commands, an[d] Steve* **put up** *a token show of obedience.* SPL

put up[6] [B1iii pass] offer. **O:** (stout) resistance, (good) fight, struggle □ *The smuggler* **put up** *a fight but was finally overcome and carried off t[o] jail.* DS □ *Very little resistance was* **put up** *b[y] the surrounded men.*

put up[7] [B1iii pass] state, advance, advocate. **O:** case, argument, proposal □ *He supported th[e] case which scientists were* **putting up** *in Washington.* NM □ *I'll see that your suggestion is* **pu[t] up** *at the next meeting of the Board.*

put up[8] [B1iii pass] advance, lend. **O:** capital, funds, cash, money □ *When we'd spent this hug[e] sum, they* **put up** *another half-million.* DS □ *A well-wisher had* **put up** *the money.* TC □ *Ho[w] much can you* **put up**? UTN

put up[9] [B1iii pass] prepare and provide (to be eaten). **O:** meal, snack; picnic lunch; sandwiches □ *Get the hotel to* **put up** *some cold chicken fo[r] the journey.* □ *'It's late, but I think we can* **pu[t]** *you* **up** *a cold meal.'* □ note the position of the Indirect Object in the last example.

put up[10] [A1 B1i pass] take food and lodging, provide food and lodging. **S:** [A1] **O:** [B1] visitor, traveller; friend, relative. **A:** at a guest house, hotel; with relatives; for the night, a weekend □ *They* **put up** *at the monastery rest-house.* ARG □ *Mother will* **put** *you* **up** *for the night.* SML □ a put-you-up is a convertible sofa on which occasional visitors can be put up.

put sb's back up [B1ii pass] (informal) offend sb, make him angry (usu by clumsy or insensitive conduct). **S:** rudeness, thoughtlessness □ *If yo[u] had pressed him for a reply, you would have* **pu[t] his back up**. PW □ *After having to listen to thes[e] jeers and catcalls for half an hour* **their back[s]** *were really* **put up**. ⇨ get sb's back up.

put the fear of death/God up [B2 pass] ⇨ put the fear of death/God in/into/up.

put one's feet up [B1ii] (informal) rest, relax, on a bed or in a chair (though not necessarily wit[h] one's feet supported) □ *'***Put your feet up** *fo[r] five minutes: you've earned a rest.'* □ *'I shoul[d] advise you to* **put your feet up** *and sleep it off.* ASA

put one's hand up [B1i pass] raise one's han[d] in order to attract attention, or to indicate one ca[n] answer a question etc. **S:** pupil, member o[f] audience □ *'***Put up your hand** *if you think yo[u] know the answer.'* □ *Someone at the back tried t[o] catch the chairman's eye by* **putting his han[d] up**. □ *The French teacher asked if there was an[y] support for another trip to Paris, and severa[l]* **hands** *were* **put up**. ⇨ (one's) hand be up.

put one's hands up [B1i] raise one's hand[s]

above one's head as a sign of surrender. **S:** soldier, criminal, fugitive □ *'Drop your weapons and **put your hands up**.'*

put the wind up [B2 pass] (informal) scare, frighten. **S:** illness, relapse, accident; disturbance, demonstration □ *'Mrs Batey, I wish you'd stop trying to **put the wind up** Virginia.' 'That child is ill, young man,' replied Mrs Batey.* AITC □ *The sudden appearance of this wasted figure **put the wind up** everybody.* ⇨ get/have the wind up.

put up (for)[1] [B1ii pass B3 pass] propose, nominate (for). **O:** present holder, 'sitting member'. **o:** (re-)election; secretary, chairman; membership; club, society □ *They'd like to **put** him **up**, but he won't accept nomination.* □ *We'll **put** him **up for** treasurer at the next committee meeting.* □ *He was **put up** twice, but didn't attract enough support.* ⇨ be/come up for; next entry.

put up (for)[2] [A1 A3 B1ii B3] offer oneself as a candidate (for election). **S:** (all patterns): (party) member, officer. **O:** oneself. **o:** (re-)election; membership □ [A3 B3] *John is **putting** (himself) **up for** election to the committee.* □ [A3] *She isn't **putting up for** re-election to Parliament.* ⇨ previous entry.

put up for auction/sale [B3 pass] offer for sale, put on the market. **O:** house, flat; site, plot; furniture, jewellery □ *That corner-site is being **put up for sale** next week.* □ *He's **putting** the family jewels **up for auction**.* ⇨ be/come up for auction/sale.

put up to[1] [B3 pass] prepare sb for a job or task, instruct sb in a job. **O:** trainee, apprentice, novice. **o:** job, work; handling a machine, running the plant □ *Get an expert to **put him up to** the job in as short a time as possible.* ⇨ (not) be up to, feel up to.

put up to[2] [B3 pass] encourage to behave mischievously or unlawfully. **o:** it; prank, escapade; trouble-making, skullduggery. □ *He wants to get off income-tax. Somebody **put him up to** it.* PW □ *He's not been out of trouble all term, and he's been **put up to** it by some of the older boys.* ⇨ be up to[1], get up to[2].

put up with [A3 pass adj] (informal) bear, tolerate; stand for[2] (q v). **o:** noise, disturbance; bad manners, inconsiderate behaviour □ *He just wasn't going to **put up with** all the caterwauling.* TC □ *There are some things that are not easily **put up with** — and his damned impertinence is one.* □ often neg, with *will/would.*

put pressure upon [B2 pass emph rel] ⇨ put pressure on/upon.

put a strain upon [B2 pass emph rel] ⇨ put a strain on/upon.

puzzle out [B1i pass] solve a problem, obtain an answer, by careful reasoning or experiment. **O:** how it works, why he did it, where the trouble started; answer, result, solution □ *He spent the afternoon trying to **puzzle out** what had gone wrong with his car.* □ *She found everything interesting, though she was quite without curiosity and never tried to **puzzle** things **out**.* HD □ *Follow that line of inquiry and I think you'll **puzzle out** an answer.*

puzzle over [A2 pass adj] think carefully about a problem etc in an attempt to solve or understand it. **o:** matter, difficulty; document, plan, diagram □ *He'd **puzzled over** the figures for hours without making head or tail of them.* □ *His scheme has been talked about in the press, and much **puzzled over** by the men who must provide the financial backing.*

Q

quail (at) [A2 rel] become fearful, feel dismay (when thinking of sth unpleasant which seems likely to happen). **o:** ⚠ the prospect, possibility; thought □ *The tunnel on the left might lead deeper into the side of the mountain rather than back towards our starting point. We **quailed at** the thought.* □ *Then there was the possibility that Jenkins might fill the vacancy left by Harrison's retirement — a prospect **at** which we all **quailed**.*

qualify (as) [A2] pass examinations, and take the title, enabling one to practise a calling or profession. **o:** accountant, dentist, teacher □ *He **qualified** (**as** a doctor) a couple of years back.* □ *He **qualified** in London **as** a teacher of English overseas* (cf *He **qualified** in London to teach English overseas*).

qualify (for)[1] [A2 emph rel] reach, or be of, the standard required for a post, civil right, reward etc (by passing a test, reaching a particular age etc); deserve by one's actions. **o:** post, career; membership, associateship; vote; pension, grant □ *You **qualify for** the vote, but your brother won't **qualify** till he's eighteen.* □ *David has already **qualified for** promotion by passing through staff college.* □ *'A few more remarks like that and you'll **qualify for** a punch on the nose.'* ⇨ next entry.

qualify (for)[2] [B2 pass emph rel] enable sb to undertake; make sb fit or eligible for. **S:** exam, test; diploma, degree; age, experience. **o:** job, post; reward, pension □ *'I'm afraid that this certificate doesn't **qualify** you **for** admission.'* □ *But **for** this kind of course his ordinary degree did not **qualify** him.* ⇨ previous entry.

quarrel with [A2 emph rel] dispute, question closely. **o:** statement, account, version (of what happened); estimate, figure □ *'You claim that you were somewhere else at the time. Well, we won't **quarrel with** that.'* □ *'I won't **quarrel with** your estimate of costs: it seems reasonable enough.'* □ usu with *will/would* + *not.*

quarrel (with) (about/over) [A2 emph rel] disagree violently (with sb), argue angrily (with sb) (about sth). **o:** (*with*) friend, colleague, workmate, wife □ *George is always **quarrelling with** his wife.* (This does not imply necessarily that she **quarrels with** him; cf *George and his wife are always **quarrelling**.*) □ *There are few people **with** whom he hasn't **quarrelled** at some time or another.* □ *'That's just like Frank and Jane, isn't it? Always **quarrelling about** something or other.'*

queen it over [B2] (informal) (of a woman) behave in a superior way towards. **S:** housekeeper, cook; matron. **o:** (lesser, other, junior) servants, staff □ *'She's not the kind of girl to let promotion go to her head. Not the sort to* ***queen it over*** *the ordinary nurses.'* ⇨ lord it over.

query (with) [B2 pass emph rel] ask questions about sth with the aim of getting a clear answer, an authoritative ruling etc. **O:** order, instruction; invoice, bill. **o:** superior; manager, accountant □ *'I'm not sure that I can issue the replacements on this authority. I shall have to* ***query*** *the request* ***with*** *head office.'*

quest for [A2 rel] (formal) seek, search (for) (q v). **S:** explorer, hunter, collector. **o:** gold, precious stones; ruins, remains □ *The travellers pushed inland,* ***questing for*** *signs of human settlement.*

queue (up) (for) [A1 A2 pass rel A3 pass rel] form a line (= (US) stand in line), to get transport, buy food etc; line up[2] (q v). **o:** bus, taxi; cinema, theatre; bread, fruit □ [A2] *She* ***queued*** *to get in the shop, and then* ***queued*** *again* ***for*** *her vegetables.* □ [A1] *Over seven hundred animals quietly* ***queued up*** *to drink.* NS

quibble (about/over) [A2 pass] (informal) ask trifling questions, raise petty doubts (about sth). **o:** unimportant details; small sums of money, a matter of a few pence; who should be given precedence □ *'I'm not questioning your claim for travel expenses. It's such a small amount that it's not worth* ***quibbling about****.'* □ *When we got down to discussing the details of the agreement we found that they were* ***quibbling over*** *the precise meaning of quite unimportant clauses.*

quicken up [A1 B1i pass adj] become, make (much) faster; speed up (q v). **S:** [A1] **O:** [B1] pace, rate; trade, commerce; activity, movement. **S:** [B1] leader, officer, director □ *The order came back to* ***quicken up*** *the pace of advance.* □ *We've noticed a distinct* ***quickening-up*** *in the turn-round of shipping.* □ *The whole process needs to be* ***quickened up****.*

quiet(en) down [A1 B1ii pass] become, make, more quiet and calm. **S:** [A1] **O:** [B1] meeting, assembly, crowd; class, child. **S:** [B1] chairman, steward; teacher, parent □ *The meeting* ***quieted down*** *after repeated warnings from the chair that the hall would be cleared.* □ *'****Quieten*** *those children* ***down****: I can't hear myself talk.'*

quiver (with) [A2] shake, tremble (esp with strong emotion). **o:** rage, fury, indignation □ *Peter* ***quivered with*** *scarcely concealed rage. What right had these people to cast doubt upon results which it had taken him years to achieve?*

quote (from) [A2 pass adj emph rel B2 pass emph rel] repeat, write, words used by another person, esp an author. **O:** extract; page, verse. **o:** play, poem; speech □ *Shakespeare is perhaps the author most frequently* ***quoted from****.* □ *I shall* ***quote from*** *the address you made at Brighton on Friday.* □ ***From*** *'Hamlet' he* ***quoted*** *the best-known soliloquy.*

R

race around/round [A1] go quickly from place to place, usu on some urgent task (e g warning people of danger) □ *The children have been* ***racing round*** *all day, collecting signatures for the petition.* □ *As soon as the alarm went, the crew* ***raced around*** *shutting the watertight doors.*

race up (into/to) [A1 A3] rise rapidly (to a particular level); shoot up[2] (q v). **S:** temperature, pressure; consumption, inflation. **o:** (***into***) the sixties, eighties; (***to***) a new level, an all-time high □ *The temperature of the outer parts of the atmosphere'll go* ***racing up to*** *hundreds of thousands of degrees.* TBC □ *Expenditure* ***raced up and up to*** *an unprecedented level.*

radiate (from) [A2 emph rel] spread outwards (from), have as its source. **S:** heat, light; authority; charm, friendliness. **o:** sun, radioactive material; fire; face, eyes; personality, character □ *Dangerous emissions* ***radiate from*** *plutonium* (or: *Plutonium* ***radiates*** *dangerous emissions*), *necessitating the use of protective clothing.* □ *I was greatly impressed by the way he* ***radiated*** *confidence and kindness* (or: *by the way confidence and kindness* ***radiated from*** *him*). MFM

radiate from [A2 emph rel] point outwards at various angles from a centre. **S:** spoke; road, railway; cable, wire. **o:** hub; capital, terminus; communications centre, switchboard □ *Most of Britain's motorways* ***radiate from*** *London.* □ ***From*** *this underground headquarters* ***radiated*** *the communications system which kept airfields informed of the movements of enemy aircraft.*

rage against/at [A2 emph rel] be violently angry about. **o:** illness, disability; confinement, restriction, frustration □ *He* ***raged*** *helplessly* ***against*** *the disability which kept him confined to a wheelchair.* □ *This nonsense at the customs post was the kind of bureaucratic pettiness* ***at*** *which he had always* ***raged****.*

rage through [A2 emph rel] pass, sweep, violently through. **S:** army; storm, hurricane; fire; plague, pestilence. **o:** street, town, country □ *A storm* ***raged through*** *the village, uprooting trees and flattening crops.* □ *The state of the house suggested that some madman had* ***raged through*** *it. Curtains were torn down and furniture smashed.*

rail against/at [A2 emph rel] (formal) reproach sb bitterly (for sth); protest bitterly against/at sb or sth. **o:** God, fate; condition, state; restriction, frustration; penalty, imposition □ *The elderly* ***railed against*** *further cuts in their standard of living.* □ *Many general practitioners* ***rail*** *vehemently* ***at*** *the volume of paperwork connected with the running of a surgery.*

rail in [B1i pass adj] enclose with railings or a fence; fence in[1] (q v). **O:** field, garden; herd, flock □ *They* ***railed in*** *part of the pasture to prevent the cattle from wandering.* □ *Behind the house was a small* ***railed-in*** *garden.*

rail off (from) [B1i pass adj B3 pass emph rel] separate one place from another by means of rails or a fence; fence off (from) (q v). **O:** garden, orchard, field. **o:** path, road □ *The bottom of the garden was* ***railed off*** *to stop the children straying into the road.* □ *They* ***railed*** *the meadows* ***off from*** *the new railway cutting.*

railroad into [B2 pass] (informal) persuade sb, by heavy or improper pressure, to do sth. **S:** commercial interests, pressure group; (impatient, ambitious) colleague, associate. **O:** government, council; company, firm. **o:** (hasty, precipitate) action, decision; buying, selling □ *'You can cut out the sales talk, John. I'm not going to be* ***railroaded into*** *joining a company with a shady past and a still more dubious future.'* □ *In the course of the evening he was* ***railroaded into*** *throwing down spiced-beef hot dogs, cream cakes and sparkling wine.* ILIH

railroad through [B1ii pass B2 pass] (informal) enact, put through[2] (q v), legislation, by applying improper pressure. **S:** government; clique, junta. **O:** Bill, Act; scheme. **o:** legislature, chamber □ *The Bill giving emergency powers to the military government was* ***railroaded through*** *with little respect for established parliamentary niceties.*

rain down (on/upon) [A1 A3 B1i pass B3 pass] (cause to) fall in showers, fall thick and fast (on). **S:** [A1 A3] **O:** [B1 B3] stones, masonry; arrows, spears, shells; blows, curses □ [A1] *He would hammer a nail into the wood with a series of blows that continued to* ***rain down*** *long after the head was flush with the boards.* DF □ [A3] *Bits of plaster* ***rained down on*** *our heads from the ceiling, filling our hair and eyes.* □ [B3] *From these positions accurate mortar fire was* ***rained down upon*** *reinforcements moving up through the valley.*

rain upon [A2 emph rel B2 pass emph rel] be offered, offer, abundantly, in great quantities to; shower upon (q v). **S:** [A2] **O:** [B2] hospitality; gift, present; food, drink; compliment. **S:** [B2] host; visitor, petitioner □ *We couldn't complain of our reception: food and drink* ***rained upon*** *us from the moment we entered the house.* □ *The distinguished guest was visibly embarrassed by the fulsome compliments that were* ***rained upon*** *him.*

raise one's voice against [B2 pass emph rel] speak firmly, boldly, in opposition to sth. **o:** sale of arms, traffic in drugs; neglect of the old; capital punishment □ *Not* ***many voices*** *were* ***raised against*** *that decision.* SC □ *He* ***raised his voice against*** *the lack of provision for the mentally sick.* □ *This was an undoubted social evil* ***against*** *which* ***many voices*** *were to be* ***raised****.* □ voices (pl) may be modified by *many, several, few, no.*

raise from the dead [B2 pass] restore to life, usu by supernatural means □ *Among the tribal elders was one credited with the power of* ***raising*** *people* ***from the dead****.* □ *A common theme in horror stories is of a monstrous creature* ***raised*** *by supernatural power* ***from the dead****.* ⇨ rise from the dead/grave.

raise a/one's glass to [B2] drink a toast to sb, thus signalling one's approval or admiration of him. **o:** friend, benefactor, host □ *'Mr Charlton, I think we should* ***raise a glass*** *(or:* ***our glasses****)* ***to*** *our hostess.'* DBM □ *We* ***raised our glasses to*** *the memory of a great man.*

raise one's hat to [B2] indicate one's approval of or admiration for sb (without literally removing one's hat); take one's hat off to (q v) □ *If you're prepared to work in that hospital for so little money, I* ***raise my hat to*** *you.* □ *That was a fine gesture: something worth* ***raising one's hat to****.* □ take one's hat off to is usu preferred.

raise an objection (to) [B2 pass emph rel] express one's disapproval (of); object (to) (q v). **adj:** no, (not) any; serious. **o:** statement; draft, wording; proposal, scheme □ *'If you won't* ***raise any objections****, I'm going to buy the champagne.... O.K?'* SML □ *There was nothing in the first draft* ***to*** *which one could* ***raise any objection****.* □ ***To*** *this part of the scheme* ***several objections*** *were* ***raised****.*

raise to the peerage [B2 pass] confer noble rank upon sb, give to sb the rank and title of peer. **O:** commoner, knight □ *Sir Peter Stainer was* ***raised to the peerage*** *in the Birthday Honours List* (a list of honours made public on the Queen's official birthday).

raise to the surface [B2 pass] bring up from the bottom to the surface of the sea, river etc. **O:** wreck; sunken ship, submarine □ *Divers place an inflatable jacket around the wreck as it lies on the seabed. Then by filling the jacket with air we can* ***raise*** *the wreck* ***to the surface****.* ⇨ rise to the surface.

raise (with) [B2 pass emph rel] introduce a subject in a discussion (with sb); bring up[3] (q v) when talking (to). **O:** ⚠ the issue, matter, point, question, subject □ *These matters have been* ***raised****, notably* ***with*** *the Canadians, before.* OBS □ *He is likely to* ***raise*** *a number of important questions* ***with*** *President Eisenhower.* SC □ *'I took the liberty, sir, of* ***raising*** *the subject* ***with*** *his lordship just now when I brought him his tea.'* EM

rake about/around/round (for) [A1 nom A3 rel] search carefully here and there (for sth). **o:** trace, sign, evidence □ *He spent the afternoon* ***raking around*** *in the attic* ***for*** *some old family photographs.* □ *The police had a good* ***rake-round*** *in the cellar, but they didn't turn anything up.*

rake in [B1i pass] (informal) take as the proceeds of one's business. **O:** a few pounds; the shekels, a lot of money, a good percentage □ *How much do you expect to* ***rake in*** *over the weekend?* □ *The dealers can* ***rake in*** *another ten or fifteen per cent on the takings.* TT

rake-off [nom (B1)] (informal) share of profit, fee, commission, esp in an illegal deal □ *The gang could get rid of the loot through a crooked dealer in London, but of course he would expect a fat* ***rake-off*** *for his trouble.* □ *'You could try selling your car through Jeff, but his usual* ***rake-off*** *is about ten per cent.'*

rake over old ashes [B1iii pass] revive (possibly unpleasant) memories of the past □ *'I don't want to* ***rake over old ashes****, Norah, but whilst we are discussing personal matters, have you heard from Jim at all lately?'* TT □ *He stood by in silent embarrassment as* ***old ashes*** *were* ***raked over****.*

rake round (for) [A1 nom A3 rel] ⇨ rake about/around/round (for).

rake through [A2 nom pass] examine documents etc carefully in search of evidence etc. **o:**

book, paper; report, transcript; clothing, possessions □ *The police* ***raked through*** *every possible hiding-place to find the weapon.* □ *We'll give the place another* ***rake-through*** (or: ***raking-through***) *before we give up the search.*

rake up [B1i pass adj] (informal) revive sth which is now forgotten (and which is best left forgotten); drag up² (q v). **O:** one's past, unpleasant memories; old grievances, past enmities □ *Old scores were* ***raked up****. Before I knew where I was, I had a fight on my hands.* DIL □ *'Why did you have to* ***rake up*** *his political past? He's a reformed character now.'*

rally round [A1 A2] unite, come together, in the face of hardship or danger and make a joint effort to face it. **S:** soldiers; country; family. **o:** commander; flag; leader; head (of the family) □ *Carrying the regimental colour* (i e flag) *in battle had a purpose: in moments of crisis, the troops* ***rallied round*** *it.* □ *When their mother fell ill, the children* ***rallied round*** *and helped with household chores and expenses.* □ *The Visual Aids Group had* ***rallied round*** *and made no end of slides and a filmstrip.* TT □ *The Prime Minister's speech ended with an appeal to party loyalists to* ***rally round*** *the flag.*

rally to the support of [A2] combine, come together, to support sb or sth at a time of crisis. **S:** followers, supporters, members; backers, investors. **o:** (political) party, leadership; industry, currency □ *When party unity is threatened, the rank and file can be depended on to* ***rally to the support of*** *their leader.* □ *During the monetary crisis, several European bankers* ***rallied to the support of*** *the pound.*

ram down [B1i pass adj] strike sth firmly so that its parts pack tightly together (usu by applying force at the end of a rod). **O:** (explosive) charge; stones, pebbles, ballast □ *In muzzle-loading fire-arms, ball and powder were placed in the barrel and* ***rammed down*** *with a steel ramrod.* □ *Broken bricks were* ***rammed down*** *in the trench to make a base for the concrete.*

ram down sb's throat [B2 pass] (informal) repeat sth often in the hope of impressing it upon the hearer; force/stuff down sb's throat (q v). **O:** view, opinion; history, science; moral, truth □ *He's* ***rammed*** *his opinions* ***down my throat*** *so many times that I could repeat them in my sleep.* □ *There's no point in trying to* ***ram*** *abstract information* ***down the throats of*** *young children.*

ram home [B1i pass] (informal) make a point absolutely clear by example or illustration. **S:** accident; fall, (car-)crash; loss, bankruptcy. **O:** lesson, moral; urgency, necessity (of sth) □ *The loss of all his belongings* ***rammed home*** *the need to insure against fire and theft.* □ *His point about sound navigation was* ***rammed home*** *by the disappearance of an aircraft over the sea.*

ram into [A2 pass rel B2 pass rel] drive (one's vehicle) with great force into. **S:** [A2] **O:** [B2] car, van, lorry. **S:** [A2 B2] driver, motorist □ *His car was* ***rammed into*** *from behind by a lorry with faulty brakes.* □ *She turned too sharply and* ***rammed*** *the car* ***into*** *a gatepost.*

ramble on [A1] continue to speak or write in a wandering, incoherent way □ *'We did think of asking Peter to make the speech of welcome, but he does* ***ramble on****, doesn't he?'* □ *Mark's tutor had difficulty in reducing his draft chapter to coherent shape. The original had* ***rambled on*** *for fifteen pages.*

range against [B2 pass emph rel] assemble, array, in opposition to. **O:** (strong) forces, army; tanks, artillery; strength, resources □ *We had* ***ranged against*** *us elements from several enemy divisions.* □ ***Against*** *us in this area were* ***ranged*** *the resources of two major oil companies.*

range from to [A2] cover the range from one stated limit (to another); vary from to (q v). **S:** price, cost; demand, yield; mood, reaction. **o:** (***from***) ten pounds; 20 000 tons; elation, optimism; (***to***) fifty pounds; 1 m tons; gloom, pessimism □ *Increases in compulsory contributions* ***range from*** *thirty pence* ***to*** *one pound.* □ *Reactions to the news that a new oil terminal is to be built* ***range from*** *bitterness and hostility* ***to*** *cautious optimism.*

range in (on) [A1 A3 pass B1i pass] (military) establish the exact range between one's guns and an enemy position; zero in (on)¹ (q v). **S:** artillery. **O:** [B1] **o:** [A3] target, position □ [A3] *'We still hadn't been* ***ranged in on*** *from the ground. It was a very peaceful atmosphere, really pastoral.'* ST □ [B1] *'They had both shores* ***ranged in****. The moment a barge set out from one shore there'd be a terrific barrage on it.'* ST

range over [A2 rel] cover, include, move about among. **S:** talk, discussion; book, article; interest, experience. **o:** (several) fields, topics, areas □ *His lecture* ***ranged over*** *a variety of topics.* □ *It would be difficult to list all the fields* ***over*** *which his experience* ***ranges****.*

rank among/with [A2 B2 pass] be in, place in, the same class or category as; rate among/with (q v) □ *I wouldn't* ***rank*** *it* ***with*** *the very finest white wines from Burgundy.* □ *He* ***ranks among*** *the best tactical commanders of the last war.* □ *He can be* ***ranked among*** *the best students of his year.*

rank as [A2 B2 pass] have the qualities or standing of; consider sb or sth to have such qualities or standing; rate as (q v). **o:** (great) statesman; painter, novelist; masterpiece □ *He* ***ranks as*** *one of the outstanding presidents of our time.* □ *It's an exceptionally fine novel, but it can't be* ***ranked as*** *a work of genius.*

rap at/on [A2] make a sudden, sharp, blow upon. **o:** door, window, table □ *He* ***rapped*** *sharply* ***on*** *the table with his knuckles and the room fell silent.*

rap on/over the knuckles [B2 pass] (informal) reprimand, reprove, sb for sth □ *My report fell short in some parts of its record and he very properly* ***rapped*** *me* ***over the knuckles*** *for it.* SD □ *Some final-year students were* ***rapped on the knuckles*** *for not submitting their theses on time.*

rap out¹ [B1i pass adj] signal a message by means of a number of sharp taps (e g on a Morse key). **O:** message; sentence, (a few) words □ *The prisoners communicated with each other by messages* ***rapped out*** *on the heating pipes.* □ *It is claimed that at seances spirits send the messages* ***rapped out*** *on the table.*

rap out² [B1i pass] utter suddenly and sharply. **O:** order, command; oath, curse □ *'Stand still!' he* ***rapped out****, in a voice that froze the troops on parade.* □ *He always* ***raps*** *his instructions* *out, as though he were still in the army.*

rat (on) [A2 pass] (informal) betray, inform against/on (q v); withdraw from an agreement or undertaking. **o:** friend, mate; promise, bargain, agreement □ *Nobody likes being* ***ratted on****, especially when so much depends on keeping things secret.* □ *We thought we could count on him backing us with cash but he* ***ratted on*** *the deal at the last minute.*

rate among/with [A2 B2 pass] be in, place in, the same class or category as; rank among/with (q v) □ *'Would you* ***rate*** *him* ***with*** *the best of the bunch?'* □ *He* ***rates among*** *the best heavyweight boxers of the past fifty years.*

rate as [A2 B2 pass] have the qualities or standing of; consider sb or sth to have such qualities or standing; rank as (q v). **o:** (good) scholar, sportsman, pilot, sailor; (very) able, competent □ *He is* ***rated as*** *very capable by the best judges.* □ *He* ***rates as*** *one of the best runners over the distance.*

rate at[1] [B2 pass rel] place at, consider to be at, a particular level (of power, capacity etc). **O:** motor, engine; output, capacity, horsepower; income, fortune. **o:** (so many) kilowatts; tons, cubic feet; pounds, dollars □ *'What would you* ***rate*** *the engine* ***at****?' 'About twelve horsepower.'* □ *Output was* ***rated at*** *about 5000 bales per working day.*

rate at[2] [B2 pass rel] value (property) for the purpose of assessing rates (in GB a kind of local tax on land and buildings). **O:** house, shop, cinema □ *His house was* ***rated at*** *£300 a year* (cf *His house had a* ***rateable*** *value of £300 a year*).

rate with [A2 B2 pass] ⇨ rate among/with.

ration out [B1i pass adj] distribute as rations, or fixed allowances, in a time of shortage. **O:** food, water; clothing □ *The remaining stores of tinned milk were carefully* ***rationed out*** *among the children.* □ *They had to* ***ration*** *the petrol* ***out****: five gallons to each motorist while stocks lasted.*

rattle away (at/on) [A1 A3 rel] operate sth energetically and with a sharp, rhythmical noise. **o:** typewriter, teleprinter; loom □ *Half-a-dozen typists were* ***rattling away*** *in a corner of the office.*

rattle off [B1i pass] say, or repeat, sth in a fast, rhythmic, sometimes careless way. **O:** report, story; poem; list □ *I got potential criminal Lamb on to the subject of agents, and he* ***rattled off*** *a few names for me.* JFTR □ *'Now read the poem again, and this time don't* ***rattle*** *it* ***off*** *like a machine-gun.'* □ *He could* ***rattle off*** *a page of the telephone directory if you asked him.*

rattle on[1] [A2 emph rel] strike sharply upon, one after the other. **S:** rain, hail; stone, pebble; finger. **o:** roof, window; key □ *A shower of rocks and stones* ***rattled on*** *the roof of the dug-out.* □ *His fingers* ***rattled on*** *the keys of the piano.*

rattle on[2] [A1] continue to talk in a sharp, fast and usu thoughtless way □ *I always found her company unendurable. She could* ***rattle on*** *for hours about absolutely nothing at all.*

rave about/over [A2 pass emph rel] (informal) talk with foolish enthusiasm of. **o:** holiday, trip; art, architecture; food, wine □ *She* ***raved about*** *her little dressmaker, who could copy a Paris model for next to nothing.* □ *The unspoiled fishing-village they'd* ***raved about*** *so endlessly turned out to be a run-of-the-mill holiday resort.* □ *Their house in the country is nothing to* ***rave over****.*

rave against/at [A2 emph rel] oppose sb or sth violently, wildly, possibly incoherently. **o:** young people, (supposed) criminals, imaginary enemies; loose morals, lax standards □ *The aging tyrant* ***raved against*** *his closest friends, accusing them of unimaginable crimes.* □ *There seemed no end to the hidden enemies* ***at*** *whom he* ***raved****.*

rave-up [nom (A1)] (slang) wild party, outing etc, esp for young people, and often with pop music □ (caption to a picture) *It's a great day for a* ***rave-up*** *— Julie takes in the scene with other pop fans at a show at Chelmsford, Essex.* DAILY EXPRESS

raze to the ground [B2 pass] flatten, reduce to ruins (esp by fire or explosives). **S:** fire; shell, bomb; bomber, artillery. **O:** city; house, factory □ *Fires swept through the outskirts, where the houses, being mostly of wood, were* ***razed to the ground****.*

reach down [B1i pass] fetch sth from a higher point by stretching one's hand. **O:** book, magazine; cigarette, match □ *'Would you mind* ***reaching down*** *my knitting from the top shelf?'* □ *One or two dusty papers were* ***reached down*** *from the top of the cupboard.*

reach for [A2] stretch out one's hand to grasp a weapon. **o:** weapon; gun, knife □ *One or two false alarms had the men* ***reaching for*** *their guns.* □ *He was overpowered before he could* ***reach for*** *his knife.*

reach out (for) [A1 A3 rel B1i pass B3 pass rel] extend one's hand etc (to take sth); stretch out[1] (q v); make an effort to grasp. **O:** ⚠ a hand, an arm, a finger. **o:** glass, knife; opportunity, opening □ [A1] *David* ***reached out*** *and took down a small leather-bound book.* □ [B3] *'Would you mind* ***reaching*** *an arm* ***out for*** *my tobacco pouch?'* □ [A3] *All manner of opportunities will come your way, but you must* ***reach out for*** *them.* □ [A3] *The farm means ease and security and wealth. I think that's what I've been* ***reaching out for****, really.* RFW

reach out (to) [A1 A3 emph rel] try to communicate (with), to make contact (with). **S:** regime, (political) party; church. **o:** masses, rank and file; poor, underprivileged □ *The worker-priest movement was a largely unofficial attempt from within the Catholic Church to* ***reach out to*** *the urban working class.* □ *A party which doesn't* ***reach out*** *and take account of grass-roots feeling is like a head without a body.*

reach (to) [A2 rel] stretch as far as. **S:** voice, music; wire; carpet, curtain; dress, coat. **o:** the back of the hall; wall; floor; below the knee □ *'Your voice won't* ***reach to*** *the back of the auditorium; we'll have to use an amplifier.'* □ *He'll fit an extension so that the flex can* ***reach (to)*** *the socket.*

react against [A2 pass emph rel] respond to a system, or a set of influences, by acting in a contrary or hostile way. **o:** regime, government; parents, upbringing □ *Children can generally be relied upon to* ***react against*** *their early upbringing, even when this is benevolent.* □ *People* ***reacted against*** *a period of austerity by frivolous spending.*

react on/upon [A2 pass emph rel] have a particular effect on/upon (esp to change in some way). **S:** acid; heat, light; mood, temper; personality. **o:** metal, wood; audience, surroundings □ *Heat **reacts upon** certain substances to change their chemical composition.* □ *Strong personalities **react on** others, while weaker personalities are **reacted on**.*

react (to) [A2 pass emph rel] act in response to sth or sb by behaving differently (e g in a kinder or more lively fashion); respond (to) (q v). **S:** organism, plant; listener, viewer; patient. **o:** light, heat; display, drama; treatment □ *Observe carefully how the bacteria **react to** this stimulus.* □ *Children **react** well **to** a lively teacher.* □ *'How is your patient **reacting to** the course of treatment?'*

read about [A2 pass rel B2 pass rel] read (sth) concerning, on the subject of. **O:** something, a little; article, letter □ *I know it's true, because I **read about** it in the official report.* □ *The heart transplants have been **read about** and discussed everywhere.* □ ***About** this particular development I have **read** very little.* □ (newspaper-seller's cry) *'**Read** all **about** it!'*

read around/round the subject/topic [A2] read works that will provide a background (e g in history or art) to a subject (e g literature) which one is studying □ *It's not enough to have read the poet's life and works. You must **read around the subject** and see how far he reflects more general movements in literature.*

read back [B1i pass] read aloud a message that has just been received so that the sender may check its accuracy. **O:** telegram; paragraph, section □ *When you send a telegram by phone, the operator will normally **read** it **back** to you.* □ *Do you mind **reading back** the text of my message?*

read between the lines [A2 B2] gather meanings from a text that are not actually stated but implied □ *I **read between the lines** of her letter that she had driven him out, and I rejoiced.* ASA □ ***Reading between the lines**, it was obvious the poor chap was desperately anxious about the future.* ASA

read for [A2] study in order to obtain a qualification, or the right to practise as a barrister. **o:** ⚠ a degree, a diploma; the Bar □ *He spent three years **reading for** a degree in history.* □ *He **read for** the Bar in his spare time.*

read from [A2 rel B2 pass emph rel] read (usu aloud) part of a book etc. **O:** passage, extract; chapter, poem; letter. **o:** novel; anthology; newspaper □ *Before the children went to bed, Father would **read from** their favourite book of stories.* □ *Dickens **read** extracts **from** his novels before audiences in the theatre.* □ ***From** the plays of Shakespeare he **read** some of the best-known speeches.*

read into [B2 pass] find sth in the words of a speaker or writer which he did not intend. **O:** implications, ideas; things. **o:** book, letter; statement, account □ *'Now don't go **reading** things **into** my stories which I didn't put there!'* □ *Too much should not be **read into** the minister's statement: we can't expect a sudden easing of the situation.*

read off [B1i pass] read completely (aloud or to oneself). **O:** message; figure, measurement; temperature □ *Frank tore open the envelope, **read off** the brief message it contained and picked up the telephone.* □ *'I want you to sit down in front of those dials and **read off** any fluctuations that occur in oil pressure.'*

read out [B1i pass] read aloud (to an audience) sth of interest to them, or of which they must take special notice. **O:** announcement, instruction; article □ *'If it's a letter from Mary, **read it out** (loud), Mother!'* □ *After morning prayers, important notices are **read out** to the assembled school.*

read over/through [B1ii pass] read completely, from beginning to end. **O:** report, account; statement, evidence □ *He lifted out the topmost two letters, and though he knew what he would see, he **read** them **through** again.* PW □ *'**Read** the report **over** to yourself, and see if you can spot anything odd.'* □ *He had to **read** the passage **through** several times before he could understand it.*

read round the class/room [A2 B2 pass] (of individual pupils or members of a group) read a text aloud one after the other, each continuing at the point where the last leaves off. **O:** text, author □ *I like 'Treasure Island'. We **read** it **round the class** last term.* □ *'We'll begin by **reading round the class**. Then I shall ask you some questions about the passage.'*

read round the subject/topic [A2] ⇨ read around/round the subject/topic.

read oneself to sleep [B2] read with the intention or in the hope of falling asleep; read so much, or so late at night, that one falls asleep □ *He felt wideawake in bed — he'd drunk too much coffee — so he tried to **read himself to sleep**.*

read up [B1i pass] acquire a knowledge of a subject through reading. **O:** facts, details, elements □ *There's no need to attend classes in theory: you can **read** it **up** for yourself in the library.* □ *I knew nothing of the subject, but I could **read up** enough to pass a simple test.*

read up on [A3 pass] improve one's knowledge of sth by reading, bring one's knowledge of sth up to date by reading. **o:** details, facts; events, what has happened □ *I must **read up on** developments in this field; I'm getting badly out of touch.* □ *We've so much to **read up on** in the subject; it's easy to get behindhand with one's knowledge.*

realize (from/on) [B2 pass emph rel] get as a price for, or as a profit on. **O:** (handsome) profit, return; sum, price. **o:** (the sale of) furniture, painting, jewellery □ *We didn't **realize** as much as we'd hoped **on** the china figures.* □ ***From** overseas sales he's **realized** enough to equip a new workshop.*

reap (from) [B2 pass emph rel] gather a crop (from); derive, enjoy profit (from). **O:** wheat, oats; (rich, poor) harvest; benefit, dividend. **o:** field; investment, savings □ *He **reaped** handsome dividends **from** all the hard work he'd put in earlier.* □ *This is an investment **from** which we expect to **reap** a very good return.*

rear (up) [A1] rise (high) on its hind legs (from fear and/or to attack an enemy). **S:** ⚠ the horse, stallion; the beast □ *For no apparent reason the horse **reared up**, almost unseating its rider.*

reason into [B2 pass rel] persuade sb by reasoned argument to do sth. **o:** membership, participation; agreement, dissent; doing sth, behaving thus □ *This is something he can be*

***reasoned into**, given time.* □ *Let me try to **reason** him **into** joining us.*

reason out [B1i pass adj] obtain, arrive at, (an answer) through careful reasoning. **O:** solution, result; that sth is the case □ *The police **reasoned out** that if the men had left by the midday train, it would be easy to pick them up at the terminus.* □ *It's easy to **reason out** what the consequences of* that *action will be.*

reason out of [B2 pass rel] persuade sb by reasoned argument not to do sth, or to leave or abandon sth. **o:** joining, taking part; mood, temper, stubbornness □ *We tried to **reason** him **out of** this course of action, but without success.* □ *These were deeply held convictions and he couldn't be **reasoned out of** them very easily.*

reason with [A2 pass rel] argue with sb reasonably in the hope of convincing him □ *Have you tried **reasoning with** him?* □ *She won't be **reasoned with*** (i e she won't listen to reasoned arguments that sth is unwise).

rebel (against) [A2 pass emph rel] oppose by force of arms; protest strongly (against). **S:** subject; follower, soldier. **o:** (established) authority, regime; (new) demand, increase, imposition □ *The new tax laws led the inland tribes to **rebel against** the central government.* □ ***Against** measures such as these almost anyone would **rebel**.* □ *The nurses **rebelled against** an increase in their hours of work.*

rebound (from) [A2 emph rel] bounce back (from). **S:** ball; stone, pebble □ *The dart struck the board sideways on and **rebounded** (**from** it).*

rebound upon [A2 emph rel] (formal) return to and affect (perhaps for the worse) the person responsible; recoil on/upon (q v). **S:** (evil, thoughtless) action, deed. **o:** oneself; the doer □ *Take care not to carry this through; the mischief may **rebound on** your own heads.* □ *Bad deeds, as well as good, may **rebound upon** the doer.*

recall (from) [B2 pass emph rel] call back, summon back, to the home country (from abroad). **O:** envoy, attaché, consul □ *Their High Commissioner has been **recalled from** London.* □ *An official spokesman named a number of countries **from** which it had been decided to **recall** our missions.*

recall to [B2 pass] (formal) make one aware, conscious, once again of sth that has been forgotten. **S:** event; tragedy, loss; occasion, company. **o:** ⚠ a sense of duty, of propriety □ *The dangers that suddenly threatened **recalled** him **to** a sense of duty.* □ *They were **recalled to** a sense of propriety by the presence of visitors whom they dared not offend.*

recall (to mind) [B2 pass] remember, recollect. **O:** face; words; what he looked like; his saying anything; that he did so □ *After so many years I find it hard to **recall** all their names **to mind**.* □ *I can't **recall (to mind)** that he said anything about payment.*

recede (from) [A2 emph rel] (formal) move away (from); be lost (from). **S:** shore, coastline; face, voice; memory. **o:** sight, view; mind □ *As we gained height, the ground **receded from** view.* □ *As the months passed, her expressions and gestures **receded from** his mind.*

receive back into the fold [B3 pass] admit again as a member of a body sb who has left it. **S:** (political) party, church, club □ *The party was glad to **receive** Stevens **back into the fold** because of his wide contacts and influence in the city.* □ *The committee was willing to let Philip attend meetings again — as a guest — but Philip was too proud to be **received back into the fold** on such grudging terms.*

receive (from) [B2 emph rel] get (from), have sent or given to one (by). **O:** gift; parcel, letter; kindness, insults □ ***From** his employers he **received** a generous pension.* □ *I expect to **receive** nothing but empty promises **from** him.*

receive into [B2 pass] admit as a member (of a religious body). **o:** ⚠ the (Catholic) Church, faith □ *John's was a late conversion: he was **received into** the Church when he was already an old man.*

reckon among[1] [B2 pass] include as one of, count among (q v). **o:** experts, judges, critics; (most) able, competent (people); one's acquaintances, friends □ *He can be **reckoned among** the best guides to form in racing.* □ *I dislike him, but I wouldn't **reckon** him **among** my enemies.* □ *We'd **reckon** these two correspondents **among** the best on the paper.*

reckon among[2] [B2 pass emph] consider particular member(s) of a group to be best, worst etc. **o:** students; applicants, candidates □ *I'd **reckon** him (to be) the least suitable **among** those coming forward for places.* □ *He was **reckoned** best **among** the new recruits.* □ ***Among** those submitting applications I'd **reckon** him (the) least qualified to do research.* □ the Object is followed by an Object Complement — usu an adj or pp, e g *best, most able, least acceptable, best suited (to do sth).*

reckon (as) [B2 pass] consider (to be), regard as (q v). **O:** agriculture, industry; farm, factory; expenditure, saving. **o:** efficient, wasteful; (good) investment, security; declining, running to waste □ *Development in this area is **reckoned as*** (or: ***reckoned** to be) money poured down the drain.* □ *We don't **reckon** this work **as** vital in the national interest.* □ *The garage was **reckoned as** forming* (or: ***reckoned** to form) part of his rateable property.*

reckon in [B1i pass] include as part of a bill, estimate etc. **O:** cost, expense □ *When you submit your claim, don't forget to **reckon in** the money spent on petrol.* □ *'Don't bother to tip: the service charge has already been **reckoned in**.'*

reckon on/upon [A2 pass emph rel] make one's plans in the sure knowledge that sth will happen, or be the case; depend on/upon[2] (q v). **o:** support, help; kindness, generosity □ *He will always help in time of need; **on** this you can **reckon**.* □ *His promises can't always be **reckoned upon**.* □ *You needn't **reckon on** my future.* NM □ *The next five years will show whether Nkrumah still has a political future **on** which he can **reckon**.* OBS

reckon up [B1i pass] find the sum, total, amount, of. **O:** expenses, outgoings, takings; losses, damage □ *A mechanic **reckoned up** the cost of repairing the damage to my car.* □ *When you **reckon up** the wastage* (i e loss) *of female staff through marriage it's quite a total.*

reckon with[1] [A2 pass emph rel] consider, assess carefully; include in one's calculations. **o:** (possible, likely) difficulty, obstacle; cost, weight, size □ *I had not **reckoned with** the facts of my temperament, training and habits.* DOP □ *He is a man to be **reckoned with*** (i e whose qualities need to be considered before one acts). □ *I hadn't **reckoned with** the possibility of his turning up so soon.* ⇨ reckon without.

reckon with[2] [A2 pass emph rel] tackle, overcome. **o:** hardship, privation, danger □ *When you consider all the petty irritations and shortages they had to **reckon with**, it's a wonder they kept their sense of humour.* □ *All these problems had to be **reckoned with** as they arose, before they grew large enough to hinder progress.*

reckon with[3] [A2 pass] punish, deal with[3] (q v). **S:** police; authorities. **o:** enemy, dissenter, traitor □ *Anyone not obeying the decrees of the new military junta could expect to be **reckoned with**.* □ *The police **reckoned**, in a horrible fashion, **with** all those suspected of supporting the government in exile.*

reckon without [A2 pass] not include in one's plans or calculations. **o:** weather, climate; (chance of) slump, depression; help, intervention □ *The organizers of the garden party had clearly **reckoned without** the possibility of a freak thunderstorm.* □ *I'd **reckoned without** their being prepared to lend me the money.* □ *He's not the sort of man you can afford to **reckon without**.* ⇨ reckon with[1].

reclaim (from) [B2 pass emph rel] make available for use, restore to use (by draining off water, using fertilizers etc); restore sb to a healthy state. **O:** acres; flooded land, waste land; drunkard, drug addict. **o:** sea, flooding; addiction, (life of) crime □ *In Holland thousands of hectares have been **reclaimed from** the sea and turned over to arable land and pasture.* □ *A convert to the faith was considered to have been **reclaimed** by God **from** a life of sin.*

recognize (as)[1] [B2 pass] be willing to accept that sb or sth has the rank or authority that are claimed for him or it. **O:** son, brother; claimant, contender; government, regime. **o:** rightful heir, lawful descendant; legally constituted □ *The break-away committee has not been properly constituted, and will not be **recognized as** such.* □ *It is not certain that the Court will **recognize** him (**as** his father's rightful successor).*

recognize (as)[2] [B2 pass] regard, consider (to be). **o:** an authority, the last word; authentic, genuine; eminent, distinguished □ *This has long been **recognized as** the standard work on the Napoleonic period.* □ *In years to come they will **recognize** him **as*** (or: ***recognize** him to be*) *one of the great founder-figures of our movement.*

recoil (from) [A2 pass emph rel] withdraw sharply, and with displeasure, in horror etc from sth that appears suddenly, which one is asked to do; reel back (q v) from. **o:** sight, prospect; action, deed □ *The leading companies **recoiled from** the murderous crossfire from the pillboxes.* □ *Her nature **recoils from** anything that will cause pain.* □ ***From** the things they were asked to do, most active consciences would **recoil**.*

recoil on/upon [A2] (formal) strike back at the doer of an action (perhaps for the worse); rebound upon (q v). **S:** greed, meanness, cruelty □ *An evil deed may **recoil on** the head of the doer.* □ *Neglect of his children **recoiled upon** him when he was of an age to need their support.*

recommend (to) [B2 pass emph rel] say that sb is suitable or qualified for a post etc. **S:** teacher, tutor; (previous) employer. **O:** applicant □ *'I feel quite confident in **recommending** Mr Jackson **to** you for the vacant post of research assistant.'* □ *A new man will be joining the project next October. He's been strongly **recommended to** us by the head of our Manchester office.*

recompense (for) [B2 pass emph rel] repay, reward, sb (e g for some good he has done); make good (a loss), compensate (for) (q v). **A:** amply, fully, richly. **o:** help, services, loyalty, support; damage, suffering □ *You will be amply **recompensed for** for your loyal support.* □ *The company now presents itself as the innocent victim of the Second World War, and has been handsomely **recompensed for** its injuries.* OBS

reconcile to [B2 pass emph rel] come to accept, bring sb to accept sth unpleasant; resign (oneself) to (q v). **o:** humble status, low wages; poverty, obscurity □ *He couldn't easily be **reconciled to** the prospect of a falling income.* □ *He **reconciled** himself cheerfully **to** a modest livelihood in a small country town.*

reconcile (with)[1] [B2 pass emph rel] bring people together after a quarrel, an angry separation etc □ *Friends managed to **reconcile** him **with** his wife after years of estrangement.* □ *He was **reconciled with** his brothers* (or: *He and his brothers were **reconciled***) *after a fierce family quarrel.*

reconcile (with)[2] [B2 pass emph rel] make one fact etc match, be consistent with, another; square with (q v). **O:** action, event; decision, statement; principle, tenet. **o:** claim, profession (of goodwill); philosophy, theory □ *I can't **reconcile** what he says here **with** statements in the earlier parts of the book.* □ *How can their aggressive actions be **reconciled with** their talk of peace and brotherhood?* □ *The two sets of figures can't be **reconciled*** (***with** each other*). □ with *can/could*; often neg.

record (from) (on/onto) [B2 pass emph rel] make a sound or video recording (esp onto tape). **O:** broadcast; speech, music; interview, play. **o:** (***from***) radio, disc; (***on/onto***) (audio-/video-)tape □ *'We managed to **record** the whole of the concert **from** a live studio broadcast.'* □ *Jack has a set of Billie Holiday numbers **recorded from** the original 78s **onto** tape.* □ *The language teaching plays were put out live but also **recorded** in the studio **on** video-tape, so that they can be shown again and again.*

recover (from)[1] [A2 pass emph rel] get well again, be restored (after some kind of set-back); get over[3] (q v). **o:** illness, operation; depression, slump; shock, surprise □ *She's still **recovering from** a bout of 'flu.* □ ***From** this kind of set-back, the industry is always slow to **recover**.*

recover (from)[2] [B2 pass emph rel] regain (from sb) sth lent or lost; □ *He **recovered** his football **from** the neighbours' lawn.* □ *Several of the missing coins were **recovered from** the bed of the river.*

recruit (into) (from) [B2 pass emph rel] enlist, enrol sb (as a member of a particular force or body) (from a particular source). **o:** (***into***) army, navy; (***from***) another service, industry □ *During the war, a number of young men were **recruited***

***into** the mining industry as 'Bevin Boys'.* □ *The wartime government first **recruited** men (**into** the forces) **from** non-essential industries.*

recur to [A2 rel] be recalled by sb, come again into his mind. **S:** idea, thought; memory, recollection; experience, event; it... how he was always ready to listen □ *The memory of the days we spent together often **recurs to** me.* □ *It **recurs to** me that he was the first person to help us in those difficult times.* □ *The tune **recurred to** me while I was having my bath.*

redeem (from)[1] [B2 pass rel] obtain again, recover, an article (from a pawnshop) by paying money. **O:** clothing, furniture, jewellery. **o:** ⚠ pawn, hock □ *He **redeemed** his one and only suit **from** pawn to attend a wedding.*

redeem (from)[2] [B2 pass rel] (religion) rescue, make free (from sin) by sacrifice (esp the Sacrificial Atonement of Christ). **S:** Christ; Christ's sacrifice, blood. **O:** mortal; sinner. **o:** ⚠ sin, death □ *We are **redeemed from** sin by the blood of Jesus.*

redeem (from)[3] [B2 pass emph rel] preserve, save (from falling to a low level). **O:** occasion; party, meal; performance, spectacle. **o:** (total) failure, disaster, ignominy; (downright) farce, comedy, tragedy □ *It was John who **redeemed** the occasion **from** utter failure by telling some of his funny stories.* □ *The second act was **redeemed from** farce by the performance of one of the supporting actors.*

redound to [A2] (formal) promote, enhance. **S:** action, deed; success, exploit. **o:** fame, honour, credit, reputation □ *Your achievements will **redound to** the good name of the whole school.* □ *His bravery **redounds to** the fame of the regiment.*

reduce (from) [B2 pass emph rel] ⇨ reduce (to) (from).

reduce to[1] [B2 pass emph rel] obtain the chemical constituents of sth; break down[7] (q v). **O:** wood; cloth, paper; gas, liquid. **o:** pulp, splinter; rag, shred; atom, molecule □ *A crushing machine **reduces** the logs **to** pulp.* □ *Water can be **reduced to** oxygen and hydrogen by electrolysis.*

reduce to[2] [B2 pass] change, convert a sum of money (in a calculation) to smaller values. **O:** amount, sum; dollars, pounds. **o:** cents, pence □ *You can **reduce** the amount in pounds **to** new pence by quite simply multiplying by 100.*

reduce to[3] [B2 pass] make sth (appear to be) of no value or importance, by revealing its faults, inconsistencies etc. **O:** argument, case; claim, pretension. **o:** shreds, tatters; nothing □ *Our case was argued by an able barrister, who **reduced** the prosecutor's submissions almost **to** nothing.*

reduce to[4] [B2 pass emph rel] bring down to a low or undignified position or state. **o:** (pretty) pass, (parlous) state; such straits, indignities; beggary, serfdom; begging, borrowing, mortgaging □ *A succession of bad harvests had **reduced** the small farmers **to** penury.* □ *You apologize to the one who ought to apologize to you — **to** such straits does love **reduce** dignity and common sense.* SPL

reduce to[5] [B2 pass] weaken the physical or nervous condition of sb to a grave extent. **o:** ⚠ a (nervous, physical) wreck, a skeleton, skin and bones, a shadow □ *Weeks in an open boat had **reduced** the surviving crew members **to** skin and bones.* □ *Anxiety about the fate of his family **reduced** him **to** a nervous wreck.*

reduce to[6] [B2 pass emph rel] state in a more concise form, summarize as. **O:** chapter, book; paper, report; case, argument. **o:** notes, headings; (a few) pages; essentials, bare bones □ *I think we can **reduce** his rather lengthy statement **to** one or two essential points.* □ *Take the complications of modern marriage in your stride. Try and **reduce** it **to** its simplest essentials.* DIL □ *Give us the basic facts **to** which you've **reduced** his argument.*

reduce to order [B2 pass] arrange in a tidy, systematic manner; organize. **O:** affairs; papers, documents; accounts, finances □ *He employed an accountant to **reduce** his money affairs **to** some semblance of **order**.* □ *All these details must be **reduced to order** before the annual inspection.*

reduce to the rank of/to the ranks [B2 pass] (military) deprive of one's present rank (as a punishment). **O:** Warrant Officer, non-commissioned officer □ *In the British army, a Warrant Officer may only be **reduced to the ranks** by Court-martial* (by the order of a special military court). □ *A sergeant may be **reduced to the rank of** lance-corporal by the order of his Commanding Officer.*

reduce to silence [B2 pass] make sb stop talking, complaining etc, through one's (moral) authority or force of personality. **O:** crowd, audience; rabble, mob. **adj:** total, complete, absolute □ *The dignity of his appeal **reduced** the loudest of critics **to silence**.* □ *His appearance on a platform could **reduce** even the professional hecklers **to** total **silence**.*

reduce to tears [B2 pass] affect sb so deeply that he cries. **S:** performance, performer; anger, fit of temper; speech, appeal. **O:** audience, listener □ *His emotional language **reduced** many of that open-air audience **to tears**.* □ *While she was feeling so overwrought, the slightest cross word or ill-judged remark could **reduce** her **to** floods of **tears**.*

reduce (to) (from) [B2 pass emph rel] lower, decrease (from one level to another). **O:** pressure, temperature, volume, weight, speed □ ***Reduce** the speed of your car **to** 30 mph when entering a built-up area.* □ *It was our opinion that we must **reduce** the tempo of our operations* (i e **from** its existing high level). MFM

reef in [B1i pass adj] (nautical) reduce the area of a sail by gathering up part of it. **O:** (main)sail, canvas □ *When a strong wind blows up, the sails have to be **reefed in** to prevent the boat from capsizing.*

reek of[1] [A2] have the strong (and unpleasant) smell of. **S:** room, house; food; breath. **o:** smoke; onion, garlic; whisky, beer □ *'Open a window: the place **reeks of** stale cigarette smoke.'* □ *It was stiflingly hot inside the bus, which **reeked of** petrol.* BM

reek of[2] [A2] suggest strongly sth unpleasant. **S:** atmosphere; talk. **o:** corruption, intrigue; snobbery □ *His conversation **reeks of** the literary world.* HAA

reel back [A1] move back out of control, stagger back (after receiving a powerful blow or shock); recoil (from) (q v). **S:** army; soldier, boxer □ *Two other Armies **reeled back** in a state of acceler-*

ating disorder. B □ *I felt rather as though I had been kicked in the face by a horse, and **reeled back**, momentarily blinded by the pain and stunned by the force of the thrust.* DF

reel in [B1i pass] wind a fishing line onto the reel fastened to the end of the rod, causing the line to rise from the water. **O:** line; fish □ *'You've got something on the end of your line: **reel** it **in**.'*

reel off [B1i pass] (informal) say or repeat sth rapidly and smoothly. **O:** list, catalogue; names, figures, facts □ *Without apparent effort, he **reeled off** the names of those who had been associated with him in those early days.* □ *'I think your father's marvellous. Fancy being able to **reel** all that **off**!'* ASA

refer back (to) [B1i pass B3 pass emph rel] pass, submit, a matter for further examination (to sb who has already considered it). **O:** letter; application, claim. **o:** office, department □ *Accounts Dept keep **referring back** our travel claims. We're claiming five pence a mile for official journeys, and they insist we're only entitled to three pence.* □ *'I've had my application for a vacation grant **referred back to** the University. Apparently, I should have asked my tutor to write a few words in support.'* ⇨ refer to[4].

refer to[1] [A2 pass emph rel] mention, allude to (q v). **o:** matter, question; need, importance, urgency □ *I have already **referred to** our guest's services to the party.* □ *The minister **referred to** the importance to the nation of increased exports.* SC □ *The shortage **to** which he **referred** has already been alleviated.*

refer to[2] [A2 emph rel] affect, concern; apply (to)[1] (q v). **S:** remark, statement; rule, restriction □ *'What I have to say **refers to** all of you.'* □ *There are few categories of workers **to** whom this order does not **refer**.*

refer to[3] [A2 pass emph rel] consult, look at, to refresh one's memory. **S:** announcer, actor. **o:** notes, script □ *'I've given you all copies of the script; but you shouldn't need to **refer to** them after the first week's rehearsals.'* □ *He carried a bundle of notes, **to** which he frequently **referred** during the course of the talk.*

refer to[4] [B2 pass emph rel] hand or pass sb or sth to another person or body for help or a decision. **O:** customer, inquirer; matter, case; dispute; claim. **o:** (another) branch, department; tribunal, court of inquiry □ *Somebody at the reception desk **referred** me **to** the manager.* □ *Their claim for higher wages was **referred to** the Prices and Incomes Board.* □ *'If he gives any more trouble **refer** him **to** me.'*

reflect on/upon[1] [A2 pass emph rel] think carefully about, consider carefully. **o:** position, state; (next) move; reply, response; how to react, what to do □ *He **reflected upon** the likely consequences of this course of action.* □ *The likely reactions of the market would need to be **reflected on** before we acted.*

reflect on/upon[2] [A2 pass] indicate, suggest, that sb or sth is sound, unsound etc; make sb or sth appear in a good, bad etc light. **S:** remark; report; recommendation. **o:** courtesy, good breeding; ability, skill. **A:** well, favourably; adversely, unfavourably □ *This mysterious man asked questions and made recommendations which **reflected on** their efficiency.* DS □ *Be careful to do nothing which **reflects** (adversely) **upon** the reputation of the department.* □ *The establishment of factories in Eastern Europe **reflects** very well **on** the vigour and enterprise of the Italian car industry.* □ when no adv is present the implication is that events etc reflect *badly* on sb or sth.

reflect credit on/upon [B2 pass emph rel] be good for the reputation of sb, enhance the good name of sb. **S:** behaviour, conduct; success, triumph; result, outcome. **adj:** some; no (not) any/much, little; great. **o:** participant, member; player, competitor □ *The success of the meeting **reflected** the greatest **credit on** all concerned.* □ *The naturalness of this proceeding **reflected credit on** both parties.* AH □ *Considerable **credit** is **reflected on** the police for their part in the operation.*

refrain (from) [A2 pass emph rel] not begin to do, stop doing (sth unpleasant or antisocial). **o:** bad language, vulgar behaviour; aggression, hostilities □ *I wish he would **refrain from** scattering his ash all over the carpet.* □ *Please **refrain from** smoking during the performance.*

refund (to) [B2 pass emph rel] return (to sb) money which he has already paid for goods or services (usu because those goods etc cannot be supplied). **S:** shop, cinema; local authority, college. **O:** cost (of goods, of admission); payment, fee. **o:** customer, patron; student □ *The management regret the cancellation of the programme, which is due to factors beyond their control. If patrons will kindly go to the booking office the cost of tickets will be **refunded to** them.* □ *The University is unable to **refund** tuition fees **to** students who fail to complete the course.*

regain (from) [B2 pass emph rel] obtain once again (from). **O:** land, possessions; freedom, independence □ *The island was **regained from** the French during a minor eighteenth-century war.* □ *These territories maintain trading links with the states to which they were subject, and **from** which they have now **regained** their independence.*

regale with [B2 pass emph rel] press, oblige, sb to accept, consume or listen to sth. **o:** gift, present; food, drink; song, story □ *Don't imagine that when you go on a trade mission overseas our customers will **regale** you **with** champagne and cigars.* □ *I'm a little tired of being **regaled with** accounts of young Michael's exploits every time we go to visit your sister.*

regard as [B2 pass] consider sb to be, reckon that sb is; reckon (as) (q v). **O:** son, brother; addition, improvement; machine, process. **o:** rightful owner, legitimate heir; useful, valuable; inferior □ *They never **regard** us, the children, **as** proper Catholics, because our father is a Protestant.* □ *He is generally **regarded as** the foremost authority on the subject.*

regard with [B2 pass emph rel] consider sb or sth with a particular attitude, in a certain light. **o:** approval, favour; caution, hesitation; disapproval, disfavour □ *If you would care to put in an application I am sure it will be **regarded with** sympathy.* □ *His intervention at that point was **regarded with** some disfavour.* □ ***With** such open hostility was this move **regarded** that the Government was forced to reconsider its general policy for the island.*

register with [A2 rel B2 rel] leave a formal

record of one's name, address etc, with the civil authorities. **O:** one's name; oneself, one's family. **o:** police, Home Office □ *Overseas students normally* ***register*** (themselves) ***with*** *the police shortly after their arrival in the country.*

reign (over) [A2 emph rel] rule as the king or queen (over). **o:** people, country □ *He was forced to leave the country* ***over*** *which he had* ***reigned*** *for twenty years.* □ *Victoria* ***reigned over*** *a great variety of peoples and lands.*

reimburse (for) [B2 pass emph rel] repay to sb the money he has spent for a particular purpose, or the value of sth he has lost. **o:** breakage, loss; moving, travelling □ *We shall be glad to* ***reimburse*** *you* ***for*** *sending us the papers* (or: ***reimburse*** *you the cost of sending* etc). □ *He considered himself amply* ***reimbursed for*** *the theft of his typewriter.*

rein in [B1i pass] check or restrain a horse by pulling on its reins. **O:** horse, mount, pony □ *The scout* ***reined in*** *his horse, dismounted, and ran towards us with his message.*

reissue (to) [B2 pass emph rel] ⇨ next entry.

reissue with [B2 pass emph rel] return, issue again, sth that has been temporarily withdrawn. **S:** firm, office; clerk, storekeeper. **o:** document, pass; overall, apron □ *The men were* ***reissued with*** *warm clothing after an unexpected change in the weather* (or: *Warm clothing was* ***reissued to*** *them after* etc). □ *The office will* ***reissue*** *you* ***with*** *your cards when the details have been checked.*

rejoice (at/over) [A2 pass emph rel] (formal) be very glad (about), be joyful (about). **o:** news, announcement; success, victory □ *The British* ***rejoiced over*** *the end of food rationing, which marked an important stage in the lifting of austerity.* □ *I'm sure John's not making fun of us. He's not the kind of man to* ***rejoice at*** *other people's misfortunes.*

rejoice in [A2 rel] (jocular) be called, have the style or title of; glory in[2] (q v). **o:** ⚠ the name, title, style (of) □ *Our unpleasant friend* ***rejoices in*** *the name of Minister of Justice.* SC □ *I can't recall the title* ***in*** *which he* ***rejoiced*** *at the time.*

relapse (into) [A2 rel] be overcome (by) again, sink back (into). **o:** illness, fever; vice, sin, heresy; (bad) ways, (old) habits □ *After a short burst of enthusiasm, he* ***relapsed into*** *his usual apathy.* □ *Nothing could rouse him from the black mood* ***into*** *which he had* ***relapsed.***

relate to [A2 rel] form personal ties with, form a natural relationship with. **o:** colleague, workmate; the opposite sex; doctor, analyst □ *She finds it difficult to* ***relate to*** *her tutors and fellow-students.* □ *It was not his kind of world: there were very few in his immediate circle* ***to*** *whom he could* ***relate.***

related to [pass (B2)] (be) connected to sb by blood or marriage; belong to the same species as. **o:** family, house; order, species □ *The present Queen is* ***related,*** *directly or by marriage,* ***to*** *most of the other royal families of Europe.* □ *The zoologist's classification by families, genera, and so on, shows how the animals known to man are* ***related to*** *each other.*

relate (to/with) [B2 pass emph rel] show a link or connection between; connect (with). **O:** event, phenomenon, occurrence; fact, detail □ *I find it hard to* ***relate*** *these events* ***with*** *the story as it has emerged so far.* □ *The recent price increase is not* ***related to*** *alterations in the tax structure* (cf *The increase and the alterations are not* ***related***).

relax one's grip/hold (on) [B2 pass emph rel] allow one's grip or control to become less tight or severe. **S:** dictator, tyrant; (strict) parent; weather. **o:** people, country; family; countryside □ *Frank continued to talk quietly and soothingly to the girl until* ***her*** *frightened* ***grip on*** *his arm was* ***relaxed.*** □ *Winter had* ***relaxed its*** *iron* ***grip on*** *the landscape.* □ *Better times ahead may persuade the Chancellor to* ***relax his hold on*** *the economy.*

relay (to) [B2 pass emph rel] pass, convey (to sb) a message etc which originates from sb else. **S:** radio station, switchboard; messenger, secretary. **O:** signal, message; order, instruction □ *Sub-stations were asked to* ***relay*** *the message* ***to*** *all receivers tuned to their networks.* □ *A standard procedure ensured that orders were* ***relayed*** *with minimum delay* ***to*** *all sub-units in the division.*

release (from) [B2 pass emph rel] let go (from); set free (from). **O:** bomb, rocket; captive, prisoner; servant, priest. **o:** aircraft; detention, prison; promise, bond, obligation □ *He was re-arrested on a fresh charge two days after being* ***released from*** *gaol.* □ *This payment will* ***release*** *you* ***from*** *any further obligation to the company.*

relegate (to) [B2 pass emph rel] place in a lower or inferior position. **O:** wife, servant, employee; team. **o:** (lower) status, rank; (third) division □ *He never involves his senior staff in decision-making: they feel* ***relegated to*** *the status of office boys.* □ (League football) *Our local team is struggling to avoid being* ***relegated*** (***to*** *the second division*).

relieve of[1] [B2 pass rel] take sth away from sb (to help him, lighten his burden etc). **O:** traveller, visitor; colleague. **o:** luggage, load; responsibility, workload □ *'Let me* ***relieve*** *you* ***of*** *that case: it looks terribly heavy.'* □ *He was happy to be* ***relieved of*** *some of the detailed paperwork connected with the project.*

relieve of[2] [B2 pass rel] dismiss sb from; remove (from)[2] (q v). **O:** general; civil servant. **o:** command; post □ *The Commander-in-Chief was* ***relieved of*** *his command for concerning himself with questions that were properly the responsibility of the politicians.*

relieve of[3] [B2 pass] (jocular) steal sth from sb. **o:** money, valuables □ *Some light-fingered rogue had* ***relieved*** *him* ***of*** *his wallet.*

rely on/upon [A2 pass emph rel] (be able to) trust sb or sth to behave or function well. (q v). **o:** him etc; help, aid, support; machine, instrument □ *She had proved that she could be* ***relied on*** *in a crisis.* DC □ *You can't* ***rely on*** *his assistance* (or: ***on*** *him for assistance;* or: ***on*** *him to assist you*). □ *Most industry within Cornwall can be* ***relied on*** *to produce only modest growth.* OBS

remain behind [A1] stay where one is, after others have left; stay behind (q v), stop behind (q v). **S:** student, participant; (member of, several of the) class, audience □ *Some of the committee offered to* ***remain behind*** *to help clear up after the meeting.* □ *'If you interrupt the lesson any more, John, you'll have to* ***remain***

behind *when the others have gone home.'*

remand (in custody) [B2 pass] (legal) order sb to be sent back to prison while further inquiries are made about him. **O:** accused, prisoner □ *The accused was* ***remanded in custody*** *for a further week to await the outcome of police investigations into a drugs racket in which he was said to be involved.*

remark upon [A2 pass adj] notice and comment on. **o:** absence, lateness; appearance, dress; conduct, habit □ *The quality of his work has often been* ***remarked upon*** *by his superiors.* □ *One of his most* ***remarked-upon*** *faults is a lack of tact and discretion.*

remember in one's will [B2 pass] leave money or property to sb in one's will (testament) □ *I hope the old man will* ***remember*** *the whole family* ***in his will.*** □ *I don't expect to be* ***remembered in her grandfather's will.***

remember to [B2 pass emph rel] give one's greetings, best wishes, to. **o:** family, friend, colleague □ ***Remember*** *me* ***to*** *everyone at home.* □ *He asked to be* ***remembered to*** *all his friends in the department.* □ often imper.

remind (of) [B2 pass emph rel] cause sb to remember, recall to sb's mind. **S:** colleague, friend; letter, souvenir. **o:** date, appointment; holiday, happy time □ *It was fortunate that you* ***reminded*** *me* ***of*** *my meeting with Jones* (or: ***reminded*** *me that I had to meet Jones*). □ *'I keep the book in the drawer of my desk and look at it sometimes. It* ***reminds*** *me a bit* ***of*** *our talks.'* UTN

remind of [B2 pass] suggest that sb is like sb else. **S:** he etc; face, manner. **o:** father, brother; celebrity, actor □ *The way he behaves when he is angry* ***reminds*** *me* ***of*** *his father.* □ *I am trying to think who he* ***reminds*** *me* ***of.***

remit (to) [B2 pass emph rel] (banking) send, transfer, money (to sb), usu by regular instalments, and by arrangement with a bank, post office etc. **O:** money; part, a proportion (of one's salary, one's pay); allowance □ *Soldiers serving overseas arrange to* ***remit*** *part of their pay* ***to*** *their wives and families.* □ *The Bank will be glad to* ***remit*** *your repayments* ***to*** *the hire-purchase company by monthly Banker's Order.*

remonstrate (with) [A2 emph rel] (formal) try to persuade sb, by strong argument, that a course of action is wrong □ *We tried* ***remonstrating with*** *him over his treatment of the children.* □ *There's little point in* ***remonstrating with*** *John. He won't listen to reason.*

remove (from)[1] [B2 pass emph rel] make sth disappear by cleaning. **O:** mark, stain. **o:** coat, table-cloth □ *Act promptly to* ***remove*** *spots* ***from*** *these fabrics. The longer you delay the more indelible will the marks become.* □ *All traces of rust should be* ***removed from*** *the metal before you begin to apply paint.*

remove (from)[2] [B2 pass emph rel] dismiss sb (from); relieve of[2] (q v). **O:** officer; minister; manager. **o:** command; post, office; control, management (of a business) □ *Timoshenko was quietly* ***removed from*** *command and transferred to the north-western front.* B □ *The new managing director* ***removed*** *Manning* ***from*** *his position as head of Sales Division.*

rend to [B2 pass] dismember, break, with strong, tearing movements; rip to (q v). **S:** tiger, eagle; machinery. **O:** deer, mouse; wood, metal. **o:** ⚠ pieces, shreds; matchwood, tatters □ *Whole logs are fed into the jaws of the machine and* ***rent to*** *pieces in a matter of minutes.*

render down [B1i pass adj] turn (a solid substance) into liquid, fat, usu by applying heat. **O:** lard, (solid) fat; carcase □ *The whale blubber is* ***rendered down*** *to make oil.* □ *You can* ***render*** *the chicken carcase* ***down*** *to make stock* (for soup, gravy).

render into [B2 pass emph rel] (formal) put into another language; translate (from) (into) (q v). **O:** text; play, novel. **o:** foreign tongue □ ***Into*** *how many languages have the plays of Shakespeare been* ***rendered?*** □ *It was a collection of short stories, badly* ***rendered into*** *English.*

render (to) [B2 pass emph rel] (formal) give in return for sth; provide as a gift or favour. **O:** thanks, tribute; help, assistance, benefit. **o:** God, Caesar; the aged; stranded ship □ ***Render*** *thanks* ***to*** *God for all His blessings.* □ *Young volunteer workers* ***render*** *a valuable service* ***to*** *the community* (or: ***render*** *the community a valuable service*). □ *'****Rendering to*** *Caesar the things that are Caesar's' means meeting one's proper obligations as a citizen — for example, paying one's taxes.*

render up (to) [B1i pass B3 pass] (formal) hand to the enemy in admission of defeat; surrender (to)[1] (q v), yield up[1] (q v). **O:** stronghold, fortress; town, city □ *After a prolonged siege, the town was* ***rendered up*** *to the insurgents.*

repay (by/with) [B2 pass emph rel] perform a mean or ungenerous action in return for a generous one. **O:** hospitality, generosity, kindness; sacrifice, service. **o:** (***by***) behaving badly, acting meanly; (***with***) ingratitude; indifference □ *'And how do they* ***repay*** *our hospitality?* ***By*** *drinking all our whisky and playing that radio to all hours of the night.'* □ *The hospital workers thought themselves badly used by the government. It was a case of long hours of work* ***repaid with*** *low wages and a niggardly pension.* ⇨ next entry.

repay (for) [B2 pass emph rel] give sth to sb in return (for). **A:** handsomely, generously. **o:** generosity, kindness; effort, hard work □ *We must do something to* ***repay*** *him* ***for*** *helping us.* □ *I felt amply* ***repaid for*** *all the extra hours I had worked.* ⇨ previous entry.

repel (from) [B2 pass emph rel] (formal) force to withdraw (from), repulse (from) (q v). **O:** enemy; invader. **o:** lines, trenches; island □ *Assault troops were* ***repelled from*** *the west bank of the river before they were able to establish a firm bridgehead.*

repent (of) [A2 pass rel] (formal) be full of regret (for), be very sorry (for). **o:** wickedness, misdemeanour, folly, foolishness □ *He deeply* ***repented (of)*** *his foolish actions.* □ *The man should not be reproached for errors* ***(of)*** *which he has fully* ***repented.***

replace (by/with) [B2 pass rel] put, use, in the place of. **O:** coal, gas; horse; turboprop engine. **o:** electricity, nuclear power; motor-transport; jet engine □ *They've* ***replaced*** *most of the old looms* ***with*** *brand-new ones imported from the States.* □ *On the finance committee Smith has been* ***replaced by*** *Brown* (cf *Brown has* ***replaced*** *Smith* etc). □ *There is nothing left in stock* (***with***

*which) to **replace** the damaged machinery.*

reply (to) [A2 pass emph rel] speak or write in answer (to). **o:** questioner, interrogator; accuser; correspondent; question, inquiry; letter □ *At the end of his talk the visitor spent ten minutes **replying to** questions put to him by the audience.* □ *I've written to the manufacturer three times to complain about delays in the supply of spare parts. None of my letters have been **replied to**.* □ *The prisoner will have the opportunity to **reply to** these accusations in due course.*

report (for duty/work) [A2] arrive at one's place of work etc, and tell the person in charge that one is ready □ *He **reported for work** a few minutes before the night shift went on.* □ *'Corporal Smith **reporting for duty**, Sir!'*

report (on/upon) [A2 pass adj emph rel] give news, information (about). **o:** event, development; crisis, disaster; meeting, gathering □ *The local newspaper **reported** very unfavourably **on** the recommended route for the new by-pass.* □ *There are few aspects of Far Eastern affairs **on** which he has not **reported** for our readers.*

report (to)[1] [A2 rel] announce that one has arrived and is ready for duty, work etc. **S:** newcomer; recruit; new boy. **o:** manager, duty clerk; orderly sergeant; housemaster, prefect □ *On arrival, new recruits should **report to** the orderly room.*

report (to)[2] [A2 rel] be responsible to, be controlled by. **S:** salesman, executive. **o:** area manager, managing director □ *'I'm sending you to the North on a fact-finding trip. Now, you won't have any dealings with the area managers: you **report** direct **to** me here in London.'*

report (to)[3] [B2 pass emph rel] inform sb in authority that an accident etc has occurred. **O:** loss, breakage, discrepancy. **o:** manager, domestic bursar □ *Any serious fluctuations in pressure should be **reported** at once **to** the engineer in charge.* □ *You must **report** the disappearance of these keys **to** the hotel manager.*

report (to)[4] [B2 pass emph rel] complain about sb, or sth he has done, to a person in authority. **O:** employee; soldier; shopkeeper; oneself; conduct, impertinence. **o:** management; officer; board, association □ *'I'm **reporting** you **to** the police for dangerous driving.'* □ *'Go and **report** yourself **to** the Headmaster. He will deal with you.'* □ *'Your impertinent remarks will be **reported to** the manager.'*

report (upon) [A2 pass adj emph rel] ⇨ report (on/upon).

repose in [B2 pass emph rel] (formal) trust sb to behave, or manage affairs, well. **O:** ⚠ (great, a good deal of) trust, faith, confidence. **o:** him etc; promises, good intentions; ability, powers □ *We **repose** great confidence **in** his ability to handle the negotiations.* □ ***In** his tact and discretion, especially, we had always **reposed** great trust.*

represent (as) [B2] portray sb, make sb appear, in a particular position or role, or as having certain qualities. **S:** painter, sculptor; writer; picture, report; leader, statesman. **O:** subject, patron; landscape; event, incident; oneself. **o:** youth, athlete, scholar; outline, blur; tragic, unavoidable; lacking in discretion, possessed of all the virtues □ *In this early portrait the prince is **represented as** a young Grecian warrior.* □ *How are these Victorian fathers **represented** to us? **As** rather terrifying figures of authority.* □ *In his public appearances the candidate was careful to **represent** himself **as** a man of the people.*

reproach (for) [B2 pass emph rel] criticize sb, or oneself, because of sth he, or one, has failed to do. **O:** colleague, husband; oneself. **o:** forgetfulness, idleness; neglecting one's family, spending too freely □ *You've done nothing to **reproach** yourself **for**.* □ *'You shouldn't **reproach** the children **for** forgetting birthdays. You're pretty bad at remembering dates yourself.'* ⇨ next entry.

reproach with [B2 pass emph rel] name a fault etc as a reason for criticizing sb. **O:** friend, colleague. **o:** fault, failing; neglect, laxness □ *The Government cannot be **reproached with** neglect of those on fixed incomes.* □ *She's not mean or vindictive. That's the last thing **with** which one could **reproach** her.* ⇨ previous entry.

reprove (for) [B2 pass emph rel] (formal) criticize sternly, chide (for). **O:** people, flock; follower, member. **o:** indolence, backsliding, extravagance □ *Southerners are **reproved** (by Northerners) **for** their indolence and moral laxity.* □ ***For** all these shortcomings they should expect to be sternly **reproved**.*

repulse (from) [B2 pass emph rel] (formal) force to withdraw (from), repel (from) (q v). **O:** enemy; attacker, invader. **o:** position, shore □ *The enemy broke through the front line, but were firmly **repulsed from** the higher ground by cavalry.*

request (from) [B2 pass emph rel] (formal) ask sb for sth, ask sth of sb, in a polite but formal way. **O:** fact, detail; help, advice. **o:** office, agency, department □ *The sales manager **requested** up-to-date information **from** his men in the field* (or: ***requested** them to send up-to-date information*). □ *The secretary presented a list of charitable trusts **from** which we had **requested** financial support* (or: *which we had **requested** to give financial support*).

require (from/of) [B2 pass rel] (formal) expect, demand, of sb as a duty or obligation. **O:** obedience, conformity, good manners; that one should behave, be punctual. **o:** employee, child, pupil □ *All he **requires of** a class is that they should be clean, punctual and submissive.* □ *He did all that was **required** (**of** him) by the regulations.* □ *To ask for cleanliness and tidiness is to **require** a good deal **from** a small child.*

requisition (from) (for) [B2 pass emph rel] (military) demand sb to supply goods or services for military use, esp during an emergency. **S:** the military; officer. **O:** stores; billet; fodder. **o:** (***from***) civilian; farmer, villager; (***for***) troops; horses □ *A sergeant went from door to door **requisitioning** billets **for** the men.* □ *The army **requisitioned** horses **from** the farmers **for** their baggage train* (or: *They **requisitioned** the farmers **for** horses to equip their baggage train*).

rescue (from) [B2 pass emph rel] deliver, set free (from); preserve (from). **O:** child, (helpless) person; captive; criminal, down-and-out; author, book. **o:** danger, drowning; prison; misery, indigence; oblivion □ *The fire brigade **rescued** three children **from** the top floor.* □ *The film had been branded as 'uncommercial' by the major distributors. **From** this judgement no* *amount of critical acclaim could **rescue** it.* □ *By unearthing and identifying manuscript scores, musical scholars have **rescued** several minor composers of the period **from** oblivion.*

research into [A2 pass emph rel] study, analyse, sth to discover answers to problems, extend knowledge etc. **S:** (social, natural) scientist, historian. **o:** custom, habit; structure, system; period, reign □ *He is **researching into** the reading problems of young school children.* □ *This is an important problem **into** which too few social scientists have **researched**.*

reserve (for)[1] [B2 pass emph rel] keep in store, keep back, for later use. **O:** food, ration; energy, strength. **o:** later; the winter; emergency □ ***Reserve** some energy **for** the last lap of the course.* □ *A very bright future is **reserved for** you* (= is in store for you).

reserve (for)[2] [B2 pass emph rel] book a place, or indicate that one is being kept free (for sb), esp on public transport, or in a theatre, stadium or restaurant. **O:** seat, place, table. **o:** passenger; latecomer, special guest □ *'Try to **reserve** a seat **for** me* (or: ***reserve** me a seat*) *on the Saturday afternoon coach.'* □ *The front row is **reserved for** overseas visitors.* □ *'Do you mind if I sit here?' 'I'm sorry, I'm **reserving** the place **for** a friend.'*

reside in [A2 emph rel] (formal) be represented by, be embodied in (q v). **S:** authority, power. **o:** body, chamber; king, president, court □ *The highest judicial authority **resides in** the Supreme Court.* □ ***In** which of the two Houses does the legislative power really **reside**?*

resign (from) [A2 emph rel] (formally) relinquish a post etc; give up[2] (q v). **o:** post, seat, place; the civil service, magistrature □ *He has **resigned (from)** his post as Permanent Secretary.* □ *They are intending to **resign from** the committee.* □ from is deletable before *post, job* etc, but not before *committee, panel* etc.

resign (oneself) to [B2 pass emph rel] accept, though not happily, sth which cannot be avoided. **o:** consequences, outcome; fate, destiny; not succeeding in sth, losing sb □ *He must **resign himself**, in fact, **to** the loss of a percentage.* PL □ *'There's no escaping death, it catches you in the end; my end is here and now, and now I'm **resigned to** it.'* HSG □ *With less than a week to go before I left, I had **resigned myself to** not being able to add a Golden Cat to the collection* (i e of wild animals). BB □ passive, as in the second example, with *be, become, seem.*

resolve into [B2 pass emph rel] present in detail as, analyse into. **O:** problem, task; body, organization; organism, substance. **o:** factors; components, constituents, elements □ *The task confronting us may be **resolved into** three basic requirements.* □ *The meeting **resolved** itself **into** a number of working committees.*

resolve (on/upon) [A2 pass emph rel] (formal) decide firmly to have or do sth; agree (on/upon) (q v). **o:** action; attack, advance; success; expansion, growth □ *The general **resolved on** an approach by night to recapture the lost ground.* □ *A plan was **resolved on** which avoided a major restructuring of the school system.*

resort to [A2 pass adj emph rel] use, adopt, a particular means (usu unpleasant) to achieve one's ends; have recourse to (q v). **o:** guile, trickery; force, violence □ *Terrorists **resorted to** bombing city centres as a means of achieving their political aims.* □ *These are means we have never **resorted to** to obtain information.*

resound in/through [A2] ⇨ next entry.

resound (with) [A2 emph rel] echo loudly (with), ring (with) (q v). **S:** hall, house, church. **o:** cry, singing, music □ *The streets **resounded with** happy voices* (cf *Happy voices **resounded in/through** the streets*). □ *The tower **resounded with** the clamour of bells.*

respect (for) [B2 pass emph rel] honour, esteem (for). **o:** courage, integrity; not yielding to pressure, standing by one's promises □ *'There aren't many who would endanger their political careers, as he did, over an issue of principle. **For** this one must **respect** him.'* □ *The qualities **for** which he is chiefly **respected** are his ability to make quick decisions and his tenacity in following them through.*

respond (to) [A2 pass emph rel] behave in answer to, or as a result of, sth; react (to) (q v). **S:** body; muscle, limb; livestock, pets; plane, car. **o:** exercise, fresh air, good food; careful handling □ *The patient is **responding** well **to** the new course of drugs.* □ *Their envoys show no sign of **responding to** our proposals.* □ ***To** this kind of teaching the class had always **responded** badly.*

rest on one's laurels [A2] pause to enjoy the fame one has earned by one's work (usu the suggestion is that one should be going on to harder achievements) □ *There is no sense in **resting on your laurels**. You still have difficult problems to face.* □ *It might be better for his reputation if he stopped writing and **rested on his laurels**, as some other novelists had.* PW

rest upon [A2 emph rel] have as its basis, be based on (⇨ base on/upon). **S:** case, argument, contention; fame, reputation. **o:** (sound, poor) evidence, hearsay; writing, speeches □ *Keats' reputation as a poet **rests** largely **upon** the Odes and the later sonnets.* □ ***Upon** such slender evidence as this did his case **rest**.* □ *All our hopes **rested upon** this venture.*

rest with [A2 emph rel] be sb's responsibility, be in sb's hands. **S:** choice, decision; result, outcome. **o:** elector; manager, doctor; consumer □ *Whether the talks are successful or not **rests with** a small number of men.* □ *It **rests with** you to settle your differences as best you can.* □ Subject may be a clause introduced by an inf, or *when, whether, how* etc.

restore in [B2 pass emph rel] give back to sb the belief that sb or sth is powerful, efficient etc. **O:** ⚠ faith, belief, confidence. **o:** government, civil service, police; currency, economy □ *These measures have helped to **restore** a belief **in** our capacity to manage our affairs.* □ *The victories in Africa had **restored** public confidence **in** the ability of the Army to achieve results.* MFM

restore (to)[1] [B2 pass emph rel] let sb have his property again. **O:** money, jewellery; book, picture. **o:** owner, trustee; collection □ *The stolen paintings have been **restored to** their rightful owners.* □ *I'll see to it that your property is **restored** (**to** you).*

restore (to)[2] [B2 pass emph rel] give back (to sb) a post, honour etc which he has lost. **O:** title, honour; position, office; command, rank. **o:** (public) servant; minister; officer □ *The officer was acquitted by a higher court and had his rank* ***restored to*** *him.* □ ***To*** *those servants who had remained loyal the king* ***restored*** *their former titles.* ⇨ restore to.

restore (to)[3] [B2 pass emph rel] establish order etc once again (in a place). **O:** calm, peace, (law and) order. **o:** country, city □ *It will be some years before peace is finally* ***restored*** (***to*** *our country*). □ *Stewards struggled to* ***restore*** *order* ***to*** *the meeting.*

restore (to)[4] [B2 pass] rebuild, repair, redecorate etc, sth so that it is as it once was. **O:** building, quarter; painting, sculpture. **o:** (former, earlier) state, condition; splendour □ *The palace gardens have been* ***restored to*** *their former grandeur.* □ *The portrait has been carefully* ***restored*** (***to*** *its original state*) *by museum experts.*

restore (to)[5] [B2 pass] treat sb skilfully so that he becomes healthy again. **O:** patient, (sick, disturbed) person. **o:** ⚠ (full, sound) health, sanity □ *He feels completely* ***restored*** (***to*** *health*) *after a period of intensive care.*

restore to [B2 pass rel] put sb back in a place of responsibility (from which he was removed). **O:** employee, officer. **o:** post, command □ *The officials freed under the amnesty have been* ***restored to*** *their posts.* □ *He seems in danger of losing the command* ***to*** *which he was recently* ***restored.*** ⇨ restore (to)[2].

restrain (from) [B2 pass emph rel] prevent sb, by firm control (from doing sth). **O:** spectator, crowd; follower; child. **o:** violence, mischief; doing harm, injuring oneself □ *The police had difficulty in* ***restraining*** *the crowd* ***from*** *rushing onto the* (football) *pitch.* □ *Sometimes children must be* ***restrained*** (e g ***from*** *touching things*) *in their own interests.*

restrict (to)[1] [B2 pass emph rel] keep sth below a certain level, or within particular limits; limit (to) (q v). **O:** traffic; output, intake; discussion, debate. **o:** 30 mph; ten kilos, five litres; (certain) topics, questions □ *The doctor has* ***restricted*** *my smoking* ***to*** *ten cigarettes a day.* □ *'I'm afraid we shall have to* ***restrict*** *discussion* ***to*** *matters arising from the document.'*

restrict (to)[2] [B2 pass rel] order, ensure, that only specified people see certain materials. **O:** document, paper, file; film, tape. **o:** (senior) officer, official, minister □ *The information in that booklet is* ***restricted to*** *military personnel.*

result from [A2 emph rel] happen as a consequence of, be the result of. **S:** accident, injury; loss, damage; improvement, success. **o:** inattention, neglect, absence; help, involvement □ *The goal* ***resulted from*** *a misunderstanding between two defenders.* □ *Much good may* ***result from*** *his intervention in the dispute.* ⇨ next entry.

result in [A2] have as an outcome or consequence. **S:** talks, negotiations; match; help, participation; failure, absence. **o:** agreement, stalemate; victory, draw; improvement; disaster, accident □ *The talks have* ***resulted in*** *a lessening of suspicion.* □ *The game* ***resulted in*** *a goalless draw.* ⇨ previous entry.

retail (to) [B2 pass emph rel] repeat (to), pass on (to)[1] (q v), in detail. **O:** story, tale; news, gossip. **o:** all and sundry, everyone who would listen; reporter, police □ *'I shouldn't share any confidences with her, if I were you. Before you know where you are they'll be* ***retailed to*** *half the street.'* □ *Investigations revealed that a senior executive in the company had been* ***retailing*** *industrial secrets* ***to*** *a rival concern.*

retail (to) (at) [A2 rel B2 pass rel] be sold, sell, retail (i e from a shop direct to the customer) (at a certain price). **S:** [A2] **O:** [B2] goods, merchandise; article; soap, sugar. **o:** (***to***) customer, shopper; (***at***) (special, bargain) price; discount □ *What do the family-size cartons* ***retail at?*** □ *Supermarkets can afford to* ***retail*** *cigarettes* ***at*** *a couple of pence below the price charged by most tobacconists.*

retain (on/over/upon) [B2 pass emph rel] continue to influence, control, dominate etc. **O:** control, dominance, hold, influence. **o:** child, wife; public, electorate; game, match □ *The generals struggled to* ***retain*** *their control* ***over*** *a very fluid battle.* □ *This great player* ***retains*** *his strong hold* ***on*** *the affections of the crowd.*

retaliate (against) [A2 pass] hurt, punish, sb in return for some offence or injury one has suffered. **o:** attack, incursion; bandit, hooligan, tough; conspiracy □ *The regular forces would* ***retaliate*** *swiftly* ***against*** *guerrilla attacks from across the border.* □ *Boycott* ***retaliated against*** *some pugnacious bowling by driving the next two balls past the bowler for four.*

retire (from) [A2 rel] leave, because of age, fatigue etc. **o:** job; the civil service, business; fight, struggle □ *He's thinking of* ***retiring from*** *his post several years before the normal age* (of retirement). □ *Jones* ***retired from*** *the 10 000 metres after completing only four laps of the track.*

retire (from) (to) [A2 rel] (military) move back (from one position) (to another) (usu in an orderly manner); retreat (from) (q v) □ *We* ***retired to*** *prepared positions behind the river line.* □ *The enemy were careful to destroy the fortifications* ***from*** *which they were* ***retiring.***

retire (to bed) [A2] (formal) go to bed □ *The old people would* ***retire to bed*** *early, to save fuel and light.*

retreat (from) [A2 emph rel] move back (from), because of a threat of defeat, capture etc; withdraw (from) (q v). **S:** army, troops; dealer, agent, prospective buyer; negotiator. **o:** line, position; deal, arrangement □ *The positions* ***from*** *which the enemy had* ***retreated*** *were extensively booby-trapped.* □ *Through excessive caution, we felt, our backers* ***retreated from*** *a firm undertaking to meet the entire cost of building.*

retrieve (from) [B2 pass emph rel] find, recover, sth which was believed lost. **O:** belongings, furniture; letter; valuables. **o:** fire; wreck, ruin □ *Some of the passengers were able to* ***retrieve*** *their luggage* ***from*** *the wrecked aircraft.* □ *He* ***retrieved*** *the papers* ***from*** *the dusty files where they had lain for years.*

return to[1] [A2 pass emph rel] consider again, go back to (in the course of an argument or exposition). **o:** theme, point, proposal □ *In the course of my remarks I shall* ***return*** *several times* ***to*** *this statement.* □ *'I wonder if we could* ***return*** *for a moment* ***to*** *what you were saying earlier.'*

return to[2] [A2 pass emph rel] resume, adopt, again. **o:** (former, old) ways, habits, style of life; tactics, methods □ *After going straight for a bit, he will* ***return to*** *petty thieving.* □ *The Chan-*

*cellor has **returned to** the familiar mixture of credit restriction and higher personal taxation.*

return to[3] [A2 rel] go back to a previous state. **S:** farm, estate; arable land. **o:** desert, scrub, bush □ *West African farmers may cut a new farm from the bush every one or two years, allowing the land previously cultivated to **return to** forest.*

rev up [A1 B1i pass adj] (informal) increase the speed of revolutions of an engine (usu before moving off). **S:** [A1 B1] driver, motorist. **S:** [A1] **O:** [B1] engine; car, lorry □ *I could hear the cars of the soldiers and the diplomats **revving up**.* QA □ *Soon we hear the sound of the lorry **revving up** and moving off.* ITAJ

reveal (to) [B2 pass emph rel] make known (to sb) sth that was previously hidden. **O:** fact, detail; truth, falsehood; hopelessness, inadequacy □ *These reports have **revealed to** the insurgents the precariousness of their position.* □ *He is not the sort of person **to** whom such important policy decisions should be **revealed**.*

revel in [A2 pass rel] take great pleasure or delight in. **o:** display, ceremony; mischief, gossip; poking fun, taking risks □ *As a student, he **revelled in** mildly dangerous escapades, such as climbing university buildings at night.* □ *He wanted to go out on night patrol alone; that was the kind of situation of personal risk **in** which he **revelled**.*

revenge (oneself) on [B2 emph rel] satisfy one's pride by hurting sb in return for an injury one has suffered from him; take revenge (on) (for) (q v) □ *In some societies it is a point of honour to **revenge oneself on*** (or: *be **revenged on***) *somebody who has insulted a member of one's family.*

revert to[1] [A2 pass emph rel] (formal) consider again, go back to (in the course of an argument or exposition); return to[1] (q v). **o:** statement, argument; question, matter □ *The Minister **reverted to** the point several times in the course of his speech.* □ *'I must ask the Court's indulgence as I **revert** again **to** the events of that Friday evening.'*

revert to[2] [A2 pass emph rel] (formal) adopt, resume, again; return to[2] (q v). **o:** (old, former) ways, habits; methods, policies □ *Following the resignation of the Northern Ireland Executive, the UK Government has in effect **reverted to** a system of direct rule from Westminster.*

revert to[3] [A2 rel] (formal) go back to a previous state; return to[3] (q v). **S:** land, farm. **o:** desert, scrub □ *The fields which it is no longer profitable to cultivate have been allowed to **revert to** moorland.*

revert to[4] [A2 rel] (legal) become the property of sb again at some time or under certain conditions. **S:** property; estate, land. **o:** original owner; State, Church, Crown □ *If he dies without leaving an heir, his lands will **revert to** the Crown.* □ *When the lease on your house runs out, the property will **revert to** Smith and Sons.*

revolt (against) [A2 emph rel] set oneself in opposition to authority; rebel (against) (q v). **S:** nation, people; youth, women. **o:** leader, government; tyranny, oppression □ *Women were **revolting against** the restrictions on job opportunities.* □ *Youthful enthusiasts may feel frustrated if there is nothing **against** which they can **revolt**.*

revolt against/from [A2 emph rel] feel disgust or horror at, be revulsed by. **S:** sensitive, decent, compassionate (person). **o:** cruelty, injustice, corruption □ *My soul **revolted against** this way of doing business, and I made that very plain.* MFM □ *Humane observers **revolted from** the employment of young children in the mines* (or: *were **revolted by** the employment* etc).

revolve about/around [A2 emph rel] have as its centre, have as its chief topic or concern, centre on/round (q v). **S:** one's life; argument, debate, discussion; dispute; struggle. **o:** family, work; question, matter; admission, exclusion (of sb); priority, method □ *Mary has no outside interests at all. Her whole life **revolves around** her husband and the children.* □ *The dispute at the moment **revolves around** whether other delegates should attend.* □ *This is the point **about** which discussion now **revolves** and on which it has always been inconclusive.*

reward (for) [B2 pass emph rel] pay sb in return for sth he has done. **O:** staff, employee; finder (of lost property). **o:** work, services; honesty, loyalty; giving sth back □ *Miners feel they are inadequately **rewarded for** the dangerous work they do.* □ *Anyone returning the necklace will be handsomely **rewarded*** (***for*** *doing so*).

rhyme (with) [A2 rel B2 pass emph rel] (of words, or parts of words, at the ends of lines of verse) have the same sounds (as each other); set at the ends of lines words etc, having the same sounds. **S:** [A2] **O:** [B2] morn; striding; air. **o:** dawn; riding; there □ *'Seen' **rhymes with** 'been'* (or: *'Seen' and 'been' **rhyme**); they are also close in spelling.* □ *In an early sonnet Keats **rhymes** 'eyes' **with** 'surmise'* (or: ***rhymes** 'eyes' and 'surmise'*).

rid of [B2 pass rel] free sth or sb of. **O:** country, town, house; friend; oneself. **o:** bandit, criminal; pest, rodent; burden, illness □ *The Pied Piper promised to **rid** Hamelin **of** its rats.* □ *She would like to **rid** herself **of** these terrible fears* (or: *be/get **rid of** these terrible fears*). □ *At last we are **rid of** him!*

riddle (with) [B2 pass emph rel] make many holes in sth (esp by shooting at it). **O:** building, fortification; vehicle, aircraft; body. **o:** shot, bullets, splinters □ *The balloon was **riddled with** anti-aircraft fire and sank burning to the ground.* □ *With his first burst the flight commander missed, **with** the second he **riddled** the bomber's port wing.*

riddled (with) [pass (B2)] (be) full of holes, weaknesses etc. **S:** floor, panelling; curtain, carpet; argument, case. **o:** holes; termites, woodworm, moth; faults, inconsistencies □ *'Have you seen the joists under the bathroom floor? They're **riddled with** fine holes.'* □ *'Yes, I've read the report and I don't think much of it. It's **riddled with** the most elementary errors.'*

ride down [B1i pass] direct one's horse at sb as if to knock him down. **S:** troops, police. **O:** spectator, onlooker □ *Opponents of the Bill would try to break up meetings by threatening to **ride down** supporters of reform.*

ride for a fall [A2] act so recklessly that disaster is likely □ *He has survived many escapades, but this will be his last: he's **riding for a fall**.* □ continuous tenses only.

ride out [B1iii pass] survive, weather, safely. **S:** ship, aircraft; country, government. **O:** storm, tempest; crisis, emergency □ *Is his boat strong enough to* **ride out** *the storms of the Cape?* □ *Commentators doubt whether the Minister can* **ride out** *the present tense situation.* □ *That Friday night was the last time the Executive felt it had the strength to* **ride out** *the Loyalist strike.* ST

ride to hounds [A2] (sport) go fox-hunting □ *In the Eighteenth Century, the clergy, like the nobility and gentry, often* **rode to hounds**. □ *He paid a subscription to the Hunt but never* **rode to hounds**, *though his daughter always did.* DBM

rig out [B1i nom pass adj] provide, supply, with clothes, kit etc; dress for a special occasion, or in a strange manner. **O:** crew, staff; oneself □ *He* **rigged** *the children* **out** *in special boots and trousers for their climbing holiday.* □ *She was* **rigged out** *in an ancient green skirt of her mother's.* □ *Some of the crew were very oddly* **rigged out** (or: *had a very odd* **rig-out**).

rig up [B1i pass adj] mount, place in position, assemble, ready for use; make sth from materials perhaps not intended for the purpose. **O:** record-player, stereo; camera, lights; shelter, hut, raft □ *Then we got the recording machine and* **rigged** *it* **up** *near the rattlesnakes's lair.* DF □ *On one side of the room they had* **rigged up** *a small bar.* SML

ring about/around/round [B1i pass] form a circle around sb or sth, esp to defend or imprison him or it. **S:** bodyguard, security man; enemy, intriguer. **O:** president; palace; town, fortress □ *The security services took care to ensure that the President was* **ringed around** *by a party of exceptionally tall policemen.* □ *Germany in 1914 was not* **ringed about** *with enemies, as Kaiser Wilhelm claimed, but it was faced with the possibility of war on two fronts.*

ring around/round [A1 A2] telephone one address after another, esp to find which of a number of tradesman can provide the cheapest, or best, service. **S:** householder, shopkeeper, motorist. **o:** shop, store; dealer □ *Before you start ordering oil for the central heating* **ring around** *the suppliers to see who will offer you the best terms.* □ *'Maybe we'd better have the party tomorrow, instead of on Saturday. I'll* **ring round** *to find out who's free to come.'*

ring back[1] [A1] telephone sb again (e g having failed to contact him a first time) □ *'I'm afraid Mr Thomson isn't in at the moment. Would you like to* **ring back** *later in the morning?'*

ring back[2] [B1ii pass] after speaking to sb on the telephone, telephone him again later (e g to give him more information) □ *'I haven't got all the details with me at the moment, Peter. Can I* **ring** *you* **back** *in about ten minutes?'*

ring the curtain down/up [B1i pass] (theatre) signal for the curtain to be lowered or raised; (generally) mark the end or beginning (of) □ *When* **the curtain** *was* **rung down** *on the first performance, the audience broke into enthusiastic applause.* □ *With the arrival in England of William of Orange,* **the curtain** *was* **rung up** *on a new epoch in our history.*

ring (for) [A2 pass rel] summon a servant etc by ringing a bell. **o:** maid, butler, waiter; service; tea, breakfast □ *'Would you mind* **ringing for** *some more hot water?'* □ *'If there's anything you need, all you have to do is* **ring** (**for** *it*).*'*

ring (in) [A2] ⇨ ring (with).

ring in the New (Year) (and) ring out the Old (Year) [B1i pass] announce, or celebrate the end of one year and the beginning of the next by ringing bells (or, by giving a party etc) □ *I bought another whisky and put gloom out of my mind: I was* **ringing a New Year in** *as well as* **an Old Year out**. SML □ *The subject of this week's cover* (of the 'Radio Times') *is the* **ringing out** *of* **the Old** *and the* **ringing in** *of* **the New**. RT

ring off [A1] end a telephone conversation by replacing the receiver □ *'I'll have to* **ring off** *now: I have a train to catch.'* □ *'Damn your dinner,' I heard him howl as I* **rang off**. CON

ring the changes (on) [B2 pass emph rel] keep varying one's choice from a range of things. **o:** clothes, wardrobe; style, cut; act, performance □ *They give cooks a whole range of interesting new flavours* **on** *which to* **ring the changes**. TO □ *After a week at the hotel I had* **rung** *all* **the** *possible* **changes on** *their limited menu.*

ring out[1] [A1] make a sudden, sharp noise. **S:** shot, cry, scream □ *A sudden report* **rang out** *— like the sound of a car backfiring.*

ring out[2] [A1] (of a subscriber's number being obtained by the operator) give the 'ringing' tone. **S:** call; number □ *'Hello, caller. The number you wanted is* **ringing out** *now.'* (Pause) *'I'm afraid they're not answering. Would you like to try again later?'*

ring out the Old (Year) [B1i pass] ⇨ ring in the New (Year) (and) ring out the Old (Year).

ring round[1] [B1i pass] form a circle round. ⇨ ring about/around/round.

ring round[2] [A1 A2] telephone one address after another. ⇨ ring around/round.

ring up[1] [A1 B1i pass] call sb on the telephone □ *'I do wish he'd get out of the habit of* **ringing** *me* **up** *at mealtimes.'* □ *'I'll* **ring** *(you)* **up** *some time during the week.'*

ring up[2] [B1i pass] record the amounts being paid for goods by pressing keys or buttons on a cash register. **O:** sale, purchase; goods, groceries □ *In the village store our weekend groceries were* **rung up** *on an old-fashioned cash register.*

ring the curtain up [B1i pass] ⇨ ring the curtain down/up.

ring (with) [A2] be filled with a ringing sound; resound (with) (q v). **S:** hall, street; ears, head. **o:** shout, cry □ *The playground* **rang with** *children's cries.* □ *Our ears* **rang with** *their insults* (cf *Their insults* **rang in** *our ears*).

rinse (out) [B1i nom pass adj] wash sth with clean water, in order to remove impurities etc. **O:** clothing; pot, basin; mouth □ *After washing them in soapy water,* **rinse** *the clothes* **(out)** *thoroughly.* □ **Rinse** *your mouth* **(out)** *well* (or: *Give your mouth a good* **rinse(-out)**) *to get rid of the taste.* ⇨ next entry.

rinse out/out of [B1i pass B2 pass] remove impurities etc by washing sth in clean water. **O:** dirt, impurities; soap; coffee-grounds. **o:** clothes; pan, cup □ *Be careful to* **rinse** *all the soap* **out of** *your hair.* □ *Don't* **rinse** *the tea-leaves* **out** *into the sink: you'll clog the drain.* ⇨ previous entry.

rip across [B1ii pass] divide sth in two by pulling at it sharply and with force; tear across (q v). **O:** paper, letter; sheet, shirt □ *In a particularly fierce tackle one player had his shirt* ***ripped across****.* □ *Without a word he* ***ripped*** *the report* ***across*** *and threw the halves into the basket.*

rip apart [B1ii pass] dismantle with sharp, forceful movements; disarrange a place (esp when searching for sth); tear apart[1] (q v). **O:** garment; book; room, flat □ *'For Heaven's sake, get my paper away from the kittens before they* ***rip*** *it* ***apart****.'* □ *'The electrical wiring in the house will all need to be replaced, and I dare say the house will be* ***ripped apart*** *in the process.'*

rip away (from) [B1i pass B3 pass emph rel] take away, remove, (from) with a sharp, forceful movement. **O:** curtain, cover; cloak, veil (of secrecy etc). **o:** wall, bed; talk, activity □ *He* ***ripped away*** *the faded hangings* ***from*** *the wall.* □ *With one remark he had* ***ripped away*** *the mask of pretence which covered their activities.*

rip down [B1i pass adj] take down with a sharp, forceful movement from a higher level; cause to fall by pulling sharply at the base; tear down (q v). **O:** curtain, picture; hut, fence; undergrowth, tree □ *The crowd* ***ripped down*** *posters depicting their political opponents.* □ *The coarse grass and dry shrubs were* ***ripped down*** *by the blades of the cutter.*

rip in half/two [B2 pass] separate in two parts with a sharp, tearing movement; tear in half/two (q v). **O:** paper, cloth; document, form; shirt □ *John* ***ripped*** *the letter* ***in two*** *and threw the halves in the fire.* □ *'That last tackle was a bit dirty. The winger nearly had his shirt* ***ripped in half****.'*

rip into [A2 pass] make a hole in, with a vigorous, tearing movement; make a vigorous attack upon; tear into (q v). **S:** saw, cutter; bulldozer; boxer. **o:** tree; plaster, wall; opponent □ *The animal's teeth* ***ripped into*** *the meat we had thrown him.* □ *Bullets from his wing guns* ***ripped into*** *the fuselage of the bomber.* □ *In the fifth round the champion* ***ripped into*** *his opponent with short jabs to the body.*

rip off[1] [B1i pass adj] remove, separate, with a sharp tearing movement. **S:** gale, wind; saw. **O:** roof; branch; limb □ *Both wings of the aircraft were* ***ripped off*** *in the crash.* □ *He* ***ripped off*** *one end of the thick envelope and pulled out the letter.*

rip off[2] [B1i nom pass adj] (slang) steal; rob; knock off[6] (q v). **O:** money, car; bank, shop □ *Is it surprising to find students* ***ripping off*** *books* (cf ***ripping off*** *a bookshop*)? □ *'Gerry* ***ripped off*** *two old ladies in the street yesterday. He makes more out of* ***rip-offs*** *in one day than I earn in a week.'*

rip out/out of [B1i pass adj B2 pass rel] take, remove, from the centre of sth with a sharp tearing action; tear out/out of (q v). **O:** page, enclosure; middle, heart. **o:** magazine; city □ *He* ***ripped out*** *and destroyed any news items referring to the theft.* □ *The planners have* ***ripped out*** *the maze of narrow streets and old buildings which formed the centre of the city.*

rip to [B2 pass emph] destroy with vigorous tearing movements; rend to (q v); attack critically, demolish. **O:** cloth, paper; wood; argument, speech. **o:** ⚠ pieces, shreds, matchwood, tatters □ *Wooden buildings on the front were* ***ripped to*** *matchwood by the gale.* □ *'Can't you see your story doesn't stand up to close examination? Anyone could* ***rip*** *it* ***to*** *shreds.'*

rip up[1] [B1i pass adj] destroy by pulling vigorously; tear up[1] (q v). **O:** paper, document; cloth; wood; road-surface, tarmac □ *The machine* ***rips up*** *old cloth to provide fibres for new material.* □ *'Do you get free coupons for soap stuck through your letterbox?' 'Yes, and I* ***rip*** *them* ***up*** *and throw them in the waste-bin.'*

rip up[2] [B1i pass] vigorously renounce, abandon, sth; tear up[2] (q v). **O:** treaty, agreement □ *Very little faith can be placed in these bargaining processes if agreements can be* ***ripped up*** *when the ink is hardly dry on the paper.*

rise above [A2 pass rel] show that one is superior to sth and can abandon it; surmount, overcome. **o:** meanness, greed; strife, squabbling; difficulty, hardship □ *Surely we can* ***rise above*** *petty personal jealousies.* □ *It must be hoped that the MCC* (cricket club) *will* ***rise above*** *this anxiety.* G

rise from the ashes [A2] return to its former state after having been badly damaged or destroyed. **S:** country, city; industry, economy □ *After a few years of active reconstruction, many famous cities* ***rose from the ashes*** *of war.* □ *New factories were everywhere* ***rising from the ashes*** *of the old.*

rise from the dead/grave [A2] reappear alive after having been believed dead; become conscious after having supposedly died □ *Jones had disappeared at sea a week before — now here he was, as if* ***risen from the dead****.* □ *No one could emerge from that avalanche alive, unless one believed that men could* ***rise from the grave****.* ⇨ raise from the dead.

rise from the ranks [A2] (military) become a commissioned officer (in the armed services) after having served, usu for some time, as a NCO □ *Before the Second World War it was unusual to find a British officer who had* ***risen from the ranks*** *— most were the products of the military academies.*

rise in the world [A2] reach, achieve, a higher social and economic position in society □ *The customs officer explained that he had once been a radio engineer, but it was difficult to understand whether he had* ***risen*** *or fallen* ***in the world*** *by local standards.* BM □ *He has* ***risen*** *far* ***in the world****, financially, without however widening his interests or his sympathies.*

rise to a/the bait [A2 rel] respond to sth aimed at interesting or attracting one; fall into a trap prepared for one □ *She would wear her new perfume — this was* ***a bait to*** *which he had always* ***risen*** *in the past.* □ *They left food and ammunition on the track — but would the enemy* ***rise to*** *so obvious* ***a bait****?*

rise to the challenge/occasion [A2 rel] show the daring, imagination etc which fits a particular occasion □ *Her breath was clean and fresh. I* ***rose to the occasion*** *like a shot. 'Kiss me, my sweet,' I said.* SPL □ ***The challenge*** *of risk or adventure was one* ***to*** *which he could be expected to* ***rise****.*

rise to one's feet [A2] stand up (usu to make a speech, propose a toast etc). **S:** chairman, member, guest □ *Someone* ***rose to his feet*** *to question the chairman on a point of order.* □ *He* ***rose***

unsteadily ***to his feet*** *to reply to the speech of welcome.*

rise to the surface [A2] come to the surface of a lake, sea etc; become visible (after having been hidden). **S:** fish, submarine; fact, circumstance □ *Great waves formed and spread as the hulk* ***rose to the surface.*** □ *Certain unpleasant aspects of this case are now* ***rising to the surface.*** ⇨ raise to the surface.

rivet on [B2 pass emph rel] give one's whole attention to, look very attentively at. **O:** ⚠ one's attention, eyes, gaze. **o:** scene, spectacle □ *His whole attention was* ***riveted on*** *the little drama unfolding before him.* □ *He* ***riveted*** *his eyes* ***on*** *the door from which the procession was to emerge.*

rivet to the ground/spot [B2 pass] cause to remain completely still; root to the ground/spot (q v). **S:** news; shock, explosion. **O:** spectator, onlooker □ *The sudden roar of low-flying aircraft* ***riveted*** *us* ***to the spot.*** □ *He stood* ***riveted to the ground*** *— it was some minutes before he could respond to the message.*

roam about/around [A1 A2] move about in an aimless way. **S:** vagrant; explorer; cattle, sheep. **o:** country, world; plain, prairie □ *He was always a rather footloose character,* ***roaming about*** *all over the place, picking up odd jobs, but never settling to anything.* □ *Before the fencing of the open range the herds* ***roamed around*** *freely.*

roar (at) [A2 pass rel] address in a loud, deep voice (like that of a lion). **S:** crowd, mob; sergeant, teacher. **o:** speaker; squad, class □ *I dislike being* ***roared at*** *as though I were a recruit on parade.* □ *The Liverpool captain waved to the crowd and the fans massed behind the goal* ***roared*** *back* ***at*** *him.*

rob (of)[1] [B2 pass rel] steal sth from sb. **o:** money, watch, wallet □ *He was* ***robbed of*** *his week's wages by a pickpocket.* □ *'It's a bit unfair to* ***rob*** *you* ***of*** *a cigar and then ask you personal questions into the bargain.'* HD

rob (of)[2] [B2 pass rel] prevent sb from enjoying sth that is within his grasp. **o:** success, victory; rest, sleep □ *Arsenal were* ***robbed of*** *victory in the last minutes of play.* □ *'That confounded cat* ***robbed*** *me* ***of*** *a good night's sleep.'*

rock to sleep [B2 pass] send sb to sleep by rocking his cradle, chair etc. **O:** baby, child □ *David was* ***rocked to sleep*** *in his mother's arms.* □ *The movement of the ship* ***rocked*** *us* ***to sleep.***

roll about [A1] (informal) enjoy oneself, laugh, hilariously. **S:** audience; spectator, listener. **A:** helplessly; in their seats, in the aisles □ *The comedians of the silent movies don't seem to lose their appeal. They can still have an audience* ***rolling about*** *in the aisles.*

roll one's eyes at [B2] (informal) move one's eyes about so as to attract or seduce. **S:** girl, woman □ *'Stop* ***rolling*** *your* ***eyes at*** *every good-looking man that comes into the room!'*

roll away [A1] move away, recede, steadily. **S:** cloud, fog, mist, smoke □ *A stiff breeze got up and the thick smoke* ***rolled away.***

roll back[1] [B1i pass adj] remove sth by bending and turning it over and over. **O:** cover, tarpaulin, carpet □ *The car has a soft hood, which can be* ***rolled back*** *in fine weather.* □ *'Let's* ***roll back*** *the carpets and have a dance.'*

roll back[2] [A1] move back in steady succession. **S:** ⚠ the tide, waves □ *The waves* ***rolled back*** *to reveal a black wooden box, half embedded in the sand.*

roll back[3] [A1 B1i pass] (cause to) move back, retreat, in a steady, uniform way. **S:** [A1] **O:** [B1] enemy; tide, wave (of disaffection, unrest) □ *The battle line* ***rolled back*** *and forth with neither side being able to claim a clear victory.* □ *The new administration is confident of* ***rolling back*** *the tide of unrest which is sweeping the country.*

roll back[4] [A1 B1iii] (of a time in the past) return, recall it, steadily to one's consciousness. **S:** [A1] **O:** [B1] ⚠ the years, centuries □ *As his father spoke, the years* ***rolled back*** *and John saw himself as a small boy again, playing on the beach at Sandgate.* □ *History as well narrated as this can* ***roll back*** *the intervening centuries and set the period vividly in focus.*

roll by [A1] pass in steady succession. **S:** ⚠ time; (the) months, years □ *Months and then years* ***rolled by*** *until the most optimistic of the prisoners gave up hope of a reprieve.* □ *Many years had* ***rolled by*** *since I last sat talking to her.*

tear(s) roll down [A2] fall in a steady stream. **o:** ⚠ cheeks, face □ *As his voice rose the* ***tears*** *began to* ***roll down*** *her cheeks.*

roll in[1] [A1] arrive in a steady stream. **S:** money, gift, donation; offer, promise (of help etc) □ *Since the appeal was launched, cheques, postal orders and cash have kept* ***rolling in.*** □ *A flood of specimens* (of wild life) *would soon be* ***rolling in.*** BB

roll in[2] [A2] (informal) have a good deal of. **o:** money; jewels, furs □ *'What do the Americans want with £250? They're* ***rolling in*** *dollars.'* RM □ continuous tenses only.

roll off [B1i pass] print, duplicate, by passing paper etc through the rollers of a machine. **O:** copy, print, sheet □ *You can quickly* ***roll off*** *some extra copies of the exercise on the duplicating machine.* □ *'I'll* ***roll*** *you* ***off*** *a couple of dozen prints.'* □ note the Indirect Object (*you*) in the second example.

roll on [A1] (informal) (a stated wish or hope) may that day etc come quickly! **S:** Tuesday; next year, month; my time; death □ *If the next few months are going to be as hard as this, then all I can say is:* ***roll on*** *death!* □ *'**Roll on** my time!'* (i e the time when a soldier's active service ends) □ Subject placed after roll on.

roll-on/roll-off [nom (A1)] kind of ferry onto which, and from which, fully laden goods vehicles can be driven (thus saving the time and expense involved in transferring goods from a vehicle to an ordinary cargo vessel) □ *One alternative which has been suggested for the Eastern Wharf is the provision of a* ***roll-on/roll-off*** *ferry terminal.* SC □ *Little has been heard of the* ***roll-on/roll-off*** *development since the question of North Sea oil arose.* SC □ used attrib, as in the examples; a hyphen can replace the oblique: roll-on-roll-off.

roll out [B1i pass adj] make flat and smooth by pressing with a roller, or rolling-pin. **O:** dough, pastry □ *Spread some flour on the table and* ***roll*** *the pastry* ***out*** *very thin.*

roll over [A1] move to one side, esp in bed, by turning over □ *Every time Stephen* ***rolled over*** *he pulled more of the bedclothes to his side.* □ (children's song) *'There were ten in a bed and the little one said* ***"Roll over!"*** *They all* ***rolled over*** *and one fell out....'*

roll up[1] [B1i pass adj] form a flat object into a cylinder by bending and turning it. **O:** carpet, linoleum; map, chart □ *The paintings were taken from their frames and* ***rolled up*** *for storage.* □ *She was tapping me with her* ***rolled-up*** *napkin.* THH

roll up[2] [B1i pass adj] (military) drive the flank of an enemy line back and round. **O:** line, position; flank □ *If we can put a company on the enemy's weak flank, we can* ***roll up*** *his entire position without engaging our main force.*

roll up[3] [A1 emph] (informal) arrive, turn up[3] (q v), in some strength; arrive in an impressive or self-important way. **S:** crowd; dignitary, official □ *The whole family* ***rolled up*** *to their daughter's first appearance on the stage.* □ *They'll be putting up the price of food when they see us* ***roll up*** *in this car.* DBM □ (cry of a 'barker' outside a fair or circus) ***'Roll up! Roll up!*** *Second performance now beginning!'*

roll one's sleeves up [B1i pass] (informal) prepare oneself for serious work □ *It's time you* ***rolled up your sleeves*** *and did an honest day's work.* □ *The girls* ***rolled their sleeves up*** *and got to work on her. 'You must get him out of your system,' they said.* RATT

romp home [A1] (racing) win easily. **S:** horse; runner □ *The favourite* ***romped home*** *several lengths clear of the rest of the field.*

romp through [A1 A2] (informal) complete, pass, with no difficulty. **o:** course; test, exam; paper □ *Patrick* ***romped through*** *his geography paper.* □ *It's a hard course: nobody* ***romps through.***

roof over [B1i pass adj] put a roof over, cover with a roof. **O:** balcony, drive, approach □ *They've* ***roofed over*** *an area at the back to make a sun-lounge.* □ *A walk* ***roofed over*** *with glass led to the greenhouse.*

root for [A2] (informal) strongly express one's support for sb. **S:** crowd, spectators; family, friends. **o:** contender, underdog □ *'Come on, Jeff, let's see some of the old form. You know we're all* ***rooting for*** *you.'* □ *In the last Presidential election, the young, the intellectuals and the racial minorities were* ***rooting for*** *McGovern.*

root out [B1i pass] get rid of, destroy, eliminate. **O:** slacker, parasite; unreliable, dissenting (element) □ *Agents were sent to* ***root out*** *elements hostile to the regime.*

root to the ground/spot [B2 pass] cause to stand fixed and unmoving; rivet to the ground/spot (q v). **S:** fear, shock; noise, explosion □ *Terror* ***rooted*** *him* ***to the spot.*** □ *He stood* ***rooted to the ground,*** *listening for the telltale rustling in the undergrowth.*

root up [B1i pass] pull from the ground with the roots, uproot. **O:** tree, shrub, flower □ *They cut down the big trees and* ***rooted up*** *the stumps.*

rope in/into [B1i pass B2 pass] (informal) persuade to join, enlist in, some body. **O:** member, follower. **o:** group, organization; joining sth, being a member □ *She had* ***roped in*** *a recruit to the Women's Institute.* PW □ *Organizing the office party — now that's something you should avoid being* ***roped into.*** □ *He tried to* ***rope*** *me* ***in*** *on that swindle.* DBM

rope off [B1i pass adj] separate or enclose an area with a rope fence. **O:** field, pitch, paddock □ *The judges' enclosure was* ***roped off*** *from the spectators.* □ *The horses paraded in a small* ***roped-off*** *area.*

rope up [B1i pass adj] tie a rope around sth, thus making it secure. **O:** bale, bundle, crate □ *His cases and trunks were* ***roped up*** *for additional safety.*

rot away [A1] decay to the point where it breaks up, disintegrates, completely. **S:** body, flesh; limb, branch, tree □ *Slates had been dislodged, and the wood underneath was* ***rotting away.*** □ *She would gradually* ***rot away*** *until she was as thin and dry as the boughs.* DC

rot off [A1] fall off, separate (from the main body) because of decay. **S:** branch, limb □ *The ground is covered with stiff, dry branches which have* ***rotted off*** *as the trees die.*

rough in [B1i pass adj] enter roughly or in outline on a drawing. **O:** detail, shape, mass □ *I* ***roughed in*** *one or two figures to give some idea of the finished drawing.* □ *The plan showed a few* ***roughed-in*** *trees and buildings.*

rough out [B1i pass adj] make a rough or outline plan. **O:** scheme, plan; route, itinerary □ *So they* ***roughed*** *it* (the future) ***out:*** *Ned was going into the army and Robert into the navy.* CON □ *I've* ***roughed out*** *some arrangements for the move tomorrow.*

rough up [B1i pass adj] (informal) push sb about, tear and dirty his clothes etc (usu with the intention of frightening him, though not of hurting him badly). **S:** hooligan, ruffian □ *A gang of youths set on him outside a pub and* ***roughed*** *him* ***up.*** □ *Keegan* (a footballer) *alleged that he had been* ***roughed up*** *by officials.* BBCR

round down [B1i pass] bring a price, weight etc to a round figure by lowering it. **O:** figure; price, cost □ *Most shopkeepers don't like halfpennies and would even prefer to* ***round*** *their prices* ***down*** *if they can't round them up to the next penny.*

round off [B1i pass adj] make round and smooth. **O:** (sharp) edge, corner, angle □ *Take a piece of sandpaper and* ***round off*** *the edges of the frame.*

round off (with) [B1i pass adj B3 pass rel] end, complete, suitably or satisfactorily. **O:** remarks, speech, sentence; meal, feast; performance, show. **o:** reference (to sth), mention (of sth); port, brandy; speech, sing-song □ *The affair was pleasantly* ***rounded off with*** *a surprising resolution of thanks.* SD □ *This somewhat abstract description is* ***rounded off with*** *a number of examples.* SNP

round on/upon [A2 pass emph rel] turn to sb in sudden anger or irritation. **o:** companion; guard, questioner □ *Stanley was irritated and* ***rounded on*** *his son: 'Why were you so late last night?'* FFE □ *He* ***rounded upon*** *her with an exasperated cry: 'Why must you keep following me?'*

round out [B1i pass adj] make fuller, more complete. **O:** story, narrative; sketch, painting □ *Your narrative is rather thin: it needs* ***rounding out,*** *filling with interesting detail.* □ *The original scheme has now been* ***rounded out*** *with ideas from his colleagues.*

round up[1] [B1i nom pass adj] assemble, collect together (people or animals who are scattered, or who have fled etc). **O:** cattle, herd; fugitive, escapee, enemy; team, panel, party □ *'**Round up** the rest of the committee.'* WDM □ *The enemy were still there, though they should have been **rounded up** by that time.* MFM □ *I have asked for the whole squad to be **rounded up*** (or: *for a **round-up** of the whole squad*).

round up[2] [B1i pass] bring a price or weight etc to a round figure by raising it. **O:** price, cost; amount □ *When a decimal system is introduced, an existing price (e g £1 2s 6d) may be rounded down to, say, £1.12; however, it is more likely to be **rounded up** to £1.13.*

round upon [A2 pass emph rel] ⇨ round on/upon.

rout out/out of [B1i pass B2 pass rel] drive, chase, vigorously from. **O:** children; fugitive; pest. **o:** house, hiding-place, lair □ *'You can **rout** the children **out of** my study; I won't have them throwing everything into disorder.'* □ *We were **routed out of** our beds at three in the morning for a fire practice.*

rub along (together) [A1] (informal) live together smoothly, without friction. **S:** couple, colleagues □ *They're **rubbing along** the same as ever.* OI □ *She and her boss have **rubbed along together** for years — for all the world like an old married couple.*

rub away [B1i pass adj] remove by continuous rubbing or friction. **O:** mark, letter; pain, stiffness □ *The paint had been **rubbed away** from the arms of his chair.* □ *You need a good course of massage to get the aches and pains **rubbed away**.*

rub down[1] [B1i nom pass adj] prepare a surface for painting, distemper etc, by rubbing it with sandpaper etc. **O:** surface; woodwork; door, wall □ *Give the doors a coat of primer, and then **rub down** well before applying the top coat.* □ *He **rubbed down** the old paintwork* (or: *He gave the old paintwork a **rub-down***) *before putting on a coat of emulsion.*

rub down[2] [B1i nom pass adj] dry oneself thoroughly (after a shower etc); dry a horse vigorously after exercise □ *'**Rub** yourself **down** properly after your swim; I won't have you catching cold.'* □ *The horses get a thorough **rub-down** after their morning gallop.*

rub sb's nose in it [B2 pass] (informal) remind sb forcibly of sth unpleasant he has done □ *'I know that I let you down badly over the arrangements for the party, but don't **rub my nose in it** in front of my friends.'* □ *People have no imagination. You've got to **rub their noses in it** before they'll recognize that they've offended someone.*

rub in/into[1] [B1i pass adj B2 pass emph rel] force sth into a material by rubbing it over the surface of the material. **O:** oil, polish, cream; ointment, linament. **o:** wood; furniture; skin, pores □ ***Rub** linseed oil **into** the blade of your bat to prevent it from cracking.* □ ***Rub** some of this cream **into** your skin to protect it from the sun.*

rub in/into[2] [B1i pass B2 pass] (informal) constantly remind sb that he is unfortunate, inferior or dependent in some way. **O:** the fact, it; (it...) that he'd failed; how successful one is □ *She first arranged to meet me and then changed her mind: I called that **rubbing** it **in** a little too far.* SPL □ *There's no need to **rub** (it) **in** that we lost by three goals.* □ *Father never failed to **rub** it **into** the family how much they depended on his money.*

rub off[1] [B1i pass adj B2 pass] remove sth from a surface by rubbing. **O:** mark, letter, drawing; oil, paint; skin. **o:** blackboard, wall; table, shelf; knee, elbow □ *'**Rub** those words **off** the board before the teacher sees them.'* □ *The plating on the spoons was so thin that it easily **rubbed off*** (i e *one could easily **rub** it **off***).

rub off[2] [A1 A2 B1i pass B2 pass] (cause to) appear less bright, remarkable, praiseworthy etc. **S:** [A1 A2] **O:** [B1 B2] gloss, glitter, shine. **o:** achievement, success □ [A1] *With the passing of time some of the glitter of the achievement has **rubbed off**.* □ [B2] *The news of rigged ballots has **rubbed** some of the shine **off** their election victory.*

rub off onto/on to [A3] (informal) pass from one person or thing to another by contact or close association. **S:** quality; fame, success; nastiness, unpleasantness. **o:** family, associate, colleague □ *Stay with him for a while, and let some of the glory **rub off on to** you.* TT □ *If he remains in the group, some of his warmth and outgoingness may **rub off onto** the shyer people.*

rub out[1] [B1i pass adj] remove, by rubbing, sth which is deeply or firmly marked or embedded in a fabric etc. **O:** dirt, stain, mark □ *If you spill coffee on the carpet try to **rub** it **out** immediately with a damp cloth.* □ *She tried to remove the mark from his jacket with a cleansing fluid, but it wouldn't **rub out*** (i e *she couldn't **rub** it **out***).

rub out[2] [B1i pass] (US slang) kill, murder. **O:** gangster, cop, boss □ *A couple of mobsters were **rubbed out** in a fracas with the law.*

rub up[1] [B1i nom pass adj] polish sth until it is clean and shiny. **O:** silver, brasswork; table; leather □ *Those chairs will look fine once they've been given a good **rub-up*** (or: *once they've been well **rubbed up***). □ *'Dust the mantelpiece and **rub up** the ornaments.'*

rub up[2] [B1i pass] (informal) refresh one's knowledge of a subject that has been neglected for some time; brush up (q v). **O:** French, Polish; maths, statistics □ *If I'm to spend two weeks in Italy, I'd better **rub up** my knowledge of the language.* □ *Your shorthand is a bit rusty: you'd better **rub** it **up**.*

rub up the right way [B1ii pass] (informal) handle sb in a careful, soothing way (so as to get the best from him) □ *He was careful to **rub** Mason **up the right way**, saying how invaluable his services had been to the club, and so on.*

rub up the wrong way [B1ii pass] (informal) treat sb clumsily, tactlessly (so as to anger or offend him) □ *He's so easily **rubbed up the wrong way**: everything you say he seems to take offence at.* □ *'Don't **rub** me **up the wrong way**: I'm in a foul temper this morning.'*

rub shoulders (with) [B2 rel] (informal) be on easy, intimate, terms (with), mix on terms of equality (with). **o:** great, distinguished (people) □ *This is not the sort of club where the great **rub shoulders with** the humble* (or: *where the great and the humble **rub shoulders***). □ *He had freely ventured into the very heart of the industrial provinces and **rubbed shoulders with** the abori-*

gines (= the local people). CON

ruffle up [B1i pass adj] (informal) disturb sth, make it untidy; annoy, irritate sb. **O:** hair, feathers; friend, colleague □ *'I've just had my hair set, Henry, and I can't bear you to **ruffle** it **up**.'* □ *'You look rather **ruffled up**. Has anything happened to upset you?' 'I'm not in the least **ruffled up**. I've never felt better in my life.'*

rule against [A2 pass] (legal) make an official, or legally binding, decision that sth is not to be allowed. **S:** court, magistrate; council, committee. **o:** admitting evidence; allowing visitors □ *The chairman **ruled against** admitting the press to this meeting.* □ *He will not be allowed to make his submission: the court has **ruled against** it.*

rule off [B1i pass adj] separate one part of a page etc from another by drawing a line with a ruler. **O:** drawing, footnote, heading □ *Write out the figures in a column and **rule off** neatly at the bottom where you want the total to go.* □ *Put your name to one side of the page, leave a margin and then **rule this off**.*

rule out [B1i pass] regard as impossible or undesirable; dismiss; forbid. **O:** possibility, chance; occurrence, appearance □ *The possibility cannot be **ruled out** that improvement is largely due to absence of fatigue.* SNP □ *I'm sure that Dr Macgregor would **rule out** visits from you as much too exciting for the patient.* RM

rule (over) [A2 pass emph rel] govern, have authority (over). **S:** king, president, elected chamber. **o:** empire, country □ *European powers no longer **rule (over)** great overseas dominions.* □ *They resent being **ruled over** by a dictatorial boss.*

rule with a rod of iron [B2 pass emph] govern, manage, with great firmness or severity. **O:** people; employee; family, children □ *A small kingdom **ruled** by herself **with a rod of iron** was what she liked.* ASA □ *'How does he **rule** his department?' '**With a rod of iron.**'*

rumour about/abroad [B1i pass] spread about news which is based on hearsay and is not very accurate. **O:** news; report, story (that he is leaving); it... that he has been dismissed □ *It's **rumoured about** that he's been given a job in Scotland.* □ *To stop the wrong sort of story being **rumoured abroad**, they've issued an official statement.* □ *I suppose somebody in the Department first **rumoured** it **about** that Harry was leaving.*

runabout [nom (A1)] (informal) small car, esp of a kind in which one can make short journeys easily in towns □ *'We're getting rid of the station-wagon. We can never park it in town. What we need is a cheap little **runabout** that'll nip in and out of the traffic.'*

run across [A2 pass] meet sb, or discover sth, by chance. **o:** (old) friend, acquaintance; reference, allusion; picture, record □ *I **ran across** one of my former colleagues on a visit to London.* □ *I **ran across** one of his earliest recordings in a second-hand shop.*

run after[1] [A2] run to try to catch sb or sth (e g because he has forgotten sth, because it has escaped etc) □ *'Quick, **run after** him: he's left his wallet on the counter.'* □ *'Don't bother **running after** the bus — you'll never catch it.'*

run after[2] [A2 pass] (informal) follow persistently, pursue (in the hope of attracting). **o:** (attractive) girl, (eligible) man □ *She had never before **run after** a man, and she was not very good at doing it seriously.* H □ *I hate to feel that I'm being **run after**: it only makes me run in the opposite direction.*

run one's head against/into a brick wall [B2] (informal) attempt sth in the face of immovable opposition; bang one's head against a brick wall (q v) □ *To try to change the political convictions of these people would be like **running your head into a brick wall**.* □ *You may get your proposal accepted next year; at the moment you're **running your head against a brick wall**.*

run aground (on) [A1 A3 emph rel B1i pass B3 pass emph rel] (nautical) touch, and become fixed on, rocks, or on the seabed in shallow water. **S:** [A1 A3] **O:** [B1 B3] ship; tanker, liner. **o:** rock, sandbank □ [A3] *Oil is gushing from the tanker which **ran aground on** the Seven Stones (reef).* OBS □ [B1] *'Keep us out into the centre of the stream or you'll **run** us **aground**.'* ⇨ go aground (on).

run along [A1] (command to a junior, or familiar) go away, be off with you (because the person is being tiresome, or because one is busy) □ *'Be a good girl and **run along**: Daddy's busy.'* AITC □ *'For God's sake **run along**,' Robert snapped. 'You're dissipating my creative mood.'* CON

run around [A1] (informal) move restlessly from one lover to another □ *When is he going to stop **running around** and settle for one girl?* □ (American Negro blues) *She treated me right, she didn't let me down. But I wasn't satisfied, I had to **run around**.*

run-around [nom (A1 B1)] (informal) behaving towards sb in a fickle, deceitful or cunning way, so hurting or upsetting him □ *He's certainly been getting the **run-around** from Sheila. He doesn't know where he stands from one moment to the next.* □ *Mogul is taking over the firm that is giving them the **run-around** in plastics production.* BBCTV

run rings around/round [B2] (informal) perform so skilfully that one's opponent looks clumsy or foolish. **o:** opposition, competition □ *The visitors were so expert in every aspect of the game that they **ran rings round** the home team.* □ *Don't pick a fight with Roberts: he'll **run rings around** you.*

run at [A2] run towards sb as if to attack him, or towards sth with the aim of jumping over it. **o:** adversary; fence, wall □ *A big fellow **ran at** me with a knife.* □ *He set his horse to **run at** the fence.*

run away (from)[1] [A1 A3 emph rel] escape (from), usu because the life is unpleasant. **o:** school, home □ *He **ran away from** home when he was sixteen and went to sea.* □ *He **ran away** twice **from** his boarding school; he hated being cooped up in an institution.*

run away (from)[2] [A1 A3 pass emph rel] avoid sth or sb because one is shy, frightened, lacking confidence etc. **o:** difficulty, challenge; grown-up, teacher □ *'Don't **run away**. I shan't eat you!'* □ *Difficulties shouldn't be **run away from**; they should be faced resolutely.*

run away (with) [A1 nom A3 rel] leave home (with) (usu in the hope of marrying without parental consent). **o:** daughter, girlfriend □ *John has* ***run away with*** *the boss's daughter* (or: *John and the boss's daughter have* ***run away*** *together*). □ *After making a* ***runaway*** *marriage, Elizabeth seemed to settle down to a fairly conventional life as a suburban housewife.* □ runaway only used attrib, as in the second example. ⇨ run off (with).

run away with[1] [A3] steal and carry away; run off with (q v). **o:** cash, takings; jewels; papers □ *Someone in the office* ***ran away with*** *the plans of the new engine.*

run away with[2] [A3] consume, use up (q v), a great deal of sth. **S:** scheme, project; machine, appliance. **o:** money; gas, electricity □ *Holidays abroad* ***run away with*** *a lot of money.* □ *Those new heaters* ***run away with*** *a lot of electricity.*

run away with[3] [A3] win clearly or easily. **o:** match, game, tournament □ *The Brazilian team* ***ran away with*** *the first match in the series* (cf *The team scored a* ***runaway*** *win in the first match,* where ***runaway*** is [nom (A1)]).

run away with[4] [A3] gain complete control of, dominate. **S:** feelings, emotion, imagination □ *You tend to let your feelings* ***run away with*** *you.* TT □ *He is not a good man for the job: he lets a fondness for intrigue* ***run away with*** *him.*

run away with the idea/notion [A3] (informal) be misled by an idea, accept an unfounded idea □ *Don't ever* ***run away with the idea*** *that bankruptcy is a joke.* TGLY □ *The audience could be forgiven for* ***running away with the idea*** *that economic recovery was at hand.* □ *often in neg imper constructions, as in the first example.*

run back [B1i pass] wind a film etc in reverse so that it can be shown or heard again. **O:** film, tape, film-strip □ *'Just wait a minute while we have that sequence* ***run back.'*** □ *'****Run*** *that excerpt* ***back*** *to the beginning and replay it in slow motion.'*

run back over [A3 rel] review, reconsider. **o:** events; career; year, month □ *'I should like to* ***run back over*** *the past term, singling out events of particular importance.'* □ *If you* ***run back over*** *the season, you can't pick out a game in which he played badly.*

run behind [A1 A2] not keep pace with one's timetable (for a meeting, radio programme etc). **S:** interviews, oral examinations; programme. **m:** five minutes, half an hour. **o:** ⚠ schedule, time □ *'Please tell Miss Williams to cancel my appointment for eleven o'clock. We're* ***running*** *about fifteen minutes* ***behind*** *as it is.'* □ *'If we* ***run*** *more than a few minutes* ***behind*** *schedule the whole evening's viewing will be thrown out of gear.'*

run counter to [A3 pass] contradict, not match; conflict (with) (q v). **S:** statement, behaviour, event. **o:** principle, professed belief, code □ *This result* ***runs counter to*** *a very basic principle of human learning.* SNP □ *The situation* ***runs counter to*** *ordinary logic.* SC

run down[1] [A1 B1 pass adj] (cause to) suffer a loss of power, through neglect, age etc. **S:** [A1] **O:** [B1] engine, motor; clock; battery; industry, economy □ *'If you leave the car lights on all night you'll* ***run*** *the battery* ***down.'*** □ *The crusading spirit disappeared: there was the sensation of a machine that was* ***running down.*** MFM □ *Through a drying-up of capital investment much heavy industry in the area was in a thoroughly* ***run-down*** *state.*

run down[2] [A1 nom B1i pass adj] decline, reduce, in numbers or size. **S:** [A1] **O:** [B1] strength, forces; establishment, sales team. **S:** [B1] government, management □ *The farm labour force is* ***running down*** *steadily* (or: *There is a steady* ***run-down*** *of the force*). OBS □ *We are* ***running down*** *our military presence in this area.*

run down[3] [B1i pass] knock to the ground, collide with. **S:** car, bus; liner, tanker. **O:** pedestrian, bicycle; boat □ *I didn't get to her before she died. She'd been* ***run down*** *by a lorry.* LLDR □ *The destroyer was* ***run down*** *by an aircraft-carrier while manœuvring across her bows.*

run down[4] [B1i pass] find eventually after a long search. **S:** search-party, police. **O:** missing person, escaped convict □ *I had a bit of trouble* ***running*** *Anderson* ***down.*** AITC □ *The suspect was finally* ***run down*** *at the home of one of his associates.*

run down[5] [B1i pass] criticize unkindly, belittle, disparage. **O:** family, friend; attempt, achievement □ *'The food had better be good after all that talk.' 'That's enough of* ***running down*** *my cooking,' she said.* TT □ *She's always* ***running*** *her husband* ***down*** *in public. I'm surprised he puts up with it.*

run down[6] [pass adj (B1)] (be) tired and in poor condition, because of overwork, lack of sleep etc □ *'You look thoroughly* ***run down.*** *Why don't you take a week's holiday?'* □ *He emerged from his ordeal in a completely* ***run-down*** *condition.* □ passive with *be, feel, look, seem.* ⇨ run down[1].

run-down [nom (B1)] (informal) (giving of) information, a briefing □ *'I've asked Mr Phillips to join us at this meeting because he can give us a* ***run-down*** *on the latest developments.'* □ *'Go over to headquarters and try and get a* ***run-down*** *on the situation.'*

run down to [A3 rel] stretch as far as, extend to. **S:** garden, estate. **o:** river, road □ *The grounds at Hampton Court* ***run down to*** *the water's edge.*

run (for) [A2 rel] (esp US) offer oneself as a candidate (for); stand (as) (for) (q v). **o:** mayor, governor □ *Then Eisenhower retired from the United States Army; he had decided to* ***run for*** *President.* MFM

run for dear life/one's life [A2] leave, escape, quickly because one's life is in danger □ *With pieces of burning masonry falling all around him, he* ***ran for dear life.*** □ *Office workers* ***ran for their lives*** *as an earth tremor shook the centre of town.*

run for it [A2] escape from danger by moving quickly □ *At first he was a bit suspicious and ready to* ***run for it*** *should the animal attack him.* DF □ *'Never mind your bloody boots.* ***Run for it.'*** UTN

run a mile (from) [B2] (informal) try hard to avoid sb (because he is boring, conceited etc) □ *I could have been made into a boring, heartless* (social) *climber whom everyone* ***ran a mile from.*** HAA □ *'I assure you I* ***run a mile from*** *people* (or: ***run a mile*** *to avoid people*) *unless I have to do business with them.'* ASA

run in[1] [B1i pass] (informal) arrest and take to a police station. **O:** vagrant, loiterer, drunk □ *Trevor was* ***run in*** *for dangerous driving on Saturday night.* SPL □ *If you throw eggs at the speaker, you are liable to get* ***run in*** *for causing a breach of the peace.*

run in[2] [B1i pass adj] prepare an engine (esp of a motor car) for use by driving it slowly and carefully for a certain distance. **O:** car; engine □ *'Don't expect me to get you home quickly — I'm still* ***running*** *my car* ***in****.'* □ *The point of* ***running*** *your engine* ***in*** *carefully is not to cause excessive friction between the new working parts.*

run in the family [A2] be a feature (e g physical, moral) which keeps appearing in successive generations of a family. **S:** hair, nose, eyes; temper, courage, obstinacy □ *We expect him to go into the navy: the tradition* ***runs in the family****.* □ *He refused to fill in personal details on some form. This idiosyncracy appears to* ***run in the family****.* BM

run into[1] [A2 B2 pass] (cause to) strike, collide with. **S:** [A2] **O:** [B2] ship; bus, lorry. **S:** [B2] captain; driver. **o:** bank; wall, hedge □ *He lost control of his car and* ***ran*** *it* ***into*** *a lamp-post.* □ *The prow of the boat* ***ran into*** *a bank of soft mud and stuck fast.* □ *Russian counter-attacks during the afternoon had* ***run into*** *the full strength of the 4th Panzer Army.* B

run into[2] [A2 B2 pass] (cause to) meet, encounter. **S:** [A2] **O:** [B2] country, firm, department. **S:** [B2] (bad) management, advice. **o:** trouble, difficulty; debt □ *His wild extravagance is* ***running*** *his family* ***into*** *the red* (i e debt). □ *We expect to* ***run into*** *a few snags before the machine is ready for production.*

run into[3] [A2] meet, enter, an area of bad weather. **S:** ship, plane. **o:** storm, blizzard □ *Climbing higher, we* ***ran into*** *a patch of thick mist which blotted out our route.* □ *Our boat* ***ran into*** *a force-nine gale in the Channel.*

run into[4] [A2] meet by chance. **o:** (old) friend, acquaintance □ *I* ***ran into*** *my old English master while on holiday in Scotland.* □ *If you visit the studio, you may well* ***run into*** *someone you recognize from the cinema.*

run into[5] [A2] be of the size or order of, extend to. **S:** income, return, figure; book. **o:** hundreds, thousands (of pounds), five figures; (several) editions, printings □ *The sum involved in the negotiation* ***runs into*** *five figures* (i e tens of thousands of pounds). □ *His latest novel has* ***run into*** *three editions within the year.*

run into the ground [B2 pass] (informal) (cause to) move, work, play etc so energetically that one is near to exhaustion. **S:** [A2] **O:** [B2] troops, transport; team, player. **S:** [B2] general; captain, coach □ *While the Germans were slowly* ***running*** *all their divisions* ***into the ground*** *with fatigue and casualties the Red Army was building up a formidable reserve.* B □ *Ball is such a strong and willing player that in a key match he can be expected to* ***run*** *himself* ***into the*** *ground.* □ often reflex.

run one's head into a brick wall [B2] ⇨ run one's head against/into a brick wall.

run off[1] [A1 B1i pass adj] (cause to) flow from a vessel etc. **S:** [A1] **O:** [B1] liquid; wine, dye, fat □ *'The oil in your engine looks very dirty — get the garage to* ***run*** *it* ***off****.'* □ *When the temperature reaches melting point, the metal* ***runs off*** *as a liquid and flows into special moulds.*

run off[2] [B1i nom pass adj] reproduce, duplicate, print. **O:** copy, photocopy, print □ *I have to* ***run off*** *a few hand-outs on the duplicating machine.* □ *'****Run*** *me* ***off*** *some copies of his electoral address* (or: *Do me a* ***run-off*** *of his address*).*'*

run off[3] [B1i pass] cause to be run, contested (esp at an athletics meeting). **O:** race, heat; 100 metres □ *The heats of the 200 metres are being* ***run off*** *tomorrow.* □ *The final of the 5 000 metres was* ***run off*** *in blazing heat.*

run off his feet [B2 pass] (informal) make sb work hard and/or move about a lot, thus tiring him. **S:** customer; patient; child, pupil. **O:** assistant; nurse; parent, teacher □ *During the New Year sales rush, the girls in the clothing departments are* ***run off their feet*** *all day.* □ *'Mother needs a holiday: the children do* ***run*** *her* ***off her feet****, you know.'*

run off the rails [A2] (informal) begin to lead a wild or unconventional life. **S:** son, daughter □ *Since his girl went to art college, she's* ***run*** *completely* ***off the rails****, dressing like a gypsy and coming home at all hours.* ⇨ go off the rails.

run off (with) [A1 A3 rel] leave in the company of sb (having left one's husband, family etc). **o:** lover; (someone else's) wife, husband □ *He decided that Art could only be some man or other that Rosemary had* ***run off with****.* DBM □ *Mary has* ***run off with*** *her music teacher* (or: *Mary and her music teacher have* ***run off*** *together*). ⇨ run away (with).

run off with [A3 rel] steal and carry away; run away with[1] (q v). **o:** receipts, takings; plan, secret □ *'Someone's* ***run off with*** *the keys to my safe.'* □ *If you leave your money lying about, somebody's sure to* ***run off with*** *it.*

run on[1] [A1 emph] flow, continue without a break (often monotonously or annoyingly). **S:** voice; words, speech □ *'How that woman's tongue does* ***run on****!'* □ ***On*** *he* ***ran****, until most of his audience were restless with impatience.*

run on[2] [A1 B1i pass adj] (cause to) continue, without indenting to mark the beginning of a paragraph; (in verse) allow a sentence to continue from one line, stanza etc to another. **S:** [A1] **O:** [B1] matter, text; sentence; sense □ ***'Run on'*** *is an instruction to a printer to ignore a paragraph indentation.* □ *In romantic poetry it becomes more normal to* ***run*** *the sense-groups* ***on*** *from one line to the beginning or middle of the next.*

run on[3] [A2 emph rel] have as its subject, be concerned with. **S:** discussion, argument; thought, address. **o:** subject, matter; event, occurrence; line, path □ *His talk* ***ran on*** *recent developments in the industry.* □ *His thinking* ***runs on*** *familiar lines.* □ *Brigit's mind kept* ***running*** *foolishly* ***on*** *the same theme.* DC

run out[1] [A1] be finished, exhausted. **S:** supply, stock (of wines, cigarettes etc); patience; time □ *If his rice has* ***run out*** (or: *If he has* ***run out of*** *rice*) *he goes to the paddy-stores.* NDN □ *Our time is* ***running out*** *and I think we ought to say something about the ending* (or: *We are* ***running out of*** *time* etc). ART ⇨ run out/out of.

run out[2] [A1] expire, be no longer valid. **S:** lease, contract, agreement □ *The lease on their*

London flat ***runs out*** *in a few months.* □ *The foreign companies seem well protected, until their concessions* ***run out*** *towards the end of the century.* T

run out[3] [B1i pass adj] (cricket) dismiss a batsman by striking his wicket while he is running □ *Jones was* ***run out*** *in the final over of play before lunch.* □ *Peters* ***ran*** *his partner* ***out*** (i e caused him to be ***run out*** by the other side) *by calling for a run when there was none to be had.*

run out at [A3] (informal) reach a particular amount; work out at (q v). **S:** expenses, cost, estimate. **o:** £5 000; a good deal, more than we can pay □ *What does the cost of converting the present building* ***run out at****?* □ *The actual bill* ***runs out at*** *considerably more than the original estimate.*

run out/out of [A1 A3] finish, exhaust. **o:** supply, stock (of commodities); ideas; patience □ *'There's been a tremendous demand for that brand. We've* ***run out****.'* □ *'Stop at the next garage. We're* ***running out of*** *petrol* (or: *The petrol's* ***running out***)*.'* ⇨ be out of[3], run out[1].

run out of steam [A2] (informal) move more slowly, or halt, because the original driving force is lacking. **S:** campaign, advance, attack; movement, crusade □ *Unless we can supply our forward units, the advance is in danger of* ***running out of steam****.* □ *House-to-house canvassing started in a fit of enthusiasm, but pretty soon* ***ran out of steam****.*

run out (on) [A1 A3 pass] desert, abandon, sb who needs or expects one's support. **o:** friend, ally, associate; family, children □ *If he refuses help, he will be accused of* ***running out on*** *the Federal Government.* OBS □ *The aid did not arrive on the promised date, giving us the unpleasant feeling of having been* ***run out on****.*

run over[1] [A1] overflow. **S:** tank, jug □ *'You'd better fetch the plumber: the cistern is* ***running over****.'* □ *'Don't fill the kettle too full: it'll* ***run over****.'*

run over[2] [B1i pass] knock sb down and pass over (part of) his body. **S:** car, bus. **O:** pedestrian, animal □ *Two children were* ***run over*** *at that road junction last month.*

run over[3] [A2 pass] read or say sth quickly, aloud or to oneself, in order to learn it or refresh one's memory. **o:** notes, minutes; script, part (in a play) □ *'Just* ***run over*** *my lines with me before the rehearsal begins.'* □ *He* ***ran over*** *in his mind what he was going to say at the meeting.* EM

run an/one's eye over [B2 emph rel] (informal) examine sth or sb closely in order to estimate its or his merits or value. **S:** dealer, buyer, critic. **o:** livestock, goods; applicant, newcomer □ *'Just* ***run your eye over*** *these materials and tell me if there are any you like.'* □ *I had the chance of* ***running my eye over*** *the new members of the company during rehearsal.*

run over with [A3 rel] show an abundance of, overflow with. **o:** enthusiasm, joy; ideas, schemes □ *The children are* ***running over with*** *energy and mischief — I can't keep them still for five minutes.*

run rings round [B2] ⇨ run rings around/round.

run through[1] [A2] pass quickly through. **S:** murmur, whisper; thought, tune. **o:** crowd, throng; head □ *An angry murmur* ***ran through*** *the audience.* □ *A snatch of their conversation kept* ***running through*** *his head.*

run through[2] [B1ii pass] play (part of) a film etc by passing it through a machine. **O:** film, tape; sequence, excerpt □ *'Will you* ***run*** *that bit of tape* ***through*** *again? I didn't hear it the first time.'* □ *'I'll* ***run*** *the whole of that sequence* ***through*** *again. Watch the action carefully.'*

run through[3] [A2 nom pass] review, summarize; pass over[5] (q v). **o:** argument, point, feature □ *Let's* ***run through*** *the main points of the Budget so far* (or: *Let's have a* ***run-through*** *of the main points* etc). BBCTV □ *'I think I've grasped your main proposals, but would you mind* ***running through*** *them once again?'*

run through[4] [A2 nom pass B2 pass] (cause to) act, perform (esp at rehearsal). **S:** [A2] **O:** [B2] actor, cast. **S:** [B2] producer, director. **o:** play, scene □ *There'll be a* ***run-through*** *of the whole play at seven o'clock.* □ *'I'd like to* ***run*** *you* ***through*** *that scene you have with Paula.'*

run through[5] [A2 pass] spend all that one has quickly and foolishly. **o:** fortune, inheritance, allowance □ *He* ***ran through*** *no end of money while he was up at University.* □ *The money inherited from his father was quickly* ***run through****.*

run a comb through one's/sb's hair [B2 pass] (informal) comb the hair quickly (e g to improve one's appearance for a visitor) □ *'I must just dash upstairs and* ***run a comb through my hair****.'* □ *'****Run a comb through the child's hair*** *— he can't go to a party looking like that.'*

run one's fingers/hand through one's hair [B2] (informal) pass one's fingers etc nervously through one's hair □ *I could see from the way he kept* ***running his fingers through his hair*** *that the big occasion had tensed him up.* □ (stage direction) *She winces as she feels the pain in her arm. She* ***runs her hand through her hair****.* LBA

run through (with) [B1ii pass B3 pass emph rel] pierce sb's body (with a weapon). **O:** enemy, rival. **o:** sword, spear □ *He attacked the post with grenades and* ***ran*** *the survivors* ***through with*** *the bayonet.* □ *One soldier was* ***run through with*** *a spear* (or: *had a spear* ***run through*** *him*).

run to [A2] be enough to cover, be sufficient for; afford, have enough money for. **S:** fund, allowance, budget; he etc; management, treasury. **o:** luxury, extras; holiday, outing; wine, cigar □ *The budget would not* ***run to*** *champagne.* BFA □ *I'm afraid we can't* ***run to*** *central heating in all rooms.*

run to earth/ground [B2 pass] (informal) find, after a long and difficult search. **O:** quarry, (escaped) prisoner; book, document; house, shop □ *Eventually, I was* ***run to earth*** *by a panting Ben, who reproached me for disappearing.* BB □ *We* ***ran*** *the bird shop* ***to earth*** *eventually, on one side of an enormous square.* DF □ *He was not in his office and I eventually* ***ran him to ground*** *in the lavatory.* MFM ⇨ go to earth/ground.

run to fat [A2] (tend to) become too fat (through neglect, overeating etc) □ *Her mother was wealthy and discontented,* ***running to fat*** *and losing her looks from idleness.* AITC □ *After a year in a desk job, and only occasional weekend exercise, he was starting to* ***run to fat****.*

run to seed [A2] drop lower than a previous high standard, deteriorate (usu through neglect). **S:** appearance, looks, figure; business, estate; economy □ *At one time she must have been a handsome woman, but now she had* ***run*** *slightly* ***to seed.*** DF □ *It annoyed him that his daughter should let her looks* ***run to seed*** *in that sort of academic dowdiness.* ASA

run together [A1 B1ii pass] (of two or more separate things) be combined, combine. **S:** [A1] **O:** [B1] colours; sounds, words; pictures □ *'I shouldn't wash those shirts in the same water, or else the colours will* ***run together.****'* □ *'Don't gabble, Lucy, I can't understand when you* ***run*** *your words* ***together.****'*

run up[1] [B1i pass] hoist, raise. **O:** flag, banner, standard □ *The admiral* ***ran up*** *a signal ordering all ships to close with the enemy.* □ *Then the white flag was* ***run up****: the post had surrendered.*

run up[2] [B1i pass adj] make, construct, quickly, and possibly from any materials that are near at hand (e g to meet a sudden emergency). **O:** dress, fancy-dress costume; shed, shelter □ *She hadn't been able to get a bathing-costume to fit her. She had consequently* ***run up*** *two for herself.* BFA □ *To deal with the overcrowding problem, they were exhorting him to* ***run up*** *an annexe or lean-to.* ILIH

run up[3] [B1i pass] cause to rise sharply in amount. **O:** bill, account; overdraft, deficit □ *She's been* ***running up*** *accounts at half a dozen big stores.* □ *The extra grant will only just cover the deficit that we've* ***run up*** *already.* OBS

run up[4] [A1 nom] (sport) run towards a bowling-crease, or jumping-off point, so as to increase the speed of one's delivery or jump. **S:** bowler, (long-, high-)jumper □ *Trueman is now* ***running up*** *to bowl the last ball before lunch.* □ *The spin bowlers take quite a short* ***run-up.*** ⇨ next entry.

run-up [nom (A1)] (informal) period just before an important event (and in which that event is prepared for) □ *Labour must in the* ***run-up*** *to the election reawaken its supporters' loyalty.* OBS ⇨ previous entry.

run up against [A3 pass] meet, encounter, come face to face with. **o:** obstacle, difficulty, problem; misunderstanding, incomprehension □ *These were some of the snags we expected to* ***run up against.*** □ *The same opposition had been* ***run up against*** *when we last tried to introduce the measures.*

fools rush in (where angels fear to tread) [A1] (proverb) foolish men act over-hastily, and without considering the consequences of their actions □ *'Despite all our warnings, he had to go off and invest in that tin-pot venture. I suppose it's a case of* ***fools rushing in where angels fear to tread.****'*

rush into [A2 pass B2 pass rel] (cause sb to) undertake sth too quickly, and without considering the consequences. **o:** buying, selling; partnership, take-over □ *'Don't let anybody* ***rush*** *you* ***into*** *joining; think it over.'* □ *We may eventually become members; but this is not something that should be* ***rushed into.*** □ *He didn't want to marry — she* ***rushed*** *him* ***into*** *it.*

rush into print [A2] publish sth too quickly (e g without weighing one's evidence carefully) in order to beat one's competitors, capture a ready market etc. **S:** author, writer; hack(-writer) □ *I deplore the writing of so-called military history by people concerned with* ***rushing into print*** *so as to catch a market that is still fresh.* MFM

rush through [B1i pass adj B2 pass] cause to become official policy, the law etc very quickly. **S:** government, assembly, committee. **O:** law, Bill □ *The Chamber has* ***rushed through*** *legislation making the carrying of firearms a serious offence.* □ *Two Private Members' Bills were* ***rushed through*** *Parliament before the end of the session.*

rush to conclusions [A2] form an opinion too quickly, i e without waiting to consider all the evidence; jump to conclusions/the conclusion (q v) □ *'You were there last night. I saw your hat and coat.' 'Now don't start* ***rushing to conclusions.****'* □ *'You were talking to Stevens at lunch. I wouldn't mind betting he offered you a job.' 'That would be* ***rushing to conclusions.****'*

rush to hospital [B2 pass] take sb to hospital very quickly (because of serious illness or injury). **O:** patient, casualty □ *Two passengers were* ***rushed to hospital*** *suffering from severe head injuries.*

rustle up [B1i pass] (informal) prepare (e g for an unexpected guest); gather, collect, together (e g to meet a special need). **O:** meal, snack; support, help; friend, guest □ *'Make yourself comfortable. I'll see if I can* ***rustle up*** *a few sandwiches.'* □ *My list of girls, from whom I might have* ***rustled up*** *one for such an occasion, seemed to have dispersed.* SML

S

saddle up [A1 B1i pass] put a saddle on one's horse (a command to this effect being a signal to prepare to move off). **S:** trooper; patrol, squadron. **O:** horse, mount □ *We got the order to* ***saddle up*** *just after dawn.* □ *The horses were* ***saddled up*** *and ready to move.*

saddle with [B2 pass rel] place a particular burden on sb, give to sb the responsibility of looking after sb or sth. **S:** employer, colleague, husband. **o:** job, task; burden, responsibility; family, child □ *I'm always being* ***saddled with*** *extra duties.* □ *The government played some part in* ***saddling*** *industry* ***with*** *a heavier load.* SC □ *'It was you who invited the Smiths to stay, and now you're* ***saddled with*** *them!* (i e they are your responsibility, and you can't get rid of them).'

sail in/into [A1 emph A2] (informal) enter an argument or dispute energetically; attack sb vigorously or angrily (usu with words). **o:** discussion, dispute, fray; him etc □ *Just as we thought the heat had gone out of the discussion, Mrs Hughes* ***sailed in.*** □ *A back-bench critic of the official line* ***sailed into*** *the Minister at this point, his temper clearly roused.*

sally forth/out [A1] (formal, jocular) emerge suddenly (usu from a position where one is surrounded) and attack the enemy. **S:** (besieged, beleagured) army, force □ *The citizens* ***sallied out*** *in an attempt to break the siege.* □ *An army of housewives* ***sallied forth*** *to do battle in the annual sales at the big stores.*

salt away [B1i pass] (informal) save, invest, for the future. **O:** part of one's income, salary; profits, earnings □ *He's got a few pounds* ***salted away*** *for his retirement.* □ *Now's the time to* ***salt*** *something* ***away*** *for your old age.* □ *Allegations have been made that 'millions of pounds are being* ***salted away****' illegally in the Channel Islands by speculators.* OBS

salvage (from)[1] [B2 pass emph rel] recover sth which is undamaged and still usable (from a place which has suffered damage). **O:** furniture, machinery; box, bale. **o:** wreckage, debris; blaze, fire; (damaged) factory □ *The walls were of wood and the flames spread rapidly. All that could be* ***salvaged from*** *the ashes was a small metal box containing instruments.*

salvage (from)[2] [B2 pass emph rel] rescue, preserve, sth worthwhile (from a situation that has deteriorated). **O:** some shreds of respectability, one's self-respect. **o:** (collapse, failure of) one's marriage, business, career □ *There was very little, morally, that John had* ***salvaged from*** *the breakdown of his marriage. His self-confidence was so shaken that he was chary of forming any new relationship.*

sand down [B1i pass adj] remove rough parts of a surface by rubbing it with sandpaper. **O:** paintwork; wall, door □ *The surface should be thoroughly* ***sanded down*** *before you apply any paint.*

saturate (with) [B2 pass emph rel] fill with a liquid, soak (with). **O:** ground, soil; cloth, rag. **o:** water, oil □ *Press the sponge into the liquid until it is* ***saturated*** (***with*** *it*). □ *We lay in the sun until our bodies felt* ***saturated with*** *the heat.*

save (from) [B2 pass emph rel] make, keep, sb safe (from). **o:** loss, injury; drowning, being burned □ *By arriving when you did you* ***saved*** *her* ***from*** *more serious injury.* □ *He needs* ***saving from*** *the consequences of his own foolishness.*

save (up) (for) [A1 A2 pass emph rel A3 pass emph rel] put money in reserve (gradually, little by little) to obtain sth. **o:** car, bicycle, radio; holiday □ *How can you manage to marry, she said, at your age? I told her I'd been* ***saving up for*** *her all my life.* KLT □ *This sea cruise was something* ***for*** *which he'd been* ***saving*** *for years.* □ *They couldn't buy a car tomorrow, but it could be* ***saved for****.* □ *'We're* ***saving up*** *to get married.'* TOH

savour of [A2] (formal) suggest, indicate some (unpleasant) feeling or attitude on the part of the speaker. **S:** suggestion, plan, proposal. **o:** malice, mischief, ill-will □ *The speaker's words* ***savoured*** *strongly* ***of*** *intolerance.* □ *Your remarks* ***savour of*** *impertinence.*

saw down [B1i pass] fell, bring to the ground, using a saw. **O:** tree, post, mast □ *Some of their trees had to be* ***sawn down*** *and sold for their valuable timber.*

saw into [B2 pass] divide in pieces using a saw. **O:** tree, timber. **o:** lengths, planks, battens □ *The trees are stripped of their bark and mechanically* ***sawn into*** *planks.* □ ***Saw*** *this board* ***into*** *pieces, each a foot long.*

saw off [B1i pass adj B2 pass] remove part of sth with a saw. **O:** branch; piece, length □ *If you* ***saw*** *six inches* ***off*** *the legs of the table, you can use it to rest the television on.* □ *'Would you* ***saw*** *me* ***off*** *a piece two metres by one?'* □ *He* ***sawed*** *an inch* ***off*** *the barrel of his revolver to make it easier to draw* (cf *a* ***sawn-off*** *barrel*). □ note Indirect Object construction in the second example.

saw up [B1i pass adj] cut into pieces with a saw. **O:** tree, plank, board □ *All the spare timber was* ***sawn up*** *to make logs for the fire.* □ *Get the carpenter to* ***saw*** *the wood* ***up*** *to your requirements.*

say (about) [B2 pass emph rel] make comments, observations (about). **S:** reporter; newspaper, article; reference book. **O:** a lot, plenty; nothing, very little; what. **o:** event, accident, case; musician, painter □ *'What does the 'Times' leader* ***say about*** *the prospects of a settlement in the rail dispute?'* □ *'The physics master tells me you've not been exerting yourself this term, Walker. Now, what have you to* ***say about*** *that?'* □ (film review) *It's a thriller from the John Le Carré novel, with plenty to* ***say about*** *people.* OBS

scale down [B1i pass adj] reduce in relation to sth else. **O:** wage, salary; investment, expenditure; output, production □ *Imports will have to be* ***scaled down*** *until exports begin to rise again.* □ *The effect of all this* (i e inflation) *is to* ***scale down*** *people's spending plans.* BBCR □ *Armies should be* ***scaled down****, but not if it meant giving one country an advantage over any other.* BBCR

scale up [B1i pass adj] increase in relation to sth else. **O:** income, earnings; benefit, bonus □ *The salaries of teachers should be* ***scaled up*** *to correspond to those of people in comparable professions.* □ (statement of director after securing a large order) *'It is now a matter of* ***scaling up*** *production, of making 30 000 retort stands instead of 1 000.'* ST

scar over [A1] close, heal, leaving a scar on the skin. **S:** wound; cut, gash □ *The cut on his finger will eventually* ***scar over****.*

scare away/off [B1i pass] cause sb to stay at a distance, or go away, by frightening him. **S:** security arrangements; guard-dog, police; manner, voice; price, luxury. **O:** burglar, intruder; visitor; shopper □ *Strangers never call at that house. I think the bulldog* ***scares*** *them* ***away****.* □ *A lot of potential visitors are* ***scared off*** *by the look of the place — it seems too luxurious for them.*

scare out of his wits [B2 pass] (informal) frighten very badly. **S:** atmosphere; noise, silence; appearance, face; film, show □ *'Don't go through the cemetery at night — it* ***scares*** *the girls* ***out of their wits****.'* □ *'Never take me to a horror film again. I was* ***scared out of my wits****.'*

scatter about/around/round [B1ii pass B2 pass] leave, throw, things here and there in a haphazard or untidy manner. **O:** clothes, books, toys. **o:** place, room □ *'I know the children have been playing here: there are toys* ***scattered about*** *all over the carpet.'* □ *'I've* ***scattered*** *some ashtrays* ***around*** *the room so that* *cigarettes don't get trodden into the floor.'*

scheme (for) [A2 pass emph rel] make plans (usu secret and dishonest) to achieve some end. **S:** rival, rebel. **o:** downfall, overthrow; power, control □ *They came perilously near to achieving the ends* ***for*** *which they had been* ***scheming.*** □ *He had been* ***scheming for*** *a bigger share* (or: *to have a bigger share*) *in the running of the business.*

school (in) [B2 pass emph rel] teach sb the elements or principles of sth (usu the teaching is informal and by example; its purpose may be sinister or antisocial). **O:** child; follower, disciple. **o:** diplomacy, statecraft; cunning, double-dealing □ *The young king was carefully* ***schooled in*** *the art of balancing one force in the kingdom against another.* □ *Movement at night, staying concealed, living off the land — these were all skills* ***in*** *which they had been well* ***schooled.***

scoop out [B1i pass adj] remove sth using a deep, rounded shovel (or one's hand shaped as one); form a hole by removing soil etc in this manner. **S:** (burrowing) animal. **O:** soil, sand; hole, cavity, trench □ *He* ***scooped out*** *a little of the earth, being careful not to disturb anything that was underneath.* □ *This small rodent can* ***scoop out*** *a long, narrow tunnel in a very short time.*

scoop up [B1i pass adj] raise sth in a deep, rounded implement or vessel (or in one's hand shaped as one). **O:** liquid; dust; filings, shavings □ *He cupped his hands and* ***scooped up*** *a little water.* □ *He took a spoon and* ***scooped up*** *a few grains of the gold dust.*

score (for) [B2 pass] (music) include parts for particular instruments in a musical composition. **S:** composer. **O:** piece; concerto, symphony. **o:** strings, woodwind, brass □ *Beethoven's Fifth is the first major symphony to be* ***scored for*** *trombones.* □ *He* ***scored*** *one quintet* ***for*** *two violas and the other* ***for*** *two cellos.*

score off[1] [A2 pass rel B2 pass rel] (cricket) score runs by striking the deliveries of a particular bowler. **S:** batsman. **O:** run; fifty. **o:** bowler; bowling □ *'He made fifty before lunch, and as you know, Carter is not easily* ***scored off.'*** □ *Edrich* ***scored*** *a quick century, mainly* ***off*** *the medium-pace bowling.*

score off[2] [A2 pass] (informal) make sb appear foolish, inadequate etc e g by a witty or unkind remark, or by one's own success. **o:** friend, rival, opponent □ *'You can cut the cheap cracks. It's too easy to* ***score off*** *poor old Fred.'* □ *If he had wanted to* ***score off*** *Robert, there were so many better ways than this.* CON

score out [B1i pass adj] cancel sth by drawing a line through it. **O:** line, mark, figure, letter □ *Three of the names on the list had been* ***scored out.*** □ *The paper was covered with untidy drawings and* ***scored-out*** *calculations.*

scour off [B1i pass B2 pass] remove by rubbing with a rough brush, powder, wire pad etc. **O:** rust, grease, burnt food. **o:** pan, pot; stove □ *See that all the burnt potato is* ***scoured off*** *the bottom of the pan.* □ *If the bath is stained, don't try to* ***scour*** *the stain* ***off:*** *you'll only scratch the enamel.*

scour out [B1i pass] rub the inside of sth with a rough brush etc, so as to remove dirt etc. **O:** (sauce)pan, pot, jar □ *The boilers will have to be* ***scoured out*** *to remove the calcium deposits.* □ *She makes a regular point of* ***scouring out*** *the pots and pans.*

scout about/around (for) [A1 nom A3 rel] hunt, search, carefully (for). **o:** food, shelter, fuel □ *'**Scout around for** a few bits of firewood.'* □ *'I know he's not here; go and have a* ***scout-around*** *in the garden* (or: *go and* ***scout around*** *in the garden*).'

scrabble about (for) [A1 A3 rel] search, grope, in a blind, clumsy way (for sth) □ *He* ***scrabbled about*** *under the counter for a minute, and came up with a small green bottle.* □ *Children* ***scrabbled about*** *on the floor* ***for*** *pennies that had been thrown to them.*

scramble for [A2 rel] struggle in rather a disorderly, undignified way to get more of sth than one's competitors. **S:** country, company, trader; spectator. **o:** possessions, market; seat, place □ *The families that had enriched themselves in the previous generation now* ***scrambled for*** *official posts and honours.* □ *The European powers* ***scrambled for*** *trading posts in the areas that had been opened up.*

scrape along (on) [A1 A3 emph rel] (informal) manage for some time to live on very little money etc. **o:** a low wage, a few pounds (a week) □ *She spent three years at college,* ***scraping along on*** *an allowance from her parents.* □ *They paid him a low salary,* ***on*** *which he was quite content to* ***scrape along*** *in the hope that something better would turn up.*

scrape by (on) [A1 A3 emph rel] (informal) manage to live (and esp to survive a difficult period) on very little money etc. **o:** small allowance, low grant, what one has saved □ *The most difficult time was the winter, when we had all the fuel bills to pay, but we managed to* ***scrape by*** *with a little money in hand.* □ *The first year in the new house was the hardest, but they just* ***scraped by on*** *a loan from the bank.*

scrape in/into [A1 A2] (informal) just manage to enter a school etc (i e by getting the lowest acceptable marks). **o:** school, college, university; army, civil service □ *If he just* ***scraped into*** *secondary school, he'll be lucky to get a place at university.* □ *'How on earth did he get into the Foreign Service?' 'He must have* ***scraped in*** *by the barest margin, or perhaps he has influence among the selectors.'*

scrape off [B1i pass adj B2 pass] remove sth from a surface e g by passing a blade between it and the surface or by (accidentally) rubbing the surface against a rougher one. **O:** paint, tar; jam, butter; skin. **o:** wall, door; floor, table; hand, elbow □ *'**Scrape** those bits of putty* ***off*** *the window pane.'* □ *He* ***scraped*** *the skin* ***off*** *his knee on a piece of corrugated iron.*

scrape out [B1i pass adj] empty, or clean, the inside of a vessel by passing a blade etc along its surface. **O:** dish, bowl; pipe, channel □ *'Would you like to* ***scrape out*** *the jam-jar? Here's a spoon.'* □ *Once in a while the bowl of his pipe is thoroughly* ***scraped out.***

scrape through [A1 A2] just manage to pass (a test etc), pass with the lowest acceptable mark. **S:** student, candidate. **o:** test, examination; selection board □ *He got a comfortable pass in zoology, but barely* ***scraped through*** *in botany.*

□ *She **scraped through** in the written papers, but may make up her marks in the oral.*

scrape together/up [B1i pass] (informal) save with difficulty; collect together (with difficulty) money from various sources, to meet an emergency. **O:** money; cash, funds, capital □ *'Well, you'll have to **scrape** the money **up**. I'm not going to dip into my funds to save you from a scandal.'* HD □ *'Can't we just try to **scrape together** a few pounds for a holiday?'*

scrape up an acquaintance (with) [B1iii pass B3 pass rel] (informal) get to know sb with difficulty and/or superficially (because he is shy and aloof, or because you know no one in common etc). **adj:** some; slight, nodding, superficial □ *I managed to **scrape up an acquaintance with** some of the single passengers, but the married ones tended to keep to themselves.* □ *He would nod over the garden wall once in a while and after a month we'd **scraped up** some kind of **an acquaintance**.*

scratch about (for) [A1 A3] dig here and there with sth sharp (in order to find sth). **S:** chicken, monkey; farmer, miner. **o:** corn, fleas; (signs, traces of) water, gold □ *Sparrows were **scratching about** in the damp soil **for** worms.* □ *'If you want to get through this rock, there's no sense in **scratching about** with a pick. You'll have to use explosive.'*

scratch (from) [A2 emph rel B2 pass emph rel] (sport) (cause to) withdraw from a sporting contest (e g because of illness). **S:** [A2] **O:** [B2] horse; runner, long-jumper. **S:** [B2] owner; manager. **o:** race; event □ *Two competitors have **scratched from** the 10 000 metres with torn leg muscles.* □ *There will only be five runners in the 3.30 at Newbury as three horses have been **scratched** (**from** the race) at the last minute.*

scratch out [B1i pass adj] remove, cancel, by making a deep, scoring mark (with a sharp, narrow instrument). **O:** line, mark; name □ *I looked at the list: somebody had **scratched** his name **out**.* □ *His essay was disfigured by many blots and **scratchings-out**.*

scratch sb's eyes out [B1ii pass] (informal) (threaten to) make a violent physical attack on sb (usu said by or of a possessive or jealous woman). **S:** wife, girlfriend □ *'Be careful, Harry: she'll **scratch your eyes out** if you so much as glance at another woman.'* □ *'You'll stop fooling around with Mike if you don't want to have **your eyes scratched out**!'* □ often with *will/would*.

screen (from) [B2 pass rel] shelter, protect (from). **O:** eyes, face; table, bed; ceremony, procession; child, pupil. **o:** sun, daylight; watcher; view, gaze; influence □ *Use a hood to **screen** the lens of your camera **from** direct sunlight.* □ *During her childhood she had been carefully **screened from** contact with 'undesirable' children.*

screen off [B1i pass adj] separate (e g from the rest of a room) by means of a screen. **O:** bed, table; patient, invalid □ *He would retire to a desk, **screened off** from the rest of the room by a heavy bookcase.* □ *'**Screen off** her bed and make sure she's not disturbed.'*

screw down [B1i pass adj] fasten a cover to a box etc with screws. **O:** lid, cover; hatch □ *After the mourners have paid their last respects, the undertaker **screws down** the lid of the coffin.*

(have) one's head screwed on [pass (B1)] (informal) (be) wise, sensible, of sound judgement □ *'I'm sorry you're all so easy to fool. You ought to **have your heads screwed on** right, with all your experience of the trade.'* CON □ *There's a lad with **his head screwed on** — he had the sense to buy in while the price was low.* □ *The next time you go into partnership, make sure the other fellow**'s got his head screwed on** the right way.*

screw on/onto [B1i pass adj B2 pass rel] fasten one thing to another, either with screws, or by a screw-thread cut into each. **O:** plate, board; top, lid; handle, knob. **o:** wall, door; jar, bottle; shaft □ *The carpenter came along and **screwed on** a shining brass plate: C. R. JONES, M.B., B.Ch.* □ *Don't forget to **screw** the lid back **onto** the jar.*

screw out of [B2 pass] (informal) get money etc from sb by undue **screw out of** [B2 pass] (informal) get money etc from sb by undue persuasion, pressure etc. **O:** money; cash, pound; promise, guarantee □ *'Can't you manage to **screw** a bit extra **out of** your parents?'* □ *He's so unscrupulous that he'd **screw** the last penny **out of** a widow.*

screw up[1] [B1i pass adj] make into a tight ball in the hands. **O:** paper; letter, bill □ *With an impatient exclamation Peter **screwed up** the second draft of his letter to the bank and threw it into the wastepaper basket.* □ *At the end of a normal morning's work the study floor would be littered with **screwed-up** bits of paper.*

screw up[2] [B1i pass] tighten the muscles of the face (so shading one's eyes, expressing surprise etc). **O:** ⚠ one's eyes, features, face □ *Even under the broad brim of my hat I had to **screw up** my eyes against the ferocious glare.* DF □ *Janice **screwed** her face **up** into an expression of the utmost seriousness.* PW

screw up[3] [B1i pass adj] (informal) make sb nervous, tense; tense up (q v). **S:** occasion; waiting; fear, anxiety. **O:** patient, examinee; soldier, prisoner □ *The last few minutes before going on stage always **screw** him **up**, so he has a cigarette and a chat with someone in the dressing room to help him relax.* □ *'Going to the dentist never seems to bother my wife, but I get terribly **screwed up** at the mere thought.'*

screw up[4] [B1i pass adj] (slang) mishandle, mismanage; mess up (q v). **S:** manager, organizer; agency, office. **O:** planning, arrangements; deal □ *'We should never have left the arrangements to Smithers. He **screwed** the whole thing **up** from start to finish.'* □ *The opening stage of the attack was badly **screwed up** with the soldiers getting bunched into too narrow a front.*

screw up one's courage [B1iii] force oneself to be brave □ *I've been **screwing up my courage** to tell you.* EHOW □ *'Don't stand there — **screw up your courage** and jump.'*

scrub off [B1i pass B2 pass] remove sth from a surface etc by rubbing it with a stiff brush, soap and water. **O:** dirt, oil, glue, paint. **o:** hand; wall, floor □ *'**Scrub** that mud **off** your fingers before you sit down to lunch.'* □ *I got paint on my hands and it won't **scrub off*** (or: *I can't **scrub** it **off***).

scrub out[1] [B1i pass] remove a mark etc which is lodged in a fabric etc, by rubbing it with a stiff brush, soap and water. **O:** mark, stain; oil, tar; coffee □ *When you spill ink on the carpet, remove it straight away — you won't be able to* ***scrub*** *it* ***out*** *later* (or: *it won't* ***scrub out*** *later*).

scrub out² [B1i pass] clean a place by rubbing the surface with a stiff brush, soap and water. **O:** room, hall; cupboard □ *As soon as they moved in, they started* ***scrubbing out*** *the rooms* (i e scrubbing the floors clean) *and washing down the walls.*

scrub out³ [B1i pass] (informal) cancel a future event, or sth which affects it; regard as invalid sth which has occurred. **O:** instruction, order; arrangements, programme; practice, trial □ *The whole exercise has been* ***scrubbed out****; you will receive fresh orders shortly.* □ *We've* ***scrubbed out*** *event 1; move on to the next event.* □ *The researchers had to* ***scrub out*** *the first set of results and start again.* □ scrub alone sometimes used in this sense: *We've* ***scrubbed*** *event 1* etc.

scrub round [A2 pass] (informal) not apply, waive, sth; avoid, circumvent, sth. **o:** rule, regulation; difficulty, obstacle □ *It says here that an applicant should have three years' experience, but I think we can* ***scrub round*** *that.* □ *The entrance requirements are strictly applied: don't think you can* ***scrub round*** *them.*

scuffle (with) [A2 rel] fight, struggle (with sb) in a confused way. **S:** spectator, demonstrator, marcher. **o:** police, troops □ *One or two hecklers on the edge of the crowd* ***scuffled with*** *the stewards.*

scurry for [A2] hurry in a nervous, excited way towards. **o:** ⚠ the door, exit; shelter, cover □ *A sudden shower of rain sent them all* ***scurrying for*** *shelter.* □ *As the plaster cascaded onto the tables, the guests* ***scurried for*** *the door.*

seal off [B1i pass adj] close the entrance to sth, so that nothing can move in or out. **O:** channel, passage; exit, entrance □ *We reached the Baltic and thus* ***sealed off*** *the Danish peninsula with about six hours to spare.* MFM □ *It did not seem to occur to the police to* ***seal off*** *the entrances or order nobody to leave.* OBS

seal up [B1i pass adj] close, fasten tightly. **O:** parcel, letter; hole, opening □ *They* ***sealed up*** *the cracks in the window to stop the icy wind from blowing in.* □ *Make sure the parcel of examination scripts is properly* ***sealed up****.*

search (for) [A2 emph rel B2 pass emph rel] look carefully about a place, examine sb carefully, in order to find sth. **S:** rescue party; plane, helicopter; detective. **O:** area, neighbourhood; house; drawer, cupboard; pockets. **o:** missing climber, airman; weapon; papers, keys □ *Police and tracker dogs* ***searched*** *the woods* ***for*** *the missing boy.* □ *'I've been* ***searching*** *everywhere* ***for*** *those scissors. Where did they get to?'* □ *At last the evidence* ***for*** *which they had been* ***searching*** *came to light.*

search out [B1i pass] (try to) discover, reveal, bring to light (q v), by looking carefully for it. **O:** author, maker; culprit, one responsible; cause, eventually ***searched out*** *a dusty portfolio.*

search through [A2 pass] look carefully for sth by moving steadily from one part of a room etc to another. **o:** drawer, cupboard; belongings; paper, book □ *You can* ***search through*** *his autobiography without finding a single reference to his first wife.* □ *There's no point in looking there: his personal papers have all been* ***searched through****.*

secede (from) [A2 emph rel] (formal) withdraw from membership (of). **S:** state, province, region. **o:** union, federation □ *The problem is to stop the richer provinces* ***seceding from*** *a federation most of which is poor.*

second (to) [B2 pass rel] transfer sb from his normal post (to another) for special duties. **O:** soldier, officer; official. **o:** staff, research establishment □ *Major Smith has been* ***seconded to*** *us to advise on the new signals procedure.* □ *He enjoyed the small, up-country post* ***to*** *which he had been* ***seconded****.* □ note the placement of stress: /sɪˋkond/.

secure (against) [B2 pass rel] make safe (against), strengthen (against). **O:** house; window, door; position, defences. **o:** intruder, thief; attack □ *They* ***secured*** *the house* ***against*** *entry on either floor.* □ *Having placed some troops over to the right he was* ***secured against*** *sudden attack from that flank.*

seduce (from) [B2 pass rel] (formal) tempt sb to neglect or forget his duty etc. **o:** duty, (a life of) virtue, respectability □ *The new government included two ministers from the centre parties,* ***seduced****, as some would say,* ***from*** *their traditional loyalties by the attraction of Cabinet rank.* □ *He regretted the passing of the simple life* ***from*** *which ambition had* ***seduced*** *him.*

see about [A2 pass] act to achieve, remedy etc, sth. **o:** cleaning, decorating; tax, insurance; damage, breakage □ *That was how I got the idea of the market-garden, though I didn't get round to* ***seeing about*** *it till now.* PW □ (advertisement) *You're so pretty, Linda, it's a pity you neglect your breath. Why don't you* ***see about*** *it?* WI

see across [B1ii pass B2 pass] guide, escort, sb across. **O:** child, old person. **o:** road, street □ *'Ask a grown-up to* ***see*** *you* ***across*** *the main road.'* □ *I was there to make sure the children were* ***seen*** *safely* ***across*** *the road.*

see beyond [A2] (be able to) foresee and understand events etc which are at some distance in space or time; be farsighted. **o:** the immediate present, the here and now, the next few hours/days; one's own family circle; one's own immediate concerns □ *He's not the man to put in charge of the food supply: he can't* ***see beyond*** *where the next meal's coming from.* □ *A man responsible for a large business must be able to* ***see beyond*** *short-term goals. He may need to plan for several years ahead.* □ with *can/could*; often neg.

see beyond the end of one's nose [A2] (informal) (be able to) understand more than is present and obvious □ *'No one would think he's your son. You treat him abominably. Just because you can't* ***see beyond the end of your*** *stupid, commonplace* ***nose****.'* FFE □ *'I've got an idea of offering Pelican a directorship,' Robin said. 'It'll be a bit tricky with my fellow directors. Pelican'd be the hell of an asset, but they can't* ***see beyond the end of their noses****.'* ASA □ with *can/could* and usu neg. ⇨ previous entry.

see in a new etc light [B2 pass] regard, understand sth or colleague, brother. **adj:** new, fresh, different; best, more favourable, more flattering ı *'We are all under somewhat of a strain, and in 'he morning we will probably* ***see*** *things* ***in a*** *:otally* ***different light****.'* TT □ *Most people want 'o be* ***seen in the best light****.* SNP

ee of [B2 pass pass(o) rel] meet, have contact vith sb often, seldom etc. **O:** a lot, a good/great leal; more, less; (not) much, anything. **o:** each other, one another; friend, colleague, boss □ *'You've got the ready answer ready, haven't you?' she said. 'We'll have to* ***see*** *more* ***of*** *each other, I can see.'* HAA □ *Nothing was* ***seen of*** *him for six months, and then he turned up as large as life at our flat.* □ *Baker was the new man from London who was to transform everything by sheer force of personality. In fact he wasn't* ***seen*** *much* ***of*** *outside his office.*

ee an end of/to [B2] witness the ending of sth usu sth unpleasant). **o:** event, development; conflict, dissention; squabbling, bickering □ *The most consistent opponents of Dr Verwoerd wish to* ***see an end of*** *violence in Africa.* SC □ *Perhaps with the appointment of our new managing director we would* ***see an end to*** *the inter-departmental rivalries and quarrels of the previous year.*

ee off[1] [B1ii pass] say, bid, farewell to sb (e g at the railway station); send off[2] (q v). **O:** relative, friend □ *A number of friends and well-wishers came to* ***see*** *him* ***off*** *at the airport.*

ee off[2] [B1ii pass] drive, chase, away. **S:** guard, dog; defence. **O:** intruder, prowler; attacker □ *Some boys came round hoping to steal apples, but the farmer* ***saw*** *them* ***off*** *with a few well-chosen words.* □ *If the enemy failed to* ***see*** *us* ***off*** *on the beaches, he would try to rope us off* = encircle us) *inland.* MFM

ee out/out of [B1ii pass B2 pass] lead, guide, sb out of a building □ *'Don't bother to come down. I can* ***see*** *myself* ***out****.'* □ *'Miss Jones will* ***see*** *you* ***out of*** *the building.'*

ee over/round [A2] visit and examine a place. **S:** visitor; prospective buyer. **o:** house; exhibition, show □ *'I shall need to* ***see over*** *the house and grounds before I can make you any kind of offer.'* □ *It took us two hours to* ***see*** *right* ***round*** *the Boat Show.*

ee through[1] [A2 nom pass] (be able to) see from one side to the other of sth (because it is transparent). **o:** window, partition; fabric, garment □ *'Would you mind moving to one side? I can't* ***see through*** *your head, you know.'* □ *Barbara was wearing one of those* ***see-through*** *blouses; in fact it was so* ***see-through*** *that she needn't have been wearing one at all.* □ see-through usu attrib, as in the first part of the second example.

ee through[2] [A2] (informal) understand the true nature of sb beneath a pleasant, deceptive appearance. **o:** him etc; act, show, manner; charm, glibness □ *She learnt to* ***see through*** *the smooth exterior to the real person underneath.* □ *'Don't think you can fool me — I can* ***see*** *right* ***through*** *you!'*

ee through[3] [B1ii B2] ensure that sb passes safely through a difficult time. **S:** friendship, support; skill, bravery. **o:** crisis, bad patch, troubled time □ *She had known he might come back and trusted to him to* ***see*** *her* ***through****.* PW □ *His courage and good humour has* ***seen*** *him* ***through*** *worse times than these.* □ *'I shall need more than a couple of drinks to* ***see*** *me* ***through*** *one of her ghastly parties.'*

see through[4] [B1ii] (informal) handle a situation and bring events to a happy conclusion. **O:** ⚠ it, the thing, things □ *Together the whole team will* ***see*** *this thing* ***through*** *to the end.* MFM □ *Depend on him to* ***see*** *things* ***through****.*

see to [A2 pass] take care that sb is properly received, that sth is made, tended etc. **o:** visitor, guest; horse; room, bed □ *'Jo, go and* ***see to*** *that coffee!'* TOH □ *Large sums of money would continue regularly to be moved, and their security must be* ***seen to****.* T

see an end to [B2] ⇨ see an end of/to.

see to it (that) [A2] ensure, take care (that sth happens, is the case etc) □ *Matron has* ***seen to it that*** *the nurse did day duty only.* WI □ *Here concealment was impossible. I simply had to hope that some kindly deity would* ***see to it that*** *I met nobody.* UTN □ *'I promise to get everything finished on time.' 'Well,* ***see to it*** *you do!'* □ followed by finite (*that*) clause. □ see to.

see eye to eye (with) (about/on) [A2 emph rel] have the same views, sympathies etc, (as); agree (with) (q v) sb (about sth). **o:** (***with***) husband, child; employer; (***about/on***) money, housework, holidays; wages, hours (of work), conditions □ *'He wasn't a member of the Party either. He never* ***saw eye to eye with*** *Pollitt* (or: *He and Pollitt never* ***saw eye to eye***).' PP □ STANLEY: *Clive, as you know, your mother and I didn't* ***see eye to eye about*** *sending you to University.* FFE □ *'Patrick and I* ***see*** *pretty well* ***eye to eye on*** *most things.'* TGLY □ eye to eye is an adv phrase; often neg.

seek (for) [A2 pass adj emph rel] try to find, look (for) (q v). **o:** answer, solution; cause, explanation □ *You should* ***seek (for)*** *a reason in the statements he has made over the past year.* □ *Talks have brought the results* ***(for)*** *which we were all* ***seeking****.* □ *Among the successes were some long* ***sought-for*** *changes in working conditions.* □ for may be omitted, except in the adj form: sought-for.

seek out [B1i pass] come looking for sb (e g to ask for help, pass on news etc). **O:** friend, colleague, confidant □ *Supposing he* ***sought*** *her* ***out*** *again and he asked her what she really did mean?* PW □ *When Marlowe returned from lunch the secretary* ***sought*** *him* ***out****. 'Cable for you, Dr Marlowe.'* TBC

seethe (with) [A2] be restless (with), be agitated (by) (like water in a kettle coming to the boil). **S:** country, town; population. **o:** discontent, unrest; anger, fury □ *The square was now fully alight and* ***seething with*** *still more revellers converging on the cafes.* BM □ *By now John was* ***seething with*** *indignation and we gathered round trying to pacify him.*

seize on/upon [A2 pass emph rel] choose in a keen, alert way some aspect of sth for special comment or criticism; fasten on/upon (q v). **o:** detail, feature; fault, flaw □ *He quickly* ***seized on*** *a basic flaw in the argument I was developing.* □ *Any weakness in their position will be* ***seized upon*** *and exploited.*

seize up [A1] become fixed or jammed because of overheating etc. **S:** engine, motor; car □ *'If you never bother to lubricate your engine of course it will* ***seize up****!'* □ *I've been wagging my* *chin so fast these last months it'll* ***seize up*** *soon.* TGLY

seize with both hands [B2 pass] grasp sth eagerly, be quick to exploit sth. **O:** opportunity, chance, opening; offer, invitation □ *An opportunity is presented to each one of us; some of us are not aware of the full significance of what has happened, and the moment is lost. Others, alert and enthusiastic,* ***seize*** *the opportunity* ***with both hands*** *and turn it to good advantage.* MFM □ *This offer was* ***seized*** *by Ernest Bevin* ***with both hands*** *and he organized a conference in Paris the next month.* MFM

sell (at) [B2 pass rel] give in exchange at a particular price level. **o:** price, figure; gain, loss; discount; £100, ten dollars □ *'What price are they being* ***sold at****?'* □ *I can't afford to go on* ***selling*** *several of my lines* ***at*** *a loss.* □ *He's* ***selling*** *his ties* ***at*** *a ten per cent discount below the normal retail price.* □ one sells at a point on a scale (e g of loss or gain); one sells for (q v) a particular amount or sum of money.

sell down the river [B2 pass] (informal) betray the interests of one's own people, of members of one's party, trade union etc. **S:** minister, leader; delegate, representative. **O:** country; union, member □ (letter to Editor) *Sir: The phrase '****sold down the river****' is American, and refers to the Mississippi. Before the Civil War the treatment of slaves in the northern tier of slave States was generally better than that further south. Consequently, the practice of* ***selling*** *recalcitrant slaves '****down the river****' developed.* OBS □ *At a mass meeting of car workers called by shop stewards the official leadership was accused of* ***selling*** *the rank and file* ***down the river****.*

sell (for) [B2 pass rel] give in exchange for a particular sum of money. **o:** £100; less than one gives, next to nothing □ *'I'm thinking of* ***selling*** *the car.' 'Oh, how much* ***for****?'* □ *I can't remember what I* ***sold*** *the collection* ***for****.* ⇨ (footnote at) sell (at).

sell off [B1i pass] get rid of by sale, goods which have not sold well, or plant which is inefficient, so as to free the money invested in them. **O:** stock, line; holding, share; factory, store □ *We are going to* ***sell off*** *some of the lines which have been cluttering up our storeroom for so long.* □ *Mogul have already undertaken to* ***sell off*** *Vornkind plastics* (a subsidiary company). BBCTV

sell out/out of [A1 A2 pass] sell one's entire stock (of a particular article). **S:** shopkeeper; store. **o:** cigarettes; bread; petrol □ *'I'm sorry, all the Sunday papers have gone: we've* ***sold out****.'* □ *'We seem to have* ***sold out of*** *your size. Can you come back next week?'*

sell out (to) [A1 nom A3] (informal) betray one's cause, one's side (to sb). **o:** enemy, opposition □ *They spoke of people who had* ***sold out to*** *the enemy.* NM □ *The union leaders were accused of* ***selling out to*** *the employers* (or: *of a* ***sell-out to*** *the employers*). □ *The meeting broke up amidst cries of '****Sell-out****!'* BBCR

sell up [A1 B1iii pass] sell a business, house etc to pay one's debts, or because one is moving or retiring. **O:** property; shop, factory; all one has □ *Before* ***selling up*** *their Clerkenwell place, they tried to borrow more money.* OBS □ *They're* ***selling up*** *next week, so go round if there's anything you want to collect before the sale.*

send about his business [B2 pass] tell sb to mind his own business; tell him to stop interfering in the affairs of others. **O:** onlooker, bystander; ghoul, busybody □ *'I soon sent hi[m] packing. Soon* ***sent*** *him* ***about his busines[s].*** *Now would you like to go and lie down for [a] while?'* TGLY □ *Anybody taking too close a[n] interest in what went on in the laboratories wou[ld] soon be* ***sent about his business****.* ⇨ go abou[t] one's business.

send across (to) [B1i pass B2 pass B3 pass] send sb or sth from one side to the other of intervening water etc. **O:** messenger; delegate, salesman; freight, mail. **o:** (***across***) the road; th[e] Channel; (***to***) shop, bank; France □ [B1] *'Th[e] evening paper hasn't come yet.' 'Oh,* ***sen[d]*** *Michael* ***across*** *for it.'* □ [B2] *Reinforcemen[ts] were* ***sent across*** *the river under cover of darkness.* □ [B3] *The cross-Channel ferries are [a] quick and convenient means of* ***sending*** *good[s]* ***across to*** *the Continent.* ⇨ get across[1], go take across (to).

send after [A2 B2 pass] ask sb to follow a person, to tell him he has left sth behind etc □ *M[r] Smith had left without his umbrella, so I* ***sen[t]*** *one of the boys* ***after*** *him.* □ *'Nobody told him t[o] leave.* ***Send after*** *him and bring him back.'*

send ahead/ahead of [B1i pass B2 pass emph] dispatch sb in advance of a main part[y] etc, to inquire, find lodgings etc; send sth so tha[t] it arrives sooner than one does oneself. **O:** patrol scout; advance party; luggage, furniture. **o:** mai[n] force; the others, the rest □ *Armoured cars wer[e]* ***sent ahead of*** *the main body of the division t[o] spot enemy troop movements.* □ *'I'm* ***sending*** *m[y] trunks* ***ahead*** *by rail so that I'm not too loade[d] down for the journey.'* ⇨ go ahead/ahead of.

send away [B1i pass] make sb leave, depart remove himself from one's presence □ *'And that boy comes around distributing trade leafle[ts] again* ***send*** *him* ***away*** *and tell him not to com[e] back.'* □ *'I wish you'd got home five minutes earlier. I had to* ***send*** *the milkman* ***away*** *without th[e] money we owe him.'* ⇨ go away[1].

send away/off (for) [A1 A3 pass rel] pos[t] money, a coupon etc to a dealer to obtain a special offer, free gift etc; write away/off (for) (q v). **o:** wall chart, map; (set of) glasses, mats (advertiser's 'blurb') *Have you* ***sent off*** *yet fo[r] your special guide to space-age exploration? He* ***sent away*** *to one of the daily papers* ***for*** *[a] free fisherman's almanac.* ⇨ send for[2].

send back [B1i pass] return sth to a shop (e g by post) because one is dissatisfied with it; ask [a] waiter to take food back to the kitchen because i[t] is unsatisfactory. **O:** dress, blouse; book; soup fish □ *'This coat is too short in one sleeve.* ***Sen[d]*** *it* ***back*** *to the shop.'* □ *Don't accept poor service If the wine is not at the right temperature,* ***send*** *[it]* ***back****.*

send down [B1i pass] dismiss from a university (usu for misconduct). **O:** student, undergraduate □ *Several students were* ***sent down*** *afte[r] incidents during the visit of a foreign Prim[e] Minister.* ⇨ be/come down (from); g[o] down[8].

send for[1] [A2 pass B2 pass] send sb to fetch help etc, or a message asking for it. **S:** parent householder. **o:** police, fire brigade, doctor help, assistance □ *A doctor advises at what stag[e]* *parents with ailing children should **send for** professional advice.* OBS □ *'The plumber's been **sent for**. In the meantime help me mop up the water.'* ⇨ go for[2].

send for[2] [A2 pass] make a request, or order (usu through the post) for sth. **o:** catalogue, brochure; form; sample □ *I'm going to **send for** that book on wild birds.* □ *Don't delay. **Send** now **for** a free catalogue.* ⇨ send away/off (for).

send in[1] [B1i pass] submit sth to a judge or assessor (in the hope of winning a prize, being accepted etc). **S:** competitor. **O:** entry, coupon; answer, solution □ *Entries should be **sent in** to arrive by 1st August.* □ *I shan't bother to **send in** the manuscript; it's sure to be rejected.*

send in[2] [B1i pass] submit sth to an official, or one's superior, to inform him or obtain his approval. **O:** application, claim; information; report, statement □ *If you want a visa, be sure to **send in** your application in good time.* □ *Situation reports were **sent in** three times a day, at 8 a m, 1 p m and 6 p m.* OBS

send off[1] [B1i pass] dispatch, post; start sb on a journey. **O:** letter, parcel; goods, consignment; wife, child □ *'Why haven't you got my letter? I **sent** it **off** last week.'* □ *Mother always makes sure the children are **sent off** with a good breakfast inside them.*

send off[2] [B1ii nom pass] bid sb farewell (e g at a railway station); see off[1] (q v). **O:** friend, relative □ *The whole family arrived on the quayside to **send** him **off**.* □ *He was given a good **send-off*** (or: *got a good **send-off***) *when he left for America.*

send off (the field) [B1i pass B2 pass] (sport) order sb to leave the field of play; order off (the field) (q v). **S:** referee. **O:** player □ *'Now don't try arguing with the ref. You'll only get **sent off**.'* □ *Two players were **sent off the field** for persistent fouling.*

send off (for) [A1 A3 pass rel] ⇨ send away/off (for).

send on[1] [B2 pass rel] dispatch sb for the purpose of. **o:** holiday, vacation; tour, safari; course □ *This year the school is **sending** a number of senior boys **on** an Outward Bound course.* □ *'John's company have been very good to him. Last year, when he was seriously ill, they **sent** him **on** a fortnight's convalescence.'* ⇨ go on[1].

send on[2] [B1ii pass] ask, get, sb to continue a journey ahead of others □ *The marketing director had pressing business which kept him in Leeds, so he **sent** his deputy **on** to represent him in Edinburgh.* □ *The damage to the truck would keep us busy for a least an hour, and we **sent** the boys **on** to explain that we would be late back to camp.* ⇨ go on[3].

send on[3] [B1i pass] dispatch, forward, letters etc, after sb has left so that they reach him at his new address. **O:** mail, post; letter, bill □ *'Would you be kind enough to **send on** any mail to my new address?'* □ *Students are asked to leave their vacation addresses with the secretary so that examination results can be **sent on**.*

send out [B1i pass] emit, radiate; transmit. **S:** lamp, bulb; sun; stove; (signalling) station. **O:** light; heat; signal □ *The oil-lamp **sent out** a gentle beam when you touched the knob.* THH □ *Long disused antennae **send out** and receive all kinds of messages.* PW

send out (for) [A1 A3 B1i pass B3 pass] ask sb to go from an office, shop etc (to fetch sth). **O:** secretary, messenger, office-boy. **o:** newspaper; coffee, sandwiches □ [A3] *'The coffee they make over the road is so much better than the foul stuff we brew up in the cupboard. Why don't we **send out for** some?'* □ [B1] *'I forgot to pick up the flowers on my way in to the office. I suppose we could always **send** Anne **out** to collect them?'*

send out/out of [B1i pass B2 pass] tell, ask, sb to leave a place (e g as a punishment, at the start of a game etc). **O:** pupil, child. **o:** class; room, office □ *'What are you doing out in the corridor, Mason?' 'Mr Naylor **sent** me **out** for throwing paper darts, sir.'* □ *'Let's begin with a game of Hide the Thimble, shall we? Now, who shall we **send out of** the room?'*

send to [B2 pass rel] arrange for sb to attend a particular school, college etc. **O:** son, ward. **o:** public school, State school; Oxford □ *There was no question of **sending** the boys **to** a public school. Paul disapproved, somewhat priggishly, of all forms of privilege in education.* □ *In the days when the expenses of a university education had largely to be met by parents it made some sense to talk of '**sending** one's children **to** university'. Now, with government help available in the form of grants this is no longer the case.* ⇨ go to[1].

send to bed [B2 pass] make sb go to bed (e g because he is ill, as a punishment etc) □ *'John's been complaining of severe stomach pains all day. You'd better **send** him **to bed** and call the doctor.'* □ *'If I get another cheep out of you two children you'll be **sent to bed** without any supper!'* ⇨ go to bed.

send to his death [B2 pass] act in a way, whether consciously or not, that will cause sb's death. **O:** soldier, policeman; fireman, lifeboatman □ *Generals who, as young officers in the First World War, had seen thousands **sent to their** certain **death** in attacks on strongly held positions were much more chary of risking their own men's lives in foolhardy ventures.* □ *'You're looking pleased with yourself,' Beatrice said. 'Doesn't it occur to you that you may be **sending** a man **to his death**?'* OMIH □ note pl forms in: *Men were **sent to their death/deaths**.*

send to sleep [B2 pass] make sb fall asleep. **S:** (mother's) singing, cooing; rocking motion (of a cot, a boat); hot drink; (boring, tedious) speech, harangue; play, concert □ *The gentle lapping of the waves against the side of the boat **sent** him **to sleep**.* □ *If there's anything calculated to **send** me **to sleep** it's a party political broadcast on television.*

send up[1] [B1i pass] cause to rise. **S:** shortage, transport costs, strike; power failure, loss of oil. **O:** price, cost; temperature □ *Any increase in production costs is bound to **send up** prices.* □ *A rise in temperature will **send up** the pressure inside the casing.* ⇨ be up[1], go up[2], put up[4].

send up[2] [B1i pass] destroy, esp by fire or explosion; blow up[4] (q v). **S:** direct hit, salvo; bomber. **O:** building; ship; ammunition dump. **A:** in flames, in smoke; with a bang, with a roar □ *A convoy of petrol lorries a mile to the rear was **sent up** in flames.* ⇨ go up[5].

send up[3] [B1i nom pass] (informal) ridicule by means of a mock-imitation, satirize. **S:** cartoonist, singer, comedian. **O:** society, the monarchy; pop-singer, hippy □ *In their most recent satirical sketch they* ***send up*** *fashionable young women who work for charitable causes* (or: *do a* ***send-up*** *of young women* etc). □ *His amusement turned to delight when those* ***send-up*** *songs rocketed into the hit-parade.* H

send up the wall [B2 pass] (informal) infuriate sb, annoy him unbearably; drive round the bend/up the wall (q v). **S:** noise, commotion; chatter, quarrelling □ *'How much longer are the builders going to be blasting away with that damned drill? It's enough to* ***send*** *anyone* ***up the wall!'*** ⇨ go up the wall.

sentence (to) [B2 pass rel] (legal) declare that sb is to have a certain punishment. **S:** court; judge, magistrate. **o:** six months, ten years; life (imprisonment); death □ *The judge* ***sentenced*** *him* ***to*** *ten years' hard labour.* □ *Those convicted of murder are no longer* ***sentenced to*** *death.*

separate (off) (from) [B1i pass B2 pass emph rel B3 pass emph rel] divide one thing from another, set a barrier between persons or things. **O:** group, class; part, fraction; area, space. **o:** another, the rest; the whole □ *'See to it that the trouble-makers are* ***separated off*** *and given something special to do.'* □ *These tests and practical exercises are intended to* ***separate*** *the sheep* ***from*** *the goats* (i e the more able from the less able). □ *Two huts at the end of the camp were* ***separated off from*** *the rest by a wire fence.*

separate out [A1 B1i pass] (cause to) become distinct from each other. **S:** [A1] **O:** [B1] oil and water; cream and milk; elements, strands □ (note in cooking instruction) *This pudding* ***separates out*** *in the cooking into a custard layer with a sponge topping* (cf *The custard layer and the sponge pudding* ***separate out***). □ *I have trouble in* ***separating out*** *the two parts of your argument.*

serve as [A2 B2] be suitable or useful for a particular purpose. **S:** stick, knife; weakness, absence. **o:** toothbrush, screwdriver; excuse, pretext □ *A hollowed-out stick* ***served*** *him* ***as*** *a spoon and a flat shell* ***as*** *a plate.* □ *His unpunctuality* ***served as*** *an excuse to get rid of him.*

serve on[1] [A2 emph rel] act as a member of. **S:** administrator, academic, councillor. **o:** committee, board □ *Sir John* ***serves on*** *the boards of several companies.*

serve on[2] [B2 pass emph rel] (legal) deliver a notice of the court to sb. **O:** ⚠ a writ, summons, notice to appear (in court), warrant □ *A summons was* ***served on*** *him to appear at the next Quarter Sessions.* □ *They've* ***served*** *a writ* ***on*** *him* (or: *They've* ***served*** *him* ***with*** *a writ*).

serve under [A2 emph rel] be a member of a force, organization etc under the leadership of sb. **o:** (famous) leader, general □ *He's not the sort of man I'd like to* ***serve under.*** □ *There was a move afoot to replace Forrest,* ***under*** *whose command we were* ***serving*** *at the time, with a younger general from England.*

serve up [B1i pass] offer (food) to sb; offer sth to sb for his consideration, entertainment etc. **O:** first course, pudding; same mixture (as before); nonsense, rubbish, tripe □ *Mother was just* ***serving up*** *the meal as I walked in.* □ *Why do the television networks keep* ***serving up*** *the same diet of old movies and second-rate variety programmes?*

serve with [B2 pass] ⇨ serve on[2].

set about[1] [A2 pass] begin a task, undertake it purposefully and energetically. **o:** job, task; preparing, buying, selling □ *We then* ***set about*** *the job of putting the animals into their travelling boxes.* DF □ *How could she* ***set about*** *finding him when she was lying helpless in bed?* DC ⇨ go about[3].

set about[2] [A2 pass] (informal) attack (with the fists or verbally) □ *'I'd* ***set about*** *them with this custard-ladle if we have any trouble,' said Mrs Fountain.* TT □ *A gang of boys* ***set about*** *a supporter of the other team.*

set against[1] [B2 pass] cause people who may be related, or close friends, to become enemies or rivals. **S:** war, politics, business; ambition, greed. **O:** father, brother. **o:** son, brother □ *Competing for the favours of a woman often* ***sets*** *friend* ***against*** *friend.* □ *In France, the Dreyfus Affair divided many families,* ***setting*** *father* ***against*** *son and brother* ***against*** *brother.*

set against[2] [B2 pass emph rel] consider, weigh, sth as a piece of evidence balancing sth that has already been suggested. **O:** evidence, factor, consideration; cost, saving, economy. **o:** argument, case; expense, wastage □ ***Against*** *the initial cost of buying a new car, you can* ***set*** *the considerable saving on repairs and servicing.* □ *I know it's dearer to buy than rent a house, but you must* ***set against*** *that the fact that I own what I pay for.*

set apart (from) [B1ii pass B3 pass emph rel] make sb or sth special or unusual. **S:** family, birth; distinction, (noble) character; intelligence, talent. **o:** others, ordinary people, the normal run of people □ *Exceptional gifts* ***set*** *him* ***apart from*** *other sculptors of his generation.* □ *For reasons he could not explain he was made to feel different,* ***set apart, from*** *the other boys.*

set aside[1] [B1i pass] place to one side, put aside[1] (q v). **O:** book, newspaper; task; knitting, sewing □ *Peter* ***set aside*** *the papers he was marking and reached for his cigarettes and matches.* □ *Work on the library extension had to be* ***set aside*** *while labour was diverted to more urgent projects.*

set aside[2] [B1i pass] (legal) cancel, annul, quash. **S:** higher court, court of appeal. **O:** decision, verdict, judgment □ *The judge's verdict was quashed and their prison sentences* ***set aside.*** BBCTV □ (interview with trade union leader) *'There is a clause which says the Minister can* ***set aside*** *the decision of the Pay Board.'* BBCTV

set aside[3] [B1i pass] get rid of, make oneself free of; suspend, dispense with[2] (q v). **O:** difference; hostility, bitterness, strife; protocol □ *In dealing with the man, he tried to* ***set aside*** *an instinctive mistrust of him.* □ *In these discussions, all formality was* ***set aside.***

set aside (for) [B1i pass B3 pass emph rel] save, reserve; name, select (for a particular purpose). **O:** money; time; minute, day. **o:** emergency, contingency; reading, play; trial, tournament □ *Don't eat all the tinned food.* ***Set*** *something* ***aside for*** *a possible emergency.* □ *He tried to* ***set aside*** *a few minutes each day* ***for*** *his exercises.* □ *This was the day* ***set aside for*** *his execution.* WI

set one's cap at [B2] (esp of a woman) try to attract, arouse, the sexual interest of sb (esp with a view to eventual marriage). **o:** eligible bachelor, unattached male, new boss □ *'She'll be jealous of you, you know, jealous of the good turns you've done me. She'll* **set her cap at** *you, I dare say.'* □ now rather dated; prefer (*try to*) get off with (q v).

set sb's mind at ease/rest [B2 pass] dispel, lighten, sb's anxieties about sth. **S:** adviser; doctor, solicitor, tutor □ *Robert could become a fashionable money-making artist, just another version of Ned, only more repulsive because of his greater pretensions. That ought to* **set Ned's mind at ease.** CON □ *The specialist said Mrs Barnes need have no misgivings about her daughter's progress. In fact he could* **set her mind** *completely* **at rest**: *the new treatment was a total success.* □ note pl form in: *Let me* **set your minds at rest**.

set back[1] [B1i nom pass] hinder the progress of sth, or reverse it (by a certain amount). **O:** programme; progress, advance, development □ *Difficulties in raising money have* **set back** *our building programme.* □ *Work on the new theatre has been* **set back** *three months.* □ *Shortage of the right materials has* **set us back** (cf *We have suffered a* **setback** *because of the shortage* etc). □ *Two years later, at the mid-term elections, his party suffered a very serious* **setback**. OBS

set back[2] [B1ii pass] (informal) be an expense to sb, cost him sth; knock back[2] (q v). **S:** house, car; party, celebration □ *His daughter's wedding* **set him back** *a few pounds.* □ *If you have dinner there it'll* **set** *you* **back** *five pounds a head.* □ back usu followed by an adv phrase of degree: *quite a bit, a fair bit* etc.

set back[3] [B1i pass] place, situate, some distance away from a road etc. **O:** house, stable, greenhouse □ *They've* **set** *the workshops well* **back**, *out of sight of the house.* □ *The house is* **set back** *some distance from the main road.* □ usu passive; back usu followed by adv phrase of degree: *some way, a fair distance* etc.

set great etc store by/on [B2 pass emph rel] regard as having a particular value or importance; attach to[1] (q v). **adj:** great, little; much, more, less, no. **o:** (outward) show, manner, appearance, dress; efficiency, competence, originality; kindness, tolerance □ *Martin* **set more store by** *official honours than I did.* NM □ *It is odd that one so susceptible to the clash and glare of the theatre should* **set so much store by** *personal privacy.* RT □ *'My wife, too,* **sets great store on** *the boys being at home.'* ASA

set down[1] [B1i pass] allow to alight (from a vehicle). **O:** passenger, fare □ *'Would you mind* **setting** *me* **down** *at the next corner?'* □ *The bus stops regularly to* **set down** *and pick up passengers.* ⇨ put down[3].

set down[2] [B1i pass] note, record, on paper. **O:** idea, thought, reflection □ *I'll* **set down** *one or two points while they are fresh in my mind.* ⇨ be down[3], get down[4], go down[9], put down[8], take down[3].

set down[3] [B1iii pass] (legal) choose, name, a day when a case is to be heard. **O:** day, date; trial, hearing □ *The day* **set down** *for the trial has still to be announced.* □ *'You knew the hearing was* **set down** *for today.'* BBCTV

set sail (for) [B2 rel] (nautical) begin a journey by sea (to a certain place). **o:** America, France; New York, Lagos □ *My speculations were suddenly interrupted by recalling that Tom had postponed his* **setting sail for** *the land of liberty.* SPL □ *The boat leaves Liverpool on the fifteenth, but before we* **set sail** (**for** *New York*) *I have to spend a few days in Scotland.*

set the stage (for) [B2 pass emph rel] make the preliminary arrangements (for), prepare (for what follows). **S:** government, minister; designer, inventor, planner. **o:** development, expansion; introduction, provision; discussion, argument, debate □ *He was associated with the establishment of the blood transfusion service in the Middle East, and* **set the stage for** *the application of chemo-therapy to the wounded soldier as soon after wounding as possible.* T □ *When the Bill came up for a second reading at the end of March* **the stage** *was* **set for** *a first-class row — which duly materialised.* MFM

set forth[1] [A1] (formal) leave home, base etc at the start of an expedition, campaign etc □ *David* **set forth** *to do battle with Goliath.* □ *We* **set forth** *on the last stage of our climb.* □ set out (on) (q v) is more usual.

set forth[2] [B1i pass] (formal) present, outline. **S:** secretary, accountant; document, manifesto. **O:** figure, cost; programme, aim, policy □ *These figures are more clearly* **set forth** *in tabular form.* PL □ *The Prime Minister* **set forth** *the aims of his government in a speech to party workers.*

set in[1] [A1] begin and seem likely to continue, gain a hold and seem likely to spread. **S:** winter, autumn; freeze, thaw; decay, gangrene; habit, fashion □ *The rails that remained looked as if the dry-rot had* **set in**. CON □ *The cold weather had* **set in**. HD □ *A new vogue in hats seems to have* **set in**. SC

set in[2] [pass (B2)] have fixed, established ways of behaving, reacting etc. **o:** one's behaviour; one's habits, ways, customs; a way, method (of doing sth); one's reactions, responses □ *I think I expected her to refuse. I just thought of her as* **set in** *her ways, and this sort of thing certainly wasn't among her habits.* CON □ *The old ruin had got so* **set in** *this habit of drinking in the Grapes* (a public house) *every lunch-time that he would have been lost without it.* CON □ passive with *be, get, seem.*

set foot in [B2 pass(o) rel] enter, arrive in. **o:** the place; France; house □ *She had never* **set foot in** *a place as grand as this before.* SML □ *No sooner had Isabel* **set foot in** *the house than she felt her mother's influence seeping into her.* PW □ *I had hardly* **set foot in** *England before somebody or other exclaimed, 'Oh, but you don't look in the least like your books!'* AH □ often in a subordinate clause introduced by (*from*) *the moment, as soon as, no sooner had he... than, he had hardly... before.*

set in motion [B2 pass] make sth begin to move; initiate. **O:** procession, parade; avalanche; campaign, invasion; debate, meeting □ *With such efficient communications armies at some distance from each other can be* **set in motion** *at the same time.* □ *Suppose the Soviets lost control of the events they had* **set in motion**? OBS □ *There followed a wave of selling on the Stock*

Market, ***set in motion*** *by the rumour that the currency was to be devalued.*

set one's (own) house in order [B2] restore one's business, one's family life etc to a proper state by removing disharmony, abuses etc; put one's (own) house etc (q v) □ *'Our brothers in the docks industry should* ***set their own house in order*** *before venturing to criticize the members of this union.'* □ *The Press must* ***set its own house in order*** *before the ultimate disaster of having order imposed upon it.* SC □ often in the form of a recommendation introduced by *should/ought to/must*; note pl form in: *They must* ***set their own houses in order.***

the rot set in [A1] (informal) (of a decline, deterioration) begin □ *Smith made a few runs at number six and then* ***the rot*** *really* ***set in*** (i e wickets fell cheaply). □ *Since Humphries was appointed Headmaster,* ***the rot*** *has* ***set in.***

set off[1] [B1i pass] cause to explode. **O:** bomb, mine; charge, explosive □ *The slightest spark can* ***set off*** *the explosive stored here.* □ *If the TNT is shaken or roughly handled it will be* ***set off.*** ⇨ go off[5], let off[4].

set off[2] [B1iii pass] cause, prompt, stimulate. **S:** news, report; discovery, invention. **O:** rumours, speculation; investment, developments □ *The threatened action by miners may* ***set off*** *sympathy strikes by transport workers.* □ *The further decline of the pound as reported today has* ***set off*** *a fresh wave of selling in the City.*

set off[3] [B1i pass] make sth appear more attractive by contrast. **S:** hair, lips; garden; carpet. **O:** complexion, pale skin; brick, stone; wall, curtain □ *The outfit* ***set off*** *her dark red hair.* PP □ *The formal beauty of the groves was* ***set off*** *by the perfection of the grey stonework.* HD

set off (against) [B1i pass B3 pass emph rel] balance, match (one thing against another). **O:** loss, expenditure; quick temper, shyness. **o:** (salary) increase, award; generosity, determination □ *The recent withdrawals from his account can be* ***set off*** *by a refund of income tax.* □ *You can* ***set*** *these heavy expenses* ***off against*** *a probable increase in salary.* □ *Yes, he is a difficult man at times. But you must* ***set off against*** *that his great kindness to the family when we really needed support.*

set off (on)[1] [A1 A3 rel] start to move, begin a journey; set out (on) (q v). **S:** runner, cyclist, explorer. **o:** race, journey; lap, stage □ *The cars* ***set off*** *in a cloud of dust.* BM □ *The police* ***set off*** *in hot pursuit.* BB □ *Look, education is like* ***setting off on*** *an expedition into the jungle.* FFE ⇨ be off[3], get off[3].

set off (on)[2] [B1i pass B3 pass] start sb telling stories, laughing etc; start off (on)[2] (q v). **S:** remark, joke; reminiscence. **o:** tale, account □ *'Don't say anything, John. You'll only* ***set*** *him* ***off on*** *one of his interminable war stories.'* □ *That* ***set*** *all of them* ***off*** *laughing again.* EM □ *The look on his face is enough to* ***set*** *you* ***off!*** ⇨ be off (on).

set on [A2 pass B2 pass] (cause to) attack. **S:** [A2] **O:** [B2] dog; gang, follower □ *He* ***sets*** *his dog* ***on*** *anyone who comes near the house.* □ *He was* ***set on*** *and beaten up in a dark alley.*

set eyes on [B2 pass(o) rel] perceive, sight; lay eyes on (q v). **o:** each other; (new) home, place of work □ *It seemed to me as if we'd done nothing but row and suffer like this from the moment we* ***set eyes on*** *each other.* LLDR □ *He had fallen victim to a jealous suspicion of all other men who might even* ***set eyes on*** *his wife, let alone speak to her.* AH □ often in a subordinate clause introduced by *(from) the moment, as soon as, no sooner had he... than, he had hardly... before.*

set on his/its feet [B2 pass] help to return to health, prosperity; put on his/its feet (q v). **S:** rest, holiday; doctor; loan, advance; bank. **O:** patient, sick man; business, industry □ *You are aware of how much help you need to* ***set*** *you* ***on your feet.*** WI □ *The ship-building industry needs more than occasional injections of capital to* ***set*** *it back* ***on its feet.***

set on fire[1] [B2 pass] cause sth to burn, set it alight. **S:** careless, negligent person; spark, heat; incendiary bomb, shell. **O:** place; house, barn; corn, hay; one's clothes □ *'How many times have I got to warn you against* ***setting*** *the place* ***on fire?'*** HD □ *The blaze was fanned by a stiff breeze and in this way all the farm outbuildings were* ***set on fire.*** □ it is often things (not persons) which set sth on fire; the action tends not to be deliberate if caused by a person: *'Stop emptying your pipe into the wastepaper basket: you'll* ***set*** *the house* ***on fire!'*** ⇨ set fire/light to.

set on fire[2] [B2 pass] arouse great interest and excitement (in a place, in people). **S:** actor, singer, writer; newcomer, recruit (to industry etc). **O:** the place, the world; literary London, the West End □ *'Tomorrow is another day. Don't let's try to* ***set*** *the world* ***on fire*** *tonight.'* AITC □ *She was a lady who once* ***set*** *the whole of the literary world (if not the Thames)* ***on fire.*** MM

set great etc store on [B2 pass emph rel] ⇨ set great etc store by/on.

set one's heart on [B2 pass emph rel] (informal) long deeply, with all one's heart, to do or achieve sth. **S:** student; scientist; athlete. **o:** career, prize; discovery, achievement; record □ *She was mad on show-jumping;* ***her heart*** *was* ***set on*** *horses.* DBM □ *To take part in the Olympics — this was an ambition* ***on*** *which he had* ***set his heart.*** □ *Isabel, Jeremy, and Janice would enjoy material benefits too, and Isabel,* ***whose heart*** *was* ***set on*** *bringing this about, would be appeased.* PW □ note pl form: set their hearts on.

set the seal on [B2 pass emph rel] mark in some appropriate way the high or final point of one's progress etc. **S:** ceremony; formal reception, investiture (with a medal or honour); election, admission (to a society); marriage. **o:** career, life's work; progress, recovery □ *Sir Francis Chichester's knighthood* ***set the*** *final* ***seal on*** *the remarkable career of this airman and lone yachtsman.* □ *'Once a man marries a girl like you, I find it impossible to think of him as a fellow citizen. He's* ***set the seal on*** *his success today.'* CON

set one's sights on [B2 pass emph rel] have as one's goal or objective. **o:** job, career; championship, gold medal; breaking the record, winning the geography prize □ *It was not that Virginia had a consuming passion to work on a women's magazine. She had* ***set her sights on*** *it because there was a chance for her in this place.* AITC □ ***John's sights*** *were* ***set on*** *acquiring the controlling interest in a group of stores.*

(s)et sb's/the teeth on edge [B2 pass] cause an unpleasant sensation in the teeth (as when one scrapes a fingernail on metal); annoy, irritate. **S:** the scrape of chalk on a blackboard; voice, accent; conversation □ *'The man I killed—I know him. He was Russian and he was very thin. I scraped the bone when I pushed the steel in. It **set my teeth on edge**.'* OMIH □ *'You say things that **set these people's teeth on edge**. You make them feel you're getting at them.'* SML

(s)et the Thames on fire [B2] (informal) arouse considerable excitement; achieve a remarkable success. **S:** actor, singer, conductor; manager, executive □ *She was a lady who once **set** the whole of the literary world (if not **the Thames**) **on fire*** (i e who achieved a limited, not a spectacular, success). MM □ *'Take young Jeffries, now. You wouldn't say he's the kind to **set the Thames on fire**, would you?'* ⇨ set on fire[2].

(s)et out[1] [A1] begin work with the intention of achieving a particular aim. **Inf** to climb Mt Everest, to win support for his scheme □ *The Mexican peasant **sets out** to burn an acre of woodland in order to plant his maize.* HAH □ *When I really **set out** to take care of somebody, I usually do the job properly.* TOH □ always followed by an inf.

(s)et out[2] [B1i pass adj] arrange items on a table, board etc; present material in an orderly manner. **O:** wares, goods; stall; idea, point; essay, argument □ *Michael **set out** the pieces on the chessboard.* □ *The ties were attractively **set out** to draw in the customers.* □ *I've seldom read such a well **set-out** piece of work from a student.*

(s)et out[3] [B1i pass adj] declare, state. **S:** chairman, secretary; delegate; paper. **O:** conditions, terms; objection, criticism □ *The staff side have already **set out** the safeguards which they think should be observed.* T □ *Recent changes in the tax law are **set out** in the enclosed booklet.*

(s)et out (on) [A1 A3 rel] start to move, begin a journey, leave on a journey; set off (on)[1] (q v). **S:** traveller; convoy, procession. **o:** trip, tour; stage, circuit □ *Vanity made you **set out** after the King, when you didn't care for him.* WI □ *The reporters **set out** in high spirits.* TBC □ *This morning, competitors **set out on** the last stage of the round-Britain cycle race.*

(s)et to[1] [A1] begin doing sth vigorously, go to work (on) (q v); begin eating hungrily □ *He is the fastest worker and **sets to** straight away, not stopping until his station is ready.* TK □ *She **set to** to do all the housework.* UL □ *The pair of them **set to** and demolished a pork pie.*

(s)et to[2] [A1 nom] begin to fight or argue. **S:** boxers; politicians; housewives □ *When those two women **set to** (or: have a **set-to**), the fur will really fly.* □ *What began as a mild discussion developed into a regular **set-to**.*

(s)et fire/light to [B2 pass(o) rel] apply a flame to sth, to burn it. **o:** rubbish, dried leaves, wastepaper; house, factory; store, dump (of food); one's clothes □ *The Dutch **set fire to** all their military installations.* TO □ *In the retreat, wooden houses were **set light to** and stone buildings destroyed by explosives.* □ a person or a thing (*hot ash, an incendiary bomb*) may set fire/light to sth; the action may be deliberate or accidental; cf *John **set fire to** the papers. Hot ash from John's pipe **set fire to** the papers.* ⇨ set on fire.

set one's mind to [B2 pass] give one's full attention to; put one's mind to (q v). **o:** task, job; finishing on time, repairing the damage □ JO: *I can do anything when I **set my mind to** it.* TOH □ *'Now just you **set your mind to** meeting these orders on time.'*

set to work [A2] begin working □ *After breakfast we **set to work** and made a cage for the armadillo.* DF □ *The floor was so encumbered with objects that I had to **set to work** to clear myself a space.* UTN

set the world to rights [B2] (informal) discuss, argue about, important problems, so creating the illusion that they have been solved. **S:** armchair critic, self-styled expert □ *An intense-looking group had gathered at one end of the bar, **setting the world to rights**, no doubt.* □ *'Do come round some time and talk about old times and,' she giggled slightly, '**set the world to rights** again.'* HAHA

set up[1] [B1i pass adj] place in position, erect. **O:** stall; mounting, tripod; telescope, range-finder; post, flag □ *I **set** the camera **up** in a small patch of shade.* DF □ *Nearby, he or one of his family **set up** an imposing Celtic cross.* SD

set up[2] [B1i pass] establish, institute. **S:** government, trades union, board of directors. **O:** office, centre; committee, commission; inquiry, investigation □ *An operations room was **set up** in the Home Office with teleprinter links and weather charts.* OBS □ *The Minister of Commerce **set up** an emergency committee today to ensure the maintenance of bread supplies.* OBS □ *The same period would be required to **set up** the international control system.* OBS

set up[3] [B1iii pass] begin to shout, protest etc, loudly. **S:** crowd; audience, class. **O:** commotion, caterwauling, din □ *As soon as he appeared on stage the crowd **set up** such a commotion that the show had to be stopped.*

set up[4] [B1iii pass] cause, produce. **S:** diet, climate. **O:** infection; swelling, rash □ *Smoking **sets up** an irritation in the throat and bronchial passages.* □ *The doctor has no idea how the condition was first **set up**.*

set up[5] [B1ii pass adj] (informal) make sb healthier, stronger, more lively etc. **S:** holiday, rest, break; diet, air □ *'Alice says that the sea air'll **set me up**. But I don't know.'* ASA □ *'Marry me, Helen. I'm young, good-looking and well **set up*** (i e healthy and vigorous).' TOH

set up[6] [B1i pass] (sport) establish a record speed, time, distance etc in a sporting event. **O:** ⚠ a record, a time (of 2hrs 8min 33·6sec) □ *Stewart **set up** a new Commonwealth Games record in the 10 000 metres.*

set-up [nom (B1)] organization, structuring (of a business, government department, household etc) □ *The **set-up** in the business was far too hierarchical.* THH □ *It took him some time to find out what the **set-up** was at head office.* □ *By all accounts, this **set-up** has functioned with superbly improvised efficiency.* OBS ⇨ set up[2].

set up shop [B1iii] (informal) establish a business (shop, large store, agency etc); begin practising a particular trade or profession □ *Ackroyd **set up shop** as a retail tobacconist in the High Street.* □ *Then eventually he **set up shop** as a freelance photographer.*

set up (as)[1] [A1 A3 B1i pass B3 pass] establish oneself in a business or trade; make it possible for sb to do so by providing the money etc. **o:** grocer, baker; locksmith, innkeeper □ [B3] *There was enough money left to **set** the youngest boy **up as** a photographer.* □ [A1 A3] *His father moved to London and **set up** at the 'Golden Lion'* (i e ***as** an innkeeper*).

set up (as)[2] [A1 A3 B1ii pass B3 pass] consider, reckon sb (or oneself) to be special in some way; have pretensions to being such a person. **O:** him etc, oneself. **o:** authority, scholar; superior, something special □ [A3] *I didn't want to **set up as** better than anyone else.* NM □ [B3] *He's not the wise, all-knowing father he **sets** himself **up as**.* □ [B3] *He's **set up as*** (or: *to be*) *something remarkable. We shall see.* □ set up *to be* may be used instead of set up as [A3 B3].

set up (in) [B1i pass B3 pass rel] make it possible for sb to start a business, buy a house etc, by providing the money. **O:** wife, brother; mistress; oneself. **o:** business, shop; flat, house □ *One could do some things which otherwise could not be thought of, like **setting up** an unmarried daughter **in** a shop.* UL □ *Perhaps he could take a flat for her in Downhaven, and **set** her **up** there.* PW □ *If I have a big win on the Football Pools I shall be **set up** for the rest of my life!*

set up house (together) [B1iii] live together as man and wife (whether married or not) □ *Military wives were not to be in the same area as their husbands, i e they were not to **set up house together**.* MFM

settle back [A1] lean comfortably back in one's chair □ *The lights dimmed, the curtain went up, and we **settled back** to enjoy the play.* □ *'Now, Mother, you're not to help with any of the housework. Just **settle back** in your armchair and read a magazine.'*

settle down[1] [A1] subside, lessen. **S:** noise, hubble; excitement, panic □ *Don't come back for a day or two until the noise and commotion have **settled down**.*

settle down[2] [A1 B1ii pass] become or make calm, peaceful. **S:** [A1] **O:** [B1] guest, child, patient; house, place; things □ *It was two days after the attack. For the moment, things had **settled down**.* SD □ *'Go away a minute while I try to **settle** Mary **down**.'*

settle down[3] [A1] seat oneself comfortably (usu for some quiet, prolonged activity) □ *Then they came back to their positions and **settled down** to watch again.* TO □ *We **settled down** to a quiet discussion of English slang.* EM

settle down[4] [A1] marry, and begin the routine, stable life usu associated with that state □ *'He isn't married, you know. I don't know why, but writers often don't **settle down** like other people.'* PW □ *He's no intention of **settling down** yet.*

settle down (in) [A1 A3 rel] establish oneself in a (permanent) job. **o:** trade, job □ *Before you **settle down** to being an honest electrician, consider this offer.* EHOW □ *He's a man whose one aim is to **settle down in** a safe job.* CON

settle for [A2 emph rel] (be ready to) accept sth simple, undemanding etc, because one has modest tastes, or is lacking in ambition etc. **o:** the simple life; low-paid work, routine job; plain fare; ordinary girl □ *She was not prepared to **settle for** being an ordinary housewife.* □ *He wants to make a quick sale, so he'll **settle for** a low price.*

settle in/into [A1 A2 rel B1ii pass B2 pass rel] (cause to) move into a new place and make oneself comfortable or at home there. **S:** [A1 A2] **O:** [B1 B2] family, child; pupil, student. **o:** district, area; house, flat; school □ [A1] *We're a little disorganized after the move, but do come and see us when we've **settled in**.* □ [B2] *We'd hardly **settled** the children **into** a new school when we were posted to another district and had to uproot them again.*

settle on[1] [A2 pass rel] decide or agree to take, buy, use etc. **o:** date, rendezvous; meeting; house, car □ *After some discussion we **settled on** a date in early July.* □ *'Now that the meeting-place has been **settled on**, can we talk about the agenda?'*

settle on[2] [B2 pass emph rel] give, leave, money or property under the terms of a will etc. **O:** sum, amount; estate, fortune. **o:** wife, child □ *The greater part of his fortune was **settled on** his three sons.* □ *It ought to have been enough to **settle** a lump sum **on** her, even if that might have meant mortgaging the place.* WI

settle up (with) [A1 A3 pass] pay the money one owes before leaving a hotel, restaurant etc; square up (with) (q v). **o:** manager; waiter, porter, doorman □ *'I'm tired of this place: let's **settle up** and go.'* □ *'I'm short of cash. Have you enough to **settle up with** the waiter?'*

settle with [A2 pass B2 pass] punish sb for an injury one has suffered, get even with; square one's accoun/accounts with (q v). **O:** ⚠ accounts, (old) scores; one's/an account, one's/a score □ *'He may think he has the better of us, but we'll **settle with** him before the week's out.'* □ *'I hear Steve's back in town. It's just as well: I've got a score to **settle with** him.'*

sew down [B1i pass adj] with needle and thread, fasten completely to a surface sth which is already partly attached to it. **O:** pocket, flap, lapel □ *The flaps of his jacket pockets were **sewn down** so that they did not crease or wrinkle.*

sew on/onto [B1i pass B2 pass rel] attach accessories etc to a garment with needle and thread. **O:** button, zip-fastener; pocket, sleeve. **o:** coat, trousers; suit □ *Medal ribbons are usually **sewn onto** a uniform above the left pocket of the jacket.* □ *'The zip has broken. Will you **sew** me a new one **on**?'* □ note the Indirect Object (*me*) in the second example.

sew up[1] [B1i pass adj] seal or close an opening by drawing the edges together with thread etc. **O:** cut, slit; wound, incision □ *The cut in his finger was **sewn up** with a piece of fine silk.*

sew up[2] [B1i pass] (informal) organize an area etc, esp for purposes of trade; arrange, settle, a deal etc. **S:** salesman, agent. **O:** region, district; market, trading; deal, contract □ *Give me a good assistant and I'll have the area **sewn up** for you inside six months.* □ *The deal was **sewn up** over drinks in the hotel bar.* □ usu passive.

shack up (together/with) [A1 A3] (slang) live in an informal, Bohemian style with sb to whom one is not married, and whom (possibly) one does not intend to marry □ *'Who is he **shacking up with** these days?'* □ *My parents would have a fit if they knew that their darling daughter was*

shacking up with *a long-haired poet* (or: *their daughter and a poet were* ***shacking up together***). □ usu indicates disapproval on the part of the speaker.

shackle with [B2 pass rel] impose some control or check on sb, so that he is not free to act. **O:** citizen, householder; trader, manufacturer. **o:** taxation, mortgage; control, regulation □ *He's a bit young to* ***shackle*** *himself* ***with*** *the responsibilities of a family.* □ *Family doctors are anxious to provide a proper service for their patients, but they can't give them the attention they need if they're* ***shackled with*** *paperwork.*

shade (off) into [A2 A3] (of one colour adjoining another) merge gradually into that colour. **S:** red; blue. **o:** pink; green □ *In the spectrum, what we call, or name as, distinct colours* ***shade*** *imperceptibly* ***into*** *each other.*

shake by the hand [B2 pass] shake sb's hand (esp to thank or congratulate him). **O:** rescuer; winner □ *I should like to* ***shake*** *you and your men* ***by the hand****, and thank each one of you personally for all you have done.* MFM □ *'Some day the world will know and acclaim, and then you, Virginia, will be able to say: "I knew him before you did. I saw his works in manuscript," and people will* ***shake*** *you* ***by the hand****.'* AITC

shake down [A1 nom] (informal) settle properly into position or running order; settle into harmony with one's companions etc. **S:** (new) machinery, engine; staff, students; course-members, participants □ *Following extensive modifications after the accident to the turbine blades, the liner underwent further trials at sea to ensure that everything* ***shook down*** *properly* (cf *underwent further* ***shake-down*** *trials*). □ *The delegates were from many different backgrounds, but they quickly* ***shook down*** *in their new surroundings.* □ shake-down used attrib, as in the first example.

shake off[1] [B1i pass] by taking avoiding action, get rid of pursuers etc. **S:** ship, aircraft; fugitive, escapee. **O:** attacker, pursuer □ *Our pilot dived into a bank of cloud in an attempt to* ***shake off*** *the enemy fighters.* □ *Walter* ***shook off*** *her unwelcome attentions and rushed into his room.* FFE

shake off[2] [B1i pass] get rid of, be cured of. **O:** cold, fever; mood □ *I wish I could* ***shake off*** *this confounded cold.* □ *He went out to the pub with a few friends, hoping to* ***shake off*** *the depression which had seized him.*

shake the dust (of sth) off one's feet/shoes [B2] leave an unpleasant place, trying consciously to rid oneself of its associations. **o:** (*of*) home, school, army life □ *However, it was not very long before I was called up for military service, and I* ***shook the dust of*** *the school* ***off my shoes*** *for ever.* SPL □ *'If he wants me to work in his London office, he won't need to ask twice. I shall be glad to* ***shake the dust of*** *this one-horse town* ***off my feet****.'*

shake out [A1] (military) move into a more open formation (to offer less of a target to enemy gunners etc). **S:** troops; company, battalion □ *'The way your battalion* ***shook out*** *into artillery formation, company by company... was the most beautiful bit of parade-ground drill I've ever seen.'* R GRAVES: GOODBYE TO ALL THAT

shake-out [nom (A1 B1)] (industry) a vigorous redistribution of staff, fresh use of resources etc, aimed at making an industry more efficient □ *Much of manufacturing industry is in incomparably better shape than a few years ago, largely as a result of the notorious* ***shake-out*** *in management and manpower of Heath's first year.* ST

shake out of [B2 pass] make sb change his normal way of life, attitudes or feelings by giving him a sharp shock. **o:** (set) ways, habits; complacency, apathy □ *Perhaps this was the adventure that would* ***shake*** *him* ***out of*** *the neurosis of routine.* NM □ *He hoped to be* ***shaken out of*** *the ruts of ordinary perception* (i e by taking drugs). DOP

shake up[1] [B1i nom pass] move a bottle etc to and fro vigorously, thus mixing the contents well. **O:** mixture, medicine, tonic □ *The contents should be well* ***shaken up*** *until all the sediment disappears.* □ *All the ingredients get a good* ***shake-up*** *in this new electric mixer.*

shake up[2] [B1i nom pass] shake a cushion etc after sb has been sitting on it, to restore it to shape. **O:** cushion, pillow, bolster □ *As soon as the visitor was announced, Mother bustled around,* ***shaking up*** *the cushions and tidying away the newspapers.* □ *'Give the pillows a bit of a* ***shake-up*** *and smooth the sheets.'*

shake up[3] [B1i nom pass] disturb, make uncomfortable, by shaking. **S:** journey; plane, tram. **O:** passenger, traveller □ *When the aircraft finally landed, most of us felt badly* ***shaken up****.* □ *Don't go on the roller-coaster at the fair unless your bones can stand a thorough* ***shake-up****.*

shake up[4] [B1i nom pass] discipline idle or unruly people by handling them vigorously. **S:** teacher, officer. **O:** pupil, soldier □ *'What these recruits need is half an hour's drill on the square — that'll* ***shake*** *them* ***up****.'* □ *After the lethargy of the last headmaster's rule, the place was ready for a* ***shake-up****.*

shame into [B2 pass rel] cause sb to behave well by making him feel ashamed of his earlier wrongdoing. **o:** apology, confession, admission; giving up his privileges, donating money □ *Mary stared at him hard and eventually* ***shamed*** *him* ***into*** *giving up his seat to the old lady.* □ *'Don't imagine that he can be* ***shamed into*** *admitting it was all his fault.'*

shape (into) [B2 pass rel] give to material a particular form or shape. **O:** metal, clay, stone, wood. **o:** figure, vessel □ *The wet clay is patted onto the wire framework and* ***shaped into*** *the body of an animal.* □ *You can* ***shape*** *the plastic* ***into*** *bowls or buckets by moulding it under pressure.*

shape up [A1] (informal) develop, progress. **S:** pupil, student; musician; athlete; economy, industry, currency □ *'How are the new boys in your team* ***shaping up****?'* □ *I've been coaching two long-jumpers for the next meeting and they're* ***shaping up*** *very nicely.* □ *The pound didn't* ***shape up*** *very well against other European currencies.* BBCR

share out (among) [B1i nom pass B3 pass rel] give a share of sth to each of a group of people. **O:** money; food, clothing; booty, spoils □ *At the end of each day, they met for a formal* ***sharing out*** *of the money they had earned.* HD □ ***Shared out among*** *five people, the food won't* *go very far.* □ *After tonight's show, we'll have a* ***share-out*** *of the takings.*

share (with) [B2 pass rel] give to one or more persons a part of what one has; use facilities in common with one or more other people. **O:** food, tobacco, drink; bedroom, bathroom. **o:** relative, team-mate; guest, visitor □ *'**Share** the toffee **with** your brother and sister.'* □ *'Would you mind **sharing** a bedroom **with** another guest?* (or: *Would you and another guest mind **sharing** a bedroom?)'*

shave off [B1i pass] remove with the razor a growth of hair that has been allowed to develop. **O:** moustache, sideboard(s), beard □ *It might be a good idea to **shave off** your beard before going to London for the interview.*

shed light on [B2 pass emph rel] clarify, explain; throw light on (q v). **adj:** no, (not) any/much, little; fresh, new, additional. **o:** event, incident; mystery, enigma; theft, disappearance □ *Considerable **light** was **shed on** recent events by his statement to the police.* □ *Government sources were refusing to **shed** any more **light** than appeared yesterday **on** the television interview with M Georges Bidault.* SC

shed tears over [B2 pass] express one's regrets esp about a person or over an event which do not merit them. **adj:** no, (not) any/much; few. **o:** ruffian, layabout, crook; failure, collapse (of an enterprise) □ *'You're not going to **shed** any **tears over** my Sandy, are you?'* EHOW □ *'The famous Templar family is bankrupt.' 'I don't believe it.' 'I'm afraid it's true. The great and mighty Saunders wouldn't **shed tears over** anything but lack of money.'* DC □ usu neg or interr.

sheer away (from) [A1 A3 rel] move sharply away from sb or sth dangerous or unpleasant. **o:** bore, drunk, incessant talker; pitfall, trap □ *If peers were unpopular, people would **sheer away from** them, would not want their daughters to marry them.* T □ *This was a topic **from** which he always **sheered away**, as though unwilling to face the embarrassment it caused.*

sheet down [A1] (of rain) fall heavily, in sheets. **S:** ⚠ the rain; it □ *We sat gloomily by the hotel window, watching it **sheet down**.* □ *The wind blew, the rain **sheeted down**, and we were all soaked.*

shell out [A1 B1i pass] (informal) pay, meet (the cost); spend, donate (a sum). **S:** parent; firm, organization. **O:** money; cost; subscription, donation □ *I know that when the collection box comes round I shall be expected to **shell out** the most.* □ *I'm tired of **shelling out** on repairs to this car.*

shelter (from) [A2 emph rel B2 pass emph rel] use sth as cover or protection (from); offer or afford cover (from). **S:** [A2] **O:** [B2] child; soldier; animal. **S:** [B2] tree, porch; trench, bunker; hedge, shed. **o:** rain, storm; bombardment □ *They huddled in a shop doorway to **shelter from** the rain.* □ *They covered the roof with earth and rock, thick enough to **shelter** the men **from** gunfire.*

shelve down (to) [A1 A3 rel] slope gently (towards), slope down (to) (q v). **S:** bank, cliff, shore. **o:** sea, water's edge □ *At this point, the chalk cliffs **shelve down to** the beach.*

shield (from) [B2 pass emph rel] give protection (from). **S:** metal plate, glass screen, spectacles; police; parent. **O:** eye, face; (dead) body; children. **o:** sun, glare; spectators; harmful influence □ *In winter your eyes should be **shielded from** light reflected from the snow.* □ *You are not helping your child if you try to **shield** him **from** every danger.*

shift for oneself [A2] manage to earn a living, run a home etc, without help from others □ *If you're marooned on an island, I won't be able to help you — you'll have to **shift for yourself**.* □ *If he hadn't been able to **shift for himself** when his parents died, he would have starved.*

shift the blame/responsibility onto [B2 pass emph rel] claim that sb else is to blame for sth unpleasant. □ *When his plans miscarry, he always looks around for somebody to **shift the blame onto**.* □ *Much of **the responsibility** for the disaster was **shifted onto** Menzies, and this was quite undeserved.*

shin up [A2] (informal) climb up. **o:** wall, drainpipe, rope □ *Thieves probably got into the house by **shinning up** a drainpipe and forcing open the window.*

shine out [A1] give out a bright light; be clearly noticeable, outstanding, because of one's qualities. **S:** sun, light; virtue; integrity, generosity □ *The curtains were suddenly drawn and a bright light **shone out** across the lawn.* □ *Among so much backsliding and indecision his courage and resolution **shine out** like a beacon.*

ship off [B1i pass] send, dispatch, esp by sea or air. **O:** load, consignment; goods, merchandise; reinforcements, drafts □ *A dozen crates were **shipped off** by air freight last week.* □ *A younger son for whom there were no prospects at home might be **shipped off** abroad to make a career for himself.*

ship out[1] [A1] (nautical) go to sea as a crew-member □ *Men from New England ports **shipped out** in these sailing vessels.* BBCTV

ship out[2] [B1i pass] (nautical) send, carry, from a port as cargo. **S:** maker, supplier; ferry, tanker. **O:** cargo, load; cement, iron-ore, oil □ *The oil company will **ship out** piping and heavy equipment* (i e to the oil rig). SC □ *We have to suck in vast quantities of raw materials before we can convert them into exports and **ship** them **out** again.* ST

shoot a glance (at) [B2] look quickly at sb, and then away again; dart a glance/look at (q v). **adj:** curious, suspicious, hostile □ ***The glance** he **shot at** Charles from beneath his straggling white eyebrows was, of all things, a slightly envious one.* HD □ *The clerk at the hotel desk **shot an** inquisitive **glance at** the young man near the newspaper kiosk* (cf ***shot** the young man **an** inquisitive **glance***).

shoot down [B1i pass adj] cause to fall to the ground (usu out of control). **S:** fighter, anti-aircraft gun. **O:** bomber, transport □ *Three out of a formation of eight were **shot down** in flames.* □ *You'd be lucky to **shoot** a fighter **down** with a light machine-gun.*

shoot in [B1i pass] (military) give covering fire for infantry assaulting an enemy position. **S:** tank, self-propelled gun, artillery. **O:** infantry, assault troops □ *In this campaign, the tanks were often used in a support role, **shooting in** the infantry as mobile artillery.*

shoot one's mouth off [B1ii] (informal) speak

in a loud, and indiscreet or boastful, way □ *'We were hoping to keep the party a secret — it was meant to be a surprise for Jane. What made you go and* **shoot your mouth off** *about it?'* □ *'It's going to be one of those awful hearty evenings, with Bill swigging his beer and* **shooting his mouth off!**'

shoot out [B1i pass] (cricket) dismiss rapidly; (informal) expel, evict (from a house etc). **S:** bowler; landlord. **O:** team, batsman; tenant, occupant □ *The Surrey team were* **shot out** *before lunch, thanks to a fine piece of spin bowling by Travers.* □ *Won't the Ministry of Agriculture people have something to say if they're* **shot out** *and we're moved in?* TBC

shoot it out [B1ii nom] fight to a conclusion, or decision (usu with small-arms) □ *Since one man had no pistol, they agreed to* **shoot it out**, *on horseback, with rifles.* □ *There is always the risk of civilians being caught in the crossfire when terrorists and soldiers* **shoot it out** (or: *when there is a* **shoot-out** *between terrorists and soldiers*).

shoot out/out of [A1 emph A2 emph rel] emerge swiftly and suddenly (from). **S:** rabbit, snake. **o:** burrow, grass □ *The lizard's tongue* **shot out** *and scooped up the fly.* □ *The dog* **shot out of** *the gate and was half-way across the field before we knew it.*

shoot up[1] [A1] (informal) grow, increase in size, quickly. **S:** plant, child □ *'My word, you have* **shot up** *since I saw you last.'*

shoot up[2] [A1] rise, increase, sharply; race up (into/to) (q v). **S:** price, cost, rent; temperature, pressure; applications, attendance □ *We shall do what we can to stop prices* **shooting up** *still further.* □ *My pulse rate would suddenly* **shoot up** *alarmingly.* DIL

shoot up[3] [B1i pass] (informal) terrorize a place by moving through it and firing into the air, at houses etc. **S:** bandit, gangster. **O:** town; saloon □ *'Nobody can scare them off: they'll come back and* **shoot** *the place* **up**, *just for kicks.'*

shop around [A1] (informal) go from one shop, dealer etc to another until one finds the best value for money; examine claims, programmes, of various firms, colleges etc before deciding which to join □ *It will pay you to* **shop around** *a bit before deciding which car to buy.* □ *'Has Peter decided which universities he's going to apply to?' 'Not yet. He's* **shopping around** *for a course with a good choice of options.'*

shore up [B1i pass adj] support, prevent from falling down, with wooden props or pillars; protect (the economy etc) by fiscal or other means. **O:** house; wall, tree; economy, currency □ *It only needs a heavy storm to bring the whole house down. We'll have to* **shore it up**. BM □ *The nations reacted blindly in 1929,* **shoring up** *their national defences and then standing by helpless as the tide of demand ebbed away.* OBS

shorn of [pass (B2)] have sth removed or cut away from it. **S:** book, document; legislation, Bill; proposal, scheme. **o:** passage, section; clause; provision □ *The story is* **shorn of** *its individualizing features, the descriptive passages lose most of what peculiarities of style and content they possess, and the original phrasing is replaced by current, commonplace clichés.* MFF □ *In its passage through the House the Land Acquisition Bill was* **shorn of** *its most controversial provisions.*

shot up [pass adj (B1)] (military) (be) injured, damaged or reduced in numbers by enemy action. **S:** tank, plane; division, regiment □ *John's regiment had been badly* **shot up** *in the last attack and was due to be relieved.* □ *The area just inside the enemy perimeter was littered with* **shot-up** *tanks and trucks.* □ passive with *be, get, seem, look.*

shoulder aside [B1i pass] push sb to one side with the shoulder □ *A big fellow rushed from the store,* **shouldering aside** *anyone who got in his way.*

shout down [B1i pass] prevent a speaker from being heard by shouting while he is speaking. **S:** crowd; faction, claque. **O:** speaker; representative, leader □ *An angry meeting* **shouted down** *one of the committee as he tried to address them through a loud-hailer.* □ *'Don't try to talk to them in their present mood: you'll only get* **shouted down.**'

shout out [A1 B1i pass] call in a loud clear voice. **O:** name, address; price; abuse □ *'If you know the answer, don't* **shout out** *— wait till I ask you.'* □ *The first person to complete a card* **shouts out** *'Bingo!' at the top of her voice.*

shove down sb's throat [B2 pass] (informal) repeat sth often in the hope that it will be learnt, accepted etc; ram down sb's throat (q v). **O:** lesson; history, Latin; view, opinion; merit, worth (of sth) □ *'You're always* **shoving it down my throat** *that you're the one with the job, but it's not so wonderful. I'm working far harder than you.'* AITC □ *He'd had French* **shoved down his throat** *for five hours a week. No wonder he grew to hate it.*

shove off[1] [A1] (nautical) move a boat away from the shore (by pushing the shore with a pole etc); push off[1] (q v) □ *'Is everybody safely aboard? Right,* **shove off!**'

shove off[2] [A1] (informal) go away, leave (usu indicating boredom, irritation etc on the part of the person leaving or asking another to leave); push off[2] (q v) □ *'Well, you've said your piece. Now why don't you* **shove off** *and leave us alone?'* □ *'I can't stand his company any longer: let's* **shove off** *somewhere and have a drink.'*

show around/round [B1i pass B2 pass] take visitors on a tour of a place, guide them round a place; show over (q v). **S:** guide, receptionist. **O:** party, delegation; visitor, tourist. **o:** house, garden; factory, site □ *If you are free at two o'clock on Friday, I shall be delighted to* **show** *you* **around** *the place.* □ *'Mr Jones is busy at the moment. He's* **showing round** *a party of visitors.'*

show-down [nom (A1 B1)] (cards) moment when the cards in all hands are revealed; (esp informal) moment, in a trial of strength, when one side reveals the weakness, pretensions etc of the other and/or its own strength □ *There is too much easy talk in the press of the Government forcing a* **show-down** *with the Unions.* □ *If it comes to a* **show-down** *with the bank we can point to the encouraging trading forecast for the next six months.*

show in/into [B1i pass B2 pass rel] lead, conduct, sb into a place. **S:** secretary, servant. **O:** caller, visitor; customer. **o:** waiting-room, drawing-room □ *'When the guests arrive please* ***show*** *them* ***into*** *the sitting-room.'* □ *'Don't keep Mr Rodgers waiting.* ***Show*** *him* ***in****!'*

show off[1] [B1i pass] display sth, make it appear, to advantage. **S:** setting; room, frame, mounting; clothes. **O:** jewel; furniture, painting; figure, shape. **A:** well, admirably; to advantage □ *The room, very plain, formal and grey, was intended primarily to* ***show off*** *the drawings that were hung there.* ASA □ *The cut of her dress* ***shows off*** *her figure to perfection.*

show off[2] [B1i pass] display, draw people's attention to, sb or sth (esp out of pride or vanity). **O:** son, daughter; skill, trick; song, poem; clothes, car □ *You'll have to practise that trick a little more before you can* ***show*** *it* ***off****.* DC □ *Her aunt liked to boast about her and* ***show*** *her* ***off*** *when she came home in uniform.* DC

show off[3] [A1 nom] display one's own abilities etc in order to impress people □ *'Do stop* ***showing off****, Andrew. Nobody's impressed.'* □ *He* ***shows off*** *tremendously* (or: *He's a tremendous* ***show-off****) in front of the ladies.*

show out/out of [B1i pass B2 pass] lead, conduct sb from a place. **S:** butler, secretary. **O:** visitor, caller. **o:** house, office □ *'I think that just about concludes our discussion. Miss Jones, will you please* ***show*** *our visitor* ***out****?'*

show over [B2 pass] take visitors on a tour of a place, show around/round (q v). **O:** customer, buyer. **o:** plant, works □ *'I'll get a guide to* ***show*** *you* ***over*** *the factory.'*

show round [B1i pass B2 pass] ⇨ show around/round.

show through [A1 A2 rel] be visible underneath a covering. **S:** colour, texture; nature, character. **o:** paper, covering; façade, formal manner □ *I've sprayed the bonnet, but the marks and scratches* ***show through*** *the paint.* □ *She has acquired a very good French accent, but her English speech habits still* ***show through****.*

show up[1] [A1 B1i pass] be easily visible, apparent; make visible, reveal clearly. **S:** [A1] **O:** [B1] line, wrinkle; mistake, imperfection; workmanship; (true) nature, character. **S:** [B1] light; (close) examination; stress, crisis □ *Close study of the surface of the picture* ***shows up*** *a network of fine cracks.* □ *At times like these the true character of the man* ***shows up****.*

show up[2] [B1ii pass] (informal) make sb feel embarrassed by behaving badly in his company. **S:** child; pupil; friend □ *I can take our children anywhere. I'm never afraid that they're going to* ***show*** *me* ***up*** *in some restaurant.* □ *'That's the last time that you* ***show*** *me* ***up*** *in public!'*

show up[3] [A1] (informal) appear, arrive (often after some delay); turn up[3] (q v). **S:** guest, visitor □ *Her place was laid for lunch and again for dinner. But she didn't* ***show up****.* PW □ *'We've been waiting for hours for you to* ***show up****!'*

show up (as/for) [B1ii pass B3 pass] reveal that sb is, show sb to be (sth inferior, unpleasant etc). **o:** weakling, coward, blackguard, cad □ *Should we expect him to tell the truth about himself if that truth would* ***show*** *him* ***up as*** *a rather poor sort of fish* (or: ***show*** *him* ***up*** *to be* etc). SNP □ *Don't* ***show*** *yourself* ***up for*** *what you are!* TOH

shower upon [A2 emph rel B2 pass emph rel] be given, give to sb, freely, in abundance; rain upon (q v). **S:** [A2] **O:** [B2] gifts, presents; food, wine; compliments, praise. **o:** guest, visitor; hero, victor □ *From the moment we arrived, hospitality was* ***showered upon*** *us.* □ *We were quite embarrassed by people's kindness: offers of meals and shelter* ***showered upon*** *us.*

shrink back (from) [A1 A3 pass emph rel] move back, withdraw (from sb or sth) out of fear, sensitivity etc. **o:** challenge, threat, danger; violence, disturbance □ *Nicky* ***shrank back****: he couldn't bear sharp voices.* DC □ *Always he* ***shrank back from*** *actual commitment: he would rather be uninvolved.*

shrink up [A1] try to make oneself small and inconspicuous (e g out of shyness). **S:** awkward girl, shy teenager; stranger, newcomer □ *He had a tendency to* ***shrink up*** *whenever attention was focused on him.*

shrivel up [A1] dry and curl up through old age, heat, frost etc. **S:** leaf, shoot, blade (of grass); skin; face □ *In the long drought, the leaves* ***shrivelled up*** *and died.* □ *If you never give scope to your feelings, you'll* ***shrivel up*** *before you're forty.*

shrug off [B1i pass] dismiss sth as not deserving one's attention. **O:** protest, objection, complaint; whistles, catcalls □ *He had a way of* ***shrugging off*** *criticism as though it were beneath his notice.*

shuffle off (onto) [B1i pass B3 pass] (informal) in a furtive way, try to pass one's responsibility for sth onto sb else. **O:** ⚠ the blame, responsibility; (feelings of) guilt □ (political broadcast) *He's running away because that is the only opportunity to* ***shuffle off*** *his responsibility.* BBCTV □ (political broadcast) *He tried to* ***shuffle off*** *his own responsibility* ***onto*** *the men who dig the nation's coal.* BBCR

shut away (in) [B1ii pass B3 pass rel] enclose, confine (in a secure or quiet place). **O:** oneself; prisoner, hostage. **o:** country; castle □ *Jeremy* ***shut*** *himself* ***away*** *for a month to catch up on his academic work.* □ *'What made him* ***shut*** *himself* ***away in*** *the heart of the country?'* □ *Important military prisoners were* ***shut away in*** *a remote mountain village.*

shut down [A1 nom B1i nom pass adj] close, cease production at (permanently or for a time); close down (q v). **S:** [A1] **O:** [B1] plant, factory, workshop. **S:** [B1] owner, manager □ *The commission has ordered two mines to be* ***shut down*** (or: *has ordered the* ***shut-down*** *of two mines*). □ *Some businesses will have to* ***shut down*** *if there is a recession.* □ *The threat of a* ***shutdown*** *in the newspaper industry has not been averted.* BBCR

shut in [B1i pass adj] enclose, surround. **S:** mountain, forest; fog, snow □ *For four months in the year the snow virtually isolates them and they are* ***shut in*** *upon themselves.*

shut off [B1i pass] stop, interrupt. **O:** supply; gas, water, steam □ *'I haven't had a bath for days — they've* ***shut off*** *the hot water supply.'* □ *Domestic supplies may be* ***shut off*** *at times of heavy demand.*

shut out/out of [B1i pass B2 pass] prevent sth or sb from entering or being seen. **O:** light, sun, warmth; sound; view; visitor, spectator. **o:** room, studio; museum; ground □ *The window was open, but the rain* ***shut out*** *the air as effectively as a curtain.* HOM □ *Ticket-holders who* *arrive late may find themselves* ***shut out of*** *the stadium.* □ *He tried hard to* ***shut*** *all thoughts of her* ***out of*** *his mind.*

shut one's eyes to [B2] pretend that one does not see sth; turn a blind eye (on/to) (q v). **o:** suffering, distress; crime, corruption; infidelity □ *'I can't help remembering how much I had to* ***shut my eyes to*** *in Godfrey. Lipstick on his handkerchiefs.'* MM □ *The company has to* ***shut its eyes to*** *petty pilfering, if only because it would be too expensive to prevent.*

shut up[1] [B1i pass] shut the windows and doors of a building securely (e g before leaving it at night); close up[2] (q v) **O:** office, shop, house □ *I* ***shut*** *my room* ***up*** *securely and left the key with the porter.*

shut up[2] [A1 B1i pass] (informal) (cause to) be quiet (e g stop talking, making a noise); dry up[5] (q v). **S:** [A1] **O:** [B1] speaker, chatterbox; pest, nuisance □ *'For heaven's sake,* ***shut*** *him* ***up****: he's said quite enough already.'* □ *Generals were in the greatest awe of him and* ***shut up*** *like an oyster in his presence.* MFM

shut up (in) [B1i pass B3 pass emph rel] hold, confine, sb under lock and key as a prisoner; put sth away under lock and key for safe keeping. **O:** enemy, suspect; madman; valuables, jewellery. **o:** cell, dungeon; safe □ *So let Catherine lie* ***shut up in*** *Kimbolton Castle, where it's said you're having her poisoned.* WI □ *He's mad as a hatter, poor chap, and* ***shut up*** *somewhere.* PW □ *The vital documents are kept* ***shut up in*** *a strongbox.*

shy away (from) [A1 A3 pass emph rel] avoid, move away from, out of shyness, prudery, fear etc. **o:** contact, involvement, commitment; danger, threat □ *Clive* ***shies away from*** *the thought of contact as Stanley makes to touch his shoulder.* FFE □ *Modern English writers tend to* ***shy away from*** *using the stage for direct autobiographical expression.* ITAJ

sick up [B1i pass] (informal) vomit, bring up[6] (q v). **O:** food; meal; breakfast □ *He can't keep anything down: he* ***sicked up*** *what little breakfast he had.*

sicken of [A2 pass emph rel] become weary of, disgusted with. **o:** old life, former companions; violence, cruelty; cant, hypocrisy □ *After a few weeks working for him I* ***sickened of*** *his methods.* □ *The casual violence of the gang—this was something* ***of*** *which we* ***sickened*** *early on.*

side with [A2 pass] put oneself on the same side as sb, take sb's part. **o:** (weaker/stronger) faction, party; enemy, opposition □ *He will always* ***side with*** *a minority against the official or established line.* □ *They're careful to* ***side with*** *the party most likely to win.*

sidle up (to) [A1 A3 pass] approach in a nervous or furtive way □ *A small man* ***sidled up to*** *him and pressed a piece of paper into his hand.* □ *If someone* ***sidles up*** *and offers to buy currency, pay no attention.*

sign away [B1i pass] surrender, relinquish, sth by signing a document etc. **O:** property, estate; livelihood, career; right, privilege □ *Read the document carefully, so that you know what you are* ***signing away****.* □ *With one stroke of the pen he had* ***signed away*** *his country's independence for a decade.*

sign in/into [B1i pass B2 pass] by signing one's name as a member enable a non-member to enter a club etc. **O:** friend, guest. **o:** club, discotheque □ *'It's not worth while paying the membership fee for one evening. I'll* ***sign*** *you* ***in*** *on my card.'*

sign off [A1] (informal) announce, mark in some way, the end of a radio programme. **S:** announcer, compère, disc-jockey (DJ) □ *'And this is your resident DJ,* ***signing off*** *with our signature tune.'*

sign on[1] [A1 B1i pass] (cause to) sign an agreement or undertaking to work for sb, or join a ship's company or the armed services for a specified period. **S:** [A1] **O:** [B1] man; labourer; recruit; seaman; footballer. **S:** [B1] employer; recruiting-sergeant; shipowner; manager □ *Men who came forward as volunteers agreed to* ***sign on*** *for the duration of hostilities.* □ *We need to* ***sign on*** *some more deck-hands for the next trip.*

sign on[2] [A1] register one's name, when unemployed, at the local office of the Department of Employment (in Britain). **S:** workman; fitter, labourer □ *A lot of men* ***signed on*** *at the Employment Exchange the week that they closed the big pit.*

sign on the dotted line [A2] (informal) sign a document which legally binds one to work etc for sb, or which is a marriage certificate, a bill of sale etc □ *'Now, Sir, if you will just* ***sign on the dotted line*** *the car becomes yours.'* □ *'You have to give Liza credit for persistence. She's been trying to get James to* ***sign on the dotted line*** *for over three years.'*

sign out/out of [B1i pass B2 pass] show by signing one's name that one has left, or intends to leave, a place. **O:** oneself; friend, workmate. **o:** camp; college, hall of residence □ *'I shan't be dining in college tonight. Would you mind* ***signing*** *me* ***out****?'* □ *After basic training the soldiers were allowed to spend weekends at home, provided they* ***signed*** *themselves* ***out of*** *camp.*

sign over [B1i pass] indicate, or confirm, a sale by signing papers. **O:** goods; consignment, load; property, land □ *A senior executive* ***signed over*** *a delivery of six aircraft on behalf of his company.* □ *The top floor of the building was* ***signed over*** *for use as offices.*

sign up [A1 B1i pass] (cause to) join a club, enrol for a course. **S:** [A1] **O:** [B1] player; footballer, cricketer; member; student. **S:** [B1] club; secretary; registrar □ *Arsenal have* ***signed up*** *a number of promising youngsters this season.* □ *Before you* ***sign up*** *for a course, make sure that the school is attached to an established employment agency.* H

silt up [A1 B1i pass adj] (cause to) become blocked with mud, sand etc. **S:** [A1] **O:** [B1] mouth (of river), cove, bay, harbour. **S:** [B1] sea; sand, shingle □ *Places which were harbours in Roman times* ***silted up*** *long ago and are now some distance inland.* □ *The drains got* ***silted up*** *with mud and bits of twigs.*

simmer down [A1] (informal) become calm, calm down[1] (q v), after being angry, excited, critical etc. **S:** excited, irascible man; situation; things □ *'Give him a minute to* ***simmer down*** *—he's always like this when we discuss politics.'* □ *When things have* ***simmered down*** *a bit more, talks can be started.* BBCTV

sin (against) [A2 pass emph rel] break, transgress, some moral or religious law; offend (against) (q v). **o:** the Holy Ghost; decorum, propriety □ *What is this unwritten law she is accused of* ***sinning against****?* □ *He is a man more* ***sinned against*** *than sinning* (i e he does less harm to others than they do to him).

sing to sleep [B2 pass] make (a child) fall asleep by singing to him. **S:** mother, nurse. **O:** baby, infant □ *If the child grew restless, she would take him out of his cot and* ***sing*** *him* ***to sleep****.*

sing up [A1] sing more loudly □ *'****Sing up****, fellows, this is supposed to be a celebration, not a funeral!'* □ *'Tell the people at the back to* ***sing up****: I can't hear them.'* □ usu direct or indirect command.

single out [B1i pass] choose, pick, one person or thing from among several for special comment, treatment etc. **O:** assistant, companion; victim, prey; incident, event □ *I imagine that to be* ***singled out*** *by the Captain for a farewell luncheon is indeed an honour.* WI □ *He* ***singles out*** *in human nature the ugly elements — the elements that hurt him.* PW

sink in[1] [A1] be fully absorbed and understood. **S:** announcement, statement; idea, suggestion □ *He said nothing; he stood without moving, while the news* ***sank in****.* WI □ *Something good may result after all if the warnings* ***sink in****.* T

sink in[2] [B2 pass emph rel] invest capital etc (heavily) in some venture. **S:** investor, speculator. **O:** (a good deal of) capital, investment; personal savings, fortune. **o:** mining, transport, canning □ *A lot of their money had been* ***sunk in*** *mineral shares that everybody had warned them not to buy.* □ ***In*** *this particular tin-pot venture he'd* ***sunk*** *half the sum left him by his father.*

sink into [A2 emph rel] fall fast asleep; fall to a lower physical or moral level. **o:** (deep) sleep; trance, coma; depressed state, black mood □ *For a moment, Yusef seemed about to* ***sink*** *again* ***into*** *drugged sleep.* HOM □ *Nobody could rouse him from the mood of black depression* ***into*** *which he had* ***sunk****.*

sink into/to one's boots [A2] (informal) become low, depressed. **S:** ⚠ one's heart; one's spirits, courage □ *He got through his little scene with Jessica quite well till the moment for the song came, when his courage* ***sank to his boots****.* WDM □ *Was this the girl that he was to spend the evening with? Jeremy's heart* ***sank into his boots****. She was immensely tall and must have weighed all of fourteen stone.*

siphon off (from) (into)[1] [B1i pass adj B3 pass emph rel] draw liquid (from a tank) by sucking it through a tube. **O:** petrol, oil, water □ *If you're short of petrol you can* ***siphon off*** *a gallon* ***from*** *my tank.*

siphon off (from) (into)[2] [B1i pass adj B3 pass emph rel] (informal) transfer from one place, area of responsibility etc, to another; (esp) transfer funds from one person or account to another for dishonest purposes. **O:** work, job; money, funds □ *There is a lot of pressure now to* ***siphon off*** *the motoring cases* ***into*** *a court of their own.* TO □ *There is no doubt that a good deal of the money paid into the campaign fund has been* ***siphoned off*** *(****from*** *it)* ***into*** *private pockets.*

sit about/around [A1] lounge idly, sit doing nothing □ *School discipline is very largely relaxed, and you have time to* ***sit about*** *and gossip.* CON □ *The foreign correspondents seemed to spend most of their time* ***sitting around*** *in bars.*

sit at the feet of [A2 rel] (jocular) go to learn from some real, or would-be, authority. **o:** (*of*) master, seer, guru □ *'I was a Red (= communist) myself once. I even* ***sat at the feet of*** *Waterman and he was a phoney old prophet if you like.'* PP □ *The talk was given by an elderly don* ***at whose feet*** *Peter had* ***sat****, many years before, at Cambridge.*

sit back [A1] relax (usu after strenuous activity); be inactive; do nothing (when action is needed) □ *After a long walk, it's pleasant to* ***sit back*** *with a drink and look out at the view.* □ *Now it was all over, we could* ***sit back*** *with our feet up.* EHOW □ *'When we needed your help, all you did was* ***sit back*** *and twiddle your thumbs.'*

sit down [A1 nom B1ii pass] be seated (e g in an armchair); (cause sb to) take a seat □ *When I came in, the others were already* ***sitting down****.* □ *'I'll bandage your foot up and you can have a* ***sit-down****.'* ARG □ *'****Sit*** *your guests* ***down*** *and give them a drink.'* □ *'****Sit*** *yourself* ***down****. I shan't keep you waiting more than a minute.'*

sit-down (demonstration/strike) [nom (A1)] demonstration in which people sit down in the street, in the entrances to buildings etc, thus preventing others from passing; strike during which employees sit down in their place of work □ *Groups advocating civil disobedience attempted to organize* ***sit-down demonstrations*** *in Whitehall. These formed part of the wider movement against nuclear weapons.*

sit down under [A3] endure, suffer, sth without protest or resistance. **o:** conditions; slight, insult, humiliation □ *I couldn't* ***sit down under*** *things any longer.* NM □ *He is a patient man, but not even he could* ***sit down under*** *that kind of provocation.*

sit for [A2 rel] take an examination. **o:** examination, college entrance, Finals □ *A number of sixth-formers came up that week to* ***sit for*** *university entrance.*

sit in [A1 nom] sit on the ground in, occupy, the building where one is employed etc, in protest against conditions, the action of authorities etc. **S:** worker, student, civil-rights campaigner □ *A company admitted this week that it had passed information on to the Special Branch on certain workers* ***sitting in*** *at its factory.* ST □ ***Sit-ins*** *were staged at lunch-counters known to have refused service to Negroes.*

sit in judgement (on/over) [A2] judge the actions, character etc of sb. **S:** parent, teacher; critic, pundit. **o:** charge, pupil; work, conduct □ *Virginia imagined that the woman knew the whole story, and was* ***sitting*** *there* ***in judgement****.* AITC □ *'Don't set yourself up as some great moral authority, Ben. You know you're in no position to* ***sit in judgement on*** *any of us.'*

sit on[1] [A2 rel] serve as a member of. **o:** committee, board, jury □ *A number of distinguished academics and teachers* ***sat on*** *the committee which recommended the expansion of higher education.* □ *This was only one of the many bodies* ***on*** *which he had* ***sat*** *during his life of* *public service.*

sit on[2] [A2 pass] (informal) neglect, suppress, a complaint etc; do nothing about sth (so as to avoid further complications). **S:** company, department; manager. **o:** letter; complaint, inquiry □ *For weeks they did nothing about my case: they just* **sat on** *it.* □ *Jenkins* **sat on** *those students' applications for a month. I suppose it fed his sense of power to think he could obstruct them.*

sit on[3] [A2 pass] (informal) handle firmly sb who behaves impertinently etc; put in his place (q v). **o:** impertinent, conceited, opinionated fellow □ *That young man is becoming insufferable: he needs to be* **sat on** *firmly.* □ *I wish someone would* **sit** *hard* **on** *Rogers — he'll be telling me how to run my department next.*

sit on the fence [A2] hesitate between, not decide between, two opposite lines of action, sets of beliefs etc. **S:** council, committee; businessman, director □ *It was my view that he always* **sat on the fence**, *never committed himself, and never gave a decision.* MFM □ COLONEL: *I think you may take after me a little, my dear. You like to* **sit on the fence** *because it's more comfortable and more peaceful.* LBA

sit out[1] [B1i pass] (at a dance) leave the floor for one dance and sit down with one's partner. **O:** number; waltz, rumba □ *'Let's* **sit** *this one* **out**, *shall we? I'm afraid I tango very badly.'*

sit out[2] [B1i pass] remain in one's seat till the end of a performance (even though one may find it unpleasant). **S:** audience, public. **O:** play, concert; match, bout □ *I found the show tedious — I don't know how I managed to* **sit** *it* **out**. □ *'***Sit** *the first bit* **out** *patiently — the game will liven up later.'* ⇨ next entry.

sit through [A2] remain in a theatre etc till the end of a performance (even though one may dislike it). **o:** play, film; concert; meeting □ *'I'm not coming to the cinema if it means* **sitting through** *some awful supporting feature first.'* □ *'Yes, I did* **sit through** *the entire programme. I didn't find it as bad as you seem to think.'* ⇨ previous entry.

sit up[1] [A1] move into an upright position after lying flat; sit straight upright after lounging in one's seat □ *I think the patient is well enough now to* **sit up** *in bed.* □ *'Don't slouch over your breakfast.* **Sit up** *straight!'*

sit up[2] [A1] move to an upright position, in a tense, alert way, usu from fear or surprise □ *She* **sat up**, *clapping her hands to her mouth, her eyes wide with fear.* DC

sit up[3] [A1] stay awake and out of bed till past one's usual bedtime (to wait for sb, keep sb company etc); stay up [2] (q v) □ *They* **sat up** *till the small hours, exchanging gossip.* □ *He had insisted on Nurse Ellen* **sitting up** *with her, although the need for a night nurse was past.* DC □ *'I shall get back very late, so don't* **sit up** *for me.'*

sit up and take notice [A1] (informal) become suddenly and keenly aware and interested. **S:** opponent, rival; critic, sceptic □ *But when she married the delightful Colonial Bishop, now Canon Joram, the County and the Close suddenly* **sat up and** *began to* **take notice** *and now no party in Barchester was complete without her.* WDM □ *'Just you wait. In the New Year we'll spring our new sports model on them. That'll make them* **sit up and take notice**.*'*

size up [B1i pass adj] (informal) form a judgement or opinion of sb or sth. **O:** newcomer, stranger; situation; competition □ *I was trying to* **size** *you* **up**, *and failing because you didn't fit into any type I knew.* HD □ *He attempted to* **size up** *the reaction of the audience: how were they being received?*

skate on thin ice [A2] (informal) handle a delicate situation skilfully; venture into a situation where there are risks, and where therefore one has to act carefully □ *The managing director explained as carefully as he could that with the fall in demand we might be forced to lay people off, but of course he's used to* **skating on thin ice** *and managed the situation as well as could be hoped.* □ *'If I were you, I shouldn't come in here telling experienced staff their business: you're* **skating on** *very* **thin ice**.*'* □ continuous tenses only.

skate over [A2 pass] move over the surface of sth, i e without really dealing with it or tackling it; slide over (q v). **o:** surface; problem, difficulty, issue □ *He's so cautious and evasive: always* **skating over** *the surface, never coming to grips with the issues underneath.* □ *'This is not something that can be* **skated over** *— let's get down to brass tacks.'*

sketch out [B1i pass adj] give a rough, outline picture of sth. **O:** plan, proposal, design; (housing) development, precinct, centre □ *'Give me a pad and pencil and I'll* **sketch out** *what I have in mind.'* □ *He showed me a hastily* **sketched-out** *plan of the road system.*

skim off[1] [B1i pass] remove sth floating on the surface of a liquid. **O:** cream, clots; oil, fat; scum, slime □ *The gravy is too greasy:* **skim off** *some of the fat before you serve it.*

skim off[2] [B1i pass] take the best, the most able, part of a group. **S:** special school, elite university; specialist arm, service (in the armed forces). **O:** cream; most able, best qualified □ *In some areas, Direct Grant and maintained grammar schools are still able to* **skim off** *the most able of the secondary school entry.* □ *The cream of manpower was* **skimmed off** *into the 'workers' battalions'.* B

skim through [A2 nom pass adj] read quickly through sth, getting a general impression of its contents. **o:** book, article; chapter, section; notes □ *'Give me a moment to* **skim through** *these notes before the meeting.'* □ *Don't read the book in detail:* **skim through** *it to get the general picture.* □ *'Leave the essay with me: I'll give it a quick* **skim-through** *before lunch.'*

skip off [A1] (informal) leave furtively (esp to avoid some unpleasant task) □ *'Trust the men to* **skip off** *and leave us to do the clearing away.'* □ *'I notice he* **skipped off** *pretty smartly when the moment came to pay the bill.'*

skirt around/round [A2 pass] go round the edge of sth, avoid it. **o:** question, matter; problem, difficulty □ *'Let's not* **skirt round** *the awkward questions — let's try and answer them.'* □ *'The question of who is to pay has been* **skirted around**. *I suppose that's because you assume I will foot the bill.'*

skittle out [B1i pass] (cricket) dismiss the opposing batsmen in quick succession. **O:** side, team; batsmen □ *The tourists were **skittled out** for 161 runs.* ITV □ *Kent **skittled out** Surrey on a green wicket that gave the ball plenty of lift.*

slacken off [A1] become less intense, less active; ease off (q v); weaken. **S:** trade, commerce; student, athlete; drama, tension □ *Business usually **slackens off** at this time of the year.* □ *The one problem of the book is that the density and texture **slacken off** somewhat in the later pages.* G

slam down [B1i pass] put down, replace, violently and noisily. **O:** (telephone) receiver, window, hatch; money, paper □ *Mr Gibbs was fighting a wild desire to **slam down** his receiver.* DF □ *He **slammed** a dirty bundle of notes **down** on the counter and walked out of the shop.*

slam the door in sb's face [B2 pass] (informal) shut the door violently to prevent sb unwelcome from entering, or to show he is unwelcome; reject some approach or initiative in a hostile way. **o:** (***of***) salesman, pedlar, beggar; visitor; negotiator, delegate □ *In my name, we'd gate-crash everywhere — cocktails, weekends, even a couple of houseparties. I used to hope that one day, somebody would have the guts to **slam the door in our faces**, but they didn't. They were too well-bred.* LBA □ *He was a door-to-door salesman for a bit, but he soon got tired of having **the door slammed in his face**.*

slam the brakes on [B1i pass] (informal) apply the brakes of a vehicle abruptly and strongly; jam the brakes on (q v) □ *Peter made the mistake of **slamming the brakes on** as he entered a tight corner, and slid into the path of an oncoming car.* □ *'If you find yourself losing control on a slippery surface don't, for Heaven's sake, **slam on the brakes**.'*

slam to [B1ii pass] close violently and noisily. **O:** door, gate, window □ *At this point, he became speechless with rage, **slammed** the gate **to**, and strode away.* □ *I didn't get a chance to speak to her — the door was **slammed to** in my face.*

slap down[1] [B1i pass] put down firmly (with the sound of a flat palm striking a surface). **O:** envelope, packet; money, banknotes □ *A boy in uniform came into the shop, **slapped** a telegram **down** on the counter, and went out without waiting for a reply.* □ *The fishmonger picked up an enormous skate and **slapped** it **down** in front of the customer.*

slap down[2] [B1i pass] (informal) check, suppress, firmly a rebellious, venturesome (etc) person □ *'Anyone who speaks out of turn in the Old Man's presence is liable to be **slapped down**.'* □ *'Getting admitted to that club is likely to be tough for upstarts like you and me. You can try it if you don't mind being **slapped down**.'*

slap on/onto[1] [B1i pass B2 pass] (informal) apply sth vigorously to a surface (making a dull, flat sound). **O:** paint, distemper; mud, clay. **o:** wall, fence; frame □ *'You'll need to **slap** a bit of creosote **on** those posts before you stick them in the ground.'* □ *'The oil tank will rust unless you do something to protect it. So **slap on** a couple of coats of red lead.'*

slap on/onto[2] [B1i pass B2 pass] (informal) add sth to the price etc of sth (in a way, or to an extent, that is unwelcome); clap on/onto (q v). **O:** tax, surcharge; levy; increase of 50 pence. **o:** beer, tobacco; betting; price, cost □ *'Before we had time to recover from the last rise, the building societies **slapped** another one per cent **on** our interest repayments.'* □ *Tourists arriving at the airport for their charter flights found that the tour operators had **slapped** a £10 surcharge **onto** the cost of their holidays.*

slave away [A1] work continuously, like a slave. **S:** housewife, servant □ *'Why should I **slave away** at a hot stove for half my life?'* □ *'Look at them, we **slave away** and they play cards.'* DPM

sleep around [A1] (informal) move casually from one lover to another, have intercourse with a succession of men without becoming involved with any (usu said of a *woman* who behaves in this way) □ *Men may not insist that their bride is a virgin any longer but they'll still avoid a girl who is known to have **slept around**.*

sleep in [A1] sleep on the premises where one works; live in (q v). **S:** porter, caretaker □ *Most of the hotel staff **sleep in**.*

sleep off [B1i pass] (informal) lose, get rid of sth, by sleeping. **O:** indigestion, hangover; headache □ *The clubroom seems to be used only by surgeons **sleeping off** official luncheons.* DIL □ *'I know he's in an evil mood, but let's give him a night to **sleep** it **off**, shall we?'*

sleep on it [A2] (informal) have a night's sleep before making a difficult decision □ *The thing to do with a problem is to **sleep on it**.* TGLY □ *I went back to my flat in Half Moon Street and sat down to write a letter to Janet Prentice. I **slept on it**, tore it up, wrote it again, **slept on it** the next night, and wrote it a third time.* RFW

sleep together/with [A1 A2] (informal) have sexual intercourse with □ *She's a very strictly brought-up girl; I doubt very much if she's **sleeping with** her boyfriend* (or: *I doubt if she and her boyfriend are **sleeping together***).

slew around/round [A1 B1i pass] (usu said of a heavy, awkward piece of machinery) turn around to face in a new direction. **S:** [A1] **O:** [B1] crane, rig; gun, tank; car, lorry. **S:** [B1] operator, driver □ *It took time to **slew** the guns **around** to engage fresh targets.* □ *The car **slewed around** in a complete circle on the icy road.*

slice into [A2 pass] insert a knife into sth to cut a slice from it. **o:** loaf, pie, sausage; arm, leg □ *I like to **slice into** a loaf when it's fresh from the oven.* □ *'Don't draw the knife towards you when you're carving: you might **slice into** your own finger.'*

slice off [B1i pass] remove as a slice (from some larger object). **O:** end; crust, steak, cutlet; finger, toe □ *The machine **sliced off** thin rounds of copper into a bin.* □ *He **sliced off** a thick crust and bit into it hungrily.*

slice up [B1i pass adj] cut into slices. **O:** loaf, cake; sausage, side of bacon □ *The long loaves were **sliced up** ready for making into sandwiches.*

slick down [B1i pass adj] flatten down one's hair close to the head with oil etc. **O:** hair; wisp, lock □ *Hair was drawn up from the side of his head and **slicked down** over the bald patch on top.* □ *Hair thickly **slicked down** with grease suggests the rock-and-roll fashions of the 1950s.*

slide over [A2 pass] move quickly over sth without really tackling it, skate over (q v). **o:** surface; (delicate) question, problem, issue □ *He **slid over** the events of the previous day, wishing to spare his guests any embarrassment.* □ *'This is not a matter that can be **slid over**; let us discuss it openly.'*

slip away [A1] leave quickly and quietly (without attracting attention). **S:** guest, spectator, prisoner □ *'If you want to **slip away**, now's a good time: everyone is dancing.'* □ *Availing herself of the diversion caused by the landlord's appearance, the barmaid had **slipped away**.* PW

slip down [A1] be swallowed smoothly and easily. **S:** drink; medicine; beer, liqueur; ice-cream, porridge □ *John was handed a glass filled with a thick, green liquid. It **slipped down** pleasantly enough.*

slip in/into[1] [A1 A2] enter quickly and quietly (without being noticed). **o:** room, garden, street □ *Later, Mother **slipped into** the children's room to make sure they were all asleep.* □ *Aunt Annabel had **slipped in** early with three cats playfully following the trailing cord of her dressing-gown.* DC

slip in/into[2] [B1i pass B2 pass emph rel] mention sth important in conversation etc, so carefully that one does not appear to be drawing special attention to it. **O:** word, remark; reference, allusion. **o:** speech, address; conversation □ *He liked, very casually, to **slip in** references to the important work he was doing.* □ *One or two appeals for funds were **slipped into** his opening address.*

slip into [A2 pass] put on, with a quick, easy movement. **o:** jacket, pair of trousers; dress, skirt □ *She got up, **slipped into** a dressing-gown, and peered out of the window.* □ *They're an old pair of shoes I can **slip into** to do the gardening.* ⇨ next entry.

slip on [B1i pass] put on, with a quick, easy movement. **O:** jumper, shirt; slacks, trousers; shoes □ *He **slipped on** a sweater and a pair of slacks and went down to open the door.* □ *'**Slip** your overcoat **on**; it's getting chilly.'* ⇨ previous entry.

slip out/out of [A1 A2] leave quickly and quietly (without being noticed). **o:** room, office, theatre □ *He had suggested to Robert that they might **slip out** for a drink before lunch.* HD □ *'I didn't see him leave: he must have **slipped out of** the room while we were talking.'*

slip over [B2 pass] pass a garment over some protruding part of the body so that it covers that, or some other part. **O:** shirt, sweater; sash, armlet. **o:** head, shoulders, arm □ *'It's a cool evening, so do **slip** a shawl **over** your shoulders.'* □ *'You **slip** this kind of life-jacket **over** the head, so that the parts which provide bouyancy rest on the chest and back.'*

slip past [A1 A2 B1i pass B2 pass] (help, cause, to) pass, without being noticed, sb who is watching or guarding a place. **S:** [A1 A2] **O:** [B1 B2] prisoner, refugee, escapee; contraband; alcohol, tobacco; blow. **S:** [B1 B2] organization, gang; smuggler; boxer. **o:** guard; customs officer □ [A2] *A well-staged diversion in the huts enabled two prisoners to **slip past** the men on the gate.* □ [B2] *He managed to **slip** one or two good punches **past** his opponent's guard.*

slip through [A1 A2 B1i pass B2 pass] (enable to) pass through, elude, sth which is intended to control or check such movement. **S:** [A1 A2] **O:** [B1 B2] article, product, specimen; suspect, captive. **S:** [B1 B2] dealer, agent. **o:** checkpoint, control-point; customs; net, trap; hands, fingers, clutches □ [A1] *We are unable to prevent a small number of defective parts **slipping through**.* □ [A2] *Some valuable information has **slipped through** the security network.* □ [B2] *They are **slipping** very few aircraft **through** our defensive screen.* □ [A2] *There isn't a woman yet born who let her quarry **slip through** her fingers.* HSG

slip up [A1 nom] (informal) make a mistake, blunder. **S:** manager, organizer □ *Somebody must have **slipped up** badly* (or: *made a bad **slip-up***) *in your report. They seem to have left out her stage name.* EGD □ *There is a slightly uncomfortable feeling of somebody having **slipped up*** (or: *of there having been a **slip-up** on sb's part*). L

slit up [B2 pass] make a narrow opening at the back etc of a garment. **O:** coat, dress, shirt. **o:** back, front, side □ *His jacket is **slit up** the back to make it more comfortable to wear when riding.* □ *Get your dressmaker to **slit** the skirt **up** the side seams a little more.*

slobber over [A2 pass] (informal) show too much sentimental feeling for. **o:** child, dog □ *'I am always embarrassed by the way he **slobbers over** small children.'*

slog away (at) [A1 A3 rel] (informal) work continuously, and in a hard, determined fashion (at sth). **o:** lesson, book; task, problem □ *Nick's been **slogging away at** his multiplication tables all morning.* □ *'Keep **slogging away**! You've nearly broken the back of the problem.'*

slog it out [B1ii] (informal) struggle, fight, until a conclusion is reached. **S:** contestants, opponents □ *The audience were on the edge of their seats as the heavyweights **slogged it out** in the final round.* □ *I enjoy a good old intellectual rough and tumble, and I only wish I could stay and **slog it out** with the two of you.* EGD

slop about/around[1] [A1] (of a liquid) move about heavily (esp in a confined space). **S:** water, paint, petrol □ *A couple of gallons of water were **slopping around** in the bottom of the boat.*

slop about/around[2] [A1] (informal) move about in a lazy, casual way; slouch about/around (q v) □ *'I've tried to get the boy interested in decorating the house, but all he does is **slop around**, picking at jobs and not settling to anything in particular.'*

slop over [A1] (of liquids) spill heavily over the edge of a vessel etc. **S:** water; coffee, tea □ *A saucepan fell into the basin, and dirty water **slopped over** onto the kitchen floor.*

slop out [A1] (of prisoners in gaol) empty away dirty water, dregs, urine etc from vessels which have been kept overnight in the cells □ *In the morning, prisoners in older gaols have to take their basins and buckets to the latrine for **slopping out**.*

slope down (to) [A1 A3 rel] form a slope stretching down from one point to another; shelve down (to) (q v). **S:** garden, lawn, field. **o:** river, road □ *At the back, a flower garden **slopes down to** a line of poplar trees.*

slope off [A1] (informal) go away rather furtively, usu to avoid doing sth unpleasant □ *'Don't think that you can **slope off** just because my* *back's turned!'* □ *'Let's* ***slope off*** *somewhere quiet and have a cigarette.'*

slosh on [B1i pass B2 pass] (informal) apply paint etc in a rough, vigorous way. **O:** paint, distemper; paste. **o:** wall; canvas; paper □ *'Don't be afraid —* ***slosh on*** *plenty of bright colour.'* □ *'Careful, you're* ***sloshing*** *paste* ***on*** *your jersey!'*

slouch about/around [A1] move about in a lazy, slovenly way; slop about/around[2] (q v) □ *'I do wish the boy would stop* ***slouching about*** *with his hands in his pockets.'*

slough off [B1i pass] get rid of, abandon. **O:** responsibility; worry, anxiety; habit, practice □ *He had* ***sloughed off*** *all the petty cares of home and work.* RFW □ *One's obligations to one's work and colleagues can't easily be* ***sloughed off.*** □ lit, of a snake, discard its old skin.

slow down[1] [A1 B1i pass] (cause to) move more slowly, decelerate. **S:** [A1] **O:** [B1] car, lorry; machine; pace, action. **S:** [B1] driver, police; operator; director □ *At first he drove rather fast and then* ***slowed down*** *to a silent crawl.* DBM □ *'The motor's overheating. Can't you* ***slow*** *it* ***down****?'* □ *'Don't* ***slow down*** *the movement in this scene: it's tending to drag.'*

slow down[2] [A1 B1i pass] (cause to) live, work etc in a less active and intense way (usu because one's health is in danger) □ *'You really ought to* ***slow down*** *— all these late nights are doing you no good.'* □ *'If I could find some way of* ***slowing*** *my father* ***down*** *I would; he's taking on far too much work.'* ⇨ next entry.

slow up [A1] act, work etc less energetically or effectively because of age, poor health etc. **S:** worker, sportsman, writer □ *I think he's beginning to* ***slow up*** *— his latest book is much weaker than the previous one.* □ *He's over sixty, but he shows no signs of* ***slowing up.*** ⇨ previous entry.

sluice out [B1i pass adj] clear, clean, sth by using a heavy flow of water. **O:** channel; drain, sink, gutter □ *If the pipe gets blocked try* ***sluicing*** *it* ***out*** *with hot water.* □ *The stables were* ***sluiced out*** *with water from a hose.*

smack of [A2] have a flavour of, suggest. **S:** life; conduct, behaviour; language. **o:** corruption, immorality; treason, heresy □ *I never went to race meetings, which to me always* ***smacked of*** *the idle rich.* SML □ *To me, his suggestion* ***smacks of*** *underhand methods.*

smarten up [A1 B1ii] become or make more smart (i e cleaner, better-dressed etc). **O:** oneself; place □ *'You'll spend the rest of your life in the ice-cream factory if you don't* ***smarten*** *yourself* ***up*** *a bit.'* ASA □ *He's* ***smartened up*** *considerably since I last saw him.* □ *The shop will have to be* ***smartened up*** *a bit if you want to cater for the top end of the market.*

smash in [B1i pass adj] make a hole, dent or wound in sth by striking it a violent blow. **O:** window, door; wing, boot (of car); ribs, face, head □ *The explosion had* ***smashed in*** *all the ground-floor windows.* □ *A single blow from an adult bear could* ***smash in*** *your rib-cage.*

smash sb's face in [B1ii pass] (informal) (threaten to) make a violent physical attack on sb (e g to stop him interfering) □ *'If you mess my girl about, I'll* ***smash your face in!'*** □ *Anyone trying to muscle in on* (q v) *the gang's territory would get* ***his face smashed in.*** □ often with *will/would.*

smash up [B1i nom pass adj] damage badly in a serious accident etc. **O:** car, lorry; train; furniture, crockery □ *The place was badly* ***smashed up*** *in the air-raids.* □ *There has been a serious* ***smash-up*** *on the motorway, involving a container lorry and three cars.*

smear on [B1i pass B2 pass rel] apply a sticky or oily substance to sth. **O:** grease, ointment; paint; butter. **o:** hand, face; wall □ ***'Smear*** *some of this cream* ***on*** *your face before putting on the grease-paint.'* □ *The children had* ***smeared*** *jam* ***on*** *the walls* (or: *had* ***smeared*** *the walls* ***with*** *jam*).

smear with [B2 pass rel] ⇨ previous entry.

smell of[1] [A2] have, give out, the smell of. **S:** house, room; dinner, meat; breath **o:** damp, decay; garlic; whisky □ *The stew* ***smelt*** *deliciously* ***of*** *herbs and onion.* □ *His breath* ***smelt*** *suspiciously* ***of*** *drink.*

smell of[2] [A2] strongly suggest. **S:** conduct, behaviour; suggestion, offer. **o:** intrigue, double-dealing; treason □ *'If I were you, I should leave his offer alone. It* ***smells*** *strongly* ***of*** *shady dealing.'*

smell out [B1i pass] discover, detect, by means of one's sense of smell; discover by noticing and understanding certain clues. **S:** dog; patrol, search-party. **O:** rat, rabbit; fugitive □ *'Lead the way with the tracker-dog; he'll soon* ***smell*** *the fellow* ***out.'***

smell to high heaven [A2] (informal) have, give off, a strong, unpleasant smell; strongly suggest dishonesty, corruption etc; stink to high heaven (q v). **S:** place; hall, cellar; deal, business □ *'When was the last time you cleaned out the parrot's cage? It* ***smells to high heaven.'*** □ *'Of course there's been dirty dealing over the allocation of building permits. The whole thing* ***smells to high heaven.'***

Fortune smile upon [A2 rel] (formal) be lucky, fortunate. **o:** him etc; endeavours, enterprise, venture □ *He is the kind of man* ***upon*** *whom* ***Fortune*** *seldom* ***smiles.*** □ *'May* ***Fortune smile upon*** *you in your new life together.'*

smoke out/out of [B1i pass B2 pass] drive from hiding by means of smoke or through cunning etc. **O:** insect, snake, fox, rabbit; terrorist, fugitive. **o:** greenhouse, hole, lair, burrow; hiding □ *We used a piece of pipe connected to a car exhaust to* ***smoke*** *the rats* ***out.*** □ *'I came back too late,' he said. 'You wouldn't have come at all if I hadn't* ***smoked*** *you* ***out.'*** TLG

smooth down[1] [B1i pass adj] make sth flat which is standing up (esp by stroking downwards). **O:** fur, feathers; lapel, pocket (of a coat) □ *John straightened his tie,* ***smoothed down*** *his unruly hair, and went to welcome the first guest.*

smooth down[2] [B1i pass adj] restore (by soothing words etc) feelings which have been upset or disturbed. **O:** ruffled feelings, susceptibilities; angry boss, husband □ *'Father's in a dreadful temper, Sarah. Do what you can to* ***smooth*** *him* ***down.'*** □ *The rooms allocated to the visitors were found to be already occupied, and it took the intervention of the manager to* ***smooth down*** *injured national pride.*

smooth out[1] [B1i pass adj] make a surface smooth by removing irregularities. **O:** sheet, table-cloth; fold, wrinkle □ *Mother brushed off* *the bread-crumbs and **smoothed out** the cloth.* □ *His face was suddenly young again, the lines of strain and fear temporarily **smoothed out**.* DC

smooth out[2] [B1i pass adj] remove difficulties etc, thus making a situation easier for sb. **O:** obstacle, snag, teething-trouble; situation □ *The director has **smoothed out** some of the formalities, so you will get your certificate as arranged.* □ *There are some technical problems to be **smoothed out** before we can fly.*

smooth over [B1i pass adj] calm sb, settle a quarrel etc, by acting calmly and diplomatically. **O:** argument, disagreement, difference; crisis □ *This was a genuine attempt to placate him and **smooth** this thing **over**.* CON □ *They were now arguing furiously, with James standing by and trying to **smooth** the quarrel **over**.*

smother (in/with) [B2 pass rel] cover thickly (with). **O:** hall, table; fire; visitor, guest. **o:** flower, decoration; earth, ash; gift, present; kisses, praise □ *The general's chest was **smothered in** orders and medals* (or: *Orders and medals **smothered** his chest*). □ *We were **smothered with** soot and ashes cascading from the fireplace* (or: *Soot and ashes **smothered** us*). □ *The welcoming committee would always **smother** him **in** compliments — an embarrassing moment which he tried to cut short.*

smuggle in/into [B1i pass adj B2 pass] bring goods illegally into a country (i e without declaring them to the customs); pass sth illegally to sb in prison. **O:** whisky; watch, camera; letter, tool. **o:** country; camp, prison □ *A strict watch is kept to prevent the **smuggling in** of drugs.* □ *Equipment was **smuggled into** the cell under the very noses of the warders.*

smuggle out/out of [B1i pass adj B2 pass] take goods illegally out of a country; get sth, illegally, out of prison. **O:** currency, literature; message. **o:** country; camp, gaol □ *The penalties are severe for people caught **smuggling** banknotes **out of** the country.* □ *Information was **smuggled out** by a friendly guard.*

smuggle past [B1ii pass B2 pass] take goods illegally past a control point; get sb or sth past a guard etc without detection. **O:** wine, tobacco, perfume; message, food. **o:** customs; sentry □ *'You're very optimistic if you think you can **smuggle** five litres of wine **past** the customs.'* □ *A couple of prisoners were **smuggled past** the sentries on the gate in empty swill bins.*

snap at [A2 pass] try to grasp sth with the teeth by closing them sharply around it; try to seize by accepting, agreeing etc, quickly. **S:** dog, fish; buyer, negotiator. **o:** leg, ankle; bait; offer, bargain □ *She must stop her dog **snapping at** visitors to the house.* □ *He'd **snap at** an opportunity to go abroad for us.*

snap one's fingers at [B2] (informal) treat sb or sth with contempt, derision etc. **o:** authorities, boss; rule, regulation; convention, established practices □ *He is not, by their standards, in the Sixth or entitled to wear First XV colours, and yet he **snaps his fingers at** their most cherished taboos.* T □ *No petty official was going to stop Philip from getting into the enclosure. He would just **snap his fingers at** them.*

snap into it [A2] (informal) get started (e g on a job); start moving quickly □ *'I said I wanted that stuff moved. Now come on, **snap into it**!'* □ *'We haven't got all day. **Snap into it**. Move!'* □ usu direct or indirect command.

snap sb's head off [B1ii pass] (informal) react sharply and angrily to sth that sb has said or done; bite sb's head off (q v) □ *'Don't ask him why he's come in late again — you'll only get **your head snapped off**.'* □ *I can't mention her boyfriend's name without her **snapping my head off**.* □ note pl form in: *If they spoke out of turn they would get **their heads snapped off**.*

snap out [B1i pass adj] exclaim in a sharp, unpleasant tone. **O:** reply, retort; instruction □ *The colonel suddenly **snapped out** the information.* QA □ *'I don't see why I should tell you anything,' she **snapped out** in reply.*

snap out of it [A2] (informal) briskly get rid of, shake off[2] (q v), a mood (esp depression, or a sense of defeat) □ *'All that self-pity, my dear! He really ought to **snap out of it**.'* PW □ *Quitting is a bad way to embark on life, and that young person had better **snap out of it**.* NEW YORKER □ usu direct or indirect command.

snap up [B1i pass adj] seize, buy quickly and eagerly; enrol, employ, marry sb (before sb else can do so). **O:** food, consumer item (in short supply); picture, antique; bargain; candidate; wife □ *In this time of austerity, nylon stockings were **snapped up** as soon as they came into the shops.* □ *She'd stay with me rather than let herself be **snapped up** by a lousy provincial artist.* CON

snarl (at) [A2 pass] make an unpleasant, growling sound (at sb), speak (to sb) in this way. **S:** dog; boss; husband □ *He has an unfortunate way of **snarling at** complete strangers.* □ *'I'm not used to being **snarled at** — change your tone!'*

snarl up[1] [A1 nom B1i nom pass adj] (informal) (cause to) become blocked or jammed in a confused way. **S:** [A1] **O:** [B1i] traffic; car, lorry; communications; telephone/radio network, switchboard. **S:** [B1] controller; operator □ *Private traffic **snarled up** completely on the approach road to the docks.* □ *Extra demand at these hours **snarls up** the whole system* (or: *causes a **snarl-up** of the whole system*).

snarl up[2] [A1 nom B1i nom pass adj] (informal) (cause to) become entangled, confused; get (sb) involved in a close, and possibly confused, way. **S:** [A1] **O:** [B1] talks, discussions; affairs, relations; colleague, member □ *They* (businessmen) *can plan in the knowledge that ministers and civil servants are not busy setting traps, scoring points and looking for every chance to **snarl up** their affairs.* ST □ *Against all the odds, he* (the Secretary for Trade) *has got Labour all **snarled up** in the referendum commitment on Europe* (i e tightly involved in the commitment to hold a referendum). ST

snatch at [A2 pass] try to grasp by putting out one's hand suddenly; try quickly to seize or take advantage of. **o:** purse, handbag; hand; rope; chance, opportunity, opening □ *A man darted from a doorway and **snatched at** his briefcase.* □ *He **snatched at** the rope-ladder, but it eluded his grasp.* □ *There are a few vacancies on the production side every year, but they come and go quickly. You have to **snatch at** them.*

snatch away [B1i pass] remove quickly (out of discourtesy, fear, suspicion, dislike etc). **O:** dish, tray; hand; child □ *I dislike having my plate*

snatched away *before I've half finished eating.* □ *In an uncontrollable nervous reaction, she* ***snatched*** *her hand* ***away***. DC

snatch from/out of [B2 pass rel] remove sth or sb from quickly (out of fear, greed etc). **O:** paper, book; hand; occupant, passenger. **o:** friend; grasp, hand; fire, wreckage □ *The letter was* ***snatched out of*** *my hand before I could read it.* □ *He was one of the few to be* ***snatched from*** *the holocaust.*

sneer (at) [A2 pass adj rel] show that one thinks little of sb or sth by smiling or talking in a mocking, superior way. **o:** effort, attempt; achievement, work □ *She constantly* ***sneers at*** *his efforts to improve himself.* □ *It's very discouraging to be* ***sneered at*** *all the time.*

not sneeze at [A2 pass] (informal) not consider lightly; take seriously. **o:** offer, proposal; chance, opening □ *'Mason says the new job carries an increase of £500 a year. That's good money. Certainly* ***not*** *something to be* ***sneezed at****.'* □ *'If you got the opportunity of working with his research team, you'd* ***not sneeze at*** *it, would you?'* □ usu with *would*.

(not) sniff at [A2 pass] (informal) (not) reject, (not) dismiss sth as unworthy of one's attention. **o:** offer; proposal, suggestion; idea □ *'You should****n't sniff at*** *this opportunity — you may not get another like it.'* □ *The agreement the employers proposed was certainly* ***not*** *to be* ***sniffed at****. The union leaders showed interest and undertook to report back to their executive.* □ usu neg or interr.

sniff out [B1iii pass] (informal) find by using the sense of smell; find by searching, investigating etc. **S:** dog; investigator; traveller. **O:** rat, rabbit; crime, racket; danger, excitement □ *It's his job to* ***sniff out*** *abuses of power.* SC □ *He's off on his travels again,* ***sniffing out*** *adventure in Tunisia.* THH

snip off [B1i pass adj] cut off, separate, with short, quick movements of scissors etc. **S:** tailor, cutter, dressmaker. **O:** (loose) thread, end, piece □ *The seamstress runs over the finished garment with the scissors,* ***snipping off*** *the loose threads.*

snipe (at) [A2 pass] (of a concealed marksman) fire (at); make sudden, sharp attacks (on). **S:** crack shot; rival, opponent; journalist □ *Our position was being* ***sniped at*** *from a clump of bushes to the right.* □ *He is seldom irritated when newspapermen* ***snipe at*** *him in their columns. It's a matter of patience born of long experience.*

snoop around [A1 A2] (informal) search, in a persistent, irritating way, for sth (esp signs that people are breaking rules, misbehaving etc). **S:** (prison) guard, warder; inspector □ *The man from the Ministry's* ***snooping around*** *again, trying to find out if we have a licence for one small chicken!* □ *The house prefects* ***snoop around*** *the dormitories at night.*

snort (at) [A2 pass emph rel] express contempt, annoyance etc, by puffing air sharply through the nose. **o:** interruption, delay; claim, conceit □ *'You can't come in here.' John* ***snorted at*** *the doorman: 'We'll soon see about that!'* □ *There was another long delay.* ***At*** *this Peter* ***snorted*** *angrily.*

snowed off [pass adj (B1)] (sport) (be) cancelled, or abandoned, because of heavy snow. **S:** match, game; race □ *Several fixtures in the League programme have been* ***snowed off****.* □ *They are now playing the match which was* ***snowed off*** *at Manchester last Saturday.* BBCR

snowed under (with) [pass (B1 B3)] (informal) (be) overwhelmed (with), have a heavy load (of). **S:** staff; business; office. **o:** work; order, commission; letter; appeal, application □ *'Don't give me any extra jobs: I'm* ***snowed under*** *already.'* □ *Don't be a clock watcher... be willing to work late if he's* ***snowed under with*** *work.* WI □ *At that time we were being* ***snowed under with*** *requests for medical aid.*

snowed up [pass adj (B1)] (be) isolated by heavy snow, be unable to leave the house etc for this reason. **S:** house; occupant, traveller, guest □ *We were* ***snowed up*** *for three days in our cottage in the mountains.* □ *The staging camps higher up the mountain would be* ***snowed up*** *if this blizzard continued.*

snuff out [B1i pass adj] extinguish, put out[10] (q v); kill, suppress. **O:** candle, lamp; hope, optimism; rising, revolt; enemy □ *The candles on the long table were* ***snuffed out****.* □ *The authorities* ***snuffed out*** *the rebellion almost as soon as it began.*

snuggle down [A1] (informal) move under the bedclothes, to get warm and comfortable □ *'Now,* ***snuggle*** *right* ***down*** *and I'll tuck you up.'* □ *The child* ***snuggled down*** *with its doll and was quickly asleep.*

snuggle up (to) [A1 A3 pass] (informal) press up close to another person for warmth or comfort, or out of affection or desire; cuddle up (to) (q v). **S:** child; lover □ *The children* ***snuggled up to*** *one another in the strange bed.* □ *She* ***snuggled up to*** *her boyfriend in the darkened cinema.*

soak (oneself) in [B2] absorb as much as possible of; steep (oneself) in (q v). **o:** history, lore, tradition □ *During these long summer visits he had* ***soaked himself in*** *the traditions and customs of the place.*

soak off [B1i pass B2 pass] remove sth by soaking it in water. **O:** (postage-)stamp, transfer; wallpaper □ *Rather than paint over the paper you'd do better to* ***soak it off****.* □ (instruction in plastic model kit) ***Soak*** *the transfers carefully* ***off*** *the backing paper and slide them onto the model.*

soak through [B1ii pass] make sb (including his clothes) thoroughly wet. **S:** rain; storm, downpour □ *'Don't stand out there: you'll be* ***soaked through****.'*

soak to the skin [B2 pass] make sb's clothes wet right through. **S:** rain; downpour, cloudburst □ *A storm burst over them as they slept in a field and they were* ***soaked to the skin****.* ASA □ *A passing bus swept through a large puddle by the side of the road and* ***soaked*** *us* ***to the skin****.*

soak up[1] [B1i pass adj] absorb, take up[2] (q v). **S:** sponge, cloth; ground. **O:** water, tea □ *If you spill ink on the carpet,* ***soak*** *it* ***up*** *straight away.* □ *This sandy soil* ***soaks up*** *moisture very quickly.*

soak up[2] [B1i pass adj] assimilate, absorb. **S:** student, class. **O:** information; figures, facts □ *'There's no holding the boy: he* ***soaks up*** *new information like a sponge.'*

soap down [B1ii pass] rub soap over one's body □ *After a hard game, it is refreshing to* ***soap***

oneself ***down*** *and then stand under a hot shower.*

sob out [B1i pass] tell a story etc while crying bitterly. **O:** (sad) tale, story, account □ *We listened sympathetically while she* ***sobbed out*** *the whole sorry tale.*

sob one's heart out [B1ii] (informal) (from pain or distress) cry bitterly, drawing in the breath sharply and noisily □ *When she heard her husband was leaving, Mary just* ***sobbed her heart out****.* □ *There seemed no way of comforting the boy. He sat there* ***sobbing his heart out****.*

sober down [A1 B1i pass] (informal) (cause to) become calm and serious after a period of lighthearted or irresponsible behaviour; make sb calm and serious. **S:** [A1] **O:** [B1] child; student; reveller, party. **S:** [B1] parent; teacher □ *'Now just* ***sober down****, everybody. I've important news for you.'* □ *He doesn't take as many risks on the road as he used to. I suppose one bad crash and two near misses would* ***sober*** *most people* ***down****.*

sober up [A1 B1i pass adj] (informal) (cause to) leave, recover from, a drunken state; (of sb who is being foolish or thoughtless) become, make, serious or thoughtful □ *'Put his head under the cold tap — that'll* ***sober*** *him* ***up****.'* □ *When he finally* ***sobered up****, he found that his wallet had been taken.* □ *I stopped grinning; not out of politeness but because what he said really did* ***sober*** *me* ***up****.*

sod off [A1] (taboo) leave, go away; clear off[1] (q v) □ *'Don't stand for any trouble from him. Tell him to* ***sod off****.'*

soften up [B1i pass] (informal) weaken a place (by shelling etc) for later attack; weaken the resistance of sb whom one wishes to persuade, convert, seduce etc. **S:** bomber, artillery; salesman, preacher, (amorous) young man. **O:** position, trench system; housewife, audience, girl □ *The beach defences were* ***softened*** *up before the landing craft* ***went in****.* □ *'She's* ***softening*** *me* ***up****, you see, so that I will be amenable by the time she gets here.'* AITC

soldier on [A1] continue to serve as a soldier; continue to work, function etc, resolutely □ *My regular engagement ends soon, but I'm thinking of* ***soldiering on****.* □ *Diesel engines failed badly in the freeze-up while electrics and steam* ***soldiered on****.* OBS

solicit for [A2] (formal) ask people for their custom (e g by calling on them, leaving handbills etc). **S:** shopkeeper; decorator, gardener, odd-job-man. **o:** trade, business, work □ *Tradesmen used to call at the houses of newcomers to a district —* ***soliciting for*** *custom. This is almost unheard of now.*

sop up [B1i pass] raise, remove liquid by pressing sth absorbent over it. **O:** water, milk, tea, ink □ *'Get a towel and* ***sop up*** *the water before it runs over the floor.'* □ *I dislike his habit of* ***sopping up*** *the gravy with a piece of bread.*

sort out[1] [B1i pass adj] put, arrange, in groups, classes (according to size, shape etc). **S:** storekeeper, packer; teacher. **O:** part, fitting; box, tin; pupil, material □ *She spent a happy afternoon* ***sorting out*** *her coins and stamps.* □ *Members of the armed forces have been* ***sorted out*** *by trades and occupations.* MFM

sort out[2] [B1i pass] settle; order, set straight; straighten out[2] (q v). **O:** dispute, quarrel; matter, problem; tangle, muddle, confusion □ *You'd better send somebody over to* ***sort*** *the situation* ***out****.* □ *It's his job to* ***sort out*** *real grievances.* SC

sort out[3] [B1i pass] (informal) organize sb, make him behave in an orderly, disciplined way. **S:** leader, manager, teacher. **O:** force, unit; staff; class □ *'I'll give you a week to* ***sort*** *your men* ***out****, then I expect things to run smoothly.'* □ *I'll need time to* ***sort out*** *the office staff — they're hopelessly disorganized at the moment.*

sort out[4] [B1i pass] (informal) punish, chastize; handle, deal with[3] (q v), (in a fight). **S:** police, guard. **O:** trouble-maker, hooligan, bully □ *'If you don't stop that din, I'll come in and* ***sort*** *you* ***out****!'* □ *He went after the big fellow and really* ***sorted*** *him* ***out****.*

sort oneself out [B1ii pass] (informal) get organized, settle into a normal pattern. **S:** newcomer, trainee; situation, things; business, trade □ *It's no good standing back and waiting for things to* ***sort themselves out****.* □ *You can sleep here till you get yourself fixed up… get* ***yourself sorted out****.* TC □ the passive is formed with *get*.

sort out from [B3 pass] separate, distinguish, one thing from another. **O:** good, true, clever; truth, news. **o:** bad, false, stupid; falsehood, comment □ *Her difficulty lies in* ***sorting out*** *what's 'right'* ***from*** *what's 'natural'.* H □ *I have picked out a few fields of study in an attempt to* ***sort out*** *the chaff* ***from*** *the wheat.* SNP □ the Object, when it is a noun or noun phrase, follows out.

sort ill/well with [A2 emph rel] (formal) (not) match or fit, (not) be in accord with. **S:** statement, declaration; conduct, action. **o:** record, history; character □ *His actions* ***sort ill with*** *his claim to be the champion of the oppressed.*

sought after [pass adj (A2)] (be) wanted, desired, in demand. **S:** (attractive) man, woman; property, house; china, jewellery □ *At the time she was* ***sought after*** *by most of the eligible men about town.* □ *Houses in this area are very much* ***sought after****.* □ *We have acquired a much* ***sought-after*** *piece of Georgian silver.*

sound off[1] [A1] (military) blow a 'call' or signal (e g reveille, lights out) on a bugle. **S:** bandsman, drummer (who may also be a bugler, in the British army) □ ***'Sound off****, drummer!'* (i e blow a particular call).

sound off[2] [A1] (informal) talk noisily and boastfully (about sth); speak loudly and pompously (on some topic) □ *I wonder when he will stop* ***sounding off*** *about this fabulous house he's building.* □ *'Please don't raise that topic: you'll start George* ***sounding off*** *on his pet theory.'*

sound out [B1i pass] try to discover or elicit sb's feelings or opinions on a question. **O:** colleague, partner; staff, employee; wife, family □ *'Have you* ***sounded out*** *your wife on the move to Australia yet?'* □ *'Where does he stand on this issue?' 'I don't know; I must* ***sound*** *him* ***out****.'*

soup up [B1i pass adj] (informal) improve the performance of a motor-car by modifying its engine. **O:** engine; production saloon □ *'If you* ***soup up*** *the engine, you'll have to do something to the suspension and brakes to take care of all that extra performance.'* □ *'The boy spends all his time batting around in a* ***souped-up*** *sports* *car. He'll get himself killed one of these days.'*

souse (in) [B2 pass rel] put a lot of liquid on sth; place sth in salt water etc to preserve it. **O:** food, meal; herring, mackerel; cucumber. **o:** vinegar, (bottled) sauce; brine □ *He **souses** everything he eats **in** tomato ketchup.* □ *Roll-mops are raw herrings cleaned and boned and **soused in** brine.*

space out [B1i pass adj] place, position, at intervals; set spaces between. **O:** post, pole; section, paragraph; output; children □ *'You've put the figures in this sum too close together; **space** them **out** clearly.'* □ *Contraceptive methods enable couples to **space out** their families in a way that is not burdensome to them.*

spare (for) [B2 pass emph rel] manage to find or give sth for a special purpose. **O:** money, time; thought, feeling. **o:** charity, activity; poor, unfortunate □ *I'd like to join you in France, but I can't **spare** the time **for** a holiday.* □ (child asking for money to buy fireworks for Guy Fawkes' Night) *'**Spare** a penny **for** the guy, please, Mister!'*

spark off[1] [B1i pass adj] cause to explode, detonate. **S:** stone, metal. **O:** charge; explosion □ *The explosive was **sparked off** by someone striking the iron heel of his boot on the stone floor.*

spark off[2] [B1i pass adj] cause sth violent, disturbing etc to begin; touch off[2] (q v), trigger off (q v). **S:** action; appearance, intervention; remark, speech. **O:** war; argument, row; debate; trouble, controversy □ *Local fighting might **spark off** a major war.* MFM □ *First are the miners, whose demands for £20 a week could **spark off** an uncontrolled wages rush in the autumn.* ST □ *The notorious third Reith lecture **sparked off** the present wave of preoccupation on the subject of sex.* SC

sparkle (with) [A2 rel] send out sudden, sharp flashes of light, intelligence etc. **S:** clothes, hair; eyes; conversation, writing. **o:** gem, ornament; mischief, excitement; wit, humour □ *The dinner tables **sparkled with** silver and crystal.* □ *This was the one dull interlude in a speech **sparkling with** witticisms.*

spatter on/onto [B2 pass emph rel] cause liquid to fall in drops on sth. **S:** car, lorry; mechanic, painter. **O:** (drops of) water, mud; oil, paint. **o:** shoe, coat; floor □ *A passing lorry **spattered** mud **onto** my new coat* (or: ***spattered** my new coat **with** mud*). □ *Green paint was **spattered on** the tiles* (or: *The tiles were **spattered with** green paint*).

spatter with [B2 pass rel] ⇨ previous entry.

speak about [A2 pass emph rel] discuss, talk about[1] (q v), talk of[1] (q v); mention □ *'What were you **speaking about** when I came into the room?'* □ *There was a rule that her late husband should never be **spoken about** in her presence.*

speak against [A2 rel] make a speech opposing sth. **S:** member, councillor, delegate. **o:** motion, proposal □ *Earlier he had **spoken against** bringing the law in; now he was inclined to support its introduction.* □ *This was a measure **against** which he had **spoken** and campaigned vigorously.*

speak for[1] [A2 rel] speak (e g in a debate, at a meeting) on behalf of others, be their spokesman. **S:** delegate, representative. **o:** member, constituent; majority, few □ *'I know I am **speaking for** all of us when I say how grateful we are to our hosts.'* □ *The Minister wondered whether the Opposition's record gave them any special right to **speak for** pensioners.*

speak for[2] [A2 rel] make a speech in support of sth. **S:** member, councillor, delegate. **o:** motion, proposal □ *Certain Members would be prepared to **speak for** the reintroduction of the death penalty for violent crime involving the use of explosives.*

speak for itself/themselves [A2] (informal) be so clear and impressive that any further comment is unnecessary. **S:** record, report; figure, profit □ *There is little need to comment on this record; it is true to say that it **speaks for itself**.* SNP □ *'I think you will agree, gentlemen, that the company's quarterly returns **speak for themselves**.'*

speak volumes for [B2] (informal) indicate a good deal about the nature of sb or sth, be strong evidence that sb or sth is of a particular character. **S:** action, conduct; appearance, manners; absence, silence. **o:** character, courage, honesty; upbringing □ *'They were mostly girls of impeccable morality — married in fact.' 'It **speaks volumes for** their husbands.'* TT □ *It **speaks volumes for** his kind disposition that he did not go straight out of the room and bang the door.* WDM

speak for yourself/yourselves [A2] (informal) don't speak or make decisions on my/our behalf □ *'I think we've done enough drinking for one evening.' '**Speak for yourself**, John!'* □ *'Perhaps it's time we were leaving.' '**Speak for yourselves**, darlings.'* □ only imper.

speaking for myself/ourselves [A2] (informal) in my/our view or opinion □ *'**Speaking for myself**, I've got a feeling that you are in danger of oversimplifying things a bit.'* TBC □ v in the *-ing* form; the expression is a non-finite adv clause.

speak on [A2 rel] give a talk, make a speech, on a particular subject. **o:** topic, subject; education, sociology, Dickens, Victorian painting □ *At our next meeting, Mr McDonald will be **speaking on** the early development of printing.* □ *The lecturer provided a list of topics **on** which he was prepared to **speak**.*

speak out (against) [A1 A3 pass] speak bravely and with conviction (on a particular question). **o:** corruption, scandal; immorality, vice; drugs, pornography □ *I am glad that someone has had the courage to **speak out against** these abuses.* □ *We've been silent for too long: it's time to **speak out**.*

speak to[1] [A2 pass rel] address, talk to[1] (q v), to exchange news etc □ *'Have a word with grandmother — she doesn't often get a chance of **speaking to** young people.'* □ *'Don't speak until you're **spoken to**!'*

speak to[2] [A2] have a word with sb, in the hope of getting sth done (e g of obtaining a favour for sb else). **o:** manager, director, producer □ *'There's something wrong with the plumbing. I'll have to **speak to** the landlord about it.'* □ *'Did you manage to **speak to** the Bursar about my salary?'* ⇨ speak about.

speak to[3] [A2 pass] scold, reproach sb, with a view to changing his conduct for the better; talk to[2] (q v). **S:** father, teacher. **o:** child, pupil □

*'You must **speak to** the children, Henry: they never listen to a word I say.'* □ *'I'm not letting those rascals trample over my garden again. They'll have to be **spoken to**.'*

speak to[4] [A2] (formal) (at a meeting of a committee, council etc) make a statement on a particular question. **S:** member, councillor, deputy. **o:** question, item (on the agenda), matter □ *'The next item is student accommodation. Mr Peters, might I ask you to **speak to** this?'* □ *Patrick **spoke to** this question for some time, accommodating various points raised by Martha.* TGLY

speak up [A1] speak in a loud, clear voice, so that one can be heard □ *'**Speak up**; we can't hear you at the back!'* □ *I do wish he'd stop mumbling and learn to **speak up**.*

specialize (in) [A2 emph rel] study, or work in, one narrow part of a general field (e g logic within the more general field of philosophy). **S:** student, research worker, scientist. **o:** biophysics; paediatrics; criminal law □ *In the second year of the degree course you can choose one of four areas to **specialize in**.* □ *In the Sixth Form you can **specialize in** the humanities or the natural sciences.*

speculate (about) [A2 pass emph rel] form and state opinions about sth (with incomplete knowledge). **o:** future, fate, destiny; (possible) outcome, consequences □ ***About** such matters it is useless to **speculate**; what we need is exact knowledge.* □ *At the moment all they can do is **speculate about** the future of the department — nothing is firm and definite.*

speculate (in) [A2 rel] buy and sell stocks and shares in the hope of profiting through changes in their market price. **S:** broker, investor. **o:** stock, share, bond; commodities, copper, rubber □ *He made a fortune **speculating in** tin shares, and lost almost all of it in cocoa futures.*

speed up [A1 nom B1i nom pass adj] (cause to) go faster, increase its speed; quicken up (q v). **S:** [A1] **O:** [B1] train, engine; action, movement; process, procedure; production, delivery. **S:** [B1] driver, operator; plant, factory; management □ *The water **speeded up** and hit the back of the funnel.* PM □ *There is now a system designed to **speed up** the work of factory inspection departments.* NS □ *The new road will ensure a **speed-up** in the movement of traffic to the docks.*

spell (for) [B2] indicate, mean, that trouble etc will ensue (for sb). **S:** arrival, appearance (of sb); change, deterioration (in the weather); strike, lay-off. **O:** trouble, disaster, ruin; suspension, delay; hunger, hard times □ *His sight was now so bad that the line of each eye crossed and converged some distance in front of him. At the cinema he was forced down to the front row, and it **spelt** ruination **for** any football match.* LLDR □ *The appointment of a new Head **spelt** disappointment **for** any boy hoping for an easy passage through the middle school.*

spell out[1] [B1i pass adj] read slowly, going laboriously over each word. **O:** passage; page, chapter □ *It was painful to hear him **spelling out** a page of an elementary textbook.* □ *'I want him to digest the contents of the letter fully, even if you have to **spell** it **out** word by word.'*

spell out[2] [B1i pass adj] make clear or explicit the full meaning or implications of sth. **S:** speaker; article, book; statement, speech. **O:** policy, philosophy; intention, proposal; consequence. **A:** word for word, in detail □ *His speech will **spell out** in some detail a short-term and a long-term strategy for growth.* OBS □ *The possible economic benefits of the treaty were **spelt out** in his recent book.*

spend (on) [B2 pass emph rel] pay money, give time, to achieve some object. **O:** money; fortune, pounds; time; hour, evening. **o:** house, car; family, girlfriend □ *He has **spent** a small fortune **on** improving his property.* □ *Every spare minute he gets is **spent on** the car.*

spend-up [nom (B1)] (informal) occasion when money is spent in a carefree and even reckless manner; a spending spree □ ALBERT: *I was thinking of having a bit of a **spend-up**.* HAROLD: *Well, you do that, you deserve it, you've worked hard for it.* BBCTV

spew out [A1 B1i pass adj] (cause to) come out, issue, in a thick, unpleasant stream. **S:** [A1] **O:** [B1] liquid; waste, effluent; gas. **S:** [B1] factory; pipe, exhaust □ *Several of our rivers have been polluted by factories **spewing out** their waste products into the water.* □ *They heard nothing but propaganda, **spewed out** over the air from a dozen stations.*

spice (with) [B2 pass emph rel] add sth to food, conversation etc to give it a more interesting flavour. **O:** dish; stew, gravy; story, conversation. **o:** herb; thyme, rosemary; joke, wit □ *They ate a green salad, strongly **spiced with** garlic and pepper.* □ *I try to remember some of the anecdotes **with** which his conversation was **spiced**.*

spill out/out of[1] [A1 A2 B1i pass B2 pass rel] (allow to) overflow, run over the side of a container. **S:** [A1 A2] **O:** [B1 B2] water, oil, paint; flour, powder. **o:** tin, jar, bucket □ [B1] *'Mind how you carry that pot: you'll **spill** some of the water **out**.'* □ [A2] *Seeds **spilled out of** the packet onto the floor.*

spill out/out of[2] [A1 A2] emerge suddenly, and in a scattered, disorganized way. **S:** passenger; audience, class □ *The excursion train pulled in, and dozens of schoolchildren **spilled out** onto the platform.*

spill over [A1 nom] be greater than, exceed, the number that a town or city can accommodate. **S:** population, inhabitants; town, suburb □ *New towns will have to be built to house the population of those boroughs which have **spilled over**.* □ *This estate takes the **spill-over** from decaying areas in the centre of the city.* □ alt, and more usual, nom form is **overspill**.

spin-off [nom (A1 B1)] (technology) the wider marketing of a product or material developed for a high technology project, or the application in other industries of a new process; general economic benefits resulting from the creation of new industries etc □ *The defence and aero-space industries are obvious sources of **spin-off** because of their advanced technology.* T □ *The need for facilities for oil rig service vessels could give Dundee some of the **spin-off** from the North Sea discoveries.* SC

spin out [B1i pass adj] make sth last as long as possible; extend, prolong. **O:** money, income; time, period, session; story, tale □ *My wife is always saying she doesn't know how to **spin** my money **out**.* TT □ *Robert couldn't think of any* *way of **spinning out** the conversation, so he called for the bill.* CON

spiral up [A1 emph] rise in a continuous curve, or spiral. **S:** smoke; aircraft, bird; employee □ *Smoke from the camp-fires **spiralled up** into a clear sky.* □ *He was going to **spiral up** to being head of the design department as soon as he knew how things were run.* CON

spirit away/off [B1i pass] (informal) make sb or sth disappear quickly and mysteriously. **S:** host; porter, waiter. **O:** guest, visitor; coat, suitcase □ *We were ushered smoothly to a table in the centre of the restaurant, and our coats and hats were **spirited away**.* □ *He was **spirited off** by some official before we had a chance to talk to him.*

spit at [A2 pass rel] direct saliva from the mouth at sb, as a sign of contempt or defiance. **S:** crowd, mob; prisoner. **o:** dignitary, leader; captor, tormentor □ *He was being **spat at** and reviled by the people who had once supported him.* □ *A cat will **spit at** a snake as much out of fear as defiance.*

spit in sb's eye [A2] (informal) make a gesture of contempt towards sb, esp, though not necessarily, by spitting at him □ *'Walk straight in, sit where you used to sit with him and **spit in his eye**.'* RATT □ *With us it will be different, only* other *people make mistakes, we can **spit in the eye of** society.* TT

spit out[1] [B1i pass] send out sharply, eject, from the mouth. **O:** medicine; vinegar; pip, seed □ *He took one sip of the wine and **spat** it **out**. 'It's turned to vinegar,' he said.*

spit out[2] [B1i pass] say sth sharply and angrily, as if spitting. **O:** word; oath, curse; name □ *'If I see you here again, I shall have you thrown out.' He **spat** the words **out** venomously.*

spit it out [B1ii] (informal) say what one has to say (e g deliver a message, make a request) quickly □ *'What are you trying to say? Come on, **spit it out**, man.'* □ usu imper.

splash about (in) [A1 A3 rel] sit or stand in water and make it fly about with one's hands or feet. **S:** child, swimmer. **o:** bath, swimming-pool □ *I left the children happily **splashing about in** their bath.* □ *A party of boys was **splashing about** at the shallow end of the pool.*

splash down [A1 nom] (space technology) (of a space capsule which has re-entered the earth's atmosphere) strike the surface of the sea. **S:** astronaut; module, capsule □ *The Apollo astronauts are scheduled to **splash down** at 3 p m local time* (cf ***Splashdown*** *is scheduled for 3 p m local time*).

splash on/onto[1] [B1i pass B2 pass rel] apply paint etc (to sth) with a brush in a vigorous or carefree way. **O:** paint, distemper. **o:** wall, fence; canvas □ *Don't be timid. Take a big brush and **splash** the paint **on**.*

splash on/onto[2] [A2 rel B2 pass rel] (cause to) fall in heavy drops onto. **S:** [A2] **O:** [B2] water, (liquid) mud; oil, paint. **S:** [B2] bus, car; mechanic, decorator. **o:** clothes, table, floor □ *A passing launch **splashed** water **onto** our deck.* □ *Don't **splash** any paint **on** your clothes* (or: *Don't **splash** your clothes **with** paint*).

splash out (on) [A1 A3] (informal) spend money (on sth) in an impulsive, carefree way. **o:** (new) clothes; furniture, equipment; entertainment □ *Before you start **splashing out on** books and records think of the bills you have to pay.* □ *'He's **splashing out** tonight, isn't he? First double whiskies, and now champagne all round.'*

splash with [B2 pass rel] ⇨ splash on/onto[2].

split away/off (from) [A1 A3 emph rel] (cause to) separate, divide (from a larger body). **S:** twig, branch; section, faction, wing. **o:** tree; party, organization □ *The wood is cracking in the heat, and pieces are **splitting away**.* □ *Their problem is to prevent the more militant elements **splitting off from** the official union organization.*

split (on) [A2 pass] (informal) give information about sb (e g of his breaking school rules) that will get him into trouble; tell (on) (q v). **o:** friend, accomplice □ *'Don't **split on** me, don't give me away!'* □ *Somebody must have **split on** him to a teacher.* □ usu said of one child by another.

split up [A1] (informal) (of a married or engaged couple) end their relationship; break up[6] (q v) □ *'Who told you that Mary and I had **split up**?'* □ *There's nothing in the rumour that they're **splitting up**.*

split up (into) [A1 A3 rel B1i pass B3 pass rel] (cause to) divide into parts. **S:** [A1 A3] **O:** [B1 B3] meeting, gathering, party; work, subject. **S:** [B1 B3] host, organizer; teacher. **o:** committee, group; section □ [B3] *For art and craft lessons the class is **split up into** small groups.* □ [A3] *About four-fifths of the boys leave school, the others **split up into** Science and Arts.* CON

spoil for a fight [A2] (informal) be eager to fight. **S:** soldier, boxer □ *We have well-trained troops, who **are spoiling for a fight**.* MFM □ in continuous tenses only.

sponge from [A2 rel B2 pass rel] (informal) get money etc from sb without giving, or intending to give, anything in return. **O:** cash, a fiver; meal, drink □ *In London he could stay with a friend **from** whom he'd **sponged** a meal from time to time.* □ *'Don't keep **sponging from** your father! His money won't last for ever, and neither will his patience.'*

sponge on [A2 pass rel] (informal) live at sb else's expense, taking money and assistance that one does not intend to return. **o:** family, friend □ *We're getting a little tired of being **sponged on** by our relatives.* □ *He calculated that if things went badly and he was out of a job for six months, he could always **sponge on** his parents.*

spoon out [B1i pass] serve, distribute sth, using a spoon. **S:** cook, hostess. **O:** potatoes, peas; plums; flour, sugar □ *She **spooned out** a few mouthfuls of rice into each of the plates.* □ *The relief supplies of beans and flour were **spooned out** from the back of a truck.*

spoon up [B1i pass] raise, take up sth, esp to the mouth, with a spoon. **O:** food; dinner; soup, pudding □ *He **spooned up** his soup hungrily and came back for more.* □ *She tried to **spoon up** a blob of potato that had fallen on the floor.*

spout (from) [A2 emph rel] come (from sth) in a thick, powerful stream. **S:** water, oil, blood. **o:** rock, soil; pipe, tube, vein □ *Dirty oil **spouted from** the damaged sump of his car* (or: *The damaged sump **spouted** dirty oil*). □ ***From** a crack in the rocks **spouted** a stream of clear water.*

sprawl about [A1] sit or lie somewhere in a casual, sloppy manner (e g with one's feet over the arms of a chair) □ *I wish I could teach the children not to* ***sprawl about*** *on the furniture.* □ *He found his students* ***sprawling about*** *on the steps of the library.*

sprawl out [A1] sit or lie with the arms and legs loosely and comfortably extended □ *I just feel like* ***sprawling out*** *in the sun for a couple of weeks.* ⇨ next entry.

sprawled out [pass adj (B1)] (be) lying with the arms and legs extended and relaxed □ *We found him* ***sprawled out*** *on the lawn behind the house.* □ *The feet of a* ***sprawled-out*** *figure appeared from beneath a large umbrella.* ⇨ previous entry.

spray on/onto [B2 pass rel] send liquid in a stream of tiny drops (onto sth). **O:** paint, varnish; perfume; disinfectant, weed-killer. **o:** wall; skin; plant □ *The gardener* ***sprayed*** *insecticide* ***on*** *the rose-bushes* (or: ***sprayed*** *the rose-bushes* ***with*** *insecticide*). □ *Insect repellent should be* ***sprayed onto*** *the skin to discourage mosquitoes* (or: *The skin should be* ***sprayed with*** *insect repellent* etc).

spray with [B2 pass rel] ⇨ previous entry.

spread on [B2 pass rel] place sth on a surface and extend it (e g by unfolding or pressing) thus covering the surface. **O:** cloth, rug; butter, jam. **o:** bed, table; bread, roll □ *An embroidered blanket was* ***spread on*** *the sofa* (or: *The sofa was* ***spread with*** *an embroidered blanket*). □ ***Spread*** *the butter thickly* ***on*** *the rolls* (or: ***Spread*** *the rolls thickly* ***with*** *butter*).

spread out[1] [B1i pass] open the hands and extend the arms (in a gesture of surprise, helplessness etc). **O:** ⚠ one's arms, hands □ *'I may possibly delay my departure.' He* ***spread out*** *his hands. 'Just by a fortnight.'* SPL □ *He* ***spread*** *his arms* ***out*** *theatrically. 'What can I do about it?' he said.*

spread out[2] [A1 B1i pass adj] (of individuals in a group) (cause to) move away from each other, disperse, so as to cover a wider area. **S:** [A1] **O:** [B1] soldiers, hunters; search-party □ *The peasants were riding* ***spread out*** *in a long line, with the cart in the middle.* DF □ *'****Spread out*** *more. Don't bunch up on the centre.'*

spread over [A1 A2 B1ii pass B2 pass] extend in time, over a period of time. **S:** [A1 A2] **O:** [B1 B2] course, studies, training; loan, mortgage □ [B2] *'I'll ask my bank manager if the repayments can be* ***spread over*** *two years.'* □ [A1] *The grammar lectures* ***spread over*** *into the next term.*

spread (to) [A2 rel B2 pass rel] (cause to) extend itself more widely, affecting other people and places. **S:** [A1] **O:** [B1] fire, flood, epidemic; disturbance, riot; revolt, disaffection. **o:** area, district; tribe, class □ *What can we do to prevent the disease from being* ***spread to*** *other countries?* □ *The strike is* ***spreading to*** *other groups of municipal workers.*

spread with [B2 pass rel] ⇨ spread on.

spring back [A1 nom] return to its previous position after having been pushed (because it is attached to a spring or counterweight) □ *Be careful when somebody goes through the door that it doesn't* ***spring back*** *in your face.* □ *The loose-leaf binder* ***springs back*** *and grips the sheets of paper* (i e it is a ***spring-back*** *binder*). □ spring-back is usu attrib.

spring from[1] [A2] (informal) appear so suddenly and unexpectedly that others do not know where one has come from. **o:** where; somewhere, anywhere, nowhere; I don't know where □ *'Where on earth did you* ***spring from****?'*

spring from[2] [A2 emph rel] have as its source or origin. **S:** curiosity, interest; restlessness, irritation. **o:** desire, wish; frustration, (thwarted) ambition □ *Her interfering ways* ***spring from*** *a desire to see her daughters comfortably married.* □ *The authorities failed to remedy the grievances* ***from*** *which these disorders* ***sprang****.*

spring on [B2 pass] (informal) present, introduce, sth to sb suddenly, so that he is surprised, and maybe unprepared. **S:** employer; government. **O:** arrangement, method, schedule; election, ballot. **o:** staff; electorate □ *'Don't expect me to make the thing work immediately — I've just had the job* ***sprung on*** *me.'* □ *The Headmaster* ***sprang*** *a revision of the timetable* ***on*** *us half-way through the term.*

spring out [A1 emph] appear suddenly from behind cover, with the intention or effect of frightening sb. **S:** thief, kidnapper □ *'You did give me a fright,* ***springing out*** *at me like that!'* □ *A masked man* ***sprang out*** *from a doorway.*

spring to attention [A2] (military) come sharply to the position of 'attention' (i e with the heels together and the arms pressed to the sides of the body). **S:** soldier; squad, platoon □ *As the general's car reached the gate, the sentry* ***sprang*** *smartly* ***to attention****.*

spring to sb's defence [A2 rel] move quickly to defend sb from (physical or verbal) attack □ *Till now he had ignored the lady* ***to whose defence*** *Mason had so gallantly* ***sprung****.* □ *The stockbroker's wife* ***sprang to her husband's defence****.* HAA

spring to one's feet [A2] jump up quickly from where one is sitting or lying. **S:** class, squad; porter, sentry □ *As the headmaster entered the classroom, 4B* ***sprang*** *noisily* ***to its feet****.* □ *Henry* ***sprang to his feet*** *to help his mother with the heavy dish.*

spring to life [A2] suddenly become active, begin to act vigorously □ *A bundle shape in the corner moved and* ***sprang to life****.* DC □ *Many dormant branches of our organization are now* ***springing to*** *active* ***life****.*

spring up [A1] arise, develop, grow, quickly. **S:** breeze, wind; weed, corn; factory, school, hospital; organization, relationship; suspicion, doubt □ *Towards evening a cold wind* ***sprang up****.* □ *Milk bars have* ***sprung up*** *all over the place.* SC □ *Friendship* ***springs up*** *between people.* SC

sprinkle on/onto [B2 pass emph rel] throw a fine shower of particles or drops onto (a surface). **O:** water; sand; pepper, salt. **o:** flower; floor; food □ *A cart went by* ***sprinkling*** *water* ***onto*** *the dusty streets* (or: ***sprinkling*** *the streets* ***with*** *water*). □ *Ink was once dried by* ***sprinkling*** *fine sand* ***onto*** *the writing paper* (or: ***sprinkling*** *the paper* ***with*** *sand*).

sprinkle with [B2 pass rel] □ previous entry.

spruce up [B1i pass adj] (informal) make sb, or oneself, clean and smart □ *I decided to go home and* ***spruce*** *myself* ***up*** *— to let everyone know that life had not got me down.* SML □ *The girls were all* ***spruced up*** *for the great occasion.* □ *'Tell the children to get* ***spruced up*** *for the* *guests.'*

spur on (to) [B1i pass adj B3 pass emph rel] drive, strongly encourage, sb to do better, to achieve more. **S:** rider; teacher, coach; ambition, greed. **O:** horse; pupil, athlete; politician, businessman. **o:** greater success, higher things □ *He was constantly* ***spurred on*** *by a fear of failure.* □ *James would have been content with a modest level of success, but she kept* ***spurring*** *him* ***on to*** *something 'higher' or 'better'.*

spurt (out) (from) [A1 emph A2 emph rel A3 emph rel] come out in a sudden burst. **S:** water; blood; flame. **o:** pipe; artery, wound; building □ [A1] *The surgeon lanced the boil and a mixture of pus and blood* ***spurted out.*** □ [A2] *As we watched, flame and smoke* ***spurted from*** *an upstairs window.*

sputter out [A1] stop burning after making sharp, spitting sounds; come to an end gradually and quietly. **S:** flame; candle; fire, heater; demonstration, rebellion □ *The last match* ***sputtered out****, leaving us in total darkness.* □ *The demonstration* ***sputtered out*** *in a few half-hearted scuffles with the police.*

spy on/upon [A2 pass] watch the activities of others secretly, with the aim of informing the authorities, other governments etc. **S:** agent, informer. **o:** colleague, employer, fellow-worker □ *He is paid by the police to* ***spy on*** *other students.* □ *The research centre was so security-conscious that we all ended up* ***spying on*** *each other.*

spy out [B1iii pass] spot, identify, detect sth illegal etc, and report it to the authorities. **S:** agent, snooper. **O:** dissent, heresy, opposition □ *These editors and writers have for years been ready to* ***spy out*** *dangerous novelty and deviation in works of art.* OBS □ *Disagreement arises, and it must be* ***spied out*** *as it occurs.*

spy out the land [B1i] assess the situation, see how matters stand (e g in a battle, in industry, in the home) □ *He sent forward a few scouts to* ***spy out the land.*** □ *I'm thinking of sending someone down to our Plymouth branch to* ***spy the land out.***

squabble (with) [A2 rel] have a petty, noisy quarrel (with). **o:** sister, wife; neighbour, workmate □ *'I always arrive home to find you* ***squabbling with*** *your brother* (or: *you and your brother* ***squabbling***)*.'* □ *'How like them: always* ***squabbling with*** *each other over trifles!'*

square off [B1i pass adj] give sth a square shape or outline; divide a surface into squares. **O:** piece, block (of wood, metal); pack, haversack; paper, page □ *For inspections, soldiers used to* ***square off*** *their packs by fitting pieces of wood inside.* □ ***Square*** *the page* ***off*** *with your ruler, then you'll be able to copy the drawing accurately.*

square up to [A3 pass] (informal) prepare to fight sb (i e by raising the fists etc); confront sb or sth resolutely. **o:** opponent, attacker; problem, task □ *He's not used to being* ***squared up to****: he may change his mind about a fight if you look fierce enough.* □ *Opposition speakers accused the Chancellor of not* ***squaring up to*** *the realities of a major trade recession.*

square up (with) [A1 A3] (informal) pay the money one owes before leaving a hotel, restaurant etc; settle up (with) (q v). **o:** waiter, tradesman; friend □ *'Can I leave you to* ***square up with*** *the waiter?'* □ *'It's high time I* ***squared up with*** *you* (or: *you and I* ***squared up***)*.'*

square with [A2 emph rel B2 pass emph rel] be, make, consistent with; reconcile (with)[2] (q v). **S:** [A2] **O:** [B2] account, story; action, practice. **o:** evidence, fact; principle, theory □ *I wonder how he* ***squares*** *this attitude* ***with*** *his criticism of the government?* SC □ *There are certain aspects of this case* ***with*** *which his statement does not quite* ***square.***

square one's account/accounts with [B2 pass rel] repay one's debts to sb; punish sb for an injury one has suffered; settle with (q v). **o:** creditor; bank, shop; rival, traitor, spy □ *I should manage to* ***square accounts with*** *the bank before the end of the quarter.* □ *I've no further quarrel with him;* ***my account with*** *him is* ***squared.***

squash in/into [A1 A2 B1i pass B2 pass] (cause to) press tightly against one another into a small space; squeeze in/into (q v). **S:** [A1 A2] **O:** [B1 B2] passenger, commuter; fruit, vegetable. **S:** [B1 B2] driver, guard; packer. **o:** car, train; lift; box, case □ [B2] *'I think we can* ***squash*** *a few more* ***into*** *the back of the van.'* □ [B2] *We were* ***squashed into*** *the compartment like sardines in a tin.* □ [B1] *'If you try to* ***squash in*** *any more peaches they'll get bruised.'*

squash up (against) [A1 A3 B1i pass B3 pass] (cause to) press tightly (and uncomfortably) against another person; squeeze up (against) (q v). **S:** [A1 A3] **O:** [B1 B3] passenger, spectator □ [B3] *There were four of us* ***squashed up against*** *each other on one seat.* □ [A1] *'You'll have to* ***squash up*** *to make room for the others.'*

squat down [A1 emph] sit on one's heels, or with the legs drawn up under or close to the body □ *The porters* ***squatted down*** *with their loads at the edge of the road.* □ ***Down*** *he* ***squatted*** *on the front porch, and defied anyone to move him.*

squeeze in/into [A1 A2 B1i pass B2 pass] force oneself or sb into a small space; squash in/into (q v). **S:** [A1 A2] **O:** [B1 B2] passenger, spectator. **S:** [B1 B2] driver, manager. **o:** car, compartment; lift; theatre; ground □ [A1] *'****Squeeze in*** *and try to get a seat near the window.'* □ [B2] *'If you* ***squeeze*** *any more* ***into*** *the back of the car you'll be stopped by the police.'*

squeeze out/out of[1] [B1i pass B2 pass rel] by pressing, force liquid etc from a container. **O:** water, juice, liquid soap, detergent, toothpaste. **o:** bottle, tube □ *'The lemon looks dry to me, but you may be able to* ***squeeze out*** *a few drops.'* □ *We have reached the point where cheese and meat-paste can be* ***squeezed out of*** *tubes.*

squeeze out/out of[2] [B1i pass B2 pass rel] (informal) get money from sb by applying pressure of various kinds (e g threats, harsh legislation). **S:** government, Inland Revenue; party, association; blackmailer. **O:** money; tax, revenue; donation, levy. **o:** tax-payer; member; victim □ *This government will* ***squeeze*** *every penny it can* ***out of*** *the unfortunate tax-payer.* □ *If you give in to the blackmailer, he will return to* ***squeeze out*** *another hundred later.*

squeeze through [A1 A2 pass rel] pass through a narrow passage etc, by pressing in the sides of one's body. **o:** tunnel, passageway, shaft; door, entrance □ *'Turn your shoulders* *round the other way and you'll manage to* ***squeeze through****.'* □ *There was a small slit* ***through*** *which one could just* ***squeeze*** *by lying flat on one's stomach.*

squeeze up (against) [A1 A3 B1i pass B3 pass] (cause to) press tightly (and uncomfortably) against another person; squash up (against) (q v). **S:** [A1 A3] **O:** [B1 B3] passenger, traveller; spectator, audience, crowd □ [A1] *'****Squeeze up*** *a bit more and let the others sit down.'* □ [B3] *Several hundreds were* ***squeezed up against*** *each other in one corner of the stand.*

squint at [A2] (of a crosseyed person) look at; look at through half-shut eyes. **o:** sun, arc-light □ *He came out on the steps,* ***squinting*** *a little* ***at*** *the bright sunlight.*

squirm (with) [A2] twist about, wriggle (because of some unpleasant feeling). **S:** audience, listener, companion. **o:** shame, embarrassment, unease □ *His remarks were so ill-judged that I* ***squirmed with*** *embarrassment.*

squirt out/out of [A1 emph A2 B1i pass B2 pass] (cause to) come out of a container with some force, and in a thin jet or stream. **S:** [A1 A2] **O:** [B1 B2] soda, beer; liquid soap, detergent; foam. **o:** bottle, jar, can; extinguisher □ [A1] *He struck the can hard with an opener and juice* ***squirted out*** *over his jacket.* □ [B2] *You* ***squirt*** *foam* ***out of*** *a nozzle and direct it at the base of the fire.*

stab at [A2 pass] aim a blow with a knife at sb, try to strike him with a knife □ *The big man* ***stabbed at*** *the security guard with a knife and grazed the ribs.*

stab in the back [B2 pass] (usu of sb who is known and trusted) attack sb's position, good name etc, while he is busy with sth else. **S:** friend, colleague, partner □ *The Minister of Defence complained to his friends that he had been* ***stabbed in the back*** *by his Chiefs of Staff.* MFM □ *While the country was engaged in the north with one enemy, it was* ***stabbed in the back*** *by another.*

stack against [B2 pass] (informal) make it unlikely that sb will succeed. **S:** poor background, lack of family connections; behaviour, attitude. **O:** ⚠ the odds, chances; chips, cards □ *'Making an enemy of the office manager must have* ***stacked*** *the cards* ***against*** *his rising any higher than a tea boy.'* □ *John had always claimed that the odds were* ***stacked against*** *him from the start, but then he was the kind to blame everything on circumstances.*

stack up [B1i pass adj] place in a pile, one upon the other. **O:** plate, dish; chair, desk; record □ *He was ushered into a dusty office, with the files* ***stacked up*** *against the wall.* □ *It's convenient to have chairs that will* ***stack up*** (or: *can be* ***stacked up***).

staff up [B1i pass adj] increase the staff of sth; bring the number of staff to the proper level. **O:** department, bureau □ *'Of course they are understaffed and we are* ***staffing*** *them* ***up****.'* BBCR □ *The project can't get under way without a fully* ***staffed-up*** *research section.*

stagger about/around [A1] move about in an unsteady, uncontrolled way (because of illness, injury, drunkenness etc). **S:** patient, casualty; drunkard, addict □ *The effect of the heart-attack was to make him* ***stagger about*** *with no sense of direction.*

stake off [B1i pass adj] separate, mark the limits of, an area by means of stakes. **O:** field, meadow □ *They've set aside a small area as a children's playground, and* ***staked*** *it* ***off****.*

stake on[1] [B2 pass emph rel] bet, place money with a bookmaker in the hope that a team, horse etc will win; put on[8] (q v), wager (on) (q v). **S:** racegoer, punter. **O:** money; fortune. **o:** horse, dog; team □ *I'm not prepared to* ***stake*** *money* ***on*** *a horse that's lost three times in a season.*

stake on[2] [B2 emph rel] be so confident that sth is the case, that one is prepared to sacrifice a good deal if one is wrong. **O:** ⚠ (one's) life, all, career, reputation. **o:** innocence, integrity, honesty; sb's being involved □ *If old Philip had been honest, you wouldn't be living in a West End house, you can* ***stake*** *your life* ***on*** *that.* DC □ *The system can hardly be inaccurate, or the Government would not* ***stake*** *its reputation* ***on*** *backing it.* NS □ *It's genuine —* ***on*** *that I'll* ***stake*** *my life.*

stake out [B1i pass adj] mark, with stakes, the boundaries of land etc in which one has a special interest. **O:** holding, farm; area, field (of interest, of study) □ *He's* ***staking out*** *a bit of land at the top end of the valley.* □ *No one can emulate him in this field: it is as though he has* ***staked out*** *this bit of biology as his own.*

stake (out) a/one's claim (on/to) [B1iii B2 B3] mark, as one's own, the limits of land where one wishes to farm, look for precious metals etc; declare a special interest in sb or sth. **S:** farmer, miner, prospector. **o:** land, area, territory; job, department; girl □ *We'll go North and* ***stake a claim****. The great uranium fever is sweeping the world.* DPM □ *He's* ***staked out a claim to*** *Susan.* RATT □ *In the absence of the Inspector General, various subordinate departments began to* ***stake out their claims on*** *industrial production.* B

stamp on [A2 pass rel] bring one's foot down heavily on sth, thus crushing it; seek to control or suppress by rigorous action. **o:** beetle, spider, wasp; book, china; rebel, dissident □ *In her rage, she would throw his papers on the floor and* ***stamp on*** *them.* □ *Anyone who stepped out of line in this period of minority government could expect to be* ***stamped on*** *by the party whips.*

stamp on/onto [B2 emph rel] print sth on a surface (with ink, dye, paint etc). **O:** name, trademark, insignia; pattern, motif. **o:** box, bale, roll; cloth, paper □ *A machine* ***stamps*** *the names and addresses of subscribers* ***onto*** *envelopes* (or: ***stamps*** *envelopes* ***with*** *the names* etc). □ *His initials were* ***stamped on*** *the brief-case in black.*

stamp out [B1i pass] eliminate, get rid of, vigorously or by force. **S:** government; police, army; fire brigade, health authorities. **O:** rebellion; dissent, heresy; malaria, cholera □ *The police and the medical profession were trying to* ***stamp out*** *the increasing wave of drug addiction in young people.* SC □ *All resistance to the regime had been ruthlessly* ***stamped out****.*

stamp out/out of [B1i pass adj B2 pass rel] cut pieces from a sheet of metal etc, by striking it with a shaped tool; punch out/out of (q v). **O:** square, disc; coin, medal □ *The older badges were shaped by hand; nowadays they are*

***stamped out of** gunmetal.* □ *The machine can **stamp out** hundreds of components in an hour.*

stamp with [B2 pass rel] ⇨ stamp on/onto.

stand about/around [A1] be still, doing nothing (because one is idle, does not know what to do etc). **S:** visitor; student, worker □ *The guests were **standing about** after dinner, smoking and talking quietly.* □ *'Don't just **stand around** doing nothing: give me a hand with the luggage!'*

stand head and shoulders above [A2] be much more able, gifted etc than sb else. **o:** one's fellows, contemporaries, companions □ *She knows there is still a long way to go before she **stands head and shoulders above** her rivals.* H □ *'Of course we had to give the girl an interview. On paper, she **stands head and shoulders above** the other applicants.'* □ head and shoulders is an adv phrase of degree.

stand apart (from) [A1 A3 emph rel] place oneself (through shyness, pride etc) at a distance (from sb); hold aloof (from sb). **o:** one's fellows, other people □ *Unlike Napoleon, Wellington tended to **stand apart from** his men, partly because he was naturally reserved, and partly because he found it profoundly distasteful to court popularity.*

stand (as) (for) [A2 rel] be a candidate (as representing a particular party or interest) (for sth). **o:** (***as***) Liberal, Nationalist; executive nominee; (***for***) election; Parliament, local council; seat, place □ *Is he prepared to **stand for** the vacant seat on the committee?* □ *At that stage in his career, there were few offices **for** which George was not prepared to **stand**.* □ *Mr Francis is **standing as** the official nominee **for** the post of District Secretary.*

stand aside[1] [A1] move to one side, move out of the way (e g to let sb pass). **S:** crowd; onlooker, spectator □ *People on the pavement were asked to **stand aside** to let the procession through.*

stand aside[2] [A1] remain at a distance from events, not be involved in them □ *He **stands aside** and lets the current of events sweep past him.* □ *Don't **stand aside** and let others decide the important issues.*

stand back (from)[1] [A1 A3] be situated at a distance (from). **S:** building; house, church. **o:** road, street □ *The school **stands** well **back from** a busy thoroughfare.* □ *The big house **stands back** about half a mile **from** the main gates.*

stand back (from)[2] [A1 A3 rel] distance oneself (esp mentally) from sth in order to understand or judge it better. **S:** writer; artist, teacher, organizer. **o:** work; painting; events, hurly-burly □ *The artist **stood back** (**from** the portrait) the better to judge the general balance of the composition.* □ *Sometimes an administrator must **stand back from** day-to-day business to grasp the wider pattern of events.*

stand back (from)[3] [A1 A3 rel] withdraw, retreat, from making decisions, influencing events etc. **S:** leader; teacher, father. **o:** decision-making; argument, controversy □ *In my own case, two matters cannot have been right: both due to the fact that my mother ran the family and my father **stood back**.* MFM □ *These were vital discussions **from** which he couldn't afford to **stand back**.*

stand between [A2 emph] exist as an obstacle between sb and sth he wishes to achieve. **S:** hurdle, obstacle; examination, test; shortage lack. **o:** (sb and) success, triumph; career expansion □ *Only two men **stood between** hir and a coveted place on the board.*

stand by[1] [A1] observe events which require ar active response without doing anything. **S:** country, government; army; partner, friend □ *A ma may not **stand by** and watch another destro himself.* ARG □ *We cannot **stand** idly **by** whil children go hungry.*

stand by[2] [A1 nom] be ready to act, be on th alert. **S:** police, troops; fire services, ambulanc crews □ *The Government ordered the Guards t **stand by**.* AH □ *Troops are on **standby** aler tonight.* BBCTV □ *Publishers of books **stand by** ready to turn out a huge new edition.* UTN

stand by[3] [A2] (be prepared to) support, help sb stick by (q v). **o:** colleague, friend, family, ally one another □ *He's the sort of friend who wi **stand by** you through thick and thin.* □ *Our sup porters continued to **stand by** us when the goin was hardest.*

stand by[4] [A2] be true or faithful to. **o:** promise undertaking, guarantee; principle, code; wha one has promised □ *I must **stand by** what I hav said.* RM □ *'I **stand by** every word of what wrote,' I said aloud.* SPL

stand down[1] [A1] (legal) leave the witness bo (i e after giving evidence). **S:** witness, prisoner □ *'Unless you have any further questions for him, think this witness may **stand down**.'*

stand down[2] [A1 B1i pass] (military) disband end its life as an active unit. **S:** [A1] **O:** [B1] regiment, corps □ *Certain regiments have chosen t **stand down** rather than be amalgamated wit other units.*

stand down[3] [A1 B1i pass] (military) relax return to other duties after having been alerted o 'stood to' (⇨ stand to) (esp at dawn or dusk) **S:** [A1] **O:** [B1] troops; company, platoon **S:** [B1] officer □ *The troops were **stood dow** only when it was clear that no attack was forth coming.*

stand down[4] [A1] withdraw one's application resign one's position etc (esp in favour of sl else). **S:** candidate; chairman, member □ *If Ton wants the job I'll **stand down**.* EHOW □ *Th secretary is proposing to **stand down** in favou of a younger man.*

stand (for) [A2 rel] ⇨ stand (as) (for).

stand for[1] [A2 rel] represent; be an abbreviatio of. **S:** church, party; faith; office, firm; letter initial. **o:** values, principles; integrity, honesty John, Paul □ *I dislike the man and all he **stand for**.* □ *'What does your second initial **stan for?'***

stand for[2] [A2] (informal) tolerate, bear; put up with (q v). **S:** authorities; teacher, parent. **o:** nonsense, impertinence, rowdiness □ *They had bee wearing pyjamas until noon. Fiorella wouldn **stand for** it.* ARG □ *If there's one thing I won' **stand for**, it's being treated like an office boy.* □ usu neg; often with *will/would*.

stand in good/better stead [B2 pass] serv sb well, be of value to sb. **S:** knowledge experience; ability, gift; connection, relationshi □ *He had a pictorial imagination, which **stoo** him **in good stead** in the first hasty shaping c the new museum.* SD □ *This circle of peopl **stood** him **in** far **better stead** with his younge* *friends.* HAA

stand in sb's way/in the way of sth [A2] prevent sb from doing sth, stop sth happening. **S:** employer, headmaster; tradition, precedent; difficulty □ *'If you want to go overseas to teach, I certainly shan't* ***stand in your way.'*** □ *No difficulty under heaven could* ***stand in the way of*** *that moment which he and Sonia so valued.* HAA

stand in (for) [A1 nom A3] (in a film) take the part of a regular actor or actress during certain sequences □ *A professional stunt-man is* ***standing in for*** *the male lead during the car chase at the end of the film.* □ *In some minor scenes, her part is played by a* ***stand-in.***

stand in towards [A3] (nautical) move towards the shore. **S:** ship; fleet. **o:** shore, coast, beach □ *It was arranged that the MTB* (motor torpedo boat) *should lie there for two hours, and she would then* ***stand in towards*** *the town upon a certain bearing.* RFW

stand off[1] [B1i pass adj] dismiss workers (e g during an economic depression); lay off[3] (q v). **S:** owner, manager. **O:** labourer, craftsman, office worker □ *If the slump continues, more men will be* ***stood off.***

stand off[2] [A2] (nautical) remain stationary at a distance from the shore etc. **S:** ship; fleet, convoy. **o:** shore, beach; Dover, Beachy Head □ *The bigger landing craft were forced to* ***stand off*** *the beaches until the tide turned.*

stand-off [nom (A1)] (rugby) half-back who, with the scrum-half, forms a link between the forwards and the three-quarters; the scrum-half obtains the ball from scrums etc, the stand-off (half) (also called *fly-half*) distributes it to the three-quarters □ *The French* ***stand-off*** *gathered a bouncing ball and kicked deep for touch.* □ *The Cardiff* ***stand-off*** *worked a dummy scissors with one of his centres and opened up a gap.* ST

stand on ceremony [A2] be too formal in one's behaviour (e g in entertaining sb) □ *I don't like too much* ***standing on ceremony*** *at a simple party like this.* □ *'Now I'm going to kiss you too, just to show we don't* ***stand on ceremony*** *here.'* TGLY

stand on one's dignity [A2] insist that one should be treated with respect, that one's feelings, age, position etc should be taken into account. **S:** mayor, alderman; actor, singer □ *I went to bed feeling what a wonderful man he was — too big to* ***stand on his dignity.*** MFM □ *She was* ***standing on her dignity*** *as a promising young actress.* CON

stand on its head [B2 pass] reverse the stated or expected order of sth. **O:** case, argument, proposition; course, order (of things) □ *John* ***stood*** *the curator's argument* ***on its head,*** *saying that charging admission to museums would attract more, not fewer, people to them.* □ *In this, as in so many other ways, telepathy and clairvoyance seem to be intent on* ***standing*** *the ordinary, accepted and understandable course of nature* ***on its head.*** SNP

standing on one's head [A2] (informal) easily, without effort □ *Mr Wickam, their agent for many years past, said if he kicked the bucket* (= died) *Mrs Merton could run the place* ***standing on her head.*** WDM □ *'Please Miss, I've finished three sums,' said Ron Bailey — very good at arithmetic, will get his eleven plus* ***standing on his head.*** TT □ a non-finite adv clause of manner; always in final position after a finite v.

stand on one's own (two) feet [A2] be independent, self-sufficient. **S:** child, pupil; (emergent) country, industry □ *If he doesn't* ***stand on his own feet*** *at his age, he'll lose his self-respect.* HAA □ *I* ***stood*** *squarely* ***on my own feet*** *— I became to a large extent financially independent of my father.* SD

stand out (a mile) [A1] be striking, noticeable, prominent; stick out a mile (q v). **S:** fact, evidence; reason, explanation; remedy, answer; (it...) what has to happen □ *The first thing that* ***stands out*** *from the hold-up is that the routine precautions gave the bandits little trouble.* T □ *It* ***stands out a mile*** *what has to be done.* NM

stand out against [A3 pass] be firm, unmoved, in one's opposition to sth. **S:** employer, trade union; delegate. **o:** increase, reduction (in wages); change, modification (of terms of work) □ *The union leaders are* ***standing out against*** *the abolition of the piece-work system, which enables them to renegotiate wage-rates whenever a new job or process is introduced.* □ *The Unionist Party in Northern Ireland has* ***stood out against*** *any policy which it feels might lead to the political unification of North and South.*

stand out (against/in contrast to) [A1 A3 emph rel] be clearly seen, because of a contrast of colour or tone with sth else. **S:** figure, shape; tone, shade. **o:** background; sky, landscape □ *The black smoke* ***stood out in*** *sharp* ***contrast to*** *the white fountains sent up by enemy shells.* SD □ ***Against*** *a pale blue evening sky, the vapour trails* ***stood out*** *clearly.*

stand out for [A3 pass] (informal) delay reaching an agreement in the hope of getting sth one wants; hold out for (q v), stick out for (q v). **S:** negotiator; delegate; committee. **o:** increase (in wages), reduction (of working hours), removal (of grievances) □ *Our executive is* ***standing out for*** *the original claim of twenty pounds a week.* □ *Students are* ***standing out for*** *a revision of the constitution.*

stand out (from) [A1 A3 emph rel] be of high quality, be pre-eminent. **S:** school, college; scholar, scientist; factory. **o:** rest, others; fellow, contemporary □ *Among modern universities some* ***stand out*** *with a special attractiveness.* TES □ *In this list two names* ***stand out*** *particularly* (or: *are particularly* ***outstanding***). □ *Even as a schoolboy player, he* ***stood out from*** *the rest of the team.* □ *(be) outstanding* is an adj equivalent in meaning to stand out [A1].

one's eyes stand out of one's head [A2] (of the facial expression) show, express, extreme fear, surprise etc □ *'Give him two double whiskies.'* ***My eyes stood out of my head:*** *I had never tasted whisky before.* SD

stand out to sea [A3] (nautical) move out from the shore towards the open sea. **S:** ship; fleet, convoy □ *A destroyer, doubtless part of the local navy, was* ***standing out to sea.*** ILIH □ *They were ordered to* ***stand*** *well* ***out to sea,*** *out of the range of shore batteries.*

stand outside [A2] not be sth which one wishes to consider, discuss etc. **S:** matter, question; compensation, re-housing. **o:** scope, range; (main) argument, discussion □ *The question of* *where these people are to be resettled has been allowed to* **stand outside** *the scope of the development plan.* ⇨ be/fall outside.

stand over[1] [A2 pass] supervise, watch over, closely. **S:** foreman, supervisor; teacher. **o:** worker, apprentice; pupil □ *I hate being* **stood over** *when I'm trying to do a job of work.* □ *'You'll have to* **stand over** *the new man until he learns the routine.'*

stand over[2] [A1 B1ii pass] postpone, defer; hold over (q v). **S:** [A1] **O:** [B1] business, matter, item; discussion, debate. **S:** [B1] chairman, committee □ *'There's no urgency about this matter: it can* **stand over** *till next week.'*

stand to [A1 nom B1ii pass] (military) (cause to) be on the alert, with weapons ready, against enemy attack. **S:** [A1] **O:** [B1] troops; company, squad. **S:** [B1] officer, sergeant □ *The men were* **standing to** (or: *were on* **stand-to**) *half the night.* □ *Units in the field are normally* **stood to** *just before dawn and dusk.*

stand to attention [A2] (military) stand in an alert posture, with the feet together, be at attention (q v); adopt this position, come to attention (q v). **S:** soldier; company, battalion □ *Perhaps it was the absence of water which made one sweat vicariously, sweat for the troops* **standing to attention** *through the long speeches.* QA □ *'***Stand to attention** *when the officer speaks to you!'*

(it) stands to reason [A2] (informal) it is only to be expected, it follows naturally, given that sth else is already the case □ *'Delicate made he is, and only a boy.* **Stands to reason** *he couldn't rough it with the others.'* ASA □ DAVIES: *All these big sports grounds,* **it stands to reason**, *they need people, to keep the ground, that's what they want.* TC □ *To Doris's great disappointment she did not find them holding hands, though she made several unexpected forays into the dining room in expectation of the same. But* **it stood to reason** *at their age, and madam was married too.* WDM □ simple tenses only; often introduces a finite clause, as in the first two examples.

stand together [A1] be united (e g in the face of some outside threat); stick together (q v). **S:** family, firm, team □ *Social classes whose interests are usually in conflict may respond to appeals to* **stand together** *if there is some danger from outside, which seems to threaten them all.*

stand (up) [A1] rise to the feet (possibly as a sign of respect); get up[2] (q v). **S:** audience, public; employees, children □ *When the Headmaster entered the room, the class would* **stand up** *as a mark of respect.* □ *I* **stood up** *to let my neighbour leave the theatre.*

stand up for [A3 pass] take the side of sb, support him, in a quarrel or fight; support or champion a particular cause; stick up for (q v). **o:** (younger) brother; underdog, weaker side; oneself; rights, liberty □ *Despite his dislike of Robin, he had always* **stood up for** *him if some other boy at school attacked him.* ASA □ *Do you claim what is due to you and* **stand up for** *your rights?* WI

stand up (to)[1] [A1 A3 emph rel] last well, remain sound, despite severe treatment. **S:** metal, fibre; chassis, bodywork; cloth, garment; health, constitution. **o:** (rough) handling, (harsh) treatment; heat, pressure; exile, imprisonment □ *Structurally the desks are sound, and will obviously* **stand up to** *a good deal of wear and tear.* TES □ *How will his party's morale* **stand up to** *what could prove to be several years of bad news?* OBS

stand up (to)[2] [A1 A3] withstand, survive, some form of test. **S:** document; claim, argument, theory; acting, poetry. **o:** ⚠ a test; scrutiny, examination, analysis □ *She knew that an hysterical letter from an old dying woman wouldn't* **stand up** *in any court of law.* DC □ *Even if this possibility did not* **stand up to** *close scrutiny, Pavlov's theory would still be valid.* SNP □ *I think this poem does* **stand up** *because this is brilliant descriptive writing.* BBCR

stand up to [A3 pass] (be ready to) resist boldly. **o:** (petty) dictator, officious person; pressure, threat, intimidation □ *How will Sarah* **stand up to** *her partner's antagonism?* WI □ *He thought of her as someone to be proud of, yet someone to be* **stood up to** *on occasion.* PW

stand (well) with [A2] have a good relationship with sb, be on good terms with sb. **o:** teacher, employer, bank manager □ *What did she get out of it, why did she put up with so much vexation of spirit? Was it just to* **stand well with** *Jeremy, whom, though often defying, she really adored.* PW □ *To proceed with the next phase of their programme they would need more capital. And whether they got the support they needed would depend on how* **well** *they* **stood with** *their overseas backers.*

stare (at) [A2 pass adj rel] look intently (at sb or sth). **A:** intently, closely; critically. **o:** stranger, newcomer; spectacle, parade; clothes, jewels □ *He looked round the room for support, but they* **stared at** *him stonily.* HD □ *Dr Hasselbacher opened his eyes and* **stared** *straight* **at** *him.* OMIH □ *If she wears a short skirt in that country, she gets* **stared at** *every time she goes out.*

stare down [B1ii pass] look intently at a curious or ill-mannered person who is doing the same, and continue looking until he is forced to lower his eyes (often a playful trial of strength between two children) □ *An inquisitive small boy looked at us from one corner of the railway compartment. Our eldest son looked back as intently at him, and did his best to* **stare** *him* **down**. ⇨ stare out.

stare in the face [B2] be so clear, or so obvious, that one should not miss seeing or grasping it. **S:** building, monument; (lost) money, purse; truth, fact; disaster, crisis. **O:** scientist, politician □ *'No wonder you woke up, with that piece of gold plate* **staring** *you* **in the face**.*'* DC □ *This logic* **stares** *anyone* **in the face** *who knows the economic needs of this country.* ASA

stare out [B1ii pass] look intently at a curious or ill-mannered person who is doing the same, and continue looking until he is forced to stop (often a playful trial of strength between two children) □ *The term began with an attempt at baiting the new teacher. One boy stared fixedly at the newcomer as if she were some strange object. The teacher, for her part, sat calmly at her desk and* **stared** *him* **out**. ⇨ stare down.

start for [A2] leave one place to go to another. **o:** home, work □ *'What time do you* **start for** *school in the morning?'*

start from scratch [A2 B2 pass] (informal)

art (sth) from the very beginning, esp when uilding or developing sth. **S:** industry, country; usinessman, artisan, scientist. **O:** everything, e whole thing □ *The company lost all its plant rough enemy bombing, so that in 1945 they* ***tarted*** *absolutely* ***from scratch.*** □ JIMMY: *I'll ose that damned sweet-stall, and we'll* ***start*** *verything* ***from scratch.*** *What do you say? Ve'll get away from this place.* LBA □ *His busi-ess was* ***started from scratch*** *with £200 he'd anaged to borrow from a relative.*

art in (on)[1] [A1 A3] (informal) begin to do sth. (one's) homework, research; (the) climb, earch; cooking the meal, cleaning the yard □ *I ought a nearly-new car dubiously at an inflated rice from a young doctor, and* ***started in*** *to ook for Janet Prentice.* RFW □ *Andy, one of the uides, was reading the mail. He put it aside hen I came in, brought me a beer, and we* ***tarted in*** *to analyse the climb* (or: ***started in n*** *analysing the climb*). BM □ [A1] pattern fol-wed by inf.

art in (on)[2] [A1 A3] (informal) begin to criti-ze, scold, harangue etc sb. **S:** orator, preacher; ther, boss. **o:** following, faithful; slacker, mis-eant □ *The team were hardly settled in the essing-room before the manager* ***started in on*** *em for slovenly, unaggressive play.* □ *Without iving anyone a chance to draw breath, Nolan* ***tarted in*** *to berate the sales force for the worst et of figures in months.* □ [A1] pattern followed y inf.

art off [A1] (informal) begin, open one's marks (or actions) by saying (or doing) sth spe-al □ *He* ***started off*** *by pointing out the dangers volved in rock climbing.* □ *They had* ***started ff*** *saying that the accommodation wasn't as ad as we'd been told.*

art off (on)[1] [A1 A3 rel B1i pass B3 pass rel] ause to) begin working on sth. **S:** [A1 A3] : [B1 B3] class; pupil, athlete. **S:** [B1 B3] acher, coach. **o:** Latin, calculus; apparatus, mple climbs □ [B3] *It's a bright class: I can* ***tart*** *them* ***off on*** *German in the second year.* □ 3] *'What made him* ***start off on*** *this weekend ycling craze?'*

art off (on)[2] [A1 A3 B1i pass B3 pass] (cause) begin talking, story-telling etc, in a way that steners find tedious; set off (on)[2] (q v). **S:** [A1 3] **O:** [B1 B3] bigot, bore, chatterbox. **o:** tirade, miniscences, tale of woe □ [B3] *'Don't for leaven's sake* ***start*** *him* ***off on*** *one of his golfing tories.'* □ [B1] *'You know that once she's been* ***tarted off,*** *it's almost impossible to stop her.'* > be off (on).

art off on the right/wrong foot (with) [A3] nformal) begin sth (esp a relationship) in the ght/wrong way; get off on the right etc (q v). **S:** on-in-law, visitor, tenant; (new) student, recruit *I want the girl to* ***start off on the right foot vith*** *my mother.* RFW □ *'Don't light a cigarette hen you meet the boss: you'll* ***start off on the vrong foot.'***

art out [A1] begin a journey, leave a place. **S:** iker, cyclist, car □ *The small party of explorers* ***tarted out*** *with high hopes.* □ *Ten machines* ***tarted out*** *on the last leg; only four finished.*

art out of [A2 B2 pass] (cause to) awake sud-enly, emerge quickly, from one's daydream etc. : [A2] **O:** [B2] listener, pupil. **S:** [B2] crash, explosion; pain. **o:** sleep, dream, reverie □ *The appearance of the teacher at his side* ***started*** *John* ***out of*** *his happy daydream.* □ *The audience was* ***started out of*** *its somnolence by a sudden crash on the drums.*

start up [B1iii pass] get going, set in motion. **O:** engine; business, service; acquaintance, conver-sation □ (order to aircraft mechanic) *'All right,* ***start*** *her* ***up!'*** □ *He* ***started up*** *a successful car hire firm.* □ *There was no danger of* ***starting up*** *some stumbling conversation with them.* CON

start up (in) [A1 A3 rel] begin a career, a work-ing life. **o:** business, teaching, dentistry □ *Twice he had raised the money and* ***started up in*** *engineering.* ARG □ *They were thinking of* ***start-ing up in*** *the fruit and vegetable trade.*

to start with[1] [A2] at the beginning, initially; to begin with[1] (q v) □ *I pulled hard* ***to start with;*** *but after a time I began to lose interest and I let go of the rope.* MFM □ *The bottom of the atmosphere, the part where we live, will be cool* ***to start with.*** TBC □ an adv expression with no object; it may occur at the beginning or end of the sentence.

to start with[2] [A2] in the first place, first and foremost; to begin with[2] (q v) □ *'****To start with,*** *Jones is a hopeless organizer. And as if that wasn't enough, he goes out of his way to annoy everybody.'* □ *'Well,* ***to start with,*** *you can put out of your mind the notion that there's money to be made out of teaching.'* □ an adv expression with no object; usu occurs at the beginning of the sentence.

starve into [B2 pass] force sb to surrender by cutting off his food supply. **O:** country, city; gar-rison. **o:** ⚠ submission, surrender, capitulation □ *They imagine that by blockading our ports they can* ***starve*** *us* ***into*** *submission.*

starve of [B2 pass emph rel] keep sb or sth short of; deprive of (q v). **O:** country, city; popu-lation; industry. **o:** essential foods, raw materials □ *The railways are* ***starved of*** *first-class tech-nical men.* NS □ *They had* ***starved*** *the work-shops* ***of*** *vital components.* □ *His children felt* ***starved of*** *affection.* □ often passive.

starve out/out of [B1i pass B2 pass] force sb to leave a hiding-place etc, by cutting off his food. **S:** invader; hunter. **O:** population, army; rodent. **o:** city; lair, burrow □ *Having failed to bomb the occupants out, the enemy resolved to* ***starve*** *them* ***out.***

stash away [B1i pass] (informal) store, deposit, sth in a place where others are unlikely to find it. **O:** food, sweets; loot, contraband; money, profits □ *'Fatty Smith always* ***stashes*** *his food parcels* ***away*** *at the back of his locker so he won't have to share them with the others.'* □ *'I suppose the Syndicate has a few millions* ***stashed away*** *in a numbered account somewhere.'*

stave in [B1i pass adj] crush the side or covering of sth, making a dent or hole in it. **S:** rock, pole; blow, impact. **O:** hull, body (of car); rib-cage □ *Repeated batterings on the rocks had* ***staved in*** *one side of the craft.* □ *He was admitted to hospi-tal with two of his ribs* ***staved in.***

stave off [B1i pass adj] prevent sth from over-whelming one. **S:** news, conversation, joke; ration, supply. **O:** misery, despair; defeat, disas-ter; hunger, thirst □ *Only the sure prospect of relief* ***staved off*** *utter despair.* □ *He stuffed* *down quantities of bread, trying to* ***stave off*** *increasing stabs of hunger.* BFA

stay abreast (of) [A1 A3] remain level (with), not slip behind; remain informed (about). **S:** car, boat; company, department; scholar, scientist. **o:** competition, field; (latest) development, discovery □ *Over the first five laps, Bedford* ***stayed abreast of*** *the Belgian runner.* □ *It's difficult to* ***stay abreast*** *in one's reading when so much is being published in this country and the States.* ⇨ keep abreast (of).

stay ahead/ahead of [A1 A2] not lose one's position in front (of others), retain the lead. **S:** horse, car; industry, manufacturer; thief. **o:** (rest of the) field; competitor, rival; police □ *'To begin with, it won't be a matter of* ***staying ahead of*** *our European rivals: it'll be a question of catching them up.'* □ *Occasionally, George is a few pounds down at the end of a week's gambling, but more often than not he* ***stays ahead*** *and goes into the next week several pounds in credit.* ⇨ keep ahead/ahead of.

stay (at) [A2 rel] live, take board and lodging, (at). **o:** hotel, boarding house, hostel □ *He travelled through the North,* ***staying*** *for a few nights at a time* ***at*** *small hotels.* □ *'Where are you* ***staying****?' '****At*** *the Grand.'*

stay at home [A2] have the settled, unadventurous qualities associated with sb who spends all his (leisure) time at home □ SARAH: *Hymie's all right. He's got a business. His children are married and he* ***stays at home*** *all the time.* CSWB □ *The younger son doesn't get about much. He prefers to* ***stay at home*** (or: *to be a* ***stay-at-home***) *and fiddle around with bits of machinery.* □ *Kate's a quiet, conventional,* ***stay-at-home*** *sort of girl.* □ nom form stay-at-home may be attrib, as in the last example.

stay away (from)[1] [A1 A3 rel] not be present (at), not appear (at); stop away (from) (q v). **S:** worker, student, child. **o:** meeting, lecture, class; home □ *That term, John* ***stayed away from*** *school for weeks at a time.* □ *If the visitors do* ***stay away*** *there is a very strong case for giving Cornwall some assistance.* OBS ⇨ keep away (from).

stay away (from)[2] [A1 A3] not interfere (with), keep one's distance (from). **S:** official, inspector; busybody; seducer. **o:** office, shop; wife, daughter □ *'I don't want men in bowler hats snooping around the place; tell them to* ***stay away****!'* □ *We were aware of the kind of reputation the man had. If he knew what was good for him, he would* ***stay away from*** *our sister.* ⇨ keep away (from).

stay behind [A1] remain at a place after others have left (to help tidy up etc); remain behind (q v), stop behind (q v). **S:** visitor, spectator, member (of group or audience) □ *Several students* ***stayed behind*** *after the lecture to ask questions.* □ *'Will somebody* ***stay behind*** *to help with the washing-up?'*

stay down[1] [A1] remain in a lowered position. **S:** handle, lever, switch □ *'Both of these switches above the boiler have to* ***stay down*** *if you want the radiators to be on as well as the hot water cylinder.'* □ *'Something's wrong with the gear lever. It won't* ***stay down*** *in fourth; it keeps popping up into neutral.'* ⇨ leave down.

stay down[2] [A1] remain in the stomach (rather than be vomited). **S:** food; solids; medicine *The baby clearly had an upset stomach. mother tried all kinds of special foods, but no of them would* ***stay down****.* ⇨ keep down[7].

stay for/to [A2] remain at sb's house to have meal; stop for/to (q v). **S:** visitor, guest. **o:** mea lunch, dinner □ *They had decided to* ***stay*** *lunch, and Brigit had fussed because there w not enough food.* DC □ *'Catch the last train, a you can* ***stay for*** *supper.'*

stay in[1] [A1] remain at school after others ha left, as a punishment; stop in (q v). **S:** clas form; culprit □ *'If this noise goes on for ve much longer you'll all have to* ***stay in*** *aft school!'* ⇨ keep in[3].

stay in[2] [A1] remain in position, remain where is. **S:** damper, plunger; passage, note, referen □ *The damper* ***stays in*** *and reduces the flow air but does not put the fire out completely. Gerald didn't very much care if the references his old chief did offend the greybeards in t Ministry. Whatever he cut from his manuscri those references would* ***stay in****.* ⇨ leave in.

stay in[3] [A1] (cricket) remain at the wicket, n be dismissed. **S:** batsman; opening pair, la man. **A:** all afternoon, throughout the morning *Turner* ***stayed in*** *for the four hours as the mo aggressive member of two productive partne ships.*

stay in/indoors [A1] remain in the hou (because one is ill, the weather is bad etc); st in/indoors (q v). **S:** family, (hotel) guest □ *W* ***stayed in*** *all that week, while the rain pour down outside.* □ *'****Stay indoors*** *for a few da until your cold is better.'* ⇨ keep in[1], kee indoors.

stay off [A2] not eat, drink, smoke etc, thin which, if taken in excess, may be bad for one health. **o:** beer, whisky; potatoes, sweet stu women □ *'Harry's wife would have had an easi time of it if he'd managed to* ***stay off*** *the bottl* □ *'You'll have to* ***stay off*** *sweets and chocolat if you want to reduce weight.'* ⇨ keep off[4].

stay on[1] [A1 A2] remain in position on top sth. **S:** lid, cover. **o:** pot, pan □ *You can't lo any very large parcels onto the roof rack. Th won't* ***stay on*** *in a strong wind, or if you're dri ing fast.* ⇨ leave on[1].

stay on[2] [A1] remain alight, keep burning. light; fire; television □ *'Of course the depa ment's electricity bills are going to be high if h the lights are allowed to* ***stay on*** *after people home at night.'* ⇨ leave on[2].

stay on (at) [A1 A3] remain at a place of stud with an employer etc, after others have left; st on (at) (q v). **S:** pupil, student; employee. school, college; the works, bank; party, dance *He's* ***staying on at*** *grammar school to take 'A' levels.* □ *A medical student becomes a sen figure in college as he* ***stays on*** *year after ye* HD ⇨ keep on (at/in).

stay on top (of) [A1 A2] remain in a superi healthy etc state; remain in control (of sth). opponent, rival; job □ (Milk Marketing Boa advertisement) *'Pick up a pinta* (= pint of mil ***Stay on top****!'* □ *The teachers need to be liv and resourceful to* ***stay on top of*** *these youn sters.* ⇨ keep on top (of).

stay out[1] [A1] remain outside the house (e after dark); stop out[1] (q v). **S:** child, husband

'*You* **stayed out** *after midnight last night. What* *appened to you?'* □ *She lets the children* **stay** **out** *half the night.*

ay out² [A1] remain in the open. **S:** car, icycle; washing □ *'I'm sure it's laziness, but I ust can't be bothered to put the car in the garage. It'll have to* **stay out** *tonight.'* ⇨ leave out.

ay out³ [A1] (industrial relations) remain on strike, continue a stoppage of work; stop out² (q v). **S:** worker; miner, postman. **A:** on strike; in sympathy □ *The electricians' leaders said the men were prepared to* **stay out** *until their grievances were remedied.*

ay out of [A2] remain at a point where sb cannot reach one, or sth cannot affect one. **o:** range, each; earshot; danger, harm's way, trouble □ *I'd been looking for him for years, but always he managed to* **stay** *just* **out of** *reach.* □ *Father hoped we'd* **stay out of** *trouble in the big city.* ⇨ keep out of¹.

ay to [A2] ⇨ stay for/to.

ay up¹ [A1] not fall or sink. **S:** building; trousers; swimmer □ *'I'm surprised that some of these packing-case houses* **stay up** *as long as they do.'* □ *'If you do fall out of the boat, your lifejacket will help you to* **stay up** *until we can fish you out.'* ⇨ keep up¹.

ay up² [A1] remain awake and out of bed (e g o wait for sb); stop up² (q v) □ *'Will you let us* **stay up** *till he comes?' 'Yes, if it's not too late.'* PW □ *She liked listening to records and* **staying up** *half the night.* SPL ⇨ be up⁴, keep up⁹.

tay up³ [A1] remain in a position where it has been mounted, hung etc. **S:** picture, decorations; curtain, hanging □ *'Your notice can* **stay up** *for a week, but then, I'm afraid, it'll have to come down to make room for others.'* □ *Christmas decorations* **stay up** *until the sixth of January (Twelfth Night). Then, according to tradition, they have to be taken down.* ⇨ leave up.

tay (with) [A2 rel] be a guest (at sb's house). **o:** friend, relative □ *At half-term we had planned to* **stay with** *my sister at her house near London.* □ *The family* **with** *whom Michael was* **staying** *at the time had welcomed his father to their house over twenty years previously.*

tay with [A2] (informal) continue to listen to sb, even though one may be tempted to go away etc, so giving him the chance to make himself clear □ *'Just* **stay with** *me a minute longer. I'm sure I can convince you that we have a reasonable case.'* □ *'***Stay with** *me just one moment, ladies and gentlemen, while I tell you about our new rub-on rub-off carpet cleaner!'*

teal a glance (at) [B2 pass rel] take quick, secret looks at sb one finds attractive. **o:** visitor, suitor □ *From time to time* **she stole a glance** *from under her long eyelashes.* □ *The man's wife chattered on,* **stealing** *occasional* **glances at** *Peter.* CON

teal away [A1] leave quietly (and possibly also furtively). **S:** guest, spectator; shy, embarrassed person. **A:** furtively, noiselessly, on tiptoe; like a thief in the night □ *He* **stole away** *from his seat in the back row while the attention of the others was engaged.*

teal a march (on) [B2] do sth before sb else, so gaining an advantage over him. **o:** neighbour, competitor, (business) rival □ *Neither of you wants to look as if the other one had* **stolen a march on** *him.* CON □ *And while you're not employing them, other people are* **stealing a march on** *you in some other trade.* ART

steal over [A2] gradually fill or take possession of sb. **S:** mood, feeling; depression, sadness; relief, liberation □ *The party feeling, the community spirit was beginning to* **steal over** *her.* PW □ *A sense of futility* **stole over** *him.*

steal up on [A3] advance quietly and carefully to a place, thus taking the occupant by surprise; (of a mood etc) come to one gradually, without one knowing. **S:** patrol, scout; feeling; melancholy, depression; old age. **o:** position, camp; him etc □ *A small party* **stole up on** *the bridge under cover of darkness.* □ *I must not let madness* **steal up on** *me and take me by surprise.* PM

steam across, along, away etc [A1 A2] move across etc under steam power (and possibly emitting puffs of steam). **S:** ship, train □ *The London to Edinburgh express* **steamed into** *Newcastle right on time.* □ *Convoys carrying essential supplies and munitions* **steamed** *continuously* **across** *the Atlantic.* □ *We arrived on Platform 10 just as the Rome train was* **steaming out**.

steam off [B1i pass B2 pass] remove one piece of paper etc from another by passing steam over them. **O:** (postage-)stamp, label. **o:** letter, box □ *Before you can mount the stamps in your album, you must* **steam** *them* **off** *their envelopes.*

steam up [A1 B1i pass adj] be covered, cover, with condensed steam. **S:** [A1] **O:** [B1] glass; window, mirror □ *The insides of the car windows* **steam up** *very quickly in wet weather.* □ *The glass doors of the kitchen were* **steamed up** *— a sure sign that the kettle had been boiling for a long time.*

steamed up [pass adj (B1)] (informal) (be) excited, enthusiastic, worked up (⇨ work up (into/to)) □ *'You come on half-naked to get them all* **steamed up** *about you, so why grumble when you succeed?'* PE □ *My mother came back all* **steamed up** *about modern decor, and painted the doors crimson.* RFW □ usu passive, with *be, get, look, seem,* but note: *a* steamed-up *condition, state.*

steel oneself (against/for) [B2 emph rel] harden, toughen, oneself in preparation (for sth). **o:** shock, blow, impact; disappointment, failure; (price) increase, (wage) cut, tax □ *Citizens will probably* **steel themselves for** *a further levy.* SC □ *They had* **steeled themselves against** *possible failure in the examination.*

steep (oneself) in [B2 pass] absorb as much as possible of; soak (oneself) in (q v). **o:** tradition, lore, ritual □ *During his year in Florence Stephen had* **steeped himself in** *the painting and sculpture of the early Renaissance.* □ *A trained soldier, who is* **steeped in** *all the rituals of kit inspections and parades, is put in charge of new recruits.*

stem from [A2 emph rel] arise from, have as its source or cause. **S:** (political) movement, agitation, unrest; dissatisfaction, anxiety; faith, hope, inspiration. **o:** (harsh) conditions, unemployment, hunger; statement, policy; tradition, (peasant) background □ *The present wave of strikes* **stems from** *discontent among the lower-paid.* □ *Significantly, he has not challenged my analysis* (of the situation) *— only the solution* *that **stems from** it.* OBS

step aside [A1] move to one side (e g to let sb pass). **S:** passenger, pedestrian, spectator □ *'Would you mind **stepping aside** to let this lady off the bus?'*

step back [A1] move backwards (from surprise, shock, etc) □ *'Take her in your arms.' At that Nicky **stepped back**, his face stiff with distaste.* DC □ *She **stepped back**, hardly able to believe her ears.*

step down [A1] resign (usu from a position of importance). **S:** chairman, president, director □ *If they disagreed seriously while I was chairman, I would at once **step down**.* MFM □ *If the people want him to form a new party he will do so, or even **step down** if they say so.* T

step forward [A1] present oneself (e g to give information, to offer help); come forward[1] (q v). **S:** witness; volunteer, would-be helper □ *When the appeal went out for volunteers to help with **ward**.*

step in [A1] intervene (to help or hinder). **S:** government, ministry; owner, editor; (union) leader □ *Seeing that I was lost for an answer, John **stepped in** to save the situation.* □ *The union leadership **stepped in** and made the strike official.*

step inside [A1] enter a house, an office etc. **S:** visitor, caller □ *'Would you care to **step inside** for a moment?'* □ *He was invited to **step inside** and take a seat.*

step into the breach [A2] help to run an organization, business etc, by filling the place of sb who is absent. **S:** (junior) colleague, assistant, understudy □ *Douglas couldn't attend the meeting, but Martin **stepped into the breach** at the last minute.* □ *Kathleen **stepped into the breach** with a generous devotion.* SD

step into sb else's shoes [A2] assume, take control of, a responsible task or post from sb else. **S:** son, nephew; assistant, deputy □ *Then Father handed over control, and Geoffrey **stepped into the director's shoes** with the confidence of someone who had been measuring himself carefully for the responsibilities involved.*

step off[1] [A2] leave, get off or out of, a vehicle etc. **o:** bus, train, boat; pier, dock □ *As he **stepped off** the plane, he was surrounded by photographers.* □ *He **stepped off** the pavement, and was nearly knocked down by a taxi.*

step off[2] [A1] (military) begin to march. **S:** troops; company, squad □ *'Now when you **step off**, take a full pace of thirty inches!'*

step off on the wrong foot [A3] (informal) begin a task, a relationship etc, in the wrong way □ *After all the care we took to prepare the ground, he has to **step off on the wrong foot**.* □ *With girls, the first approach is important: don't **step off on the wrong foot**!*

step on sb's corns/toes [A2] (informal) behave (e g when taking up a new job) without proper regard for the feelings of others □ *'As a new boy here, I'm anxious not to **step on anyone's toes**, but it seems to me that something ought to be done about the tremendous losses through pilfering.'* □ *He walks into every new situation with the sensitivity of an ox, **stepping on people's corns** right and left.*

step on it/the gas [A2] (informal) press down the accelerator of a car to increase speed; hurry, go faster. **S:** driver, motorist □ *'Tell the driver **step on it** — we don't want to be late!'*

step out [A1] lengthen one's stride so as to mov[e] more quickly □ *'Tell the people at the front **step out** — we'll never be back in time for sup[-] per.'*

step outside [A1] (informal) (invite sb to) leav[e] a private party, bar etc to have a fight □ *'**Ste[p] outside** and repeat to me what you've just said* □ *Brother Nigel asked me to **step outside** wh[en] I told his mother she was evil-minded.* LBA

step over [A2 pass] raise one's feet to cross a[n] obstacle. **o:** rope, barrier; feet □ *We had to **ste[p] over** rows of outstretched legs to reach our sea[ts] in the stalls.*

step up [B1i nom pass adj] increase; improv[e] enhance. **S:** government, industry, informatio[n] services, army. **O:** effort, campaign; productio[n] delivery; broadcast, propaganda; drive, offensiv[e] □ *Resources allotted to these operations shou[ld] be **stepped up**.* MFM □ *One effect of the lesso[n] proved to be **stepped-up** attendance figure[s]* TES □ *Their social position had been muc[h] **stepped up**.* PW □ *We hope for a sharp **step-u[p]** in production.*

stew in one's (own) juice [A2] (informa[l]) (leave sb to) bear the unpleasant consequences [of] his own actions □ *'Johnson's been trying to st[ir] up trouble between the two of us for months an[d] now his scheming has bounced back on him' 'Well, don't feel obliged to make things comfor[t-] able for him. He can **stew in his juice** for a bit* □ *Let Ella **stew in her own** self-centred, neu[-] rotic **juice**, she thought.* HAA

stick about/around [A1] (informal) remain in [a] place waiting for sth to happen, sb to arrive etc *'**Stick around** for a while — the boss will soo[n] be back.'* □ *I didn't want to **stick about** waitin[g] for the bomb to explode.*

stick at [A2 pass] (informal) work steadily an[d] persistently at sth. **o:** work; task, job □ *I **stick a[t]** my painting five or six hours a day, but nothin[g] comes of it.* □ *'You can get the report writte[n] inside a week, but you'll need to **stick at** it.'*

stick at nothing [A2] (informal) (be ready t[o]) behave in an unscrupulous way to get what on[e] wants; stop at nothing (q v) □ *'Like you? O[f] course he doesn't like you. He'll **stick at noth[-] ing** to get you out of the way!'* □ *He'll **stick a[t] nothing** if ruthlessness is the difference betwee[n] staying in the middle and getting to the top.* □ us[u] with *will/would*; often followed by an inf.

stick by [A2] (informal) support loyally, stan[d] by[3] (q v). **o:** friend, colleague □ *His wife h[as] **stuck by** him in good times and bad.* □ *The olde[r] staff would **stick by** the firm through thick an[d] thin.*

stick down[1] [B1i pass adj] fasten the cove[r] flap etc of sth with glue, paste etc. **O:** fla[p] flange, edge; envelope □ *'Don't forget to put th[e] postal order in before you **stick down** the enve[-] lope.'* □ *The corner of the page has been **stuc[k] down**; I can't read what's written there.*

stick down[2] [B1i pass] (informal) place on th[e] floor etc, put down[1] (q v). **O:** bag, case; parce[l] chair □ *'You can **stick** the table **down** in [a] corner for the time being.'* □ *'Where does th[e] mail go?' 'Oh, **stick it down** over here.'*

stick down[3] [B1i pass] (informal) write o[n] paper. **O:** name, address, 'phone number

*'**Stick down** your names at the top of the form.'* □ *He'd **stuck** the formula **down** on the back of an old envelope.*

stick in [B1i pass B2 pass] fix, fasten sth into a book etc with glue, paste, etc. **O:** photograph, postcard, cutting. **o:** album, scrapbook □ *The children spent a rainy morning **sticking** stamps **in** their albums.*

stick in sb's craw [A2] (informal) be so unpleasant, painful etc that it cannot easily be borne or accepted. **S:** behaviour; treachery, deceit; rudeness, insensitivity □ *When I thought about marrying Myrtle — yes, there were many, many moments when I did think of marrying her — this angry hurt recurred. I could not get over it. It **stuck**, as they say, **in my craw**.* SPL □ *'What really **sticks in my craw** is hearing that odious man claim all the credit for himself.'*

stick one's heels in [B1ii] (informal) resist, oppose, firmly sb's attempt to ignore one's rights, dictate to one etc; dig one's heels/toes in (q v). **S:** taxpayer, consumer, commuter □ *The Education authority wanted to move the school to new buildings, but parents and children **stuck their heels in**.* □ *Hundreds of tenants are **sticking their heels in** over the new rent increases.*

stick in sb's/the mind [A2] be vividly remembered; be frequently recalled to the conscious mind. **S:** event; death, sacrifice; words, speech □ *There are passages in that play which still **stick in my mind** twenty years after the first performance.* □ *It is the unheroic sacrifices of ordinary people that chiefly **stick in the mind**.* □ *His words on that day must have **stuck in the minds of** many people.*

stick on [B1i nom pass B2 pass] fasten sth to a surface with paste, glue etc. **O:** label, picture, cut-out. **o:** trunk, case; wall □ ***Stick** a few exotic labels **on** your suitcase if you want to make it look as though you're much travelled.* □ *Pictures of football stars were **stuck on** the wall by his bed.* □ the kind of label one sticks on luggage is a stick-on label.

stick out[1] [A1] project, jut out (q v). **S:** rock, cliff; nose, chin □ *I could see a pair of feet **sticking out** at the end of the blanket.* □ *We parcelled up the material securely, without leaving any ends **sticking out**.*

stick out[2] [B1i pass] cause to project, thrust forward. **O:** head, chest, tongue □ *Someone **stuck** a foot **out** and tripped me up.* □ *'Don't **stick** your tongue **out** at me — I'll tell your father.'*

stick it out [B1ii] (informal) endure sth unpleasant □ *He swore he'd **stick it out**, and stay unemployed, until he got something really worth while.* EGD □ *He hated life in the city, but he would **stick it out** a bit longer for the sake of his family.*

stick out (a mile) [A1] (informal) be strikingly clear; stand out (a mile) (q v). **S:** motive, intention; origins, background; it... that he intends to seize control □ *He tried to disguise the purpose of his visit, but his real intentions **stuck out a mile**.* □ *'It **sticks out a mile** that he's hoping to take over your job.'*

stick one's neck out [B1ii] (informal) behave in a bold, adventurous and possibly dangerous way (e g by expressing novel ideas, criticizing authority etc) □ *'I'm not sure of the answer myself, but I'll **stick my neck out** and say that John's solution is correct.'* □ *'You can support the campaign if you want to, but I'm not **sticking my neck out** for anybody.'*

stick out for [A3] refuse to yield now, in the hope of getting sth better later on; hold out for (q v), stand out for (q v). **S:** worker, employee; union; striker. **o:** higher wage, bigger bonus □ *The men are in a fighting mood; they are **sticking out for** the full amount of their wage claim.* □ *We're going to **stick out for** fuller representation on the Council.*

stick to[1] [A2] not move, stray, wander, from. **S:** speaker, lecturer. **o:** subject, facts; point (at issue), argument □ *I find his lectures very confusing: he never **sticks to** the point.* □ *The music pursued its course, never **sticking to** the same key for two bars together.* DOP □ *'This is getting us nowhere. Let us **stick to** the facts. Mrs Carstairs has died — from cyanide poisoning.'* EM

stick to[2] [A2 pass] not abandon or change; hold to[1] (q v). **o:** choice, decision; principle, belief □ *'Once we've sorted out a programme of events, let's for Heaven's sake try to **stick to** it.'* □ *Flying is simple if you **stick to** the rules.* DM

stick to sb's fingers [A2] (informal) (of sb else's property) stay in one's possession, be stolen. **S:** money, jewels □ *A million pounds went through his hands, and around forty thousand **stuck to his fingers**.* DS

stick to one's guns [A2] (informal) defend one's rights, point of view etc, stubbornly, refuse to give way on a point of principle. **S:** speaker, author; politician, academic □ *I **stuck to my guns** and refused to be over-ruled by my political masters.* MFM □ *'If you think you have a reasonable case, don't give way: **stick to your guns**.'*

stick to one's last [A2] confine oneself to the work one is trained to do □ *Don't play around with jobs that are really outside your field: **stick to your last**.*

stick together [A1] (informal) be united (in the face of some threat); stand together (q v); keep the same company and offer mutual assistance. **S:** family, political party; old boys (of a school), members (of a club); (religious, racial) minority □ *'We've been in worse situations than this before. If we keep calm and **stick together**, we shall be all right.'* □ *'You can feel that Old Downhamians* (= former pupils of the same school) *even in this wild and distant part **stick together**.'* HOM □ *New arrivals in a community are sometimes accused of **sticking together**. This may be because they are given little encouragement to feel at one with their neighbours.* ⇨ stick with.

stick up[1] [B1i pass] fasten sth with glue, nails etc to an upright surface, pole etc. **O:** picture, poster; effigy, statue; flag □ *Supporters of the government **stuck up** pictures of the Prime Minister in their front windows.* □ *The heads of traitors were once **stuck up** on London Bridge.*

stick up[2] [B1i nom pass] (informal) using firearms, force people to keep their hands in the air while one robs them or their place of work. **O:** train, stage-coach; bank, insurance office □ *Masked bandits **stuck up** a bullion train yesterday.* □ *'Nobody move — this is a **stick-up**!'*

stick 'em/your hands up [B1ii] (informal) hold your hands above your head; put one's hands up (q v) (command used by bandits etc in thrillers and cowboy films) ▫ *'All of you, **stick 'em up** and get back against that wall!'*

stick up for [A3 pass] (informal) take sb's side in a quarrel or fight; support a particular cause; stand up for (q v). **o:** brother, mate; oneself; rights ▫ *'If you don't occasionally **stick up for** yourself, nobody will **stick up for** you.'* ▫ *He's always **stuck up for** the lower-paid workers in industry and that's won him a lot of grass-roots support.*

stick with [A2] (informal) stay close to sb (in the face of some danger or to ensure one's future well-being). **o:** the others; (the rest of the) group, party; Labour, the Liberals ▫ ***Stick with** the gang on those beach parties. There's safety in numbers.* H ▫ *'**Stick with** the Party you know you can trust!'* ⇨ stick together.

sting (for) [B2 pass] (informal) collect money from sb which he is unwilling to give. **S:** club, society; treasurer; collector (for charity). **O:** public; member. **o:** subscription, donation, contribution ▫ *On Boxing Day in Britain the milkman and dustman come round and **sting** the public **for** a pound or so.* ▫ *At the airport he was **stung for** a few quid for having excess luggage.*

stink the place out [B1ii] (informal) fill a room, house, laboratory etc with an unpleasant smell ▫ *'You're **stinking the place out**. You don't belong in a nice place like this.'* TC ▫ *Ever since he got that chemistry set, he's been **stinking the place out**.*

stink to high heaven [A2] (informal) have, give off, a strong, unpleasant smell; strongly suggest dishonesty, intrigue, corruption etc; smell to high heaven (q v). **S:** place; garage, barn; yard; deal, sale; the whole thing ▫ *'I'm sure the cats have messed in the small bedroom: the place **stinks to high heaven**.'* ▫ *'It's pretty certain that money changed hands under the counter* (= secretly) *so that Phillips could get first claim on the land. The whole business **stinks to high heaven**.'*

stint (of) [B2 pass emph rel] give sb a small supply (of), keep sb short (of). **S:** employer, parent. **O:** workers, children; oneself. **o:** food, money, luxury ▫ *Money was short in those days, and the family were **stinted of** all the things that made life easy and pleasant.* ▫ *He envied people who enjoyed the comforts **of** which he'd had to **stint** himself for so long.* ▫ *'They don't **stint** themselves **of** anything, so why should you go short?'*

stir in/into [B1i pass B2 pass emph rel] add sth to a liquid etc, and mix everything together by stirring. **S:** cook; decorator. **O:** herb, stock, purée; water, turpentine. **o:** soup, stew; emulsion, paint ▫ *Add a tin of tomatoes to the mixture and **stir** them **in** well.* ▫ *You can **stir** a small amount of thinner **into** the paint.*

stir to the depths [B2 pass] move deeply, profoundly. **S:** address, speech; sight, spectacle ▫ *It seemed to me incredible that I must constantly be passing quite ordinary men in the street whose natures were **stirred to the depths** by the sight of newly-born infants.* SML ▫ *Still calm, still not **stirred to any** damaging or ennobling **depths**, he felt a tranquil and comforting sense of being welcome and in his right place.* HD

stir up [B1i pass] excite, stimulate, provoke. **S:** orator, agitator; teacher, leader, priest. **O:** hatred, unrest, trouble; it; follower, flock ▫ *He is blamed for **stirring up** hatred between nations.* SC ▫ *'Don't go round to that house **stirring it up** between Peter and Mary.'* ▫ *The new priest had a quiet, placid parish—people badly in need of **stirring up**.*

stitch on/onto [B1i pass adj B2 pass emph rel] attach sth to a garment etc, with stitches made by needle and thread. **O:** pocket, patch, button. **o:** blouse, coat ▫ *One of the sleeves of the jacket had been **stitched on** very badly.* ▫ *Ask Mother to **stitch** the badge **onto** your blazer.*

stitch up [B1i pass adj] close, seal, an opening with stitches made with needle and thread. **O:** seam; tear, rip; incision, wound ▫ *The deep cut he'd made in his finger had to be **stitched up**.* ▫ *'Don't mend the tear by hand—**stitch** it **up** on the machine.'*

stock up (with) (for) [A1 A3 rel] obtain, accumulate, supplies (for some occasion or purpose). **S:** shop, store; housewife; garrison, expedition. **o:** (***with***) food, wine, fuel; (***for***) Christmas, New Year; weekend, holiday; siege, winter ▫ *Housewives started to **stock up** when a shortage of oranges was reported.* ▫ *Father is **stocking up with** wine and brandy **for** the New Year party.* ▫ ***Stock up with** coal **for** a long winter.*

stoke up (with) [A1 A3 rel B1i pass adj B3 pass rel] put fuel on a fire, esp of an enclosed type (e g stove, furnace); fill oneself with food. **O:** stove, furnace; boiler; oneself. **o:** coal, anthracite; food, drink ▫ [B1] *It's his job to see that the boilers are **stoked up** last thing at night.* ▫ [A3] *He would **stoke up with** food and drink for thirty-six hours.* CON ▫ [A1] *She was **stoking up** as though this meal was going to be her last.*

stoop to [A2 emph rel] make oneself so low (morally) as to do sth; descend to (q v). **o:** intrigue, blackmail, cheating; anything ▫ *He would **stoop to** anything to further his career.* ▫ *There is no folly **to** which she would not **stoop**.*

stop (at) [A2 rel] live, take board and lodging (at); stay (at) (q v). **o:** hotel, inn; one's parents' house ▫ *We **stopped** for a fortnight **at** a camping site on the southern shore of Lake Garda.*

stop at nothing [A2] (informal) (be ready to) behave in a ruthless, unscrupulous way to get sth; stick at nothing (q v) ▫ *He'd **stop at nothing** to get a big part in the play.* ▫ *'Is he ambitious?' 'He wants to get to the top, and he'll **stop at nothing**.'* ▫ usu with *will/would*; often followed by inf.

stop away (from) [A1 A3 rel] not be present (at), be absent (from); stay away (from)[1] (q v). **o:** lecture, seminar; school, home ▫ *'What made you **stop away from** that particular talk? It was one of the best he's given.'*

stop behind [A1] remain after a meeting etc has ended, to ask questions etc; remain behind (q v), stay behind (q v). **S:** audience; member ▫ *The audience was invited to **stop behind** to discuss the play with its author.* ▫ *'Will a few of you **stop behind** to help clear the chairs away?'*

stop by [A1] (esp US) call at sb's house, call (in) (at) (q v). **S:** friend, relative ▫ *'Ask him to **stop by** and talk things over.'*

stop down [A1] (photography) reduce the size of the aperture on a camera through which light passes before falling on the film □ *'The sun's just come out: you'll have to **stop down** a bit.'*

stop for/to [A2] remain at sb's house to have a meal; stay for/to (q v). **o:** meal; lunch, dinner □ *'Why don't you **stop for** supper? I dare say the stew will stretch to feed four.'*

stop (from) [B2 pass] prevent (from), hinder (from). **S:** authorities; parent, teacher, employer. **O:** public; child, ward, pupil; staff. **o:** trespassing, stealing; disturbing, playing □ *Someone tried to **stop** us **from** parking* (or: ***stop** us parking*) *in the square.* □ *'I wish you'd **stop** him **from** playing that trumpet!'*

stop in [A1] remain at school after others have left, as a punishment; stay in[1] (q v). **S:** child, pupil; trouble-maker □ *'If I have any more of this nonsense the entire class will **stop in** after four o'clock.'*

stop (dead) in one's/his tracks [A2 B2 pass] (cause to) stop sharply, suddenly. **S:** [A2] **O:** [B2] traveller, hunter; animal. **S:** [B2] sight, spectacle; shock, surprise □ *What I saw as I opened the door made me **stop dead in my tracks**.* UTN □ *At most places the Ethiopians were **stopped in their tracks** by rifle fire.*

stop in/indoors [A1] remain inside a building, e g because the weather is bad; stay in/indoors (q v) □ *It poured with rain all day and we had to **stop indoors**.* □ *I **stayed in** all weekend trying to shake off that damned cold.*

stop off [A1] break one's journey by car, rail etc, to rest, visit friends etc □ *'We'll **stop off** for a few days in Paris to visit your cousins.'* □ *David **stopped off** on his journey north to have a meal and a drink.*

stop on (at) [A1 A3] remain at a place of study etc after others have left; stay on (at) (q v). **o:** school, college □ *Peter **stopped on** for an extra year in the Sixth to take a University Scholarship.* □ *Some of the senior girls won't **stop on at** school for a month later than they have to.*

stop out[1] [A1] remain out of doors (esp after dark); stay out[1] (q v). **S:** son, husband; guest □ *'If you're going to **stop out** half the night there's really not much point in your living at home.'*

stop out[2] [A1] (industrial relations) remain on strike, continue a stoppage of work; stay out[3] (q v). **S:** worker; fitter, boilerman. **A:** on strike; in protest against sth □ *The Union decided to **stop out** until their demands were met.*

stop (out of) [B2 pass emph rel] (informal) deduct a sum of money (from sb's income). **S:** government, Inland Revenue, employer. **O:** tax, subscription, donation. **o:** pay, wages □ *Students pay the college a deposit, and the cost of breakages is **stopped out of** that.* □ *He's paid twenty pounds a week, and **out of** that about three pounds are **stopped** for tax and National Insurance.*

stop over [A1 nom] break one's journey by air, for sightseeing etc, afterwards going on by another aircraft □ *These are pictures of the Jumbo-jet passengers when they **stopped over** in Rome.* BBCTV □ *I'm buying a **stop-over** ticket for the return journey* (i e *one which will enable me to **stop over** at one or more places*).

stop to [A2] ⇨ stop for/to.

stop up[1] [B1i pass adj] fill a (small) hole etc. **S:** carpenter, decorator. **O:** crack, nail-hole □ *'You'll have to **stop up** those holes you've made in the skirting-board before you start painting.'*

stop up[2] [A1] not go to bed until after the usual time; stay up[2] (q v). **S:** parent, wife □ *We **stopped up** late to hear the midnight news.* □ *'I shall be in late, but don't bother to **stop up** for me.'*

store away [B1i pass adj] put away, accumulate, in a safe place for use later. **O:** food, water, ammunition; note, quotation □ *Survival rations are **stored away** in waterproof boxes.* □ *He **stored away** everything for future use — every scrap of information that came his way.*

store (in) [B2 pass emph rel] keep as a stock (in). **O:** food, wine; information, fact. **o:** pantry, refrigerator; brain, computer □ *The squirrel **stores** nuts **in** his burrow.* □ *You can **store** a lot of kit **in** this locker* (cf *This locker will **store** a lot of kit*).

store up[1] [B1i pass adj] accumulate supplies etc (e g for an emergency). **S:** dealer, shopkeeper, housewife. □ *Mother had **stored up** enough food to last through a siege.*

store up[2] [B1i pass adj] allow bad feelings to develop, fester etc; harbour, nourish such feelings. **S:** rival, opponent. **O:** bitterness, resentment, hatred, jealousy □ *'I know Bob's had more than his share of lucky breaks, but you're not doing yourself any good by **storing up** resentment.'*

storm in/into [A1 emph A2 emph rel] enter a room etc noisily and aggressively □ *John **stormed into** the meeting waving a piece of paper about.* □ *Just when we thought we had the matter nicely settled, **in stormed** Alan, claiming that the vote was irregular.*

stow away [A1 nom] hide aboard a ship or aircraft, in the hope of travelling free to another country □ *At the age of sixteen, he **stowed away** on a cargo-boat bound for America.* □ *The crew found three **stowaways*** (i e people who had ***stowed away***) *in the hold.*

straighten out[1] [A1 B1i pass adj] (cause to) lie in a straight line or form a straight line. **S:** [A1] **O:** [B1] string, rope; tie, cloth □ *'Get all the wires **straightened out**, so that we know which is which.'* □ *After much tugging, the rope untangled itself and **straightened out**.*

straighten out[2] [B1i pass] settle, resolve; order, put right; sort out[2] (q v). **O:** quarrel, misunderstanding; mess, confusion □ *We have inherited a very confused situation, which we are now trying to **straighten out**.* □ *The disagreement between them will not be **straightened out** overnight* (or: *will not **straighten** itself **out** overnight*).

straighten out[3] [B1i pass] (informal) remove the doubt, ignorance etc in sb's mind, make sb understand how matters stand. **S:** adviser, parent, teacher. **O:** client, child, pupil □ *He seriously misunderstands certain aspects of our plan; I'd like to **straighten** him **out** on these.* □ *The police would have charged me with a traffic offence if my local guide hadn't **straightened** them **out**.*

straighten (oneself) up [A1 B1ii] make the body straight, e g after being in a crouching position □ *The old man bent to pick up a piece of paper, and had some difficulty in **straightening up*** (or: ***straightening himself up***).

strain after an effect [A2] try in a forced, unnatural way to make sth seem impressive. **S:**

author, director, actor ▫ *The playwright does something remarkable in this scene, but without any impression of* ***straining after an effect.*** ▫ *'Read the speech naturally: don't* ***strain after effects.'***

strain (at) [A2] exert effort or energy by pulling at something. **o:** rope, mooring; oar; lead, leash ▫ *The crew* ***strained at*** *the oars to keep the boat clear of the rocks.* ▫ *The dog is so powerful that every time it* ***strains at*** *its lead it nearly pulls me off my feet.*

strain at the leash [A2] (informal) pull against some restriction (e g of one's home background) in the desire to be free, make progress etc ▫ *She was planning to go to England, and* ***straining at the leash*** *to get away.* RFW ▫ *We hoped to keep these young scientists with us, but could see that they were* ***straining at the leash*** *to move to better jobs.* ⇨ previous entry.

strain away/off [B1i pass adj] separate liquid from solid matter by placing both together in a wire mesh, vessel with holes etc. **O:** water, gravy, juice ▫ *When you've boiled the cabbage,* ***strain off*** *the water through a colander.*

strap on/onto [B1i pass B2 pass emph rel] fasten one thing to another by means of straps. **O:** equipment, pack, haversack; radio; watch. **o:** back, wrist ▫ *The soldiers' greatcoats were* ***strapped onto*** *their packs.* ▫ *The climbers* ***strapped on*** *a variety of equipment.*

strap up [B1i pass adj] keep sth closed, secure it, with straps; bind up a wound, limb, with bandages. **O:** case, trunk, bundle; arm, leg ▫ *All the luggage was* ***strapped up*** *and waiting to go to the station.* ▫ *'Don't get dirt in that cut: ask somebody to* ***strap*** *it* ***up*** *for you.'* ▫ *George didn't play rugby that Saturday. He was sitting on the terraces with a heavily* ***strapped-up*** *shoulder.*

stray from [A2 pass emph rel] leave, move from (e g through absent-mindedness, moral laxness etc). **S:** speaker, writer; follower, adherent. **o:** point, issue; the right path, the true faith, the strait and narrow (way) ▫ *We are* ***straying from*** *the subject, which is what action is Maria likely to take.* OMIH ▫ *Some members are* ***straying from*** *a firm allegiance to the party.* ▫ *These regulations form the bedrock of our wages policy, and are not to be* ***strayed from.***

stream down [A1 A2 rel] flow continuously down (sth). **S:** water, rain; tears, sweat. **o:** wall, window; face ▫ *In the basement, water* ***streams down*** *the walls* (or: *the walls* ***stream with*** *water*). ▫ *Sweat* ***streamed down*** *the miners' bodies* (or: *Their bodies* ***streamed with*** *sweat*).

stream with [A2 rel] ⇨ previous entry.

stretch away [A1] extend to a great distance. **S:** plain, prairie, steppe; wood. **A:** into the distance, as far as the eye can see ▫ *A day's journey brought them to the coastal plain, which* ***stretched away*** *to a distant blue haze.*

stretch out[1] [B1i pass] extend the hand etc, e g to greet sb, or take sth; reach out (for) (q v). **S:** onlooker; beggar, suppliant. **O:** ⚠ a hand, an arm, a finger ▫ *The child* ***stretched out*** *its hands to seize the toy.* ▫ *The official walked coldly by, ignoring the* ***outstretched*** *hands of the crowd.* ▫ adj form is **outstretched**.

stretch out[2] [A1 B1i pass] (make sth) last, be sufficient to cover one's needs. **S:** [A1] **O:** [B1] money, housekeeping (allowance); food, fuel ▫ *I don't see how I can* ***stretch out*** *the housekeeping to the end of the month.* ▫ *'Will the food* ***stretch out****? We've got two extra guests for dinner.'*

stretch (oneself) out [A1 B1ii pass] relax by lying at full length ▫ *He* ***stretched himself out*** (or: ***stretched out***) *on the floor, and fell asleep.* ▫ *A few holiday-makers were* ***stretched out*** *in the sun outside the window* (i e *they had* ***stretched themselves out*** *in the sun*).

strew on/over [B2 pass emph rel] throw sth down so that it forms a covering. **S:** crowd, onlooker; mourner. **O:** branches, leaves, flowers. **o:** route, path; grave ▫ *Rubbish was* ***strewn*** *all* ***over*** *the back yard* (or: *The back yard was* ***strewn with*** *rubbish*). ▫ *The villagers had* ***strewn*** *flowers* ***on*** *the simple grave* (or: *had* ***strewn*** *the simple grave* ***with*** *flowers*).

strew with [B2 pass emph rel] ⇨ previous entry.

strike (against) [A2 emph rel] (industrial relations) stop work in protest (against sth). **S:** miner, docker, clerk. **o:** (bad) conditions, low wages ▫ *The proposed change from piece-work arouses strong feelings and is certainly something* ***against*** *which the men are prepared to* ***strike.*** ▫ *The nurses* ***struck against*** *the Department of Health's refusal to grant an interim pay increase* ⇨ **strike (for)**.

strike as [B2] appear, occur, to sb as having certain qualities. **S:** idea, suggestion, proposal; voice, manner; newcomer, guest. **o:** excellent, ridiculous; the very thing, just what was wanted; strained, pretentious ▫ *Long after the idea, whatever it was, had ceased to* ***strike*** *her* ***as*** *funny, she went on giving peal after peal, just for practice.* CON ▫ *Mr King does not* ***strike*** *a stranger* ***as*** *a deeply religious man, but rather as a determined cleric preoccupied with social reform.* OBS

strike at [A2 pass] aim a blow at, try to hurt or damage. **S:** law; action; proposal. **o:** root, basis, foundation; principle, right ▫ *By acting now, we hope to* ***strike at*** *the root cause of the trouble.* ▫ *The Opposition's view has always been that the proposed Act* ***strikes at*** *the basic freedoms of the citizen.*

strike down [B1i pass] make sb incapable of leading an active life, lay sb low. **S:** (serious) illness; thrombosis, paralysis ▫ *Many active professional men at the peak of their careers have been* ***struck down*** *by heart disease.*

strike (for) [A2 emph rel] (industrial relations) stop work in order to gain sth. **S:** docker, dustman. **o:** higher wages, (better) conditions ▫ *Assembly workers are* ***striking for*** *an improvement in their overtime earnings.* ▫ *The men never expected to win all the concessions* ***for*** *which they were* ***striking*** ⇨ **strike (against)**.

strike home (to) [A1 A3 emph rel] strongly impress sb (as being true, worthwhile etc). **S:** force, truth, validity (of sb's remark, argument, plea) ▫ *The full measure of his detachment had for the first time really* ***struck home to*** *me.* SML ▫ ***To*** *cost-conscious managers the value of having a manufacturing base in Europe must surely* ***strike home*** *very forcibly.*

strike into [B2 emph rel] make sb afraid, esp by sudden, vigorous action. **S:** arrival, appearance;

ıttack, drive; prospect, outlook. **O:** terror, dread, ear. **o:** enemy; hearts □ *Meeting one's first class 'n a tough London school has* ***struck*** *cold fear* ***'nto*** *many young teachers.* □ *'I can't talk about ny driving test. The mere thought* ***strikes*** *terror* ***'nto*** *me!'*

trike off[1] [B1i pass] remove with a sharp blow, :ut off. **O:** head, limb; branch, twig □ *He* ***struck*** ***off*** *the head of the dandelion with a swish of his :ane.*

trike off[2] [B1i pass adj B2 pass] remove sb 'rom the membership of a professional body. **O:** loctor, solicitor, barrister. **o:** ⚠ the Medical Register, the Roll □ *Before the law was changed, a British doctor might be* ***struck off*** *for procuring an abortion.* □ *The Law Society ordered that their names be* ***struck off*** *the roll of solicitors.* T

trike out [B1i pass adj] remove sth by drawing ı line through it; cross out (q v). **O:** word, name; 'eference, mention □ *The offending parts of the article have been* ***struck out.*** □ (instructions on a 'orm) ***Strike out*** *any questions which do not apply.*

trike out (at) [A1 A3 pass] aim a blow sud-lenly and vigorously (at sb). **o:** friend, wife; :aptor, tormentor □ *If the animal feels trapped he will* ***strike out*** *wildly.* □ *My wife had* ***struck out at*** *me again.* QA

trike out for/towards [A3] move in a vig-orous, determined way towards sth. **S:** swimmer, oarsman; patrol, expedition. **o:** shore, bank; home □ *Without hesitating, he* ***struck out*** *strongly* ***for*** *the beach.* □ *She stood looking up and down before she* ***struck out for*** *the bus-stop.* AITC

trike through [B1ii pass] draw a line through sth, thus cancelling it. **O:** paragraph, sentence; word, name □ *If you disagree with anything I have written,* ***strike*** *it* ***through.*** □ *Their names had been* ***struck through,*** *and were almost illegible.*

trike up [A1 B1iii pass] begin to play. **S:** band, musicians. **O:** tune, march □ *The Russian band would* ***strike up,*** *playing waltzes.* BM □ *She* ***struck up*** *the first carol on the grand piano.* ASA

trike up (with) [B3 pass emph rel] begin a friendship etc by casually meeting and talking to sb. **O:** ⚠ a friendship, an acquaintance; a conversation □ *I'd first* ***struck up*** *an acquaintance* ***with*** *him while waiting for a train* (or: *We'd first* ***struck up*** *an acquaintance* etc). □ *He'd* ***strike up*** *conversations* ***with*** *people to hear them speak in the local accent.* CON

tring along [B1ii pass] (informal) mislead, deceive sb into doing sth he might not otherwise do. **O:** colleague, partner □ *'I've a feeling that the young man is just* ***stringing*** *us* ***along.*** *Check his credentials.'* □ *The governors felt that they were being* ***strung along*** *by their advisers.* T

tring along (with) [A1 A3 pass] (informal) stay with sb, accompany him (in work, pleasure etc). **o:** (older) friend, (experienced) colleague □ *Take my advice —* ***string along with*** *me. I know this business inside out.* EGD □ *If you're celebrating, what about* ***stringing along with*** *me?* TC □ *'Can't you stop them* ***stringing along*** *— they're such dreadful bores!'*

tring out [A1 B1i pass adj] (cause to) be positioned, or move, at a distance from each other. **S:** [A1] **O:** [B1] (members of) team, squad, patrol; vehicles; horses. **S:** [B1] leader, commander □ *The captain got his defenders to* ***string out*** *across the width of the field.* □ *6th Army had got badly* ***strung out*** *and would have little prospect of mounting a successful attack.* B

string together [B1i pass] combine words etc to form meaningful statements. **O:** words, phrases, sentences □ *It was as much as he could do to* ***string together*** *a few words of French.* □ *His sentences were so badly* ***strung together*** *that it was difficult to grasp their meaning.*

string up[1] [B1i pass] hang sth (e g as a decoration) from a line or cord. **O:** flag, banner, bunting, streamer □ *He was* ***stringing up*** *gay lines of flags about and among the tents.* DBM □ *A makeshift notice was* ***strung up*** *above the do?r.*

string up[2] [B1i pass] (informal) put to death by hanging. **S:** executioner; mob. **O:** traitor, rebel; suspect □ *Two of the rebel leaders were* ***strung up*** *as a warning to the others.*

strip away/off[1] [B1i pass] remove sth which has been attached to a surface. **O:** wallpaper; paint □ *Using solvent and a palette knife John* ***stripped*** *four coats of paint* ***off.*** □ ***'Strip away*** *that awful patterned paper, fill the cracks with plaster, rub them down well, apply a couple of coats of emulsion, and you might then have a reasonable-looking room.'*

strip away/off[2] [B1i pass] remove sth which is hiding the true nature or intentions of sb. **O:** pretence; mask, façade; fine words □ *You have to* ***strip away*** *the affected manners and speech to get at the real man underneath.* □ ***'Strip off*** *the platform rhetoric and what are you left with?'*

strip down [B1i pass adj] take an engine etc to pieces, dismantle it. **O:** motor; gearbox, carburettor; clock □ *Parts of a* ***stripped-down*** *engine were spread out on the bench.* □ *'I'll have to* ***strip down*** *the mechanism to trace the fault.'*

strip down (to) [A1 A3] take all one's clothes off; remove all but a few garments. **o:** underclothes; the skin □ *He* ***stripped down to*** *his underpants and leaped into the stream.* □ *Like the rest of the women she had* ***stripped down to*** *her brassiere.* DBM

strip of [B2 pass rel] take sth of value away from sb. **O:** statesman, soldier, civil servant. **o:** honours, titles, rank □ *Having been* ***stripped of*** *all his titles, he disappeared from public life.*

strip off[1] [A1 B1i pass] remove one's clothing. **O:** clothes; shirt, pants □ *The boys* ***stripped off*** *behind the bushes and dived naked into the river.* □ *Patients were asked to* ***strip off*** *their clothes, put on dressing gowns and take a seat in the waiting-room.*

strip off[2] [B1i pass adj B2 pass] remove, take off, the covering from sth. **O:** skin, peel, bark; lining, backing. **o:** fruit, tree; jacket □ *Thieves had* ***stripped*** *the lead* ***off*** *the church roof.*

strip off[3] [B1i pass] remove sth which has been attached to a surface. ⇨ strip away/off[1].

strip off[4] [B1i pass] remove sth hiding the true nature or intentions of sb. ⇨ strip away/off[2].

strive after an effect [A2] = strain after an effect.

strive (against) [A2 pass emph rel] (formal) fight to overcome or resist. **o:** enemy, oppressor; adversity, hardship; ignorance, disease □ *The crew* ***strove against*** *wind and tide to bring the* *ship to a safe anchorage.* □ *The terms which the Government sought to impose should not have been accepted tamely but resolutely* ***striven against****.* ⇨ struggle (against) which is less formal, and more commonly used.

strive (for) [A2 pass emph rel] (formal) fight to obtain or achieve. **o:** freedom, human rights; (better) standard, conditions □ *The material improvements* ***for*** *which their fathers had* ***striven*** *were now gradually coming about.* □ *Personal freedoms are worth* ***striving for****.* ⇨ struggle (with) (for) which is less formal, and more commonly used.

struggle (against) [A2 pass emph rel] fight to overcome or resist. **o:** tyrant, regime; system, conditions □ *Official statements could not disguise the attempt to reintroduce measures* ***against*** *which we had* ***struggled*** *successfully in the past.* □ *Troops moving through Burma had to* ***struggle against*** *an appalling climate, which could render the primitive roads impassable.*

struggle with [A2 pass emph rel] fight inwardly with; wrestle with (q v). **o:** uncertainty, doubt; problem, question □ *Matthews* ***struggled*** *briefly* ***with*** *his conscience before making the false entries in the accounts book.* □ *The staff difficulties he'd had to contend with, the supply problems* ***with*** *which he'd* ***struggled*** *— all this now seemed a thing of the past.*

struggle (with) (for) [A2 pass emph rel] fight, try to overcome, sb (to obtain or achieve sth). **o:** (***with***) intruder, assailant; employer, government; (***for***) gun, knife; (higher) wages, (improved) conditions □ *Two men were* ***struggling*** *(****with*** *each other)* ***for*** *the possession of a small jewel box.* □ *In the middle of the floor, Billy was* ***struggling*** *furiously* ***with*** *a boy twice his size.* □ *He is* ***struggling for*** *a bigger say in decision-making.* □ *Several times the same rights have been* ***struggled for*** *and lost.*

strung up [pass adj (B1)] (informal) (made) tense or nervous □ *He was* ***strung up*** *by having to attend so many official parties.* □ *On the evening of his big speech he didn't seem at all* ***strung up****.* □ passive with *be, seem, feel, look, get.*

strut about/around/round [A1 A2] walk about in a pompous, self-important way; suggest pomposity, solemnity by one's style of walking. **S:** official, guard, leader; goose, chicken, peacock □ *No sooner had the man been appointed team leader than he was* ***strutting about*** *the place like some pint-sized field-marshal.*

stub one's toe (against/on) [B2 rel] catch, strike, one's foot on sth which projects. **o:** stone; kerb, step □ *I* ***stubbed my toe on*** *your front step: it was very painful.*

stub out [B1i pass adj] extinguish, put out, a cigarette by striking it against sth. **O:** cigarette, cigar □ *'Don't* ***stub*** *your cigarettes* ***out*** *on my mantelpiece!'* □ *The place was littered with empty glasses and* ***stubbed-out*** *cigarettes.*

stuck in [pass (B1)] (informal) (become) really busy, closely involved in a task □ *The painter got* ***stuck in****: nice firm strokes, no paint wasted, sure hands.* TT □ *'Get* ***stuck in****, United!'* (encouragement to footballers to play hard) □ usu with *get.*

stuck up [pass adj (B1)] (informal) (be) snobbish, full of (unwarranted) social pride. **S:** social climber, the nouveaux riches □ *'I don't know what they've got to be so* ***stuck up*** *about. Perhaps they think they've done us a favour by moving in next door.'* □ *The next customer was a very* ***stuck-up*** *lady with a painfully refined voice.* □ passive with *be, seem, sound.*

stuck with [pass (B2)] (informal) (be) obliged to accept sth or sb irksome, unpleasant etc. **o:** (onerous, tedious) job, task; handicap, disability; presence, company (of); (tiresome) guest, neighbour □ *We were* ***stuck with*** *the job of addressing a thousand envelopes by the following morning.* □ *'It's my face and I'm* ***stuck with*** *it!'* H □ *Here the sites are leased by the Ministry for 5[...] years and we are* ***stuck with*** *some of these edifices until the end of the century.* OBS

study (for) [A2 pass emph rel] give time and effort to learning sth for a special purpose (e[g] passing an exam). **o:** qualification; diploma; degree; test, exam; the Bar □ *He's* ***studying for*** *a degree in Economics in his spare time.* □ *'The next stage is A-levels,* ***for*** *which he'll need to* ***study*** *very much harder.'*

stuff down sb's throat [B2 pass] (informal) force sb, esp by tedious repetition, to accept or learn sth; force/ram sth down sb's throat (q v). **O:** opinion, view; morality, religion; French, math[s] □ TONY: *What are the words — don't say I've forgotten them, they've been* ***stuffed down my throat*** *all my life — liberty, democracy, brotherhood.* EHOW □ *'For a start, he can stop* ***stuffing*** *his revolting opinions* ***down people's throats****.'*

stuff into [B2 pass rel] press, pack, tightly into. **O:** kit, clothing; padding, lining; food. **o:** bag, sack; space, hole; child □ *All kinds of gear have been* ***stuffed into*** *their kitbags* (or: *Their kitbags have been* ***stuffed with*** *all kinds* etc). □ *That child has been* ***stuffing*** *food* ***into*** *himself all morning* (or: *He has been* ***stuffing*** *himself* ***with*** *food* etc).

stuff up [B1i pass adj] close, block, sth by pushing material etc into it. **O:** ear, nose; vent, hatch, window □ *'****Stuff up*** *your ears — there's going to be an almightly bang!'* □ *We had to* ***stuff*** *the ventilator shafts* ***up*** *to stop the smoke entering the room.*

stuffed up [pass adj (B1)] (of one's nose) (be) full of mucus (because one has a bad cold) □ *'Don't come near me — my* ***nose*** *is terribly* ***stuffed up*** *today.'* □ *'I shan't come to the party. You don't want to take along a girl with a* ***stuffed-up*** *nose.'*

stuff with [B2 pass rel] ⇨ stuff into.

stuff sb's head with [B2 pass] (informal) fill sb's mind with information (esp of a useless or harmful kind). **o:** facts; nonsense, rubbish □ *'How can you expect these children to exercise their minds?* ***Their heads*** *have been* ***stuffed with*** *pap from the television.'* □ *The press* ***stuffs the people's heads with*** *dreary, and largely false, statistics for industrial production.*

stumble across/on/upon [A2 pass] discover by chance, come across[1] (q v) **o:** evidence, clue, manuscript, remains □ *Karl had* ***stumbled on*** *just the right contact, and arranged a series of fruitful meetings.* DS □ *They* ***stumbled across*** *the entrance to an underground passage, half covered by ivy.*

stumble over [A2 pass emph rel] hesitate awkwardly when speaking. **o:** words, lines speech, address □ *The man's voice was rather low, and the most important part of what he had to say was* ***stumbled over****, so we're really no wiser than we were before.* □ *The company chairman must have felt embarrassed at reading out such an abnormally low set of figures, because he* ***stumbled over*** *that section of his report.*

stump across, along, away etc [A1 A2] move across etc heavily (and often in anger or irritation) □ *Throwing down his paper with a snort of impatience, Bill* ***stumped across*** *to the door.* □ *Uncle Saunders went* ***stumping up*** *to bed at his usual time, followed presently by Aunt Annabel.* DC

stump up [A1 B1iii pass] (informal) pay a sum of money required; pay up (q v) (the suggestion is that the person finds it hard or irksome to pay). **S:** parent; taxpayer, debtor □ *'You get into trouble and I have to* ***stump up*** *the money for a fine to get you out of it.'* □ *He's tired of* ***stumping up*** *for school fees, books and uniform.*

subject to[1] [B2 pass rel] make oneself the master of (e g by conquest). **S:** power, nation; aggressor; army. **O:** neighbour, (weaker) country. **o:** rule, control, sway, dominion, domination □ *In two brilliantly conducted campaigns, the Romans* ***subjected*** *half the country* ***to*** *their control.* □ *Armed resistance showed that a minority at least was not prepared to be* ***subjected to*** *foreign rule.*

subject to[2] [B2 pass rel] apply force etc to materials. **S:** physicist, engineer. **O:** metal, wood, cloth; bar, strip. **o:** force, strain; temperature; pressure □ *The metal plate was* ***subjected to*** *intense pressure.* □ *On this test-track, the makers deliberately* ***subject*** *standard production cars* ***to*** *rough treatment.*

subject to[3] [B2 pass rel] make sb experience or undergo. **O:** speaker, author; prisoner, victim; animal. **o:** criticism, questioning; humiliation; torture, grilling □ *The visiting speaker was* ***subjected to*** *very close questioning.* □ *It is remarkable how this one man in his small boat survived the hardships and privations* ***to*** *which he was* ***subjected****.*

submit (to)[1] [B2 pass emph rel] present (to sb) for discussion, decision etc. **S:** author; architect, engineer; union. **O:** manuscript; plan, proposal; claim. **o:** publisher; committee, panel; arbitration □ *Some students have not yet* ***submitted*** *their essays* ***to*** *their tutors.* □ *After various delays he eventually came face to face with the official* ***to*** *whom he had* ***submitted*** *his application for planning permission.*

submit (to)[2] [A2 pass emph rel] give way in the face of pressure. **o:** pressure; bullying, intimidation; enemy □ ***To*** *such threats as these we have no intention of* ***submitting****.* □ *Need a Church* ***submit to*** *a silence imposed by the State?* SC

submit oneself to [B2 emph rel] place oneself under the control of sb. **S:** student, priest, disciple. **o:** discipline, rule; authority, master □ *No one becomes a monk who is not prepared to* ***submit himself to*** *the rules of his Order.*

subscribe (to)[1] [A2 pass emph rel B2 pass emph rel] give money for charitable purposes, donate (to). **S:** philanthropist, benefactor. **O:** sum, amount. **o:** charity, (good) cause, fund □ *Two local businessmen have* ***subscribed*** *large sums* ***to*** *the rebuilding fund.* □ *This is a cause* ***to*** *which he has* ***subscribed*** *generously in the past.*

subscribe (to)[2] [A2 pass emph rel] pay in order to have a newspaper etc regularly and for some time. **o:** paper, (learned) journal, magazine □ *He* ***subscribes to*** *a number of journals concerned with his subject.* □ *The library committee decides whether publications* ***to*** *which we* ***subscribe*** *are to be ordered for a further year.*

subscribe to [A2 pass emph rel] (formal) support, agree (with) (q v). **o:** philosophy, code; belief, opinion □ *His is a pessimistic view of man* ***to*** *which I have never* ***subscribed****.* □ *How could anyone* ***subscribe to*** *such an inhuman code?*

subsist (on) [A2 emph rel] stay alive, sustain life (on). **o:** bread, potato, rice □ *There are whole villages* ***subsisting on*** *corn meal and a little milk supplied by the relief organizations.* □ ***On*** *this largely carbohydrate diet a working adult barely manages to* ***subsist****.*

substitute (for)[1] [B2 pass emph rel] put, use, sth in the place of sth else. **O:** margarine, synthetic fibre; word, phrase. **o:** butter, natural wool; original text □ *'The recipe does specify butter, but vegetable oil will do just as well. So* ***substitute*** *oil* ***for*** *butter at that stage.'* □ *Copies have been* ***substituted for*** *the original manuscripts to save wear and tear on the latter.*

substitute (for)[2] [A2 B2 pass] (sport) enter, bring into, a game in the place of sb else. **S:** [A2] **O:** [B2] player; striker, sweeper □ *Chivers* ***substituted for*** *Clarke just after half-time when it appeared that the injury to Clarke's knee was affecting his performance.* □ *A striker was* ***substituted for*** *a midfield player in the last half-hour of play in the hope that increased pressure on the Scottish defence would produce the winning goal.*

subsume under [B2 pass emph rel] (formal) place in a class, under a heading etc. **O:** item, article; example, instance. **o:** heading, rubric, rule □ *These various trades may all be* ***subsumed under*** *the general heading of 'distributive'.* □ ***Under*** *which category should these items of expenditure be* ***subsumed****?*

subtract (from) [B2 pass emph rel] take one number (from another). **O:** 20, 32 kilos; 13 cents. **o:** 29, 36 kilos; one dollar □ *At this age, he should be able to* ***subtract*** *one fraction* ***from*** *another* (or: *he should be able to* ***subtract*** *fractions*). □ ***From*** *this amount you need to* ***subtract*** *something to cover fixed overheads.*

succeed (in) [A2 emph rel] do what one sets out to do, achieve one's aim. **o:** aim, intention; passing (a test), climbing (a mountain) □ *He usually* ***succeeds in*** *anything he really puts his mind to.* □ *The new marketing team promised to push up sales, and* ***in*** *this they certainly* ***succeeded****.*

succeed (to) [A2 rel] take a title etc on the death of its previous holder. **S:** heir; son, cousin. **o:** throne, title; estate □ *The present Queen* ***succeeded to*** *the throne upon the death of her father.*

succumb (to)[1] [A2 pass emph rel] give way (to sth), without conscious intention but through weakness etc. **o:** pressure; flattery, persuasion, blandishments □ *If manufacturers spend as much as they do on advertising, it must be because people are known to* ***succumb to*** *persuasion* *through the media.*

succumb (to)[2] [A2 emph rel] die from physical strain, overexposure to the natural elements etc. **o:** injuries; (low) temperature □ *The climbers would have to face extremes of climate,* ***to*** *which many had* ***succumbed*** *before.*

suck down/under [B1i pass] draw, pull down, below the surface of sth. **S:** undertow, current; bog, marsh □ *We were able to pass a rope to him before the bog* ***sucked*** *him* ***under****.* □ *The whirlpool* ***sucks down*** *everything floating on the water.*

suck up [B1i pass adj B2 pass] draw liquid etc up a tube by making a vacuum at its upper end. **O:** milk, juice; grain, flour. **o:** straw, pipe □ *The chemist* ***sucked up*** *20 cc of acid into a pipette.* □ *Great quantities of grain are* ***sucked up*** *into the elevators through flexible tubes.* □ *The dredger in the middle of the channel was* ***sucking*** *gravel* ***up*** *huge pipes and discharging it into a barge moored alongside.*

suck up (to) [A1 A3 pass] (slang) try to please sb important or powerful by praising him, doing favours etc. **S:** schoolboy, student; (ambitious) junior, (young) executive. **o:** teacher, professor; boss, manager □ *'I can't stand the way that Spinks always* ***sucks up to*** *the prefects.'* □ *'Don't try to impress the new boss — he hates being* ***sucked up to****.'*

sue (for) [A2 rel B2 pass rel] (legal) make a legal claim against sb for injury to oneself, neglect of one's interests etc. **S:** employee, customer; wife. **O:** firm, shop; husband. **o:** costs, damages, compensation; divorce □ *If you broke your leg as a result of their negligence, you can* ***sue*** *them* ***for*** *damages.*

suffer from [A2 rel] be regularly afflicted by; have as a weakness. **S:** patient, inmate; plan, proposal, production. **o:** backache, gout, insomnia; (bad) execution, (faulty) planning □ *He* ***suffers*** *terribly* ***from*** *hay fever in the summer.* □ *His presentation of the play* ***suffers from*** *an over-close attention to the detail of the text.*

suggest itself/themselves (to) [B2 emph rel] come into the mind, occur to one. **S:** idea, thought; plan, scheme □ *'Two possibilities* ***suggest themselves to*** *me at the moment. One is that he's been misleading us all along.'* □ *A more promising way out of our difficulties then* ***suggested itself to*** *me.*

suit (down) to the ground [B2 B3] (informal) be perfectly suitable for sb. **S:** job, work; arrangement, schedule; room, flat □ *Joe had got himself a job as one of the gardeners. Literally and metaphorically it* ***suited*** *him* ***down to the ground****.* TBC □ *I have a nice line in tin coffins that would* ***suit*** *you* ***down to the ground****.* DPM

suit to [B2 pass] make sth suitable or appropriate for sth or sb. **O:** language, dress, behaviour. **o:** topic, occasion, audience □ *His approach was well* ***suited to*** *the sophistication of his listeners.* □ *Take care to* ***suit*** *the punishment* ***to*** *the offence.* □ *'Do you really think this work is* ***suited to*** *a class of beginners?'*

suited (to) [pass (B2)] (of a person) (be) fitted, right in one's nature for sb or sth. **S:** wife; partner, colleague. **o:** husband; life, routine □ *'It's no surprise to me that Roger and Elaine are breaking up. I've never felt that they were particularly well* ***suited to*** *one another.'* □ *Robert was not temperamentally* ***suited to*** *the tedium of life in a small country town.* □ passive with *be, seem, feel.*

suit the action to the word/suit one's actions to one's words [B2 pass] follow a threat, invitation, promise etc with suitable action □ *'Politicians should learn to* ***suit their actions to their words****. Of course, I say this more in hope than expectation.'* □ *'There's nothing we can do except give you a drink.' He* ***suited the action to the word****.* PW □ *On this occasion* ***the action*** *was* ***suited to the word****. A cheque arrived by the next post.*

sum up[1] [A1 B1i pass] (at the end of a speech etc) give the main points of what has been said; state people's feelings in a few words. **S:** chairman, lecturer. **O:** address; account, analysis; debate, discussion; feelings □ *I find it hard to* ***sum up*** *after such a wide-ranging debate.* □ *Wendy* ***sums up*** *the way the members feel in a few words.* H

sum up[2] [A1 B1i pass] (legal) review, and comment upon, the main points of a law case. **S:** judge, magistrate. **O:** case; evidence, arguments □ *In a packed and silent court-room the judge began to* ***sum up*** (or: *began his* ***summing-up***).

sum up[3] [B1i pass] form, pass, a judgement or opinion on sb or sth. **O:** acquaintance, colleague; situation, place □ *A difficult fellow to* ***sum up*** *— you never know what he's thinking.* □ *'A quiet American.' I* ***summed*** *him* ***up*** *as I might have said, 'A blue lizard.'* QA

summon (to) [B2 pass emph rel] (formal) call, require, sb officially to be present. **S:** ruler, employer, (magistrates') clerk. **O:** subject, official, witness. **o:** court, office, law-court □ *Ambassadors were* ***summoned*** *hastily* ***to*** *their home countries.* □ *A message arrived* ***summoning*** *him* ***to*** *the director's office.*

summon up [B1iii pass adj] evoke, prompt; gather strength etc (e g to meet a crisis). **O:** picture, souvenir, thought; energy; resolution □ *We find it hard to* ***summon up*** *thoughts of Venice at the sight of the lake today.* T □ ***Summoning up*** *his last ounce of strength, he flung himself over the finishing line.*

superimpose (on/upon) [B2 pass emph rel] (formal) place one thing upon another. **O:** picture, slide, cut-out; (one) culture. **o:** another (picture etc), background; preceding (one) □ *The negative showed that one snapshot had been* ***superimposed on*** *another.* □ *From archaeological evidence it is apparent that each group* ***superimposed*** *its ideas and culture* ***on*** *the previous one — Quimú on Moche, Huari on Quimú, but with all finally being absorbed or destroyed by the Incan Empire.*

supply (to) [B2 pass emph rel] give (to sb) for his use; furnish (to) (q v). **S:** school, firm, army. **O:** food, clothing, weapon; excuse, pretext. **o:** pupil, employee, soldier; critic, rival □ *Overalls have been* ***supplied to*** *everyone* (or: *Everyone has been* ***supplied with*** *overalls*). □ *The family* ***supplies*** *the basic necessities* ***to*** *them* (or: ***supplies*** *them* ***with*** *the basic necessities*).

supply with [B2 pass emph rel] ⇨ previous entry.

surge up [A1 emph] rise up in a wave. **S:** feeling; anger, longing, frustration □ *She felt the desire to burst into tears* ***surging up*** *within her.*

□ *His feelings could not be constrained:* ***up*** *and* ***up*** *they* ***surged***.

surrender (to)[1] [A2 emph rel B2 pass emph rel] (military) place oneself, one's soldiers etc in the enemy's hands, in admission of defeat. **S:** [A2] **O:** [B2] troops; army, force. **S:** [B2] commander □ *Through the interpreter the officer tried to persuade us to* ***surrender to*** *the 'heroic German army', as defence was useless and we would not be able to hold our positions any longer.* B □ *Positions* ***surrendered to*** *our troops earlier in the day had now to be prepared against the inevitable counter-attack.*

surrender (to)[2] [A2 emph rel] weaken, give way, in the face of some pressure. **o:** appeal, plea; argument, persuasion; (one's own) feelings □ *'In an emergency, keep cool. Don't* ***surrender to*** *panic.'* □ *Blackmail was one kind of pressure* ***to*** *which they were not prepared to* ***surrender***.

suspect (of) [B2 pass emph rel] feel, sense, that sb is guilty (of sth). **O:** colleague, employee. **o:** lying, cheating; treason, theft □ *We* ***suspected*** *him* ***of*** *removing the cash-box* (or: ***suspected*** *that he had removed* etc). □ *He was* ***suspected***, and accused, ***of*** *selling state secrets.*

suspend (from)[1] [B2 pass emph rel] hang (sth) from. **O:** lamp, ornament; rope, cord. **o:** ceiling, beam, hook □ *The pot was attached to a chain* ***suspended from*** *the ceiling.* □ *He* ***suspended*** *a rope-ladder* ***from*** *the rail of the ship.*

suspend (from)[2] [B2 pass rel] remove sb, usu temporarily (from a post etc). **O:** official; player. **o:** post, job; team □ *Two tax officials were* ***suspended*** *(****from*** *their posts) pending investigations into charges of corruption.*

swab down [B1i pass adj] clean the floor from one end to the other with water and a swab (or mop). **S:** sailor, charwoman. **O:** deck, floor □ *The crew were ordered to* ***swab down*** *the decks.*

swab out [B1i nom pass adj] remove dirt from (the floor of) a room etc with a swab and water. **O:** yard, latrine, stable □ *The soldiers had to* ***swab out*** *the barrack-room* (or: *give it a* ***swab(-)out****) before inspection.* □ *The place was freshly* ***swabbed out*** *and disinfected.*

swallow up[1] [B1i pass] make sb disappear, as if taking him in like food. **S:** earth, forest, jungle. **O:** expedition, traveller, vehicle □ *They had only to move a short distance to be* ***swallowed up*** *by the undergrowth.* □ *There was no gaping dark hole that would* ***swallow up*** *bad people.* DC □ *She was so embarrassed, she wished the earth would open and* ***swallow*** *her* ***up***.

swallow up[2] [B1i pass] consume, exhaust. **S:** project, scheme; bill, debt, expense. **O:** resources, manpower; money, income □ *Pay increases are no use if they are instantly* ***swallowed up*** *by rising prices.* □ *His reserves of men were soon* ***swallowed up*** *in the spring offensive.*

swamp with [B2 pass] send sth in a great volume to sb. **O:** office, radio-station, school, factory. **o:** letter, request, application, order □ *Indignant viewers* ***swamped*** *the television company* ***with*** *complaints.* □ *Dealers have been* ***swamped with*** *orders for the new car.* □ usu passive.

swap for [B2 pass] (informal) exchange one thing for another. **O:** car, flat; stamp, coin; seat, place; job. **o:** minibus, house; another, sb else's, a better one □ *I certainly wouldn't* ***swap*** *my life* ***for*** *his.* □ *'Who wants to* ***swap*** *a ham sandwich* ***for*** *a cheese and tomato?'* □ alt spelling: swop for.

swap over/round [A1 B1i pass] (of two persons) change places with one another; put one thing in the place of another; change events so that one takes place at the time of the other. **O:** chair, plate; wire, plug; time, period; lecture □ *'Go on,* ***swap over*** *and let Jane sit next to him!'* □ *'David, I've given you the wrong plate. Do you mind* ***swapping round*** *with Daddy, please?'* □ *'I want Mary to sit here and Bill there, so* ***swap over*** *the chairs.'* □ *'No wonder the set isn't working. Somebody has* ***swapped*** *two of the valves* ***round***.*'* □ alt spelling: swop over/round.

swap (with) [B2] (informal) give sth to sb in return for a similar thing. **O:** clothes; places; jobs. **o:** friend, colleague □ *I* ***swapped*** *jackets* ***with*** *John to get a better fit* (or: *John and I* ***swapped*** *jackets* etc). □ *'Can you* ***swap*** *seats* ***with*** *Joan? She can't see the screen* (or: *Can you and Joan* ***swap*** *seats* etc).*'* □ alt spelling: swop (with).

swarm over/through [A2] gather or move in large numbers (like a swarm of bees). **S:** reporter, photographer, policeman; rodent, pest. **o:** building, site; field, crop □ *The crowd* ***swarmed over*** *the pavements, trying to catch a glimpse of the President's car.* □ *Locusts* ***swarmed over*** *the landscape* (or: *The landscape* ***swarmed with*** *locusts*).

swarm with [A2] ⇨ previous entry.

swathe in [B2 pass] wrap sth tightly around sb. **O:** child; body; arm, leg. **o:** towel, blanket, bandage □ *Michael emerged from the bathroom* ***swathed in*** *a towel.* □ *'Don't* ***swathe*** *the fellow* ***in*** *bandages. Put on a simple dressing.'*

swear (at) [A2 pass] direct bad language or curses at sb. **o:** wife, pupil, staff □ *'There's no need to* ***swear at*** *me — control your language!'* □ *He resented being* ***sworn at***, *even if he* had *made a mistake.*

swear (by) [B2 emph] appeal to sb or sth sacred in saying that sth is the case. **O:** that one is innocent, that sth is true. **o:** ⚠ Almighty God, all the gods, all that is sacred, holy, all one holds sacred □ *He* ***swore by*** *all that is holy that he'd been elsewhere at the time.* □ (oath taken in court) *'I* ***swear by*** *Almighty God to tell the truth.'* ⇨ swear (on).

swear by [A2] (informal) have great confidence in sth as a remedy etc. **o:** medicine; pill, lotion, ointment □ *'Take these tablets if you feel run down: I* ***swear by*** *them.'* □ *He* ***swore by*** *some twopenny-ha'penny tonic a quack had recommended to him.*

swear in [B1i pass adj] make sb take an oath to be truthful, fair etc (in court); admit a member to a society by making him take an oath. **S:** clerk; president. **O:** witness, jury; new member □ *The defence counsel objected to the jury, so that a new one had to be* ***sworn in***. □ *The full committee has to attend when a new member is* ***sworn in*** (or: *attend the* ***swearing-in*** *of a new member*).

swear off [A2 pass] (informal) promise to abandon, stop doing, sth. **o:** drink, smoking, gambling □ *'No, I won't have a cigarette, thanks. I've **sworn off** them on doctor's orders.'*

swear (on) [B2 emph] appeal to sb or sth sacred in saying that sth is so. **O:** that he is lying, that I wasn't there. **o:** ⚠ the Bible, my son's head □ *He'd **swear on** all the Bibles in the world that he wasn't after her money.* ⇨ swear (by).

swear to [A2] (informal) be certain that sth is the case, is right. **o:** having seen sb, having heard sth; figure, sum; it □ *Had there been a voice? Now, in the silence, she could not **swear to** it.* DC □ *I wouldn't **swear to** any figure for smuggling — it's just grown with the diamond industry.* DS □ with *can/could* or *will/would*; usu neg.

swear to secrecy/silence [B2 pass] make sb promise not to reveal important information. **O:** committee, board, department; gang □ *Everyone connected with the project was **sworn to secrecy**.*

sweat out [B1i pass] wrap up warmly, and by sweating get rid of a cold etc. **O:** fever, cold, 'flu □ *When you feel 'flu coming on, get into bed and **sweat** it **out**.*

sweat one's guts out [B1ii] (informal) work extremely hard. **S:** worker, tradesman, athlete □ *'Why should I **sweat my guts out** for twelve pounds a week?'* □ *Normally, I **sweated my guts out** on a milling-machine with the rest.* LLDR

sweat it out [B1ii] (informal) keep going, persevere, in an unpleasant situation; suffer, endure, such a situation □ *'Don't throw up your job: **sweat it out** a bit longer.'* □ *The climbers will just have to **sweat it out** until we can get a rescue team to them.* □ *'The exam results won't be posted till six. We'll have to **sweat it out** for another hour.'*

sweep aside [B1i pass adj] dismiss comment etc, continue as if it had not been made; brush aside[2] (q v). **S:** speaker, organizer, salesman. **O:** argument, criticism, objection □ *He was so full of his own schemes, that he **swept aside** reasonable doubts.* □ *Interruptions were **swept aside** with a wave of the hand.*

sweep away[1] [B1i pass] remove, carry away, with great force. **S:** storm, flood, avalanche. **O:** bridge, dyke, dam □ *Farmhouses and buildings were **swept away** in the avalanche.* □ *The floodwaters **swept away** part of a road.*

sweep away[2] [B1i pass] remove, abolish, by vigorous action. **S:** reformer, revolutionary. **O:** system, society; convention, practice; inequality, injustice □ *Successive left-wing governments have promised to **sweep away** the last vestiges of privilege in education.* □ *Newspaper editorials spoke of the need to **sweep away** corrupt practices in local government.*

sweep in/into[1] [A1 emph A2 emph] enter in a proud, lordly way. **S:** king, chief; bandit, braggart. **o:** hall, room □ *The procession **swept into** the hall, preceded by trumpeters.* □ *Peter **swept in**, with his dignity and insolence.* DC

sweep in/into[2] [A1 A2 B1i pass B2 pass] return, be returned, to office, easily, by a clear majority. **S:** [A1 A2] **O:** [B1 B2] Labour, the Conservatives. **o:** ⚠ office, power □ [A1] *Labour **swept in** on a tide of discontent over rising prices.* □ [B2] *The administration **swept into** power in the election of 1945 was to remain in office for over six years.*

sweep off his feet [B2 pass] (informal) fill with enthusiasm; captivate (a girl), make her fall suddenly in love with one. **S:** orator, actor, hero. **O:** audience; girl □ *His speeches were calculated to **sweep** uncommitted people **off their feet**.* □ *After one meeting she was completely **swept off her feet**.*

sweep out [B1i nom pass] remove dirt from a place, with a broom. **O:** hall, room, attic □ *This room needs to be well **swept out*** (or: *This room needs a good **sweep-out***).

sweep out/out of [A1 emph A2 emph] leave in a proud, lordly way. **S:** king, duchess; actor. **o:** room, house □ *Without a word, she turned and **swept out of** the room.*

sweep under the carpet [B2 pass] (informal) hide sth which might cause a scandal, trouble, for oneself etc. **O:** findings, evidence, truth □ *Unpleasant episodes in his early career were **swept under the carpet**.* □ *'There's enough hard evidence **swept under the carpet** to start a couple of major scandals.'*

sweep up [A1 nom B1i nom pass adj] lift, collect, dirt etc with a broom (and dustpan). **S:** housewife, maid. **O:** mess; crumbs, cigarette-ends □ *'Don't leave me to **sweep up** after the party!'* □ *This place needs a bit of a **sweep-up**.*

swell up [A1] rise to form a bulge on the skin. **S:** boil, blister □ *'Don't prick that boil; allow it to **swell up** and burst.'* □ *The flesh around the ankle had **swollen up**.*

swerve (from) [A2 emph rel B2 pass emph rel] (cause to) change one's direction or aim. **S:** [A2] **O:** [B2] disciple, follower. **o:** way, path; purpose, aim □ *'You needn't waste time trying to persuade him. He won't be **swerved from** his course once his mind's made up.'* □ *Eventually he returned to the official line — **from** which he had often **swerved**.*

swill out [B1i nom pass adj] clean a container etc by pouring water in and out of it; rinse (out) (q v). **O:** tub, pot, basin; mouth □ *'**Swill out** the saucepan — it's still got stale food in it.'* □ *Make sure the yard gets a good **swill-out*** (or: *is well **swilled out***).

swindle out of [B2 pass emph rel] (informal) get money from sb by fraud or deceit. **O:** citizen, customer, heir. **o:** money; donation, investment; inheritance □ *He's just the kind that would stoop to **swindle** old people **out of** a few pence* (or: *to **swindle** a few pence **out of** them*). □ *'Of course he's hopping mad. He's been **swindled out of** thirty quid!'*

swing (at) [A2 pass B2 pass] swing one's fist etc in an arc in an attempt to hit sb or sth. **O:** fist; bat, club. **o:** chin, jaw; ball □ *'I didn't try to start a fight. I made a harmless remark to some guy at the bar and he **swung at** me.'* □ *He **swung** hard **at** the next delivery, got an outside edge, and was well caught in the slips.*

swing round [A1] turn round suddenly (e g to answer sb, argue etc) □ *He **swung round** to confront the thin-faced man, and seized him by the collar.* □ *Saunders **swung round** on his wife. 'I won't have those police in my house again,' he said.* DC

swing round (to) [A1 nom A3 emph rel] turn to face in another direction; come to hold quite different opinions etc. **S:** wind; weather-vane; public, electorate. **o:** east, south-west; (opposite) view, position □ *The breeze had **swung round**, so that now instead of fighting against it we were being borne along by it.* □ *Since the last election public opinion has **swung round** completely* (or: *there has been a complete **swing-round***) *on the question of allowing heavy traffic into the centre of cities.*

swipe (at) [A2 pass] (informal) aim a vigorous blow at sth. **S:** golfer, cricketer. **o:** ball; wasp, mouse □ *'Every time you **swipe at** the flies you knock over the marmalade.'* □ *He doesn't enjoy being **swiped at*** (= clumsily attacked) *in the local paper.*

swirl about [A1 A2 B2 pass] move about in thick masses, constantly changing speed and direction. **S:** [A2] **O:** [B2] smoke, clouds, dust; crowd, dancers; leaves, clothes □ [A1] *Thick clouds of dust **swirled about**, getting into our food and water.* □ [A2] *Happy people linked arms and **swirled about** the streets.* □ [B2] *Inside the launderette old ladies dozed in front of their washing-machines or gazed vacantly through the glass windows at the drums **swirling** their dirty washing **about**.*

swish off [B1i pass] remove, cut off, with a stick etc which makes a hissing sound. **S:** he etc; scythe, sword, cane. **O:** leaf, stalk, head (of plant) □ *He **swished off** the tops of the grasses with a neat flick of his cane.*

switch around/round [B1i pass] alter the positions of people or things relative to each other. **O:** furniture, dishes; staff □ *His parents are always redecorating the rooms and **switching** the furniture **around**. The flat is never the same for two months on end.* □ *It's part of company policy to **switch** its young trainees **round** within departments and between departments. The idea is to give them early experience of all sides of the business.*

switch off[1] [B1i pass adj] disconnect an appliance; disconnect a supply (of gas or electricity); turn off[1] (q v). **O:** (gas-)fire, (electric) stove, radio; power; gas, electricity □ *Television sets have the great advantage that they can be **switched off**.* OBS □ *Make sure the current is **switched off** at the mains before you leave on holiday.* ⇨ switch on[1].

switch off[2] [B1i pass adj] (informal) make sb dull, lifeless, unresponsive; turn off[2] (q v). **S:** loud music, card games; company, conversation; drink, drugs □ *Parties switch him on, but they seem to **switch** her **off**!* □ *He's the most **switched-off** guy you ever met.* ⇨ switch on[2].

switch on[1] [B1i pass adj] connect an appliance; connect a power supply; turn on[1] (q v). **O:** light, lamp, washing-machine; current, power □ *She had come to **switch on** the lights and light the fires.* DC □ *The transmitters were **switched on** during December.* TBC ⇨ switch off[1].

switch on[2] [B1i pass adj] (informal) make sb lively, excited (by providing some stimulant); turn on[2] (q v). **S:** pop-music; alcohol, drugs; company, atmosphere □ *Her conversation doesn't **switch** me **on**—it leaves me cold.* □ *There are always plenty of **switched-on** people at their parties.* ⇨ switch off[2].

switch over (to) [A1 nom A3 B1i pass B3 pass] (cause sb to) do one job instead of another; (cause sth to) use one kind of power etc rather than another. **S:** [A1 A3] **O:** [B1 B3] worker; factory; household. **S:** [B1 B3] director, Board, Council. **o:** (another) job; distribution, production; electricity, gas □ [A3] *Peter **switched over to** teaching* (or: *made a **switch-over to** teaching*) *in mid-career.* □ [B3] *The aim is to **switch** the whole country **over to** natural gas.* □ [B1] *All the petrol pumps on our forecourt have been **switched over** to show decimal values.*

switch round [B1i pass] ⇨ switch around/round.

switch through (to) [B1i pass B2 pass] connect an outside caller to sb on an internal network, put through (to) (q v); transfer an incoming call from one extension to another on the same network. **S:** operator; switchboard. **O:** call; caller □ *'I have a caller from London on the line, Mr Jeffries.' 'All right, Joan, **switch** him **through**.'* □ *'Operator, would you mind **switching** this call **through to** Mr Martin on extension 7049?'*

swoop (down) (on) [A1 A2 pass A3 pass] descend suddenly to seize or attack; attack suddenly, descend upon (q policeman. **o:** prey, target; enemy, gang □ *A dozen hands **swooped down** and snatched the pieces of bread.* □ *Detectives **swooped down on** a gambling club and made several arrests.*

swop for [B2 pass] ⇨ swap for.

swop over/round [B1i pass] ⇨ swap over/round.

swop (with) [B2] ⇨ swap (with).

swot (for) [A2] (informal) study hard (for a particular purpose). **S:** pupil, student, apprentice. **o:** exam; Finals, GCE □ *He's **swotting** every evening **for** his Bar exams.*

swot up [A1 B1i pass] (informal) by hard study, learn or revise sth; mug up (q v). **S:** student, candidate. **O:** maths, physics; table, formula □ *'You'll need to **swot up** your irregular verbs during the holiday.'* □ *'I seem to spend most of my time **swotting up**!'*

T

tack down [B1i pass adj] fasten with small nails (esp to a floor). **O:** carpet, mat; corner, edge □ *'You'd better just **tack down** the edge of the carpet: people keep tripping over it.'*

tack on/onto[1] [B1i pass adj B2 pass emph rel] attach with long, loose stitches (esp before finally assembling a garment with a sewing-machine). **O:** sleeve, collar, skirt. **o:** jacket, bodice □ *The lining has been **tacked on** too loosely—it keeps coming unstitched.*

tack on/onto[2] [B1i pass adj B2 pass emph rel] become, make sb, a member or part of sth larger; add sth to (the end of) a document etc. **O:** oneself; name; paragraph, appendix. **o:** (end of the) line, queue; list; document, report □ *John **tacked** himself **onto** the end of a long queue at* *the bus-stop.* ◻ *The Bill was not allowed to go forward without further modification. Another clause was* ***tacked on*** *at the last minute.*

tackle (about/on/over) [B2 pass] speak to sb frankly and boldly (about sth that one is troubled by). **O:** neighbour; landlord; (school, local) authorities. **o:** disturbance, nuisance; (high) rents, repairs; (provision of) amenities ◻ *'He's always playing his radio at full blast: it's high time we* ***tackled*** *him* ***about*** *it.'* ◻ *At the last meeting, the headmaster was* ***tackled over*** *his policy of allowing some boys to proceed to 'O' level in four years.*

tag along (after/behind) [A1 A3] (informal) accompany, follow, in a tame, dependent way. **S:** child; henpecked husband; would-be member. **o:** parent; wife; gang-leader ◻ *She gives these ghastly parties and poor Robin has to* ***tag along****.* ASA ◻ *Some of these men — we used to knock about together sometimes. I used to* ***tag along*** *on some of their evenings.* TC ◻ *Wherever the three Party leaders went in their election campaigning a gaggle of press and TV reporters was sure to* ***tag along behind****.*

tail off[1] [A1] decrease gradually; taper off[2] (q v). **S:** output, supply, demand; spending, investment ◻ *We expect production to* ***tail off*** *at this time of the year. Ours is a seasonal business.* ◻ *There's some* ***tailing off*** *in the demand for new cars at the end of the summer holidays.*

tail off[2] [A1] fade into silence (usu because the speaker is shy or embarrassed). **S:** speaker; voice, words ◻ *John was clearly overwhelmed by the occasion. After a few sentences, his voice* ***tailed off*** *into complete silence.*

tailor to [B2 pass rel] make, devise, in such a way that it fits particular needs; adapt to (q v). **O:** scheme, plan; product. **o:** need, requirement, purpose ◻ *Our insurance policies are specially* ***tailored to*** *the earnings pattern of the insured at different stages in his career.* ◻ *Experience has taught us to* ***tailor*** *our merchandise* ***to*** *the particular requirements of each overseas market.*

take aback [B1ii pass] surprise (and upset or dismay) sb. **S:** criticism, reproof; answer, retort ◻ *The reply* ***took*** *him so much* ***aback*** *that for a moment he was lost for words.* ◻ *Looking back, I'm surprised I wasn't more* ***taken aback*** *by the whole thing.* TC ◻ *He was somewhat* ***taken aback*** *by the news that the police intended to prosecute him.* ◻ usu passive.

take aboard [B1i pass B2 pass] take on board a ship or aircraft; take on[1] (q v). **o:** lifeboat, fishing-vessel; plane ◻ *The vessel had to jettison some of the cargo* ***taken aboard*** *at Liverpool.* ◻ *Passengers may only* ***take aboard*** *the aircraft a minimum of hand luggage.* ⇨ come/go aboard. go aboard.

take umbrage (about/at) [B2] feel displeased, annoyed, offended (by sth); take offence (at) (q v). **o:** remark, comment; neglect, slight ◻ *'He's like the rest of you, forever* ***taking umbrage about*** *something.'* US ◻ *Although Steve was given to lying, he never* ***took umbrage at*** *being accused of it.* SPL

take abroad (with) [B1i pass B3 pass] take to a foreign country (with one). **O:** wife, family; car, caravan; money, foreign currency ◻ *Restrictions have been eased on the amount of currency a British holiday-maker may* ***take abroad with*** *him.* ◻ *'Are you thinking of* ***taking*** *your car* ***abroad*** *again this year?'* ⇨ go abroad.

take across (to) [B1ii pass B2 pass B3 pass] take sb or sth from one side to the other. **O:** child, blind person; vehicle; goods. **o:** (*across*) road, busy crossing; the Channel, the North Sea; (*to*) France, the Continent ◻ [B1] *There ought to be someone posted at this point to* ***take*** *the children* ***across*** *in the morning.* ◻ [B2] *'Would you mind* ***taking*** *me* ***across*** *the street?'* ◻ [B3] *'Have you tried* ***taking*** *a caravan* ***across to*** *France yet?'* ⇨ get across[1]; go/send across (to).

take after [A2] resemble a parent in looks and/or character. **o:** father, mother; grandfather ◻ *'You must* ***take after*** *father. I don't. I long to have lashings of cash.'* DC ◻ HELEN: *You're not fond of work, are you?* JO: *No. I* ***take after*** *you.* TOH

take aloft [B1ii pass] take into the air on board an aircraft. **S:** pilot; plane. **O:** passenger, stowaway; load ◻ *There were at least two cases of soldiers being* ***taken aloft*** *hanging on to the undercarriage or tail wheel in desperation.* B

take apart[1] [B1ii pass] dismantle, reduce to its component parts; take to bits/pieces (q v). **O:** car, radio, clock ◻ *Nick had* ***taken*** *the fuel gauge* ***apart*** *and spread the bits all over the carpet.*

take apart[2] [B1ii pass] (informal) defeat utterly, punish severely; criticize harshly. **S:** team; bowler, forward, boxer; critic; the press. **O:** opponents, visitors; performer, artist ◻ *He had a rough time in his first fight. He was drawn opposite a real old pro who* ***took*** *him* ***apart*** *inside two rounds.* ◻ *His first novel had rave notices; his second was* ***taken apart****.*

take around/round (with) [B1i pass B3 pass] take as a companion, wherever one goes. **O:** mother, younger brother; dog ◻ *He's beginning to teach his son the business. He* ***takes*** *him* ***around with*** *him in the car when he calls on customers.* ◻ *It's as though he can't let the girl out of his sight. He* ***takes*** *her* ***around*** *all over the place.* ⇨ go around/round (with).

take aside/to one side [B1ii pass B2 pass] lead sb away from a group in order to talk privately to him ◻ *I shall have to* ***take*** *the boy* ***aside*** *one of these days and warn him against the company he's been keeping.* ◻ *'Will you* ***take*** *Mrs Stevens* ***to one side*** *and tell her that some important news has come through on the phone?'* ⇨ go aside.

take at (his/its) face value [B2 pass] treat, evaluate, sb or sth according to what he or it appears to be on the surface. **O:** stranger, visitor; dealer, salesman; remark, statement; goods ◻ *These people respect an artist. They* ***take*** *everybody* ***at his face value****.* CON ◻ *I can* ***take*** *nothing you say* ***at face value****.* TC ◻ *The truth is that few titles* (i e of nobility) *can be* ***taken at their face value****.* T

take a look (at) [B2] examine, look at[1] (q v). **adj:** close, good, quick, careful. **o:** face, features; letter, report; evidence, signs, traces ◻ *'Those drawings, did you examine them?' 'I sent them straight on.' 'Well,* ***take a*** *good* ***look at*** *them now.'* OMIH ◻ *He* ***took a*** *quick* ***look at*** *his notes.* OMIH

take offence (at) [B2 pass emph rel] be offended (by). **o:** manner, tone (of voice); remark, (supposed) insult ◻ *If she was going to* ***take offence at*** *everything he said, she had got* *to be put right straight away.* AITC □ *I couldn't* ***take offence at*** *his tone, but I resolved to be more careful in front of him in future.* RATT □ *They then devised an entertainment* ***at*** *which no one could possibly* ***take offence.***

take umbrage (at) [B2] ⇨ take umbrage (about/at).

take at his word [B2 pass] behave as though sb is speaking the truth. **O:** speaker, official, employer □ *'Why not* ***take him at his word*** *and act accordingly? When has he ever given you any reason to doubt him?'*

take sb's breath away [B1ii pass] surprise, startle. **S:** (sudden) arrival; (unkempt, tattered) appearance; injuries; expense, cost □ *'Please don't come too close* (i e to kiss me). *You* ***take my breath away,*** *and you know how much I love talking.'* DPM □ *The appetite with which he consumed, during these next few days, really* ***took my breath away.*** CON □ *It* ***takes one's breath away*** *to see how much the place has changed in a few years.*

take away (from)[1] [B1i pass B3 pass emph rel] cause sb to leave a place, or a person to whom he was entrusted etc. **O:** child, ward. **o:** school, children's home; foster parents □ *Father was convinced that Peter was unhappy at boarding school, and made arrangements to* ***take*** *him* ***away.*** □ *He can't be accused of* ***taking*** *the baby* ***away from*** *its mother irresponsibly. For various reasons, she's unable to look after the child.*

take away (from)[2] [B1i pass B3 pass emph rel] remove sth from sb (e g because it is dangerous, no longer deserved etc). **O:** gun, knife; plaything, sweets; privilege, office. **o:** intruder, bandit; child; official, prefect □ *One unit of the army has had its fire-arms* ***taken away*** *following the recent mutiny.* □ *He's always been a slave to women — who* ***take away*** *with one hand while they give with the other.* PW ⇨ get away from.

take away (from)[3] [B1i pass B3 pass emph rel] make a feeling or sensation disappear (from). **O:** joy, fun; pain, distress. **o:** existence, life; experience; body, leg □ *This queer worry and apprehension had* ***taken away*** *all her pleasure in her regained mobility.* DC □ *'Now, I'll give you some tablets to* ***take away*** *the pain.'*

take away (from)[4] [B1i pass B3 pass emph rel] (mathematics) subtract a smaller sum from a larger. **O:** (smaller) number, digit. **o:** (larger) number, total □ *'****Take away*** *this number* ***from*** *that, and tell me how much you have left.'* □ (a child is speaking) *'I can do adding up, but we haven't done any* ***taking away*** *yet.'*

take away/out [B1i nom pass] buy and carry away, from a special restaurant or shop, cooked dishes for consumption at home. **O:** meal, snack; curry, chop suey □ *'They do a very good curry here, and you can* ***take*** *stuff* ***out*** *if you want.'* □ *There's a small* ***take-out*** *on the corner, where you can get baked potatoes with various fillings.* □ *'Incidentally, I hope nobody's eating Chinese* ***take-aways*** (or: ***take-away*** *meals) for breakfast.'* BBCR □ each of the nom forms take-away and take-out can refer both to the meal etc and to the place where it is prepared.

take back[1] [B1i pass] cause to return. **O:** child; (stray) animal; (borrowed) book, record, camera □ *'It's nearly time for afternoon school. Margaret, do you mind* ***taking*** *the children* ***back*** *in your car?'* □ *'Some of these library books are long overdue. I really must* ***take them back.'*** ⇨ be back[1], bring back[1], come back[1], get back[1], go back[1].

take back[2] [B1i pass] agree to accept or receive sth which one has sold, or sb whom one has dismissed. **S:** shopkeeper, store; wife. **O:** (shoddy, defective) article; (errant) husband □ *There's something seriously the matter with this car. Under their guarantee, the dealers are obliged to* ***take*** *it* ***back.*** □ *After all his wife has gone through, I think Frank will be extremely lucky if she* ***takes*** *him* ***back.*** ⇨ have back[2].

take back[3] [B1i pass] withdraw, retract. **O:** remark, statement; accusation; it all; what one has said □ *I wanted you to ask me to marry you, and you did. Now* ***take*** *it* ***back,*** *if you want to.* H □ *He would have given anything to be a small boy, who by saying '****Take back*** *what I said' could erase a whole conversation.* ASA

take back (to) [B1ii pass B3 pass] recall earlier experiences to sb; carry back (to) (q v). **S:** conversation, reminiscences; music, voice; smell. **o:** his etc early days, childhood □ *'Just chatting over a drink like this — it certainly* ***takes*** *you* ***back,*** *doesn't it?'* □ *Seeing Mike again* ***took*** *me* ***back to*** *my first years as a teacher overseas.*

take before [B2 pass] make sb appear in a court etc to explain his actions, to be punished etc. **O:** offender, accused; schoolboy; soldier; case. **o:** magistrate; headmaster; company commander □ *Prefects could deal with minor breaches of the school rules; serious offenders were* ***taken before*** *the headmaster.* ⇨ be before[2], bring before, come before[2], go before[2], put before[2].

take below [B1i pass] (nautical) lead sb, carry sth, to a cabin etc from the deck of a ship. **O:** passenger, visitor; gear, tackle □ *The rescued seamen were* ***taken below*** *and given some hot food and dry clothes.* ⇨ be below[3]; go below (decks).

take the bit between the teeth [B2] (informal) settle to a hard task in a determined way. **S:** athlete; climber, swimmer; worker, student □ *I wouldn't have given him much credit for determination, but he's* ***taken the bit between the teeth,*** *and now there's no holding him.*

take by [B2 pass] in grasping sb or sth, take hold of a particular limb, or part. **O:** him etc; pot, kettle, dish. **o:** hand, elbow; scruff of the neck, seat of the pants; handle □ *He* ***took*** *Mary gently* ***by*** *the wrist, and drew her aside.* □ *'I'll have you* ***taken by*** *the scruff of your neck and thrown out of this club.'* □ *Don't* ***take*** *the knife* ***by*** *the blade;* ***take*** *it* ***by*** *the handle.*

take the bull by the horns [B2 pass] (informal) handle a difficult, or dangerous, situation by facing it boldly and directly □ *'You won't get the financial support you need by staying here.* ***Take the bull by the horns.*** *Go and speak to your bank manager.'*

take down[1] [B1i pass] lower, drop; remove from a high level (e g on a wall or shelf). **O:** flag, bunting, streamer; picture, curtain rail; book, ornament □ *An old tradition has it that Christmas decorations must be* ***taken down*** *before Twelfth Night.* □ *I* ***took down*** *my copy of 'The Tibetan Book of the Dead' and opened it at random.* DOP

⇨ come down[1].

take down[2] [B1i pass] dismantle. **O:** scaffolding; crane, derrick □ *They've* ***taken down*** *the iron railings on this side of the park.* □ *The ornamental gates have been* ***taken down*** *and sold as scrap.* ⇨ come down[1].

take down[3] [B1i pass] record in writing, write down (q v). **O:** lecture, speech; remarks, statement □ *We were sitting about listlessly while the Bloater* (a teacher) *droned out some stuff we were supposed to be* ***taking down***. CON □ *These occasions are ghastly enough without feeling that what one says may be* ***taken down*** *and used against one.* ASA (cf the form of official caution used by the police when taking a statement: *...anything you say will be* ***taken down****, and may be used in evidence.*) ⇨ be down[3], get down[4], go down[9], put down[8], set down[2].

take down a peg (or two) [B1ii pass] (informal) humble an arrogant or conceited person □ *'I've never heard such pretentious rubbish: he needs to be* ***taken down a peg or two****.'* □ a peg (or two) is an adv phrase (of degree).

take (for) [B2 pass] mistakenly assume that sb is sb (or sth) else. **o:** his brother; (genuine) official, member of staff; local person, foreign visitor; fool, idiot □ *'I'm sorry I spoke to you so familiarly: I* ***took*** *you* ***for*** (or: ***took*** *you to be*) *a close friend.'* □ *He speaks English so well, that he's often* ***taken for*** *a native.* □ *'So!' he said, in a surprised tone. 'And yet, Briggs, I should not have* ***taken*** *you* ***for*** *a coward.'* EM

take credit for [B2 emph rel] be recognized as, accept that one is, the person who has acted well in a certain situation. **adj:** some (of the), all the, a lot of the; full, due. **o:** saving, rescuing (sb), restoring (sth); success, revival □ *'He will also* ***take*** *the* ***credit for*** *getting rid of a dangerous agent.'* OMIH □ *'Of course the exhibition was a tremendous success, and* ***for*** *this you must* ***take*** *full* ***credit****.'* ⇨ give credit for, give credit (to) (for).

take for granted[1] [B2 pass] assume that sth is true, is the case, and act on that assumption. **O:** nothing, no facts; a lot, too much; his reliability, trustworthiness; his help, co-operation; it... that he speaks the truth, it... that the room is available □ *Cyril Robertson was a stimulating, provocative man who* ***took*** *nothing whatever* ***for granted***. OBS □ *There are certain standards of civilized behaviour in international relations which it should be possible to* ***take for granted*** *in the family of nations.* SC □ *'Then if it's* ***taken for granted****, let's get on with it. We might as well commit the crime if we're certain to receive the punishment.'* TBC

take for granted[2] [B2 pass] assume that sb's reactions can be known in advance and therefore act without making due allowance for them. **O:** wife, colleague, partner □ *'You might consult me before making these arrangements: I do resent being* ***taken*** *so much* ***for granted****.'* □ *She knew that she was in danger of* ***taking*** *him too much* ***for granted***. PW

take revenge (for) [B2 emph rel] ⇨ take revenge (on) (for).

take for a ride [B2 pass] (informal) fool, dupe, outwit, get the better of, sb (in a business deal, a legal transaction etc). **O:** customer, consumer; client; partner, shareholder □ *'If you paid more than £500 for that car, you've been* ***taken for a ride****!'* □ *Vin was the sharp, clever boy who wasn't to be* ***taken for a ride*** *by anybody, the boy who knew all the answers.* ASA

what do you take me for? [B2] (informal) the speaker is asking, rhetorically, whether another person supposes that he is foolish, immoral etc □ *'Of course I wouldn't walk out on you and the children.* ***What*** *on earth* ***do you take me for?****'* □ *'Would you like me to kiss her?' 'Don't be disgusting, Harold,* ***what do you take me for?****'* PW ⇨ take (for).

take sb's word for it/that [B2] accept on sb's authority that sth is the case □ *'Oh, don't worry to explain, Gerrie, I'll* ***take your word for it*** *that it's important.'* ASA □ *'They can do without you,* ***take my word for it****. But without them, you're lost—nothing.'* EGD □ *'And as Ada says,' Mr Blearney went on, 'she's only a woman. I have to* ***take her word for that****, mind you.'* HD □ it introduces, or refers back to, a finite clause.

take from[1] [B2 pass emph rel] choose, extract, a text for reading or study from a larger work. **S:** priest, preacher; student, scholar. **O:** reading, text, passage □ *The vicar preached a short and effective sermon,* ***taking*** *his text* ***from*** *St Mark's Gospel.* □ *'I am going to* ***take*** *an extract* ***from*** *some recordings I've made of bird songs, and play it over to you.'*

take from[2] [B2 emph rel] (informal) suffer, be the target of, attacks etc, from. **O:** abuse, insults; a lot, too much, not... any more □ *I've* ***taken*** *more than I can stand* ***from*** *those two.* □ *For the sake of general harmony, he was someone* ***from*** *whom I was prepared to* ***take*** *a certain amount of sniping and petty jealousy.*

take from[3] [A2] lessen, weaken, the effect or value of sth; detract from (q v). **S:** scarcity, expense, poor quality (of labour, materials); voice, manner. **o:** attractiveness, feasibility (of a project); success, effectiveness (of a speech) □ *His appearance in a shabby dressing-gown* ***took*** *somewhat* ***from*** *the impression of stern authority he wished to convey.*

take heart (from) [B2 emph rel] be encouraged or heartened (by), esp in difficult times. **o:** news; knowledge, realization (that...); words, remarks □ *Whenever I spoke of the Bushman a look of wonder would come into their eyes, and I* ***took heart from*** *that.* LWK □ *But let them* ***take heart*** *(****from*** *this): it might have been worse. So far we have had neither frost nor snow.* T

take it from me/us [B2] (informal) (one may) believe or assume, on the speaker's authority, that sth is the case. **O:** it... that the worst is over; it... he won't come back □ ***Take it from me****: your troubles are nearly over.* □ *He can* ***take it from me*** *that the magistrate is usually lenient in such cases.* □ usu imper, or after *can*.

take it from the top [B2] (theatre) (an instruction to) play, repeat, a scene from the beginning □ *'Right, everybody. When you've settled down, can we* ***take it from the top****, please.'*

take one's pick (from/of) [B2 emph rel] (informal) (be free to) choose what one likes from a selection. **o:** (***from***) range, assortment (of articles); variety, mixture; (***of***) ties, shirts; horses, dogs (in a race); partners, girls □ *Ask the chemist for our product, and* ***take your pick***

from eight romantic shades. H □ *He was handed a list, and told he could* ***take his pick of*** *the drinks available.*

take home [B1iii nom pass] (industry) have as net wages after deductions have been made for tax, national insurance etc. **O:** wage; pay; £40 □ *Miners, after that many hours underground,* ***take home*** *£31 a week after deductions.* T □ *I have to work continuous nights to earn a gross wage of £35, and a* ***take-home*** *pay of £29.* T □ *Men employed labouring in the oil-related industries are earning a basic of £50, with a* ***take-home*** *of £75 plus.* OBS

take in[1] [B1iii] receive, admit, lodgers for payment. **O:** lodger, paying-guest; student, commercial traveller □ *Many households in the neighbourhood of the University add to their income by* ***taking in*** *students.*

take in[2] [B1iii] accept work for payment to be done in one's own home. **O:** washing, sewing, mending □ *Mrs Peters, who is a widow with young children,* ***takes in*** *washing to supplement her pension.*

take in[3] [B1i pass] make narrower, alter, to fit a thinner person. **O:** dress, trousers □ *The dress is not a bad fit, but it needs* ***taking in*** *a little at the waist.* □ *'I'll have the waistband* ***taken in*** *for you a couple of inches.'*

take in[4] [B1iii pass] include, cover. **S:** (field of) study, discipline; work, responsibilities; district, area. **O:** branch, speciality; teaching, research; (many) villages □ *Forensic science* ***takes in*** *criminology, which covers the causes of crime.* NS □ *These tours* ***took in*** *every part of the British Empire.* MFM □ *Her accusation* ***took in*** *not only Mrs Curry, but Mrs Craddock also.* HAA

take in[5] [B1i pass] observe, note visually. **O:** surroundings; room; contents, occupants. **A:** at a glance, at once □ *Scrodd was* ***taking in*** *with his short-sighted glance the general area within which his interlocutor might be found.* HD □ *Her eyes were* ***taking in*** *nothing but the telephone.* NM

take in[6] [B1i pass] (hear or read and) understand or absorb. **O:** talk, lecture; words, remarks; (difficult) material, subject □ *Isabel wondered how much Irma was* ***taking in*** *of what was said.* PW □ *Halfway through the chapter I stopped. I wasn't* ***taking in*** *a single word.* RATT □ *She couldn't* ***take in*** *this new situation or size up what Irma's revelation meant to her.* PW ⇨ go in[5].

take in[7] [B1i pass] (informal) fool, delude, dupe. **S:** salesman; quack doctor; magician; politician. **O:** customer; patient; audience □ *I'm sorry you're all so easy to* ***take in****. You ought to know better with all your experience of the trade.* TC □ *The public must be pretty gullible to be* ***taken in*** *so easily by door-to-door salesmen.*

take in hand[1] [B2 pass] undertake, begin work on. **O:** project, scheme, programme □ *We are just now* ***taking in hand*** *a massive programme for the redevelopment of the city centre.* □ *The plans which have been laid before you will be* ***taken in hand*** *by the autumn.* ⇨ be/have in hand.

take in hand[2] [B2 pass] (informal) assume responsibility for sb, with the aim of training him, changing his character etc. **O:** (unruly, delinquent) child, youth; horse, dog. **A:** firmly, seriously □ *'Why don't you go to a decent school?' 'I've never been to any school.' 'You need* ***taking in hand****.'* TOH □ *Clearly somebody new had* ***taken*** *Madge* ***in hand****, somebody far more expert than Sammy.* UTN

take a hand (in) [B2 emph rel] become involved, intervene, in events. **S:** authorities, police, army. **o:** events, proceedings; what is happening □ *A salesman who is doing the rounds in Newtown seems to be too clever for the law—that is until Sgt Watt* ***takes a hand in*** *events.* RT

take an interest in [B2 pass emph rel] interest oneself in, become interested in. **S:** scientist, scholar; businessman; teacher; police. **adj:** (not) any/much, no, little; keen, lively, added. **o:** field, topic; developments, opportunities; organizing playgroups, studying the locality, reducing the accident-rate □ *You never* ***took any interest in*** *what he did.* AITC □ *Ex-Superintendent Williams was* ***taking a*** *keen* ***interest in*** *George's affairs.* PE □ *Rock-climbing is an activity* ***in*** *which more and more young people are* ***taking an interest****.*

take one's life in one's hands [B2] (informal) run a serious risk of being killed. **S:** motorist, pilot, diver □ *It may soon be true to say that you* ***take your life in your hands*** *every time you move into the fast lane of a motorway.* □ *The swimmers are conscious of* ***taking their lives in their hands*** *whenever they venture into these waters.*

take part (in) [B2 emph rel] be involved (in), lend one's support (to). **adj:** some; (not) any/much, no, little; (a) leading, prominent, decisive, useful. **o:** festival, celebrations; demonstration, strike; contest, struggle; supporting sth, achieving sth □ *The Union decided to warn all their shop stewards not to* ***take part in*** *unofficial strikes.* SC □ *They were asked to* ***take*** *a* ***part in*** *organizing the emergency preparations that were gaining momentum.* TBC □ *The Scottish TUC have* ***taken*** *a leading* ***part in*** *efforts to strengthen the economy.* SC

take pride in [B2 pass emph rel] be proud of, draw satisfaction from. **adj:** such, some; (not) any/much, no; little, great, considerable. **o:** work; appearance; achievement, success; being fashionably dressed, looking smart □ *Nurse Ellen sewed beautifully and* ***took*** *great* ***pride in*** *her work.* DC □ *He seems to* ***take*** *a* ***pride in*** *being offensive to everyone he meets.* □ *I can assure you: I* ***take*** *no* ***pride in*** *the way some of our employees have behaved.*

take refuge in [B2 emph rel] use something as a mask, or cover, for embarrassment, inefficiency etc. **o:** daydreams, fantasy; lies, excuses; silence; pretending not to understand □ *Bill, feeling at a disadvantage,* ***took refuge in*** *words.* HAA □ *Mrs Curry* ***took refuge*** *for a moment* ***in*** *licking her little lips.* HAA □ *The fiction that there are 'foreign agitators' wishing to destroy the country, is one* ***in*** *which many governments have* ***taken refuge****.*

take in one's stride [B2 pass] manage a difficult situation without strain. **O:** obstacle, difficulty; examination; setback, failure; mood, temper; (difficult, unfamiliar) person □ *She might not like to be the wife of a factory hand; but to his surprise she* ***took it in her stride****.* AITC □ *This over-response to an emotional situa-*

tion — Dr Clements ***took*** *it all* ***in his stride***. HAHA

take in/into [B1i pass B2 pass] receive into one's house, offer shelter and hospitality to. **O:** child, orphan; vagrant; stray animal. **o:** house, home □ *You've been a good friend to me. You* ***took*** *me* ***in***. TC □ *Several families in the area have* ***taken*** *overseas students* ***into*** *their homes at Christmas.*

take into account/consideration [B2 pass] consider, include in one's study, calculations etc; take account of (q v). **O:** factor, circumstance; pressure, light; view, attitude □ *The third reason why Birkhoff went wrong lies in his failure to* ***take into account*** *some additional complexities.* SNP □ *In this case there are special features to be* ***taken into account***. SC □ *In your proposals you haven't* ***taken into consideration*** *the special needs of old people.*

take into one's confidence [B2 pass] share with sb, confidentially, one's plans, problems etc; confide in (q v). **O:** colleague; staff, workpeople □ *He had contemplated* ***taking*** *Mr Mackay* ***into his confidence****, and asking his advice about his difficult position.* RM □ *Much of the success of the project is due to the fact that the unions were* ***taken into the employers' confidence*** *from the outset.*

take it into one's head that [B2] (informal) form the idea that, reach the conclusion that (esp with the suggestion that one is foolish or ill-informed). **O:** it... that one is being watched, that money was to be made, that the law is one's vocation □ *Somehow he'd* ***taken it into his head that*** *his wife was trying to poison him.* □ *'Try to stop them* ***taking it into their heads that*** *we're planning any big organizational changes.'*

take it into one's head to do sth [B2] (informal) decide to do sth, form the intention of doing sth. **O:** it... to move, change jobs; it... to argue, disagree □ *If I should* ***take it into my head to tell*** *what I had heard, tremendous mischief could result.* AH □ *I watched a troop of little birds, which every so often* ***took it into their heads to move*** *on a few yards.* SPL

take the law into one's own hands [B2] act as a policeman, judge, etc because one believes that the machinery of law is slow or ineffective. **S:** vigilante, Citizens' Defence Committee; (irate, intemperate) citizen □ *Where troops and police have to operate against urban guerrillas, it may be hard to prevent sections of the public* ***taking the law into their own hands***.

take matters into one's own hands [B2] act on one's own behalf when the person responsible does not act for one □ *The headmaster was plainly going to do nothing to ensure my allowance was paid, so I* ***took matters into my own hands*** *and went to see someone at the Education Office.* □ *'Don't* ***take matters into your own hands****: make your application through the usual channels.'*

take account of [B2 pass pass(o) emph rel] include in one's assessment or reckoning of a situation etc; take into account/consideration (q v); pause to check or weigh sth (after activity). **adj:** (not) any/much, no; small, little; careful. **o:** factor, circumstance; speed, light; change, movement; economy, expenditure □ *Have you* ***taken account of*** *possible shifts in demand?* □ *Future movements of population cannot be* ***taken account of***. □ *The time comes for a country to* ***take account of*** *its situation.* BBCTV

take advantage of[1] [B2 pass pass(o) emph rel] use well, properly etc, opportunities which one has at a certain time. **adj:** (not) much/any, no; little; full, ample, proper. **o:** (social) service, benefit, allowance; opening, opportunity □ *The careers master urged boys who were leaving to* ***take*** *full* ***advantage of*** *facilities for further education.* □ *Proper* ***advantage*** *is not being* ***taken of*** *this splendidly equipped sports hall.* □ *The Headmistress hoped that the newly expanded library was fully* ***taken advantage of***.

take advantage of[2] [B2 pass(o)] (informal) use one's strength, or another's weakness, to get what one wants from sb; seduce (a woman) □ *'I don't like people who* ***take advantage of*** *me while my back is turned: hand back the money.'* □ *In flirting with him she had gone to such lengths that three times he had wished to* ***take advantage of*** *her.* SNP □ *'Miss Elliott is much too nice a girl to be* ***taken advantage of*** *by you.'* TT

take care (of) [B2 pass(o)] make sure that sb is well and happy; care for[2] (q v), look after (q v); assume responsibility for making plans, paying bills etc. **adj:** good, proper. **o:** children, elderly relatives; patient, invalid; oneself; bills □ *There had been no accident that afternoon and Guy said, 'Didn't I tell you? Nurse Ellen can* ***take care of*** *herself.'* DC □ *Don't worry about the children while you're away: they'll be* ***taken*** *good* ***care of***. □ *'I haven't been able to book into a hotel yet.' 'That's all right, we've already* ***taken care of*** *all that.'* □ *'I've* ***taken care of*** *the waiter* (i e tipped him).'

take charge (of) [B2 emph rel] assume the leadership of, or responsibility for (sth developing *or* fixed). **S:** officer, executive; agency, ministry. **o:** campaign, project; planning, selling; district, area □ *Eisenhower told me that he wanted me to* ***take*** *complete* ***charge of*** *the land battle.* MFM □ *'Make sure that she's the right type. Someone capable of* ***taking charge of*** *the technical side.'* OMIH ⇨ be in charge (of).

take control (of) [B2 emph rel] assume a position where one manages or regulates the behaviour of sb, or the movement or progress of sth. **S:** teacher, father; pilot, skipper; director, manager. **o:** pupil, child; plane, vessel; operation, situation □ *It's not the easiest task to* ***take control of*** *a class of young children.* □ *Surely she would* ***take control of*** *the situation; after all she was a professional.* OMIH ⇨ be in control (of), have control of/over.

take heed (of) [B2 pass pass(o) emph rel] note sth (and draw from it any lesson it may contain). **adj:** (not) much/any, no; little; proper, sufficient. **o:** warning, threat; portent, sign; advice, recommendation □ *Fog warnings are clearly displayed on motorways, but many drivers still* ***take*** *no* ***heed of*** *them.* □ *No* ***heed*** *was* ***taken of*** *the many reminders sent about his overdue account.* □ *There are indications, and I hope they are* ***taken heed of****, that we are heading for an economic recession.*

take one's leave (of) [B2 rel] (formal) bid farewell (to). **o:** host, guest; country □ *The sound of drums, flutes and rattles heralded the arrival* *of the Fon to* ***take his leave of*** *me.* BB □ *It was going to be very difficult, after such a close working partnership, to* ***take our leave of*** *each other.*

take leave of one's senses [B2] behave in a wild, irrational way □ *'You must have* ***taken leave of your senses*** *to talk to your father in that way!'* □ *'What did you mean by rushing off like that without telling anyone? Had you* ***taken leave of your senses****?'* □ usu perfect tenses.

take note of [B2 pass pass(o) emph rel] note, record; consider, when making a decision or taking action. **o:** factor, circumstances; statement; request, submission; feelings; preference □ *Your remarks have been* ***taken*** *careful* ***note of****, and I hope soon to give a detailed reply to each of them.* □ *The Authority will* ***take note of*** *a teacher's stated preference for one posting rather than another, though it cannot undertake to send every teacher to the school of his first choice.*

take notice (of) [B2 pass pass(o) emph rel] give one's attention to sb or sth. **adj:** some, no, (not) any/much; not... a blind bit of. **o:** him etc; child, parent; advice, comment; appearance, dress □ *Don't* ***take*** *any* ***notice of*** *your friends' criticism or advice.* WI □ *'****Take*** *no* ***notice of*** *him, Nan. To hell with him and what he said to you.'* WI □ *I am angry that so little* ***notice*** *is* ***taken of*** *these warnings.* □ *She's a charming child, but she's never* ***taken*** *any* ***notice of*** *at home.* □ usu neg or interr.

take the/this opportunity (of) [B2 pass] use a favourable chance offered by circumstances to do sth. **adj:** first, earliest. **o:** expressing one's views, challenging his decisions, making good one's escape □ *Mr Nehru may* ***take the opportunity of*** *pointing out* (or: ***take the opportunity*** *to point out) that the effect of China's conduct is to unite Asia, as well as the rest of the world.* SC □ *The Government should* ***take the opportunity of*** *demanding a more forward-looking attitude from the British Transport Commission.* NS □ object is the *-ing* form of a v.

take one's pick (of) [B2 emph rel] ⇨ take one's pick (from/of).

take a poor etc view of [B2 pass emph rel] (informal) regard, consider, in a particular way. **adj:** poor, dim, sombre, pessimistic; optimistic, sanguine, bright. **o:** future; events, circumstances □ *The federation* ***takes a gloomy view of*** *the prospects for the economy in the months to come.* T □ *Most other road-users* ***take a stern view of*** *the private motorist.* SC

take stock (of) [B2] after a period of activity, pause to weigh or assess sth. **adj:** calm, careful; hasty, quick. **o:** supplies, ammunition; situation, position □ *We had been out three days,* ***taking stock of*** *the huts in this valley and making them secure.* BM □ *Dennis* ***took stock of*** *the odds. Though he had been under fire, he had no experience of attack.* ARG

take a/its toll (of) [B2 pass emph rel] damage; reduce the numbers or strength of. **S:** crisis, shortage; fever, malnutrition; bomb, shell; attack. **adj:** severe, serious, heavy. **o:** (small) business, trader; population; armour, transport □ *On the London Stock Exchange, the threat of a credit squeeze has been* ***taking its toll of*** *business.* SC □ *He* (the enemy) *is now being 'written off', and heavy* ***toll*** *is being* ***taken of*** *his divisions by ground and air action.* MFM

take off[1] [B1i pass B2 pass] remove, detach (esp sth fastened to a surface or edge). **O:** fitting; knob, handle, knocker; door; paint. **o:** car; door, window; hinges; wall □ *Before the body of the car can be properly repaired, all the external fittings must be* ***taken off****.* □ *The intense heat* ***took*** *most of the paint* ***off*** *the doors.* ⇨ be off[2], come off[2].

take off[2] [B1i pass B2 pass] remove. **O:** coat, hat; tablecloth, bedspread. **o:** him etc; table, shelf, divan □ *'****Take*** *your shoes* ***off*** *and dry your feet.'* □ *The wardrobe door was shut on the outdoor clothing which someone had* ***taken off*** *her.* DC ⇨ get off[4].

take off[3] [B1i pass] amputate. **O:** limb; leg, toe □ *Gangrene was far advanced, and the leg had to be* ***taken off*** *above the knee.*

take off[4] [B1i pass B2 pass] remove from service. **O:** bus, train. **o:** route, run □ *They've had to* ***take*** *two of the evening buses* ***off*** *this route because of a shortage of crews.* □ *There is no night-flight to Lisbon at this time. The service was* ***taken off*** *at the end of the summer.*

take off[5] [B1i pass B2 pass] transfer to another vessel, rescue. **S:** lifeboat, helicopter. **O:** crew, passenger. **o:** (stranded, shipwrecked) vessel □ *The crew of the tanker which ran aground last night were* ***taken off*** *by helicopter.*

take off[6] [B1i pass B2 pass] ask, order, sb to leave one job (usu to do another). **O:** executive, assistant; journalist; policeman. **o:** job, assignment; case □ *Two detectives have been* ***taken off*** *the inquiry to help with a murder case.* ⇨ come off[7].

take off[7] [B1i pass B2 pass] cause to lose weight. **O:** pounds, stones □ *At the Health Farm they guarantee to* ***take off*** *at least a stone in one course of treatment.* □ *'She's slimming.* ***Taken off*** *pounds.'* BFA □ *'We'll* ***take*** *a bit of surplus weight* ***off*** *you before you finish basic training.'*

take off[8] [B1i pass B2 pass] reduce a price; remove (part of) a tax etc. **O:** £10, fifty pence; tax, levy, surcharge. **o:** price, total; car, washing-machine; import □ *It's not so much a case of what taxes will be* ***taken off*** *in the next Budget as what new taxes will be put on.* □ *There is little prospect of the present levy being* ***taken off*** *betting.* ⇨ come off[8].

take off[9] [B1i pass B2 pass] remove an item from a menu (in a restaurant). **O:** fish, chicken. **o:** menu, bill of fare □ *'We're running low on steak: you'll have to* ***take*** *it* ***off*** *the menu.'* □ *My favourite dish has usually been* ***taken off*** *just before I get to the restaurant.* ⇨ be off[5].

take off[10] [B1ii] have as a break from work, as a holiday. **O:** (a few) days, week, weekend; Easter, Bank Holiday □ *'You need a break. Why not* ***take*** *a fortnight* ***off*** *from work?'* □ *Everyone* ***takes*** *Christmas* ***off****.* FFE

take off[11] [B1i pass B2 pass] withdraw, no longer perform. **O:** production; play, show, opera □ *The play was* ***taken off*** *after libel charges had been laid against its author.*

take off[12] [A1 nom] leave the ground; cause (an aircraft) to leave the ground. **S:** plane, aircraft; pilot; passenger □ *Another lot of tracks showed that the plane had started down the beach on its* ***take-off*** (or: *to* ***take off****).* DS □ *The pilot made a smooth* ***take-off*** (or: ***took off*** *smoothly).* □ *The*

Prime Minister's party ***takes off*** *for Brussels this morning for the next round of talks.* □ *The Government has ordered ten more vertical* ***take-off*** *aircraft* (i e ones which ***take off*** vertically; also known as VTOL (vertical take-off and landing) aircraft; cf also STOL (short take-off and landing) aircraft).

take off[13] [A1 nom] (commerce) begin to improve markedly; begin to show a profit. **S:** economy; sales campaign; product, commodity □ *Following a low-key launch with minimum advertising, the product suddenly* ***took off*** *and had soon captured a quarter of the market.* □ *The Government is clearly reluctant to throttle down* (q v) *expansion now that the economy is reaching its* ***take-off*** *point.*

take off[14] [A1] (informal) move off, leave, hurriedly (e g to keep an appointment) □ *I grabbed my hat and* ***took off*** *for the Town Hall.* TST □ *The moment he saw a police car turn the corner, Bloggs* ***took off*** *in the opposite direction.*

take off[15] [B1i nom pass] (informal) mimic, imitate (esp in an amusing or satirical way). **S:** comedian, satirist. **O:** politician, minister, trades union leader □ *Bill* ***took off*** *Winston Churchill to perfection* (or: *did a perfect* ***take-off*** *of him*).

take the edge off [B2 pass] blunt, lessen, the sharpness or force of. **o:** blade; knife, axe; blow, disappointment, criticism; pleasure; hunger, appetite □ *'If you keep using that chisel as a screwdriver you'll* ***take the edge*** *right* ***off*** *it.'* □ *There won't always be an adoring mother to* ***take the edge off*** *the blows. It's just one of the prices of growing up.* HAA □ *Stocker was half-way through his lunch, and had* ***taken the edge off*** *his appetite sufficiently to talk.* CON

take one's eyes off [B2] stop looking at. **o:** stage, television screen; match, fight; pretty girl □ *If you* ***take your eyes off*** *the dials for one instant, you may miss an important change in temperature.* □ *'That dark girl in the corner—she's lovely. I can't* ***take my eyes off*** *her.'* □ usu neg and with *can/could*.

take the gilt off the gingerbread [B2] (informal) (of bad news or events following upon good) reduce or cancel the pleasant feelings aroused by good news etc □ *It* ***takes the gilt off the gingerbread*** *when you arrive on holiday only to find that the rooms you've booked have been allocated to someone else.* □ *Increased mortgage payments coming on top of a salary rise—that's really* ***taking the gilt off the gingerbread.***

take off sb's hands [B2 pass] (informal) remove from sb (e g by purchase) the expense and responsibility of looking after sb or sth. **O:** daughter, elderly parent; guest; house, car □ *With other girls, he had not cared whether they cheated him or not: it was a relief when another man* ***took*** *them* ***off his hands.*** AITC □ *We've not let a single one of those flats in six months; I should be glad if a buyer* ***took*** *the entire block* ***off our hands.*** ⇨ be off one's hands.

take a load/weight off sb's mind [B2 pass] (informal) relieve sb of his anxiety. **S:** news, announcement; reduction (in cost), cuts (in taxation); escape, rescue. **adj:** great, tremendous □ *It* ***took a load off my mind*** *to know he was alive and well.* □ *A reduction in the interest charged on bank loans* ***took a weight off the minds of*** *many small borrowers.*

take sb's mind/thoughts off [B2 pass] help sb not to think about sth (esp sth worrying or distressing). **o:** himself; accident, illness, bereavement; examination, ordeal; law-suit, trial □ *At least, wondering about Prissie's secret, real or imaginary,* ***took Brigit's mind off*** *herself.* DC □ *He played cards, read, went for a walk—anything to* ***take his thoughts off*** *the decision he knew he must make.* □ *'Let's put the radio on. It might* ***take our minds off*** *the big match.'*

take oneself off [B1ii] (informal) leave, remove oneself (often with the suggestion that one is no longer needed, or in the way) □ *A quarrel was developing between husband and wife: it was high time I* ***took myself off.*** □ *'Now, why don't you* ***take yourself off*** *to the pictures while I try and get through this correspondence?'*

take the smile off one's/sb's face [B2 pass] (informal) make sb suddenly become serious. **S:** (stern) teacher, parent; drill-sergeant; (spectacle, experience of) suffering, hardship □ *'And you can* ***take those smiles off your faces,*** *or I'll take them off for you!'* □ '(You can joke about) *me and my unmarried mothers' hostel. Would you like to come with me one evening? It would* ***take the smile off your face.'*** TT

take the weight off one's feet [B2] (informal) sit down and relax (after tiring work or exercise) □ *'Now here's the most comfortable chair. Sit down and* ***take the weight off your feet.'*** ⇨ get the weight off one's feet/legs.

take years off [B2] (informal) make sb appear younger. **S:** holiday; life abroad; diet, course of treatment, exercise; change of job □ *I never imagined that an outdoor life could do so much for a man: it's* ***taken years off*** *him.* □ *Moving to London may have* ***taken*** *five* ***years off*** *her, but it's put ten years on him.*

take off (to) [B1i pass B3 pass emph rel] lead, accompany, away from one place to another. **O:** family, team, party; friend, relative; suspect, prisoner. **o:** seaside, mountains; France, London; police station □ *The French Master is planning to* ***take*** *a party of boys* ***off to*** *Paris at Easter.* □ *One of the police officers* ***took*** *her* ***off*** *for questioning.* OBS □ *Grandfather greatly resents being* ***taken off to*** *an Old People's Home.* ⇨ go off[1] (q v).

take one's hat off to [B3] (informal) express admiration for (without literally removing one's hat); raise one's hat to (q v). **o:** rescue team, fire brigade; missionary, parish priest, doctor □ *I* ***take my hat off to*** *anyone who is prepared to work underground for long hours.* □ *He was doing important work for very little money, and I* ***took my hat off to*** *him.* □ usu first person; present or past simple tenses.

take on[1] [B1i pass] take on board a ship or aircraft; take aboard (q v). **O:** fuel; stores, provisions; cargo; passengers □ The fuel oil we ***took on*** *at Freetown will be enough to get us to Tilbury.* □ *The pilot refuses to* ***take*** *any more passengers* ***on:*** *he's overweight for take-off as it is.*

take on[2] [B1i pass] employ as staff; enrol as a student or pupil. **O:** staff, personnel; assistant, secretary; trainee, pupil □ *They no longer have to* ***take on*** *large numbers of temporary staff to do the checking.* TES □ *Six candidates were to be* ***taken on*** *for three months' trial, after which* *three of the six would be selected for permanent employment.* SD □ *You come here recommending yourself as an interior decorator, whereupon I* ***take*** *you* ***on****.* TC

take on[3] [B1i pass] undertake, assume, a burden or responsibility. **O:** work; contract, engagement; patient, invalid, problem family □ *He blamed his own weakness for letting her* ***take on*** *too much work.* ASA □ *I'm beginning to regret that I* ***took*** *the job* ***on****; I'm working overtime every evening.* □ *I don't think I want anything more to do with love. Any more. I can't* ***take*** *it* ***on****.* LBA

take on[4] [B1iii] change in appearance, sound, form, meaning etc. **S:** face, body; walk, posture; street, house, garden. **O:** look, appearance; suppleness, elegance; colour, fragrance □ *Now her hair has* ***taken on*** *a healthy shine.* WI □ *Our lives had* ***taken on*** *a certain regularity.* AH □ *In this context the words of Socrates, in the Phaedo,* ***take on*** *a new significance.* HAH

take on[5] [B1i pass] take as one's opponent, tackle. **S:** team; boxer, footballer; government, employer. **O:** tough opponents; a heavier man; union, shop steward □ *In the first round of the FA Cup, several minor league teams will be* ***taking on*** *clubs near the top of the First Division.* □ *A member of the union executive remarked that in* ***taking on*** *the miners the Government was faced with the toughest fight of the present industrial crisis.*

take action (on) [B2 pass emph rel] act so as to achieve an aim, to resolve difficulties etc. **adj:** some; (not) any, no; swift; firm, resolute. **o:** recommendation, proposal; plan; matter, issue □ *The Party would not be able to* ***take action****, in one Parliament,* ***on*** *all the proposals now before the annual Conference.* □ *The Government has promised to* ***take*** *swift* ***action on*** *the energy crisis* (i e to resolve the crisis).

take a chance (on) [B2 emph rel] gamble, run the risk, that sth one hopes for will happen, or that sth unpleasant will be avoided. **o:** his agreeing to pay, his willingness to co-operate; the door being unlocked, the guard being asleep □ *'He'll pay up all right. Anyway, I'm prepared to* ***take a chance on*** *it'.* PE □ *Are you willing to* ***take a chance on*** *the petrol running out before the end of the journey?* □ object is usu the *-ing* form of a v.

take pity on [B2 pass(o) rel] show kindly feeling, or sympathy, for. **adj:** (not) any/much, no; (very) little, great. **o:** poor, hungry, homeless, deprived (persons) □ *She was so vexed with curiosity, that Virginia* ***took pity on*** *her and restored her peace of mind.* AITC □ *She would bring into the house stray animals* ***on*** *whom she had* ***taken pity****.*

take (right) on the chin [B2 pass] (informal) receive a blow in a sensitive and vulnerable place (lit or fig); receive a hard blow without flinching or complaining. **O:** blow, punch, knock; it □ *He felt dazed and groggy, like a boxer who has* ***taken*** *a hard one* ***on the chin****.* PE *Our industry has* ***taken*** *a few nasty ones* ***on the chin*** *since the new financial controls were introduced.* □ *He must have felt acutely disappointed when his job went to another man, but he never said a word: he* ***took*** *it* ***right on the chin****.*

take on (so) [A1] (informal) express strong feelings, esp of sorrow or displeasure □ *'Poor darling, you mustn't* ***take on so****. You don't see it now, but it* (his mistress's death) *was all for the best.'* RATT □ *'It's no good your* ***taking on****, because the matter's settled, signed and sealed.'* PW

take on trust [B2 pass] assume that sb may be trusted; assume that sth one reads or hears is reliable. **O:** him etc; statement, claim, version of the facts, report □ *'Sarah* ***takes*** *everyone* ***on trust****, just like you do. Nicky is more like me.'* DC □ *You don't have to* ***take*** *everything he says* ***on trust****. Do a little checking up occasionally.* □ *He's wrong if he thinks a teacher's report on a child is to be* ***taken*** *more or less* ***on trust****.*

take on (at) [B1i pass B3 pass] accept as an opponent (esp in a sporting contest). **O:** anybody, everybody; the (whole) world; champion, record-holder. **o:** billiards, darts, chess □ *With that amount of liquor in him he felt fit to* ***take on*** *the whole territory.* BM □ *You can't expect to* ***take*** *a professional* ***on at*** *tennis the first time you go out on the court.*

take revenge (on) (for) [B2 emph rel] act against sb in return for some injury (real or imagined) which one has suffered from him; revenge (oneself) on (q v). **o:** (*for*) offence, crime, injury; murder; insult, slight □ *To* ***take revenge for*** *acts of revenge was merely to extend the horror and call it justice.* ARG □ *The Medici* ***took revenge on*** *the Pazzi family by slaughtering as many as they could find and forcing the rest into exile.*

take a (firm) stand (on/over) [B2 pass emph rel] behave in a firm, unyielding way over some issue. **S:** government, minister; employer, trades union; teacher, coach. **o:** question, matter, issue (of); inflation, incomes policy; productivity, redundancy; indiscipline, slackness □ *The Government is forced to* ***take a firm stand on*** *the cost of living issue.* □ ***Over*** *whether shipping can move freely through these waterways we shall of course* ***take a*** *very* ***firm stand****.*

take a (firm) grip/hold on/upon oneself [B2] (informal) control oneself, calm oneself, in a difficult situation □ *'Now let's just* ***take a firm grip on ourselves****. I know the car's stuck in the mud, but we should be able to get it out again.'* □ *Miss Murphy* ***took a hold upon herself*** *and tried to think. The thing to do was to stop someone. There did not seem to be any pedestrians. But there were cars.* ARG

take out[1] [B1i pass] obtain, by payment, a document that will ensure some kind of service in the future. **O:** subscription (to a journal); (personal, vehicle) insurance; (dog, driving) licence; permit □ *It's now more expensive, because of postal costs, to* ***take out*** *an annual subscription than to buy the periodical from a newsagent.* □ *Road-fund licences may be* ***taken out*** *for four months or a whole year.*

take out[2] [B1i pass] (military) destroy, neutralize. **S:** artillery, rockets; tank, aircraft. **O:** strongpoint, pillbox □ *Had the initiative been Israel's, the Air Force would have spent the first 48 hours or so attacking airfields and* ***taking out*** *the missile screens.* OBS

take out[3] [B1i nom pass] buy from a special restaurant cooked dishes for consumption at home. ⇨ take away/out.

take out (against) [B1iii pass B3 pass] (legal)

issue a document calling upon sb to appear in court. **S:** police; injured party. **O:** ⚠ a writ, summons, petition □ *The police have decided to* ***take out*** *a summons* ***against*** *the drivers of both cars involved in the accident.*

take out (for/to) [B1ii pass B3 pass] conduct, accompany, sb somewhere for exercise or recreation. **O:** wife, child; girlfriend; school party; dog. **o:** (*for*) drive, walk, ride; (*to*) cinema, theatre □ *'I thought the nurse was looking after you.' 'No, she* ***took*** *the children* ***out*** *this afternoon.'* DC □ *I'll* ***take*** *her* ***out to*** *the pictures.* AH □ ***'Take*** *the dog* ***out for*** *a walk: he needs the exercise.'* ⇨ be out (at); come/go out (for/to).

take it out in [B3 pass] (informal) be given goods etc to the value of money which one is owed. **o:** goods; trading stamps, vouchers; savings certificates □ *When I returned the appliance, the manager would not refund the cost, but he did let me* ***take it out in*** *vouchers redeemable at the shop.*

take out/out of[1] [B1i pass B2 pass] lead sb, or carry sth, from a place. **O:** child; animal, pet; chair, carpet; car. **o:** house, room; garage □ *'Will you* ***take*** *this dog* ***out*** *at once? It's chewing the carpet.'* □ *As danger threatened, young children were* ***taken out*** *of the major cities and into the country.* ⇨ be out/out of[1], bring out/out of, come out/out of[1], get out/out of[1].

take out/out of[2] [B1i pass B2 pass] withdraw, extract sth, from an inner or enclosed space. **O:** nail, screw; tooth; cup, plate; money. **o:** wall; gum; cupboard; bank, safe □ *Then she unbuttoned her navy-blue coat, and* ***took out*** *the ball from the pocket.* TT □ *I* ***took out*** *a packet of cigarettes and offered the man one.* CON □ *Cash was* ***taken out of*** *my account without my knowledge.* ⇨ be out/out of[2], come out/out of[2], get out/out of[2].

take the easy etc way out/out of [B1ii B2] (informal) escape from a difficult situation by a simple, painless course. **adj:** ⚠ easy, simplest, quickest, coward's. **o:** difficulty, dilemma, crisis □ *As the embarrassment of the guests deepened, he* ***took the quick way out*** *by offering them all another drink.* □ *'This is not a situation you can* ***take the easy way out of.*** *You'll have to explain the whole thing and pray he's in a good mood.'*

take out of [B2 pass] deduct a sum of money owed, a debt incurred etc, from a particular source. **O:** cost; breakages; subscription, donation. **o:** expense account; pay, wages, salary □ *'Don't you pay for the meal.* ***Take*** *it* ***out of*** *this* (ie a £5 note).' □ *Contributions to a pension scheme are* ***taken out of*** *a teacher's monthly salary.*

take out of sb's hands [B2 pass] remove from sb the responsibility for dealing with sth. **O:** matter, issue; responsibility; job, task; inquiry, investigation □ *'I shall have to make a report to my office. Then if you don't co-operate, it'll be* ***taken out of my hands.'*** DBM □ *As matters are developing, the CID will step in and* ***take*** *the inquiry* ***out of our hands.***

take sb out of himself [B2 pass] (informal) make sb forget his worries, problems etc. **S:** change (of scene), holiday; companionship, party □ *One of the things about a surprise or shock is that it is said to* ***take one out of oneself.*** SML □ *The experience meant an enlargement of the spirit that would* ***take her out of*** *and above* ***herself.*** PW

take it/a lot out of [B2] (informal) make sb physically or nervously tired. **S:** nursing, teaching; domestic crisis, accident □ *Keeping on the alert* ***took it out of*** *him.* ILIH □ *Getting turned down in marriage must have* ***taken a lot out of*** *you.* SML

take a leaf out of sb's book [B2 pass] copy sb else, base one's conduct on what he does □ *The new teacher* ***took a leaf out of his colleague's book.*** *Instead of teaching anything fresh, he asked the boys to do silent revision.*

take the mickey/piss (out of) [B2 pass] (slang/taboo) mock, ridicule, sb (in the hope, or with the effect, of irritating him) □ *Larrie's face flushed and his eyes blazed. 'You're not going to* ***take the mickey out of*** *me,' he cried.* ASA □ *I can see perfectly well that you are trying to* ***take the piss out of*** *me. Only it won't work.* CON □ *Every time the new teacher walks into a classroom he gets* ***the mickey taken out of*** *him.* □ the passive is usu formed with *have* or *get*.

take a/the rise out of [B2 pass] (informal) chaff, make fun of, sb, with the aim of irritating him. **o:** brother, friend, colleague □ *'He didn't seriously mean that you were a bad driver: he was just trying to* ***take the rise out of*** *you!'* □ *'If there's one thing I can't stand, it's having* ***the rise taken out of*** *me by a pipsqueak like you!'* □ the passive is usu formed with *have* or *get*.

take the sting out of [B2 pass] (informal) make sth seem more pleasant or bearable. **S:** kindness, sympathy; (pleasant) manner, tone. **o:** disappointment, setback; reproach, criticism □ *Once you've resigned yourself to marriage you can* ***take*** *a lot of* ***the sting out of*** *it by grabbing one of the really good girls as she comes past.* TGLY □ *The smile which accompanied it* ***took the sting out of*** *the reproof.* RATT ⇨ go out of[1].

take the wind out of sb's sails [B2 pass] (informal) disturb sb's balance or self-confidence; humble an overconfident or pompous person □ *To hear an ordinary member of the public criticize his policies so effectively* ***took the wind*** *right* ***out of the Minister's sails.*** □ ***The wind*** *was* ***taken out of his sails*** *by her remark, but he collected himself sufficiently to ask: 'And may I call you Irma?'* PW

take out on [B3 pass] (informal) make sb else the scapegoat for sth one has done or suffered; work off (against/on) (q v). **O:** it, things; one's disappointment, frustration, irritation. **o:** wife, child; dog □ *Feeling obscurely that she had better not* ***take*** *things* ***out on*** *Mrs Jones, she decided to* ***take*** *them* ***out on*** *Daniel.* US □ *'I know how you must be feeling, but there's no need to* ***take*** *your resentment* ***out on me.'***

take out (to) [B1ii pass B3 pass] ⇨ take out (for/to).

take (over) [B2 pass emph rel] spend a certain length of time in doing sth. **O:** ⚠ too long, a long time, ages. **o:** job, task; meal □ *Would his work on the doctorate ever come to an end? He had already* ***taken*** *three years* ***over*** *it.* □ *'Make your phone call, but don't* ***take*** *too long* ***over*** *it.'* ⇨ be over[3].

take over [A1 B1i nom pass] (commerce,

industry) acquire control of a firm, esp by obtaining the support of a majority of its shareholders. **O:** business, company □ *A London publisher is bidding to **take over** (or: is making a **take-over** bid for) an important national newspaper.* □ *British industry should give as much status to the scientist as it does to the **take-over** bidder and advertising manager.* T □ *The City pages are full of news of company mergers and **take-overs**.*

ake a (firm) stand over [B2 pass emph rel] ⇨ take a (firm) stand on/over.

ake pains/trouble over [B2 pass emph rel] show diligent care in performing, completing, a task. **adj:** some, such; (not) any, no; great, considerable, enormous. **o:** arrangement, organization; project, essay; plan, drawing; finishing, preparing (sth) □ *It's worth **taking** some **trouble over** getting the two sections perfectly aligned.* □ *He enjoyed the assembling and painting best. **Over** that part he'd really **taken** great **pains**.* □ to take pains over sth is to *be painstaking about* it.

ake one's time (over) [B2] (informal) not be in a hurry (to do sth), do sth at a leisurely pace. **o:** meal, drink; bath; getting ready to leave, finishing one's work □ *I **took my time over** this book, with the result that I was able to shape it exactly as I wanted it.* AH □ *'You **took your time** coming back from Vienna, Middleton,' said Sir Edgar gruffly* (cf *'You **took your time over** the journey'*). ASA

take over (from) [A1 A3 pass rel B1iii pass B3 pass rel] assume the direction or control of sth, in place of sb else. **S:** (new, younger) man; pilot, skipper; specialist, expert; runner, car. **O:** management, direction; controls, helm; case, inquiry; lead, first place. **o:** (retiring) director; crew member; assistant; competitor □ [A1] *Some fellow has suddenly been taken ill, and I've got to **take over**.* WI □ [A3] *Prissie was saying that she could **take over** very well **from** Nurse Ellen.* DC □ [B1] *My father was asked to **take over** the London office of his newspaper.* SD □ [B3] *30 Corps had now **taken over** the lead **from** 10 Corps.* MFM

take over (to) [B1i pass B3 pass] conduct, convey sb, carry sth, to a place in another part of a large town etc, or across intervening water. **O:** family; passenger, fare; goods. **o:** one's parents' house; park, swimming pool, shops; island, mainland □ *I was thinking of **taking** the children **over to** my mother's this weekend.* □ *Prissie has **taken** them **over to** Harrods to shop.* DC □ *'Ask the boatman what he charges to **take** passengers **over to** the island.'* ⇨ go over (to).

take round [B1i pass B2 pass] conduct sb on a tour of. **O:** visitor; delegate, customer. **o:** building; college, factory □ *When you arrive inside the gate an official guide is waiting to **take** you **round**.* □ *The Press Secretary is **taking** a Chinese delegation **round** the University this afternoon.* ⇨ go round².

take the hat round [B1i pass] (informal) collect money (e g at work, for sb who is sick etc); pass the hat round (q v) □ *The miners' leaders appealed from the platform for contributions to the strike fund and a couple of stewards **took the hat round**.*

take round (with) [B1i pass B3 pass] ⇨ take around/round (with).

take through [B2 pass] read sth with sb, repeat it to him, so that its accuracy can be checked; (theatre) help sb to rehearse a scene etc. **S:** detective, official; director. **o:** story, statement; argument; scene, text □ *'Now, I'll just **take** you **through** your application for benefit, to check the details, and then you can sign at the bottom.'* □ *'I want to **take** you **through** your scene with Sheila again. There are one or two things that are not quite right.'* ⇨ go through⁵.

take to¹ [A2] go away to a place, esp to escape from an enemy. **S:** population; townspeople, villagers; guerrillas. **o:** hills, mountains; woods, forests □ *He was Caodist Chief of Staff, but he's **taken to** the hills to fight both sides, the French and the Communists.* QA □ *As the enemy advance continued, whole families would **take to** the forests carrying all their belongings.*

take to² [A2] adopt as a habit, practice, pastime etc. **o:** drink(ing), drugs, smoking (a pipe); interrupting, waving one's hands; golf, bowls □ *Some men would go off their heads. Others'd **take to** drink. My form of escapism is to roar at politicians.* TBC □ *As Harold became more an acquaintance, almost a stranger, Isabel **took to** noticing him more.* PW

take to³ [A2 pass] (informal) form a liking for sb or sth. **o:** newcomer, visitor; place, house. **A:** right away, quickly, instantly □ *It was embarrassing if the mother did not **take to** you. It looked as though it were your fault.* AITC □ *I **took to** him immediately.* SML □ *As Robert had reached the age of forty-four without getting married, it was obvious that he was not the sort of man who **takes to** matrimony like a duck to water.* SML

take to (one's) bed [A2] go to bed, esp to recover from an illness □ *Half the boys in the form had **taken to their beds** with streaming colds.* □ *If everybody with a disordered metabolism **took to bed** it would never do.* AH

take to bits/pieces [B2 pass] reduce a complex machine etc to the parts which make it up; take apart ¹ (q v). **O:** car; motor, gearbox, dynamo; radio, television; clock □ *The gas-fitter **took** the stove **to pieces** before Virginia had a chance to cook supper.* AITC □ *He's **taken** the record-player **to bits**. The question is: can he put it together again?*

take to one's bosom [B2 pass] (fig, jocular) embrace, draw affectionately to oneself. **O:** (the) poor, needy, homeless □ *Did he cherish wart-hogs and dote on hyenas, did he **take** the skunk **to his bosom**?* AH □ *His Italian listeners were **taken to his bosom**, and their hearts beat with his.* SD

take to court [B2 pass] (legal) begin legal proceedings against sb (leading to a court action). **O:** dealer, tradesman; case □ *If you have agreed specifications with the builder which he fails to carry out, you can **take** him **to court**.* TO □ *'You can **take** me **to court** if you want to. There's nothing in writing.'* DM

take exception to [B2 pass pass(o) emph rel] be much offended by. **adj:** grave, serious, strong. **o:** remark, statement; smear, innuendo; accusation, charge □ *This remarkable gift made us nickname her Dormouse, a name that she **took** grave **exception to**, but which nevertheless stuck.* DF □ *We in Obaig **take** strong **excep-***

***tion to** the attack on Mr Mackay made by your anonymous correspondent.* RM □ *The strongest **exception** is **taken to** the suggestion that our actions were politically motivated.*

take a fancy to [B2] (informal) form a liking for, be attracted by, sb or sth. **adj:** big, great; decided. **o:** girl, man; house, ornament, car □ *'I met this young man in the train, and I've **taken a** big **fancy to** him already.'* HD □ *There's this new kind of pocket transistor set that I've rather **taken a fancy to**.*

take to heart [B2 pass] be greatly affected in one's feelings by sth. **O:** disappointment, setback, loss; things; it, everything. **A:** very much, too much, so □ *'Come now, we have been through much together. Do not **take** a little incident so much **to heart**.'* ARG □ *The reader should not **take** it too much **to heart** if he finds that he gives 20 or more 'yes' answers* (to the questionnaire). SNP

take to one's heart [B2 pass] (informal) give a warm, enthusiastic reception to, show affection for. **S:** crowd, audience; staff, membership. **O:** actor, comedian; (new) director, leader □ *It was when the Liberal candidate began to talk about local problems, in language that the farmers could understand, that they **took** him **to their hearts**.* □ *The public, bless them, **took** me **to their hearts**, right from the first.* HD

take to one's heels [A2] flee, run away. **S:** (shy, nervous) child, girl; animal □ *Then I doubled back into Welbeck Street and **took to my heels**.* UTN □ *A few of the antelope caught our scent, and in a matter of seconds the whole herd had **taken to their heels**.*

take to one side [B2 pass] ⇨ take aside/to one side.

take a shine to [B2] (slang) come to like, be attracted to. **o:** stranger, visitor; girl, fellow □ *In prison, a likeable rascal called Sammy **took a shine to** him.* DS □ *He was a susceptible fellow, **taking a shine to** every pretty face or neat figure that he saw.*

take to task [B2 pass] criticize, reprimand, sb for an error, failure etc. **O:** colleague, assistant; child, pupil □ *We were sure that the gate had been left unlocked. We would **take** the night-watchman **to task** over it.* □ *The Minister was **taken** severely **to task** about his decision to close uneconomic railway lines.*

take under one's wing [B2 pass] behave protectively towards sb, act as his patron or mentor. **S:** (older, more experienced) teacher, worker, sportsman. **O:** newcomer, novice □ *The Bannions were resident in Portugal and had evidently **taken** the Marchants **under their wing**.* ILIH □ *He took care to bring Ned into the conversation a good deal. But here he ran into another problem; Ned didn't need to be **taken under anybody's wing**.* CON

take up[1] [B1i pass] lift, raise. **O:** pen, book; carpet, floorboard □ *The electricians had to **take up** the skirting board to lay new electric wires.* □ *She was expecting that Brigit, like the young man in the Bible, would **take up** her bed and walk.* DC

take up[2] [B1i pass] absorb, soak up[1] (q v). **S:** sponge, flannel; blotting-paper. **O:** liquid; milk, ink □ *The cloth is saturated: it can't **take up** any more of the liquid.*

take up[3] [B1iii pass] adopt as a pastime. **O:** gardening, golf, stamp-collecting □ *I should have **taken up** singing — everybody used to tell me so.* TOH □ *Why not **take up** some outdoor sport as a relaxation from office work?*

take up[4] [B1iii pass] start a job, begin work. **O:** office, employment, one's duties □ *I would be required on **taking up** my duties in Whitehall to give my views and assist in making decisions.* MFM □ *Charley threw up his job to **take up** more respectable, more sensible employment.* BFA

take up[5] [B1i pass] adopt as a protégé, patronize. **S:** impresario, actor-manager, conductor. **O:** (promising, young) singer, actor, soloist □ *A young actor will find it hard to make his way on the London stage unless he is exceptionally talented or has someone established to **take** him **up**.*

take up[6] [B1i pass] join in, add one's voice to. **O:** song, chant; chorus, refrain □ *It was Pop who started the song, and everyone **took** it **up** in shrill voices.* DBM □ *Someone started to sing 'For he's a jolly good fellow,' and the chorus was **taken up** by all the others.* PE

take up[7] [B1iii pass] continue a story which has been interrupted, or left unfinished by someone else; pick up[15] (q v). **O:** tale, story; (narrative) thread □ *He **takes up** the tale at the outbreak of war in 1939.* NM □ *We were back at our posts again and Ned was **taking up** the thread. Even Randall was listening.* CON

take up[8] [B1i pass] raise, mention, a topic in order to consider or discuss it. **O:** question, matter, issue, point □ *Much in the story has interesting parallels to the present time. I shall not **take** these **up**, however.* SNP □ *There are one or two points of detail that should be **taken up** before we move on.*

take up[9] [B1ii pass] interrupt sb in order to disagree or criticize him. **A:** sharply, short □ *'I wonder if you'll find them likeable?' 'What's the difference?' he **took** me **up** sharply.* CON □ *'Not hungry?' the old man **took** him **up**. 'Are you ill or something?'*

take up[10] [B1i pass] occupy, fill. **S:** desk, cupboard; work, study; question, matter. **O:** space, room; time, hours; attention □ *'How can you move about in here? The bed **takes up** half the room.'* □ *Some very important issue was **taking up** all his attention.* CON

take up[11] [A1 nom B1iii nom pass] gather onto itself, by winding, a long thread or ribbon. **S:** spool, bobbin. **O:** thread; cotton, silk; (magnetic) tape, film □ *The spool on my tape recorder isn't **taking up** very well: the tape's spiralling all over the floor.* □ *The reel which **takes up** the film after it has been projected* (i e *the **take-up** reel), is below and behind the lamp.*

take up the challenge [B1iii pass] accept a challenge. **S:** runner, boxer, golfer; industry, trade □ *As one athlete after another **took up the challenge** of the front-runners, the pattern of the 5000 metres race was constantly changing.* □ *Some sections of the motor industry are complacent about the increase in foreign imports. **the challenge** is not being **taken up**.*

take up a position [B1iii pass] (esp military) occupy ground suitable for defence, or from which an attack could be made; adopt an attitude or line of argument. **S:** general; army, force;

speaker, advocate □ *The evening before the battle, Wellington* **took up a** *defensive* **position** *along, and to the rear of, a long ridge.* □ *'Now, while the fieldsmen are* **taking up their positions** *for the left-hander, I'll bring you up to date on the score-card.'* □ *'Sit back and I'll talk you out of* **any position** *you've decided to* **take up**.*'* CON

take up residence [B1iii] (formal) begin to live somewhere. **A:** overseas, in the country, at the palace □ *For part of the year, the Queen* **takes up residence** *at Sandringham.* □ *Snakes sometimes* **take up residence** *in the disused portions of the nest.* DF

take up the slack [B1iii pass] straighten a sagging rope; (industry) make men and plant which are now idle or under-used active and productive again. **S:** crewman; climber; industry; government, ministry; policy, decision □ *As the yacht tacked to gain full advantage of the change of wind, the crew stood by their stations ready to* **take up the slack** *in the ropes.* □ *Such a move would* **take up the slack** *which now exists in our economy.* BBCTV □ *There's a good deal of* **slack** *to be* **taken up** *before we have reached full productive capacity.*

take up arms (against) [B1iii B3 emph rel] go to war (with), begin to fight (against). **S:** nation, power; minority, peasantry. **o:** neighbour, invader; oppressor, tyrant □ *His people and the Emperor Charles would* **take up arms against** *him if he killed either the woman or her daughter.* WI □ *The country would certainly* **take up arms** *in its own defence.*

take up on [B3 pass] (informal) get sb to prove or confirm sth which he has claimed or offered. **o:** it, that; claim, boast; offer □ *'What's more I can drink as much beer as you.' 'I'll* **take** *you* **up on** *that.'* RATT □ *The insurance company guarantees to replace any parts of the car which are stolen: you should* **take** *them* **up on** *their guarantee.*

take up with[1] [B3 pass rel] raise a matter, for critical comment, with the person(s) most involved or responsible. **O:** issue, question, matter, problem. **o:** authorities; manager, shopkeeper; official, teacher □ *I* **took** *the matter* **up** *at once* **with** *M Coulet, and was informed that he had received no complaint.* MFM □ *My son is being given too much homework; I shall* **take** *things* **up with** *his form-master.*

take up with[2] [A3] (informal) begin to keep company with (sb one should perhaps avoid). **o:** crank, reprobate, half-wit; (disreputable) man, woman; gang, set □ *His conventional parents were alarmed to find that he had* **taken up with** *a group of 'long-haired anarchists'.* □ *She's* **taken up with** *a man old enough to be her father.*

take a (firm) grip/hold upon oneself [B2] ⇨ take a (firm) grip/hold on/upon oneself.

take liberties (with) [B2 pass] (informal) behave in an over-familiar or presumptuous way (towards sb); handle too freely sth that belongs to, or has been made by, sb else. **adj:** such, many; (not) any, no; few; great. **o:** sb's sister, wife; one's friend, colleague; (original) work; text, score □ *'Don't start* **taking liberties with** *my old mother, let's have a bit of respect.'* TC □ *Cane Rats would not hesitate to bury their large incisors in your hand if you tried to* **take liberties with** *them.* BB □ *The film was a largely successful adaptation of the stage play, though there were times when one felt that the scriptwriter had* **taken** *rather too many* **liberties with** *the original text.*

take the rough with the smooth [B2 pass] (informal) accept adversity along with good fortune □ *If you want to enjoy the pleasure of living far from the madding crowd* (i e far from cities) *you have to* **take the rough with the smooth**. RM □ *She knew what the future would be like, and how different it would be from what she had hoped. She must learn to* **take the rough with the smooth**, *just like everybody else.* TGLY

take turns (with) [B2] share a task with sb, working turn and turn about. **o:** (messy, unpleasant, tiring) job, chore; cleaning, washing; supervision, checking; keeping watch, steering □ *We drove to the South of France in a day,* **taking turns with** *the driving.* □ *Some working-class husbands will share the washing-up if their wives go out to work, or will* **take turns with** *the baby if their job releases them early and not too tired.* UL

talk about[1] [A2 pass adj rel] discuss, exchange thoughts about; speak about (q v), talk of[1] (q v). **o:** weather; trade, business; family □ *He brought out a bottle of whisky, and began to* **talk about** *old times.* SPL □ *The road-accident rate is a much* **talked-about** *topic; but how much good does talking do?*

talk about[2] [A2 pass adj rel] discuss in an inquisitive, slightly shocked way. **S:** newspapers, gossip writers, fans. **o:** clothes, car; love life, affair □ *'Why must she go about with that dreadful man? She's beginning to get herself* **talked about**.*'* □ *What has made our new, candid series for adult readers the most* **talked-about** *event in Fleet Street?*

talk about[3] [A2 pass rel] propose, consider, a possible course of action (though usu without acting in fact); talk of[2] (q v). **o:** going to live abroad, buying a larger house, decorating the kitchen □ *'Of course, for years they'd* **talked about** *moving to the country, getting away from the stress of city life, but nothing ever came of all the talk.'*

talk about[4] [A2] (informal) an idiom which humorously reinforces or underlines a statement, either by exaggeration (first example) or by apparently denying what one has just said (second example) □ *At the first sign of trouble, my old headmaster used to haul boys into his study for a good caning —* **talk about** *a Reign of Terror!* (i e he ruled through the fear of punishment). □ *First the Government promises to reduce prices, then it gives way to inflationary wage demands —* **talk about** *consistency!* (i e the Government is not consistent).

talk above/over sb's head [A2] (informal) talk of matters, or in a way, that others cannot understand. **S:** specialist, expert; lecturer, teacher □ *The lecture was highly technical — the man was* **talking** *way* **above our heads** *for most of the time.* □ *If only he had lived up to his philosophy of life, they would not have minded his* **talking over their heads**. HAA

talk at [A2 pass] (informal) address sb as though he were an object, or an audience, instead of an individual. **S:** self-important bore, pompous ass □ *'Don't* ***talk at*** *me, talk to me: you're not in the classroom now!'* □ *There we were, being* ***talked at*** *for two hours by the great man, and quite unable to escape.*

talk back [A1 nom] reply, answer. **S:** audience, reader, listener □ *This weekly programme gives viewers the chance to* ***talk back*** *to producers on aspects of broadcasting that displease them.* □ *His self-confident fluency left her no room to* ***talk back.*** □ 'Talk-back' is the name of a BBC television programme in which viewers are able to talk back.

talk down [B1ii pass] (aeronautics) bring a plane in to land by giving the pilot instructions over the radio. **S:** control tower, air traffic control. **O:** aircraft; pilot □ *There is a particular need to* ***talk*** *aircraft* ***down*** *when visibility is poor or when several pilots are waiting to land.*

talk down (to) [A1 A3 pass] (informal) address sb as though he were a social or intellectual inferior. **S:** (office) manager, (shop) assistant, house agent; lecturer. **o:** customer, client; audience, class □ *'Credit the child with some intelligence; try to avoid* ***talking down.****'* □ *Whatever their technical knowledge may be, adult students have a good deal of practical experience: they greatly resent being* ***talked down to.***

talk into [B2 pass] by talking, persuade sb to do sth. **O:** (prospective) buyer, member, recruit. **o:** selling, joining, signing on; membership, participation □ *'I know you've got a smooth tongue, so don't even start to* ***talk*** *me* ***into*** *buying.'* □ *He had better see the lawyer before anyone could say he had been* ***talked into*** *anything.* NM

talk of[1] [A2 pass adj rel] discuss, exchange thoughts about; speak about (q v), talk about[1] (q v). **o:** weather; business; crisis, disaster; this and that □ *For weeks, the BBC's correspondents in the United States could* ***talk of*** *little else except the Watergate hearings.* □ *At the time, he was very much* ***talked of*** *as a likely contender for the Presidency.*

talk of[2] [A2 pass adj] consider, discuss, a possible plan of action (though usu without following it); talk about[3] (q v). **o:** giving up one's job, emigrating to Canada, getting a divorce □ *At one stage he* ***talked of*** *throwing up his job in advertising — but nothing much came of it.* □ *Then there was the much* ***talked-of*** *plan to open a travel agency.*

talk one's/sb's head off [B1ii] (informal) speak at great length; tire or irritate sb by speaking to him at great length □ *'Don't expect me to sit here like a good boy while Smithers is up there* ***talking his*** *fat* ***head off!'*** □ (a child is speaking) *'When me and Jeremy are by ourselves, he talks, he talks, he* ***talks my head off.****'* PW

talk the hind leg(s) off a donkey [B2] (informal) (be able to) talk endlessly □ *He would obviously do very well in politics — he could* ***talk the hind legs off a donkey.*** □ *I dried her tears and exercised an old man's privilege of* ***talking the hind leg off a donkey.*** DIL

talk out of [B2 pass] by discussion, argument etc, persuade sb not to do sth. **S:** adviser, agent; colleague; wife. **o:** buying, selling; resigning, leaving; (hasty) decision □ *It's my own decision entirely. In fact, she's just been trying to* ***talk*** *me* ***out of*** *it.* LBA □ *He's rather impulsive, but he can sometimes be* ***talked out of*** *making over-hasty moves.*

talk over sb's head [A2] ⇨ talk above/over sb's head.

talk over (with) [B1ii pass B3 pass emph rel] discuss sth fully (with sb). **O:** things, the (whole) thing; matter, question; project, scheme □ *I would suggest a line that you may care to consider and* ***talk over*** *at our next appointment.* RFW □ *He* ***talked*** *things* ***over with*** *his wife* (or: *He and his wife* ***talked*** *things* ***over.***) DS

talk round[1] [B1ii pass] persuade sb to do sth (to which he was at first opposed). **O:** partner, colleague, associate □ *He thought he could* ***talk*** *me* ***round*** *like last time, when he had me voting for some candidate who refused to stand.* ART □ *He's not the easiest man to win over; he'll need some* ***talking round.***

talk round[2] [A2 pass] in conversation, avoid approaching a subject directly (e g through shyness, the wish to keep sth secret etc). **o:** subject, topic; issue, problem □ *'Don't try to put me off this time. I don't want to* ***talk round*** *the subject, I want to talk* about *it.'* □ *'With him, you never get a direct discussion of the point that's bothering you. He'll always* ***talk round*** *it.'*

talk through [B1i nom pass B2 pass] (theatre, cinema, TV) during rehearsal, guide sb through the movements he must make. **S:** director, floor manager. **O:** cast, actor. **o:** scene; bit □ *'Stay on stage for a minute — I want to* ***talk*** *Mary* ***through*** *her scene with Bill.'* □ *After a few* ***talk-throughs,*** *a few rehearsals, she said, 'Let's make it an equal concert'* (i e one with two performers appearing together). BBCR

talk to[1] [A2 pass rel] address, speak to[1] (q v), to give or exchange news, gossip etc. **o:** friend, neighbour; oneself □ *She always complains that there's nobody living near that she can* ***talk to.*** □ *'I've called to* ***talk to*** *you about our latest product.'* □ *Sarah is struggling to fill out an official form — she* ***talks*** *a lot* ***to*** *herself.* CSWB

talk to[2] [A2 pass] reproach, scold; speak to[2] (q v). **o:** child, pupil; tradesman, workman □ *'There's something the matter with this television. I'll have to* ***talk to*** *the shop about it.'* □ *'That child needs to be* ***talked to,*** *and you're the person to do it.'* □ *He jumped from his chair, arms akimbo as though to deliver him a* ***talking-to.*** ASA □ note the nom form in: *give sb/get a (good)* talking-to.

tally (with) [A2 emph rel] match, correspond (to/with) (q v). **S:** figure, sum; account, version □ *You'll be hard put to it to make this set of figures* ***tally with*** *that* (cf *make the two sets* ***tally***). □ *'What you are now saying does not quite* ***tally with*** *your statement to the police officer.'*

tamp down [B1i pass adj] drive sth down (so that it is firmly packed) with repeated light blows. **O:** tobacco; packing, wadding □ *Unless the tobacco is well* ***tamped down*** *in the pipe it will burn too quickly.*

tamper with [A2 pass adj] handle sth which is not one's concern (so breaking or disturbing it). **o:** paper, document, letter; catch, lock, hinge; wiring, plumbing □ *Don't let an untrained person* ***tamper with*** *the electrical circuits.* □ *'You can see someone has tried to break into the flat;*

the lock's been ***tampered with****.'*

angle with [A2] (informal) come into conflict with, be involved in a dispute with. **S:** striker, demonstrator, marcher; consumer, customer. **o:** police, troops; supplier, manufacturer □ *'Don't try and* ***tangle with*** *him — he's bigger and tougher than you.'* □ *This is not the first time he's* ***tangled with*** *the Gas Board over excessive charges.*

ank up [A1 B1i pass adj] (slang) (make sb) drink a great deal of alcohol □ *A couple of the fellows were already at the bar,* ***tanking up*** *on lager.* □ *'Now don't for heaven's sake get me* ***tanked up****. Remember I've got to drive home.'*

ap (for) [B2 pass] (informal) (try to) extract sth from sb. **O:** friend, parent, employer. **o:** money; donation, loan; advice, information □ *I managed to* ***tap*** *father* ***for*** *a few pounds towards our holiday fund.* □ *'You could try* ***tapping*** *Mr Young* ***for*** *a few hints as to how the exam went.'*

ap off [B1i pass adj] draw liquid from a cask etc through a tap. **O:** beer, cider, wine; bottle(ful), jug(ful) □ *He keeps a barrel of the local red wine in his cellar and* ***taps off*** *a couple of bottles every day.*

ap (on) [A2 emph rel] give a quick, sharp blow (on). **o:** door, window; shoulder, arm □ *'Who's that* ***tapping on*** *the window?'* □ *A policeman* ***tapped on*** *his shoulder* (or: ***tapped*** *him* ***on*** *the shoulder*).

ap out [B1i pass adj] produce a rhythmic succession of sounds with the fingers etc. **S:** signaller, telegraphist; drummer. **O:** message; beat, rhythm □ *A trained signaller can* ***tap out*** *messages at great speed on the Morse key.*

aper off[1] [A1 B1i pass adj] become, make, narrower towards one end. **S:** [A1] **O:** [B1] plank, batten, strut; boat, vehicle □ *The stern of the vessel* ***tapers off*** *sharply.* □ ***Taper*** *the plug* ***off*** *a bit with the chisel so that it will fit into the hole.*

aper off[2] [A1 B1i pass adj] (allow, or cause, to) grow less intense, active, productive etc; tail off[1] (q v). **S:** [A1] **O:** [B1] production, output; investment; unemployment □ *There has been some* ***tapering off*** *in demand following the price increases.* □ *Production of small vehicles was deliberately* ***tapered off*** *to allow for re-tooling of part of the works.*

art up [B1i pass adj] (slang) make a woman, or a place, smart so that she or it attracts in an obvious and vulgar way. **O:** oneself; appearance; cottage, pub; street □ *'I didn't expect you to* ***tart*** *yourself* ***up*** (or: *get* ***tarted up****): we're going to an official reception, not a students' dance!'* □ *Whole streets of unpretentious cottages in Chelsea have been transformed into* ***tarted-up*** *boxes for the smart set.*

aste of [A2 rel] have the flavour of. **S:** soup, stew; pudding, pie. **o:** garlic, onion; vinegar □ *The ice-cream* ***tasted of*** *soap. The plums were sour.* HD □ *'The filling in the buns* ***tastes of*** *cream cheese.' 'It is cream cheese.'*

aunt (with) [B2 pass emph rel] refer in a cruel and mocking way to sth (supposedly) shameful about sb. **o:** cowardice, desertion; family background, illegitimacy □ *Right-wing critics* ***taunted*** *him* ***with*** *his membership, earlier in life, of a revolutionary party.* □ *Enemies on the Left* ***taunted*** *him* ***with*** *having become a safe, middle-aged liberal.*

tax with [B2 pass rel] bring sb face to face with sth he is believed to have done, and ask for an explanation. **O:** employee; dealer, manufacturer. **o:** loss, discrepancy; decline, deterioration (in quality) □ *I suspected that he had sold me defective goods, but when I* ***taxed*** *him* ***with*** *this he strenuously denied it.* □ ***Taxed with*** *the difference between the two statements, the girl broke down and confessed.*

teach-in [nom (A1)] teaching session consisting of contributions from experts and general discussion, and usu on a subject of topical interest or concern □ *A* ***teach-in*** *on student participation in university government will take place in the Union on Wednesday next.* □ *The Trust have organized a weekend* ***teach-in*** *on the preservation of the rural environment.* ⇨ **sit in, work-in.**

team up (together/with) [A1 A3] (informal) join or form a group for a common purpose (e g business, leisure activities). **o:** relative, neighbour; singer, musician □ *Very soon I found some other people to* ***team up with*** *and we began to write songs.* T □ *John then* ***teamed up with*** *a boat builder* (cf *They* ***teamed up (together)***) *and began making cabin cruisers.*

tear across, along away etc [A1 A2] (informal) move across etc quickly, and with a sense of urgency □ *'The next time you* ***tear across*** *the road like that you'll go under a bus!'* □ *He* ***tore out of*** *the room waving a piece of paper.* □ *A large saloon* ***tore past*** *without even bothering to signal that it was overtaking.*

tear across [B1ii pass] divide sth into two by pulling sharply at both sides. **O:** paper, letter; circular, bill □ *He was so furious with the tone of the letter that he* ***tore*** *it* ***across*** *and flung it in the fire.* □ *The usherette in the cinema* ***tears*** *your ticket* ***across*** *and gives back one half to you.*

tear apart[1] [B1ii pass] dismantle using considerable force; completely disarrange a place (esp when searching for sth). **O:** place; house, flat □ *I cannot wait to get out before the workmen come and start* ***tearing*** *the place* ***apart****.* BM □ *'I'll find the evidence I want even if we have to* ***tear*** *the whole house* ***apart****.'*

tear apart[2] [B1ii pass] divide painfully; upset, disturb severely. **S:** strife, antagonisms; (religious, linguistic) differences; spectacle, experience (of suffering). **O:** state, society; onlooker □ *The country was* ***torn apart*** *by fierce tribal hostilities.* □ *Angela didn't think she could sit through the film again. It was so harrowing, it* ***tore*** *her* ***apart****.*

tear at [A2 pass emph rel] try to pull sth open, or pull it to pieces, with the fingers etc. **o:** collar, jacket; fastening, catch; fruit, bread □ *The irritation of his burns was so intense that the patient kept* ***tearing at*** *the bandages.* □ *Margaret* ***tore*** *hungrily* ***at*** *the grapes.*

tearaway [nom (A1)] (slang) impetuous, reckless and (sometimes) violent young person □ *'The people round here think that every kid on a motorbike is a* ***tearaway****. But only one or two youngsters are ever in trouble with the police.'* □ *Bus conductors have complained of* ***tearaways*** *getting on late at night and terrorizing the other passengers.*

tear away (from) [B1ii pass B3 pass rel] (informal) leave, stop doing sth, with great unwillingness; make sb leave sth despite his reluctance to do so. **O:** oneself; child. **o:** work, pleasures; book, toy; meal; companion □ *I found the programme absolutely fascinating. I couldn't* ***tear*** *myself* ***away*** *— even to finish an urgent letter.* □ *'If you could* ***tear*** *Patrick* ***away from*** *his game perhaps we could all go out for a drive.'*

tear away/off[1] [B1i pass] remove (from a surface) by pulling sharply. **O:** wallpaper, curtain; plaster; pocket, label □ *You could* ***tear away*** *some of the panelling with your fingers — it was so badly eaten by woodworm.* □ *'You caught the pocket of your coat on a nail: it's nearly* ***torn off****.'*

tear away/off[2] [B1i pass] remove some superficial quality. **O:** mask (of pretence), cloak, veil (of secrecy) □ *If you* ***tore away*** *that elaborate manner he puts on for everybody, you wouldn't find much underneath.* □ ***Tear off*** *the rhetorical top-dressing from his speech and you find there's very little solid content.*

tear down [B1i pass adj] bring to the ground by pulling sharply. **O:** fence, barrier; wall, house □ *Streets of terrace houses have been* ***torn down*** *to make way for blocks of council flats.* □ *A heavy lorry skidded across the fast lane of the motorway and* ***tore down*** *a section of the crash barrier on the central reservation.*

tear in half/two [B2 pass] divide sth into two parts by pulling sharply. **O:** ticket, coupon; letter; coat □ *The ticket-collector* ***tore*** *my ticket* ***in two*** *and handed back the return half.* □ *Nick emerged from the fight with his shirt* ***torn*** *nearly* ***in half****.*

tear into [A2 pass] make a hole in sth with a strong, tearing movement; make a vigorous attack (physical or verbal) on sb or sth. **S:** saw; bulldozer; boxer; critic. **o:** plank; bank, hillside; challenger; writer □ *Explosive shells* ***tore into*** *the walls of the strongpoint.* □ *The dog was half starved. He positively* ***tore into*** *the dish of meat.* □ *The treatment meted out to his second play was savage. That he could survive being* ***torn into*** *to write another is a tribute to his resilience.*

tear off[1] [B1i pass B2 pass] remove (a garment) with urgent movements. **O:** coat, shirt □ *The policeman* ***tore off*** *his jacket and plunged into the river.*

tear off[2] [B1i pass] write or draw rapidly; dash off (q v). **O:** note, letter; sketch □ *He* ***tore off*** *a letter to his family while waiting in the airport lounge.* □ *'Don't give me something you've* ***torn off*** *in an odd moment: I want a carefully considered plan.'*

tear off[3] [B1i pass] remove (from a surface). ⇨ tear away/off[1].

tear off[4] [B1i pass] remove some superficial quality. ⇨ tear away/off[2].

tear sb off a strip; tear a strip/strips off sb [B1iii pass B2 pass] (informal) reproach, admonish severely. **S:** boss; foreman, supervisor; sergeant; magistrate. **O:/o:** workman; soldier; prisoner □ *Why did she feel frightened of Anna, as if the other was going to start* ***tearing a strip off*** *Jenny's family* (or: ***tearing them off a strip****)?* TGLY □ *'You've been a long time with the boss. Hasn't been* ***tearing you off a strip****, has he?'* (or: ***tearing a strip off*** *you*) RATT □ the passive forms are: [B1] *He was* ***torn off a strip****.* [B2] ***A strip*** *was/****Strips*** *were* ***torn off*** *him*; or: *He had* ***a strip/strips torn off*** *him.*

tear out/out of [B1i pass adj B2 pass re[l]] remove, separate, by pulling sharply. **O:** page, sheet; picture, diagram. **o:** book, magazine □ *Th[e] walls were decorated with pictures* ***torn out*** *[of] colour magazines.* □ *He scribbled the addre[ss] down in his notebook,* ***tore*** *the page* ***out****, an[d] handed it to me.*

tear to pieces/shreds[1] [B2 pass] reduce, des[troy], by pulling sharply; tear up[1] (q v). **O:** paper, letter, magazine; cloth, garment □ *Materi[al] passed through this machine is* ***torn to shre[ds]*** *by a set of powerful blades.* □ *Slowly and delib[erately] he* ***tore*** *her letter* ***to pieces****.*

tear to pieces/shreds[2] [B2 pass] (informa[l]) destroy, demolish, by critical argument sth whic[h] a person has said or written. **S:** teacher, tutor, critic. **O:** essay, thesis; argument, case □ *She ha[d] reached the point where she couldn't face havin[g] another piece of work* ***torn to pieces*** *by he[r] tutor.* □ *'Your case would never stand up i[n] court; a good criminal lawyer would* ***tear*** *it* ***t[o] shreds****.'*

tear up[1] [B1i pass adj] destroy by pulling shar[p]ly; tear to pieces/shreds[1] (q v). **O:** letter, bil[l], ticket □ *'Did you mean me to keep the receip[t]? I'm afraid I've* ***torn*** *it* ***up****.'* □ *'Daddy hasn't g[ot] your letter at all. I have. I took it and* ***tore*** *it* ***up****[.']* DC

tear up[2] [B1i pass] vigorously renounce, aban[don]. **S:** state; employer, trades union. **O:** treaty, agreement □ *The other side clearly doesn['t] regard such agreements as binding: they can b[e]* ***torn up*** *at will.*

tee off [A1] (golf) drive the ball from the tee (th[e] point from which (part of) a game begins) □ *Th[e] first player* ***teed off*** *into a strong cross-wind.*

tee up[1] [A1 B1i pass adj] (golf, football et[c]) settle the ball in a good position before striking [it] □ *Golfers usually* ***tee*** *the ball* ***up*** *on a sma[ll] wooden or plastic peg before driving off.* □ (dis[cussion]) cussion following a football match) *'You don['t] have time to* ***tee*** *the ball* ***up*** *and then hit it[.']* BBCTV

tee up[2] [B1i pass adj] (informal) arrange, organize. **O:** (sales) drive, campaign; (military) offensive; things, the (whole) thing □ *While th[e] reinforcement was moving to the left flank, w[e]* ***teed up*** *the blitz attack which was to go in whe[n] it arrived.* MFM □ *'Now is everything proper[ly]* ***teed up*** *for your trip to Holland?'*

teem in [A2] be present in large numbers. **S:** wi[ld] life; fish, insects, bacteria; idea, image. [o:] forest, stream; head, brain □ *Grubs and insec[ts]* ***teem in*** *the rich soil around the roots of the tr[ee]* (or: *The soil* ***teems with*** *grubs* etc). □ *Ideas f[or] new plays and short stories* ***teemed in*** *his hea[d]* (or: *His head* ***teemed with*** *ideas* etc). □ simpl[e] tenses are used with teem in; simple and cont[i]nuous tenses with teem with.

teem with [A2 rel] ⇨ previous entry.

telescope (into) [B2 pass emph rel] simplify, shorten, sth so that it fits a limited time or spac[e]. **S:** lecturer; author, editor; speaker. **O:** course, syllabus; (series of) lectures, books; remarks. [o:] five days, half a term; single volume; brief inte[r]view □ *The publishers have* ***telescoped*** *th[e] large reference dictionary* ***into*** *a paperback ed[i]tion suitable for college students.* □ *He had a l[ot] to explain, and no time for more than a sho[rt] meeting. Thus a lengthy briefing had to be* ***tel[escoped]***

scoped into half an hour.

ell (about) [B2 pass] give sb information (concerning sb or sth). **O:** wife, family; reporter, interviewer; audience. **o:** success, loss; incident, occurrence; experience □ *'There's something I've not* ***told*** *you* ***about*** *yet. I can't find the air tickets!'* □ *'I could see the driver of the lorry was in difficulties.' 'Yes?* ***Tell*** *us* ***about*** *that.'*

ell against [A2] be sth which hinders or hampers sb, prevents him from succeeding etc; weigh against (q v). **S:** (one's own) height, weight; youth; inexperience, immaturity. **o:** him etc; survival, success □ *He's a very brave, aggressive player, but his weight is bound to* ***tell against*** *him in a game against a heavy pack of forwards.* □ *Martin tends to act impulsively, without consulting people higher up. That'll* ***tell against*** *him in an old-fashioned firm, where they play everything by the book of rules.*

ell apart [B1ii] (be able to) distinguish between two similar persons or things. **O:** twins, (two) brothers; animals, birds; buildings; programmes, courses □ *Every day is identical with the one before. I literally can't* ***tell*** *them* ***apart*** (or: *I literally can't* ***tell*** *one* ***from*** *the other*). HAHA □ *Even when magnified, the two organisms are difficult to* ***tell apart***. □ with *can/could*. ⇨ next entry; tell from.

ell the difference (between) [B2] (be able to) distinguish between two similar persons or things. **o:** (two) people, animals; butter and margarine, burgundy and claret; one performance and another □ *The twins' mother reminded me that Stephen had the darker hair, but for the life of me I still couldn't* ***tell the difference between*** *them.* □ *'How can I* ***tell the difference between*** *Scotch* (i e Scotch whisky) *and Bourbon?'* OMIH □ with *can/could*. ⇨ previous entry; tell from.

ell (by/from) [A2 emph rel B2 emph rel] judge, deduce (by observing sth). **O:** (probable) result, outcome; reaction; that he's an honest man, how far they can be trusted. **o:** look, expression; remark, comment; listening, taking note □ *You can* ***tell*** *just* ***from*** *looking at him that he's nobody's fool.* □ *'He'll make enemies in this department.' 'How can you* ***tell****?' 'Oh, just* ***by*** *listening to what people say.'* □ ***From*** *monitoring the radio traffic you could* ***tell*** *that heavy reinforcements were moving up behind the enemy lines.* □ with *can/could*.

ell from [B2] (be able to) distinguish one person or thing from another (which may be similar to, or different from, the first). **O:** truth; order, democracy; male, older (one). **o:** lying; anarchy, tyranny; female, younger (one) □ *I was less capable than Dominguez of* ***telling*** *truth* ***from*** *falsehood.* QA □ *On the beach she could hardly* ***tell*** *him* ***from*** *the other fathers.* PW □ with *can/could*. ⇨ tell apart, tell the difference (between).

ell sb where he gets off/where to get off [A1] ⇨ entry after get off[7].

ell off (for) [B1i pass B3 pass] (informal) reproach, reprimand sb (for sth he has done); dress down (q v). **O:** employee; pupil; (girl/boy)friend. **o:** being late, leaving work undone, making a fool of oneself; negligence, slovenliness □ *I was ten minutes late and she* ***told*** *me* ***off*** *in front of everyone.* H □ *He didn't like being* ***told off for*** *something he hadn't done.* □ *That child needs a darned good* ***telling-off***. □ nom form is telling(s)-off.

tell off for [B3 pass] (military) choose sb to perform, detail off (q v) for, a certain task. **O:** squad, platoon. **o:** guard duty, fire picquet, cookhouse fatigues □ *The smartest men were* ***told off for*** *guard duty at Government House.* □ usu passive.

tell (on) [A2] (informal, esp among children) report sb for sth he has done wrong; split (on) (q v). **S:** brother, sister; form monitor; sneak, toady □ *'I won't ever do it again. I swear. Please don't* ***tell on*** *me!'* RATT

tell on/upon [A2 emph rel] have an effect on the health or condition of. **S:** strain, tension; overwork, long hours; responsibility. **o:** health, nerves, temper □ *He's looking distinctly run down. All those late nights are beginning to* ***tell on*** *him.* □ *Hard driving over bad roads will soon* ***tell upon*** *the suspension of the car.*

temper with [B2 pass emph rel] (formal) modify, soften, an action etc, by doing sth which contrasts with it. **O:** severity, harshness, rigour (of an action, mood). **o:** mercy, compassion, humour □ *The academic rigour of his lectures is fortunately* ***tempered with*** *wit.* □ ***With*** *these few concessions to the tax-payer the government hopes to* ***temper*** *the bleakness of its new measures.*

tempt (into) [B2 pass] (try to) persuade sb to act wrongly or unwisely. **O:** rival, opponent, competitor. **o:** (making) a false move, (taking) the wrong decision □ *By varying his pace and spin, the bowler tried to* ***tempt*** *Smith* ***into*** *an over-hasty stroke.* □ *This was a course of action he was not to be* ***tempted into*** *(following).*

tend towards [A2 rel] be inclined to develop in a certain way. **S:** industry, retail trade, building; government, management. **o:** what is safe, conventional, profitable; (newer, different) form, framework □ *As far as supermarkets are concerned, we are* ***tending towards*** *much larger units, often on the edge of towns.* □ *New housing still* ***tends towards*** *the traditional. Few buyers want something really unusual.*

tender (for) [A2 pass rel] (industry, commerce) make a formal offer to do work, or supply goods, at a stated price. **S:** contractor, supplier. **o:** construction, building, erection (of sth); supply, furnishing (of sth) □ *Several major firms are known to have* ***tendered for*** *the construction of the new airport.* □ *Offers have been invited, but the work has not yet been* ***tendered for***.

tense up [A1 B1i pass adj] (informal) (of nerves) become strained; strain; screw up[3] (q v). **S:** [A1] **O:** [B1] athlete, footballer; traveller; examinee □ *A runner exercises before a race to prevent his muscles from* ***tensing up***. □ *She is never* ***tensed up*** *or nervous before a big event.* H □ *He dislikes oral exams most of all: they always* ***tense*** *him* ***up***.

terrify into [B2 pass] drive sb, through fear, to do sth; frighten into (q v). **S:** tyrant, bully; prospect, likelihood (of failure, of disaster). **o:** surrender, submission; giving way, granting sb's demands □ *The thought that the children might be in danger had* ***terrified*** *her* ***into*** *handing over the safe keys.* □ *Let us not be* ***terrified into*** *anything — their threats are probably a bluff.*

test out [B1i pass adj] find, by experiment or

practical use, whether sth is valid or effective. **O:** idea, theory; process, mechanism; machine, device □ *Now that he had a post as scientific adviser to the Air Ministry, Jeffries would be able to* ***test out*** *his theories under the stress of war.* □ *'We're not ready to go into production yet. The new switch mechanism isn't fully* ***tested out****.'*

testify (to) [A2 pass emph rel] (formal) give evidence (of sth); bear witness to (q v). **o:** truth, reliability, genuineness; ability, talent; good character, sound moral qualities □ *'I would be prepared to* ***testify to*** *the reliability of the witness* (cf ***testify*** *that he is reliable).'* □ *Experts had* ***testified to*** *the machine's excellent performance at extremes of heat and cold.*

thank (for) [B2 pass emph rel] express gratitude to sb (for sth). **O:** participant, helper, donor. **o:** help, co-operation; gift, subscription □ *'I should like to* ***thank*** *all of you* ***for*** *your support at a difficult time.'* □ *He's been* ***thanked*** *enough* ***for*** *an action that was after all, in his own interests.*

thaw out[1] [A1 B1i pass adj] (cause to) become warm, liquid or soft. **S:** [A1] **O:** [B1] (frozen, icy) hand, foot; (frozen) chicken, vegetables □ *'Just give me a minute to* ***thaw out*** *in front of the fire — then we can talk.'* □ *Deep-frozen meat or poultry needs to be* ***thawed out*** *— preferably over night — before it is cooked.*

thaw out[2] [A1 B1i pass adj] (informal) become more relaxed or friendly. **S:** [A1] **O:** [B1] official, dignitary; (stern) father, teacher □ *'Let's all sit down,' said Isabel, 'if Daddy's thoroughly* ***thawed out****.'* PW □ *'Offer the visitor a drink. That will* ***thaw*** *him* ***out****.'*

theorize (about) [A2 pass emph rel] discuss, talk about, sth in theory (as distinct from practice); construct theories in an attempt to explain sth. **o:** construction, development (of motorways, of railways); language, human development, the nature of living matter □ *'We can't allow ourselves the luxury of simply* ***theorizing about*** *the development of city centres: circumstances press us into making practical decisions.'* □ *Linguists* ***theorize about*** *the relationship between the structure of language and the ways in which language is used.*

thin down [B1i pass adj] make (a liquid) less dense. **S:** decorator; turpentine, water. **O:** paint; emulsion □ *You can apply the emulsion in one thick coat, or* ***thin*** *it* ***down*** *with water and put on two coats.*

thin out [A1 B1i pass adj] become, make, fewer or more widely scattered, over an area. **S:** [A1] **O:** [B1] hair; crop; crowd, traffic. **S:** [B1] age, disease □ *Periodic major floods had* ***thinned out*** *the population.* □ *The traffic had* ***thinned out*** *by then — we were out of London.* CON

think (about) [A2] consider, contemplate in the mind, sth (e g a past event) which requires no action. **o:** childhood, schooldays; holiday, work; (sb's) kindness, generosity □ *I was just* ***thinking about*** *the time when old Fred fell into the river.* □ *'What are you* ***thinking about****?' 'Oh, nothing in particular.'* □ *We've no idea what's happened to them; but their probable fate under the new regime doesn't bear* ***thinking about****.* □ usu continuous tenses.

think about [A2 pass rel] consider, examine, sth to see whether one should take action; think of[2] (q v). **o:** offer, proposal; plan, scheme resigning, moving □ *I'm interested in buying your house, but I'd like more time to* ***think about*** *it before making a decision.* □ *He'd* ***thought about*** *selling up and emigrating at one stage.* □ *This is something that needs to be* ***thought about*** *very carefully.*

(not) think twice (about) [A2] (not) pause for long or careful reflection before acting. **o:** informing, betraying, recommending (sb); selling, acquiring (sth) □ *'There's no need for you to* ***think twice about*** *it, is there? There's nothing for you if you don't take the offer.'* RATT □ *The day after Martin's piece of persuasion I did what, at any previous time, I should* ***not*** *have* ***thought twice about****.* NM □ *'I'd* ***think twice about*** *entrusting my savings to that company.'*

what (to) think (about) [B2] hold particular views (on), react in a certain way (to). **o:** statement, declaration; decision; action, move □ *'You've heard that he's offered his resignation. Now,* ***what*** *do you* ***think about*** *that?'* □ *I don't know* ***what to think about*** *their decision to close the school.* □ direct and indirect questions only.

think ahead (to) [A1 A3] cast one's mind forward to, anticipate, an event. **A:** five weeks, ten hours; far, a long way. **o:** (possible, probable) outcome, consequence, result; event, contingency □ *I carried out certain movements which were, at the time, merely precautions, i e, I was* ***thinking ahead****.* MFM □ *In this business it's wise tactics to* ***think*** *some way* ***ahead****.* □ *We're already* ***thinking ahead to*** *our next move.*

think back (to) [A1 A3] recall and reconsider sth in the past. **A:** a long way, some way. **o:** remark, statement; occurrence; change, development; time, moment □ *'Do you remember when we first met?' 'That's* ***thinking back*** *a long way.'* □ ***thought back*** *a few years* ***to*** *the last occasion when the issue had been raised.*

think of[1] [A2 pass] anticipate; consider, weigh. **o:** (likely, probable) effect, outcome; cost, expense; wife, family; oneself □ *He's a wonderful organizer: he* ***thinks of*** *everything!* □ *We'd like to go to Portugal this summer, but* ***think of*** *the cost!* □ *He never* ***thinks of*** *anyone but himself.* □ *'That sounds a good idea, but have all the possible snags been* ***thought of****?'* □ usu with the simple tenses.

think of[2] [A2] contemplate, consider the possibility of (without yet reaching a decision, or acting); think about (q v). **o:** travelling, visiting, asking, inviting; trip, holiday □ *'Margot, are you* ***thinking of*** *marrying Jim?'* H □ *They were* ***thinking of*** *calling for a final bottle of champagne, when there came a new and disconcerting blow.* OBS □ *'Why don't we buy that flat in town?' 'Oh, I was* ***thinking of*** *a little place in the country.'* □ often with the continuous tenses; object is often the *-ing* form of a v.

think of[3] [A2] call to mind, recall. **o:** name, address; date, time. **A:** at the moment, at this precise/exact moment □ *'I can't* ***think of*** *his name, but he was a tall chap with glasses.'* □ with *can(not)*.

think of[4] [A2 pass] propose, suggest; invent, devise; think up (q v). **o:** name, title; scheme, project □ *We're still trying to* ***think of*** *a suitable* title for the book. □ *'**Think of** a number, double it, and add your age.'* □ *'I know the prospect is a little bleak at the moment, but don't worry, we'll **think of** something.'* □ not usu with the continuous tenses.

think of[5] [A2 pass adj rel B2 pass rel] have a certain opinion of, regard in a particular way. **A:** [A2] well, highly. **O:** [B2] a great deal; little, not much; the world. **o:** colleague, associate; work, achievement; writing, poetry; design, craftsmanship □ *I know my dear brother doesn't **think** so highly **of** me.* ASA □ *In Wales we **think** a great deal **of** our bards.* PW □ *He's well **thought of** in government circles.* □ *'I know you don't **think** much **of** him, although you've hung around him for ages, but I **think** the world **of** him.'* AITC □ simple tenses only.

think better of [A2 pass(o)] reconsider a possible action, and decide not to take it. **o:** it; action, step; intervention; interfering, interrupting □ *Whatever retort Dr Bottwink was about to make, he **thought better of it**.* EM □ *He'd clearly **thought better of** intervening in a situation which was already highly charged.*

never/not think of [A2 pass] not entertain a particular idea, not allow as a possibility. **o:** allowing, permitting; interfering; giving way □ *'Why don't you let me pay for the meal?' 'I wouldn't **think of** it!'* □ *He'd **never think of** letting the boy decide for himself.* □ *'We could cut our losses by selling that side of the business.' 'No, that's **not** to be **thought of**.'* □ with could/would.

think nothing of [B2] not regard as important or significant; not consider to be a special achievement. **o:** friendship, affair, connection; working all night, walking twenty miles □ *Some would have thought these large transfers of money highly suspicious, but at least his colleagues **thought nothing of** it.* □ *During training, these athletes **think nothing of** running eighty miles a week.*

think nothing of it [B2] a politely reassuring remark to sb who feels he has behaved rudely □ *'I'm sorry if I interrupted your meal.' 'Oh, that's all right. **Think nothing of it**.'* □ *'**Think nothing of it**,' he said, when Virginia apologized for keeping him out of his bed.* AITC □ the sentence is in the imper form.

think out [B1i pass adj] consider, examine, carefully sth that may affect the future; plan sth carefully, stage by stage. **O:** proposal; scheme, project; play, novel; things, the (whole) thing □ *There is little opportunity to **think out** what the long-term solution may be.* NS □ *A work (of art) may have been **thought out** in the medium or be a translation from a painting or a drawing.* G □ *Mother and I had bought the dress together on one of our well-**thought-out** expeditions to the West End Stores.* THH ⇨ next entry.

think over [B1ii pass adj] review past events in one's mind; consider carefully sth that may affect the future. **O:** events, happening; things, it all; offer, suggestion □ *With the beginning of a new day he had to **think** things **over** again, reconsider his position, see where he was now.* PE □ *She had **thought** the plan **over**; it was important that he would think it had been his idea.* H ⇨ previous entry.

think up [B1i pass adj] invent, devise; think of[4] (q v). **O:** idea, scheme, plan; story, tale; excuse, apology □ *There were one or two fellows who **thought up** ideas of their own.* CON □ *He would have to **think up** some more catchy names for these designs.* HD □ *He offered some quickly **thought-up** pretext for being there.*

thirst for [A2 rel] desire ardently, long (for) (q v). **o:** chance, occasion; revenge, vengeance; knowledge, adventure □ *He was surrounded by savages **thirsting for** his blood.* PE □ *These advertisements are calculated to appeal to young men **thirsting for** adventure.*

thrash about[1] [A1] move about, stir, in an agitated, restless way; stir water etc violently with one's limbs □ *Stephen was **thrashing about** in bed with a high temperature.* □ *We left the children **thrashing about** happily in the shallow end of the pool.*

thrash about[2] [A1] act in a nervous, restless way (often without aim or success) □ *Alan was getting all worked up over his maths homework — **thrashing about** for the answer to a quite simple problem.*

thrash out [B1i pass adj] solve, remove, by thorough discussion; find, arrive at, in this way. **O:** difficulty, obstacle; problem, issue; answer, solution □ *He was worried enough to call a meeting at the Windsor Hotel to **thrash** the problem **out**.* OBS □ *The top level should now be brought in to **thrash out** the whole business.* MFM □ *We can leave the second part to them, and lastly we can **thrash out** our conclusions.* TBC

thread one's way through [B1ii B2 rel] move with difficulty, and in an indirect way, through. **o:** crowd, throng; trees, undergrowth □ *I **threaded my way through** the crowd with the dog at my heels.* UTN

threaten (with) [B2 pass emph rel] (formal) hold out sth as a possible punishment or danger. **O:** victim, prisoner; subject, employee, servant. **o:** punishment, torture; penalty, dismissal □ *We were **threatened with** the severest penalties for failing to report on time.* □ *The treatment **with** which they were **threatened** did nothing to alter their views.*

thrill to [A2] feel excitement at. **o:** (the sound of) sb's voice, sb's touch □ *She **thrilled to** the sound of his footsteps on the stairs.* □ usu associated with the style of popular women's magazines.

thrive on [A2 emph rel] grow strong, prosper, by taking or using sth. **S:** child, animal; business, industry. **o:** milk, eggs; competition, hard work □ *He **throve on** a pure meat diet for some time.* DF □ *This is the style of life **on** which he seems to **thrive**.* □ *'Say something nice to Muriel. She **thrives on** compliments.'*

throttle down [A1 B1i pass] make a vehicle move more slowly by supplying less petrol to the engine; reduce the rate of movement or growth of sth. **O:** engine; car; expansion, development □ *'**Throttle down** a bit on these sharp bends — the tail of the car is swinging out.'* □ *It is absurd that the United States should be compelled to **throttle down** economic growth.* T

throw one's money about [B1ii] (informal) spend money in a reckless and conspicuous way □ *The pub is full of spoilt young men-about-town who like to **throw their money about**.* □ *Sailors tend to **throw their money about** on their first night ashore.*

throw one's weight about [B1ii] (informal) behave in an arrogant, overbearing way so that others are made to feel small and unimportant □ *'You come in here, **throwing your weight about** as though you were the big boss himself.'* □ *Tell him not to **throw his weight about** when he starts his new job. He can sit back quietly and pick up a few ideas from the others.*

throw around/round [B2 pass emph rel] surround, encircle sth, to control movement in and out. **S:** police, army. **O:** cordon; ring (of troops, armour). **o:** area, zone □ *The state government has **thrown** a cordon **around** the stricken area to contain the spread of the epidemic.* □ *A tight security ring was **thrown round** those parts of Southern England where invasion troops were concentrated.*

throw (at) [B2 pass] direct a missile (at sth or sb) with a sharp movement of the arm. **O:** stone, brick, mud. **o:** window, car; police □ *'He had a brick **thrown at** him at that meeting. He's got concussion.'* UTN

throw the book (of rules) at [B2 pass] (informal) remind sb forcefully of the correct procedure to be followed in some task (and perhaps punish him for not following it). **S:** officer, superintendent, foreman. **o:** pilot, constable, worker □ *'If you spend more than £50 on that account again without referring the matter to me, I'll **throw the book at** you.'* □ *'I know I'm **throwing the book of rules at** you, as you call it, but, believe me, you're never going to be happy without it. I tried throwing it away all these months, but I know now it just doesn't work.'* LBA

throw oneself at [B2] (informal) make over-eager advances to a man (usu in the hope of catching him as a husband). **o:** (any, every) man, the first man one meets □ *'You couldn't wait, could you? You had to **throw yourself at** the first man you met, didn't you?'* TOH

throw away[1] [B1i nom pass] get rid of, discard. **o:** carton, can, box, packet; ticket, receipt □ *Beer is now often sold in cans that can be **thrown away*** (cf *sold in **throw-away** cans*). □ *Don't **throw** your bus ticket **away** — the inspector may want to see it.* □ throw-away is used attrib.

throw away[2] [B1i pass adj] lose, let slip, by foolishness or neglect; give away[4] (q v). **O:** lead, advantage; match, game; life, career □ *The visiting team built up an impressive lead in the first half, then **threw** it **away** by loose defensive play in the second.* □ *More was loyal to him, and incorruptible, but he surely was worldly enough not to **throw** his life **away** for nothing.* WI

throw away[3] [B1i nom pass] (theatre, broadcasting) speak sth casually, under-emphasize it, for deliberate effect. **O:** ⚠ a line; a word, remark □ *'Something special is usually made of those lines. But don't play them up — **throw** them **away**.'* □ *The minister replied with a neat **throw-away** remark which made his interviewer smile in admiration.* □ nom form is often attrib: throw-away *line* etc.

throw away on [B3 pass rel] waste sth, or oneself, in foolish ventures, on undeserving people etc. **O:** money; capital, investment; oneself, one's life. **o:** (wild, madcap) scheme, project; (unsuitable, unworthy) partner, lover □ *'Think carefully. You may be **throwing** yo savings **away on** shares that will be worthless a few years.'* □ *Mrs Knighton thought that Isab had **thrown** herself **away on** Harold.* PW □ *A advice you might give is clearly **thrown awa on** Bill.*

throw back[1] [B1i pass] return with a shar movement of the arm or wrist. **o:** ball; boo magazine; box, packet □ *The ball was throw **back** underarm to the bowler.* □ *He **threw** th bundle of papers **back** across the desk. 'Every thing seems in order,' he said.*

throw back[2] [B1i pass] raise, remove, with sharp movement. **O:** bedclothes, bedsprea hangings, curtain □ *She sat up in bed and thre **back** the bedclothes.* DC □ *The curtains we **thrown back** to reveal a small boy cowering b the french windows.*

throw back[3] [B1i pass] repulse, repel, vig orously. **O:** enemy; infantry, armour; assaul attack □ *The attackers were **thrown back** in series of fierce engagements.*

throw-back [nom (B1)] sb who recalls phys ically, or in his character, a generation earlie than his parents; sth which recalls an earlie period □ *'Well, I suppose there's a **throw-bac** in every family.'* DBM □ *Some of the cloth young people are wearing seem to be a **throw back** to Victorian styles.*

throw back at [B3 pass] (informal) remind s reproachfully of sth he has done or said (esp afte he has been shown to be wrong); throw in sb' face (q v). **O:** past record, previous history loyalty, connection, affiliation; belief, convic tion □ *'Why should you of all people **throw** m decisions **back at** me? You agreed with me at th time.'* □ *Now that things are not going so wel Peter is sure to have all his earlier slips an blunders **thrown back at** him.*

throw back on [B3 pass] force sb to use, c resort to, sth as a defence or support. **S:** change shift (in events); (sb's) attitude, reaction. **o** defence, excuse; stratagem, device; one's ow resources □ *The failure of this policy **threw** th party leaders **back on** a scheme which had bee put forward some time previously.* □ *John se cretly enjoyed a situation in which he wa **thrown back on** his own reserves of shrewdnes and stamina.*

throw down the gauntlet [B1iii] issue a chal lenge. **S:** enemy, rival; contender (for a cham pionship) □ *The champion will soon have t defend his title again — a young American con tender has **thrown down the gauntlet**.*

throw in [B1iii pass] (informal) include as a fre or unexpected extra. **O:** carpets, furniture; (cos of) fitting, installing; (musical) encore, (the atrical) act, turn □ *'If you're set on buying th house, we'll **throw in** the carpets and curtains a no extra cost.'* □ *There was all that, and Barbar impersonating her mother **thrown in**.* ILIH

throw (the ball) in [B1ii nom pass] (footbal put the ball back into play (after it has crossed th touch-line) □ *'And it's Moore to **throw the ba in*** (or: *to take the **throw-in***) *near the half-wa line.'* □ *The linesman has given the **throw-in** t Leeds.*

throw in sb's face [B2 pass] remind sb re proachfully or insultingly of sth he is, or has don (esp when it seems to explain sth that is nov

;oing wrong); throw back at (q v). **O:** (past) ıction, decision; friend, associate; family back-ground □ *'The last thing I want to do is to* ***throw*** *a man's past* ***in his face*** *unless he's a double-dyed villain.'* DS □ *'My education, which you* ***throw in my face****, was an education along humane lines that didn't leave me with any illusions about the division of human beings into classes.'* HD

row one's hand in [B1i] (cards) leave, withdraw from, a game; (informal) abandon, give up, sth in which one is engaged □ *After a run of bad cards, James decided he had lost enough money and* ***threw in his hand****.* □ *'I warned you. I told you I was* ***throwing my hand in****. Now didn't I?'* TOH

row in the towel/throw up the sponge B1iii] (boxing) acknowledge defeat (by throwing a towel or sponge into the ring); (informal) abandon the struggle; admit defeat □ *After his man had been knocked to the floor twice for a count of eight, the second decided he'd had enough, and* ***threw in the towel****.* □ *'I know you've been going through a tough time, but it's a bit early to* ***throw up the sponge*** *yet, isn't it?'*

row in one's lot with [B3 rel] join, become an associat of, sb in an enterprise. **o:** government, opposition; Labour, the Conservatives; trader, dealer; venture, expedition □ *After years in the political wilderness, Stephens has* ***thrown in his lot with*** *the new party leadership.* □ *He was hoping to convey the impression that he had been encouraged to* ***throw in his lot with*** *Bunder, and was hesitating.* HD

row in/into [B1i pass B2 pass emph rel] insert into the course of, add as a contribution to. **O:** remark, comment, suggestion. **o:** conversation, discussion, debate □ *'Could I just* ***throw in*** *the reminder that all these arrangements must be finally tied up by next week?'* □ *'He could never take these official meetings seriously — always* ***throwing*** *some outrageous comment* ***into*** *the proceedings.'*

row into [B2 pass emph rel] confuse, disorganize, upset etc, by sudden or violent action. **S:** (sudden) arrival, appearance; announcement, statement; change, development. **O:** place; office, department; staff; plan, scheme. **o:** ⚠ confusion, disarray, disorder □ *This unexpected change of plans* ***threw*** *everyone* ***into*** *confusion.* □ *Our arrangements were* ***thrown into*** *complete disarray by that interfering fool from head office.*

row oneself into [B2 rel] undertake, become involved in, sth with enthusiasm. **A:** vigorously, wholeheartedly, enthusiastically. **o:** work, job; arrangements, organization; building, developing (sth) □ *She tried again to* ***throw herself*** *with a will* ***into*** *life.* PW □ *The Bafutians had obviously* ***thrown themselves*** *wholeheartedly* ***into*** *the task.* BB

row into relief [B2 pass] through contrast, make sth appear sharp and clear. **S:** light; colour; background, setting. **O:** shape, form; carving, moulding; house; tree □ *The roofs of the city are* ***thrown into*** *sharp* ***relief*** *against the evening sky.* □ *Skilfully placed lights* ***throw*** *the marble figures* ***into*** *clear* ***relief****.* □ *Details of private behaviour are* ***thrown into*** *high* ***relief*** *against backgrounds of doom and disaster.* AH

hrow off[1] [B1i pass] remove with a quick movement. **O:** clothes; coat, scarf, hat □ *He* ***threw off*** *his shirt and trousers and plunged into the cool water.*

throw off[2] [B1iii pass] discard, get rid of, sth which prevents others from seeing one as one really is. **O:** mask, disguise; manner, pretence □ *If only he would* ***throw off*** *that carefully cultivated manner!*

throw off[3] [B1iii pass] get rid of a person who, or a thing which, troubles or irritates. **O:** pursuer; tout, beggar; cold, 'flu □ *The visitor has to* ***throw off*** *the swarm of guides and hotel touts who cluster round the station entrance.* □ *'I can't manage the meeting tonight. I'm still trying to* ***throw off*** *this wretched cold.'*

throw off[4] [B1iii pass] compose quickly and without effort; knock off[4] (q v), toss off[2] (q v). **O:** poem, satire, epigram □ *The two men sat down over a bottle of wine and* ***threw off*** *a few songs and sketches for the evening's concert.*

throw off (his) balance [B2 pass] upset, disturb, sb's mental composure. **S:** news, announcement; realization, awareness (of sth); shock □ *The news that someone else had been given the job* ***threw*** *him momentarily* ***off balance****.* □ *Not even the shock of passing his final examinations had upset Grimsdyke. But Nikki seemed to* ***throw*** *him* ***off his*** *psychological* ***balance****.* DIL

throw off the scent/the track [B2 pass] do sth that will prevent a pursuer from following one. **S:** fugitive; (escaped) convict, prisoner. **O:** pursuer; police, troops □ *The gang broke up into four groups in the hope of* ***throwing*** *the police* ***off the track****.*

throw light on [B2 pass emph rel] make clearer, or easier to understand; shed light on (q v). **S:** discovery, findings; research, investigation. **adj:** no, (not) any/much; a lot of, little; fresh, new. **o:** problem, question; mystery, puzzle, riddle □ *The real importance of the* (Dead Sea) *Scrolls lies in the* ***light*** *they* ***throw on*** *Palestinian history.* OBS □ *Hugo's inquiries rarely failed to* ***throw*** *an extraordinary amount of* ***light on*** *whatever he concerned himself with.* UTN

throw oneself on/upon sb's mercy [B2] beg for kind or lenient treatment. **S:** captive, prisoner; accused □ *The accused was clearly guilty; all he could now do was* ***throw himself upon the mercy of*** *the court.*

throw out[1] [B1i nom pass] discard, get rid of, sth because it is no longer useful. **O:** old clothes; took, toy □ *There are some bundles of old magazines here that I want to* ***throw out****.* □ *Not all your* ***throw-outs*** *are useless rubbish. The metal, paper and glass may be useful scrap.*

throw out[2] [B1i pass] reject, dismiss. **S:** council, committee, board. **O:** Bill; amendment; proposal, suggestion □ *A proposal to extend the motorway into the City Centre was* ***thrown out*** *in committee.* □ *The idea was put up to the Faculty Board, but they* ***threw it out****.*

throw out[3] [B1iii pass] (military) extend one's position by moving men to a flank; deepen it by placing men in front. **O:** wing, screen, line □ *The commander* ***threw out*** *a thin screen of motorized troops to protect his exposed flank.* □ *In Wellington's time a line of sharpshooters was usually* ***thrown out*** *in front of the main defensive position.*

throw out[4] [B1iii pass] utter, express (in an indirect, tentative or casual way). **O:** threat, (dark) hint; suggestion; (possible) solution, answer □ *When last I spoke to him, he was* ***throwing out*** *dire warnings of a financial crisis.* □ *I wasn't offering a positive answer. All I was doing was* ***throwing out*** *a few suggestions as to how we might proceed.*

throw out[5] [B1iii pass] be a source of. **S:** sun; fire, radiator. **O:** heat, warmth □ *His new gas central heating is very effective — it* ***throws out*** *a lot of heat.*

throw out[6] [B1ii pass] cause an error in sth; put out[12] (q v). **O:** student, pupil; scientist, research worker; result, sum □ *'Go and play your guitar somewhere else. I've nearly got this sum right, and I don't want you to* ***throw*** *me* ***out****.'* □ *A tiny variation in temperature can* ***throw*** *us* ***out*** *in our results.* □ *It* ***throws*** *their calculations totally* ***out****.* BBCTV

throw out/out of [B1i pass B2 pass] (informal) remove forcibly; dismiss, expel. **O:** intruder, trespasser; drunk, troublemaker. **o:** park, gardens; club, pub □ *'Now that you know why I'm here, am I to be allowed to stay or are you going to* ***throw*** *me* ***out****?'* TBC □ *'You know that Bill got* ***thrown out of*** *college for failing his exams?'*

throw the baby out with the bathwater [B3 pass] when getting rid of sth undesirable or unpleasant also reject sth of real value □ *We must be careful not to* ***throw the baby out with the bathwater****. Our task now is to control technology, not to turn away from it.* ST □ *To relinquish all of modern science in order to get rid of the necessity of having to admit psychical phenomena is like* ***throwing out the baby with the bathwater****.* SNP

throw over [B1ii pass] (informal) end a relationship (esp a love-affair) with. **O:** girl/boyfriend, mistress, lover; (political) party, church □ *This young Circe seduced him and taught him to drink, and then lightheartedly* ***threw*** *him* ***over****.* PE □ *'What happened to his long-standing love-affair with politics?' 'Oh, he* ***threw*** *the party* ***over*** *years ago.'*

throw overboard [B1ii pass] (informal) abandon, reject. **O:** rule, regulation; principle, standard; procedure, protocol □ *We were* ***throwing overboard*** *the principle of concentration of effort.* MFM □ *Nobody knows how to proceed in these discussions — the book of rules seems to have been* ***thrown overboard****.*

throw round [B2 pass emph rel] ⇨ throw around/round.

throw caution/discretion to the winds [B2 pass] abandon caution, not behave discreetly, when acting or deciding to act □ *After the guests had had a few drinks,* ***discretion*** *was* ***thrown to the winds*** *and a good deal of malicious gossip flew about.* □ *Sometimes, when a downward slope favoured it, it* (the lorry) ***threw caution to the winds*** *and careered along in a madcap fashion at twenty-five miles per hour.* BB

throw together [B1i pass] (informal) assemble, roughly or hurriedly; compose, compile, in this way. **O:** clothes, books; ingredients; brick, plank; essay, exercise; meal; house □ *'Give me five minutes to* ***throw*** *a few clothes* ***together****, then we'll be off.'* □ *You can't* ***throw*** *a couple of good ideas* ***together*** *and expect a wel[l]-constructed essay somehow to emerge.*

throw up[1] [B1i pass] (informal) abandon[,] resign. **O:** job, post; (military) commission[,] assignment □ *Charley had enough sense t[o]* ***throw up*** *his job at the tax inspector's offic[e].* BFA □ *She had planned to do a manageme[nt] course but since then she had* ***thrown*** *it* ***u[p].*** THH

throw up[2] [A1 B1i pass] (informal) vomi[t,] bring up[6] (q v). **O:** meal; food □ *Robert gorge[d] like a man driven insane by hunger. I was afra[id] he'd* ***throw*** *it all* ***up*** *over the table-cloth, but h[e] didn't.* CON □ *'How horribly servile and ingra[tiating] that man is. He makes me want to* ***thro[w] up****!'*

throw up[3] [B1iii pass] produce, witness, th[e] appearance or development of. **S:** country, dis[trict]; generation; movement, organization. **O:** leader, organizer; inventor, artist □ *I was anxio[us] the Unions should grow naturally; this polic[y] would ensure that the right leaders would b[e]* ***thrown up*** *gradually.* MFM □ *Not every gener[ation]* ***throws up*** *a composer of his remarkab[le] gifts.*

throw up the sponge [B1iii] ⇨ throw in th[e] towel/throw up the sponge.

throw oneself upon sb's mercy [B2] ⇨ throw oneself on/upon sb's mercy.

thrust across, along, away etc [B1i pass B[2] pass] move sth across etc suddenly and force[fully.] **O:** parcel, box; plate, cup; knife, swor[d;] hand □ *With an impatient gesture he* ***thrust*** *t[he] food* ***away*** *from him.* □ *With his hands* ***thrus[t]*** *deep* ***into*** *his pockets, he walked restlessly abo[ut] the room.*

thrust at [A2 rel B2 pass rel] aim, direct onese[lf] or sth or sb, by moving (it) forward suddenly an[d] forcefully. **O:** oneself; finger, hand; stick, swor[d;] paper, parcel □ *'Please don't* ***thrust at*** *me wi[th] that umbrella* (or: ***thrust*** *that umbrella* ***at*** *me[;] it's bad for my nerves.'* □ *He had a printed for[m]* ***thrust at him*** *by an unpleasant official.*

thrust upon [B2 pass rel] oblige or force sb [to] accept or undertake. **O:** oneself; (one'[s]) presence, company; (extra) work, duties; visito[r,] guest □ *He felt she was trying to* ***thrust*** *herse[lf]* ***upon*** *him — her attentions were too insistent [to] mean anything else.* □ *I hope it hasn't put yo[ur] housekeeper out having three extra guests su[d]denly* ***thrust upon*** *her.* WI

thud into [A2] strike, and partially enter, with [a] dull sound. **S:** fist; bullet, arrow, knife. **o:** bod[y;] wall, door; parapet, embankment □ *Shell fra[g]ments* ***thudded into*** *the earth piled in front [of] their trench.*

thumb through [A2 nom pass] scan a boo[k] etc, turning the pages with a quick movement [of] the thumb; flick through (q v). **o:** magazin[e,] report; (pile of) photographs □ *I was* ***thumbin[g] through*** *an old copy of a colour suppleme[nt] when a secretary came in to say that Mr Ma[t]thews was ready to see me.* □ *He took down [a] standard textbook and had a quick* ***thumb through*** *to get a general idea of the lay-out.*

thump out (on) [B1i pass B3 pass rel] pro[duce,] play, by striking sth heavily; beat out (o[n]) (q v). **O:** tune, rhythm; message. **o:** drum; table [□] *A man in the corner of the pub was* ***thumpi[ng] out*** *a tune* ***on*** *an old piano.*

thunder across, along, away etc [A1 A2 rel] move across etc with a heavy, continuous rumbling noise. **S:** train, engine; aircraft; lorry, cart □ *The London express* ***thundered across*** *an iron bridge.* □ *A flight of jet fighters* ***thundered past.***

thunder against [A2 pass rel] (formal, jocular) speak in a loud and fierce voice to criticize or condemn; fulminate (against) (q v). **S:** preacher; church. **o:** sin, vice; excess, laxity, corruption □ *A back-bench MP* ***thundered against*** *what he called extravagant spending on the social services.* □ *The sins of the flesh were* ***thundered against*** *from every pulpit.*

tick away [A1] make light, regularly repeated sounds, so indicating the passage of time. **S:** clock, watch; meter; bomb □ *A grandfather clock* ***ticked*** *solemnly* ***away*** *in the hall.* □ *The taxi driver had left his meter* ***ticking away*** *while I dashed into the house. When I emerged there was an extra 50 pence to pay.*

tick away/by [A1] pass, go by (esp to the accompaniment of the sounds of a clock or watch). **S:** hour, minute, second □ *The minutes* ***ticked away*** *interminably. How much longer would we be held up at the frontier?* □ *Half his life had* ***ticked by*** *with little happening to disturb its even course.*

tick off[1] [B1i pass adj] put a small mark against sth written down (to show that sth has been dealt with, that sb is present etc); cross off (q v). **S:** clerk, storekeeper; receptionist, housekeeper. **O:** item, article; entry; name □ *'Why did you* ***tick*** *these stores* ***off*** *in the inventory when you haven't checked that they're actually in stock?'* □ *Those two jobs can be* ***ticked off****. I've already done them.*

tick off[2] [B1i pass adj] (informal) rebuke, reprimand. **S:** boss; parent; commander. **O:** employee; child; subordinate □ *If I went too fast again, I was quite prepared to be sent for and* ***ticked off****.* MFM □ *The Captain gave me a hell of a* ***ticking-off*** *for firing at all.* RFW □ nom form is **ticking(s)-off**.

tick over[1] [A1 nom] (of an internal-combustion engine) turn relatively slowly (e g before the gears are engaged and the vehicle moves off). **S:** engine, motor; car, lorry □ *Buses and taxis* ***tick over*** *rather noisily* (or: *have a rather noisy* ***tick-over***). □ *If an engine* ***ticks over*** *too slowly or too fast an adjustment must be made to the carburettor.*

tick over[2] [A1] (informal) live or function quietly, without achieving much success or making great progress. **S:** pupil, worker; shop, industry, department □ *'How is business?' Isabel asked. 'Oh, not too bad, just* ***ticking over****.'* PW □ *How are you* ***ticking over*** *these days? How is the big bad world treating you?* THH

tickle to death [B2 pass] (informal) greatly please or amuse sb. **S:** news, announcement; story, joke; it... to see, to hear, to realize sth □ *It* ***tickled*** *me* ***to death*** *to hear how his wife had locked him out all night to cool off, but it can't have pleased him.* □ *First he's in despair because she comes back, and now he's miserable because she's gone away. He should be* ***tickled to death*** *and yet he isn't.* PW

tide over [B1ii pass B2 pass] (informal) help sb to live through, or manage, a difficult period. **S:** loan, gift, allowance; (temporary, part-time) work; lodging, flat. **o:** year, month; crisis, bad time; illness, convalescence □ *'Give me something, just to* ***tide*** *me* ***over*** *till I can get a decent, steady job,' said Robert.* CON □ *Sarah could have found work other than nursing, to* ***tide*** *them* ***over*** *the years till the children could support themselves.* WI

tidy away [B1i pass] put sth away (e g in a drawer or cupboard) so that a room etc appears neat and orderly. **O:** book, letter, paper; toy; clothes □ *'Do* ***tidy*** *your papers* ***away****; your desk looks in a terrible mess.'* □ *It was difficult to tell that anyone had stayed at the cottage. Plates, cups, knives and forks had been carefully* ***tidied away****.*

tidy out [B1i pass] remove sth from a place, so making it neat and orderly. **O:** drawer; desk, cupboard □ *The boys spend part of the last day of term* ***tidying out*** *their desks and handing in their books.*

tidy up [A1 nom B1i nom pass adj] make sth, oneself, or sb neat. **O:** room, office; desk; oneself; child □ *Mary got rather tired of constantly* ***tidying up*** *after the children.* □ *We need to* ***tidy*** *the place* ***up*** *a bit* (or: *give the place a bit of a* ***tidy-up***) *before the guests start arriving.* □ *I ought to have found a wash-room and* ***tidied*** *myself* ***up****, perhaps even had a shower and a shampoo.* CON

tie back [B1i pass adj] draw back sth that is free or loose and attach it in place. **O:** hair; plant; vine, rose □ *The girl had her long blonde hair* ***tied back*** *in a neat bun.* □ *'****Tie*** *the gate* ***back*** *— it keeps banging to and fro in the wind.'*

tie down[1] [B1i pass adj] fix in a low position with string, cord etc. **O:** branch; hand, foot; awning, cover □ *There was such a gale blowing that we had to* ***tie*** *the caravan* ***down*** *to prevent it overturning.* □ *Prisoners were* ***tied down*** *hand and foot to pegs in the ground.*

tie down[2] [B1ii pass] limit, restrict, sb's freedom of action or movement. **S:** family; work; debt, mortgage □ *I'd like to take a job overseas, but there are too many things* ***tying*** *me* ***down*** *here.* □ *They were the rebellious few, the vagabonds, who were not* ***tied down*** *by a wife and family.* AITC

tie down[3] [B1i pass] (military) occupy, engage, the attention of sb, so that movement is difficult. **S:** forces, troops; artillery, air force. **O:** reserves, reinforcements □ *Partisans operating from the mountains were able to* ***tie down*** *three enemy divisions.* □ *Armour coming up in support was* ***tied down*** *by air strikes.*

tie down to [B3 pass rel] oblige sb to follow or conform to. **O:** employee, client; company, firm. **o:** terms, conditions; contract, agreement; text, script □ *During the candidate's pre-election tour, his agent found it impossible to* ***tie*** *him* ***down to*** *the programme of visits he had prepared.* □ *John hates being* ***tied down to*** *a regular work schedule.* ⇨ tie down[2].

tie in with [A3 B3 pass] match, fit; (make sth) correspond (to/with) (q v). **S:** [A3] **O:** [B3] statement, story; plan, project. **A:** well, badly; scarcely, fully. **o:** our version; the overall design, existing proposals □ *This evidence* ***ties in*** *very well* ***with*** *the picture which detectives have already built up.* □ *'Blind drunk, did you say?'*

*That doesn't **tie in with** what I know of his habits.'* □ *We managed to **tie in** our holiday arrangements **with** my work programme for the early summer.*

tie on [B1i nom pass adj B2 pass rel] attach sth with string, cord etc. **O:** flag, pennant; label, badge; basket, bag. **o:** mast, pole; case, box; jacket; bicycle □ *His shoes were **tied on** with old bits of string.* □ *Use stick-on labels for your trunk and **tie-on** labels* (or: ***tie-ons***) *for your hand luggage.*

tie up[1] [B1i pass adj] fasten, bind, together with string, cord etc. **O:** parcel, packet, bundle; sticks, twigs □ ***Tie** the paintbrushes **up** into bundles and put them away carefully.*

tie up[2] [B1i pass adj] (informal) complete (the arrangements or organization of). **O:** things, the (whole) thing; trip, visit; business, deal □ *I like to get all the arrangements for a holiday **tied up** a month in advance.* □ *'I'm glad I got that all **tied up**, Sarah. I never did like to see any ends sticking out, I always liked to finish things.'* WI

tie up[3] [B1i pass] (informal) keep busy or occupied. **S:** work; accounts, calculations; social engagements □ *'As far as I can tell, this editing will **tie** me **up** for the next fortnight.'* □ *'I'm sorry, I shan't be able to get to your party after all. I'm a bit **tied up** at the moment.'*

tie up (in) [B1i pass B3 pass rel] (informal) have money etc invested in sth, so that it is hard to draw upon for other purposes. **O:** capital, savings, reserves. **o:** property; long-dated stocks □ *It's unwise to **tie up** all your capital **in** one enterprise.* □ *Most of the family money is **tied up in** land.*

tie-up/tied up (with) [nom pass (B1) pass (B3)] (informal) connection, relationship; (be) connected, related (to). **S:** [pass] firm, company; government; army, process, development; idea □ *A good deal of British car manufacture is closely **tied up with** the continental industry* (cf *There is a close **tie-up** between the one and the other*). □ *We can now look forward to a much closer **tie-up** between the educational systems of Western Europe.*

tighten up [B1i pass] make more strict or effective. **S:** government, local authority; manager, commander. **O:** law, regulation; control; system □ *He should be responsible for reorganizing and **tightening up** the local administrations.* SD □ *When a national currency is in difficulties, the rules governing the amount of money one can take abroad are generally **tightened up**.*

tilt at windmills [A2 rel] attack imaginary enemies, supposing them to be real ones □ *'So let us stop bickering within our ranks. Stop **tilting at windmills**. Stop talking of victories over our colleagues and concentrate instead on winning victories over the Tories.'* OBS □ *He is strong in body, of outstanding courage, and fortified by magic. The things **at** which so strong a man **tilts** cannot be **windmills**.* NDN

tinker (with) [A2 pass] work on sth in a casual way, often for pleasure and sometimes with the effect of making matters worse. **o:** car; engine, suspension; watch; radio □ *'Have a look at the engine if you like, but don't **tinker with** it. If something is really the matter I'd rather take the car to a garage.'* □ *'No wonder the lights don't work — Harry's been **tinkering with** the switches.'*

tip into [B2 pass emph rel] by tilting or overturning a vessel, empty its contents into sth. **O:** contents; salt, flour; sand; water; passenger. **o:** dish, bowl, bucket; river □ *The cook **tipped** the reminder of the flour **into** a mixing-bowl and added two eggs.* □ *A sudden gust of wind overturned the dinghy, **tipping** the crew and their gear **into** the water.* ⇨ tip out/out of.

tip off [B1i nom pass] (informal) inform, warn, sb that sth is about to happen (esp that a crime is going to be committed). **S:** (police) informer; spy, agent. **O:** police; customs, inland revenue; bank □ *Mr Bevins denied that the Post Office had been **tipped off** that a raid on the train was planned.* G □ *We'd been **tipped off*** (or: *been given a **tip-off***) *by London that a man of this name was believed to have arrived in Nairobi.* DS

tip out/out of [B1i pass B2 pass] by tilting or overturning a vessel, remove its contents. **O:** clothes; flour, salt; seed, grains; passenger. **o:** suitcase; tin, bowl; bucket; boat □ *Buckets rise on a long chain from the well, and the water is **tipped out** into irrigation channels.* □ *The train stopped with a violent jerk, nearly **tipping** me **out of** my bunk.* ⇨ tip into.

tip up [A1 B1i nom pass adj] (cause to) turn upwards around a hinge or pivot. **S:** [A1] **O:** [B1] seat, shelf, table □ *Many theatres and cinemas have seats that can be **tipped up*** (i e *have **tip-up** seats*). □ *If you press this catch, the bunks will **tip up** and fold back into the wall.*

tire of [A2 emph rel] no longer be interested in or attracted by; weary of (q v). **A:** soon, quickly, never. **o:** experience, activity; (city, country) life; friend, lover; company, conversation; living alone, being flattered □ *He never seems to **tire of** the sound of his own voice.* □ *The things **of** which he **tires** least are good company, gardening and music.* ⇨ next entry.

tired of [pass (B2)] (become) weary of, irritated with, fed up (with) (q v). **o:** routine, daily round; waiting, wasting time; being ordered about □ *He finally got **tired of** sitting in an office all day. He longed for a more active life.* □ *'I'm **tired of** being reminded of what I should have done. Have you never made any mistakes?'* ⇨ previous entry.

tire out [B1i pass adj] exhaust sb (physically or mentally). **S:** task; walk, climb; question, discussion; neighbour, relative. **O:** staff; traveller; student; oneself □ *By midnight Janet was **tired out**, but there was no respite for anyone.* RFW □ *I'm thinking about the future. I won't be **tiring** myself **out** dodging trouble.* JFTR

toddle along [A1] (informal) leave, go away (esp after talking to friends, being at their house, etc) □ *'It's eleven o'clock, time I was **toddling along**.'* □ *'There's not much else we can do now, is there?' 'No, that's right.' 'Don't you think we ought to **toddle along**?'* YAA

tog (oneself) up [A1 B1ii pass] (informal) dress, esp in fine clothes (for a party, dinner etc) □ *'I don't want to go to the party if it means **togging up** in a dinner jacket.'* □ *'Get **(yourself) togged up** — we're going out to celebrate.'* □ passive with *be, get*.

toil over [A2 pass rel] work hard and continuously at; labour over (q v). **o:** task, chore; manuscript; corrections, accounts □ *'I feel that I've been **toiling over** these exam scripts for weeks. There seems to be no end to them.'*

tone down [B1i pass adj] make sth appear milder or less extreme. **S:** author, critic; reporter, commentator. **O:** account, story; description; view, opinion; adjective □ *Ian Fleming had to **tone down** a few of my rather critical opinions.* DS □ *The editor eventually accepted a **toned-down** version of the correspondent's dispatch.*

tone up [B1i pass adj] make more vigorous, lively, alert etc. **S:** exercise; walk, swim; shower-bath, dip (in the sea). **O:** him etc; body, system, muscle □ *More exercise and a change of diet — that's what you need to **tone** you **up**.* □ *After a quick dip and a brisk rub-down his whole system felt **toned up**.*

tool up [A1] (industry) equip a factory with new machine-tools (as when a new product or model is to be manufactured). **S:** industry; plant, factory □ *The real cost in car-making isn't design or raw materials, but the expense of **tooling up**.* OBS

top out [A1 B1i pass] (building) perform a ceremony (with speeches, drinks etc) to mark the completion of a high building. **O:** tower-block, office-block, hotel □ *The Minister was present at the **topping-out** of London's Post Office Tower.* □ *When we **top out**, there will be beer for everyone who has worked on the site.*

top up[1] [B1i nom pass adj] fill a glass etc which has been partially emptied. **S:** host; waiter. **O:** him, you etc; glass, tankard □ *'Can I **top** that drink **up** for you?'* ILIH □ *We weren't given a chance to finish our wine; the waiters were constantly on the move, **topping up** the glasses.* □ *'Let me **top** you **up*** (or: *Let me give you a **top-up**).'*

top up[2] [B1i nom pass adj] fill a petrol tank which is partially empty; add water, oil etc (esp to part of an internal-combustion engine), to bring the level back to what is normal. **O:** tank, battery, radiator, engine □ *The cells of a car battery need to be **topped up** with distilled water.* □ *Keep the engine **topped up** with the right grade of oil.* □ *In the early days of the fuel crisis, many cases were reported of motorists calling at a garage for a **top-up** worth a few pence. Many drove with **topped-up** tanks from fear of imminent petrol rationing.*

torn between [pass (B2)] (be) mentally or emotionally divided by conflicting thoughts, feelings etc. **o:** (two, several) aims, purposes; opposing impulses, emotions □ *You are **torn between** two tendencies — your wish to indulge your personal fancies, while at the same time keeping within your resources.* WI

toss for [A2 B2] decide sth (with sb) by spinning a coin in the air. **o:** (best, most comfortable) place, position; bed, chair; ends (of the field, in football) □ *'Who's going to sleep on the top bunk?' 'Let's **toss for** it.'* □ *'To prevent any argument, I'll **toss** you **for** who does the washing-up.'* ⇨ toss up.

toss off[1] [B1i pass] drink sth straight down. **O:** glass (of sth); beer, whisky □ *I never met a man who could **toss off** so many drinks in so short a time.*

toss off[2] [B1i pass] produce, compose, sth with little thought or effort; knock off[4] (q v), throw off[4] (q v). **O:** remark, answer; poem, song, story, article □ *It isn't enough in this job to be able to **toss off** a few bright remarks. It calls for real thought and understanding.*

toss up [A1] decide sth (esp in a sporting contest) by spinning a coin in the air □ *At the start of a football match the referee **tosses up** to decide which team will kick off.* □ *In cricket the two captains **toss up** to see who will bat first and who will field.* ⇨ toss for.

toss-up [nom (A1)] (informal) (be) a matter of doubt, (be) sth which could be decided either way □ *It's a **toss-up** which of the two yachtsmen will cross the finishing-line first.* □ *I'm not sure whether the headmaster will throw him out or give him a second chance. It's a complete **toss-up**.*

tot up [B1i pass] (informal) find the total of; add up[2] (q v). **O:** figures, amounts; marks, scores □ *Every fortnight the form-masters had to **tot up** the marks scored by each boy and write out their names in a competitive list.* CON □ *Over breakfast we **totted up** our balance and found we had a fiver each to play with.* BM

touch down [A1 nom] land (at an airfield etc) after a flight; reach the shore after a journey at sea. **S:** aircraft; pilot, passenger; boat; landing-craft □ *We **touched down** at Galena. We made as good a landing as could be expected.* BM □ *The first of the assault divisions **touches down** on the beaches at 6 a m (cf **Touch-down** for the first of the divisions is at 6 a m).*

touch (the ball) down [A1 nom B1ii pass] (Rugby football) ground the ball behind one's opponent's, goal line to score a try, or behind one's own to prevent an opponent from doing so. **S:** forward, three-quarter, full-back □ *The winger kicked the ball over the opposing full-back's head, calculating that he could beat him to the **touch-down**.* □ *Williams broke through the centre to **touch down** right between the goal-posts.*

touch for [B2 pass] (slang) borrow money from sb (without necessarily intending to pay it back). **o:** loan; (a few) quid, bob □ *He's a bit tight with his money; definitely not the sort of man you can **touch for** a few bob.* □ *John had been **touched for** 'a small loan' before; he wasn't going to be caught a second time.*

touch in [B1i pass] add small details carefully, to improve or complete sth. **O:** line, shape, shading □ *The small figure to the right of the painting seems to have been **touched in** at a later date.* □ *You need to **touch in** a few patches of colour with a fine brush.*

touch off[1] [B1i pass] discharge; cause to explode. **O:** cannon; explosive charge; guncotton, dynamite; explosion □ *This explosive needs to be handled very carefully; the slightest jolt will **touch it off**.* □ *Field guns were formerly **touched off** by a slow match being applied to a hole near the breech.*

touch off[2] [B1i pass] cause some violent action to begin; spark off[2] (q v), trigger off (q v). **S:** speech, harangue; appearance, intervention (of police etc). **O:** riot, disturbance; (violent) quarrel, argument □ *Fresh violence was **touched off** when police moved in to disperse the crowd.* □ *Argument continued as to what exactly **touched off** the disturbances.*

touch on the raw [B2 pass] offend, upset, sb

by referring to sth about which he is sensitive □ *I had **touched** him **on the raw** somewhere, so I got up and said I was sorry to have taken up his time.* PP □ *He was teasing me out of kindness, but **touched** me so accurately **on the raw** that I barely held back any retort.* LWK

touch on/upon [A2 pass] treat a matter briefly or superficially. **S:** writer, speaker; book, article; lecture, lesson. **o:** subject, topic, question □ *Your correspondent had only **touched upon** the fringe of the matter.* NS □ *Let me now deal more fully with the important question that was **touched on** earlier.*

touch up [B1i pass adj] alter sth by adding, or removing, small details. **O:** painting, photograph; portrait, landscape; article, essay □ *These photographs appeared on front pages of the dailies, in some cases after a generous degree of **touching up**.* TBC □ *He has two short articles almost ready for publication; they just need to be **touched up**.*

toughen up [A1 B1i pass] (cause to) become tough. **S:** [A1] **O:** [B1] athlete; swimmer, boxer; child □ *He needs a meat diet and plenty of hard exercise to **toughen him up**.*

tout about/around [B1i pass] (informal) offer for sale or acceptance in a furtive, underhand manner (since what is offered may not have been honestly acquired). **O:** (football, theatre) tickets; currency; (scarce) components, spares; trinket, jewel; idea, scheme (for making money) □ *'If you'll take my advice, you'll try **touting** that money **around** somewhere else. If you stay here, the police will pick you up for black market dealing.'* □ *'Is he still **touting about** those unsavoury opinions of his?'*

tower above/over [A2 emph rel] stand much taller or higher than sb or sth; be of greater moral or mental stature than sb. **o:** brother, colleague; house, street; (other, one's fellow) scientists, politicians □ ***Above** the Victorian houses and shops **tower** the monster office blocks of the redeveloped centre.* □ *As an original contributor to socialist thinking, and as a spell-binding orator, he **towered above** other members of the party.*

toy with[1] [A2 pass] handle in a casual, absent-minded way; play with[1] (q v). **o:** chain, bracelet, key-ring, pen, pencil □ *He sat well back in his chair, his feet on the desk, **toying with** a glass paperweight.*

toy with[2] [A2 pass] treat lightly or frivolously; dally with[2] (q v), play with[2] (q v). **o:** her etc; feelings, affections □ *'He makes a great show of being fond of her in front of other people — just to show he's not altogether heartless — but he's only **toying with** her really.'*

toy with[3] [A2 pass] consider, though not in a serious way, some course of action; dally with[1] (q v), play with[3] (q v). **o:** idea, scheme, plan □ *He **toyed with** the idea of going back to his university town and getting a contract from his college.* HD □ *He could still go to Australia. That was something he'd often **toyed with** but never done anything positive about.*

trace back (to)[1] [B1ii pass B3 pass emph rel] find the source or cause of sth by going back over a series of events etc. **O:** story, rumour; incident, event; illness, fear, phobia. **o:** author, instigator; source, root; childhood, infancy □ *She **traced** her irrational fear of birds **back to** something which had happened to her as a child.* □ *The police have **traced** her disappearance **back** as far as a day in April.*

trace back (to)[2] [B1ii pass B3 pass] be able, going back in time, to name one's ancestors in succession. **O:** ⚠ one's family; one's descent; one's (family) line, lineage. **o:** Norman conquest, Huguenot settlement; twelfth, sixteenth century □ *'How far **back** can he **trace** his family?'* □ *On his father's side, he can **trace** his descent **back to** Elizabethan times.*

track down [B1i pass] find, discover (esp by following evidence that has been left behind). **O:** fugitive, runaway; (lost, escaped) animal; truth, facts □ *'Mrs Templar is taking the children in the park. They might **track down** that starved cat.'* DC □ *It was almost 48 hours before the Army **tracked down** the facts: there had been a series of brawls, involving 30 soldiers.* OBS

trade (for) [B2 pass] barter; give in exchange for sth else. **O:** salt, tobacco, hides. **o:** knife, gun, cloth □ *Early European visitors to the North of Canada **traded** manufactured goods **for** furs and skins.* □ *'I'll **trade** you five comic books **for** your scout knife.'* □ in the second example, trade for represents American usage; British speakers would use swap for (q v).

trade in[1] [A2 rel] be a dealer in (esp natural, untreated products). **o:** furs, skins; precious metals, stones; timber, rubber □ *In West Africa there are a number of businesses **trading** on a large scale **in** palm products, cocoa and rubber.*

trade in[2] [B1i nom pass adj] hand to a dealer a used article in part payment for a new one. **O:** car, motorbike; television, washing-machine □ *He keeps a car for two years, then he **trades it in*** (or: *does a **trade-in***). □ *'Did you get a good **trade-in** on your sewing machine?'* □ in the second example, the trade-in is the amount of money realized.

trade on/upon [A2 pass emph rel] use, exploit, sth unfairly to get sth for oneself. **o:** (one's) charm, beauty; weakness, illness; (sb else's) generosity, forgiveness □ *When are you going to stop **trading on** your helplessness — offering yourself all day to be petted and stroked?* FFE □ *His easy, forgiving nature was something **upon** which she was only too ready to **trade**.*

traffic in [A2] be a dealer in (usu sth illegal). **o:** drugs, heroin, marijuana; illicit alcohol; arms, explosives □ *People **trafficking in** obsolete rifles and pistols clearly still find a ready market for them.*

trail across, along, away etc [A1 emph A2 emph rel] move in line, slowly and wearily, in a particular direction. **S:** procession, column; prisoner, refugee □ *Miss Jeffries came first; **behind** her **trailed** a dismal crocodile of small girls in uniform.* □ *The army **trailed back** from the front in complete disorder.*

trail away/off [A1] fade into silence. **S:** voice, words, sounds □ *'He happens to have fallen in love, and wants to...' Her voice **trailed away**.* PW □ *Before the intimidating glare of the form-master his words **trailed off** into silence.*

train (for) [A2 emph rel B2 pass emph rel] (cause sb to) study, do practical work, exercise etc, in preparation for. **S:** [A2] **O:** [B2] student, pupil; athlete. **o:** profession, calling; race, match, contest □ *A number of older men are coming forward to* ***train for*** *the priesthood.* □ *This was not work* ***for*** *which he had been* ***trained***. □ *The coach believes in* ***training*** *the team hard* ***for*** *every match.*

train on/upon [B2 pass rel] point sth towards an object, so as to hit it, make it visible etc; aim at[1] (q v). **O:** howitzer, field-gun; telescope, binoculars. **o:** target; enemy; view □ *Anti-tank weapons were* ***trained upon*** *all possible approaches to the bridge.* □ *I prised the glasses from her reluctant grasp and* ***trained*** *them* ***on*** *the distant scene.* DF

train up (to) [B1i pass B3 pass] raise sb to a particular standard by giving instruction and practice. **O:** child; pupil, apprentice; soldier. **o:** standard, level, pitch □ *They are unable to* ***train up*** *their successors* ***to*** *any higher standard than their own.* SD □ *All the technical staff are* ***trained up to*** *a high level of efficiency.*

traipse across, along, away etc [A1 emph A2 emph rel] (informal) walk slowly, heavily and wearily in a given direction. **S:** (tired) shopper, traveller □ *She's been* ***traipsing back and forth*** *across the world.* EHOW □ *'It means* ***traipsing upstairs*** *to the bar if you want anything stronger than fruit juice.'* HAA

tramp across, along, away etc [A1 emph A2 emph rel] walk across etc with heavy steps. **S:** soldier, policeman □ *The delivery man* ***tramped in*** *with a sack of potatoes across his shoulders.* □ *The bridge shook as the column of troops* ***tramped across***.

trample down [B1i pass adj] flatten, crush, sth by moving about heavily on it. **S:** cattle, elephant. **O:** grass, corn, flowers □ *A flock of sheep had got into the garden and* ***trampled down*** *his prize begonias.*

trample on [A2 pass rel] move about heavily on sth (so as to crush it); behave in a clumsy, insensitive way (so as to hurt sb). **o:** foot, flower; feelings, sensibilities □ *Avoid the London Underground in the rush hour — you'll be buffeted about and have your toes* ***trampled on***. □ *His attack on traditional family life was so intemperate that everything they most valued seemed* ***trampled on***.

transfer (from) (to)[1] [A2 emph rel B2 pass emph rel] move from one place to another, esp to conduct a business, take up a post etc. **S:** [A2] **O:** [B2] employee; manager; civil servant; office, branch, department. **o:** city, provinces □ *With the reorganization of the Post Office's research and development, many employees have had to* ***transfer to*** *a new centre in Suffolk.* □ *After two years in one appointment, staff officers are usually* ***transferred to*** *another department.*

transfer (from) (to)[2] [B2 pass emph rel] take sth from one person or place and give it to sb else, or put it elsewhere. **O:** interest, enthusiasm; loyalty, affection; (bank) account, investments; business, trade. **o:** issue, (good) cause; friend, lover; bank, company □ *His wife suspects that he has* ***transferred*** *his attentions* ***to*** *a younger woman.* □ *If there is no improvement in the standard of service, I shall have my account* ***transferred from*** *that bank.*

transform (into) [B2 pass rel] change the form, nature or quality of sth (into sth else); make into (q v). **S:** heat, stress, pressure; experience; ordeal, suffering. **O:** substance, material; character, personality □ *The training centre* ***transforms*** *some rather unpromising material* ***into*** *skilled craftsmen.* □ *Under war conditions children may be* ***transformed*** *overnight* ***into*** *men.*

translate (from) (into) [A2 rel B2 pass emph rel] put, render, sth spoken or written into another language. **O:** text; book, letter; poem, play; speech, address. **o:** English, French, Russian □ *Interpreters employed by international agencies must be able to* ***translate*** *instantaneously* ***from*** *one language* ***into*** *another.* □ *Do you feel that his poems can be* ***translated*** (or: *can* ***translate***) ***into*** *German?* □ ***Into*** *how many languages have his novels been* ***translated****?*

transliterate (into) [B2 pass rel] write sth in the characters of a different language. **O:** word, sentence, passage. **o:** (foreign) script, characters, letters □ *'Sputnik' is an example of a Russian word which has been* ***transliterated into*** *Roman script.*

transmit (to)[1] [B2 pass emph rel] (radio) send (to), signal (to). **O:** message, signal; news, information □ *On board ship, telephone messages may be* ***transmitted to*** *the shore by radio.*

transmit (to)[2] [B2 pass emph rel] convey (to), pass on (to). **O:** heat, electricity; quality, characteristic; disease. **o:** house, consumer; child, descendant □ *A special generator* ***transmits*** *electricity* ***to*** *all parts of the factory.* □ *None of his finer qualities seem to have been* ***transmitted to*** *his children.* □ *An illness such as German measles will not be* ***transmitted to*** *an unborn child, though it may affect its normal development.*

trap into [B2 pass] make sb act as one wishes by setting a trap for him. **o:** admission, confession; revealing sth, betraying sb □ *'Think carefully before you answer his questions. You may be* ***trapped into*** *giving away vital information.'*

travel in [A2] (be employed to) move from place to place selling a certain product. **o:** textiles, machinery, domestic appliances □ *'Her husband is a salesman of some kind. I think he* ***travels in*** *office stationery.'*

travel over [A2 emph rel] look at, survey, consider, one by one. **S:** eyes, gaze; mind; thoughts, speculations. **o:** audience, crowd; subject, topic, field (of study) □ *His eyes* ***travelled*** *slowly* ***over*** *the rows of faces in front of him.* □ *There are few problems* ***over*** *which his mind has* ***travelled*** *more searchingly than this one.*

tread down [B1i pass adj] flatten or crush sth by putting one's feet on it. **O:** flower, vegetable; earth □ *The soil around the plants should be well* ***trodden down***, *so that they are firmly rooted.* □ *The floor of the hut was of* ***trodden-down*** *red earth.*

tread on [A2 pass] put one's foot, or feet, down on sth (so as to move, spoil or damage it). **o:** clean floor, loose plank; flower-bed, young plant; foot, toe □ *John* ***trod on*** *the head of the broom and the handle flew up and hit him in the face.* □ *'Don't* ***tread on*** *that part of the floor — I've just finished varnishing it.'*

tread on air [A2] be lighthearted, joyful (as after receiving good news) □ *So the young man really was interested after all. He was calling for her that evening. All afternoon Margaret* ***trod on air***. □ *We seemed to* ***tread on air*** *— work was* *over for a month, the bank had been understanding about a loan, and the next day we were off to France.*

tread on sb's corns/toes [A2 pass] (informal) behave insensitively towards sb, so that he is offended; step on sb's corns/toes (q v) □ *Someone has* ***trodden on your*** *pet* ***corns*** *and you're never going to speak to him again.* TT □ *Robert, of course, hated Baxter from the first. But Ned arranged it so that they didn't* ***tread on each other's toes.*** CON □ *'I'm rather used to having* ***my toes trodden on*** *by now, so I don't get upset.'*

treat (for) [B2 pass rel] (medicine) give sb medical or surgical care (so as to cure a certain illness). **O:** patient; the sick. **o:** diabetes, bronchitis, malaria □ *The doctor had been* ***treating*** *Mrs Jones* ***for*** *chronic headaches; she herself was convinced that something much more serious was the matter.* □ *If a family doctor finds that a patient needs to be* ***treated for*** *a serious ailment, he generally passes him on to a specialist.*

treat of [A2 rel] (formal) have as its subject, deal with[4] (q v). **S:** book; essay, thesis; lecture. **o:** event; progress, development; incidence, distribution □ *The second volume of the series* ***treats of*** *social changes between the wars.* □ *His doctoral thesis* ***treated of*** *the kingship system in a Nigerian city.*

treat to [B2 pass] (informal) give or offer sth to sb that will afford him special pleasure (e g as a reward for hard work). **O:** child, pupil; audience, spectators; oneself. **o:** holiday, outing; drink, ice-cream; (fine) spectacle, performance □ *The whole school was* ***treated to*** *an extra half-holiday after the Governors' annual visit.* □ *I remembered the second-hand Austin Seven which the Chief Treasurer had just* ***treated*** *himself* ***to.*** RATT

treat (with) [A2 emph rel] (formal) discuss terms of peace, an armistice etc (with sb). **o:** (neighbouring, rival) state, kingdom; enemy; invader, conqueror □ *Though beaten almost to its knees, this small country had no thought of* ***treating with*** *the invader.*

trespass on/upon [A2 pass rel] (formal) interfere in activities which are sb else's concern. **o:** (sb's) privacy, preserves, ground, sphere (of interest) □ *Smithers had no wish, he said, to* ***trespass on*** *my area of responsibility, but he felt he ought to point out one or two omissions in my report.* □ *No one's privacy is so sacred that it can't be* ***trespassed upon*** *occasionally.*

trick into [B2 pass rel] by deceit, make sb do as one desires. **O:** customer, client; employee, servant; girl. **o:** buying shoddy goods, giving away one's money, accepting low wages □ *Don't let some backstreet trader* ***trick*** *you* ***into*** *signing a hire-purchase agreement.* □ *She was* ***tricked into*** *a disastrous marriage with a charming but quite unscrupulous young man.*

trick out [B1i pass adj] decorate, ornament. **O:** gown, blouse, hat; table, sideboard; banner □ *She wore a floppy straw hat,* ***tricked out*** *with a yellow ribbon.* □ *We speedily produced a liberal edition of the pamphlet,* ***tricked out*** *prettily in red, white and blue, and ending with a resounding 'God Save the King'.* SD

trickle in/into [A1 A2] enter in a thin stream. **S:** audience, spectators; money; donations, gifts; letters. **o:** theatre, stadium; bank; office □ *The vote-counters are now* ***trickling in*** *and waiting for the ballot boxes to arrive.* BBCTV □ *Cancellations are* ***trickling in*** *at Newquay which takes about a quarter of Cornwall's 2·2 million holidaymakers.* OBS

trickle out/out of [A1 A2] leave in a thin stream. **S:** blood, water, oil; spectators; news, information. **o:** wound, crack; theatre, cinema; agency, (government) department □ *Blood was* ***trickling out of*** *a cut near his right ear.* □ *Someone had cut a hole in the bottom of the bag and sugar was* ***trickling out*** *over the floor.*

trifle with [A2 pass] treat in a light, frivolous or insincere way. **o:** feelings; love, affections; offer, proposal □ *'Stop* ***trifling with*** *our affections.'* SC □ *'I'm in no mood to be* ***trifled with!'***

trigger off [B1i pass] (informal) cause, stimulate, an event (esp one which is disturbing or violent); spark off[2] (q v), touch off[2] (q v). **S:** disagreement, argument; remark, accusation; visit, journey. **O:** fight, strike; (angry) exchange, discussion; tale, poem □ *The present dispute was* ***triggered off*** *by a rumour that some workers were to lose their jobs.* □ *Most of his stories are* ***triggered off*** *by word associations, or some odd juxtaposition of ideas.* ARG

trim down [B1i pass adj] lessen, reduce, the bulk of sb or sth by removing excess matter. **O:** bulk, size; figure, waistline; budget, expenditure □ *Mary was made aware how much her figure needed* ***trimming down*** *when she tried on last year's winter suit.* □ *In a year of great financial stringency, the department will have to* ***trim down*** *its spending on stationery and duplicating services.*

trim off [B1i pass adj B2 pass] make smaller, make neat and trim, by cutting, clipping etc. **O:** hair, sideboards, fringe; fat, gristle; (ragged) edge, border □ *'You'll have to get some of that hair* ***trimmed off*** *before you go for your interview.'* □ *'Ask the butcher to* ***trim*** *the excess fat* ***off*** *the joint.'* □ *'The finance department has* ***trimmed*** *about £1 000* ***off*** *our travel budget for the year.'*

trip across, along, away etc [A1 A2] move with quick, light steps in a particular direction. **S:** child, girl, dancer □ *The principal dancer* ***tripped forward*** *to the front of the stage and made a deep curtsey.*

trip over [A1 A2] stumble, and possibly fall, because of some obstacle near the ground. **o:** step, kerb; tree-root, low branch □ *He* ***tripped over*** *someone's foot in the darkened cinema and almost fell.* ⇨ next entry.

trip up[1] [A1 B1i pass] (cause to) stumble and fall. **S:** [A1] **O:** [B1] footballer, runner, wrestler □ *'Would you mind getting that dog out of the way? That's twice it's nearly* ***tripped*** *me* ***up.'*** □ *He went into the kitchen,* ***tripping up*** *twice over his own feet.* RATT ⇨ previous entry.

trip up[2] [A1 B1i pass] be caused, cause sb, by a deliberate action to make a mistake, reveal a secret etc. **S:** [A1] **O:** [B1] examinee, candidate; prisoner, accused. **S:** [B1] interviewer; counsel, prosecutor, police officer □ *'Be careful — there may be questions in the paper designed to* ***trip*** *you* ***up.'*** □ *The witness* ***tripped up*** *rather badly under close cross-examination.*

triumph (over) [A2 pass emph rel] (formal)

win a clear victory (over sb); convincingly overcome sth. **o:** enemy, opponent; difficulties, adversity, handicap □ *This embattled people had* **triumphed over** *everything the enemy could send against them.* □ *He ended his first year of work confident that every new hardship could be* **triumphed over**.

troop across, along, away etc [A1 emph A2 emph rel] move across etc in a group. **S:** audience, crowd; children, pupils □ *The door opened and* **in trooped** *his first class of the afternoon.* □ *The cricketers* **trooped off** *the field at the end of a long day in the sun.*

trot across, along, away etc [A1 emph A2 emph rel] move across etc at a pace between a walk and a run or gallop. **S:** horse, dog, sheep □ *Her husband always follows at a discreet distance, like a small round dog* **trotting after** *its mistress.* □ *Gleeson is now* **trotting in** *to bowl the first ball of a new over.*

trot out [B1iii pass] (informal) state, produce, quickly and easily (and often without careful thought). **O:** idea, thought, theory; remark, comment; story □ *I said that my theory seemed improbable when I first* **trotted** *it* **out**. TBC □ *The accountant* **trotted out** *a few figures in support of his argument.*

trouble (for) [B2] (informal) ask sb to do or give sth. **o:** match, light; the (correct) time; score (in a game) □ *'Can I* **trouble** *you* **for** *the time? My watch seems to have stopped.'* □ always in questions, with *can/could.*

trudge across, along, away etc [A1 emph A2 emph rel] move across etc in a heavy, weary way. **S:** soldier, refugee; procession, column; expedition □ *In the early afternoon the first of the casualties began to* **trudge into** *the dressing-stations.* □ *Progress was slow, as we had to* **trudge through** *deep mud.* □ *Joe marvelled at the picture of himself as a solid breadwinner,* **trudging off** *to the station in the morning light.* AITC

trump up [B1iii pass adj] invent, construct, sth in order to make sb appear guilty. **S:** police; authorities. **O:** ⚠ a case, charge; evidence □ *The case against the prisoner was clearly* **trumped up**; *the authorities had evidently decided that an example should be made of a leading opposition figure.* □ *Others felt to be involved in the conspiracy were arrested on* **trumped-up** *charges.* □ often passive.

truss up [B1i pass adj] (pin and) bind the wings of a fowl to its body before cooking it; bind sb's arms and/or legs tightly to his body. **O:** chicken, duck, turkey; prisoner □ *The poultry is sold* **trussed-up** *and ready for the oven.* □ *The captives were* **trussed up** *hand and foot and dumped in the back of a lorry.*

trust (for that) [A2] (informal) confidently expect, from what one knows of sb, that he will act shrewdly, do sth difficult etc □ *Alec got the house rebuilt when licences were almost unprocurable —* **trust** *him* **for that** (or: **trust** *him to do that*)! PW □ *'Last night's meeting just left a beastly taste of spite and malice.' 'Yes,* **trust** *Sherman* **for that**.*'* HAA □ used in an imper sentence, as in the examples.

trust in [A2 emph rel] have confidence in sb or sth, feel sure that sb or sth will serve one well. **o:** God; leader, organizer; judgement, sense of values, integrity □ *'I told you it didn't pay to* **trust in** *him — he's let us down again.'* □ *We felt that we could* **trust in** *his wide experience of the property market.*

trust to [A2] leave the result or progress of events to be decided by chance or by the unreasoning part of one's mind. **o:** ⚠ chance, luck, fate, fortune; instinct, intuition □ *You must have the whole project carefully planned in advance — don't just* **trust to** *luck.* □ *There's not much room for cold analysis in judging human character — you have to* **trust to** *intuition.*

trust with [B2 pass rel] confidently allow sb to take care of, use or share. **O:** employee; junior, child; pupil. **o:** money; key (to a safe, house); car, bicycle; secret □ *He's not the sort of man you can* **trust with** *large sums of money.* □ *'Is Peter reliable enough to be* **trusted with** *the details of the scheme?'*

try for [A2] attempt to win or secure. **o:** prize, medal; (speed, distance) record; bursary, scholarship; post, position □ *Two Ugandan runners will be* **trying for** *the 5000 metres title at this afternoon's meeting.* □ *I don't think I have a particularly good chance of getting the job, but it's certainly worth* **trying for**.

try on [B1i pass] put a garment on to see if it fits, looks well etc. **O:** coat, suit, dress; necklace, bracelet □ *She* **tried on** *ten pairs of shoes before she found any that suited her.* □ *She gave a wonderful personality display while having her hair done and* **trying on** *her jewellery.* OBS □ *'Would you like to* **try** *this jacket* **on** *for size, sir?'* (i e to find out whether it is the right size).

try on (with) [B1ii nom B3 emph] (informal) act in a bold or impudent way to see if one's conduct, attentions, advances etc will be welcomed. **O:** ⚠ it; anything, something. **o:** girl, woman; teacher, prefect; boss, foreman □ *She was just waiting for you to* **try** *it* **on** *so she could slap your face.* ILIH □ *You needn't think you can* **try** *anything* **on with** *the new form-master: he's a strict disciplinarian.* □ *'Don't pay attention to all that sweet talk. If I know him, it'll just be a* **try-on** (or: *he'll just be* **trying** *it* **on**)*.'*

try out[1] [B1i nom pass adj] use, handle, sth to see if it functions well. **O:** car, lawn-mower, razor, typewriter □ *'Does the pen I gave you write well?' 'I don't know, I haven't had the occasion to* **try** *it* **out** *yet.'* □ *These products give good cooks a whole range of interesting new flavours.* **Try** *them* **out** *for yourself.* TO □ *Give the machine a thorough* **try-out** *before you buy.*

try out[2] [B1i nom pass] test sb's abilities or character (e g before employing him). **O:** applicant, candidate; player, competitor □ *Fisher was* **tried out** (or: *given a* **try-out**) *in the marketing section before a decision was made about his future.* □ *'I wonder if you can solve this problem.' 'I shan't know until you* **try** *me* **out**.*'*

try out on [B3 pass rel] test the effectiveness of sth on sb. **O:** song, trick; disguise; invention, gadget. **o:** family, friend □ *'You've been waiting to* **try out** *the Beethoven Opus 106* **on** *us. Now's your chance.'* TBC □ *The new margarine has already been* **tried out on** *a small sample of London housewives.*

tuck away[1] [B1i pass] (informal) consume great quantities of food; put away[4] (q v). **O:** pie, cake; meat, vegetables □ *Between them, the children*

tucked away *a small Christmas pudding and a plate of mince pies.*

tuck away[2] [B1i pass] put sth in a box, drawer etc, because one has finished using it or wants to hide or protect it; put away[1] (q v). **O:** dress, clothes; doll, toy; jewellery □ *She brought out the dress in which she had been christened and, after allowing us to examine the very fine lace, wrapped it carefully in its tissue paper and* ***tucked*** *it* ***away*** *in the bottom of the trunk again.* ⇨ next entry.

tucked away [pass (B1)] (be) stored, hidden and perhaps difficult to find; (informal) have money saved in a secretive way. **S:** (antique) furniture; village, house; (a tidy bit of) money, fortune □ *Art dealers are always hoping to find some forgotten masterpiece* ***tucked away*** *in a little old lady's attic. Sometimes they are lucky.* □ *We eventually located the cottage —* ***tucked away*** *behind an unprepossessing row of shops and approached up a cart-track.* □ *'What does he do with his money? He never seems to spend a penny on anything.' 'I don't know, but he must have a fair bit* ***tucked away*** *somewhere.'* ⇨ previous entry.

tuck in [B1ii pass] settle sb in bed by pushing the sheets and blankets tightly under the mattress. **O:** child; patient □ *'Get into bed and I'll be up in a moment to* ***tuck*** *you* ***in****.'* □ *She calmly went on with her task of smoothing the bed and* ***tucking*** *Brigit* ***in****.* DC ⇨ next entry.

tuck in/into[1] [B1i pass adj B2 pass] press, push, sth loose into a narrow space. **O:** shirt, blouse; banknote, letter; pistol. **o:** trousers, skirt; wallet, pocket; belt, waistband □ *'Your shirt's hanging out:* ***tuck*** *it* ***in****!'* □ *He had a villainous-looking knife* ***tucked into*** *his belt.* □ ***Tuck*** *the sheets and blankets* ***in*** *well.*

tuck in/into[2] [A1 nom A2] (informal) (begin to) eat heartily. **o:** meal; breakfast, dinner; pie, stew □ *'Dinner's on the table.* ***Tuck in****!'* □ *We had a good* ***tuck-in*** *before settling down for the night.* □ *He was offered a beer and invited to* ***tuck into*** *a plate of cold turkey.*

tuck up [B1i pass adj] raise sth loose and fold or roll it around itself. **O:** sleeve, trouser-bottom, skirt □ *He* ***tucked up*** *his sleeves and reached down into the water.*

tuck up (in bed) [B1ii pass B3 pass] make sb comfortable in bed by drawing the sheets etc up around him. **O:** child; patient, invalid □ *Nurse Ellen had* ***tucked*** *her* ***up*** *and left her to sleep.* DC □ *The children are all safely* ***tucked up in bed****.*

tug across, along, away etc [B1i pass B2 pass] draw sth or sb heavy or resisting in a particular direction. **O:** cart, sledge, boat; (unwilling) child □ *A day in town isn't much fun if you have to* ***tug*** *a couple of children* ***around*** *with you.*

tumble across, along, back etc [A1 emph A2 emph rel] fall, collapse, in a sudden, uncontrolled way, and in a certain direction □ *We* ***tumbled*** *gratefully* ***into*** *bed at the end of an exhausting day.* □ *A large jar* ***tumbled off*** *the shelf, spilling its contents over the floor.* □ *The coach came to a halt and* ***out tumbled*** *a party of schoolchildren.*

tumble to [A2] (informal) realize the true character of sb; understand what is being done, planned etc. **o:** him etc; plan, scheme, trick; what is going on, what sb is up to □ *'I'm not a very nice chap, I suppose. You* ***tumbled to*** *it about the phone call, didn't you?'* TGLY □ *He tries to keep his intentions well hidden, but it doesn't take too long to* ***tumble to*** *him.*

tune in (to)[1] [A1 A3 rel B1i pass B3 pass rel] (radio) adjust the controls of a set so that one receives a certain station. **O:** radio; set, receiver. **o:** London, Hilversum; Radio 3 □ [A1] *'Don't forget to* ***tune in*** *next Sunday at the same time, when we present another programme of old favourites.'* □ [A3] *'You won't get the cricket scores: you've* ***tuned in to*** *the wrong station.'*

tune in (to)[2] [A1 A3 B1i pass adj B3 pass] (informal) become, be made, sympathetically aware of sb's feelings, reactions etc. **o:** class, audience; wife, friend □ [A3] *He hasn't the knack of* ***tuning in to*** *people.* □ [B1 B3] *The lecturer could see from the expressions on the faces of his audience which students were really* ***tuned in*** *(****to*** *what he was saying).* □ for [B1] and [B3] the passive patterns are more usual than the active.

tune up [A1 B1ii] (music) adjust musical instruments so that they can play together in tune. **S:** [A1 B1] **O:** [B1] instruments; violins. **S:** [A1] players, musicians □ *The orchestra were already* ***tuning up*** *when we reached the concert hall.*

turf out/out of [B1i pass B2 pass] (informal) forcibly remove (from), put out[2] (q v). **S:** steward, doorkeeper, bouncer. **O:** hooligan, troublemaker; intruder, gatecrasher. **o:** theatre, cinema, dance-hall □ *'I was just looking, Miss,' he said. 'And then Mr Woodgate* ***turfed*** *us all* ***out****, and he was properly wild.'* TT □ *The meeting was marred by a noisy disturbance and the ringleaders had to be* ***turfed out of*** *the hall.*

turn about [A1 emph B1i pass] (military) (cause to) face in the opposite direction. **S:** [A1] **O:** [B1] troops; company, platoon. **S:** [B1] sergeant, corporal □ *The company* ***turned about*** *and marched ten paces to the rear.* □ *'Squad will retire.* ***About turn****!'* □ about turn is the form used in commands.

turn against [A2 B2 pass] (cause to) oppose, be hostile to. **S:** [A2] **O:** [B2] father, colleague, friend □ *He had the distinct impression that everyone was* ***turning against*** *him.* □ *'What* ***turned*** *her* ***against*** *me, do you think? The child I suppose, horrid little creature.'* DC

turn around/round[1] [A1 B1ii pass] (cause to) face in the opposite direction. **S:** [A1] **O:** [B1] car, aircraft; procession, parade □ *He* ***turned around*** *to find a policeman eying him suspiciously.* □ *'We've come on too far;* ***turn*** *the car* ***round*** *and go back to the last village.'*

turn around/round[2] [A1 nom] (finance, commerce) reverse, begin to show an opposite trend or movement. **S:** (money, stock) market; economy; sterling, the dollar □ *The American market* ***turned round*** *very sharply about a week ago.* BBCR □ *It is already too late to expect a* ***turn-round*** *in the balance of payments in the first half of next year.* G

turn away (from)[1] [A1 A3 emph rel] stop facing or looking at sb or sth (esp because one finds him or it unpleasant, painful etc). **S:** passer-by, onlooker; spectator. **o:** sight, spectacle □ *She* ***turned away*** *in horror at the sight of so much blood.* □ *It was tempting to* ***turn away from*** *such a daunting task.*

turn away (from)[2] [B1i pass B3 pass emph rel] refuse entry, hospitality, help etc to sb. **S:** manager, organizer; police; hotel keeper. **O:** (would-be) spectator, visitor; car, coach. **o:** theatre, concert-hall; show, festival □ *All seats were sold out in advance; many people hoping for last-minute cancellations had to be* ***turned away.*** □ *The Salvation Army hate to* ***turn away from*** *their hostels anyone in need of food and shelter.*

turn back[1] [A1] return, go back, the way one has come. **S:** car; climber, explorer □ *One of the party* ***turned back*** *to help a friend who had sprained an ankle.* □ *The sight of the Castle was the end of her walk, and meant she must* ***turn back.*** PW □ *We have come so far in our programme of reorganization that there can be no* ***turning back.***

turn back[2] [B1i pass adj] fold one (smaller) part of sth over another (larger) part. **O:** sheet, bedspread, cover; cuff; corner, edge □ *He* ***turned back*** *the coverlet and slipped between the sheets.* □ *'Don't* ***turn back*** *the corner of the page to mark your place.'* ⇨ turn down[1].

turn (down) [A2] enter a (minor) road leading off from the one on which one is travelling. **S:** driver, pedestrian; car; procession. **o:** side street, alley, passage-way □ *You go straight along the High Street for about a mile and* ***turn*** *left* ***down*** *a narrow side-street.*

turn down[1] [B1i pass adj] fold one part of sth over another (esp over sth which is lower down). **O:** collar, neck (of a garment); brim (of a hat); sheet; blanket; corner (of a page) □ *He* ***turned down*** *the brim of his straw hat to keep the sun out of his eyes.* □ *A leaf (= page of a book)* ***turned down*** *showed that she was in the middle of 'Two Gentlemen of Verona'.* OMIH ⇨ turn back[2].

turn down[2] [B1i pass adj] refuse sb who applies, sth which is submitted etc. **S:** board, committee; school; company, publisher. **O:** applicant, candidate; offer, bid; manuscript □ *Mr Pelican was* ***turned down*** *by a large majority vote at the board meeting.* ASA □ *'I'm always proposing to you and you always* ***turn*** *me* ***down.'*** EHOW □ *You'd had a couple of stories* ***turned down*** *by the highbrow magazines.* ASA

turn down[3] [B1i pass adj] make less bright, intense or loud. **O:** light, flame; fire; gas, electricity; radio, television; sound, volume □ *I* ***turned down*** *the gas.* BM □ *He* ***turned*** *the wireless* ***down.*** UTN

turn down[4] [A1 nom] (finance, commerce) become weaker, decline. **S:** (stock, money) market; economy; investment □ *The economy was* ***turning down*** *of its own accord.* BBCTV □ *Wall Street reports a* ***turndown*** *in the economy.* BBCTV □ *The province was beginning to experience a* ***downturn*** *in industrial production and consumer spending.* ST □ note the two nom forms turndown and (more usu) downturn.

turn from [A2 emph rel] leave, abandon. **o:** life, career; study, consideration; problem □ *He had no intention of going back to the life* ***from*** *which he had finally* ***turned*** *after so much indecision and struggle.* □ *At this point we* ***turn from*** *simple observation and enter the realm of speculation.*

turn in[1] [A1 B1i pass adj] face or curve inwards (naturally); cause to face inwards. **S:** [A1] **O:** [B1] ⚠ one's toes, feet, knees □ *His big toe* ***turns in*** (i e towards the other toes on that foot). □ *His feet* ***turn in*** (i e towards each other).

turn in[2] [B1i pass] return, because it is no longer needed, serviceable etc. **O:** uniform, equipment, bedding; radio, washing-machine □ *'I'll give the machine one more week to behave itself. And if it doesn't then I'll* ***turn*** *it* ***in*** *for another.'* DBM □ *'Don't forget to* ***turn in*** *all your camping gear before you leave.'*

turn in[3] [B1i pass] hand, submit, to sb (e g for study or publication); achieve, attain. **O:** essay, exercise; article, contribution; performance □ *'That was a terrible piece of work you* ***turned in*** *the other day. I could hardly believe it was yours.'* □ *At yesterday's athletics meeting, Thompson* ***turned in*** *a personal best time which is only two seconds outside the European record set up last year.*

turn in[4] [B1i pass] (informal) surrender (e g to the police); turn over (to)[1] (q v). **O:** prisoner; runaway, escapee; suspect □ *'I know you think I probably deserve it, but please don't* ***turn me in,*** *please!'* □ *The farmer was in two minds whether to* ***turn*** *the poachers* ***in*** *or let them go.*

turn in[5] [B1i pass] (informal) abandon, leave; renounce. **O:** job; night work, early shift; smoking, drinking □ *Peter had to* ***turn in*** *his evening paper-round: he found he had too much homework to do.* □ *'All this travelling about the country is doing your health no good. Why don't you* ***turn*** *it* ***in****?'*

turn in[6] [A1] (informal) go to bed □ *'It's late — time I was* ***turning in.'*** □ *A week from the date, you began refusing second helpings,* ***turning in*** *early, and the rest of it.* CON

turn in one's grave [A2] (of sb already dead) be likely to be offended or displeased. **S:** father, ancestor; founder (of a company); writer, composer □ *'Whether I'm in this or any Conservative club,' I said, 'my father'd* ***turn in his grave*** *if he could see me.'* RATT □ *I hear that somebody has written a pop version of Mozart's G minor Symphony. No doubt the composer is still* ***turning in his grave.*** □ often with *would.*

turn it in [B1ii] (slang) stop behaving in a way which irritates, annoys etc; knock it off (q v), pack it in (q v), pack it up (q v). □ *'Oh,* ***turn it in,*** *Robert. Can't you see that these people aren't the least bit interested in what you're saying?'*

turn in upon oneself [A3 B3 pass] move away from contact with others and become unhappily preoccupied with one's own problems. **S:** [A3] **O:** [B3] (hospital) patient; prisoner; divorcee, widow. **S:** [B3] life, experience; illness, bereavement □ *Nothing was built, every activity was delayed, and the villagers* ***turned*** *bitterly* ***in upon*** *themselves, hoping for nothing better than food and peace.* BN □ *Avoid him. He's one of those bitter, disillusioned men who will* ***turn*** *you* ***in upon*** *yourself.*

turn inside out [B1ii pass] make the inside of sth face outwards; search a place thoroughly (with the result that things are in disorder). **O:** umbrella; sock, jumper; bag, sack; room, drawer □ *'Are you quite sure you haven't got the key on you?* ***Turn*** *your pockets* ***inside out.'*** □ *'If you don't give us the evidence we want, we'll* ***turn*** *the place* ***inside out.'*** □note that inside out functions like a single particle here.

turn into[1] [A2] become, be changed into. **S:** water; wine; milk; caterpillar; youth, girl. **o:** ice, steam; vinegar; cheese; butterfly; man, woman □ *From an animal pacing within the area of his defended posts, the goalkeeper **turned into** a leaping ape.* LLDR □ *A rather skinny, spotty adolescent had **turned into** a confident, presentable young man.* ⇨ next entry.

turn into[2] [B2 pass] cause to become, change (into). **S:** experience, hardship, suffering; travel; builder; magician; heat. **O:** boy, girl; recruit; room, house; pumpkin; water. **o:** man, woman; veteran; workshop; fairy, coach; steam □ *She had thought that being happy would **turn** him **into** a normal confident person.* DC □ *She's **turned** the top floor **into** a temporary nursery and bedrooms.* DC □ *The magic spell **turned** the frogs and rats back **into** men.* HD ⇨ previous entry.

turn off[1] [B1i pass] disconnect; stop the flow of; switch off[1] (q v). **O:** light, fire; radio, television; shower; supply; electricity, gas, water □ *'Don't forget to **turn** all the lights **off** before you come up to bed.'* □ *The electricity supply must be **turned off** at the mains before you alter the lighting circuit.* □ *Sarah goes to **turn off** the music.* CSWB ⇨ be off[6], go off[7].

turn off[2] [B1ii pass B2 pass] (informal) make sb lose the appetite for, or interest in, sth or sb; switch off[2] (q v). **S:** visit, journey; smell, sight, sound. **o:** cooking, drink; tobacco, drug; music □ *One sniff of his breath was enough to **turn** you **off** drink for good.* □ *Pop music may turn you on, but it **turns** me **off**!* ⇨ be off[8], go off[4], put off[5].

turn off[3] [A1 nom A2] leave one road for another. **o:** road, motorway, track □ ***Turn off** about a mile further on.* □ *We **turned off** the motorway at exit 31.* □ *'You must have missed the **turn-off*** (i e the road which ***turns off***) *to Northampton. You'd better take the next exit.'*

turn on[1] [B1i pass] connect; start the flow of; switch on[1] (q v). **O:** light, fire; radio, record player; bathwater; gas, electricity □ *'I think we'll **turn on** a bar of the electric fire — it's a little chilly this evening.'* □ *'I've **turned on** your bath.'* FFE ⇨ be on[8], go on[15], put on[2].

turn on[2] [B1ii nom pass] (informal) stimulate, excite; switch on[2] (q v). **S:** singer, actor; girl; music; drug □ *'I think she's a marvellous girl — she really **turns** me **on**!'* □ *I'm not impressed by their choice of candidate. He's not likely to **turn** the voters **on**.* □ *'This little fellow came out and he reached to about here'* (indicating her navel). *'It was terrible because I'd always thought of him as a really fruity **turn-on**'* (i e *the kind of man who **turns** you **on***). ST

turn on[3] [A2 pass] become hostile towards, attack sb (verbally or physically), esp to blame or reproach him for sth. **o:** leader, organizer; wife, child □ *I lost the son you wanted; what a fine excuse you have at last for **turning on** me.* WI □ *'There's no need to **turn on** me just because rain spoiled the picnic.'*

turn on[4] [A2 emph rel] be decided by, follow logically from; depend on/upon[4] (q v); have as its main topic. **S:** result, outcome; decision, verdict; discussion, debate. **o:** factor, circumstance; (previous) record, convictions; what was to happen, how things were to be arranged □ *The question of a reprieve may **turn on** the age of the victim.* OBS □ *Our conversation **turned** mainly **on** what was to be done when the battle was over.* MFM

turn one's back on [B2 emph rel] not face or confront; reject, desert. **A:** firmly, finally, decisively, irrevocably. **o:** problem, difficulty; family, friend, ally □ (horoscope) *You really haven't much business sense, and you **turn your back on** material problems.* WI □ *The unions have **turned their backs** firmly **on** the government's incomes policy.* □ *Britain must not **turn her back on** Europe.*

turn the key on [B2 pass] lock a door behind sb. **S:** guard, goaler. **o:** captive, prisoner □ *I was thrown into a cell and the sentry assured me, as he **turned the key on** me, that my head would be cut off in the morning.* LWK

turn the tables (on) [B2 pass emph rel] gain an advantage (over sb) after having been at a disadvantage. **o:** rival, competitor, opponent □ *He enjoyed matching his wits against hers, allowing her to think that she was fooling him, and **turning the tables on** her eventually.* PE □ *If he were not expecting any attack, he would be at the mercy of a quick approach. But since he was expecting it, **the tables** were **turned on** the attacker.* ARG

turn a blind eye (on/to) [B2 pass emph rel] pretend to ignore or overlook; shut one's eyes to (q v). **S:** authorities; (school) staff; police. **o:** proceedings, goings-on; fault, error; misdemeanour, misconduct; rule, regulation □ *The Liberians **turned a blind eye on** the diamond traffic.* DS □ *By **turning a blind eye to** the small faults of juniors, your popularity and prestige should grow.* WI □ *These are petty infringements, **to** which the officials usually **turn a blind eye**.*

turn out[1] [B1i pass] extinguish. **O:** (electric) light, (gas, oil) lamp □ *'Make sure all the lights are **turned out** before you come up to bed.'* ⇨ be out[10], go out[5], put out[10].

turn out[2] [A1 nom] appear, be present, attend. **S:** crowd; supporter, follower, member; voter, elector □ *A large crowd **turned out*** (or: *There was a large **turn-out***) *to welcome the royal visitors.* □ *The weather prevented people from **turning out** in large numbers to watch the athletics meeting.*

turn out[3] [A1] develop, progress, in a certain way. **S:** events, things; child, pupil. **A:** well, all right, for the best; badly; how □ *She realized that perhaps what they all said was true — that Margot wasn't **turning out** very well.* H □ *I don't like it when I know from the start how things will **turn out**.* HD □ *We needn't have worried. Everything **turned out** all right in the end.* □ adv or adv phrase is present.

turn out[4] [B1i nom pass] empty the contents from (esp to find sth). **O:** pocket, wallet, briefcase, satchel, drawer □ *'But you must have the tickets on you somewhere. **Turn out** your pockets again.'* □ *I must give my files a good **turn-out*** (or: *have a good **turn-out** of my files*).

turn out[5] [B1iii pass] produce; develop, train. **O:** goods; car, van; yarn, fabric; student, pupil; athlete □ *Why go up to the manager in my own factory and tell him the stuff I'm **turning out** is shoddy and vulgar?* FFE □ *The press is ready to*

***turn out** a huge new edition.* UTN □ *The most useful function of any nursing school is **turning out** a supply of fully trained doctors' wives.* DIL

turn out[6] [B1ii nom pass adj] dress smartly etc. **O:** child, pupil; oneself. **A:** smartly, elegantly, beautifully □ *She always **turns** her children **out** beautifully.* □ *The troops were smartly **turned out** for the drill parade.* □ *The boys were complimented on their neat **turn-out**.* □ *A chic, well **turned-out** young lady of seventeen minced demurely towards us.* BM

as it/things turn(s) out [A1] as is shown or proved by later events □ ***As it turned out**, it was not snakes that disturbed us that evening.* DF □ ***As things turned out**, he had to tone down a few of my rather critical opinions.* DS

turn out (that) [A1] come to be known (that), transpire (that). **S:** it... (that) he knew all along, (that) he was already married, (that) there was no money left □ *It **turned out** he was born in the Caledonian Road.* CON □ *It **turns out that** this method does not work well* (or: *This method **turns out** not to work well*). NS ⇨ next entry.

turn out to be sb/sth [A1] prove (eventually) to be. **S:** stranger, visitor, newcomer; message, warning. **Inf** to be a cousin, to be false; to have lost his way □ *The symptom she had taken to the doctor hadn't **turned out to be** a false alarm.* PW □ *This **turned out to be** none other than the passport officer's respectable relative* (or: *It **turned out that** this was none other than* etc). BM □ *The girls would probably **turn out to be** models already* (or: *It would probably **turn out that** the girls were* etc). H ⇨ previous entry.

turn out (the guard) [A1 B1iii pass] (military) (of the soldiers guarding the regimental prisoners, the entry to barracks etc) (cause to) parade with rifles in front of the guard-room □ *The visiting general complimented the duty officer on **the guard's** quickness in **turning out**.* □ ***The guard** always dislikes being **turned out** in the middle of the night.* □ ***'Turn out the guard!'*** □ the last example shows the form of command used on these occasions.

turn out/out of [B1i pass B2 pass] expel sb, drive him out (by force, threats etc). **O:** intruder, invader; resident; worker. **o:** country; house, chair; job, post □ *We would have to get a good lodgement before the enemy could bring up sufficient reserves to **turn us out**.* MFM □ *I was **turned out of** my own office.* AITC

turn over[1] [A1 B1ii pass] (cause to) face in another direction by rolling. **S:** [A1] **O:** [B1] sleeper; body; car □ *'You bet you weren't listening* (i e *to me*). *Old Porter talks, and everyone **turns over** and goes to sleep.'* LBA □ *The child had been sleeping face down. His mother **turned** him **over** and tucked up the sheets.* □ *The aircraft struck the ground and **turned over** and **over**.*

turn over[2] [B1iii nom pass] (commerce, industry) do business to a particular amount; sell and replace (all) one's stock. **S:** trader; business, shop. **O:** amount, sum; £500, £2 000; stock □ *With my type of business the **turn-over** can vary considerably. One year I might **turn over** £1m — the next only £100 000.* OBS □ *The two men argued as to what sum, in a first year of market gardening, could be considered a reasonable **turn-over**.* PW □ *This supermarket chain **turns over** its stock very rapidly.*

turn-over [nom (B1)] (rate of) movement of workers into and out of a job or industry □ *The **turn-over** of labour is very rapid in some sections of the catering trade.* □ *Industries which need a stable workforce try to discourage a high **turn-over** of staff.*

turn over a new leaf [B1iii] change one's way of life for the better □ *I want to settle down, **turn over a new leaf**.* DPM □ *It is due to his protection and advice that I remained at Sandhurst, **turned over a new leaf**, and survived to make good.* MFM

turn over in one's mind [B3 pass] consider, think about, sth carefully and at length; reflect on/upon[1] (q v). **O:** offer, proposal; idea, scheme □ *He had the air of a man who is **turning over** a number of things **in his mind**.* CON □ *He had plenty of time before him to **turn** the idea **over in his mind**.* PW

turn over (to)[1] [B1i pass B3 pass] pass the control or running of sth (to sb else). **O:** control, direction, management; business, company. **o:** brother, partner, associate □ *The day-to-day management of the firm has been **turned over to** someone appointed from outside the company.*

turn over (to)[2] [B1i pass B3 pass] give into the custody of; turn in[4] (q v). **O:** captive, prisoner; (escaped) convict. **o:** authorities; police □ *'How do you know he isn't wanted by the police.' 'Why should he be?' 'If he is we ought to **turn** him **over**.'* ART □ *'I am quite sure that you have no intention of **turning** me **over** to any of them.'* T

turn round[1] [A1 B1ii pass] (cause to) face in the opposite direction. ⇨ turn around/round[1].

turn round[2] [A1 nom] (finance, commerce) reverse. ⇨ turn around/round[2].

turn round[3] [B1ii nom pass] (nautical) discharge passengers and/or cargo and get ready to sail again. **O:** ship; liner, tanker □ *One of the factors in the profitability of passenger ships is speed of **turn-round*** (cf *is how quickly they can be **turned round***).

turn round and do sth [A1] (informal) say or do sth which surprises and displeases the listener (because it suggests ingratitude, conceit etc) □ *Then the owner **turned round and said** we couldn't have the house after all, because he'd promised it to a friend.* □ *'You bring them* (i e children) *up, and they **turn round and talk** to you like that.'* TOH

turn to[1] [A2 pass emph rel] go to sb or sth for help, advice, information etc. **o:** father, teacher, priest; dictionary, guide, calendar □ *The child felt there was no one he could **turn to** with his problems.* □ *The parish priest was someone **to** whom everyone could **turn** in difficult times.* □ *It would have taken hours to work the sum out, so I **turned to** my pocket calculator.*

turn to[2] [A1] begin to work vigorously. **S:** family; staff; crew □ *There was nothing for it but to shift the load by hand, so everyone **turned to** with a will.* □ *The children **turned to** and cleared the dishes away.*

turn a blind eye (to) [B2 pass emph rel] ⇨ turn a blind eye (on/to).

turn a deaf ear (to) [B2 pass emph rel] try, or pretend, not to hear. **o:** complaint, criticism; moaning, caterwauling, commotion □ (horoscope) *Affairs should move extremely well provided that you **turn a deaf ear to** the chatter of a* *frustrated female.* WI □ ***To** all these accusations of foul play the referee **turned a** resolutely **deaf ear**.*

turn one's hand to [B2] (be able to) undertake (esp sth practical). **o:** task, job; carpentry, decorating; sewing, dressmaking □ *I'm not an interior decorator, but I could always **turn my hand to** most things.* TC □ *I know you've always thought that you could do anything you **turned your hand to**, and mostly you could.* AITC □ with can/could.

turn to one's (own) advantage [B2 pass] use, exploit, sth in a way which favours oneself. **O:** situation; crisis; shortage; misunderstanding □ *The Minister saw how the quarrel between his two senior colleagues could be **turned to his own advantage**.* □ *The swift stream hampered bridge building, but we could **turn it to advantage** by floating men across from up-river.*

turn up[1] [B1i pass adj] cause to face or point upwards. **O:** collar, sleeve, hat-brim □ *The collar of his overcoat was **turned up** against the bitter wind.*

turn up[2] [B1i pass] expose, make visible (esp by digging). **S:** plough, spade, excavator. **O:** bone, pottery, ornament □ *A tile from a Roman villa was **turned up** during the recent restoration work at York Minster.* □ *Relics from the First World War are still being **turned up** by farmers in Northern France.*

turn up[3] [A1] arrive, appear (often after some delay); show up[3] (q v). **S:** guest, visitor; bus, taxi □ *'Guy will **turn up**. If he isn't here by morning we can start some inquiries.'* DC □ *'The young scoundrel never had any thought for anyone. He shall hear about this from me when he **turns up**.'* DC

turn up[4] [A1] be found (esp by chance) after it has been lost. **S:** ring, watch, key □ *Her purse eventually **turned up**. The boy who took it had got scared and dropped it behind some lockers.*

turn up[5] [A1] present itself, become available (without one doing anything to create it). **S:** opportunity, chance; job, vacancy; something □ *I've been putting off a decision, and trying not to think about it, hoping that something would **turn up**.* RFW □ *He stayed in the North, hoping that an opening would **turn up** in textiles.*

turn up[6] [B1ii] (informal) make sb feel physically sick; repel sb morally or emotionally. **S:** sight, smell; blood; cruelty, neglect □ *The mere thought of flying **turns** her **up**.* □ *It **turned** me **up** to think of children being made to suffer.*

turn up[7] [A1] (finance, commerce) improve; rise, increase. **S:** (stock) market; economy; investment □ *Investment is **turning up** sharply, including a flood of new projects flowing into the regions on the back of the Industry Act.* ST □ *But the next **upturn** in the firm's fortunes came with the arrival of a Canadian manager.* BBCR □ nom form is upturn.

turn-up(s) [nom (B1)] trouser bottom which is permanently folded up □ ***Turn-ups** seem to be coming back into fashion.* □ *'Watch it,' I said to Ned. 'If she gives you any coffee, pour it into your **turn-ups**.'* CON ⇨ turn up[1].

turn-up (for the book) [nom (A1)] (slang) sth unusual or unexpected □ *'Fancy Jones getting a steady job after a lifetime of crime — now that's a **turn-up for the book**!'*

turn it up [B1ii] (slang) abandon a job etc, give up[2] (q v); stop doing or saying sth which offends other people □ *I wish I could **turn it** all **up** and get away abroad for a bit.* ILIH □ *'**Turn it up**. You're upsetting the poor girl.'*

turn up trumps [A1] (informal) act in a helpful or dependable way in difficult times □ *Trust John to **turn up trumps** when we're short of cash.* □ *He can always be depended on to **turn up trumps** in a crisis.*

turn one's nose up (at) [B1i B3] (informal) behave in a superior way (towards). **o:** (ordinary, working-class) people; tradesmen; (foreign, provincial) voice, manners □ *I know it's only sausages and mash again, but there's no need to **turn your nose up at** it.* □ *Some people **turn up their noses** if you say your father was a miner or a docker.*

tussle (with) [A2 pass] fight, struggle (with). **o:** solicitor, bank; problem, difficulty □ *She had to **tussle with** the lawyers for years before she could win custody of her daughter.*

twiddle (with) [A2] turn, handle, aimlessly; play with[1] (q v). **o:** control, knob, button; bracelet, necklace □ *He could quite happily spend hours **twiddling with** the knobs on his radio.*

twine around/round [B2 pass emph rel] wind sth thin and supple around. **O:** (cotton, woollen) thread, yarn. **o:** spool, bobbin, reel □ *As she spoke, Susan idly **twined** a piece of wool **round** her finger.* □ *The brambles were **twined around*** (cf *had **twined** themselves **around***) *the garden fence.*

twist around/round [B2 pass emph rel] wind sth thin and stiff around. **O:** (piece of) grass, wire. **o:** branch; spool, coil; leg, finger □ *A bamboo support was driven into the ground alongside the cherry tree and a length of raffia **twisted around** them both to hold them together.* □ *A thin piece of wire had got **twisted round*** (or: *had **twisted** itself **round***) *his ankle.*

twist around/round one's little finger [B2] (informal) by charm and guile persuade a man to do what one wants; wind around/round one's (little) finger (q v). **S:** daughter, wife □ *I believe, if she wanted to, she could **twist** anyone **round her little finger**.* DC □ *'You could even **twist** my uncle **around your little finger**.'* WI

twist off [B1i pass B2 pass] remove by turning. **O:** top, cap, cover; knob; button. **o:** pot, jar, bottle; door; coat □ *'You try to **twist** the cap **off** this jar. My hands are too slippery.'* □ *The handles can be **twisted off*** (cf: *The handles **twist off***).

twist up [B1i pass adj] contort, distort. **S:** pain; disgust, contempt; envy, greed. **O:** him etc; expression; face, body; inside, character □ *Every time he tried to move, a sudden stab of pain **twisted** him **up**.* □ *'He's a rather pitiful character, really — all **twisted up** with fear and jealousy.'*

type in/into [B1i pass adj B2 pass] include, insert, sth in a text by typing it. **O:** (omitted, additional) word, phrase. **o:** text, script □ *'Don't bother to do the notice over again. You can **type** the missing name **in** above the line.'* □ *'You'll notice I've **typed** a few afterthoughts **into** the margin of this letter.'*

type out [B1i pass adj] produce sth on the typewriter (i e without having first written it by hand); make a typewritten copy of a handwritten text. **O:** list, notice, application; speech □ *'If you wait a minute, I'll* ***type*** *you* ***out*** *a proper receipt.'* □ *'Would you mind* ***typing out*** *a list of first-year students?'* □ *A secretary was* ***typing out*** *the candidate's election address.* □ the first example contains an Indirect Object (*you*).

type up [B1i pass adj] make a 'fair' typed copy of a handwritten text; make, in typescript, a fuller, better organized version of rough notes etc. **O:** manuscript; book, thesis; notes, rough draft □ *The final draft of his thesis has been approved by his supervisor. Now he must take it to be* ***typed up*** *and bound.* □ *Mary spent the evening* ***typing up*** *the notes of her laboratory experiment.*

U

unaccounted for [pass adj (A2)] (be) unexplained. **S:** loss, disappearance; (missing) men, aircraft □ *A discrepancy in the miscellaneous earnings column remains* ***unaccounted for.*** □ *There is an* ***unaccounted-for*** *gap of several minutes on the tape-recording of his telephone conversation.* □ *Serious concern that 'some' Sam-7 anti-aircraft missiles are '****unaccounted for****' in Europe was expressed here by Administration sources.* T ⇨ account for[1,2].

unbosom oneself (to) [B2 emph rel] (formal) reveal, disclose, one's secret thoughts, anxieties (to). **o:** friend, mother, lover □ *Here was somebody to whom she could speak freely,* ***to*** *whom she could* ***unbosom herself.***

unburden oneself (to) [B2 emph rel] (formal) reveal to sb anxieties, sorrows etc which are a burden to one's thoughts or conscience. **o:** friend, relative □ *She longed for a sympathetic person* ***to*** *whom she could* ***unburden herself.*** □ ***To*** *him she might* ***unburden herself*** *fully of the anxieties which beset her.*

uncalled for [pass adj (A2)] not (be) desirable or necessary. **S:** remark, comment; insult, rudeness; intervention, intrusion □ *His remarks on that occasion were quite* ***uncalled for.*** □ *His* ***uncalled-for*** *criticisms upset quite a number of people.* ⇨ call for.

uncared for [pass adj (A2)] not (be) properly tended or looked after. **S:** house, garden; child; appearance, hair, clothes □ *Since the break-up of his marriage he has looked distinctly haggard and* ***uncared for.*** □ *The house was allowed to go to rack and ruin and the children were poorly fed and* ***uncared for.*** ⇨ care for[2].

undreamed/undreamt of [pass adj (A2)] (be) unimaginable. **S:** sum, amount (of money); riches, fortune; success, fame □ *Investment on that sort of scale was* ***undreamed of*** *when I first joined the company.* □ *'£3 000 a year? That was* ***undreamt-of*** *wealth to his father's generation.'*

unfit for [B2 pass emph rel] make sb unable to fulfil a particular task, duty etc. **S:** injury, illness; instability; temper, rudeness. **o:** work, duty; membership □ *'I am afraid that his attitude to authority* ***unfits*** *him* ***for*** *work on this project.'* □ *He was* ***unfitted for*** *flying by the loss of his legs.*

unfold (to) [B2 pass emph rel] (formal) make known (to), reveal (to) (q v). **O:** plan, intention, scheme. **o:** colleague, associate □ *The board listened in silence as the details of the scheme were* ***unfolded to*** *them.* □ *The few men* ***to*** *whom he had* ***unfolded*** *the arrangements for the next day were sworn to secrecy.*

unguessed at [pass adj (A2)] (be) unsuspected. **S:** presence, existence; threat, danger (of invasion, absorption); size, gravity (of the problem) □ *The presence of invasion forces along the frontier went* ***unguessed at*** *for several months.* □ *The imminence of the oil embargo was* ***unguessed at*** *even in government circles.*

unheard of[1] [pass adj (A2)] (be) unknown. **S:** writer, composer, actor □ *He was virtually* ***unheard of*** *before he had his first part on the West-End stage.* □ *With a young,* ***unheard-of*** *poet and a first book of verse, the publisher is taking a risk.* ⇨ hear of[1].

unheard of[2] [pass adj (A2)] (be) without previous example, without precedent. **S:** achievement, feat; (it...) for sb to achieve so much □ *It's* ***unheard of*** *for a boy of his age to gain university entrance.* □ *Combining a career with the responsibilities of running a house — this was an almost* ***unheard-of*** *achievement fifty years ago.*

unite (in) [A2 B2 pass] join with others in expressing particular feelings or views. **S:** [A2] **O:** [B2] country, (political) party, association. **o:** praise (for); condemnation (of), opposition (to), protest (against) □ *The Trade Union leaders were* ***united in*** *deploring the unprecedented rise in food prices.* □ *The employers had* ***united in*** *condemning excessive wage demands.* □ *The harsh, repressive, policies adopted by the invader had* ***united*** *the country* ***in*** *resistance to the occupation forces.*

unite (with) [A2 emph rel B2 pass emph rel] join with another to form one unit. **S:** [A2] **O:** [B2] country, province, region □ *Scotland was* ***united with*** *England* (or: *Scotland and England were* ***united***) *in 1707.* □ *There are many ties that* ***unite*** *our two countries* (or: ***unite*** *your country* ***with*** *mine*).

unleash (against/on/upon) [B2 pass emph rel] release sb or sth in a powerful attack (on). **O:** dog, hound; army, forces; tanks, aircraft. **o:** stranger, intruder; country, people □ *'I'm not going anywhere near his front gate if it means having that great bulldog* ***unleashed on*** *me.'* □ *When enemy forces at the centre had spent themselves with hard fighting, our reserves would be* ***unleashed against*** *their flanks.*

unload onto [B2 pass emph rel] (informal) pass a heavy or irksome burden onto sb else. **O:** work, responsibility; stock, share □ *There is always somebody in the office* ***onto*** *whom the really unpleasant jobs are* ***unloaded.*** □ *'The value of your holdings is falling. Better try to* ***unload*** *them* ***onto*** *someone else.'*

unlooked for [pass adj (A2)] (be) unexpected because it has not been sought. **S:** opportunity, break, chance; benefit, bonus □ *Then came an* ***unlooked-for*** *blessing in the form of a salary increase.* □ *The welcome was all the more pleasant for being quite* ***unlooked for.***

unprovided for [pass adj (A2)] having no money saved for him or her by a parent, guardian or husband. **S:** widow, child; relative, dependent □ *His unmarried sisters were left quite* ***unprovided for*** *in the will.* ⇨ provide for[1].

unthought of [pass adj (A2)] (be) unthinkable, (be) inconceivable (and thus likely to arouse disapproval). **S:** step, move, initiative; questioning, criticizing (one's elders); to act independently; choosing one's own wife □ *In Victorian times it was* ***unthought of*** *for a middle-class girl to seek a professional career, except perhaps as a governess or schoolmistress.* □ *The younger son had decided to marry a girl without money — an* ***unthought-of*** *undertaking in such a property-conscious family.*

used to [pass (B2)] have learned to accept or expect; (be) accustomed to (q v). **o:** heat, cold, damp; uninteresting food, poor service, royal treatment; being ignored, having the best of everything □ *It was some time before my eyes got* ***used to*** *the gloom in Stanley's workshop.* □ *'I'm not too upset by the news. By now, I'm* ***used to*** *adjusting to sudden changes of plan.'* □ passive with *be, become, get.*

use up [B1i pass adj] use until no more is left, exhaust. **O:** supply, stock; fuel; ink; strength, energy □ *he* ***used up*** *his reserves in fruitless counter-attacks during the spring.* □ *'There isn't any more coal: it's all been* ***used up.****'*

usher in [B1i pass] announce, signal the start of. **O:** time, period, epoch □ *It is the happy custom for the Viennese to* ***usher in*** *the New Year with a concert of music by Strauss.* RT □ *It would be unwise to assume that the July elections will* ***usher in*** *a new millenium.* OBS

usher in/into [B1i pass B2 pass rel] conduct, lead (in). **S:** butler, maid □ *We were* ***ushered into*** *a waiting room lined with uncomfortable chairs.* □ *The room* ***into*** *which we were* ***ushered*** *looked out onto the gardens.*

usher out/out of [B1i pass B2 pass rel] conduct, lead (out). **S:** butler, maid □ *He was* ***ushered out of*** *the charge office by two policemen.* □ *And he opened the door and* ***ushered her out.*** TT

V

vacillate (between) [A2 emph rel] be uncertain as to which of two courses to choose; move restlessly from one emotional extreme to another; waver (between) (q v). **o:** action and inertia, hope and despair, greed and disgust □ *At the moment we seem to be* ***vacillating between*** *positive action and doubt that any good can come of such action.* □ *Total gloom and foolish optimism — these are the moods* ***between*** *which he keeps* ***vacillating.***

value (at) [B2 pass emph rel] set the money value of sth at a particular figure. **S:** estate-agent, auctioneer. **O:** property, estate; house, farm. **o:** amount, sum □ *The house has been* ***valued at*** *around £20 000.* □ *I'm not prepared to sell below the price* ***at*** *which the flat has been* ***valued*** *by the agents.*

vamp up [B1i pass adj] (informal) make sth superficially attractive without making any genuine changes underneath. **S:** owner, manager. **O:** appearance; presentation, packaging; decorations, paintwork □ *The front office has been* ***vamped up*** *with strip lighting and a new coat of paint.* □ *There's no real change in the content of his lecture course — he's* ***vamped*** *it* ***up*** *a bit with one or two tricks of presentation.*

vanish (from) [A2] suddenly cease to be visible or present. **o:** sight, view; our presence, midst; the face of the earth □ *The horseman* ***vanished from*** *sight behind a clump of trees.* □ *The destruction of the village was ruthless and total. It was as though the place had* ***vanished from*** *the face of the earth.*

varnish over [A2 pass adj B1i pass adj] cover with varnish; cover sth unpleasant with a smooth surface. **o:** table, chair; appearance, manner □ *Scrape the old paint off, sand the surface down, and then* ***varnish over*** *it* (or: ***varnish*** *it* ***over***). □ *The cracks and flaws in his old performance have been skilfully* ***varnished over.***

vary (between) [A2] ⇨ next entry.

vary from to [A2] move up and down, fluctuate between certain limits; range from to (q v). **S:** temperature, pressure; takings, profit; demand, expenditure; mood, response. **o:** (***from***) (maximum) level, point; one extreme; (***to***) (minimum) level; another extreme; rock bottom □ *Consumption of domestic fuel oil* ***varies from*** *150 gallons a month at the height of winter* ***to*** *practically nothing in July–August* (or: ***varies between*** *150 gallons* etc *and practically nothing* etc). □ *'One never knows quite how one's going to find him. His moods can* ***vary from*** *black introspection* ***to*** *wild exuberance* (or: *can* ***vary between*** *black introspection and wild exuberance*)*.'*

vent (on) [B2 pass emph rel] (formal) express, get rid of, by attacking one person, the anger etc one feels against another. **O:** anger, fury, temper; spite, spleen, bitterness. **o:** wife, child; subordinate; dog □ *He longed to* ***vent on*** *George all the spite he felt against his former associates.* PE

venture on/upon [A2 pass emph rel] (formal) attempt, undertake, sth involving risk or danger. **o:** undertaking, operation; journey, expedition; explanation, criticism □ *The hope of making further discoveries led them to* ***venture upon*** *a second voyage.* □ *The company secretary, who had never liked the scheme, but who also knew that stronger voices would be raised in support of it,* ***ventured*** *cautiously* ***on*** *a statement of the risks involved.*

verge on/upon [A2] come close to, approach. **S:** company, trader; idea, proposal; behaviour, condition. **o:** ruin, bankruptcy; lunacy, foolhardiness □ *He had taken over an old company* ***verging on*** *liquidation.* □ *She was not in that state* ***verging on*** *hysteria all the time.* DC

vest in [B2 pass emph rel] (formal, official) legally confer rights etc on a person or body. **S:** sovereign, legislature; constitution. **O:** right, power, authority. **o:** official, public servant; Senate □ *In the United States, the power to declare war is **vested in** the Senate* (or: *the Senate is **vested with** the power* etc). □ *'By the powers **vested in** me, I declare you duly elected.'*

vest with [B2 pass emph rel] ⇨ previous entry.

vie (with eachother/one another) [A2] try to surpass one another (in doing sth). **S:** (two, several) firms, departments; comedians; sportsmen □ *Two engineering companies were **vying with each other** to capture this valuable market.* □ *The members of the Military Board **vied with one another** in telling me agreeable things, and I kept looking around at them in astonishment.* OBS □ usu followed by an inf or a prep + *-ing* form.

visit with [A2] (US) call at the house of sb to talk etc; visit (GB). **o:** friend, neighbour, relative □ *Weekends we usually **visit with** my husband's family.*

volunteer (for) [A2 emph rel] offer oneself as willing to serve in the armed forces, or to do a particular task. **o:** infantry, tank corps; flying duty, overseas service; work on the land □ *The arm of the service **for** which he'd **volunteered** already had its full complement of men.* □ *'I can't get any of the children to **volunteer for** work in the garden.'*

vote (against) [A2 pass emph rel] show that one opposes sb or sth by ballot or by a show of hands. **S:** member, delegate; elector(ate), country. **o:** leadership; proposal, motion; Bill □ *He **voted against** the government party at the last election.* □ *The Chamber **voted** overwhelmingly **against** changing the law.* □ *'Which way did you **vote**?' '**Against** the Bill.'*

vote down [B1i pass] reject sth, or defeat the person advocating sth, by ballot or show of hands. **O:** motion, proposal; member □ *Someone proposed that the proceedings of the meeting should be recorded on tape, but the suggestion was **voted down**.*

vote (for) [A2 pass emph rel] show one's support (for sb or sth) by ballot or by a show of hands. **S:** member, delegate; elector, country. **o:** leader; policy; proposal, motion; Bill □ *The government were not implementing the policies **for** which he'd **voted** in the last election.* □ *Whether you **vote for** or against the proposal doesn't seem to matter very much.*

vote in/into [B1i pass B2 pass] elect sb to serve in Parliament, on a local council etc; put in[6] (q v). **O:** Labour, the Conservatives; MP, councillor. **o:** ⚠ office, power □ *Labour was **voted in** for a second term of office, though with a greatly reduced number of seats.* □ *The Democrats were **voted into** power on a programme of wide-ranging social reform.*

vote (on) [A2 pass emph rel] express one's support of, or opposition to, sth by ballot or show of hands. **S:** chamber, assembly; meeting. **o:** motion, proposal; Bill □ *We are now **voting on** a motion to adjourn the meeting.* □ ***On** this Bill every member is free to **vote** as his own conscience dictates.*

vote on/onto [B1ii pass B2 pass] make sb a member of some official body by ballot or show of hands. **O:** specialist, expert; (additional) member. **o:** committee, board, panel; council □ *'He has more experience of fund-raising than anyone, so we'll **vote** him **on** for a start.'* □ *An accountant and an architect were **voted onto** the committee in the hope that they would contribute their expert knowledge at the planning stage.*

vote out/out of [B1i pass B2 pass] remove from office by casting one's vote at an election. **O:** Labour, the Republicans; minister; member, representative. **o:** ⚠ office, power □ *If the present Government is **voted out** it will be on its general handling of the economic situation.* □ *'If you don't like the way the Council are going about things, you can always **vote** them **out of** office.'*

vote through [B1i pass] approve, make legal, by ballot or a show of hands. **S:** House, chamber; meeting. **O:** legislation, Bill, Act □ *The Bill was **voted through** by both Houses with little delay.*

vouch for [A2 pass emph rel] support the truth of sth, by producing evidence, indicating that one was present etc; express one's confidence in a person. **o:** truth, reliability, accuracy; prisoner, the accused □ *One application of 'primitive' medicine, **vouched for** by modern anthropologists, goes back beyond the reach of human memory.* SNP □ *I can definitely **vouch for** it that Robert and his Italian girl are washed up* (i e no longer lovers). CON

W

wade in/into [A1 A2 pass] (informal) attack sb or sth vigorously. **o:** opponent, adversary; task, job □ *He just **waded into** the bigger boy with both fists flying.* □ *He didn't stand about looking at all the jobs to be done: he **waded** straight **in**.*

wade through[1] [A1 A2] walk through some thick liquid substance which reaches some way up one's legs. **o:** mud, slush; grain; oil; pond □ *Rescue teams **waded** knee-deep **through** the flooded streets.* □ *Every time our youngest daughter, Sarah, comes to a deep, muddy puddle she has to **wade through** it.*

wade through[2] [A1 A2] (informal) proceed slowly and with difficulty with some task. **o:** paperwork, marking, accounts, files □ *'I shan't be able to get away this weekend: I've got six sets of exam scripts to **wade through**.'*

wage war (against/on) [B2 pass emph rel] fight, conduct, a war against; try to control by vigorous action. **o:** nation, state; inflation, rising prices □ *For almost a year they had **waged** a **war** of nerves **on** their neighbours; now it was to be war in earnest.* □ *The government promised to **wage** a ceaseless **war against** price increases.*

wager (on) [B2 pass] bet money on a horse etc,

hoping that it will win; put on[8] (q v), stake on[1] (q v). **O:** large sum, fortune. **o:** horse, dog; boxer □ *'There's nothing in this race I'd be prepared to* ***wager*** *more than a few pence* ***on****.'* □ *A lot of money was* ***wagered on*** *a good-looking horse in the second race.*

wager on [A2 B2 pass] (informal) (be prepared to) agree confidently that sth is the case, or will occur. **O:** ⚠ anything, (too) much, a lot. **o:** it, that; John arriving in time; prompt delivery, good response □ *'He promised me a fabulous holiday in the Bahamas.' 'Well, I wouldn't* ***wager*** *too much* ***on*** *that.'* □ *'I suppose he might settle his bill at the end of the month, but I shouldn't* ***wager on*** *it, if I were you.'* □ usu neg, with *should/could*.

wait about/around [A1] stay in a place (usu idly and impatiently, because sb who is expected has not arrived etc); hang about/around (q v) □ *'I'm furious: you've kept me* ***waiting about*** *here for a whole hour.'* □ *'Show the visitor in as soon as he arrives. Don't make him* ***wait around*** *in the corridor.'*

wait at table(s)/on tables [A2] bring food and drink to guests at their table(s), remove dishes etc □ *I got holiday jobs in guesthouses, washing dishes and* ***waiting on tables****.* DC □ ***Waiting at table*** *is a skilled job, requiring careful training.*

wait behind [A1] remain in a room etc after others have left □ *'John, you can* ***wait behind*** *when the class is dismissed: I want to have a word with you.'* □ *One or two students* ***waited behind*** *to put more questions to the lecturer.*

wait for [A2 rel] stay where one is until sb comes or sth happens; await an event hopefully. **o:** train, bus; end, beginning; better things, improvement □ *A queue of people were* ***waiting for*** *the last bus.* □ *The climax of the film is something worth* ***waiting for****.* □ *The birth of a son was an event* ***for*** *which they had* ***waited*** *and prayed.*

wait for it [A2] (informal) (a warning not to) speak, move etc, before the proper moment has come □ *'Yes, I know what happened then: Mike fell out of bed.'* ***'Wait for it****, can't you? Who's telling the story, you or me?'* □ *By her side the old Chief said quietly,* ***'Wait for it****. Remember, don't look at the tracer, just keep looking at the sights* (i e of the gun)*, and mind what I told you.* ***Wait for it****.'* RFW □ imper only.

wait on tables [A2] ⇨ wait at table(s)/on tables.

wait on/upon sb hand and foot [A2 pass] act as a servant to sb, answering to his every need. **S:** servant; wife, daughter □ *He lived in great style —* ***waited on hand and foot****.* □ *At home the boys never lifted a finger. We girls had to* ***wait on them hand and foot****.*

wait out [B1ii] await calmly and patiently the end of an unpleasant period. **O:** ⚠ it; a storm, crisis □ *The storm showed no sign of abating. We'd have to be patient and* ***wait*** *it* ***out****.* □ *Don't interfere when they are like this — stay in a corner and* ***wait*** *it* ***out****.*

wait up (for) [A1 A3 pass] stay awake and out of bed until sb comes home. **S:** parent, wife □ *The old folks always go to bed about ten. They don't* ***wait up for*** *me.* TC □ *'I shan't get in till after midnight, so don't bother to* ***wait up****.'*

wake up [A1 B1i pass] (cause to) become conscious after a sleep □ *I drowsed off and* ***woke up*** *to hear Bob talking to some fellow who was new to the place.* BM □ *'Don't make a noise — you'll* ***wake*** *the baby* ***up****.'*

wake up (to) [A1 A3 pass] realize, become aware (of), sth important. **o:** danger, threat; the fact, realization… that times have changed, that one is no longer young; (an awareness of) oneself □ *They should* ***wake up*** *and see the problems they've got on their hands* (or: *They should* ***wake up to*** *the problems* etc). □ *It's time I* ***woke up to*** *myself. I had a good look in the mirror just now, and it's not flattering.* RFW

walkabout [nom (A1)] (informal) a tour on foot (esp by a politician, or visiting dignitary) to meet and talk to people informally □ *Jeremy Thorpe launched the Liberal campaign yesterday with a damp but cheery* ***'walkabout'*** *at Richmond, Surrey.* ST □ *New Zealanders are understandably proud that the Queen chose their country for the first-ever* ***walkabout*** *eleven years ago.* BBCTV □ *This time there will be no nonsense from Harold Wilson, playing around in a low key campaign, showing himself in quiet* ***walkabout*** *chats in the High Street.* ST □ may be attrib, as in the last example.

walk abroad [A1] (formal) spread far and wide. **S:** disease, pestilence; murder, arson □ *There death and destruction had already* ***walked abroad****.* SD

walk away with [A3] (informal) win a contest easily. **S:** player, team; (political) party, candidate. **o:** game, match; election □ *'It's no good — they've lost. They should have* ***walked away with*** *the game.'* LLDR □ *The official Labour Party candidate* ***walked away with*** *the election: his majority was about ten thousand.*

walk in/into [A1 A2] enter a place easily, because it is not properly locked or guarded. **o:** shop, office □ *The security is so bad here that anyone could simply* ***walk in*** *and take what he wanted.*

walk into [A2] receive a blow, shock etc, because one is inattentive or careless. **o:** blow, punch; trap, ambush □ *For a second his attention wavered, and he* ***walked*** *straight* ***into*** *a right hook.* □ *'He loves to set traps for the unwary: you wouldn't be the first to* ***walk into*** *one.'*

walk off [B1i pass] remove, reduce, by walking. **O:** some weight, a few pounds; (the effects of a) heavy lunch, business dinner; mood □ *I'll have to get out into the country more, and* ***walk off*** *some of this fat.* □ *We started back in a mood of deep depression, but had* ***walked*** *it* ***off*** *before we got home.*

walk off his feet [B2 pass] (informal) make sb walk so fast and so far that he is exhausted □ *'Let me sit down for a moment: the children have been* ***walking*** *me* ***off my feet****.'* □ *'If you want a leisurely stroll through the museum, don't take that guide — she'll* ***walk*** *all of you* ***off your feet****.'*

walk off with [A3] take, carry away, sb's property, either intentionally or by mistake. **o:** purse, bag, briefcase; coat, hat □ *'This isn't* ***my*** *mac — some idiot must have* ***walked off with*** *it.'* □ *'Don't leave your suitcases unguarded. Somebody may* ***walk off with*** *them.'*

walk on [A1 nom] (theatre) have a small part, appear briefly, in a play □ *When he first joined* *the company, Christopher was happy just to be able to* ***walk on*** *— to play the butler or the policeman.* □ *She's had a couple of* ***walk-on*** (or: ***walking-on***) *parts in West End productions — and that's about all.* □ nom forms usu attrib, as here.

walk out[1] [A1] (military) leave barracks with permission during off-duty hours. **S:** soldier, NCO □ *During the first weeks of basic training recruits are not permitted to* ***walk out***. □ *Soldiers are normally allowed to* ***walk out*** *in uniform or plain clothes* (= civilian dress).

walk out[2] [A1 nom] (industrial relations) leave one's place of work to protest, to obtain sth etc; come out[1] (q v). **S:** worker; docker, fitter □ *Building workers* ***walked out*** (or: *staged a* ***walk-out***) *during the morning in protest at the sacking of a bricklayer.*

walk out/out of [A1 nom A2] leave a meeting, organization etc as an expression of disapproval, protest etc. **S:** delegate, representative; delegation. **o:** conference, meeting; talks; committee □ *The Minister of Employment is attempting to call a fresh meeting following yesterday's* ***walk-out*** *by union delegates.* □ *At various times, both teams of negotiators had* ***walked out of*** *the peace talks.*

walk out on [A3 pass] (informal) leave, abandon, sb (esp when he is in difficulties and expecting help); leave sb because the relationship is at an end, or difficult to bear. **o:** friend, child, colleague; wife, boyfriend, girlfriend □ *'You've got his baby; you can't just* ***walk out on*** *him because he doesn't get on with your family.'* ASA □ *'So you're* ***walking out on*** *the job, are you? You're just a louse like the rest of them.'* HD □ *'So things didn't work out then?' 'No, I've just* ***walked out on*** *him, for better or for worse.'* EGD

walk out (with) [A1 A3 rel] form a serious relationship (spending a lot of time in one another's company etc), usu leading to marriage □ *'Is she engaged to him?' 'That I don't know, but they are* ***walking out***.*'* PW □ *He understood that this was a definite invitation from her. She was prepared to* ***walk out with*** *him.* HD □ *John is* ***walking out with*** *Mary* (or: *John and Mary are* ***walking out*** *(together)*). □ usu rural and/or lower-class.

walk-over [nom (A1)] (informal) victory that is easily won, success that is easily achieved □ *'It won't be a* ***walk-over*** *this time: the champion has a tough fight on his hands.'* □ *'Now, stop worrying about those exams. You've got all the answers at your finger-tips, so relax. It's going to be a* ***walk-over***.*'*

walk all over [A2] (informal) defeat thoroughly, punish severely (as in a contest); behave towards sb in an inconsiderate, domineering way. **S:** boxer, team; boss, father. **o:** novice, opposition; staff, children □ *The replay wasn't much of a contest: Liverpool* ***walked all over*** *them.* □ *'Imagine trying to stand up to the woman. It'd be like doing battle with a tank. She'd* ***walk all over*** *you.'*

walk over (the course) [A1 nom A2] (horse-racing) in a race where there is no other starter, walk the length of the course to be adjudged the winner □ *Danny Boy and Morning Star scratched from an already reduced field in the 3.15, so Running Wild got the* ***walk-over***.

walk through [B1ii nom pass B2 pass] (theatre) show sb the movements he must make in a scene etc, and make him copy them. **S:** director. **O:** cast, actor. **o:** scene, act □ *'Don't worry too much about lines. I just want to* ***walk*** *you* ***through*** *part of Act I.'* □ *'After lunch I want to do a* ***walk-through*** *of the ghost scene.'*

walk up [A1] (invitation to) enter a circus etc (from a man posted outside the ticket office) □ *'****Walk up****! ****Walk up****! The greatest show on earth is about to begin!'*

wall in [B1i pass adj] enclose with a wall; surround sb so that he is not free to move. **O:** garden, park, yard; fugitive, quarry □ *Behind the house was a neat* ***walled-in*** *garden.* □ *The mass of faces pressed closer,* ***walling*** *him* ***in***.

wall up [B1i pass adj] close, seal, with a wall (of brick, plaster etc). **O:** space; door(way), window □ *When the central-heating was installed, the fireplaces were* ***walled up***.

wallow in [A2 rel] roll about (pleasurably), usu to get or stay cool; sink oneself into a particular emotion (usu self-indulgently or perversely). **S:** elephant, buffalo; neurotic. **o:** water, mud, slime; self-pity, remorse; corruption, sensual delights □ *The rhinoceroses* ***wallow in*** *the soft mud at the edge of the river.* □ *The longer she* ***wallows in*** *feelings of guilt the harder it will be for her to make a fresh start.*

waltz off with [A3] (informal) win a prize etc, esp by beating others easily; run away with[3] (q v). **S:** athlete; schoolboy. **o:** cup, medal; scholarship, prize □ *Later in the week, the Kenyans* ***waltzed off with*** *gold medals in the 5000 metres and the steeplechase.* □ *The head prefect* ***waltzed off with*** *the maths and science prizes.*

wander about [A1 A2] move about without any sense of where one is going. **S:** traveller, expedition; (lost) child □ *'I was the one who found your little boy* ***wandering about*** *on the edge of the crowd and took him to the police station.'* □ *The survivors* ***wandered about*** *the jungle for days before being picked up by a search party.*

wander from/off [A2 rel] move, stray, in an absent-minded way from the subject one is concerned with. **S:** speaker; mind, thoughts. **o:** ⚠ the (main) point, issue, subject, matter □ *Don't let your mind* ***wander off*** *the main point at issue.* □ *Someone seated at the chairman's elbow would need to bring him back to the subject under discussion —* ***from*** *which he all too easily* ***wandered***.

(not) want for [A2] (not) require, (not) need, (not) lack money, or the means to a good life. **S:** family, wife, parents. **o:** ⚠ anything, (very) much; nothing □ *His children* ***don't want for*** *anything — they're well provided for.* □ *He makes sure that his widowed mother* ***wants for*** *nothing.*

want out/out of [A1 A2] (US informal) wish to be freed from sth unpleasant, not wish to be involved any longer. **S:** husband, wife; partner; company, country. **o:** involvement, commitment; risk; war □ *'Don't imagine that you can depend on my support any longer; I* ***want out***.*'* □ *The ordinary people* ***want out of*** *their government's involvement in the war.*

ward off [B1iii pass adj] defend, protect,

oneself against. **O:** attack; blow, thrust; feeling; depression, despair □ *He flung up an arm to **ward off** the blow.* PE □ *To **ward off** the feeling, I drank the whisky quickly.* SML

warm to [A2] become more lively about, enthusiastic about sth (as one proceeds with it). **o:** work, task; subject, theme □ *Sensing the interest of the audience, the chairman **warmed to** his topic, giving the most entertaining, and convincing, speech of the evening.* □ *Pierre grew ruder and louder as he **warmed to** his work.* BFA

warm towards [A2] feel a sympathetic interest in □ *I felt myself **warming towards** this big friendly man who had done so much to help us.* □ *She's not the sort of girl one **warms towards** easily — rather cold and aloof.*

warm up[1] [A1 B1i pass adj] become, make, warm, or warmer. **S:** [A1] **O:** [B1] food, liquid; house, room □ *'Just a minute while I **warm up** some milk on the gas.'* □ *Why is it this room always takes so long to **warm up**?* □ *'Don't serve me **warmed-up** food* (i e which has been cooked, allowed to get cold and then reheated).'

warm up[2] [A1] reach the point (after particular parts are warm and working smoothly) where the whole machine etc can function properly. **S:** machine, motor; car; television (receiver), radio □ *In cold weather pull the choke out half-way, and let the engine **warm up**, before you move off.* □ *A transistorized radio takes no time to **warm up**.*

warm up[3] [A1 nom] (sport) take exercises to loosen one's muscles etc, before a game etc. **S:** athlete, footballer □ *The German manager has one of his substitutes **warming up** on the touch-line now.* □ *The runners are having a quick **warm-up** before the race.*

warm up[4] [A1 B1i pass] become, make, more lively and interested. **S:** [A1] **O:** [B1] audience, spectator; contest, game; party, celebration □ *The comedian told a few quick jokes to get his audience **warmed up**.* □ *We agreed about the port and whisky: it would **warm** them all **up**.* BFA

warn (about/against) [B2 pass emph rel] tell sb to be wary of, or avoid, sth harmful, undesirable etc. **O:** public; consumer; child, pupil. **o:** (danger, risk of) infection, poisoning; (excessive) smoking, drinking; swimming out of one's depth, travelling without a guide □ *Travellers to the tropics are generally **warned against** drinking water that has not been filtered or boiled.* □ *A Government notice on each packet **warns** the public **about** the dangers of cigarette smoking.*

warn off [B1ii pass B2 pass] prohibit from advancing, trespassing, intruding etc. **S:** company, landowner; police; father. **o:** property, land; looking into the case; seeing too much of his daughter □ *'That's twice I've had to **warn** you **off** my land. The next time I'll report you for trespassing.'* □ *A reporter had got hold of some new information about an old political scandal. He wanted to follow it up, but the editor **warned** him **off**.*

wash away [B1i pass] remove by striking repeatedly; carry away to another place. **S:** sea; breaker, wave; flood. **O:** cliff; road, railway; hut □ *The base of the cliff had been **washed away** in the continuous gales.* □ *The river flooded its banks **washing away** part of the main railway line.*

wash away sb's sin(s) [B1iii pass] (religion) by an atoning sacrifice, remove from sb his guilt at having broken God's laws. **S:** God; Christ; the blood of Christ, of the Lamb □ *If you sincerely repent, then God will **wash away your sins**.* □ ***Their sins** are **washed away** by Christ's atoning sacrifice.*

wash down (with)[1] [B1i nom pass adj B3 pass] clean dirt from a surface (using water etc). **O:** wall, door; paintwork; car; deck (of a ship). **o:** jet, spray (of water); hose, brush □ *On Sundays, he **washes** his car **down with** the garden hose.* □ ***Wash** the walls **down** well* (or: *Give the walls a good **wash-down***) ***with** soap and water before putting on the distemper.*

wash down (with)[2] [B1i pass B3 pass] drink sth after, or at the same time as, taking a solid meal. **O:** meal; meat and potatoes; bread and cheese. **o:** beer, wine □ *We ate sausage, and **washed** it **down with** a whisky.* TC

wash one's hands of [B2 emph rel] say, show, that one no longer wishes to be responsible for, or involved in. **S:** parent, teacher; manager; shop, department. **o:** one's children, dependants; (the whole) affair, matter, business □ *'Very well,' John got up and looked out of the window, 'I **wash my hands of** it. If you and Larrie want to fuss over the wretched bird, do.'* ASA □ *'If you're going to regard every suggestion I make as a criticism, then I must **wash my hands of** the whole matter.'* ASA

wash off [B1i pass B2 pass] remove sth from the surface of a material etc, by washing it. **O:** dirt, grime; mark; grease, paint □ *'**Wash** that dirt **off** your fingers before coming to the table.'* □ *I tried to remove the grease spots from the wall but they wouldn't **wash off*** (or: *I couldn't **wash** them **off***).

wash out[1] [B1i pass] wash (the inside of) sth so as to remove the dirt etc from it. **O:** clothing; pot, basin; mouth □ *'I just want to **wash out** one or two dish-cloths.'* □ *When you've cleaned your teeth, **wash** your mouth **out** with clean water.* ⇨ wash out/out of.

wash out[2] [B1i nom pass adj] (sport) bring play to an end; prevent it from starting. **S:** rain; downpour, cloudburst; storm. **O:** game, match □ *Heavy rain this weekend **washed out** five league fixtures.* □ *Our mid-week match was completely **washed out*** (or: *was a complete **wash-out***). ⇨ next entry.

wash-out [nom (B1)] (informal) failure; disappointment. **no:un** party; meeting; show, film. **adj:** total, complete, absolute □ *If you launch a sales campaign now, when there's so little money about, I guarantee a total **wash-out**.* □ *'Did you enjoy the party?' 'No, I thought it fell flat — a bit of a **wash-out**.'* ⇨ previous entry.

washed out [pass adj (B1)] (informal) (be) very tired, (be) lacking in spirits □ *'I thought Mike was looking a bit **washed out**.' 'I'm not surprised, with all those late nights.'* □ *Mary was in very bad shape — a dreadful **washed-out** appearance, with none of the old sparkle.*

wash out/out of [B1i pass adj B2 pass] remove dirt etc from sth by washing it. **O:** dirt, umpurities; grease, paint. **o:** clothes; brush □ ***Wash** all the blue **out of** your brush before starting on another colour.* □ *'If you'd **wash** the* *sleep* ***out of*** *your eyes, you might be able to see what was going on.'* □ *He wore* ***washed-out*** *blue overalls* (i e from which some of the dye had been removed by repeated washing). ⇨ wash out[1].

wash over [A2] (informal) take place all around sb, be expressed, without greatly affecting him; flow over (q v). **S:** noise, disturbance; quarrels, tensions; backbiting □ *The kids were making a tremendous din, and he sat there quietly typing his report. It all* ***washed over*** *him.* □ *'He doesn't seem to mind what people say, does he? All the recent criticism seems to have* ***washed*** *right* ***over*** *him.'*

wash overboard [B1ii pass] (nautical) sweep over the side of a ship into the sea. **S:** (heavy) sea, wave. **O:** passenger, crew; cargo □ *A huge wave* ***washed*** *a deck hand* ***overboard.*** □ *Some of the cargo lashed to the forward deck was* ***washed overboard*** *in the gale.*

wash up[1] [A1 B1i pass adj] wash the dishes, cutlery etc after a meal. **O:** dishes, knives and forks; tea/dinner things □ *He had helped Edith with the* ***washing up*** *on the maid's day out.* HD □ *After supper we'd* ***wash up*** *and she'd sit by the fire.* ITAJ □ *He lunged across to the sink and snatched the* ***washing-up*** *bowl.* HD □ the nom form as in: *do the* washing up; attrib use in: washing-up *liquid* (i e liquid soap etc used for washing up).

wash up[2] [B1i pass adj] (of the movements of the sea) carry to shore floating objects or substances. **S:** sea, tide, waves. **O:** survivor, body; debris, wreckage; driftwood; oil □ *The incoming tide* ***washed up*** *cargo from the wrecked coaster.* □ *The surveyors department — with men switched from drawing boards to beaches — were coping deftly with any oil* ***washed up.*** OBS

washed up [pass adj (B1)] (informal) (be) finished, at an end; (be) ruined, a failure. **S:** marriage, affair; couple, friends □ *'Your marriage was* ***washed up*** *long before Gilbert left: you should never have married him.'* ASA □ *'Robin and I aren't lovers any more. We're* ***washed up,*** *as they say in the movies.'* ASA

waste away [A1] grow unhealthily thin (through illness, poor feeding etc) □ *Matthew was looking dreadful the last time I saw him — he's* ***wasting away*** *to skin and bone.*

watch out [A1] be careful to avoid danger, not to upset others etc; look out[1] (q v), mind out (q v) □ *'You need to* ***watch out*** *here. The ground's a bit boggy on either side of the path.'* □ *'You'll be in dire trouble if you don't* ***watch out.'*** □ often in the clause: *if he doesn't/you don't* ***watch out.***

watch out (for) [A1 nom A3 pass rel] be alert, so that one notices sb or sth important; look out (for) (q v). **S:** authorities; police, customs. **o:** intruder, trouble-maker, smuggler; movement, change, sign □ *I said I should be sick, and that I must* ***watch out for*** *symptoms.* PM □ *'Keep a sharp* ***watch-out for*** *anybody trying to come in this way.'*

watch over [A2 pass adj] be responsible for the health, safety etc of. **S:** parent, teacher, doctor; policeman, security guard. **o:** safety, security; well-being; pupil, patient; passenger □ *The security of passengers travelling on routes favoured by hijackers needs to be* ***watched over*** *more vigilantly.* □ *A new minister has been appointed to* ***watch over*** *the welfare of disabled people.*

water down [B1i pass adj] dilute, make weaker, by adding water; make arguments etc less forceful or extreme, weaken them. **O:** beer, brandy; idea, philosophy; policy, programme □ *There was no more whisky left, not even a drop to* ***water down.*** DBM □ *I have considerably* ***watered down*** *Blaize's criticisms of the guilty men.* DS □ *They have presented a* ***watered-down*** *version of their Trades Union policy.*

wave away/off [B1i pass] show, with a motion of the hand, that sb must move or stay away. **S:** policemen, bodyguard; doorman, butler. **O:** onlooker; reporter, photographer; tout, door-to-door salesman □ *John wanted to take a closer look at the silver Rolls, but a uniformed chauffeur appeared, and* ***waved him off.*** □ *Nobody was allowed near the wreckage of the plane. Even those with press cards were* ***waved away.***

waver (between) [A2 emph rel] be unsure which of two alternative courses to choose; move restlessly from one emotional state to another; vacillate (between) (q v). **o:** action and inaction; a house and a flat; attraction and revulsion, tolerance and bigotry □ *At the moment he's* ***wavering between*** *a smart coupé and a large family saloon.* □ *You never know what mood you're going to find him in — always* ***wavering between*** *despair and elation.*

wean (away) (from) [B1i pass B2 pass emph rel B3 pass emph rel] lead sb away gradually from sth which appears pleasant, but which is no longer suitable for him. **O:** pupil, student; follower. **o:** idea, belief; association □ [B3] *His son needs to be* ***weaned away from*** *the notion that everything will come easily to him.* □ [B2] *These were serious misconceptions* ***from*** *which, gradually and tactfully, we were trying to* ***wean*** *him.*

wear away [A1 B1i pass adj] disappear, remove, through constant pressure, friction etc. **S:** [A1] **O:** [B1] hill, cliff; step, pavement. **S:** [B1] weather, elements □ *Wind and rain have* ***worn away*** *the sharp ridges of these mountains.* □ *With the passing of the years, the finer detail of the carvings has almost* ***worn away.***

wear down[1] [A1 B1i pass adj] become, or make, shorter or lower, through continuous pressure, friction etc. **S:** [A1] **O:** [B1] point (of instrument), tread (of tyre), heel (of shoe) □ *Get the cobbler to fit metal studs to your boots: they won't* ***wear down*** *so quickly.* □ *'Your back tyres are badly* ***worn down:*** *you should fit new ones.'*

wear down[2] [A1 B1i pass adj] become, or make, weaker by constant (moral) pressure or attack. **S:** [A1] **O:** [B1] resistance, opposition; conviction, faith. **S:** [B1] argument, speech, sermon □ *He might be* ***wearing down*** *her superstitious belief in the punishment by constantly belittling it.* ARG □ *Under so much pressure from her parents, her will to independence was slowly* ***wearing down.***

wear off[1] [A1 B1i pass] (of the surface, or sth applied to the surface) disappear, remove, through continuous pressure, friction etc. **S:** [A1] **O:** [B1] nap, pile (of carpet); paint, plating (on cutlery). **S:** [B1] (rough) use, rubbing □ *'Don't polish those badges: the gilt will* ***wear off*** *in time if you do.'* □ *Don't buy a cheap carpet; children* *running in and out will soon **wear** the pile **off**.*

wear off² [A1] disappear, no longer affect one. **S:** newness, novelty; feeling, sensation; tiredness, depression □ *The children lingered among their presents, feeling the strangeness **wear off** and the thrill of ownership begin.* PW □ *The drink inside them had **worn off**, leaving only a sour feeling in the stomach.* HD

wear on [A1] proceed slowly or tediously. **S:** day, week, month; meeting, party □ *The gloomy afternoon **wore on**.* LWK □ *The fields were covered with ice and, as September **wore on**, the noisy rivers were gradually silenced.* TBC

wear out¹ [A1 B1i pass adj] become, make, unusable through continuous wear, handling etc. **S:** [A1] **O:** [B1] clothing, shoe; engine, motor □ *Children's clothes **wear out** very quickly — they get so much rough treatment.* □ *Existing aircraft will already be **worn out**.* SC

wear out² [B1i pass adj] exhaust. **S:** movement, excitement; tension, stress; company, conversation □ *Anne, **worn out** with anxiety and strain, followed from one house to the next.* WI □ *I've seen plenty of girls **wear** themselves **out** trying to run a home and a job.* AITC

weary of [A2 rel] no longer be interested in or attracted by; become irritated by; tire of (q v). **o:** girl, companion; attachment, love-affair; experience, pastime; chatter, nagging □ *He'd spent too long in the same job, and was beginning to **weary of** it.* □ *Eventually one **wearies of** this constant bickering between political leaders.*

weave in and out/out of [A1 A2] advance by moving sideways around obstacles. **S:** car, bicycle; procession. **o:** traffic; crowd □ *He goes to work on a motor-bike, **weaving in and out of** the traffic jams.* □ *The cart moved over the dew-soaked grass, **weaving in and out** among the giant thistles.* DF

weave (up) (from) [B1i pass B2 pass rel B3 pass rel] make cloth from threads by weaving them together. **O:** length, piece; (cotton, woollen) cloth. **o:** yarn, thread □ [B2] *The curtains were **woven** on a hand loom **from** local cotton.* □ [B3] *'I **wove** this length **up from** hanks of cotton which I dyed myself.'* ⇨ next entry.

weave (up) (into) [B1i pass B2 pass rel B3 pass rel] make threads into cloth by weaving them together. **O:** yarn, thread; cotton, wool. **o:** cloth; blanket, covering □ [B1] *'I've no yarn left; it's all been **woven up**.'* □ [B2] *Threads of different colours and textures were **woven into** an intricate pattern.* ⇨ previous entry.

wed (to) [B2 pass emph rel] combine one thing or quality with another. **S:** author, designer, builder. **O:** simplicity, strength, utility. **o:** feeling, grace, spaciousness □ *In the design for the church, he has **wedded** a traditional ground plan **to** (or: and) modern structural methods.*

wedded to [pass (B2)] (be) so attached to, or absorbed in, sth that one finds no room for anything else. **o:** work; studies, research; car, gardening; view, opinion □ *He spends most evenings at the office. You could say he's **wedded to** the job.* □ *She won't be shifted — she's **wedded to** her prejudices.* □ passive with *be, become, get, seem.*

weed out [B1i pass adj] get rid of parts which weaken or injure the whole; improve the whole by doing this. **S:** farmer, breeder; commander, manager. **O:** runt, weakling; malcontent, dissident; herd, flock; group, unit □ *We shall have to **weed** the herd **out** carefully if we hope to improve the breed.* □ *Officers who couldn't stand the strain were to be **weeded out** and replaced.* MFM

weep for joy [A2] cry with happiness □ *The news of his release came as such a surprise that she **wept for joy**.*

weep over [A2 pass] express regret at sth or for sb; cry over (q v). **o:** loss, misfortune; past failings; his resignation, embarrassment, disgrace □ *There's not much point in **weeping over** what's past.* □ *If they sent Johnson packing tomorrow, I don't suppose his departure would be **wept over** very much.*

weigh against [A2] tend to make people disfavour or reject sb; tell against (q v). **S:** age; immaturity, lack of experience; evidence, testimony; criticism. **o:** him etc; candidate, applicant; his being selected □ *'The landlady's evidence will **weigh** heavily **against** him. I'm not optimistic about the verdict.'* □ *The fact that a man has taught overseas for several years ought not to **weigh against** his getting a senior post in Britain.*

weigh down¹ [B1i pass adj] (of a weight) make sb or sth bend or sag. **S:** load, burden; box, parcel; crop. **O:** porter, shopper; plant, tree □ *'Get this bundle off my back; it's really **weighing** me **down**.'* □ *The branches were **weighed down** almost to the ground with ripe fruit.* alt form: **weight down**.

weigh down² [B1ii pass adj] lower sb's spirits, make him sad and anxious. **S:** responsibility, charge; care hardship □ *He doesn't let the cares of parenthood **weigh** him **down**.* □ *John seems altogether **weighed down** by all the extra work they're pushing on him.*

weigh in (at) [A1 nom A3] (sport) have one's weight measured before a race or boxing match. **S:** jockey; boxer. **o:** 200 lbs, 12 stone 8 lbs □ *The boxer **weighed in at** more than the limit for his class and had to sweat off a few pounds.* □ *A number of reporters were present at the **weigh-in*** (i e *the time of **weighing in***).

weigh in (with) [A1 A3] (informal) lend one's weight or support to an enterprise; bring forceful arguments to bear in a discussion. **S:** firm, bank; member, supporter; delegate, councillor. **o:** donation, loan; speech, reply □ *The whole family **weighed in with** offers of help.* □ *All of us will **weigh in** one hundred per cent to do what you want.* MFM □ *One man leapt to his feet and **weighed in with** a forceful appeal for an all-out strike.*

weigh on sb/sb's mind [A2 emph rel] worry, make anxious. **S:** responsibility, burden; loss, debt; disgrace, dismissal □ *'Don't disturb your father; he has so many things **weighing on his mind**.'* □ *Didn't Nurse Ellen's accident **weigh on** her at all?* DC □ *He's the sort of man **on whom** setbacks **weigh** very heavily.*

weigh out [B1i pass adj] measure a quantity of sth by weight. **S:** chemist, grocer, cook. **O:** substance; flour, sugar; gram, kilo, pound □ *The ingredients for the cake were all carefully **weighed out**.* □ *She **weighed out** small quantities of dye to make up a colour.*

weigh up¹ [B1i pass] assess, judge; consider

carefully before forming a judgement. **O:** situation; prospects, chances □ *In a split second Mr Charlton had everything **weighed up**.* BFA □ *When you come to **weigh** things **up**, there isn't any practicable alternative to this Government.* ILIH

weigh up[2] [B1i pass] form an opinion, make a judgement, of sb's character. **O:** visitor, newcomer □ *Father usually has someone **weighed up** within a few minutes of meeting him.* □ *The children hadn't **weighed up** their new teacher yet.*

weigh up[3] [B1i pass] consider alternatives carefully before choosing one of them. **O:** alternatives, pros and cons; whether to go or stay □ *He was **weighing up** whether to stay with us or not.* SML □ *Parents can then **weigh up** whether their child should leave or try for an apprenticeship.* OBS

weigh with [A2 emph rel] be regarded as important by sb, be seriously considered by sb. **S:** factor, element; output, efficiency; talent, industry; evidence, opinion. **o:** director, consumer; selector; judge □ *Trade considerations in particular are bound to **weigh** heavily **with** us.* SC □ *The social background of the applicants does not **weigh** at all **with** the interviewing panel.*

weight down [B1i pass adj] = weigh down[1].

welcome back [B1i pass] greet sb enthusiastically on his return. **S:** crowd, supporter, fan. **O:** king, president; player, actor, siger □ *A large crowd gathered at the airport to **welcome back** the national football team.*

welcome in/into [B1i pass B2 pass] greet a visitor to one's home etc, warmly. **O:** (foreign) visitor, student; delegate, envoy. **o:** house, office □ *The bride and groom stood by the door to **welcome in** their guests.* □ *A number of families **welcome** overseas students **into** their homes at Christmas.*

weld together [B1i pass] unify, combine, strongly or solidly. **S:** leader, movement. **O:** element, force; people, tribe □ *The regime has succeeded in **welding together** many diverse elements — religious, racial and linguistic.* □ *The nation has been **welded together** by the shared experience of exile and persecution.*

well up [A1] rise like water in a well; (of sound) grow louder. **S:** water, tears; hubbub, chatter; passion □ *Tears suddenly **welled up** in her eyes.* □ *The bath has filters through which hot water **wells up** and the waste drains away.* WI □ *Strong feelings **welled up** within him.*

welsh (on) [A2 pass] (sport) leave a race-course without paying winnings to those who have placed bets with one; repudiate an obligation or agreement previously entered upon. **S:** bookmaker ('bookie'); he etc; the Government. **o:** race-goer, punter; debts; deal; election programme □ *'Don't lay any bets with one of the small bookies on the course: he may **welsh on** you.'* □ *At the very last moment his main backer **welshed on** the deal leaving him high and dry with no money to satisfy his creditors.*

wheel in/into[1] [B1i pass B2 pass] push a wheeled truck etc (or sb/sth mounted on one) into a place. **O:** truck, trolley; stretcher; patient; tea things □ *The door opened and a waiter **wheeled in** the tea trolley.* □ *The patient was anaesthetized before being **wheeled into** the theatre.*

wheel in/into[2] [B1i pass B2 pass] (informal) conduct, escort, sb into a place where he is to be interviewed, questioned etc. **O:** applicant, visitor; prisoner □ *'Who's next on the list, Miss Jones?' 'A Mr Davis.' 'All right, **wheel him in**.'*

while away [B1i pass] (do sth to) make the time pass pleasantly. **S:** reading, sewing; radio, television. **O:** time; afternoon, evening; (few) days, hours □ *He had a volume of Pascal open on his desk to **while away** the time.* QA □ *I was glad of his company to **while away** an hour until the train came.*

whip away [B1i pass] remove (e g from a flat surface) with a sharp, snatching movement. **O:** cloth, cover; cup, plate; newspaper □ *The conjuror **whipped away** the cover to reveal two live rabbits.* □ *The waiter **whipped** my cup **away** before I'd finished my coffee.*

whip back [A1] return sharply, with the action of a whip. **S:** branch; boom (of a sailing boat); swing door □ *Stephen was pushing through the wood just ahead of me, and a thin branch **whipped back** and cut me just below the eye.*

whip off [B1i pass B2 pass] take off, remove, with a sharp, snatching movement. **S:** wind, draught; intruder, thief. **O:** hat; paper, letter. **o:** desk, shelf □ *As the boss entered, the men **whipped** their hats **off** and shuffled their feet unesily.* □ *Gales uprooted trees and **whipped** the slates **off** roofs.*

whip on [B1i pass] make an animal go faster by striking it with a whip; drive sb to go faster, work harder etc by means of curses, threats etc. **S:** rider, jockey; escort, gang-leader; employer. **O:** horse; convict, navvy; work force □ *The horses flashed past the post, **whipped on** furiously by their jockeys.* □ *The fugitives wanted to rest, but the fear of capture **whipped** them **on**.*

whip out/out of [B1i pass B2 pass] take out, produce, with a sharp, snatching movement. **O:** gun; wallet, letter. **o:** holster; pocket, drawer □ *How would you react if someone entered your shop and **whipped out** a revolver?* □ *He **whipped** a piece of paper **out of** his pocket and waved it in our faces.*

whip round [A1 nom] (informal) appeal to colleagues etc for money to help in a good cause. **S:** department, shop, office □ *I'll **whip round** and raise a few pounds for the office party.* □ *He's suggesting a **whip-round** to subscribe to a new statue.* RM □ usu nom.

whip up (to)[1] [B1i pass adj B3 pass] beat ingredients vigorously until they are solid, thoroughly mixed etc. **O:** mixture; eggs, cream □ ***Whip up** the eggs and flour **to** the consistency of a smooth paste.* □ *When the cream is well **whipped up** it should stick to the fork.*

whip up (to)[2] [B1i pass adj B3 pass] arouse, excite, by vigorous action, public speaking etc; work up (into/to) (q v). **S:** demagogue, rabble-rouser. **O:** crowd, audience; feeling; anger, support □ *A party orator **whipped** the crowd **up to** a state of frenzy.* □ *Competitive journalism had **whipped up** public interest in a rather strange stunt.* SD

whisk away [B1i pass] drive away with a small brush (like a horse's tail) etc. **O:** fly, mosquito □ *He **whisked** a wasp **away** from his food with a rolled newspaper.*

whisk away/off (to) [B1i pass B3 pass] take sb or sth away suddenly, as if by magic etc. **S:** car, ambulance; police; waiter, attendant. **O:** guest, patient; prisoner; dish. **o:** hospital; gaol □ *Stop him* ***whisking away*** *the remains of the meal.* OMIH □ *Our special holiday issue* ***whisks*** *you* ***off*** *on a magic carpet* ***to*** *Starland.* WI

whisk up (to) [B1i pass adj B3 pass] mix, change the thickness of, ingredients by beating them with a whisk (a single or double coil of wire). **O:** eggs, cream. **o:** smooth paste, creamy consistency □ *To make meringues, you first take the whites of several eggs and* ***whisk them up****.*

whisper about/around [B1i pass B2 pass] pass about, secretly circulate, stories which damage a person's good name or position. **S:** neighbour, gossip. **O:** tale, rumour, scandal; it... that sb has been in prison, that he is divorced □ *It doesn't take long for such stories to be* ***whispered about*** *this neighbourhood.* □ *It was* ***whispered about*** *that he had a conviction for drunken driving.*

whistle for [A2] (informal) hope in vain for sth. **S:** creditor, tradesman. **o:** money, loan □ *John borrowed two of my books, and as far as he is concerned, I can* ***whistle for*** *them.* □ with *can/could; may/might.*

whittle away[1] [B1i pass] remove the outer part of sth in small pieces, using a knife. **O:** bark, veneer □ *'Make this plug smaller for me, but don't* ***whittle away*** *too much wood.'*

whittle away[2] [B1i pass] remove, take away, one by one or little by little. **S:** Chancellor, the Inland Revenue; inflation, escalating costs; legislation. **o:** gain, increase (in wages, profits); rights, privileges □ *We had a pay rise in October but increases in the cost of fuel and food have* ***whittled away*** *the extra money, so that we're more or less back where we started.*

whittle down[1] [B1i pass adj] make sth thinner by removing fine slices with a knife. **O:** stick, post; branch, twig □ *He took a square block of wood and* ***whittled*** *it* ***down*** *to form the hull of a model boat.*

whittle down[2] [B1i pass adj] reduce the size or importance of sth by degrees. **S:** employer, department; investigator. **O:** staff, work force; privilege, benefit; field, suspects □ *The research team has been* ***whittled down*** *considerably to staff other projects.* □ *The detective couldn't be expected to fool the smuggler unless his status was* ***whittled down****.* DS □ *We've* ***whittled down*** *a mass of evidence and produced two clear leads.*

whiz(z) past [A1 A2] pass, go past, making a high, whistling noise. **S:** shell, bullet; car, aircraft. **o:** head, ear; house □ *An arrow* ***whizzed past*** *and stuck in a tree.* □ *All these cars* ***whizzing past*** *my front window keep me awake at night.*

whoop it up [B1ii] (informal) celebrate in a cheerful, noisy way □ *The bar stayed open late and groups of holidaymakers were still* ***whooping it up*** *after midnight.* □ *Trafalgar Square is a favourite place for* ***whooping it up*** *on New Year's Eve.*

win back [B1i pass] get back, recover, after a struggle. **S:** country, industry; boxer, sprinter. **O:** territory, market; title, cup □ *As a result of the 1914–18 war, France* ***won back*** *Alsace and Lorraine.* □ *Valuable orders have been* ***won back*** *from our competitors.*

win (from/off) [B2 pass emph rel] get from sb as a result of a contest, game etc. **O:** money; bracelet, watch; title, crown. **o:** bookmaker, tote; opponent □ *He* ***won*** *a gold watch* ***off*** *someone he met in a pub.* □ *Supporters celebrated noisily when Ajax* ***won*** *the European cup* ***from*** *Inter Milan.*

win out/through [A1] (informal) come successfully through a difficult period. **S:** patient, invalid; applicant, examinee; army, expedition □ *He fought his trouble down and I thought he was going to* ***win out****.* TBC □ *Do you look business-like? If so you may* ***win out*** *over some more experienced applicant.* H □ *He settled to his task with a good will, and with his help we* ***won through****.* SD

win over (to) [B1i pass B3 pass rel] persuade sb to agree, to be on one's side etc. **O:** parent, colleague; rival, rebel. **o:** cause, persuasion, way of thinking □ *She wanted to marry, but her mother could never be* ***won over****.* ARG □ *After some argument, they were eventually* ***won over to*** *our side.* □ *This is a specious philosophy* ***to*** *which too many have been* ***won over****.*

wind around/round [B2 pass emph rel] twist, fold, yarn or material etc round sth or sb. **O:** string, wool; blanket, towel. **o:** spool, bobbin; post; waist, neck □ *She was absent-mindedly* ***winding*** *a length of thread* ***around*** *her finger.* □ *A strip of bandage was* ***wound round*** *his ankle.*

wind itself around/round [B2 pass emph rel] become twisted, entangled, around sth or sb. **S:** cable, wire; hair, thread; creeper. **o:** engine; spindle, cog; post, tree □ *When your car is being towed, keep the tow-rope taut, otherwise it may* ***wind itself around*** *your front wheels.* □ *Pieces of wool had got* ***themselves wound round*** *the rollers of the vacuum cleaner.* □ passive with *get,* as in the second example.

wind around/round one's (little) finger [B2] (informal) through feminine charm, flattery etc, persuade sb to do what one wants; twist around/round one's little finger (q v). **S:** wife, girlfriend, daughter □ *He almost admired her for the way she had succeeded in* ***winding*** *Utterson* ***round her*** *cunning* ***finger****.* US □ *She knows full well she can* ***wind*** *her father* ***round her little finger****.*

wind back [A1 B1i pass] bring back a section of film etc for re-showing, by turning the spool on which it is mounted. **S:** operator, projectionist. **O:** film, film-strip, tape □ *'****Wind*** *the film* ***back*** *a few frames. I want to see that sequence again.'*

wind down[1] [B1i pass adj] lower, bring down by turning a handle or wheel. **O:** window, shutter, screen □ *He* ***wound down*** *the window of his car and leant out to ask the way.*

wind down[2] [A1] (of a clock-spring) become slack, causing the clock to lose time and stop. **S:** clock, watch □ *It's a one-day clock; the spring* ***winds down*** *in 24 hours.*

wind down[3] [A1] move more slowly, or with less energy, lose momentum. **S:** movement, operation; offensive, drive □ *The enthusiasm of the sales staff weakened and the whole campaign* ***wound down****.*

wind in [B1i pass] draw a fishing-line from the water and coil it around a reel attached to the rod; bring a fish to land by doing this. **O:** line; fish, catch □ *You play a fish by letting it have a bit of line, and then* ***winding*** *the line* ***in*** *sharply.*

wind on [A1 B1i pass adj] move a film etc forward (so as to expose, or show, the next portion). **S:** photographer, cameraman. **O:** film, film-strip, tape □ *If you don't* ***wind on*** *after taking a picture, your negative will be double-exposed.*

wind round [B2 pass emph rel] ⇨ wind around/round.

wind itself round [B2 pass emph rel] ⇨ wind itself around/round.

wind round one's (little) finger [B2] ⇨ wind around/round one's (little) finger.

wind up[1] [B1i pass adj] raise, bring up, by turning a handle, wheel etc. **O:** bucket; window, roller-blind □ *They drove along with all the car windows* ***wound up.***

wind up[2] [B1i pass adj] tighten the spring of a watch etc, to make it function. **O:** spring; watch, clock; (clockwork) motor □ *She* ***wound up*** *the toy mouse and set it running across the carpet.* □ *'Have you* ***wound up*** *the alarm?'*

wind up[3] [B1i pass adj] raise sb to a pitch of excitement. **S:** orator, agitator. **O:** audience, follower □ *By this time, he had* ***wound*** *the crowd* ***up*** *to fever pitch.* □ *In any political discussion he always gets terribly* ***wound up.*** □ usu passive.

wind up[4] [A1 B1i pass] (of a speech or meeting) close, terminate. **S:** speaker, chairman. **O:** remarks, address; debate, discussion; session □ *'This is the way I see it, in a nutshell,' said Ned,* ***winding up.*** CON □ *As we walked along, Blaize* ***wound up*** *his story.* DS □ *Mr Jenkins* ***wound up*** *the debate for the Opposition.*

wind up[5] [A1 B1i pass adj] (cause to) stop functioning, cease its activities; stop, cease. **S:** [A1] **O:** [B1] department, firm; business; exercise, project, scheme. **S:** [B1] director, manager □ *We hope that when the campaign* ***winds up*** *officially its educational service will carry on.* TES □ *The smuggling organization* ***wound up*** *its activities and prepared to disband.* DS

wind up one's affairs [B1iii pass] finally settle one's (business, personal) affairs before leaving, retiring etc □ *In the last month I was* ***winding up my affairs*** *in England and saying goodbye to all my friends.* RFW □ *I can't go on holiday until* ***my affairs*** *are properly* ***wound up.***

wind up (with) [A1 A3] (informal) as a result of one's work, manner of life etc, get or experience sth unusual (and usu unpleasant). **o:** depression; ulcer, hangover □ *'Don't carry on living at this pace: you'll* ***wind up with*** *nervous exhaustion.'* □ *'You'll keep your nose out of my affairs, unless you want to* ***wind up*** *in hospital.'* □ *'Mark my words, one day he'll* ***wind up*** *running the company.'*

wink (at) [A2 pass] close and open one eye as a sign of friendship or invitation (e g to a girl) or as a secret signal (at some shared joke) □ *After making some outrageous remark, which no one except George would understand, he would turn to George and* ***wink*** *broadly* ***at*** *him.* □ *Nice girls don't always like being* ***winked at.***

wink at [A2 pass] (informal) deliberately ignore, overlook. **S:** parent, teacher, employer. **o:** offence, mischief, slackness □ *Her extravagance is usually* ***winked at;*** *her husband thinks he's buying a quiet life.* □ *In this department, the manager* ***winks at*** *petty theft.*

winkle out/out of[1] [B1i pass B2 pass] (informal) remove, dislodge, slowly and with difficulty. **S:** soldier; farmer. **O:** sniper, pocket of resistance; rabbit, rat □ *Enemy troops hiding in the cellars had to be* ***winkled out*** *one by one.* □ *'I've dropped a coin between the floorboards; try to* ***winkle*** *it* ***out of*** *there.'*

winkle out/out of[2] [B1i pass B2 pass] (informal) extract information etc with difficulty from sb. **O:** news, story; gossip, scandal. **o:** witness, interviewee □ *'See if you can* ***winkle*** *anything* ***out of*** *the wife; I'll question the husband.'*

wipe away [B1i pass] remove, clean, by rubbing with the hand, a cloth etc. **O:** tear, sweat; mark, spot □ *He* ***wiped*** *the sweat* ***away*** *from his brow with the back of his hand.*

wipe down [B1i nom pass] clean from top to bottom (from end to end) by rubbing with a cloth. **O:** window, shop-front; table, dresser □ *When you've washed the car,* ***wipe*** *it* ***down*** *well* (or: *give it a good* ***wipe-down***) *with a shammy leather.* □ ***Wipe*** *the walls* ***down*** *with a soapy cloth.*

wipe off [B1i pass B2 pass] remove, take off, by rubbing with a cloth etc. **O:** drawing, sentence, formula. **o:** blackboard; door, wall □ *'****Wipe*** *that drawing* ***off*** *the board before the teacher sees it.'* □ *Paint won't* ***wipe off*** (i e can't be ***wiped off***).

wipe off one's/sb's face [B2 pass] (informal) stop smiling, grinning (in a self-satisfied way). **O:** ⚠ the smile, grin, smirk □ *'I'd be grateful if you'd* ***wipe*** *that silly grin* ***off your face.'*** □ *The smile could be* ***wiped off the Government's face*** *if the economic winds changed for the worse.* OBS

wipe off the face of the earth/off the map [B2 pass] remove, obliterate, by violent action. **O:** town, village; competitor, opponent □ *Whole villages were* ***wiped off the map*** *as a reprisal for alleged atrocities.* □ *'We'll* ***wipe*** *that company* ***off the face of the earth.'*** *She spoke with cruel satisfaction.* UTN

wipe out[1] [B1i pass] clean the inside of a vessel by rubbing with a cloth. **O:** bath, basin; dish, cup □ *'Make sure the inside of the coffee pot is thoroughly* ***wiped out.'***

wipe out[2] [B1i pass] clear, repay; cancel out (q v). **S:** borrower; company; theatre, club. **O:** deficit, overdraft □ *The museum's financial debt had been* ***wiped out.*** SD

wipe out[3] [B1i pass] nullify, reduce to nothing. **S:** counter-attack, thrust; price increase, rising costs. **O:** gain, benefit, advantage □ *An attack on the central front* ***wiped out*** *the gains of the previous winter's fighting.* □ *Escalating costs will almost certainly* ***wipe out*** *within a year the benefits of the latest salary increases.*

wipe out[4] [B1i pass adj] destroy completely. **S:** fire, disease, drought; bombing. **O:** village, farm; stock, crop; population □ *A summer fire can* ***wipe out*** *all the pasture feed.* RFW □ *The whole of life on the earth might be* ***wiped out*** *with little compunction.* TBC

wipe out[5] [B1i pass] abolish, cleanse society of. **S:** government, system; science, technology. **O:** crime, disease, poverty □ *Many people still believe that wars, strikes and crime could be* ***wiped out*** *as if by some magic wand.* SNP □ *In many areas once infested by mosquitoes, men* *have* ***wiped out*** *malaria.*

wipe over [B1ii nom pass] pass a cloth etc over sth, so cleaning it, but not thoroughly. **O:** table, shelf; wall, window □ *There wasn't time to clean the windows properly, so Jane just* ***wiped*** *them* ***over*** *with a damp cloth.* □ *'The table's a bit sticky. I'll give it a quick* ***wipe-over*** *before we lay the cloth.'*

wipe up[1] [B1i pass] remove, pick up, with a cloth (esp sth that has fallen or been left on a table or floor). **O:** mess; beer, milk; food, gravy □ *'Don't let the coffee sink into the carpet:* ***wipe*** *it* ***up****!'* □ *'You can just go and* ***wipe up*** *the mess you've made in the kitchen.'*

wipe up[2] [A1 B1i pass] dry crockery etc after it has been washed; dry up[2] (q v). **S:** housewife, kitchen staff. **O:** dishes; plate, knife □ *'Would you mind helping me to* ***wipe up*** (or: *helping me with the* ***wiping-up****)?'* □ *'Don't bother to* ***wipe up*** *the dishes; stack them on the draining-board.'*

wire (for) [B2 pass] fit a building with wires to carry electric current. **O:** house, room. **o:** electricity; power, lighting □ *'Has the studio been* ***wired for*** *sound yet?'*

wise up (to) [A1 A3 pass B1ii pass adj B3 pass] (informal) become, make, aware of the true nature of sb or sth. **o:** intrigue, game, plan, tactics; newcomer, neighbour □ [A3] *By this time, I had fully* ***wised up to*** *their little game.* □ [B3] *The new store detective was quickly* ***wised up to*** *the shoplifters' favourite methods.* □ [A3] *He was new here, but it didn't take him long to* ***wise up to*** *what was going on.*

wish away [B1i pass] (try to) get rid of sth by wishing it did not exist. **O:** problem, difficulty; increase, deficit □ *The rising numbers seeking places in higher education cannot simply be ignored or* ***wished away****.* UL

wish (for) [A2 pass] desire, long to have, sth (which is difficult to obtain, or can only be had by extreme good fortune). **o:** opportunity, opening; wealth, success □ *She* ***wished for*** *something to happen* (or: ***wished*** *that something would happen) to remove her from her drab surroundings.* □ *'Why should the children want to leave home? They have everything they could possibly* ***wish for****.'* □ *'I couldn't* ***wish for*** *a better wife than I've got.'*

wish on/onto [B2 pass] (informal) pass to sb some unpleasant burden which one is unwilling to bear oneself. **S:** colleague, relative. **O:** guest, visitor; pupil, infant; responsibility, task □ *The school has had ten extra infants* ***wished on*** *it by the Education Office.* □ *'How like grandma to* ***wish*** *Aunt Maud* ***onto*** *us for the Easter holidays!'*

withdraw (from) [A2 emph rel B2 pass emph rel] (cause to) move back from, because of a threat of defeat, retreat (from) (q v); no longer (allow to) take part (in) (because of difficulty etc). **S:** [A2] **O:** [B2] troops; contestant, team. **S:** [B2] commander; owner, manager. **o:** position; race, contest □ *Our men were* ***withdrawn from*** *a position made untenable by heavy shelling.* □ *Some runners have* ***withdrawn from*** *the race as a political gesture.*

wither away [A1] gradually disappear. **S:** state; organ, institution (of government) □ *Marxists talk of the* ***withering away*** *of the state under Communism.*

withhold (from) [B2 pass emph rel] (formal) not allow sb to know or have; keep back (from)[2] (q v). **O:** news, information; promotion, privilege; passport □ *Teachers* ***from*** *whom salaries have been* ***withheld*** *are organizing a protest.* □ *Visas have been* ***withheld from*** *some members of the delegation.*

wobble about [A1] move unsteadily from side to side (from weakness or lack of skill) □ *John came into sight,* ***wobbling about*** *on an old bicycle.* □ *He still* ***wobbles about*** *a bit after his recent fall.*

wolf down [B1i pass] (informal) eat hungrily or greedily. **O:** food; supper □ *He went into the kitchen in search of food and* ***wolfed down*** *a pie.*

wonder (about) [A2] be curious (about), ask oneself questions (about). **o:** (absent) friend, relation; (sb's) marriage, life together □ *'So Peter's in hospital? I was* ***wondering about*** *him.'* □ *Now that we've finished this project, I am* ***wondering about*** *our next move* (or: ***wondering*** *what our next move should be*). □ with continuous tenses.

wonder at [A2 pass] (informal) (not) be surprised (if/that). **o:** his resigning, her refusal; it... if he resigns, it... that she refuses □ *Can you* ***wonder at*** *it that people get angry if they live in these conditions?* □ *It's not to be* ***wondered at*** *that he should want to pack up and go.* □ *'So she's finally left him? I don't* ***wonder at*** *it.'* □ in neg or interr sentences.

work one's way across, along, back etc [B1ii B2] move, progress, usu in the face of obstacles, in a given direction □ *Porters laden with stores were now* ***working their way*** *slowly* ***across*** *a rope bridge.* □ *He managed to* ***work his way back*** *through the crowd of guests with two glasses of champagne.*

work against [A2] affect negatively, impede. **S:** attitude; prejudice, ignorance; conditions; climate, disease. **o:** change; progress, understanding □ *The lack of investment in new machinery has* ***worked against*** *any rise in productivity.* □ *His poor grasp of the basic processes* ***works against*** *his progress in mathematics.*

work (among) [A2 rel] practise a profession, provide a service, in (and for) a community. **S:** priest, doctor, teacher. **o:** people; the homeless, the poor; outcasts □ *She has been* ***working among*** *down-and-outs in the East End of London.* □ *His early life was spent* ***working among*** *lepers.*

work around/round to [A3 pass] (informal) come gradually and indirectly to face or tackle sth; get around/round to (q v). **o:** problem, decision; paying, speaking, acting □ *By the time he* ***works round to*** *asking for a salary increase, it will be too late.* □ *'Don't worry about the correspondence: I'll* ***work around to*** *it in time.' 'That's what you were saying this time last month.'*

work at [A2 pass] give thought, energy etc to getting rid of or solving sth. **o:** problem, task, sums, tables □ *'You'll crack this problem if you really* ***work at*** *it.'* □ *'There's no easy way round the difficulty: you'll just have to* ***work at*** *it.'* □ work on.

work away (at) [A1 A3 pass] give continuous effort, thought etc to sth. **o:** maths, German; car pentry, decorating □ *I found him **working away** in the library.* □ *Chemistry was a subject he didn't mind **working away at**.*

work-in [nom (A1)] (industry) form of industrial action in which workers occupy and run a factory etc (often one which is threatened with closure during a trade recession) □ *During the **work-in** at the Clydebank shipyards a committee elected by the work force made the day-to-day management decisions.* □ *They* (i e the Lip watchmakers) *organized a **work-in** and enlisted the support of the powerful left wing in France.* BBCTV

work in/into[1] [B1i pass B2 pass] insert sth gradually, by moving it from side to side etc. **O:** bolt, shaft, key. **o:** socket, hole □ *She **worked in** the key and opened up the classroom.* TT

work in/into[2] [B1i pass B2 pass] include sth by showing special care or cunning. **O:** bit, section; humour, romance, liveliness. **o:** account, story □ *You won't get the story published unless you **work in** a bit of human interest.* □ *He always contrives to **work** his war experiences **into** the conversation.*

work off [B1i pass] get rid of sth extra or burdensome by exercise etc. **O:** energy, steam; fat; debt, overdraft □ *'If you feel like **working off** steam, go and dig the garden.'* □ *'It will take months to **work off** this bank loan. In the meantime, how can we possibly afford to take a holiday?'*

work off (against/on) [B1i pass B3 pass] get rid of an unpleasant feeling (at sb else's expense); take out on (q v). **O:** frustration, irritation; anger, spleen. **o:** wife, child; junior; cat □ *One generally has to **work off** one's irritation **on** somebody.* MFM □ *'There's no need to **work** your disappointment **off on** me.'*

work on [A2 pass] give thought, effort etc to making or discovering sth. **o:** book, play; Milton, Tolstoy; radio, rocket-motor; improvement □ *For his doctorate, he's **working on** the use of dialect speech in the Victorian novel.* □ *The manufacturers are **working on** a modification to the steering.* ⇨ work at.

work on/onto [B1i pass B2 pass] place one thing gradually around another, by moving it from side to side etc. **O:** ring; nut, washer. **o:** finger; bolt, spindle □ *When he tried to **work** the nut **onto** the spindle, he broke the threads.*

work out[1] [B1i pass adj] plan, devise. **S:** committee, team; engineer, architect; artist, philosopher. **O:** scheme, programme, theory □ *A sub-committee has been appointed to **work out** a new constitution for the club.* □ *Religious thinkers may **work out** a new interpretation of life.* AH □ *Staff officers presented a fully **worked-out** plan of attack.*

work out[2] [B1i pass adj] calculate. **S:** accountant, bursar. **O:** pay, allowance, pension; cost; that it will cost £100, how much to pay him □ *We have computers to **work out** our salaries these days.* □ ***Work out** how much one needs to spend in shops to earn these 'free gifts'.* T □ *Have you **worked out** the number of man-hours lost through illness?* ⇨ work out at.

work out[3] [B1i pass adj] solve, find the answer to; get out[5] (q v). **O:** problem, sum; riddle, code □ *You seem to have the problem nicely **worked out**. All the details are in place.* TC □ *See if you can **work** this puzzle **out**.*

work out[4] [B1ii] (informal) understand the nature of sb; make out[4] (q v). **O:** relative, colleague; Peter □ *'You are funny: I shall never **work** you **out**.'* ILIH □ *For as long as I've known him, I've never been able to **work** Martin **out**.* □ usu with *can/could + not.*

work out[5] [A1] (informal) develop well/badly, prove successful/a failure; pan out[2] (q v). **S:** arrangement, relationship; things, it. **A:** all right, well; badly, unhappily; that way □ *I hoped that you'd get married. But it doesn't seem to be **working out** that way.* RFW □ *I'm glad that things are **working out** so well for them in Australia.*

work out[6] [A1 nom] (sport) (esp of a boxer) train for a contest by skipping, sparring etc. **S:** champion, heavyweight □ *Mohammed Ali spoke to reporters after **working out** at the gym this morning.* □ *After breakfast, he had an intensive **work-out**.*

work things out [B1ii] (informal) settle personal problems. **S:** (married) couple, family □ *'I wish their parents would leave them to **work things out** for themselves. You know how young people hate interference from their elders.'* □ *Have you managed to **work things out** with your wife?* ⇨ next entry.

things work themselves out [B1ii] (informal) (of personal problems) be resolved, settled □ *These **things** have a way of **working themselves out** in time.* □ *'These **things work themselves out**, you know.'* SPL □ a remark meant to comfort sb in trouble. ⇨ previous entry.

work out at [A3] be equal to, be calculated as; come out at (q v). **S:** pay, pension, contribution. **o:** ten pounds, fifty dollars □ *His take-home pay **works out at** £26 a week.* □ *What does his share of the bonus **work out at**?* ⇨ work out[2].

work over [B1ii pass] (slang) beat sb all over, to extract information, as a punishment etc; beat up (q v). **S:** thug, gangster. **O:** informer, prisoner □ *A couple of the boys **worked him over*** (or: *gave him a **working-over***) *in a dark alleyway.*

work round (to) [A3 pass] ⇨ work around/round to.

work (one's way) through [A2 pass emph rel B2 emph rel] complete, finish, a task by giving steady attention to it. **S:** student, class. **o:** exercise, problem; course, text; meal □ *He **worked through** the theorems of Euclid when still quite young.* □ *He was **working his way** steadily **through** an enormous steak.*

work to [A2 pass rel] be guided, governed, by a plan etc when doing sth. **S:** builder, student. **o:** blueprint, pattern; timetable, deadline □ *See that you are careful with money and **work to** a budget.* WI □ *Magazines, photographers and dress houses **work to** tight schedules.* H

work to rule [A2] (industrial relations) follow strictly the rules laid down for a job (as a form of protest, or in an attempt to secure higher wages). **S:** railwayman, docker, electrician □ *The national executive of the union has ordered its members to **work to rule*** (or: *ordered a **work-to-rule***).

work towards [A2 emph rel] strive to reach or achieve. **S:** delegate, negotiator; trades union, church. **o:** settlement, agreement; understanding, amity □ *We have been **working towards** a new wages structure in the industry.* □ *'There's no* *reason why we shouldn't reach a settlement. After all, we're **working towards** common objectives.'*

work under [A2 rel] do a job under sb's direction or guidance. **S:** scientist, engineer; student. **o:** (able) director, head, professor; direction □ *The new headmaster's a very good man to **work under**.* □ *'He's always been a lone wolf, you know — he hates to **work under** supervision.'*

work up[1] [B1i pass] develop, extend, gradually. **S:** trader, shopkeeper. **O:** trade, business, market □ *It took Smith some years to **work up** a market for his products.* □ *The retail side of the business was **worked up** by his father.*

work up[2] [B1i pass] increase sth in numbers or strength. **S:** movement, union, party. **O:** support; a following, membership □ *Local organizations are trying to **work up** more support for the party before the election.*

work up[3] [B1i pass] stimulate, make more keen. **O:** appetite, thirst; interest □ *I went out for a brisk walk to **work up** an appetite for lunch.* □ *He doesn't seem to be able to **work up** any enthusiasm for his studies.*

work (one's way) up (from) [A1 A3 B1ii B3] (informal) rise, move, to more responsible positions by one's own efforts. **S:** director, manager, officer. **o:** office-boy, the shop floor, private soldier; the bottom □ [B3] *The chairman of the company claims to have **worked his way up from** delivery boy.* □ [B1] *Major Burton joined the army as a boy entrant and **worked his way up**.*

work up (into) [B1i pass adj B3 pass] gradually change the shape or nature of sth, by thought, effort etc. **O:** wood, metal, stone; idea, note. **o:** figure, trinket; book, thesis □ *The mass of clay was **worked up into** a reclining figure.* □ *He's **working up** his notes on child language **into** a dissertation.*

work up (into/to) [B1i pass adj B3 pass rel] raise sb or oneself to a high point of excitement (about sth); whip up (to)[2] (q v). **S:** orator, agitator. **O:** crowd, follower; oneself. **o:** (***into***) state, frenzy; (***to***) (such an) extent, pitch, point □ *She didn't say when she was coming back. Alec got quite **worked up** about it.* PW □ *He can **work** the crowd **up to** the point where they would kill for his sake.* □ *Don't get yourself all **worked up** over something which can easily be put right.* TT □ *She's **working** herself **up into** a dreadful state over nothing.*

work up to [A3] develop what one is doing or saying to a high point. **S:** orchestra, singer, orator. **o:** crescendo, high note, climax □ *I felt, as he **worked up to** a climax, an impulse to stand up and shout.* CON □ *He took her out, all over the place. He was **working up to** a proposal of marriage.* YAA

worm oneself/one's way into [B2 rel] (informal) move gradually and cunningly into. **S:** adventurer, careerist. **o:** position; favour, prominence; (sb's) confidence □ *He **wormed his way into** a position of trust at Court.* □ *For the sake of his career it was important for Brown to **worm himself into** the director's confidence.*

worm out of [B2 pass emph rel] (informal) extract, obtain, sth from sb slowly and cunningly. **S:** wife, girlfriend. **O:** information; story, secret □ *She was **worming out of** him shameful secrets about the Templar family.* DC □ *There are few details of his private life that aren't **wormed out of** him sooner or later.*

worry (oneself) about/over [A2 emph rel B2 emph rel] cause oneself anxiety over, trouble oneself about. **A:** ⚠ sick, silly; to death. **o:** family, work, health □ *He **worries himself** sick **over** his eldest daughter.* □ *'Look after yourself, my dear, and don't **worry about** me.'* HOM □ *He **worries about** the slightest thing* (cf: *The slightest thing **worries** him*). □ *sick* etc only present in reflexive and passive patterns.

wrangle (about/over) [A2 pass emph rel] argue, dispute, noisily and keenly over sb or sth. **S:** brother, partner, wife. **o:** rights, money, children □ *In that family they are always **wrangling about** something.* □ *'This business is not so important that it needs to be **wrangled over**. Sit down and discuss things calmly.'*

wrap around/round [B2 pass emph rel] wind sth in thick folds around sth or sb. **O:** bandage, dressing; towel, blanket. **o:** finger, wound; baby □ *He **wrapped** a clean rag **around** his ankle.* □ *The mayor had a tricolour sash **wrapped round** his waist.*

wrapped in [pass (B2)] (be) thickly covered by sth (so that nothing is visible). **o:** fog, mist; darkness, obscurity □ *The signposts along the route were **wrapped in** fog.* □ *The events of those days are **wrapped in** mystery.*

wrap up[1] [B1i pass adj] (informal) close, conclude; wind up[4] (q v). **S:** chairman, announcer. **O:** programme, meeting □ *'Well, I think that just about **wraps up** our business for this evening.'*

wrap up[2] [B1i pass adj] (informal) conclude successfully. **S:** salesman, executive; firm. **O:** business, deal; sale, merger □ *The sales team flew in at ten o'clock, **wrapped up** a couple of deals before lunch, and caught the afternoon plane back to Stuttgart.*

wrap (it) up [A1 B1ii] (slang) be quiet, shut up[2] (q v). **S:** speaker, musician □ *'**Wrap up**, Dad,' he said, 'you'll bust a gut!'* TT □ *'**Wrap it up**, will you, stop ringing those bells!'* LBA

wrap (up) (in)[1] [B1i pass adj B2 pass rel B3 pass rel] cover with paper etc for presenting to sb or sending through the post. **O:** gift; book, dress; parcel. **o:** paper, foil □ [B1] *Mother **wraps up** the children's presents on Christmas Eve.* □ [B2] *'If the packet isn't **wrapped in** strong paper and sealed, it'll come open in the post.'*

wrap (up) (in)[2] [A1 B1i pass adj B2 pass rel B3 pass rel] put on warm clothing so that it enfolds one (completely). **o:** scarf, blanket □ [A1] *'Now **wrap up** warm: it's freezing outside.'* □ [B3] *The children were warmly **wrapped up in** scarves and anoraks.* □ [B2] *The nurse carried in a baby **wrapped in** a thick shawl.*

wrapped up in [pass (B3)] (be) completely absorbed by, closely involved in. **o:** each other; his own little world; friendship, love; reflections; work, reading □ *Annabel became **wrapped up in** a society dedicated to the welfare of animals.* DC □ *I must have been **wrapped up in** my thoughts.* TC □ *I got **wrapped up in** the book.* JFTR

wrap (up) in cotton wool [B2 pass B3 pass] (informal) overprotect sb from danger or risk. **S:** mother, nurse. **O:** child, pupil □ *She keeps her children **wrapped up in cotton wool**.* □ *'Don't* *wrap* ***the boy in cotton wool*** *— let him play with the others!'* ⇨ wrap (up) (in)[2].

wreathe (itself) around/round [B2 pass emph rel] wind (itself) in a coil or wavy line around sth. **S:** smoke, mist; ivy, rose-bush; snake. **o:** house, tree; window □ *Creeping plants had* ***wreathed themselves around*** *the trellis* (cf: *The trellis was* ***wreathed in*** *creeping plants*). □ *A garland of flowers had been* ***wreathed round*** *his head.* ⇨ next entry.

wreathed in [pass (B2)] (be) surrounded by coils or wavy lines of. **o:** smoke, mist; ivy, creeper □ *His head was* ***wreathed in*** *cigar smoke.* □ *His funeral bier was* ***wreathed in*** *flowers.* ⇨ previous entry.

wrench off [B1i pass adj B2 pass] take off, remove, with a powerful, twisting movement. **O:** door; handle, grip. **o:** hinges, frame; door □ *By placing a piece of steel pipe over the car door, the thief was able to* ***wrench*** *it* ***off***. □ *The house was a shambles, with windows broken and doors* ***wrenched off*** *their hinges.*

wrest from [B2 pass emph rel] (formal) obtain, win, from by a hard struggle. **S:** worker, farmer; invader; interrogator. **O:** living, livelihood; city, castle; admission, secret. **o:** job, land; owner, inhabitant; prisoner □ *Here one finds a few peasants,* ***wresting*** *a poor living* ***from*** *the harsh soil.* □ *The citadel was* ***wrested from*** *its defenders only after a hard struggle.*

wrestle with [A2 pass emph rel] fight inwardly, morally, with; struggle with (q v). **o:** doubt, dilemma, problem; conscience □ *He was still* ***wrestling with*** *uncertainty over his religious faith.* □ *These questions, long* ***wrestled with***, *were now resolved.*

wriggle out of [A2 pass] (informal) escape sth unpleasant by careful or cunning movements. **o:** responsibility, task; being present, giving help □ *'I notice that he's* ***wriggled out of*** *his share of the washing-up.'* □ *He was asked to supervise an examination, but somehow he's* ***wriggled out of*** *it.*

wring from/out of [B2 pass emph rel] get sth from sb, extract sth, by applying moral or physical pressure. **O:** story, account; confession, secret □ *An admission was* ***wrung from*** *the bank messenger that he had prior knowledge of the raid.* □ *'Have you tried* ***wringing*** *a donation* ***out of*** *him? It's like getting blood from a stone.'*

wring out [B1i pass adj] force water from clothing, by twisting it or passing it through rollers. **O:** clothes; skirt, towel □ *She has a few garments to* ***wring out*** *and hang on the line.* □ *Charles dipped the wash-leather in the pail and then* ***wrung*** *it* ***out***. HD

write (about/on) [A2 pass emph rel B2 pass emph rel] produce books etc on a particular subject. **S:** author, playwright. **O:** novel, play; much, a good deal. **o:** childhood, home, family; love, war; Spain, Africa □ *He's an expert on breeding dogs — he's* ***written*** *several books* ***on*** *the subject.* □ *These events have been argued about and* ***written about*** *so much that I know them by heart.* □ *This was a theme* ***on*** *which he'd* ***written*** *more than once.*

write (against) [A2 pass B2 pass] produce articles etc critical of sb or sth. **S:** journalist, pamphleteer. **O:** article, book. **o:** state, regime, system □ *Several novelists were called to account for supposedly* ***writing against*** *the state.* □ *A great deal was* ***written against*** *the penal system, without however changing anything.*

write away/off (for) [A1 A3] send an order for sth offered as a free gift, for sale etc; send away/off (for) (q v). **S:** reader, customer. **o:** catalogue, list; sample; map, book □ ***Write away*** *now* ***for*** *the free album offered to every new subscriber.* □ *I've* ***written off*** *to order the second edition of his textbook.*

write back (to) [A1 A3 rel] write (and send) a letter in reply to sb. **S:** relative, customer. **o:** office, shop, factory □ *I* ***wrote back*** *straight away to thank John for his kind invitation.* □ *If the supplier sends you the wrong goods,* ***write back to*** *them at once.*

write down [B1i pass adj] record on paper (often as an aid to memory); put down[8] (q v). **O:** name, address; detail, particular □ *'****Write down*** *my phone number in your diary before you forget it.'* □ *I* ***wrote*** *a few important notes* ***down*** *on the back of an envelope.*

write in [B1i nom pass] (politics, esp US) add to the ballot paper the name of a candidate not already printed there. **O:** name; candidate □ *British voting procedure does not normally provide for the* ***writing in*** *of candidates' names.* □ *There was a heavy* ***write-in*** *vote for a candidate not officially sponsored by the Republicans.*

write in/into[1] [B1i pass adj B2 pass] include, insert, sth in a written text. **O:** correction, amendment, comment; line, word, passage. **o:** article, book □ *Any alterations should be* ***written in*** *neatly to one side.* □ *The editor had* ***written*** *numerous suggestions* ***into*** *the margins.*

write in/into[2] [B1i pass B2 pass] make a part of, embody in, a legal document; build in/into[2] (q v). **O:** provisions, terms; guarantee. **o:** Bill; contract, agreement □ *A guarantee to protect pension rights has been* ***written into*** *their contracts.* □ *The agreement would not be signed unless it contained* ***written-in*** *assurances that the work force would not be further reduced.*

write in (to) [A1 A3 rel] address an inquiry, complaint etc to some central office or agency. **S:** listener, viewer; motorist, consumer. **o:** BBC, newspaper office, advice bureau □ *Indignant viewers have been* ***writing in*** *to complain of the moral content of plays.* □ *To qualify for your free sample, all you do is* ***write in to*** *this address.*

write off[1] [B1i pass] recognize that sth is a loss, cannot be recovered etc. **S:** creditor, bank, accountant. **O:** sum, amount; debt, loss □ *The firm has* ***written off*** *two thousand pounds' worth of bad debts.* □ *It is inevitable that losses should have to be* ***written off***. SC

write off[2] [B1i nom pass adj] damage sth so badly that it has no value; recognize that sth is so badly damaged that it is no longer economic to pay for its repair. **S:** motorist, pilot; insurance company. **O:** car, plane □ *The car was completely* ***written off*** (or: *was a complete* ***write-off***) *and the driver seriously injured.* □ the write-off value of a vehicle is the amount paid by its insurer when it is written off.

write off[3] [B1i nom pass adj] (informal) regard sth as a failure, beyond recovery etc. **O:** friendship, partnership, marriage; meeting, party, dance □ *Everyone they spoke to had* ***written off*** *the marriage before it began.* □ *It looks as though* *tonight's going to be a complete **write-off**.* TBC

write off as [B3 pass] regard sb or sth as unimportant, not worth listening to etc (because he or it is thought to be wild, foolish etc). **O:** speaker, author, preacher; opinion, statement, claim. **o:** simpleton, charlatan; absurd, nonsensical; hysteria, propaganda □ *He can't just be **written off as** an eccentric recluse.* AH □ *His political philosophy tends to be **written off as** an outmoded fantasy.* AH

write off (for) [A1 A3] ⇨ write away/off (for).

write (on) [A2 pass emph rel B2 pass emph rel] ⇨ write (about/on).

write out [B1i pass adj] write in full, complete. **O:** cheque, claim; statement, confession; imposition □ *'I haven't got cash, but I can **write** you **out** a cheque.'* □ *'**Write out** one hundred times: "I must not be impertinent to prefects."'* □ note the Indirect Object in: ***Write** me **out** a full account.*

write (oneself) out [B1ii pass] reach the point where one is no longer original, creative. **S:** novelist, playwright □ *He was still comparatively young and there was no reason to think he had **written himself out**.* PW □ *What were the critics saying about him? '**Written out** at the age of thirty'.*

write out/out of [B1ii pass B2 pass] remove a character from a dramatic series on radio or TV (e g by arranging for him to 'die'). **S:** author, script-writer. **O:** character, part. **o:** script, story □ *An actor who has been booked for a long series on television may be alarmed to hear that his part is being **written out of** the script.*

write up[1] [B1i pass adj] rewrite sth in a fuller, better organized way; give a full, written account of sth. **S:** student, research-worker. **O:** note, observation; experiment, project □ *The basic experimental work has been done; what I have to do now is **write** it all **up**.* □ *'For homework you can **write up** the rough notes you made in class.'*

write up[2] [B1i nom pass adj] write a review of a play etc (usu for a newspaper). **S:** critic, reviewer. **O:** play, film; novel □ *You can go home afterwards and **write** the film **up** in the paper.* CON □ *His latest book got an enthusiastic **write-up** in the quality press* (or: *was given an enthusiastic **write-up***).

wrought up [pass adj (B1)] (be) nervously strained, tense □ *'Calm down, you're getting terribly **wrought up** over nothing.'* □ *Spreading rumours would merely get people **wrought up** to no purpose.* TGLY □ *He came in with a deadly serious, **wrought-up** look on his face.* □ passive with *be, get, seem.* ⇨ work up (into/to).

Y

yank off [B1i pass B2 pass] (informal) take off, remove, with a sharp pull. **O:** handle, lock; cupboard. **o:** door, wall □ *He seized my hand in his great clasp and nearly **yanked** it **off**.* □ *Lids had been **yanked off** desks and lay scattered about the floor.*

yank out/out of [B1i pass B2 pass] (informal) extract with a sharp tug. **O:** tooth; nail, screw, bolt. **o:** jaw; plank □ *I have to go to the dentist to have a few teeth **yanked out**.* □ *Tap the nails up from the back, and **yank** them **out** with pincers.*

yearn (for) [A2 pass adj emph rel] (formal) desire strongly (sb or sth from which one is separated); long (for) (q v). **o:** lover, family; sight, touch, smell □ *How he **yearned for** her whenever they were separated.* □ *She **yearned for** a sight of* (or: ***yearned** to see*) *her dear ones.*

yell out [A1 B1i pass] (informal) cry or shout aloud (e g to attract attention, show pain etc). **O:** name; order □ *When the sergeant **yelled out** my number, I had to rush forward.* □ *'Don't squeeze his hand: it makes him **yell out** in pain.'*

yield (to) [A2 emph rel] allow oneself to be overcome by pressure; give in (to) (q v), give way to[2] (q v). **S:** shopper, tenant, striker. **o:** (sales, economic) pressure, argument, persuasion; force; emotion, anger □ *'If they won't **yield to** reason we shall have to try other methods.'* □ *Blackmail was a weapon **to** which they were not prepared to **yield**.* □ ***To** such persuasive arguments they had to **yield** eventually.*

yield up[1] [B1i pass] (formal) hand to the enemy in admission of defeat; surrender (to)[1] (q v), render up (to) (q v). **S:** governor, garrison. **O:** fortress, citadel; town; oneself, one's prisoner □ *The city would only be **yielded up** when ammunition and food supplies were exhausted.* □ *Did Calais **yield up** the burghers to the English?*

yield up[2] [B1i pass adj] (formal) deliver; reveal, disclose; give up[4] (q v). **S:** earth, sea; rock, soil; oracle, clairvoyant. **O:** wealth, treasure; secret □ *In that year of plenty, the seas **yielded up** a rich harvest of fish.* □ *What new mysteries will be **yielded up** to the scientist?*

Z

zero in (on)[1] [A1 A3 pass] (military) find the exact range from one's guns to an enemy position; range in (on) (q v). **o:** position, emplacement; crossroads, bridge □ *With first light, the artillery **zeroed in on** the road junctions, making it a nerve-testing journey for the men who had to bring through the barges.* ST

zero in (on)[2] [A1 A3 pass] (informal) position oneself so as to grasp or profit from. **S:** banker, investor, industrialist. **o:** opportunity, opening; market □ *The City of London is never slow to **zero in on** an opportunity of this magnitude, and already certain parties are positioning themselves to get in on the act.* T

zip along [A1] progress, move along, at a fast,

lively pace. **S:** car, train; (action of a) play, film; game. **A:** really, fairly □ *'The car **zips along**, all right, but have you noticed how bad the bodywork is?'* □ *The game got off to a sluggish start, but after half-time it fairly **zipped along**.*

zip up [B1i nom pass adj] close by means of a zip-fastener. **O:** pocket, fly-front; purse, bag □ *He packed his books into his briefcase and **zipped** it **up**.* □ *His flying jacket **zips up*** (i e can be ***zipped up***) *at the front.* □ nom used attrib as in zip-up *jacket.*

zone off [B1i pass adj] make a separate zone of (e g where traffic is restricted) esp in a town or city. **O:** city centre, shopping precinct □ *The business and commercial centre has now been **zoned off**: private cars are prohibited, and delivery vans may only enter and leave at specified times.*

zoom across, along, away etc [A1 emph A2 emph] move across etc swiftly, with engine(s) roaring. **S:** aircraft; jet, bomber; car, bus □ *A flight of fighter aircraft **zoomed** low **over** the saluting base.* □ *A heavily-laden minibus **zoomed past** in a cloud of dust.*

zoom in (on) [A1 A3] (cinema, TV) by adjusting the 'zoom' lens on a camera, gradually change from a distant shot to a close-up (of sb or sth). **S:** cameraman; camera. **o:** table, bed; face, hand □ *'Camera 3, **zoom in** a bit more. That's fine — hold it there.'* □ *After an 'establishing' shot of a waiter carrying drinks on a tray, the camera **zooms in on** a couple seated at the bar.*

zoom out [A1] (cinema, TV) by adjusting the 'zoom' lens on a camera, move gradually from a close-up to a longer shot □ *'Camera 2. I want you to **zoom out** until you've got a head-and-shoulders shot of John and the girl.'*

Index of nouns etc used in headphrases

This index lists the nouns, adjectives and adverbs which appear in the headphrases in the dictionary, whether as part of an entirely fixed expression (e g *lot* in *cast in one's lot with*), or as an optional part of an expression which is otherwise fixed (e g *right* in *take (right) on the chin*), or as alternative elements in an expression (e g *ease*, *rest* in *set sb's mind at ease/rest*). Also listed are the less fixed, but still 'restricted', elements of an expression which, though not included in the headphrase itself, are marked with the sign ⚠ in the group of collocating words of an entry (those listed after **S:**, **O:**, **o:** etc), e g **o:** ⚠*the opportunity, the chance, the offer* in the entry *leap at*. ⇨ Introduction, 6.

In addition some verbs are included in this index because they are not in the normal alphabetical sequence in the dictionary (e g *done* in *be over and done with*) or because they are subordinate to the main verb + particle/preposition entry (e g *take* in *sit up and take notice*).

The index will help the user find an entry by means of the non-verbal elements of the idiomatic expression, when he is unsure of the verb or of the construction in which it is used. Thus he may also explore the relationship of a noun with different verbs (e g *chance* with *jump at*, *leap at*, *leave to* etc).

The arrangement of the index is as follows:

1 Each index word (printed in **bold** type) is listed alphabetically and followed by the headphrase(s) (printed in light type) in the form in which it appears in the dictionary, a tilde (~) being used for the indexed word:

fall
pride goes before a ~
ride for a ~

The headphrases themselves are arranged in the order in which they appear in the dictionary, and the user will be able to find the main entries by their verb + preposition elements (*go* + *before*; *ride* + *for*). ⇨ Introduction, 2.

2 When the indexed word does not appear in the headphrase but is one of the collocates in the dictionary entry, the tilde representing the indexed word is shown inside square brackets to mark it off clearly from the actual headphrase entry:

blazes
blow to² [~]

confidence
restore [~] in

The actual headphrases here are *blow to²* and *restore in*. In some cases, when the collocated word is (part of) a complex variation on the original headphrase, perhaps replacing one word in it or extending the idiom, this is shown by giving the variation in full, followed by a colon and the actual headphrase to which it is linked:

blazes
go to ~: go to hell etc

cackle
cut the ~ and get the horses/'osses: get to¹

3 In some entries particular meanings (printed in *italic* type) or parts of speech are recorded for the sake of greater clarity:

bed
put to ~ (*printing*)

right (*adj, adv*)
be [~] out⁹

right/rights (*n*)
be within one's ~s

make no ~s about
reduce to[5] [skin and ~s]
book/books
get into sb's black ~s
go by the ~/rules
take a leaf out of sb's ~
throw the ~ (of rules) at
(a) turn-up (for the ~)
bootlaces
pull oneself up by one's own ~/bootstraps
boots
[one's heart etc] sink into/to one's ~
bootstraps
pull oneself up by one's own bootlaces/~
bosom
take to one's ~
both
make the best of ~ worlds
make the worst of ~ worlds
seize with ~ hands
bottom
the ~ drop out of the market/ price
get to the ~ of
knock the ~ out of
bounds
keep within ~
bows
be down by the ~/stern
brain/brains
have on the ~
beat one's ~s out
beat one's/sb's ~s out
dash one's/sb's ~s out
brake/brakes
jam the ~s on
put a/the ~ on
slam the ~s on
brass
get down to ~ tacks
brave
put a bold/~/good face on
breach
step into the ~
break
make a ~ for it
breast
make a clean ~ of it/ the whole thing
breath
gasp for ~
take sb's ~ away
brick
bang one's head against a ~ wall (*also* beat, knock *etc*)
run one's head against/into a ~ wall
bridge (= *card game*)
make up a four (at ~)
brief
hold no ~ for

brimstone
call [fire and ~] down on sb's head
bud
be in ~/leaf
come into ~/leaf
nip in the ~
bull
take the ~ by the horns
bump
bring down to earth [with a ~]
come down to earth [with a ~]
Burton
go for a ~
bush
beat about the ~
business
be about[1] [one's ~]
do ~ (with)
get down to ~
go about one's ~
go out of ~
poke one's nose in/into [(sb else's) ~]
put out of ~
send about his ~
cackle
cut the ~ and get to the horses/'osses: get to[1]
call
be/go beyond the ~ of duty: go beyond one's duty
put a ~ through (to)
canaries
put the cat among the ~/ pigeons
candle
not hold a ~ to
cans
live out of ~/tins
canter
break into[1] [a ~]
cap
put one's thinking ~ on
set one's ~ at
capital
make ~ (out) of
capitulation
starve into [~]
cards
lay one's ~ on the table
put one's ~ on the table (*also* place *etc*)
stack [the ~] against
care
take ~ (of)
career
carve out a ~ for oneself
stake [one's ~] on[2]
careful
keep a ~ eye on: keep an/one's eye on

caring
be beyond/past ~
carpet
sweep under the ~
cart
put the ~ before the horse
case
[the ~] be on[7] (*legal*)
[the ~] come on[2] (*legal*)
make out a ~
trump up [a ~] (*legal*)
cat
let the ~ out of the bag
put the ~ among the canaries/pigeons
cause
give ~ for
caution
throw ~/discretion to the winds
centuries
the ~ roll back/roll back the ~: roll back[4]
ceremony
stand on ~
certain
have [(~) misgivings/ reservations/qualms/ scruples] about
challenge
fling down a ~
rise to the ~/occasion
take up the ~
chance/chances
jump at [the ~]
leap at [the ~]
leave to ~
stack [the ~s] against
take a ~ (on)
trust to ~
change/changes
get no ~ out of
ring the ~s (on)
channels
go through (the) proper ~
charge
be in ~ (of)
bring a ~/(against) (*legal*)
clear (of) [the ~] (*legal*)
take ~ (of)
trump up [a ~] (*legal*)
check
keep in ~[1,2]
cheeks
tear(s) roll down [one's ~]
chest
get off one's ~
puff one's ~ out
chew (*v*)
bite off more than one can ~
child
get with ~

nouns etc used in headphrases

chin
chuck under the ~
come up to sb's ~/shoulder
keep one's ~/pecker up
take (right) on the ~
chips
stack [the ~] against
chump
be off[9] [one's ~]
go off[8] [one's ~]
Church
receive into [the (Catholic) ~]
cinder/cinders
burn to [a ~/~s]
circulation
get back into ~
claim
lay ~ to[1,2]
peg out a ~
stake (out) a/one's ~ (on/to)
class
read round the ~/room
clean
make a ~ breast of it/the whole thing
climax
bring to a ~
come to a ~
clock
put the ~ back
close *(n)*
draw to a ~
close *(adj)*
keep a ~ watch on
keep an ear/one's ear(s) (~) to the ground
clouds
be up in the ~
clover
lay down to [~]
clutch
let the ~ in
coals
haul over the ~
cobwebs
blow the ~ away
cold
break out in a ~ sweat
fix with [a ~ stare]
collision
be in ~ (with)
come into ~ (with)
collusion
be in ~ (with)
colours
nail one's ~ to the mast
coma
fall into[2] [a ~]
pass into[3] [a ~]
comb
run a ~ through one's hair
comfortably
be ~ off (for): be well etc off (for)
commas
put in inverted ~ *(also place etc)*
company
impose oneself/one's ~ on/upon
part ~ (with)
compassion
have ~/pity on
concerns
poke one's nose in/into [(sb else's) ~]
conclusion/conclusions
bring to a successful ~
come to a successful ~
jump to ~s/the ~
rush to ~s
confidence
have ~ in
repose [~] in
restore [~] in
take into one's ~
confinement
clap in/into [solitary ~]
confusion
cover in/with ~/shame
throw into [~]
consideration
leave out of [~]
take into account/~
construction
put a ~ on *(also place etc)*
contact
be in ~ (with)
bring into ~ (with)
come into ~ (with)
get in ~/touch (with)
lose ~/touch (with)
contempt
be beneath ~
glare ~/defiance/hate (at)
pour [~] on
contrast
stand out (against/in ~ to)
control
be in ~ (of)
be under ~
bring under ~
get under ~
have ~ of/over
keep under ~
take ~ (of)
conversation
bring [the ~] round to
strike up [a ~] (with)
convictions
have the courage of [one's ~]
corner
drive into a ~
corns
step on sb's ~/toes
tread on sb's ~/toes
cotton
wrap (up) in ~-wool
counsel
profit by [sb's ~]
count
be down for a ~ of ...
be out[9] [for the ~]
lose ~ (of)
country
go to the ~ *(i e hold an election)*
live off the ~
coup
bring off[2] [a ~]
courage
have the ~ of [one's convictions etc]
pluck up ~
screw up one's ~
[one's ~] sink into/to one's boots
course
walk over (the ~)
court
laugh out of ~
pay ~ (to)
take to ~ *(legal)*
cover
scurry for [~]
coward
take the ~'s way out/out of: take the easy etc way out/ out of
crack
have [a ~] at
craw
stick in sb's ~
credence
give ~ to
credit
give ~ for
give ~ (to) (for)
reflect ~ on/upon
take ~ for
crisis
wait out [a ~]
crisp
burn to [a ~]
criticism
be above[1] [~]
crowds
pack in[3] [the ~]
crunch
if/when it comes to the ~/ push
crush
have a ~/pash on
crying
burst out ~/laughing
curiosity
[~] eat up[2]
currency
give ~ to
current
[the ~] pull under
curses
call ~ down on sb's head
curtain
[the ~] go up[6]

ring the ~ down/up
custody
remand (in ~)
cut (*v*)
~ the cackle and get to the horses/'osses: get to[1]
daisies
push up (the) ~
dance
make a song and ~ about/over
dark
keep in the ~
dash
make a bolt/~ for
date
be up to ~/the minute
get up to ~ (with)
daylights
knock hell/the living ~ out of
days
the ~ close in
[the ~] draw in
[the ~] draw out[2]
fall on/upon evil ~/hard times
live out one's ~/life
dead
be at a ~ end
be [~] out[9]
bring to a ~ end
come to a ~ end
cut out (the) ~ wood
give up for ~/lost
leave for ~
raise from the ~
rise from the ~/grave
stop (~) in one's/his tracks
deaf
fall on ~ ears
turn a ~ ear (to)
deal
make a ~ (with)
make a good ~ of play with: make great etc play with
dear
run for ~ life/one's life
dearly
pay [~] for
death
bleed to ~
bore to [~]
burn to ~
crush to ~
do to ~
drink oneself to ~
flog to ~
freeze to ~
frighten to ~
gore to ~
lie at ~'s door
put the fear of ~/God in/into/up
put to ~
redeem (from)[2] [~]

send to his ~
tickle to ~
worry (oneself) [to ~] about/over
debt
be up to[4] [here/his ears/ eyes/neck in ~]
decay
fall into ~
decks
go below (~)
declaration
bring out[7] [a ~]
[a ~] come out[9]
decline
fall into a ~
deep
fall into a (~) depression
fall into[2] [a ~ sleep]
get into ~ water
go off the ~ end
pass into[3] [a ~ sleep]
defence
spring to sb's ~
defiance
glare contempt/~/hate (at)
degree
read for [a ~]
demands
make ~ (of/on)
demonstration
(a) sit-down (~/strike)
dent
make a ~ in
depression
fall into a (deep) ~
depth/depths
be out of one's ~
get out of one's ~
stir to the ~s
descent
trace [one's ~] back (to)[2]
description
answer to the ~ (of)
designs
have ~ on
desires
have the courage of [one's ~]
despair
drive to ~/desperation
desperation
drive to despair/~
details
[(the) ~] come in[8]
devices
leave to his own ~
devil
play the ~/hell (with)
Devil
call up the ~
the ~ get into sb: get into[6]
go to the ~: go to hell etc
diet
go on (to)[2] [a ~]
difference

make a ~ (to)
tell the ~ (between)
dignity
be beneath one's ~
stand on one's ~
diploma
read for [a ~]
direct
give the lie (~) to
disarray
throw into [~]
discretion
throw caution/~ to the winds
discussion
bring [the ~] round to
disfavour
fall into ~: fall from/out of favour
disgrace
fall into ~
disorder
throw into [~]
disrepair
fall into ~
disrepute
bring into ~
fall into ~
distance
bring within [striking ~]
get within [striking ~]
keep at arm's length/a ~
distraction
bore to [~]
disuse
fall into [~]
dodges
be up to[2] [all his ~]
dogs
call off[2] [the ~]
go to the ~
done
be over and ~ with
get over and ~ with
donkey
talk the hind leg(s) off a ~
door
keep the wolf from the ~
lay at sb's ~
lie at death's ~
lie at sb's ~
scurry for [the ~]
slam the ~ in sb's face
dotted
sign on the ~ line
doubts
have ~ about
dozen
(not) exchange more than a few/half a ~ words (with)
dread
have [a ~] of
drink
drive to ~
dumps
be down in the ~/mouth

get down in the ~/mouth
dust
kick up[2] [a ~]
shake the ~ (of sth) off one's feet/shoes
duty
go beyond one's ~ [*also:* the call of
recall to [a sense of ~]
report (for ~/work)
each
cancel (~ other) out
go at[1] [~ other (hammer and tongs etc)] vie (with ~ other/one another)
ear
give an ~/eye to
go in (at) one ~ and out (at/of) the other
grin from ~ to ~
have an ~/eye/a nose for
keep an ~/one's ~(s) (close) to the ground
turn a deaf ~ (to)
early
get in[3] [~]
ears
be up to[4] [his ~ in debt/work]
crash about one's ~
din in sb's ~
fall about one's ~
fall on deaf ~
fall on/upon sb's ~
jangle on/upon [sb's ~]
keep an ear/one's ear/~ (close) to the ground
prick one's ~ up
earshot
be out of[2] ~
be within[1] ~
bring within ~
come within ~
get within ~
earth
bring down to ~
come down to ~
go to ~/ground
run to ~/ground
wipe off the face of the ~/off the map
ease
put at his ~
set sb's mind at ~/rest
easy
take the ~ etc way out/out of
edge
have an/the ~ over
set sb's/the teeth on ~
take the ~ off
edgeways
get a word in (~)
effect
come into ~
have an ~/impact (on/upon)
put into ~
strain after an ~ (*also* strive *etc*)
effective
make ~/good use of
put to ~/good use
efforts
concentrate [one's ~] (on/upon)
focus [(one's) ~] (on)
eggs
put all one's ~ in one basket
elbow
not know one's arse from one's ~
else
poke one's nose in/into [(sb ~'s) affairs etc]
step into sb ~'s shoes
'em (= *them*)
stick ~/your hands up
emphasis
lay ~/stress on
employment
be out of[1] [~]
end
be at a dead ~
be at an ~
bring to a dead ~
bring to an ~
come to a bad etc ~
come to a dead ~
come to an ~
get hold of the wrong ~ of the stick
go off the deep ~
keep one's ~ up
put an ~/a stop to
see beyond the ~ of one's nose
see an ~ of/to
endurance
be beyond/past (one's) ~
energy/energies
burst with [~]
concentrate [one's energies] (on/upon)
expend ~ (on)
focus [one's energies] (on)
enough
not have ~ imagination/intelligence/sense to come in out of the rain
~/something to go on with
enthusiasm
burst with [~]
envy
[~] eat up[2]
escape
cut off[4] [every avenue of ~/sb's ~ route]
evening/evenings
[the ~s] draw in
[the ~s] draw out[2]
make an ~/a night/weekend of it
pass [the ~] away
events
~ fall out (thus): fall out[1]
put a bold/brave/good face on ~
ever
not (~) clap eyes on
every
cut off[4] [~ avenue of escape]
drink in[1] [~ word]
hang upon [(sb's) ~ word]
everything
[~] be over and done with
carry all/~ before one
chuck up [~]
~ falls out (thus): fall out[1]
evidence
give ~ of[1,2]
trump up [~] (*legal*)
evil
fall on/upon ~ days/hard times
examination
stand up (to)[2] [~]
example
hold up as an ~
make an ~ of
exception
take ~ to
exempt (*adj*)
be ~ from: exempt from
exhibition
make an ~ of oneself
existence
be in being/~
bring into being/~
come into being/~
exit
scurry for [the ~]
expectations
be up to[5] [(sb's) ~]
come up to [(sb's) ~]
experience
profit by [one's ~]
expression
[one's ~] glaze over
extreme/extremes
go to the other ~/go from one ~ to another/the other
go to ~s
eye
cast an ~/one's eyes over
[his ~] fall on/upon[3]
get one's ~/hand in
give an ear/~ to
have an ear/~/nose for
have one ~ on
have one's ~ on
keep one's ~/hand in
keep an/one's ~ on
keep one ~ on
(not) look in the ~/face
pass one's ~ over
run an/one's ~ over
see ~ to ~ (with) (about/on)

stick to sb's ~
finish
be in at the ~/kill
finishing
put the final/~ touches to
fire
call [~ and brimstone] down on sb's head
open ~ (on)
play with ~
set on ~[1,2]
set the Thames on ~
set ~/light to
firm
keep a ~/tight grip/hold on
take a (~) stand (on/over)
take a (~) grip/hold on/upon oneself
first
get in[3] [~]
get to ~ base with
fishy
fix with [a ~ stare]
fit
fly into [a (~ of) temper etc/ an angry ~]
fix
get into a ~
flair
have a ~/gift for
flames
burst into ~
flat
fall ~ on one's face[1,2]
go into a (~) spin
flight
put to ~/rout
floor
be in on the ground ~
come in on the ground ~
get in[3] [on the ground ~]
flower
be in blossom/~
bring into blossom/~
burst into[2] [~]
[a ~] close up[1]
come into blossom/~
focus
be in ~
be out of ~
bring into ~
come into ~
go out of ~
fold
receive back into the ~
folklore
pass into[2] [~]
fool/fools
make a ~ of
make a ~ of oneself
~s rush in (where angels fear to tread)
foot
get off on the right/wrong ~
put one ~ before/in front of the other
put one's ~ down[1,2]
put one's best ~ forward
put one's ~ in it
set ~ in
start off on the right/wrong ~ (with)
step off on the wrong ~
wait on/upon sb hand and ~
footsteps
follow in sb's ~
force/forces
be in ~
be out in [~]
bring into ~
come into ~
join ~s (with)
put into ~
fore
be to the ~
bring to the ~
come to the ~
fortune
trust to [~]
Fortune
~ smile upon
four
make up a ~ (at bridge)
friend/friends
make a ~ of
make ~s (with)
friendship
strike up [a ~] (with)
front
put up[5] [a ~]
fruition
bring to ~
come to ~
full
do (ample/~) justice to
draw oneself up to one's ~ height
restore (to)[5] [(~) health]
fun
make ~ of
poke ~ at
fury
draw [sb's ~] down (upon one's head)
[the ~] go out of[1]
fuss
kick up[2] [a ~]
make a ~ about/over
make a ~ of
gallop
break into[1] [a ~]
game
the ~ be up
give the ~/show away
garden
lead up the ~ path
gas
step on it/the ~
gatepost
(be) between you, me and the ~: be between ourselves/ you and me
gauntlet
throw down the ~
gaze
[his ~] fall on/upon[3]
fix [one's ~] on/upon
rivet [one's ~] on
gift
have a flair/~ for
gift-horse
(not) look a ~ in the mouth
gilt
take the ~ off the gingerbread
gingerbread
take the gilt off the ~
glance
dart a ~/look at
flash [a ~] (at)
shoot a ~ (at)
steal a ~ (at)
glare
fix with [a terrifying ~]
glass
raise a/one's ~ to
glory
blow to[2] [~]
go (*n*)
burst with [~]
have [a ~] at
make a ~ of
God
call [the wrath of ~] down on sb's head
draw [the wrath of ~] down (upon one's head)
pray (to ~) for
put the fear of death/~ in/ into/up
swear (by) [almighty ~]
gods
swear (by) [all the ~]
gold
come off the ~ standard
good
be on to a ~ thing
be up to[1] [no ~]
come to no ~ end: come to a bad etc end
get off to a ~ etc start
hold (~/true) (for)
make effective/~ use of
make a ~ etc job of
make a ~ deal of play with: make great etc play with
put a (~) word in
put a bold/brave/~ face on
put to effective/~ use
stand in ~/better stead
grab
make a ~ (at)
grace
fall from ~
lapse from ~

grain
go against the ~

granted
take for ~[1,2]

grasp
be within one's ~

grass
lay down to [a]

grave
rise from the dead/~
turn in one's ~

great
make ~ etc play with
set ~ etc store by/on

grief
come to ~

grin
wipe [the ~] off one's/sb's face

grindstone
get back to the ~
keep one's nose to the ~

grip
get a ~ on
keep a firm/tight ~/hold on
relax one's ~/hold (on)
take a (firm) ~/hold on/upon oneself

grips
be at ~ with
bring to ~ with
come to ~ with
get to ~ with

groove
get out of the ~/rut

ground
be in on the ~ floor
bring to the ~
come in on the ~ floor
come to the ~
cut the ~ from under sb's feet
fall to the ~
get in[3] [on the ~ floor]
go to earth/~
keep an ear/one's ear(s) (close) to the ~
lose ~ (to)
raze to the ~
rivet to the ~/spot
run into the ~
run to earth/~
suit (down) to the ~

grudge
have a ~ against

guard
be on one's ~ (against)
put on his ~
turn out the ~ (*military*)

guffaw
burst into[1] [a ~]

guilt
clear (of) [~]
lay [the ~] at sb's door
[the ~] lie at sb's door
purge (of) [~]
shuffle [the (feelings of) ~] off (onto)

guns
stick to one's ~

guts
sweat one's ~ out

habit/habits
fall into[3] [the ~ of doing sth/ bad/undesirable ~s]
get into[4] [the ~ (of doing sth)]
get out of[2] [the ~ (of doing sth)]
make a ~/practice of

Hades
go to ~: go to hell etc

hair
keep one's ~/shirt on
let one's (back) ~ down
plaster one's ~ down
run a comb through one's/ sb's ~
run one's fingers/hand through one's ~

half
(not) exchange more than a few/~ a dozen words (with)
rip in ~/two
tear in ~/two

half-cock
go off at ~

halt
be at a ~/standstill
bring to a ~/standstill
come to a ~/standstill
grind to a ~

hammer
go at[1] [(it/each other) ~ and tongs]
go under the ~

hand
be in ~
be well in ~
be out of ~
one's ~ be up
cross sb's ~/palm with silver
dive (one's ~) into
eat out of sb's ~
get one's eye/~ in
get out of ~
have in ~
have a ~/part in
have well in ~
keep one's eye/~ in
never/not lay a finger/~ on
put one's ~ up
reach [a ~] out (for)
run one's fingers/~ through one's hair
shake by the ~
stretch out[1] [a ~]
take in ~[1,2]
take a ~ (in)
throw one's ~ in
turn one's ~ to
wait on/upon sb ~ and foot

handkerchief
bury one's face/head in [one's ~]

handle
fly off the ~

hands
be off one's ~
bury one's face/head in [one's ~]
fall into sb's/the right etc ~
get one's ~ on[1,2]
go through sb's ~
have on one's ~
have time on one's ~
join ~ (with)
keep one's ~ off
lay one's ~ on[1,2,3]
play into sb's ~
put one's ~ up
seize with both ~
spread out[1] [one's ~]
stick 'em/your ~ up
take one's life in one's ~
take the law into one's own ~
take matters into one's own ~
take off sb's ~
take out of sb's ~
wash one's ~ of

handy
come in ~/useful

hang
get into[4] [the ~ of it]
get the ~ of
get out of[2] [the ~ of it]

hard
be ~ at it/work
be ~ up
bear ~/severely on/upon
bring up the ~ way
come up the ~ way
~ done by
fall on/upon evil days/ ~times

harm
come to ~

harmony
be in accord/~/tune (with)

harness
get back into ~

harsh
[the (~) note/tone]

hash
make a ~/mess of

hat
keep under one's ~
pass the ~ round
raise one's ~ to
take one's ~ off to
take the ~ round

hatches
batten down the ~

hate

glare contempt/defiance/~ (at)

hay
make ~ of

head
bang one's ~ against a brick wall (*also* beat, knock *etc*)
be above one/one's ~
be off[9] [one's ~]
bite sb's ~ off
bother one's ~ about
bring to a ~
bury one's face/~ in
call down on sb's ~
come to a ~
crow one's ~ off
draw down (upon one's ~)
eat one's ~ off
fling one's ~ back
get into one's ~
get out of one's ~/mind
go off[8] [one's ~]
go to sb's ~
hit the nail on the ~
keep one's ~ above water
knock sb's block/~ off
knock on the ~
laugh one's ~ off
make ~ or tail of
put the idea/thought into sb's ~
put ideas into sb's ~
run one's ~ against/into a brick wall
(have) one's ~ screwed on
snap sb's ~ off
stand ~ and shoulders above
stand on its ~
standing on one's ~
one's eyes stand out of one's ~
stuff sb's ~ with
swear (on) [(my son's) ~]
take it into one's ~ that
take it into one's ~ to do sth
talk above/over sb's ~
talk one's/sb's ~ off

heads
knock their ~ together
put our/your/their ~ together

health
[(one's) ~] break down[8]
bring back to ~/life
burst with [~]
restore (to)[5] [(full) ~]

hearing (*legal*)
[(the) ~] be on[7]
[(the) ~] come on[12]

heart/hearts
cry one's eyes/~ out
eat one's ~ out
(not) find it in oneself/one's ~ to do sth
[one's ~(s)] go out to
go to the ~ of [the matter etc]
heave (one's ~) up
learn off (by ~/rote)
put one's ~ and soul into
set one's ~ on
[one's ~] sink into/to one's boots
sob one's ~ out
take ~ (from)
take to ~
take to one's ~

heat
[the ~] go out of[2]
put on[9] [the ~]

heaven
smell to high ~
stink to high ~

Heaven
call [the vengeance of ~] down on sb's head

heavily
pay [~] for

heavy
make ~ weather of

heed
pay ~ (to)
take ~ (of)

heel
be down at ~
bring to ~
come to ~

heels
dig one's ~/toes in
kick up its ~
stick one's ~ in
take to one's ~

height
draw oneself up to one's full ~

hell
go at[1] [(it/each other) ~ for leather]
go to ~ etc
knock the ~/the living daylights out of
play the devil/~ (with)

help
come to sb's aid/assistance/~

here
be up to[4] [~ in debt/work]

high
be for it/the ~ jump
hold in ~/low regard
smell to ~ heaven
stink to ~ heaven

hind
get up on one's ~ legs
talk the ~ leg(s) off a donkey

history
go down to ~/posterity
pass into[2] [~]

hit
make a ~ (with)

hives
come out in [~]

hock
redeem (from)[1] [~]

hold
get ~ of
get ~ of the wrong end of the stick
have a ~ over
keep a firm/tight grip/~ on
lay ~ of
lose one's ~ on/over
relax one's grip/~ (on)
take a (firm) grip/~ on/upon oneself

holes
pick ~ in

holy
swear (by) [all that is ~]

home (*n*)
(*note that* home *as a particle* (*e g in* take home) *is not indexed here*)
eat out of house and ~
make tracks (for ~)
stay at ~

honest
make an ~ woman of

honour
be on one's ~
put on his ~

hook/hooks
fall for (~, line and sinker)
get one's ~s into/on
let off the ~

hope/hopes
build one's ~s on
come up to [sb's ~s]
give up (all) ~
hold out[3] [(the) ~]
live in ~ of

horns
draw one's ~ in
take the bull by the ~

horror
fling one's arms up in ~
have [a ~] of

horse/horses
[the ~s] be off[10] (*racing*)
cut the cackle and get to the ~s/'osses: get to[1]
put the cart before the ~
[the ~] rear (up)

hospital
rush to ~

hot
get into ~ water

hounds
call off[2] [the ~]
ride to ~

house
be about/around[1] [the ~]
bring the ~ down
eat out of ~ and home
put one's (own) ~ in order
set one's (own) ~ in order
set up ~ (together)

nouns etc used in headphrases

think nothing of ~
try [~] on (with)
turn ~ in
as ~/things turn(s) out
turn ~ up
wait for ~
wait [~] out
whoop ~ up
wrap [~] up
itself
blow ~ out
lend ~ to[1, 2]
speak for ~/themselves
suggest ~/themselves (to)
jail
clap in/into [~]
jealousy
[~] eat up[2]
jeopardy
be in ~
put in ~ (*also* place *etc*)
Jericho
go to ~: go to hell etc
jerk
bring up[7] [with a ~]
job
be out of[1] [a ~]
buckle down to [the ~]
chuck up [one's ~]
hold a/the ~ down
lie down on the ~
make the best of a bad ~
make a good etc ~ of
joint
put sb's nose out of ~
joke
be beyond a ~
go beyond a ~
Joneses
keep up with the ~
joy
weep for ~
judgement
sit in ~ (on/over)
juice
stew in one's (own) ~
jump
be for it/the high ~
justice
do (ample/full) ~ to
keeping
be out of[4] [~ with the occasion]
key
turn the ~ on
kick
get a ~ out of (*also* from)
kill
be in at the finish/~
kindly
~ disposed towards: well etc disposed towards
kindness
kill with ~
kingdom come
blow to[2] [~]
knees
beat to his ~
fall on/to one's ~
go down on one's ~ (to)
one's ~ knock together
one's ~ turn in/turn one's ~ in: turn in[1]
know (*v*)
I don't ~ what gets into him: get into[6]
knuckles
rap on/over the ~
ladder
get to the top (of the ~/tree)
land
live off/on the fat of the ~
spy out the ~
language
play on/upon[1] [~]
large
be out in [~ numbers]
last
stick to one's ~
laughing
burst out crying/~
fall about (~/with laughter)
laughter
burst into[1] [~]
fall about (laughing/with ~)
laurels
look to one's ~
rest on one's ~
law
keep on the right side of the ~
lay down the ~
take the ~ into one's own hands
lawsuit
[the ~] be on[7]
[the ~] come on[2]
leaf
be in bud/~
come into bud/~
take a ~ out of sb's book
turn over a new ~
lease(hold)
[the ~] fall in[3]
leash
strain at the ~
leather
go at[1] [(it/each other) hell for ~]
leave
take one's ~ (of)
take ~ of one's senses
leg/legs
get the weight off one's feet/~s
get up on one's hind ~s
talk the hind ~(s) off a donkey
legend
pass into[2] [~]
length
keep at arm's ~/a distance
let (*v*)
~ sb get on with it
liberties
take ~ (with)
lid
put the (tin) ~ on it/things
lie
give the ~ (direct) to
life
bring back to health/~
bring to ~
choke the ~ out of
come to ~
give [one's ~] for
go in fear of one's ~
lay down one's ~ (for)
live out one's days/~
make an attempt on sb's ~
mark for ~
~ pass by
pester the ~ out of
run for dear ~/one's ~
spring to ~
stake [one's ~] on[2]
take one's ~ in one's hands
light/lights
be out[9] [like a ~]
bring to ~
come to ~
make ~ of
[the ~s] go up[6]
make ~ of
see in a new etc ~
set fire/~ to
shed ~ on
throw ~ on
line/lines
be in ~ (with)
be out of ~
bring into ~ (with)
come into ~ (with)
draw the ~ (at)
fall for (hook, ~ and sinker)
fall into ~ (with)
keep in ~
read between the ~s
sign on the dotted ~
throw [a ~] away[3]
trace [one's (family) ~] back (to)[2]
lineage
trace [one's ~] back (to)[2]
lip/lips
hang upon [sb's ~s]
pay ~ service to
put a/one's finger to one's ~s (*also* place *etc*)
little
count for ~
go for nothing/very ~
twist around/round one's ~ finger
wind around/round one's (~)

piss
take the mickey/~ (out of)

pity
have compassion/~ on
take ~ on

place/places
be about/around[1] [the ~]
be out of[4] [~]
be all over the ~
change ~s (with)
fall into ~
feel out of ~
give ~ to
have a ~ in
keep in his ~
put in his ~
put oneself in sb's ~/shoes
stink the ~ out

play
be in ~
be out of ~
bring into ~
come into ~
go out of ~
make a/one's ~ for
make great etc ~ with

point
bring around/round (to)[2] [his ~ of view]
come around/round (to)[2] [his ~ of view]
come to the ~
make a ~ of
not to put too fine a ~ on it
raise [the ~] (with)
wander from/off [the (main) ~]

police
go to the ~

polls
go to the ~

poor
take a ~ etc view of

position
chuck up [one's ~]
put in an awkward ~ (*also* place *etc*)
take up a ~

possession
be in sb's ~
come into sb's ~

possibility
hold out[3] [the ~]
quail (at) [the ~]

post
chuck up [one's ~]

posterity
go down to history/~

pot
go to ~

power
be in ~
come into ~
fall from ~
put into ~
sweep into ~: sweep in/into[2]
vote into ~: vote in/into
vote out of ~: vote out/out of

practice
make a habit/~ of

pranks
be up to[1] [his ~]

preferences
not account for ~/tastes

premium
put at a ~ (*also* place *etc*)
put a ~ on (*also* place *etc*)

present
live in the ~

press (*printing*)
go to ~

pressure
(the) ~ be on
pile the ~ on
put ~ on/upon (*also* place *etc*)

pretty
bring to a ~ pass/such a pass
come to a ~ pass/such a pass

price/prices
the bottom drop out of the market/~
cut (~s) to the bone

pricks
kick against the ~

pride
~ goes before a fall
take ~ in

print
rush into ~

prison
clap in/into [~]

problem
go to the heart of [the ~]
put [the ~] in a nutshell

proceedings
put a bold/brave/good face on [~]

professional
keep a ~ eye on: keep an/one's eye on

prominence
bring into ~
come into ~

proper
go through (the) ~ channels

propriety
recall to [a sense of ~]

prospect
hold out[3] [the ~]
quail (at) [the ~]

pulse
keep one's finger on the ~ of

punch
get a blow/~ in

punishment
hand it/(the) ~ out

push
if/when it comes to the crunch/~

qualms
have [(some/serious/certain) ~] about

quarrel
pick [a ~] (with)

question
go to the heart of [the ~]
put [the ~] in a nutshell
raise [the ~] (with)

quick
be ~ off the mark
cut to the ~

quickest
take the ~ way out/out of: take the easy etc way out/out of

rack
go to ~ and ruin

rag
get one's ~ out

rage
fly into [a (fit of) ~]

rails
go off the ~
keep on the ~
run off the ~

rain
not have enough imagination/intelligence/sense to come in out of the ~
[(the) ~] come on[8]
[the ~] keep off[1]
[the ~] pour down
[the ~] sheet down

range
be out of[2] [~]
be within[1] [~]
bring within [~]
come within [~]
get within [~]

rank/ranks
reduce to the ~ of/to the ~s
rise from the ~s

rash
bring out in [a ~]
come out in [a ~]

raw
touch on the ~

rays
[the (sun's) ~] beat down (on)

real
[the (~) truth] come out[7]

rear
bring up the ~

reason
(it) stands to ~

reckoning
leave out of [the ~]

record
set up[6] [a ~]

recourse
have ~ to

refuge
take ~ in

regard
be beneath [(one's) ~]
hold in high/low ~
Register
strike off[2] [the Medical ~]
relief
throw into ~
remark/remarks
drink in[1] [his ~s]
throw [a ~] away[3]
reply
hang upon [sb's ~]
report
[a ~] come in[8]
reproach
be above[1] [~]
reproof
be above[1] [~]
reputation
stake [one's ~] on[2]
rescue
come to sb's/the ~
resemblance
bear a ~ to
reservations
have [(some/serious/certain) ~] about
residence
take up ~
resources
leave to one's own ~
responsibility
clear (of) [~]
lay [the ~] at sb's door
[the ~] lie at sb's door
shift the blame/~ onto
shuffle [the ~] off (onto)
rest
bring to ~
come to ~
lay to ~[1,2]
set sb's mind at ease/~
retreat
cut off[4] [sb's ~]
revenge
take ~ (on) (for)
review
pass in ~
ribbons
cut to pieces/~/shreds
ribs
dig in the ~
ride
take for a ~
ridicule
hold up to ~/scorn
pour [~] on
right (*adj, adv*)
be [~] out[9]
come out on the ~/wrong side
get off on the ~/wrong foot
give [one's ~ arm] for
keep on the ~ side of
keep on the ~ side of the law
move ~ down
rub up the ~ way
start off on the ~/wrong foot (with)
take (~) on the chin
right/rights (*n*)
be within one's ~s (to do sth)
have a ~ to sth/to do sth
put to ~s
set the world to ~s
rings
run ~ around/round
ripe
live to a/the ~ old age (of)
rise
give ~ to
take a/the ~ out of
river
sell down the ~
rocker
be off[9] [one's ~]
go off[8] [one's ~]
rod
rule with a ~ of iron
role
play a part/~ (in)
Roll (*of solicitors*)
strike off[2] [the ~]
roof
live under the same ~ (as)
room
make ~ (for)
read round the class/~
roots
put down ~
rot
the ~ set in
rote
learn off (by heart/~)
rough
cut up ~
take the ~ with the smooth
rout
put to flight/~
route
cut off[4] [sb's escape ~]
routine
go into one's act/~
row (= *noise*)
kick up[2] [a ~]
ruin/ruins
go to rack and ~
lie in ~s
rule/rules
go by the book/~s
throw the book (of ~s) at
work to ~
run/runs
break into[1] [a ~]
pile on ~s (*cricket*)
rut
get into a ~
get out of the groove/~
sacred
swear (by) [all that is ~/all one holds ~]
safe
to be on the ~ side
sail
clap on ~
set ~ (for)
sails
take the wind out of sb's ~
sale
be up for auction/~
come up for auction/~
put up for auction/~
same
come to the ~ thing (as)
live under the ~ roof (as)
sanity
[one's ~] break down[8]
restore (to)[5] [~]
say
have a ~/voice in
saying
it/that goes without ~
scene
be on the ~
come on the ~
scent
put off the ~/track/trail
throw off the ~/track
schedule
run behind [~]
scope
give ~ for
score/scores
settle [one's/a ~/(old) ~s] with
scorn
draw [~] down (upon one's head)
hold up to ridicule/~
pour [~] on
scratch
be up to[5] [~]
bring up to [~]
come up to [~]
start from ~
screw/screws
put [the ~/~s] on[9]
scruples
have [(some/serious/certain) ~] about
scrutiny
keep under[4] [~]
stand up (to)[2] [~]
sea
[the ~] get up[5]
[the ~] go out[7]
go to ~
stand out to ~
seal
set the ~ on
seams
come apart at the ~
season
be in ~
be out of ~

come into ~
secrecy
swear to ~/silence
secret
[the ~] be out[7]
let into a/the ~
make a ~ of
seed
go to ~
run to ~
sense
not have enough imagination/intelligence/~ to come in out of the rain
knock (some) ~ into
make ~ of
recall to [a ~ of duty/propriety]
senses
bring to his ~
come to one's ~
take leave of one's ~
sentence (*legal*)
pass ~ (on)
serious
have [(~) misgivings/reservations/qualms/scruples] about
service
be in ~/use
be out of ~/use
bring into ~/use
come into ~/use
go into ~/use
go out of ~
pay lip ~ to
severely
bear hard/~ on/upon
shade
put in the ~
shadow
reduce to[5] [a ~]
shame
cover in/with confusion/~
purge (of) [~]
put to ~
shape
lick into ~
sharp/sharply
bring up[7] [~/~ly]
draw up ~/~ly
keep a ~ eye on: keep an/one's eye on
shell
bring out of his ~
come out of one's ~
shelter
scurry for [~]
shift
make ~ (with)
shilling
cut off with a ~
shindy
kick up[2] [a ~]
shine
take a ~ to
ship
when one's ~ comes in
shirt
keep one's hair/~ on
put one's ~ on
shoes
put oneself in sb's place/~
shake the dust (of sth) off one's feet/~
step into sb else's ~
shop
set up ~
short
bring up[7] [~]
shot
have [a ~] at
shoulder/shoulders
come up to sb's chin/~
rub ~s (with)
stand head and ~s above
show
give the game/~ away
put up[5] [a ~]
shreds
cut to pieces/ribbons/~
rend to [~]
rip to [~]
tear to pieces/~[1,2]
sick
worry (oneself) [~] about/over
side
to be on the safe ~
come out on the right/wrong ~
get on the wrong ~ of
get out of bed (on) the wrong ~
keep on the right ~ of
keep on the right ~ of the law
laugh on the other ~ of one's face
let the ~ down
pass by on the other ~
put on one ~[1,2] (*also* place *etc*)
take aside/to one ~
sight/sights
be in ~/view
be out of[2] [~]
be within[1] [~]
bring into ~/view
bring within [~]
burst into ~/view
come into ~/view
come within [~]
disappear (from ~/view)
get out of sb's ~
get within [~]
go out of ~/view
heave in ~
keep in ~[1,2]
keep in ~ of
know by ~
line up in one's ~s
lose ~ of[1,2]
set one's ~s on
silence
reduce to ~
swear to secrecy/~
silly
worry (oneself) [~] about/over
silver
cross sb's hand/palm with ~
simplest
take the ~ way out/out of: take the easy etc way out/out of
sin/sins
one's ~(s) will find one out
live in ~
purge (of) [~]
redeem (from)[2] [~]
wash away sb's ~(s)
sinker
fall for (hook, line and ~)
situation
bring around/round (to)[2] [his assessment of the ~]
come around/round (to)[2] [his assessment of the ~]
six
knock for ~
size
cut down to ~
skates
get one's ~ on
skeleton
reduce to[5] [a ~]
skin
get under sb's ~
reduce to[5] [~ and bones]
soak to the ~
sky
the ~ cloud over
slack
take up the ~
sleep
cry oneself to ~
fall into[2] [a deep ~]
get off (to ~)
lull to ~
(not) lose any ~ about/over
pass into[3] [a deep ~]
put to ~
read oneself to ~
rock to ~
send to ~
sing to ~
sleeve/sleeves
laugh up one's ~
roll one's ~s up
smile
flash [a ~] (at)
take [the ~] off one's/sb's face
wipe [the ~] off one's/sb's face

smiling
come up ~
smirk
wipe [the ~] off one's/sb's face
smithereens
blow to[1] [~]
smoke (*v*)
put that in one's pipe and ~ it
smooth
take the rough with the ~
snap (= *photograph*)
blow up[6] [a ~]
snow
[(the) ~] come on[8]
[the ~] keep off[1]
so
take on (~)
sobs
burst into[1] [~]
sock/socks
pull one's ~s up
put a ~ in it
soft
have a ~/weak spot for
solitary
clap in/into [~ confinement]
solution
find an answer/a ~ (to)
some
give (~ etc) thought (to)
have [(~) misgivings/ reservations/qualms/ scruples] about
knock (~) sense into
something
~ be up
be up to[1] [~]
[~] be up (with)
[it has/we have] come to ~ [when ...]
do ~ to
~ get into sb: get into[6]
enough/~ to go on with
have ~ on sb: have on[4]
put ~ across sb: put across[2]
put ~ over (on sb): put over (on)
try [~] on (with)
son
swear (on) [(my ~'s) head]
song
burst into[1] [~]
go for[6] [a ~]
make a ~ and dance about/over
soul
keep body and ~ together
put one's heart and ~ into
sound
break through the ~ barrier
restore (to)[5] [(~) health]
sour
[the (~) note/tone] go out of[1]
speed
pick up ~
spell
fall under sb's/the ~
have in one's ~
spilt
it's no use crying over ~ milk
spin
go into a (flat) ~
spirit/spirits
enter into the ~ (of)
knock the ~/stuffing out of
[one's ~s] sink into/to one's boots
spite (*v*)
cut off one's nose to ~ one's face
spoke
put a ~ in sb's wheel
sponge
throw in the towel/throw up the ~
spot/spots
bring out in [~s]
come out in [~s]
have a soft/weak ~ for
knock ~s off
rivet to the ground/~
squeeze
put [the ~] on[9]
stab
have [a ~] at
stage
go on the ~
hiss off (the ~)
set the ~ (for)
stake
have a ~ in
stallion
[the ~] rear (up)
stand
take a (firm) ~ (on/over)
standard
be up to[5] [~]
bring up to [~]
come off the gold ~
come up to [~]
standstill
be at a halt/~
bring to a halt/~
come to a halt/~
stare
fix with [a fishy ~]
stars
[the ~] be out[5]
[the ~] come out[5]
[the ~] go down[1]
[the ~] go in[2]
[the ~] peep out
start
get in[3] [at the ~]
get off to a good etc ~
make a ~ (on)
state
keep in (a ~ of) suspense
statement
bring out[7] [a ~]
[a ~] come out[9]
stead
stand in good/better ~
steam
blow off ~
get up ~
let off ~
run out of ~
step
fall into ~ (with)
keep one ~ ahead/ahead of
keep in ~ (with)
stern
be down by the bows/~
stick
get hold of the wrong end of the ~
sticky
come to a ~ end: come to a bad etc end
sting
[the ~] go out of[1]
take the ~ out of
stitches
cast off (~)
cast on (~)
stock
take ~ (of)
stone
get blood out of a ~
kill two birds with one ~
stools
fall between two ~
stop/stops
pull out all the ~s
put an end/a ~ to
store
lie in ~ (for)
set great etc ~ by/on
storm
[a ~] get up[5]
wait out [a ~]
story
[a ~] come in[8]
[the (whole) ~] come out[7]
straight
keep to the ~ and narrow (path)
strain
put a ~ on/upon (*also* place *etc*)
straw
catch at a ~ (*also* clutch *etc*)
grasp at a ~
streets
go on the ~
strength
be out in [~]
stress
lay emphasis/~ on
stride
get into one's ~
put off his ~/stroke
take in one's ~

nouns etc used in headphrases

strike
(a) sit-down (demonstration/~)
striking
bring within [~ distance]
get within [~ distance]
strip/strips
tear sb off a ~; tear a ~/~s off sb
stroke
put off his stride/~
struggle
give up the fight/the (unequal) ~
stuffing
knock the spirit/the ~ out of
style
keep in[5] [~]
rejoice in [the ~ of]
subject
raise [the ~] (with)
read around/round the ~/topic
wander from/off [the (main) ~]
submission
cow into ~
crush into ~
starve into [~]
success
make a ~ of
successful
bring to a ~ conclusion
come to a ~ conclusion
such
bring to a pretty pass/~ a pass
come to a pretty pass/~ a pass
summons
serve [a ~] on[2]
take out [a ~] (against)
sun
[the ~] be out[5]
the ~ be up
[the ~('s rays)] beat down (on)
[the ~] break through[2]
[the ~] come out[5]
the ~ come up
the ~ glare down
[the ~] go down[1]
[the ~] go in[2]
[the ~] peep out
support
rally to the ~ of
surface
raise to the ~
rise to the ~
surrender
starve into [~]
surveillance
keep under[4] [~]
suspense
keep in (a state of) ~

suspicion
be above[1] [~]
clear (of) [~]
sweat
break out in a cold ~
[(the) ~] pour off
swing
go with a bang/~
swords
cross ~ (with)
sympathy
[one's ~] go out to
system
get out of one's ~
tab/tabs
keep a ~/~s/a tag on
table/tables
drink under the ~
get round the ~
lay one's cards on the ~
put one's cards on the ~ (*also* place *etc*)
turn the ~s (on)
wait at ~(s)/on ~s
tacks
get down to brass ~
tag
keep a tab/tabs/a ~ on
tail/tails
have their ~s down/up
make head or ~ of
take (*v*)
~ (sth) lying down: lie down under
sit up and ~ notice
tangent
go off at a ~
task
buckle down to [the ~]
take to ~
tastes
not account for preferences/~
tatters
rend to [~]
rip to [~]
tear/tears
blink away/back (one's) ~s
bore to [~s]
burst into[1] [~s]
dash away a ~/one's ~s
reduce to ~s
~(s) roll down
shed ~s over
teeth
get one's ~ into
give [one's back ~/eye-~ for
give ~ (to)
kick in the ~
set sb's/the ~ on edge
take the bit between the ~
temper
fly into [a (fit of) ~]
tension
[the ~] go out of[2]

terms
come to ~ with
terrifying
fix with [a ~ glare]
terror/terrors
have no fears/~s for (*also* hold *etc*)
have [a ~] of
test
put to the ~
stand up (to)[2] [a/the ~]
Thames
set the ~ on fire
that
[~] be between ourselves/you and me
[~] not be on
be well out of it/~
[~] be over and done with
if it come to ~
cut it/~ out
it/~ goes without saying
leave it at ~
how make ~ out
put ~ in one's pipe and smoke it
take sb's word for it/~
trust (for ~)
them (⇨ also 'em)
knock ~ in the aisles
pack [~] in[3]
themselves
speak for itself/~
suggest itself/~ (to)
things work ~ out
they
[~ (= *race-horses*)] be off[10]
thin
skate on ~ ice
thing/things
be on to a good ~
bring [the ~] off[2]
bring [~s] to a head
come to the same ~ (as)
[~s] come to this
[~s] fall out[1]
feel out of it/~s
fix it/~s up (with)
have a/this ~ about[1,2]
make a clean breast of it/the whole ~
put [the whole ~] in a nutshell
put a bold/brave/good face on [~s]
put the (tin) lid on it/~s
see [the ~/~s] through[4]
as it/~s turn(s) out
work ~s out
~s work themselves out
thinking
bring around/round (to)[2] [his way of ~]
come around/round (to)[2] [his way of ~]

Index of nominalized forms

This index covers all the nominalized forms (i e nouns derived from verbs + particles/prepositions) recorded in the main part of the dictionary (usually but not always the base form of the verb + particle/preposition, with or without a hyphen). For a full treatment of these forms ⇨ Introduction, 3.

Nominalized forms consisting of the *-ing* form of the verb + particle/preposition (e g *(a) dressing-down*, *(a) summing-up*, *(a) telling-off*) are not recorded here; the more common examples are noted in the dictionary.

Each nominal form is listed alphabetically and is followed by the headphrase(s) of the entry (or entries) in which it appears in the main text:

change-over change over (from) (to); change over/round[2]

output put out[7, 8]

When the nominalized form is a headphrase itself, this fact is noted as follows:

fall-out *(main entry)*

(There is no finite verb + particle expression in regular use from which *fall-out* derives: a sentence such as **The nuclear tests fell out over a wide area* is unacceptable.)

When a nominalized form is generally used attributively, a noun with which it commonly occurs is given in parentheses after it:

(a) knock-down (price) knock down[4]
knock-down (furniture) knock down[5]

Hyphenation or lack of it (i e nominalized forms printed as one word with or without a hyphen) tends to be a matter of printing convention or individual usage. The entries in the dictionary and in this index generally show the most accepted form in British usage, but variations are recorded where appropriate, e g *(a) poke(-)about/around.*

back-up back up[1]
balls-up balls up
(a) **bat around** bat around
blackout black out[1, 2, 3, 4]
blast-off blast off
blowout blow out[2]
blowout[1, 2] *(main entries)*
blow-up blow up[6]
bog-up bog up
botch-up botch up
(a) **break-away (group)** break away (from)[2]
(a) **break-away (state)** break away (from)[3]
break-back break back[2]
breakdown breakdown[4, 5, 6, 8]
break-in break in/into
break-out break out/out of
breakthrough break through[1, 3]
break-up break up[6]
brew-up brew up
(a) **brush(-)down** brush down[1]
brush-off brush off[2]
build-up build up[1, 4]; build up (to)[1, 2]
bully-off bully off
burn-up *(main entry)*
bust-up bust up
bust-up *(main entry)*
call-up call up[2]
carry-on carry on[2]
carve-up carve up
casher-in cash in (on)
castaway/cast away *(main entry)*
cave-in cave in[1, 2]
change-down change down
change-over change over (from) (to); change over/round[2]
change-round change over/round[2]
change-up change up
check-in check in (at)
check-out check out/out of
check-up *(main entry)*
chucker-out chuck out/out of
clamp-down clamp down (on)
clawback claw back
clean-out clean out
clean-up clean up[1, 2]; clean (oneself) up
clear-up clear up[1]
climb-down climb down[2]
clip-on (ear-rings) clip on/onto
clock-in (time) clock in/out
clock-out (time) clock in/out
clock-off (time) clock off/on
clock-on (time) clock off/on
close-down close down
cock-up: cock up[2]
come-back come back[2]
come-back[1, 2] *(main entries)*
come-down *(main entry)*
(a) **come-hither (look)** *(main entry)*
come-on *(main entry)*
come-uppance *(main entry)*
count-down count down
cover-up cover up (for)
crack-down crack down (on)
crack-up crack up[1, 2]

cutback, cut-back cut back[2]
cut-off[1, 2] *(main entries)*
cut-out cut out[6]
(a) **cut-out (picture)** cut out/out of
dig-in dig in/into[2]
(a) **doss(-)down** doss down
(a) **down (on sb)** be down on[1]
down-and-out(s) be down and out
downpour pour down
downturn turn down[4]
drawback *(main entry)*
(a) **drive-in (movie theater)** *(main entry)*
drop-out drop out
fade-out fade out
fall-out *(main entry)*
feedback feed back (into/on)[1, 2]
fill-up fill up[2]
flare-up flare up
flashback *(main entry)*
(a) **flick(-)through** flick through
(a) **flip(-)through** = flick through
flyover *(main entry)*
flypast fly past
follow-on follow on
follow-through follow through[2]
follow-up follow up[1]
foul-up foul up
frame-up frame-up
freak-out freak out
freeze-off freeze off
freeze-up *(main entry)*
freshen-up freshen up
fuck-up fuck up
gadabout gad about
getaway get away (from)[1]
get-together get together[1]
get-up get up[7]
give-away give away[1, 3]
glance-over, -through glance over/through
(the) **go-ahead (to do sth)** go ahead[1]
(a) **go-ahead (organization)** go ahead[2]
go-between *(main entry)*
go-by *(main entry)*
grown-up(s) grow up[1]
hand-me-downs hand down[1]
hand-off hand off
hand-out hand out[1, 2]
hand-over hand over[2]
hang-out hang out[2]
hangover/hung over *(main entry)*
hang-up/hung up *(main entry)*
hideaway hide away (in)
hold-up, holdup hold up[1, 2]
hook-up *(main entry)*
(a) **hose down** hose down
(an) **in (style)** be in[1]
jump-off jump off[1, 2]
kick-back *(main entry)*
kick-off kick off[2]
kip-down kip down
(a) **knock-about (comedy)** knock about[2]
(a) **knock-down (price)** knock down[4]
knock-down (furniture) knock down[5]
knock-on knock on[3]
(a) **knock-on (effect)** *(main entry)*
knock-out knock out[1, 2]
knocker-through knock through
knocker-up knock up[2]
knock-up *(main entry)*
lace-up(s) lace up
lash-out lash out (at)
layabout *(main entry)*
layby *(main entry)*
lay-off lay off[3, 4]
lay-out lay out[3]
lead-in lead in
lean-to *(main entry)*
leaseback lease back
let-down let down[2, 4]
let-out let out[3]
let-up let up
lie-down lie down
lie-in lie in[1]
lift-off lift off
(a) **lift(-)up** lift up[1]
limber-up limber up[1]
line-out *(main entry)*
line-up line up[3]
link-up link up (with)
listen-in listen in (to)
lock-out lock out
lock-up[1, 2] *(main entries)*
(a) **look around/round** look around/round[1, 2]
look-in *(main entry)*
looker-on look on
look-out[1, 2] *(main entries)*
(be) **sb's look-out** *(main entry)*
(on the) **look-out (for)** look out (for)
look-over look over[1]
look-through look through[2]
make-up make up[4, 5, 7]
makeshift(s) make shift (with)
march-past march past
mark-up mark up[1, 2]
marry-up marry up
mess-up mess up
mix-up mix up (with)[2]
mock-up *(main entry)*
muck-up muck up
(a) **nose(-)about/around** nose about/around
offprint print off[2]
onlooker look on
outbreak break out
outcast cast out
outfit, outfitters fit out
outlay lay out[1]
outpouring pour forth/out
output put out[7, 8]
overspill spill over
passer-by pass by
paste-up paste up[2]
pay-off pay off[3, 4]
peel-off peel off[2]
(a) **phone-in (e g radio programme)** phone in
pick-me-up pick up[1 2]
pick-up pick up[3, 6, 7]
(a) **pick-up (truck)** *(main entry)*
pile-up pile up[1, 2]
pin-up pin up
play-back play back[1]
play-off play off
(a) **poke(-)about/around** poke about/around
(a) **pop-up (book)** pop up[2]
(a) **potter(-)about/around** potter about/around
print-off print off[1, 2]
print-out print out
pull-in pull in/into[2]
(a) **pull-out (magazine-section)** pull out[2]

pull-out pull out/out of[4]
pull-up pull up[1]
punch-up punch up[2]
push-off push off[1]
push-over (*main entry*)
put-you-up put up[10]
(a) **rake(-)around/round** rake about/around/round (for)
rake-off (*main entry*)
rake-through rake through
rave-up (*main entry*)
rig-out rig out
rinse-out rinse (out)
rip-off rip off[2]
(a) **roll-on/roll-off (ferry)** (*main entry*)
round-up round up[1]
rub-down rub down[1,2]
rub-up rub up[1]
runabout (*main entry*)
run-around (*main entry*)
(a) **runaway (marriage)** run away (with)
(a) **runaway (victory)** run away with[3]
run-down (e g of numbers) run down[2]
run-down (= briefing) (*main entry*)
run-off run off[2]
run-through run through[3,4]
run-up (in sport) run up[4]
run-up (= preparation) (*main entry*)
(a) **scout about/around** scout about/around
(a) **see-through (blouse)** see through[1]
sell-out sell out (to)
send-off send off[2]
send-up send up[3]
setback set back[1]
set-to set to[2]
set-up (*main entry*)
(a) **shake-down (cruise)** shake down
shake-out (*main entry*)
shake-up shake up[1,2,3,4]
share-out share out (among)
shoot-out shoot it out
show-down (*main entry*)
show-off show off[3]
shut-down shut down
sit-down sit down
(a) **sit-down (strike)** (*main entry*)
sit-in sit in
(a) **skim(-)through** skim through
slip-up slip up
smash-up smash up
snarl-up snarl up[1,2]
speed-up speed up
spend-up (*main entry*)
spill-over spill over
spin-off (*main entry*)
splashdown splash down
(a) **spring-back (binder)** spring back
standby stand by[2]
stand-in stand in (for)
stand-off (*main entry*)
stand-to stand to
(a) **stay-at-home (girl)** stay at home
step-up step up
(a) **stick-on (label)** stick on
stick-up stick up[2]
stop-over stop over
stowaway stow away
sun-up the sun be up
(a) **swab(-)out** swab out
sweep-out sweep out
sweep-up sweep up
swill-out swill out
swing-round swing round (to)
switch-over switch over (to)
(a) **take-away (meal)** take away/out
take-home (pay) take home
take-off take off[12,13,15]
(a) **take-out (meal, restaurant)** take away/out
take-over take over
(a) **take-up (reel)** take up[11]
talk-back talk back
talk-through talk through
teach-in (*main entry*)
tearaway (*main entry*)
(a) **throw-away (can)** throw away[1]
(a) **throw-away (remark)** throw away[3]
throwback (*main entry*)
throw-in throw (the ball) in
throw-out throw out[1]
(a) **thumb(-)through** thumb through
tick-over tick over[1]
tidy-up tidy up
(a) **tie-on (label)** tie on
tie-up/tied up with (*main entry*)
tip-off tip off
(a) **tip-up (seat)** tip up
top-up top up[1,2]
toss-up (*main entry*)
touch-down touch down
trade-in trade in[2]
try-on try on (with)
try-out try out[1,2]
tuck-in tuck in/into[2]
turn-around turn around/round[2]
turndown turn down[4]
turn-off turn off[3]
turn-on turn on[2]
turn-out turn out[2,4,6]
turn-over (of money) turn over[2]
turn-over (of staff) (*main entry*)
turn-round turn round[3]; turn around/round[2]
turn-up(s) (*main entry*)
(a) **turn-up (for the book)** (*main entry*)
upbringing bring up[1]
upkeep keep up[4]
uplift lift up[2]
upturn turn up[7]
walkabout (*main entry*)
(a) **walk-on (part)** walk on
walk-out walk out[2]; walk out/out of
walk-over (*main entry*)
walk-over walk over (the course)
walk-through walk through
warm-up warm up[3]
wash-down wash down (with)[1]
wash-out wash out[2]
wash-out (*main entry*)
weigh-in weigh in (at)
whip-round whip round
wipe-down wipe down
wipe-over wipe over
work-in (*main entry*)
work-out work out[6]
(a) **work-to-rule** work to rule
write-in write in
write-off write off[2,3]
write-up write up[2]
(a) **zip-up (jacket)** zip up